RURAL SOCIOLOGY IN INDIA

BY THE SAME AUTHOR

Indian Feudal States and National Liberation Struggle

Gandhi's Truth and Non-violence X'Rayed

Social Background of Indian Nationalism

Recent Trends in Indian Nationalism

Rural India in Transition

Essays on Modernisation of Underdeveloped Societies (2 Vols.) (Ed.)

Slums and Urbanization (with S. Devadas Pillai)

A Profile of an Indian Slum (with S. Devadas Pillai)

State and Society in India

A Positive Programme for Indian Revolution (Ed.)

Peasant Struggles in India

Urban Family and Family Planning in India

India's Path of Development

Violation of Democratic Right in India

RURAL SOCIOLOGY IN INDIA

A. R. DESAI

POPULAR PRAKASHAN
BOMBAY

POPULAR PRAKASHAN PRIVATE LIMITED
301, Mahalaxmi Chambers, 22 Bhulabhai Desai Road,
Mahalaxmi Mumbai 400026.

Fourth Revised Edition, 1969
Fifty Edition, 1978
Fourth Reprint, 1990
Reprinted, 1992
Reprinted, 1994
Reprinted, 1995
Reprinted, 1997
Reprinted, 1999
Reprinted, 2009

First three editions were published by
The Indian society of Agricultural Economics, Bombay
in 1938, 1959 and 1961

(3188)
ISBN 978-81-7154-154-6

PRINTED IN INDIA
by Saurabh Printer Pvt. Ltd., A-15-16, Sector-4, Noida
and Published by Ramdas Bhatkal For Popular Prakashan Pvt. Ltd.
301, Mahalaxmi Chambers, 22 Bhulabhai Desai Road, Mahalaxmi 400026.

PREFACE TO THE FIFTH EDITION

The present edition is a reprint of the Fourth Revised Edition published in 1969. It has been only reprinted for a number of reasons. The Fourth edition was out of print for a number of years. The constant and growing demand necessitated a quick reprint.

There is a heavy pressure on good printing presses. The difficult technical situation for printing and publishing new works, as well as the fear of upsetting the schedules of new publications apprehended by publishers, lead us to a conclusion that it was advisable and practical to reprint the book as it would facilitate quicker availability of the volume already in great demand.

A number of friends and advisors were of the opinion that the Fourth edition, was so revised and altered that it did reveal the major long-term tendencies of the changes that were experienced by rural India. In fact the logic of the subsequent unfoldment in the Indian countryside, according to them, had been effectively highlighted in the previous edition.

I also felt that the developments in the Indian agrarian set-up that took place after 1969, hinted at in a number of selections, were forecasted in the author's own papers and sectional introduction and the underlying causes clearly analysed in my own writings included in the earlier edition. Revision, alteration or addition, however tempting and otherwise useful, would have caused inordinate delay in the availability of the book without basically affecting the major thrust of the logic underlying the work.

During this period, I was involved in preparing a book on *Peasant Struggles in India*, a companion volume to the present work. Preoccupation with that work, left me little time to undertake alterations and additions in the present work. Desire to make the two volumes *Rural Sociology in India* and *Peasant Struggles in India* available simultaneously also refrained me to revise the present work, which in its earlier form was considered adequate for highlighting the major long-term trends of agrarian social transformation.

It is my submission that availability of these two volumes simultaneously would help to stimulate both the students and activists who are attempting to understand and transform the Indian society which is experiencing unparalleled titanic, and stormy convulsions into a better and higher form of social order.

I again express my sense of gratitude to all whose writings have made this volume so productive.

To my young friend Mr. Ramdas Bhatkal I express my thanks for undertaking to publish this volume in such elegant form, inspite of his numerous commitments.

I feel a sense of satisfaction that *Rural Sociology in India* is constantly in demand and is being received as a useful work. I wish the present edition will receive the same welcome. I shall feel obliged if I receive suggestions and comments on my work to enable me to improve my understanding of the Indian situation and thereby improve my efficacy in contributing to the process of those basic qualitative, transformative processes, which may usher in a new, non-exploitative, socialist India.

A. R. DESAI

Jaykutir
Taikalwadi Road
Mahim
Bombay 400 016
9th October 1978

PREFACE TO THE FOURTH EDITION

THE PRESENT volume is the fourth revised and enlarged edition of *Rural Sociology in India.* This work was originally published in 1949 as *Introduction to Rural Sociology in India* by the Indian Society of Agricultural Economics. It was the fourth publication in the series "Readings in Agricultural Economics". At that stage the purpose of this work was to focus the attention of scholars, administrators, political and social workers on the importance of studying systematically the domain of social reality which had not received sufficient attention. In the subsequent editions the scope and content of the work was substantially changed. It no longer merely emphasized the need for scientific approach but actually delineated the picture of rural society in India emerging out of various studies of its numerous aspects.

The third edition was published in 1961. It was warmly received and was out of print within 3 years. The publication of the present volume, due to certain unavoidable and unforeseen circumstances, has been delayed for about 5 years. The delay in the publication has its own advantages. As a result of the availability of more time, I could look into the rapidly increasing literature on the subject and could insert very valuable selections which were published during this period.

Rural society in India has acquired a new significance after Independence. India is now no longer considered as a mere raw material-producing hinterland. The agrarian sector provides the very morphological framework to the underdeveloped Indian society. The Government of the Indian Union is making a vigorous effort to transform the underdeveloped Indian society in conformity to the basic postulates of progress embodied in the Constitution of India and concretely formulated in the first three Five-Year Plans. Agrarian social structure which provides the very anatomy to the Indian society is attempted to be re-shaped with a greater thoroughness. From the inception of the First Five-Year Plan, a huge endeavour is being made to overhaul the very productive base of the rural society as also its institutional and ideological superstructure. Serious efforts are being made to transform its ecological framework, the mode and motif of its economic production, the pattern of class relationships prevailing in it, the type of social institutions and associations composing it, the configurations of political power, and the very value-systems underlying cultural life. Indian rural society is subjected to the pressures of actively operating agencies of social change. It has been hurled into the whirlpool of unprecedented change. However shapeless the rural social order may appear, Indian society and its rural sector have been acquiring a design. This design requires to be comprehended.

It is heartening to note that a number of institutions, sponsored both by the Government and other agencies as well as a large number of academicians and reformers have started observing and analysing the transformation that is taking place in the structure, functions, power-relations, regulative systems and cultural norms within rural society. They have also begun to analyse the institutional, associational, and ideological changes that are taking place in rural society. Nay, eminent scholars belonging to different disciplines like sociology, anthropology, social psychology, archaeology, economics, politics, history, and others have launched studies which throw fresh light on the Indian civilization, past and present. These studies which have been increasing in number are helping, on the one hand to rediscover the true characteristics of "the classic Agrarian Civilization" of India and, on the other to evolve a picture of the rapidly changing present society. Unfortunately, most of the literature is in monographs and articles. A large body of it is not easily available. A considerable portion of it attempts to portray only segments of total reality. Some of it is photographically static in its narration. There are very few efforts to evaluate the total scene. The perspective of the total format, however dim or sketchy in outline it may be, to evolve out of the innumerable intimate and valuable studies of trees that are made, has become absolutely urgent. It is the author's feeling that such an outline is now possible even on the basis of the available literature.

This work is prepared with a view to subserving the following purposes :

(1) It attempts to focus the attention on the need of a sociological perspective in studying rural life.

(2) It attempts to outline the approach to study the rural society.

(3) It attempts to make accessible in one volume, the significant among the numerous studies that have been made regarding rural society. These studies reveal the various viewpoints and the diverse methods and techniques that have been adopted to study the different domains of rural society. It thereby draws attention to the growing body of literature germane to rural society.

(4) It further attempts to portray the picture of the multi-sided and complex rural life as is emerging in India and as is mirrored in the growing literature.

(5) It also tries to locate the major trends that are at work in the rural society which according to the author are becoming increasingly discernible on the basis of various studies.

The present edition like the earlier one is composed of two parts. The first part, as indicated in the earlier edition, gives an outline of Rural

Sociology, as viewed by me. I have kept the outline intact as desired by many scholars who found it very useful as an introduction to the subject. The second part is comprised of readings chosen from the writings of others. This part is considerably altered and expanded in the present edition. The writings have been grouped into 16 sections instead of 12 as in the third edition and 10 in the second edition. Each section is prefaced by the sectional introduction as in the third edition. The readings in the present edition not only attempt to provide considerable amount of factual information on various aspects of Indian rural society but also contain discussions on some of the most controversial issues connected with the various aspects of Indian agrarian social system.

The Section, xvi, 'Theories of Agrarian Development' is a novel feature in this volume. The 10 selections embodied in this section provide the crucial theoretical projections about future of not merely agrarian social order but of the entire underdeveloped countries as a whole because all the underdeveloped countries are overwhelmingly agrarian. Eminent scholars like Prof. Wertheim, Ernest Germain, Late Prof. Baran, Prof. Nunez, Prof. Surendra Patel, Prof. Dandekar, Prof. Dantwala and others have been seriously cogitating over the likely trend of development in underdeveloped countries. This section, I believe, will provide valuable material in connection with the path of development—for progressive improvement of conditions of masses in these countries. Which path will lead these countries from underdevelopment to affluence—Capitalist or Socialist? This is the crucial question posed for examination. On the right answer depends the fate of the "Third World" and of the humanity as a whole. The present volume attempts to provide a picture of the development that is taking place on Capitalist mixed-economy path in a country which contains one-fifth of humanity. It will, I am sure, be useful to develop a proper sociological perspective for developing countries.

In re-shaping and altering the third edition into the present form I have tried to improve upon my studies on the basis of the suggestions made by scholars and reviewers. It was very heartening to me that many scholars from many domains and many countries warmly communicated with me with regard to the third edition of my work and encouraged me to take up certain aspects for future editions. I am deeply grateful to them for their suggestions. I hope in this edition I have met some of their wishes. The present edition is comparatively larger than the third one. Even then I feel the readings are indicative and not comprehensive. It is very painful to decide which of the growing material be selected. I know my selections may not satisfy all. There are still very interesting and significant writings which could have been selected for this volume. However, inaccessibility of some of the literature, copyright difficulties and others, forced me to limit the choice of selection. It is encouraging for me to find that "Rural Sociology in India" is receiving unusual response. In the process of revising the edition I am realising how profound and complex is the subject which I have attempted to understand. Indian rural society with its complex and rich historical past is passing through a great transition. The drama of rural life is fascinating and involves one-fifth of humanity. I have attempted in my humble manner to work out the selections in such a manner that it may help the readers to draw an outline of the design of living that is emerging in rural India. If my work stimulates interest in sharper and better minds to conduct deeper studies, my endeavour would be rewarded.

It is not necessary to mention that such a venture cannot be undertaken except on the basis of support from friends. They are too numerous to be individually thanked.

However, I must express my deep sense of gratitude to late Shri Manilal B. Nanavati, who initiated me into this venture. I must also express my sense of gratefulness to Prof. D. G. Karve, Prof. M. L. Dantwala, Shri Jakhade, Dr. M. B. Desai, Dr. C. H. Shah and others who were connected with the Indian Society of Agricultural Economics, for encouraging me to explore this study. The earlier three editions were published by the Indian Society of Agricultural Economics. The Society, due to unavoidable circumstances, could not undertake to publish the fourth edition. However, I am thankful to the authorities of that institute for permitting me to publish it through Popular Prakashan.

I express my thanks to the staff of the library of Bombay University for their willing and prompt co-operation in supplying me with the necessary literature. I am deeply grateful to Dr. Udaya Mehta and Shri M. N. V. Nair for their valuable suggestions and technical assistance. I again acknowledge my deep sense of obligation to the authors and institutions from whose writings and reports I have selected the readings. They have been responsible for my increased understanding of the problem.

Indian society is experiencing unparalleled, titanic, stormy convulsions. I trust the revised edition will stimulate the students attempting to understand the drama of Indian rural life to undertake studies which would answer some of the crucial questions raised in the present epoch. I hope the present edition will also receive the same favourable response. I will be obliged if the readers would help me by sending their comments with a view to improving my own understanding of this fascinating subject.

Department of Sociology A. R. DESAI
University of Bombay
Bombay
May 1969

ACKNOWLEDGEMENTS

OUR THANKS are due to the following authors, institutions and publishers for their kind permission to quote extracts from their articles, reports, monographs etc.

The Editor, *Economic Weekly*, The Reserve Bank of India, Indian Society of Agricultural Economics, Planning Commission, Government of India, The All India Rural Credit Survey, The Editor, *Journal of the American Folklore*, President, The Indian Society of Agricultural Economics.

Hamza Alavi; Representatives of late A. S. Altekar; Yogesh Atal; Representatives of late Paul A. Baran; Acharya Vinoba Bhave; N. K. Bose; D. Chattopadhyaya; P. K. Chaudhari; Manmohan Choudhari; Bernard S. Cohn; Y. B. Damle; V. M. Dandekar; M. L. Dantwala; M. B. Desai; S. C. Dube; D. R. Gadgil; Ernest Germain; G. S. Ghurye; E. Kathleen Gough; Hugh Gray; Arun Chandra Guha; Sulekh Chandra Gupta; P. C. Joshi; Irawati Karve; G. J. Khudanpur; A. M. Khusro; V. Y. Kolhatkar; Representatives of late D. D. Kosambi; S. B. Mahabal; Representatives of late D. N. Majumdar; H. D. Mala- viya; David G. Mandelbaum; Uday Mehta; Ramakrishna Mukherjee; Shantibhushan Nandi; Lucio Mendiea Y. Nunez; T. K. Oommen; Martin Orans; Surendra J. Patel; B. T. Ranadive; P. S. Sanghvi; Representatives of late C. G. Shah; S. M. Shah; K. S. Shelvankar; Yogendra Singh; Surajit Sinha; O. H. K. Spate; M. N. Srinivas; Representatives of late B. Subbarao; Representatives of late S. Thirumalai; Daniel Thorner; D. S. Tyagi; Myron Weiner; W. F. Wertheim.

CONTENTS

PART I

INTRODUCTION TO RURAL SOCIOLOGY IN INDIA

CHAPTER I

STUDY OF RURAL SOCIOLOGY IN INDIA

RURAL INDIA NOT INERT

A SYSTEMATIC study of the rural social organization, of its structure, function and evolution, has not only become necessary but also urgent after the advent of Independence. The very process of achieving national freedom and transfer of power from the British to the Indians as also the colossal and very significant consequences which have followed this achievement, have revealed the signal importance of a careful, all-comprehensive, and methodical study of the rural society in our country.

The extensive participation of the rural masses in the long drawn out national liberation struggle; the devastating communal frenzy which swept over the rural social world and resulted in the uprooting of a great section of the village population in a number of provinces; the deep ferment which is, at present, seething in the agrarian area and which frequently bursts out in varied forms of struggles between different strata of the people; the numerous prejudices which are corroding the life of the rural people and which manifest themselves in various caste, linguistic, provincial and other forms of tension, antagonism and conflict; and similar other phenomena reveal that rural India is not so inert and quiescent as it was once assumed to be.

OBJECTIVES OF THE NEW STATE

The grave problems pertaining to rural society outlined above have been brought to the forefront in the post-independence period. The Constitution of the independent India has already fixed the goal towards which Indian society is to develop. A secular state, based on universal franchise and with the welfare of its citizens as its prime objective as provided for in the directive principles of the Constitution, is the national ideal which has emerged after the transfer of power. The realization of such an ideal, however, is a most complex and stupendous task which a people can set to itself.

To evolve a truly secular state in a country which is a citadel of the most stubborn religious prejudices rampant among its people; to create a social and cultural atmosphere for the intelligent exercise of universal adult franchise by the citizens who are living within the traditional, authoritarian, joint family, caste and semi-feudal social framework and the overwhelming majority of whom are illiterate; to develop a welfare economy in a country where the entire productive system is increasingly deteriorating; to implement such directive principles of the Constitution which accept the need to provide such rights as the right to work, the right to social security, and the right to education to citizens when even the task of providing primary necessities to them is increasingly becoming more and more difficult;—to fulfil such a programme it is vitally necessary to have a precise and thorough understanding of the Indian social structure and its developmental tendencies.

Predominantly Agrarian Backward

Those who desire to strive for such a creative social transformation have to bear in mind that India is overwhelmingly an agrarian country; that not less than three-fourths of her population is engaged in agriculture; and that the agricultural economy, which forms the material basis of the life of this vast mass of the population, determines their social organization (the institutional matrix within which their life processes flow) as well as moulds their psychological and ideological life. Further, since the rural society forms the major sector of the Indian society, the specific programme of the re-casting of the former must inevitably play a decisive role in any scheme of transformation of the latter on a higher economic and cultural basis.

Urban Bias of Scholars

Statisticians, economists, sociologists, social workers and government agencies have, hitherto, overwhelmingly focussed their attention on the study of the phenomena and problems of the urban society, though by far the greater portion of the Indian humanity lives in the rural area amidst conditions of immense material and cultural poverty. Even the literature dealing with the factual data about the life of the rural people is very meagre. It is true that there has grown a literature, though insufficient, devoted to the study of different kinds of soil, manure, seeds, techniques of agriculture, land holdings, land tenures, processes of marketing of crops and other matters pertaining to agrarian economy. There are even some fragmentary studies delineating the life history of some castes and tribes and indicative studies of some villages. However, uptil now, neither the problems of the rural society have been formulated in all their bewildering complexity and variety, nor have scientific diagnosis and solutions to these problems been offered.

The study of the Indian rural society, which varies from state to state, from even district to district, due to their extreme geographical, economic, historical, ethnic and other peculiarities, hitherto made has been spasmodic, insufficient and often superficial. Such a study cannot give an authentic, composite picture of the variegated landscape of the rural life, nor can it serve as a guide for evolving a scientific programme of reconstruction of the rural society, so essential for the renovation of the entire Indian society.

In fact, a concrete and comprehensive study of the rural society in all its aspects, ecological, morphological, institutional and cultural, has hardly begun.

STUDY OF RURAL SOCIETY, REASONS

It is, however, urgently necessary to make a scientific and systematic study of the rural society, of its economic foundation and social and cultural superstructure, of its institutions and their functions, of the problems arising from the rapid process of disintegration which is undergoing and which even threatens its breakdown.

(1) India is a classic land of agriculture. Its long past history, its complex social organization and religious life, its varied cultural pattern, can hence be understood only if a proper study is made of the rise, growth crystallisation and subsequent fossilisation and break up of the self-sufficient village community, the principal pivot of the Indian society only till recently.

(2) Due to historical reasons, the existing Indian rural society has become a veritable mosaic of various types of rural societies and hence reveals a diversified cultural pattern. The culture of the hunting and food gathering tribes; the culture of the primitive hoe-agriculturists; further, all the varied cultures of peoples engaged in agrarian production with the plough and the bullock, as also the modern culture of a rural people influenced by new technical and economic forces—all these cultures are juxtaposed in the contemporary rural India. Further, the Indian rural humanity is also being influenced by the ideological currents of the modern era. Consequently we find in the Indian rural world today, the persistence of primitive cults of magic and animism, polytheism, pantheism of the ancient world, monotheism and other idealistic philosophic world outlooks inherited from the ancient medieval periods as also a minor current of modern rationalist world view. This has transformed it into a veritable museum of different and even conflicting cults and ideologies.

(3) The unique agrarian socio-economic structure of India experienced a decisive transformation as a result of the impact of the British conquest and rule. On the eve of the British conquest of India the Indian rural society was composed of a multitude of villages. Each village lived almost an independent, atomistic, self-sufficient social and economic existence. The village represented a closed society based on economic autarchy and social life governed by caste and community rules.

In the economic sphere, the village experienced a steady transformation during the British period. Its economic self-sufficiency was dissolved. It slowly began to produce for the Indian and the foreign market and, not as before, for meeting the needs of the village population. The village economy became increasingly an integral part of the national and even world economy. The influx of cheap foreign and, subsequently, of indigenous industrial goods into the village, progressively undermined the village artisan industries. The old self-sufficient economy based on an equilibrium between the village agriculture and the village artisan industry was thus disrupted.

In the social field, the rule of custom enforced by the joint family, the caste and the village panchayat, was gradually replaced by the reign of laws made by the centralized British state in India and administered by its own revenue, executive and judicial officials posted in the village. This considerably undermined the powers of the joint family, the caste and the village panchayat.

The introduction of the modern means of transport and communication accelerated the processes mentioned above.

Every aspect of the village life, social, economic, political and cultural, experienced a steady transformation. The old pattern of village life, the old structure of village society, became appreciably changed.

Since the transformation was mainly brought about by a foreign power to serve its own political and economic interests, it resulted in the destruction of the old type of the rural society without its being replaced by a socially healthy, economically progressive and culturally more advanced new type. The transformation culminated in the emergence of the present impoverished and culturally backward village which, moreover, lacked stability and a definite structural design.

The Indian agrarian economy is at present in a state of acute crisis. This has resulted in the unbearable economic misery of the rural people. The agrarian situation has consequently become almost explosive.

It is, therefore, vitally necessary to focus attention on the crisis of the rural economy. The solution of the crisis is the essential pre-condition not only for eliminating poverty of the rural population but also for building a prosperous national economy which can guarantee a higher material standard of life to all citizens.

It should be noted that the role of social institutions in accelerating or retarding the fulfilment of an advanced programme of agrarian reconstruction is greater in India than in any other country. Programmes and policies of rural renovation based on pure economic factors have not, therefore, met with appreciable success. The role of such institutions as the caste and the joint family organization in thwarting such programmes and policies has not been hitherto properly grasped. The necessity of *Rural Sociology* becomes all the more important in India.

Rural Sociology, Its Urgent Need

To reconstruct such a rural society on a higher basis, it is urgently necessary to study not only the economic forces, but also the social, the ideological and other forces operating in that society. It is a complex and colossal task.

As referred to above, only stray, spasmodic efforts have been hitherto made to study the life processes of the Indian rural society. No systematic study has still been launched to study that society in all its aspects, to study its life processes in their movement and, further, in their interconnections.

In fact, Indian Rural Sociology or the science of the laws governing the specific Indian rural social organism has still to be created. Such a science is, however, the basic premise for the renovation of the Indian rural society, so indispensable for the renovation of the Indian society as a whole.

CHAPTER II

RURAL SOCIOLOGY, ITS ORIGIN AND SCOPE

Its Origin

Rural Sociology or the science of the laws of development of rural society in general has come into being only in recent times.

Early Reflections

Reflections on rural society, indeed, are as old as the rural society itself. In the past, social thinkers had made attempts to comprehend the life processes of the rural world and to advance solutions of the problems arising therefrom. A comprehensive survey of the views of eminent thinkers belonging to various countries in the past epochs regarding rural life and its problems as they emerged in the changing rural society in various stages of development has been made in the "Systematic Source Book in Rural Sociology" Vol. I, edited by Sorokin, Zimmerman and Galpin. It reveals how some of the basic features of rural society and urgent problems of changing rural life had commanded the interest and attention of earnest social thinkers of ancient, medieval and early modern periods and impelled them to make sociological reflections, though they would betray to the well-equipped modern rural sociologists a lack of scientific methodology.

Systematic Observations from XIXth Century

It was since about the middle of the ninteenth century that more systematic observations on the history of the origin and transformation of rural society have been advanced. The impact of the capitalist industrial civilization upon the rural economy and social structure, in various parts of the world, forced the attention of scholars to the study of the trends of rural social development. Research in the subject of the origin and the nature of village communities which were undergoing transformation was launched.

Olufsen, Maurer, Maine, Hexthausen, Gierke, Elton. Stemann, Innes, Coulanges, Nasse, Laveleye, Baden Powell, Ashley, Pollock, Maitland, Lewinski, Seebohm, Gomme, Guiraud, Jubainville, Slater, Vinogradoff, Meitzon and others are some of the outstanding scholars who have thrown light on rural society from various angles.

Subsequently eminent scholars, professors and others interested in the phenomena of the rural life have published in various countries enormous material dealing with its various aspects.

As an Organized Discipline in the U.S.A.

However, rural sociology as an organized discipline consciously developed, is of very recent origin. Due to historical reasons it has originated in the U.S.A. and slowly tends to draw attention elsewhere as its importance is being realized. During what is called "Exploiter Period" of American society (1890-1920), a period when the American rural society witnessed allround decay, a considerable literature, describing and analysing the problems arising out of its growing crisis, came into existence. This literature, however, did not explore, locate, and formulate the fundamental laws governing the development of rural society. It created the prerequisites for the birth of the science of rural society but did not still create that science. However, the beginnings of rural sociology may be traced to those "streams" of publications.

The first valuable work on the subject was the Report on the Country-life Commission appointed by President Theodore Roosevelt in 1907. A number of Doctorate theses based on the study of the rural community comprised further significant literature dealing with problems of rural life and providing, revealing information thereon. Finally a group of rural church and school studies made by individuals interested in an investigation of maladjustments in rural life constituted the third "stream" of publications. This literature served as the basis for creating the science of rural sociology in the U.S.A.

The Countrylife Commission, under the chairmanship of Dean Bailey, the eminent scholar of rural problems, circulated 5,00,000 questionnaires to farmers and leaders of rural life and received nearly 1,00,000 replies. The Commission, on the basis of this investigation, published a report in which they attempt to analyse and diagnose the defects and deformities of rural society. "This report actually provided what might be called a charter for Rural Sociology."

"An American Town," "Quaker Hill" and "A Hoosier Village," of which James Michel Williams, Warren H. Wilson and Newell L. Sims were respectively authors, represented further studies of the American rural community. These studies were based on statistical and historical data and field-interview techniques and were submitted as research documents at the Columbia University between 1906 and 1912. Dr. Warren Wilson, along with others interested in the processes of rural life, carried on a number of rural church studies. These studies, together with some rural school studies and "The Social Anatomy of an Agricultural Community" by Dr. C. J. Galpin based on an investigation into rural life made by him at the Agricultural Experiment Station of the University of Wisconsin in 1915, comprised additional literature germane to rural sociology until 1916.

"Rural Sociology" by Prof. John M. Gillettee published in 1916 served as the first college text book on the subject. Subsequently, a number of writers devoted themselves to the study of rural life and published valuable works which also enriched the literature on the subject. The publication of " A Systematic Source Book in Rural Sociology " in 1930 recognised as an " Epoch-making " work contributed decisively to accelerate the advance of rural sociology.

Later on, other intellectuals also focussed their attention on the subject and helped its further development.

Sorokin, Zimmerman, Galpin, Taylor, Kolb, Brunner, Sims, Dwight Sanderson, Landis, Redfield and Smith are some of the outstanding social thinkers in the U.S.A. whose intellectual labour resulted in a phenomenal advance of the new science of rural sociology.

The founding of the journal "Rural Sociology" in 1935 (at present a monthly) and the establishment of "Rural Sociological Society of America" in 1937 were further landmarks in the history of its growth.

In the U.S.A., rural sociology, though a new science and still in a state of immaturity, is commanding wider and wider interest among social thinkers to-day. More than eight hundred professors and research workers are engaged in developing that science in that country.

Its Present State

In other countries also, increasing attention is being paid to study and systematise this branch of study.

The various studies organized by the League of Nations and embodied in a number of monographs, together with the recent studies made by such organizations as UNO, UNESCO, FAO and others, have also contributed to the rapid advance of rural sociology.

Such is the history of the genesis and growth of rural sociology, the youngest amongst all sciences. It has started taking roots and is slowly but securely spreading itself in various parts of the world including India which needs it the most in view of its very large rural population with innumerable complex problems.

Its Scope

As in the case of every young science, especially of a young social science, a great controversy has taken place over the question of the definition and scope of rural sociology among scholars engaged in the endeavour to develop it.

Controversies

Is rural sociology a distinct science or is it merely an application of the general principles of sociology (or the science of society as a whole) to the sphere of rural social phenomena ? Should rural sociology restrict its scope merely to the life processes of rural society or should it also include as an integral part, a study of rural and urban social life, comparative as well as in their mutual inter-connection and interaction and, further, have as its central concept what Zimmerman describes as "The mechanism and effects of urbanization and ruralization upon a population" ?

Further, should rural sociology only provide scientific knowledge about rural society and laws governing its development or should it also serve as a guide and suggest practical programmes of reform or reconstruction of that society in the economic, social or cultural fields ? In short, should rural sociology merely give an objective authentic composite picture of the changing rural life in all its multifold and multiform aspects or also function as an ideological instrument to remould it according to a social purpose and a practical plan ?

These are some of the principal problems over which extensive controversy is at present raging among sociologists. Such a disagreement among social scientists is not a characteristic peculiar to the field of rural sociology. Even regarding sociology in general, neither a clear, universally accepted definition nor a unanimous view of the scope of its study have as yet emerged among sociologists. The sub-domains of the single concretely whole domain of social life are so intermingled, interacting and even overlapping, that it is difficult to isolate one of them, study it and evolve a distinct science disclosing the laws of its structure and its evolution. Hence it is that disputes take place among social thinkers regarding the method and approach to be adopted to evolve a social science.

Basic Agreement

In spite of a wide divergence of views among rural sociologists regarding the definition, scope, and objective of rural sociology and also about the emphasis to be laid on this or that factor of the rural society as the point of departure of its study, there also exists a number of basic agreements among them.

All rural sociologists recognize that the social life of the community is divided into two distinct segments, rural and urban. Though these segments interact among themselves, each is sufficiently distinct from the other.

All of them hold the view that social life in rural setting exhibits characteristics and tendencies which are peculiar to it, which constitute its specificness and which, therefore, sharply distinguish it from social life in urban setting.

All of them unanimously declare that the prime objective of rural sociology should be to make a scientific, systematic and comprehensive study of the rural social organization, of its structure, functions and objective tendencies of development, and, on the basis of such a study, to discover the law of its development. Since every science, social or natural, has for its aim the discovery of the hitherto hidden law of development of a domain of nature or society, the basic task of rural sociology, they unanimously declare, is to discover the law of development of rural society.

CHAPTER III

RURAL–URBAN DIFFERENCES

AFTER BRIEFLY referring to the origin and the scope of rural sociology, we will endeavour to locate and study the distinctive features of the two types of social phenomena, rural and urban.

NEED TO DISTINGUISH RURAL-URBAN SETTINGS

Social life in the countryside moves and develops in a rural setting just as social life in the urban area moves and develops in an ubran setting. Their respective settings considerably determine rural and urban social life.

A correct comprehension of the specific characteristics of the rural framework is, therefore, indispensable for a proper grasp of the distinct features of rural social life. Such a study constitutes the first task of the rural sociologist and can be accomplished by studying in contrast the distinctive features of rural and urban settings. A brief outline of the principal points of contrast between the rural and urban settings will show how the different structures and life-processes of rural and urban societies are to a great extent the consequence of the difference between those different settings.

SIGNIFICANT CRITERIA TO DISTINGUISH THEM

Outstanding sociologists have laid down a number of significant criteria for distinguishing the rural social world from the urban social world, such as the social composition of population, "the cultural heritage," the magnitude of material wealth, social stratification of the population, the degree of the complexity of social structure and social life, the intensity and variety of social contact and others. They have finally attempted to trace the sharp differences and contrasts between the two types of social phenomena, rural and urban, largely to the basic differences between the rural and urban settings.

The following are the most important criteria for distinguishing the rural social world from the urban social world :

(1) Occupational differences.

(2) Environmental differences.

(3) Differences in the sizes of the communities.

(4) Differences in the density of the population.

(5) Differences in the homogeneity and heterogeneity of the population.
(6) Differences in the social mobility.
(7) Differences in the direction of migration.
(8) Differences in the social differentiation and stratification.
(9) Differences in the system of social interaction.

The following table reproduced from " Princples of Rural-Urban Sociology"[1] reveals the decisive differences between the rural and the urban worlds :

	Rural World	Urban World
Occupation	Totality of cultivators and their families. In the community are usually a few representatives of several non- agricultural pursuits.	Totality of people engaged principally in manufacturing, mechanical pursuits, trade, commerce, professions, governing, and other non-agricultural occupations.
Environment	Predominance of nature over anthropo-social environment. Direct relationship to nature.	Greater isolation from nature. Predominance of man-made enviroment over natural. Poorer aid. Stone and iron.
Size of community	Open farms or small communities, " agriculturalism" and size of community are negatively correlated.	As a rule in the same country and at the same period, the size of urban community is much larger than the rural community. In other words, urbanity and size of community are positively correlated.
Density of population	In the same country and at the same period the density is lower than in urban community. Generally density and rurality are negatively correlated.	Greater than in rural communities. Urbanity and density are positively correlated.

(contd.)

[1] P. A. Sorokin and C. C. Zimmerman : " Principles of Rural-Urban Sociology. " pp. 56-57.

	Rural World	Urban World
Heterogeneity and homogeneity of the population	Compared with urban populations, rural communities are more homogeneous in racial and psychological traits (Negative correlation with heterogeneity).	More heterogeneous than rural communities (in the same country and at the same time). Urbanity and heterogeneity are positively correlated.
Social differentiation and stratification	Rural differentiation and stratification less than urban	Differentiation and stratification show positive correlation with urbanity.
Mobility	Territorial, occupational and other forms of social mobility of the population are comparatively less intensive. Normally the migration current carries more individuals from the country to the city.	More intensive. Urbanity and mobility are positively correlated. Only in the periods of social catastrophy is the migration from the city to the country greater than from the country to the city.
System of interaction	Less numerous contacts per man. Narrower area of the interaction system of its members and the whole aggregate. More prominent part is occupied by primary contacts. Predominance of personal and relatively durable relations. Comparative simplicity and sincerity of relations. "Man is interacted as a human person."	More numerous contacts. Wider area of interaction system per man and per aggregate. Predominance of secondary contacts. Predominance of impersonal casual and short-lived relations. Greater complexity, manifoldedness, superficiality and standardized formality of relations. Man is interacted as a "number" and "address."

CHAPTER IV

VILLAGE, ITS HISTORY

VILLAGE, A HISTORICAL CATEGORY

AFTER HAVING surveyed the chief characteristic differences between the rural and urban segments of social life, we will now proceed to analyse the structural pattern of the rural society since it provides the matrix within which the whole drama of rural life is unfolded.

The village is the unit of the rural society. It is the theatre wherein the quantum of rural life unfolds itself and functions.

Like every social phenomenon the village is an historical category. The emergence of the village at a certain stage in the evolution of the life of man, its further growth and development in subsequent periods of human history, the varied structural changes it experienced during thousands of years of its existence, the rapid and basic transformation it has undergone during the last hundred and fifty years since the Industrial Revolution—all these constitute a very fascinating and challenging study.

PLOUGH AGRICULTURE, ITS SIGNIFICANCE

The rise of the village is bound up with the rise of agricultural economy in history. The emergence of the village signified that man passed from the nomadic mode of collective life to the settled one. This was basically due to the improvement of tools of production which made agriculture and hence settled life on a fixed territorial zone possible and necessary.

How humanity, in different parts of the world, passed from the nomadic hunting and food gathering stage to that based on roving hoe agriculture and thereafter, on settled plough agriculture carried on by means of draft animals, has been one of the most difficult and complex problems in the field of social research.

With the invention of the plough, man could develop stable agriculture, the basic source of assured food supply. Man's nomadic mode of life ceased. No longer men roamed in herds from place to place in search of means of subsistence. They settled on a definite territory and organized villages based on agricultural economy. Agrarian communities with villages as their fixed habitation and agriculture as their main occupation came into existence. This event marked a landmark in the history of mankind, inaugurating a higher phase of social existence. Agriculture assured the community, for the first time, a relatively stable food supply in contrast to previous stages of social life. While food supply derived from such sources as hunting, fishing, fruit gathering and migratory hoe agriculture had always been insufficient and precarious, grain and other types of food products derived from plough agriculture could be counted upon and also be stored for use in periods of emergencies, thereby assuring relative food security for the future.

In the agricultural phase the struggle for existence became relatively less acute for man. Further, at a certain stage of the development of agricultural economy, due to the greater productivity of agriculture, a section of the community could be liberated from the necessity of participating in food production and could therefore concentrate on secondary industrial or ideological activity. This gave momentum to the growth of technology, arts, sciences and philosophy. It also brought about, though slowly, the significant transition in the social organization of humanity, from an organization founded on kinship and clan to that based on territorial ties. With the development of agriculture at a certain level, mankind took a leap from totemistic collectivist clan society to territorial civil society with its distinct multi-class social structure and the resultant institution of the state.

Civilization thus began with the development of agriculture. The village—the first settled form of collective human habitation and the product of the growth of agricultural economy—thus historically gave birth to rural society, and from the surplus of its food resources, nourished the town which subsequently came into existence.

Different Types of Village Aggregates

In the history of different peoples living in different parts of the world, different types of villages emerged with the rise and spread of agriculture. This was mainly due to differences in geographical environments in which those peoples lived. Further, the early village of a people also underwent changes in time due to its subsequent technical, economic, and social evolution as well as due to the impact of other societies on it.

The history of the village, in time and space, reveals such diverse village types as the Saxon viallge, the German Mark, the Russian Mir, the self-sufficient Indian Gram, the village of the feudal Europe which was an integral part of the manor; and finally the modern village, which is an integral part of national and world economic systems, with its variants such as the U.S.A. village, the typical West European village, the village of the backward modern countries of Asia, the village of the Soviet Union based on collectivized agricultural economy and others.

Hence the student of rural society should study the village, the basic unit of rural society as it originated and underwent a constant state of development and change due to the action of its own developing internal forces as also due to its interaction with other societies.

CRITERIA TO CLASSIFY VILLAGE AGGREGATES

Eminent sociologists have advanced a number of criteria to classify village communities.

(1) According to one criterion the village aggregates have been classified according to the types which evolved during the period of the transition from man's nomadic existence to settled village life. Thus villages have been divided into three groups : (i) the Migratory agricultural villages where the people live in fixed abodes only for a few months; (ii) the Semi-permanent agricultural villages where the population resides for a few years and then migrates due to the exhaustion of the soil; and (iii) the Permanent agricultural villages where the settled human aggregates live for generations and even centuries.[1]

(2) According to the second criterion villages have been classified into grouped (or nucleated) villages and dispersed villages. In grouped villages the farmers dwell in the village proper in a cluster. They work on the fields which lie outside the village site. Since they dwell together in a single habitat, they develop a compact life. In the case of the non-nucleated dispersed village type, the farmers live separately on their respective farms. Their habitats being thus dispersed, their social life assumes a different form.[2]

(3) Village aggregates have been also classified according to a third criterion, that of social differentiation, stratification, mobility and land, ownership.[3]

According to this criterion, village aggregates have been grouped into six broad types *viz.* (1) that composed of peasant joint owners; (2) that composed of peasant joint tenants; (3) that composed of farmers who are mostly individual owners, but also include some tenants and labourers; (4) that composed of individual farmer tenants; (5) that composed of employees of a great private landowner; and finally (6) that composed of labourers and employees of the state, the church, the city or the public landowner.

NEED FOR SYSTEMATIC CLASSIFICATION IN INDIA

A systematic classification of Indian village aggregates on the basis of the above criteria and a study of their history will provide valuable information about village communities in India, about varied types of social institutions which have come into being in rural India, and also on the complex cultural patterns which have influenced and been influencing life processes of the Indian rural people.

An exhaustive survey of Indian villages co-relating the village types classified according to three principles will help to disclose the laws of

---

[1] "Encyclopaedia of Social Science" Vol. 15, "Village Community" by Harold J. Peake. P. 254.

[2] Systematic Source Book in Rural Sociology. Vol. I, p. 263.

[3] *Ibid*, p. 560.

the rise and development of Indian village communities. It will also help historians and sociologists to locate the laws of the peculiar development of Indian society and, further, will assist rural workers to evolve scientific programmes of rural reconstruction.

CHAPTER V

REGIONAL APPROACH TO RURAL SOCIETY

SIGNIFICANCE OF REGIONAL APPROACH

ONE OF the important aspects from which rural social life is increasingly being analysed is the aspect of its spatial organization.

What factors determine the growth of varied types of villages, what factors operate to combine a cluster of villages into an agrarian region, what factors tend to transform an agrarian region into a cultural, linguistic or political region, and how do regions evolve into a province–these problems are of considerable significance in the study of rural society.

FACTORS GENERATING REGIONAL VARIATIONS

Sociologists have attempted to locate the factors explaining this process. According to them, some of the important factors, which have determined the structural pattern of the village, the formation of regional and other bigger units and the interrelations of the village with those units, are as follows:

(1) Natural conditions like relief, configurations, soil, water resources and others; (2) the stage of agrarian economy, whether it is the nomadic stage, the stage of fixed subsistence agriculture or that commercial agriculture; and (3) the nature of social conditions such as needs of defence, forms of property and others.

GROUPED AND DISPERSED HABITATS

The first great division which has been made of village communities from the ecological angle is that of nucleated or grouped villages and dispersed habitats. This distinction is vital from the point of view of the study of the entire social life of the rural community. The members of a rural community who dwell in villages have generally stronger social urges, exhibit a stronger feeling of social cohesion, and possess greater ability for co-operation than those who are dispersed and live on their respective farms. Each type of habitat furnishes a different framework for social life. The nucleated village is marked by " proximity, contact, community of ideas and sentiments" while in dispersed habitats "everything bespeaks separation, everything marks the fact of dwelling apart."

STUDY OF LARGER RURAL REGIONS, DIFFICULTIES

The study of the emergence of a larger rural area is one of the most baffling problems confronting the student of rural society. The factors which have combined to evolve homogeneous rural regions demand a very careful examination. Again we find that the larger rural regions change their characteristics with the change in the techno-economic, socio-economic and socio-political forces. The epoch of self-sufficiency evolved one category of regions. Under the impact of Industrial Revolution and production for market, a totally new type of rural areas came into being. The change from market economy to planned economy, where the agrarian sector is consciously developed as a part of the total life of the community, is creating in some countries and will create in other countries a new type of regional units. And, above all, the gigantic development of productive forces which is evolving an international economic and cultural community in the modern epoch is forcing the students of human society and especially of rural society to discover the appropriate variety of rural regions which will be in consonance with this development.

Efforts are being made to define economic, linguistic, administrative, religious and cultural regions in various countries. Efforts are also being made to find out where these regions coincide and also to study the laws which bring about this concurrence.

The works of Sanderson, Kolb, Taylor and others which embody an intensive study of rural economic and cultural zones in the U.S.A. have thrown considerable light on the phenomenon of the development of such zones. Various studies of primitive tribes—their geographical milieu, technical equipment, economic organization, social institutional structure, religion, arts and culture and, further, their transformation under the impact of communities belonging to various stages of civilized life—also furnish rich material for discovering the laws of rural development. Works dealing with the role of geographical factors—such as mountain, river, desert, sea, rainfall, various species of trees and animals—in indirectly or directly influencing the nature of economic organization, social institutions, styles of architecture, and beliefs and other ideological elements of man's life, also provide valuable clues for a correct understanding of the emergence of varied rural cultures.

The environmental and regional approach will help to distinguish chief village types and village social structures. It will also assist in scientifically classifying principal regional, district and provincial units. It will also aid in locating the underlying factors which have operated to create distinct culture-areas. And finally it will help to evolve a systematic account of the evolution of Indian society as a whole.

Ecological Map of India, An Urgent Need

A detailed map of India indicating various natural and economic regions; indicating the areas inhabited by populations living in various stages of economic development; showing linguistic regions including regions based on different dialects as well as different variations of the main language; and showing, further, religious regions based on different religious beliefs prevailing among the people; will throw great light on some of the most burning problems of Indian society and will also assist those engaged in the difficult task of reforming rural society to locate some of the fundamental causes of the present crisis of that society.

CHAPTER VI

RURAL PEOPLE

THE FIRST task confronting the rural sociologist is to define the rural people and distinguish them from the urban population. Various approaches have been suggested for that purpose by eminent thinkers. Classification adopted by Government Census Departments in various countries is, however, generally accepted as the most convenient, though it may vary from one country to another.

RATIO OF RURAL-URBAN POPULATION

The next task before the student of the rural people is to determine the ratio of rural and urban populations. In many countries, this ratio in a great measure indicates the level of living of the people as a whole since it shows the relative proportion of industry, and agriculture and hence the total wealth of the people. The ratio, further, considerably influences the apportionment of social amenities within the country. It thereby serves as a guide for evolving a correct programme for social advance. One of the great mistakes committed by a number of reformers and social engineers is to transplant mechanically the techniques adopted for reform in a country inhabited by a small agrarian population and with a vast area of land to a country inhabited by an overwhelmingly agrarian population and with scarce land resources. The recent effort to introduce measures adopted to improve the agrarian sector of the U.S.A. which is overwhelmingly industrial to predominantly agrarian backward countries of Asia is an instance of such an error. Even within the same country a detailed study of the ratios of rural-urban population in different regions is essential because these differences considerably alter the nature of problems relating to those regions. For instance, the problems of Gujarat and those of Bihar are different as there is a difference in the proportion of rural-urban population of these states.

DENSITY OF RURAL PEOPLE

The next important problem is that of the density of the people living on land. Sociologists, after adequate investigation, have reached the conclusion that the average density beyond a particular limit indicates an undesirable over-concentration of the people in that area. This is because the density of the population affects production and distribution and also generates various social reactions which greatly influence the total life of a society. The density of the population further affects the level of the standard of living of the people.

A systematic study of the density of the population in different regions and districts in India and also of the proportion of various groups belonging to diverse castes, religions, and vocations which comprise the population, will unfold the variegated picture of the complex social life of the Indian people with all its multiple tensions, antagonisms as well as mutual adjustments among these groups.

Birth and Death Rate

The study of birth rates, death rates, rates of suicides, specific bodily diseases and such other matters regarding the rural population is another important aspect of a demographic study of the rural society as it reveals the quantitative and qualitative growth or decline of the rural people. Further, when this study is correlated to that of the social, economic and religious life processes of various social groups, it provides intelligent and correct criteria of evaluating the norms of those groups.

General Health and Longevity

Aprat from a study of the death and survival rates prevailing among the rural people, there are also other means to determine their vitality such as a study of their general health and longevity. Further, estimates of mortality prevailing among separate groups such as infants, females and old people; upper, lower and middle social strata; and land labourers, farmers, artisans, and other social categories, will give a detailed picture of the vitality of various sections of the rural people.

Age and Sex Groups

Another aspect of the life of a population which requires a close study is their distribution in age and sex groups. The analysis of age groups gives us a correct understanding of the proportion of the people who are of productive age and those who are to be sustained by the society. The preponderance of children and the aged over the working section of the people would considerably influence their economic and social life.

Similarly the analysis of the sex composition is also essential, since it is generally recognized by sociologists that "sex mores, social codes, social rituals, and social institutions are all likely to be affected where extremely unbalanced sex ratios are found."

Other Aspects of the Composition of the People

Caste, race, nationality and religious composition of the people has a great social significance. It gives rise to a rich, complex, diversified social life and varied patterns of culture. More often it breeds animosities, antagonisms and conflicts. We know how in India in recent years the multi-religious composition of the Indian people engendered ghastly communal Hindu—Muslim riots. We know how nationality conflicts are steadily corroding the body politic of India.

A very peculiar type of social grouping which is found in India is the caste grouping. A student of the Indian society who fails to study closely and carefully this variety of social grouping will miss the very essence of that society. Looking to its important role in India a separate chapter has been devoted to the sociological significance of caste elsewhere.

A systematic, co-ordinated and inter-related study of the rural people from various angles is an urgent need.

CHAPTER VII

ECONOMIC LIFE OF THE RURAL PEOPLE

AGRICULTURE, ITS SPECIFICNESS

SINCE ECONOMIC production is the basic activity of a human aggregate, the mode of production (productive forces and social relations of production) plays a determining role in shaping the social structure, the psychology and the ideology of that human aggregate.

Rural society is based predominantly on agriculture. Village agriculture is sharply distinguished from urban industry by the fact that it is based on direct extraction from Nature by man.

Land is the basic means of production in the countryside. Land is a part of Nature, though made arable by human labour. From land, the rural people produce, by means of technique and their labour power, such a variety of agrarian products as food, cotton, jute, tea, coffee, tobacco and others.

Urban industry only transforms the products of agriculture into industrial products. In city factories and mills, such agricultural products as cotton, jute and sugarcane are transformed into cotton and jute cloth and sugar respectively.

This basic difference between agriculture and industry plays a significant role in shaping the social institutions, the psychology and the ideology of the rural and urban populations.

Further, the level of production and the way in which the products are distributed among the different strata of a society, determine the level of the material prosperity of the society as a whole and of the various socio-economic groups comprising it. They also, to a very large extent, mould the institutional set up of that society as well as the cultural life of its people.

For instance, in India, the primitive nature of agriculture, the resultant low level of agricultural production and the specific types of land relations which determine the differing shares of agricultural products among the social groups composing the rural society, explain the general poverty of the rural people, their hierarchic gradation into a pyramidal system of socio-economic groups and, further, their distinct social institutions and cultural backwardness. They also largely fix their customs, conceptions, and social mores.

MOTIF OF PRODUCTION

The rural sociologist should find out whether, in the given society, agricultural production has for its objective the direct satisfaction of the subsistence needs of the rural aggregate or is carried on for the market and profit of the producers who do not themselves consume their products. This means whether the agricultural economy is a subsistence or a market economy.

For instance, in pre-British India, village agriculture mainly produced for meeting the needs of the village population. This subsistence village agricultural economy was transformed into a market economy during the British period. This was due to a variety of causes. The British Government created private property in land in the form of ryotwari and zamindari. In the ryotwari area, it introduced the system under which the peasant producer had to pay to the state land tax in cash instead of in kind. The land tax grew progressively heavy resulting into the increasing indebtedness of the agriculturist. In the zamindari area, the burden of increasing rent imposed on the tenant producer by the zamindar impoverished the tenant and saddled him also with the ever expanding burden of debt. Largely due to the necessity for cash for the payment of land tax, rent and debt, the agriculturist, the peasant proprietor or the tenant, was more and more constrained to produce for the market. Thus village agriculture increasingly ceased to produce for directly satisfying the needs of the village population and began to produce for the national and subsequently even world market.

There is a third and new conception of the objective of agricultural production. According to it, not only should agriculture produce to meet the needs of the community but also it should be adapted to the *consciously assessed needs* of the total community. The exponents of this view argue that this will not only eliminate the competitive market intervening between the producers and the consumers but will also transform agriculture into planned agriculture, a planned sector of the social economy conforming to the needs of the community. They further declare that planned agriculture together with planned industry will transform the entire social economy into a planned economy which alone would make the maximum use of the natural, the technical and human labour resources of the community possible with the result that the material wealth of society would enormously increase and hence the standard of life of the people would rise higher and higher. The rural sociologist needs to devote greater attention to this aspect of the study of agricultural production. This is because not only the technique of agriculture but also the motif of agricultural production determine the level of that production and the resultant wealth of the agrarian community and, therefore, its standard of life.

Techniques of Production

The history of agriculture reveals that a variety of implements have been employed by rural communities. Generally speaking, we can divide the rural technical cultures into the following three types :

(1) *Hoe culture* : During this phase of mankind's existence, even the plough had not been invented. It was the early stage of agriculture when it was carried on only through the hoe operated by the human hand.

(2) *Plough culture* : During the next historical phase, man invented the plough. Being technically superior to the hoe, the plough enabled the agricultural community to produce more with the expenditure of the same amount of human labour power. The plough culture implied the use of animals in agricultural operations. Though our country has advanced beyond hoe culture centuries ago, the hoe still lingers in the existing phase of plough culture in some agrarian areas.

(3) *The higher technical cultural phase of tractors and fertilizers* : The invention of power-driven machinery in modern times resulted into the production of such amazing labour-saving agricultural machines as tractors and fertilizers. Though this new agricultural technique is used on a large-scale in a number of advanced countries at present, it has not yet displaced the plough to any appreciable extent in our country.

The productivity of the labour of the agriculturist and hence the volume of agricultural products have increased in proportion to the advance of agricultural technique. The extent of the material wealth of rural society, therefore, depends mainly upon the technical basis of agriculture.

It may be noted that the power basis of agriculture has also changed in history. As pointed above, the hoe excludes the use of draft animals or any kind of power. The plough is worked with the aid of draft animals. The tractor eliminates even the necessity of draft animals and is propelled by oil power.

The technique of production also determines the division of labour among the members of a society actually engaged in the production process. It gives rise to a definite number of functions in the production process. This results in the emergence of various working groups, each of them attending to a particular function in production.

Thus we have a greater division of labour where the technique employed in production is higher. Correspondingly, we have a greater number of working groups.

Where agriculture is based on the plough, the division of labour is limited. The whole process of agricultural production in various stages is carried on by a peasant family on the basis of the simple and restricted division of labour among its members. In contrast to this, where agriculture is carried on by means of tractors and fertilizers, we have not only a larger physical unit of agriculture (land) but also a greater technical division of labour. We have then such working groups as engineers, electricians, chemists, tractor drivers and others.

The rural sociologist requires to study the various working groups determined by the technique used in agriculture as a part of the study of the rural population.

Land Relations, Their Role

Next, in the course of the study of the economic life of the rural society, it is vital to understand the land or property relations within the framework of which agricultural production is carried on.

While technique strictly determines the techno-economic division of labour and the resultant number of specific working groups, it does not, as we find from our study, of history always lead to the rise of the same property relations. For instance, the plough was the technical basis of agriculture carried on within the framework of such different land relations as existing in slave and feudal societies. It has also remained the technical basis of agriculture, in modern times, in under-developed capitalist societies of countries like India, Burma, Indo-China, and others. Again we find that such advanced techniques as tractors and fertilizers are used in agriculture within the famework of such diametrically opposite types of land relations as capitalist and collectivist which exist in the U.S.A. and Soviet Union respectively.

Thus, while techno-economical relations based on functional division of labour correspond to the existing technique of agriculture, land relations or socio-economic relations of production do not always conform to the technique in the form of a single pattern. Hence even when agriculture is carried on with the same plough, we find such varied socio-economic groups as serfs and barons, zamindars and tenants, peasant proprietors, and labourers and others. And, further, when it is worked by tractors and other kinds of modern machinery, even then we observe such diverse groups as wage workers, capitalist landowners, agriculturists who are members of state-owned collective farms and others.

(1) The nature of land relations determines the share of various socio-economic groups associated with agriculture in the total agricultural wealth. For instance, in the zamindari area, the zamindar receives by far the larger share of agricultural income than the cultivating tenant. The staggering disparity between the colossal income of the former and the meagre income of the latter is basically due to the zamindari type of land relations. Further, the agrarian economy based upon a specific type of land relations has its own logic, its own law of development. Hence we find that the general tendency of the agrarian economic development in the zamindari zone is to accentuate the economic contrast. The cultivating tenant, in spite of a series of reforms, is being increasingly impoverished.

To take another instance, where full-fledged capitalist agriculture exists, a wage worker gets from the capitalist owner of land a wage determined by the state of the labour market.

Thus land relations determine the mode of distribution of the agricultural wealth among the various sections of the rural population just as technique determines the volume of that wealth.

(2) As a consequence of the above, land relations determine the degree of enthusiasm and interest of various groups bound up with

agriculture, in the process of production.

For instance, in zamindari area, the cultivating tenant has meagre incentive to work since he has to surrender a big share of the crop, the fruit of his labour, to the zamindar and his agents. This is in contrast to the peasant proprietor in the ryotwari area, who feels appreciable incentive since he retains the whole product of his labour. However, even in his case, if he feels the burden of land tax and debt too heavy, his enthusiasm for agricultural effort would decline.

(3) Land relations play a decisive role in determining the degree of homogeneity or heterogeneity of the rural population.

In the zamindari area, the rural society is mainly divided into such groups as zamindars, non-cultivating tenants and sub-tenants, and finally cultivating tenants. In the ryotwari area, there are generally peasant proprietors of various grades and landless workers. In the case of large-scale capitalist agriculture, there exist such groups as agrarian capitalists, farm managers, technicians, wage labourers and others.

(4) The nature of land relations which determines the share of material wealth of various sections engaged in agriculture thereby also determines the respective specific weight of those sections in the social, political and cultural life of rural society. The class of rich zamindars or capitalist landlords, by virture of its wealth can have leisure and material means whereby it can establish its hegemony over the life of rural society in all spheres. The mass of poor cultivating tenants or land labourers can hardly have any say in shaping it.

(5) The nature of land relations will also decide the degree of stability and social harmony in the agrarian area. For instance, in the zamindari area, due to the extensive contrast between the wealth of the zamindars and utter poverty of the cultivating tenants, there will exist a permanent condition of bitter struggle between the two classes. If poverty becomes unbearable, the struggle may even take forms which would undermine the stability of the existing rural society. In fact, contemporary India is rapidly becoming an amphitheatre of such struggles.

If we survey the past and the present history, we find that the rural society has been the arena of numerous struggles which had their genetic cause in the existing land relations. During the French Revolution the serfs wanted to abolish feudal land relations and become free peasant proprietors. The success of the communists in China is also largely explained by their skilful solution of the land problem.

The question of land relations has become the crucial question in all backward countries of the world to-day.

Thus the degree of stability or instability of the rural society is largely determined by the nature of extant land relations.

(6) Wealth is the material means to get access to education and culture specially in modern commodity society. Land relations, by basically determining the share of various agrarian social groups in the total agricultural wealth, therefore, also decide how much scope each of

these groups will have for education and culture. Land relations, thus, play a big role in determining the degree of the intellectual and cultural development of various strata of the rural people and their individual members since this development largely depends upon the education they have received and the culture they have assimilated.

The points mentioned above reveal and emphasize the great significance of land relations in moulding the economic and hence the social, the political, the intellectual, and the cultural life of the rural people.

Standard of Life

The standard of life of a village community and its sections will indicate the amount of wealth at its disposal and the manner in which it is distributed among those sections. The volume of wealth of the rural community depends primarily on agriculture, and in final analysis, on the technique used in agriculture since the higher is the technique, the greater is the productivity of agriculture. Land relations determine, as we saw above, the share of various groups comprising rural society in the total agrarian wealth. Yet even where they engender sharp contrasts of wealth among these groups, the absolute share of even the lowest group will be at a high level if the total wealth of the rural aggregate, due to advanced technique of agricultural production, is considerable. For instance, in the U.S.A. where agriculture is mechanised and, therefore, creates great agrarian wealth, in spite of the fact that agrarian capitalists make millions, the income of the wage workers on land is on a much higher level than that of the agriculturist in India.

The problem of the standard of life of the rural population has been keenly studied by eminent sociologists like Sorokin, Zimmerman, Sims, Kirpatrick and others. The criteria and methods laid down by them for such a study can serve as a useful guide to the students of rural society in India.

It is observed by these scholars that the standard of life of the rural people on an average is lower than that of the urban people. This is because the income of the rural people on the average is lower than that of the urban people. "Further, the standards of living of the rural population and its various groups (owners, tenants, croppers and labourers) are more homogeneous than those of the urban classes."

It has also been noted that the standard of life of the farmers approximates more to that of the lower strata of the city population.

Though income is the primary factor determining the standard of life of a social aggregate, there are other factors also which influence it. "To be sure, income may be chiefly responsible for the existence of classes; but wholly apart from material possessions, there are class norms and values dictated by tradition." For instance, in India, the Middle class strives to adopt a standard of life according to its own specific conception of life. This is reflected in their choice of food, dress, recreations, cultural amenities and other things. Their standard of life is thus determined not merely by their economic position but also by their specific group outlook, temperament and taste. The role of caste in India as a determinant of the group standard of living demands special study.

It has been further observed that the degree of civilization existing in a society also influences the standard of life of the people. For instance, such institutions as well-furnished libraries, cultural and sport clubs, radio, telephone, cinema and theatre, swimming pools, restaurants and others, do not generally exist in the rural zone of India. Hence the standard of life of the rural people is not affected by them unlike that of the urban people.

However, due to the interaction of the rural and urban societies and the resultant growth of mutual contacts, the rural people are slowly but inevitably influenced by the urban. They begin to develop a predilection and craving for such amenities. They also tend to adopt the food and dress habits of the urban population. Bicycles, modern footwear, games like cricket and football, schools, libraries, cinema, and other things associated with urban life, begin to penetrate the village. This results in gradually modifying the mode of life of the rural people.

In his study of the economic life of the rural people, the rural sociologist needs to study the impact of the more powerful influences of urban life on the rural society and hence on the standard of life of the rural people. Further, he should not take a static view of their standard of life. Human needs are not an immutable entity. They grow from phase to phase.

Rural Poverty, A Crying Problem

A very big section of the rural population has been living in varying states of poverty in all countries. Even in the U.S.A., the most prosperous country of the world to-day, the poverty of a large stratum of rural society has become a crying problem. As Sims remarks, "Although students of rural conditions have long been aware of the existence of country slums and of disadvantaged or submerged classes, such as the share croppers of the south (U.S.A.) no one fully realised how precarious the lot of a large part of the country population was and how quickly millions could be plunged into a state of destitution until the industrial depression revealed the true situation," and further, "all in all, it is estimated that more than one-third of the rural families of the nation have suffered poverty."

When, as seen above, a large section of the rural population of even such an economically advanced country like the U.S.A. suffers from poverty, it is no wonder that chronic poverty is rampant among the agrarian population in India, an economically much less developed country.

The immense poverty of the Indian agriculturist is proverbial and presents the fundamental problem of the programme of national economic reconstruction.

The principal causes of the rural poverty in India have been, in general, laid bare by eminent Indian economists and sociologists. Primitive agricultural technique, insufficient irrigation system, land fragmentation, uneconomic holdings, overpressure on agriculture, alarming rural indebtedness and, above all, the existing land relations are some of its principal causes.

It is necessary to study the problem of poverty not merely of the rural people as a whole but also of its different strata and, that too, in detail.

Poverty adversely affects not only the health and vitality of the rural people but also explains their backward social and cultural conditions. If the rural people are ignorant, superstitious, uncultured, it is mostly because they are abysmally poor and cannot afford to pay for education. They, thereby, remain excluded from any access to scientific knowledge of the natural and social worlds imparted by educational and cultural institutions.

Economic prosperity is the basic pre-requisite for a flourishing social and cultural life. Hence the problem of rural reconstruction at a high social and cultural level is organically bound up with the problem of the eradication of rural poverty.

CHAPTER VIII

RURAL FAMILY

Rural Family, Its Signal Importance

Among the institutions that compose rural society, the family is the most important. It has been its very foundation. It plays a decisive role in the material and cultural life of the rural aggregate and in moulding the psychological characteristics of the rural individual as well as the rural collectivity. In fact, according to some thinkers, family and familism impress their stamp on the entire rural structure. Familism permeates it from top to bottom.

A systematic study of rural family, of its structure, functions, evolution, and interrelations with other institutions of the rural society is vitally necessary for the rural sociologist.

The Indian rural society provides a classic field for the study of the institution of rural family. Within it are found many types and patterns of family organization which humanity has hitherto evolved.

Four Main Patterns of Family Organization

Prof. Rivers has distinguished four types of institutions which have been designated by the term family, *viz.*, the clan, the matrilocal joint family, the patrilocal joint family and the individual family composed of only parents and minor children.

According to one group of sociologists, these four types reveal four main stages of the evolution of the family form corresponding to four stages in the evolution of society. The first type corresponds to the hunting and food gathering stage of social evolution; the second to the phase of hoe agriculture and the beginnings of domestication of animals; the third—a classic type—to the phase of agricultural economy based on the plough and domestication of animals, and, finally, the fourth type to the modern industrial capitalist phase of human existence. As a result of the growth of market economy in the agrarian area and of the impact of urban socio-economic forces on the rural society, the last type is increasingly becoming predominant today.

The Indian rural society provides a great laboratory to test this view, since it includes within its fold the relics of the clan as well as matrilocal and patrilocal family types and the recent individual family group also. A methodical study of the structure and functions of these various family types and their correlation with the stages of civilization to which they correspond will throw a floodlight on the history of Indian humanity and will enable Indian historians to evolve a correct sequence of the developmental phases of the Indian society.

Patriarchial Joint Family, Its Characteristics

In almost all fully developed agrarian societies depending on plough agriculture, patriarchial joint family has been found to be the predominant family form in rural areas. Outstanding rural sociologists have made a close study of the characteristics of this type of family. They have observed the basic structural, psycho-social, and functional features of this type of the rural family which distinguish it sharply from the urban family. They are as under :

(1) *Greater Homogeneity* : The rural family is far more homogeneous, stable, integrated and organically functioning than the urban family. The ties binding the members of the former, for instance the husband and the wife, parents and children, are stronger and last longer than those in the case of the urban family.

A glance at the Indian countryside will corroborate this view. The Indian village still remains a cluster of joint families though, due to a number of historico-economic causes, the joint family has been exhibiting a tendency of slow but steady disintegration.

The rural family is composed not only of the members of the family but also frequently includes distant relations which hardly happens in the dovecotes of the urban society.

(2) *Based on Peasant Household* : Another essential characteristic of the rural family is that it is generally based on the peasant household. All its members are engaged in the agricultural occupation. Work is distributed among them mainly on lines of age and sex distinctions. " The Community house, common land and common economic functions along with the common kinship bond create the peasant household."

Since the members of the rural family form a single economic unit and constantly co-operate with one another in agricultural operations, since they hold property in common usually managed by the eldest member of the family, since also they spend most of their time together, the psychological traits they develop are very similar.

(3) *Greater Discipline and Interdependence*: The rural family is characterised by greater discipline among its members than the urban family. Further, since there is considerably less state or public provision for meeting the educational, cultural, or social needs of the people in the rural area than in the urban, the rural family attempts also to satisfy these needs of its members. It thus serves as a school, a recreation centre, as well as a maternity or a non-maternity hospital.

(4) *Dominance of Family Ego*: The interdependence of the members of the rural family and the dependence of its individual member on it are, therefore, far greater than in the case of the urban family. This

welds its members into a homogeneous, compact, egoistic unit, strengthens emotions of solidarity and co-operation among them and fills them with family pride. They develop more collectivist family consciousness and less individualistic emotion.

In a rural society, a family is discredited if any of its individual members perpetrates an infamous act. Similarly the glory of his or her achievement also accrues to the family from which he or she springs.

The urban family in contrast to the rural family, is less authoritarian of the family even at the cost of their lives.

(5) *Authority of the Father*: Since the rural family is a more integrated and disciplined unit than the urban family, the head of the rural family exercises almost absolute power over its members. It is he who distributes the work of the peasant household among the family members on lines of sex and age differences; arranges marriages of sons, daughters, nephews and nieces; administers the joint family property according to his wisdom; and trains the youngsters for future agricultural work and social life. All initiative and final authority are vested in him. In fact " the head of the family has had the rights and authority to be the ruler, the priest, the teacher, the educator and the manager of the family. "

Thus, the family, through its head, subordinates its individual members to itself. The latter are completely submerged in the family; hence they hardly develop any individuality or personality.

Such a family type can only be a nursery for the growth of family collectivism but not of individuality.

The urban family in contrast to the rural family, is less authoritarian but also less co-operative. This is due to a variety of reasons. First, it is not a single productive unit administered by the family head since its adult members are mostly engaged in occupations unconnected with, and outside the home. Further, educational, recreational and a number of other needs of its members are satisfied by extra-family institutions like school, club, and others. Property of its earning members, too, tends to be individual, since it is derived out of extra-family occupations. In the sphere of marriage also, its members are increasingly exhibiting indepedence and marry persons of their own choice.

(6) *Closer Participation in Various Activities*:—One striking feature of the rural family lies in the fact that its members, being engaged in work connected with the peasant household, spend practically the whole day together. In contrast to this, the members of the urban family engaged in different occupations or being educated outside home, spend only a small portion of the day together. Even their recreational centres such as clubs and others lie outside the home. Hence the home becomes only a temporary nightshed for the members of the urban family.

Impact of Urbanisation on Rural Family

Rural society has been increasingly urbanised in modern times. In proportion to its urbanization it exhibits the characteristics of urban society. The rural family more and more develops centrifugal tendencies. Its economic homogeneity based upon a single cumulative economic activity of its members declines. Joint family property tends to be disrupted since its individual adult members begin to demand its partitioning. Being increasingly engaged in different occupations, they earn independent separate incomes which they retain as their own. They live less and less together and spend only a fraction of the day in association. They begin to seek extra-familial centres like clubs, hotels, unions, associations, cafeteria, which are also slowly growing in and around rural areas. All this results in the growth of individualistic psychology among them which weakens family emotion and egoism so vital for the vigorous functioning of a homogeneous family.

The individual hitherto submerged in, and subordinated to, the family tends to become atomistic. He more and more breaks away from the family restrictions. He develops his own initiative and independence. This inevitably results in the weakening of the family authority, family ties, and the family itself.

Familism, Gestalt of Rural Society

According to the views of such eminent sociologists as Sorokin, Zimmerman and others, the social and political organization of all agrarian societies during their subsistence stages bears the fundamental traits of rural family, the basic unit of rural society. These traits they characterise as familism.

"Since the family has been the basic social institution of the rural social world, it is natural to expect that the whole social organization of agricultural aggregates has been stamped by the characteristics of the rural family. In other words all the other social institutions and fundamental social relationships have been permeated by, and modelled according to, the patterns of rural family relationships. Familism is the term used to designate this type of social organization......Familism is the outstanding and fundamental trait in the gestalt of such a society."[1]

These sociologists enumerate a number of important characteristics of such societies bearing the stamp of familism. They are as under :

(1) *Marriage Earlier and its Higher Rate*: The members of these rural societies marry at an earlier age than those of urban societies. Further, the rate of marriage in the former is higher than that in the latter.

(2) *Family, unit of Social Responsibility*: Since family is the unit of rural society, it is the family collective that pays the taxes and discharges social responsibilities. The individual is also appraised according to the status of the family to which he or she belongs.

(3) *Family, Basis of Norms of Society*: Further, ethical codes, religious doctrines, social conceptions and legal norms governing rural societies have always condemned anything which would weaken the

---

[1]Systematic Sourcebook in Rural Sociology, Vol. II, p. 41.

stability of the family. They have preached implicit obedience to parents on the part of sons and daughters and to husband on the part of wife.

(4) *Family, Its Impress in Political Form*: The political organizations of those rural societies have been also based on the conception on which rural family rests. Their political ideology has conceived the relation between the ruler and the ruled as that between the head of the family and its members, i.e., paternalistic. "King, monarch, ruler, lord have been viewed as an enlarged type of family patriarch.........the predominant type of political organization in the rural community is represented by the institution of the village elder, the head, elected by the peasants as the family elder is either openly or tacitly elected by the family members. The whole character of the village chief's authority and administration is a mere replica of the paterfamilia's authority and administration."[2]

(5) *Co-operative rather than Contractual Relations*: The relations between the members of the rural society are basically co-operative in contrast to those between the members of the urban society which are preponderatingly contractual. This difference, according to the view of the outstanding sociologists, is the result of the difference between the rural and urban families. "In a rural family the solidarity of its members is organic and spontaneous.........It springs up of itself—Naturally as a result of close co-living, co-working, co-acting, co-feeling and co-believing. Any contractual relationship between its members would be out of place and contradictory to the whole tone of family.........it is no surprising, then, that purely contractual relationships have been but little developed in familistic societies."[3] The members of the urban family on the other hand have separate interests as well as individualistic psychologies. They have more or less lost collective family feeling. The urban society bears this characteristic of the urban family. Spontaneous co-operation and solidarity-feeling are found to be appreciably less among the urban people than among the rural people.

(6) *Family, Unit of Production, Consumption and Exchange* : The economic structure of the rural society also bears the traits of the rural family. It is based on family ownership. The production and consumption are familistic. The market is less developed. Exchange has more the characteristics of simple barter than of full-fledged monetary transactions. The entire code of laws regulating the economic relationships within such a society bears the stamp of familism. In contrast to this, the urban economy is predominantly a commodity economy and therefore the economic and hence the general social relations between the members of the urban society are competitive and contractual.

(7) *Dominance of Family Cult and Ancestor worship* : The idelogy and the culture of rural society also exhibit traits of familism. The cult of family dominates. Religious and other ceremonies have for their

---

[2]*Ibid.*, p. 46.

[3]*Ibid.*, p. 46.

object the security and property of the family. Ancestor worship is almost universally prevalent. Even the relationships between its gods and goddesses are familistic, they being related to one another as father, mother, brother, sister, etc.

(8) *Dominance of Tradition*: As a result of all these factors rural society is marked with much less mobility than urban society. Tradition severely governs its life processes. It undergoes change with extreme slowness.

Rural Family in India, Its Trends

To sum up, until the impact of the Industrial Revolution and the competitive market economy, familism was the heart of village communities. Subsistence agrarian economies and rural societies based on them were familistic through and through. However, the rise and development of modern industries sreadily undermined subsistence agrarian economy and brought the rural economy within the orbit of capitalist market economy. This transformation together with the growing pressure of various urban forces brought about the increasing disintegration of the old rural family. The rural society, too, more and more lost its familistic traits.

In India, due to lack of sufficient industrial development, the forces of urban society have not penetrated rural society to the same extent as in the U.S.A., Great Britain and other industrially advanced countries. The rural family consequently retains its specific traits to a far greater extent in India. Urban industrial development affects the rural family in many ways. It creates new occupations such as those of factory and workshop workers, of clerks, typists, and others. The members of the rural family develop a desire to take to those occupations, demand their share in the joint family property and migrate to towns and cities. This process undermines the joint family based on a common occupation of its members and joint family property, income and expenditure.

Modern industries produce a number of articles cheaply and on a mass scale. They reach out to the village population who purchase them. Thus the peasant family which was formerly producing cloth and other necessities with primitive techniques more and more ceases to produce them now. Thus it loses a number of its economic functions with the result that the scope of the collective labour of its members narrows down.

Capitalist economic development transforms the social and political environments of a people also. In India, British capitalism transformed the socio-economic structure of the Indian society and, further, established a centralized State. This resulted in a number of consequences. Private and State agencies increasingly established schools, dispensaries and administrative and judicial machinery in the village. The rural family which served as the school for its members no longer functioned as such, since its members now began to receive education outside the family. Also not the grandfather or the grandmother, the embodiment of traditional medical knowledge, but the doctor appointed by an agency unconnected with family, now increasingly treated the members of the family. Caste and panchayat councils were deprived of their functions as guardians of law and dispensers of justice. The customary law was replaced by the new law of the centralized state which operated through its administrative and judicial organs. The process progressed in proportion as the urbanization of the country advanced.

The historical tendency of the rural family is towards its increasing disintegration and loss of functions. The more this tendency grows, the more the family ego and solidarity feeling cradled in and nourished by the collective labour and life of its members weaken and atomistic individualistic psychological traits develop among them.

During the last hundred and fifty years, the traditional joint family and the familistic rural framework have been undergoing a qualitative transformation. The basis of rural family relationships is shifting from that of status to that of contract. The rule of custom is being replaced by the rule of law. The family is being transformed from a unit of production to a unit of consumption. The cementing bond of the family is being changed from consanguinity to conjugality. Further, the family is ceasing to become an omnibus social agency, it being shorn of most of its economic, political, educational, medical, religious and other social and cultural functions. Instead, it is becoming a specialized and affectional small association. From a massive joint family composed of members belonging to a number of generations, the family is increasingly shaping as a tiny unit composed of husband, wife and unmarried children. Familism, too, is gradually dropping off. The rural society is acquiring quite a new *gestalt*.

A systematic study of the rural family from many angles has never been so necessary as at present in India. Its methodical, intensive and extensive study will provide proper direction for evolving a programme of appropriate measures to realise grand objectives that are embodied in the Constitution of the Indian Union. Rural sociologists in India require to launch a very comprehensive campaign of study to locate the laws of the transformation of one of the most classic familistic civilizations that has emerged in the history of humanity.

CHAPTER IX

CASTE SYSTEM IN RURAL INDIA

CASTE SYSTEM, ITS UNIQUE SIGNIFICANCE

A VERY peculiar type of social grouping which is found in India is the caste grouping. A student of the Indian society, who fails to closely and carefully study this variety of social grouping, will miss the very essence of that society. In India, caste largely determines the function, the status, the available opportunities as well as the handicaps for an individual. Caste differences even determine the differences in modes of domestic and social life, types of houses and cultural patterns of the people which are found in the rural area. Even land ownership exists frequently on caste lines. Due to a number of reasons, administrative functions have also been often divided according to castes, especially in the rural area. Caste has, further, determined the pattern of the complicated religious and secular culture of the people. It has fixed the psychology of the various social groups and has evolved such minutely graded levels of social distance and superior-inferior relationships that the social structure looks like a gigantic hierarchic pyramid with a mass of untouchables as its base and a small stratum of elite, the Brahmins, almost equally unapproachable, at its apex. The Hindu society is composed of hundreds of distinct self-contained caste worlds piled one over the other.

The increasing spread of the modern means of communication, the introduction of the British system of administration and laws, and the growth of modern capitalist competitive economy which shattered the subsistence economy of the self-sufficient village community, undermined more and more the functional basis of caste. However, the transformation of self-contained rigid castes into modern mobile classes has taken place in a peculiar manner. Certain castes have been monopolising the position of the privileged upper classes of modern society. Certain castes have been loosing previous status and functions and slowly submerging into the lowest class groups of modern society. This development has created a peculiar social structure in modern India with the result that, within the existing Indian society, class struggles have been often assuming the form of caste-struggles. The student of rural society is here confronted with one of the most complex types of social transformation in the socio-economic as well as in the ideological spheres. The caste system composed of caste groups in a state of increasing decay and undergoing a transformation into modern classes in a confused way and offering stubborn resistence to it, presents the epic spectacle of a social Cyclopes writhing in violent death agonies.

Caste Matrix, Essential for Sociological Study in India

One of the most urgent tasks before the student of rural society in India is to evolve an approach which will be able to appraise the social and cultural processes of that society within the matrix of caste structure.

Failure to develop such a perspective has, in spite of an immense accumulation of economic and other factual data, obstructed the elaboration of a living composite picture of rural society. The rural sociologist should concentrate on the following vital problems:

Caste and Economic Life

The economic life of rural society should be studied in context of caste, in its interrelation and interaction with caste.

(1) *Production*: In the field of production the rural sociologist should study the extent to which functional and propertied groups correspond to castes.

Such a study, for instance, as that of Bhuvel has revealed how far the new economic and political forces have undermined the homogeneous functional basis of old castes and also the distribution of property among them. It will thereby disclose the degree of distintegration and alteration of the status, privileges, and social and political significance of various castes. Secondly, it will enable us to comprehend the attitude of the Hindu as well as the Indian Mahomedans too, who are affected by the caste phenomena, towards the hierarchically graded caste structure of society as well as their reaction to the process of change which it is experiencing.

Such a study, for instance, as that of Bhuvel has revealed how in some parts of the Central Gujarat, the Rajputs who owned land are declining in their social and economic status being increasingly supplanted by the Patidars.

(2) *Consumption*: In the field of consumption the rural sociologist requires to study how castes greatly mould the pattern of consumption of respective caste groups. For instance, caste appreciably fixes the food and dress habits or the choice of utensils and other articles of its members. This caste-determined mode of consumption reacts on and influences production. The pure economic theory of consumption would be misleading and result into incorrect conclusions unless its modification due to the intervention of the caste institution is taken into account.

(3) *Indebtedness* : The rural indebtedness, a striking feature of rural economic life, also requires to be studied in context of caste. Dr. R. K. Nehru has vividly pointed out in his exploratory study of a few villages what close relation exists between caste and indebtedness and credit in the rural area. Certain castes are predominantly composed of members who are almost hereditary debtors; some others of those who are mainly

creditors. The rural sociologist should study the social and economic millieu and find out why it is so.

(4) *Habitat* : Caste also largely determines the type of houses its members reside in, their housing habits and the choice of village area where these houses are located. The village is generally divided into areas, each inhabited by the members of a particular caste. Further, even when some members of a caste cease to pursue the caste-determined vocation, they generally continue to reside in the same area and socially interact with other members of their caste.

(5) *Mobility* : Another significant problem which requires to be studied is the co-relation between caste and economic mobility of the rural people. As a result of the operation of the forces of economic evolution of Indian society, a slow but steady and constant inter-change of functions among various castes has been taking place. Members of a caste gradually cease to perform the caste-determined function and take to occupations which other caste groups are engaged in. Further, for the same reason some castes slide down the economic ladder while some castes go up the ladder. Since these changes have an effect on the development of the rural economy and its nature, their specific study is necessary.

Caste and Joint Family Life

The study of the rural society should include the study of how caste and joint family—its two dominant social institutions—influence the social life of the rural individual and the rural aggregate. They are powerful forces determining their social activities and thereby play a big role in moulding their psychology and ideology. As observed eleswhere, a caste in the rural area is generally a cluster of joint families. Hence, the caste moulds the nature of the lif e of those families.

Caste and Educational Life

Caste also largely determines the attitude of the rural man towards education and even fixes the nature of the education which he intends to receive. A Brahmin child will, due to caste tradition generally receive education and that too predominantly religious in contrast to the Bania child who will be given secular education and the child of a depressed class who would forego all education. Further, it must be noted that education is not evaluated from the standpoint of individual development or social advance but from that of the caste tradition.

Caste and Religious Life

How religious life is determined rigorously by caste, especially in the rural area, also deserves to be studied. While in cities religious practices are slowly shrinking, in villages they flourish luxuriantly even now. It is the caste that rigidly determines the place of its member in the religious life of the people.

CASTE AND POLITICAL LIFE

Caste influences the political life to a greater extent in the rural area than in the urban centres. This is because caste consciousness is stronger among the rural people than among the urban people. Choice or rejection of candidates as well as the nature of propaganda in political elections are determined by caste considerations more in villages than in towns and cities. Caste ego is stronger among the rural people and hence exerts a powerful influence in shaping the political life of the rural aggregate. In contrast to this, extra-caste considerations considerably influence political prejudices and predilections of the urban population.

CASTE AND VALUE SYSTEMS OF THE COMMUNITY

Since caste largely determines the ideals and patterns of life of the rural social groups, it also considerably shapes the value systems prevailing in the rural society. The value patterns of the rural society bear a far greater impress of caste traditions than those of the urban society where extra-caste institutions and ideologies operate.

CASTE AND TYPES OF RURAL LEADERSHIP

Caste plays a big role in determining the nature and the personnel of the leadership of the rural society. Caste leaders are generally leaders also of the social, economic, political and ideological life of the rural society. As a consequence of this, caste struggles are often co-eval with social, political, economic and ideological struggles in the rural zone.

The study of the role of caste in the life of the Indian rural aggregate in all its spheres is thus vitally necessary for getting a correct picture of the Indian rural society and its life processes.

MUTUAL ATTITUDES OF CASTE GROUPS, THEIR SIGNIFICANCE

It is further necessary to study the actual functioning of the caste and the subjective reactions of its members to that functioning. A proper study of such subjective reactions of different caste groups to the almost all-pervasive functioning of caste will enable the rural sociologist to comprehend that fundamental social phenomenon called social distance in the Indian rural society. It will explain the emergence and development of various grades of social superiority and inferiority complexes rampant among the rural people. It will also disclose how those subjective reactions of various groups crystallize as different group psychologies which express themselves in various cultural patterns.

CASTE SYSTEM, A LABORATORY TO STUDY SOCIAL DISTANCE

The study will also enable him to comprehend what type of consciousness arises out of a social life mainly moving within the caste matrix. It will also aid the rural sociologist in his indispensable study of those socio-historic forces, which, across centuries, brought into existence the most complex and elaborate, the most systematised and logically worked out structure of orgnised and minutely graded group inequality, *viz.*, the caste system in India.

The New Constitution and Its Impact on Caste

The problem has acquired a special significance for the contemporary Indian people for a number of reasons. First, the Constitution of the Indian Union has assumed as its postulate the individual citizen and not caste as the unit of Indian society. Secondly, it has laid down equality of citizens and not hierarchically graded privileges based on the caste as the principle of State legislation. It has chosen as its objective a democratic social order free from inequality and special privileges. Finally, the existing socio-economic structure is also based on the principle of contract between free and equal individuals and not on caste privilege. Individual contract and not caste status is the basis of all rights and responsibilities today.

Caste and Hinduism

This shift from the caste to the individual as the unit of society has brought about convulsive changes in Indian society transforming old social relations. It has been dealing shattering blows to the orthodoxy of Hinduism and the caste social order of the Hindus. The socio-psychological patterns, the religio-ethical norms and even the philosophical outlook of the Hindus determined by the old Hinduism are being increasingly undermined as the process of the transformation of the social relations advances. A democratic conception of social relations in all fields, social, legal, political, economic and cultural, is progressively replacing the former hierarchic conception of those relations. A study of the caste and of the process of its steady dissolution today will, further, inevitably make it necessary for the rural sociologist to study the historical genesis of caste and also of the Hindu religion and the Hindu culture which are closely bound up with it. It will also show whether Hinduism can survive as an ideology without the existence of caste, the social institutional expression and concretization of Hinduism.

A research in the subject of the origin of caste will also require a study of (i) past economic evolution of Indian society which at a certain stage made caste historically inevitable, (ii) its subsequent role as a formidable obstacle to further economic and cultural development of Indian society and (iii) contemporary forces which are steadily undermining caste and therefore also probably weakening Hinduism as an ideology and a culture.

Joint Family, Caste, and Village Community, Their Interrelationship

Joint family, caste and village community were the basic social institutions of the pre-British Indian rural society. It is the task of the rural sociologist to study the relations between them.

The process of dissolution of those institutions, however slow, commenced, as previously stated, with the impact of British contact after the conquest of India. It must be noted that the autarchic village had been the socio-economic unit of Indian society during the period of agrarian civilization based on a subsistence economy which intervened between the food gathering phase of social existence and the modern phase of competitive nation-scale capitalistic civil society founded on national economy and mobile classes. One unique feature of social evolution in India was that primitive food gathering tribal society was not historically succeeded by a society based on a slave mode of production as in Greece and Rome or by a society based on a feudal mode of production with serf labour which developed in the Western Europe during the Middle Ages. Slavery or serfdom was never the basis of social production in the long history of Indian society though the phenomenon of slavery might have crept in here and there. Due to complex ecological and socio-historical reasons, primitive collective tribal society seems to have been superseded in India by a unique type of society which persisted for a remarkably long period. It began to disintegrate only after the contact with the capitalist West in modern times.

Extensive historical research dealing with the most remote periods of past history of the Indian people together with the utmost exercise of the power of historical inference guided by a scientific theory of social development, are needed to trace the causes of the genesis of village communities in India. It is necessary to locate the peculiar ecological and socio-historical factors which brought about the emergence of a unique type of social structure based on those autarchic and collectively land-possessing village communities in India. Thereafter, it is necessary to probe into the problem whether caste arose as a socio-economic institution adapted to the exigencies of such a social formation.

Doctrine of Casteism and Brahminic Supremacy

The next problem which the rural sociologist should investigate is whether the doctrine of immutable casteism propagated by the Brahmins was the inevitable theoretical outgrowth of a society which remained unaltered and stationary for a remarkably long period as a result of unchanging technique and resultant unvarying division of labour. Was it because caste persisted for ages and subsequently became rigid and ossified, that an illusion was generated in the consciousness of the Hindu humanity that it was immutable ?

It is also vital to comprehend why the Brahmin caste exercised ideological and social dictatorship over the Hindu people for centuries with rare episodic interruptions like the challenge of Buddhism and a few others. Was it because the Hindu people living in such a stationary society as mentioned above developed an organic predisposition to docilely accept and submit to authority and tradition ? Was it, therefore, that they surrendered themselves to the social and ideological sway of the Brahmins who were not only the architect of authoritarian social and religious philosophies but were also the repository and monopolist of whatever scientific knowledge, astronomical, agronomical, medical and other, which existed in the past ? Even regarding the uncanny forces of nature, they were the Brahmins who alone were supposed to have the religio-magical power of propitiating and mastering them through rites, incantations and other devices.

Study of Origins of Caste, Its Vital Significance

Numerous theories have been advanced to explain the origin, development, crystallization and ultimate petrifaction of the caste system. Most of them have been offered in the spirit of surmises only. The rest, though they have illuminated the problem, have given partial solution of it. A consciously planned out, systematic and still deeper study of the problem of caste, historically and in its complex interconnections with other social developments, has still to be made.

To unravel this problem it is necessary to study the ecological conditions of India in the past, which resulted in the peculiar economic development of Indian society and gave rise to the peculiar type of social formation as the village community. This may provide a valuable clue to the solution of the problem of the origin of caste. Then alone the significance of caste which has played such a powerful role in past Indian society and which is still playing considerable role in the life of the Indian people in general and the Indian rural people in particular can be fully grasped.

CHAPTER X

POLITICAL LIFE OF THE RURAL PEOPLE

POLITICAL ASPECT OF RURAL LIFE, INSUFFICIENTLY STUDIED

ONE OF the vital problems which requires to be intelligently studied by the rural sociologist is the political life of the rural people. Writers on rural problems as well as social workers in the rural area have generally paid insufficient attention to this aspect of the rural life. They have often presumed that the agrarian population is politically almost an inert mass and have attempted to evolve and work out schemes of better villages on that premise. However, nothing is more unreal in modern times than the hypothesis of the political inertness of the rural people. When we study modern history, we find that the agrarian masses, predominantly composed of farmers, have participated in mighty political movement in a number of countries. For instance, in India, large sections of peasants and artisans supported and joined the great National Revolt of the Indian people against the British rule in 1857. Subsequently peasant struggles like the Deccan Peasant Riots and others directed both against the money-lenders and the government broke out in some parts of the country. In more recent times, increasing sections of the peasantry participated in a series of national political movements like the Non-co-operation Movement of 1919-24, Civil Disobedience Movement of 1930-34, a number of political satyagraha campaigns in different districts, Quit India Movement and others. After 1934 the peasant masses even started building their own class organizations like kisan sabhas and launched a number of struggles against the government and landlords. During and immediately after the partition of India, the peasant discontent and restlessness found a distorted political expression in bloody communal clashes which occurred in a number of provinces.

Recent history also records such peasant struggles as took place in Telangana and in portions of Bengal and Assam.

In other countries, too, the agrarian masses have taken part, sometimes even decisive, in political movements. Tens of millions of peasants participated in such world shaking revolutions as the Russian and the Chinese. Large sections of Indonesian and Burmese peasantry also took part in a series of political struggles having national independence as their objective. Peasant masses constituted the preponderant social force of the resistance movements in France, Yugoslavia, Poland, Hungary and other European countries which developed during the period of occupation of those countries by Nazi Germany. Also in recent decades the agricultural populations of Spain, Italy, Latin American countries and others have exhibited considerable political awakening, formed sometimes their own political parties and have launched numerous political struggles.

These events explode the misconception that agrarian population is politically a passive force.

In fact, the growth of political consciousness among peasant populations and their increasing political activity are striking features of the political life of mankind to-day.

The agrarian areas of a number of countries have been transformed into storm centres of militant political activity of the rural people.

Its Study in India, a Vital Need

The following are the two main reasons why it becomes imperative for the rural sociologist in India to study the political life of the rural people to-day.

(1) The Constitution of the now independent India has provided universal adult suffrage to the Indian people. Tens of millions of peasants who constitute the majority of the population thereby acquire a political status. Their will expressed through the ballot box would now considerably influence the political life of the nation. This is a unique event in the long history of the Indian humanity, for, it is for the first time that the people including the rural masses have secured the democratic right to determine who will rule them. The theory of the divine right of the king or a "providence ordained" imperialist power to rule the people has been ousted by that of the democratic right of the sovereign people to determine their political destiny. Universal adult suffrage serves as a powerful ferment in the life of the rural people making them politically conscious to a phenomenal degree. It is a momentous event in the history of the rural society.

The new situation has posed a number of fresh questions for the rural sociologist. How will the rural people, illiterate, ignorant and superstitious in the main, exercise their franchise ? What social, economic, and ideological influences will determine their voting ? What types of political organisations will the peasant masses throw up for implementing a programme embodying their conception of a good society by legislative means ? What political parties will emerge in the rural area, corresponding to various layers of the existing stratified rural society? What repercussions will take place in the sphere of social and ideological life of the rural people due to the mass-scale growth of political consciousness and activity among them due to their acquisition of adult suffrage ? How will this political equality affect caste and other social as well as cultural and economic inequalities ?

The study of these new problems will form an integral part of the study of the Indian rural society.

(2) A proper understanding of the political life of the rural people is necessary also for another reason. Unlike in the pre–British period, the modern state plays a decisive role in determining the life of the rural society. During the pre-British phase, the village, as we have seen previously, was an autarchic and almost autonomous unit. During the British period, it experienced a basic transformation. Its self-contained subsistence economy based on self-sufficient agriculture and artisan industry was undermined

Further, the British Government established a centralized State with an administrative machinery which penetrated the hitherto autonomous village. This basically changed the political physiognomy of the village. It became a unit of the countrywide political and administrative system.

The consequences of this economic and political transformation were far-reaching. The village population no longer lived an almost hermetically sealed existence but was drawn into the wider whirlpool of the national and international economic and political life. Thenceforward the economic, political, and other problems of the rural community had to be considered in the wider context of national and world politics and economy as well as of the policies of the Central Government.

Three Main Lines of Study

A systematic study of the rural political life may be made on the following lines :

(a) The study of the governmental machinery in the rural area.

(b) The study of the non-governmental political organizations in the rural area.

(c) The study of the political behaviour of the rural people and its various sections.

A few observations on each of these are made below :

(a) Governmental Machinery

The study of the governmental machinery can be divided into two parts: (i) the study of the structure of the administration and its functioning within the village and (ii) the study of the administrative machinery of larger units like Talukas. Districts, Regions and States.

In the pre-British period, when the state did not interfere in the life of the village beyond claiming a portion of the village produce as land revenue and occasionally levying troops, the village administration was carried on by the village panchayat composed of elected or customary representatives of various castes, generally elders of the castes, or by village headman with the panchayat as the consultative body. The village panchayat was the link between the village population and the higher authority. The panchayat and the headman maintained peace in the village, settled disputes among the villagers, looked after the sanitation and other matters of common concern of the village population, determined and collected the share of the farmer family in the collective land-revenue to be paid to the State on behalf of the village, and also regulated the use of collectively owned pasture land and forest area in the periphery. Thus from the standpoint of administration the village was autonomous.

The administrative, judicial, policing, and economic functions of the village were, as seen above, performed by the village panchayat and the headman. So far as the personal, social and religious life of the village people was concerned, the customary law governing it was operated by various caste councils which regulated the behaviour-patterns of respective castes.

The disintegration of empires did not affect the administrative autonomy and general internal life of the village. This was because the State, even the Imperial State, restricted its intervention in the internal affairs of the village to the mere gathering of the tribute and the levying of the troops generally in war time. The State or the king looked after the inter-village administration and other vital matters affecting the people of the kingdom as a whole such as coinage, irrigation, and the maintenance and development of the network of roads.

With the advent of the British rule in India, as we have stated before, the Indian society began to experience a fundamental economic and political transformation. The new administrative machinery evolved and organized by Britain in India supplanted the old one which had functioned for centuries with little variation. The new state, the organ of British rule in India, stationed its own revenue, judicial, police and other officials in the village. The village lost its administrative autonomy and the caste councils, their penal powers. In the new political set up, the village became the basic administrative unit of a hierarchically graded country-wide administrative system.

The local village officials were independent of any control over them by the village population. Thus if the forest had to be cleared, wells to be dug or roads to be built in the village, it was not now the village panchayat which independently and of its own will evolved a scheme and mobilized the village population for implementing that scheme. It was the new village administration, itself a unit of the national administrative system and subject to the latter's control, that decided those questions.

Henceforward the social, political and economic life of the rural people, was largely determined by the State. Village problems became an integral part of the total problems of the nation and could not be solved in isolation by the initiative of the village community.

The character and policies of the government appreciably determined how those problems would be solved and hence what type of life the rural people would live.

After independence, the Indians retained the centralized State apparatus elaborated by the British in India. The rural sociologist needs to study the working of the administrative system inherited from the British in the new national situation. It should be noted that this administrative system had been devised by them as a lever to suppress or restrict the initiative of the people. A critical evaluation of this system from the standpoint of the solution of such problems of the rural population as their general economic advance, universal spread of education, cheap expeditious justice, awakening and play of the local initiative within the framework of the national plan, and others, has, therefore, to be made and a scheme of reconstruction of the existing administrative system evolved.

The study of the administrative system raises the following problems :

(i) How far the administrative machinery is responsive to the opinions and wishes of the people.

(ii) How far the people are associated with it and participate in its functioning.

(iii) How far it is cheap, efficient, and sensitive to the problems of the people.

(b) NON-GOVERNMENTAL POLITICAL ORGANIZATIONS

It is further necessary to note that the governmental activity is only one aspect of the political life of the village population. Non-governmental political organizations also have emerged and are functioning in the rural area in modern times. Political parties thrown up by the rural people are principal among them.

It is very essential to study the various political parties operating in the rural area. These parties express the specific interests and aspirations of various classes and socio-economic groups composing of rural people such as landlords, tenants, land labourers, peasant proprietors and others. They voice their desire and determination to secure political power and use it to modify or overhaul the existing social system in consonance with their own interests and social objectives. The rural area becomes the arena of struggle between these parties. To have a concrete composite picture of the political life of the rural people it is, therefore, vitally necessary to study closely the ideologies, the programmes and the policies of these political parties and trace their roots. The general elections recently held in our country on the basis of the new Constitution have revealed the extensive growth of political consciousness among the rural people, the expansion of the old political parties and the emergence of new ones in the rural area and, above all, large scale participation of the rural people in the elections. Paradoxically enough, voting in some rural areas even exceeded that in urban zones. Further, large sections even of illiterate peasant women registered their vote, an event of great political significance.

The student of rural society should also study the changing political moods of the rural people and the resultant increase or decline in the influence of different political parties among them. He should further investigate, by means of a sociological analysis, the causes which bring about the rise and fall of political parties in the rural area. He can predict on the basis of such a study the tendency of the development of the political life of the rural people. Such a study is very vital since the victory of a political party in a country implies its capture of government machinery which it intends to use as an instrument to alter or replace the existing socio-economic structure of society in the interest of the class or the group which it represents. For instance, in India, the Socialist or the Communist Party desires to win political power so that it can use it to abolish capitalism and establish socialism. The Hindu Mahasabha aspires for political power to establish the Hindu Raj and reconstruct Indian society in conformity with the Hindu ideals. The Indian National Congress, the ruling party in India is working for a society based on a mixed social economy with two sectors, private and state owned, and Secular democracy.

(c) Political Behaviour of Rural People

Another aspect of the rural political life deserving study is the political behaviour of the rural people. The study must be made from two angles.

Programmes

First, the rural sociologist should study the various programmes which various strata of the rural people or the rural people as a whole are striving to fulfil.

These programmes will disclose the basic social aspirations and the immediate needs of the rural people and its various sections. The nature of these aspirations and needs will also disclose the psychologies and ideologies of the rural people and its constituent groups at a given historical moment.

For instance, some decades back, the cultivating tenants in the zamindari tract considered the zamindari system as immutable and merely desired and asked for a humane treatment from the zamindars. Subsequently, increasing sections of them questioned the zamindari system itself and put forth the demand for the abolition of landlords and transfer of land to themselves. They also aspired for a workers' and peasants' Raj which they previously did not even conceive of.

The rural sociologist is required to concentrate special attention on the study of the programme and the political behaviour of peasantry since it constitutes the major section of the rural people and, therefore, would exert decisive influence on the future of the rural society. The peasant movements in a number of countries in recent times have been transforming the entire social, political, and economic landscape in the agrarian area.

Secondly, the rural sociologist should make a thorough study of the methods which the rural people have been adopting to realize their aims.

Methods to Implement Programme

Different sections of the rural people make use of different methods to implement their programmes at various times.

Indian rural society provides a classical laboratory for the study of a rich variety of these methods. The following are the principal among them.

1. Petitioning.
2. Voting.
3. Demonstrations and marches.
4. Hijrats or mass emigrations.
5. Satyagraha, passive resistance.
6. No-rent and no-tax campaigns.
7. Spontaneous elemental revolts.
8. Organized armed struggles.
9. Guerilla warfare.

Peasant populations in different countries in the present epoch have been employing diverse methods to implement their programmes. In India, too, as previously stated, these varied methods have been used in varying degrees by the agrarian population in different parts of the country in different periods. In the second half of the ninteenth century a section of the Maharashtrian peasantry took to spontaneous armed struggle known as the Deccan Peasant Riots against moneylenders and the government. Mahatma Gandhi organized a number of no-tax campaigns of the peasantry in various parts of India. Subsequently a series of peasant demonstration and marches have been organized by the Kisan Sabhas and the Socialist party of India. In Telangana, a combination of the methods of open armed struggle and guerilla warfare was adopted by the peasantry led by the Communist Party only a few years back.

In the two General Elections held very recently, the rural population including millions of peasants, men and women have utilized the method of the ballot box and elected representatives to the State Assemblies and the House of the People.

Thus the rural people have used at various times parliamentary as well as extra-parliamentary methods of struggle to achieve their aims and demands.

A sociological analysis of the programmes of the rural people as a whole and its constituent strata as well as of the varied methods employ ed by them specially becomes necessary when the agrarian society is in a state of deep crisis and is simmering with great discontent of the rural masses in the major part of the world including India.

Role of Land Relations in Rural Politics

Since agriculture is the pivot of the rural economy and land is the most important means of production in agriculture, the struggle between the various groups of the rural society has mainly revolved round the question of the ownership of land. As has been almost universally recognized by sociologists and statesmen all over the world, the problem of land relations is the basic problem in all backward or semi-backward countries of Asia and even of some countries of Europe like Spain and Italy. The peasant movements in those countries have had as their basic objective the abolition of feudal or semi-feudal forms of land ownership and transfer of land to the actual tillers.

Struggle over the question of land has, in fact, provided the main dynamic to the political life of the rural society in the present period.

Different sections of the rural people hold different views on the land problems which are determined by their differing specific position in the socio-economic structure of the rural society. The view-points of the landlords, the tenants, the land labourers, the peasant proprietors, and the moneylenders and the merchants to whom the peasant debtors have mortgaged their land, vary widely. The divergence of views which expresses divergence of material interests of these groups, is the genetic cause of the economic and political struggles between them, struggles which now-a-days form an essential part of the political life of the rural people.

This inter-group struggle among the various sections of the rural people revolving round the land problem has not been adequately and scientifically studied hitherto by the student of the rural society. A historically progressive solution of the land problem is a crucial need since the future of the rural society, its retrogression of further advance, depends upon it.

Political Movement and Caste

In the Indian rural area where the occupational homogeneity of the caste is not still seriously undermined and where caste consciousness among the people remains stronger than in the urban centre, caste influences the political life to a much greater extent than it does in towns and cities. In recent times, however, due to the growth of class consciousness among various groups into which the rural population is divided on economic lines, the influence of caste on the political life is slowly diminishing. For instance, non-Brahmin landlords will politically ally with Brahmin landlords rather than with his non-Brahmin tenants since both the Brahmin and the non-Brahmin landlords stand for the defence of landlordism, their common economic interest. Similarly, the Brahmin and the non-Brahmin tenants will more and more come together and form a Kisan Sabha or a peasant party with the programme of abolition of landlordism and transfer of land to the tillers of land, both Brahmin and non-Brahmin.

In India, where the old caste system of the Hindus still exists and is strong, special attention should be paid to its role in determining political life. Often even when a caste is not occupationally homogeneous and does not, therefore, correspond to a socio-economic group, the caste allegiance among its members is so strong that they may politically support caste leaders who belong to another socio-economic group.

It should, however, be noted that, due to historical reasons, the caste and the socio-economic group often correspond to a great extent in various parts of the country. For instance, a good proportion of the farmers-tenants in Maharashtra happen to belong to the non-Brahmin caste while a good proportion of the landlords to the Brahmin caste. Due to this the party of the peasantry has an overwhelmingly non-Brahmin social composition. This often blurs the fact that, judged from the standpoint of the basic aim and demands of the organization, it is the party of a socio-economic group, a class. Caste in this case obscures the class content of the party. The specific weight of caste in the political life of the rural people is still great and the rural sociologist has to assess it carefully.

CHAPTER XI

RURAL RELIGION

Study of Rural Religion, Reasons

A Thorough study of rural religion and its significant role in determining the life processes of the rural society should form an essential part of the study of that society. The following are the principal reasons for this :

First, it has been observed by sociologists all over the world that rural people have a greater predisposition to religion than what the urban people have. The dependence of agriculture—the basic form of production in the countryside—on the hitherto unmastered forces of nature like rains and the near absence of scientific culture, which provides a correct understanding of the natural and social worlds, among the rural people are two main reasons for the greater degree of religiosity among them. Traditional religion composed of the crudest conceptions of the world holds their mind in its grip. Animism, magic polytheism, ghost beliefs and other forms of primitive religion, are rampant among the rural people to a far greater extent than among the urban people.

Secondly, the religious outlook of the rural people overwhelmingly dominates their intellectual, emotional and practical life. It is difficult to locate any aspect of their life which is not permeated with and coloured by religion. Their family life, caste life, general social life, economic and even recreational life, are more or less governed by a religious approach and religious norms. Religious conceptions also largely dominate their ethical standards; the form and content of their arts like painting, sculpture, architecture, folk-songs and others; as also their social and economic festivals.

This is specially true of societies based on subsistence economies of the pre-capitalist epoch when religion was almost completely fused with social life and when even the then existing secular scientific knowledge of man—physiology, medicine, astronomy, mathematics, agronomy, mechanics, sociology, ethics, etc.—was clothed in religious garb and was the monopoly of the priestly caste.

Thirdly, in societies based on subsistence economies, the leadership of the village life in all domains was provided by the priestly group, in India the Brahmins. Mores, which this group laid down for the individual behaviour as well as for social control were determined by the traditional religious concepts. Hence the life of the village aggregate in all spheres was moulded in the spirit of religious ideas and dogmas and was controlled by religious institutions and leaders.

Fourthly, a new development took place in modern times in India after the advent of the British rule. The social, economic and political life of the village, as stated elsewhere, experienced a progressive transformation. The development and spread of capitalist economic forms led to the disintegration of the subsistence economy of the autarchic village. Further, a new and secular centralized state took over the administration of the village from the village panchayat and caste councils whose outlook was essentially religious and who were generally guided by religious conceptions and criteria even in secular matters.

In the new economic and political environs, new norms, basically non-religious and secular and derived out of a liberal democratic philosophy, emerged and began increasingly to supersede the authoritarian religious norms which for ages had governed even the secular life of the village population. The village people for the first time in history felt the impact of secular, and democratic and equalitarian ideas on their consciousness. A new ferment began to spread among them which has been steadily affecting their life and outlook hitherto coloured with religion. Also new secular institutions and associations, new secular leadership and social controls, began to emerge within the rural society.

This has resulted in a slow but steady decline in the hegemony and control of the leaders of religion over the life of the rural population.

It must be noted that, even then, religion still continues to exercise a powerful hold over the mind of the rural people and determines their behaviour in a number of secular fields. However, as a result of the operation of such material and ideological forces as modern means of transport like buses and railways and democratic secular ideas, as also due to the growth of secular economic and political movements of the rural masses, the historical tendency, though admittedly very slow, is towards a dereligionizing of increasing sectors of secular life of the rural people as also of their attitude towards purely secular matters.

The contemporary rural society in India has become a battle ground of struggle between the forces of religious orthodoxy and authoritarian social conceptions on the one hand and those of secular democratic advance on the other. It is essential for the student of Indian rural society to follow this conflict.

Rural Religion Vs. Urbanized Religion

Crude forms of religion comprising animism, magic, polytheism, mythology, ghost beliefs and others, which exercise sway over the mind of the rural population, should be distinguished from the refined and subtle types of religion and religious philosophy which are prevalent in cities among the urban intelligentsia. These refined and subtle religions and religious philosophies have been elaborated by great idealistic thinkers out of daring philosophical speculations on basic problems of life such as the problems of the nature of ultimate reality, the genesis of human knowledge and others, which markedly distinguish them from the naive religious beliefs generated in the rural atmosphere.

While rural religion tends to be crude and concrete in form, urbaniz ed religion has tended to be abstract. While the rural population worships and falls prostrate before a multitude of gods and goddesses derived out of their animistic conception of the universe, the cultured educated section of the urban humanity subscribes to the idealistic view of the universe and discusses such categories as the nature of Brahman, Free Will and others.

Further, even critical rationalism and philosophical materialism as minority philosophical currents flourish in urban centres.

The rural sociologist needs to distinguish between the crude, almost static, rural religion and the refined and highly abstract urbanized religion which soars in the stratosphere of speculative thought and grapples with ontological, epistemological and other basic problems of philosophy. Further, he should also note that rationalist and materialist philosophical thought currents found in the urban society are almost absent in the rural area.

The roots of rural religion lie principally in the great, almost abysmal, ignorance and resultant fear of the forces of environment prevailing among the rural people. Refined urban religion, even if based on the erroneous idealistic interpretation of the world, is not born of mere fear. This distinction regarding the psychological roots of rural and urban religions is important.

Three Aspects of Rural Religion

The rural religion should be studied in its following three important aspects :

1. Rural religion as providing a specific world outlook, a specific view of the universe;
2. Rural religion as prescribing a body of religious practices to the rural people; and
3. Rural religion as an institutional complex.

Each of these three vital aspects of the rural religion needs a few observations.

1. As A World Outlook

The world outlook provided by the rural religion includes such ingredients as (a) magical conceptions, (b) animism, (c) the conception of a bizarre world peopled by spirits, (d) the conception of a posthumous world of dead ancestors who have to be worshipped, and (e) mythology.

The most striking feature of the rural religion is its dynamic conception of the universe, i.e., the conception of the universe as a theatre of the interplay of conscious freely acting elements. The rural religion unfolds such worlds as *Pitrulok*, *Pretlok*, *Devlok*, and *Vaikunth Dham*, i.e., the worlds of dead ancestors, disembodied spirits, gods and goddesses, as also the celestial world. It also, in addition, conjures up worlds peopled by such deities as those of fertility, various epidemics, rivers and forests. In fact, the rural religion sees spirits practically behind all phenomena and creates a phantasmagoria of numerous uncanny worlds of spirits.

Such a world outlook is fundamentally born of the profound ignorance of the forces of nature and of the nature of man. Ignorance breeds fear and these two are the interrelated twin sources of the world outlook fashioned by the crude rural religion.

Since the world outlook, consciously or unconsciously, largely determines the social, ethical and other views of the individual and the social aggregate as well as their behaviour, its study forms an indispensable part of the study of the rural society.

2. As a Body of Practices

The body of religious practices prescribed by the rural religion is imposing. These practices may be divided into the following three groups:

(a) *Prayers*: The individual is enjoined to offer prayer to various deities at home as well as outside the home. At home he is required to pray to the family god or goddess. The prayers are offered by the members of the family at the family alter.

Every caste generally worships a special deity and maintains, if possible, caste temples where the deity is installed. All members of the caste are exhorted to regularly offer prayers to the deity, a god or a goddess.

Further, every street or locality in the village has its own deity, generally Goddess *Moholla Mata* to whom the people residing in the locality have to offer prayers, specially during the *Navaratra* religious festival.

There is also the village temple in which the village god is installed. Community prayers have to be offered to him.

Further, prayers are offered also to the river goddess if the village is situated on a river, to the forest deity and to other deities of the locality.

In addition, prayers have to be offered also to some or all gods and goddesses common to all Hindus.

The prayer and worship aspect of the rural religion deserves a careful study because, in recent times, sections of the Hindus—the depressed classes—who were denied the right of temple entry, organized a number of struggles to secure that right. The issue of the right to enter public temples and worship and offer prayers to deities became even a political issue.

(b) *Sacrifices*: The rural religion prescribes a variety of sacrificial acts to its adherents, which range from the sprinkling of some drops of water and scattering of leaves or grains in front of various deities to the offering of animal and, though rarely, even of human sacrifices to them.

The rural religion is composed of various sub-religions and each sub-religion prescribes to its followers a particular set of sacrificial acts.

Sacrifices are offered to a variety of gods and goddesses. There are the food god (*Annadevata*), the gods of different diseases (*Baliakaka and others*), the rain god, the river goddess, and a plethora of others. Sacrifices are offered to propitiate them and thereby disarm their wrath or win their favour.

A sociological analysis of sacrifices is valuable for comprehending the conceptions of the rural people of the cause of diseases, floods and other devastating phenomena. It can also provide a clue to their social habits and styles of living. It will reveal their attitudes to the world and life. It may assist the rural sociologist to grasp how various castes practising different kinds of sacrificial acts, thereby, develop a hierarchic conception of the caste series. Such a study can further help him to explain certain psychological and cultural traits of different social groups. And finally it may aid him in tracing the past-history of Indian society, social, economic and cultural, of which the concept and practice of sacrifice were an organic outgrowth. Sacrifices to particular deities have a specific character and hence presupposed a specific concept of each deity. Those deities were born in the field of human consciousness at a certain stage in the socio-economic development of society. Mythology, in fact, is the history of society in terms of symbolism and since society changes, the pantheon of gods and goddesses too changes.

The rural society has at present become the amphitheatre of the struggle between the conservative and the reformist religious tendencies and movements. The conservative social groups strive to preserve old religious practices while the reformist social groups are characterizing those practices as irrational and mentally deadening. They counsel a rational approach to problems of life. A study of sacrifices becomes essential if one were to properly understand this struggle, particularly because they play a very significant role in the life of the rural people. The culture of the rural people is predominantly religious and sacrifices also form the theme of the rural folklore which constitutes the major part of their culture.

(c) *Rituals* : One of the significant features of the life of the rural people is its meticulous domination, even in details, by rituals. The conception of purity had been elaborated in the past Indian society to such an extent that it became a veritable principle. Rituals are the religious means by which the purity of the individual and the social life becomes guaranteed. The inherited rural religion prescribes a complex pattern of behaviour for the individual as well as for various social groups in all spheres of life, complex because rituals are associated with their numerous significant and even insignificant activities. Particular sets of rituals are dictated to a particular caste or sub-caste group so much so that distinct differences in the respective rituals which those social groups and sub-groups follow enable one to distinguish them from one another. Social condemnation and even the threat of ex-communication provide sanction for the strict enforcement of rituals among their members.

Rituals are associated with most of the life activities of the rural people. A ritual is prescribed whenever the individual or the social group initiates an activity even though the activity may be, like food-taking, repeated in future. Before an individual Brahmin starts consuming the food in the dish, he is required to draw a magic circle round the dish and apportion some grains of cooked rice to the god or gods. There are rituals prescribed for a number of such ordinary mundane and secular activities. There are the bath ritual, the occupational ritual, the ritual to be performed when a person occupies a residential premises. There are separate rituals when the farmer begins sowing and harvesting. All landmarks in the process of agricultural production have been associated with specific rituals.

Rituals have been prescribed for auspicious days and also for the start of a new season. When a child for the first time goes to the school, there is also ritual to be performed.

In fact, the life of the rural human is a succession of rituals corresponding to a succession of activities he is engaged in from morning to night, from month to month and year to year, almost from birth to death. Even the dead person is not to be left alone. Specific rituals have to be performed in the posthumous period for some days.

In fact, we may remark that it is very difficult to locate in the Hindu society where religious observances end and secular practices begin.

3. As An Institutional Complex

The Hindu religion, which a preponderant section of the rural population subscribes to, is a conglomeration of numerous sub-religions and religious cults.

A number of these sub-religions and religous cults have been institutionalized. Corresponding to these institutionalized sub-religions and religious cults there exists a number of religious organizations.

Some of these religious organizations function on a national scale, some on the provincial and others on the local basis. They maintain Maths, Ashrams and temples where their adherents flock to worship and to pray to various deities as also to listen to religious discourses.

These religious bodies own property, often substantial. They maintain a permanent staff of priests and preachers who spread the doctrines of their respective sub-religions and religious cults among the people.

Thus we have in the country such religious organizations as those headed by Shankaracharya, descendants of Ramanuj, Vallabha, Sahajanand and others, all differing again in subtle points of philosophy and rituals.

Some of the sub-religions and religious cults have not been institutionalized. Their protagonists and preachers have not been integrated into regular organizations.

The absence of state religions has been one striking characteristic of religion in India. This is in contrast to Christianity and Islam which became state religions in a number of countries of Europe and Asia. Religion in

India was considered the concern of the community and not of the state. The religious organization was always distinct and separate from the state though a Hindu or a Muslim king might favour and support his respective religion.

In Europe, as history records, it was otherwise. There existed, in the Middle Ages, Catholic and subsequently Catholic and Protestant states. Till Kamal Pasha separated the state from religion, Turkey was a theocratic Muslim State.

Hence we do not find in Indian history such struggles as that between the Pope, the head of the organized international Catholic religion, striving to maintain a system of Catholic states and Henry VIII who rebelled against Catholicism and transformed the English state into a Protestant one.

One significant feature of the life of Indian society in the past lay in the fact that great democratic mass movements took the form of religious movements led by outstanding religious leaders popularly known as *Bhaktas* (Sants). Since religion was a community and not a state matter in India these movements were not directed against the state (in contrast to Protestantism in Europe) but aimed at winning over the people to their programmes and, through their initiative and action, bringing about the reform of society.

The popular democratic character of those *Bhakti* movements is evidenced by the fact that they generally stood for democratization of the Hindu society (liquidation of castes or caste inequalities) and for equal access to God and religious culture by all, including women, without the intermediary of the priestly Brahmin caste. Further the *Bhaktas* developed the vernaculars or the languages which the common people knew and spoke and themselves created a vast literature in those languages. Thus they also brought culture to the common people.

It must, however, be noted that a Hindu, a Buddhist or a Muslim king would often utilise his state power and state resources for the extensions of the particular religion he subscribed to. The state, however, had not a Hindu or a Muslim character. Religion was not a department of the state.

We will next refer to the group of men exclusively devoted to religion. This group can be divided into two categories, priests who have a fixed domicile and *sanyasis* who travel from place to place.

There are various kinds of priests. There are family priests who serve the religious needs of the family; the caste and sub-caste priests who cater to the needs of various castes and sub-castes; and the village priest who looks after the village temple and meets the religious requirements of the village community as a whole.

These priestly groups exercise a powerful influence over the life of the rural people, both religious and secular, since secular life processes are coloured by religion and before being undertaken, require to be hallowed by religion through rituals. Religion is even now largely interwoven in the texture of the secular life of the rural people.

The historical tendency, however, is towards a decline of the domination of the secular life of the rural people by the priestly group.

There are, in our country, in addition to priests, a large number of roving religious men (*Sanyasis*) who mostly tour in the rural area. Some of them are preachers of the religious cults to which they belong. Others are just holy men who hallow the village by their visit and deign to taste the hospitality of the villagers for a while.

Significance of Temple in Rural Area

We will next evaluate the role of the village temple in the life of the rural people. This is because the temple has not only functioned as a place of worship and prayer but also has served as the main centre and initiator of village activities. It plays a significant part in the village life even to-day.

The temple has been associated with education in the village. For ages it maintained a school where the village youngsters of higher castes received religious and secular education. It organized for the village people religious discourses as well as *Kathas* narrating the past history of the Indian people.

The temple did philanthrophic and social welfare work in the village. It collected money and goods from the villagers with which it used to bring relief to the needy among them.

The temple organized collective social and religious functions. Under its auspices marriages were performed, social and religious festivals including village dinners were organized, and significant days like the New Year's Day were celebrated. In fact, a good proportion of the collective life of the village, religious and secular, moved round the temple.

The temple also embodied and was the guardian of all traditional culture, literary and artistic. Sometimes it even attached to itself and maintained singers, dancers and musicians. It must be borne in mind that the past culture was largely religious and even its secular part was clothed in the religious raiment. Hence, this inherited culture was associated with and guarded by the temple. Thus the village temple became the predominant centre of village culture; and the cultural life of the village, religious and secular, artistic and literary, moved round the temple.

The temple was the source of ethical values which regulated the life of the village people. The head of the village temple was the inexorable moral critic and controller of the actions of the villagers, though in recent times the control has been diminishing.

The temple played and also plays today an important role in the economic life of the village. All turning points in the process of agricultural production such as sowing, reaping, and others are signified by religious rituals. When an artisan starts his occupation, there is the inevitable ritual linked with the event. The temple through its priestly representative hallows the farmer's plough and the artisan's instruments, when they are first put to use, by means of appropriate religious rituals. Thus, the temple, the visible expression of the rural religion, plays an important role also in the economic life of the rural society.

The temple occasionally dispenses justice too. It adjudicates disputes between villagers with the authoritative voice of religion. It prescribes religious methods of expiation for even heinous secular offences.

Not only that. The temple further makes forecasts of future events through the priestly representative.

The temple serves as a social centre also. Even village gossip is largely carried on within the precincts or the periphery of the temple.

Public meetings are generally held near or in the temple since it is the most significant and spacious place in the village.

The temple provided largely in the past and provides to a less extent now, teachers, physicians, medicine men, ethical leaders, songster, experts in narrating past history before village audiences (*Kathakars*), scribes, astrologers, astronomers, and soothsayers to the village.

There is a rich variety of temples in the village. There are caste and sub-caste temples as well as temples consecrated to deities worshipped by the village people in common with the entire Hindu community as a whole. There are also temples for the worship of deities of specific religious cults like the *Shakti* cult and others. There are, further, temples where local village deities are enshrined.

Some of the village temples are owned publicly ; others are owned privately.

Need to Study Rural Religion

The study of contemporary rural religion is very essential for having a composite picture of the past cultural evolution of the Indian people. The history of Indian culture is still scrappy, is still in a fragmentary state. A controversy is still going on regarding the genesis of Indian culture and further phases of its subsequent development. Varied views have been advanced on the subject. Also problems such as, where the Indian culture originated and how it spread in different parts of India, also remain in the domain of debate.

Need to Study Regional Rural Religion

A study of various rural religions in various rural regions of India reveals certain common characteristics such as common patterns of gods and goddesses, common objects of worship, common rituals as well as almost common religious conceptions and myths. A number of these characteristics, however, exhibit regional variations.

Further, a regional rural religion also possesses features which are distinct and its own which it does not share with others.

This discloses two striking facts. First, the common characteristics of these rural religions indicate that they had their origin in a common Indian culture in the past and, in spite of regional variations, constitute a varied pattern of a single Indian rural culture even today. Secondly, in spite of common ancestry they are also distinct rural religions of various rural areas since they possess certain independent traits and elements.

A careful sociological analysis of this rich diversity of contemporary regional rural religions will assist to trace their evolution. It will, further, help to discover the genesis of these rural religions which spread along with great and frequent migrations of peasant communities from one part of India to others.

Even the varied geographical conditions of India have played a big role in determining Indian rural religion and its regional variations. Mighty rivers, mountainous territories, decisive trade routes, have influenced the character and content of those religions. The spread of modern railways, which have greatly neutralized the topographical and geographical factors in conditioning the cultural life of the people in modern times, makes it difficult for us to comprehend the significance of these factors in shaping the past Indian culture.

An inventory of the various religious beliefs, rituals and pantheons of gods and goddesses of various regional rural religions and a study of their common characteristics as well as their regional variations will help to evolve a scientific history of the Indian rural culture as it developed and spread for many centuries.

The study of the Hindu rural religion is particularly fascinating because of the rich variety of its content. Hinduism is a colossal diversified complex of religious beliefs and rituals. In its contemporary form it is an aggregate of religious dogmas and practices almost of all phases of development of human society.

Study of Rural Religion, Aid to Evolve Scientific Indian History

Further, a sociological investigation into Indian rural religion will disclose, though in a symbolic form, the past social, political, economic and ethnic history of India. It will unveil the history of economic and other clashes as well as of various social, political and cultural amalgamations of conflicting social groups in the past.

This is because the shadow world of religion reflects the real movement of society.

The studies of Egypt, Babylonia, Greece and other countries by eminent scholars like More, Maspero, Breasted, Frankfort, Gordon Childe, Thomson and others have shown how a systematic study of the evolution of gods from tribal totems and fetishes to national pantheons unfolds the process of the transformation of tribal society into territorial political society. A study of the ideology and mythology of the rural religion in India may also unlock the secrets of changes in the Indian society in various stages of its evolution.

The rural sociologist in India has to study such problems as to why *Shaivism* spread in certain parts of India, how *Vaishnavism* spread in certain regions, why the *Shakti* cult took various forms in various zones. Migrations of gods and goddesses signify the migrations of peoples too. Fusion of gods and goddesses reveals the historical process of the fusion of peoples. The hierarchy of gods and goddesses and the branding of some deities as villainous and extolling of others as beneficient, unfold, though in mythological terms, struggles among ethnic groups and peoples and the subordination of some to others in real historical conflicts.

It must be noted that in addition to Hinduism which we have extensively discussed on account of its preponderance, other religions like Islam, Christianity and Zoroastrianism also have existed in the Indian rural society. It is, therefore, also necessary for a rural sociologist to make their study on similar lines for a thorough assessment of the role of religion in the life of the rural people.

Rural Religion Under the Impact of Modern Forces

Further, the study of the rural religion is also very vital because, due to the impact of modern economic, social, political and rationalist forces, the rural society is experiencing a transformation, however, slow, in the present period. The transformation is taking place in all spheres of rural life including the sphere of rural religion. The ideology, the institutions, the rituals, the ethics, and the aesthetics of the rural religion are undergoing a change, though gradual, under the pressure of new material and cultural forces. It is the task of the rural sociologist to study this process to be able to predict the future of the rural religion which exercises a great sway over the mind of the rural people and the life processes of the rural society.

CHAPTER XII

RURAL EDUCATION

EDUCATION, ITS SIGNIFICANCE IN MODERN TIMES

THE SIGNIFICANCE of education in modern societies cannot be overestimated. A literate and educated people are a prerequisite both for maintaining and further developing these societies. The crucial need of education for the people in various spheres of modern social life (economic, political, social, ethical and others) has been unanimously recognized. We will see why this need arises.

1. ECONOMIC REASONS

In contrast to the multitude of self-sufficient village economies which mainly constituted the economic life of the pre-modern communities, the economy of a modern people has a national basis. Further even this national economy has been largely outmoded in recent decades and has become an integral part of the single world economy. The national economy, in fact, produces industrial, agrarian and other commodities, both for the national and international markets. Consequently, it is the world price movement of various commodities which finally determines the volume and the price of products in different production centres. An intelligent and correct understanding of the complex economic life of mankind as a whole therefore becomes necessary for all producers.

It was not so in pre-modern societies. In pre-British India, as observed earlier, the village farmer group produced just enough to meet the requirements of the village population and of the land revenue to be paid by the village collectivity to the state. In post-British India the village farmer group has been producing for the local, national and even international market. If the village agriculturist is not to be a victim of the vicissitudes of the world market, he needs to be educated enough to follow the movement of national and world economies.

2. POLITICAL REASONS

Education is necessary for the modern rural aggregate also for political and administrative reasons. Formerly, as mentioned before, the state exercised nominal sovereignty over the village. Its administrative machinery did not penetrate and function in the village. The village panchayat and caste committees regulated the life of the people. After the modern society evolved, the village has become an integral part of the political and administrative machinery of a highly centralized state. Since the modern state appreciably shapes the economic, social, and cultural life of the people, it is indispensable for the rural people to study its mechanism. The rural man needs to know a minimum of law, governing judicial and administrative processes as well as powers of various state organs. Further, in recent decades, various political parties have sprung up in the rural area. These parties struggle among themselves to win the support of the rural people with a view to gaining control over the state. It is, therefore, also necessary for the rural people to study the programmes and policies of these political parties. Both these reasons make it obligatory for them to have education.

3. Social Reasons

Education is essential for the rural people also for the broad social reason, *viz.*, that all social relations between citizens are, in the modern society, governed by the principle of contract and not by status as in the former epoch. Contractual social relations are complex and multifold demanding from the citizen an understanding of the basic structure of the modern society and hence this need for education. The economic relations between citizens, the relations between the members of the family and other types of social relations, which in their totality form the complex variegated pattern of the modern society, are governed by laws based on the principle of contract. Only an educated citizen can have a comprehension of such a diversified system of contractual relations.

4. Ethical Reasons

There is another reason why the rural man must be an educated man. In the modern society the ethical life of the individual as well as of the social aggregate is increasingly being based on secular and humanist instead of on religious principles as in the medieval society. Equality of all men, individual liberty, development of human personality, reason as the determinant of human conduct—such are some of the principal conceptions which have been progressively determining the behaviour of the individual and the social aggregate. Modern education is absolutely necessary to comprehend these basic conceptions.

5. Cultural Reasons

Education is also the prerequisite for the study and assimilation of the rich culture which has developed in the contemporary age. Human knowledge of the natural world has registered a phenomenal advance in modern times, giving man a greater mastery over nature. Similarly knowledge in the sphere of social life too has immensely grown, thereby enabling man to mould his collective social life more consciously. Further, there has been a tremendous advance in the field of artistic culture also. A part of this rich modern culture has even acquired the character of a world culture. Education is indispensable for assimilating this mighty world culture so vital for enriching the intellectual and emotional life of the individual and thereby increasing his capacity to contribute to the advance of society. The best part of modern culture lays strong emphasis on individual liberty and social co-operation both of which are so essential for the development of the individual's personality and powers and for social progress. The citizen who imbibes such a culture will feel an inevitable urge to work for the creation of a society free from social antagonism and discord and based on social solidarity and individual freedom.

6. Other Reasons

For the agriculturist, education is, in addition, necessary for understanding of the advantages of the use of such advanced agricultural techniques as tractors, fertilizers, harvesters and thrashers.

It must be also noted that the modern society throws up specific problems which only modern knowledge can successfully solve. For instance, the economic or political science embodied in *Arthashastra* by Chanakya cannot aid in solving the economic and political problems emerging from the soil of contemporary society. And modern education is the only means to acquire modern knowledge.

Just as old knowledge cannot assist in solving modern problems, educational methods of gaining old knowledge cannot help to assimilate modern knowledge. Modern science of pedagogy, modern methods of instruction and modern schools are required for imparting modern knowledge.

A shockingly large portion of the Indian rural population is submerged in gross ignorance and illiteracy. The problem of transforming tens of millions of those illiterate rural humans into educated and well-informed citizens is a problem of herculean proportion and still has to be resolved if the Indian society is to advance materially and culturally.

Education in Pre-British India, its Basic Features

We will first delineate the main features of education in the pre-British Indian rural society based on subsistence economy.

Education in the agricultural, industrial, and other occupational arts was imparted to the members of the growing young generation not in schools but in the process of their direct empirical participation in those occupations under the guidance of family elders.

Social education or education in the arts of social behaviour and adaptations was imparted to them by the family and the caste as the social life of the village people mainly moved within the family and the caste matrix.

The growing young generation received its moral and intellectual education largely from the priests, the *Kathakars* and saints, and also, to some extent, from the family.

The multitude of secular and religious functions, festivals and celebrations, which the family, the caste, and the village community organized and in which the youngsters of the village participated, served as the school for the aesthetic education of those youngsters.

The world outlook inculcated by that education was fundamentally religious. It propagated the concept of the divine origin of the world and of God's free will determining all phenomena and happenings. In addition to one supreme God it also taught the belief in a pantheon of gods and spirits behind all phenomena, significant and insignificant. Eclipses and earthquakes, floods and epidemics, were not scientifically explained but were declared to be the result of the wrathful actions of malevolent gods and goddesses. For instance, the eclipse signified the temporary suppression of the Sun-God by the two demons, *Rahu* and *Ketu*. The earthquake was the consequence of the movement of *Shesh Nag* who supports the earth on its colossal hood. The eruption of small-pox was the result of the ire of the deity *Balia Kaka* who, therefore, had to be propitiated by a proper ritual. Education, then, also encouraged belief in animism in tree gods, mountain gods and river goddesses.

Thus the rural people of the pre-modern society had a religious unscientific conception of the world.

The history of the past Indian society taught to the young generation was largely mythology. It dealt with the superhuman feats of god-kings. Even gods participated in the terrestrial battles between these god-kings. Such a history could not give a consistent continuous account of the development of the social, economic and political life of the people in the past and explain all historical transformations by means of secular causes.

The social education adapted the individual to the exigencies of joint family, caste and village communal life. Since the social structure was authoritarian, the social education was authoritarian too in spirit. It exhorted the individual to completely subordinate himself to the joint family, the caste or the village community. It disciplined him in the service of these institutions. Such a social education could hardly serve individual liberty or help the development of human personality.

All education including agricultural and craft education consisted of empirically acquired and hereditarily transmitted body of knowledge from the past. It was imparted to the young orally, mostly in the process of practice in arts, crafts and agriculture and participation in social life. There did not exist any technical institutes, musical and other art academies or schools of social sciences in the village. It was only in some distant urban centres that some educational and training institutions existed and functioned.

Education Under the British Rule, its Chief Characteristics

Impact with the west in general and Britain in particular and the resultant rise of modern society in India led to the spread of modern education among our people.

The new education was essentially secular and, on the whole liberal in spirit and content. This signified a shift from the religious and authoritarian to secular and liberal character of education. The spread of the modern education was, however, extremely slow and mainly restricted to middle and upper strata of the urban society. Very few villages had schools, and, even where they existed, the stark poverty of the rural people made it impossible for them to take advantage of the educational facility due to high cost. Further, since the modern education was introduced in India by the British mainly to meet the need of the personnel for their administrative machinery and economic enterprises, its liberal aims remained hazy or were even distorted. It did not set to itself the ideal of turning out citizens armed with modern knowledge who would use that knowledge for the untrammelled material and cultural advance of the nation to which they belonged. It was bereft of nationalist spirit and ideals. Nevertheless, it must be recognised that in spite of these serious flaws, the introduction of the new education brought the Indian people in contact with the liberal, democratic and rationalist ideologies of the modern west. Supersession of the pre-British education, authoritarian in spirit and largely superstitious in content, by the modern education, however defective, was an event of great significance in Indian history. Radhakrishnan's University Commission Report vividly depicts the achievements as well as the limitations of the system of modern education introduced during the British period.

As we have stated before, the benefits of the modern education hardly extended to the rural India. The problem of education in the rural area was almost completely ignored by the British as is evidenced in the fact that, even after a hundred and fifty years of the British rule, 86 per cent of the total Indian population, including its advnaced urban section, still remained illiterate.

A number of agencies worked for the spread of the modern education in India. The British Government, various foreign missionary bodies, Indian social reform organizations and subsequently political institutions like the Indian National Congress, were the chief among these agencies.

All these agencies, however, failed to achieve any appreciable result in the rural area.

The problem of rural education, it must be said, was not even thought out in all its complexity.

PROBLEMS OF EDUCATION IN INDEPENDENT INDIA

With the advent of national independence, the problem of rural education has assumed urgent importance and new significance. The free Indian people have set to themselves the task of building up of a democratic, progressive, national life, which surely cannot be achieved when tens of millions of rural people are illiterate, ignorant and superstitious.

Campaign against the mass illiteracy among the rural people is the urgent task to-day. Further, treasures of rich modern knowledge have to be brought within their reach if they are to be effective participants in the creative work of national reconstruction.

For successfully evolving a comprehensive and scientific programme of rural education a number of problems germane to it have to be resolved.

We enumerate these problems below :

1. Objective of Education.
2. Structure of the Machinery of Education.
3. Technical and other Means for its Spread.
4. Finance and Personnel.

. OBJECTIVE OF EDUCATION

It is now recognized by eminent educationists that the present system of urban education lays unduly greater emphasis on the training of intellect than on the development of the physical, emotional, and moral aspects of the pupil's personality. Such education results in the one-sided and therefore defective development of the young generation. It fails to evolve an integral human being with an all-sided development of his personality.

The present system of urban education is further criticized on the ground that, during the long period of schooling which extends from childhood to almost adulthood, the role of general knowledge is over-emphasised. It is not related to concrete problems of real life. Consequently the educated youth, when he enters the arena of life after completing education, finds it difficult to grapple with the concrete problems of real life.

Various views have been advanced in the field of controversy over the question of education.

There are some who emphasise that education must have the liberal and humanist ideal before it. Others lay greater stress on the technical and practical aspects of education.

There are some who declare that the basic aim of education should be the development of the individual's personality. There are others who give greater importance to the cultivation of the virtues and qualities of an ideal citizen in the pupil.

There are some who desire secular education to be reinforced by religious training. There are others who sharply disagree with this view and uncompromisingly stand for purely secular education.

There is a group of educationsists who are the exponents of a synthetic type of education which would help the development of all sides of the pupil's nature, intellectual, emotional, moral, and social, and help him to evolve into a synthetic man.

The view is gaining ground among a large number of social thinkers that the present education, which at the lower level, concentrates on the three R's, thereby concerns itself only with the development of the intellectual side of the pupil. They recommend that, instead of this, education should focus on three H's, *i. e.*, education of hand, heart and head. This will guarantee, they observe, the all-sided development of the pupil. Such education will result into the emergence of citizens, physically healthy and strong, emotionally rich, intellectually alert and capable of social co-operation. They will be valuable assets to the society.

The new Constitution of the Indian Union has stated in its Preamble that it aims at creating a democratic society based on "justice, social, economic and political; liberty of thought, expression, belief, faith and worship; equality of status and opportunity." Further it aims at promoting among all citizens "Fraternity, assuring the dignity of the individual and unity of the Nation."

It implies the creation of a society free from all forms of inequalities and exploitation and based on individual liberty and social solidarity and co-operation.

For the realization of such an objective, it is necessary that the conception and the programme of education should be in harmony with and be derived out of it.

In his University Education Report, Dr. Radhakrishanan has given an elaborate picture of the social ideal depicted in the Constitution and has further described how it should be paraphrased and expressed in terms of the educational ideal of the nation.

Reconstruction of the Indian society as a whole in the spirit of the social ideal embodied in the Constitution would imply also the reconstruction of the Indian rural society in the spirit of the same ideal. Rural education should be therefore adapted to the needs of creation of the new and higher type of rural society envisaged in the future.

The study of a society reveals that the prevailing system of education serves the needs and ideals of that society. The educational system of a society based on self-sufficient economy serves the needs and ideals of that society. Similarly the present educational system subserves the requirements of the existing capitalist society based on a competitive and market economy and its social ideals.

A new educational system will have to be evolved if a new society based on co-operative socio-economic relations is to be created. It will have to instil virtues of social solidarity and social co-operation in the members of the young generation, uproot anti-social individualism, infuse social passions, and build up the ability for social co-operation among them.

The type of rural society which is programmed for construction should determine the educational system to be elaborated for the rural people.

The rural sociologist has to give the most earnest attention to this fact while making suggestions for a new system of education for the rural people.

2. Structure of the Machinery of Education

The success of an educational scheme like that of all schemes depends upon the machinery evolved for implementing that scheme. The scheme may be scientific and adapted realistically to social conditions and, further, the social ideal conceived by it may be noble, yet, if the appropriate machinery for its implementation is not forged, it will meet with failure.

The task of elaborating the organizational machinery for a scientific and comprehensive educational plan for millions of illiterate and ignorant villagers is a stupendous task. This is obvious when we consider that even the problem of creating a machinery for carrying out the minimum programme of the abolition of illiteracy among the rural people presents formidable obstacles.

The task raises a number of problems. What type of primary schools should be established for children? How will they be co-ordinated with such schools started for adult illiterates? In what manner will the primary schools be linked with secondary schools and the latter with higher educational institutions ?

Further, should the schools in the rural area be open air or single room schools? Should they be specialized and differentiated or omnibus institutes? And, finally, how should the school time be adjusted to the exigencies of agricultural and artisan labour in which not only village adults but also youngsters participate ?

The educational scheme will also raise such problems as those of the graded system of schools, suitable curricula to be evolved in the spirit of the social ideal in view, and the graded system of courses.

3. Technical and Other Means for Its Spread

During the last two hundred years, humanity has made amazing progress in the domain of technology. It has invented railways, steamships, aeroplanes, telephone and telegraph, radio, cinema and other marvellous technical devices. These devices constitute the valuable material means of integrating humanity into a single unit as well as of building up of a rich unified economic and cultural life on a national and even international scale.

Formerly the school was practically the only effective lever of education. After those astonishing inventions, the school can be reinforced by other means also.

These modern means, it must be noted, have not yet been sufficiently utilised for educational and cultural purposes in our country.

We will enumerate below some of the principal among these means which along with the school, are available for the rapid advance of education and cultural enlightenment of our people:

(a) School.
(b) Library.
(c) Museum.
(d) Movie.
(e) Radio.
(f) Mobile Van.
(g) Gymnasiums and Sport Centres.

A maximum and simultaneous utilization of these means will undoubtedly accelerate the process of extension of education and culture among the rural people.

We will refer very briefly to the specific role of these various means.

(a) *School* : The school should remain the principal lever of education. It can serve as the medium of formal education, patterned and planned.

(b) *Library* : The library adequately equipped with books scientifically dealing with varied subjects; with newspapers and magazines of local, national and even international significance; and with charts and maps; can be a rich reservoir of variegated knowledge, social, political, technical, economic and cultural. It can also enable the villager to follow decisive national and international happenings. The art section of the library can help him to develop a refined aesthetic sense and artistic taste. The library, when properly made use of, will help him to broaden his outlook, enlarge his vision extend the frontiers of his knowledge and to visualise local developments as an integral part of one single organic world development. He will thereby steadily build up a national and even international consciousness.

The library is particularly necessary in the village to-day, because, due to its absence, a large number of even those few, who have become literate through elementary village school education, cannot maintain their ability to read and hence lapse into illiteracy. As in the case of a bodily organ, a capacity atrophies when it is not continuously exercised.

The programme of providing the library to the rural area raises a number of problems. A veritable legion of them will be required for tens of thousands of villages in our country. Further, a good section of the village library should comprise literature adapted to the specific psychology, lower cultural level, and requirements of life of the village people. The production of such literature will itself present a task of stupendous proportion. The problem of fixing its content will bring headache even to expert educationists.

(c) *Museum* : The role of the museum as a source of knowledge is not often sufficiently realized even by the educated man. The various studies prepared by the League of Nations in the past vividly demonstrate the great significance of the museum in the educational programme for the rural people. Even a museum with a local scope has a great value for the enlightenment of the villager. It can bring him rich information about the geography, the geology and the topography of the local territory, its flora and fauna, racial stocks inhabiting it, its arts and crafts as well as its past embodied in historical records and relics. This would enable the villager to get a vivid composite picture of the life and culture of the local people of whom he is a part, in various stages of their development. It would thus help him to develop a historical sense and thereby recognize the causal connection between the past and the present. It would further deepen and vivify his imagination, enhance his sense of appreciation and strengthen his habit of observation. It would also deepen his interest in the social and natural worlds in which he lives. This would engender in him the urge to transform those worlds.

The museum will prove a valuable reinforcement to the school and library in the complex of means of disseminating education and culture among the rural people. It will not only improve the quality and quantity of education but will also, further, serve as a priceless additional source of material and factual data for preparing an authentic, multi-sided history of the people.

(d) *Movie* : It is very difficult to realize the hidden potentialities of the cinema, one of the most outstanding inventions of modern times, for creative social use. It can be a most powerful means of disseminating the modern protean culture among the people on a mass scale. It can be a classic weapon of mass education. It is one of the most effective means precisely because it enables hundreds of persons simultaneously to imbibe education and culture visually. In minimum of time the cinema can transmit maximum of instruction and cultural information. Further, since it operates through a succession of visual images interpreted through words, it accentuates interest in the educational and cultural content of those images. It is, in addition, the most economical method of spreading knowledge because it does not involve the necessity of engaging a large personnel of instructors.

This marvellous instrument has not still been utilized for mass education in India. It should be adopted as rapidly as possible as a means for educating the rural population in the briefest possible time and also for making accessible to them the immense wealth of contemporary artistic and intellectual culture.

(e) *Radio* : Radio is another remarkable invention which, too, can reinforce the school as an auxiliary means of the education of the rural people. Ideally, each village should be equipped with a radio in the central place. Songs of great artists relayed by the radio will not only have recreational and emotionally nourishing value for the villager but will also develop his aesthetic faculty. Radio will further keep him acquainted with day-to-day events, both national and international. Further, talks given on radio on various themes by eminent experts and specialists will bring valuable knowledge to the village people.

(f) *Mobile Van* : Mobile vans, equipped with loudspeakers, radio, films, libraries and cultural objects, will greatly accelerate the spread of knowledge among the rural population. They can travel from village to village and bring enlightenment at the very door of the rural people. This would draw even its inert section, which lacks sufficient enthusiasm to visit schools or libraries into the orbit of modern culture.

(g) *Gymnasiums and Sport Centres* : The role of gymansiums and sport centres as valuable means of physical culture and recreation should not be underestimated. They help to build up a physically sturdy and vivacious rural people. Further, by drawing the people in the sphere of vital and pleasant collective activities, they develop such qualities as social solidarity, co-operative habits, and social discipline among them. This is recognized by educationists and sociologists all over the world. The technique both of physical culture and sport has appreciably grown in quantity and quality in modern times due to the great advance of general technique. The modern gymnasiums are equipped with more complex and varied instruments than those of the previous societies. In the world of sport too, new games like cricket, lawn and table tennis, badminton, hockey and others have been added to the old ones.

Further, in former times, gymnastics and sports were isolated local activities only. In contrast to this, in modern times they have acquired a national and even international scope as is proved by national and international contests which are organized to-day. Not only are modern games and sports more specialized, differentiated and consciously planned but they have also become a permanent feature of the life of the society. This is unlike in former times when games and sports were only episodic phenomena mainly associated as subsidiaries with important social and religious functions.

It must, however, be noted that modern games, which have been practically transplanted from the West, have not still penetrated the rural area. This is primarily due to their expensive character.

Indigenous games and gymnastics bequeathed from pre-modern India still exist in the rural area.

One of the tasks confronting the rural educationist is to evolve a synthetic physical and sport culture which would be a creative amalgam of the best elements of pre-modern and modern physical and sport cultures.

The establishment of gymnasiums and sport centres, conceived in the spirit of such a scheme of synthetic physical and sport culture, in villages should be a part of the educational programme for the rural people.

This in brief is a survey of the role of various means, available in the modern age, for carrying out a comprehensive scheme of education and culture for the rural people. The problem is complex and the task colossal. However, the solution of this problem is vitally necessary for evolving a generation of sturdy people equipped with modern knowledge who alone can be the architect of a rural society based upon democratic and co-operative socio-economic relations and pulsating with rich cultural life.

For accomplishing this signal task it is necessary to abandon not only the old conception of rural education but also of the machinery to spread it. It is not only necessary to create schools and libraries in the rural area but also to establish museums, cinemas exhibiting educational films, radio sets relaying topical news and gymnasiums and sport centres, and, further, to organize a numerous fleet of mobile vans equipped with libraries, films and loudspeakers constantly engaged in their peripatetic educational and cultural campaign.

4. Finance and Personnel

The principal prerequisites for a successful fulfilment of the programme of rural education and culture outlined before are first, the mobilization of the necessary finances and secondly, the creation of the personnel to man the gigantic venture.

The financial resources at the disposal of a nation for implementing progressive plans in various spheres of life, in final analysis, depend on the productive power of the social economy which, in its turn, is determined by the natural resources of the country, the technique of production in industry and agriculture, and above all, by the character of the social economy within which the production process is carried on. The extant social economy may help or hinder the free and rapid development of the productive forces of a society. The rural sociologist has, therefore, to be interested in the economic system prevailing in a country, study it, and decide whether it requires to be modified or even overhauled in the interests of the economic advance of the people and the resultant expansion of their material wealth. Only then the community can set apart finance requisite for the realization of comprehensive reform or reconstruction programmes including that of the rural education. Material prosperity and social and cultural advance of a people are indissolubly bound up. Culture is the spiritual perfume of the social economy.

The problem of teaching and directing personnel is another baffling problem. An enormous number of cadres of instructors, who have imbibed modern culture and who are, further, fired with social passion, will be needed for fulfilling the comprehensive educational plan.

Rural Education, A Herculean Task

Only when all the above mentioned factors—a comprehensive scientific educational and cultural plan, a properly elaborated organizational machinery, various modern technical devices, a large personnel trained in modern knowledge and, finally, adequate financial resources—are created, it is possible to liquidate illiteracy among the rural people and also to bring treasures of modern knowledge and culture to them.

The problem of the rural education—its scope, methods, means, agencies, finances and personnel—is one of the most vital problems confronting the student of rural society in India.

CHAPTER XIII

AESTHETIC CULTURE OF THE RURAL PEOPLE

AESTHETIC CULTURE, ITS CHIEF INGREDIENTS

AESTHETIC CULTURE is an integral part of the total culture of a society. It expresses, in art terms, the ideals, the aspirations, the dreams, the values, and the attitudes of its people, just as its intellectual culture reveals its knowledge of the natural and social worlds which surround them.

A systematic study of the aesthetic culture of the Indian rural society, in its historical movement of the dissolution of old types and the emergence of new ones, is vital for the study of the changing pattern of the cultural life of the rural people. Further, since art reflects social life and its changes, such a study will help the rural sociologist to comprehend the movement of the rural society itself as it progressed from its past shape to its present one. It will also reveal the changes in the psychological structures of the rural people and its sub-groups.

Eminent sociologists have enumerated the following principal arts comprising the aesthetic culture of rural society:

(1) Graphic Arts such as Drawing, Painting, Engraving and others which have two dimensional forms.

(2) Plastic Arts which "involve the manipulations of materials to yield three dimensional forms—that is to say—carving and modelling in high and low relief and in the round."

(3) Folklore comprised of "myths, tales, proverbs, riddles, verse together with music."

(4) Dance and drama which combine the three forms mentioned above and therefore are "synthetic" arts.

ITS CHIEF CHARACTERISTICS IN SUBSISTENCE SOCIETIES

Outstanding rural sociologists like Herskovief, Sorokin, Zimmerman, Galpin, and others have also located a number of specific characteristics of the aesthetic culture of the rural people living in society based on subsistence economy. The following are the important among them:

(1) *Art was fused with life*

As Sorokin remarks, "The arts were not sharply differentiated from religion, magic, intellectual pursuits, and other activities. Aesthetic elements penetrated to practically all daily occupations including agricultural work and they were an inseparable part of religious and other cultural activities."[1]

(2) *The people as a whole took part in artistic activities*

This is in contrast to the situation in the present society where the people are divided into artists who perform art and the audience which enjoys it. This antithesis was not known to earlier society.

A social group, a family, or the village people as a whole, did not break itself into actors and spectators when they engaged themselves in artistic activity. Men, women, and children of the group, all participated in it; "they were both the actors and the audience." There were very few professional artists in that society. In the social division of labour artistic work was not still separated from the total social work so as to create a special body of social workers like artists.

(3) *Art was predominantly familistic*

As seen in the previous chapters, in the pre-modern society, the life of the rural aggregate had familistic character. Consequently, the rural art, which was fused with the life of the rural people, also bore the impress of familism. "The significance, the manifestations, the content and the symbolism of rural aesthetic activities were permeated with familism. Births, marriages, deaths and sickness of members of the family were the main subjects of rural art."[2]

(4) *The technique of art was simple*

This was due to comparatively low level of general technique of the period, on which the technique of art depends.

The instruments of rural art were the products of the village artisan industry. Often the family itself made some of these in the home.

This is in contrast to the instruments of modern art which are the products of modern industries and are therefore complex, highly specialised, varied and multifold.

A simple drum (*Dhol Nagara*, *Dholak*, *Duff*, *Khanjri*, *Nobati*); a flute made out of simple reeds or handy wood; a few stringed instruments not complicated in structure (*Ektar*, *Ravanhatha*); some metal instruments of simple design like gongs, bells, *Manjiras*; some wooden instruments like *Kartal*; ordinary metal vessels of domestic use like *Thali*, *Gagar*, *Lota* or drinking pot, tongs; such natural objects as branches of trees, feathers of birds, shells, conches;—these constituted the technical prerequisites of art in the pre-modern Indian rural society. Further, art performances were organized not in theatres and concert halls as in modern times but either in domestic premises or in open village spaces. The village drama was enacted not on any imposing stage equipped with colourful curtains, spotlights, and rich scenery in the background. Much of the realism was achiev-

---

[1] Systematic Sourcebook in Rural Sociology: Vol. II p. 445.

[2] *Idid.*, p. 446

ed not by suggestive or symbolic artifice but was created by histrionics.

(5) *Art had agrarian life processes as its main content*

Since art was fused with life, it depicted the life of the rural people in its various aspects, economic, social and religious. For instance, "The most common of the work songs of nonurbanized agricultural peoples were those that accompanied collective agricultural occupations, hunting and fishing, grain grinding and milling, flax-thrashing, corn-thrashing, ploughing and seeding, fruit-picking and so forth.........Some of their religious and magical songs were concerned with love, death, mourning, health and fertility, others dealt with agricultural activities and were sung as a part of the religious and magical rites connected with spring, summer fall and winter festivities, still others honoured the grove, wood, field and corn deities...... Both work songs and religious songs were inseparably connected with daily life and with the religion and magic that centred in agriculture."[3]

Even a cursory survey of the songs of the Indian rural people corroborates the above view. Agricultural work processes like sowing, reaping, and harvesting; or other work processes like the fetching of water from the well by women; or sentiments of gratitude to gods for successful agricultural operations or plaintive appeal to them for their fruition, form the main thematic content of those songs.

Dance, another form of art, had also, for its predominant content the real agrarian life processes. Similarly, the folklore composed of legends, myths and stories, mostly dealt with the same theme either in a direct or symbolic form.

Ornamental and decorative rural arts also bore the impress of the rural environmental and social milieu. The specific flora and fauna found in the rural area provided material for design. Rural artistic creations in these and other spheres "are based on rural environment and occupation; trees, flowers and plants, horses, cattle and other animals, birds and fish and peasant houses."[4] Further, geometrical designs characterizing those arts had a magical meaning bearing on various agrarian life processes.

The rural sociologists have also observed that "Agricultural characteristics are most clearly mainfest in songs, music, dances, stories, proverbs, riddles, literature, pantomimes, festivals, dramatic performances, and similar forms of the arts; they are less conspicuous in designs, ornamentations, architecture and sculpture, but even here if properly interpreted, the agricultural stamp is noticeable."[5]

(6) *Art creations were predominantly collective creations, collective in spirit*

This is one of the most striking features of the rural art. While in the urban area, songs, stories, dramas, and such other art pieces, have been the products of individual artists, practically the entire folklore of the rural

---

[3] *Idid*: p 451.

[4] *Idid.*, p. 453.

[5] *Idid.*, p. 458.

people, comprising rural songs and tales as well as rural dramas, has been the collective creation of generations of rural artists. Their authorship cannot be traced to individual artists since no individual artists created them. They remain, therefore, almost always anonymous in origin.

As a result of this, the rural art has been overwhelmingly collective in spirit. It has expressed the fears, joys, aspirations, and dreams of the collectivity even more than most of the social art of the urban society. Further, it has been marked with profound natural-dreams of the collectivity even more than most of social art of the urban society. Further, it has been marked with profound naturalness, sincerity, and spontaneity. This is in contrast to the urban art which is either commercialized and, therefore, caters largely to the emotions of its potential buyers or is super-individualistic (ivory tower art) and embodies the individualistic caprices and momentary emotions of the artist. Further, rural art has expressed the sentiments and life experiences of countless generations. It has been, therefore, also more organic and durable than most of the urban art.

(7) *Rural art was non-commercial*

In agrarian societies based on self-sufficient economies, products have not the character of commodities. Thinkers and artists create their intellectual and artistic products not for the market but for the direct consumption of the village rural aggregate that looks after their needs. Rural art, hence, is not commercialized. Since the rural artist is not motivated by the urge to make profit through his art creations, his artistic activity is urged on only by the artistic aim. The urban artist, in contrast to this, is torn between two urges; one, the urge for artistic selfexpression and the other, the need to make livelihood in a competitive economic environs by producing for the market and hence by adapting his art to the tastes of those who can buy it. This dualism disrupts his artistic personality and tends to distort his art. The rural artist does not suffer from these contradictory motives and his art is, therefore "harmonious."

Here we must strictly guard ourselves against the danger of idealizing rural art and the self-sufficient society which generates that art. In such a society, the individual is not still differentiated from the collectivity, be it the joint family, the caste, or the village community. The individual is subordinated to these groups. The structure and environment of such a society do not, therefore, provide freedom for the development of the creative individuality of its members or scope for them to strike out new unconventional paths of thought and craftsmanship. This puts a limitation on the rural art though its collective spirit should be properly noted and valued.

The competitive socio-economic environs of the modern society, on the other hand, while differentiating and liberating the individual from the pressure of the collectivity on his free development, tends to weaken his social urges. Most of the urban art is, therefore, individualistic. It mostly portrays the struggles of the individual against the stifling forces of the unplanned competitive society. Excepting for a growing minority art current which mirrors the dream of, and struggle for a higher co-operative society, the exisitng urban art is, largely, socially sterile, morbid or escapist.

(8) *Artistic craftsmanship and culture were transmitted from generation to generation orally.*

This was due to the fact that there existed no printing press which would produce literature on art. Further, there did not exist any schools or academies of art in self-sufficient societies. Hence, they were mainly the family elders who trained the youngsters in the knowledge and execution of arts like folk songs, folk dances and others.

We have referred elsewhere to the process of the transformation of the old rural society into the new modern society.

Transformation of Rural Aesthetic Culture

We will briefly summarize the most striking features of this transformation in the sphere of rural aesthetic culture. Art gradually became a specialized activity of the artist. The village population increasingly became differentiated into artists and the rest. Individual artist or a group of artists sang and danced on festive occasions, the rest of the village people constituting the audience. The technique of art also slowly altered, became more complex, thanks to the ability of modern industry to produce complex art instruments. Above all, since commodity production extended to the village also, art itself became a commodity and the artist, a seller of the artistic goods. Pecuniary gain became the main motif of artistic creation.

Art, moreover, became gradually separated from life. Its thematic content changed. It began to draw its themes and imagery from new sources such as the travails of the individual struggling against the pressures of a competitive socio-economic environment. Formerly, it dealt with the vicissitudes of the life of the village collectivity; now it concerned itself with the fate of the individual. Thus art increasingly ceased to be a collective activity of the village group as a whole dealing with its collective life processes and became the individual activity of the artist dealing with the problems of the individual struggling in a competitive world. Further, the traditional practice of handing down art from generation to generation also began to decline since the printing press made it possible to perpetuate art techniques and art creations like folk songs and village tales in the printed form.

The modern cinema with its film songs and film stories, the gramophone with its song records, together with the radio, slowly began to penetrate the rural zone and became new means of aesthetic delight for the rural population.

These developments led to the increasing urbanization of the rural aesthetic culture. Thus under the impact of the technical and economic forces of modern society, not only did the socio-economic structure of the rural society undergo a single transformation but its aesthetic culture with its specific characteristics also suffered an increasing change.

The Indian rural society, for the last one hundred and fifty years, has been experiencing a historical change. The change has not, however, advanced to the same extent as in some other countries since a foreign power which ruled India during this period retarded the process of rapid industrialization and resultant modernization of our country. In West European countries and the U. S. A. the urbanization of the old rural society and its aesthetic culture have advanced to a far greater degree than in India. It must, however, be noted that even in those advanced countries the aesthetic culture of the rural society possesses a number of specific characteristics which distinguish it from the aesthetic culture of the urban society.

It is essential for the Indian rural sociologist to study the aesthetic culture of the contemporary rural Indian people and the transformation it is undergoing. Such a study will enable him to comprehend the transformation of the life of the rural people and their struggles, dreams and aspirations. Art reveals life through more subtle nuances and often provides a more authentic picture of life than what even history books can give. The French society of Balzac's period is more vividly and truthfully laid bare when viewed through the prism of his great realistic novels than as revealed by the French historians in their works.

As Mr. Morris observes:

"To a superlative degree the arts express the qualities which an age prizes, the human actions which it cherishes, and the ideals which it ennobles......In the aesthetic attitude, a culture can be captured and held, not as a set of bare facts to be statistically tabulated, but as a function of the travail of human minds."

The aesthetic culture of the rural people should be next studied from the standpoint of (1) its content and (2) its form.

Content of Rural Aesthetic Culture

The rural aesthetic culture, a rich complex of myths, legends, folk songs, folk tales, riddles and proverbs, dances, dramas and pantomimes, and graphic and plastic arts, transmitted from generation to generation, embodies directly or symbolically the world outlook, social conceptions and ethical norms of the rural people as they emerged and changed across ages. It can serve as a very valuable source material for a rural sociologist of imagination and insight to build up a concrete vivid picture of the technical, economic, social, religious, moral and cultural life of the rural aggregate in various periods. Since the rural aesthetic culture was always anchored in the life of the rural people, was fused with it and, further, artistically mirrored it, it would reveal what technique they employed in material production in a particular period, what weapons they used in warfare, what ornaments and costumes they wore, what houses they built and lived in, what socio-economic system prevailed during that period, what social classes comprised it, what social conflicts rent it, what type of family and other social institutions then existed, what customs ruled the people, what views and attitudes they held on diverse problems, what norms and criteria determined their social conduct. It will thus not only lay bare the social structure and life of the people in a past period but will also disclose their social, ethical and religious conceptions as well as their material and ideal aspirations and aims. It will also reveal the story of their brave social endeavour, also of their reverses and victories.

The enormous rich material comprising the rural aesthetic culture has to be first assembled, analysed and classified. The next task for the rural sociologist is to interpret it with deep historical imagination and sociological insight. This alone will help him to achieve a living objective picture of the rural society and the rural life as they existed in the past. This is specially necessary because no detailed written history is available.

The Indian rural society is divided into a number of regional rural societies.

A comparative study of the contents of the aesthetic cultures of these units will disclose elements common to them such as a number of common folk songs, folk tales, myths, proverbs, riddles and other, though generally to be found with regional variations.

Such a discovery will help to comprehend the process of the diffusion of culture which had taken place in various rural zones of India in the past. It will also help to get an adequate picture of the historical process of the contacts and collisions, amalgamation or even assimilation, among numerous tribes and communities which lived in India in past epochs. A veritable past history of the Indian rural society and the Indian rural humanity can be composed through such a comparative study of the various rural aesthetic cultures of the various rural zones today.

Such a history of the Indian rural society is indispensable for evolving the history of the Indian society as a whole.

There are various means of deciphering the past history of the Indian people. The study of the variegated and massive content of the aesthetic cultures of the regional agrarian groups and its evaluation will serve as perhaps one of its most fruitful means for that purpose. Nevertheless, all the varied means should be utilised in mutual co-ordination.

Form of Rural Aesthetic Culture

After studying the content of the rural aesthetic culture, it is necessary to study the specific forms in which this culture is expressed.

There exists an organic relationship between the content and the form of art. It consists in the unity of its form and content, the content determining the form.

The specific content of the rural aesthetic culture outlined previously determines the specific forms of that culture. It determines the styles of painting, engraving, sculpture and architecture; the designs of costumes and ornaments; the tunes of folk songs and the rhythms of folk poetry; the structures of folk tales, dances and dramas. Further, a good proportion of that culture is marked with symbolism and it is the task of the rural sociologist to penetrate through the symbols and uncover the hidden significant ideas conveyed in an art work.

The Indian rural aesthetic culture comprising various regional rural cultures exhibits a variety of styles, patterns and modes. For instance, we have such varied forms as Sorathas, Dohas, Chaupais, and Chhappas, Kirtans, Bhajans, Abhangas, Pavadas, Deshis, Horis, Kajaris, Kawalis and others in the domain of poetry and song; Rasas, Garbas and others in the sphere of dance; and Bhavais, Ramlilas, Tamasas and other in the field of drama. Similarly the words of other rural arts also reveal a rich diversity of forms.

The study of different forms of the art cultures of different regional rural communities will help us to distinguish them as distinct cultural units. Further, since the agrarian life possesses certain common characteristics, though with local and regional variations, such a study will also reveal how basically the same life content has been variously handled in the sphere of art by different agrarian communities.

A considerable amount of specialization is found in the agrarian arts mainly because the art is fused with concrete activities like sowing, reaping, harvesting and others or with such articles of utility as ornaments and earthenware. Again, since the art creations maintain a thematic continuity, the arts dealing with them are enriched from generation to generation. There is thus continuous improvement of agrarian arts, their forms, styles and patterns.

A study of the forms of various regional aesthetic cultures discloses the significant fact that a number of them are essentially the same with regional variations only. This would assist the rural sociologist to resolve the problem of the diffusion of art forms, and of the migrations of a number of rural arts.

The Indian rural people have a long and rich history of aesthetic culture. Musical concerts and dramas were a feature of the rural life during the Maurya period and have been, as A. S. Altekar states, described as "Preksha," by Chanakya and "Samaja" by Ashoka. They were an integral part of the celebrations of religious festival such as Ram-Navmi, Gokul-Ashtami, Dasera, Ganesh Chaturthi, and Holi. They were also organised at village and inter-village fairs which were great social occasions in premodern times.

Trends of the Changes in Aesthetic Culture

Since the advent of the British in India, as previously seen, a process of the fundamental alteration of Indian society began. As a result of this the psychology of the rural people also changed. The old aesthetic culture began to decline. The process is still continuing. The old arts have been gradually declining though the new modern ones have not been replacing them with the same tempo.

The rural sociologist is confronted with the problem of a renaissance of the rural aesthetic culture. He has to resolve a number of problems germane to a programme of such a renaissance. What will be the nature of the new aesthetic culture ? What will be its content and form ? Will the new rural arts be fused with the new rural life ? Will the organic unity of art and life, the basic characteristic of the old aesthetic culture, be preserved in the new art ? Will the new rural art retain the sincerity and the spontaniety of the old one or will it be sophisticated as a good section of the modern urban art is ? What will be the ideology informing it ? Will it be a mass art in which the people participate or will it be a distinct domain of the professional artists ? Will it be a commercialized art produced by artists who subordinate their self-expression to the needs of the market or an ivory tower art where the artists create solely for their own satisfaction, or an art which is social and still provides free self-expression for the artists ? These are some of the vital problems which the rural sociologist has to investigate.

Further, modern humanity has at its disposal an advanced technology which can create a complex and multifold technique of art. The material means and resources available today for such arts as painting, music, drama architecture and others are simply astounding. They can serve as the material prerequisite for the creation of a rich and variegated artistic mass culture which can express profound social ideas and portray individual and mass emotions in all their complexity and variety. The new art by means of the material technique accessible to it can work up not merely a few simple collective ideas and emotions as the old rural art did, but also the multifold and complex collective as well as individualized ideas and emotions which the modern rural humanity even today conceives and feels under the impact of a changing agrarian world. With the steady transformation of the rural society, the social relations are being constantly recast engendering new conceptions and feelings, new social passions, dreams and aspirations.

The existing rural aesthetic culture is in a state of increasing disorganization. This, in the final analysis, is the result of the increasing disorganization of the rural society itself of which it is the aesthetic reflex. The crisis of culture is the product of the crisis of society.

The problem arises whether the process of increasing disorganization and dissolution which the present rural aesthetic culture is undergoing will culminate into the emergence of a new historically higher aesthetic culture.

It depends on how the crisis of the present rural society is resolved. If the present rural society is replaced by one materially and culturally more advanced and based on co-operative social relations, a higher aesthetic culture will spring as a beautiful flower on the tree of such a higher type of society.

As mentioned before, the rural aesthetic culture has been declining and some of the rural arts even disappearing. From the stand-point of the history of the evolution of the Indian art, it is necessary to preserve the knowledge of the present rural aesthetic culture. Further, this is also necessary because, in absence of the written history of the early phase of the Indian society and insufficiently recorded history of subsequent phase, the rural aesthetic culture with its myths and legends, folk tales and folk songs, dances and dramas, paintings, engravings and statues, can provide a clue to the life of the Indian people in past epochs.

Modern technical means such as printing press, gramophone, camera, film and others can be made use of for preserving the rural songs and stories, statuary and architecture, fables and legends, through printing, recording and photographing.

For all these reasons a careful study of the rural aesthetic culture is indispensable for the student of the rural society.

CHAPTER XIV

CHANGING RURAL WORLD

Rural Society, Changing

LIKE ALL other phenomena the rural society too has been changing since its emergence. Its technology, economy and social institutions, its ideology, art and religion, have undergone a ceaseless change. This change has sometimes been imperceptibly slow, sometimes strikingly rapid, and at some moments even qualitative in character resulting into the transformation of one type of rural society into another type.

To discern change in a system, to recognize its direction, to understand the objective and subjective forces which bring it about and, further, to consciously accelerate the process of change by helping the progressive trends within the changing system—this constitutes a scientific approach to and active creative intervention in the life of a system.

Rural Change, Factors Responsible

We will now refer to the forces and factors, conscious or unconscious, which bring about change in rural society.

Close investigators of rural society have enumerated a number of these forces and factors, the following being the principal among them.

Natural Factors

Natural forces such as floods, earthquakes, famines and others affect the territorial zone in which the rural people live. They have a disastrous effect on the flora and the fauna of the zone which often considerably influences the economic life of the people, and, in the case of earthquakes of dangerous intensity, even sometimes results in large-scale loss of human life and material devastation. The rural collectivity lives in the midst of a specific geographical and geological milieu and manipulates them through agriculture, mining and other operations. Hence a profound change in earth structures modifies or sometimes even convulses its life processes.

These are the natural forces which bring about change in rural society. There are human factors, too, which operate to alter that society.

Technological Factors

As observed earlier, man carries on his struggle against the environment by means of tools. He has, therefore, been ceaselessly engaged in improving the old tools and inventing new ones. Though the inventors create new tools consciously, they are unable to prognosticate the social consequences of their inventions which are sometimes far-reaching. The invention of new tools, new means of transport and communications, and the discovery of new materials such as iron, new chemical substances and others, result in the change in the life of the rural people, in their economy and even in the structures of their social and political relations. The far-reaching economic, social and political outcomes of outstanding inventions like the plough, the steam engine and others, were not and could not be predicted by their inventors.

As Prof. Ogburn observes, the invention of radio led to about 150 major changes in social life.

The invention of steam-driven machinery in England resulted in the evolution of modern industries, which, at a certain stage of their development, needed foreign market. This led to the political and the economic expansion of Britain and the rise and growth of the British Empire. Once the power-driven technique was invented, it was adopted by other nations also. Western nations, in steady succession, developed modern industries and, due to the need of foreign market for their industrial products, conquered other countries and built up empires. This changed the economic and political life of those nations as well as of those who were subjected to them. The societies of the countries of both the dominant as well as the subject nations were either completely transformed or appreciably modified.

What is true of the national societies is also true of the rural society since it is an integral part of the national society.

Various Conscious Methods

Next we will survey the methods and devices adopted by social groups and organizations to consciously bring about the alteration or transformation of the rural world.

Eminent sociologists like Sims and others have collected and mentioned various techniques and methods used by these groups and organizations. The following are the chief among them :

(1) *Persuasive Method* : The protagonists of this method seek to convince the rural population of the necessity of effecting changes in the rural society in various spheres, technical, economic, social and others, through organized propaganda campaign. They endeavour to popularise among them various rural reforms or rural reconstruction programmes and exhort them to implement these programmes.

The distinguishing characteristic of this method lies in the fact that its proponents restrict their effort only to the propaganda of their programmes. They do not themselves initiate or participate in implementing the programmes. They leave this to the rural people themselves.

This is because the exponents of this method have almost limitless faith in the force of argument. They hold the view that it is possible by means of a suitable argument to convince the rural people of the need for change in the rural social structure, to kindle in them the urge for such a change, to popularise among them an appropriate programme of rural reform or reconstruction and, through this, to rouse them to practical activity for the accomplishment of that programme.

(2) *Demonstrative Method*: This method is also known as the method of propaganda through example or by deed. The exponents of this method endeavour to popularise their programme of rural reconstruction or specific reform by themselves implementing it on a miniature scale. They declare that the rural population would be more easily convinced of the advantages of a programme of rural change if the advantages of such a programme are demonstrated in action. They consider this method more effective than that of mere oral and written propaganda.

For instance, they organize demonstration farms to convince the farmers of the superiority of a new technique and new and better methods of agricultural production.They start model agricultural colonies based on the co-operative principle to rouse the farmers to the recognition of the economic advantages of co-operative farming so that they themselves, on their own initiative, may combine or integrate their individual uneconomic or semi-economic holdings and embark on the road to co-operative or collective agriculture. They establish a few educational and health centres so that the rural population may recognize the benefits of education and hygiene and, thereafter, themselves start schools and health centres in the entire rural area.

(3) "*Compulsory*" *Method*: The state itself often intervenes and, through legislation, brings about changes in the rural life or the rural social structure. It is not the will and the initiative of the rural people but of the state that determine and accomplish those changes. During the War, "To rural America, along with the rest, coercive measures were applied. Among other things, production was made compulsory, prices were fixed, the disposal of food stuffs prescribed and time of labour regulated by law."

In India, a number of states have recently enacted anti-zamindari laws to alter land relations in the rural areas.

Such "compulsory" intervention of the state in the life of the rural people has been increasing in modern times.

(4) *Method of Social Pressure*: This method is adopted by a rural individual, a group or a class to achieve a desired change in the life of the rural people or in the rural social or economic structure. The means resorted to may vary widely. They may include petitioning, passive resistance, individual and group satyagraha, processions and marches, strikes and demonstrations, even individual terrorism (for instance killing of money lenders or landlords by farmers or tenants), mass revolts, revolutions and others.

These forms of pressure and struggle have been growing more and more prevalent in modern times.

The rural sociologist has to carefully analyse and study these forms of struggle since they have been playing a significant role in transforming rura societies of various countries in the contemporary epoch.

(5) *Contact Method* : "It is generally recognized that one of the most effective means of social change is found in contact of cultures......where peoples of different cultures come in touch with one another, cross-fertilization takes place."

In the medieval age, the town and the village lived almost independent social, economic and cultural existence. This separatism was increasingly undermined as a result of the extension and wider and wider ramification of modern means of transport and communication all over the country and resultant closer and closer contact of urban and rural populations. Further, the village economy was transformed and became an integral part of the national and even international economy. This created and multiplied the points of contact between the rural and urban societies and their populations. This increasingly led to the changes in the socio-economic structure of the rural society and the life of the rural people.

The historical tendency is towards a growing urbanization of the rural society due to the stronger impact of the urban forces on the latter.

(6) *Educational Method* : The increasing spread of modern education among the rural people through the establishment of schools and other educational institutions has been one of the very effective means to bring about changes in the rural life and the rural social structure. The village people, when they are initiated in scientific knowledge of life and the world, would find it easy to break with superstition which affects their consciousness and keeps them conservative.

A group of social thinkers invest the educational method with decisive importance in bringing about the rural change.

CONCLUSION

We have referred above to some of the principal methods observed by some of the eminent rural sociologists, which have been operating to bring about the rural change.

These methods should be carefully studied by those who desire to evolve a programme of rural reform or reconstruction. They should assess the value of these methods and assign them a proportional significance while elaborating such a programme.

CHAPTER XV

RURAL SOCIOLOGY, A GUIDE TO RURAL RECONSTRUCTION

THREE SCHOOLS OF RURAL RECONSTRUCTION

THERE ARE numerous individuals and groups who desire and strive for improvement of the material and cultural life of the rural people.

They can be broadly divided into the following three categories :

(i) The Philanthropic group;
(ii) The Reformist group; and
(iii) The Revolutionary group.

THE PHILANTHROPIC GROUP

The Philanthropic group does not view the problem of the material and cultural poverty of the rural people in the context of the institutions and the basic structure of the rural society. It holds the conviction that it is possible to ameliorate the position of the rural people through direct humanitarian effort, without changing those institutions and structure. It evolves economic, educational and other programmes of village uplift which embody such items as creation of charity funds to help the village needy, moral appeals to landlords and such other groups to relax their pressure on peasants, establishment of hospitals and schools, and others.

The basic feature of the standpoint and the programmatic approach of this group to the problem lies in the fact that it attempts to improve the conditions of the rural population within the matrix of the existing institutions and structure of the rural society, by means of purely humanitarian endeavour.

THE REFORMIST GROUP

The Reformist group subscribes to the view that it is the malfunctioning of the existing rural social system and its institutions (and not the social system and its institutions in their basic essence), which is the social-genetic cause of the economic misery and social and cultural backwardness of the rural people. They therefore, work for a healthy functioning of the social system and its institutions, or, at most, for reforming them. They assert that once this institutional reform is accomplished, it will result in the all-sided betterment of the life of the rural population.

The distinguishing characteristic of the standpoint and the programmatic approach of this group to the problem lies in the fact that for elevating the conditions of the rural people at present it does not regard it necessary to replace the existing social system and its institutions by new ones but strives only to reform them.

THE REVOLUTIONARY GROUP

Finally, there is a third group whose standpoint and programmatic approach to the problem are based on a revolutionary conception. They think that the abysmal poverty, crass ignorance, and cultural backwardness of the mass of the rural people are fundamentally due to the existing social system and the institutions which are its organs to sustain that system. The social system and its institutions, they feel, cannot but breed these evils. They declare, therefore, that both the programme of individual aid and relief and that of institutional reform will be unable to achieve the desired end. They contend that no reform can appreciably liberate the rural people from want, disease, illiteracy, and lack of culture. They argue that new wine cannot be filled into the old bottles.

Thus, according to this group, the evils of the rural society are not the result of any malfunctioning of the rural social system or its institutions but are inherent in this system and institutions themselves, are the inevitable product of the natural functioning of the present social order. This group, therefore, evolves and attempts to carry out a programme of a revolutionary transformation of the rural social structure from its economic base upward.

While laying decisive emphasis on its social revolutionary objective, this group includes in its programme a number of items of the first two programmes. It however, links its struggle to implement those items with the struggle for the change of the entire social system.

These three groups with their diverse and even conflicting programmes are at present struggling for hegemony in the agrarian area.

RURAL RECONSTRUCTION PROGRAMMES, THEIR PRINCIPAL WEAKNESSES

Various individual groups, associations and parties, each according to its own light, are thus engaged in the movement of rural uplift and reconstruction. Among them are individual philanthropists and philanthropic bodies; social, political, religious, economic and educational organizations including welfare associations; missionary groups; Governmental institutions and others.

We will make a few observations regarding the work of these groups and organizations.

(1) *Exclusive Concentration on One Aspect of the Rural Life*

Some of them exclusively concentrate on one single aspect of the rural life like education, economic welfare, sanitation, crusade against reactionary social customs and practices, religious superstition, ethical uplift or fight against disease. They isolate one aspect of the rural life from its other aspects. The organic unity of the rural life and the interrelations and interdependence of its many aspects are thus lost sight of.

This results either in the abortion or limited success of their programme even when dealing with one single aspect of the rural life.

(2) *Predominantly Emotional Approach*

Most of these groups and organizations, while inspired by ethical and humanitarian motives, lack scientific training for the work they undertake. They forget that an objective study of the rural society and its conditions is vital for evolving a correct programme and methodology of work and that merely good intentions are no guarantee of successful social work. They forget that a patient gathering of factual data pertaining to the life of the rural people and a detailed concrete study of their specific prerequisites for formulating a correct programme of rural work. A study of the psychological traits, ethnic and communal composition, customs and beliefs of the rural aggregate, is also indispensable for the purpose. Further, these groups and organizations require to have a concrete knowledge of the economic structure of the rural society, the specific system of land tenure prevailing in it, the various socio-economic groups bound up with its economy and with different and even conflicting interests, the religious and other ideologies which have a hold over their mind, the particular types of family and other social institutions existing there and many other things. Such knowledge is necessary because the task before them is not the renovation of a vague and vast rural society, in general, but of a specific type of rural society; not the amelioration of the abstract rural people but of a particular rural people with local limits, defined past and crystallized present conditions. It is, therefore, essential to study the particular rural society and its people in concrete details. Then alone, it is possible to evolve an appropriate programme of rural work for the recuperation of a particular rural society and the advance of the specific rural aggregate living in that society. Then alone, also, it is possible to locate the specific social, economic, psychological, ideological and other obstacles in the way of the fulfilment of that programme. A rural aggregate in Gujarat is different from that in Saurashtra, Bihar or Maharashtra.

Many individuals and organizations oriented to the work of rural reconstruction and uplift lack this understanding. They evolve naive programmes of rural work which, not being based on concrete detailed knowledge of the specific rural society and its people, fail or meet with partial success. This breeds the sentiment of defeatism among them and results sometimes in their abandoning of the rural work altogether.

(3) *Lack of Co-ordination of work*

Lack of co-ordination of activities in various spheres marks the work of some organizations and groups. Further, their activities are often based on conflicting value systems.

This, too, is detrimental to the success of the programme. It is obvious that all activities should be co-ordinated and should constitute a single organic stream of total work. Also it is evident that a single principle must determine and permeate the diverse activities in diverse fields. Otherwise there will ensue mutual negating of activities.

(4) *Insufficient Ability to Assess the Results*

Some groups and organizations exhibit insufficient ability for a proper assessment of the results of their efforts in various domains of rural work. Since they have, therefore, no adequate conception of the cumulative result of their activities, they get a hazy notion regarding their advance towards their objective. Inability to properly evaluate their work in terms of productivity also denies them that power of self-criticism which is also vital for a correct planning of next stages of work.

When work is not properly planned and correctly assessed, there is also the danger of deviating from the correct road to the goal.

Sporadic and unplanned forms of rural welfare work are also sometimes launched. In a number of instances, they degenerate into mere fads. This reveals unconscious lack of earnestness or absence of scientfic understanding of the problem on the part of their sponsors. We find a mushroom growth of such efforts embarked upon by individuals and even institutions in the rural area. This tends to make the picture of the rural reconstruction work chaotic to some extent, and often leads the rural people to become victims rather than beneficiaries of such endeavours since they yield unstable and distorted results.

(5) *Absence of Proper Sociological Perspective*

The principal weakness characterizing these organizations however, generally lies in their lack of proper sociological understanding of the problem of rural reconstruction. To evolve a successful programme of rural reconstruction at a higher level, it is quite necessary to know the law governing the development of the rural society. The structure, the functioning and the objective tendencies of development of the existing rural society, the interconnectedness and the interdependence of various elements of that society (technical, economic, social, political, ideological), and the relative significance of those elements in determining the life of the rural society and their respective role in the total social change, require to be comprehended.

To change society consciously, we must have a science of society. Rural sociology is the science of rural society. The laws of the structure and development of rural society in general can aid us in discovering the special laws governing a particular rural society. Without the science of rural society, it is not, therefore, possible to get an authentic picture of a particular rural society. Rural sociology alone can provide a correct, organic, synthetic and multi-sided knowledge of a specific rural society and the tendency of its further evolution.

Rural Sociology, an Indispensable Guide

Rural sociology will help the rural worker to make a correct diagnosis of its ills and will, further, enable him to evolve a correct prescription or programme to overcome those ills. If the diagnosis of the ills is erroneous or imperfect, the prescription itself will be unscientific and therefore futile. The uniformed rural worker will adopt unhistorical and inappropriate means to cure the defects and deficiencies of the rural social organisms. The social ills may have a deep-seated cause in the very social system itself and may be merely symptoms proclaiming the general disease of the social organism. Not knowing this, the rural worker will engage himself in a symptomatic treatment of the social ills which, as all physicians know, gives no relief or gives only a partial and temporary relief.

There is another grave danger for a rural worker who is ignorant of rural sociology. The present social evils are the features of the present society and therefore cannot be overcome by methods adopted to cure the social evils of bygone societies. For instance, solutions of the evils of self-sufficient society would not be adequate for the solution of the maladies of the present competitive commodity society. If the rural worker is unaware of this fact, he will attempt to graft the former on the present society. He will recommend the resuscitation of the techniques, political systems or ethical concepts of the past societies to overcome the crisis of the present one. Such a view is unscientific. The evils of the present rural society arise out of its own inner structure and can be cured by means determined by its own trend of development.

The programme of rural reconstruction should be derived from a strict sociological analysis of the actual conditions and tendencies of the actually existing rural society and evaluation of the actual forces at work within it.

Here comes the decisive creative role of rural sociology which is as indispensable for the purpose of rural reconstruction as the science of medicine is to a medical practitioner.

CHAPTER XVI

CONCLUSION

Need for Rural Sociology

In conclusion a few observations may be made.

As observed at the outset, the study of rural society has become extremely urgent today when in a number of countries rural social structure is passing through an acute and even organic crisis; when its economy is rapidly disintegrating, unfolding the perspective even of utter collapse; when social antagonisms and resultant conflicts between various social classes and groups comprising the rural humanity are being aggravated; in fact, when the rural social world is increasingly being transformed into a theatre of a far-reaching social revolution. In such a situation pregnant with mighty developments, it is the task of the rural sociologist to discover the law of development of rural society, to make a historico-theoretical analysis of that society and to locate the dynamics of its development.

Cognizance of the specific law of the development of the rural society is the basic prerequisite for its reconstruction. Its necessity for a correct grasp of the forces at work in the rural world in their interrelations and mutual interactions cannot be overstressed.

Only when the social programme and the social action undertaken in pursuance of that programme are based upon and guided by the scientific social theory, they are successful.

Present Volume, its Aim

The present volume has the aim of, first, emphasizing the vital need of studying the life processes of the rural society analytically and synthetically and, secondly, suggesting some of the appropriate lines of approach for such a study.

An indication of the more significant among the various aspects of the rural life in their complex and variegated interconnections has been attempted here. Further, an effort has been made to point out how a composite picture of the multi-sided rural life process has yet to be built up.

Enormous research and theoretical labour are necessary to get a proper insight into the process of structural and functional transformations which the rural society has experienced in the past and the present. Such an insight is absolutely essential to assess the specific weight and role of various factors whose actions and mutual interactions have provided movement to the rural society at various times.

Only such a study of the past and present rural social structures can help to generalize the total movement of the rural society into a single law of its development. Then alone rural sociology can become a science. And then alone a scientific programme of the reconstruction of the rural society and a scientific plan for its realization can be evolved.

Though the task is herculean, disconcertingly baffling, there is no ground for pessimism. And that for a variety of reasons.

Growing Awareness of the Problem

First; there is a growing awareness, on the part of the earnest section of the intelligentsia, of the urgency of the problem of the agrarian crisis and its solution. This section is increasingly realizing the futility, nay, even the harmful consequences, of sentimental, one-sided and other unscientific approaches to the problem. Such realization is generally the result of a deeper sociological investigation of the problem or of the practical failure of various plans of rural social reform or reconstruction.

Growing Literature on the Problem

Secondly, there has accumulated in recent times enormous statistical and other factual material providing illuminating information about the rural society, past and present. Individual scholars—historians, economists, sociologists, anthropologists—as well as governmental and non-governmental bodies have made studies of the various aspects of the rural life and published considerable literature on the subject. The existence of this literature implies that the precondition for the discovery of the law of evolution of the rural society, so vital for a correct approach to the problem of the present debacle of that society, has been appreciably created. The student ... of the rural society has, at his disposal, enormous and varied material for scientific analysis and conclusions.

There exist today such sources of rural information as the Imperial, Provincial and District Gazeteers, the Government Census Reports, the Settlement and Survey Reports, the Reports on the Castes and Tribes of India, the Economic and other Surveys by various Governmental bodies and Commissions, the Archaeological, Linguistic and other Surveys, the yearly Economic, Political, Educational and other publications, the recent research studies of Bureaus of Statistics and Economics and others. These are some of the sources of concrete information about the Indian rural life. With careful indexing and editing, this literature can be of great value.

The works published on the Indian rural society by numerous scholars, Indian and foreign, since the time of Sir Henry Maine, constitute still another source of information on the subject. They deal with various aspects of the Indian rural life. This group of writers includes eminent historians, economists, politicians, administrators, social reformers, anthropologists and sociologists. However, as we stated, no comprehensive scientific history of the Indian rural society tracing its origin and development in successive historical stages and dealing with various aspects of the rural life in reciprocal interaction and historical movement, has still been written. The works of these scholars will, however, prove of considerable value for preparing such a history.

The literature on the Indian rural life in general and on the rural economy in particular published by the Indian National Congress, the Kisan organizations and other political parties, though meagre, also provides useful data about the life conditions of the rural people. The information lies scattered and hence requires to be assembled, classified and co-ordinated, so that it can be utilized for building up a composite picture of the rural scene.

Another source of information is provided by the studies in the form oi various theses on different rural problems prepared by students for M. A. and Ph. D. degrees of various Indian Universities. The theses are the product of strenuous study, inquiries, and fieldwork. A number of othei educational and research agencies have also published literature or the subject.

The primary data gathered by various welfare organizations and welfare workers is also voluminous and, being based on case work, is detailed anc living. These institutions and workers, however, generally make a purely empirical approach to the study of rural social phenomena. The materia collected by them, hence, has to be sifted and generalized so that the histo-rical tendency of the movement of the rural society can be detected.

The mass of material collected by the various above mentioned agencies lies in an unorganized form. It has to be very carefully catalogued, classi-fied, summarized and edited so that it could be made available in a coherent form to those who are exploring the laws of that society.

New groups and institutions are also springing up in various parts of the country which have for their objective a thorough and detailed study of our rural world. Some of these bring with them a new social outlook and adop new methods of social research promising more fruitful results.

It is also necessary to refer to the growing literature on the rural societ in the international world in recent decades. A part of this literature ha great theoretical and historical value. It deals with the genesis of the rura society and its transformation in different periods in a number of countries A part of this literature is also devoted to the investigation of the existing rural societies in various countries. The student of Indian rural society may get useful theoretical hints and practical suggestions from a study of thi literature for solving the Indian rural problems.

Its Insufficient and Lop-Sided Nature

It must, however, be noted that the literature on the rural society, inter national and Indian, is insufficient for an adequate understanding of th origin and development of the Indian society in the past and as it exist today with all its numerous provincial, district and local variants. Whil utilizing this literature, it is vitally necessary to organize further systemati field-studies of this society and its variants with a correct sociological approach. The basic defect characterising the existing literature is the absence of a co-ordinated study of the various aspects of the rural life process in their reciprocal interactions. This is due to the weakness of the methodology used in the investigation.

Need for a Planned Research

An authentic picture of the Indian rural society, its origin, development and the existing state, can be built up only when a number of experts of different disciplines collaborate and synthesize the fruits of their labours in separate spheres of the rural life. It is the task of the rural sociologist to generalize the results of studies of the various experts at work on separate aspects of the rural life into a law of the movement of the rural society. Then alone an objectively true picture of the Indian society as a whole, its emergence and subsequent evolution through successive stages right upto the present, is also possible.

This alone can assist to visualize the problems arising from the crisis of the rural society in proper sociological perspective and evolve a correct programme of their solution. It will mean a programme of reconstruction of rural society in conformity with the real objective movement of the rural society and, therefore, lifting it to a higher level of material and cultural existence.

It is first necessary to evolve an all-India Plan for the study of the rural society. An appropriate delimiting of rural zones should be made and a team of experts for each zone selected, who would organize a co-ordinated study of the various aspects of the rural society of that zone and evolve an integrated picture of that society. They can, then study it historically, as the last link hitherto in the chain of the evolutionary series of the rural social structures of that zone which succeeded one another from stage to stage.

The study of the rural social structures of the different agrarian zones, of their origin and historical evolution, will pave way for the study of the Indian rural society, its origin and historical evolution, as one organic whole.

Such a historical, co-ordinated and systematic study of the Indian rural society is the prime prerequisite for a scientific understanding of its life processes today and for evolving an adequate programme of its reconstruction on a more advanced economic, social and cultural basis.

field studies of this society and its variants with a correct sociological approach. The basic defect characterising the existing literature is the absence of a co-ordinated study of the various aspects of the rural life process in their reciprocal interactions. This is due to the weakness of the methodology used in the investigation.

NEED FOR A PLANNED RESEARCH

An authentic picture of the Indian rural society, its origin, development and the existing state can be built up only when a number of experts of different disciplines collaborate and synthesize the fruits of their labour in separate spheres of the rural life. It is the task of the rural sociologist to generalize the results of studies of the various experts at work on separate aspects of the rural life into a law of the movement of the rural society. Then alone an objectively true picture of the Indian society as a whole, its emergence and subsequent evolution through successive stages right upto the present, is also possible.

This alone can assist to visualize the problems arising from the crisis of the rural society in proper sociological perspective and evolve a correct programme of their solution. It will mean a programme of reconstruction of rural society in conformity with the real objective movement of the rural society and, therefore, lifting it to a higher level of material and cultural existence.

It is first necessary to evolve an all-India plan for the study of the rural society. An appropriate delimiting of rural zones should be made and a team of experts for each zone selected who should organize a co-ordinated study of the various aspects of the rural society of that zone and evolve an integrated picture of that society. They should also study historically the evolution hitherto in the course of the evolutionary series of the rural social structures of that zone which succeeded one another from stage to stage.

The study of the rural social structures of the different cultural zones, of their origin and historical evolution, will pave way for the study of the Indian rural society, its origin and historical evolution, as one organic whole.

Such a planned co-ordinated and systematic study of the Indian rural society is the prime prerequisite for a scientific understanding of its dynamic process of change and for evolving an adequate programme of its reconstruction on a more advanced economic, social and cultural basis.

PART II

READINGS IN RURAL SOCIOLOGY

SECTION I

INTRODUCTORY

THIS SECTION contains two selections by the author. The purpose of this section is first to provide an overall statistical picture of the Indian society and more particularly of the Indian rural society and, secondly, to indicate the major sociological implications of the conscious transformation that is being attempted to be brought about by the Government of independent India through its planned economic programme, founded on the principle of a mixed economy.

The Indian society has been considered a classic agrarian society. The Government of India is trying to reshape this society into highly industrially developed one. It has, therefore, consciously initiated a number of measures and also accelerated a number of processes like industrialization, commercialization, monetization, and production for competitive market which were generated haltingly by the British predecessors. This effort to change the structural basis of the Indian society is making a number of old institutions disfunctional, thereby creating a peculiar phenomenon called anomie. It has been also creating numerous sociological problems as a result of introducing new and varied institutions and associations without however providing adequate economic and other means for their proper functioning. Consequently, a peculiar situation, anxiously described as overurbanization, has emerged and it is our belief that any study of life of the rural society cannot be adequate without keeping this framework in mind. The article on the sociological problems of economic development attempts to pinpoint this crucial framework (*Author*).

1

SOCIOLOGICAL ANALYSIS OF INDIA

A. R. DESAI

THE ACHIEVEMENT of Independence of India was a great landmark in the history of the Indian society. However, the way in which Independence was granted, the shape which free India acquired, and the problems which the Indian Union was confronted with were unique.

Socially, India has been one of the most complex countries. It has a continuity of history and cultural heritage which extends back to millenniums. It is a country which has probably the largest number of pre-historic tribes. It has been a stage on which an immense drama of contact and conflict, fusion and fission, of a number of ethnic stocks, primitive tribes belonging to all stages of development, civilized communities and religious and linguistic groups has been enacted with an intensity and duration, probably unparalleled in any country except China. Its heritage includes legacy from Paleolithic and Neolithic groups, from civilized societies speaking the Dravidian Branch of language, from the Indo-Aryan stocks, from the Huns, the Saks, the Scithians, the Bactrians, the Greeks, the Muslims, the Christians and others. It has witnessed the growth of systems of social organization like the caste, the joint family and the village communities based on self-sufficient village economy, and also of diverse types of feudal order and variegated feudal culture which are unique and which have left impression, nay have determined to a great extent the specific contour of the contemporary social organization.

Indian social landscape has been kaleidioscopic because of its changing pattern across ages.

Unless this unique past and its legacy are properly comprehended, it will be difficult to understand the complicated process of the economic, political, social, cultural and ideological developments, that have been taking place in the Indian Union after Independence.

However, for a proper study of the economic, political, social, institutional, cultural and ideological problems confronting the Indian people, it is necessary, as a first step, to acquaint ourselves with the composition of the population of the Indian Union. A systematic analysis and study of the population of the Indian Union from various angles, therefore, is a prerequisite to properly appreciate the scope, the scale and the depth of the process of transformation of the life process of this immense section of mankind.

The present essay represents an attempt to make a brief analysis of the population of the Indian Union from various angles with a view to provide a background on the basis of which the numerous social currents and cross-currents that are agitating the extant Indian society may be adequately comprehended.

We will first draw a statistical picture of India's population from various angles. We will then indicate from that analysis some of the principal forces which provide momentum to the Indian society.

Indian Humanity

India, next to China, is the world's most populous country. According to the Census of 1951, it has a population of 35,68,29,485 human beings. The population is further increasing at an average rate of 13 per thousand per annum. The average density of population in India is 312 per sq. mile though varying considerably from State to State. On an average, India has 947 females for every 1000 males.

Ethnologically, most of the major types of ethnic groups of mankind are represented in the country. According to physical appearance, as indicated in India Year Book 1956 the following five types could be easily distinguished: (a) The Negritoes of the Andaman Islands, having physical affinity with Asian and Oceanic peoples like Semangs of Malaya, and Popuans of New Guinea, but not with the African Negroes or Negritoes; (b) The Veddids or Proto—Australians—majority of the tribal peoples of the Central and Southern India. Genetically, they are supposed to be related to the Australians and the Europeans; (c) The Mongoloids found in the mountain zones of North and North-East India; (d) The Mediterraneans of Melanids are found in the Plains of South India. Generally, the word Dravidian was used for these groups incorrectly; (e) The Indids are found mainly in North India, Central Deccan and the West Coast. Genetically and physically, they are considered by Anthropologists as forming a part of the South European Stock.

Broadly, the Indid type predominates in North India and Melanid type in South India. However, it should be remembered that the Indian population has emerged from the intermingling of these various ethnic groups. Physical Anthropologists, Ethnologists, Culture historians and linguists are trying to evolve a picture of the Indian society and its complex culture traits on the basis of correlating the cultures and languages of the Indian people with these ethnic stocks and thereby trace the positive interaction as well as frictions which have been occurring even today as a result of the still advancing process of inter-living of these groups. Interesting insights are being elaborated to study Indian history from this type of analysis.

India, Overwhelmingly Rural

India is overwhelmingly rural. Out of 35·7 crores of people inhabiting the territory, 29·5 crores or 82·7 per cent live in 5,58,089 villages. Only 17·3 per cent, i. e., 5·2 crores, have urban setting provided by some 3,018

TABLE 1

(in thousands)

Age Group	Total		Unmarried		Married		Widowed or divorced	
	Male	Female	Male	Female	Male	Female	Male	Female
Below 1 year	5,821	5,668	5,821	5,668	—	—	—	—
1-4 years	17,939	17,908	17,939	17,908	—	—	—	—
5-15 "	44,703	41,989	41,804	35,737	2,833	6,118	66	134
15-24 "	30,672	30,052	16,627	5,184	13,660	24,041	384	827
25-34 "	27,875	26,633	3,701	733	23,122	23,731	1,052	2,129
35-44 "	22,032	19,528	1,150	304	19,323	15,346	1,559	3,178
45-54 "	15,719	13,898	604	173	13,076	8,314	2,038	5,412
55-64 "	9,064	8,624	299	89	6,777	3,334	1,998	5,201
65-74 "	3,867	3,976	104	37	2,533	1,092	1,230	2,847
75 and over	1,630	1,756	46	18	883	370	701	1,367
Age not stated	111	117	51	60	46	42	14	15
Total population (excluding displaced persons).	1,79,433	1,70,149	88,146	63,911	82,253	82,388	9,042	21,110

towns. It should be further noted that the overwhelming majority of the villages, viz., 3,80,020 of them contain less than 500 persons. We will refer to the implications of this rural setting subsequently.

Predominance of Juveniles, Child Marriages

The following Table portrays the distribution of population according to age, sex and civil conditions :—

The presence of a large proportion of juveniles and a very low proportion of persons above the middle age eloquently reveal the complicated social problems which the Indian society has to face. The enormous number of child marriages and equally significant numerous eharacter of child widows bring into the forefront the decisive need and the resultant herculean task of overhauling the Indian society.

Land of Religions

India is a land of numerous religions. It is inhabited by people belonging to almost all major religious and derivative religious cults providing rich complexity of other-wordly beliefs, rituals, sacrifices and institutional diversity. Even the Hindu Religion, which is followed by the vast bulk of people reveals great regional variations as well as religio-ideological diversity. The Table below indicates the composition of the population as distributed according to various religious beliefs.

TABLE II

Population according to Religion

Religion	Number (in lakhs)	Percentage to total population
Hindu	3,032	85·00
Muslim	354	9·92
Christian	82	2·30
Sikh	62	1·74
Jain	16	0·45
Buddhist	2	0·06
Zoroastrian	1	0·03
Other religions (tribal)	17	0·47
Other religions (non-tribal)	1	0·03
All religions	3,567	100·00

India's Multi-lingual Population

India presents a spectacle of a museum of tongues. According to the 1951 Census Report, there are 845 languages or dialects in the country. These include 720 Indian languages each spoken by less than a hundred thousand persons and 63 non-Indian languages. However, it should be noted that 91 per cent of the total population, i. e., about 32·4 crores of people speak one or the other of the fourteen languages specified in the Constitution. The following Table indicates the percentage of population speaking these fourteen languages.

TABLE III

Language	Number of persons (in lakhs)	Percentage to total
Hindi, Urdu, Hindustani, Punjabi	1,499	46·3
Telugu	330	10·2
Marathi	270	8·3
Tamil	265	8·2
Bengali	251	7·8
Gujarati	163	5·1
Kannada	145	4·5
Malayalam	134	4·1
Oriya	132	4·0
Assamese	50	1·5
Kashmiri	0·05	
Sanskrit	0·01	

LINGUISTIC CONFLICTS

These fourteen languages have a long historic past. They have reached a high stage of development. Rich literatures expressing the dreams, the aspirations, the emotions and the thoughts of various peoples speaking these tongues have come into being. They are further considerably localised in specific territorial zones thereby transforming various Indian Linguistic groups into separate nationalities within the Indian Nation. Some of these languages like Tamil, Telugu, Kannada and Malayalam are associated with a body of traditions which have a predominantly Dravidian cultural background, differing in some respects qualitatively from the Indo-Aryan Group of languages. The difficulties involved in evolving a national language for the Indian Union can be appreciated only if this background is kept in mind. The great ferment, which has exploded into veritable tempests in contemporary India on the issue of the Reorganisation of States within the Indian Union, the objective of which has been to evolve administrative units composed of linguistic groups occupying specific territorial segments of India could be understood only if, as a preliminary step, this Linguistic composition of the Indian population is properly kept in mind. "About 1·2 crores of persons (3·2 per cent) speak one or the other of the 23 tribal languages and nearly 1·8 crore persons (5·0 per cent) speak one or the other of the other Indian languages (or dialects) spoken by a lakh or more persons." The problem of providing scripts to these tongues, and the further issues involved in the supply of appropriate material and technical resources to help their development have to be intensely thought over in the general background of the poverty and scarce resources available to the society.

Dark Cloud-Illiteracy

According to the Census Report of 1951, 16·6% of the people were literate. The significance of the enormity of the situation where 83·4% of the citizens lacking the elementary instrument of culture needs no elaborate discussion. It means great reliance on vocal medium for the bulk of the people. It means enormous influence of that category of the means of spread of culture, which we call oral propaganda. It means the rise and disproportionate influence of those groups of leaders who wield great demagogic powers. It also indicates the significance of spoken languages and dialects for assimilating and shaping the cultural heritage by the bulk of the population. The problem of the proper medium of instruction and communication at different stages of the educational ladder takes on a new complexion in the multi-tongued population when it is visualised that a beginning has to be made for 83% of the population. It also raises the unpleasant problem of the cost of education and its proper apportioning at various stages of education and among various tongues. The problem of priorities with regard to the sharing of the limited resources acquires acute complexity in the light of the above situation.

The specific policy of spreading literacy in India will determine which castes, which lingual groups, which social strata of the society will gain initial advantages. Will the groups so privileged utilise these advantages for their own sectional interests or for the benefits of all ? How will they influence the quality and the nature of education ? The problem of illiteracy linguistic group, socio-economic stratification and the motives of the mode of life are highly inter-connected. Their implications are great in terms of the trend of social development.

Caste Hierarchy

The institution of caste which emerged in India many centuries ago, which has a hoary history and has survived numerous political upheavals and military convulsions and which has been still persisting, though slowly losing vitality, due to the pressure of the forces of modern, social, economic and political developments is a unique institution unparalleled in the history of mankind. The considerable role which this institution still plays in influencing the life of the Hindus, by far the largest section of the Indian people, makes it obligatory for an investigator of the life processes of the Indian society to carry on an intimate study of this institution in all its protean functioning. Caste decides to a great extent the social status and the vocation of a member of the Hindu community, which is heirarchically graded in numerous castes and sub-castes. It largely determines the opportunities accessible to him for material and cultural self-advancement. A Hindu is a prisoner of the caste or sub-caste to which he is shackled with all its traditional handicaps, and taboos. The life of a Hindu is essentially and considerably lived within the matrix of the particular caste or sub-caste to which he is affiliated. This largely moulds his consciousness, keeping it at a petty level.

Further caste differences also engender different patterns of domestic and social life, different cultural complexes, even differences in the type of houses which various caste groups inhabit. Not only that. Due to historical reasons, property rights exist, markedly in agrarian area, on caste lines as also administrative functions and occupations. It must also be noted that the massive and complicated inherited religious and secular culture of the Hindu community which still holds almost decisive sway over their mind is caste contoured. It has fixed the psychology of the various social groups and has evolved such minutely graded levels of social distance and superior-inferior relationships that the social structure looks like a gigantic heirarchic pyramid with a mass of untouchable as its base and a small stratum of elite, the Brahmins, almost unapproachable, at its apex. The Hindu society is composed of hundreds of distinct self-contained caste worlds piled one over the other.

Classification of Caste during British Rule

During the British period, these castes were broadly grouped into four categories, viz., the higher castes, the intermediate castes, the backward castes and the scheduled castes. After Independence, the Constitution of India has abolished all caste distinctions. However, this *de jure* abolition does not mean *de facto* abolition of the caste system in real life. The caste matrix of the Indian population has been deliberately omitted in the Census of 1951, except for some special groups. This has drawn a curtain over the most vital aspect of the Indian social life. Instead of utilising the census data for properly correlating the factor of caste with property ownership, wealth and linguistic, educational as well as other factors of vital social concern by eliminating the caste factor from the census study, the framers of the census have veiled the operation of a decisively important force which operates very subtly in retarding the growth of democratic social relations between the citizens of the Indian Union. Even more than that, this ostrich like ignoring of the caste has prevented the proper understanding of those forces which are evolving various devices to perpetuate a hierarchic and unjust social order.

Caste Monopoly of Power

It has been observed by a number of students of the social life of the Indian people that there is a close correlation between the position of caste in the hierarchy of the Hindu social order and the respective status of its number with regard to wealth, economic rank, class position, political power and accessibility to education and culture. It has been pointed out by some outstanding students of the Hindu society that a couple of dozens of castes in India hold the monopoly of economic resources, political power, and educational and cultural facilities available. As has been indicated by a number of studies, an overwhelming majority of agrarian labourers or unprivileged classes of the Indian society spring from untouchables, some of the backward castes and the uprooted scheduled tribes.

Caste and Democracy

This point has to be properly borne in mind for a number of reasons. It alone gives clue to the like processes, both of contacts and conflicts, which provide dynamics to the Indian social life. It helps us to understand a number of movements that erupt in different parts of the country such as the Anti-Brahmin movement in South, the anti-Bhatji and Sethji (Anti-Brahminic and anti-Businessmen) movements in Maharashtra. It also helps us to gain an insight into numerous linguistic, communal and class conflicts wherein the comingling of certain castes with certain exploiting classes symbolically representing certain communal or linguistic groups operate as an under-current in these movements. It also raises a significant problem. Will it be possible to abolish caste system and caste hierarchy in fact without adopting measures of basic changes in the economic structure ? Could cultural and other forces be released such as would create economic security and extend cultural facilities to the lowest strata, and abolish the caste system and caste hierarchy in reality ?

Emerging Small Family Pattern

Village self-sufficient community, caste system and joint family were the three pivotal social institutions on which the Hindu social structure was reared. A general feeling about the family system prevailing in India is that it is still largely joint based on the joint living of members belonging to three generations. However, the findings of the Report of the Census of 1951 reveal a different reality.

The census differentiates 4 types of households : one having three members or less as a 'small' household; one which has 4, 5 or 6 members as a 'medium' household; one which has 7, 8 or 9 members as a 'large' household; and one which has 10 or more members as a 'very large' household. The Table given below indicates how many households of each type are found in a typical village and a typical town.

TABLE IV

Type of household	No. of households in a	
	Typical Village	Typical Town
Small	33	38
Medium	44	41
Large	17	16
Very Large	6	5
Total ...	100	100

The fact that nearly 77% of the households in village constitute small and medium households and further that every third household in the village constitutes a family having three or less than three persons clearly discloses the fact that the traditional joint family of the Hindu society is rapidly experiencing distintegration. The habit of breaking away from the joint family and setting up small families has been growing. Though some Sociologists have doubted the sharp formulation of the Census Authorities, it is admitted by all that the traditional joint family is disintegrating and is creating varied types of family structures which have lost their old vitality and functions and which have still not crystallized themselves into healthy nuclear family types.

Disintegration of the Joint Family—Its Implications

The traditional joint family was a universe in itself, performing all the important economic, political, social, religious, recreational and cultural functions in the old society. The joint family has broken down. However, in India, the functions which should have been taken over by the other specialised associations and groups are not shouldered by these bodies either effectively or in a sufficient measure thereby hurling the individual into a whirlpool of social and cultural ferment unprotected. The policies of the present government are also so moulded that they generate the forces which would accelerate this process of disintegration of joint family. What are the implications of this process in terms of economic security, political stability, social solidarity and co-operative endeavours, cultural designs and personality and character integrity ? How far the Indian society which has lost its old stability and design will create a new equilibrium of various institutions and associations ? What measures will really generate a new progressive and higher harmony of interpersonal relations ?

These are some of the problems which emerge from the analysis of the family composition of the Indian population as it exists today.

Class Stratification of Indian Society

As observed earlier India is overwhelmingly rural. It is a poor under-developed country with a national income of Rs. 9,950 crores in 1953-54, and a *per capita* income in the same year of Rs. 266·5 both computed at 1948-49 price level.

Under the impact of the British rule and its economic policies, India has been transformed from a feudal to a capitalist country. The Indian society is now stratified into new classes like capitalists (commercial, industrial and financial), professional classes like lawyers, doctors and others, fairly large-sized middle class employees and an overwhelming section of the urban proletariat living on wages in urban areas. While in rural areas we find the society regrouped into classes of agrarian landlords, peasant proprietors, tenants and agricultural labourers along with strata of ruined artisans and a group of money-lenders and traders. It is unfortunate that a proper analysis of the distribution of wealth among various classes has not been tabulated either in the Census Report of 1951 or in the India Year Books.

Rural Class Structure

We will briefly portray the class composition as it prevails in agrarian area. We will also indicate the concentration of land that has taken place there. It will reveal how the agrarian India which was founded on a balanced self-sufficient village economy on the basis of equilibrium of agriculture and artisan industry and functioning through village panchayat, caste councils and joint family and producing for subsistence before the advent of the British rule has undergone a qualitative transformation. The following statements unfold this class configuration that has taken place in agrarian areas.

The available cultivable land *per capita* is only ·9 acres. It indicates the enormous pressure of population on land. About 75 per cent of the total sown area is under food crops. "The gross value of these crops is only almost equal to that of cash crops though the latter are sown on merely 25 per cent of the land. About 35 per cent of the total produce is sold by the cultivators. In nearly two-thirds of these sales transactions the commodity is delivered to the trader in the village itself." "The marketing of agricultural produce is largely in the hands of a body of men, who, as distinguished from Government and Co-operatives, represent private interests, and who control both the sources of credit and disposal of the produce. Often enough, therefore, the cultivators' position is that of having to bargain, if he can, with someone who commands the money, commands the credit, commands the market and comes with transport." This point is emphasised to highlight the immense power of the new class of creditors and traders in an under-developed rural economy which is switching on from production for subsistence to that of market. In the peculiar environment based on the hierarchic caste system, the combination of superior caste prestige and this economic hold needs to be properly understood.

The following is the picture of the rural class structure as it has emerged after the British withdrawal :—

Agricultural landowners	...	22·2 per cent.
Agricultural tenants	...	27·2 "
Agricultural labourers	...	30·4 "
Non-agriculturists	...	20·2 "

The inequality of cultivators' holdings is also considerable. "Holdings below one acre formed about 17 per cent; those between 1 and 2½ acres about 21 per cent; and those between 2 acres to 5 acres another 21 per cent. These accounted respectively for 1·0, 4·5 and 9·9 per cent of the total area. At the other end of the scale 16 per cent were in the group 10 to 25 acres accounting for 32·5 per cent of the area and another 5·6 per cent above 25 acres covering about 34 per cent of the area and further. The medium cultivator, numerically two-fifths of the cultivators, has less than a third of the sown area under him. There is an even steeper descent when we come to the small cultivators; his sown area is just a little more than a tenth of the total area sown by the cultivators."

The Unprivileged in the Indian Society

The rise of the agrarian proletariat, the existence of a large section of uneconomic holders of land, and the prevalence of an enormous group of ruined artisans who constitute the bulk of the non-agricultural section of the rural population reveal the tragic tale of the miserable economic life lived by the large section of rural population in the Indian Union.

Viewed from the standard of economic stratification, India contains the following categories of people whose problems are becoming explosively urgent :—

(1) Vast groups of Scheduled Tribes who are almost living the life of agrarian serfs or debt slaves.

(2) Agricultural labourers whose grim tale of existence is portrayed in the studies conducted by agricultural Labour Enquiry Committee.

(3) The cultivators of uneconomic holdings gripped in the evertightening princer of unprofitable deficit production, taxation, claims of the money-lender and market fluctuations.

(4) A large majority of artisans and craftsmen who are progressively being ruined due to the blows of competitive market economy.

(5) The bulk of the petty producers who just produce enough in normal times to make both ends meet.

(6) The bulk of rural unemployed or under-employed whose position and horrible helpless mode of existence is indescribable.

(7) In urban areas, the unemployed, the wage labourer, the bulk of middle class employees, handicraftsmen and petty shopkeepers and traders constitute the bulk of the population who form the economically under-privileged groups living a precarious, insecure existence. Along with these sections it would be proper to mention the group of displaced refugees whose by far the largest section still lives a very unstable and economically precarious life.

Wealth Concentration in India

Thus India is not merely poor and under-developed but is having a class stratification wherein a few capitalists (financial, industrial and commercial), a few money-lenders and traders (many a time fused with either urban capitalist groups or with landowning sections in the rural India), a small section of the upper stratum of the professional groups, a layer of big landlords, prosperous capitalist agricultural farmers and the top stratum of the peasant proprietors, have concentrated wealth and economic resources among themselves.

This peculiar class configuration is very subtly correlated with the groups with specific linguistic, caste and educational stratifications, making the problem of economic, social and cultural progress of the Indian people as a whole complex and difficult.

Problems Before Independent India

What should be the nature of economic planning in India ? What should be the nature of the institutional devices which would assist the transformation of the present population into economically secure, politically equal, socially non-hierarchic and culturally equipped with values which are embodied in the aspirations laid down in the Preamble of the Constitution? What will be the nature of levers for accomplishing such a transformation of the Indian society ?

These and a number of other issues emerge when we make even a cursory sociological analysis of India.

2

SOCIOLOGICAL PROBLEMS OF ECONOMIC DEVELOPMENT

A. R. Desai

The object of this essay is to indicate, in a very brief manner, the sociological problems involved in the process of economic development that has been launched by the Government of the Indian Union.

Meaning of Sociological Problems

By sociological problems, we mean here, the problems of replacing the old social organization, modifying or discarding old social institutions, altering or removing old forms of social controls and revising or liquidating old agencies of social change, with a view to overcome their retarding role in the economic development of the Indian people. Further, we also mean, by this, the problems connected with the evolving new web of social relations, new types of social institutions, new devices of social control and also new agencies and factors of social change which would be appropriate for a rapid and harmonious development of the economic life of the Indian people.

Like a number of Colonial and Semi-Colonial Countries which were under the domination of various Imperialist Powers, India was also kept under-developed by British Imperialism. It was kept predominantly as an agrarian, raw material producing appendage of British Imperialism. Its industrial development was predominantly regulated to suit the needs of British Capitalism. Heavy industries were not permitted to grow. Even regarding light industries, only those were allowed to develop which either did not compete seriously with similar home industries or which provided better and more profitable opportunities for the investment of British Capital. In fact the British and other foreign capital dominated Indian industries during the British period. Indian economic development was carried on under the dictatorship of British Imperialism.

This, as is well-known, led to a lop-sided, unsymmetrical, dependent and weak development of the country. The British rulers thus weakened the old motif, the old technique and the old organization of production but did not replace them by healthy new ones to any extensive degree. They introduced the Capitalist mode of production in India but only to the extent that subserved the interests of the British economy and not sufficiently enough to organically wield the entire mechanism of production of the country within the Capitalist economic framework. They introduced mechanization in production which proved just effective enough to dislocate the old pre-British economy for their own purpose but not sufficiently extensive as to make it the basis of the entire national economy. They initiated commercialization of production and money economy in the country but only to the extent that would subserve their exploitative interest and not the organic developmental economic needs of the Indian society. Thus, under the Biritsh rule, a hybrid national economy developed in India composed of two inharmoniously interconnected sectors, viz., a sector organized for market and an inherited sector which predominantly survived and functioned for subsistence.

While the British rulers thus distorted and retarded the free harmonious development of the Indian economy, they also made a peculiar dent into the social organization, social institutions and social outlooks of the Indian people.

The traditional self-sufficient village community, which was based on equilibrium of agriculture and artisan industry, which operated through the village panchayat, caste and joint family institutions and was governed by custom and which subscribed to other-wordly, fatalistic, stationary outlooks, was almost fatally undermined. However, it was not replaced by a new social framework, a new institutional matrix, a new outlook corresponding to and in harmony with the new type of economy. In fact, in absence of these, the introduction of the new legal system resulted only in disorganizing the then prevailing social relations and introducing chaos in these. The old principle of co-ordination and co-operation (though based on hierarchy, inequality and authority) on which the pre-British community was based, was replaced by the principle of competition which set into motion a whirlpool in the social structure. Further, the restricted, insufficient and deformed development of the new economy prevented the full blossoming of a new form of social unity and solidarity (national in character) and a new modern outlook. Every development in the material, social and ideological domain, exhibited mainly two characteristics, hybridness and under-development.

Such was the economic and social legacy of the British rule left to the Indian people at the time of the achievement of National Independence.

Social Problems of Economic Development

The Government of the sovereign and free Indian Union has earnestly set to itself the herculean task of the reconstruction of the economy of India. Its policy of economic development is slowly taking shape through its Five-Year Plans.

We shall divide the sociological problems confronting the Indian Government for a successful implementing of its schemes of economic development into two categories.

PROBLEMS OF NEGATIVE CHARACTER

The first category of problems are of a negative character. They arise out of various types of social legacies which work as an obstacle to the progressive achievement of the economic developmental programme. They are due to the immense deadweight of social, institutional and ideological superstructure which may have corresponded to the past authoritarian, and traditional society based on the mainly subsistence economy but which still persists and works as a shackle on the developing new economy. This group of problems arise out of the persistence of old social institutions like caste, authoritarian joint family, tribes, traditional religious organizations and serfdom and others. They also emerge out of old forms of social control like supernatural sanctions, authoritarian norms, complicated and intricate caste, family, tribal, religious and other customary sanctions permeating almost every core of the life of the Indian humanity. They also arise out of the old world outlook which was basically religious, other-worldly, fatalistic and anti-democratic in content. They spring also from the strong parochial interpersonal ties leading to sectional, petty-tribal, kin, caste, family, religious or regional loyalties detrimental to national and broad human emotions. They further emanate from large-scale illiteracy, ill-health, unemployment, under-employment or weightage of employment in favour of certain castes or certain regional groups.

PROBLEMS OF POSITIVE CHARACTER

The second category of the sociological problems arise from the very nature of the economic development which has been inaugurated by the Indian Government.

They arise out of the policy of industrialization, of commercialization, of the introducing of money economy in every corner of the country. They arise out of its agrarian policy and from the very character of the economic order which it wishes to establish. The government has become the biggest single agency of economic development. It thereby generates currents of social processes which are of unique significance as we shall observe subsequently.

SOCIAL OBSTACLES TO ECONOMIC DEVELOPMENT

We shall now survey the sociological problems in relation to the economic development in greater detail to have a clearer view of them.

In an interesting report published by the United Nations dealing with "Processes and Problems of Industrialization in Under-developed Countries" it has been pointed out that among the three basic obstacles to economic development in under-developed countries, the social and institutional framework and values inherited from the past constitute an important obstacle.

CASTE SYSTEM—AN ILLUSTRATION

The caste system in India provides one of the best examples of this. The retarding role and the reactionary significance of this institution is still very insufficiently realized by the students of India's economic development.

Though this institution was affected during the British rule, and though it has been abolished theoretically and juridically by the Constitution of Free India, its significance in real life, its influence on the economic development, its direct effect upon the patterns of property relations and patterns of consumption, and its impress upon the configurations of power structure in the economic, political, social and cultural fields is still not properly comprehended and hence gravely under-estimated.

Caste prevents mobility of the people so essential for dynamic economic development. It prevents certain groups from taking to certain vocations, certain patterns of economic behaviour, certain forms of consumption. It obstructs the growth of a socially mobile population which would be conducive to easy and quick manning of various vocations.

One of the interesting findings by some of the scholars of Indian society is that most of the controlling positions in economy, administration, and cultural pursuits are monopolized by a few castes all over India. Not merely that. Some of the castes of a few regions today even control the destiny of the entire people of the country, leading to a number of caste, economic, and regional tensions.

This monopoly position of certain castes and groups of a certain linguistic zones has generated a peculiar unrest in the modern competitive social setting. It engenders and keeps alive a bitter competitive struggle among the privileged groups themselves as well as between them and the unprivileged groups also. This struggle exercises a highly detrimental effect on the development of a healthy national economy.

A closer study of a number of tensions which have emerged and which are rampant in India, when properly investigated, reveals, as one of the important causes, the caste background.

Persistence of Backward Types of Loyalties

Another sociological implication of the legacy of the caste and other pre-industrial social institutions is the persistence of backward types of loyalties resulting into factionalism and division of the Indian people into groups with petty caste and other group egos to the detriment of the growth of a highly developed national consciousness.

As pointed out by the UNO Report on 'Processes and Problems of Industrialization in Under-developed Countries,' "Another characteristic of pre-industrial society found in all its sub-divisions and at all levels, is factionalism that is the tendency of the society to be divided by caste and class cleavages, ethnic and religious distinctions, differences in cultural traditions and social pattern, kinship loyalties and regional identifications, and so on. These divisions tend to inhibit the development of a feeling of unity in the society and of identity among its members and as a result the individual's sense of personal loyalty and duty may be limited to the members of a very narrow social environment; his family, his clan, local community, or parochial circles and groupings. The normative pressure rooted in such an environment may profoundly affect the conduct of the individual in external situations and relations. In particular they may pose difficult problems for personnel recruitment and management."

This parochial mentality together with the old outmoded institutions in an under-developed country, obstructs the proper economic development in a number of ways.

(1) First, it leads to the practice of nepotism. Not efficiency and merit but ingroup loyalty often becomes the basis of the selection of personnel. It leads to favouritism, corruption, monopolization, all those practices which militate against healthy economic progress of the nation.

(2) It also results in the growth of the harmful practices of wrong (unproductive) investment patterns and wrong consumption patterns. Such fields of activity as speculation, hoarding, money-lending, landowning and trading attract capital with far greater temptation than industrial enterprises. A considerable amount of wealth is also squandered in conspicuous consumption. Traditional outlooks, social mores and institutional compulsions on the background of the scarce resources are largely responsible for this. The herculean efforts made by the Government of the Indian Union to plough back these resources from those unhealthy economic activities and to divert them in proper industrial channels bear eloquent testimony to the pernicious impact of old social institutions and old outlooks on the healthy economic development of the Indian society.

(3) It also generates distorted attitudes to work, to the problem of efficiency, to the selection of vocations, also to the allocation of resources and patterns of production and consumption. It further prevents the rapid growth of those secular, positive, scientific, and technologically oriented approaches which are so vital for the expansion and development of an economic system.

(4) It also obstructs the growth of those mores and sanctions which are basic to a developing economy in modern times, viz., mores and sanctions founded on law, respect for personality, concept of equal citizenship and also based on contract.

There are a number of other sociological problems of this group which relate to economic development. Limitation of space, however, precludes discussion on these.

Economic Development and Sociological Problems

We will now briefly survey the sociological problems which arise as a result of the positive implementation of the policy of economic development which has been launched by the Government of the Indian Union.

It is unfortunate that while a number of evaluation and progress reports of the economic measures adopted by the Government of the Indian Union have been published, no serious attempt has still been made to evaluate the sociological implications of these measures.

We shall hazard our views on this on the basis of some findings of a few scholars as well as on that of the findings of some international associations which have studied the sociological problems involved in the efforts to transform under-developed countries into prosperous ones. UNESCO publications in the Tensions and Technology series indicate a number of sociological problems of economic development.

We will mention a few typical instances.

Industrialization, mechanization, commercialization and spread of money economy are the four-fold devices by means of which economic development is attempted to be worked up.

Industrialisation, Mechanisation and their Social Consequences

It has been found that industrialisation uproots the old division of labour, creates new occupational patterns demanding new training, new discipline, new routine, and a new mode of living. It has been found that "in introducing a programme of industrialization or building of great public works and large factories, such countries have introduced radical change in the standards of living, drastically curtailing consumers' goods. Usually the effects have been much more far-reaching and costly in human welfare than this statement implies."

Further, "Mechanisation itself, whether in agriculture or in industry, separates man from the traditional processes and techniques of his social units, from the skills which he learned as an aspect of his belongingness with his family or of his identification with his father or line of ancestors. Finally, even on small farm, where even cash crops have been introduced, the effect of the new money economy have often been of the same kind as with the introduction of industrial wages."

Commercialisation and its Social Significance

Commercialization also creates numerous problems. It brings about a shift in power and authority in the village. Not the farmers and producers but owners and administrators are becoming the ruling groups. The centre of political power of the village shifts from elders and old gentry to usurers, merchants, landlords, prosperous capitalist farmers, and the group of officials. As pointed out by an UNESCO report, "Commercialisation unaccompanied by healthy system of production is thus shown to be a deteriorating factor...........although it at first brings a transitory period of prosperity."

Implication of Monetization in Agriculture

Similarly, spread of money economy is also fraught with numerous sociological problems. As Mr. Sengupta has pointed out, "it has been shown that higher monetisation of different sectors absolutely and relatively creates several dangers of which the authority should be aware. These dangers are: (i) greater susceptibility to internal and external propagation of cyclical ups and downs with relative deterioration of the agriculturist, (ii) greater money illusion and hence more uneven distribution of burdens of fluctuating prices, (iii) greater proportion of expenditure on non-food item, and non-necessities, (iv) greater fluctuation in land values, (v) greater price-spreads of food articles, (vi) lower percentage of village retention and (vii) greater propensity to stock for mediate links in the economy and uneven land concentration. Monetary and fiscal policy in future must take account of the implied threat of putting more money into the economy, some spilling out to villages." And further as observed by a scholar, "The introduction of money economy has usually meant atomization of the individuals within family, complete destruction of the structuring of family relationships, and of the social and economic system of the group............the money economy has meant secession and revolt, the undermining of parental authority and the authority of the tradition and this has resulted in the rise of the 'young generation' as a class apart. Marriage is often no longer a contract between families but............one between a man and a woman."

Thus industrialization, mechanization, commercialization and introduction and development of money economy which are attempted to be extended and made universal in our country as a part of policy of economic development are generating sociological problems.

If the ultimate object of economic development is the raising of the levels of living, the provision of higher standards of nutrition, housing and health, of a larger *per capita* volume of manufactured goods and liesure, occupational and income security and greater cultural facilities, its fulfilment will demand great and drastic social changes. New property institutions will be required to be built up, new family organization will have to be evolved. Provision of cultural and social amenities, which will be a substitute for the loss of old form of mutual aid and customary co-operation shall have to be made. India is overwhelmingly rural. To transform this agrarian country into an industrial one, a fast network of new institutions, new forms of co-operative social activities, new forms of secular, equalitarian and democratic norms and mores and new techniques of overhauling the outlook of the people will have to be created. New appropriate organizations and structural patterns to compensate for the loss of old stability assured by caste and joint family shall have to be conceived and brought into being.

Thus the programme of economic development launched by the Government of the Indian Union raises numerous positive sociological problems.

Two Directions of Development

How far this Government will be able to successfully resolve the problems arising out of the needs of the healthy economic development will depend upon whether its aim of the economic development itself is to evolve a society founded on the objective of production for the profits of few, or that of production for the satisfaction of the needs of the people.

The two different objectives of economic development will engender two qualitatively different groups of sociological problems.

SECTION II

REGIONAL

Introduction

THE PRESENT section is comprised of four selections embodying some valuable empirical and general studies which try to correlate the diversified geographical background of the Indian society and varied type of cultures which have emerged in that society. Unfortunately, a systematic investigation into this problem has hardly begun. However, eminent archeologists like Subbarao and others, geographers like Spate and others, eminent Anthropologists like Prof. N. K. Bose and others, economic historians like Daniel Thorner and others as also various Census Reports have launched the exploration of the problem on these lines. Professor Subbarao's selection provides us a brief interesting background of how different geographical factors have also been operating in shaping different cultural zones of India. The selection from Spate provides essential information about the major natural regions which, according to him, should be properly studied as the separate and total background of cultural development that has taken place in India as a whole and its constituent regions. Prof. N. K. Bose, in his introduction to Peasant Life in India, has emphasised unity in Diversity of Indian Culture by an empirical research in material cultural traits in various regions of Rural India. Daniel Thorner has attempted to give a comparative picture of four major efforts (including his own) of demarcating various agrarian regions of India which, in the context of administrative and linguistic classification as portrayed by the Census Report of 1951, provides a valuable guide for elaborating a more systematic and fruitful, study of regionalism. The correlation between the natural factors, administrative units, linguistic demarcation, and general cultural patterns and their growth studied on the basis of the framework provided by the four articles will assist a proper study of the rural society and the changes that are taking place therein.

This regional approach has become all the more necessary in the context of quick and rapid transformation that is taking place at present as a result of the implementing of the conscious policies of economic and social change launched by the Government. It has also a relevance in the light of the emerging regional consciousness and resultant struggles for regional reorganisation. (*Author*).

1

GEOGRAPHICAL FACTORS IN INDIAN HISTORY*

B. SUBBARAO

FOR AN intelligent understanding of the pattern of development of cultures in India, one should begin with the geographic factors.

The pioneer of geographic studies in India was F. J. Richards, who indicated the main trans-continental communication system and the pattern of migrations based on it, by a brilliant analysis of Indian history. Outside the sub-continent, the most important region at the "dawn of civilization" was the Afrasian dry zone covering the great river valleys of Western Asia and North Africa. The great cultural developments in that area and the progressive desiccation has resulted in radial migrations of people to the east. This position has made India a zone of constant immigration, owing to its location on the margin of the Eurasian continent. But the magnitude of the alluvial plains of Indus and Ganges and the relative solidity of the physical barriers have, to a great extent, offset the disadvantage of her location. It is idle to speculate at the state of our kowledge of human evolution in general and of early man in India in particular, about the beginnings of human life in this sub-continent. But in the subsequent periods, it is well-known that every new wave of people, who entered the Indo-Gangetic plains as conquerors or fugitives, very rapidly lost their individuality in this melting pot of cultures and added their own indistinguishable element that has gone into the composition of this Indian Culture Complex. The greatest example of this is the Indus Civilization itself with its obvious affinities, specially at the initial stages, to those of Western Asia, but with the distinct stamp of the great river valley in whose lap it flourished. But it left its deep imprint on the whole development of the Indian Civilization of the succeeding ages.

INFLUENCE OF COAST LINES

The next important factor is India's long coast line with its convenient anchorages. This has played no mean role in the interchange of cultures as it has kept a window open to the great civilization of Western Asia and the Mediterranean region. But it must be emphasised here that in our present state of knowledge of Indian Archaeology, we are not in a position to corroborate the vague references which occur in literature—Indian

* Reproduced from 'The Personality of India', by B. Subbarao, pp. 5-11.

and foreign—to maritime trade and other contacts. We get definite and palpable material evidence of these contacts only in the early centuries of the Christian Era.

Refuge Zones

Within the country, the wide inviting alluvial plains, opening on to the main gateways to Western Asia, an older land mass of Peninsular Indian cut up into important river valleys separated by ridges of hills and forests. This feature, in particular, has enabled the earlier inhabitants to isolate hemselves in what may be called '*cul de sacs*' or refuge zones.

In this feature, India stands midway between Europe on the one hand and Africa and Australia and Oceania on the other. In Europe, there were continuous cultural impacts from Western Asia and the Mediterranean region. Besides, "every dominant civilization imposed its cultural pattern on all people within its orbit" and as pointed out by Prof. Haimendorf, "the geographic conditions did not favour isolation of refuge areas." In Africa, on the other hand, the two wide deserts of Sahara and Kalahari with the huge equatorial forests in between have completely isolated a large portion of the continent, and the inhabitants have not advanced beyond the stages of primitive agriculture, stock raising and hunting. Only the coastal belts facing the Mediterranean and the Indian ocean have to some extent escaped this fate. Besides, with the intensive exploitation of North African belt during and prior to the Roman Empire, man lent his evil hand to Nature in turning it into a desert, making it more or less a blind alley of civilization. Australia and Oceania were completely isolated, and but for small-scale island-hopping adventurers, their isolation was broken only with the much later European colonial expansion.

Chief River Basins

India displays both these phenomena, and stands midway. The chief river basins of the country; Indus, Ganges, Narmada, Tapi, Godavari, Krishna and Kaveri, were in turn penetrated and exploited by large-scale agricultural communities, driving the older and static people in a more primitive economy, into the forested mountains where they have survived to this day. The main river basins of the country with a rainfall between 20 and 40 inches, which can sustain large-scale agricultural communities, have been colonized or occupied. One can notice a fine correlation between this optimal rainfall zone and vegatation map of the country showing areas cleared for cultivation.

Areas of Relative Isolation

In between these two categories of areas of attraction of perennial nuclear regions and the area of isolation or *cul de sac*, we have what may be called, areas of relative isolation. These, on account of their location away from the main trans-continental communications, display a different pattern of development but their isolation was broken up slightly later than the areas of attraction.

Pattern of Development of Material Culture

Accepting this fundamental concept of areas of attraction, relative isolation and isolation, the whole pattern of development of material culture, can be defined as one of horizontal expansion of the higher cultures, leading to a displacement, contraction and isolation of the lower cultures in different parts of the country, at different periods, and at different cultural levels. The divergence in the country is due to the difference in the cultural milieu of the first large-scale agricultural communities, in the different regions. Naturally, this cultural development in space and time was closely controlled by the geographic features of the individual regions and the relative effectiveness of the barriers—physical and human. This interaction has given rise to a very interesting pattern which can be seen in the fundamental unity of Indian culture with its associated variety. Following Ratzel and Vidal De La Blanche, we can describe these smaller nuclear zones as "Provincial States" within a "National State." The former may be defined as "complicated economic units, opening on to the same routes, converging on the same river, commanding one another and finding it necessary to exchange their produce and their means of defence: in short, societies for mutual protection, moral and physical solidarity."

Concept of Regions

What is the criterion of this sub-division ? Various methods have been tried by different authors. This old concept of regions has received a new life in the hands of modern geographers. According to E. W. Gilbert, "Geography is the art of recognizing and describing the personalities of regions." Among the systems based on pure geomorphological features, the most satisfactory one seems to be that of Professor M. B. Pithawala. It is based on the main physiographic sub-divisions: Himalayan uplands, Indo-Gangetic plains and Peninsular India. These are again sub-divided on geological and morphological features. But from the point of view of cultural studies, the finest analysis of Indian geographic regions is contained in Spate's recent work on India and Pakistan. But since we have already explained the function of hill and jungle belts, we can proceed on that basis. It is very difficult to determine the linear boundaries and hence an attempt is made here to ascertain the foci of the various zones. This system has the advantage of defining regions academically and not suit the convenience of the politicians. The most important belt, running right across the country from the west coast to the delta of the Ganges, may be described as the Vindhyan complex, comprising the Satpuras, Vindhyas, Mahadeo hills, Gavaligarh, Maikal range, Hazaribagh range, the Chota Nagpur, Singhbhum and Manbhum plateaus. This is also the most populous tribal belt sheltering Bhils, Dangs, Gonds, Santals, Uraons, Baigas, Gadabas, Marias and a host of other tribes. Running almost at right angles to this system at its western end, is what may be called the Western belt beginning with the Aravallis (almost touching Delhi), the Sahyadris, and the long chain of Western Ghats up to the southern tip of the peninsula. Beginning in a geographic order, we have Bhils, Dangs, Worli, Toda, Kurumbar, Kadar, Puliyan, Muthuvan, etc., inhabiting this zone. At its eastern end, the Vindhyan complex is joined by the Eastern Ghats, which run right across more or less parallel to the east coast upto 13°N latitude and then take an oblique turn south-westwards to join the Western Ghats, south of the Mysore plateau. The most important tribes living in this belt are Savaras, Baiga, Chenchu, Reddi, Irulas and Yenadis, etc.

The ethnographic studies in India based on modern methods have not yet made sufficient progress. But one can see the close relation between the thick jungle and rain forests and the main centres of the so called primitive tribes. There is a harmonious adjustment of their physical and cultural environment, which has enabled them to survive. The significance of these belts of jungles and hills cannot be exaggerated. Depending on the depth of these belts, they have managed to survive the pressure of expansion of the people of the plains. While the villages of the plains are generally nucleated we get the dispersed type of settlements in the uplands.

Regions and Their Foci

Now working on this system, we can easily define the regions and their foci. Bounded by the Aravallis and the desert of Rajaputana on the east, and the Sulaiman and Kirthar ranges in the west, is the Indus basin draining the Central Himalayas. This can be roughly sub-divided at the point, where the hills from the west and the desert from the east converge near the Bugti country into the upper and the lower, corresponding to Punjab and Sind respectively. Beginning with the Delhi gap, where the Aravallis converge towards the Himalayas, the Gangetic basin runs east from the narrow divide. On its south lies the Vindhyan Complex. The lower deltaic region of Ganges, as it leaves the Vindhyan Complex, is Bengal. The Valley of Brahmaputra is Assam. Forming as it were a little triangle constituted by the Aravallis in the west and the Vindhyas running obliquely towards the Gangetic basin, is the plateau of Malwa, drained by the rivers—Chambal, Banas, Sipra and Son. Lying south of the Vindhyas and constituting the upper basins of the rivers Krishna and the Godavari and more or less co-extensive with the Deccan Trap area, is Maharashtra. The lower basins of these two great rivers constitute Andhra. The southern part of the Krishna basin more or less constituting the rocky triangle formed by the Eastern and the Western Ghats, viz., the Mysore plateau, is Karnatak. At its southern end, it is drained by the river Kaveri. Beginning from the constriction of the Nagar hills and the Pulicat lake and running right along the east coast is Tamilnad. The narrow coastal plain on either side of the Palghat gap in the Western Ghats is Kerala. The Valley of Mahanadi surrounded by hills and plateaus all round constitutes Orissa. The northern part of the West coast and the peninsula of Saurashtra, abutting on the desert of Rajaputana is Gujarat. Rajaputana really consists of two natural regions: Mewar and Marwar on either side of the Aravalli ranges. Mewar, drained by the river Banas, falls into the Gangetic basin and is more or less an extension of the Malwa plateau. The semi-arid desert country, Marwar lies to the west of the mountain range.

Geographic Division Coincide with Linguistic

It may be noted that each of these regions started with a well endowed focus, around which the neighbouring areas merged. Hence, it is no accident that these areas correspond more or less to the linguistic divisions of the country. After all, language is the product of a social tradition and in itself reacts on other modes of thinking. The very genesis of our modern linguistic units in their historical setting, is one of the most important proofs of these latent and dormant geographic factors, which in a proper political environment led to the present pattern. This process resulted sometimes in the division of larger units (Krishna-Godavari basins) and at other times in the fusion of contiguous units (Gujarat). A very interesting example of the former type is the division of the Krishna-Godavari basins into Maharashtra and Andhra, both occupying the either end of the valleys. As Spate puts it, "...the boundary of Maratha speech shows a striking accordance with the edge of the Lavas; hence the division of the State (Hyderabad) into Marathwada and Telangana, is a rare instance of official recognition of regionalism."

It may be stated at once that these cultural and linguistic zones have very often defined and survived political history. As Spate has shown, there was a tendency throughout Indian History, for political boundaries to coincide with nuclear regions, yet, they never always did.

But whenever they have coincided in the history of these zones, we see a fine flowering and consolidation of the cultural forces. For example, under the aegis of the Eastern Chalukyan dynasty, that ruled a major part of the Andhra for four centuries, the latent geographic forces have helped the assertion of its individuality. This manifested itself in the unmistakable appearance of the Telugu language in the records of the 8th century and by 11th century, it assumed the status of a literature. This consolidated the cultural homogeneity of Andhra.

2

DIVERSITY AND UNITY IN THE SUB-CONTINENT*

O. H. K. Spate

The isolation of India, then, is but relative; yet isolation there is, and within the girdle of mountains and seas has developed the almost incredibly complex culture of Hinduism : not unaffected by outside influences, certainly, but, insofar as we can dimly descry the origins of some of its yet existing cults in the earliest Indus civilization, native to this soil. Hinduism gives, or until very recently has given, a certain common tone to most of the sub-continent, but it contains within itself a vast range of diversities, not to mention the enclaves of primitive tribes and the fossils of ancient faiths, such as the Jains, the Parsees, the Jews of Cochin, the 'Syrian' Nestorian Christians whose traditions go back to St. Thomas the Apostle. Confronting it, and ever drawing strength from its bases in arid Asia, is the great rival creed of Islam. For millennia the Peninsula has been virtually a *cul-de-sac* into which peoples and cultures have infiltrated or been driven, retaining much of their ancient rules of life and yet ceaselessly reacting upon one another, and, for the most part, if not welded together at least held together in the iron clasp of the caste system, a unique solution‡ to the problems of plural society, which are in essence resolved by recognising, cannalising, and in fact sanctifying the plurality. It is no exaggeration to say that among the peoples of India are groups at levels of economic development from that of junglefolk barely out of the Stone Age to that of monopoly capitalism, with a tinge at least of state planning. The difficulties of building no more than two nations out of this heterogeneous human stuff are obvious.

This human heterogeneity is seconded by more purely geographical factors, which give some colour to the generally accepted description of India as a 'sub-continent'. The concept of a sub-continent is far from clear, but the term has its uses, especially now that 'India' as the name or a state is the name of but a part of the old India, and it will often recur in the following pages. So far as it has a meaning distinct from the shorthand usage just mentioned, 'sub-continent' conveys and idea of size and numbers, and these India certainly has : the Empire covered an area of 1,581,410 square miles and the 1951 population of India and Pakistan together was

* Reproduced from India and Pakistan, A General and Regional Geography by O. H. K. Spate, pp. xxx—xxxii.

‡ Unique at least in degree of development.

about 438,000,000. This is possible more than that of China, so that what Herodotus wrote may still be true : "of all the nations that we know, India has the largest population." This great population is of course unequally distributed : the sub-continent contains, in the deserts of Baluchistan and the Thar and in the high desolation of outer Kashmir, tens of thousands of square miles almost devoid of inhabitants, while in Bengal, Dacca Division has twice the population of Belgium on an area one-third greater, and this with only four towns of any size and with practically no industry.

It is only to be expected that so vast an area, bordered by incomparably the most massive mountains of the world, intersected by rivers of the first rank, should contain very considerable physical diversity. In essence the sub-continent falls into only three macro-regions : the Extra-Peninsular Mountain Wall; the Indo-Gangetic Plains; the old Peninsular Block. But these contain a multitude of distinctive pays within themselves. Even in the broad alluvial monotony of the Indo-Gangetic Plains factors of climate, soil, aspect, and hydrology give rise to clear, if not clearly marked, regional divisions; and although the transitions, like those in a suite of fossil echinoderms, are almost imperceptibly gradual, the extremes are extreme indeed: from the desert environs of Karachi to the almost unbelievably dense stipple of homesteads between Calcutta and Dacca.

Yet there is a sort of massive architectural simplicity in the pattern of the three great divisions : the old Peninsular platform, wrapped found by the great trough from the Indus to the Ganges Delta, a trough filled with the debris of the mountains which again enfold it on three sides. This is not accidental, since it is the rigid resistance of the old block which has moulded the frozen waves of the mountains, though their onset has in turn wrapped the foot of the Peninsula to form the scraps and ranges from Gujarat to Chota Nagpur. It is aesthetically fitting that the historic heart of India should lie on the divide between Indus and Ganges, which is also the passage between the Aravallis and the Himalayas, perhaps the oldest surviving and the youngest ranges on the globe. This is the great node of Delhi, for over two thousand years, since the far-off legendary battles of the Mahabharata epic, the key to power in Hindustan.

Underlying the life of India is one great common factor, expressed it is true in divers modalities and degrees: the rhythm of the monsoonal year. The peoples of India are predominantly agrarian, and even most of the past, is after of today, like the great dynastic achievements of the past, is after all built upon the ancient foundation, the toil of the dwellers in 650,000 villages. The tapestries of their lives are wrought in various colours—the lush green of the deltas, the drab khaki of the deserts—but nearly everywhere the fundamental lineaments of the patterns are similar, and are controlled by seasonal cycle in which the great bulk of the rainfall comes in the warmer half of the year : this is so whether the annual fall is 450 ins. on the Assam Plateau, or under 15 in the Punjab, the only really large exception being the Tamilnad coast in the S. E. There is also—away from mountains—a certain sameness in the regimes of temperature, annual or diurnal; but here, though we commonly think of India as 'tropical', it must be remembered that half of the area and over half of the population are N of the Tropic of Cancer. To a large extent, however, this is offset by the mountain wall forming an insulated compartment; and although in the Punjab night frosts bring the mean January temperatures down to the level of an English May, clear skies and intense insolation raise day temperatures to a tropical level, so that all beneath the Himalayas is essentially tropical, despite latitudes of 25-30°. Outside the Himalayas agriculture is nearly everywhere tropical in type, and it is rain, not temperature, that essentially decides what crops shall be grown.

3

UNITY IN INDIAN DIVERSITY*

N. K. Bose

As one goes through separate sections of the present report, one is struck by a general accordance between the findings in regard to various items of material culture in rural India. Firstly, there is a certain measure of local differentiation; and there is also a considerable amount of interpenetration in almost every case. Secondly, the boundaries of the culture areas or sub-areas do not tally with Grierson's boundaries of either linguistic families like Indo-Aryan and Dravidian or of branches within either of these families. Material items of culture seems to have independent extensions of their own; and these, very roughly, tend to be in accord with one another. On their basis, India becomes divided very roughly into two distinguishable, but overlapping, regions meeting at a broad zone which runs from Maharashtra to Bihar in some cases and to Orissa or Bengal in others. This broad belt has also been the area where several material traits have interpenetrated again and again bringing about changes in form or function.

Thus, for instance, village plans in India have a certain rough distinction between North and South. The North is the area of shapeless clusters, often broken up into dispersed units, while Southern villages are, on the whole, distinguished by the presence of open streets as an integral part of the lay-out. Oil-presses too can be divided into the Peninsular and Northern types. A certain amount of infiltration has taken place which has sometimes modified form and sometimes function. Yet, a broad regionalism is evident. The form of the plough also yields to a kind of geographical classification. Here, however, the types are not Northern and Southern; but what prevails in the South extends way up into Bihar. Some less extensive styles are localized in both north-eastern and north-western India. The wheels of bullockcarts similarly show a regional distinction; and this comes closer to the plough in distribution than to either village types or to oil-presses.

It will also be noticed in many cases that styles present in India have affiliation with styles in neighbouring countries. The presence of one or two special varieties of the plough and yoke, and of portable multi-socketed wooden mortars for husking paddy take us over to some portions of

* Reproduced from *Peasant Life in India.*

South-East Asia. And similar affinities can be drawn in relation to domestic architecture between India and Sumatra.

A very important item has been deliberately left out in the present preliminary report. This is, methods of pottery manufacture, as well as the forms of earthen vessels. Work is now proceeding on this subject.

From the information which has already been gathered in regard to these items, it appears that relationships can be established on their basis as much with South-East Asia as with countries lying to the west and north-west of India. This is not strange, for India has been in historical contact with countries lying both to the west and east for many centuries of her history. Our guess is that this relationship stretches back into the pre-historic past; for simple methods of pottery manufacture by hand, or processes of cooking food, etc. must have been practised long before the rise of urban civilization. And these help us in establishing cultural relationships which have been overlaid by later movements.

India has been a land where cultures have mingled after flowing in from both the west and the east. But what is original is that new combinations have taken place here, and sometimes even new inventions. It is not our purpose at the present moment to enter into the depths of cultural history, but to indicate in the beginning of the present series of surveys that broad regional distinctions are even now discernible in the material culture of India, as well as sufficient proof of their interpenetration.

Two things, again, stand out clearly in relation to this aspect of the question. One is that this regionalism seems to be on the whole independent of language as well as of physical types. This means that the plough or the husking mortar and pestle the unsewn cloth worn and regarded as ritually pure by women, the forms of villages, of oil-presses and methods of cooking food in oil,etc. etc. show a kind of kinship between the peasant folk, the weaver, the potter, etc. of various parts of India which is quite likely to be overlooked.

The second observation which can be made here is however, not in relation to the material traits which have been classified and geographically located as in the present report. But that is with reference to other kinds of traits which the Anthropological Survey of India has a desire to investigate more fully, and in which pilot schemes have already been set in operation.

Let us take the case of caste and the productive organization with which it became intimately associated and identified to a certain extent. From the little work which has already been accomplished it appears that there is a slight distinction between a Northern and Southern type of the organization of caste. Similarities are many; so that distinctions are based on finer shades only, quite unlike the distinctions which mark off common material objects of life from one another. Yet, it appears possible to draw a subtle distinction as one looks at selected aspects of the organization of caste as it has survived to the present day.

What is even more assuring is that, as one considers other spheres of life, namely things like laws which guide inheritance or define the rights and duties of individuals in a kin group, or if one rises to higher reaches of life confined to ideals or faiths or art, the differences which one has noticed at the material level of life gradually become feebler and feebler. They are eventually replaced by a unity of beliefs and aspirations which gives to Indian civilization a character of its own.

The structure of Indian unity can therefore be compared to a pyramid. There is more differentiation at the material base of life and progressively less as one mounts higher and higher. It is needless to say that the implication is not that village people are more different from one another than city people or sophisticated and propertied classes: but that, whether it is villager or a dweller of Indian towns, there is more variety in regard to some aspects of life and less in relation to others.

And, as we have said already, even the distinctions at the level of material culture override our language boundaries again and again. There is more unity in India's variety than one is likely to admit in moments of forgetfulness. And if this lesson can be brought home by means of the labours of the Anthropological Survey of India, every worker in that department will feel amply rewarded.

A deep acquaintance with the facts of life is perhaps the best introduction to any form of social science.

4

DEMARCATION OF AGRARIAN REGIONS OF INDIA: SOME SUGGESTIONS FOR FURTHER STUDY*

DANIEL THORNER

BY REDUCING the number of States in India and increasing their average size, the States Reorganization of 1956 has invited fresh attempts at demarcating the economic regions of India. Prior to 1956 efforts to differentiate regions came up against the dilemma of running counter either to economic considerations or to administrative considerations. The helter-skelter juxtaposition of State boundaries, especially in the case of the smaller units, made it difficult to devise analytically valid regions which could be equated with or confined within the individual States. In indicating regional groupings, therefore, the Census of 1951, the Rural Credit Survey, and various studies by individual scholars cut repeatedly across state lines.[1]

From the point of view of administrative policy and action, however, the individual States have been continually hungry for economic data presented according to State lines. In response to this pressure, students of regional variations have felt compelled to furnish such data, even while noting, for example, that "averaging of the data for the State as a whole may give results which may not be very meaningful for the pruposes of inter-regional comparisons.".[2]

Study of the map of India since the State Reorganization of 1956 indicates that it may perhaps now be possible both to take due account of socio-economic factors and at the same time to respect State boundaries. We must, of course, bear in mind the severe qualifications to which all efforts at the regionalization of India remain subject.[3] In very rough terms we may

*This is an extract from a revised version of my article " Demarcation of Agrarian Regions of India : Some Preliminary Notes, " originally published in the Seminar Series, Vol, I, of the Indian Society of Agricultural Economics, *Rationale of Regional Variations in Agrarian Structure of India* (Bombay, 1957), pp. 46-67.

[1] See the maps printed in my article " Demarcation of Agrarian Regions of India," *Rationale of Regional Variations* etc., pp. 49-52.

[2] M. L. Dantwala, " Regional Variations in Agricultural Employment and Wages," *Rationale of Regional Variatians, etc., p.* 98.

[3] Cf., O. H. K. Spate, *India and Pakistan : A General and Regional Geography,* 2nd Edition (London, 1957), Ch. XIII, " The Regions of the Sub-Continent, " esp. at pp. 353-54.

suggest that the following nine States form sufficiently distinctive areas for each of them to be considered as a separate region : Assam, West Bengal, Orissa, Punjab, Kashmir, Rajasthan, Kerala, Mysore, and Madras. Four other States may best be considered as composed of two major regions each : Uttar Pradesh (West U. P. and Central and Eastern U. P.), Bihar (North Bihar and South Bihar), Andhra Pradesh (Coastal Andhra and Inland Andhra), and Madhya Pradesh (Chhattisgarh and Malwa-Bundelkhand). Bombay, India's largest State, would appear to be the most varied and, at a minimum, should be considered in terms of three regions: Gujarat Saurashtra Bombay-Deccan plus Berar-Nagpur, and Konkan. In this way we obtain a total of twenty broad economic regions which may be listed as follows :

State		*Regions*
ANDHRA	...	Coastal Andhra
		Inland Andhra
ASSAM	...	Assam
BIHAR	...	North Bihar
		South Bihar
BOMBAY	...	Gujarat-Saurashtra
		Berar-Deccan
		Konkan
JAMMU and KASHMIR	...	Jammu and Kashmir
KERALA	...	Kerala
MADHYA PRADESH	...	Malwa-Bundelkhand
		Chhattisgarh
MADRAS	...	Madras
MYSORE	...	Mysore
ORISSA	...	Orissa
PUNJAB	...	Punjab
RAJASTHAN	...	Rajasthan
UTTAR PRADESH	...	Western Uttar Pradesh
		Central & Eastern Uttar Pradesh
WEST BENGAL	...	West Bengal

The reader may rightly ask, what are the criteria which have been used to demarcate these twenty regions. Before answering this, I should like to direct attention to the broad agreement which has been reached in three previous efforts to demarcate the regions of India : the Census of 1951, the Reserve Bank's Rural Credit Survey, and the study by Dr. Chen Han-seng, *Agrarian Regions of India and Pakistan*. This agreement, it should be noted, has been reached despite the employment of somewhat diverse criteria. The Census of 1951 divided the country into five regions and fifteen sub-regions on the basis of topography, soil and rainfall.[4] The Rural Credit Survey sponsored by the Reserve Bank of India in 1951-52 grouped its seventy-five districts into thirteen regions "on the basis of certain consi-

[4] Census of India, 1951, Vol. I, India : Part I-A, Report (Delhi, 1953), p. xi.

derations of contiguity and of similarity of physical, climatic or other natural and demographic conditions."[5] Dr. Chen Han-seng, in his as yet unpublished monograph on the *Agrarian Regions of India and Pakistan*, prepared in 1948-50, used five criteria to separate India into sixteen regions. He has set forth his criteria as follows : "topographical situation, agricultural water supply (both rainfall and irrigation), crop system, land system, and general economic development."[6] The accompanying chart shows the striking similarity of the three sets of regions.

Rural Credit Survey	*Dr. Chen Han-seng*	*Census of* 1951
Assam—Bengal	Assam	Eastern Himalyan
Bihar—Bengal	North Bihar	Lower Gangetic Plains
	W. Bengal—S. Bihar	,, ,, ,,
Eastern Uttar Pradesh	East U.P.	,, ,, ,,
Western Uttar Pradesh	West U. P.	Upper Gangetic Plains
Punjab—PEPSU	Punjab	Trans-Gangetic Plain
		Western Himalayan
Rajasthan	Rajputana	The Desert
		North West Hills
Central India	North Madhya Pradesh and Vindhya Pradesh	North Central Hills and Plateau
Orissa and E. Madhya Pradesh	S.E. Madhya Pradesh and Orissa	N.E. Plateau
Western Cotton Region	Gujarat—Khandesh	Gujarat—Kathiawar
North Deccan	Maratha Region	North Deccan
South Deccan	Southern Deccan	South Deccan
East Coast	North-east Madras	North Madras and Orissa Coastal
,, ,,	Tamil Region	South Madras
West Coast	Malabar Coast	Malabar—Konkan
,, ,,	Konkan	

The set of twenty regions which I have presented above is quite consonant with the basic regions of the 1951 Census, the Rural Credit Survey, and Dr. Chen's study. There are only two noteworthy changes that I have introduced. The first is in the eastern tract comprising Bengal-Bihar-Chhota Nagpur-Orissa, which is not treated exactly alike in any two of the above studies. My procedure has been to separate Chhattisgarh as a region from the rest of Madhya Pradesh; to treat North Bihar and South Bihar as distinct regions; and to consider West Bengal and Orissa each as a region.

The second important change that I have made relates to Mysore and

[5] All-India Rural Credit Survey Vol. I, The Survey Report : Part I (Rural Families) (Bombay, 1956), p. II.

[6] Agrarian Regions of India and Pakistan, (Philadelphia, 1950—ms.), p. ii.

Andhra. I have taken the whole of the new Mysore State as a region, but have considered coastal Andhra as a separate region distinct from inland Andhra. It should be stressed that the demarcation of these twenty regions is highly provisional and subject to modification.

The criteria which I am using have been determined by the nature of my interest in the regional analysis of India. This centres on the classic agrarian problem namely, the interrelation of the institutional framework on the one hand, with the level of output and the distribution of the product on the other.

Accordingly, I have been attempting to make use of the following seven criteria :

1. Socio-economic systems (e. g.—tribal ways of life such as we find in Assam or Chhattisgarh; settled agriculture carried on primarily by subsistence-oriented peasant households as prevalent in the villages of Coastal Orissa or Rayalaseema; cash-crop farming as typified by sugarcane producers of Meerut or cotton-growers of Berar).
2. Types of landholding and concentration of control.
3. Labour supply: family labour, unfree labour, free labour.
4. Control of credit, marketing, processing, shopkeeping.
5. Geographic factors: topography, soil, climate, water supply and drainage.
6. Crop patterns and cultivation units.
7. Overall degree of modernization: industrialization, urbanization, population growth.

The value of these regions for purposes of analysis will have to be tested by trial breakdowns of the available empirical data. If the boundaries have been defined appropriately, the variations within a given region, in terms of these criteria, should be less than the variations from the given region to the neighbouring regions.

A number of these regions, it will be noted, are very large, both in area and in population. Madras, for example, although much reduced from its former size and diversity still extends to some 50,000 square miles in which live about 30 million people. Others, such as Assam, Punjab, or Western Uttar Pradesh include hill districts with characteristics of their own. The existence of these important differences within some of our major regions suggests the need for a more detailed regional breakdown. Consequently, taking as my point of departure the twenty regions listed above, I have prepared a second set of forty divisions. Four of these divisions refer to India's metropolitan areas or, more pedantically, the "conurbations" of Calcutta, Bombay, Delhi, and Madras.

Seven of the divisions represent areas taken over intact from our previous list; these include the States of Kerala and Kashmir, and five regions: Coastal Andhra, North Bihar, Gujarat-Saurashtra, Konkan, and Chhattisgarh. There has not seemed to me to be sufficient reason for dividing further any of these.

The principal innovation has been with respect to the thirteen remaining regions of my original list. Ten of these regions have been split into two divisions each, while three of our largest regions—Rajasthan, Mysore and Malwa-Bundelkhand—have been broken into three divisions each.

The present scheme can be summed up as a two-stage breakdown with 20 major regions each consisting of a single State or a part of a State, and 40 divisions (4 urban and 36 overwhelmingly rural), each constituting a region or a part of a region. In order to indicate more precisely the territorial extent of these regions and divisions, I have specified the districts assigned to each division in the chart given below.

I should like, in conclusion, to emphasize that the entire scheme is tentative and preliminary in nature, and is put forward primarily to elicit criticism from other research workers.

REGIONS/DIVISION	DISTRICTS IN EACH DIVISION
Coastal Andhra	
Coastal Andhra	Srikakulam. Vishakapatnam, East Godavari, West Godavari, Krishna, Guntur, Nellore.
Inland Andhra	
Telengana	Adilabad, Nizamabad, Karimnagar, Medak, Warangal, Khammam, Nalgonda, Mahbubnagar, Hyderabad.
Rayalaseema	Kurnool, Anantapur, Cuddapah, Chittoor.
Assam	
Assam Hills	All Hill and Frontier districts, including N.E.F.A. and Manipur and Tripura.
Assam Valley	Cachar, Goalpara, Kamrup, Darrang, Nowgong, Sibsagar, and Lakhimpur.
North Bihar	
North Bihar	Saran, Muzaffarpur, Champaran, Darbhanga, Saharsa, Purnea, Monghyr *North.*
South Bihar	
South Bihar	Shahabad, Patna, Gaya, Bhagalpur, Monghyr *South.*
Chhota Nagpur	Palamau, Hazaribagh, Dhanbad, Santhal Parganas, Ranchi, Singhbhum.
Gujarat-Saurashtra	
Gujarat-Saurashtra	Kutch, Banaskantha Mehsana, Sabarkantha, Jhalawar, Halar, Madhya Saurashtra, Sorath, Amreli, Gohilwad, Ahmedabad, Kaira, Panch Mahals, Baroda, Broach, Surat.

Region / Sub-region	Districts
Berar-Deccan	
Khandesh-Berar	West Khandesh, East Khandesh, Dangs, Buldana, Akola, Amraoti, Yeotmal, Nagpur, Wardha, Bhandara, Chanda.
Bombay Deccan (including Marathwada)	Nasik, Aurangabad, Parbhani, Nanded, Ahmednagar, Bhir, Poona, Osmanabad, Satara North, Satara South, Sholapur, Kolhapur.
Konkan	
Konkan	Thana, Kolaba, Ratnagiri.
Greater Bombay	Greater Bombay.
Jammu and Kashmir	
Jammu and Kashmir	All districts
Kerala	
Kerala	Malabar, Trichur, Kottayam, Quilon, Trivandrum.
Malwa-Bundelkhand	
Malwa-Nimar	Mandasaur, Rajgarh, Ratlam, Ujjain, Shajapur, Jhabua, Dhar, Dewas, Indore, Nimar-I, Nimar-II.
Gwalior-Bundelkhand	Morena, Bhind, Gwalior, Shivpuri, Datia, Guna, Tikamgarh, Chattarpur, Panna, Satna, Rewa.
Narmada	Bhilsa, Sehore, Raisen, Saugor, Damoh, Jabalpur, Hoshungabad, Betul, Narsinghpur, Seoni, Mandla, Chhindwara.
Chattisgarh	
Chattisgarh-Baghelkhand	Sidhi, Shahdol, Surguja, Bilaspur, Raigarh, Balaghat, Durg, Raipur, Bastar.
Madras	
Coromandal Coast	Chingleput, South Arcot, Pondicherry, Tanjore, Ramnad, Tinnevelly, Kanyakumari.
Inland Madras	North Arcot, Salem, Nilgiris, Coimbatore, Tiruchirapalli, Madura.
Madras City	Madras City.
Mysore	
North Karnatak	Bidar, Gulbarga, Bijapur, Belgaum, Dharwar, Raichur, Bellary.
Mysore	Shimoga, Chitaldrug, Chickmagalur, Hassan, Tumkur, Bangalore, Kolar, Mandya, Mysore.
Kanara-Coorg	Kanara, South Kanara, Coorg,
Orissa	
Coastal Orissa Inland Orissa	Balasore, Cuttack, Puri, Ganjam. Sundergarh, Sambalpur, Keonjhar, Mayurbhanj, Bolangir, Phulbani, Dhenkanal, Kalahandi, Koraput.

Region	Districts
Punjab	
Punjab Hills-Himachal	Kangra, Simla, Chamba, Mandi, Sirmoor, Mahasu, and Bilaspur.
Punjab-Plains	Gurdaspur, Amritsar, Hoshiarpur, Kapurthala, Jullundur, Ferozepur, Ludhiana, Bhatinda, Sangrur, Patiala, Ambala, Hissar, Karnal, Rohtak, Gurgaon, Mohindergarh.
Delhi State	Delhi State.
Rajasthan	
Jodhpur-Bikaner	Ganganagar, Bikaner, Churu, Jaisalmer, Jodhpur, Nagore, Barmer, Jalore, Pali.
Jaipur-Ajmer	Jhunjhunu, Sikar, Jaipur, Alwar, Bharatpur, Ajmer, Tonk, Sawaimadhopur.
Mewar-Kotah	Bhilwara, Kotah, Bundi, Jhalawar, Chittorgarh, Sirohi, Udaipur, Dungarpur, Banswara.
Western Uttar Pradesh	
Kumaon-Garhwal	Garhwal, Tehri-Garhwal, Nainital, Almora, Dehra Dun.
Meerut-Agra-Rohilkhand	Saharanpur, Bareilly, Bijnor, Pilibhit, Rampur, Kheri, Muzaffarnagar, Meerut, Bulandshahr, Aligarh, Mathura, Agra, Mainpuri, Etah, Budaun, Moradabad, Shahjahanpur, Etawah, Farrukhabad.
Central & Eastern Uttar Pradesh	
Oudh-Jhansi	Sitapur, Hardoi, Bara Banki, Lucknow, Kanpur Unao, Rai-Bareli, Jalaun, Hamirpur, Fatehpur, Banda, Jhansi, Pratapgarh, Allahabad, Sultanpur, Faizabad.
Banaras-Gorakhpur	Bahraich, Gonda, Basti, Gorakhpur, Deoria, Azamgarh, Ballia, Jaunpur, Ghazipur, Banaras, Mirzapur.
West Bengal	
Darjeeling-Duars	Darjeeling, Jalpaiguri, Cooch Behar, (Sikkim).
Lower Bengal	West Dinajpur, Malda, Murshidabad, Birbhum, Purulia, Bankura, Burdwan, Nadia, Hooghly, Midnapore, 24-Parganas.
Calcutta	Calcutta-Howrah-Chandernagore.

SECTION III

HISTORICAL

INTRODUCTION

THE PRESENT section is comprised of four selections. A great controversy has been raging over the nature of the pre-British Indian society. Eminent scholars have been trying to decipher its characteristics and distinguish it from the pre-capitalist societies as they existed in Europe and other parts of the world. Extensive discussion has been going on over the question of the distinction between European feudalism from which modern Western capitalist society emerged and Indian feudalism which was replaced by a colonial capitalist social order created in India by the British conquerors. The two articles by Shelvankar attempt to reveal the nature of the bond which retained the unity of the pre-British Indian society as well as the peculiar character of Indian feudalism which distinguished it from European feudalism. The distinction pointed out by him between the military fiscal feudalism of India and the baronial feudalism of the West deserves careful attention. Professor Kosambi, in his work, *An Introduction to the Study of Indian History* has also attempted to understand the pre-British Indian society and culture and has compared and contrasted Indian and European feudalisms. Prof. Debi Prasad Chattopadhaya, while surveying the literature on the village communities in Pre-British India has thrown light on the same subject.

An adequate comparative investigations of some of the great civilizations such as those of India, China and others having a continuous history from the neolithic to the modern times has become very necessary for a proper comprehension of the various trends of social development that are taking place in those countries. Without a proper methodical exploration into the structural framework of the pre-British Indian society with its peculiar caste system, self-sufficient village community and the tribute-gathering feudal class, as well as the forces which generated this framework, one is not likely to grasp the peculiar socio-historical development which took place in India during British period as well as the social-developmental trend that is taking place after Independence. The study of India's peculiar past is indispensable for a proper understanding of the recent trends. The four articles have been selected with a view to indicating how a historical study of the Indian agrarian social order should be simultaneously launched along with the study of its contemporary trend of development. To our mind, the four selections are valuable for such a historical study of the Indian agrarian society and the laws of its development (*Author*).

1

THE UNITY OF INDIA*

K. S. Shelvankar

The Unity of a Pre-Capitalist Culture

As many Hindu writers have pointed out, the concept of the fundamental unity of India is an important element in the Hindu heritage.

But this religious and, as it were, ideological unity—fostering the love of the land "as a sacrament of a culture which it embodies"—was based on the minute social differentiation that goes by the name of caste. This is a system that can be related to no coherent idea, not even perhaps least of all—to what is stated in the Hindu scriptures to be its true foundation. It represents actually a confusion of all manner of distinctions, racial and occupational. The one thing that can be said about it with certainty is that it segregates the castes by forbiding inter-marriage and restricts each caste to a particular vocation. It implies not only the negation of equality but the organisation of inequality exclusively on the basis of inheritance. Differences there will be in any imaginable society—differences of function, at all events. It is not in recognising their inevitability that caste is peculiar; it is in the method it adopts to systematise and control them. You are a Brahmin (priest) because your father was a Brahmin; or a butcher or scavenger, weaver or washerman, for the same reason. Birth is all.

What is more, the system was clothed with all the sanctions of religion. Indeed, it was the Hindu religion and this massive and complex social structure which was declared to be rooted in the eternal order of things. And Hinduism asked of the ordinary individual not so much the acceptance of any precise intellectual or mystical dogma, but rather that he should adapt himself to the social position in which he was born, i. e., his place in the caste hierarchy—and be diligent in his observance of the traditional duties and restrictions it imposed on him. "Each caste and sub-caste was a separate centre with its own particular interest of various kinds, with its own stray likes and dislikes, with its rigid wall that hindered all real and practical identification with the intersts and likes of other castes and with the wider self of the body-politic."

Thus while Hinduism unified India, it obstructed the further development of unity by upholding on religious grounds a social system composed of bits and pieces, of interlocked fragments, like a Chinese puzzle. The

---

*Reproduced from *The Problem of India,* by K. S. Shelvankar, pp. 19-23.

obstruction might have been broken down if economic development had demanded it. But the economic system was stabilised at a low level. It was based on the village community which was a more or less self-sufficient unit, combining agriculture and handicrafts. Production was everywhere on a small-scale, and for consumption rather than exchange. Technology was backward, communications were poor, money was scarcely needed, and every thing moved in narrow, well-worn grooves fixed by custom. It was, in short, a precapitalist economic system parochial, static and, in many respects, primitive. There was indeed, a market of varying dimensions for different commodities; but it was not a self-expanding dynamic market binding together the whole country, or even any very large areas of it, in a process of continuous and vital commodity exchange.

In these circumstances the emergence of a political organisation identifying an "Indian nation" with an "Indian State" was naturally out of the question. Frontiers fluctuated from time to time, dynasties rose and fell, wars and invasions ravaged some part of the land or other. But they left the life of the people largely unaffected, for it was governed ultimately not by the laws of the State but by caste, codes of function and privilege, by caste organisation, and by virtually autonomous bodies such as the local guilds and village communes.

Secondly, as a result of military disturbances and calamities like floods and famines, the fabric of caste was shaken and reshaken, and progressively lost whatever element of rationality it ever had. In the realms of politics and military affairs it played little or no part; individuals frequently broke through its bonds; new castes were formed; but in all essentials the system nevertheless remained unchanged. Thirdly, since no social or economic regime is absolutely static, new cultural, linguistic and sectarian groups and sub-groups arose in different regions of India; partial crystallisations, as it were, within the wide stream of Hindu culture—the Marathas, Tamils, Kashmiris, Gujaratis, Bengalis, the votaries of Siva and of Vishnu, etc., while completely outside the pale of Hinduism but not uninfluenced by it there came into existence religious minorities such as the Moslems and Sikhs.

Unity and the British Conquest

The British conquest initiated and enforced a series of interrelated changes. Each of them by itself would have been revolutionary enough in its consequences, but, occurring simultaneously as they did, they shattered once for all, within the space of a few decades, the foundations of a civilisation that had endured for well nigh three thousand years. There was a new land system, a new revenue system and a new system of administration. Railways were built, trade was encouraged and markets were widened. The transition to a money economy was speeded up. A uniform system of coinage was introduced and the use of money, that most potent dissolvent of ancient ties, was made obligatory. At the same time, law more and more tended to replace the customs which had for so long kept India tethered to her immemorial past.

Underlying and dominating these changes was the political unification of the country. Nationalist writers sometimes argue that this had been achieved in earlier period of Indian history. There is a grain of truth in the contention but it is not of much importance. For there is an essential, qualitative difference between the unity which enables the Government in India today to exercise at need a direct and immediate control over any village or hamlet in any part of India and the sort of general and in the main nominal overlordship exercised by Asoka or Akbar.

The basis of this unity was three-fold. In part it was technological; railways, telegraphs, etc. In part it lay in the character of British power in India: it was not, as in the case of the Turks and Moguls, the power of a body of military adventures acting on their own behalf and for their personal gain, hence liable to fall out among themselves, but of rulers who were the nominees and agents of a foreign Government—of the highly organised and unified British Government and the capitalist class which supported it. It was made possible, above all, through the disruption, by the various social and economic forces released by the British conquest, of institutions such as caste]and the village commune which had formerly barred the road to the political unification of India.

Stated in the broad terms, the transformation was an episode, one of the major episodes, in the history of capitalism. The breakway from the feudal order welded England into a national state dominated by the capitalist class. The subsequent extension of British power to India was admittedly dictated by economic motives, by the desire to exploit the trade and industry of India. Exploitation required, and meant in practice, the construction of railways, the reorganisation of the land system, the stimulation of commerce, etc. The direct object of these measures was to increase the profitability of India to British capital, but they inevitably had the effect of destroying the precapitalist social and economic system of the country. They paved the way for the evolution of India on capitalist lines and thereby also created the technological and economic conditions for the attainment of a degree of unity such as they had not known at any period in her history.

2

INDIAN FEUDALISM*

D. D. KOSAMBI

INDIAN FEUDALISM differs so much from its European counterpart, at least, as regards superficial manifestations, that the very existence of feudalism in India has sometimes been denied, except to describe the Muslim and Rajput military hierarchies. The main characteristics of European (specifically English) feudalism may be summarised as follows: (1) "A low level of technique, in which the instruments of production are simple and generally inexpensive, and the act of production is largely individual in character; the division of labour.........being at a very primitive level of development." This is true of India at all stages, including the pre-feudal. (2) "Production for the immediate need of household or a village-community and not for a wider market." In a broad sense, this is also true here, though increasing commodity production in metals, salt, coconuts,cotton *tambule* (*pan, Piper betle*), areca nuts, and the like has to be noted. (3) "Demesne-farming; on the lords estate often on a considerable scale, by compulsory labour service." This is decidedly not true of India. The manorial system had begun to come into existence only towards the end of the feudal period, in India. The reason was that the Mauryan empire had nothing to correspond to the villas and slave economy of classical Rome. The unit of settlement was the village. It has been shown that its expansion into tribal areas took place in general by far more peaceful methods than under Rome, or Charlemagne, or feudal barons. Nevertheless, the later Indian feudal lords tried always to cultivate some lands directly so as to be independent of the villagers, whose united resistance or failure to produce a crop in bad years might bring disaster to the lord. The armed retainers of the baron had to be assured an independent food supply for emergencies. These seigneurial lands were often cultivated by slaves. Slavery now took on a new importance though still not indispensable to the means of production. (4) "Political decentralization" is common to both India and Europe, beginning in the period of feudalism from above. The Mauryan theory that all land belongs to the king was reinforced by the tribal concept of land as territory (not property) held in common by the tribe, whose symbol and expression was the chief; this chief would be replaced by the king (Arth. 11·1) or turn into a king, or be converted into a feudal tributary by a conqueror who might at need support the chieftain

*Reproduced from *An Introduction to the Study of Indain History* by D. D. Kosambi, pp. 326-328.

against his former tribesmen. In time, the functions of the village councils were more and more usurped by the nearest feudal lord. The exception was of villages paying taxes directly to the king. For them, and for their individual landowners, some separate form of ownership or tenure-rights were recognised. (5) "Conditional holding of land by lords on some kind of service-tenure." This is particularly noticeable among Rajputs, whose chief profession was of arms; and among the earlier Muslims, whose chiefs were invaders and who used the common religion to keep themselves, converts included, apart from the rest of the population. The Gangas seem to have been the first to develop it in the south (Amma 1, 10th century). Later, all lords were required to serve but their jagirs shifted from time to time. It is important to note that the military hierarchy at the centre was not hereditary in general. The emperor would be sole heir to the court-noble whose children might be reduced to penuary at the will of the autocrat. The high courtiers might even be slaves. (6) "Possession by a lord of judicial or quasi-judicial functions in relation to the dependent population." This came in part by the lord's sole possession of armed force over the disarmed village, in part from displacement of the older village council. One might trace this back to the Manusmrti princeling who dispensed justice directly as raja, or to Mauryan absolutism in the extensive *sita* crown lands. Both of these contributed to the development of later feudalism, inevitable as long as the village had no armed force of its own. Three notable characteristics further distinguish Indian from European feudalism; the increase of slavery, absence of guilds, and the lack of an organized church. Caste replaced both guild and church, being symptom and cause of a more primitive form of production.

The question "who owns the land?" could not be answered because ownership had totally different meanings under Indian feudalism and the European bourgeois or proto-bourgeois mode. The "lumberdars" held responsible for payment of taxes, soon found it possible to claim ownership rights of the new type, though they had only been representatives of the commune. The answer, therefore, lay in the creation of a new type of guaranteed property in land, essentially bourgeois property under various traditional outward forms. This was not accomplished at one stroke; but it was done, irrevocably. Later feudal tax-collection had degenerated into plunder of the cultivators, without protection except such little as might derive from their communal solidarity behind ancient custom (FCM 1·378·80). The new revenue settlement resulted in direct assessment and taxation of the owner class whose possession was subject to the same laws as other personal property, and could be transferred by a financial transaction as for trade goods. The rights were maintained by an efficient judiciary and a compact police force, both paid regular salaries, independent of any feudal nobility, with the same powers over all classes of people as regards the law—bourgeois law.

3

INDIAN FEUDALISM, ITS CHARACTERISTICS*

K. S. SHELVANKAR

THE TRIPLE CONFLICT OVER LAND

WHAT INDIAN agrarian development created was thus a multiplicity of simultaneous and co-ordinate claims on the land. They were broadly of three kinds: the customary claims of the peasants in the village; the delegated or derivative claims of the intermediary; and the superior claims of the sovereign. Private property in land, as ordinarily understood, can only arise when this triple claim has been systematised and unified in some form or other. It involves a clarification of the position (a) as between the overlord and the intermediaries as a body; (b) as between the intermediaries and the village; (c) among the peasants themselves.

In Western Europe, too, the elements of agrarian history are the same as in India: the villages, more or less collectivist in character, with a real or putative basis in tribal kinship; on top of them a tribal chief whose power, through conquest and other means, is extended over a larger territory and greater numbers; and the development, based on technical deficiencies and military necessities, of a class of fief-holders, intermediaries, between overlord and village. But owing to the difference in the relations between these constituents of the agrarian scheme, their development led in one case to a definite system of private property, while in the other it did not.

INDIAN FEUDALISM: ITS CHARACTERISTICS

There were in the main three reasons why agrarian development in India proceeded on different lines.

(1) On the plane of theory, the difference is rooted in different conceptions of monarchical power. The king under European feudalism combined in himself authority over all persons and things in his kingdom. When the king's dominium was delegated under vows of allegiance to a number of barons and fief-holders of different degrees, and a hierarchy of authority was created, the power and the rights that were passed on from superior to inferior were power and rights over things (over the land of a given area) as well as over the persons connected with it.

In India there was nothing analogous to the Roman conception of dominium and the sovereign's power was not until a late period, regarded as

*Reproduced from *The Problem of Iudia*, by K. S. Shelvankar, pp. 96-102, 139-143.

absolute and unlimited over the agricultural land of the kingdom. The king did not, in theory, create subordinate owners of land because he himself was not in theory the supreme owner of the land. What he delegated to the intermediaries was not even his sovereignty understood in this restricted sense, but only the specific and individual rights of zamin, the revenue-collecting power.

Hence there did not occur, as in England, a conflict between the king and his baronage, with the baronage endeavouring to delimit and circumscribe the claims which the king could make upon them in virtue of his exercise of the supreme dominium. The king was not *primus inter pares*; and the baronage were not co-sharers with him of sovereignty. From the beginning they held no more than a fairly well-defined title of the collection of taxes, or rents, and they could escape this condition not by fighting with the king for the clarification and settlement of their mutual relationship—which was precise enough—but by taking up arms against him and, if they were powerful enough, by themselves assuming the insignia of royalty. The conflict between the king and his feudatories did not therefore lead to political and constitutional developments within the framework of the State, but merely to the creation of a new State in no way dissimilar to that from which its ruler had torn himself apart.

(2) In order to resist, when necessary, the overlord's terms or conditions made even on the narrow ground of the zamin power, a principle of cohesion was necessary, and that was lacking among the intermediate baronage. They were intermediaries of different grades, different powers, different environments and languages, whose allegiance was never centralised and focused on a single person or institution, and who were, moreover, scattered widely over an immense territory. They could never, as an organised and coherent body, resist a common overlord and impose checks on him, partly because there was no common overlord to whom all of them had sworn allegiance, and partly because they themselves were rent asunder, were scattered and had each a different historical antecedent.

(3) Save in some exceptional cases the intermediary in his relations with the peasantry and the village had no occasion to convert his zamin rights into one of *de facto* dominium in the European sense by any attempt directly to influence the course of rural operations. Indian feudalism remained fiscal and military in character, it was not manorial. There was in general none of the intermingling of peasant land with demesne land in a common village, nor interdependence for labour services such as marked the manorial system. The peasant was not the lord's serf, nor was the lord directly interested in cultivation. There was therefore nothing similar to the direct conflict between the manorial lord and the peasantry over the disposal and cultivation of the land and of labour services which agitated Europe from the twelfth to the eighteenth centuries.

When there was a conflict, it was over the share of the agricultural produce to be retained by the peasant or surrendered to the lord. The foundations of agriculture themselves were not affected. Nor was there any such widespread and general rise in prices or the temptation of greater income by turning arable into pasture, to lead the baronage to assert their power in a manner capable of introducing fundamental changes in the rural economy. Even as late as the eighteenth century there was an abundance of land, and the hard-pressed peasant could always abscond on the open plains of the Ganges. The lord therefore was in general satisfied to exact his utmost from the peasant in the shape of produce, without concerning himself with economic and technical questions of increasing production......

There was no security or safeguard for a right against the State, as critics sometimes observe, for the simple reason that the right was in fact and manifestly a concession of the State, a delegation of its political revenue collecting power. But this applies only to the non-cultivating classes. As for the village and the peasantry, they had strictly neither rights nor safeguards—except such as were grounded in custom. They tilled the land not because it was a right or a duty, but because it was the matter of their fathers. And no one was foolish enough to try to evict them, because there was plenty of other land to which they could go. What their masters wanted was not the peasant's land, but his surplus value.

None of the major conflict in Indian history had for its object the exercise of rights over the village. They were conflicts between overlords of various grades for the right or power to get a payment from the peasant, not to seize his land. European history, on the contrary, reveals a conflict between the peasantry and the manorial lords because the latter not only demanded a share of the produce, but desired to retain a particular method of cultivation—by forced labour—or to introduce new methods of cultivation (enclosures, large-scale farming). The Indian conflict was one between lords who were concerned not at all with methods of cultivation, but only to draw an income from the peasantry. If all ownership of land rests ultimately either on the claim of the sword or the claim of the plough, the issue in India was never fought out between the claimants of the plough and the claimants of the sword. The issue was always between different claimants of the sword, the village and the peasantry remaining throughout the passive subject of conflict, the booty over which the rival powers fought each other....

The Cause of Frustration

This frustration, this incapacity to outgrow itself which weighed down the productive system of India, may be explained, to begin with, in terms of the village community.

Owing to the direct combination of domestic industry and agriculture that it represented, and the resultant economies, the village was able to preserve its equilibrium and offer the strongest resistance to disruptive influences. The manor, it is true, was in some respects similar to the Indian village, but it was a less stable organisation. It was based on serfdom and ruled over by a feudal baron; and to serf and baron alike the development of urban trade and industry held out advantages, either of personal freedom or pecuniary gain. Hence, when these forces came into play, the manor succumbed, not perhaps without a struggle, but in a comparatively short period.

The village, on the other hand, which had in general no room either for serfdom or baronial exploitation, was the more firmly articulated in its inner structure and therefore succeeded, where the manor had failed in maintaining its distinctive character. When we consider that, in the nineteenth century, it withstood the assault even of mass-produced goods—"which are everywhere perforated by the dead expenses of their process of circulation" —and broke down finally under the cumulative pressure of political and economic changes, we cannot be surprised at the tenacity it displayed for so long.

The dogged resistance of the village is, however, only a part of the explanation. We must take into account also the political and social weakness of the Indian bourgeoisie, a weakness of which the most striking proof is the absence in Indian history of anything comparable to the town economy of the European Middle Ages.

"During this period the whole of the commercial and industrial life of the time was concentrated in, and indeed confined to, the town; was controlled, assisted and limited by municipal regulations. ......The policy of self-interest pursued by the towns was directed not only against burgesses of other towns, but also in relation to the inhabitants of the surrounding agricultural areas. ......Every town expected to obtain for its own consumption the surplus food grown in the country around, and sought to prevent the rustics from engaging in any industry which could compete with its own manufactures"....

In India, too, there were guilds—craft as well as trade guilds. (Something like a loose federation of trade guilds existed in South India for many centuries).

It is certain, in any case, that the merchants and handicraftsmen, the bourgeoisie as a class organised in its guilds, never attained the ascendancy that its European counterpart won for itself when it seized political power in the towns. In India the town was nearly always an outpost of the territorial State, governed by prefects or boards appointed from the centre.

Why, it will be asked, did the European bourgeoisie overcome this obstacle? Why did they triumph over the State machine, driving it out of or assimilating it into the towns? The answer takes us to the heart of the question. There was an essential difference in the inter-relations which prevailed in Europe and India between the State, town and country. For the agrarian system of India, public works and irrigation works were a necessity. It could only be met by an organisation with the resources and the authority of the State. And to control, regulate and supervise public works, and the collection of the land-tax, the State was compelled to station its agents at the various local centres, which were the towns.

Feudal Europe also was an agrarian society, perhaps more completely so than India. But irrigation and irrigation works were of negligible importance; and the towns, such as they were, were primarily fortresses and judicial and administrative centres; they were not vitally related to the productive organism. The capture of these key points by industrial and commercial interests divorced from agriculture did not, accordingly, present any threat to the stability of rural production. (Actually, it served as a stimulus). In Indian conditions, however, where it would have presented such a threat, the State, whose fortunes were bound up with the land, never relaxed its hold on the towns which were the bases of its action.

That is why commerce and guilds and towns—if we leave aside the circumstances of their origin at an early and obscure period—had no revolutionary significance in India: they did not bring about a new division of labour between town and country, concentrating industry and trade in one and agriculture in the other. That is why, again, although not only administrative but geographical, military, strategic and religious factors helped to determine the character of the towns, few of them derived their importance exclusively from trade and industry.

It was the existence of the town and of an urban population requiring goods and services, which drew trade and industry towards it. And the Indian bourgeoisie, lacking the means to break down the opposition of the village and turn the countryside into its market, as the European burgeoisie had been able to do, had perforce to submit to this situation and resign itself to playing a subordinate role to the courts and noblemen, the soliders, officials, priests and pilgrims, who collectively constituted the consumer class and who were in possession of the towns. It was in the main their wealth that the Indian bourgeoisie tried to tap......

For these reasons—the invincible toughness of the village and the political importance of the burgeoisie—the evolution of Indian economy was inhibited and the spontaneous emergence of a capitalist order was rendered impossible.

4

VILLAGE COMMUNITIES*

D. CHATTOPADHYAYA

SMALL AND SELF-SUFFICIENT village communities had been a very conspicuous feature of the traditional Indian social system. We are going to discuss these insofar as they reveal the relics of tribal society.

Following is Marx's famous description of the village communities :

Those small and extremely ancient Indian communities, some of which have continued down to this day, are based on possession in common of the land, on the blending of agriculture and handicrafts, and on an unalterable division of labour, which serves, whenever a new community is started, as a plan and scheme ready cut and dried. Occupying areas of from 100 upto several thousand acres, each forms a compact whole producing all it requires. The chief part of the products is destined for direct use by the community itself, and does not take the form of a commodity. Hence, production here is independent of that division of labour brought about, in Indian society as a whole, by means of the exchange of commodities. It is the surplus alone that becomes a commodity, and a portion of even that, not until it has reached the hands of the State, into whose hands from time immemorial a certain quantity of these products has found its way in the shape of rent in kind. The constitution of these communities varies in different parts of India. In those of the simplest form, the land is tilled in common and the produce divided among the members. At the same time, spinning and weaving are carried on in each family as subsidiary industries. Side by side with the masses thus occupied with one and the same work, we find the 'chief inhabitant', who is judge, police, and tax-gatherer in one; the book-keeper, who keeps the accounts of the tillage and registers everything relating thereto; another official, who prosecutes criminals, protects strangers travelling through and escorts them to the next village; the boundary man, who guards the boundaries against neighbouring communities; the wateroverseer, who distributes the water from the common tanks for irrigation; the Brahmin, who conducts the religious services; the schoolmaster, who on the sand teaches the children reading and writing; the calendar-Brahmin, or astrologer, who makes known the lucky or unlucky days for seed-time and harvest, and for every other kind of agricultural work; a smith and a carpenter, who make and repair all the agricultural implements; the potter, who makes all the pottery of the village;

*Lokayate : Village Communities in India., pp. 186—198.

the barber the washerman, who washes clothes, the silversmith, here and there the poet, who in some communities replaces the silversmith, in others the schoolmaster. This dozen of individuals is maintained at the expense of the whole community. If the population increases, a new community is founded, on the pattern of the old one, on unoccupied land. The whole mechanism discloses a systematic division of labour; but division like that in manufactures is impossible, since the smith and the carpenter, &c., find an unchanging market, and at the most there occur, according to the sizes of the villages, two or three of each, instead of one. The law that regulates the division of labour in the community acts with the irresistible authority of a law of Nature, at the same time that each individual artificer, the smith, the carpenter, and so on, conducts in his workshop all the operations of his handicrafts in the traditional way, but independently, and without recognizing any authority over him. The simplicity of the organisation for production in these self-sufficing communities that constantly reproduce themselves in the same form, and when accidentally destroyed, spring up again on the spot and with the same name–this simplicity supplies the key to the secret of the unchangeableness of Asiatic Societies, an unchangeableness in such striking contrast with the constant dissolution and refounding of Asiatic States, and the never-ceasing changes of dynasty. The structure of the economical elements of society remains untouched by the storm-clouds of the political sky.

Co-operative life, and even more important than that, the absence of private ownership of land among these communities, we are going to argue, were the survivals of the tribal system.

However, the validity of Marx's description is questioned. The key point of the controversy centres round the ownership of land.

Earlier writers like Wilks, Campbell and Maine, arguing mainly on the Reports of Revenue and Settlement—the detailed registers 'of all rights over the soil in the form in which they are believed to have existed on the eve of the conquest of annexation' concluded that the traditional Indian village communities, like the Marks or Townships of early Europe as studied by Von Maurer, exercised joint ownership over land. As Maine put it :

"The village-community of India exhibits resemblances to the Teutonic Township which are much too strong and numerous to be accidental. It has the same double aspect of a group of families united by the assumption of common kinship, and of a company of persons exercising joint ownership over land. The domain which it occupies is distributed, if not in the same manner, upon the same principles; and the ideas which prevail within the group of the relations and duties of its members to one another appear to be substantially the same. But the Indian village-community is a living, and not a dead institution. The causes which transformed the Mark into the Manor, though they may be traced in India, have operated very feebly; and over the greatest part of the country the village-community has not been absorbed in any larger collection of men or lost in a territorial area of wider extent."

This comparison of the Indian community to the Mark as studied by Von Maurer was significant, though it over-looked the point, already clearly explained by Marx and Engels, that this joint ownership of land which characterised the ancient Teutonic Mark was nothing but a survival of the tribal system. Before Maine wrote the above, Engels, in answer to Duhring's fantastic claim (viz., that the serfs are necessary, because in order that man can bring nature under control the exploitation of landed property in tracts of considerable size is to be carried out, and who but the serfs work ing for the landed proprietors could carry on this exploitation of the land?), wrote :

If we confine ourselves to the exploitation of landed property on a large scale, the question arises: whose landed property is it? And then we find in the early history of all civilized peoples, not 'the great landlord,' whom Herr Duhring interpolates here with one of his customary tricks of legerdemain, which he calls 'natural dialectic', but tribal and village communities with common ownership of the land. From India to Ireland the exploitation of landed property in tracts of considerable size was originally carried out by such tribal and village communities; sometimes the arable land was cultivated jointly for account of the community, and sometimes in detached parcels of land temporarily allocated to families by the community, while woodland and pasture-land continued to be used in common. It is once again characteristic of the 'most exhaustive specialised studies,' made by Herr Duhring 'in the domain of politics and law' that he knows nothing of all this, that all his works breathe total ignorance of Maurer's epoch-making writings on the primitive constitution of the German Mark, the basis of all German law, and of the ever increasing mass of literature, chiefly stimulated by Mauer, which is devoted to proving the primitive common ownership of the land among all civilized peoples of Europe and Asia, and showing the various forms of its existence and dissolution.

It needs to be noted that Engels spoke of the 'tribal' and the 'village communities,' implying thereby that according to his understanding, the two separate, though the 'primitive common ownership of the land,' originally a characteristic of the pre-class or tribal social organisation, continued to persist in the village communities of India, even as late as on the eve of the British conquest. This is an important point. For all the peoples all over the world, insofar as they have tribal past, had also the history of the common ownership of the land behind them; the merit of Maurer's writings, called 'epoch-making' by Engels, consisted in tracing this history of common ownership behind the German Marks. Similarly the merit of the works of Wilks, Campbell and Maine consisted in showing that the early British Reports on Revenue and Settlement were evidences of the fact that this characteristic of the primitive pre-class society, namely the common ownership of land, continued to persist as a living feature of the Indian village communities, even when these communities were much ahead of the strictly tribal stage.

But the fact of this common ownership was vigorously questioned by some writers, foremost of whom was Baden-Powell. We shall therefore begin with an examination of some of his observations and arguments.

At any rate I think that we have every right to insist that the distinct existence of a type of Indian village in which 'ownership in common' cannot be proved to be a feature either of the past or present should be duly acknowledged; and that it is hardly possible to appeal to 'the Indian village-community' as evidence in any general question of archaic land custom or of economic science, if we first obtain a single type by leaving out of view the wide area of a country which furnishes divergent forms or features.

The type of the Indian villages which, according to him, disproved the evidence of ownership in common was the ryotwari one. But according to his own admission, there was another type of villages in India, which he called the joint village and to which Maine's description did apply. According to Baden–Powell's estimate, the total area covered by these two types of villages were as follows : Joint Villages-2,18,170 square miles; Ryotwari Villages-5,75, 313 square miles. Therefore, even granting his own assumption that the ryotwari type of villages presented no feature of common ownership, we cannot deny that extensive areas of the country retained this feature. But his assumption is not beyond doubt. For even the villages of the ryotwari type were observed to retain strong relics of tribal equality and, therefore, ultimately of the tribal collective life. Thus, for example, Baden-Powell himself observed that the arable land of such villages, though divided into household estates, were periodically redistributed. This periodic redestribution was meant to ensure equality, and as such it was a relic of the pre-class tribal society. This had been a universal primitive practice.

In Palestine, Transjordan, and Syria still another form of semi collective ownership exists......When the tribes settled originally, the arable land of each village was allotted between members equally, each member receiving a piece of land in different zones of the village, and to maintain equality between the members, the land was re-allocated at intervals.

Thomson, on the authority of Seebohm and Vinogradoff, has shown that this primitive practice of ensuring equality by annual redistribution of land characterised the early English villages too. As they put it, the practice rested directly on the principle that 'the soil was not allotted once for all to individuals but remained in the ownership of the tribal community, while its use for agricultural purposes was apportioned according to certain rules among the component household, strips for cultivation being assigned by lot.'

Many more parallels have been quoted by Thomson, the significance of which can hardly be overlooked. The point is that, periodic redistribution of the land by lot was universal of the early agricultural villages all over the world.

And if the type of ryotwari villages, too, preserved this feature down to the beginnings of British rule, which it did according to Baden-Powell himself, then far from being evidences against joint ownership of land, this type of villages also are to be looked at as possessing strong relics of the tribal past.

Strangely enough, Baden-Powell, though so anxious to disprove collective-ownership of land, did not argue against the survival of the tribal elements in these villages of ryotwari type. On the contrary, one of the specific points of his criticism of Maine was that the latter overlooked the tribal survivals in these villages.

> In this fact, I find the explanation of the total omission in Sir H. S. Maine's pages of any specific mention of the ryotwari form of village, and the little notice he takes of the tribal or clan constitution of Indian races in general, and of the frontier tribal villages in the Punjab.

Again, referring to the ryotwari type of villages he said :

> In the countries marked by the prevalence of villages of this type we are almost always able to note evidences of a tribal state of society... There were clan divisions of territory containing a number of villages each under its own headman or chief.

But what was meant by the clan composition and the tribal state of society ? Evidently, largely because of this neglect of Morgan, Baden-Powell suffered from a rather peculiar notion about it; he overlooked the fact that the genuinely tribal state of society and private ownership of land were concepts irreconcilable. Private ownership emerged only at comparatively later state of social progress. As Hobhouse generalised:

> We may express the whole tendency best by saying that the communal principle predominates in the lower stages of culture and retains a small preponderance among the pastoral peoples, and that private ownership tends to increase in the higher agricultural stages, but partly in association with the communal principle, partly by dependence on the chief, or in some instances by something in the nature of fedual tenure. We seem in fact to get some thing of that ambiguity as between signorial and popular ownership that we find at the beginning of our own history. Over and over again, at the stage in which barbarism is beginning to pass into civilization, the communal, individual, and signorial principles are found interwoven......and it seems to be next stage upwards in civilization that gives its preponderance to the lord.

Baden-Powell, however, wanted to work on a hypothesis which, in fact, made this historical process topsyturvy. His thesis obviously is that the type of ryotwari villages with private ownership of land was there at the beginning and the system of joint ownership was superimposed on it in certain areas by those that conquered the country. Referring to the ryotwari villages he wrote :

> It is quite possible that when the first Dravidian and other tribesmen formed villages of this pattern, there was some general idea of tribal union, and that every member of the clan was entitled to receive an allotment sufficient for his wants; but there is no trace of common holding of the land occupied; the several portions of the village are allotted or taken up severally, and are enjoyed quite independently from the first.

Common ownership, according to Baden-Powell, was introduced into these villages much later. This is how he wanted to explain the origin of the joint villages :

The body of owners who thus, whether their lands are partitioned or not, still hold together and have a certain joint interest in the village, arises in various ways. I wish first to repeat once more that in all cases they are either a ruling, conquering, and often non-agriculturist caste, who have taken the superior or landlord position over an earlier existing village group of cultivators, usually of aboriginal or some mixed or humbler descent; or else they have founded their own village in the virgin waste, either by their own exertions, if agriculturist by nature, or by aid of tenants and dependants.

As an inversion of the historic process, this must be manifestly false. Apart from what is known in general about the development of the institution of private property, a large number of specific cases are known in India in which individual or private ownership of land was introduced into originally tribal villages by those that established their rule over these.

We now leave these modern Western writers and turn to consider certain older evidences which show that the private ownership of land had not been a prominent feature of the traditional agrarian India.

It is remarkable as Maine pointed out, that the law-codes of such a predominantly agricultural country as India, presented 'a singular scarcity of rules relating especially to the tenure of land, and to mutual rights of the various classes engaged in its cultivation'. Instead of that we come across laws concerning the revenue to be collected by the kings from the villages, which were usually one-sixth of the total produce of the village as whole, called bhaga or kara by Manu.

This evidence of the ruler's right to a part of the village produce, together with the exaggerated epithets usually applied by the law-books to the kings, led some writers to imagine that the land was not owned by the cultivators at all; instead it was owned by the kings. 'The native law of India,' said Smith 'has always recognised agricultural land as being crown property.'

The only serious argument so far adduced in favour of this theory of crown-ownership, however, is not the evidence of the Indian legal literature, but rather the account of the early Greek travellers. But Wilks already showed how little we can depend on such account.

Therefore, Jayaswal was quite right in retorting Smith :

The native law of India as laid down by its own lawyers of unquestioned and unquestionable authority is the other way. It may be the native law of any other land; it is certainly not the native law of India.

However, the evidences mentioned by scholars like Jayaswal and others in disproof of the theory of crown-ownership were considered by them to be proofs of private property in the soil, and this in the sense of individual ownership as contrasted with collective ownership.

A critical review shows that though all these were really evidences against crown-ownership, there is nothing in these to prove private ownership or to disprove collective ownership. In fact, private ownership (or property in the modern sense), is not the only possible alternative of crown-property. There remains the other alternative, namely collective ownership, i.e., ownership in the ancient or tribal sense, the strong relics of which survived in the Indian village communities.

Jayaswal began with a quotation from Colebrooke's essay on Mimamsa.

At certain sacrifices such as that which is called Viswajit, the votary for whose benefit the ceremony is performed is enjoined to bestow all his property on the officiating priests. It is asked whether a paramount sovereign shall give all the land, including pasture ground, highways and the sites of lakes and ponds, a universal monarch the whole earth, and a subordinate prince the entire province over which he rules ? To that question the answer is: The monarch has not property in the earth, nor the subordinate prince in the land. By conquest kingly power is obtained, and property in house and field which belonged to the enemy. The maxim of the law, that 'the king is the lord of all excepting sacerdotal weatlh, concerns his authority for correction of the wicked and protection of the good. His kingly power is for government of the realm and extirpation of wrong; and for that purpose he receives taxes from husbandmen, and levies fines from offenders. But right of property is not thereby vested in him; else he would have property in house and land appertaining to the subjects abiding in his dominions. The earth is not the king's but is common to all beings enjoying the fruit of their own labour. It belongs, says Jaimini, to all alike; therefore, although a gift of a piece of ground to an individual does take place, the whole land cannot be given by a monarch, nor province by a subordinate prince, but house and field acquired by purchase and similar means are liable to gift.

The earth was not the property of the king and the land was not the property of the subordinate prince. Whose property were these then ? The crucial text quoted by Colebrooke which answered this question was Jaimini's statement that the land belonged to all alike. There was no suggestion of individual ownership here.

Jayaswal next quoted the authority of Nilakantha, which, as translated by him runs as follows :

Similarly conquest and the other (modes) are (available) for a ruler (Ksatriya) and the others. On conquest the ownership of the conqueror arises only in respect of the houses, lands, and personality, etc. of the ruler conquered. Where the latter had a right to taking taxes, the conqueror acquires that much right, and no ownership. Hence 'by an emperor the whole country and by a provincial ruler the province is not a 'deya" (a "subject of gift") is laid down in Book VI (of the Purva Mimamsa). Proprietary right in the whole land with regard to villages and lands etc., lies in their respective landlords etc. The king's right is limited to the collection of tax therefrom. Therefore what is technically called at present ' gift of land ' etc. (by the king) does not mean giving away of land, but a mere creation of allowance. If house, land, etc. are bought from the owner (by the king) proprietorship indeed can arise.

The word landlords, in this quotation, may suggest private ownership of the feudal type. But it is the result of a mistranslation. The landlords, as we understand them, being the creation of British rule, could not have existed during Nilakantha's times. The actual word used by him was *bhaumikadi*. Monier-Williams has suggested that the literal meaning of *bhauma* is ' relating or dedicated to the earth, produced or coming from the earth. ' Etymologically, *bhaumika*, in the plural, means the children of the soil; because it is the result of the suffix snik (lit., to indicate children) added to the word *bhumi* (land). Besides, it is to be noted that Nilakantha did not mention only the *bhaumikas*; he also added the word *adi*, meaning ' and others ') to it. Assuming *bhaumikas* to mean the landlords, the addition of ' and others ' makes no sense. However, from the point of view of the meaning we have suggested, the addition of this word ' adi ' is quite logical. As we have seen, apart from the actual tillers of the soil, there were the craftsmen and others in the village communities; the land and the village (*bhumi-Ksetradi*) belonged to them all, jointly.

Secondly, the mention of sale and purchase in this quotation, may create some confusion. We shall presently return to discuss the real sense of such sales and purchases.

Jayaswal next quoted some other authorities: like Madhava, Katyayana, Mitramisra and the author of the Bhattadipika. However, none of these contain any decisive evidence in favour of the individual ownership of land.

Madhava referred to the *maha-bhumi* (the great land) as the common wealth of all living beings to enjoy the fruit of their labour. The author of the Bhattadipika spoke of the purchase of houses and lands, but these were, as in Nilakantha, *grihaksetradan*, definitely contrasted to *maha-prithivi*. On this great land, there could be no right of any kind other than the right of the king to collect a portion of the produce of the cultivators. Katyayana and Mitramisra did not indicate anything more than this. We may therefore reasonably assume that according to these legal works, though the village land was not definitely owned by crown, there was neither any private nor individual ownership of these.

Kane, too, mainly on the evidence of the law-codes of Manu, argued that the ownership of the cultivable land was vested in the cultivators rather than in the king. Referring to a considerable number of passages from Manu he argued that these showed ' that Manu held that the ownership of arable land was in the cultivator himself and the king was entitled to demand a certain share in the produce.

But the question is : were the cultivators, according to the lawbooks, owning their land individually or collectively ? Kane was inclined to accept the first alternative though without adducing any definite evidence or argument in favour of it or against the second alternative. We are, therefore, not obliged to accept this point.

Jayaswal, in defence of this theory of the private ownership of land, has referred to the evidence of the inscriptions. 'Inscriptions proving to the hilt private property in the soil are extant.' But, not to speak of analysing the implications of the inscriptions, he has not even mentioned any single inscription that could prove his thesis. Instead he has referred to, in his footnote, an article in the Indian Antiquary. The same article was claimed by him to justify the following assertion.

Gupta title-deeds, inscribed on copper-plates and registered at the district officers' office, whose seals they bear, clearly prove private ownership.

This article, on the strength of which Jayaswal was proving private ownership so conclusively, was the rather well known one by Pargiter on Three Copper-Plate Grants from East Bengal. Strengely, however, the plates actually examined here are strong evidences against the view of individual ownership of land and even the author of the article thought so. Of the three charters, the first was the clearest and Pargiter thought that it went to show that the land was the joint property of the villagers. Here is the inscription :

"The leading men of the district (modern Faridpur), who were headed by Lalita, Kulacandra, Garuda, Brihaccatta, Aluka, Anacara, Bhasaita, Ghosacandra, Abamitra, Gunacandra, Kalasakha, Kulasvamin, Subhdeva Durlabha, Satyacandra, Arjunabappa, and Kundalipta, and the common fold (Prakritayah) were appraised by the agent Vatabhoga thus : 'I wish to buy a parcel of cultivated land (ksetrakhanda) from your honours and bestow it on a Brahmin ; therefore do ye deign to take the price from me, to divide (the land) in the district and give it (to me).' Wherefore, we, giving heed to this request (and being unanimous, determined (the matter) by an appraisal by the keeper of the records (pustapala) Vinayasena. There is in this district the rule established along the eastern sea (that) cultivated lands are things which may be sold according to the (rate of the) sum of four dinaras for the area that can be sown with a kulya of seed (kulyavapa) and that the evidence of a sale is by the custom of (giving) a copper plate, which custom applies immediately on seeing the counting made for the parcel of cultivated lands of such-and-such sowing (area), and thereby the feet of the emperor receive the sixth part (future taxes) (tacca parama bhattaraka padanam atra dharma-sadhbhagalabhah), according to the law here. Therefore the agent Vatabhoga having adopted this procedure, (and) having by tendering the deposit (complied with it) by the act as well as by the intentions of one who has desired to establish the fame of his own merit (and) having paid twelve dinaras in our presence we, having severed (the land) according to (the standard measure of) eight reeds (nala perhaps bamboo here) by nine (per kulyavapa) by the hand of Sivacandra, have sold to Vatabhoga a triple Kulya-sowing (area) of cultivated land in Dhruvilati by the custom of the copper plate. This very Vatabhoga who desires benefit in another world as long as (this land) shall be enjoyed, while the moon, the stars and the sun endure has joyfully, for the (spiritual) benefit of his own Parents bestowed the land on (the Brahmin) Chandrasvamin who is of the Bharadvaja gotra, who is a Vajasaneya, and student of the six angas (imprecation against violators of the grant; limits of the area donated). The third (regnal) year, 5th day of Vaisakha."

What deserves specially to be noted is that the land could be 'purchased' only on the basis of the unanimous approval of the leading men of the district as well as the common folk. This is evidenced against individual or private ownership. Nevertheless, the fact of payment as well as the terms of purchase and sale are clear and these raise interesting questions. As Kosambi has put it, 'The main question, then is : to whom was the payment made, and for what purpose ?' The payment could not be possible to those who gave their consent, for they included not only the villagers but also leading men of the whole district. Besides, 'the transaction was not for financial profit, nor an investment'; rather 'the land went to a Brahmin for spiritual merit gained by the purchaser and his parents. According to the custom of the country, a piece of land, when it went to a Brahmin for such purposes, became tax-free. What was purchased, therefore, was presumably the exemption from taxation, the traditional one-sixth of the produce. In that case, the purchase of land meant only a compensation to the state-treasury for this exemption of taxation. Kosambi rightly observed :

Thus the 'sixth part' mentioned would not be a sixth of the total price, but would indicate payment made to the treasury (or to those whom the state held responsible for the taxes) in commutation of the sixth portion of the yield, which was the standard land-tax in this period.

The copper-plate under discussion belonged to the sixth century A.D. Other inscriptions and charters belonging to other periods give us roughly the same idea concerning the ownership of land. We may quote some of the observations of Kosambi.

Chandragupta's general Amarakarddava purchased the village of Isvaravasaka in A.D. 409-10 with money furnished by certain members of the royal household and presented it, with the interest of an added sum, to the support of the Buddhist monastic order at Sanchi. The purchase could only have been from the state, in the sense of compensation to the royal treasury after which the village revenues were assigned to the monastic order by the state; but this must be conjectured, in the absence of any further date about the village, from other grants of the Gupta period in Bengal.

Indeed, purchase of any sort is unusual in these charters, and a private owner of that day selling land is unheard of. The Camodarpur plates do not indicate purchase of plots from the village council by immigrant strangers, as has sometimes been claimed. The payment there is clearly to the state, by a Brahmin or his patron, of compensation at the rate of 3 dinaras per kulyavapa for the right to cultivate family-sized holdings in hitherto unploughed, marginal (khila), waste-land, without payment of taxes. What had been purchased was freedom (in perpetuity) from taxation by a Brahmin or for a temple-plot, not the land itself; the officials concerned were ultimately responsible to the king.

The typical conditions of such freedom from taxation are to be found in an inscription of the early fifth century A. D. In this case, as in many other cases, the donor was the king but as one who was entitled to a fixed tax from the land; that is, the donation only meant forgoing the tax.

The charters dug up till now are overwhelmingly of land or village gifts made by kings to Brahmins.

But what was meant by such gifts ?

Generally, the king grants the right to tax-free cultivation; at a later stage, the village taxes themselves are also given to the donee. The taxes, being usually in kind, amount to a gift of grain. The tax donation conveys no proprietary rights in the land itself, which cannot be sold or alienated as a rule. The beneficiary is not accountable for tax-dues received, nor does he pass on some agreed fraction to the state as would be the case in later feudal times.

But even in later feudal times, whatever might have been the changes introduced into the taxation-system, private ownership of land did not develop, at least not as a universal feature of Indian economy. Even as late as the Moghul period, common ownership of land persisted over extensive areas of the country. As Wilks pointed out:

The European travellers who visited the court of Aurungazebe in the latter part of the 17th Century are unanimous in denying the existence of private landed property in India.

Evidences like these are conclusive.

It is not possible for us to go into greater details over the problem of traditional Indian land tenure. As a matter of fact, the problem remains yet to be fully solved by our historians. What is necessary for argument is already sufficiently discussed. We are trying to argue that tribal survival formed an outstanding feature of the traditional Indian social system. The Indian village communities were examples of such survivals. The co-operative life and common ownership of land, obviously relics of the tribal system, were the main features of these communities.

Hegel and Marx already noted this. Said Hegel :

The whole income belonging to every village is, as already stated, divided into two parts, of which one belongs to the Raja, the other to the cultivators; but proportionate shares are also received by the Provost of the place, the Judge, the Water Surveyor, the Brahmin who superintends religious worship, the Astrologer (who is also a Brahmin, and announces the days of good and ill omen), the Smith, the Carpenter, the Potter, the Washerman, the Barber, the Physician, the Dancing girls, the Musicians, the Poet. This arrangement is fixed and immutable, and subject to no one's will. All political revolutions, therefore, are matters of indifference to the common Hindu, for his lot is unchanged.

The individual as individual, according to Hegel, did not exist in India. But what was the reason of this ? Hegel thought that the answer was to be found in ' the character of Spirit in a state of Dream, ' as the generic principle of the Hindu Nature.

Spirit has ceased to exist for itself in contrast with alien existence, and thus the separation of the external and individual dissolves before its universality, its essence. The dreaming Indian is therefore all that we call finite and individual, and, at the same time—as infinitely universal and unlimited—a something intrinsically divine.

It was naturally left for Marx to tear off this veil of metaphysics and state the reality about the village communities in a clear and objective manner, i.e. to make Hegel stand on his feet.

SECTION IV

INDIAN VILLAGE COMMUNITY

(*i*) *Historical* (*ii*) *Ecological*

INTRODUCTION

THE PRESENT Section is divided into two sub-sections, each consisting of four selections. The Indian village community has evoked profound interest among the scholars belonging to various social disciplines. It has also, due to its unique features, attracted the attention of literateurs, historians and social workers. Stormy controversy is still raging among them over its true nature and functions. One group of thinkers has conjured up an idyllic golden age picture of the village community. Another group has advanced a sharp criticism of the static, narrow and extremely self-centred life that was provided by the village community. The Indian village community has thus become a storm-centre of extremely belligerent partisan views.

The Indian village community has been recognised as a unique entity differing widely from the village of West Europe, the mir of Russia, the German mark or the Chinese village. Various efforts are made to locate the causes of the emergence of this unique unit of rural life. Also attempts have been made to fix the salient characteristics of the village community since Henry Maine published his monumental work on the subject. In the four selections constituting the sub-section one (titled Historical) we have attempted to provide a picture of different stages of evolution of the village community, the typical characteristics of the village community and lessons drawn by the eminent scholars regarding the teaching of history about the village community. The selections are indicative and do not comprise all that is best on the subject. It is our belief that these selections will provide fairly representative material to explore the problem and conduct enquiries into the subject on different lines.

The sub-section two, composed of four articles, deals with the ecological patterns of the various types of village which have emerged in India and which have to be taken into account while reshaping these rural units according to the consciously directed general scheme of agrarian transformation. The study of different ecological patterns of Indian village is still in its infancy. An elaborate and comprehensive study of the village types in various regions on the lines indicated in these selections will unfold a fascinating picture of the rural life and also will provide fruitful clues to the understanding of the specific factors which have operated to make India a land of classic agrarian civilization with its complex and diversified features. It will also help us to study the problem of the formation, the spread and the increasing disintegration of these villages. (*Author*)

(i) Historical

1

TEACHINGS OF HISTORY*

A. S. ALTEKAR

HAVING DISCUSSED and stated the peculiarly Western features, we proceed to consider the lessons of the history we have so far narrated.

VILLAGE COMMUNITIES, NOT UNCHANGING

(1) Our history shows that the observations made by early writers like Metcalfe and Maine about Indian village communities being unchanging have to be accepted with great reservations. (a) The difference between the Western and Northern communities that were pointed out in the last section were all due to the fact that the communities in the North had changed owing to the factors that were not operating in Western India. (b) Since the days of Elphinstone and Metcalfe, we have actually noticed before our very eyes how most of the village institutions that excited their admiration have gone into oblivion. So the myth of these communities remaining unchanged must be given up. (c) Nor can it be maintained that leaving apart from consideration the changes introduced by the Moslem and British influences, there were no changes taking place in the Hindu period. For, we have seen how the influence of the Vedic Sabha dwindled down in the Brahmanic age, how under the Maurya Imperialism, the jurisdiction of the local council and Panchayat was considerably curtailed, how '*lekhaka*' or the accountant did not exist in earlier times but came into existence subsequently, how the regular council of elders was not in existence down to the Valabhi period and so on. To conclude, history, shows us that both internal and external forces have been working out changes in our village communities. The Mohammedan influence was not powerful enough, so the institutions continued to exist but their growth was arrested and efficiency weakened; the British influence, dominant and all-sided, has all but killed most of the village institutions. The headman has lost his importance the accountant has ceased to be hereditary, the village council no longer exists, the Panchayat is never heard of, the village fund has also vanished. Village life to a great extent remains the same, people still till their lands and sow their crops in the old manner; but even here changes are com-

*Reproduced from *Village Communities in Western India*, by A. S. Altekar, pp. 124-127

ing and coming fast enough. The theory therefore that the Indian village communities do not change is completely disproved by the teachings of history......

COMMUNITIES, NOT REPUBLICS

(2) Similarly, our history shows us that our village communities were never in historic times republics as Metcalfe had thought. In the Vedic times it appears probable enough that each village community was independent republic, but throughout the historic period, the community was always subordinate to and a constituent of larger political units. In the Jataka period, we have seen how the taxes and serious criminals were sent to the Central Government; the Maurya period need not be even considered; for, it was an age of imperialism par excellence; but even under the Valabhi, Chalukya, Rashtrakuta and Yadava kings, the village was a regular unit of the State and no republic. The fixed order of officials invariably mentioned in the grants shows that there was a real control from the Central Government. Were the villages republics, the grants would have been addressed only to the Gramakutas; they mention the Rashtrakutas and Vishayapatis obviously because these district and divisional officers were exercising a general supervision and control over the village administration. The Smritis also mention how the headman was to report serious cases to the officer over ten villages, the latter to the officer over twenty villages and so on, and Sukraniti enjoins the king to inspect his villages.........

We have also shown how the amount of the land revenue varied with the needs or whims of the Central Government. The defence arrangements of the community were supplemented by the police and military departments of the Central Government. The same was the case with regard to the public works where help from the Central Government in one form or another was often forthcoming. To call the village communities then as small independent republics, is hardly what the facts would justify.

COMMUNITIES NOT DEMOCRATIC, BUT SELF-GOVERNING

(3) The word republic again is very unfortunate; it conveys notions of democracy, of equal rights, of general election and so on. Nothing of the kind took place in our village communities. There was no idea of equality.

We in modern days should never forget that democratic notions were never prevalent in our village communities.

2

VILLAGE COMMUNITIES IN INDIA : A HISTORICAL OUTLINE*

H. D. MALAVIYA

COLLECTIVIST APPROACH TO PROBLEMS : THE LOCAL BODIES

THE VEDAS, and specially the Rig-Veda, signify a collectivist approach to all problems. Of special significance in this connection would be the last Sukta of the last (10th) Mandala of Rig-Veda. In this hymn Rishi Angiras offers his prayer to the deity called Samajnana or Samjnana. The erudite commentator of the Rig-Veda, Sayanacharya, explains this term as signifying the collective, general and national consciousness of an entire people, the political consciousness which is spread evenly (Sambhavenu) among all the classes, making up the total population of the country. Commenting upon this hymn, Dr. Radha Kumud Mookerji says that the deity worshipped here " may be called the deity of democracy." The assembly is conceived as " a united body. " And further : " It stands for equal right and liberties of all its members as the common assembly of the whole people, so that there should be a sense of liberty, equality and fraternity in the minds of all. "

In his pre-eminent study Hindu Polity, Dr. K. P. Jayaswal says that " national life and activities in the earliest times on record were expressed through popular assemblies and institutions. " Such gatherings are referred to as Samiti (Sam+Iti) meaning " meeting together. " That such bodies existed at all levels is indicated in Prithvi Sukta (56) of Atharva-Veda. " In the villages and forests of the lands, in the various meetings and assemblies to discuss problems, I should always, O Mother Earth, speak for your good, for your interests. " That even at this time India had come to be a nation of diverse peoples with different languages and religions, and that the sense of unity in this diversity had developed, is made abundantly clear by Prithvi-Sukta (45) : " This land which holds within its bosom men of diverse languages religions and as though they are people living in one household should like, a milch cow, profusely give us wealth and riches...... "

Vedic society was, indeed, sufficiently developed and settled to admit of an elaborate differentiation of functions. As Dr. Mookerji has listed

*Reproduced from *Village Panchayats in India* by H. D. Malaviya, pp. 43-89.

the original texts use a number of terms to designate these popular local bodies, viz, kula, gana, jati, puga, vrata, sreni, sangha, samudaya, samuha, sambhuya-samutthana, parishal, Charana......

The Ancient Indian Village : The Gramani and other Officials

What actually was the village in ancient times and who were its officials ? Valmiki Ramayana mentions of two types of villages, the Ghosh and the Gram, the former being smaller than the latter. Its officials were called Ghosh-Mahattar and Gram Mahattar. The Ramayana also mentions Gramani as another village official. He was no doubt a highly respected man, so much so that when Rama killed Ravana, the happy goods, in singing praises to him, compared him to a general and a Gramani. The Mahabharata also mentions of Ghosh and Gram. Ghoshs are indicated as being smaller in size, generally situated near forests where dwelt the Gops, that is those people who maintained cow-herds. Manu calls the village official by the name of Gramik. He says that the maladjustments in the village should be reported by the Gramik to the next higher official, the one over ten villages. This Gramik was thus responsible for the village administration, and Manu has indicated his functions as collection of the king's dues from the village inhabitants. The next higher official, the one in charge of the administration of ten villages, to whom the Gramik had to report, was called Dashi. This man had to report to another official responsible for twenty villages, called Vishanti. Over him used to be an official responsible for a hundred villages (called Shati or Shat-Gramadhipati), and above him was yet another over one thousand villages, called Sahasra-Gramadhipati.

Village Control Over the Gramani

The appointment of the Gramani by the king should not, however, be taken to mean that he was a superimposition from above and could do as he liked in the villages. On the contrary, he had to work strictly under the advice of the Village Elders, the Gram Vridhas, who were chosen by an assembly of the village. Dr. Altekar is very specific on the point. He says that these Gramanis, who he explains as the village Mukhiyas (a class in our villages which continued even through the British period, bereft, of course, of all the glory and functions of the past), and the village scribe, the record-keeper (like our patwaris, patels, kulkarnis, etc. of the day), " could not act as they like. They had to work in accordance with the advice of the Gram Vridhas. These have functioned from the earliest times as a non-official body. The Mukhiya was the executive authority, but if he ever acted against the customary practices, the Gram Vridhas used to correct him. "

Functions of the Village Panchayat and the Gramani

In the Gramani, it would appear, the relationship which developed between the State and the people found an exact expression. He was like father and mother to the village folk, and " though responsible to the State, he was essentially a man of the people and used to be ever ready to protect their interests. He was as necessary for the State as for the people. " The first duty of the Gramani was to look after village defence and he headed the crops of volunteers and guardsmen organised for the purpose. His second task was to realise the State dues and keep records of the realisations. All important papers used to be under his direct charge, and the village body of elders, as also the entire village community, co-operated with him in this task. There may have been some other functions of the Gramani, but these are the most important and significant among them, apart from the judicial ones.

JUSTICE IN THE VILLAGE

The judicial functions in Rama's court, as also in the courts of all the long line of kings that preceded him, it should be borne in mind, were essentially of the appellate type, the administration of justice being primarily the task of the ganas, kulas, etc. etc. that is, the bodies at the village level. Mahabharata (Shanti Parva) says that in ganas, " criminal justice should be administered promptly and by men learned in law, through the president. " In Shanti Parva, Bhishma tells Yudhishthira at length about these bodies, which denotes for them a period of existence and functioning before the rise of kingship. In course of time, when the customs and usages of these bodies had developed and taken roots, they entered into confederations and the institution of kingship came into being and these bodies came to owe allegiance to it. Their laws were, however, held in the highest respect in the courts of the kings, and appeals against the decisions of the village bodies were decided in accordance with current customs and practices. The kings, of themselves, imposed or promulgated no laws of their own, from which the obvious implication is that the laws of the ganas were quite comprehensive. K. P. Jayaswal points out that these laws of the ganas were called Samaya. " Samaya, literally means a decision or a resolution arrived at in an assembly, that is, the laws of the ganas were passed in their meetings."

INDIAN VILLAGES IN BUDDHIST TIMES

Indeed, glimpses of the agricultural system and references to the self-governing village communities are scattered all through Jain and Buddhist texts dating from 5th century B.C. The canonical books of the Buddhsists elaborately refer to the arrangement of villages, towns and forts. Gama, nigama, kula and nagarka are often mentioned. The Jain texts refer to settlements such as Ghosa, Kheta, Kharvata, Gram, Palli, Pattana, Samvaha, Uagara, Matamba, etc. The average village contemplated in the Buddhist Jatakas consisted of families numbering upto 1,000. The village dwellings were fairly close to one another, so much so that a fire starting in one might spread to the whole village. The villages almost invariably had a gate, the gram-dwara. Beyond this used to be the village orchard, and then the gram-kshetra, that is the cultivated area of the village. Fences, snares and field-watchmen protected the crops from pests, beats and birds. The gram-kshetra was extended, as and when need arose, by cleaning the forest. Beyond this arable area used to be the village pasture, which was invariably held in common and the cattle of the king or the commoner, all had equal rights over it. The jatakas refer to Gopalaka (meaning "protector of the flocks") a village official or employee, a sort of a common communal neathered whose task was to pen the flocks at night or, in the alternative, return it to their owners by counting heads.

The cultivated area of the village consisted of individual holdings. It would appear that the demarcation of areas was done in a well-planned manner. There seems to have obtained a system of co-operative irrigation and the water channels divided the holdings. Rhys Davids has also observed that the irrigation channels were laid by the community, the rows of boundaries were in fact the water channels and the supply of water was regulated by rule, under the supervision of the headman.

System of Landholdings and Village Organisation : The Communal Concept

The communal concept was even more pronounced in the case of the village common—the grasslands and the forests. Grazing rights and the right to pick up fallen wood was free and unfettered. As Rhys Davids had remarked : " No individual could acquire, either by purchase or inheritance, any exclusive right in any portion of the common grassland or wood land. Great importance was attached to these rights of pasture and forestry. Even when the king made a grant of some village to some priest, or some other dignitary in effect it was not a conferment of free rights over village lands. "

Maurya Period: Kautilya's Artha-Shastra

Kautilya said that village boundaries should be demarcated by river, hill, forest ditches, tanks, bunds and trees of various descriptions. Further the villages should be situated at distances of one or two Krosha (1 Krosha=2 miles) so that in times of need one village may go to the help of another. The villages were organised under unions of 10 called Samgrahana, of 200 called Karvatika, of 400 called Dronamukha, and of 800 villages constituting a Mahagrama and administratively termed Sthatnuja (from whence probably come the modern term Thana, that is the jurisdiction of a Police Station). The Sthatnuja then, as now was a centre of trade and fairs of the neighbourhood villages.

The Villages : Administrative Staff : Rules for Agricultural Promotion

The village administrative staff comprised (i) the Adhyaksha (i.e. the Headman); (ii) the Samkhayaka (i.e. the Accountant); (iii) the Sthanikas (Village officials of different grades); (iv) Anikasta (Veterinary doctors); (v) Jamgha Karika (Village couriers). Besides these, there used to be an officer to look after village sanitation (Chikitsaka) and a horse-trainer (Ashwa-Damak) with a view to build up a cavalry for needs of war. These were granted land free of rents and taxes, but they were forbidden to alienate it by sale or mortgage.

In Chandragupta's time, the villages were divided into three categories according to their population: Jyeshtha or the biggest one, Madhyama or the middling ones, and Kanishtha or the smaller ones. These in turn, were divided into four categories for purposes of State revenue, as enumerated below. First were the Gramagras, or ordinary villages, paying the usual revenues. Then came the Pariharak villages, which were revenue-free. These were given to priest and teachers, who were entitled to collect the State's demands and use it themselves, not being required to pay anything to the State. In turn they had the obligation to spread education and otherwise help the people in the pursuits of Dharma, this revenue grant was in the form of their salary. Then were the Ayudhuja villages, whichwere revenue-free by virtue of the fact that they supplied ready soldiers for the army in times of war. Lastly were villages which paid taxes in kind, not in cash, in the form of agricultural produce, animals, forest products, gold, silver, pearls, corals, conch shells and minerals extracted from earth, and in labour.

Village Communities in South India

Dr. Radha Kumud Mookerji has rightly said : "Local Government in Northern India and that in Southern India belong to the same series in the order of sociological development. Their tribal origins and rudiments may have been diverse and heterogenous but there is no mistaking the essentially Indian stamp impressed upon these institutions." And, further : "............the Southern institutions, when they first emerge into view, evince marks of a certain maturity and a certain established order, which point to a long process of silent growth in the dim twilight of the earlier centuries, unconnected though they might be with those political crises and cataclysms of State, which leave historical records behind." It would appear that in the tenth century A.D. there existed a village Uttarmerrur, which is present today also under the name of Uttaramallur in Chingleput district in Tamil area. The Chola King Parantaka I was the then ruler. It was an agrahar village, and as, Dr. Altekar puts it, "the details given about the executive of the Grama Sabha, or the constitution of the panchayat have greatly benefited history." Dr. Mathai says that the main point revealed by these inscriptions is that there existed several committees for village administration. The committees, whose designation gives an idea of the nature of their responsibilities, were as under.

(1) Annual Committee,
(2) Garden Committee,
(3) Tank Committee,

(4) Gold Committee,
(5) Committee of Justice,
(6) A Committee styled Panch-Vara.

Life in the villages was to a large extent common and based on mutual aid rather than mutual exclusiveness. Dr. Mathai has quoted as follows : "From a South Indian inscription of the tenth century A.D., it would appear that each village owned a certain number of looms in common, and the weavers who worked them were maintained out of the village fund. Any other looms would be unauthorised.

Dr. Mathai has given the following list of officers and public servants in a Madras village at the beginning of the 19th century as revealed in the 1812 Select Committee Report of the House of Commons. the famous Fifth Report.

(1) *The Headman*:—In charge of general superintendence, collection of village revenue, in charge of police work, settlement of village disputes.

(2) *The Accountant*:—In charge of keeping account of cultivation and maintenance of registers of allied affairs.

(3) *The Watchman*:—These were of two types, the superior and the inferior. The first one had to get information of crimes and to escort and protect persons travelling from one village to another. The activities of the inferior one were confined to the village and included, among others, guarding the crops and assisting in measuring them.

(4) *The Boundaryman*:—Responsible for prescribing the limits of the village and giving evidence about them in cases of disputes.

(5) *The Superintedent of the Tank and Water Courses*:—Responsible for distribution of irrigation water.

(6) *The Priest*:—Performance of village worship.

(7) *The Schoolmaster*:—Teaching village children to read and write 'in the sand'!

Besides these are mentioned the astrologer, the smith and carpenter, the washerman, the barber, the cowkeeper, the doctor, the dancing girl, and the musician and poet. " The original method of remunerating the village servants was either by giving them a grant of land free of rent and sometimes free of revenue, or by giving them definite shares out of the common heap of grain on the threshing floor or from the individual harvest of every villager, or by combining grants of land and of grain—supplemented in each case by various occasional perquisites."

3

THE SOCIAL ORGANISM

RAMAKRISHNA MUKHERJEE

THAT UPTO the advent of the British in India her social organization was predominantly characterised by the village community system has been noted by several authorities. It is true that this system was found to be absent or rudimentary in the south-western extreme of the sub-continent (such as in the present-day State of Kerala), but that in all other parts of India it was or had been the dominant institution in society is borne out from the findings of the officials of the East India Company at the early stage of expansion of the Company's power in India. Already in the last decades of the eighteenth century, the officers of the East India Company were struck by the presence of village communities in India and their reports formed the basis for the exhaustive description of this institution in British *Parliamentary Papers*. This description was essentially based on the findings of Company's officials in the Madras Presidency, wherefrom further details emanated in later years. Also in 1819, Holt Mackenzie reported the existence of village communities in northern India while in service there as the Secretary to the Board of Commissioners in the Conquered and Ceded Provinces; and further details came in 1830 from Sir Charles Metcalfe, a member of the Governor-General's Council. Likewise, Elphinstone noted the presence of village communities in the Deccan in his report, written in 1819, on the territories conquered from the Peswa; and it was further confirmed from Poona in the administrative report of Captain Robertson in 1821; etc. Similarly, the First Punjab Administrative Report, published in 1852 after the consolidation of British power in that territory, recorded that " the corporate capacities of Village Communities " used to be recognized there also. And even for eastern India (that is, Bengal, Bihar and Orissa), which Baden-Powell stated to have given the impression " that all land must have some *landlord*, with tenants under him, " the British *Parliamentary Papers* recorded quite categorically that previously the *zamindars* (that is, revenue farmers, who were turned into landlords during British rule) were essentially " accountable managers and collectors (of revenue), and not lords and proprietors of the lands," that " the sale of land by auction, or in any other way, for realizing arrears of land

---

*Reproduced from *Rise and Fall of the East India Company*, by Shri Ramkrishna Mukherjee, pp. 140-174.

revenue, appears to have been unusual, if not unkown in all parts of India, before its introduction by the British government into the Company's dominations, " and that traces still remained to show that the village community system existed also in this part of India.

In short, except in the south-western tip of the sub-continent, the village community system flourished practically all over India. Therefore, in order to understand the social organization of India in the pre-British period of her history, one should first examine what was this village community system, why it came into existence, and how it attained its stability in Indian society.

While the working of the village community system in different parts of India was described by several East India Company officers, and on the basis of some of these notes a general account was published in British *Parliamentary Papers* in 1812, it may not be an exaggeration to state that one can get the best idea of how these village communities functioned from the classic description given by Marx on the basis of the literature available to him. What he wrote in this respect while discussing "Division of Labour and Manufacture" in pre-capitalist societies is of inestimable value as a brilliant piece of scientific generalization."

"Those small and extremely ancient Indian communities, some of which have continued down to this day, are based on possession in common of the land, on the blending of agriculture and handicrafts, and on an unalterable division of labour, which serves, whenever a new community is started, as a plan and scheme ready cut and dried. Occupying areas from 100 upto several thousand acres, each forms a compact whole producing all it requires. The chief part of the production is destined for direct use by the community iself, and does not take the form of a commodity. Hence, production here is independent of that division of labour brought about, in Indian society as a whole, by means of the exchange of commodities. It is the surplus alone that becomes a commodity, and a portion of even that, not until it has reached the hands of the State, into whose hands from time immemorial certain quantity of these products has found its way in the shape of rent in kind. The constitution of these communities varies in different parts of India. In those of the simplest form, the land is tilled in common, and the produce divided among the members. At the same time, spinning and weaving are carried on in each family as subsidiary industries. Side by side with the masses thus occupied with one and same work, we find the 'chief inhabitant.' who is judge, police, and tax-gatherer in one; the book-keeper who keeps the accounts of the tillage and registers everything relating thereto; another official, who prosecutes criminals strangers travelling through, and escorts them to the next village; the boundary man, who guards the boundaries against neighbouring communities; the water-overseer, who distributes the water from the common tanks for irrigation; the Brahmin, who conducts the religious services; the schoolmaster, who on the sand teaches the children reading and writing; the calendar-Brahmin, or astrologer, who makes known the lucky or unlucky days for seed-time and harvest, and for every other kind of agricultural work; a smith and a carpenter, who make and repair all the agricultural implements; the potter, who makes all the pottery of the village; the barber, the washerman, who washes clothes, the silversmith, here and there the poet, who in some communities replaces the silversmith, in other the schoolmaster. This dozen of individuals is maintained at the expense of the whole community. If the population increases, a new community is founded, on the pattern of the old one, on unoccupied land. The whole mechanism discloses a systematic division of labour; but a division like that in manufacturers is impossible, since the smith and the carpenter, etc., find an unchanging market, and at the most there occur, according to the sizes of the villages, two or three of each, instead of one. The law that regulates the division of labour in the community acts with the irresistible authority of law of Nature at the same time that each individual artificer, the smith the carpenter, and so on, conducts in his workshop all the operations of his handicraft in the traditional way, but independently and without recognizing any authority over him. The simplicity of the organisation for production in these self-sufficing communities that constantly reproduce themselves in the same form, and when accidentally destroyed, spring up again on the spot and with the same-name—this simplicity supplies the key to the secret of the unchangeableness of Asiatic societies, an unchangeableness in such striking contrast with the constant dissolution and refounding of Asiatic States, and the never-ceasing changes of dynasty. The structure of the economical elements of society remains untouched by the storm-clouds of the political sky."

The autonomous character of these village communities is evident from the facts elicited by the scholars, that the "jurisdiction of the village authorities extended over houses, streets, *bazars* (markets), burning grounds, temples, wells, tanks, waste lands, forests and cultivable lands"; that the village council "looked after the village defence, settled village disputes, organized works of public utility, acted as a trustee for minors and collected the government revenues and paid them into the central treasury." and that the central-state governments "could eventually reach the people and discharge their functions mainly through these bodies." On the other hand, it has been stated that "the representatives of the people had a decisive voice in them" (that is, in the village councils,) for the "local executive officers were usually hereditary servants and not members of the central bureacracy; they usually sided with the local bodies in their tussle with the central government." Thus, while, on one side, almost all functions of the government, except that of organizing the army, determining foreign policy and declaring and conducting a war, were discharged through the agency of the local bodies, where the representatives of the locality had a powerful voice, on the other, the village communities were such independent and powerful societal units that: "Kings may impose any number of taxes; eventually those only could be realised which the village councils could agree to collect."......

The question that follows is why did the village community system come into existence in India? Here one should bear in mind the distinctive features of her geography which influenced the early stages of India's social development, and especially her agrarian economy. No doubt, there were several factors which worked conjointly and led to the formation of the village community system in India. But, curiously enough, among them the role of geography seems to have been constantly present, explicitly or implicitly............

Because of India's peculiar climatic and territorial conditions, artificial irrigation by canals and water-works had to be the basis of a flourishing agrarian economy. But, owing to her territorial vastness and diversity of her people, her decentralised and dispersed social configurations, and foremost of all, owing to the technical resources at the disposal of the individual peasant householders, this imperative demand could not be met by them individually, although field cultivation had by then come into vougue and with the extensive use of the plough peasant-farming on specific plots of land had become the unit of cultivation. Under the circumstances the village community system was the solution that was worked out. As Marx wrote:—

"Climate and territorial conditions, especially the vast tracts of desert, extending from the Sahara, through Arabia, Persia, India and Tartary, to the most elevated Asiatic highlands, constituted artificial irrigation by canals and water works, the basis of Oriental agriculture. As in Egypt and India, inundations are used for fertilising the soil in Mesopotamia, Persia, etc.; advantage is taken of a high level for feeding irrigative canals. This prime necessity of an economical and common use of water, which in the Occident drove private enterprise to voluntary association, as in Flanders and Italy, necessitated in the Orient, where civilisation was too low and the territorial extent too vast to call into life voluntary association, the interference of the centralising power of government. Hence an economical function devolved upon all Asiatic governments, the function of providing public works......

However changing the political aspect of India's past must appear, its social condition has remained unaltered since its remote antiquity, until the first decennium of the nineteenth century. The handloom and the spining wheel, producing their regular myriads of spinners and weavers were the pivots of the structure of that society......

These two circumstances—the Hindu, on the one hand, leaving like all Oriental peoples, to the central government the care of the great public works, the prime condition of his agriculture and commerce, dispersed, on the other hand, over the surface of the country, and agglomerated in small centres by the domestic union of agricultural and manufacturing pursuits—these two circumstances had brought about, since the remotest times, a social system of particular features—the so-called *village system* which gave to each of these small unions their independent organisation and distinct life. "..............

From the evidences furnished by the indologists and historians one is inclined to agree with the observations made by one of them that : " The advance of agrarian village economy over tribal country is the first great social revolution in India; the change from an aggregate of gentes to a society, " and that : " If the village seems to exist from ' Time Immemorial, ' it is only because the memory of time served no useful function in the village economy that dominated the country.

How did the village community system attain such a stability that it came to be regarded as existing from ' time immemorial ' ? This question should be examined from two aspects,— (i) economic and (ii) social and ideological; viz., one in relation to a village community and its outer words, and the other in relation to its internal mechanism. Regarding the former, which is essentially economic in character, one should not forget that the autonomous and self-sufficient character of the village community system as well as the simplicity of its organisation (as noted by Marx) maintained the villages as independent units of society and contributed greatly to the stability of the system over hundreds of years. As Charles Metcalfe noted so forcefully as late as in the ninteenth century :

" The Village Communities are little Republics, having nearly everything they can want within themselves, and almost independent of any foreign relations. They seem to last where nothing else lasts. Dynasty after dynasty tumbles down; revolution succeeds to revolution; Hindoo, Pathan, Mogul,Mahratta, Sikh, English, are all masters in turn; but the Village Communities remain the same. In times of troubles they arm and fortify themselves; an hostile army passes through the country; the Village Communities collect their cattle within their walls, and let the enemy pass unprovoked. If plunder and devastation be directed against themselves, and the force employed be irresistible, they return and resume their occupations. If a country remain for a series of years the scene of continued pillage and massacre, so that the villages cannot be inhabited, the scattered villagers nevertheless return whenever the power of peaceable possession revives. A generation may pass away, but the succeeding generation will return. The sons will take the places of their fathers, the same site for the village, the same position for the houses the same lands, will be reoccupied by the descendants of those who were driven out when the village was depopulated; and it is not a trifling matter that will drive them out, for they will often maintain their post through times of disturbance and convulsion, and acquire strength sufficient to resist pillage and oppression with success.

The union of the Village Communities, each one forming a separate little State in itself has, I conceive, contributed more than any other cause to the preservation of the people of India through all revolutions and changes which they have suffered, and it is in a high degree conductive to their happiness and to the enjoyment of a great portion of freedom and independence."..............

But what supplied the *social force* to this kind of vegetative existence and reproduction of the villages, and thus upheld the village community system of India for centuries as unaffected by the political clouds over the Indian sky ? This question leads one to the second aspect of stabilization of the village community system, for it was the peculiar development of the Indian social structure on the basis of the *jati*-division of society which provided the internal mechanism of the village community system and stabilized it socially and ideologically.

The *jati*-division of Indian society (strictly speaking, of the Hindu society at first) is represented by the immutable social units, demarcated from one another by the three main attributes of (i) hereditarily-fixed occupations, (ii) endogamy, and (iii) commensality, and arranged in hierarchical orders in particular societies in different parts of India, such as in Bengal, Maharashtra, Tamilnad, the Punjab, etc. These *jatis* truly represented, the Indian caste system and showed the unique character of Indian social organization (along with the village community system). For the previous division of the Aryan society into four *varnas* of Brahmins, Kshatriyaas, Vaishyas and Sudras could only present a social ranking based on birth qualification, and this, as Senart stated quite precisely, is not unknown in other parts of the world.........

The reason behind such a simultaneous development of the caste system and the village community system is that while the latter fulfilled a vital demand of the Indian society concerning its material needs, the former supplied the *social* foundation to the latter. For the village community system it was a *social* need that the village-units should not burst as under by the tension generated *within* them by contradictory aspirations of the people in social and material life; and this need was fulfilled by the *jati*-division of society, whereby everybody (however humbly or loftily placed in the societal hirerarchy) had a definite socio-spiritual position and *specific* work to do. Indeed, more than that; such positions of the respective individuals and families in the village communities remained stationary through generations. Thus, a Brahmin priest's son became a Brahmin priest, and so also his son; and it was the same in the family of a calendar-Brahmin or of other Brahmins living on distinct professions within the community. Likewise, a blacksmith's son and grandson and their later descendants, all remained blacksmiths; and so it was with all other *jatis* (castes) of artisans, traders, peasants, fishermen, hunters, the so-called " menial servants. " etc. Therefore, from one village, when it was over-saturated, households belonging to various castes (which could bring about an autonomous and self-sufficient existence in another site) would separate and form another village in the exact image of the parent one without creating discord either between different castes and occupational groups or within the village as a whole. In the same way, new villages would be formed when with the spread of civilization the people in outlying areas were brought under a stable economic life of plough cultivation and craft production; and along with it the detailed occupational groups among them as well as any ethnic or cultural differences in the assimilated communities of the local area would be located in the caste structure. A similar pattern of social mosaic would thus appear in the village community established in a new settlement.

It was in this way that the *jati*-division of society supplied the social foundation to the village community system in India by providing " an unalterable division of labour " in society, whereby " the whole mechanism discloses a systematic division of labour " is regulated " with the irresistible authority of a law of Nature. "

Moreover, the village community system was further stabilized by the spiritual sanctions accompanying the *jati*-division of sociey as contained in the doctrine of *Karma* and the theory of Reincarnation. The doctrine of *Karma* and the theory of Reincarnation taught the people that their position in society was the consequences of their work in the previous birth and that their obedience to the ethics of the society (viz., to obey the caste rules and regulations and to accept the privileges and obligations of the respective castes in which they were born) would improve or deteriorate their caste position in the next life or might even lead to their deliverance from any future wordly existence. Following this ideology not enough force could generate within the society to disrupt the standardised harmony, and if any one was fool enough to challenge this doctrine and seek his improvement in the existing rather than in the next life, he could be effectively silenced by the sanction of law. And if his crime was so great that he became an outcaste, then he was lost to the society and practically dead for all purposes. It is not difficult to imagine what a fate awaited an individual who was thrown out of the village community system and received no quarter from anywhere in the society with respect to his economic, social and spiritual needs.

Thus fulfilling the social and economic needs of the society at a certain stage of its development, the caste system played the most significant role in Indian social organization so long as the village community system dominated Indian life. And simultaneously these two institutions (namely, the caste and the village community systems) transformed a self-developing social state into a never-changing natural destiny, as it appeared to the people and still appears so to a very large number of Indians and others.

4

VICTORY OF VILLAGE*

D. D. KOSAMBI

THE FORMATION OF A VILLAGE ECONOMY

THE SMRTI foreshadows complete victory of the village, with consequences far deadlier than any invasion. The hide-bound caste system became rigid only within stagnant villages whose chief intellectual product, the Brahmin, was stamped with incurable rusticity elevated to religious dogma. For an orthodox Brahmin, travel beyond the traditional limits of arya-desa entailed penance; residence was forbidden. Let him not enter into a town, let him not allow the dust of the town to settle upon him, is another characteristic recommendation of the Baudhyana dharma sutra (2.3.33) also disobeyed regularly. This mentality killed history. It mattered little which king ruled over relatively changeless village.

The superb coinage of the Indo-Greek rulers meant as little as any other piece of silver to the countryside which lived by petty internal production, paid taxes in kind to anyone strong enough to extort them, so had very little use for currency. The passage of years had little meaning compared with the vital round of the seasons, because the villagers produced almost all they needed every year, to consume it (but for that portion expropriated for taxes) by the time of the next harvest. As a result, Brahmin scholars joined (and still engage in) bitter theological controversy about the *tithi* (lunar date) of a festival event like Rama's legandary conquest of Lanka, without troubling themselves as to the year. It is only in Jain manuscripts that the date by year and era is normally given, because the merchants were used to keeping annual records over a long period. Any unusual character produced by the village migrated to a court, or was canonized by his fellow villagers; in either case, his saga and memory were swallowed up in folklore or legend. Awareness of strangers means steady contact by travel, warfare or trade. Of these, the first was negligible, in the guise of pilgrimage. The second was impossible to the disarmed villages, the third reduced to a low minimum monopolized by exclusive, despised, professional groups. To the village priest, myth gradually became more real than whatever happened to his neighbours of low caste with whom cultural or social inter-course was low. Differences between villages were eroded by the static mode of

---

*Reproduced from *An Introduction to the Study of Indian History*, by D. D. Kosambi, pp. 243-245.

production, so that a village founded in 1500 A.D. looked about the same after century or two as one first settled over a thousand years earlier. The Indian village appeared " timeless " to foreign observers simply because memory and record of time served no useful purpose in the life of the village.

The village-kingdom of the Manusmrti had little use for the Buddhism suited to combine warring aryanized tribes into a new society, or for the earlier vedic religion. But elements from both were retained, the Brahmin preached non-violence at the same time as war, and supposedly devoted himself to vedic study. The traditional five great vedic animal sacrifices had now degenerated into symbolic offerings (Ms. 3.67-71). The hard-drinking fighter, Indra (Dionysos of Megasthenes), and the vedic gods, except Vishnu reshaped, could not be modified to suit newer needs, though the attempt had been made. New gods developed, better suited to the rustic mentality, more paying to the Brahmin. The most successful was Vishnu-Narayana-Krishna, who dominates the final redaction of the Mbh, which is closely related to the Ms. It was easy to absorb all prominent ancient or local cults as incarnations of numina of the God. This syncretism gave a unity to the Brahmins, a cultural unity to the land. It was most important for the absorption of foreigners into a caste society."

1

Ecological

THE INDIAN VILLAGE*

IRAWATI KARVE

A STRUCTURE is something concrete and visual as also something abstract and conceptual. It is objective and subjective and the grades of objectivity and subjectivity differ from people to people depending on their social conditioning. A structure has a form or gestalt which may be sharply defined and simple or indistinct and vague. For a casual observer the habitation area called a village has a gross form in most cases. This form gets disturbed and becomes indistinct in certain ways and still something called " a village " remains with its objective boundaries and its subjective feelings for those who live in a village as also for those who are its neighbours. In some recent field work in certain areas of Maharashtra (the region where Marathi is spoken) I felt forcibly the gestalt aspect of the entity we call a village. The question presented itself to me in a negative way. As I viewed certain villages and walked through them I found myself asking why the area was called a village at all.

VILLAGE TYPES ACCORDING TO THEIR STRUCTURE

It would be very difficult to experiment about the gestalt of a village but one can define certain types of villages. For a casual observer the habitation area called a village has a gross discernible form in some cases. This form tends to be obliterated in certain ways and yet a village remains a felt entity for one who lives in it. In Maharashtra there appear to be three types of villages which are differently constituted as regards their gestalt.

One type is the tightly nucleated village with the habitation clearly defined from the surrounding cultivated fields. These villages are situated on high plateau of the Deccan.

In such villages, while the habitation area is well marked, the boundaries of the village together with its fields are never perceived. The fields owned by one village merge into those owned by another except where a hillock or a stream or a highway forms the boundary.

*Reproduced from *Deccan Bulletin*, Vol. XVIII (Taraporevala Volume).

The second type of village is found on the west-coast (the Konkan) near the coast. The villages are generally strung along length-wise on the two sides of a road. The houses stand in their own compounds with their fruit and cocoanut gardens and are fenced on all sides. One walks or drives through fences on both sides of the road all the time. There are numerous tiny streams joining the Arabian sea and there are also spurs of the western mountains (the Sahyadri) coming right into the ocean. Where the streams join the sea they widen considerably, are forbidable at low tide and have on both sides strips of the salt marshes called Khajana. These natural obstacles divide one village from the other. Where these are absent one village merges into the other and a casual traveller does not become aware of having crossed from one habitatic area into another. The gestalt has changed not merely as regards form but also as regards the inter-relation of the background and the gestalt.

In such villages the exploitation of land is of two types—horticulture and agriculture. The gardens of cocoanut and arecanut palms and plantain, jack fruits and cashewnuts are planted near the house and fenced in, while the rice fields may lie a little away from the houses though in some areas they come right to the steps of the houses. There is no sharp distinction between the habitation area and the cultivated area.

The third type of the village was found in the Satpura mountains on the north-western boundary of the Marathi-speaking region. The Satpura mountains are made up of seven main east-west folds with undulating high valleys in between.

The houses are situated in their own fields in clusters of two or three huts, all belonging to a single close kinship group. They are either the huts of a father and grown-up sons or brothers and their wives. Sometimes a woman and her husband may have a hut in the same cluster as that of the father and brothers of the woman.

The next cluster of huts may be as far as a furlong or two away depending on how big the holding of each cluster is. The village boundaries are many times not defined by streams or hillocks because the houses belonging to one village are situated on separate hillocks or divided by streamlets. Added to this scattering is the habit of the Bhils to change the location of habitation on the smallest pretext ranging from a mishap to just wish to be near a friend or even just wanting a change.

In this area the village loses its gestalt completely, on all four sides. The habitation area is not distinguished from the cultivated area and the widely scattered houses of such villages are many times nearer to the houses in the next village than to the houses of its own village.

The clusters of habitation illustrated above may belong to two or three villages and but for the stone heaps erected by the revenue department to mark the boundaries it would be difficult to separate one village from the other.

Function of Roads

The function of the roads is different in these three types. In the first type (the tightly nucleated villages) there are two types of roads.

(a) The roads connecting different villages meant for inter-village communications ;

(b) Internal streets or narrow alleys connecting housing areas ; sometimes a main arterial road may pass through or near a village and owing to modern ribbon development may become the main street of the village but such cases are very few. One can generally distinguish between roads connecting villages and streets connecting internal habitation areas.

In the case of the villages of the second type, the main road in the village is generally also the main arterial road joining the villages of the coast for miles and miles in one linear direction. Such roads are seen in most villages of the west-coast from Bombay to Cape Comorin. The road from Cape Comorin to Trivandrum in the extreme south-west of India is a typical example of such a road.

In the third type of village there are no village streets because no houses are aligned along streets. There are only footpaths leading from one house cluster to another and the continuation of these leads to houses in the next village.

As a consequence of these different ways of grouping houses in habitatic areas, the individual dwelling or a cluster of dwellings gain individuality—are seen as a gestalt—to the same degree that the village or the whole habitation area loses its individuality or distinctness. In the tightly packed Deccan villages one loses sight of the individual houses which are but vaguely felt as parts of a big conglomerate. In the linear coastal village a house being situated in its own compound and separated from the next house, has a greater individuality is however blurred to a certain extent as a single house in the Deccan villages. This individuality is however blurred to a certain extent as a single house is but one in a long row of similar houses. It is the row which impresses itself on the observer rather than the individual house. In the Bhil-area the individual house or houses cluster is a gestalt whose individuality is not disturbed by the proximity of the other houses. On the other hand, the widely spaced houses or cluster are not experienced as a unity making one village separating itself from a similar unity called another village.

The first type of village is the one found all over the Maharashtra plateau as also in other parts of India like Uttar Pradesh, Gujarat, Andhra, Mysore and Orissa......

The second type of village is found as already stated all along the west coast. Whether the same type is found also on the eastern coast I do not know.

The third type of village is found in parts of the Satpura region as also along the coast slightly in the interior. There are villages of scattered homesteads in the coastal area where sometimes the only way of internal communication is walking over the narrow bunds of the tiny rice fields, a very tricky business for strangers especially when all the fields are full of water. Though this type is found in some hilly regions as also in some parts of the coast it cannot be called a jungle type or a primitive type either, as there are a number of jungle people who live in villages where the houses are clustered together in a nucleus but are not as tightly packed as in some of the Deccan villages. The Gonds and the Kolams in Maharashtra and Andhra and the Katkaris in Maharashtra, the Bette Kuruba, the Jenu Kuruba, the Erawa and the Sholega of Mysore also live in villages made up of many huts. The Warli of the west coast and the Cheachus living in the Nallamalai hills live sometimes either in an individual family house apart from others or in a cluster of a few houses which cannot rightly be called a village.

Communication in Nucleated Villages

The nucleated Deccan villages show a clear distinction between communications within one village and communications with other villages. In modern Marathi there are words which are used exclusively for roads within a habitation area. There are also words as in Sanskrit which are used for both internal and external communication arteries but there is a whole series of words which denote various types of roads inside a habitation area. *Ali*, *Galli*, *Bol* are some of these words. *Ali* is a row of houses of one caste, or one profession ; *Brahmin Ali* means a road both sides of which there are Brahmin houses, *Tambat Ali* means a road both sides of which have the workshops of the makers of brass and copper pots. *Galli* is a narrow street. " *Galli Kuchchi* " is an expression used for narrow roads full of mean houses. "Kuchchi " might have relation with word ' Kancho ' used for a certain type of communication in Gujarat.

We find that an explanation of the various words used for an internal system of communication involves reference to social structures like the family and the caste. It would appear that these words have primarily reference to a type of habitation area with the larger habitation area called a village and secondarily mean communication arteries with a village. They reflect a differentiated society, leading to a separate area for houses leading to sub-areas and hence to internal communication channels. The differentiation with an inhabited village may be based on lineage or caste and we will describe it presently.

Whatever the place name suffixes, the most common word for an habitation area in Marathi is ' Gaon ' and in Telugu it is " Oor. "

Inter-relation Between Gaon and Wadi

In Maharashtra each ' Gaon ' has habitation clusters a little away from the main habitation area. These clusters are called ' Wadi ' and are said to belong to a ' Gaon. ' In the same way in the Andhra Pradesh there are clusters of huts a little away from the main village which are called ' *Palli* ' or ' *Guda* ' which are said to belong to an ' *Oor*. ' The inter-relation of the Wadi and Gaon is manyfold. The Wadi people sometimes call the Gaon to which they belong ' Kasaba ' or ' Pethi ' words which mean an area where various types of craftsmen (Kasabi) live or where there is shopping and market centre. The hereditary village servants and village craftsmen live in the Gaon. The village headman, the Patil, also must live in the Gaon, the revenue records and office are situated in a Gaon. A Wadi is generally a cluster of agnatically connected households. It may sometimes have just one big family with its farm servants and livestock. Sometimes people live in temporary huts in Wadis and have more permanent houses in the Gaon. Sometimes a Wadi is a settlement of a particular caste which by the nature of its occupation may need a larger space than is available in a Gaon. In the eastern parts of the Satara district many villages have Banagar Wadis a few furlongs away from the main village. The Banagars are shepherds who need large compounds near their houses for their mixed heards of sheep and goats. It also seems probable that this is an immigrant element which has made a separate settlement near a village with the consent of the villagers. In the same way there are Ramoshiwadis, i.e., hamlets where only the Ramoshi live.

They were counted among criminal tribes. Wadis are called generally after clan name or after a tribe or a caste. Vagh Wadi, Shinde Wadi, Kamat Wadi are names of the first type. Banagar Wadi, Ramoshi Wadi, Brahman Wadi are of the second type.

The Wadi originally is a cluster of hutments belonging to one family or belonging to two or three families whose fields lie in the immediate neighbourhood. Sometimes these are temporarily inhabited during the sowing and the harvesting season for facility of work in the field and the necessity to guard the crop.

Sometimes when the population is growing and there is available land for new settlement and the habits of the people are semi-nomadic, an originally compact village splits into different habitation areas. Recently, I came across such a village in the jungle tract of the Shrikakulam district of the Andhra Pradesh. The village is called Devanpuram. The original village was a settlement of two tribes, the Jatapu and the Savara. The Savara went a few furlongs away and had their own settlement. The Savara settlement split and one part has gone about a mile away over the hills and has a settlement there. Devanpuram is thus an Oor with three Pallis—(1) A Jatapu palli, (2) a small Savara palli called China Savara palli and (3) a bigger Savara palli called Pedda Savara palli. This split has occurred since the last survey. If they remain in their present situations, the three parts may be acknowledged as three separate villages with the same name but separate headmen ; for example, the villages called 'Gondi.' The two villages are within a mile of each other. The one near the road is as usual Jatapu-Gondi and the one nearer the hills and a little more inaccessible is the Savara Gondi. Generally, the most important and the most independent of these Wadis or Wada is that of the fisher folk and in a recent study we found that in one village the Koli or Bhoi are successfully defying the authority of the main village.

Village—An Ever-changing Nucleus

A village is thus an ever-changing nucleus of habitations from which tiny clusters separate and remain attached or separate completely to form a new nucleus. The quality of being a 'gestalt' objectively and subjectively is thus a dynamic quality which makes it difficult to give a definition of a village which would apply to all villages. This difficulty will be more apparent when we look closer into the internal structure of a village.

Among many semi-nomadic primitive agriculturists a village may endure for as few as three years. When the soil round about is exhausted the whole village moves off to somewhere else. Villages which were registered as existing at a particular place during the last elections are no longer there.

In the plains the villages are generally permanent and of long standing and hundreds of epigraphic records have shown that villages with the same boundaries have existed for over a thousand years.

In Maharashtra, there is a great variation as regards villages and the families they contain. For a particular caste there may be only one family (with one clan-name), for other castes there may be several families so that for one caste there is village exogamy while for the other castes there may be marriage within a village.

In the South, multi-clan village is the rule. In the North, where there are no clans, villages are supposed to be peopled by descendants of one ancestor for each caste and there is strict exogamy. This exogamy applies even when people of separate ancestries and Gotras come and live in the village.

Caste and Habitation Area in a Village

Generally, a village in India is, however, socially a far more complicated structure and the complexity is reflected in the way houses are built and roads existed. A village generally has more than one caste. In the North and sometimes even in Maharashtra there may be only one lineage of a caste, but generally in the North and almost as a rule in the Dravidian South, each caste in a village is made up of more than one lineage and clan. A map of a village will show almost invariably that the habitation area of each caste is separated from that of the other by a greater or a lesser distance. A few castes may live in houses situated side by side but others live apart. The castes which are always separated from the others are those whose touch was supposed to pollute the rest—the so-called untouchables. Their habitation area has generally a distinct name. In Maharashtra there is a Maharwada in almost every village. Mang is another untouchable caste which has its dwelling cluster separate from the rest of the village and also from the Mahars. The same is the case in Andhra Pradesh where the Mala live apart from the rest of the village. The Madiga live near the Mala but have a separate cluster of houses. The Maharwada or the Mala and Madiga Wadi are generally at the end of a village, hence the sanskrit name Ante-Vasi (living at the end) and the Marathi name Vesakar (living near or outside the wall of a village). The Kumbhars (potters) also live a little away from the rest of the village and their part of the village is called Kumbhar Wada. Villages which have weavers in their population also have a separate area where weavers live. If there are a number of Brahmin houses they have an area for themselves. The shepherds live so far away that their habitation area is termed a Wadi of the village.

This tendency to have separate sub-areas for habitation within a larger unit called a village can be explained in various ways and on different grounds like caste-hierarchy, ideas of impurity and pollution, the need for certain occupations to have room for carrying out the different processes needed for their craft. The first reason applies to the house complexes generally, the second applies to the distance found between the untouchable quarters and the rest, the third applies to castes like potters, brickmakers, weavers and dyers, shepherds, wool carders and blanket makers, etc. To me it appears that there is an inherent tendency in the Indian culture to form separate groups and remain separate. The arguments listed above all strengthen this tendency and the phenomenon called 'caste,' apart from its hierarchical structure, is the direct outcome of this tendency. The primary group is the large family, sometimes unilateral sometimes bilateral. This group extends into the caste. The family as well as the caste are based on territory. The smallest territorial unit is the area in which the house and the family land are situated, the largest territorial unit in that part of linguistic area through which a caste has spread. Rarely is any area, small or big, in sole possession and occupation of a single family or a single caste so that we find in each such area a check-pattern of sub-areas belonging to families, clans, and castes. I have not seen anywhere either castes or tribes living inter-mingled. However tightly nucleated and crowded a village, the check-pattern sub-areas were always there.

This tendency is seen even among the primitives. The Bhils are divided into endogamous sub-divisions. They have villages of mixed population where sometimes allied tribes like Dhanak and untouchables live. Each of these has a separate habitation area and within each area there are house-clusters belonging to different lineages.

This is but a preliminary study of habitation areas and their structure. The way people build their houses, the way they group them, the way arteries of internal and external communication are formed would lend itself to ecological and anthropological analysis and may help to establish environmental-geographical as well as cultural zones and by linking with social institutions like the family and the caste will help to understand the meaning of the social institutions. It will perhaps reveal the fact that the unity or uniformity of Indian culture is based on tiny check-patterns fitted one into the other rather than a unicolour homogeneity.

2

THE INDIAN VILLAGE*

O. H. K. Spate

The Village in General

The great majority of the country folk live in small or large nucleated settlements, and areas of dispersed habitations are few : the Himalayan zone is perhaps the only extensive area of true dispersal, of the type found in European highlands, elsewhere, even in the hills, the normal unit is the small hamlet rather than the homestead. In the arid W this is enforced partly by the paucity of water-points, partly by the needs of defence—still visibly attested by the watch-towers of Pathan villages. In the Assam-Burma Ranges defence is also an important factor : villages are on hill-tops or spurs, often stockeded; it must be remembered that in these jungly hills the valleys are extremely malarial, and that communication is easiest along relatively open ridgeways. Bengal--especially the En delta—is *sui generis*: there is indeed much settlement that is not nucleated, but " dispersal " appears an exceedingly inappropriate term for the dense stipple of separate homesteads, hardly isolated except in the most literal sense of the word when, during the rains, each is an island on its little earthen plinth. Other more or less dispersed zones are found in the Assam jungles, or in the great floodplains by farmers using the rick khadar for high-value crops after the rains. But in both groups the very small hamlet—say 6 to 12 huts—is the rule, rather than true dispersal : and in the latter case the huts are often only temporary, inhabited during the dry weather by people normally resident in big villages on the bluffs above.

Those are anomalies : in the great homogeneous plains nucleation is almost invariable. In the past defence played its part, and in areas open to constant disturbance (e.g. the Sutlej/Jumna and Jumna/Ganges Doabs, Rohilkhand, the fringes in Central India, Khandesh, the Raichur Doab) villages are often grouped around a petty fort; and even today the close-packed houses, with blank outer walls and low doorways, massed into a ring with few entrances, present a defensive aspect. Often there is not much in the way of site selection; one place is as good as another, and the village rises are as often as not their own creation, the rubbish of generations. But any discontinuity, any break in the almost imperceptible slope, produces linear settlement patterns : especially notable are the

* Reproduced from *India and Pakistan* by O. H. K. Spate, pp. 171-181.

bluffs above flood-plains and the margins of abandoned river courses. The bluff villages tend to be larger than those on the drier interfluves; they have the advantage of two types of terrain, the upland doab and the valley-bottom with its tamarisk brakes and the excellent soil of its chars or diaras—the floodplain islands—submerged in the rains and liable to disappear completely in floods, but cropping up again sooner or later. These alluviated areas are often given over to cash crops of high value; near large towns they are often used for market gardens, easily irrigated by wells taking advantage of the high water-table.

Settlement lines tend to occur also at the marked break of slope where steep residual hills grade into a fan, which has usually a fairly high water-table. Lateritic shelves along deltaic margins are also important building sites, poor in themselves but offering rough grazing, scrubby woodland (the source of a great range of minor necessities from tiber to illicit alcohol), and providing space for dry crops, the flats below being entirely given over to paddy. They form as it were neutral ground between the jungly hills and the waterlogged paddy-plain. Here not only the general arrangement of settlements but also the village itself is often linear; islands of lateritic and older alluvium in the deltas are often completely ringed with houses. Linear settlement is also, of course, prominent in the deltas and wider floodplains themselves, strung out along levees or artificial embankments, and in places (e.g., Kerala and the Contai area of SW Bengal) along old beach ridges. Very often such sites are the only dry points in the rains and the only water-points in the hot weather.

There is in general very little that looks like a " Plan, " other than that dictated by such site factors as alignment along bluffs or levees, grouping round a fort or a tank; but within the seemingly chaotic agglomeration there is, as a rule, a strong internal differentiation, that of the separate quarters for various castes.

These points are best brought out by a close view of a specific village, not indeed ' typical ' (no single village could be that) but certainly the most random of samples. Our example is in the Deccan, more precisely in the Bombay-Karnatak.

Aminbhavi lies seven miles NNE of Dharwar; an old settlement, going back at least thirteen centuries, originally walled and moated. Essentially its site is governed by the junction of the Dharwar rocks, forming poor red soils around the mosque-crowned hill to the W, with the crystallines which have weathered into deep black cotton soils in the E. It is a typical black soil agricultural village, with a rainfall of about 24 ins. devoted mainly to dry crops (cotton, jowar, wheat, pulses, safflower, in that order), tending to become a satellite of Dharwar, the market of its dairy and agricultural produce. On the poorer land to the W is rough grazing, supporting a few shepherds, and immediately W of the village the common or *gauthana*, an essential part of its economy, the centre of all harvesting.

A Village in Detail

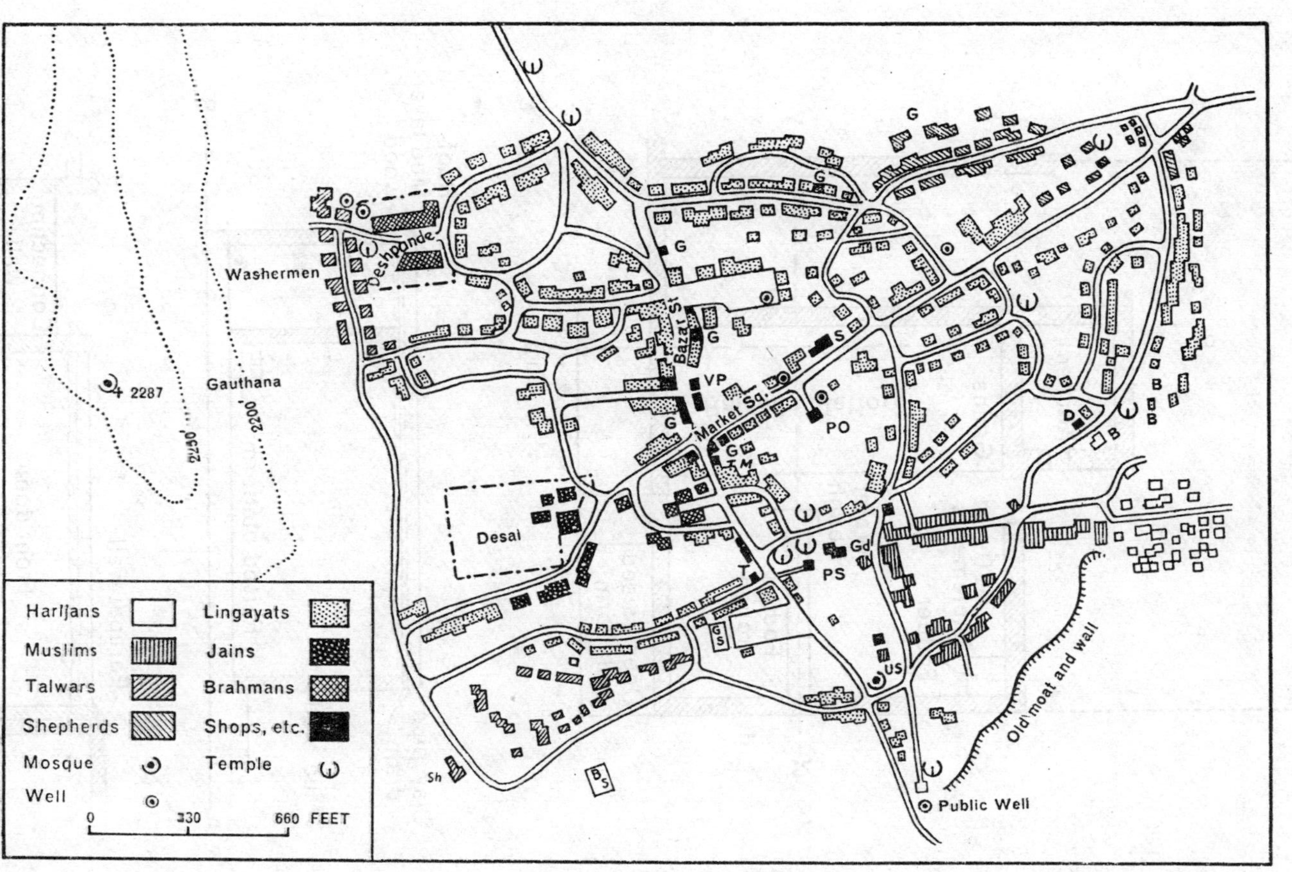

A Village in Detail : Aminbhavi, Deccan, from survey by C. D. Deshpande : BS, GS, US, Girls', Urdu School ; G. B, T Gocers', Bania's and Tea-Bidi Shops ; PO, PS, Post Office, Police Station ; D, Dispensary ; Gd, Govt. Grain Godown ; VP, Village Pancrhayat ; *M*, Lingayat Math ; *Sh*. Shikalkars.

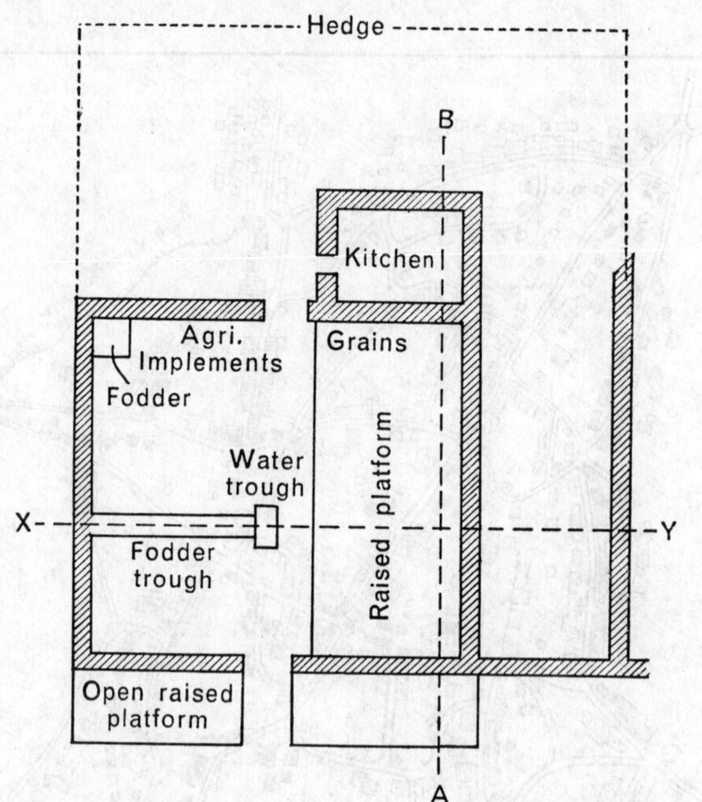

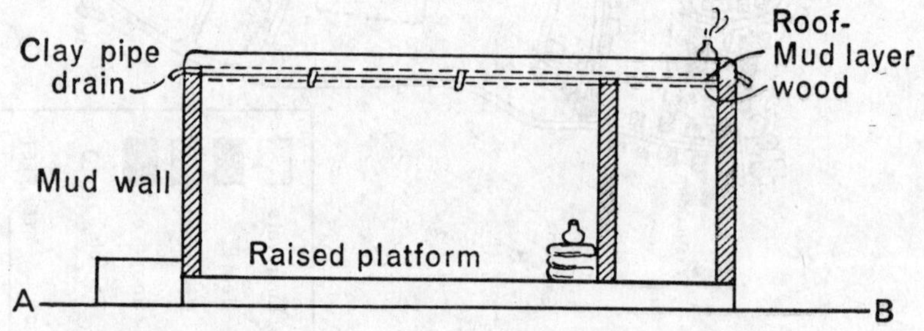

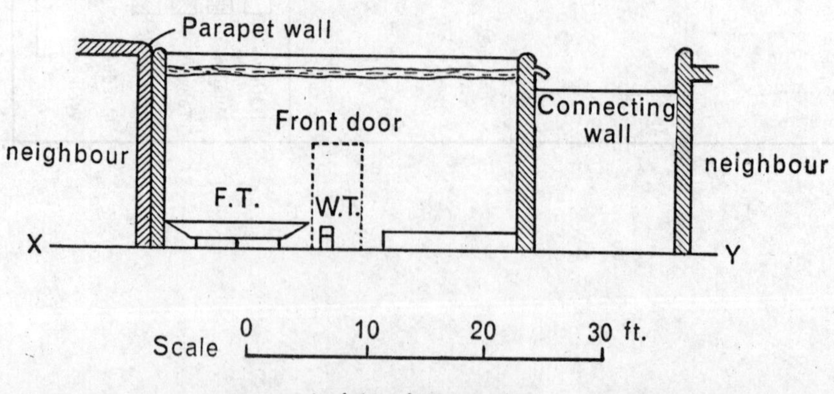

Aminbhavi House Plan

Caste and community largely govern the layout. Of its 4,106 inhabitants, Lingayats, the sturdy agricultural caste of the Karnatak, number some 2,650. Next come 550 Muslims, an unusually high proportion, but the place was of some importance in the days of the Bijapur Kingdom, and the first element in its name is indeed that of some forgotten Muslim (Aminbhavi roughly—Amin's Well). But the culturally dominant groups are the Jains (250) and the Brahmins (75); this is an Inam(landlord) village, most of it belonging to the Desai (Jain) and Deshpande (Brahmin) families, whose wadas (more or less equivalent to manor houses) stand on the best sites, within large compounds. The Desai provide the village patel or headman. For the rest, each caste tends to occupy a solid block of contiguous houses in a lane named from the caste; where, as with the leading family residing in it. Besides those mentioned, there are 300 Talwars (domestic servants and agricultural labourers), 200 Harijans (" untouchables "), and smaller groups of other low castes—Wadars (quarrymen), and so on. These groups live on the circumference of the village, or even beyond the old moat. (Fig. 34).

Occupations likewise are still mainly on a caste basis : the Lingayats provide the bulk of the tenant-farmers, Talwars and Harijans, landless agricultural labour; carpenters, smiths, cobblers, washermen, barbers are all separate castes. Apart from these crafts and agriculture, there is some handloom cotton weaving, a subsidiary occupation of the Lingayats.

Houses are generally built on to each other, or at least the mud walls of the compounds are continuous. The house layout (Fig. 35) is as standard as in any English working class street. In front is a porch (katte), used for drying agricultural produce, as a formal reception room, as " a place of female gossip when the master of the house is out, " and above all as a sleeping-room in the stifling summer nights. Behind this is the main room, some 25 ft. square, part of which is a cattle pen, at threshold level; the remainder, raised some 2 or 3 ft. is the general living-room, for sleeping, eating, more intimate entertainment of guests, and perhaps handicrafts. The most prominent object is the pile of grain stored in gunny bags and sadly depleted towards the end of the agricultural year. Behind is a separate kitchen (with a corner for the bath) and the back-yard with manure-pit and haystacks. This is the standard pattern; construction is similar in all groups (except the lowest), differences in economic status being reflected merely in size, except that the well-to-do have more separate single-purpose rooms. Jains and Brahmins do not live so tightly packed as the rest, either in the spacing of the houses or within them.

The poorest castes live in wretched one-room wattle huts with thatched roofs. Apart from these all houses have walls 1 or 2 ft. thick of mudbrick, with few (and high) or more likely no windows : Indians in general have a doubtless well-founded burglar-phobia. The flat roof is supported by wooden posts and made of mud on a framework of crude beams and babul (acacia) branches; they have rounded mud parapets and clay rain water pipes.

As for services, these are mostly grouped around the main village lane : market-place for the weekly bazar, eight shops (four grocery, two cloth, one tailor, one miscellaneous) and a number of booths selling tea and bidis, the cheap crude cigarettes of the Indian masses. Near the market-place is the room of the village panchayat or caste council, an ancient institution generally fallen into desuetude but now being fostered as the first step in local government. Associated with this tiny ' urban core ' are the government establishments—Police Station, Post Office, grain warehouse. There are three mosques, one giving its name to the Idgah hill in the W, and eight temples, including that of the Deshpandes, as well as the Lingayat math, a centre of religious and charitable fellowship. The professions are represented by an Ayurvedic (indigenous) dispensary, a Urdu school for the Muslims, and separate schools for boys and girls. The boys' school is the most modern building in Aminbhavi, its stone walls and red-tiled roof standing in sharp contrast to the monotony of mud walls.

Finally we may note the large masonry-lined public well, sunk in what was once the moat; it is no mean excavation, an apt reminder of the all importance of water-supply in Indian life.

Once more, no one village can be typical of the whole sub-continent; but many of the features detailed above can be parallelled over and over again in most parts of India. Our random sample is at least very representative.

The Village : Its Aspect and Life

The aspect of the village varies not only with the general regional setting, with building materials and house-types, but with social factors. The generally greater emphasis on caste in the S takes social fragmentation allied with spatial separation to the extreme, segregating the untouchables in outlying cheris or sub-villages, sometimes located several hundred yards from the main villages of which they are service-components. This is indeed the climax of geographical differentiation; apartheid. A typical cheri may consist of two rows of huts with a narrow central " street; " in the middle this widens to make room for a tiny temple. The huts have thick mud walls, roofed with palmyra thatch, and low mud porches scrupulously swept. To enter one must bend double; the only light comes from the door and from under the leaves and the furniture consists of a few pots and pans, a couple of wooden chests, and the essential paddy-bin, 4 to 6 ft. high and 3 to 4 in diameter, raised from the ground to escape the rats, and built up of hoops of mud. Poor as they are, these dwellings are yet homes, and obviously loved as such : their cleanliness, the surrounding mangoes, coconut and palmyra palms, redeem them from utter squalor; The nadir is reached in the bustees of Calcutta and the revolting camps of casual tribal labour found on the outskirts of the larger towns : shelters (they cannot be called even huts) of matting, of rags, of petrol tins beaten flat, on waste spaces open to the sun and reeking with filth.

A geographical study of Indian house-types would be a work vast in scope and rich in instruction; a few of the more striking instances are mentioned in the regional chapters. Social factors are no less important than environmental, at least once we go beyond the fundamental antithesis of the NW (or SW Asia) type and the thatched gable of the more humid areas. Not only the site and layout of the village, but the " geography of the house " often reflects age-old religious and magical traditions; the round huts of some lower castes in Telengana, with bold vertical stripes of white and rusty red, are clearly culturally rather than geographically influenced. At the other extreme from the rude massive huts of Bundelkhand we have the elaborate courtyard house of the richer U. P. farmer, with some pretensions to elegance—the survival of decayed traditions—in doorways and arcading. Some Indian domestic building indeed reaches a high standard of artistry: the carved timber of Kumaon or of the small towns of the Konkan, the restrained but excellent brick details and the very pleasant white bungalow-style houses, with low gables of semi-cylindrical tiles, found in small Maharashtra towns. Environmental influence is well seen in the flat-roofed blank-walled box standard in the Punjab and Wn U. P.—so strongly reminiscent of arid SW Asia, and fitting so well into the four-square planned villages of the Canal Colonies. Against these may be set the Bengal house, matting-walled, with thatched gables pitched high to shed the rain and ingeniously designed to take the strain of cyclonic gales. In Madras " We see flat-roofed stone houses in the Ceded District (Deccan), so constructed as to protect the dwellers from the severe heat of the sun, the rocks and slabs locally available being used. In contrast we find in Malabar timber entering into the construction. Here the buildings are on high ground and have sloping roofs, both necessitated by the high rainfall......... In the Tamilnad we have tiled brick houses with open courtyards, reflecting an equable climate and moderate rainfall. "

As for what life in the Indian village is really like, who knows save the Indian villager? A few officials like M. L. Darling, whose Punjab rural rides compare with Cobbett's, a few devoted social workers, Indian and European, Christian and otherwise. But even then there is the difference between living in the village from cradle to grave (or burning-ghat), and living in the village with a territorial—and social and psychological—base outside. The alien may perhaps glean something from that rich harvest of salty rural proverbs (a comparative anthology of them would be fascinating) which are as vital a part of India's cultural heritage as the lyrical and metaphysical visions of her sages. Not that this latter strain of culture is absent from the village; the great epics Ramayana and Mahabharata pass from lip to lip in folk-versions, to some extent at least every man is his own poet, and not a few of the noblest figures in India's predominantly devotional literature sprang from the village rather than the schools : Kabir the weaver, Tukaram. The things that strike the outsider, then, are not perhaps ultimately the most important : the flies and the sores, the shrill clamour of gaunt pi-dogs, the primitive implements, the utter lack of sanitation.

At its worst the Indian village is infinitely depressing: in the plains where so much ground is cultivated that the scanty village site cannot grow with its growing population, or where a few miserable huts cling to shadeless stony rises in the drier parts of central India or the Archaean Deccan. Yet cheerfulness keeps breaking in, in the most unfavourable circumstances; fatalist as he is and must be, the peasant often displays an astonishing resilience and refuses to be broken by his often bitterly hard geographical and social environment. And over much of the land the villages have their amenities, even their beauties: in the plains and deltas they rise out of the sea of cultivation, emerald or gold or drab grey in the stubble season, like dark green islands, shaded in mango or orange trees, tamarinds, bamboos, palms. The tank or the well, the shade of the great banyan or the porch of the headman's hut, are essentially free clubs for the women and the men-folk respectively. Though the substratum of life—the gruelling round of the seasons—remains and will ever remain the same, though a miserable livelihood exacts an exorbitant price in endless toil, there have been great changes, material and psychological, since Edwin Montagu, Secretary of State for India, spoke in 1918 of the "pathetic contentment" of the Indian village. Pathetic it still too often is; contented, less and less; which is as it should be. "These idyllic village communities confined the human mind within the narrowest possible compass." This is overstated; there were the epics and the proverbs; but the horizons were far too narrow for a full life. Now new motifs are changing the tempo of life in the large villages: perhaps a radio, perhaps a mobile film unit, more and more frequently a school. The mass movements launched by Congress have not always been amenable to a thus-far-and-no-farther policy: the peasant has other enemies than British imperialism, and Congress taught him organisation. All are helping to break down the isolation and lack of information which rendered the villager so helpless a prey to the money-lender, the retailer, and the grain broker—often all three being one and the same person. Perhaps the most powerful agent of change is the battered, ramshackle motor-bus, packed to the running-board and coughing its way through clouds of dust along the unmetalled roads to the nearest town. There may be loss as well as gain in all this; but it is idle to bewail the break-up of integrated codes of life—too often integrated by religious, social, and economic sanctions which were a complete denial of human dignity. In any case the disintegration set in long ago with the impact of world market; and it is high time that new horizons should be opened, that the villager should see whence the forces that have subverted his old life have their origins and what of good they may bring.

3

SOCIAL STRUCTURE AND CHANGE IN INDIAN PEASANT COMMUNITIES*

S. C. Dube

In this paper I shall outline the social structure of Indian village communities, list some of the important factors of change, and attempt a broad analysis of the major trends of change.

For an understanding of the structure and problems of Indian village society we have to view the village both as a distinct isolable entity, and as a link in the chain of a wider inter-village organization. An individual village derives some of the characteristic features of its organization from the great national tradition of India, while the traditions of the region or the culture area in which it is located also contribute substantially toward shaping its value-orientation, ethos, and general pattern of life. Notwithstanding these national and regional influences, there is much that is individual to the village; its pattern of inter-group adjustment gives a certain degree of distinctiveness to the village. The Indian village is thus sufficiently isolable, but it is not an isolate, and has therefore to be viewed as a community within a larger community.

The interplay of several different kinds of solidarities determines the structure and organization of Indian village communities. Kinship, caste, and territorial affinities are the major determinants that shape the social structure of these communities. An individual belongs to a family—nuclear, compound or joint; and the family belongs to a lineage as well as to a large group of relatives having kin or affinal ties with it. These units belong to an endogamous sub-caste or caste; in some instances we find a number of endogamous sub-castes grouped together as a caste. Non-Hindu religious groups in villages tend to function as separate castes. Most of the Hindu castes are fitted into one of the four major divisions of Hindu society, called *varna*. Solidarities provided by kin and caste tend to merge, but those of territorial affinity belong to a different level. An individual and his family belong also to a village, which is often multi-caste in its composition. The village itself is a part of a network of neighbouring villages, the region, and the nation. The structural model of Indian peasant communities can be presented in the following diagram:

---

*Reproduced from *Transactions of the Third World Congress of Sociology* Vol. I—II, pp. 259-266.

In the following diagram dotted circles show the comparatively less effective units of social structure. Non-Hindu groups also fit this scheme. In Diagram A, rather than being described as a " sub-caste " or " caste ",

Indian Village Communities

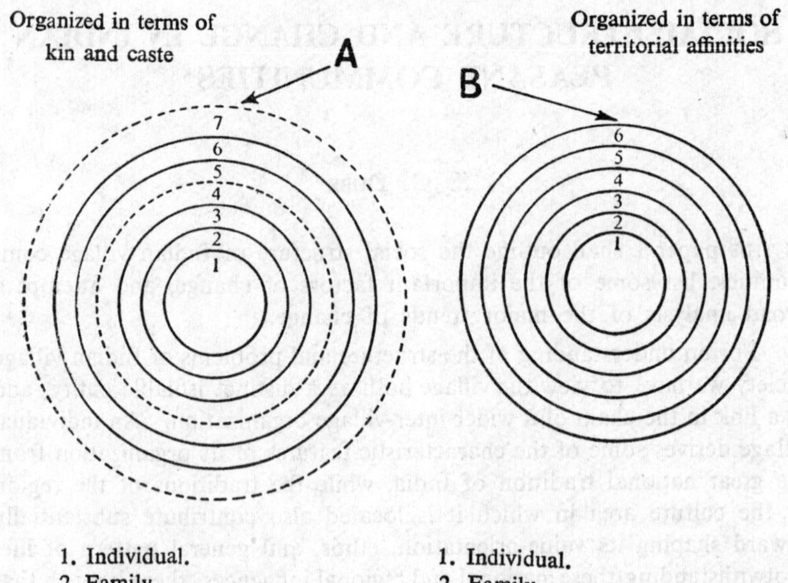

1. Individual.
2. Family.
3. Group of near kin.
4. Lineage.
5. Relatives (kin and affinal).
6. Sub-caste or caste.
7. Varna.

1. Individual.
2. Family.
3. Village.
4. Inter-village organization.
5. Region.
6. Nation.

they should be called " religious group ", and of course they are outside the *varna* organization of Hindu society.

Caste is perhaps the most important single organizing principle in these communities, and it governs to a very considerable degree the organization of kinship and territorial units. In this system of segmentary division of society the different segments are kept apart by complex observances emerging from an all-pervading concept of ritual pollution. The caste divisions are regarded as divinely ordained and are hierarchically graded. The difference between the different segments is defined by tradition and is regarded as permanent. In inter-group relations the caste structure works according to a set pattern of principles : hierarchy and social distance manifest and express themselves in rules and regulations that are calculated to avoid ritual pollution and maintain ritual purity. Marriage, commensality, and physical contacts particularly are governed by strict rules. It has been pointed out earlier that castes are endogamous. Matrimonial alliances outside the caste are viewed with disapproval and are forbidden by tradition. Complex rules of commensality specify the castes from which a particular caste may accept different kinds of food. Foods are classified into several categories, depending on the degree to which they are susceptible to pollution. Everyday interaction between the different castes is also governed by caste rules: persons from some castes should never be touched, while physical contact with some others should be avoided under special conditions, such as a state of ritual purity. Caste largely determines occupational choice: with the exception of a few " open " occupations which may be pursued by anyone irrespective of caste, a large number of crafts and occupations are caste monopolies and can be practised only by certain castes. In its functioning an individual caste generally illustrates a distinctive way of life, for different castes have different sets of prescribed norms of conduct and expectations regarding standards of behaviour. These norms and expected standards of behaviour cover such aspects of life as observance of rules of purity especially those of bathing and washing (at appropriate hours) public conduct, and even dress and speech. Another important feature of caste may also be noted in this connection. In new situations demanding group decisions and group action in recent years, caste has shown its dormant strength and has proved itself a cohesive force. Most local, and even some state and national elections were fought along caste lines, and in these the contestants depended to a great extent on the support of their caste fellows. Within a village the caste system manifests itself as a vertical structure in which individual castes are hierarchically graded and kept permanently apart and at the same time are linked and kept together by some well-defined expectations and obligations which integrate them into the village social system. The horizontal ties of a caste, too, are important, for a village caste group has strong links with its counterparts in other villages, and in several spheres of life they tend to act together. In order to be able to discharge the control functions implied in the complex norms associated with the system, castes have local and regional organizations and associations which have the authority to enforce the rules and customs of the caste.

The great diversity of forms in the family and kinship organization of Indian peasant communities makes the task of presenting a general account of them somewhat difficult. Contrary to common belief the basic unit of social organization in these communities is not the large joint family, but the nuclear family and the smaller joint family in which only a part of those who should have constituted the ideal larger joint family live together, and even the latter generally breaks up when minors attain maturity and a degree of enonomic self-sufficiency. Recent village studies have shown that large joint families are relatively few in number and they too are largely confined to the upper, i.e., the priestly, trading, and agricultural castes. In some parts of north Indian plains it has been observed that a house is shared by a number of people having close lineal ties, who live not as one family, but as distinct nuclear families organized as separate hearths or *chulhas*. However, very special ties are recognized between a family and the local group of near kin, i.e., all other families lineally related to it up to the third generation. The solidarity between this cluster of families expresses itself on ceremonial occasions and in times of stress and calamity. In the hour of need they must support each other, and mutual consultations among them in regard to all major decisions are regarded as desirable. Informally the local group of near kin functions as an effective agency of social control. The larger circle of relations has more or less the same functions, though physical distance between the different constituent units naturally makes its functioning less effective. The outlook of the people has been distinctly kin-oriented, and in an hour of need or stress they almost instinctively look to their kin for sympathy and support.

The village as a unit of social structure cuts across the boundaries of kin and caste and unites a number of unrelated families within an integrated multicaste community. Structurally the village communities can be divided into three main groups: the " single settlement " village, in which the community shares a common and compact settlement site, the " nucleated " village which has a central settlement as the nucleus around which there are a number of smaller satellite settlements, and the " dispersed " village community, in which the community consists of a series of dispersed homesteads having well-defined ties with one another. Both have a number of common features. They are stable populations generally, with a common past and a number of shared values. They recognize and emphasise their individual identity, and in certain situations act as one unit. Their economy is built largely around agriculture; economically and socially the agricultural castes are the most important, while the non-agricultural occupations are subsidiary to agriculture. Land is greatly loved and valued, and the community as a whole shares some common problems and acculturative influences. Being largely caste-structured, the community finds itself integrated in terms of traditional patterns that define the interactions between the different segments of the community in the fields of economy, socio-religious life, and village administration. Operating under traditional arrangements, artisan and other occupational castes render services to the agriculturist in their respective fields of specialization; in return the agriculturist gives them a stipulated share of the crops when they are harvested. Socio-religious life, especially ceremonials and rituals connected with birth, puberty, marriage and death, are so organized that they require participation by a large number of castes at various stages. As the rites progress, at different points small fees have to be paid to the castes that are assisting. For these purposes there are established patron-client relationships under which families of occupational castes are affiliated with families of agriculturists; for services in the socio-religious field even non-agriculturists are covered by these traditional arrangements. Among the occupational castes themselves there is often a barter of their traditional services. A similar integration of various castes and their functions is seen in the organization of village administration and village rituals, in both of which the different castes often have well-defined position and functions. A common organized authority of the village gives it a still greater unity, and besides maintaining law and order tries effectively to secure observance of village norms. This invariably consists of influential and responsible members of different castes living in the village.

4

FORMS OF VILLAGES

Santibhushan Nandi
D. S. Tyagi

A LARGE proportion of India's population lives in villages; these are more than 5½ lacs in number. Some of them are small even uninhabited, while others are large with a population reaching in extraordinary cases upto ten thousand.

The inhabitants of a village may be farmers or traders or artisans or scholars or priests; and a village can be classified according to the occupation of the majority of its inhabitants. Villages may, moreover, belong to a single tribe, or may differ from one another in caste or religious persuasion; and this may give us another means of classification of types. But one of the most useful and objective means is furnished by the physical form taken by a village. From this point of view, the following different orders can be distinguished in India. Each type has a fairly wide range of variation, so that instances may not be rare when it becomes difficult to determine if a particular example should be placed in one category or another.

These orders are:

(1) Shapeless Cluster or agglomerate with streets not forming an integral part of the design. These may be of the (i) massive or (ii) dispersed type, in which the village is reckoned to consist of an assemblage of discrete clusters of comparatively small size.

It may be noted here that in villages belonging to this order there may be a tortuous or irregular road; but this grows according to local requirements, not as part of the original design.

(2) Linear Cluster or assemblage with a regular open space or straight street provided between parallel rows of houses.

(3) Square or Rectangular Cluster or agglomerate with straight streets running parallel or right angles to one another.

(4) Villages formed of Isolated Homesteads, a number of which are treated together as a mauza for convenience of collection of rent or taxes.

Various factors are involved in the origin and character of a rural settlement. Wherever possible, these have to be taken into account during classification. Thus, an example of Shapeless Cluster may be

Fig. 1
Small Clusters of huts in the Punjab Himalayas

enclosed by a protective stone wall or wooden palisade for purposes of defence. If it lies on the top of a narrow ridge in a mountainous country it may take on an elongated form. But, after comparison with a number of other examples in the same neighbourhood, the proper course might be to regard it as belonging to the first instead of the second order. The same thing may happen when a village of the first order is built on a levee in a flooded district. Linear Clusters may, again, grow in size as population increases and parallel streets may be added or streets even set at right angles to the old streets so that, eventually, a square form results which may appear like a shapeless cluster from a distance. But the presence of open streets as an integral part of the design and the occurrence of simpler linear forms in the same neighbourhood when the settlement is of small size should help us in regarding the square as genetically

Fig. 2
Shapeless Cluster Huts with horizontal roofs—Western Uttar Pradesh

related to the linear and unrelated to the massive cluster which may by accident approximate to a square.

Parellelisms may also occur on account of a variety of geographical and other reasons. Thus, houses and farms may be isolated on high hills or deserts, or in the midst of jungles as well as in shallow islands thrown up in an estuary as a river discharges its heavy load of silt.

In the high Himalayan Range, where people live with their flocks which also help them in transporting merchandise between India and Tibet (formerly), villages tend to be clustered and sometimes there is a summer and winter encampment, each of which remains unoccupied for some months in the year. But when the same people settle down nearer the northern plains of India and begin to cultivate potato for the market, their isolated houses are set in the midst of fields which need constant attention or watching.

Fig. 3
Isolated homestead with central courtyard–Birbhum District, West Bengal

Fig. 4 ; Isolated huts with conical roofs Cuddaph District, Andhra Pradesh

Fig. 5 : Isolated Homestead Central courtyard with huts all round 24 Parganas District, West Bengal

Settlements formed of isolated farmhouses or homesteads are thus found in various parts of India irregularly. These areas include portions of the western Malwa plateau, where they occur in association with dispersed clusters, in portions of the Western Ghats stretching from Satara towards the Kerala highlands and some portions of the high Himalayan Mountains both in Kashmir and Uttar Pradesh. In the flooded districts of eastern Uttar Pradesh and Bihar we find isolates which are seasonally unoccupied in the islands thrown up in the midst of braided streams. There is no uniformity of tradition among these isolated homesteads. They seem to have grown according to the exigencies of local circumstances.

When we come to the three major orders of Shapeless Cluster and Clusters of the Linear and Square types marked by straight streets, these are confined to clearly defined contiguous expanses of land. This can hardly be due to geography, as within the areas occupied by these types, climate, soil and agricultural practices have a fairly wide range of variability and settlement types seem to have more to do with tradition then either geography or agriculture.

On an examination of the distribution map, one notices that much of the Gangetic plain, Rajasthan, the Malwa plateau and portions of Maharashtra are characterized by shapeless clusters. In Western Rajasthan, in the districts of Jaisalmar and Barmer, these occur along with villages of the dispersed type. Dispersed clusters by themselves occur over a long stretch of the Western Ghats from Thana to Kolhapur and also in portions of Kerala. The same types, namely, shapeless cluster and dispersed cluster, occur also in eastern Uttar Pradesh, portions of Madhya Pradesh and the Himalayan or sub-Himalayan districts in the north of Bihar and practically over the whole of the Brahmaputra valley. Manipur and Mizo District also have examples of the clustered type.

Fig. 6 : Shapeless Cluster Huts with tiled roofs Varanasi District, Uttar Pradesh

When we come to the linear type, the best examples are observed in the coastal districts of Orissa and Andhra Pradesh. This extends westwards into a large portion of the Telugu-speaking area of the former princely state of Hyderabad. Gujarat also shows the same type in large villages, and even smaller ones are formed of parallel rows separated by broad streets. This is true of Kutch and Saurashtra as well as of districts stretching from the South of Rajasthan to Surat.

The square development of the linear, if we may call it so, extends over a solid portion of Madras State including both the dry Rayalaseema districts as well as the prosperous agricultural districts of the coastal plain.

There is an interesting feature noticeable in coastal Orissa and northern coastal Andhra. The houses tend to be contiguous and laid in an unbroken line, adjacent ones quite often sharing a common wall between themselves. As one proceeds southwards to Madras the arrangements remain the same, but the houses become separate. A change is also noticed in the thatches and in the placement of the courtyard; but these are matters which will be taken up in the following chapter dealing with dwelling houses.

Fig. 7 : Linear Cluster Huts with horizontal roofs–Kurnool District, Andhra Pradesh

Fig. 8 : Linear Cluster Huts with central courtyard–Puri District, Orissa

Fig. 9 : Linear Cluster–Nellore District, Andhra Pradesh

Fig. 10 : Linear Cluster–Jamnagar District, Gujarat

An observation may be made at this stage. The total area covered by the linear and the square types cuts across several kinds of boundaries. In the South, it includes the Telugu-Tamil and Kanarese-speaking states, while in the north it is present in Indo-Aryan speaking Orissa, portions of West Bengal and Indo-Aryan speaking Gujarat and some tribal areas like Santal Parganas in Bihar where the language belongs to a different stock altogether. The Santals are supposed to have at one time emigrated from the northern districts of Orissa and fanned out into the north and north-east. It is not unlikely that the linear village was carried by them wherever they went.

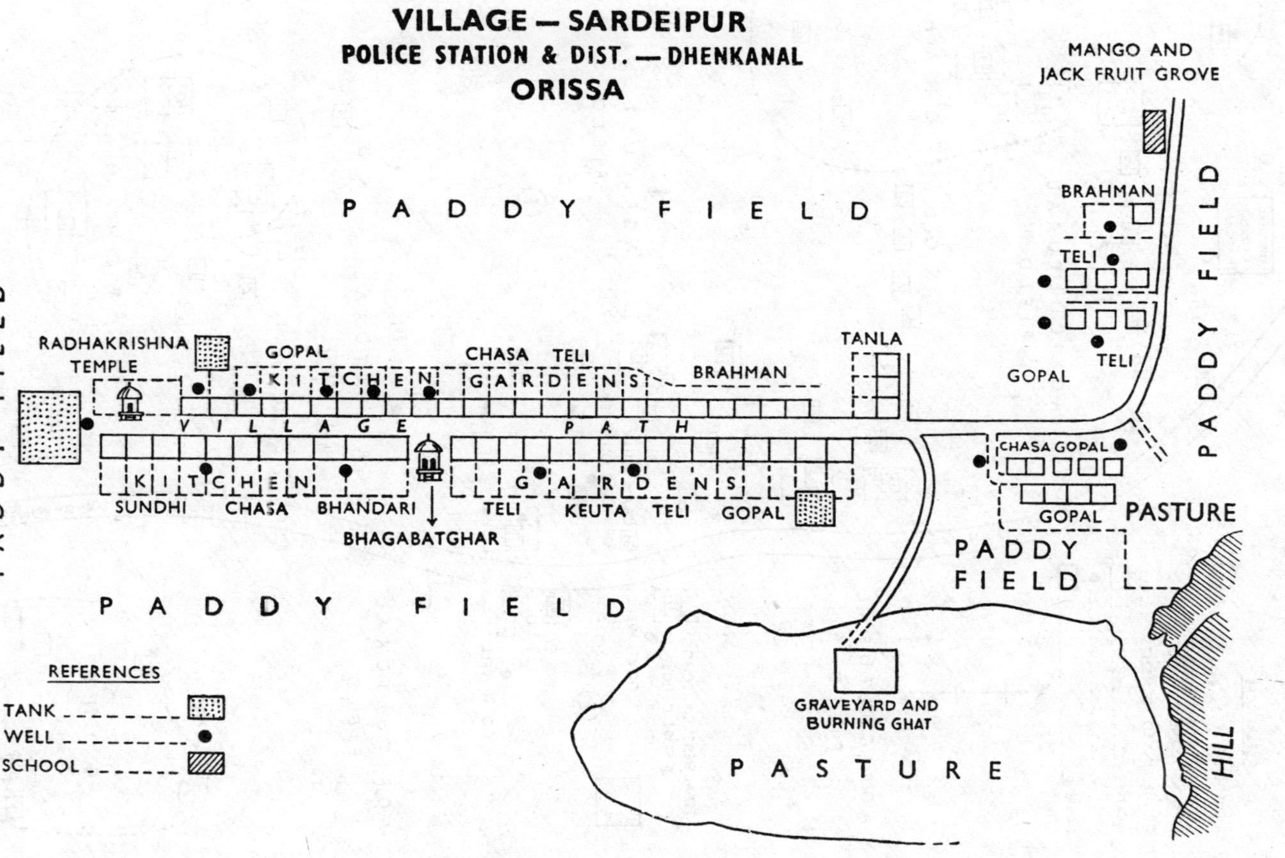

Fig. 11 : Linear Cluster Orissa

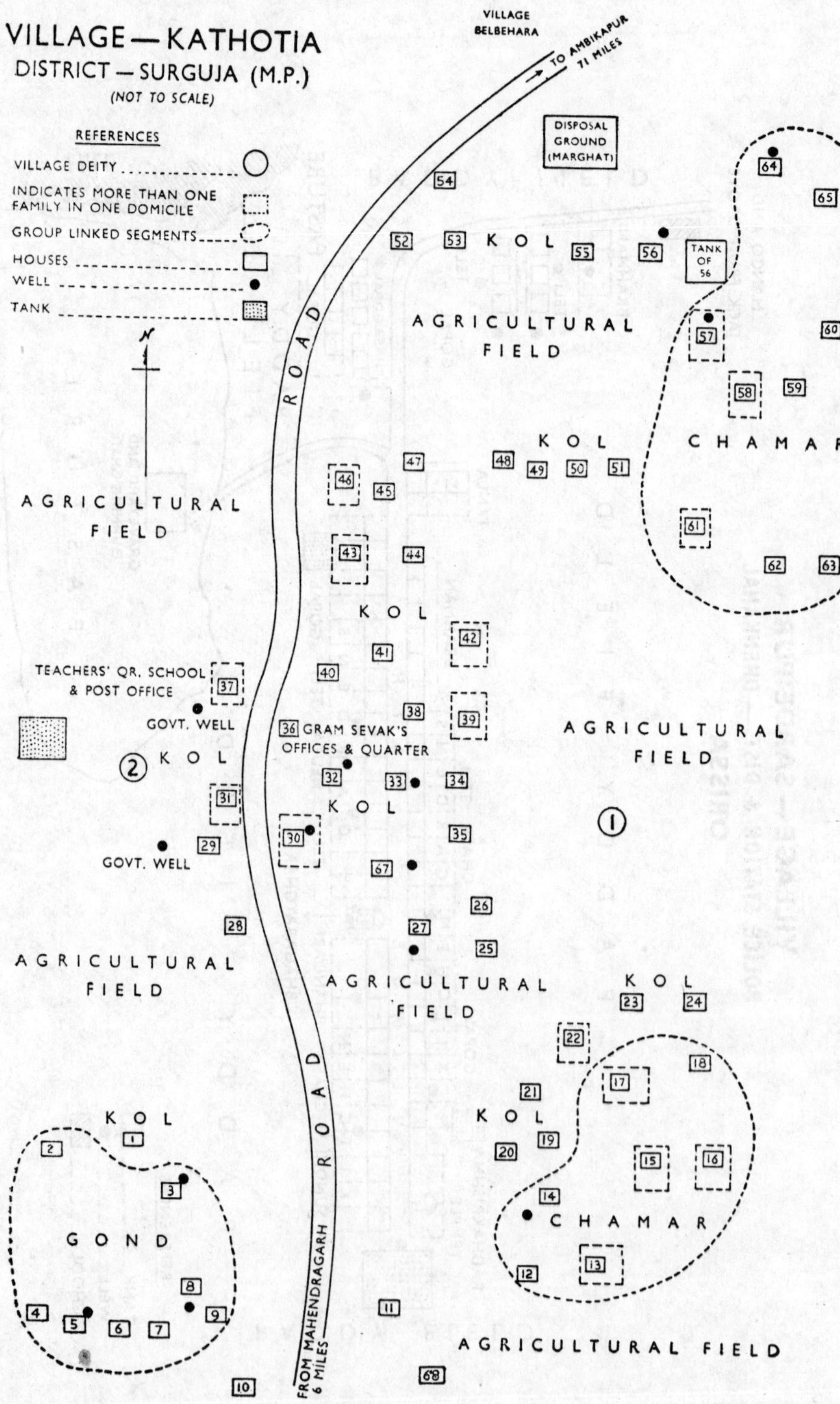

Fig. 12 : Isolated homesteads–Madhya Pradesh

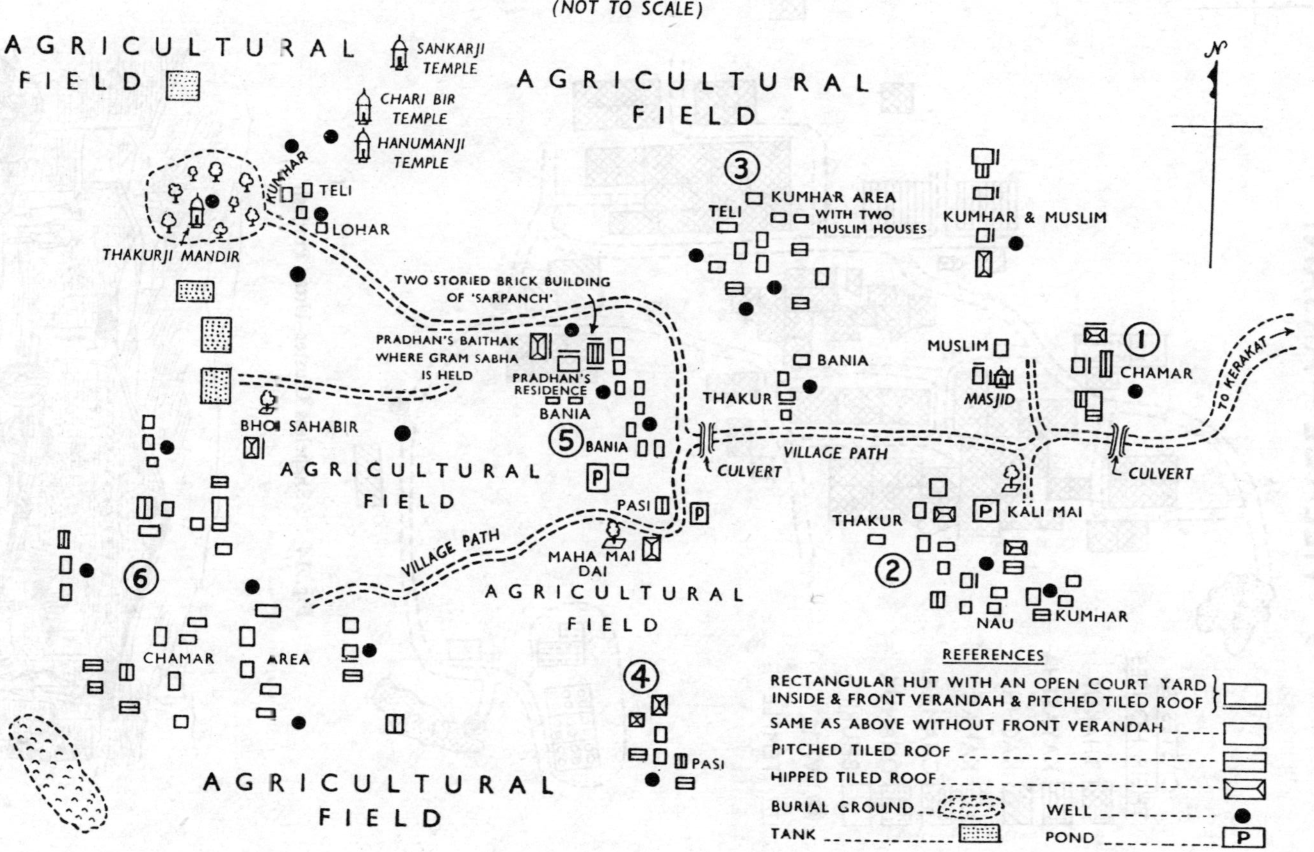

Fig. 13 : Dispersed clusters–Uttar Pradesh

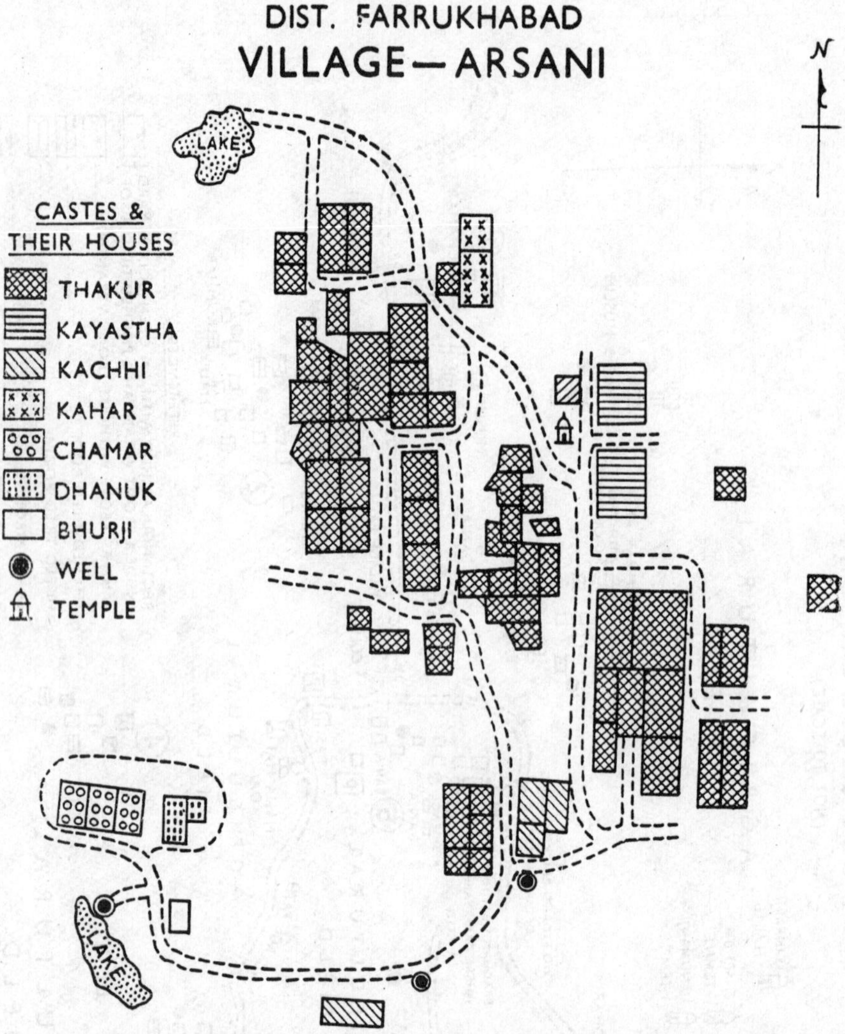

DIST. FARRUKHABAD

VILLAGE—ARSANI

N

LAKE

CASTES & THEIR HOUSES

THAKUR

KAYASTHA

KACHHI

KAHAR

CHAMAR

DHANUK

BHURJI

WELL

TEMPLE

LAKE

Fig. 14 : Shapeless Cluster–Uttar Pradesh

Fig. 15 : Linear Cluster–Sabarkantha District, Gujarat

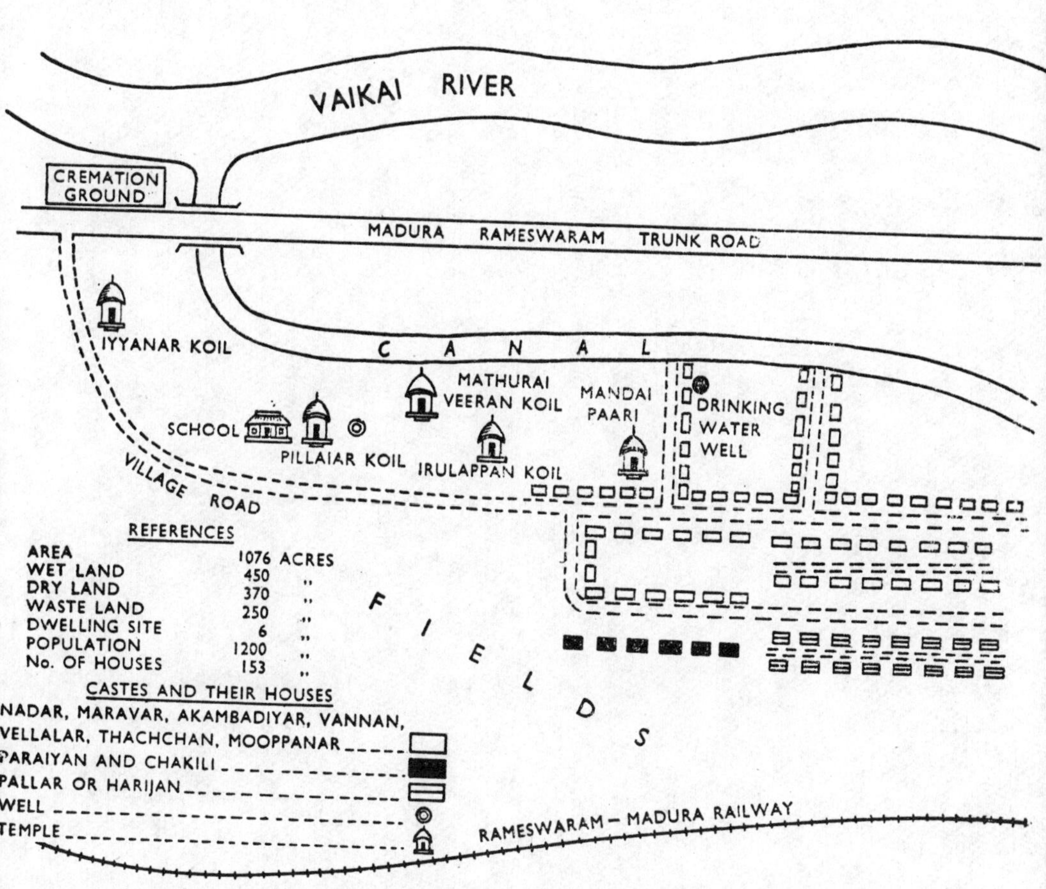

Fig. 16 : Linear arrangement of houses in a square rectangularly shaped village : Thelichathanallore Village; Ramnad District; Madras State

The tradition of laying out villages with an open street or several such streets thus giving rise to two of the orders described above seems to have little relation to the present distribution of languages in the relevant parts of the country or to boundaries of the States of India as they have been drawn after Independence.

SECTION V

TRIBES IN TRANSITION

INTRODUCTION

THIS SECTION consists of five selections. Rural India contains probably the largest number of tribes compared to any other single country of the world. According to some thinkers the development and spread of the Hindu society is nothing but a gigantic special process of absorbing the tribal population of India into the original Hindu caste system. Some of them go to the extent of asserting that the present tribes are the relics which have remained un-assimilated into the Hindu society because of the British intervention. Considerable anthropological literature regarding tribes and their cultures has emerged. Tribes have been also studied from a number of angles. The categorising of tribes as criminals, the massive conversion of a number of them by missionaries, the impact of administrative and economic policies of British government on the tribes and the numerous studies of tribes from the point of view of elaborating the history of the complexity and diversity of Indian culture—all these have stimulated controversies regarding the fate of tribals in India. After Independence, the tribal people are subjected to conscious and elaborate influence by various agencies. The tribes are in transition and are being aborbed into the matrix of a social order which is being created by political, economic and cultural forces actively inaugurated by the Government of Independent India. How do the tribes react to the various forces which are impinging upon their lives? The five selections attempt to portray certain crucial aspects of the interaction between tribes and the large society which is in the process of emergence. The various approaches and findings embodied in the selections provide fruitful insights and interesting lines of investigation of tribes in transition. We believe more elaborate studies on the lines indicated in this Section will provide a large body of empirical material which would significantly help to evolve adequate laws of social development of the rural society (*Author*).

SECTION V

TRIBES IN TRANSITION

INTRODUCTION

This Section consists of five selections. Rural India contains probably the largest number of tribes compared to any other single country of the world. According to some thinkers the development and spread of the Hindu society is nothing but a gigantic social process of absorbing the tribal population of India into the original Hindu caste system. Some of them go to the extent of asserting that the present tribes are the relics which have remained un-assimilated into the Hindu society because of the British intervention. Considerable anthropological literature on the tribes and their cultures has emerged. Tribes have been also studied from a number of angles. The categorising of tribes as criminals, the massive conversion of a number of them to Christianity, the impact of administrative and economic policies of British government on the tribes and the numerous studies of tribes from the point of view of elaborating the history of the ethnography and diversity of Indian ethnic stock have also stimulated controversies regarding the fate of tribes in India. After Independence, the tribal people are subjected to conscious and deliberate influences by various agencies. The tribes are experiencing and are being absorbed into the matrix of a social order which is being created by political, economic and cultural forces actively manipulated by the government of independent India. How do the tribes react to the various forces which are impinging upon their lives? The five selections attempt to portray certain crucial aspects of the interaction between tribes and the larger society which is in the process of emergence. The various approaches and findings embodied in the selections provide useful insights and interesting lines of investigation of tribes in transition. We believe that elaborate studies on the lines indicated in this Section will provide a large mass of empirical material which would immensely help in evolving adequate laws of social development of the rural society of India.

2

TRIBES IN TRANSITION

A. R. Desai

The problem of tribal population has acquired a new significance after Independence.

What are these tribes? How do they differ from the non-tribal population? Why have they remained at a tribal stage of social evolution? How did they fare in History? What is their present status and condition? What is their future in the context of the objectives laid down in the Constitution of the Indian Union and planned economic development inaugurated by the Government of India? All these and a number of other questions have cropped up with acute poignancy during the post-Independence period.

There is another reason which has forced the problems of the tribal population to the forefront. There has taken place a great awakening among these groups. Struggles to improve their conditions have and are being launched by various groups comprising this stratum of Indian population.

The forest Satyagrahas of various tribal groups in different parts of India, the revolts of Warlis, Dublas, Dhodias, Bhils and others in the Western India against their inhuman exploitation by landlords, contractors, moneylenders and petty officials, the organised protests started by Santhals and other tribal groups, the movement to secure Zarland and similar tribal autonomous belts in the Bihar, the M. P. and other States of the Union, and finally, the continuous, violent, almost military battles of the Nagas of Assam, for last fifteen years either for an autonomous Naga State within the Indian Union or even complete Independence—these and such other expressions of the awakening of the tribal people have elevated the problem of the tribal pupulation to a new level of acuteness.

Agencies Handling the Problem

Numerous agencies have been attempting to study and solve the problems of the tribal population.

The Indian National Congress—as the governing party—has, from the day of framing the Constitution of the Indian Union, adopted various measures to handle the tribal problems. Special clauses have been incorporated in the Constitution for the creation of Scheduled Areas for their intensive development, by granting various tribes an autonomous status for internal administration, such as N. E. F. A. (Manipur, Tripura, North Cachar hills). Further, they are provided with special representation in the Parliament, in Legislative Assemblies, Local Bodies and special privileges in the form of reservation of a certain percentage of posts in the Government services and seats in the educational institutions. In addition, the Government have established the special office of the Commissioner for Scheduled Castes and Scheduled Tribes for safeguarding their interests. It has also framed special welfare schemes exclusively for them having as its objective the bringing of these tribes on par with the rest of the Indian people.

Christian Missionaries and Hindu Social Reformers have also intensified their efforts to study and reform the conditions of the tribes. Academicians,—Anthropologists, Sociologists and others—have also launched a vigorous drive to scientifically study the situation and the problems of the tribal population. Tribal research institutes have also been sponsored to methodically explore and examine the conditions and the problems of the tribal communities. Further, various political parties have been extending their zones of activities in tribal areas. They have created numerous organizations in the tribal areas and even launched various movements to redress the grievances of the tribal population. The "vocal" educated and richer sections of the tribes in various parts of the country themselves have also started independent organizations of the tribal population, with a view to securing concessions which they feel to be beneficial to the tribes.

Tribal Population

India, it is claimed, has the largest tribal population compared to any other single country in the world. However, regarding the total strength of the tribal population inhabiting India, there exists a wide divergence of assessment by scholars, as well as Census Reports. As Professor Mamoria has pointed out, " Doubts have been expressed about the reliability of their numbers for two reasons. Firstly, because of the difficulty of classification and, secondly, because of deliberate misrepresentations as after 1909 with the inauguration of the separate religious electorates, there had been an increasing pressure on the part of religious groups to swell their number in the census. As a result of these errors, the data on the tribals are most inaccurate of all those gathered by the Census ".

However, without entering into the fascinating history of this controversy over the assessment of the numerical strength of the tribal population, we will presume that the tribal population in India ranges between about twenty millions as assessed by the 1951 Census and twenty-five millions as estimated by the Conference of Social Workers and Anthropologists held in 1948

Out of these 25 millions, 20 millions, according to these scholars, " live in the plains and are assimilated with the rest of the people, more or less, and only 5 millions may be taken as the population residing in the hills."

CONTROVERSY REGARDING DESIGNATION

Another controversy which is rampant among the scholars, reformers and administrators is regarding adequate designation to describe these groups.

Risely, Lacey, Elwin, Grigson, Shoobert, Tallents, Sedwick, Martin, A. V. Thakkar and others have described them as " aborigines ' or ' aboriginals '. Hutton called them as primitive tribes. Dr. Ghurye described them as ' so-called aborigines ' or ' Backward Hindus ' and now accepts the designation ' Scheduled Tribes ' as formulated in the Constitution of the Indian Union. Some scholars and reformers have described them as Adivasis. Dr. Das and others designated them as " submerged humanity ".

It would be very interesting and thought-provoking to probe into the reasons which prompted various scholars, administrators and reformers to adopt different designations to describe the same group. It would open up a new line of inquiry, an inquiry into the different ideologies of those scholars and administrators who were prompted to evolve different designations. However, lack of space forbids this discussion.

The Constitution of the Indian Union (Article 366) has defined "Scheduled Tribes " as " such tribes or tribal communities or parts of or groups within such tribes or tribal communities as are deemed under Article 342 to be Scheduled Tribes for the purpose of this Constitution. " Constitution Order 1950 declared 212 tribes located in 14 States as " Scheduled Tribes "

CONTRADICTORY CRITERIA

It is pertinent to point out that no single criterion has been hitherto adopted to distinguish tribal from non-tribal population. Different and even contradictory criteria have been employed by anthropologists, social reformers, Government officials, Census Commissioners and others for this purpose. Dr. Ghurye in his work. 'The Scheduled Tribes' has pointed out how factors like religion or occupation or racial features have proved inadequate to distinguish the tribal people from the non-tribal population in India.

However, the purest of the tribal groups, which have been still resisting acculturation or absorption, possess certain features which can be considered as common features once possessed by all the tribal groups. They are as follows :

(1) They live away from the civilized world in the inaccessible parts lying in the forests and hills; (2) They belong either to one of the three stocks—Nagritos, Austroloids, or Mongoloids; (3) They speak the same tribal dialect; (4) They profess primitive religion known as "Animism " in which the worship of Ghosts and Spirits is the most important element; (5) They follow primitive occupations such as gleaning, hunting, and gathering of forest produce; (6) They are largely carnivorous or flesh or meat eaters; (7) They live either naked or semi-naked using tree barks and leaves for clothing; (8) They have nomadic habits and love for drink and dance. "

Tribes in various stages

The tribal population in India belongs to various stages of cultural development. Dr. Elvin divides Tribes into four classes according to their stage of cultural development. Class I is the purest of the pure tribal groups comprising about two or three million persons. Dr. Elwin and a large section of missionary reformers and anthropologists grow lyrical over the robust, vibrant and healthy life of these tribal groups. Dr. Elwin's panegyric is worth quoting: " These Highlanders do not merely exist like so many villagers, they really live. Their religion is characteristic and alive; their tribal organisation is unimpaired, their artistic and choreographic traditions are unbroken; their mythology still vitalizes the healthy organisation of tribal life. Geographical conditions have largely protected them from the debasing contacts of the plains. It has been said that the hoot of the motor-horn would sound the knell of the aboriginal tribes. "

Contrasting Characteristics

However, a section of this category of tribes has been experiencing " contact with the plains " and consequently has been undergoing change. This group, Class II of Dr. Elvin's classification, though retaining their tribal mode of living has been exhibiting the following characteristics in contrast to the first group:

(a) Instead of communal life, this group lives a village life which has become individualistic. Their communal life and traditions, are only preserved through their village dormitories; (b) In contrast to the Class I Tribes, the members of those of Class II do not share things with one another; (c) Axe cultivation has ceased to be a way of life for them; (d) The members of these tribes are more contaminated by the outside life. They come in contact with the groups living in the periphery, which live a more complex viz., civilized life; (e) The members of these tribes (Class II) according to Dr. Elwin, are less simple and less honest than the members of the tribes belonging to class I.

The Agonies of Majority of Tribals

The tribes belonging to Class III constitute the largest section of the total tribal population about four-fifth of it, i.e., nearly twenty millions. Members of this class of tribal groups are in a peculiar state of transition. According to some investigators, they are tribals in name but have become " backward Hindus " constituting a sizeable section of the lower rung of the Hindu Society or some further constituting Christians. They have been appreciably affected by external contacts. They have been exposed to the influences of economic and socio-cultural forces of the Hindu and have been also subjected to missionary influences. But, above all, they have been most adversely affected by the British economic and political policies which resulted in dragging them into the orbit of colonial-capitalist system in India.

The members belonging to this category of tribal groups were uprooted from their tribal mode of production in the same way as millions of cultivators and artisans living in the multitude of autarchic villages of pre-British India from their self-sufficient, self-conducted village, community setting. During the British period, under the impact of new economic and new politico-administrative measures, these tribesmen lost their moorings from their tribal economy, tribal social organisation, tribal religion and tribal cultural life.

A large section of this population was reduced to the status of bond slaves or agrestic serfs of moneylenders, zamindars and contractors who emerged in Indian society as a result of the political and economic policies pursued by the British. Another section was reduced to the category of near slave labourers working on plantations, in mines, railway and road, constructions and other enterprises. They were uprooted from habitat and have been living a wretched existence. A section of these tribes were branded as criminal tribes, as the members of these tribes could survive by methods officially described as crimes because of loss of land, occupation and no accessibility to alternate occupation, as a result of the economic and political measures adopted by the British Rulers to enhance their colonial economic exploitation.

LIKE NON-TRIBALS

The vast bulk of the lower strata of the Indian Society—Hindu, Muslim, Christian and Buddhist—from the exploited sections of the Indian Society suffer from the same disabilities which the tribals suffer. They have been uprooted from their moorings in the same way as artisans and peasants were uprooted under the impact of colonial-capitalist profit-oriented economic and political forces. They have been subjected to the same groups of the new exploiting sections which emerged as a result of the new colonial-capatalist economic frame-work and subjected to the same difficulties as other groups by losing their old customary mode of living and loss of their own ancient organization like tribal councils, as other groups lost their own caste councils. They suffer from the rigours of law which were favourable to propertied classes in the same way as people belonging to lower castes in the most non-tribal population. It is one of the ironies of distorted perspective that a large number of scholars, Missionaries, social reformers and administrators have not been able to visualise the major basic common problems confronted by all the exploited strata belonging either to tribal or non-tribal groups, and are not able to locate the common origin of these common problems in the socio-economic system which ushered in India after the advent of British Rule.

Winning the Battle

The Class IV of tribals (a very small minority) consists of " the old aristocracy of the country, represented to-day by great Bhil and Naga Chieftains, the Gond Rajas, a few Binghawar and Bhuyia landlords, Korki noblemen, wealthy Santhal and Uraon leaders and some highly cultured Mundas. They retain the old Tribal names and their clan and totem rules and observe elements of tribal religion though generally adopt the full Hindu faith and live in modern and even European style. "

According to Dr. Elwin, this class of tribals have won the battle of culture contacts. It means that they have acquired " aristocratic traditions, economic stability, affluence, outside encouragement,] a certain arrogance and self-confidence characteristic alike of ancient families and modern enterprise. " This class of tribals has secured according to Dr. Elwin, the benefits of civilization, without injury to themselves.

Further, Dr. Elwin observes: " The whole aboriginal problem is how to enable the tribesmen of the first and second classes to advance direct into the fourth class without having to suffer the despair and degradation of the third. "

Regent Classifications

Anthropologists and workers who met, as the Tribal Welfare Committee, under the auspices of the Indian Conference of Social Welfare Work at Calcutta recently, suggested the following classification of the existing tribes :

" (1) Tribal communities or those who are still confined to the original forest habitats and follow the old pattern of life;

(2) Semi-Tribal Communities or those who have more or less settled down in rural areas and have taken to agriculture and allied occupations;

(3) Accultured Tribal communities or those who have migrated to urban or semi-urban areas and are engaged in modern industries and vocations and have adopted modern cultural traits; and

(4) Totally Assimilated Tribals in the Indian population. "

Dr. Ghurye in his book 'The Scheduled Tribes', in Chapter II "Assimilational Stresses and Strains" has divided the Tribes into three classes: " The so-called aboriginal tribes may be divided into three classes: First, such sections of them as the Raj Gonds and others who have successfully fought the battle, and are recognised as members of fairly high status within Hindu Society; second, the large mass that has been partially Hinduized and has come in closer contact with Hindus; and third, the hill sections, which have exhibited the greatest power of resistance to the alien cultures that have pressed upon their border. "

Reasons for Emphasising Classification

Even at the cost of incurring the odium of disproportionate delineation of these varied classifications of Tribes it is absolutely essential to emphasise this point for the following reasons:

(1) The problems of the tribal population belonging to various categories are qualitatively different and demand different solutions. Are the pristine primitives living in the forest areas, who constitute nearly two million persons, to be kept in their hilly and forest isolation amidst their semi-starving, semi-clothed, food-gathering or axe cultivating stage? It is objectively possible to keep them isolated, even if desired, in the epoch of railways, motors, electricity, radio, telephone and even aeroplanes? " If the hoot of the motor horn is sounding the death-knell of tribal existence ", can this hoot be prevented?

Inevitable Absorption

Almost every one now accepts that such a possibility is not merely utopian but even unreal moon-shine. Every corner of the land including hills and forests is being enmeshed into the web of more complex civilized network. If these tribals are to be enmeshed into larger communities, the problems posed are different, the basic problem being how to absorb them without subjecting them to exploitation.

Similarly the vast bulk of tribals who are transformed into agricultural labourers, agrestic serfs and cultivators, and/or further into labourers in mines, factories, railways, plantations and other enterprises are faced with problems which are qualitatively different from their more primitive bretheren. In fact their problems are identical with those of agricultural labourers, agrestic serfs, bond-slaves, cultivators, craftsmen and workers belonging to the non-tribal population. " The bare truth is that there is a large section of our population deriving its subsistence from agricultural pursuits, which is exploited in various possible ways by moneylenders, would-be absentee landlords, rack-renters and middlemen ". Their problems are similar and for their solution demand the reconstruction of the existing social order into a new one which will not merely protect both tribal and non-tribal population from such exploitation but will also abolish such exploitation.

Acute Controversy Regarding Tribal Absorption

(2) The classification of tribals into various categories also poses another significant issue viz., what are the forces which compel the tribals to come under the influence of the non-tribal populative living at a higher stage of technological development? If they come under the influence of civilized societies, how are their modes of life modified? Also, what are the forms of cultural contacts between civilized groups and tribal groups? An acute controversy is raging over these problems among various scholars in India. This controversy has gained momentum because it has been

claimed that the tribals are aggressively absorbed by the Hindu Society. As Prof. Haimendorf suggests, before the 19th century, there was more or less " frictionless co-existence between tribal folks and Hindu caste society in the truest sense of the word ". However, from the 19th century onwards, as a result of the spread of railways and roads, physical isolation was broken, population growth suddenly increased, land-hungry Hindu peasants and money-lenders and traders penetrated into tribal areas. They, on one side, exploited them and, on the other, compelled or coaxed them into abandoning their own cultural traditions and values.

Prof. Haimendrof's statement raises very significant problems. Was the Hindu civilization tolerant, as he formulates, up to the 19th century and became intolerant only afterwards ? It is a fact that tribal assimilation has not been going on or was only marginal during last thousands of years in India?

Studies of the history of the Indian civilization reveal how the growth and the expansion of the Hindu Society was a prolonged and complex process of assimilation, both forcible and peaceful of the tribal people into the Hindu Society.

The statement made by Prof. Haimendorf unfolds a new field of inquiry. In fact, as history discloses, various methods of tribal assimilation or absorption have been adopted in different societies in different epochs.

Prof. Bose on Types of Tribal Absorption

Prof. Nirmal Kumar Bose in his thought-provoking essay "Hindu Method of Tribal Absorption" has indicated how a study of various methods of tribal absorption deserves more careful attention than has been given upto now. By comparing the Hindu or Brahminical Method of Tribal Absorption with the Soviet Union's method of tribal acculturation he has shown how the method of acculturation of tribal population should be studied in the context of the system of the property-relations within which the tribals have been planned to be absorbed. The tribal acculturation brought about in a society like the ancient Roman Society founded on slavery will be different from that brought about in a feudal society. The mode of tribal acculturation followed in a capitalist society will be different from the above two and also from that of the society which attempts to build up a social order founded on socialist relations.

The mode of acculturation of the tribal people in India before the 19th century took place within the matrix of a different social order. After the 19th century, it occurred on the basis of a colonial and capitalist matrix. Unfortunately, a large number of missionary reformers, anthropologists and administrators are not inclined to confront this fundamental crucial fact. Similarly our larger number of tribal reformers, administrators, anthropologists who work as consultants to the Tribal Welfare organizations do not still pose the problem viz., even after independence whether the difficulties of the tribal people, as a matter of fact of all those who are considered submerged, backward, and exploited strata of the Indian society may be resolved within the framework of social order which is being founded on a mixed-economy, functional planning and profit oriented production for a competitive market.

EMERGENCE OF A SMALL PRIVILEGED SECTION AMONG TRIBES

(3) The study of the classification of the tribal population has also indicated another fact viz., that even among the tribal population, a peculiar type of stratification has been progressing. On one hand, a small privileged section has been emerging as a result of the advantages of special privileges, education, land-owning or other factors while on the other hand, the vast bulk of the tribals are being hurled into the ranks of the lowest, toiling, exploited classes of the contemporary Indian society. The stratification has crucial significance. The "vocal", "richer" "privileged" minority would inevitably utilize the benefits bestowed on the tribals in the form of special concessions in their game for power. Further they launch programmes and movements in the name of the entire tribal people, but which in reality would serve only their interests. Further, such programmes and movements may also prevent the unification of the tribal groups with non-tribal population whose grievances and demands are common. These grievances can be redressed and demands secured only by joint movements of both tribal and non-tribal population.

WELFARE PROJECTS

The Government of the Indian Union has launched various projects for tribal welfare. Some of them we have mentioned earlier. We will briefly enumerate below the principal among others :

(1) A number of multi-purpose Blocks for the tribals for their intensive development.

(2) Training-cum-production centres and subsidies for the development of cottage and village industries in tribal areas with a view to providing them with employment.

(3) Colonization of the tribals—settling of the tribals who are practising shifting cultivation on land. Introduction of improved methods of shifting cultivation which may bring more yield without doing harm to the soil.

(4) Educational facilities—scholarships, free-studentships and other educational aids.

(5) Establishment of tribal cultural institutes for studying the various cultural problems affecting tribal life.

(6) Reservation of posts in Government services for the tribals.

(7) Enactment of Regulation Acts to counteract exorbitant rates of interest of moneylenders.

(8) Establishment of the office of the Commissioner for Scheduled Castes and Scheduled Tribes for the enforcement of the safeguards provided for the tribals in the Constitution and for the evaluation of various welfare schemes.

The Second Five Year Plan allocated Rs. 91 crores for the welfare of the backward classes and about Rs. 39 crores for the welfare of the scheduled tribes.

INVESTIGATIONS

It would be instructive to study the findings of the Reports of the Commissioner for the Scheduled Castes and the Scheduled Tribes as well as the recently published Report of the study team on the Social Welfare and Welfare of the Backward classes. (To my knowledge these are the only available official documents regarding this study). We will mention the salient points about these Reports below.

(1) The progress achieved during the First Five Year Plan cannot be properly assessed because the progress made during the first two years was meagre and progress made during the subsequent three years could not be assessed as many state governments had failed to submit the progress reports.

(2) The benefits of the schemes mostly accrued to the " vocal section " of the population only.

(3) Failure of the Employment Exchange in providing jobs to a large number of educated and uneducated tribals enrolled in the register.

(4) Failure of the Tribal Research Institutes in playing a functional role in bringing about the coordination of research with the formulation of welfare planning.

(5) Persistence of exploitation of the tribals by moneylenders and contractors.

(6) Total failure of the training-cum-production centres in either providing successful training or even functioning as production units, thus resulting in the wastage of money.

(7) Meagre provision of cultivable land with other facilities in settling the tribals.

(8) Red-tapism, lack of coordination among different departments resulting in the lapse of grants and untimely supply of materials, etc.

The above observations reveal the superficial and uncoordinated nature of the aid, provided to the tribal population. Such an approach whets the appetite without satisfying it. It thereby creates more acute frustration which is exploited by the " vocal section " of the tribal population for their sectional interests.

PROBLEM OF EXPLOITATION

As stated earlier, the problems of the vast bulk of the tribal population are basically similar to and bound up with the problems of the vast mass of the exploited and uprooted non-tribal Indian population. As observed in my earlier studies—Recent Trends in Indian Nationalism and Rural Sociology in India, the problems of the masses including the intensely oppressed tribal population arise from the very character of the social order that is existing and further developing in our country. In fact their problems will only be aggravated within the existing and functioning capitalist social system. Their solutions can be found only when a non-exploitative social order is established.

The problems of the tribal population should not be treated in a superficial symptomatic way. These problems have to be viewed in the context of the present capitalist socio-economic system prevailing in India. The very pressure of the exploitative, competitive, profit oriented forces of this society will reduce the tribals into objects of capitalist exploitation.

Fundamental Issue

The desperate, violent and militant struggles which are being launched by the tribal population in various areas are the revolts directed against the inhuman conditions to which they have been subjected and which are basically perpetuated even after independence. Their problems fundamentally are not whether they should be permitted to practice the habits and customs of leaf-dresses, polyandry, and polygamy or be allowed to continue indulgence in drink or further that their primitive tribal culture including colourful dances should be perpetuated. All these aspects of their life were organically bound up with their tribal mode of subsistence, which is now in the melting pot. The fundamental problems of the tribal population are economico-political. They are problems such as security of job, decent standard of living, easy accessibility to resources of civilized life, acquisition of education which can enable them to decide what customs, what rituals and what aesthetic cultural elements they should retain, eliminate or absorb from their and other cultures. If the prevention of head-hunting practices or human sacrifices (however organic they may be with their tribal life) could be justified on the grounds of ' natural justice ', without raising the issues of relativity of morals as asserted by Prof. Haimendorf and his ilk, starvation, exploitation, clothlessness, disease, should be prevented on the same grounds.

The tribal problem is a problem which raises the fundamental issue viz., the issue of the establishment of social order founded on equality of opportunities and elimination of exploitation.

2

A TRIBAL PEOPLE IN AN INDUSTRIAL SETTING*

MARTIN ORANS

THE MAIN body of this report is divided into three sections, concerned respectively with the recruitment and commitment of the Santal portion of Jamshedpur's labour force, with changing beliefs and practices concerning witchcraft, and with quantitative variations in marriage forms.

If Jamshedpur is characterised in terms of these co-existing and intermingled traditions, it will be found to be one of the most modernised and least " great traditional " of India's major cities. It is a city as much dominated by modern industry as a medieval city was by its cathedral. Traditional institutions such as temples and organizations for the propagation of the Great Tradition exist but are relatively weakly developed. The Tata Company, the Tata Workers Union, and the town's competing regional, and national political parties are the dominant corporate groups. Caste persists as an institution for regulating marriage, for regulating employment in certain traditionally degrading occupations, and to a certain extent in structuring social interaction. But class in the traditional Western sense is increasingly displacing caste as the organizing principle of membership in social groups and in social interaction. Jamshedpur is again extreme in the proportion of leisure time spent in modern Westernised forms of diversion as compared to devotional or entertainment forms characteristic of the Great Tradition. It should be noted that modernism is more pronounced among the upper classes, but even the lower classes have absorbed more of it than people of similar status in other more typical Indian cities. This modernism which trickles down with increasing distortion through the social order, is partly the result of the relative extreme modernism of the Parsi community which fills the top positions in the company and hence in the community. It also happens to be dominant tendency among the highly skilled engineers and technicians, whatever their community.

In Jamshedpur the traits of the two primary traditions tend to remain clearly discrete and there is little self-conscious effort to shape new patterns by fusion even among the city's elite.

To the Santals, Jamshedpur offers an alluring spectacle of complex industrial machinery and gigantic industrial structures; it has superior

*Reproduced from *Journal of American Folklore* by Martin Orans, July-September 1958, Vol. 71, No. 281, pp. 422-446.

markets where a comparatively wide range of merchandise can be seen or brought. Perhaps most important for the young Santal man is the fact that its atmosphere is free from many of the strictures of the rural village.

Those who live in company houses have become attached to the unusual amenities provided with these houses, for example, water from a tap, electricity, special sanitation facilities, and a house that doesn't leak and doesn't have to be repaired. When these city dwellers (the non-Seraikela Santals) visit their villages, they find life somewhat uncomfortable and their children find it even more trying. Those who live in the *bustees*, on the contrary, live under the same conditions as they did in the village. A few of these *bustee* Santals would like to move into company houses in town. The attraction seems not so much the physical facilities provided but rather the cultural climate of the city. It is the urbanity of the city folk that they prize, and it is the vulgarity of their fellow *bustee* Santals that they wish to escape from. This vulgarity manifests itself, as they see it, particularly in the rather violent quarrels which break out in the *bustee* especially after considerable drinking, and in the sexual display indulged in for example, by men during the dance. Such Santals who disdain the life of the *bustee* are a small minority, but it is they who are most desirous of moving into town. Generally the *bustee* dweller prefers his position to that of the city dweller. He pays virtually no rent, he may have enough land for a respectable garden, and above all he is surrounded by congenial Santals rather than treacherous and hostile non-Santals (diky, particularly Hindus). With these Santals, he may enjoy all the traditional forms of behaviour that he desires, while comparatively little notice will be taken of him if he chooses not to enter into these forms. The *bustee* is congenial, familiar, and at the same time relatively permissive.

The city dwellers tend to be more firmly attached to their jobs, which are generally better paid, require more skill, and are, in a few cases, of the white collar variety, and they are deeply committed also to their new physical environment. Both groups have become more committed to their jobs through a number of special inducements offered in recent years by the various companies. One of the most effective of these inducements to the Santal is the right to name one of his sons to a job after he has served at least thirty years. As the Santals say, " Having a job at Tata is like having land, you can pass it on to your son. "

Changing Beliefs and Practices Concerning Witchcraft : The investigation of witchcraft in village, *bustee*, and town not only provides observations of changing belief and practice in the two kinds of industrial communities, but also an opportunity to test hypothesis concerning the interconnections of witchcraft with other phenomena in the village.

Generally for the village, beliefs and practice regarding witchcraft have not much changed during the last fifty years, despite the fact that a few relatively well educated Santals there hold views radically different from those of their fellows. According to the traditional view held by most village Santals, disease may be caused and treated either by natural means or by a number of supernatural means, of which witchcraft is one of the most important. Almost all treatment is administered by a Santal medicine man who is part-time specialist (*ojha*, as in Hindi). If natural methods such as root medicine fail to bring about a cure, the *ojha* will attempt to exercise evil spirits or spells by various supernatural methods. If even this fails he may suggest that a witch is responsible. While the *ojha* does not have the power to find out who the witch is, he can perform certain rites to eliminate the effects of the witchcraft. If these also fail, it becomes necessary to go to a *sokha*, who has the power, through divination, to find out the guilty witch.

Witches are always women. They obtain their power to cause sickness through certain malevolent spirits (*bonga*) who instruct them in return for various offerings. It is believed that witches are motivated by *hisa*, a concept with a variety of meanings. In Hindi the word means ' injury, ' ' malice, ' ' robbery, ' or ' murder. ' The essence of the Santali meaning is ' envy ' and or ' concealed malicious intent. ' The witch who harbours such feelings harms her victims by either eating the victim's internal organs or luring away his life spirit (*jiwi*; Hindi *jw*).

Every Santal woman is regarded as a potential witch, and this belief, plus women's ritual impurity during the menstruation, are the justifications for their exclusion from all forms of worship. As in many societies with the ideal of the patrilineal extended family, it is the women who are invariably blamed for schisms leading to the fragmentation of this unit into its component nuclear families. This projection of tension within the extended family onto women, especially wives, contributes toward the general denigration of the character from women. They are said to be of weak character, easily attracted by a shiny trinket, and hence persons in whom one cannot place trust, I suggest the hypothesis that this projection of tension is intimately connected with the view that all Santal women are potential witches.

The actual naming of a witch by a *sokha* occurs only during serious illness or after an unexplained death. The penalties inflicted on the alleged witch vary in seriousness depending upon circumstances. She may merely be chastised by the *sokha* and villagers, made to promise to discontinue her evil practices, and forced through her husband to pay a fine. If she does not confess and her husband will not testify to her guilt, they may both be beaten to extract the needed confession. In very serious cases she and her husband may be driven out of the village or even outcasted. If all of these community punishments prove unsatisfactory to the alleged victim or his family, they may themselves take action and do violence to or even take the life of the witch. For a variety of technical reasons connected with detection of crime and legal technicalities the " murderer " is seldom convicted even if brought to court. In addition the villagers may frequently take his side.

The Santals are, on the whole, a notably neat people. Unfortunately, the clean appearance of both their homes and persons is not often a hygeinic cleanliness—for example, they frequently scrub their cooking and eating utensils to a fine polish with obviously contaminated water. Hence, like their Hindu neighbours, they suffer severely from a number of, more or less, endemic diseases. Particularly devastating are malaria and a variety of dysenteries, as well as the common epidemic diseases of the area such as cholera and smallpox. A large number of illnesses are attributed to witchcraft, but it is rare that a *sokha* will be consulted and witch named. The restraints operating are the serious repercussions which may follow with their danger to village solidarity, and the fact that consulting a *sokha* is an expensive procedure.

Although any innocent looking Santal woman may secretly be a witch while the community remains unaware of it, it is possible to see witches in action. Almost every Santal has seen unexplained lights emanating from witches and a good number have actually seen a witch or two making offerings or even dancing in the sacred grove (*jaher*) where worship is held. It should be remembered that these beliefs and practices are not fundamentally different from those of many of the Santal's Hindu neighbours.

In general, belief and practice in the *bustee* regarding witchcraft are much like those in the village. Certain beliefs almost never found in the village have been added, however, to the common stock. One added belief which proved quite a surprise to me is a new idea about the elimination of witchcraft. I was told by a Santal in the *bustee* where I did most of my work that witchcraft is a bad thing, and the reason it is so prevalent among the Santal is ignorance. He added, " the educated *diku* don't have it, and with education it will disappear from our community also. " As I thought this answer implied a disbelief in witchcraft, and as he was the first Santal to have indicated such an opinion to me, I fortunately decided to press the point further When I then asked him how education could eliminate witchcraft, he gave an answer showing quite clearly that he still firmly believed in witches, but thought the practice of witchcraft would decline with education. He explained that women practise witchcraft because of *hisa*, and the reason they have this *hisa* is that they are ignorant. " When they become educated, " he said, " they will see that this *hisa* is a bad thing and will give up the practice of witchcraft. " I thought this to be a special instance of a peculiar view-point and was astonished to learn that it is the common view in the *bustee*.

A less common attitude, but one which is much more frequent in the *bustee* than in the village is skepticism about the existence of witches. A number of *bustee* Santals have told me, " Yes, I have seen lights from what are supposed to be witches, but who knows if they were really witches? I have never seen a witch myself although others say they have seen. Since I have never seen myself, how can I say whether they exist or not? "

As for accusation of witchcraft in the *bustee,* I do not yet have a record adequate for comparing the nature and frequency of such accusations in the *bustee* with those in the village. Only a couple of years ago, one woman in the *bustee* was named by a *sokha* as a witch, and she and her husband were beaten, made to pay a fine, and forced out of the *bustee*. A few years prior to this, a woman from the same *bustee* was killed while returning from market. The murderer was never apprehended, and it may well be that whoever was responsible believed her to be a witch.

In the city there are number of attitudes toward witchcraft either totally lacking or extremely rare in the *bustee* or village. The most common point of view is a kind of quasi-naturalistic interpretation. Such city dwellers hold that witchcraft motivated by *hisa* does indeed exist, as demonstrated by many observations they themselves and their fellows have made. They argue, however, that this witchcraft is not, strictly speaking, a supernatural power conferred by malevolent spirits, but rather a magical technique passed on from one witch to another. The Hindi word *jadu* is used for magic. They make it clear that it is magic in the sense of "seemingly supernatural." It is a kind of mysterious scientific technique, and the word which they frequently use to convey their view of its nature is " mesmerism. "

They have a very limited idea of what mesmerism is supposed to be, but they do know that it is a kind of scientific magic. As one Santal put it, expressing his preference for a naturalistic point of view, " How can I believe that witches can eat one's internal organs? When people are sick I never see any holes in their skin through which the organs might have been removed. If a witch really has caused the sickness it must be by the use of some kind of poison or *jadhu.* "

Another Santal, who is a student in the Jamshedpur Co-operative College, is the only Santal I know who gives a totally naturalistic explanation of witchcraft and denies the existence of witches. In the course of his studies he came across a psychology book belonging to one of his Hindu schoolmates, in which he read that people frequently imagine that they see those things of which they are very much afraid. He accepted this as a convincing explanation of witchcraft congenial to his own general outlook. This young man is the son of a Seraikela Tata employee and lives in that part of town where a number of Seraikela Santals are domiciled. As he told me this, a few of these Seraikela workers sat about and listened. Since they were completely uneducated and unintiated to the ideology involved, his explanation was totally unconvincing to them. The young student's father is also unwilling to accept his son's point of view.

To our knowledge there have been no identifications of witches among the city Santals. From this fact and the changes in belief described previously, it should not be inferred, however, that fear of witchcraft has declined much among the city Santals. While they are not much worried about it when among their city brethren, a great deal of anxiety is aroused when they visit a village. One of the most important reasons for this persistence of fear is that the city Santals believe themselves to be particularly susceptible to the *hisa* or envy of villagers. This envy is aroused because they are so much richer and more successful than the villagers.

Before attempting an interpretation of the variations in witchcraft beliefs and practices that have been described, one additional set of witchcraft beliefs must be mentioned which in some ways cuts across the village-*bustee*-city axis. The Santals have a religious teacher (*guru* as in Hindi) of high repute who has been given the title " Spiritual leader " (*maran gomke*). This guru, *Raghnat Murmu*, has founded an organization whose chief function is to ascertain the " true " beliefs of the Santals and to codify them. Only the witchraft beliefs of this *guru* and his followers can be presented here.

According to the *guru's* view, there are witches who, because of *hisa*, practise witchcraft. These witches, however, can cause sickness only in a person who has committed some sin (*pap*, Hindi; he also uses the English " sin "). He and his followers further believe that the *sokha* cannot be relied on to find out who are witches. The solution to the problem of illness caused in part by witchcraft and in part by one's own sin is to live a virtuous life and to follow the traditional religious practices and beliefs. The members of his organization all share his belief in the inefficacy of consulting a *sokha* and the value of following religious tradition, but many of them do not quite comprehend his doctrine of sin. One Santal who attended a meeting of the organization with me but who is not a member remarked, " How can sin in any way be a cause of sickness? I have sinned so much; still I am usually healthy! "

Raghnat Murmu lives today in his native village in Mayurbhanj, practising agriculture and engaging in his teaching, which also includes the propagation of an original alphabet he has developed for Santali. He is a matriculate graduate and has served several years as a high school teacher. Having learned to read Sanskrit in high school, he became deeply interested in and influenced by the Hindu Great Tradition. He has also been noticeably influenced by Christianity through contact with a Catholic missionary. His organization is headed by two uneducated Tata employees who live in a *bustee* (president and treasurer), one young student who is a Tata apprentice (secretary), and one villager from Seraikela who is also uneducated, called the priest (*nueke*) of the organization. The treasurer, though totally illiterate, is a brilliant ecstatic religious teacher who tends to dominate the organization when the *guru* himself is not present.

It is too early yet to tell how influential the beliefs of this organization will become. The evidence seems to indicate that it has picked up a few converts in the various *bustees* and has indirectly influenced the opinions of some who are not converts. The more educated city Santals, however look down on the uneducated leaders who dominate the organization, and find the *guru's* theory about witchcraft uncongenial.

In a very general way it seems that the increasing skepticism toward witchcrafts in the *bustees* and the quasi-naturalistic attitude toward it characteristic of the city, are examples of what has earlier been called " modernism " The rather striking *bustee* view of the role of education in eliminating witchcraft is an example of the syncretism of modernism and Santal traditional culture, since it is a combination of the social uplift force of education in eliminating bad social practices, and traditional beliefs regarding witchcraft. It has been stated that the " sin " theory of witchcraft is the result of a syncretism of traditional views of the Santals with those of the Hindu and Christian Great Traditions. Something of the congruence of the various witchcraft beliefs with differing ideological viewpoints has also been discussed.

It is not, however, solely ideological affinity which determines the varying Santal viewpoints on witchcraft. These affinities themselves develop in a matrix of social identification, social approval, and correlative self-approval. Although this is true of the beliefs of all people, it is especially true for the Santals, who traditionally regard the true and the good as inseparable from the shared views of their community. The idea of an internalized yardstick of the true and good, as distinct from the point of view of society, is almost totally lacking, and even among the most modernized and Hinduized it is weakly developed. The variations concerning witchcraft observed in the three kinds of communities under discussion are largely a function of differences of social identification.

The typical village Santal identifies almost exclusively with the Santal community. He is sensitive to the judgments of his fellow Santals primarily and almost exclusively—more particularly to those of his own village or region. He is satisfied with his own views and behaviour if his fellow Santals approve of them. Even if he has an ideological proclivity to differ with his fellows, he will be reluctant to express this difference in his village, and he will do all he can to modify his own beliefs so as to bring them into line with those of the community. For these reasons he is the least affected by views of the non-Santal world, even if he is made aware of them.

The *bustee* Santal is less exclusively Santal than is the villager. One powerful influence in the direction of wider identification for both the *bustee* and the city Santal is the fact that Jamshedpur and its environs are great centres of political activity. Many *bustee* and city Santals have entered into the activities of the *adibasi* Jharkhand political party. These Santals frequently identify themselves first as *adibasis* and then as Santals. From this organization particularly they have imbibed the notion of social uplift which has been shown to be connected with the *bustee* Santals, new notions about witchcraft. Both the *bustee* and city Santals have widened their social horizons even further through union activity, which causes them to recognize common interest with their fellow workers of whatever community. The increasing skepticism of the *bustee* Santals toward witchcraft, and the increasingly naturalistic viewpoint evident among the city Santals, are not only the results of increased contact with these ideas through non-Santals; they are also the result of new forms of social receptivity of ideas from the non-Santal world. The city Santals' beliefs and practices regarding witchcraft have been more influenced by the non-Santal world because their social interaction is more intensive and persistent with this world than is the case with the *bustee* Santals. Therefore their receptivity is greater.

With respect to the development of a more naturalistic viewpoint among the city Santals and to a lesser extent among the *bustee* Santals, the question might be raised of the possible effects of industrial labour itself. The first is that the creation and operation of an industrial establishment presupposes the existence in fair numbers of personnel who already have such a naturalistic view-point. These modernized individuals are observably spreaders of their point of view, making it difficult to isolate any possible effect of industrial labour itself. The second difficulty is that if there is such an effect, it is not directly observable and would have to be inferred from the evidence available with the aid of some general theory regarding the relations of various forms of labour to naturalistic or supernaturalistic orientations.

The fact that the *bustee* Santals are much less naturalistic in their orientation than the city Santals, although both perform industrial jobs, suggests that human contact is at least the more important determinant. This latter comparison, however, must be qualified by recognition that, on the whole, the city Santals hold jobs which require more skill than those held by *bustee* Santals. There can be little doubt that where more complex jobs are learned by normal training, some naturalistic orientation will be absorbed. Some Santals of the city have had such training. The question is how far they will generalize this orientation to embrace other spheres. Will it, for example, affect their attitude toward witchcraft? I do not know of an adequate general theory with which this question can be approached. It may be that, all other things being equal, the more a man knows his working life to be governed by naturalistic means, the more likely he is to extend naturalistic techniques and beliefs to his non-working life. The Santal certainly knows that all physical problems in the steel mill where he works are solved in a mechanical fashion. It is also certainly true that his working life in the factory is far more controllable and controlled than his traditional agricultural life. It must be remembered, however, that a naturalistic attitude toward witchcraft, for example, will hardly solve the problems that have generated the belief in witchcrafts, such as the tensions in the extended family and the displacement of these onto women.

It will be remembered that all specific accusations of witchcraft occur at the time of illness. All Tata workers and most employees of other firms in Jamshedpur are not only provided with free medical treatment but are required to see a doctor and obtain a health certificate whenever they absent themselves from work for health reasons. In the early days this medical care was not much appreciated, but today it is widely used. In line with differences already noted between the *bustee* and the city

Santals it is not surprising that the latter take much more advantage of this service than the former. The *bustee* Santals frequently employ a native practitioner even when they are receiving professional medical care.

In spite of the fact that the *bustee* Santals undoubtedly recover from illness more rapidly and oftener than villagers because of the professional medical care they do receive, sickness is, if anything, more frequent in the *bustee*. This is probably the result of the fact that the *bustee* is much more crowded than any village, while its physical facilities are in no way improved. The city Santals, on the contrary, not only receive better medical care but enjoy far better physical accommodations and are far healthier than either the villagers or the *bustee* dwellers. These circumstances are then perhaps another reason why belief in witchcraft and even witchcraft accusations persist in the *bustee*, while belief is greatly weakened and accusations unheard of in the city.

From the few hypothesis put forth in connection with witchcraft in the village, it follows that anything which tends to raise the status of women in Santal society or to weaken the ideal of the extended family will tend to weaken belief in witchcraft. In this connection the *bustee* Santal suggestion that the education of women will help to eliminate witchcraft may not be wrong. It is as yet too early to pronounce judgment on the persistence of the ideal of the extended family, but if industrial life does lead to its demise, this too should lead to a higher status for women and a weakening of witchcraft.

The case of the city Santals' increased identification with Hindu society raises the final point to be considered. What is it that keeps these city Santals out of the Hindu fold? While they have abandoned many of the traditional values and attitudes of their society, they cling to certain religious practices and other traditional behaviours which are distinctively Santal and will not identify themselves as Hindu. Among the most important bonds with his own society are the traditional and deeply rooted sentiments of obligation and emotional attachment to his kin. These bonds are made even more manifest for the city Santal by his dependence on kin in his native village to maintain his interest in the family land. Ordinarily these relatives cultivate his share of the land and periodically bring him rice in return for cash contributions. He is further bound to his own society by the belief or at least the fear that if certain traditional rites are not performed to ancestors and other deities he may be punished with illness. One of the most prominently mentioned dependence of the city Santal on his own society is for the traditional rites associated with death in the event that he or a member of his immediate family should die. This dependency when considered in terms of the traditional configuration of beliefs and practices concerned with death appears to be largely a symbolic representation of his ramified interconnection with the traditional Santal social order. Apart from these and a number of other internal bonds there are a number of particularly significant external institutions contributing to the maintenance of his Santal identity. One of the most important of these is the system of caste ranking. The much acculturated city Santals have decided, for the moment at least, that to become Hindu would mean to accept a low position in the caste hierarchy. They know of the movement to abolish caste but they are not yet convinced that it will triumph. As suggested earlier, the rise of the Jharkhand party has contributed to a strong new identification with all *adibasi*. In addition it has provided a new avenue of social mobility, i.e., election to public office. Through the Jharkhand party and other institutions for tribal welfare the Santal who is better educated than his fellows can gain status in an area less competitive than that of the wider Indian society. Finally there are significant practical reasons for maintaining their identity as members of a scheduled tribe. Among such benefits are scholarships, special governmental appointments and preferential industrial appointment.

This cursory treatment of the conditions contributing to Santal self identification particularly among the city Santal is obviously far from exhaustive. I have only meant to indicate that not all recent developments have contributed towards the absorption of city Santals into the Hindu fold. What he is very actively considering is the conflict between his accepted social identity and his dissatisfaction with various aspects of the traditional culture. Under the present conditions it is far more likely that he will continue his attempt to remould Santal culture to his own liking than abandon his social identity. Increasingly sensitive to the beliefs, practices and criticisms of the general Indian society, his aim is to "raise" his own society to a level where it will command the respect of the non-Santal world.

3

TRIBAL CULTURES OF PENINSULAR INDIA AS A DIMENSION OF THE LITTLE TRADITION: A PRELIMINARY STATEMENT*

SURAJIT SINHA

IN OUR discussion of tribal India, we roughly limit ourselves to fifteen million people living in and around Peninsular India, covering the hills, plateaus and the neighbouring plains of Bombay, Madhya Pradesh, Hyderabad, Orissa, southern Bihar and West Bengal. In order of their numerical importance, the principal tribes are the Gond, Santal, Bhil, Oraon, Kondh, Munda, Bhuiya, Ho, Savara Kol, Korku, Pathariya and Baiga. They represent communities at various levels of economic efficiency; the Birhor and the Hill Kharia live by dependence on hunting and collecting; the Baiga or Hill Bhuiya similarly depend on shifting cultivation while the Munda, Ho, Santal, and Bhumij practise settled agriculture. Some of these tribes living in relatively interior areas have been very lightly touched by Hinduism, namely, the Baiga or the Ho or Kolhan, while at the other extreme there are tribes such as the Bhumij of Manbhum or the Raj Gond of Madhya Pradesh, who declared themselves as Hindu in the census of 1931.

The languages of these tribal groups of Peninsular India belong primarily to two stocks, the Munda or Kherwari and the Dravidian. The Munda speaking tribes, such as the Ho, Kharia, Munda and Santal, are restricted in their distribution to Chota Nagpur plateau and surrounding areas, while the major habitat of the Dravidian speaking tribes, such as the Gond, Khond, Bisonhorn Reddi, Kadar, etc., is in central and southern India. A few of these tribes, again, like the Bhil of central India and the Bhumij of Manbhum, have used Indo-Aryan languages in place of their original tongue for quite some time.

Physical anthropologists of the past have specified the physical features of the group as follows : short to medium stature, wavy black hair, dark skin colour, dolichocephalic head and platyrrhine nose. Guha labels them Proto-Australoid as distinguished from the Mediterranean type of South India, represented mainly by the Dravidian speakers. With the exception of narrower nose, the latter's physical features are almost identical with those of the so-called Proto-Australoids. (Guha 1937).

*Reproduced from the *Journal of American Folklore*, July-September 1958, Vol. 71, No. 281, pp. 504-517.

Hutton, since the census operation of 1931, has made a somewhat arbitrary and neat speculation about racial migrations and cultural developments in India. In Hutton's view, there have been successive waves of migration of people into India, bringing in different cultures. Contemporary Indian population and civilization, according to Hutton, is an amalgam of all these. The successive series, as he sees them, are Negrito, Proto-Australoid, Early Mediterranean, and finally, the Latter Mediterranean, Alpine, and Nordic, all these having come through the north-western gateway. From the north-east came the various Mongoloid groups, about whose relative date of entry Hutton is not certain.

Arthur Keith questions Guha's and Hutton's hypothesis that the early population of India was entirely received through immigration; " Yet, strange to say, all or nearly all, who have sought to explain the differentiation of the population of India into racial types have sought the solution of this problem outside the Peninsula. They have never attempted to ascertain how far India has bred her own races.........No doubt India has been invaded over again; certain racial types are of extraneous origin. But one would venture the opinion that eighty-five per cent of the blood of India is native to the soil. At least it is urgently necessary that our eyes should be focussed more directly on the possibility of India being an evolutionary field—both now and in former times. " Following this lead of Keith, S. S. Sarkar prefers to use the term " Veddid " for the Dravidian speaking, mainly forest dwelling, tribes of South India who are, according to him, the true autochthonous of India. Within this group he tentatively includes the Urali, Kanikkar, and Muthuvan of Travancore; the Paniyan of Wynad, Malabar; the Sholga, the Kurumba and the Irula of the Nilgiris; the Chenchu of Hyderabad and the Kadar and the Malsar of Cochin. Sarkar distinguishes the autochthonous. Dravidian speaking Veddid racial stock from the Munda speaking tribes, who are regarded by him as later immigrants to the Indian soil.

In the absence of datable fossil human remains and adequate cultural data, we are not yet in a position to take too definite a stand on this controversial issue, particularly with reference to the chronological aspect of it.

We can perhaps say with some confidence that the Aryan speakers are later arrivals on the Indian scene compared to the main carriers of Munda and Dravidian languages. In all probability the basic orientation of India's primary civilization was laid before the Aryan intrusion, through prolonged interaction of the little Traditions of the Munda and Dravidian little communities. If the measurements on the Mohenjodaro skeletal remains published by Marshall, Mackay, Sewell and Guha are taken at their face value, we find evidences both of " Proto-Australoid " and " Mediterranean " types in the urbanized population. If the Mediterranean type be identified with the ancestors of modern " non-Proto-Australoid " " non-Veddid " Dravidian speakers in South India, then we may assume that the interaction started as early as about the third millenium B. C.

Leaving these historical speculations aside, let us turn to a synchronic structural comparison between the tribal cultures and the cultures of the Hindu peasantry. The data on tribal cultures is provided by various published materials and my own field work among the Munda, Bhumij, Ho, and Oraon. Broadly speaking, we shall restrict ourselves to the following communities: 1) mainly hunters and gatherers, the Hill Kharia, Pahira and Birhor of Chota Nagpur; 2) mainly shifting cultivators, the Hill Bhuiya, Juang and Khond of Orissa; the Korwa, Baiga, and Hill Maria Gond of Madhya Pradesh; the Chenchu and Bison-horn Reddi of Hyderabad; 3) settled agriculturists, the Munda, Ho, Santal, Dudh Kharia, Bathuri, Bhumij, Oraon and Savara of Southern Bihar and Orissa; the Raj Gond of Madhya Pradesh and Hyderabad.

The generalized characteristics of the Hindu peasant communities will be derived partly from my general impression of Hindu village communities in West Bengal, Bihar and Orissa, as I have seen them, and also from the recent publication on Indian peasant communities in the Economic Weekly (1951-54), and from the various articles published in Village India, edited by Marriott (1955).

The Two Kinds of Cultural Systems

In the following pages, we shall describe in broad terms some implicitly functionally related aspects of the culture pattern of the two kinds of societies, referring only occasionally to a single community or tribe. The totality of the culture pattern and its settings has been broken down into the following aspects, namely, habitat, economy, social structure, and ideological system. Our characterization will perhaps be more applicable to pre-industrial India, i.e., the India of the middle of the nineteenth century, than to contemporary India; although in all essentials it fits the contemporary picture as well.

1·1. *Habitat—Tribals* : A major portion of the tribal habitat of central India is hilly and forested. Tribal villages are generally found in away areas from the alluvial plains close to rivers.

1·2. *Hindu Peasantry* : A large portion of Hindu peasant villages are in deforested plateaus or plains. Many of these villages are crowded in the river plains.

2·1. *Economy—Tribals* : The subsistence economy is based mainly on either hunting, collecting, and fishing (e.g., the Birhor, Hill Kharia), or a combination of hunting and collecting with shifting cultivation (e.g., the Juang, Hill Bhuiya, etc.). Even the so-called plough using agricultural tribes have the tradition of having subsisted mainly by means of shifting cultivation in the past.

Specialization of crafts includes iron smelting and smithery, basket and bark rope making and weaving. It is difficult to say whether they had wheel made pottery and brass work traditionally. Some of the tribes, like the Juang or the Chenchu, have the tradition of never having used pottery in ancient times. In all probability, initially, most of the crafts were not confined to fulltime specialists. There is evidence that the Lohar blacksmiths and iron smelters once formed a part of the Munda tribe, and that the Mahali basketmakers once formed a part of the Santal tribe.

The local village community is nearly self-sufficient. Circulation of goods is based entirely on barter. There are, however, rudiments of inter-ethnic co-operation in the circulation of goods within a limited area. The wandering Birhor supplied bark ropes and honey to the Ho and Munda and other neighbouring people. The Munda procured iron implements from the Asur and various types of basketry from the Mahali. Mandelbaum describes the socio-economic symbiosis among the aboriginal Kota, Badaga, Kurumba and Toda in the Nilgiri area. There are no specialist traders among them.

There is very little incentive towards the accumulation of capital on an individual level, although a sense of individual ownership is quite developed with reference to hunted animals or collected vegetables. The hunting or collecting territory roughly belongs to the village community; and it is customary for any group not to poach upon the territory of another. Among the tribes that practice shifting cultivation, and have ample scope for expansion, there is very little competition for the covering of more land individually. Among the settled agriculturists, like the Ho, Munda, and Bhumij, however, we find a distinct incentive towards accumulation of capital in the form of land and a store of paddy.

2·2. *Hindu Peasantry* : The main subsistence economy is intensive agriculture with the help of the plough drawn by bullocks or buffaloes. There is also an intricate full-time specialization in crafts, with the development of a sophisticated tradition of artistic excellence supported mainly by a feudal aristocracy. Among the full-time specialists associated with Hindu villages, not to be found in the traditional tribal communities, may be mentioned gold and silver smith, weavers of the silk cloth, bell-metal workers, etc.

Beyond limited degree of local self-sufficiency, the village community is tied to a country-wide network of markets, ultimately related to commercial towns. Incentive towards the accumulation of capital is quite strong. Capital is mainly defined in terms of land, store of grains, cash, valuable metals, and jewelry.

3·1. *Social Structure—Tribals* : The largest significant reference group is the tribe or a segment of it, the " sub-tribe, " i.e., a single, endogamous, ethnic group occupying a more or less contiguous territory. In many cases, we find tribes like the Santal, Munda, or Ho describing themselves as Hor ' men. ' while others are Diku ' aliens. ' In actuality, we find that, among the same tribes, the latter term is not actually used with reference to a few ethnic groups with whom they have set up a traditional symbiotic relationships of long standing. Thus the Ho do not use this term for the Lohar ' blacksmith, ' Mahali ' basketmaker, ' or Gaur ' cattle tender ' within their village community.

The tribe segmented into exogamous (patrilineal in most cases), (often) totemic clans, frequently with territorial cohesion and strong corporate identity. Clans are segmented into lineages which serve as important corporate groups.

The kinship system may be labelled as " tempered classificatory " (maximal lineage setting the limit to the application of kinship terms, although terminologies, often extend to members of the village as a whole). In terminology, we find that the emphasis lies on the unilineal principle, generation and age. There is an emphasis on patrilineal descent and patripotestal authority in most groups.

The village is the most important territorial unit. Among many of these tribes, nearly twelve villages form a socio-political federation with its own council. Among a few (the Munda and the Bhumij) we also find a tendency to form even larger federations.

There is very little specialization of social roles. With the exception of role differentiation in terms of kinship and sex and some specialization in crafts already referred to, the only other role specializations are headman, village priest, and medicine man.

There is very little rigid stratification in society. (This is especially so among the tribes who practise hunting and collecting and shifting cultivation). There is, however, a tendency towards stratification along the following lines, especially among the settled agricultural groups : relative political supremacy of the numerically dominant clan, compared to other settlers; superiority in land holding of the earlier settlers, relative to later settlers; symbolic ritual superiority of one group over another, due to ritual degradation of the other in traditional terms, and tendency of the priest-headmen to form an endogamous class.

Secular and religious leaderships are combined in one person. The headman is a chief amongst equals, with no special privilege in property. He is assisted in his work by a democratic council of village elders formed by all the adult members of the village. The council's decision is final.

3·2. *Hindu Peasantry* : The largest significant reference group expands beyond the village or the caste group to the linguistic province or even farther, covering the total Hindu social universe and comprising numerous distinct ethnic groups. The bases of such extended ties beyond the little village community are varied and numerous, including connection with central administrative townships, network of markets, marriage and caste relations, and network of religious centrals and religious fairs.

The caste is usually segmented into exogamous clans which are often non-totemic. The clans are usually non-territorial and do not have any corporate identity. Clans or gotras are segmented into lineages which serve as important corporate groups.

The kinship system may be labelled as " tempered classificatory " (maximal lineage setting the limit to the application of kinship terms, although terminologies often extend to members of the village as a whole).

In terminology, we find the emphasis on the unilineal principle, generation and age. There is an emphasis on patrilineal descent and patripotestal authority among most groups.

The village is the most important territorial unit. But territorial relations extend beyond the village on various different bases, such as democratic federation of villages under a superior council, connection with a hierarchy of administrative towns, network of markets, and relationships through marriage, ties of caste, and participation in religious fairs and pilgrimages. Territories organized under such varied principles make up a complex interpenetrating country-wide network.

We have already spoken about intensive specialization of crafts and the existence of full-time traders. There is similar specialization in political roles within the feudal setting which touches the village. Religious aspects of culture demand the service of various specialists, e.g., priests (for usual life cycle rites and festivals), astrologers, genealogists, sadhus of repute and also medicine men or *ojhas*. Among such specialists, we may also mention teachers belonging to traditional schools.

Intricate stratification into hierarchically arranged, endogamous castes whose ranking refers itself to the classical ideal pattern of four orders or *varnas* is evident; while specific rank as a caste within a region seems to be determined by a combination of the following objective factors: relative economic position, especially with reference to land holding, relative political dominance, relative numerical strength, and symbolic validation in ritual habits in relation to the Great Tradition.

Besides caste ranking, there are also other principles of stratification current in society, e. g. ranking in terms of wealth or economic class, political class, political power and literary education. These various principles of stratification largely overlap and partially interpenetrate, making the overall ranking system extremely complicated.

Although secular leadership is provided with direct and indirect ritual sanctions, the two functionaries, secular and religious, are clearly differentiated. Here we often find a combination of democratic leadership by elders and direct control by the feudal aristocracy from the top, with its centre at the capital township, having its court of justice as final reference of law and order, supported by a police force and military reserve.

4.1.1. *Ideological System—Tribals—Supernaturalism* : The pantheon consists of one Sun God and a lower hierarchy of gods. Next to the Sun God, the important deities are village tutelary gods and ancestral spirits. Almost of equal importance are some nature spirits, for example, the spirits of the hills and the presiding deities of the waters.

Gods are conceived of as powerful beings. They are classified into two classes, namely, those who are habitually friendly or benevolent, and those who are malevolent. But even the benevolent gods are not considered to be repositories of ethical qualities. Gods do not necessarily demand noble or generous action from their devotee; they demand only personal loyalty.

Supernatural rites are explicitly directed towards happiness and security in this world, abundance of crops and children and avoidance of sickness and death being the supreme considerations.

There is no concept of " heaven " or " hell " or of rewards or punishments for moral or immoral acts. The soul is called back to join the ancestral spirits in the sacred domestic tabernacle. The soul turns into a malevolent spirit only in the case of an unnatural death.

There is a belief in reincarnation and transmigration of souls into various forms of life, namely, trees, birds, animals, etc. But there is no connection between ethical action and the form of reincarnation. The concept of reincarnation is not arranged in an ascending hierarchy of superior forms of life (as traditionally determined), nor is reincarnation considered inevitable.

No idol or temple in well-defined form is found; athough we do find rudiments of idolatry in the worship of unworked stones and also rudiments of the concept of the temple in the institution of the sacred grove. There is, however, no erection of a house for the deity among most of these tribes.

Animal sacrifice is an essential part of rituals, and magic and witchcraft predominate.

4·1·2·1. *Some Aspects of Value System and World Views—Man-Nature* : The natural universe is charged with impersonal and personalized supernatural power. The natural universe is significantly continuous with the human world of sentiments and social integration. Thus man, nature, and the supernatural are connected in terms of intimate relationship. (This is true with reference to both tribal and non-tribal Hindu peasant communities).

4·1·2·2. *Man-Man* : The human universe is practically limited to the tribe or, at the most, extends to a few local ethnic groups having long standing traditional symbiotic relationship. Equality and reciprocity are emphasised in human relationship. Morality of social action is always judged in terms of corporate kinship or territorial reference groups. Elders are respected. There is significant male dominance in social life, and the desire for children is strong. The good life is conceived of as a life with ample scope for indulgence in pleasure, while maintaining social obligations to corporate group or groups. We find little emphasis on cautious accumulation of wealth at the cost of pleasure.

4·2·1. *Hindu Peasantry—Supernaturalism* : This is a combination of monotheism, pantheism and polytheism. Sun worship is a very important element of Brahmanical tradition; although the Sun God is not regarded as the Supreme Being or *Bhagavan*.

The pantheon is much more elaborate in peasant Hinduism, which has some limited access to written sacred literature. It contains some of the gods of the Great Indian Tradition, as well as local spirits and deities. Reverence for mountains, ancestral spirits and village tutelary spirits is an important element in peasant Hinduism. The peasant is accustomed to classifying his gods with special reference to caste, village, lineage, family and individual, each unit having its special presiding deity.

In peasant Hinduism, magical or power connotation of the deities predominates. But, in addition, there is an emergent overtone of the gods occasionally standing for high ethical quality, *dharma*, rewarding moral behaviour and punishing sinful or immoral behaviour. When he uses the term " religious " (*dharmika*), the villager may mean a rather mechanistic concept of one who observes the traditional rituals correctly. But there is also a parallel concept of one leading a generous and selfless life, not speaking untruth, being above greed, and so on. It is believed such moral behaviour is favoured by the gods, and is also good for the soul.

Along with the predominance of concern about happiness in terms of material prosperity and health in the world, there is also a pragmatic concern about a similar kind of happiness in the other world. Austerity and renunciation are directed towards this goal.

The concepts of " heaven " and " hell " are very important. Belief in reincarnation is highly systematized through the concept of an ascending series of forms, and is loaded with ethical connotation; the form of reincarnation being determined by the ethical value of an action.

Both temples and idolatry are very important. Animal sacrifice forms an essential part of the rituals of many sects; while abstention from killing of all kinds is associated integrally with other sects. There is a predominance of magic and witchcraft.

4·2·2·1. *Some Aspect of Value Systems and World Views* : Same as in 4·1·2·1.

4·2·2·2. *Man-Man*: The human universe, after accentuation of narrow range social affiliations like lineage, local group or village, caste, and so on, expands outwards to encompass the state or even farther. Superordination and subordination is the keynote of social interaction. The morality of social action is usually judged in terms of corporate kinship territorial, or other reference groups. Respect for elders is even more intense than in the case of the tribals, this being specially so among upper castes. Male dominance is even more marked among most groups, and the desire for children is strong. Tribal hedonism is mixed with a cautious concern for economic prosperity through strenuous and steady labour, the latter attitude being supported by the puritanical streak of abstention that we find in supernaturalism.

5. Aspirational, Impressionistically, we can state that relative to the peasantry, the level of aspiration among tribal communities is comparatively lower. Even within the bounds of indigenous civilization, the peasant's world view is affected by ideals coming from the elite of the city, creating in him the desire for more land and wealth, more political power, superior social status for his family, lineage, or caste group, artistic and intellectual excellence which is recognized by an expanded audience, and so on. These surplus desires hit the peasant's mind, which is otherwise marked by a relatively passive acceptance of what he is.

5·1. *The Common Denominators* : A cursory review of the above comparison reveals significant elements of continuity between non-Hindu peasant socio-cultural systems. Among these may be mentioned the following:

Economy : Emphasis is on local self-sufficiency, with barter as an important element in trade, corporate kinship reference in economy, and symbiotic relationship with ethnic groups.

Social Structure : " Caste " and " tribe " have almost identical structural features as social units, with a belief in common descent and endogamy, exogamous clans segmented into functional lineages, a tempered classificatory kinship terminology whose maximum limit of applicability is set by the maximal lineage; relative age and generation are very important in the kinship system; the village is the most important territorial unit; there is patrilineal and patripotestal emphasis (in most cases), and finally democracy in leadership.

Ideological System : (1) Supernaturalism : There exists a polytheism, belief in a supreme being, pantheon including village tutelary gods, ancestral spirits, spirits of the hills and waters, belief in reincarnation, corporate social reference in religion; pragmatic considerations of fertility in crops and women, and avoidance of sickness, rule supreme in rituals and animal sacrifice. (2) Value-system and world-view : The natural universe is charged with personal and impersonal supernatural powers; it is contiguous with the human world of sentiments and social interactions; there is respect for elders, desire for children, male dominance in social life, and an underlying hedonism.

One question, however, arises in the pursuits of common denominators : to what extent is their commonness " apparent " or " real "? How can we be sure, for example, whether animal sacrifice, trasmigration and reincarnation of the soul and the like have the same meaning in the two cultural systems under comparison? It is the contention of the writer that while a final definite answer cannot be given to such queries in the present state of our knowledge, existing literature and the writer's ethnographic field experience point to the plausibility of such a comparison.

Many of the earlier students of tribal culture in India were aware of this fact of continuity, especially in the field of religion. Risley described Hinduism as " animism more or less transformed by philosophy, " or as " magic tempered by metaphysic, " and finally expressed the opinion that, " No sharp line of demarcation can be drawn between Hinduism and animism (i.e., tribal religions). The one shades away insensibly into other. " E. A. Gait, Census Commissioner of 1911, found it extremely difficult " to say at what stage a man should be regarded as having become Hindu, " J. J. Marten, Census Commissioner of 1921, observes : " There is little to distinguish in the religious attitude of an aboriginal Gond or Bhil from that of a number of lower Hindu castes. Both are essentially animistic. " Verrier Elwin suggests that all the aboriginal tribes except those of Assam " should be classed in the census returns as Hindu by religion as their religion belongs to the Hindu family. "

Reviewing previous comments on the cultural position of the aboriginal tribes of central India, Ghurye remarks:

It is clear from this discussion that the proper description of these peoples must refer itself to their place in or near Hindu society......... while sections of these tribes are properly integrated in the Hindu society, very large sections, in fact the bulk of them, are rather loosely assimilated. Only very small recesses of hills and depths of forests have not been more than touched by Hindusim. Under the circumstances, the only proper description of the people is that they are imperfectly integrated classes of Hindu society. Though for the sake of convenience they may be designated as tribal classes of Hindu society, suggesting thereby that they retained much more of the tribal creeds and organizations than many of the castes of Hindu society, yet in reality they are backward Hindus.

6. *The Emergent Aspects* : Now let us summarily isolate and list the " discontinuous " or " emergent " aspects in peasant cultures.

Economy : Intensive agriculture is the basis of economy, with an incentive towards accumulation of capital, a currency and intricate network of markets tied finally to commercial towns, multiple specialization of roles in production, emergence of the specialist trader group, and the differential possession of wealth leading to economic stratification.

Social Structure : There is a highly formalised stratification, more complex specialization of social roles, widening of social roles, widening of social ties involving multi-ethnic groups, interpenetrative network of territorial structure, tied to townships and cities, priestly class and literate, and the presence of formal educational institutions.

Ideological System : (1) Supernaturalism : There exist idol worship and temples, and organized priestly class moral connotation of supernaturalism with concepts of sin, heaven, and hell, and reference to a written sacred tradition. (2) Value system and world view : Emphasis is placed on superordination and subordination in social life. There is an intensive supernaturally oriented drive for moral life supported by puritanical concepts of asceticism and renunciation, and the human universe extending beyond caste, lineage or local group.

Among the above emergent items a surplus economy based on settled agriculture, the development of social stratification, and the growth of ethical religion, appear to have been most comprehensive in scope.

7. *The Transitional Aspects* : We should also note some of the transitional elements in tribal cultures in the direction of our general characterization of the peasant level of culture. In economy, for example, we find a tendency towards full-time specialization in the following crafts : basketmaking, smithery, rope-making and weaving. We also find interethnic exchange of goods and services in the aboriginal setting, for example, the case of the Birhor and the Ho, and also of the Kota, Kurumba, Badaga, and Toda. In social structure, we spoke of some tendencies towards stratification, defined by the factors of relative numerical strength, priority of arrival, ritual purity, and so on. We also found

tendencies towards feudalization of leadership among the Bhumij and the Munda.

In supernaturalism, however, we cannot identify elements of transition from " ethnically neutral supernaturalism " to " ethical supernaturalism. "

APPRAISAL

G. S. GHURYE

THE PROBLEMS and ills of the tribals may be grouped under two categories. The first category is formed by those problems which, like those of new habits, language, and shifting cultivation, are peculiar to some or many of them, and are not common to other classes of Indian population. In the second category are comprised such problems as arise from the inroads of the British system of law and revenue on their solidarity, from the forest laws, and from the loss of their land as the combined result of the British system and the rapacity of the money-lending classes. The latter kind of problems, at least many of them, these people share in common with other classes of Indian population. They are also far more important to their very existence than the problems of the first category, which in comparison may be regarded as minor ills.

One such ill peculiar to many of the tribals is that they have begun to take to more spacious clothing than they were formerly accustomed to. Though they have begun to don this civilized clothing, they are not aware of, or cannot afford, or do not practise civilized hygiene thereof. The result is that some of them have begun to suffer from skin troubles and such other diseases. It appears to us that this ill is rather made too much of. That some clothing in addition to the meagre apparel of their tribal existence is quite necessary for some of them will be admitted by all who know that in their habitat it is frosty cold in some months of the year. That they themselves feel the rigour of their climate is clear from the fact that they sleep just near a burning fire in their huts. We are not convinced that the evil of clothing is greater than the evil of sleeping in an ill-ventilated hut with a fairly big fire burning in it. Even supposing that skin diseases are being spread by the adopted clothing, it is so because these people do not carry out the regular washing of clothes which they require. They can pick up the practice of regularly washing their clothes much more easily from the same source from which Mr. Grigson believes they have adopted the habit of putting on additional clothing, i.e., by their contact with the population of the plains. Mr. Grigson himself tells us how both the Hill Marias and the Bison-Horn Marias are changing their habits about washing their bodies and their hair and are getting cleaner as a result of their contact with the plains people.

These minor ills like clothing, housing, etc., can be righted through the same agency that has given rise to them and not by segregating the people.

Another partial problem and hardship is in connection with the practice of shifting cultivation. There are some tribes like the Birhors, the Korwas, the Baigas, and the Khonds, which have not yet taken to plough-cultivation. In the case of some, like the Birhors, the Korwas, and the Khonds, no attempt at settling them as plough-culturists was ever seriously made till almost nineteen-twenties. It does not appear that they have any religious belief to prevent their being properly settled if a sympathetic attempt is made in that direction. The Baigas are perhaps the only fortunate people who were tried to be turned to plough-culture through encouragement and special help. They were also shown special consideration by the reservation of an area of about twenty-two thousand acres wherein they have been allowed to carry on their shifting cultivation under certain conditions. The problem of the Baigas is, however, complicated by their belief that to plough the land is to lacerate the breast of mother earth, which brings upon the people the wrath of the gods.

How the problem of keeping these people contented should be solved, depends not only on the feelings of the Baigas, though they ought to be given an important place in the formulation of any solution, but also to a large measure on the findings of science regarding the consequences of shifting cultivation. We have already quoted authorities to show the natural economic importance of the forests of the central belt. Forsyth long ago suggested that all " treatment irksome to their wild and timid nature which is not necessitated by the general requirements of the country " should be avoided. Dr. Elwin quotes this opinion with evident approval. We think the suggestion is broad and sound enough to be adopted as a general principle in administration of backward peoples.

The question turns on the view one takes of the effects of shifting cultivation in the present instance. That the region is valuable is not to be doubted. If it can be established beyond doubt that shifting cultivation does not cause significant damage to the forests or to the surrounding plains, then, doctrinaire uplift apart, there is no rational ground for causing these people hardship by forbidding them their practice of shifting cultivation. Dr. Elwin has tried to prove that with proper precautions the practice of shifting cultivation is almost innocuous. Mr. Grigson has added some further support, from a book on soil erosion, to the contention that shifting cultivation does no harm to the soil. He has also pointed out that in the tract in which the Baiga Chak—reservation for the Baigas—is located, it is the only form of cultivation likely to give fair means of subsistence to them. The soil is so poor that without heavy manuring or the burning of the branches as is done in the other or Gond variety of shifting cultivation, the cultivators are not likely to get even fair crops. After detailing the difficulties of raising proper crops in the soil at their disposal, he observes: " The only alternative appears to be the burning of forest-growth and raising of crops in the ashes. At least the Baiga is not being taught how otherwise to raise crops, either by the Forest, or much less, by the Agriculture Department. " He, therefore, recommends that contentment of the Baigas should be restored and preserved by giving them adequate facilities for shifting cultivation, which, in his opinion, can be done " without harm to any valuable forest. "

This is a subject on which the views of an anthropologist or an ordinary administrator, however intelligent, cannot be regarded as the final word, which must lie with forestry experts. Dr. N. L. Bor, Forest Botanist in the Forest Research Institute at Dehra Dun, in his presidential address to the section on Botany of the Indian Science Congress, 1942, observes: " Of all practices initiated by man the most noxious is that of shifting cultivation. " A writer in *Nature* reviewing the " Report of Forest Administration in the Province of Assam for the year 1940-41, " calls shifting cultivation " that most wasteful of agricultural methods. " In view of this fresh indictment of shifting cultivation from competent quarters, it is difficult to accept the argument and the statement of Messers. Elwin and Grigson regarding its harmlessness.

Even Dr. Hutton in his writing published between the two publications of Dr. Elwin, observes: " Obviously the practice of *bewar* (shifting cultivation) is uneconomic and detrimental to the interests of the Indian community as a whole, except perhaps in certain limited areas and under conditions of strict control. " On the whole, therefore, till the experts can assure us about the harmlessness of shifting cultivation we must look upon it as rather dangerous to the general life of the community of which the Baigas, the Gonds, the Khonds, etc., form a part.

The question of reserving certain forest areas for the use of the Baigas or others so that they may practise their favourite method of shifting cultivation, must be considered with great circumspection. The probable effect of that method on the peoples themselves, as well as the extent of area proposed to be set apart and the future of the other population in the area, all become relevant considerations.

A large number of the tribes, the Santals, the Mundas, the Oraons, the Khonds, the Gonds, the Korkus, speak languages which either belong to the Kherwari or Mundari group of languages or to the Dravidian family, and are, more often than not, different from the languages of the plains people among whom they have their being or with whom they have a large amount of social intercourse. The languages of the latter in most cases belong to the Indo-Aryan family. Many of these tribes, though they have preserved their tribal languages, can and very often do employ the Indo-Aryan languages of the surrounding people in their routine intercourse. Many of them thus are bi-lingual, having their own mother-tongue and having more or less acquired the language of the neighbouring people. There are others, like the Baigas, who have taken up the Indo-Aryan tongue of the locality in place of their own language, whatever it might have been. Others like the Bhils speak languages which are dialects of the local languages. In all cases the languages spoken by the so-called aborigines were till recently only spoken tongues and had no scripts of their own. Needless to say, they have had no literature, the only kind of it being what is known as folk-literature, viz., folk-songs and folk-tales. There is some poetry enshrined in some of the folk-songs. Whether the poetry is of high value or not, naturally these folk-songs make a strong appeal to the aborigines who have been accustomed from their childhood to listen to and to chant their tunes.

Christian missions, when they began to work among these people, felt the need of reducing their languages to writing in order to spread the gospel among them through their languages. The missionaries therefore prepared grammars for some of them after a close study of the spoken tongues, and wrote the languages in the Roman script. Sir Richard Temple noted in 1866 that some thought that the Devanagari alphabet would afford much better means of conveying the sounds of the words of the Gondi and other dialects, though they were being written in the Roman script. Though the missionaries benefited these people by providing grammars for their languages, they have placed them under a disadvantage by adopting the Roman script for writing them, so long as the neighbouring peoples use the Devanagari script for their languages, or in a very few cases the Telugu script. If the so-called aborigines have to learn to write the languages of their neighbours, they have to master two scripts, the Roman for their tribal language and the Devanagari for their language of social intercourse outside the tribal world. Those of them who can proceed to higher education, will find compensation for the pains they took in learning the Roman script. But the percentage of such is bound to be small. The large majority of the learners then are loaded with an unnecessary burden at the initial stage when, in order that education may spread among them, handicaps and difficulties should not be more than the irreducible minimum. This is the case if the so-called aborigines have to learn the languages of their neighbours. Dr. Hutton sees great use for them in such learning. All those who do not subscribe to the doctrine of segregation and no change, will admit the great urgency of these people learning to write the languages of their neighbours, so that they will be able to carry on their dealings with the plains people free from one of the disadvantages they have suffered from.

That the preservation of so many uncultivated languages is not very desirable should be granted by those who have to carry on the administration.

It is seen that as the so-called aborigines live amidst people using languages different from and more highly developed than their own tribal languages, it is desirable to teach them these languages, if they are to hold their own in the routine intercourse of life which they have to carry on with the non-aboriginals. It is also clear that many administrative difficulties are solved if the language of the schools in any tract is the same as the language generally used therein. It is further noticeable that in the opinion of many there is very little of value to be preserved in the tribal languages.

The solution is based on the view that the tribal languages must be looked upon as only a means to an end. The end to be achieved is speedy and effective spread of education among the so-called aborigines. Only the no-changers, who desire to segregate the tribals from the neighbouring people and to preserve them in their traditional stage of culture, will object to this end. Others will acclaim it as one of the most potent instruments of helping the so-called aborigines to live a life of comparative comfort and self-respect. To achieve this end, the tribal languages may be used, wherever the conditions make their use imperative, even as media of instruction, so that the so-called aborigines may be attracted to the schools and may derive real benefit from them. Two more or less sure results will ensue. First, very soon the so-called aborigines will show a tendency to modify some traits of their culture, and gradually they will effect a change therein. Second, they will drop their tribal languages and will adopt, in the largest number of cases, the Indo-Aryan languages which, as instruments of expression, are more highly evolved than their own languages and possess a varied literature. To have the use of a highly developed language and to be served by a varied literature is a privilege which not all people possess. All well-wishers of the so-called aboriginal people must look forward with hope and enthusiasm to the time when they can be placed in a position to enjoy these benefits.

It must be very plainly stated here that this is not a political view of the language-problem of the so-called aborigines. It is a perfectly orthodox anthropological point of view, especially as the cultural affinities of these people, through the possession of common substratum and the cultural interaction with their neighbours over a long period, are so great. In order to add to this view the weight of higher authority, we shall quote a few sentences from Dr. R. R. Marett's chapter on Language in his book called *Anthropology*. He says: " If there is a moral to this chapter, it must be that, whereas it is the duty of the civilized overlords of primitive folk to leave them their old institutions so far as they are not directly prejudicial to their gradual advancement in culture, since to lose touch with one's home-world is for the savage to lose heart altogether and die; yet this consideration hardly applies at all to the native language. If the tongue of an advanced people can be substituted, it is for the good of all concerned."

Tribal solidarity has been broken by two distinct agencies. Hinduism and its assimilative process has broken up and is breaking up various tribes, sections of which seek and acquire some nook or corner in the Hindu social world. This leaves the section, not so absorbed, rather weak and smarting or benumbed under the feeling of brokenness. If sections of tribes get assimilated in the Hindu fold they are not ushered into an altogether strange social world. Hindu castes, at least many of them, have had and still have many of the characteristics of tribal society as regards the management of their internal affairs. Tribal sections on joining Hindu society develop an internal organization of the caste pattern, and thus have the regulating and controlling power within themselves. The account given elsewhere, shows clearly that many of such tribal sections or tribes get smugly settled in the Hindu fold. Others not so fortunate strive for a proper status, and, in the effort at stabilization, they better themselves. The sections of tribes which have been left over do suffer from the loss of their brethren, but that is an inevitable consequence of a process which is natural, and which,if it can be shorn of the ugly feature of chicanery regarding land and labour, on the whole, is beneficial to the tribal people. Of course it disrupted their pristine homogeneity and unity.

But a more disruptive inroad on tribal solidarity was made by the introduction of the British rule. The collection of revenue, the establishment of the central police system, and of the judicial system have all contributed to the deterioration of the authority of tribal elders, and have established the practice of seeking escape from tribal authority through resort to British Courts. No longer the same sense of dependence on the tribe and the consequent respect for its corporate opinion are felt in the old way. That the British system of centralized administration has directly or indirectly contributed to the break-up of tribal solidarity is quite true. But this effect of the British rule in India has not been felt only by the so-called aborigines. The British system of law undermined the old sovereignty of Hindu castes, diminishing the authority of caste panchayats, and encouraging individual members of caste to seek redress for their wrongs in British courts of justice. If the system has not broken the solidarity of caste as quickly and as much as it might have done, it is because of other factors that have come into play. And the inroads on caste-sovereignty would have been much more welcome than they have been but for that fact that the agency, which operated against the solidarity of caste, has still more affected the corporate sense of life of the village. The collection of revenue over a large part of the country directly from individual proprietors, the introduction of central police system to which the village headman was subordinated, weaning him away from the village community, tended to foster individualistic tendencies in place of the sense of corporate life in the village community. Far-seeing and sympathetic administrators had protested against the introduction of the particular revenue system as well as the centralized police system. They had even pointed out the need for continuing the corporate life of the village community, which some of them had found in certain parts of the country operating more or less vigorously. Some of them even succeeded in retaining some independence for the village headman. Some judicial functions of the village panchayat were continued in truncated fashion. But the total effect was that life departed from the village community. General realization of the great harm done did not dawn on the British administrators till it was borne in upon them by the rude shock of the Deccan riots. Since then, however, tardy and half-hearted attempts were made from time to time to infuse life into the all but dead rural institutions of the past. During the last twenty years or so even more serious attempts have been made. Today it is generally recognized that the creation of a sense of corporate existence in the small local units of the Indian leviathan is a task of first-rate national importance.

Break-up of the solidarity of tribal life, which has come about through the operation of the British system of revenue and justice, is thus only one aspect of the general result, and not a peculiar phenomenon confined to the so-called aborigines. The problem created affects the larger whole and is different from the general problem of infusing a corporate sense in the local units not in kind but only in degree. It is, therefore, best tried to be solved along with the general problem. The obvious method of artificially segregating the so-called aborigines may prove to be a retrograde step rather than a solution affording scope for progress.

But the forest policy followed by British administrators in India has entailed hardships not only on the so-called aborigines but also on the settled villagers. Villages along the foot of the hills which are forested have depended and do depend upon forest produce for their complete economy. The forests adjoining the village are the natural grazing grounds for the cattle of the agriculturists, who resort to them also for collecting cowdung and firewood. The manure of the village fields is provided by the cow-dung, dry leaves, and dry wood to be procured from the forests.

Introduction of forest conservancy has meant, more often than not, very severe curtailment, if not entire stoppage, of customary rights, on the exercise of which depends agricultural prosperity. Such grievances of the agriculturists were voiced before the authorities. The non-tribal cultivators, too, have a number of grievances against the forest policy, which are connected with a vital aspect of their economy. Here, again, the problem of the so-called aborigines is not entirely different from that of the non-tribal population. It is desirable that the problems created by certain aspects of the forest policy should be considered as a whole, and a solution, giving the maximum relief to all concerned, be accepted.

In certain areas inhabited by the so-called aborigines, they are required by custom to render some compulsory labour for their landlords at such times as may be decided upon by the latter. It has been found that the chief trouble of such labour, apart from the economic loss it involves to the person whose labour is thus demanded, is that it becomes a source of vexation.

The problem created by the demand for compulsory labour is not one which is peculiar to the so-called aborigines. The system is older than the British rule in India. " Compulsory labour in the interests of the village community has been in existence in some form or other in nearly every part of India. " Describing the forms of rent paid by certain tenants to their landlords in the United Provinces, Dr. S. S. Nehru points out that the rent paid by the low-caste tenants was pitched lower than the fair rent on the understanding that the tenant, known as *razil*, would provide manual labour. He speaks of this compulsory labour, which may be paid at traditional rather than market rates of wages, as labour rent. Chamar tenants in Chattisgarh have to render similar service to their landlords.

Another evil besetting the tribals is that of bonded labour. This system consists in a person agreeing to serve out a loan he may take from a money-lender, a landlord or not. Though money-loans are small in amount, the manipulation of accounts is so arranged as to require the debtor to spend his life-time as a bondman, and not infrequently even his son may be found paying out his father's debt by similar service. Bonded labour is not restricted to the tribals. Agricultural labourers in certain parts of the Bombay Presidency, and large numbers of such labourers in the Madras Presidency, work under a system which Dr. Pillai characterizes as agrestic serfdom. The system of advancing money for purposes of marriage to a domestic or farm servant on the understanding or undertaking that he will pay it off by serving his creditor is fairly widespread on Bombay side. Bonded labour is not a unique feature of tribal life, but is to be met with very often where lower castes of suitable status are available. The *Kami-auti* system of Bihar appears to be not confined to the tribal tracts. Under that system cultivation is practically carried on by serfs. One of its causes, or perhaps the principal cause, is that a man, among these castes, has to pay for a wife. Owing to the poverty of the people the amount to be paid as brideprice can only be raised by borrowing. If the creditors were honest, the system would solve a vital problem of life for the poor people of working capacity without causing them serious hardship. As it is, the evil is fairly common, and to be successfully eradicated requires to be handled wherever it exists.

Economic servitude is not confined to agriculture, but is also met with in small artisan industries. Artisans in certain crafts take the raw materials and wherewithal for their subsistence from capitalists in advance, and contract to hand over the manufactured articles for sale to the creditor. The system works in such a way that "the debt is practically irredeemable, and the artisan is transferred from capitalist to capitalist in a manner which practically amounts to sale and purchase." It should be particularly noticed that the honesty and the ignorance of law, so often attributed to the so-called aborigines, are not altogether unknown in the agricultural and artisan sections of the population. The Royal Commissioners on Indian Agriculture observe: "The crushing burden of hereditary debt remains largely through ignorance of the legal position which is that no personal liability is transmitted and that no suit lies against the heirs of a deceased debtor except to the extent to which the property of the deceased has come into their hands by survivorship or succession."

There is another type of compulsory labour which the so-called aborigines are called upon to render. Government officers touring over the forest and hill areas can demand such labour from the people for carrying their personal luggage and such other work. They can also in some parts require the people to work on mending roads, etc., in the remote areas where regular labour is not likely to be available. For all such labour the labourer is to be paid at a certain rate which is generally lower than the market rate, and which is sometimes not paid by the petty servants of the State who exact it from the people. Such labour, if properly paid for, cannot be looked upon entirely as a tyranny. Generally such labour is expected and necessary for touring officers. A Bombay Committee, so late as 1930, received complaints that forced and unpaid labour was exacted from the members of the Depressed Classes and Aboriginal Tribes. Dishonesty and tyranny of lower servants of the State, which make compulsory labour the evil it is, perhaps press more heavily on the tribal people, to which such high officials as Dr. Hutton and Mr. Grigson have testified, the people being much more ignorant than the low castes of Hindu society, and occupying localities which may not be visited by higher officials for a long time, than on other sections of rural population; but it cannot be said that the latter are entirely free from such experience. The true remedy for this evil lies in the field of administration. If the whole administrative machinery is tuned up higher, if the practice of dishonesty comes to be detected and then severely punished, then only the people, whether tribal or non-tribal, will be properly treated by the lower staff. The idea that servants of the State are the masters of the people has become strongly rooted in the whole machinery, the lower staff only venturing to put it into open practice in out-of-way places. The essential feature of the evil of compulsory labour exacted by Government servants is thus a part of a larger problem, which is general rather than peculiar to the tribals.

The most important and general feature of the life of the people, as must be clear from the account of their doings and of the views of a number of writers given above, is that they get into debt, and that because of their simple nature and ignorance of law their debts increase beyond bounds. The classes which lend them the money take full advantage of the situation. The rights of transfer of property in land conferred by the British system of law and revenue make it possible for the tribals to be manoeuvred into selling their land to non-tribal landlords or money-lenders. Thus their lands pass on to the non-tribals. They become landless labourers. In a number of cases the headman is changed or his land bought in the same fashion, and the people suffer at the hands of the non-tribal headman.

The process of land passing from the hands of the cultivating classes into those of non-cultivating ones, who become absentee landlords, having little sympathy with the problems of their tenantry, is a feature noticeable in almost all parts of India, from the third quarter of the 19th century. For example, the money-lenders have " ousted numbers of improvident proprietors of the cultivating castes and many of them have become large landlords " in the Central Provinces. The part played by the British system of law and revenue in this process is fully recognized by the writers on the subject. Prof. D. R. Gadgil thus summarizes the situation: " The British had given rights of free transfer and absolute ownership—especially in the ' raytwari ' tracts—to the cultivators which they had never possessed before. Again the judicial system which had been adopted gave the money-lender a great power over his debtor, and finally the Limitation Act, making the renewal of the debt bond in short periods compulsory, made the position of the debtor much worse. Thus, though there was nothing in the nature of a peculiar hardship in the mere fact of an agriculturist being indebted, these other causes acting in concert had reduced the debtor, in many cases, to the position of a virtual serf. ......The ease with which the money could be recovered through the courts, had made the money-lender more ready to lend. The process had gone on during the period of prosperity, and the cultivator was quite oblivious of where he was going, but as soon as the reaction came and the money-lender began to tighten his grip on the cultivator's land, his real position was brought home suddenly to the cultivator." We have made this long quotation not only because it describes the position of the agriculturists very truly, but also because it is very reminiscent of the situation, almost in its details, described by Bradley-Birt, S. C. Roy, and others with regard to some of the tribals like the Santals, the Oraons, and the Mundas. And we venture to go a step further to suggest that the proverbial pessimism and fatalism of the Indian agriculturists is, in part at least, a cognate phenomenon to the " moral depression " sensed by Dr. Hutton, Dr. Elwin and others, among the so-called agorigines.

Sir Theodore Morison quotes the following remark made in 1869 by an observant officer: " The tendency of our rule has been greatly to increase the insecurity of the cultivator's tenure. " Discussing the system of land-tenure he speaks of the evil results of unequal competition between the landlord and the tenant which " are not confined to the immediate sufferers, but are necessarily cumulative, and tend permanently to depress and degrade these classes of tenants, so that it is well-nigh impossible for their children ever to remedy their situation. " Russell and Hiralal have observed that the introduction of the English law of contract and transfer of property have worsened the character of the money-lending business by offering a new incentive to and reward for the successful money-lender. Their description of the transaction between the money-lending creditor and the cultivating debtor is worth perusal, as it reminds one of similar description of transactions among the so-called aborigines. They observe: " The debtor signs bond sometimes not even knowing the conditions, more often having heard them, but without any clear idea of their effect or the consequences to himself, and as readily allows it to be registered. When it comes into court, the witnesses, who are the money-lender's creatures, easily prove that it was a genuine and *bona fide* transaction, and the debtor is too ignorant and stupid to be able to show that he did not understand the bargain or that it was unconscionable. In any case the court has little or no power to go beyond a properly executed contract without any actual evidence of fraud, and has no option but to decree it in terms of the deed. " Dr. Vera Anstey quotes the following observation of B. A. Collins, showing the contrast between the pre-British and post-British relative positions of the money-lender and the cultivator. " The institution of Civil Government tends to act as an engine to deprive the cultivator of his holding, and of the profits of cultivation. The verbal contracts of the past and the easy relations with a hardly more literate money-lender have given way to a formed, though one-sided, account-keeping which tends to reduce the more important party to slavery and indigence. "

The Indian landlord, in contrast to his confreres in the more progressive agricultural countries, is known to be more a rent-receiver than a person actively interested in agriculture. The landlord, thus oriented, may employ lessees who generally are strangers to the tenants. In an early report on the settlement of the Moradabad district in the U. P. they are thus characterized: " They have not even the lingering spark of scruple which may sometimes have restrained the rapacity of their principals; they do not know, and they do not care to know, the people; and in their turn they work through a hired agent, with what results it is not difficult to guess." "The effect of this sort of treatment is to impoverish and depress the people." Prof. Gadgil, writing about the conditions in the Deccan prevailing in the third quarter of the 19th century, tells us that the money-lenders, who were acquiring the land of the local cultivators, belonged to the up-country Marwari class. Russell and Hiralal observe that the money-lender in the Central Provinces is a member of a different caste and often of a different country from those of the cultivators and " has no fellow-feeling towards them, and therefore considers the transaction merely from the business point of view of getting as much profit as possible. " He was mainly restrained in these activities by the fact that he was quite often a local resident, though not permanent, and as such was under some salutary influence of public opinion and fear for his own life. But with the rise of large banking houses and consequent use of agents, even this check disappeared. And the slight personal contact that could have existed between the money-lender, though coming from a distant town, and the local cultivator ceased entirely. " The agent looks mainly to his principal, and the latter has no interest in or regard for the cultivators of distant villages. " That this phenomenon of the creditor, having no communal relation with the local cultivator, is very widespread is clear from the following observation of the Royal Commission on Agriculture in India: " That creditor is too often a landlord of a different class who has no natural or historical connection with his estate and is only interested in the immediate exploitation of the property in his control. "

The operation of all the factors ushered in by the British rule, some directly, others indirectly, has led to a large number of the peasant class being reduced to virtual serfdom, toiling away on the land only to hand over the product of their industry to their creditors, who are the legal owners of the land, and piteously waiting for the creditor's gracious bounty to supply the daily needs of their families at the most to a miserable extent.

We have already referred to the position of artisans in certain crafts in connection with bonded labour obtaining among them. Some of them find themselves precisely in the same situation as the agriculturists *vis-a-vis* their creditors. Prof. Gadgil, describing the condition of weavers working on hand-looms in the period of about twenty years before the last war, points out how, while a large proportion of the weavers, working on a bare subsistence wage for the yarn dealer, managed to keep their wretched independence, others were too heavily indebted to the dealers to retain any independence whatever. They had to pledge their very means of production, the looms, and to work for the creditors on piece-work wages.

It must be clear from the above discussion that it has been the fate of a large number of rural workers, whether agriculturists or artisans, as the combined result of various circumstances and forces that have appeared since the advent of British rule in India, to lose their very means of production and thus to be reduced to the position of wage-earners at the mercy of a rather unsympathetic class of middleman or even to that of serfs and helots. There is, therefore, nothing very peculiar to themselves in the identical condition of the so-called aborigines respecting the loss of their lands and the resultant loss of independence.

Honesty shown by the tribals in their transactions has its counterpart among the cultivators in regard not only to the acknowledgement of debt but also to the non-utilization of certain provisions of the special legislation in order to escape easily from the debt. About the use of the facility provided in the Deccan Agriculturists' Relief Act for a cultivator to get himself declared insolvent under certain conditions, Prof. Gadgil observes: "It is a striking proof of the honesty of the peasant that this provision was very rarely resorted to."

The evils arising from the operation of some laws seem to have attracted the attention of the British administrators in India fairly early. Dr. Pillai thinks that the earliest attempt to remedy some of the evils was made after the pattern suggested in Mills' work, the Bengal Rent Act (x) of 1859 being the first of its kind. Since then various laws were enacted in the different Provinces and by the Central Government to safeguard the interests of large landed estates and of tenants and landholders. Among other things legislation has sought (i) to prevent large landed estates of zamindars from passing into the hands of others through mismanagement, (ii) to secure the tenant in his tenure and the landholder in his land and to prevent the land held by tenants or owned by farmers from passing into the hands of non-cultivating classes, and (iii) to prevent debts of agriculturists becoming excessive through high rates of interest and practice of chicanery.

The second set of laws seeks mainly to secure a tenant in the tenure of his land and a landholder from exploitation, and generally speaking to prevent land passing out of the hands of the cultivating classes. It comprises principally the Tenancy Acts, the Land Alienation Acts, and the

Redemption of Mortgages Acts. Here and there, the same purpose is sought to be achieved through restricted tenures under the provisions of the Land Revenue Code. This type of legislation, except for the Bengal Tenancy Act, came into operation a little later among the non-tribal than among the tribal agriculturists. But once begun, it has gone almost with unabating speed. The Deccan Agriculturists' Relief Act of 1879 is generally considered to be the archetype of most of the legislation for the stabilization of the agriculturists. Its provisions appear to be comprehensive, even providing " a special machinery to render cheap and summary justice to the rayats. " It made possible an investigation of transactions between the agriculturists and the creditors, and empowered the courts to so manage as to avoid the sale of land of the debtor. As a last resort it provided for insolvency being granted to the agriculturist. Yet the main object of the Act is described to have been " to put the relations between agriculturists and money-lenders on a better footing. " Therefore the Bengal Tenancy Act of 1865, which was an amendment of the Tenancy Act of 1859, must be considered to be the earliest law safeguarding the interests of tenants in the lands held or occupied by them. The Punjab Land Alienation Act of 1900, however, has been the charter of the small landholder and of the cultivating classes, as against the non-agriculturists, money-lenders, and others and it has inspired similar legislation in other Provinces. The third group of laws is represented by the Agriculturists ' Relief Acts, the Usurious Loans Act, the the Debtors' Relief Acts, and the Money Lenders' Act. The principal aim of these Acts has been to prevent unnecessary and excessive indebtedness among the agriculturists through, among various devices, regulating the rate of interest. Indirectly, of course, they are meant to prevent loss of land to the agriculturist-debtors. Laws in the second category, too, many times provide for the recognition of only a reasonable rate of interest. The Deccan Agriculturists ' Relief Act properly belongs to the third category of legislation. Prof. Gadgil observes: "Looked at retrospectively, the D. A. R. Act is in the main a rural Money Lenders' Act. "

Protection through preventing high rates of interest being charged and through making difficult alienation of land in favour of creditors, money-lenders and non-cultivating classes is, at best, only negative or restrictive as long as the need for raising loans and other associated problems of agriculture remain as they are. Positive or constructive protection of agriculturists must attempt to solve their problem of getting easy credit to such an extent as is within their reasonable powers to bear the burden of, without taxing their capacity for suffering or production. Of the various methods of such positive or constructive protection, three have been so far attempted in India. First, the existing amount of debt, which is generally found to be depressingly heavy, must either be scaled down or liquidated. Leaving aside the early experiment in Bengal and the provisions of the Deccan Agriculturists' Relief Act, the first scheme of conciliation of debt was tried in the Central Provinces between 1897 and 1912.

Many of the laws classed in the third category above included provisions for conciliation and scaling down of debts. In addition, Debts Conciliation Acts, too, specially exist for this purpose. Second, to provide easy credit and enable the agriculturists to tide over certain bad periods, co-operative movement and the land mortgage banks have been fostered since 1904. Third, the State has taken up the positive duty and function of helping cultivators with the funds of the State under certain conditions. As early as 1793 Regulations were issued providing for *taccavi* advances for certain purposes. Under the Land Improvement Loans Act of 1883 and the Agriculturists' Loans Act of 1884, Local Government can, and do, advance loans at reasonable or rather low rate of interest to the agriculturists either to carry out certain improvements to their lands or to tide over periods of distress or to purchase seed or cattle, etc.

It is seen from the above discussion that both legislation and practice in regard to the safeguarding of the interests of a large section of the non-tribal agricultural population are very similar to those described above in the history of the protection of the so-called aborigines. In the literature on the subject the cultivators are, more often than not, described as ignorant and improvident. The problem regarding land and its proper cultivation is very largely the same for a large section, of our population, whether aboriginal or non-tribal. The bare truth is that there is a large section of our population deriving its subsistence from agricultural pursuits, which is exploited in various possible ways by money-lenders, would-be absentee landlords, rack-renters, and middlemen. All the people who are thus being exploited are really backward. And in the classification of the Education Departments of some Provinces, there figure in the category of backward people many more groups than the so-called aboriginal tribes, leaving aside the Scheduled or Depressed classes.

That the problems of some of the non-aboriginal people are more or less similar to those of the so-called aborigines is appreciated by some administrators, is clear from the grouping of the two together by the Bihar Government in showing the percentage of the advanced to the backward peoples in some of the districts in its proposal for treating them as partially excluded tracts. Mr. Tallent's observation, made in 1921, is clear on the point. He says: "What exactly is included in the depressed classes has never been stated, but the term would appear to include a wider range of castes and tribes than the untouchables. If it is taken to include the Hindu 'untouchables' *plus* the Animists *plus* the Hindu members of tribes which are largely Animistic, the total comes to about 10 millions or something less than a third of the population of the Province." Mr. Lacey in 1931 cut out from Mr. Tallents' enumeration some of the untouchable castes and put the number, not of the depressed classes, but of the primitive and semi-primitive people, as roughly seven million or one-sixth of the provincial population. The Bombay Government has been giving away some of the land at its disposal mostly to the members of the so-called aboriginal tribes, in the districts of Khandesh and Thana, and to some specific castes in Kanara under restricted tenure. By 1928 about a million acres were held under this tenure " mostly by members of aboriginal tribes " in the presidency, and " about a million and a half acres in Sind. " The Starte Committee in 1930, finding that land was mainly granted to members of the aboriginal tribes, made a guarded suggestion: " We agree that they have a prior claim to such lands; at the same time we consider that some share of the land should be given to the Depressed Classes, as in many respects their need is greater than that of the Aboriginal Tribes. " The Committee suggested that the category of " Backward Classes " should be formed of three sub-sections, viz., the Depressed Classes, the Aboriginal and Hill Tribes, and other Backward Classes, the last to include wandering tribes. According to the census of 1921 the Depressed Classes numbered about 15 lakhs, the Aboriginal and Hill Tribes a little over 13 lakhs, and the other Backward Classes about 10 and a half lakhs. It proposed that Government should find ways and means to see that land which was changing hands should, instead of being allowed to pass into the hands of the money-lenders or rich classes, " be secured to the members of the Backward Classes or other equally poor persons. " Mr. D. Symington suggests that *all* new land in certain areas should be reserved for members of the Backward Classes and should be granted to the non-tribals on equal terms with the aborigines. There is a considerable population, such as Malhari Kolis, Dhor Kolis, and Mahars, whose condition is similar to that of the so-called aborigines. Mr. Grigson, too, recognizes the similarity of the problems of the so-called aborigines and many other castes and tribes. Regarding the measures he remarks: " Nearly everything that I advocate for the Gond, the Korku, the Baiga, and the Bhil is necessary, if not always in the same degree, for all the castes and tribes of the backward areas, save in so far as, because of greater backwardness, inferior economic conditions or linguistic difficulties, there are problems peculiar to the ' aboriginal'.

Some of the legislation enacted for the benefits of the non-tribal cultivators was framed on the model of similar legislation for the tribals. On the other hand, as we have seen, fair protection was afforded to the Gonds, the Korkus, and other tribals in the Central Provinces with the help of the laws designed for the use of the general body of the community. The main problem of the tribals, therefore, is very similar to the problems of non-aboriginal agriculturists.

It is the problem of the backward, the ignorant and exploited people, who work on land and carry on cultivation for some time only to find sooner or later that their lands are no longer theirs. The result is brought about by a combination of many factors, viz., improvidence and ignorance of the people, passion for land and higher powers of intelligence, thrift and chicanery of the money-lending classes, and the rather complicated, costly, and inconvenient machinery of law.

The effective solution of the problem lies in strengthening the ties of the tribals with the other backward classes through their integration. How such integration may be brought about is a matter for practical administration.

SECTION VI

RURAL STRATIFICATION

Introduction

THIS SECTION is comprised of eight selections. It attempts to provide the emerging new class stratification in rural India. A student of rural society wanting to properly understand the dynamics of the rural society must understand the class structure of that society. The rural community is not comprised of homogeneous groups with identical interests but is a community comprised of diversified classes with conflicting interests. This fundamental fact has to be properly comprehended if the complex and complicated drama of rural life is to be understood properly. The economic measures adopted by the Government of India for changing the rural life have produced different effects on various classes. The overall agrarian policy of the government which is a part of its major economic plan has kept the entire agrarian area as a private sector. The elimination of certain strata like landlords (the so-called intermediaries between the peasants and the government) which are functionally parasitic in the domain of agrarian economy, the strengthening of the peasant proprietary class which would on the basis of profit incentives improve agricultural production, the curbing of money-lending groups, the provision of irrigation, seeds, fertilizers, and other facilities to the farmers to improve their conditions, are some of the important measures adopted by the government along with the interlinking of agriculture through roads, networks of communication and means of transport and markets, with the national economy.

This has transformed agricultural production and has resulted into the radical alteration of the socio-economic structure of the rural society. It has led to the reshuffling of social classes in agrarian India. The old caste stratification resting on the equilibrium of village occupations and mutual functional interdependence which was the basic characteristics of the village self-sufficient community was disturbed by the British rulers. The Government of Independent India, through its policy of mixed economy, is attempting to accelerate this process of the transformation of still almost self-sufficient village communities into a vital, prosperous, agrarian sector of a highly industrialised Indian society.

What classes are being generated in agrarian India? What classes are to acquire dominance in the rural world? What castes are dovetailing into different classes? What classes have been benefiting from the economic, social and cultural measures adopted by the Government? From what classes the power elite which controls the economy, the polity and the social, institutional and cultural life of the villages are emerging? What will be the fate of various classes in the competitive profit-oriented productive system which is being rapidly developed after Independence? All these problems are crucial for studying the rich and variegated life that is developing in rural India in recent times. It is the author's belief that a proper understanding of the caste and class matrix of the rural society will alone help to draw proper deductions about the laws of rural social development.

The eight selections indicate the lines on which a detailed analysis of the agrarian society from the standpoint of the caste and class matrix could be elaborated. They also can help to inaugurate a number of such studies in different parts of the country (*Author*).

I

AGRARIAN STRATIFICATION IN INDIA*

DISTRIBUTION OF HOLDINGS ACCORDING TO SIZE

THE INEQUALITY of cultivators' holdings is considerable in India. While the average size of the holdings was about 7·5 acres, about 70 per cent of the holdings were below this average. Holdings below one acre formed about 17 per cent, those between one and 2½ acres about 21 per cent and those between 2½ and 5 acres another 21 per cent. These accounted respectively for 1·0, 4·6 and 9·9 per cent of the total area. At the other end of the scale, 16 per cent were in the group 10 to 25 acres accounting for 32·5 per cent of the area and another 5·6 per cent above 25 acres covering about 34 per cent of the area.

The overall average size of holdings was 5·3 acres in North India (Uttar Pradesh) but the number of holdings upto 2·5 acres in size formed about 40 per cent of the total number of holdings and cover 9·7 per cent of the total area. The largest concentration of holdings, viz., 25 per cent was in the group 2·5 to 5 acres covering 16·7 per cent of the total area; 20·6 per cent were in the group 5 to 10 acres and covered 26·4 per cent of the area, while 11·4 per cent were in the group 10 to 25 acres covering 30·6 per cent of the area.

In East India zone, the overall average size was 4·5 acres. Here also, the largest concentration of holdings, namely 26·4 per cent covering 20·8 per cent of the total area was in the group 2·5 to 5 acres. However, 45·8 per cent were below 2·5 acres and covered 11·2 per cent of the area. The rest were above 5 acres.

In South India zone, as much as 55 per cent of the holdings covering 12·2 per cent of the area were below 2·5 acres, the overall average size being 4·5 acres. About 21 per cent of the holdings occupying 16·3 per cent of the area were in the size group 2·5 to 5 acres, while the rest were above 5 acres.

In West India zone, the overall average size was high, namely 12·3 acres, but 61 per cent of the holdings were below 10 acres and occupied 18·6 per cent of the area. A little above 25 per cent of the holdings covering 32·6 per cent of the area were in the group 10 to 25 acres, while 13·5 per cent covering 48·8 per cent of the area was above 25 acres.

---

*Reproduced from the *Report of the Agricultural Labour Enquiry, Rural Manpower and Occupational Structure* 1954, pp. 24 to 35.

Census Zones	Distribution of Cultivators' Holdings according to Size-groups												Average size of holdings (acres)
	Under one acre		1 acre to 2·5 acres		2·5 acres to 5 acres		5 acres to 10 acres		10 acres to 25 acres		Above 25 acres		
	Number	Area	Number	Area	Number	Area	Number	Area	Number	Area	Number	Area	
1	2	3	4	5	6	7	8	9	10	11	12	13	14
North India ...	14·8	1·4	26·2	8·3	25·1	16·7	20·6	26·4	11·4	30·6	1·9	16·6	5·3
East India ...	21·4	2·1	24·4	9·1	26·4	20·8	18·4	27·6	8·0	25·1	1·4	15·3	4·5
South India ...	28·0	2·7	27·1	9·5	20·9	16·3	14·0	21·1	7·9	25·4	2·1	25·0	4·5
West India ...	11·2	0·5	15·6	2·1	13·9	4·1	20·4	11·9	25·4	32·6	13·5	48·8	12·3
Central India ...	7·4	0·3	12·3	1·5	16·4	4·5	22·1	12·0	28·4	33·7	13·4	48·0	12·2
North-West India ...	5·4	0·2	14·4	2·0	16·9	5·1	22·5	13·4	31·0	39·3	9·8	40·0	12·6

The overall average size of holdings in Central India zone was 12·2 acres but 58 per cent of the holdings covering 18 per cent of the total area were below 10 acres. About 28 per cent were in the size group 10 to 25 acres and accounted for 34 per cent of the area, while 13·4 per cent occupying 48 per cent of the area were above 25 acres in size.

The average size of holdings was the highest, viz., 12.6 acres in North-West India zone. However, 59 per cent of the holdings occupying 20·7 per cent of the area were below 10 acres. About 31 per cent of the holdings was in the size group 10 to 25 acres and occupied 39·3 per cent of the area, while 9·8 per cent covering 40 per cent of the area were above 25 acres.

The above statement gives the percentage distribution of cultivator's holdings according to size groups in the different Census Zones.

Distribution of Holdings amongst the Different Categories of Families

The enquiry revealed that besides the cultivating owner families and tenant families the agricultural labour families as also the non-agricultural families were also cultivating holdings, smaller though, as a subsidiary occupation. Of the total number of holdings, about 35 per cent were cultivated by owners, another 35 per cent by tenants, 20 per cent by labourers and 10 per cent by non-agriculturists. The percentage distribution of the total area of the holdings as amongst these categories was 52·4 for landowners, 35·7 for tenants, 7·8 for agricultural labourers and 4·1 for non-agriculturists. While the average size of the holdings of owner families was larger, being 11·37 acres, that of the tenants 7·74 acres approximated the overall average. The average size of holdings of the agricultural workers was 2·86 acres and that of the non-agriculturists 3·10 acres. About 51 per cent of the area of the holdings were occupied by landowners and 37 per cent by tenants, while agricultural workers and non-agriculturists occupied 8 and 4 per cent respectively.

Livestock and Implements

Small farming requires livestock, implements and considerable human labour since mechanisation is possible only on large farms. Livestock such as bullocks, buffaloes and horses and to a small extent camels, are used as draught animals for ploughing, irrigating and sometimes for threshing. Bullock labour is also used for transport of manure to the fields, agricultural produce to the market, etc. Operations such as preparatory work, sowing, weeding, irrigating and threshing require many implements such as crowbars, spades, hoes, seed-drills, *charas* and persian wheels, etc. In case the cultivator does not own sufficient livestock or implements, he either borrows them or engages workers who bring their own in return for higher wages.

The number of work animals and ploughs owned are thus closely related to the number of holdings and their size. It is possible to arrive at, broadly, the average work unit for a pair of work animals and a plough in a particular region by dividing the total cultivated area by the number of pairs of work animals and ploughs separately and obtain a mean of the two sets of figures relating to average area per plough and per pair of work animals. This concept of a work unit will have some value in attempting to estimate the labour surplus in agriculture.

During the General Family Survey, data on livestock and ploughs possessed by each family living in the sample villages were collected. Table 11 in Appendix VI gives the average number of cattle, sheep and goats, poultry and ploughs according to different categories of families.

The families of agricultural landowners had 44·8 per cent of the ploughs, while those of tenants, agricultural workers and non-agriculturists had 38·2, 11·7 and 5·3 per cent respectively. On an average, there were 0·7 plough per family. The zonal figures were almost the same.

The following statement gives the zonal differences:

Average Number of Ploughs per Family

Zones		Number of ploughs per family of				
		Land-owners	Tenants	Agri-cultural labourers	Non-Agri-culturists	All families
North India	...	1·2	1·0	0·2	0·2	0·7
East India	...	1·4	0·8	0·2	0·2	0·6
South India	...	1·5	1·5	0·3	0·1	0·6
Western India	...	0·9	0·9	0·2	0·1	0·8
Central India	...	1·4	1·1	0·3	0·3	0·8
N. W. India	...	1·1	1·2	0·2	0·2	0·8
All India	...	1·2	1·0	0·3	0·2	0·7

On an average, a landowner's family had 1·2 ploughs, whereas a tenant's family had 1·1. The average number of ploughs per agricultural labour and non-agricultural family was extremely small, viz., 0.3 and 0·2 respectively. As stated already, about 50 per cent of the agricultural labourers held land. If, therefore, adjustments are made keeping this point in mind, the average number of ploughs per family would come to about 0·6. Similarly, the average number of ploughs per family of non-agriculturists having land would come to 0·7. The average number of ploughs per landowner and tenant family in South India zone was higher than that in other zones. The average was the least in West India zone.

For purposes of the Agricultural Labour Enquiry, the term 'cattle' included oxen or bullocks, cows (over 3 years), he-buffaloes and she-buffaloes. There were, on an average, 2·2 head of cattle per family taking all rural families together. The families of agricultural landowners had 3·8, tenants 3·3, agricutural labourers 1·0 and non-agriculturists 0·9 head of cattle. The zonal details are given in the statement below:

Head of Cattle per Family

Zones		Head of cattle per family of				
		Land-owners	Tenants	Agri-cultural labourers	Non-Agri-culturists	All families
North India	...	3·0	3·1	1·2	0·9	2·4
East India	...	4·1	2·5	1·1	0·9	2·0
South India	...	3·8	3·8	1·0	0·6	1·7
West India	...	3·4	3·5	0·8	1·0	2·4
Central India	...	4·3	4·7	0·8	1·1	2·6
N. W. India	...	3·7	4·3	1·2	1·1	2·9
All India	...	3·8	3·3	1·9	0·9	2·2

The average head of cattle per family of landowners and tenants varied between 3 and 4 in all the zones. But the average for agricultural labour families was about 1 and even slightly less in some of the zones.

The average number of sheep and goats per family came to 1·3, the corresponding figures for families of landowners, tenants, agricultural labourers and non-agriculturists being 1·7, 1·1, 0·8 and 1·5 respectively. The statement below gives the zonal details:

Sheep and Goats per Family

Zones		Average number of sheep and goats per family of				
		Land-owners	Tenants	Agri-cultural labourers	Non-Agri-culturists	All families
North India	...	0·4	0·6	0·5	1·1	0·7
East India	...	1·1	0·9	0·7	0·6	0·8
South India	...	2·4	1·2	1·1	0·4	1·2
West India	...	1·4	0·9	0·7	3·7	1·6
Central India	...	2·0	1·2	1·1	3·9	1·8
N.W. India	...	1·9	2·7	1·0	2·2	2·1
All India	...	1·7	1·1	0·8	1·5	1·3

The average number of sheep and goats in each category of family was comparatively small in North India zone. The average for landowners family was quite high in South and Central India zones. This was due to high averages for Mysore (5·2) and Hyderabad (3·6). The average for tenant families was also quite high (2·7) in North West India zone. This was due to high average for Rajasthan, viz., 2. 8. The relatively high average for non-agricultural families in West and Central

India was partly due to high figures for Saurashtra and Madhya Pradesh and Hyderabad respectively.

The average number of poultry per family was 0·9. The average per family of tenants, agricultural labourers and non-agriculturists was almost the same, it being 0·9, 0·8 and 0·7 respectively. The figure for landowners families was, however, relatively high being 1·2.

The following statement gives the zonal differences:

Average Number of Poultry per Family

Zones	Average number of poultry per family of				
	Land-owners	Tenants	Agri-cultural labourers	Non-Agri-culturists	All families
North India ...	0·2	0·1	0·1	0·2	0·1
East India ...	3·5	1·8	1·1	1·1	1·5
South India ...	2·1	3·2	1·0	1·0	1·4
West India ...	0·9	0·9	0·6	0·3	0·8
Central India ...	0·5	0·6	0·5	0·5	0·6
N. W. India ...	0·3	0·3	0·3	0·5	0·5
All India ...	1·2	0·9	0·8	0·7	0·9

The average for East and South India zones were much higher than that for any other zone.

Table 12 in Appendix VI gives the average area of cultivated land per plough and per pair of work animals in the sample villages. In working out the figures, however, it has been assumed that only the ploughs and the work animals owned by the families living in the same villages were utilised for the various agricultural operations, that no ploughs or work animals were brought from outside and that the ploughs and work animals owned by the families in the sample villages were not utilised by others outside the villages. The average area of cultivated land per plough and per pair of work animals in the sample villages worked out to 6·04 and 7·18. acres respectively. The relatively high figures for Saurashtra and Kutch have to be viewed in the context that the average size of holding was high and the soil sandy.

Housing Condition in Rural Areas

During the General Family Survey, information on housing was collected through a special rubric. The data collected have, however, considerable limitations. In the first place, it is very difficult to have standard definitions especially for purposes of place to place comparisons. Broadly, houses were classified into *pucca* houses and *kacha* houses. *Pucca* houses are those the walls and roofs of which are built of bricks and stones with lime and mortar. If the walls were made of bricks and stones but the roof was made of thatch, the house was called partly *pucca* and partly *kacha*. Others were classified as *kacha* houses. The nature and structure of the house differed from region to region and was determined primarily by the climatic conditions on the one hand and the building materials easily available on the other. Thus, in the hilly regions of Assam, U. P. and Himachal Pradesh the houses were mostly of wooden structure. In regions with hillocks around, the walls were usually built of stones as they were available in plenty. In villages which were situated near rivers, the reeds grown on these river banks were used as thatching material. It was also common for villagers to use dried stalks of maize, cocoanut leaves and palm leaves for making roofs.

Since the construction of *pucca* houses with bricks and mortar require substantial initial investment, only those who were relatively better off owned such houses. Thus, a few big landlords, merchants and money-lenders had *pucca* houses and the rest, working classes, the artisans and the marginal cultivators lived in *kacha* houses with mud wall and thatched roofs.

Data on the floor area of houses and the rent paid either for the house or for the ground on which it was erected were also collected. These are not, however, given here since these were not considered to be quite accurate in view of the difficulty in getting precise information from the villagers.

Nature of Housing

In the sample villages about 84 per cent of the houses were *kacha* houses. Amongst the major States, this percentage was more than 90 in U. P., the Eastern States of Assam, Bihar, West Bengal and Orissa and the Central States of Madhya Pradesh and Hyderabad. It ranged between 80 and 90 in Rajasthan and Madhya Bharat and between 70 and 80 in Punjab, Bombay, Madras and Travancore-Cochin. The position was comparatively better in Pepsu and Saurashtra, the percentage being about 60. This was so presumably due to availability of stones. The following statement shows the percentages in the different Census Zones:

Percentage of *kacha* houses occupied by important categories of families

Zones	Percenrage of *kacha* houses occupied by families of	
	Agricultural workers	All families
North India	99·7	92·5
East India	97·2	98·5
South India	90·0	78·1
West India	68·5	63·5
Central India	95·6	92·1
North-West India	88·6	76·1
All Sample Villages ...	92·6	84·1

The percentage of partly *pucca* and partly *kacha* houses was only 2·1, taking the Indian Union as a whole. Thus the percentage of *pucca* houses came to 13·8, The percentage of partly *pucca* and partly *kacha* houses was, however, relatively high, viz., about 8 per cent in North-West Zone mainly due to existence of such houses in Punjab and Pepsu.

Ownership of houses:—The houses were almost all self-owned. This meant that the plot on which the house was erected was also owned by the house owner. However, when ground rent was paid, it generally meant that only the house was owned but not the plot. Such cases were included in the owned houses. Taking all the sample villages, the percentage of rented houses was about 1·7 and varied up to 4 in the major States. In respect of the agricultural labour families in particular, this percentage was about 1·3. The details are given in the State Chapters.

Families per house:—Generally there was only one family per house. In fact the percentage of houses accommodating a single family was 95·3; those with two families formed 3·2 per cent and those with three or more families only 1·5 per cent. The same trend was observed in each of the six Census Zones. The percentage of houses having one family varied from 93·6 in North India to 96·6 in South and Central India, while the percentage of those having 2 families varied from 2·3 in South India to 4·2 in North India, and those having 3 or more families varied between 1 and 2.

Distribution of houses according to number of families living in them

Zones	Percentage of houses accommodation		
	One family	2 families	3 or more families
North India	93·6	4·2	2·2
East India	94·4	3·7	1·9
South India	96·6	2·3	1·1
West India	95·7	3·0	1·3
Central India	96·5	2·6	0·9
North-West India	94·8	3·6	1·6

Number of rooms per house :—Houses with a single room formed the largest percentage, viz., 38. Two room houses formed 28 and those having three or more rooms 34 per cent. The average number of rooms per house was 2·3. The agricultural labour families had limited accommodation, the average number of rooms per house being 1·9 and houses with one room formed the largest percentage, viz., 55, while two room houses constituted 27 per cent. The following statement gives the frequency distribution of houses according to rooms in the different Census Zones.

Taking the major States, the average number of rooms per house was 1·3 in West Bengal, 1·8 in Madhya Pradesh, 1·8 in Bombay, 1·9 in Madras and varied between 2 and 3 in the remaining States. The position in important States is given in the statement below:

Percentage Distribution of Houses According to Number of Rooms

Zone	All families			Agricultural labour families		
	1 room	2 rooms	3 or more rooms	1 room	2 rooms	3 or more rooms
North India	17·7	24·6	57·7	27·5	32·3	40·2
East India	42·0	24·7	33·3	48·8	27·5	23·7
South India	47·9	27·5	24·6	60·6	25·6	13·8
West India	42·7	38·6	18·7	54·7	33·9	11·4
Central India	48·6	30·3	21·1	63·9	27·4	8·7
North-West India	25·9	32·3	41·8	46·0	34·1	19·9
All sample villages	37·7	28·2	34·1	54·8	27·7	17·5

Number of Persons per Room: The number of persons per room depended on the number of rooms per house and the size of the family. Taking all the sampled villages, the average was about 2·3. The average generally varied between 2 and 3 as among the different States and was the highest in West Bengal being 3·6.

Number of Persons per Room

Zones	Average number of rooms per house occupied by families of	
	Agricultural workers	All families
North India	2·5	3·2
Uttar Pradesh	2·5	3·2
East India	2·1	2·4
Assam	1·9	2·6
Bihar	2·4	3·2
West Bengal	1·2	1·3
Orissa	2·2	2·9
South India	1·8	2·1
Madras	1·5	1·9
Mysore	1·8	2·1
Travancore-Cochin	2·0	2·0
West India	1·8	1·9
Bombay	1·6	1·8
Saurashtra	1·2	1·6
Central India	1·5	2·0
Madhya Pradesh	1·5	1·8
Madhya Bharat	1·5	2·3
Hyderabad	1·5	1·8
North-West India	1·9	2·8
Punjab	1·6	2·4
Pepsu	1·6	2·6
Rajasthan	2·3	2·9
All sample villages	2·0	2·3

Taking the agricultural labour families, the size of the family was generally less than that of other classes of families and still the congestion was higher in view of the limited accommodation. In most of the major States, the number of persons per room was 3 with the exception of U. P., Assam, Bihar, Orissa, Rajasthan and Travancore-Cochin where it was, 2, 1·8, 2·5, 2·2, 2·1, and 2·6 respectively. The following statement gives the average number of persons per room in the different zones:

Average Number of Persons per Room

Zone	Average number of persons per room in the houses occupied by families of	
	Agricultural workers	All families
North India	2·1	1·7
East India	2·5	2·3
South India	3·0	2·4
Central India	2·6	3·2
West India	2·9	2·8
North-West India	2·7	2·6

2

RURAL CLASS STRUCTURL IN WEST BENGAL*

RAMKRISHNA MUKHERJEE

THREE CLASSES have, therefore, been formed out of the nine occupational groups. Their descriptions and the basis for this classification are given below :

(1) The Class I is composed of the occupational groups of *land-holders* and *supervisory farmers*, that is, of the sub-infeudatory landlords and the prosperous non-cultivating or supervisory farmers whose top--most position in society is unquestioned.

(2) The Class II mainly comprises the self-sufficient peasantry, *viz.*, the *cultivators*; but the *artisans* and traders are also included in this class because, like the *cultivators*, most of them barely maintain a somewhat self-sufficient existence, partly based on land.

(3) The Class III is composed of the remaining occupational groups, *viz.*, the *sharecroppers*, *agricultural labourers*, *service-holders*, and *others*, which are formed of those people who depend for working on other members of society or in the case of a few of them on the charity of the wealthier folks.

Thus for a comprehensive study of the relation between the economic structure and the caste hierarchy, the affiliation to the three classes of the economic structure should be examined for each of the groups of " upper Caste Hindus, " " lower Caste Hindus, " Scheduled Castes, Sayyad Moslems, Moslem functional castes, Scheduled Tribes, and the " intermediate " groups like Nat, etc. But, unfortunately, from the available data it is impossible to undertake such an elaborate analysis for the whole of Bengal. Even so, it can be shown from a series of partial analysis that, in general, the " upper Caste Hindus " belong to Class I of the economic structure; the " lower Caste Hindus " and the Sayyad Moslems to Class II; the Scheduled Castes, the Moslem functional castes, the Scheduled Tribes and the " intermediate " groups to Class III. And thereby it will be realised how the caste-hierarchy (or the economic structure of society in the pre-British days) has dovetailed itself into the economic structure which emerged in Bengal during the British rule.

As regards the " upper " and " lower " Caste Hindus, the Scheduled Castes, Sayyad Moslems, the *Khulu* or oilpressing Moslems (which was

*Reproduced from '*The Dynamics of Rnral Society*' by Ramkrishna Mukherjee pp. 93-102.

the only Moslem functional caste found in these villages), the above hypothesis is substantiated by the following Table which presents the data obtained from an intensive study of six villages in the district of Bogra in north Bengal which the writer undertook during the last war.

TABLE 2·3

Classes of economic structure	"Upper" caste Hindus	"Lower" caste Hindus	Sayyad Moslems	Scheduled castes	*Khulu* Moslems
(1)	(2)	(3)	(4)	(5)	(6)
			Number of persons		
I	4	—	21	—	—
II	—	10	50	7	16
III	1	4	79	33	7
Total	5	14	150	40	23
			Precentage of total		
I	80	—	14	—	—
II	—	71	33	18	70
III	20	29	53	82	30
Total	100	100	100	100	100

In the above Table only the position of the *Khulu* Moslems appears to contradict the above hypothesis, as they are represented more in Class II than in Class III of the economic structure. But this is mainly due to the fact that, while their condition was no better (in fact, worse) than that of the Scheduled Castes, since in lieu of a better occupation many of them still followed their traditional occupation of oil pressing as their primary source of livelihood, they were classified under the category of " artisans and traders " and were thus included in Class II of the economic structure.

Comparable data are also available from West Bengal, from an intensive survey of 12 villages in the district of Birbhum, which was conducted in 1937 by the Vishvabharati Institute for Rural Reconstruction. These are shown in Table 2·3 above.

It will be noticed from the Table that except the Sayyad Moslems the other caste-groups conform to their expected position in the economic structure of society. The anomalous position of the Sayyad Moslems in this sample may be accounted for by the regional characteristic of the district of Birbhum where only a few seriously affect the above hypothesis, as is further borne out by an examination of the medium household incomes of the caste-groups. While giving the most satisfactory indication of group-characteristic, these medium values show how clearly the caste-groups are demarcated in the society in accordance with their economic positions. Thus the medium household income for the year was Rs. 334

for the "upper Caste Hindus," Rs. 262 for the "lower Caste Hindus" Rs. 195 for the Sayyad Moslems, Rs. 131 for the Scheduled Castes, and Rs. 137 for the tribals.

For the whole of rural Bengal a somewhat comparable Table including the "upper" and "lower" Caste Hindus, the Scheduled Castes, Sayyad Moslems and one group of Moslem functional castes, (*viz.*, Jolahas, who, however, have in general a better position in society than other Moslem functional castes) can be prepared from the data available from the 1931 census of Bengal. This is done in Table 2·4 below.

TABLE 2·4

Classes of economic structure	"Upper" Caste Hindus	"Lower" Caste Hindus	Sayyad Moslems	Scheduled Castes	Jolahas
(1)	(2)	(3)	(4)	(5)	(6)
			Number of persons (all figures in thousands)		
I	454	120	14	23	4
II	167	981	21	212	63
III	131	264	10	711	14
Total	752	1365	45	946	81
I	61	9	31	3	5
II	22	72	47	22	77
III	17	19	22	75	18
Total	100	100	100	100	100

The Table shows, that, except in the case of the Jolahas for the reason noted above, by and large the caste structure maintains the sort of relation with the economic structure as expected according to the stated hypothesis. Moreover, a Chi-square test applied to the above frequencies (as the data relate to a section of castes and not to all of them in Bengal) gave a value significant at the one per cent level of significance, proving thereby the reliability of the above conclusion.

The preceding all-Bengal analysis, however, did not take any account of the tribes. Therefore, on the basis of the 1951 census data for West Bengal, Table 2·5 has been prepared to show how only in one part of Bengal and at a date which can more specifically show the legacy of the past the social hierarchy is seen to maintain the sort of relation with the economic structure as enunciated before.

It is seen from the Table that although the Scheduled Tribes and the Scheduled Castes depend more on the agrarian economy than the remaining population in rural Bengal (80 and 77 per cent of their total populations, respectively, as against 73 per cent of the remaining population), they are located in very large population in Class III of the economic structure, while the remaining population in society (including the caste Hindus and the entire Moslem community) occupy mainly the Class II, with 4 to 8 times the proportion of the Scheduled Castes and Tribes in Class I of the economic structure.

TABLE 2·5

Classes of economic structure	Scheduled Castes	Scheduled Tribes	Others	Total
(1)	(2)	(3)	(4)	(5)
		Number of persons (all figures in thousands)		
I	7	1	96	104
II	1,226	326	6,363	7,915
III	1,989	588	3,343	5,920
		Percentage of total		
I	0·22	0·11	0·98	0·75
II	38·05	35·63	64·92	56·78
III	61·73	64·26	34·10	42·47
Total	100·00	100·00	100·00	100·00

Unfortunately for the " intermediate " groups, like the Nats, no data was available for rural Bengal, and, as seen from the above analysis, the Moslem functional castes also could not be adequately represented in the present study. No doubt, because of the lack of relevant data, this remains a weakness of the present course of analysis; but this may not be considered as very serious, for it is a common knowledge that members of these social groups generally live on pursuing their " traditional " occupations of petty craft production or trade or performing menial services to other members of society as well as by sharecropping the lands of landlords or by working as wage-labourers in the rural areas. In other words, as has been noted before, they belong almost entirely to the Class III of the economic structure. Therefore, even from the series of partial analysis as given above, it appears reasonable to conclude that there does exist a relation between the social hierarchy and the economic structure of Bengal in the British period of her history.

This conclusion, however, should not give the impression that the writer is inclined to prove that the proportion of sharecroppers and agricultural labourers in society (in Class III of the economic structure) is the result of differences in the social composition of the population. It is necessary to mention this, for a theory is apparently in circulation in some quarters in India according to which where the Scheduled Castes people are found in large numbers, the agricultural labourers are also there in great bulk. No doubt, such a theory looks at the situation from the wrong end of the telescope, for to say that the people placed low in the social hierarchy generally belong to Class III of the economic structure does not mean that all those in that class belong to the Scheduled Castes or the Moslem functional castes. This theory thus neglects the essential characteristics of the agrarian crisis in British India, because of which increasing numbers of Caste Hindus (though mainly " lower Caste Hindus " and Sayyad Moslems also came down to this class.

But, on the other hand, it will be quite wrong not to see, as the foregoing analysis has revealed, that the association between the social hierarchy (which was previously the economic structure of society) and the economic structure which emerged under British rule reveals some interesting features in society. Firstly, it is seen that the great majority of persons belonging to the *usurping castes*, who had previously lived on taxes and tributes from the producing and serving castes as feudal rent-receivers, now under British rule maintained their social and economic domination in society by belonging to Class I of the newly evolved economic structure. Moreover, their role in society was further stabilised, for henceforth they became *landowners* which they were not before. Secondly, it is seen that the members of the *producing castes* of pre-British days remained in large numbers in Class II of the new economic structure, that is, they persevered to continue with their " traditional " role in society as self-sufficient and self-working artisans, peasants and traders. But it is also evident that due to the ever-aggravating agrarian crisis during British rule, an appreciable proportion of them successively went down the ladder and were finally located in Class III of the economic structure, that is, in the circle of disintegrated peasantry and the like. And, thirdly, it is seen that in overwhelming numbers of the low caste people, viz., *the serving castes* of pre-British days, remained at the bottom of the society—in Class III of the economic structure. Although many of them could no more earn their living only from their " traditional " occupations of serving other members of society, they remained, as before, especially under the domination of the *usurping castes*; for, in lieu of any other source of livelihood, in increasing numbers they became sharecroppers and agricultural labourers and thus continued to live under the control of landholders.

Thus it is seen that while the previous economic structure of society lost its direct usefulness under British rule, the previous social strata did not wither away. On the contrary, they remained in society by dovetailing themselves in the newly-evolved class structure. This was possible because there was no fundamental change in the character of the economy which under colonial conditions and due to the lack of industrialisation on the one hand and the growth of landlordism on the other remained semi-feudal in all essentials. Therefore, the domination of the *usurping castes* in society (if not in such a direct form as it was before, for it had come under severe attacks from the fourteenth century onwards, as mentioned before) remained in force, and so in this new situation also both the *producing castes* and the *serving castes* remained under their control. Only mass pauperisation (which became an important trait of the economic life under British rule because of the agrarian crisis) led more and more members of the *producing castes* to come down economically to the level of the *serving castes*, and all of them began to lead a life of abject poverty and dependence on the landholders.

In this way the peculiar development of the economic structure of rural Bengal in the British period of her history gave a new lease of life to the caste system and upheld the caste-ideology in society, although its economic function had become useless. This is indeed the crux of the dovetailing of the previous economic structure of the society (or the social hierarchy in the British period of Bengal's history) into the economic structure which emerged during British rule.

3

RURAL CLASS STRUCTURE IN GUJARAT*

S. M. Shah

Ownership of land : of all the economic resources land is the chief form of capital in rural areas; and generally the less land the peasant has, the poorer he is. Ownership of land, therefore, becomes a fair index of the economic status of persons connected with agricultural industry. The economic status, moreover, puts an individual in a particular social ' station ' as well. Hence, ownership of land becomes a major determinant of the socio-economic status of an individual in the agrarian society.

The owner-cultivator and the owner-cum-tenant cultivator are the only two classes who own some land. The rest are landless, and form the agricultural proletariat group. The average ownership of land among the owners is 9·4 acres, while the owner-cum-tenants have only 5·8 acres. The part owners have, therefore, lower status than the owners.

As compared to the owners, a proportionately large number of the part owners have lower social status too. The social stratification of the agricultural classes that formed our sample is depicted in a diagram. The diagram indicates that of the total owner cultivators 4·3 per cent are from the Brahmins and the Banias. These two castes who are at the apex of the caste system do not follow agriculture as the main source of livelihood, so that when a relationship is sought to be established between caste and class, it begins with the exclusion of these two castes who are at the top of the social ladder. The part owners are drawn entirely from the " intermediate " and the " lower " castes. The proportion of intermediates is 44·4 per cent among the owners, and 37·5 per cent among the part owners. The lower castes constitute 51·3 per cent of the total owners. They constitute 52·5 per cent among the part owners. The labourers belong entirely to the lower caste. There is evidently a definite correlation between economic and social status.

The ' higher ' castes such as the Banias and the Brahmins, are at the top of literacy scale, whereas at the foot of the scale are found the ' lower ' castes. The Brahmins at the top of the caste structure have a literacy of 60 per cent, the Patels, the ' intermediates ' have 30 per cent and the Harijans have only 21 per cent. These " untouchables " till to-day had

*Reproduced from " Rural Class Structure in Gujarat, " by S. M. Shah, (an unpublished Thesis for the Ph.D. Degree in the Department of Economics, University of Bombay), pp. 205-215.

no equal access to educational institution and evens now they live in social isolation. Such a situation has led some to believe that education is the monopoly of the privileged.

Average cultivated holding (Acres)

Owner	Owner-cum-Tenant	Tenant
8·8	9·8	8·7

Size of the cultivator's holding (Acres)

Caste Group	Persons	Area under cultivated holding (Acres)	Average cultivated holding
Higher			
Banias and Brahmins	2	28·0	14·0
Intermediates			
Patels	67	853·9	12·7
Artisans	8	107·5	13·4
Rajputs	8	52·6	6·6
Lower			
Kolis	9	31·0	3·4
Patelias	10	55·9	5·6
Barias	61	331·8	5·4
Bhils	30	112·1	3·7
Harijans	34	104·2	3·1
Miscellaneous	48	159·6	3·3

Size of the holdings in relation to the size of the family

Cultivator	Average size of cultivated holding (Acres)	Irrigated holding (P.C.)	Average size of the family	Adult Male equivalent
Owner	8·8	10·3	5·93	4·98
Owner-cum-tenant	9·8	6·4	5·89	4·92
Tenant*	8·7	*Nil*	5·40	4·59

* Tenants excluding Roopgadh.

Ownership of wells (Class-wise)

Class	No. of wells	No. of families
Owner	59	117
Owner-cum-Tenant	41	80
Tenant	12	50

Caste-wise

Caste	No. of wells	p.c. to total wells
Patels	46	53·5
Rajputs, Barias, Thakardas	23	26·7
Kolis	6	7·7
Others	11	12·8

Co-operation (Caste-wise)

Caste	No. of families in the sample	No. of families in co-operative	No. of families in co-operatives as per cent to total in the sample
Brahmins, Banias	6	4	66·7
Patelias	10	6	60·0
Patels	76	45	59·2
Artisans	10	4	40·0
Muslims	11	4	36·4
Kolis	16	4	25·0
Harijans	34	6	17·6
Bhils	30	5	16·7
Barias	61	7	11·5
Rajputs	10	1	10·0
Others	52	3	5·8

Literacy (Class-wise)

Class	Combined (Males & Females)	Male	Female
Owner	18·9	28·3	8·6
Owner-cum-tenant	11·9	20·1	2·8
Tenant	9·9	17·9	1·2
Bhagia	—	—	—
Annual Labourer	—	—	—
Casual labourer	4·9	7·1	2·3
	12·9	20·2	4·7

The extent of literacy is reduced as we descend the ladder.

Caste-wise Literacy

Caste	Literacy as p.c. of Total Sample	Total Sample	Total Literate
Brahmin	60·0	5	3
Bania	40·6	10	4
Patel	29·5	302	89
Artisan	29·6	27	8
Koli	10·1	69	7
Rajput	12·5	32	4
Baria	6·2	177	11
Patelia	—	41	—
Bhil	1·0	104	1
Harijan	4·1	122	5
Muslim	2·2	45	1

Its Repercussions on Class Structure

These differences in literacy and educational standards have serious repercussions on the class structure. The above picture conveys that educational opportunities are ' closed ' to classes on the lower social and economic scale. A disparity in learning makes class distinctions more pronounced and leads to group tensions whereas a wide diffusion of education among all classes reduces class cleavage.

4

SOME ASPECTS OF INDIAN AGRICULTURE

(As revealed in recent studies)

SULEKH CHANDRA GUPTA

I

UNTIL RECENT years, agriculture in India has seldom been regarded as a business enterprise. It has been looked upon merely as a source of meagre livelihood for the mass of petty peasants, who carry on production chiefly for subsistence and largely with family labour.[1] They are of course known to be working under severe handicaps since the classes of landlords, moneylenders, and traders oppress and exploit them brutally and claim all their produce beyond a bare subsistence for the family and the cattle, often not even that. But they are generally regarded as insulated against the operation of the laws of the free market, and beyond the orbit of economic processes of commercialisation and monetization, since they are believed to have little to sell in the market for money or invest in agriculture except on the fringes.

This view of Indian agriculture has conjured up a rather simplified image of Indian agrarian society. On the top are seen only the layers of intermediaries, moneylenders, and traders, and at the bottom a mass of small peasants, more or less equal and homogeneous in their land and produce and suffering from the burdens of rack rent, usurious interest rates, and middlemen's profits in trade. The solutions derived from this image also have an appearance of naivete. It is perhaps believed that if only the intermediaries are eliminated rent-burdens reduced, interest charges regulated through co-operatives and middlemen's profits brought down through co-operative marketing, there will prevail a regime of social and economic harmony in Indian villages. And this harmoneous mass of small peasants, aided with improved seeds, fertilisers, irrigation, credit, and extension services, and somehow persuaded to join the farming co-

N. B. The views and opinions expressed in this paper are those of the author and not of the Agricultural Economics Research Centre, University of Delihi. The author is indebted to Shri M. R. Rao, his colleague, for his help in preparation of some statistical Tables.

1. P. K. Mukherjee, *Economic Surveys in Underdeveloped Countries* (Bombay, 1959), pp. 43-65; and Daniel and Alice Thorner, *Land and Labour in India*, (Bombay, 1962), pp. 3-13.

operatives, would be able to march forward smoothly towards economic prosperity and socialism.

This image of Indian agriculture might have been close to realities at some remote time in the past. But it holds sway over most minds to-day as if these realities have remained unchanged. However, in recent years, for the first time, ample data have become available which provide an altogether different picture of contemporary realities in Indian agriculture. These data show that this view of Indian agriculture is at best facile, and partial. The realities are far more complex. An attempt has been made in this paper to present these data and discuss some of their implications.

All recent studies[2] about Indian agriculture strike at the root of the mythical harmony and homogeneity of Indian agrarian society. They reveal that it is composed not merely of intermediaries, money-lenders, and traders or of a mass of petty peasants, more or less homogeneous in their social and economic conditions, but of a peasant mass, characterised by a wide heterogeneity, and bitter mutual strife. They show that the conditions of life of peasants, vary widely not merely from region to region or village to village due to natural factors but even from farm to farm and peasant to peasant[3] within the village, due to socio-economic compulsions.

The farming community of an average Indian village in these studies is found to be composed of several strata of cultivators, highly differentiated from each other in respect of the size of land owned or cultivated, number of draught and milch cattle possessed, nature and amount of capital invested in farming, types of tools and implements used, amount of family or hired labour employed, techniques of cultivation practised, extent of surplus produce sold in the market, amount of gain or loss from farming business and the volume of savings or deficits made. Moreover, the

[2] Reliance is placed here mainly on the following studies :

i. Studies in Economics of Farm Management in U. P. and Punjab, Madhya Pradesh, Bombay, West Bengal and Madras for 1954-55 and 1955-56, issued by the Directorate of Economics & Statistics, Ministry of Food & Agriculture, New Delhi.

ii. Village Reports of the Agro-Economic Research Centres at Delhi, Santiniketan, Poona and Madras, set up by the Directorate of Economics & Statistics, Ministry of Food and Agriculture, Government of India, available in a type script form.

iii. Reports of the All-India Rural Credit Survey, published by the Reserve Bank of India, Bombay.

iv. Reports of the National Sample Survey, Eighth Round, July 1954, March 1955, Numbers 10 and 30, on Landholdings in Rural India, issued by the Cabinet Secretariat, Government of India.

Reports of the Agricultural Labour Enquiries., (First and Second), issued by the Ministry of Labour, Government of India.

[3] Indian Society of Agricultural Economics, *Rationale of Regional Variations in Agrarian Structure of India*, (Bombay, 1957), pp. 142-45.

studies also reveal that these strata are no longer the 'parallel social strata' of H. S. Maine's times which were scarcely distinguishable from each other except in the length of time over which they had been absorbed in the village community.[4] On the contrary, they are today very much unlike each other in almost all aspects of their economic and social life. They present the curious spectacle of being engaged in a bitter economic and social strife which affects not only their mutual social relations but also their economic fortunes, standards of living and social welfare. And if one has to grasp the essence of contemporary developments in Indian agriculture, which often appear to pull into contrary directions, one has to look upon Indian agriculture not as a sector aggregate of small, uneconomic and subsistence peasant units of production but as one in which production units of different types and sizes with wide differences in their character of farming, techniques of cultivation, forms of employment of labour power, profitability, saving, investment and consumption, compete with each other and in which laws of the free market operate sluggishly but as ruthlessly as in the other sectors of the Indian economy. The following paragraphs illustrate these aspects with data.

The first and the foremost basis of differentiation amongst the peasants which causes differentiation amongst them even in other aspects, is the ownership and cultivation of land. The distribution of owned land in present day India is 'extremely concentrated with a small minority owning most of the land'.[5] During last few years, three nation-wide surveys, viz. the National Sample Survey, the First Agricultural Labour Enquiry and the Census of Landholdings,[6] have thrown up a mass of data on the pattern of land ownership in India. All these surveys reveal a high degree of differentiation amongst present households in respect of their ownership holdings, as shown in the following Table.

Thus, while at the bottom about three-fourths of all rural households own less than 5 acres of land, and hold less than one-sixth of the total area owned, on the top, one-fourth of all rural households hold 83·68 per cent

---

[4] H. S. Maine, *Village Communities in the East and West*, (Cambridge, 1873), p. 176.

[5] N. S. S., *First Report on Landholdings, Rural Sector*, No. 10, (Delhi, 1958), p. v.

[6] i. National Sample Survey, Eighth Round, July 1954-April 1955, No. 10, *First Report on Landholdings, Rural Sector*, (1958) and No. 30 *Report on Landholdings* (2) (*Operational holdings in rural India*), (Delhi, 1960).

ii. *Agricultural Labour Enquiry—Report on Intensive Survey of Labour*, Vol. I All India, (Delhi, 1954).

iii. Planning Commission, *The Third Five Year Plan*, (Delhi, 1961) Annexure to Chapter XIV, pp. 239-240.

Of these three surveys, the data of the N. S. S. are the most widely used since (1) the data for the census of landholds has not been aggregated for the whole of India and is available only for individual States; and (2) the report of the first Agricultural Labour Enquiry does not contain data regarding distribution of ownership holdings for all rural households and defines an ownership holding somewhat differently from the N. S. S. and the Census of Landholdings.

TABLE I

Distribution of Ownership Holdings amongst Rural Households according to size-groups Crop Season 1953-54
(Percentages)

Size-group (acres)	Household Ownership Holdings			
	p.c. of holdings to the total	Cumulative p.c. of holdings	p. c. of area to total area owned	Cumulative percentage of area
0·00*	23·09	—	—	—
0·01—0·99	24·17	47·26	1·37	—
1·00—2·49	13·98	61·24	4·86	6·23
2·50—4·99	13·49	74·73	10·09	16·32
5·00—9·99	12·50	87·23	18·40	34·72
10·00—24·99	9·17	96·40	29·11	63·83
25·00—49·99	2·66	99·06	18·63	82·46
50·00 or above	0·94	100·00	17·54	100·00
Total	100·00	—	100·00	—

* Includes households owning an area of ·005 acres or less

of the total area in size-groups above 5 acres. Even amongst them, 12·77 per cent of all the rural households hold as much as 65·28 per cent of the total owned area in size-groups of more than 10·00 acres. And in the collection of data, ownership of land was defined as ' the right of permanent heritable possession with or without right to transfer the title '[7] which means that even secure tenants of the State or of private individuals, who enjoyed rights, of permanent heritable possession, have been included as owners.

The data of household ownership holdings pertain to the year 1953-54, when the abolition of intermediaries in most parts of India was either in progress or almost completed. Thus ownership of land has remained so concentrated despite the abolition of intermediaries.[8] This may be due to an aspect of ownership which may be noted. Before the abolition of intermediaries, ownership of land was generally vested in a heterogenous class of intermediaries and was very uneven and highly concentrated. It is usually thought that these ownership holdings were almost entirely cultivated by tenants, and the intermediaries were merely a class of functionless parasites. While it was true for the large bulk of land of the intermediaries, they also held some land as their *Sir* and *Khudkasht*—also very unevenly distributed–on which theycould carry on cultivation with

7 N. S. S. Report No. 30, op. cit., p.5.

8 That the abolition of intermediaries did not make much difference in the concentration of owned land is amply revealed in a recent *Study of Land Reforms in Uttar Pradesh*, by Prof. Baljit Singh and Dr. Shridhar Misra, (Lucknow, 1962), Mimeographed. See further p. 10.

their family labour or hired labour, and in which no tenancy rights could arise, even though a small part of these lands were let out to tenants. The bulk of these lands was cultivated by the zamindars personally with family labour or hired labour.[9]

The average size of *Sir* and *Khudkasht* land varied widely between different zamindars. For instance in U. P. it ranged over 1·09 acre to 280·05 acres per zamindar.[10] With such wide differences in the extent of *Sir*, it was natural that the *Sir* lands also should have been let out especially when there were no restrictions on leasing. Nevertheless, it may be emphasised that most zamindars engaged in direct cultivation on their *Sir* and *Khudkasht* lands with their own family labour or hired labour, in addition to realising rents from their tenants. Confronted with the prospect of abolition of their privileges as landlords a couple of years before the advent of Independence, the zamindars took measures to expand the area under *Sir* and *Khudkasht* cultivation to retain the maximum possible area for personal cultivation,[11] and not let it become the property of the State. The age-old struggle of the landlords and tenants for land was thus left by the government to be fought between themselves for some years before they enacted and implemented legislation taking over the intermediaries' lands.

As a result, while the State acquired a substantial area in ownership, the zamindars also retained large areas, as unevenly distributed as before. And not many tenants acquired ownership rights by paying compensation. Consequently, no significant change in the distribution of owned land took place after the zamindari abolition.

However, an important result, generally unnoticed and scarcely written about, has been that the ex-zamindars have been forced into a new way of life, and are on their way towards changing their character as a class. Deprived of the sources of land rent and prohibited from leasing out *Sir* lands, they are obliged to take even more interest in direct cultivation of land, and gradually convert themselves into peasant proprietors or capitalist farmers depending on the size of their holdings, and their social and economic position.

A close examination of the laws relating to abolition of zamindari in most States suggests that the governments have gone out of their way to provide for their gradual conversion into cultivators of their own lands by making special provisions for resumptions, evictions, by leaving numerous loopholes and gaps in the land laws, and by delaying implementation. Provision of compensation is also a means to provide them with capital for investment in agriculture. Measures for imposition of ceilings and the manner of their implementation are also devised to compel them to take

[9] Baljit Singh and Shridhar Misra, *Study of Land Reforms in U. P.*, (Lucknow, 1962), Mimeographed. p. 48.

[10] Ibid., p. 46.

[11] Ibid., pp. 50-51.

up farming by leaving only as much land with them as may be cultivated with hired labour on the basis of the technology in vogue, and insufficient for being leased out.

Of course, all intermediaries have not responded alike to these measures. Nor have they all been affected alike since the majority are only petty intermediaries with small holdings. But the bulk of the land retained for self-cultivation is in the hands of a small minority and their conversion into entrepreneur farmers depends on a host of factors, such as the availability and extent of non-farm sources of income, caste prejudices and attitudes towards cultivation, and personal competence to take up various tasks of agricultural enterprise. And for these reasons, variations arise in different regions of the country in the extent and manner in which this small minority takes to self-cultivation.

However, several careful observers of the Indian rural economy have drawn attention to the change in the position of the ex-intermediaries since their abolition. For instance, Daniel and Alice Thorner write :

> ...there are cases where these ex-landlords have used the money paid them as compensation for the taking over of their lands to buy tractors and go in for modern-style agriculture.[12]

Dr. A. M. Khusro, summarising the group discussion held at the Annual Conference of the Indian Society of Agricultural Economics at Pilani, has observed that :

> In Punjab and U. P. a substantial fraction of ex-zamindars who became bhumidars or resumed their lands is known to have taken to managerial type of cultivation and a new brand of farming, often termed ' capitalist farming ', seems to have been emerging.[13]

Similarly Dr. Otto Schiller has remarked that :

> ...the number of tractors in......India has increased...many of them are being introduced by big landowners who have become aware of the great possibilities offered by modern techniques. With the help of tractors, they have started to farm land which previously was cultivated by tenants. As a result some of the tenants have had either to work for the landowner on a hire basis or to look for other employment unless they could find other land which they could lease.[14]

---

[12] Daniel and Alice Thorner, op. cit., p. 9; also see p. 11 where they write: ' In parts of Punjab, in Western Uttar Pradesh, in Gujarat, and in Andhra, we find numerous cases of larger peasants who carry on their production in genuine capitalistic style; that is by relying on regularly hired free labourers to grow crops for sale in organised markets with the aim of realising profits '.

[13] *Indian Journal of Agricultural Economics*, Vol. XVII, No. 1, (January-March, 1962), p. 192; also see *Report of the Foodgrains Enquiry Committee* (Delhi, 1957), p. 46; The Committee write: ' As a result of abolition of zamindari and in view of the proposed tenancy reforms many intermediaries have now become owner-cultivators'.

[14] *Proceedings of the Ninth International Conference of Agricultural Economists*, (London, 1956), p. 120.

IV

This process of conversion of erstwhile intermediaries into 'capitalist farmers' has developed unevenly and at varying speed in different regions of the country. But it has created pre-conditions for vital changes in the agrarian economy and its functioning. By narrowing the gap between ownership and cultivation of land, it has considerably diminished the scope for rack renting of the tenants in future, except covertly under the law, and provided them a sense of security. But, at the same time, it has helped the distribution of total cultivated area remain highy unequal and aggravated the differentiation of peasants in respect of the size of their cultivation. The following Table shows the distribution of cultivated area in India.

TABLE 2

Distribution of operational (cultivated) holdings amongst Rural Households according to size-groups Crop season 1953-54 (Percentages)

Size-groups (acres)	Household Operational Holdings			
	Percentage of holdings to the total	Cumulative percentage of holdings	Percentage of area to the total	Cumulative percentage of holdings
0·00*	10·96	—	—	—
0·01— 0·99	31·12	42·08	1·20	1·20
1·00— 2·49	14·07	56·15	4·38	5·58
2·50— 4·99	15·08	71·23	10·02	15·60
5·00— 9·99	14·19	85·42	18·56	34·16
10·00—24·99	10·36	95·78	29·22	63·38
25·00—49·99	3·12	98·90	19·54	82·92
50·00 and above	1·00	100·00	17·08	100·00
Total :	100·00	—	100·00	—

It is evident that the distribution of cultivated area also is concentrated in the hands of a small minority. At the bottom, as many as 71·23 per cent households cultivate only 15·60 per cent of the total cultivated land in size-groups of less than 5 acres, while at the top, a small minority of 14·48 per cent households operate upon 65·85 per cent of the total cultivated area in size groups of 10 acres and above.

The pattern of distribution of operational holdings is quite close to that of the ownership holdings. And the bold fact emerges that concentration of ownership in land signifies simultaneously a concentration of the operated area. How little has been the change in this pattern as a result of zamindari abolition is shown by the data regarding distribution of cultivated area prior to and after abolition of zamindari in some sampled villages of Western, Central and Eastern U. P. as follows :

TABLE 3

Percentage distribution of cultivating households and cutltvated area according to size of holdings before and after zamindari abolition in sample villages of U.P.[15]

Size-group	Before Zamindari Abolition				After Zamindari Abolition			
	Percentage of house-holds	Percentage of area	Cumulative percentage of house-holds	Cumulative percentage of area	Percentage of house-holds	Percentage of area	Cumulative percentage of house-holds	Cumulative percentage of area
Less than 5 acres	51·53	16·95	51·53	16·95	51·89	18·25	51·89	18·25
5 — 15 acres	37·27	40·17	88·80	57·12	37·39	43·55	89·28	61·80
15 acres and above	11·20	42·88	100·00	100·00	10·72	38·20	100·00	100·00

15 Baljit Singh and Shridhar Misra, *A Study of Land Reforms in U. P., Mimeographed,* (Lucknow, 1962), pp. 74 and 194.

V

Let us examine whether cultivation on such a highly differentiated pattern of operational holdings would really be with family labour and for subsistence, and how far, so long as this pattern remains substantially intact, the objectives of agrarian policy laid down by the Congress Agrarian Reforms Committee[16] can be really achieved.

The extent of use of family labour on different size-groups of holdings largely depends upon the number of household members. The following Table shows the relationship between the size of operational holdings and the average household size in the respective size-groups.

TABLE 4

Average Household Size by Size of Household Operational Holdings (July 1953 to June 1954)[17]

Size of Operational Holdings (acres)	Average Household Size
0·00	3·91
0·01— 0·99	4·14
1·00— 2·49	4·81
2·50— 4·99	5·24
5·00— 7·49	5·76
7·50— 9·99	6·16
10·00—14·99	6·34
15·00—19·99	6·76
20·00—24·99	6·86
25·00—29·99	7·15
30·00—49·99	7·23
50·00 and above	8·30
Average	5·01

In the Table above, the average household size shows an increasing trend with the increase in the size of household operational holding. But the increase in household size is much less (only a little more than two-fold) relatively to the increase in the size of household operational holding (about 50 fold).

16 *Report of the Congress Agrarian Reforms Committee*, (New Delhi, 1951), p. 8. The Committee recommended that the following principles should govern the agrarian policy of the country.

i. The agrarian economy should provide an opportunity for the development of the farmer's personality.

ii. There should be no scope for exploitation of one class by another.

iii. There should be maximum efficiency of production.

iv. The scheme of reforms should be within the realm of practicability.

17 N. S. S. Report No. 30, *Report on Landholdings* (2) (*Operational Holdings in Rural India*) (Delhi, 1960), p. 28.

If we assume that the proportion of family workers in an average household size of 5·01 is 2·0 and apply this proportion uniformly to all size-groups and compute the operated area per family worker in different size-groups dividing the average size of household operational holding by the number of family workers, we get the following result :—

TABLE 5

Average size of holdings, Average number of workers and operated area per worker according to size-groups of household operational holdings[18].

Size-group (Acres)	Average size of holding*	Average number of family workers per household[19]	Operated area per family worker
0·00	—	1·56	—
0·01— 0·99	0·21	1·65	0·13
1·00— 2·49	1·69	1·92	0·83
2·50— 4·99	3·62	2·09	1·73
5·00— 7·49	6·12	2·30	2·66
7·50— 9·99	8·68	2·46	3·53
10·00—14·99	12·18	2·53	4·81
15·00—19·99	17·29	2·70	6·40
20·00—24·99	22·21	2·74	8·11
25·00—29·99	27·40	2·85	9·61
30·00—49·99	37·98	2·89	13·14
50·00 and above	83·54	3·31	25·24
Average	5·43	2·00	2·71

From this Table, it is evident that the availability of cultivated land in different size-groups of holdings varies widely between 0·13 to 25·24 acres per family worker. In the higher size-groups of holdings, it is so large that family workers would find it impossible to cultivate it only by themselves and would necessarily depend on the regular use of hired labour. Moreover, if the family workers of households with large operational holdings prefer to abstain from physical participation in agricultural operations for reasons of their traditional status as zamindars, caste, etc, and remain content only with supervision and management, the need for hired labour is further aggravated.

From the data collected in the Farm Management Studies, one finds that the use of hired labour increases with an increase in the size of operational holdings, as, for instance, is shown in the following Table :—

18 Computed from the data given in N. S. S. Report No. 10, op. cit., p. 13.

19 Computed from the data in N. S. S. Report No. 30, op. cit., p. 28, on the assumption that an average size household consists of 2·0 workers and that the proportion of workers to the total members of households is uniform in all size-groups.

TABLE 6

Percentage classification of Farm Labour into Family and Hired Labour on some Sampled Holdings in U. P. (Survey Sample).[20]

Size-groups of holdings (acres)	Percentage contribution by		Total
	Family Labour	Hired Labour	
Below 5·0	87·8	12·2	100·0
5·0—10·0	79·2	20·8	100·0
10·0—15·0	68·2	31·8	100·0
15·0—20·0	58·0	42·0	100·0
20·0 and above	47·0	53·0	100·0

Now, if we regard the optimum work unit for an average household–sufficient to provide full employment for all the family workers[21] to be, on the average, between 7·5 acres and 10·0 acres[22], then, under the present distribution of operational holdings, cultivation on 65·84 per cent of the total cultivated area in India must necessarily be done with the *regular* use of hired labour, permanent or temporary, on cash or kind wages. And it is no wonder that India had 17·9 million agricultural labour households in 1950-51 which constituted 30·39 per cent of all rural households and whose major source of livelihood was wage-labour in agriculture.[23] Amongst them, bulk of the permanent farm servants were found to be employed on holdings of 10 acres or above in size, as is shown in the Table 7.

From the Table, it is evident that 64·3 per cent of total permanent farm servants are employed on farms of 10·0 acres or more, and most of the remaining, employed on farms of less than 10 acres must be usually on holdings of small intermediaries or others who either do not touch the plough for reasons of caste, traditional status as zamindars or personal incapacity, or are engaged in non-farm occupations and get their holdings cultivated by permanent farm workers.

20 *Studies in Economics of Farm Management in U. P.* Report for the year 1955-56, issued by the Directorate of Economics and Statistics, Ministry of Food and Agriculture, Government of India, p. 37; also see data for the cost-accounting sample in the same Table.

21 See A. M. Khusro, *An Analysis of Agriculture Land in India by Size of Holding and Tenure*, Mimeographed, (Delhi, 1962), pp. 23-32; also see Table 6 above. It will be seen that the percentage contribution of hired labour to the total farm labour rises significantly on holdings above 10 acres and is about one-third or more on all operational holdings 10 acres or above in size.

22 The actual size of an optimum work unit is of course liable to vary between different regions according to differences in soil, climate, crop-pattern, availability of irrigation facilities etc.

23 *Report on the Second Agricultural Labour Enquiry*, 1956-57, Vol. I, All India, (Delhi, 1960), p. 47.

TABLE 7

Percentage Distribution of Households, Operated Area and Permanent farm servants by size-groups of operational holding in India (July 1953-June 1954).[24]

Operational Holding Size (Acres)	Percentage of total number of households	Percentage of total operated area	Percentage of total farm servants
0·00 (a)	10·9	0·0	0·0
0·01— 2·49	45·2	5·9	6·5
2·50— 4·99	15·5	10·6	9·6
5·00— 7·49	8·8	10·1	10·4
7·50— 9·99	5·5	9·0	9·2
10·00—14·99	5·5	12·8	13·5
15·00—19·99	3·0	9·7	10·1
20·0 and above	5·6	41·9	40·7
Total	100·0	100·0	100·0

(a) Includes households who operate 0·005 acres or less
1. Total number of households = 63,532,000
2. Total operated area = 335,711,000 acres
3. Total No. of farm servants = 7,523,852

It thus appears that use of hired labour in Indian agriculture is not merely on the fringes or marginal but wide-spread.[25] And the prevailing pattern of distribution of operational holdings makes it impossible for the small minority of farm operators (14·8 per cent) who hold about two-thirds of the total operated area (65·84 per cent) to cultivate their holdings merely with their own resources of family labour and necessitates regular use of permanent hired labour in farm operations.[26]

Now let us examine whether agricultural production on the bulk of arable land is carried on for subsistence or for sale. If we estimate the amount of land (of average productivity) required to produce average foodgrain requirements for the average household in different size-groups holdings, we get the following result :—

24 N. S. S. Report No. 46 (Draft) Report on Landholdings (4) Rural Sector (Some Aspects of Operational Landholdings—Population zones and all India), Eighth Round, July 1954-April 1955, I. S. I. Calcutta, (January, 1960), pp. 47 and 73.

25 Use of hired labour is widespread in the sense that wage-labour is used in a major part of the total arable land, although the number of households who operate this land constitute only a small minority of all the cultivating households.

26 Of course, it is true that the necessity for use of hired labour also arises on farms less than 7·5 or 10·0 acres in size in the peak period or because holders of such farms may either have insufficiency family labour resources or may be engaged in other non-farm activities. But farms above that size, under the prevailing techniques of cultivation, necessarily use labour even outside the peak period, though they may have the average amount of family labour and may not engage in non-farm activities.

TABLE 8

Estimates of Land sufficient to produce household foodgrains requirements in different size-groups of holding and Land producing crops for sale

Size-Groups (acres)	Average size of household operational holding	Average household size	Requirement of food grains for an average household per year in Lbs.[27]	Average amount of land sufficient to produce foodgrains requirements of household.[28]	Amount of land production on which is likely to be for the market.
0·00[29]	—	3·91	1632	2·86	-2·86
0·01— 0·99	0·21	4·14	1728	3·03	-2·82
1·00— 2·49	1·69	4·81	2008	3·52	-1·83
2·50— 4·99	3·62	5·24	2188	3·83	-0·21
5·00— 7·49	6·12	5·76	2405	4·21	1·91
7·50— 9·99	8·68	6·16	2572	4·50	4·18
10·00—14·99	12·18	6·34	2647	4·64	7·54
15·00—19·99	17·29	6·76	2822	4·94	12·35
20·00—24·99	22·21	6·86	2864	5·02	17·19
25·00—29·99	27·40	7·15	2985	5·23	22·17
30·00—49·99	37·98	7·23	3018	5·29	32·69
50·00 and above	83·54	8·30	3465	6·07	77·47
Average	5·43	5·01	2092	3·66	1·77

From this Table certain interesting conclusions emerge. First of all, we find that according to our estimates, 67·0 per cent of an average household operational holding would have to be devoted for the production of the foodgrains requirements of an average size household. And thus an average peasant household would have too little land to produce any substantial amount of crops for the market. But if we look at the estimates for the different size-groups, it is evident that households with operational holdings of less than 5 acres (71·23 per cent of all rural households, and operating only 15·60 per cent of the total operated area) would not have land sufficient even to produce their foodgrains requiremen ts. But house-

[27] The average per capita consumption of foodgrains is taken as 18·3 oz. per day as estimated by National Sample Survey for 1949-50 in the First Round. N. S. S. *General Report No.* 1 *on the First Round,* October 1950-March 1951., (Delhi, 1952), p. 25.

[28] It is assumed that the productivity per acre is uniform in all the size-groups of holdings. The average yield of foodgrains per acre for 1953-54 (571 lbs) is used to compute the figures of this column. Ministry of Food and Agriculture, Directorate of Economics and Statistics, *Area, Production, and Yields per Acre of Forest Crops.* 1949-50 *to* 1959-60, (December 1960), p. 61.

[29] Includes households who operate 0.005 acres or less.

holds with holdings of 10 acres or more (14·58 of all rural households and operating 65·84 per cent of total operated area) would be devoting more than 50·0 per cent of their total holding to the production of crops for the market. It would thus appear that crop production on about two-thirds of the total land is mainly for the market.

In fact, even on holdings below 5 acres, cultivators of which do not have sufficient land for producing their foodgrains requirements, crop production is likely to be for sale. In the first instance,these households are compelled to make ' distress sale ' of their produce to meet their money obligations like land revenue, rent and debt service, and to purchase such necessities of life as salt, kerosene and cloth,[30] and for that reason, it has been estimated, that the holders of land below 5·0 acres sell a relatively larger proportion of *their* produce than the cultivators of large holdings[31]. Moreover, these cultivators, in the absence of adequate availability of foodgrains requirements for the household, try to raise cash crops with the help of which they purchase foodgrains for consumption. Such is the situation in areas like Eastern U. P. where cultivators of lands even below an acre or a half raise sugarcane and purchase paddy from fair price shops.[32] In case they resort to neither of these expedients, they depend on money incomes from non-farm sources, like wage-labour in agriculture or non-farm small jobs outside the village or petty trade. In fact, it has been found in most recent studies that small cultivators generally take recourse to subsidiary occupations.[33] For instance, we read in the Report of the All India Rural Credit Survey :

> The smaller the holding he (the cultivator) cultivates, the more is his dependence on other forms of earnings; the small cultivator,for instance, has often to resort to carting or agricultural labour.[34]

It appears that it is only a small section of the farming community cultivating 14·19 per cent of all rural households and operating in all 18·56 per cent of the total operated area, and holding lands in size-groups of 5·0 to 10·0 acres that devotes more than half of its operational holding size to the production of its own foodgrains requirements. But on the remaining 81·44 per cent of the operated area, particularly on the 65·84 per cent held in size-groups of 10 acres or more, crop-production is generally for the market.

Thus, it is evident that the character of farming, whether farming is based on family labour or wage labour, and whether crop-production is

30 Dharm Narain, *Distribution of the Marketed Surplus of Agricultural Produce by Size-level of holding in India*: 1950-51 (Delhi, 1961), p. 36.

31 Ibid., p. 35.

32 Unpublished data available from the Survey of 5 villages in District Deoria, Eastern U. P. conducted by the Agricultural Economics Research Centre, University of Delhi, on behalf of the F. A. O., United Nations.

33 See for instance the village reports (typed), prepared by the Agricultural Economics Research Centre, University of Delhi.

34 Report of the All India Rural Credit Survey, Vol. II, (Bombay, 1954), p. 371.

for subsistence or for the market—depends essentially on the size of operational holding, and that over bulk of the land, operated by a small minority of all rural households in size groups of 10 acres or more, is characterised by regular use of wage-labour and production for the market.[35]

Let us now analyse the economics of the farming business in the light of the differentiation in operational holdings, and the characteristics of farming, analysed in the foregoing paragraphs. So far, only a few studies were available in which farming as a business enterprise was examined.[36] But since these studies pertained only to a few selected holdings in small local areas, and there were wide differences in the concepts used and methods followed for collection, tabulation and analysis of data, they could hardly be used to derive general inferences about the economic efficiency of cultivation in different parts of the country. However, in recent years, a series of investigations with uniform concepts, methods and proformas were conducted into the economics of farm management in 'six' typical regions of peasant agriculture'[37] in the States of U. P., Punjab, West Bengal, Madhya Pradesh, Bombay, and Madras.[38] These have provided valuable and useful data [39] for our purpose. From these studies one can derive a fairly general picture of the economic aspects of farming business in different States of India.

---

35. It does not mean that farms below 10 acres do not use wage-labour or do not produce for the market. In fact, all size-groups of farms use hired labour and sell some portion of their produce in the market for the reasons already mentioned. This makes it extremely difficult to distinguish as to where family-based farming ends and wage-based articulture begins and necessitate the use of uniform concepts and tools of analysis for all size-groups of farms as has been done in the Studies on the Economics of Farm Management, op.cit., Cf. A. K. Sen, "An Aspect of Indian Agriculture", *Economic Weekly*, Vol. XI, No. 1, Annual Number, (February, 1962), pp. 243-246.

36. See for instance, the series of *Farm Accounts of Selected Holdings in Punjab*, published by the Punjab Board of Economic Enquiry or *A Survey of Farm Business in Wai Taluka*, by D. R. Gadgil, Gokhale Institute of Politics & Economics, Poona.

37. 'In each of the six regions, two contiguous districts have been selected for study in such a way that they represent the most important and typical soil crop complexes in the State concerned and these six regions, taken together represent the major cropping patterns in the country.' *Studies in Economics of Farm Management, Punjab*, p. 11.

38. These investigations were initially confined to the six States mentioned and were conducted for three successive years i. e. 1954-55, 1955-56 and 1956-57. In subsequent years they have been extended to other states also but the reports have not yet become available.

39. The findings of these studies have formed the nucleii of controversy over many aspects fo agriculture such as the costs and returns on different sizes of farm, and their implications for policies towards co-operativisation or imposition of ceilings on landholdings or promotion of capital formation in agriculture. But we shall refrain from drawing any policy conclusions, and confine ourselves to the presentation of data, in the belief that they reflect the economic conditions prevailing on the farm holdings studied.

These studies strikingly reveal that the economic efficiency of the farming business depends to a considerable extent on the size of the operational holding. In all States, the size of the farm has been found to have a decisive influence on the nature and extent of capital employed, forms of employment of labour, techniques of cultivation, input output co-efficients, profitability or remunerativeness of the farming business, savings and consumption expenditure of the farming household and the nature and extent of capital formation on the farm. And the relative economic efficiency on different size-groups of operational holdings has been found to be essentially in a similar direction in all States though there are quantitative variations from State to State.[40] Since our purpose is not to examine the quantitative aspects of these data but only to analyse the data bearing upon the relative economic efficiency of farming business on different size-groups of holdings, and since the findings in all States are more or less in a similar direction, we shall utilize data only for U. P. for the year 1955-56[41] for illustrating the basic economic relationships that obtain on different size-groups of operational holdings.

TABLE 9

Per Farm Resources of Land Capital and Labour on 400 holdings in districts Meerut and Muzaffarnagar of U. P. (Survey Samples) in 1955-56.[42]

Size-Groups (Acres)	Average area in acres	No. of draught[42] Cattle (units)	No. of milch cattle[43] (units)	Value of investment on[43] live-stock (Rupees)	Investment on Implements (Rupees)	Investment on Farm Buildings Rupees	Total investment on fixed assets land (Rupees)	No. of family workers (Units)
Below 2·5	1·5	1·1	0·9	354	116	270	793	1·6
2·5— 5·0	3·7	1·8	1·0	559	246	324	1138	2·0
5·0— 7·5	6·1	2·1	1·4	781	348	501	1713	2·3
7·5—10·0	8·7	2·3	1·7	1008	370	717	2357	2·6
10·0—15·0	12·1	3·0	1·7	1209	564	895	2843	2·7
15·0—20·0	16·8	3·8	2·0	1613	669	1039	3895	2·9
20·0—25·0	22·8	4·2	2·1	1812	569	1281	4539	4·0
25·0 & above	34·8	6·0	3·6	2658	1111	2643	7251	3·5
Average	9·1	2·5	1·5	977	407	690	1963	2·5

40. See A. K. Sen, op. cit., p. 243.

41. We have refrained from using the data for 1954-55 in view of ' a word of caution ' from the Committee of Direction on Farm Management Surveys, that the ' possibility of some shortcomings in first year's work particularly during the initial stages cannot be completely ruled out '. *Studies in Punjab*, op. cit., p. V.

42. *Studies in Economics of Farm Management in U. P. Report for the year* 1955-56, pp. 7, 10, 14, 15 and 17.

43. The data for livestock, both in number and value terms, are given for 597 holdings and not only for 400 holdings included in the Survey Sample.

The above Table shows the assets structure of the farms according to size groups.

In this Table, some of the important economic relationships essential for the determination of economic efficiency of farming have been shown. Per farm resources of land, labour and capital are obviously necessary for this purpose. And we find that the range of variation of these resources per farm is very wide, as is also the case for the average size per farm in different size-groups of holdings.

While the average size of farm in the sampled holdings was 9·1 acres, the lowest size farms were as small as 1·5 acres and largest size farms as big as 34·8 acres. On these farms, while the average number of draught cattle per farm was 2·5, and of milch cattle 1·5, the small farms below 5·0 acres had much less than the average number, while farms above 10·0 acres had much more than the average. The farms below 5·0 acres possessed less than even 2·0 draught cattle per farm, which is the minimum necessary for independent and efficient cultivation from an individual peasant's point of view.[44] This means that these farmers must either be sharing bullocks of others on an exchange basis, or hiring them from other farms. This would usually involve difficulties in the timely performance of farm operations like ploughing, sowing and irrigation and consequently even loss of potential produce. It would also mean delays in operations like threshing, crushing of sugar cane, and transport of produce, since they must adjust their operations to the convenience of those who provide bullocks to share or on hire. The farmers in the range of 5·0 to 10·0 acres size-groups would not suffer from such disabilities. And the farmers of 10·0 acres or more would not be handicapped in this respect in any sense.[45]

More or less similar pattern of distribution is seen in case of the milch cattle. While the cultivators of lands between 5·0 to 10·0 acres possess only the average number of milch cattle, those cultivating below 5·0 acres possess only 1·0 or even less than 1·0 milch animal and those cultivating above 15·0 acres possess 2·0 or more.

Data on the value of investment in livestock per farm indicate that while farms below 5·0 acres in size possess livestock of poor quality, much

44. A pair of bullocks has often been used as a basis to determine the size of an 'economic holding' or 'family holding'. See *Report of the Congress Agrarian Reforms Committee*, (New Delhi, 1951), p. 8; also *Second Five Year Plan.*

45. The distribution of draught cattle for the country as a whole shows that households operating farms below 2·5 acres in size possess only 95·10 working draught cattle per 100 households, i. e. even less than 1 draught cattle per household, and farms of lands between 2·5 to 5·0 acres have only as many as 142·24 working draught cattle per 100 households, which too is much less than 2·0 per household. But the cultivators of lands above 15·0 acres possess more than 2·0 per household and as many as 495·81 working draught cattle per 100 household on holdings of 50 acres or more. See N. S. S. Report No. 30, op. cit., p. 31; also see S. Bhattacharya and K. Joshi, 'A Note on the size of Agricultural Holdings and its relation with the ownership of major capital equipment and livestock in the State of U. P.', submitted to the International Statistical Conferences, held in New Delhi, 1951.

less than the average, and farms between 5·0 to 10·0 acres have livestock close to the average, the farmers of 10 acres have much better quality animals. [46]

The data of investment on implements, farm buildings and fixed assets again shows that while farms of 5·0 to 10·0 acres have made investments on these items more or less close to the average, farms below 5·0 acres show much less investment per farm, and farms above 10 acres show investment much more than the average. In fact, farms of 15·0 acres and above have invested in implements Rs. 1,111 per farm, against the average of Rs. 407, in farm buildings Rs. 2,643 against the average of Rs. 690, and in all fixed assets (including livestock, implements, farm buildings and miscellaneous equipment but excluding land) Rs. 7,251 against the average of Rs. 1,963.

The fact that value of capital investment per farm increased considerably with an increase in the size of the operational holdings suggests that the capital-intensity of large-sized farms is much more than of the small farms. *Ipso facto* they also command bulk of the total capital resources employed in farming. And thus, concentration of land simultaneously brings about a concentration of capital resources.

The data in value terms do not bring out the variations in the numbers and quality of capital employed in farms of different sizes. But it has been found that the small farms have generally a much less number of implements and of very poor quality and large farms possess more and better

TABLE 10

Percentage of Farms possessing various types of improved implements according to size of holdings.[47]

		Percentage of farms in various size-groups having			
Size-Groups (acres)	No. of farms in the size-group	Iron-ploughs	cultivators	Bullock operated chaff-cutter	Pneumatic-tyred bullock cart
Below 2·5	47	—	—	—	—
2·5— 5·0	130	2·3	3·8	—	—
5·0— 7·5	111	4·5	1·8	—	1·8
7·5—10·0	104	4·8	3·8	—	1·9
10·0—15·0	103	6·8	4·9	—	2·9
15·0—20·0	52	13·5	9·6	—	13·5
20·0—25·0	25	16·0	16·0	4·0	16·0
25·0 & above	25	8·0	24·0	12·0	32·0
Total	497	5·5	5·2	0·7	4·4

46. '...On smaller farms...the bullocks are lower in size. They are also given much less concentrates as compared with large-size bullocks maintained on bigger farms.' *Studies in Economics of Farm Management in U. P.* op. cit., p. 28.

47. *Studies in the Economics of Farm Management in U. P. op. cit.*, p. 16.

implements. For instance, in the region of U. P. under study, we find the following pattern in the distribution of some 'improved implements'.[48]

It is evident that the use of improved implements has been much more on the large-sized farms. And, in fact, large farmers have more of these improved implements per farm. For instance, 'out of 33 farms having iron ploughs, four had more than one. A farmer in the size-group of 25 acres and above has two iron cultivators'.[49]

The resources of family labour per farm also increase with an increase in the size of holding like the resources of land and labour. But the extent of increase even for the highest size-groups of farms is not more than about two-fold,[50] which is much less than the increase in per farm resources of land or capital. Consequently, need arises to employ hired labour in bigger size-groups on a regular and permanent basis. And, we have already seen that the proportion of hired labour to the total farm labour increases considerably on farms of 10·0 acres or more, and about two-thirds of all the permanent farm servants are engaged on those very farms.

However, despite an increase in the quantum of hired labour employed with an increase in the size of farm, since the resources of capital per farm increase more than proportionately to the increase in labour, the value of capital investment per worker increases with an increase in the size of farms. The Table 11 illustrates this point fully.

It is evident that on farms below 5·0 acres and even on farms of 5·0 to 10·0 acres, investment per worker is less than the average. But on farms between 10·0 acres to 20·0 acres, it is higher than the average, and highest on the farms of 20·0 acres and above. The investment per worker (excluding land) in the highest size-group is more than double of that in the smallest size-group.

From these data, and from the variations in the nature and quality of capital employed on different sizes of farms, it follows that techniques of farming on small farms are labour-intensive and tend to become relatively capital intensive as the size of farms increases. We have already seen that the proportion of hired labour in total farm labour increases considerably with an increase in the size of farms. Thus it appears that increasing employment of hired labour and increasing investment of capital per worker co-exist together. This co-existence suggests that an increase in capital investment per worker with an increase in the size of farm may

48. A similar pattern has also been found from the data of agricultural implements collected by the N. S. S. (see Report No. 10, op. cit., p. 36). If the data in the quinquennial Census of livestock and agricultural implements were collected according to the size of holdings, it would provide a crucial indicator to determine as to which size-group of farms have contributed to capital formation in agricultural implements and contributed to increase agricultural productivity thereby.

49. Ibid.

50. This situation is similar to the one we have examined for the all India data in Section V of this paper.

TABLE 11

Capital Investment (fixed and operating excluding land) per worker according to size-groups of Holdings[51]

Size-Groups (acres)	No. of workers[52] per farm	Investment of capital (fixed & operating including land) per farm[53]	Investment of capital (including land) per worker per farm[54]	Investment of capital per farm[55] (excluding land)	Investment of capital (excluding land) per worker[56]
		Rs.	Rs.	Rs.	Rs.
1	2	3	4	5	6
Below 5·0	2·0	4236	2118	1718	859
5·0—10·0	2·8	7077	2528	2059	735
10·0—15·0	2·6	13377	5145	4432	1705
15·0—20·0	3·9	20608	5284	5680	1456
20·0 & above	4·6	37445	8140	9000	1957
Average	2·9	11892	4076	3477	1199

be due to the efforts of the large farmers to increase productivity of hired labour by providing them relatively more and better capital. Since the large farmers have to pay a wage to hired labour, they like to extract the maximum output from them, and for this reason provide relatively better tools and implements, better means of irrigation and better types of inputs. A small farmer dependent only on family labour has neither incentive nor compulsion nor even resources to economise on family labour since it is surplus and there is no payment of wages. But as the size of farm increases and the share of hired labour in total farm labour increases, the farmer is obliged to consider whether it would provide him sufficient additional output to compensate for the payment of the wage.

Moreover, since bulk of production on large farms is destined for the market, large farmers are compelled to maximise their net money income by extracting maximum possible work, from their hired workers. In times before abolition of zamindari when the zamindars had almost an unbridled

51. Data in this Table relates to the Cost Accounting Sample since these data are not available for the Survey Sample.

52. Number of workers per farm includes both family and hired workers, and have been computed from Tables 3·9 and 3·18 (A), *Studies in the Economics of Farm Management in U. P.* op. cit., pp. 35 and 41.

53. Table 3·20 p. 42, Ibid.

54. Computed by dividing column (3) by column (2).

55. Total capital investment including fixed and circulating capital but excluding the capital value of land have been computed from Tables 2·10, and 3·20 on pp. 11 and 42 respectively, Ibid.

56. Computed by dividing column 5 by column 2.

and despotic command on farm labour, the exploitation of the farm worker used to be in the form of being made to work for the longest possible hours under conditions of bondage and servitude and providing forced labour himself and by his dependents. But since after the abolition of zamindari, such bondages of servitude and forced labour have practically disappeared.[57] The zamindars, being obliged to convert themselves gradually into entrepreneurial farmers, have lost their earlier overlordship of farm labour. They are now also obliged to change or modify their forms of exploitation. Despite persistence of old practices of oppressions on farm labour in some regions, they now generally seek to increase the productivity of the farm worker by employing more and better capital equipment unlike before by keeping him attached to their farm in servitude.

Of course, with such extreme concentration of total cultivated land in the hands of a small minority consisting mainly of ex-intermediaries and big peasants, plentiful supply of cheap labour and stubborn persistence of the earlier forms of exploitation of farm labour are bound to remain with us for a long time. Under these circumstances, a rapid or widespread movement for increasing productivity by investment of more capital per worker, amongst the large farmers, is hardly likely to gather momentum since the cost of labour would generally remain lower than the cost of capital until the pace of industrialisation and absorption of surplus labour from agriculture into non-farm sectors of employment becomes very fast. But the prevailing pattern of distribution of operational holdings has made such a development almost inevitable. One witnesses an increasing use of tractors and other farm machines in Indian agriculture.[58] For instance, the number of tractors in India increased from 4,524 in 1945 to 35,000 in 1961[59] about an eight-fold increase; the number of electric pumps for irrigation from 8,561 in 1945 to 46,930 in 1965,[60] a more than five-fold increase; and the number of oil engines with pumps for irrigation from 12,062 in 1945 to 1,22,230 in 1956,[61] a more than ten-fold increase. These

57. 'By and large, the force of hired labourers in Indian agriculture is now made up of free men. One could not say this a generation ago. If we go back to the turn of the century, it is probable that the bulk of the agricultural labourers were unfree men, men who were in debt bondage or some other forms of servitude', Daniel and Alice Thorner, op. cit., p. 8.

58. 'The use of improved machinery and implements such as tractors, bulldozers, sugarcane crushers, harrows, hoes, seed drills and fodder cutters is gaining popularity. Though mechanisation has made considerable headway in these fields, it is only recently that greater attention is being paid to mechanisation in farming practices. The State Government and private farm owners have begun showing considerable zeal in the use of tractors and other improved implements.' *Indian Livestock Census*, 1956. op. cit., p. xxxi.

59. *Indian Livestock Census*, 1956, Vol I. (Summary Tables), p. 4 and *Lok Sabha debates*, Vol. LIV, No. 47, Col. 12170. Of these tractors, only 3252 are held on Government account and the rest are on private account. The number of tractors in urban areas also is only 3252, and the rest are all in rural areas.

60. *Indian Livestock Census*, op. cit., p. 4.

61. Ibid., p. 4.

machines are employed mainly by the large farmers, and make their techniques of farming highly capital intensive. They replace farm labour from substantial areas and make surplus labour and unemployment accumulate amongst the lowest strata of the Indian agrarian society.[62]

Turning away from per farm resources of land, labour and capital, let us now examine the relative availability of labour and capital resources per unit of land. Despite an increase in per farm resources of labour and capital with an increase in the size of farms, per unit of land, these resources decline with an increase in the size of the farms, as shown in the Table 12 below.

These data reveal that while small farms possess much less capital and labour relative to the large farmers, they have too much capital and labour per acre,[63] relative to the large farms. One finds that farms below 5·0 acres possess resources of labour and capital per acre much above the average, farms of 5·0 to 10·0 acres a little more than the average, and farms

TABLE 12

Per Acre Resources of Land, Capital and Labour on 400 holdings in districts Meerat, Muzzaffarnagar of U. P. (Survey Sample) in 1955-56[64]

	No. of draught cattle (units)[64]	No. of milch cattle (units)[64]	Value of investment on livestock[65] Rs.	Investment on implements Rs.	Investment on farm building Rs.	Total investment on fixed assets excluding land Rs.	No. of workers (units)
1	2	3	4	5	6	7	8
Below 2·5	0·70	0·53	233	77	178	523	1·1
2·5— 5·0	0·47	0·26	150	66	87	305	0·6
5·0— 7·5	0·35	0·22	129	57	83	282	0·4
7·5—10·0	0·26	0·19	116	47	83	272	0·3
10·0—15·0	0·25	0·14	100	42	74	236	0·2
15·0—20·0	0·23	0·11	96	40	62	231	0·2
20·0—25·0	0·19	0·09	80	25	56	199	0·2
25·0 & above	0·18	0·10	76	32	76	208	0·1
Average	0·27	0·16	107	44	76	215	0·4

62. See A. S. Kahlon and S. S. Johl, ' Rationale of Family Farm ', *Economic Weekly* Vol. XIV, No. 16, p. 672.

63. Also see C. H. Shah, *Problems of Small Farmers,* (Bombay, 1958), pp. 4-5 and 108-110.

64. *Studies in Economics of Farm Management in U. P., Report for the year* 1955-56, pp. 7, 10, 14, 15 and 17.

65. The data for livestock (both in number and value terms) are given for 597 holdings and not only for 400 holdings included in the Survey Sample.

of 25·0 acres and above employ the least resources of labour and capital per acre.

This aspect of farm structure has an important bearing upon the costs of production, input-output coefficients, and profitability or remunerativeness of the farming business in different size-groups of farms. As a result of this farm assets structure, the inputs of labour and capital per unit of land decline and the costs of production per acre go down with an increase in the size of farm. In fact, the inputs per acre even of other resources such as seeds, fertilizers, manures and irrigation decline with an increase in the size of farm, leading to a considerable decline in total inputs per acre. Evidently, the output-input coefficient is more favourable on larger farms and the profitability of remunerativeness of farming increases with an increase in farm size,[66] despite a somewhat larger gross output per acre on small farms. The following Table 13 illustrates these points.

In this Table, the costs of production per unit of land, as well as per unit of output are lower on large farms, and higher on small farms. The profits per farm and net profit or loss as percentage of total output also increases with an increase in the size of farm. Thus the farming business is more economic and efficient on large farms than on the small farms.

It was further found that ' farms incurring loss are most numerous among those below 10 acres and form about 80 per cent of total number (of farms) showing loss in both samples '.[67] It thus appears that farms smaller than 10·0 acres have not merely made less profits but have also incurred losses, whole larger farms have made much greater profits and relatively suffered much less losses.

The calculation of profitability or remunerativeness of farming business by ' imputing ' values to the contribution of family labour at the current wage rate for permanent labour and including it as an input factor for calculating the output-input co-efficient has been criticised recently.[68] This is because, by following this method, much of Indian agriculture appears unremunerative. In fact, even the authors of the farm-management studies, who have done much to apply and popularise this method of calculating farm profitability, themselves felt the need to develop ' some other concept of cost which may provide the explanation for continued production in spite of sustained losses '[69] (on the basis of the method of calculation followed). However, no satisfactory concepts of cost, or criteria of economic efficiency have yet been developed. Only Dr. A. K. Sen, in very brief-in fact too brief-outline has suggested that since

---

66. The decline in the input per acre on larger farms is due to economy of size...... ' *Studies in Economics of Farm Management in U. P.* op. cit., p. 33.

67. *Studies in Economics of Farm Management in U. P.*, op. cit., p. 44.

68. See A. K. Sen, op. cit., Dr. Sen writes " As an indicator of efficiency the surplus of output over all ' cost ', including the imputed wage of family labour is worth very little. "

69. *Studies in Economics of Farm Management in U. P.* op. cit., p. 38.

TABLE 13

Input-Output relationships, Costs of Production and Profits or Losses of Farming on 400 holdings (Survey Sample) in U. P. according to size-groups of farms.[70]

Size-Groups (acres)	Average size of farm	Value of inputs per acre (Rs.): Bullock labour	Human labour	Seed	Fertilisers & manures	Upkeep of implements	Rent & Cess	Irrigation on charges	Interest on fixed capital	Total of inputs per acre	Total of output per acre	Output/Input ratio	Total amount of profit per farm	Net profit or loss as percentage of output
1	2	3	4	5	6	7	8	9	10	11	12	13	14	15
Below 5·0	3·2	137·9	56·8	18·6	8·5	17·4	9·7	9·8	10·9	269·6	291	1·08	75	8
5·0—10·0	7·2	94·3	50·2	17·0	7·4	12·3	9·5	9·0	8·2	208·9	253	1·21	314	17
10·0—15·0	12·1	76·8	45·9	16·0	7·0	11·0	10·0	9·5	6·8	183·4	241	1·31	691	24
15·0—20·0	16·8	74·4	43·8	15·5	6·8	10·1	9·3	8·3	6·7	174·9	216	1·23	678	19
20·0 & above	28·6	60·1	36·8	13·5	5·9	7·6	8·4	5·8	6·2	144·3	190	1·32	1299	24
Average	9·1	84·3	45·9	16·0	7·0	11·1	9·3	8·4	7·5	189·5	234	1·23	407	19

70. *Studies in Economics of Farm Management in U. P.*, op. cit., pp. 29-40.

' there may be no alternative employment opportunities, at the margin ' for family labour, the factor that makes the crucial difference is the system of farming viz., whether it is wage-based or family-based, and non-wage family farming has some efficiency advantages[71], since it would enable family labour to be applied to a piece of land upto the point where net marginal product of labour becomes almost equal to zero.

Even if one agrees that imputation of value to family labour at the prevailing market rate for permanent labour exaggerates the costs of the small farmer, it nevertheless remains necessary to develop a method which may provide a uniform basis for comparison of economic efficiency on different farms, so heterogenous in their assets structure, forms of employment of labour and techniques of cultivation in which it is often difficult to distinguish a purely family-based and purely wage-based farm since all farms make use of both family and hired labour though in different proportions. It appears that if instead of taking into account the profit or loss per farm in this fictional sense, we take into consideration the farm business income, also computed in the farm management studies, which ' is the measure of earnings of the farmer and his family for management, risk, their labour, and capital investment ' and is obtained by adding the family labour income, the unpaid interest on owned capital and unpaid rent on owned land, we might bet a better measure of economic efficiency of different farms.[72]

Some other measures of farm efficiency are also available in the U. P. Farm Management study. These measures are not given as alternative criteria of economic efficiency of farm business but have nevertheless been

TABLE 14

Economic Efficiency of Different Size-Groups of Farms according to different criteria.[73]

Size-Group	Farm Business income per farm Rs.	Farm Business income per acre Rs.	Farm Business income a .:c to total out-put	Output per earner Rs.	Return per worker per year Rs.	Return per labour day of family members-Rs.
1	2	3	4	5	6	7
Below 5·0	497	155·3	54	459	136	1·3
5·0—10·0	779	108·2	43	758	245	1·5
10·0—15·0	1396	115·4	47	1074	334	1·6
15·0—20·0	1520	90·5	42	1252	327	1·7
20·0 & above	2302	80·5	42	1359	595	3·1
Average	940	103·3	44	868	304	1·7

71. A. K. Sen, op. cit.

72. This might also probably meet the objections of Dr. Sen.

73. *Studies in Economics of Farm Management in U. P.*, op. cit., pp. 39-41.

calculated. And we can use them also for a comparative picture of farm efficiency according to the size-groups. These are return per labour-day of family members, output per earner, or return per worker per year (including among workers both family and hired workers).

In the Table 14, the relative efficiency of different size-groups of farms is shown according to these criteria.

Thus it appears that even if we ignore the criterion of economic efficiency in terms of profit and loss altogether, we find that large farms yield much larger total farm business income per farm, although the small farms yield more farms business income per acre than the large farms. Similarly, in terms of output per earner, return per labour day of family members or return per worker both family and hired, large farms have a distinct advantage in terms of economic efficiency and productivity of family or hired labour,and yield a much higher income per family member than the small farms, despite the fact that the proportion of hired labour on large farms increases. This means that family members obtain larger incomes for themselves even while employing hired labour and productivity per worker on large farms increases even when a larger proportion of them are hired. This fact dispels the myth that application of family labour in agriculture is inherently superior and more productive than hired labour, because the latter lacks personal interest and requires supervision.

The only advantage of small farms appears to be their ability to extract more output per unit of land, though not per unit of labour.[74] But since these farms operate within a competitive market mechanism, and compete with the produce of large farms, this advantage would only be temporary.[75] It would last only during the period until the large farms, which are slowly ascending the scale of entrepreneurial agriculture in the wake of zamindari abolition, by investing more capital, employing better tools and implements, using improved methods of farming, and raising the productivity of both hired and family workers outstep the small farms even in output per unit of land. We have seen that in a strictly economic sense, the costs on the small farms are not compensated even by higher gross output per acre. But the small farms continue in production because they do not calculate their profits or losses in the economic sense but only look to their total farm business income. And since the size of their land is extremely small, they try to extract the maximum output. But despite that they have to depress their standards of living to the lowest level and they have little to invest in land or its cultivation. Consequently, in the long-run, they are bound to lose in the race so long as their economic fortunes are determined by a competitive market system. The following data in Table 15 brings out these aspects :

74. This also appears to be the secret of their continuance in production against the large farms which are otherwise much more favourably placed in respect of their assests structure and productivity of labour.

75. See A. S. Kahlon and S. S. Johl, *Economic Weekly*, Vol. XIV, No. 16, pp. 671-72 and Vol. XIV, No. 25, pp. 985-86.

TABLE 15

Living Expenses per family and per member and savings per family on (197) holdings (cost Accounting Sample) in U. P.[76]

Size-Groups (acres)	Average number of family	Living expenses per family	Living expenses per member	Savings per family
Below 2·5	6·1	772	126	– 302
2·5— 5·0	6·5	941	145	– 132
5·0— 7·5	5·5	1399	154	– 433
7·5—10·0	7·1	1216	171	– 19
10·0—15·0	6·8	1564	230	– 360
15·0—20·0	9·5	1998	210	– 356
20·0—25·0	14·1	2404	170	+ 430
25 and above	12·5	2541	203	+ 713
Average	7·6	1446	190	– 186

It is evident that living expenses per family as well as per member are much lower in the small farms than on the large and increase with an increase in farm size. And despite such a depressed standard of living, the small farmer is unable to make both ends meet even with his total farm business income, because of his high input costs and high living expenses. Even farmers between 10·0 to 20·0 acres suffer from the same difficulty. And only farmers of lands above 20·0 acres have savings for capital accumulation or investment on land or in cultivation. Thus, despite the initial advantage of higher gross output or farm business income per unit of land, the small farmer tends to lose this advantage in course of time, because the large farms,in the meanwhile accumulate capital and improve farm productivity.

The inability of the small and the medium farmer to make any savings or capital investment is also revealed by the Rural Credit Follow-up Surveys. For instance, we read that :

> The capital formation reported by cultivators resulted, in a substantial measure, through the efforts of big and large cultivators. The performance of medium and small cultivators, especially the latter group, was poor, barring one or two districts. It is significant to note that even in the districts in which big and large cultivators found it possible to undertake substantial capital formation expenditure, the performance of medium and small cultivators was generally poor. Medium and small cultivators had generally to finance a fairly large proportion of even their small capital formation through borrowings.

And yet another place, we find that :

> The data for the four classes of cultivators clearly show that generally it was only among big and large cultivators that any net investment took place during the year. Medium and small cultivators generally

76. *Studies in Economics of Farm Management in U. P.*, op. cit., pp. 132 and 135.

recorded, disinvestments in the districts barring Mandsaur, East Khandesh, and Coimbatore.

And with disinvestments, the small and the medium farmer will not be able to retain their advantage of a higher gross output or farm business income per acre for very long.

VII

Let us now examine as to how these farming units, with such wide differences in their assets structure, costs of production, input-output co-efficients, farm business income, productivity per worker, and savings and investment potential, would fare under a competitive market mechanism. The output of all these production units competes in the market where a given price prevails.[77] And those whose costs of production per unit of output are the lowest, productivity per worker the highest, and output-input co-efficient most efficient, derive the maximum profits. The large farmers are thus very favourably placed in a competitive market for agricultural produce while the small farmers face heavy odds in competition against them. And the middle group of farmers, since they are generally average in all aspects of farming, are in a state of continuous instability and flux due to the uncertainties of the market prices which affect them for the better or for the worse from time to time. The natural tendency of a competitive market is to impoverish the small farmer, enrich the large farmer, and to push the group of average or middle farmers into contrary directions, depending upon the numerous economic group of middle farmers gets drawn gradually into the whirlpool of economic competition, and is unable to remain close to the average and is slowly and gradually split up, some of them rising in the scale to become large farmers, and others, the bulk of them, dwindling into the position of small farmers.

This view of the impact of a competitive market on different types of farming units refers only to a long-term tendency. It is only the abstraction of an extremely complicated and protracted process which passes through complex stages and manifests itself in various forms. For instance, the impoverishment and economic ruin of the small farmer may express itself—and that too after a fairly long time—not in his complete elimination from the farming business but in his increasing dependence on non-farming subsidiary occupations, increasing burden of indebtedness or increasing liquidation of his farming assests. Gradually, he might turn to leasing out his land for a crop-season or a year, and may return to farming again depending upon the regularity and adequacy of his alternative employment. He may also continue to remain in the farming business by depressing his standard of living to the lowest possible level. These processes may also take long to become manifest on a considerable scale

[77]. We have already seen that the production of most farms except those between 5·0 to 10·0 acres would be for sale. Although the Farm Management Studies do not show how much of the gross output was sold in the market and how much was consumed within the household, without entering the orbit of exchange, they furnish some indications with which one can estimate the likely magnitudes of these quantities. The Table 16 is result of this exercise.

TABLE 16

Estimates of the likely amount of output per farm sold in the market according to size groups of holdings (Survey Sample).[78]

Size of the farm	Output per farm	% of actually incurred cash & kind exp. to total output	Living expenses per family[79]	% of actual exp. in purchases and other payments.[80]	Account of output exchanged for the purpose of col. 3	Amount of output exchanged for the purpose of col. 5	Total amount of output exchanged	% of exchanged output to total
1	2	3	4	5	6	7	(6+7) =8	9
Below 5·0	918	36·7	895	38·9	337	348	685	74·6
5·0—10·0	1818	38·3	1293	40·0	696	517	1213	66·7
10·0—15·0	2904	43·9	1564	40·3	1275	630	1905	65·6
15·0—20·0	3630	39·0	1998	39·1	1416	781	2197	60·5
10·0 & above	5437	42·9	2476	44·2	2333	1094	3427	63·0
Average	2135	40·2	1446	39·6	854	573	1427	66·8

78. *Studies in Economic of Farm Manegment*, op. cit., p. 43 and 132. These computations are made on the assumption that there is no other source of money incomes except the sale or exchange of output.

79. Data for living expenses 8 per family pertains to the Cost Accounting Sample, *Studies in Economic of Farm Management*, op. cit., p. 130.

80. Of course, it assumes that a uniform price is available to all groups of farmers. In so far as the small farmers are obliged to sell their produce at lower prices and the large farmers secure higher prices by virtue of their capacity to hold produce, the gains of the latter would be still more.

in a large country like ours. Similarly, the process of gradual splitting up of the middle group of farmers into small and large farmers may never come to light in the absence of two-point studies of a selected group of middle farmers over a reasonable period of time. The enrichment of the large farmers may also proceed slowly over a long period and remain disguised for a long time in the absence of any data regarding the changes in the distribution of land, capital investment, total output, savings, and new capital formation in the contryside. But a competitive market, unchecked by any counter measures, is likely to lead into these directions, is certain and well-known. So long as the market remains an effective regulator of the economic fortunes of the farming units, the direction of the movements of the small, middle, and large farmers would be along these lines.

If this view of the competitive process be correct, we should expect a bitter economic strife to prevail amongst peasants. There must exist a movement in opposite directions in India's agrarian society—a process of economic prosperity and ruin, improvement and decay, progress and regress. Some in the rural society, possessed of ample resources of land and capital, and using hired labour for farm operations, would make large profits, accumulate capital and expand output. Propelled by the motive to maximise their net money returns, they would take all steps conducive to economise on costs, enhance productivity of labour and output including the efforts to enlarge the scale of their farming business by taking more land on lease or buying it up from others, subject to the legal maxima. Another group—designated as the middle group—though not having such large resources of land and capital, but only a little more or less than the average, would also be drawn into the process of improving output, reducing costs, and investing capital in farming in order to be able to take the maximum advantage of the competitive market mechanism. And a few who are more skilful, hard-working and enterprising amongst them, by using inexpensive techniques of farming, and improved implements would succeed in expanding their scale of farming, make some profits and accumulate some capital. But because of their limited resources of land and capital and because of the severe competition from the top-group who command the bulk of the land and capital resources and reap much larger profits per farm, most of them would be gradually sliding down the scale of economic efficiency and welfare. And lastly, the vast majority of farmers, having only a small fraction of the total resources of land and capital, and with vast resources of surplus manpower, and suffering from acute pressure of population on their small holdings, would be fighting a losing economic battle against their formidable adversaries and would gradually face economic ruin and impoverishment. Sustained losses in the farm business, and inability to depress their standards of living beyond a given minimum will drive them to seek non-farm sources of income, thus diminishing the importance of cultivation as a source of livelihood for them, even leading them to lease out their small fragments to those who are expanding their scale of farming business.

This contradictory movement is likely to proceed only if there are no counter-checks or hindrances against it. However, in actual situations, numerous hindrances arise, and many counter-checks are applied against this natural tendency. For example, in economies with a large agricultural population, a highly unfavourable man—land ratio and without any alternative avenues of employment, this process does not lead to elimination of the small farmer from cultivation despite such heavy odds against him but only intensifies his exploitation as share-cropper, tenant-farmer or agricultural worker.[81] Nor is the movement for increasing the productivity of human labour by investment of capital or by improvement of technology very rapid.

In some agrarian economies, conscious counter-measures may be planned against this movement. For instance, the State may guarantee minimum prices for agricultural produce at a level at which most of the small farmers may continue in production despite all the diseconomies of their farming business. Even though it might lead to increasing disparities of income and wealth, since the large farmers would benefit more fromthe guaranteed prices, it may at least stabilise the small farm economy and arrest the process of its decline and economic ruin. Or limits may be imposed on the expansion of scale or farming by imposition of ceilings on the size of the operational holding, thus preventing complete alienation of the uneconomic farmer from his land, despite all disadvantages. Ad hoc measures like provision of subsidised inputs—irrigation, seeds, fertilisers, manures, credit and extension—may be provided which also, to some extent, may check these contradictory processes. However, so long as production is destined for a free market, and the market plays a dominant role in determining the economic destiny of the farming units, the process must tend to assert and manifest itself.

In India, in the context of the present-day distribution of operational holdings, the process is likely to work out with particular severity. The group of large farmers with adequate resources of land and capital consisting only of those having farms of 10·0 acres or more, is extremely small—only 14·58 per cent of all rural households, which commands 56·84 per cent of total operated area. Even amongst them, only 4·22 per cent of households hold as much as 38·62 per cent of the total operateds area. And this small group is likely to ascend the economic ladder. The next group of middle farmers, holding farms between 5·0 to 10·0 acres which forms about 14·19 per cent of all rural households and holdings about 18·56 per cent of the total operated area, though drawn into the economic strife, is scarcely likely to make much headway, except for a few. And the vast mass of the small peasant households, with lands below 5·0 acres, forming 71·23 per cent of all rural households and possessing only 15·60

81. Whether he is exploited as a tenant-farmer, share-cropper, or agricultural worker depends upon the nature of the tenurial framework which prevails when the agrarian economy is drawn into the orbit of the competitive market mechanism.

per cent of the total operated area, must face economic ruin and utter impoverishment if they are left entirely to the free winds of a competitive market.

Had the pattern of land reforms been different, and the monopoly of cultivated land by a small group of persons was liquidated at the time of abolition of intermediaries, or even later, the impact of the competitive process would have been far more widespread, rapid, and much less iniquitous. The movement for improving production and productivity, improvement of technology and investment of capital in agriculture would have embraced a far larger number of peasants than at present, and some of the anomalous developments currently apace in the countryside could have been avoided. But the path appears to have been laid, and unless it is reversed, must work itself out even though slowly, sluggishly, yet tortuously.

VIII

In recent years, there has been some evidence of these opposite processes developing simultaneously in the countryside. But this evidence is relevant only for small areas since no countrywide impirical investigations have been conducted for this purpose. The data about area and agricultural production, yields per acre, livestock, agricultural machinery and equipment and national income are collected only on an aggregative basis. No serious attempt has yet been made to collect these data according to broad socio-economic groups, or by size of operational holdings, which alone can reveal changes of opposite character in case of different groups. Nor have data been gathered in the decenial census to gauge these changes, even broadly. However, there are some studies, which do reveal some aspects of these contrary processes of growth and decay. We shall analyse them for whatever they are worth.

It is well known that Indian agriculture has shown considerable dynamism during the last decade since 1950-51. The index of agricultural production has risen by 45·5 per cent[82] and agricultural output has risen at the simple rate of about 4·5 per cent per annum, or at about twice the rate of population growth. This rate of increase is in sharp contrast to the rate of growth of agricultural output during the half century before 1950-51 when it was scarcely more than the rate of growth of population.[83] However, it has been estimated that out of the total increase of Rs. 1700 crores in agricultural income during 1949-50 to 1958-59, the share of the upper-income in the agricultural sector (accounting for only about 3·0 per cent of the rural population) in the increase of income at current

[82]. Central Statistical Organisation, Government of India, *Basic Statistics relating to the Indian Economy*, (Delhi, 1961), p. 1.

[83]. K. N. Raj, 'Growth of the Indian Economy from 1900-1960', *Yojna*, October, 1961.

prices may have been Rs. 600 crores or more (35·3 per cent of the total increase).[84]

It is already wellknown that the benefits of the community projects have chiefly gone to the large landholders. For instance, we read in the Report of the Team for the Study of Community Projects and National Extension Service :

> In nearly all the facilities that have nothing to do with agriculture and animal husbandry one notices that there is a direct relationship between the size of landholdings for a group and the proportion of respondents from that group that derive benefit from the particular facility. Thus we see that 66 per cent of the large owner-cultivators, 46 per cent of the medium owner-cultivators and 22 per cent of the small owner cultivators have derived benefit from the programme of improved seed supply. The same is found to be true about manures and fertilisers, improved methods of cultivation and pesticides. This implies that the better of group of farmers tends to be represented in higher proportion among the beneficiaries of agricultural facilities.[85]

Now, if we relate these observations with the gradual conversion of ex-intermediaries and a few big peasants into entrepreneurial farmers, who seek to raise output and productivity, by employing agricultural machinery, hired labour, etc. it is natural that the large farmers should have more or less monopolised over the benefits of the Community Projects and contributed a major share in the total additional agricultural output. It has been suggested that the percentage increase (of agricultural output per acre) has most probably been greater in the bigger than in the smaller farms.[86] And it should cause no surprise since bulk of the capital investments must also have been made by the large farmers, and bulk of the increased inputs like seeds, fertilisers, irrigation etc., must have also been applied by them. The large increase in the number of tractors, electric pumps and oil engines for irrigation, iron ploughs, bullock carts

---

84. K. N. Raj, ' Some Features of Economic Growth of the Last Decade in India ', *Economic Weekly*, Annual Number, February 4, 1961. Dr. Raj has defined as ' big farmer ' or ' upper income groups ' only those who operate farms of 30·0 acres or more. But if one considers holders of farms of 10·0 acres or more as large farmers who constitute only 14·58 per cent of the total rural population and hold 65·84 per cent of the total operated area, it may well be found that almost the entire increase in the agricultural output has been contributed by this group only. See results of a resurvey in village Sohalput Gara, mimeographed by the Agricultural Economics Research Centre, University of Delhi in which the largest percentage increase in output per acre has been on holdings of 12·3 to 16·5 acres (p. 74) and there has been an actual decline in the output of small farms during a brief period of 4 years from 1954-55 to 1958-59.

85. Committee on Plan Projects, Government of India, *Report of the Team for the Study of Community Projects and National Extension Service*, (Delhi, 1957), Vol. II., p. 101.

86. K. N. Raj, ' Some Features ....' op. cit.

and other implements during the last 15 years [87] suggests that large farmers, amongst whom there are ex-intermediaries and large peasants, have made considerable capital investment in the farming business. The investments are not only large in amount but also larger in per acre terms as compared to the small farmers. For instance, we find that :

> Big cultivators, who numbered 10·0 per cent of the cultivating families accounted for more than 40 per cent of the total capital formation reported by cultivators in Ferozepur, Broach and West Godavari. In all these districts the share of big cultivators in the total capital formation was marked higher than their share in the total area of cultivated holdings.[88]

Apart from making capital investment in agriculture, large cultivators have also been taking lands on lease. For instance, the N. S. S. data show that of the total area taken on lease (which forms 21·0 per cent of the total operated area), three-fifths is with households operating farms of 10·0 acres or more, one-fifth with farmers of 5·0 to 10·0 acres size holdings, and only one-fifth with cultivators of holdings below 5·0 acres.[89] Evidently, cultivators of farms of 10·0 acres or more do not take land on lease for eking out their subsistence, for which their own holdings are more than sufficient, but for commercial cultivation.[90]

Similarly, the increasing use of hired labour in Indian agriculture, since 1950-51, is revealed in the data of the Second Agricultural Labour Enquiry. According to the Report, the total agricultural wage paid employment of agriculture since 1950-51 is revealed in the data of the 189 days per annum in 1950-51, to 194·26 days in 1956-57, despite more rigorous norms of working hours and intensity of employment having been used for determining a day of wage labour than in the First Enquiry. Again, wage paid employment for women workers in agriculture also increased during the period from 120 to 131 days per worker per annum.[91] These data show that during the six years period, there has been relatively greater availability of wage employment, even though the level of total employment per worker per annum has gone down.[92] Of course, the extent of increase

87. There have been Rs. 51.05 crores of imports of agricultural machinery in the last decade (*Basic Statistics*, ... op. cit., p. 41). In addition, the value of agricultural machinery and equipment manufactured in India has been growing significantly.

88. *Rural Credit Follow-up Survey*, 1956-57, *General Review Report*, pp. 227-228.

89. N. S. S. Report No. 30, op. cit., p. 20.

90. ' The analysis (based on N. S.S. data) should explode the belief firmly held even in the highest quarters of policy makers that those who lease in land (tenants) are necessarily small farmers and those who lease-out are big, absentee landowning cultivators ' M. L. Dantwala, Presidential Address at Chandigarh Conference, *Indian Journal of Agricultural Economics*, Vol. XVI, No. 1, p. 14.

91. Ministry of Labour, Government of India, *Report of the Second Agricultural Labour Enquiry*, (Delhi, 1960), pp. 68 and 422.

92. See the *Resurvey Case of a Village in U. P.* (*Sohalpur Gara*), op. cit., where, during 4 years,the increase in the use of hired labour has been of the order of 22·1 per cent.

is not much, but the significant aspect of this fact is that it has taken place only over six years, and within 3-4 years after the abolition of zamindari. As years roll by, its magnitude is likely to increase although in view of the plentiful supply of cheap labour, the increase in the figures of employment per worker per annum may yet be small and may not reflect its full significance.

Taking all these data together, one can form a broad view of the direction in which Indian agriculture has been moving in recent years. It is manifestly a path towards the development of the system of farming, often called, 'capitalist farming', in which a very small group of farm holders are becoming economically more prosperous and socially and politically more powerful in villages.

Unfortunately, not much data are available specifically about the relative performance of the small farmers during the last decade, since attention has been confined only to the new emergent group of prosperous farmers. Yet some symptoms of increasing economic difficulties of small farmers are seen in the N. S. S. data on the leasing out of land. For instance, it reveals that of the total area leased out, 61·38 per cent is leased out by those holding lands below 5·0 acres[93], which means that the small owners have found it difficult to continue in cultivation because their holdings are too small even to grow a bare subsistence.

A direct corollary of this situation is the dependence of small farmers on off-farm subsidiary occupations. The Rural Credit Survey found a close relationship between the size of landholding and the extent of dependence on subsidiary occupations.[94] Again, in a study into the problems of low-income farmers in Kodinar Taluke (Gujarat), [95] it was found that 83·0 per cent of the small farmers depended on off-farm labour, and a few on sale of subsidiary products. Similar observations have been made in the numerous unpublished village reports of the agro-economic research Centres and other studies.[96]

Another important aspect of the small farm economy is the liquidation of physical assets or net disinvestment over a period of time. For instance, in the Gujarat Study, it was found that during 1948-53, a period of high prices of agricultural produce, small cultivators had sold away land to finance the acquisition of other assets like implements and livestock.[97] Again, comprehensive data about investment and disinvestment was collected in the All India Rural Credit Survey and it was found that......in almost all the districts except a few the small cultivators showed a net disinvestment position, while for the medium cultivators this was the position except in respect of a large majority of the districts.[98]

---

93. N. S. S. Report No. 10, op cit., p. 23.
94. *All India Rural Credit Survey Report*, Vol. II. op. cit., p. 371.
95. C. H. Shah, op. cit., p. 58.
96. See, for instance, Baljit Singh and Shridhar Misra, op. cit., p. 229.
97. C. H. Shah, op. cit., pp. 121-122.
98. *All India Rural Credit Survey*, Vol. I (Part I), (Bombay, 1956), pp. 777-787.

The liquidation of assets or net disinvestment by small farmers only accelerates the process of their gradual alienation from the farming business and increases their dependence on borrowing and off-farm sources of income.

All these symptoms are only aspects of the basic problem, the uneconomic and unremunerative character of small scale cultivation. Since no comprehensive studies over two points on the relative performance of small cultivators in respect of agricultural output, income, capital investment, productivity per acre etc. are available, one has to depend only on these indirect symptoms of a basic malady.

However, recently resurvey investigations have been completed in several villages in different states which are expected to throw some light on the nature and extent of socio-economic changes in the farm economies of different groups of cultivators. The preliminary findings of one of these studies on the relative performance of the different size-groups of cultivators in respect of agricultural output over the years 1954-55 and 1958-59 are shown in Table 16.

From these data, it is evident that during a brief period of 4 years, significant changes have taken place in the farm economies in different size-groups of cultivators, and the small cultivators have suffered a decline in gross value of output, (both total and per acre) as well as in residual income from cultivation (total and per acre). And the farmers of lands between 12·3 to 26·5 acres have achieved the maximum increase in gross

TABLE 16

Percentage Changes in Gross Value of Output, Output per acre, and residual income (total and per acre) from cultivation (net of actually incurred expenses) at constant prices according to size of operational holdings in village Sohalpur Gara between 1954-55 and 1958-59[99]

Size-Group (acres) *	p.c. Change in the gross value of output over 1954-55	p.c. change in gross value of output per acre over 1954-55	p.c. change in residual income from cultivation over 1954-55	p.c. change in residual income per acre over 1954-55
1	2	3	4	5
Below 4·1	— 41·2	— 19·8	— 9·9	— 24·8
4·1— 8·2	— 4·1	— 2·3	+ 21·2	— 7·5
8·2—12·3	— 0·6	— 0·3	— 13·2	+ 1·8
12·3—16·5	+ 23·0	+ 12·9	+ 13·1	+ 9·1
16·5 & above	+ 6·6	+ 3·8	+ 34·2	+ 1·0
Average	+ 1·8	+ 1·0	+ 11·0	— 1·0

* The size-groups are not in accordance with the standard classification since data were collected and tabulated in terms of local units and have been converted only afterwards.

99. *Socio-Economic Change in Rural India*, 1954-55—1958-59, *Case Study of a Village in Western U. P., Sohalpur Gara District Saharanpur*, (Mimeographed), Agricultural Economics Research Centre, University of Delhi, pp. 74 and 86.

output as well as residual income. These changes have altogether changed the relative position of small farmers in terms of even gross vlaue of output and residual income per acre, and reduced them to the lowest ladder in the scale, as shown in Table 17.

TABLE 17

Changes in Gross Value of Output and Residual Income from Cultivation per acre during 1954-55 and 1958-59 according to the size of operational holdings in village Sohalpur Gara.[100]

Size-Groups (acres)	Gross Value of Output per acre 1954—55	1958—59	Residual income per acre 1954—55	1958—59
1	2	3	4	5
Below 4·1	203·3	167·1	166·05	124·80
4·1— 8·2	180·0	175·9	137·30	127·02
8·2—12·3	189·2	188·6	138·57	141·03
12·3—16·5	178·4	201·4	127·22	138·77
16·5 and above	175·6	182·2	129·98	131·22
Average	128·7	184·5	135·41	133·20

These data show that changes in opposite directions have taken place in different size-groups of operational holdings and have entirely changed their relative position. They pertain only to one village and are used here for mere illustration of the manure as to how different farms respond to the processes of a competitive market mechanism, and how the gap between the small and the large farmers widens under its impact.

The opposite process of increasing prosperity along with increasing economic ruination has its social symptoms as well. These are reflected in ' the conflict between the rural elite and the rural poor' which, according to an eminent sociologist, ' is bound to grow acute as the latter become increasingly conscious of the fact that they are not benefitting as much (?) as they should from the various development programmes. '[101] This conflict generates social tensions and intensifies caste feuds, mutual rivalries, and the struggle for economic and social power in the village.[102] And these tensions are only the reflexes of a deeper economic process penetrating into the vital pores of our rural economy and society. The whisper about increasing inequalities of income and wealth and the cry about the rich getting richer and poor getting poorer also owe their genesis to the inevitable logic of this process.

For those who are shaping the course of the current agrarian revolution in India, it is necessary first to grasp this vast and complex process, before they can muster the strength and the will to cope with the problems generated in its development.

100. Ibid.

101. M. N. Srinivas, ' Changing Institutions and Values in Modern India ', *Economic Weekly*, Annual Number, February 4, 1961, p. 315.

102. Ibid.

5

SOME ASPECTS OF CASTE IN WEST BENGAL*

NIRMAL KUMAR BOSE

BIRBHUM IS a district in West Bengal which has retained its predominantly rural character. In the heart of this rice growing country lies the village of Jajigram with a population of 2160 individuals. The name of the village is derived from *yajana*, *yajna*, Vedic 'fire sacrifice,' and *gram*, 'village,' and the fact that the place has a large Brahman population is probably the result of its ancient historical origin when a colony of Brahmans took up residence in this place. There are, altogether, twenty-eight castes in residence here, and the following Table presents the number, traditional occupation, as well as actual occupation followed by each of these castes. It may be pointed out that the census presented below was the result of a local social worker's survey undertaken in the year 1947.

Group A : Castes from whom water is not accepted by Brahmans

Name	No. of families	Individuals	Traditional Occupation	Actual Occupation
Muci	65	325	Tanning, shoe-making	Landless labour
Bhuimali	40	150	Sweeping, cleaning	T. O., landless labour; 2 peasant proprietors
Phulmali	7	25	Gardening, supplying flowers for religious offering	Landless labour
Rajbamsi	10	35	Boatmen and agricultural labour	Landless labour
Bhar	12	35	Mfg. of chapped rice, labour	T. O.
Mal	80	400	Agricultural labour	T. O.
Konai	15	350	—do—	T. O.
Bauri	1	5	—do—	T. O.
Dom	5	20	Working in bamboo (basket weaving)	T. O.
Kora Santal	25	65	Digging earth, labour	T. O.
Jele	11	55	Fishing	T. O. ; 2 peasant proprietors
Dhoba	2	10	Washing clothes	T. O.

* Reproduced from the *Journal of American Folklore*, July-September, 1958.

Group B : Castes from whom water is accepted by Brahmans

Name	No. of Families	Indivi-duals	Traditional Occupation	Actual Occupation
Goala	8	25	Milk trade and cow-keeping	T. O. and farming
Sadgop	5	10	Farming	Landless labour
Kumor	4	10	Mfg. Pottery	T. O.
Kamar	6	20	Blacksmithery	T. O.
Chutar	1	5	Carpentry	T. O.
Napit	7	50	Shaving and hair-cutting	T. O.
Bene	2	5	Trading in spices	Trade and farming
Barai	40	200	Cultivation of betel vine	T. O.; 2 grocers, 3 unskilled physicians
Bhat	2	10	?	Clerical jobs
Kayastha	28	120	Clerical work	Farming, clerical job, 2 physicians, some unemployed

Group C : High Castes

Name	No. of Families	Indivi-duals	Traditional Occupation	Actual Occupation
Rajput	4	15	Soldiers	Landless labour
Chatri	6	15	Soldiers	Farming, clerical work
Brahman	30	150	Priestcraft, teaching, etc.	Farming, clerical job, 1 physician, some unemployed
Grahacarya (Brahman)	1	5	Astrology	T. O.
Vaidya	12	50	Physician	Farming, physicians, clerical job also unemployed.
Bairagi (Vaisnava mendicant)	5	15	Religious mendicancy	1 in farming

It is observed in the Table that sixty eight per cent of the population belongs to the section from whom water is found unacceptable by "upper" castes like Brahman or Vaidya. Leather workers have mostly lost their hereditary occupation, because hides and skins have, for many years past, formed an important collection from the villages of India for purposes of export. They have gradually drifted towards agriculture and form a fair proportion of the landless labour corps of the village. Bamboo workers, i.e., basket-weavers, and fishermen alone have been able to retain their own profession; among the last, two have become peasants owning land.

Among the " clean *Sudras,* " i. e. those farming and artisan castes from whom water is acceptable to Brahmans, the change from traditional occupation has been less marked in character. These *Sudras* constitute altogether 22·6 per cent of the total population. We find that milkmen have also taken to agriculture, while one member of the blacksmith caste has joined clerical service. The comparatively more prosperous cultivators of betel vine, namely Barai, are, by and large, farmers; while two of them trade in grocery, three are physicians, and some are unemployed. The Kayasthas form in this group, an educated and professional class; while there is also some dependence among them upon cultivation through hired labourers. The Brahman (including *Grahacarya,* astrologer) and Vaidya, who claim equal status with the Brahman in society, are both dependent on farming through hired lobourers, or earn their livelihood through professions like clerical service, teaching, etc., or are unemployed. They altogether constitute about nine per cent of the total.

6

MALIKS AND MONEY-LENDERS—THEIR ROLE*

DANIEL THORNER

SOCIALLY, the resident maliks and money-lenders form a small and quite distinctive group within the village. A handful of six or a dozen families, they typically belong to Brahmin, Thakur, or other high-ranking castes; alternatively, as in Andhra, they may be members of respectable cultivating castes like the Kammas, Reddis, or Raos. They live in larger houses, wear finer clothes, and eat a better diet than the rest of the villagers. They may send their children to higher schools, subscribe to newspapers, listen to battery radios, or own bicycles—all luxuries usually quite beyond the compass of the debt ridden kisans, to say nothing of the landless *mazdurlog*.

Between these last two groups, although the community of economic interest may appear very large, there is a steep social barrier. The kisans are drawn primarily from cultivating or artisan castes; the *mazdurlog* primarily from Harijans, Scheduled, depressed or " backward " classes. Certain types of work locally considered degrading, such as ploughing in the Eastern U. P., are reserved for these lowly servitors. The rare Chamar, Mahar, Panchama or other untouchable who prospers economically and attempts to secure a foothold for his family by buying land may find insurmountable obstacles in the way of the purchase. For he is up against the deeply entrenched tradition of rural inequality—a tradition which goes back centuries if not millennia. To a considerable extent the belief that low castes are born to labour with their hands, and high castes to enjoy the fruits of others' labours,is accepted by the former as well as the latter. The separation between proprietorship and physical cultivation both draws sanction from and serves to reinforce the caste structure of rural society.

What we have here in India today, then, is an unique agrarian structure. It represents a blending of remnants from the pre-British economic order (including, above all, the claim of the State to a share of the produce of the land), together with modern Western concepts of private property. The result has been a layering of rights from those of the State as super-landlord (or ultimate owner) down through those of the sub-landlords (penultimate owners) to those of the several tiers of tenants. Both the State and the superior holders exercise the right to draw income from the soil in the form of rents, wherever possible the tenants also try to subsist by collecting rents from the working cultivators with rights inferior to their own.

---

*Reproduced from *The Agrarian Prospect in India,* by Daniel Thorner pp. 10-13.

The maintenance of this hierarchical structure of interests in the land has required, in effect, that quite a substantial proportion of the produce be reserved for persons who perform no agricultural labour. What was left to the actual cultivator, after the claims of the various superior right holders were satisfied, might still be subject to collection as unpaid debt by the money-lender. The mechanism for the enforcement of this withdrawal of the great bulk of the product from the primary producers was provided by the new body of written law, the courts, the police, the promulgation of ordinances, and so forth. In the end, the working kisan was left with no surplus to invest in better implements,improved seed or fertilizer, and in any case no real incentive to increase his productivity. Since his tenure was in most cases insecure, it was scarcely worth his while to think of undertaking long-term improvements. For the landless *mazdur*, there was even less point to any attempt to raise his efficiency.

Both the harassed small-holder and the down-trodden labourer, seeing before them little prospect of a betterment of their condition, concentrated rather on warding off a worsening. So far as any changes might be proposed, their attitude was typically one of a stubborn and suspicious conservatism. The superior right holders, from whom a more progressive approach might have been expected, were interested in agriculture only to the extent that they might continue to draw their incomes from it.

Typically they found it more profitable to rent out their lands than to manage them personally. Clearly it was not worth their while to invest capital in agricultural operations so long as these operations were to be left in the hands of the most backward and ill-educated villagers. On the other hand, as members of higher castes, they preferred not to think in terms of undertaking the " degrading " field work themselves. The primary aim of all classes in the agrarian structure has been not to increase their income by adopting more efficient methods, but to rise in social prestige by abstaining in so far as possible from physical labour.

This complex of legal, economic, and social relations uniquely typical of the Indian countryside served to produce an effect which I should like to call that of a built-in " depressor. " Through the operation of this multi-faceted " depressor, " Indian agriculture continued to be characterized by low capital intensity and antiquated methods. Few of the actual tillers were left with an efficacious interest in modernization, or the prevention of such recognized evils as fragmentation. The pattern of landholding, cultivation, and product sharing operated to hold down agricultural production. From the 1880's to the 1940's total output rose so slowly that it would not be too strong to speak of stagnation. The income of the kisans and *mazdurlog* (i. e., the overwhelming bulk of the rural population) remained at or below the subsistence level. For the newly developing urban manufacturing sector, this in turn constituted a serious handicap in the form of a severly restricted Indian home market. It is difficult to see how India's current plans for economic development can get very far without a concerted effort to remove the " depressor. "

7

TWO POWERFUL CLASSES IN AGRARIAN AREAS*

D. R. GADGIL

IT IS OFTEN said that the Indian countryside requires an economic and social revolution. It is necessary to be specific about the nature of this revolution. Economic power in the coutryside is today exercised chiefly by two elements. The first of these is represented by the trader-money-lender class who chiefly profit from all opportunities of gain connected with the finance of agricultural production and with trading in the countryside. This element is connected chiefly with the urban trading and financial communities and acts as their representative in the countryside. The other element is that of the substantial landlords and farmers, say, the top 10 per cent. These are ordinarily holders of land as also cultivators of it on a comparatively large scale and they usually wield considerable political and social power. In some instances the two elements would have much in common and may act together closely. In many areas, however, they would be separate.

The problems of change involved in the two cases are different and different types of programmes have to be devised for them. In relation to the operations of the trader-money-lending interest, the programme now adopted appears to be that of strengthening co-operative efforts in the spheres of both agricultural finance and marketing with extended emphasis on processing activities; the co-operatives are to be helped by direct State activity in storage and warehousing of agricultural produce, and, perhaps, also in purchase of agricultural products at a later stage. This programme, if successful, woulds till not affect the position of the top agriculturists. They would be left as strong as before; actually their position may become stronger as a result of the diminution of the influence of traders and money-lenders if in the co-operatives which take their place the top cultivator elements are dominant. Such domination on their part may indeed be expected and would ordinarily take place unless special efforts are made to obviate it.

The present position of the top agriculturists depends on their command of extensive land areas and will continue as long as this command lasts. Therefore, their position could be affected only by certain types of land reform proposals.

*Reproduced from the artcle " Gramdam-Implications and Possibilities, " *Indian Journal of Agrcultural Economics*, Vol. XII, No. 4. pp. 1-3.

Both these programmes, that of land reform and of co-operative development, are today largely paper programmes. It is indeed possible that they may be seriously whittled down even before they are launched. It is clear that there are today powerful forces operating at the highest level working for the retention of the trader-money-lender class in rural India. Two recent events may be noted which are of significance in this connection. The first is the keenness of many in authority to ensure the continuance of the operations of the private trader even in the handling of foodgrains. The second is the attack on the whole programme of strengthening of co-operative primary units by making their sizes economic and by supplying them initially with required financial resources by contributions from the State. The opposition takes the form of raising a cry of voluntarism. It safely ignores or deliberately shuts its eyes to the universal lesson, specially emphasised by experience in India, that the unaided activities of the poor and the weak can make no advance against the heavily entrenched position of the trader-money-lender classes. The plea for small uneconomic single village units and for denying financial aid to primaries of poor peasants, in a country where all the largest industrial units have been established through and maintained by sacrifices imposed on the consumers and have been given all kinds of State aid including concessional finance, appears no more than an unsuccessful attempt at concealing the real intentions of those who want to maintain the *status quo*. The great difficulty of doing anything effective in the matter of land reform shows the strength of the other element which is powerful in the countryside. The basic sterility of the community projects administration stems from its inability and unwillingness to do anything which will affect the position and interests of these two entrenched classes. The approach of the C. P. A. is illustrated by a recent survey which revealed that the C. P.A. was unwilling to encourage the scheduled castes to assert their constitutional guarantee of legal and civic rights.

The position may be summarised as follows. There is a general agreement that economic, political and social progress must rapidly take place in the countryside. At present there is, in fact, very unequal distribution of rural resources and the benefits of the better terms of trade for agriculture have most largely accrued to the financing, trader-money-lender classes and next, in some measure, to big cultivators. A change in this situation and a rapid movement forward in production could take place only if there is a more even distribution of productive resources, greater economic strength on the part of the smaller units leading to ability to withstand pressures from either the top cultivators' strata or the money-lender-trader classes and a concentration of the finance, trading and processing of agricultural production in the hands of the cultivating community itself. In order to achieve these ends there are planned programmes of land reform and of co-operative development and there is a special agency, the Community Projects Administration charged with the responsibility of promoting technical improvement and welfare.

Bearing the abolition of Zamindari, which in itself does not complete land reform but merely brings the problem in the older Zamindari areas conceptually to the same level as in the Ryotwari areas, no great success has yet been achieved in the programme of land reform. In many States comprehensive legislation on well established principles is itself lacking. Where legislation is satisfactory the implementation of the tenancy provisions is either weak or the local land-owning classes have successfully circumvented it. The programme of redistribution of land and the strengthening of the uneconomic units by some sort of pooling of land and other resources lags in every way, far behind even the tenancy aspect of land reform. Programmes of co-operative development in relation to finance, marketing and processing have made some headway in States where already non-official co-operation was strong and had some idea of the nature of the problem faced by it. In other States the progress is far from satisfactory and there is likelihood of the programme in this regard meeting heavy weather in the near future. The Community Projects Administration is unable to take any action which vitally affect the interests of existing powerful groups of rural society. There is no prospect, therefore, of any immediate large-scale socio-economic change in the countryside and this is so simply because there is no desire for any such change among those who hold economic and political power. It is only when pressures generate from below and discontent with existing conditions comes to surface that the formally accepted programmes could become alive.

8

THE PROBLEMS OF THE MARGINAL FARMERS IN INDIAN AGRICULTURE

UDAY MEHTA

THE AGRICULTURAL reconstruction has proved an achilles hill of planning in India. The official policy of 'betting on rich' in rural areas has only aggravated agrarian crisis in India. One of the basic prerequisites for the revitalization of agriculture is the effective resolution of problems of marginal farmers in rural India. The overwhelming majority of Indian cultivators operate on submarginal or marginal units of cultivation. The inadequate appreciation of this vital phenomenon has undermined official endeavours for rural reconstruction. An attempt is made here to unfold the deeper implications of the problems of marginal farmers within the profit-oriented matrix of Indian economy. A proper appraisal of their problems assumes greater significance in the light of the emerging trend among the experts, advocating inherent superiority of marginal farms compared to bigger units of cultivation.

TABLE 1

Distribution of ownership holdings amongst rural households according to size groups crop season, 1953-54

Size-Group	Household ownerships holdings			
	P.c. of holdings to the total	Cumulative p. c. of holdings	P. c. of area to total area owned	Cumulative p. c. of area
1	2	3	4	5
0·00**	23·09	—	—	—
0·01— 0·99	24·17	47·26	1·37	—
1·00— 2·49	13·98	61·24	4·86	—
2·50— 4·99	13·49	74·73	10·09	16·32
5·00— 9·99	12·50	87·23	18·40	34·72
10·00—24·99	9·17	96·40	29·11	68·83
25·00—49·99	2·66	99·06	18·63	82·46
50·00 or above	0·94	100·00	17·54	100·00
Total	100·00	—	100·00	—

** Includes households owning an area of ·005 acres or less.

MAGNITUDE

It is generally accepted that the cultivators whose holdings are below 5 acres, can be placed in the category of marginal farmers in the present state of agriculture in India. The vast bulk of these farmers are deficit cultivators as the farming has ceased to be a gainful occupation for them. The Table I* reveals the proportion of these farmers in the total cultivating population.

It can be seen from the above Table that nearly three-fourths of all rural households operate on holdings which are below 5 acres, and together own only one-sixth of the total area. In sharp contrast to this, the top one-fourth of households hold 83·68 per cent of the total area in size-group, above 5 acres. It can be also further observed from the above figures that, 12·77 per cent of the rural households hold as much as 65·28 per cent of the total owned area in size-groups of more than 10·00 acres. Even after implementation of land reforms the land distribution pattern has not altered in favour of marginal farmers. This fact is also confirmed by the Mahalanobis Committee Report.

We shall now examine how the laws of market economy remorselessly operate against marginal farmers and gradually worsen their plight.

PRICE STRUCTURE

The last decade witnessed unprecedented rise in the prices of manufactured articles as well as agricultural products. The recent sharp rise in the prices of foodgrains transcended all past records. This inflation of prices caused primarily by deficit financing, erodes the standard of living of masses and leads to further concentration of wealth in the hands of the richer sections. According to Prof. Gyanchand,** " Rise of the prices in the Second Five Year Plan period has been of the order of 25 per cent and since 1956 the rise has been maintained and even accelerated. This has happened in spite of the increase of 33 per cent in agricultural and 66 per cent in industrial production......The premise that in a developing economy rise of prices is inevitable is being made a cover for all errors and failings in respect of price policies......The fact that in spite of the peak of agricultural production of 76 million tons and increase of industrial production of 11·7 per cent during the course of 1960, the average level of prices has risen during the year by 6·5 per cent, of raw materials by 16 per cent. The index number of general price level at the end of war with 1939 as base was 260, the average at 1952-53, when the new base for the revised index number was adopted, was 380, and in January 1961 it was 475. In everyone of these indices are congealed un-wanted and iniquitious changes in economic relativities of different income groups, which have been known to exist but have been deliberately left unredressed owing to the extreme difficulties of righting the wrongs created by inflationary upsurge from time to time. The result has been that these inequities have

* National Sample Survey, Eighth Round, Report of Land Holdings, Rural Sector.

** '*Perspective*' June, 1961, Prof. Gyanchand's article 'Price Policy'.

accumulated and their incidence has been severe on agricultural labourers and even industrial labourers,small peasants, small traders and lower middle classes with fixed and relatively in elastic incomes. The whole income structure of the country has been gravely distorted on this account and the increasing national income has not accrued to the benefit of these classes i. e. the vast majority of our people, and they are as a matter of fact distinctly worse off than they were before the war. Any price policy which leaves this cardinal fact of the economic situation out of account follows the line of least resistance and is escapist in the worst sense of the word."

Though it may sound paradoxical, it is still true that high agricultural prices hit the marginal farmers as much as the urban population. The rise in agricultural prices benefits only the rich farmers with marketable surplus. They profit from higher prices and strengthen their economic position, at the expense of the deficit cultivators and agricultural labourers. Nearly 40 per cent of the Indian cultivators have to buy a part of their food requirements from the market and they suffer heavily from the high prices of essential commodities. Thus rise in prices only depresses the already depressed consumption standard of vast bulk of our deficit farmers. Even the exchange equivalents in the countryside are also more unfavourable to the marginal farmers than suggested by the wholesale price indices. The overwhelming proportions of small farmers are still under the firm grip of the village Shaukars, most of whom perform the combined functions of moneylending as well as trading. It is estimated that the moneylender-cum-traders' profit over the prices paid to the growers ranges from 30 to 200 per cent whereas in other countries it seldom goes beyond 15 to 20 per cent. Thus the market mechanism within the framework of underdeveloped economy intensifies the process of impoverishment of the marginal farmers. The following Table distinctly reveals the

TABLE 2*

Distribution of sales of paddy by farmers in selected villages in W. Bengal, 1942-45, 1955-57

Size group of holdings (acre)	Percentage sales of each group to total		Quantity of sales per acre of holdings (in mds)	
	1942—43 1944—45	1955—56 1956—57	1942—43 1944—45	1955—56 1956—57
upto 2·5	3·29	1·94	1·76	0·82
2·5 to 5	12·92	10·91	1·90	1·94
5 to 10	37·99	30·32	3·60	4·57
10 to 20	33·15	28·58	6·22	6·46
Above 20	12·65	28·25	5·14	10·69
Total	100	100	3·94	4·61

* Reproduced from the findings of the Survey of Agro-Economic Research Centre, Viswa-Bharti, Agricultural Situation in India, 1960.

worsening plight of the marginal farmers in terms of the quantity of sales per acre.

It is evident from the above Table that the quantity of sale by small farm registered a fall while that of the big farms relatively increased during the periods under reveiw. Similarly eminent scholars like Prof. Khusro, Dharam Narain and others have also pointed out that marketable produce as a proposition of total produce increases generally with increase in farm size.

Unremunerative and uneconomic character of marginal units of cultivation can be further elucidated from the following Table.

TABLE 3*

Per acre resources of land, capital and labour on 400 holdings in districts Meerut, Muzzfarnagar of U. P. (Survey sample) in 1955—56

Size-groups acres	No. of draught cattle (units)	No. of milch cattle (units)	Value of investment on livestock Rs.	Investment on implements Rs.	Investment on farm buildings Rs.	Total investment on fixed assets excluding land Rs.	No. of workers (units)
1	2	3	4	5	6	7	8
Below 2·5	0·70	0·53	233	77	178	523	1·1
2·5— 5·0	0·47	0·26	150	66	87	305	0·6
5·0— 7·5	0·35	0·22	129	57	83	282	0·4
7·5—10·0	0·26	0·19	116	47	83	272	0·3
10·0—15·0	0·25	0·14	100	42	74	236	0·2
15·0—20·0	0·23	0·11	96	40	62	231	0·2
20·0—25·0	0·19	0·09	80	25	56	199	0·2
25·0 & above	0·18	0·10	76	32	76	208	0·1
Average	0·27	0·16	107	44	76	215	0·4

It can be seen from the above Table that the marginal farms possess much less capital and labour compared to the larger farms. In contrast to this they exhibit too much capital and labour per acre in comparison to larger units. " This aspect of farm structure has an important bearing upon the costs of production, input output coefficients, and profit ability or remunerativeness of the farming business in different size-groups. As a result of this farm assets structure, the inputs of labour and capital per unit of land decline and the costs of production per acre go down with an increase in the size of farm. In fact, the inputs per acre even of other resources such as seeds, fertilizers, manures and irrigation decline with an increase in the size of farms, leading to a considerable decline in total in-

*Enquiry No. 6. Some Aspects of Indian Agriculture by Sulekha Gupta, pp. 32-33.

puts per acre. Evidently, the output input coefficient is more favourable on large farms and the profitability or remunerativeness of farming increases with an increase in farm size, despite a somewhat larger gross output per acre on small farms".*

Under the circumstances, it is no wonder that the under-utilization of available resources is a chronic problem faced by the marginal farms. This can be better illustrated from the under-utilization of the working capacity of bullocks on small farms. A pair of healthy bullocks is presumed to be capable of work for 8 hours each day for 350 days in a year. On this basis, it can be seen from the following figures that, the utilization of bullocks varies from 13·1 to 43·30 per cent of their available labour on holdings of different sizes.

Below 2 acres	13·14%	5 to 10 acres	36·79%
2 to 5 acres	34·12 %	10 to 15 acres	43·35%

It is evident from the above figures that the considerable amount of the working capacity of the bullocks remains unutilized on smaller farms. Dr. C. H. Shah has further highlighted this phenomenon. He observes,** 'The field survey in the Kodinar taluka reveals that the central problem of the small farmers is relatively greater imbalance of factors of production. This affects on the one hand farm production and land productivity and on the other affects his income, savings, credit and investment and through them his economic betterment. Since two aspects are interlinked they set into motion a vicious circle which with passage of time brings about deterioration of his economy. Imbalance in factor combination takes two forms. Firstly, since the quantum of family labour is given and the size of holding is inadequate to provide full employment to all working members of the family, his economy has surplus of labour, only a part of which is employed outside. Unemployed labour is a heavy drag on his small income. Secondly, a certain minimum of equipment and housing facilities is necessary but his investment is rather heavy for his size of holding. On the other hand, his equipment is inadequate for efficient farming. Further the low income leaves very little for investment in working capital, with his small holdings, he commands low credit which is inadequate to meet the requirement of working capital." The above observations of Dr. Shah distinctly reveal the paucity of resources and resultant helplessness of the small farmers in a relatively prosperous tract of Gujarat. He also prognosticates decay of small farming with the passage of time.

We shall conclude this paper, by referring to the extent of under-employment that prevails in marginal units of cultivation in the absence of opportunities for gainful employment.

The following Table provides some pertinent facts with regard to labour days and family labour income per acre for different size groups of farms in U. P. in the year 1954-55.

*Ibid.

**The Problems of Small Farmers in Kodinar Taluka—C. H. Shah.

TABLE 4*

Size group (acres)	Labour days (per acre)	Family labour income (per acre)
Below 2·5	133	83·72
2·5 to 5	114	
5 to 7·5	96	119·87
7·5 to 10	67	
10 to 15	52	91·81
15 to 20	49	111·84
20 to 25	40	124·47
25 & above	31	

The following Table reveals that the number of labour days put in per acre is more on the marginal farms. Even if it is assumed that the intensity of cultivation and reliance on mixed farming is greater on marginal units that by itself cannot explain such a wide range of difference in the number of days put in per acre which vary from 133 for the size group of 2·5 acres and below, to 31 for 25 acres and above. Therefore, it can be safely concluded that the labour input on marginal units of cultivation has very low returns. This precisely indicates that there is considerable amount of underemployment of small farms. The unremunerative character of marginal farms becomes evident from the fact that family labour income per acre increases with the increase in the size of farm though the family labour input is much smaller.

CONGLUSION

From the foregoing discussions the conclusion remains irresistable that economically, farming is a unremunerative occupation for the large bulk of marginal farmers. These farms also suffer from under-utilization of available resources and man-power. The input-output coefficient too works unfavourably against marginal farmers. Further the prevailing price structure also affects them adversely. This phenomenon viewed in context of our competitive economy, spells their disintegration, perhaps a rapid one from the Indian agriculture.

*" Farm cost studies as Aid to Economic Analysis & Policies ", M. C. Dantwala.

SECTION VII

RURAL INDIA GLIMPSES

THE PRESENT section is comprised of eight selections. They provide intimate intensive studies of villages in different parts of the country by eminent scholars. They delineate in a live manner the changes that have been taking place in different spheres of social life in villages. Kathleen Gough's selection portrays the struggle between the Brahmin land-owning class and the depressed classes who are predominantly landless labourers, revealing a conflicting situation in a typically Brahmin village of South India. The peculiar social, economic and ideological weapons adopted by the conflicting groups are described in vivid details. The attempts made by the leadership of the lower castes to elevate the status of this group through the medium of sharpening economic struggle on class lines rather than through religious reforms or through the acquisition of concessional benefits and the impact of this struggle upon both the consciousness of these castes and their cultural activities require a more intensive examination. The process revealed in Gough's village study, provides a good contrast to the process adopted by the depressed castes to change their status by self-reform and by securing concessional benefits as revealed in the study of Thakur Village of U. P. by Bernard Cohn. These two articles bring out significantly the implication of the two processes of change, *viz.*, change through class struggle and change through self-reform and securing of concessional benefits. These two processes generate different types of currents in rural society as a result of struggles of lower castes to raise their status. The first process generates currents which secularise the consciousness of the lower strata, make them more aware of their interest as a class rather than as a caste and, further, eliminate all those activities which Professor Srinivas has called *Sanskritization* and which is generally known as *Brahminisation.* The other process keeps alive caste consciousness in the lower castes, builds up numerous activities and traditions which would help those castes to appear as higher castes and also stimulate cultural practices which are followed by higher castes. A student of rural society should discriminate between these two major types of processes. More extensive studies on the lines indicated by these two papers would considerably assist those who want to understand the complex class and caste struggles that are seething in agrarian areas. Such an investigation will also assist to evolve adequate measures to combat the new wave of casteism that is growing in rural areas. The articles by Cohn, and Gough give us a picture of various social processes that are going on in rural India. The article depicting the changes in the rural life based on a comparative study in a village in 1915 and 1955 provides an interesting picture of the changes in food habits, clothing styles, housing designs and general consumption pattern which have been taking place in an Indian village and that too in the context of the caste and wealth matrix. A more elaborate examination, of the phenomenon on these lines will throw considerable light on the type of the potential market and the specific social strata which would constitute that market in rural areas. It would also reveal the changing values regarding conspicuous consumption which are emerging among different strata in rural society. The impact of styles of the urban upper strata on the emerging styles of life in rural areas and more particularly on those of the upper stratum of the rural population deserves to be noted and further studied. Professor Damle's selection is interesting from a totally different angle. It reveals how the impact of the communication of ideas, emotions and informations would be functionally dependent upon their utility to the different strata. It unfolds a new line of study. The content of massive propaganda and educational campaigns which are launched in rural areas through the medium of various agencies and various techniques requires to be examined in the light of its functional utility. Why, much of our propaganda, information and educative campaign are dysfunctional, wasteful and failing in their objective? The problem requires a more careful examination and demands more extensive research in a society which is undergoing a rapid transformation and is suffering acute shortage of resources.

The six selections indicate very fruitful lines of research on different aspects of rural society. They also provide a great incentive to elaborate various techniques and approaches to build up a methodological armoury for the social scientist in India. (*Author*).

1

SOCIAL DRAMA IN A TAJORE VILLAGE*

E. KATHLEEN GOUGH

TANJORE DISTRICT

TANJORE DISTRICT of Madras State lies on the south-eastern tip of India. It is a green, fertile country, dead flat, the delta of the Cauvery. This river, rising in the Western Ghats in Coorg, flows south-east through Mysore, Salem, and Trichinopoly, to be dispersed throughout Tanjore in a network of small irrigation channels which finally reach the sea. These irrigation devices have for the most part obviated the former evils of periodic drought and flooding. Tanjore's increased fertility over the last fifty years has attracted many immigrants from the neighbouring deficit districts of Ramnad, Trichinopoly, and Madura. Tanjore is now one of the most densely populated parts of India. Wet paddy and coconuts are the chief crops, paddy being exported to neighbouring areas. Though there are a number of large market towns, machine industry is almost entirely undeveloped.

The Hindu population of Tanjore falls into three broad sets of castes; Brahman, Non-Brahman, and Adi Dravida. Their language is Tamil, though certain immigrant Telugu, Maratha and Saurashtrian trading castes speak their own languages in the home. The Brahmans, whose ancestors must have come to South India at least early in the Christian Era, number about 200,000 in this district. They own the land and have administrative rights in about 900 out of a total of 2,611 villages.

The many Non-Brahman castes may be divided into higher castes, who traditionally own land, like Brahmans, administer villages, and lower castes, who for the most part live as tenants, artisans, and specialized labourers under land-lords of higher caste.

Adi Dravidas, or " original Dravidians ," are the lowest group, the so-called " exterior castes " of Tanjore. They include Pallans, Parayans, and Cakkiliyans. Pallan and Parayans were formerly the agricultural serfs of the land-owning castes and still do the bulk of agricultural labour.

Tanjore was of interest to me because it is, for South India, one of the main centres of the Saivite religion and of orthodox Brahmanical culture. Its magnificent temples, the best of which were built by Chola kings in the tenth and eleventh centuries, are famous throughout India. Religious

*Reproduced from the article " The Social Structure of a Tadjore Village, " in ' *Village India,* ' edited by McKim Marriott, pp. 36-52.

instrumental music and singing are much patronized: thousands flock annually to the musical festival in honour of Tyaga Raja Bhagavatar, a famous Brahman songster. The Tanjore Tevatiyans, or temple dancers until recently carried on a magnificent tradition of Bharata Nayta dancing in the large temples dedicated to Visnu or to Siva. Though public temple dancing was prohibited about fifteen years ago because of its association with prostitution, it is exhibited at private concerts, and several Tanjore dancing girls are now film stars well-known in the Tamil country. In some areas the land in whole groups of villages, comprising up to six thousand acres, is owned by important temples, dedicated chiefly to Siva and managed by Brahman trustees. Altogether the Brahmans, who number about one fifteenth of the population, are in this district more numerous, wealthy and influential than elsewhere in the Tamil country.

While Sanskrit learning has been conserved by the Brahmans, Tanjore shares with the neighbouring district of Madura an illustrious heritage of Tamil religious literature extending back to the pre-Christian Era and developed by both Brahman and Non-Brahman castes. In the last twenty years much animosity has arisen between Brahman and higher caste non-Brahman scholars, professional men, politicians, and also land-owners, so that an attempt is often made to divide into two traditions the literary and religious heritage of the Tamil country. The higher Non-Brahmans and particularly the Vellalans claim honour for indigenous Tamil literature, ignoring its debt to Vedanta philosophy and the Sanskrit Saivite texts, or Agamas. The Saivite Brahmans, by contrast, tend to emphasise their unique heritage of the Vedas and Vedanta philosophy, to some extent neglect those Tamil saints who were not Brahmans, and favour the monistic Advaita metaphysics

While so famous in religious and literary history, Tanjore is today looked down on by the more " progressive " Western-educated Tamils of neighbouring districts. Having no machine industries, Tanjore town lacks the amenities of other more industrialized district capitals such as Trichinopoly, Coimbatore, and, of course, Madras. The old-fashioned religious orthodoxy of Tanjore Brahmans, their stranglehold on much of the land, their general opposition to land reform and welfare movements among the lowest castes, and their apparent arrogance, cunning, and tortuousness in philosophical arguments are mocked in other districts. The " Kumbakonam, " the name of the second town of the district, where orthodox Brahmans are particularly influential, has come to mean " Humbug " or " Bunkum " among the educated in Madras. The wealthier Vellalan, Kallan, and immigrant Telugu Non-Brahman landowners of the district have a similar reputation for backwardness in social reforms. Among these higher castes in general (though many, since independence, pay lip service to Congress ideology) it is probably true to say that very few are ardent in implementing its policies. The comparative lethargy of the higher castes with regard to economic development, coupled with a general increase in the population over the last hundred years and a particularly marked increase owing to immigration from the neighbouring famine areas during the bad harvests of the last five years have recently created acute economic distress among landless labourers and small tenant farmers of the lower castes. The spectacular rise of the Communist party in the last five years issues partly from these circumstances. In response to angry rebellion among labourers, the Madras Government passed an emergency ordinance in September, 1952, requiring security of tenure for share-croping tenants, an increase in the tenant's share of paddy crops from approximately one-fifth to two-fifths, and for permanently employed, tied labourers, an increase in wages which in some villages amounted to a doubling of the traditional rates of pay. This ordinance, while it appeared temporarily to appease the small tenant and the permanent labourer, did nothing to change conditions for the ever increasing number of Adi Dravidas and low-caste Non-Brahman landless coolies who are hired by the day. Labour relations were still exceedingly tense when I left the district in April, 1953, and the Communist party appeared by that date to have enrolled most of the Adi Dravidas as members.

II. Kumbapettai, A Tanjore Village

Kumbapettai, the Brahman village studied, lies eight miles north of Tanjore town, about two hundred miles south-west of Madras, and three miles west of the Madras to Tanjore railway. In the centre of the village is a single street containing thirty-six occupied and twelve-unoccupied Brahman houses. The Brahmans living in the village are small landowners, apart from six families who have recently sold their lands. Holdings of wet paddy on the outskirts of the village range from three to thirty acres per family. Near the Brahman street are three streets of Non-Brahman tenants and servant castes, comprising twenty houses of Konan tenants and cowherds; seven of Kallan paddy merchants and small cultivators; twelve of Toddy-tappers, cultivators since prohibition; six of recently arrived Ahambatiyan and Pataiyatchi tenants; four of Anti-Temple Priests; three of Potters; one of Tevatiyan prostitutes and low-caste temple dancers; four of Ambalakkaran fishermen; two of Maratha coolies; one of Blacksmiths, one of Goldsmiths, and one of Carpenters; two of Barbers; one of Washermen; one of Muslim watchmen; and one of Gypsies, who are now employed by the government as road-sweepers.

The bulk of agricultural labour is done by landless labourers, formerly serfs, of the Pallan caste, who live in eighty-nine houses in five streets, beyond paddy fields, outside the village proper. Kumbapettai has no Parayans but employs two families from the next village to remove dead cattle and beat drums at funerals.

In considering the structure of social relations within this village we may take as our central problem : To what extent is Kumbapettai an isolable social unit? And to what extent is it changing in this respect? I propose to discuss this problem briefly with reference to economic organization, local administration, ritual practices at the village level, inter-castes relations of a social nature within the village and some general relations of the village to the wider community.

Within living memory, and I take as my date line the period between forty and fifty years ago, it is clear that Kumbapettai has been much more self-sufficient than it is today. Until about twenty years ago Brahman families living in the village owned all the village lands and held economic control over their tenants and Adi Dravida labourers. Forty years ago, all Non-Brahmans of Kumbapettai were either tenants of Brahmans or specialized village servants working for Brahmans and each other. Konans, the dominant Non-Brahman caste of the village at the date, leased land on an annual share-cropping tenure from Brahmans, from which they retained roughly one-fifth of the crop for their maintenance and cultivation expenses. In addition, some worked as cowherds and gardners for Brahmans and were paid monthly in paddy. Those fields not given over to tenants, that is to say, about two-thirds of the village land, were cultivated directly by Adi Dravidas among whom each man was attached as a tied labourer, or pannaiyal, to a Brahman landlord. He was paid daily in paddy and, in addition, was perpetually in debt to the landlord for extra amounts granted at marriages, births, and funerals. Both tenants and labourers received annual gifts of clothing, materials to re-thatch their huts, built on sites owned by the landlords, and extra food in time of sickness or in the summer famine months. Part of the labourer's paddy was exchanged for toddy, tapped by the Toddy-tappers, who leased their coconut gardens from Brahmans. The village servant castes of Barbers, Washermen, Goldsmiths, Blacksmiths, and Temple Priests, and the village watchmen appointed by the landlords, were paid in kind by both landlords and tenants twice annually after each harvest.

Today, Kumbapettai has moved about half-way in the transition from this relatively stationary feudal subsistence economy to a much wider-scale, expanding capitalist economy. First, one-third of the land has in the last twenty years been sold by impoverished Brahmans to more prosperous traders or professional men of Tanjore and neighbouring towns. Further, twelve Brahman families who have houses and own lands in the village have temporarily emigrated to towns, some to Madras, where they work as clerks in government offices, as teachers, or as vegetarian restaurant owners. Some of these absentee landowners come home twice annually at harvest to receive rent in kind from their tenants; other give their land on sub-tenure to Brahman kinsmen within the village, who make a small profit on the rent they receive from the tenants. None out of sixty-seven Non-Brahman men now lease land from landlords living outside the village and are no longer under the economic control of their traditional administrators.

Other Non-Brahmans have become partly or totally emancipated from the feudal system in modern forms of work. Most of the seven Kallan households, descendants of one who came fifty years ago, earn a living as paddy merchants, buying paddy from Brahmans and carting it to the mill three miles away. Two Kallans, two Toddy-tappers, one Potter, and five Konans —that is to say, ten out of sixty-seven Non-Brahman men—have managed to buy between one and four acres of land from Brahmans, which they cultivate themselves. None out of sixtyseven men work in other ways independently of Brahmans: three have teashops, and two have small grocery shops in the village; one has a teashop in the town three miles away; one Muslim is the watchman of some coconut gardens in the village which have been bought by another Muslim of Tanjore; and two men are wage-earners in a cigar factory in the nearby town. Only eleven men lease land from owners within the village, while nine are tied labourers, and ten are daily coolies. Thus, altogether only 63 per cent of Non-Brahman men are now economically dependent on Brahman landowners within the village.

Among Adi Dravidas, too revolutionary changes have taken place. Only 22 per cent now work as tied labourers for payment in kind. One family now owns one acre of land, 38 per cent have in the last ten years become share-croppers on the same terms as the Non-Brahmans, while 39 per cent work as daily coolies for whoever—Brahman, Non-Brahman, or outsider — will employ them, and receive their wages in cash. Even tied labourers, since paddy rationing was instituted in the war and landlords were subject to procurement regulations, are obliged to receive part of their pay in cash.

These economic changes within the village are accompanied by a great increase in economic transactions outside it. Members of all castes, when they can afford it, now patronize the cinema in Tanjore and in the nearby town; all travel on buses and trains to buy clothing or household goods, which have increased both in amount and in kind. Few families now receive clothing from their landlords; most are required to buy it from the town themselves. Most important, the village as a whole is now in debt to the town. In short, the village is annually participating to an increasing extent in the wider urban economy. This change, as everywhere in India, is part of the overall change from a feudal to an expanding capitalist economic system, and is the fundamental prerequisite, in my view, for most other modern changes in the pattern of social relations within the village.

In this traditional system Brahmans have administrative rights over all the lower castes. Among their Non-Brahman and Adi Dravida servants, Brahmans have the power forcibly to interfere in disputes which threaten the peace of the village and to punish rebellion in any form against their own authority. These vary between fines, paid to the temple funds; beating with sticks, administered by Brahmans; in more serious cases, the penalty of forcing the culprit to drink a pint of cowdung or even human dung dissolved in water; and in the most serious cases, eviction from the land. Sometimes whole streets or caste groups offend against village custom.

In connection with the unity of the village, the important point is that

Brahmans were until recently, by reason of their economic power, able to prevent disputes within their village from passing into the hands of the local police, or, alternatively, to negotiate with the police in such a way that their own authority, and traditional custom, were upheld.

Even murder cases have in the past been handled according to the Brahmans decision.

But today Brahmans complain that with the gradual loss of their economic power over the lower castes the loyalty of tenants and labourers is no longer what it was, and the unity of the village is declining.

In other ways, the breakdown of the feudal economic system, the emergence of lower-caste groups in economic rivalry rather than co-operation, and the widening range of social relations beyond the village have endangered the power of the Brahmans and the unity of Kumbapettai. In the past, though the headman of each lower-caste street were elected by street member, Brahmans reserved the right to depose a low-caste headman if he displeased them in any way. But in recent years it has been impossible for Brahmans to interfere in the street administration of the two newest Non-Brahman streets. In these two streets the Kallan, Konan and Toddy-tapper households are almost all economically independent of Brahmans and conduct their street affairs without consulting Brahman opinion. During y stay, when the all-India elections took place, only members of these streets dared openly to admit that they had voted for the Communists, against the Congress-supporting Brahmans. Their own Non-Brahman tenants and Pallan labourers were marshalled by the Brahmans on voting day and instructed to vote for Congress, though it was doubted whether all had complied. Shortly after I left the village, however, in September, 1952, the Tanjore Tenants' and Labourers' Ordinance increased the economic strength of tenants and Pallans and removed from them the fear of eviction by their landlords. At the next harvest, in February, 1953, I heard, while working in a second village sixty miles away, that Kumbapettai Pallans had emerged in a body against their landlords, hoisted the Communist flag in their street and refused to thresh the village paddy until higher wages were promised for daily coolies as well as for tied labourers of the village to whom the act strictly applied. In the area where I was then working in the east of the district, the Adi Dravidas of twelve neighbouring villages had already three years ago formed a Communist-controlled union in open opposition to their landlords, along the lines of their traditional street assemblies.

The unity of the village was formerly dramatized in ritual at the annual temple festival to Uritaicciyamman, the mother-goddess of the village. This goddess like all village deities, is a Non-Brahman diety; though she is worshipped by Brahmans and is regarded by them as an aspect of Sakti, the consort of Siva, it is clear that she is not one of the Sanskrit pantheon. Annually, however, at the large temple festival, all castes combine in rituals which are sponsored by the Brahmans and conducted by both Brahman and Non-Brahman temple priests. This festival dramatizes the unity of the village and also the separateness and ritual rank of each caste within it.

But in the year of my stay this festival was for the first time not conducted. Brahmans, who are responsible for organizing and collecting funds from villagers, complained that their several families, many of whose more influential members have left the village, would not co-operate together and that the state of unrest among tenants and labourers made them fear disputes and possibly violence if they attempted to enforce the traditional ranked participation of all the castes. I heard that the festival was, however, conducted the following year, but that not all castes had taken part. It is clear that village festivals of this type are dying out all over the district; in many villages in the eastern part of Tanjore District they were abandoned five years ago. At the same time, the last twenty years have seen a growth in importance of the large temple festivals to Sanskrit deities, formerly managed by Brahmans, in the major towns of the district. To these festivals, where, since the Temple Entry Act of 1947, caste rank is no longer emphasised, thousands flock by bus and train to witness the spectacle of the procession and the firework displays. Even these festivals, however, are now losing their appeal for the lower-castes, among whom they are associated with the supremacy of Brahmans and with religious doctrines in which they no longer have faith. Changes in ritual co-operation thus show a widening of social relations and a tendency toward new homogeneity in ritual practices of Brahmans and the higher Non-Brahman castes, yet at the same time the emergence of a new, low class of unbelievers who pin their faith rather to rebellious political action. Among organized Communist groups of Adi Dravidas in the east of the district the younger leaders pursue an active policy of anti-religious and anti-Brahman propaganda, and here ritual co-operation within the village is almost confined to the higher castes.

The vertical unity of the village has always been counter balanced by the horizontal unity of each endogamous sub-caste. Traditionally, each caste group of the village appears to have belonged to an endogamous sub-caste extending over some fifteen to thirty villages. For at least forty to fifty years, however, with the vast increase in population, and the influx of newcomers and movement of small Brahman and Non-Brahman groups over all parts of the district, whole streets or individual families of the endogamous sub-caste have become very widely scattered. The Brahmans of Kumbapettai thus today belong to a sub-caste of eighteen villages fairly widely scattered round the North Tanjore and Trichinopolly boundary. Many of their individual families are also now settled in towns up to one hundred miles away who are visited by bus or train at family ceremonies. The Pallan endogamous caste group is still confined largely to villages within a radius of twenty miles, but isolated families are scattered farther afield. In Kumbapettai no intercaste marriages have yet taken place, but in other respects accidental contiguity and similarity of economic status are replacing kinship ties as organizing principles within and between villages. Thus the three traditional Non-Brahman streets, once occupied respectively by cowherds, various servant castes, and Toddy-tappers, now each contains immigrant families of other castes who dine with the traditional occupants at ceremonies and combine to elect the street headman. A fourth most modern street on the main roadside, sprung up in the last eighty years,contains families of six Non-Brahman castes, about two-thirds of whom are independent of the traditional landowners, and most of whom dine together at each other's ceremonies. Pallans and Brahmans, at the two extremes, are still isolated in their streets, but each group contains two or three families of recent immigrants, of other endogamous sub-castes within the same broad caste, to whom dining rights are extended. In each wider endogamous caste, by contrast, all but the closest kinship ties are gradually being weakened by the increasing heterogenity of wealth, education, and occupation.

All these changes in the broad pattern of village organization have their effect on everyday social relations between the several castes. In Kumbapettai the fact that two-thirds of the land is still owned by Brahmans and that about 75 per cent of the population is still employed in traditional ways accounts, in contrast to some other villages, for the comparatively orthodox etiquette still preserved in relations between members of different castes. Thus Non-Brahmans and Adi Dravida labourers still come to the back door of a house to receive their wages, and Adi Dravidas still do not enter the Brahman street or, of course, the Brahman temples. Brahmans and most Non-Brahmans do not enter the Adi Dravida streets. In the last twenty years, a considerable relaxing of caste restrictions has taken place. Non-Brahmans were formerly forbidden to enter Brahman houses; both men and women now work as house servants for their landlords, though they may enter the kitchen. Non-Brahmans were formerly forbidden to wear shoes while walking in the Brahman street or standing before a Brahman. But today two Non-Brahman boys whose fathers are independent of the landlords walk deliberately in their shoes down the Brahman street to post letters in the mailbox. These boys, one Adi Dravida, and thirteen Brahman boys attend high schools three miles away, where caste discrimination is forbidden. In particular, no group now has power to ex-communicate serious offenders against caste law. But today they are condemned but not ostracized.

In the east of the district it is among Communist groups and particularly Adi Dravidas that caste restrictions have broken down most completely. Non-Brahman Communist leaders go freely into Adi Dravida streets, eat with them, and spend the night in their huts. In the second village where I worked, Pallans and Parayans of twelve villages had in the last five years completely abandoned their age-long dispute for precedence, ate freely together, assembled together at large areal Communist meetings, supported each other in strikes to gain higher wages from landlords, and within each village, together settled their disputes concerning debt and adultery. In this district, in fact, so weak is the propagation of Congress policy regarding caste, and so strong the Communist that any person who attempts to defy caste laws is promptly hailed as a Communist.

III. Conclusion

It is clear that, in general, the social structure of the Tanjore village is changing from a relatively closed, stationary system, with a feudal economy and co-operation between ranked castes in ways ordained by religious law, to a relatively " open, " changing system, governed by secular law, with an expanding capitalist economy and competition between castes which is sometimes reinforced and sometimes obscured by the new struggle between economic classes. In perhaps ten years, even if there is no Communist revolution in the meantime, it is questionable whether the village will any longer be a useful isolate for study. Certainly, it is difficult even now to speak meaningfully of modern economic relations within the village without reference to broader government policies—for example, of rice rationing, procurement of surplus paddy, admittance of students to high schools and colleges, communal representation in government employment, and government attempts to readjust the relations between landlords and tenants. It is equally difficult to speak of social and administrative relations between castes without reference to the rise of the Communist party since 1947 or to the earlier development of anti-Brahman political movements. All the more need, therefore, to record what we can of the traditional structure of village before this has quite decayed.

2

THE CHANGING STATUS OF A DEPRESSED CASTE*

BERNARD S. COHN

THIS PAPER describes attempts by the members of one " untouchable " caste in one village to raise their social status. The caste is the Camars, traditionally leather workers and agricultural labourers, who have long stood near the bottom of the rigional society of Uttar Pradesh in wealth, power, and caste position. Attempts by the Camars of Madhopur (*Madhopur*) village to achieve a higher status must be understood in relation to changes both in the village and in the outside world as well as in relation to the Camars' own internal, social and religious organization. This paper offers a preliminary analysis of some of the complex processes which are involved.

THE VILLAGE AND ITS ECONOMY

Madhopur is a large, Rajput-owned village of 1,047 acres on the level Ganges-Gomti plain. It is located in Kerakat Tahsil in the southeastern part of Jaunpur District, U. P. In Madhopur village the agricultural lands are about equally divided between the production of rice and the production of other grains such as barley and millets, with sugarcane as a leading cash crop. The village is two miles from an all-weather road and bus route which connects it with the cities of Banaras and Azamgarh, twenty-five and thirty-eight miles distant, respectively. It is four miles from the nearest railway, which provides transportation to Jaunpur, the ancient district centre (Nevill 1908 : 1-3). Kerakat town, the sub-divisional headquarters for Madhopur, having a population of about 5,000 persons, is four miles away. Description of the traditional village of Madhopur and of recent changes there have been published previously by Opler and Singh.

The Camars of Madhopur are the most numerous of the twenty-three principal caste groups which are resident there. Among the 1,852 persons enumerated by the village accountant in his census of 1948, five castes were represented by more than 50 members each: Camars (636), and Lohars (67). Eleven other local caste groups had less than 20 members each.

The twenty-three local caste groups of Madhopur are distributed in one main settlement and in nine hamlets in a manner which approximately symbolizes their relative standings in Madhopur society.

*Reproduced from the article " The Changing Status of A Depressed Caste, " from " *Village India,* " edited by McKim Marriott, pp. 53-76.

Camars, like all other castes of Madhopur, have long been subordinate in all economic and political affairs to the Thakur landlords (*Zamindars*) of the village. These Thakurs, Rajputs of the Raghubansi clan, have held predominant economic and political power in Madhopur since the conquest of the village and the region by their ancestors in the sixteenth century.

Zamindari Abolition in 1952 did little to affect the economic and political dominance of the Thakurs either in Madhopur or in the immediate region, for it expropriated the landlords only from that part of their tenanted lands which had not previously been registered as being under their own personal cultivation. In 1953, after landlord abolition, Thakur ex-landlords still owned and cultivated approximately 70 per cent of the lands of Madhopur. The few permanent tenants in the village were enaabled to buy out their parts of the Thakurs' landlord holdings by payment to the State government of ten times the annual rent, but the landlords who lost land thereby are to be compensated by the government. Some ex-landlords, moreover, continue to receive rent from their now protected tenants-at-will. Although the old legal bases of tenancy under landlords ceased to exist in 1952, most non-Thakur families continue to gain access to land only as lessees under Thakurs.

Recent Change

By the early part of the twentieth century the seeds of social change had been extensively sown; a railroad had been built near Madhopur, affording wider geographic mobility; boys had left the village to go to colleges and universities; the official courts settled more and more village disputes; the Arya Samaj movement of religious refrom grew strong; elections brought political competition on a wider scale; and the nationalist struggle became a reality for the villagers. Along with these outside influences, population in the village and surrounding area steadily rose, because of strains on the village economy, more and more residents from all castes began to seek work in the cities. Family structure, political behaviour, attitudes towards caste status, and religious customs have all undergone notable change. All these happenings are summed up by the remark often heard in the village, "A new wind is blowing."

A. Change in Family Structure

The Thakurs of Madhopur, and following them at some distance the Camars, have been slowly reshaping their respective family structures. Among the Thakurs, family ties have grown looser and the importance of clan and village has declined. Thakurs are tending to move in the direction of less formality and respect for the father, more freedom between husband and wife, and smaller household units. The stimuli of Western education and urban living have been strongly felt among them.

The small changes in family structure that can be noted among the Camars, especially among Camars who have attained some education, are not changes in the direction of a Western-influenced family but changes in the direction of a more orthodox " Hindu " family. Camars are trying to tighten the authority of the father and place restrictions on the wife. While Thakur wife is coming out of seclusion, the Camar wife is being put in seclusion. The Thakur model for the family appears to be influenced by the urban, Western family, while the Camar model is based on the family of the Thakurs fifty years ago. A similar chronological sequence and typological discrepancy is evident between Thakur and Camar models for caste observances, religion, food habits, and many other aspects of social life.

B. Political Changes

The twentieth century saw the break-up of the Thakur panchayats which had once dominated both the village of Madhopur and the whole taluka of Dobhi. The decline of these panchayats may be related to changes throughout the whole social fabric but may be attributed particularly to changes in the prestige system of the Thakurs and in the formal superstructure of government.

Since 1900 more and more Thakurs had begun to derive incomes and prestige from working outside the village as teachers, police inspectors, printers, and businessmen rather than from the traditional sources of landownership and from agnatic and affinal family ties. Such externally oriented persons were much less at the mercy of the sanctioning pressures which any rural panchayat could apply. Outcasting lost its sting for the Thakurs, for an outcaste Thakur family could with increasing ease make marriage alliances with other outcaste families or with families in good standing whose desire to establish marriage ties with a Raghubansi family outweighed their scruples about the stigma of outcasting. The legal, economic, and prestige structures of the village and taluka were ceasing to exist as a closed and integrated system, but the Thakurs were at the same time learning how to exercise their power at new and higher levels. The higher administrators, if they are not Thakurs themselves, tend to be of high caste and often of landowning backgrounds, so that their sympathies generally lie with landlords rather than with tenants.

While the authority of Thakur panchayats began to grow weaker, caste organization among the Camars if anything grew stronger. As patron-client and landlord-tenant ties have weakened, Camars have come to depend more upon themselves for the settlement of their own disputes. Camars have also grown more sensitive about their collective good name. It was a commonplace a generation ago for a Thakur man to have sexual relations with a Camar woman. This still occurs, but the caste is now trying to punish offenders. Eating and drinking restrictions for the Camars have been tightened and are strictly enforced. Although Camars formerly would eat with and take water from other untouchables, they now punish such acts by outcasting. As the Camar caste has grown stronger, outcasting by the Camar panchayat has actually become more frequent.

The beginning of elections, first for the District Board in the twenties, later for the legislative positions of the provincial and central governments in the thirties, helped further to weaken the Thakur's local and taluka panchayats, while they gave still further stimulus to action by Camars and other lower castes.

District Boards had been set up in India in the eighties to give the people some small measure of self-government. The initial electorates for these boards were very small, however, and many members of the boards were either officials or appointees of officials. Only in the twenties, when elective representation was increased, did there begin to be competition among some of the Dobhi Thakurs for election to positions on the Jaunpur District Board. To secure votes, candidates had to promise help and support to factions among the chiefs of the Dobhi Taluka panchayat. Both the Thakurs who were candidates and the chiefs of the panchayat who were allied with them lost their reputations for honesty and impartiality in these elections. Like outside employment and litigation, election to the District Board offered an extra-village and extra-taluka source of power and prestige. Members had control of rural education, sanitation, and roads as well as access to higher government officials whom they could influence to the advantage of themselves and their friends and supporters. Village and taluka panchayats became small matters by comparison, and fell into desuetude.

Provincial elections in 1937, which were won by the Congress party after an intensive political campaign, helped to stimulate subsequent political action by tenants against the Thakurs of Madhopur. Although the electorate was closely limited by criteria of property and education, a few low-caste people were entitled to vote. One of these was a Noniya, who not only voted but also actively supported the Congress candidate. The Noniya was an exceptional individual. As a boy, he had struggled to get himself an education through the eighth grade. He put his education to use by learning and studying the land laws. He quickly realized that, even before formation of a Congress ministry, the permanent tenants had possessed guaranteed rights which the Thakurs were ignoring. The tenants were so cowed and were kept in such a state of ingorance by the Thakurs that the more powerful and clever Thakurs could successfully evict even tenants who had legal right to permanency. The Noniya first defended his own lands against seizure by the Thakurs and then began to advise the other Noniyas, as well as the Camars who lived near the Noniya hamlet, as to their rights.

Not long after the elections, in 1938 the Camars made their first large-scale attack upon the Thakurs' position of power. They did so by supporting some Noniyas rather than their own Thakurs in a dispute over land. This alliance of Noniyas and Camars gave one of the first indications of the growing solidarity of the lower castes in opposition to the Thakurs. To punish them for joining the Noniyas the Thakurs decided to prevent the rebellious Camars from sowing their winter crop. A gang of Thakurs went to the fields where the Camars were working, drove off their cattle, beat the Camars, and then went to the Camars' hamlet where they ripped down the thatched roofs of the Camars' houses.

The Camars held council with Noniya who was their ally. He advised them to complain directly to the district magistrate in Jaunpur, while he himself wrote letters on their behalf to various officials in Lucknow, the State capital. The Camars, preparing for the difficult siege, took their cattle and all that they could carry of their belongings and went to Jaunpur. There the District Congress Committee fed and housed them. The Camars immediately hired a lawyer to prosecute the Thakurs who had beaten them.

The Thakurs of Madhopur supposed that the beaten Camars had simply run off to another village. When word reached them of the Camars' legal and political action, they were thunderstruck. A few of the more influential Thakurs went at once to Banaras, where they contacted a relative who was an employee in the court. Through him they were able to reach the official in Jaunpur who would deal directly with the case which the Camars were bringing against them. The Thakurs were successful in having the case delayed and then in having it taken out of the court in Jaunpur and sent to the more pliable sub-district officer's court in Kerakat. The Thakurs next bribed the police sub-inspectors of Kerakat to delay his report to that court for several months. Meanwhile, the court ordered that no one must cultivate the land in dispute in order to prevent further trouble. During all this time the Camars had to pay a lawyer, court fees, and other expenses, while they were deprived of income from their cultivation. After more than six months of postponements, the Camars agreed to a compromise with Thakurs. They dropped their case against the Thakurs, took back their lands, and obtained a written guarantee from the Thakurs that the Thakurs could not beat them.

The Thakurs had nevertheless caused the Camars great loss by attrition.

The " Quit India " movement in 1942 and the independence agitation of 1946-47 reached the village of Madhopur and even touched the Camars. These political actions were but distractions, however, from the Camars' own drive for power.

The next principal episode in the Camars' struggle and their second major defeat came about after the passing of the U. P. Panchayat Raj Act, of 1947. Under this Act, which replaced the previous official, appointed panchayat, a village council (*Gaon Sabha*) and a rural court (*panchayati adalat*) were to be elected by universal adult suffrage. The village council, with thirty-six members, was to take over a large number of local governmental power and responsibilities regarding land, sanitation, roadways, rationing, etc. The rural court was to try all minor cases from Madhopur and several nearby villages.

Elections for these new panchayats in 1948 provided the occasion for the first successful organization of all the lower castes of Madhopur against the Thakurs. The party of the lower castes was called the "Tenant (*Praja*) Party." Its leadership was provided by an Ahir, a Brahman who had been a political thug, a Kandu who had lived many years in Bombay, a Teli who prided himself on his part in the independence movement, and the Noniya who had stimulated previous legal action against the Thakurs. Several of the lower castes were brought into the Tenant party by their own caste headmen. Secret meetings were then held in the Camar hamlets. When protection was promised them against possible reprisals by the Thakurs, the Camars joined the party wholeheartedly. Some Thakurs even associated themselves with the Tenant party from the beginning, partly through friendship with its Brahman leader and partly through a desire to strike back at old enemies within their own caste.

As the time for the panchayat elections drew near, the Thakurs who had been the traditional leaders of the village saw that the Tenant party controlled the bulk of the electorate. The influential Thakur who had been the chairman of the old appointed panchayat declined to stand at all in the election lest he be defeated. Other influential Thakurs likewise withdrew from candidacy. In a final gesture of disassociation, the majority of the Thakurs refused even to vote against the Tenant majority.

The lower castes' Tenant party thus succeeded in electing both a village council and rural court made up wholly of its own candidates or sympathizers. Camars were elected to both bodies. The traditional village leadership of the Thakurs had been completely routed from formal control of Madhopur. What was more, the Tenant party's strength and its connections with the district Congress party at first prevented the Thakurs from moving directly against it.

After its initial success in winning the panchayat elections, however, the Tenant party rapidly declined in power and organization. The village council whose offices had been won proved unwieldy. Ordinances which the council passed to promote cleaning of the village paths, proper drainage and removal of manure piles could not be made effective because of the opposition of the traditional leaders who were Thakurs and of persons of other high castes. An attempt by Camars to force compliance by court action proved too expensive. The village council found itself unable even to collect its own tax. Its meetings, scheduled to be held monthly, became less and less frequent. The Tenant party was disrupted through the bribing of some of its leaders, and through law suits brought against its members individually by certain Thakurs. The low castes, and particularly the Camars, lacked the economic base for a long-term fight against the Thakurs, on whom they were dependent for a livelihood. The final act in the dissolution of the Tenant party was the murder of one of its leaders by a Thakur.

Thus, although the Camars found that with their allies they could elect a village government and for a short time could even coerce the upper castes, they found also that they could not sustain themselves in a position of effective dominance. Today, political solidarity among the lower castes of Madhopur has vanished, and there is much discouragement.

C. Efforts to Raise Social Status

For the last thirty years the Camars of Madhopur have struggled consciously to raise their status on another, related front—that of the caste hierarchy—but with scarcely greater outward success than they achieved on the political front.

At least two generations ago *Jaisvara, Camars* in the vicinity of Madhopur began to outlaw the eating of beef and the carting of manure in what proved a futile attempt to gain greater respect for the caste. Previously Camars had been thought degraded because of their eating of carrion beef; they often had been accused of poisoning cattle in order to obtain the meat. Somewhat more than thirty years ago, beef eating was banned by the Camars. Although some Thakurs suspect that a few Camar women still eat beef, Camars maintain that beef-eaters would be outcasted immediately. Thirty years ago, in opposition to their own Thakurs, some Camars of Madhopur declared also that they would no longer carry manure to the Thakurs' fields. They were compelled to leave the village to escape the Thakurs' wrath. When ultimately these Camars were permitted to return to the village and were excused from the manure work which they had perceived as degrading. Camar women in general took a further step; they refused any longer to make dung cakes for the Thakurs' households. Ultimately, they, too, secured a grudging acquiescence from the Thakurs. As for inspiring greater respect from the higher castes, such changes of caste behaviour receive at best passive recognition, certainly not approval. The gain to the Camars from these changes has been chiefly a gain in the vital dimension of self-respect.

Camars are not alone in trying to elevate their caste status. Fifteen years ago representatives of most of the *Bhars* of Kerakat Tahsil met to plan ways to raise their status. Several educated Bhars who were government officials addressed the meeting and told them that they were lowly and despised because they raised pigs. The Bhars gave up pig-raising, yet it is difficult to say that they have improved their status in the eyes of other castes. They are still regarded as " untouchable, " although they are held in better regard than are the *Khatikas* and *Pasis* of the area, who still herd swine.

Other castes have made more extreme efforts to raise their status. Fifteen years ago the Noniyas of Madhopur went so far as to put on the sacred thread and call themselves by their long-claimed title of " *Cauhan Rajput*. " Their action was met with violence by the Lords of the village, who beat the Noniyas, broke their threads, and threatened further violence if the act was repeated. Five years ago the Noniyas again put on their sacred threads, this time without overt reaction on the part of the Lords. Now the Ahirs and the Lohars of Madhopur also wear the thread of the twice-born, the Ahirs calling themselves " Yadav Rajputs " and the Lohars claiming to be " Visvakarma Brahmans. " Camars in nearby villages of Jaunpur District and also in Azamgarh District have started wearing sacred threads, calling themselves " Harijan Thakurs, " but so far the Camars of Madhopur have not joined them.

Such attempts by Camars to raise their caste status are not individual in character or effect, nor are they necessarily legislated by large, formal gatherings. Rather, a leader or group of leaders in the caste in one village may feel that some traditional behaviour should be changed, and the change is talked over in the village. Relatives and others who are visiting hear about the proposed change and carry the news to their home villages. If a local group of Camars decides to initiate the change, it decrees that any Camar who fails to conform to the new pattern will be outcasted. Active propagandizing follows from the initiating village or villages. Ultimately, the initiating Camars determine that they will no longer give daughters to or accept daughters-in-law from Camars who do not conform to the change.

While the Camars are becoming stricter about their habits of diet, dress, and occupation, the higher castes are becoming less strict. Camars have become very sensitive about such matters as accepting food from castes whom they consider to be their inferiors, while at the same time some of the Thakurs are relaxing their conformity to commensal prohibitions. Younger Camars are less prone to give outward signs of respect to Thakurs, and the younger Thakurs seem to expect such signs less.

Quite apart from changes in traditional symbols of caste status, modern secular education is playing a central role in Camars' efforts to improve their position. Camars constantly verbalize a desire for more education, and many attribute their low position to a lack of education. But those two Camars who have achieved the most education—the two Camar school teachers—have not been accorded the full degree of respect which is granted to teachers of higher caste. Teachers of higher caste are called " Master " (*Master*), while these Camar teachers are merely called " Writer " (*Munshi*). Teachers of higher caste are given a string cot or chair to sit on when they visit a Thakur's house, while these Camar teachers are given instead a stool or an overturned basket only–a better seat,however, than the floor, which is the only place for an uneducated Camar. One of these school teachers is among the leaders who are most actively attempting to make Camar behaviour accord more with the traditional behaviour of the higher castes. Education is an individual achievement, but even educated Camars cannot escape an awareness that mobility for them, too, must be a group phenomenon.

D. Religious Changes

Consistent with efforts to raise their caste status and to gain power, the Camars of Madhopur have in recent years also made conscious efforts to suppress their distinctive traditional religion, to Sanskritize their rituals still further, and to emulate the specific religious forms of the higher castes. Although they continue to propitiate the goddess *Bhagauti* jointly in ceremonies of the whole hamlet, and although they continue to worship the other village deities as do members of higher castes, yet they have made many changes in the rest of their religious practice. Camar school teachers, leading families, and especially members of the Siva Narayan sect, rather than the traditional Camar panchayat, have been the principal agents of these changes. At the same time that the Camars are becoming more concerned with the forms of their religion, however, many persons of the upper castes, most notably the Thakurs, are being drawn into a more secular culture.

Domestic ceremonies of the Camars have been modelled increasingly upon domestic ceremonies of the Thakurs and Brahmans, especially under the influence of leaders and devotees of the Siva Narayan sect. The sacrifice of a pig which formerly began the Camar wedding ceremony has now been given up and replaced by the cutting of a nutmeg. The practice of giving dowry has been introduced, although the boy's father still gives a token payment to the girl's father: here the transition between bride price and dowry can be seen in progress. Camar weddings have now been lengthened from one day to three days, so as to resemble Brahman weddings. A Brahman priest now conducts every ceremony of the wedding except the final rites. While Thakurs now marry at higher ages, Camars are marrying at lower ages: Camars of Madhopur now marry at from five to seven years of age, whereas they had previously married at from twelve to sixteen years of age. Horoscopes are now cast by Brahmans for Camar babies at the ceremony of naming, and death rituals have been altered in several ways so as to conform more closely with the practices of the higher castes. Adherence to the cult of *Pancon Pir* has been eliminated. A new emphasis on pilgrimages has helped to Sanskritize Camar religion even more fully. If the older cult of Siva Narayan may be said to have paralleled Sanskritic religion, recent changes have moved Camar religion directly toward the main stream of the great tradition of orthodox Hinduism.

Parts of the religious ideology of the Siva Narayan sect recently have been fused with the social and political aspirations of the Camars in annual celebrations of the birthday of the Camar saint, Raidas, in the month of *Magh* (January-February). Educated Camars have played an important part in the revival and transformation of these birthday celebrations. In 1953 the procession and meeting were organized by a Camar member of the Legislative Assembly, by several of the Camar school teachers in the area of Madhopur, and by Camar students from Ganesh Rai Intermediate College and from the Banaras Hindu University. Camars from all of Dobhi Taluka attended the celebration. The speakers, who included a Thakur school teacher, spoke of Raidas as a saint and pointed out the Camars' contribution to the culture and religion of India. Several of the speakers used Raidas as an example of a Camar who, through leading a "good life," gained the respect of the rest of the community. Other speakers used the opportunity to preach political action to the Camars. Saints and devotees such as Raidas are important to the Camars because they reaffirm the Camars' belief that members of their caste at one time were the equals or in some senses the superiors of the Brahmans and other high castes. The stories reaffirm the belief that it is not a person's caste status but his devotion that counts.

Summary

The Camars of Madhopur like many other peoples of the Indian subcontinent, are in the midst of processes of change. These processes of change are complex and even contradictory. While the Camars are organizing and fighting for social, political, and economic equality with the higher castes, they are also trying to borrow and to revive for themselves elements of a culture that the higher castes are shedding. As the higher castes of Madhopur become secularized and are increasingly drawn into an urban economy and culture, the Camars seem to be trying not only to benefit by the loosening of some old restrictions but also to buttress their own position by adapting these old restrictions to new uses.

3

CHANGES IN SOCIAL LIFE IN A GUJARAT VILLAGE A COMPARATIVE STUDY (1915 and 1955)*

Social Customs

During the first survey, expenses of marriage among Brahmins ranged from Rs. 1,500 to 2,500 and some parents were taking money for marrying their girls. Vaishyas had to spend larger sums on marriage and some had to " buy wives " for a price ranging from Rs. 1,000 to 2,000. The expenses of marriage among Patidars varied from Rs. 1,000 to Rs. 2,000. In all these 3 castes, there was dearth of brides; and so, sometimes brides were " sold and purchased " at a price ranging from Rs. 500 to Rs. 1,500 . However, some Patidars did not take any money for marrying their girls, but on the contrary they gave a dowry of about Rs. 500 to the bridegroom. Barias had to pay about Rs. 150 to the bride's parents while marrying their boys. Among *Dheds*, bride's parents charged about Rs. 125 if the bride was young or unmarried; and about Rs. 500 if she was " big " or a widow who knew weaving. Among Muslims a bride cost about Rs. 150 to Rs. 200. In case of deaths of old persons or persons of mature age, caste dinners were held on the 12th and or the 13th day which cost about Rs. 500 to Brahmins and Vaishyas; Rs. 100 to 300 to Patidars, and ordinarily less to persons of other castes.

Comparing the castes and customs during the first survey and the second survey, we note the following changes :—

1. The number of divisions among castes, sub-castes, sections and sub-sections has generally neither increased, nor decreased, barring a few small exceptions.

2. The institution of "*Panch*" in castes continues, but its hold, influence and power has been generally waning.

3. Some sections have written conventions, regulating caste customs and expenses and the tendency for such practice is increasing.

4. Attempts have been made to reduce amounts of money that are given as gifts on auspicious or inauspicious occasions. There have been also decisions and efforts to curtail expenses on social functions, and on occasions of *seemant*, death etc., feeding of caste fellows, and expenses have been generally decreasing; but expenses on marriage have, on the contrary increased. This increase is due partly to the rise in prices of essential commodities, etc., and partly to extravagance and luxury.

---

* Reproduced from "*Bhadkad: Social and Economic Survey of a Village,*" *A. Comparative Study* (1915 and 1955), pp. 40-55. Indian Institute of Agricultural Economics.

5. There is great laxity and freedom in the observance of restrictions in taking food prepared or touched by inferior or lower castes. But these restrictions are ordinarily observed at home and on occasions of caste dinners.

6. In case of marriage, husband and wife belong to the same caste and among higher classes, to the same section.

7. There is still dearth of brides among Brahmins, some Vaishyas and Patidars.

8. The custom of giving a send-off by parents to the daughter with her first baby, and expenses in clothes, ornaments, etc., for daughter and some of her relations on the husband's side still continues. But in modern times, some women have not to go to their father's place, for their 'first ordeal,' and in such cases, the question of observing this custom does not arise at all.

9. Boys and girls are now betrothed and married at a later age than before, and some castes have resolved to reduce expenses relating to betrothal.

10. The practice of "*Palla,*" that is gift of clothes, ornaments and money by the bridegroom's parents to the bride generally continues, and the value of "*Palla*" has increased in some higher castes.

11. For the marriage of their sons, some Patidars of Bhadkad have still to pay money to bride's parents. Some have paid Rs. 1,000 to Rs. 3,000 to bride's parents on such accounts.

12. Some Patidars of Bhadkad have taken money from the bridegroom's side, for marrying their girls; it is said that such receipts varied from Rs. 1,000 to 3,000. Some persons who take money in this way report that they take the same not as a price, but just to cover marriage expenses. On the marriage occasions, expenses regarding food, clothing, lighting, decoration, amusements, and entertainments have increased. The increase is partly due to the rise in prices.

13. Among Brahmins and Vaishyas, widows do not remarry. Marriage by widows of these castes is considered improper, immoral and irreligious. Widow marriage is not viewed similarly by some other castes, and so among them some widows do marry again; a second marriage by a widow may be due to economic or social reason.

14. Among castes which believe in *Shraddh*, practice of its performance continues.

15. "Death Dinners" have decreased, but they have not been still totally abolished.

16. Weeping and breast-beating by women in unison, has become less but is still common.

17. The custom of (purdah) veiling her face by a woman in the presence of her husband's elders has become less rigid, but generally it does persist among women even now.

Food Habits

The main differences between the food of those in good economic condition and that of those who are poor are as under :—

The well-to-do use rice and wheat more; eat more vegetables, consume more milk, ghee, sugar, oil, condiments, spices, sweets and farsans etc. The poorer sections of the people use less of rice or wheat, and more of kodri, bajri and bavta, besides taking less or going without the other items mentioned above. The quality of the food in case of the former is good or fair, and poor in case of the latter.

The following are the main changes in food during the period between the first survey and the second survey.

(1) Consumption of rice, dal and wheat has increased. Number of families eating these has also increased.

(2) Consumption of vegetables and the number of persons eating them have increased. Formerly in the summer, vegetables used to come to the village from outside at the interval of 10 or 12 days; now they come almost every day or third day.

(3) Formerly 40 to 50 families among Patidars used to eat " Bhaidka " (porridge) 4 to 5 times a week. Now hardly any Patidar family eats this.

(4) Formerly some Barias used to eat barley; now nobody among them eats the same.

(5) Formerly most of the milk in the village was exported outside for making cream. Now much less is sold outside the village. So people consume milk and ghee in greater quantities than before—at least the higher caste people and the people of means do consume them decidedly more.

(6) Pickles are eaten more than before.

(7) Consumption of sugar, molasses and condiments is greater than before.

(8) Formerly hardly in any family tea was prepared daily. Now tea is being drunk in almost all families, and some people have it twice every day. This is the chief reason for more consumption of milk and sugar in the village.

(9) Formerly there was starvation among some families, for want of sufficient food due to poverty. The number of families on starvation level has greatly decreased; but some persons in the village do starve even now.

Clothing

Among the Hindus most of the adults wear white dhotee and white *paheran* or shirt which may be white or coloured. Some of them also wear half coat or jacket which may be coloured or white. On their heads, they put on white Gandhi cap or coloured cap. Many Barias and a few others tie '*safa*' over their head, Some of the young men do not wear anything on their head. But many persons who work on the fields wear '*safa*' or dhotee over their heads to protect them from heat or cold. A large number of men wear shoes; some put on sandals, while some are barefooted for lack of means to buy footwear.

Adult women or married women wear "kabja"—blouse which covers their body over the waist, and "chania"—petticoat—which covers the lower portion of the body from waist to feet. Over this chania and kabja they wear "sari." All these three are generally coloured and sometimes printed too. A good number of women wear "Sapats" or sandals.

Boys generally wear "lengha"—pyjamas—or shorts and shirt or *paheran.* All these may be white or coloured. Some boys wear caps and some do not.

Girls wear kabja and "chania," which is called "gaghari." Some girls wear "odhani" over this. "Odhani" is a small sari with length and width smaller than sari. A full-fledged Gujarati sari measures 5 yards in length and from 45 to 49 inches in width. Instead of kabja and gaghari, some girls wear frocks which are replacing the former.

Among Muslims men wear either dhoti or lengha or pyjamas, their other clothing apparel being similar to that of Hindu men. Muslim women wear "surval" from waist to feet and "paheran" covering hands and the body from neck to ankles. Over the paheran they wear "odhani." All these clothes may be coloured or white and sometimes they may be printed also. Men wear shoes or sandals and women wear "sapats" or sandals.

Most of the cloth is mill-made. Only a few persons wear handspun khadi or cloth woven on handlooms. The percentage of persons wearing fine and superfine cloth is small, while that of persons using coarse and medium cloth is considerably large. The Brahmins, the shop-keepers and men of means use more of fine cloth while cultivators, labourers and poor persons have to use more of thicker and rougher stuff.

The apparels are generally of cotton. But Brahmin, Vaishya, Lohana and some Patidar women and some other women also keep silk or artificial silk apparel, which they wear on festive occasions. Among Brahmins men too wear silk dhotees during caste dinners and some religious ceremonies.

The clothing of Rabaries is in striking contrast to that of other Hindus. Rabari men wear very thick short dhotee, a short tight waist coat with scores of 'folds' fluttering round their waist, and long narrow sleeves extending to their waist, and a white or red '*safa*' over their head. Rabari women wear short thick wollen skirts cover their breasts with kapada and wear woollen odhani over both. Their attire is coloured, black, red yellow, etc., and is sometimes studded with small, bright pieces of sparkling '*Abarak*' or glasses. Only Rabaries have remained faithful to their ancient attire.

The following are the main differences in dress between the first and second survey :—

(1) Formerly adults were waring turbans, some daily and some on occasions. Now hardly any one wears turbans. Instead, now many men wear caps and some go bare-headed.

(2) Even the wearing of '*safa*' round the head has decreased greatly.

(3) The coloured cotton, silk or woollen caps or woollen coloured fur caps have been replaced by "Gandhi" cap which may or may not be khadi caps.

(4) Only a few men wear coats now. Long coat is hardly seen in the village.

(5) No Hindu adult male used to wear lenghas before. Now some of them do wear the same.

(6) Formerly, women used to wear "choli" or "kapadu" and later on "Porka" with short flower, like blooming bulging sleeves, keeping their chest open in Victorian fashion. Now they have forsaken polkas and wear tight kabjas with tight sleeves.

(7) In case of girls, frocks are fast replacing gagharis and kabjas.

(8) Owing to the simplicity in clothing advocated by Mahatma Gandhi, use of coats has decreased, and even "*khes*" also is hardly worn.

(9) Formerly much of cloth was foreign. Now most of the cloth is 'made in India.'

(10) In spite of the propaganda for the use of handspun khadi, consumption of handspun khadi is meagre.

(11) Consumption of the fine cloth has been increasing.

Housing

The number of houses shown against some castes such as Brahmins, Vaishyas, Lohanas, Patidars, and Barias are more than the number of families in the castes. This is because some families have been staying out of Bhadkad and some families have become extinct. Barring a few exceptions and number of houses for each caste is generally even with the number of families in that caste. Compared to the houses of Barias, Dheds and Bhangies, houses of Brahmins, Vaishyas, Lohanas, and Patidars are generally *pucca*, better and bigger. Most of the houses of the lower castes are *kachcha* and smaller; but the houses of Potter, Carpenter, Blacksmith and Barbers are *pucca* and better than those of Barias and Harijans. However, 2 houses belonging to Harijans are not only *pucca* but quite good also. A few houses belonging to Patidars have dexterous carving on wood on the front side of their buildings. But these are old ones. To have such carvings now would be quite a costly affair.

In the houses of upper castes, there is general evidence of greater affluence in the possession of articles of comfort and luxury than what we see in those of the lower castes. Moreover, in the former, there are signs of greater attention to cleanliness and orderly display than those in the latter. Poverty of the lower class is one of the chief reasons for this difference in upkeep and appearance.

The changes in housing are as under :—

(1) Many people have begun to understand the advantages of light and air; so some of them try to have as much of light and air in their houses as possible, and provide for more and bigger windows.

(2) Formerly men of means used to spend considerable money over carvings, decorations, etc., in their houses; now, instead, they use their money in providing necessary facilities and conveniences in them.

(3) Formerly there were only a few separate rooms for kitchen, now their number has been increasing.

(4) Some persons have provided separate bathrooms in their houses. This is a new noticeable feature and a great convenience. There are no latrines, except one or two which are used by ladies and during nights.

(5) In old houses, the ground used to be dressed with cattle dung. Now some of the new houses have flooring of stone, cement or tiles. Now more cement is used in building houses.

(6) Formerly there were castor-oil lights in earthen bowls. They have been replaced by kerosene lanterns.

(7) In some houses chairs and tables have usurped the place of *gadies* and *takias*. '*Pats*' are also hardly seen.

(8) Formerly all houses had roofs of "*nalias*," now many have roofs of corrugated iron sheets.

(9) In some houses kerosene stove is used, in place of firewood for preparing food and hot drinks.

(10) In a number of houses, pictures of what are called "Leaders" have been eclipsing old patriots, heroes and gods.

Sanitation and Cleanliness

Except for a small number of families who keep their houses and surroundings clean, many families keep bullocks or buffaloes in front of or near their houses with the result that the dung and urine of these cattle, along with refuse thrown here and there by residents make '*falias*', '*mohollas*' and pathways, quite dirty. Besides children, even adults seem to have no civic consciousness. Government have ceased payment of salaries to Harijan sweepers, and the latter are absolved from the duty of sweeping and cleaning the village. In the absence of alternative local arrangement, voluntary or otherwise by any agency, the village remains unswept over long period; only occasionally some leading persons in the village get the same swept by local sweepers, mostly by their personal influence.

Due to the housing of cattle in the same place, their dung, and urine, as well as other dirt, refuse etc., tend to the breeding of mosquitoes and bugs which suck the blood of men and cattle already emaciated for lack of nutritious food. Under economic pressure, a number of persons work under severe cold or in scorching heat under great physical strain. Some persons suffer through worries arising from economic or social difficulties, hardships, troubles and calamities. These are some of the main causes of ill-health and diseases in Bhadkad. During the first survey also, the village was noted for dirt, refuse etc. There were bugs, mosquitoes etc. which pestered people and cattle and affected their health. After very heavy rains, water used to collect in big pools around the village. This impeded passage and was detrimental to the health and sanitation of Bhadkad.

Prevalent Diseases

Cold, cough, malaria, asthma, lung troubles, pneumonia are the common diseases in the winter season, while in summer, people suffer from malaria, typhoid, diarrhoea, sprue and sometime cholera also. During the rainy season a number of persons are attacked by malaria and cough.

During the year 1954-55, 417 cases were registered in the Dispensary of Bhadkad, among which 261 were men and 156 women. The total number of days for which they took medicine is 1,087.

Literacy

Out of 1,516 persons in Bhadkad, 352 are literate; they can read and write fairly well. This means that the percentage of literacy is 23. Of the 832 males, 297 are literate, and of the 684 females, 55 are literate. The percentage of literacy, among men and women are 35 and 8 respectively. Among the higher castes, literacy is higher in Brahmins, Vaishyas and Lohanas whose occupations need knowledge of the "Three Rs." Literacy is not high among Patidars who are mainly agriculturists. Among the lower or backward castes, literacy is good or fair among Garasias, Dadhus, Potters, Blacksmiths, Barbers, Golas, Ravals, Dheds, and Chamars, while it is less or much less among Gosaies, Rabaries, Barias, Bhois, Shoemakers, Vagharies and Harijans. Among the 2 Chamars—one male and one female, and the 2 adult Golas, one male and one female—the males alone are literate. The high percentage of literacy noted among the backward classes is due to the comparatively less number of women in these families. Literacy is high among Muslims.

As compared to the present position, in the previous survey, there were 303 literates out of a total population of 1,218 persons. So, literacy has increased only 2 per cent (excluding the children attending school) including the children, the percentage of increase is from 25 to 34 that is 9 per cent only.

During the second survey among those who have received higher education, there is one B.A., LLB., one Chartered Accountant, and one who has studied Engineering at Kala Bhavan Technical Institute at Baroda. Besides these persons, there are a few who have received higher education in Colleges or have passed Matriculation Examination; but most of them have been staying out of Bhadkad, as they cannot find suitable gainful occupation in the village.

4

MADHOPUR REVISITED*

BERNARD S. COHN

ON FIRST RETURNING to Madhopur, a village in Eastern Uttar Pradesh, I was struck by how little had changed since I had lived and worked there for a year 1952-53. There was last October, still the tortuous journey by bus, train, *ekka*, and foot to get to the village; the fields, the houses, and even the children looked the same. I soon realized that I wasn't looking at the same children but at their younger brothers and sisters; similarly my initial impression of no change in the village gave way during my two brief visits to a more considered one that a good deal had changed since I left in 1953. In some cases these changes were the results of the passing of six years and in others they reflect some of the Government's efforts to change the lives of the Indian villager.

THE NONIYAS NOW INDEPENDENT

The lands of Madhopur, until 1951, were owned by some 50 families of Thakurs (Rajputs) who dominated the 250 other families of 22 castes living in the village. With Zamindari Abolition the Thakurs lost some of their lands to the low caste tenants who had been cultivating as permanent tenants. So it was natural to expect changes in the relations between the low castes and the Thakurs. As an illustration, I will describe some of the changes in two castes: the Noniyas, a low but clean caste, whose traditional occupation is earthworking and cultivating; and the Chamars, an untouchable caste of labourers.

The Noniyas do not live in the main settlement of Madhopur, but in a satellite hamlet a mile away Before Zamindari Abolition they were mainly permanent tenants on the Thakurs' lands, and although somewhat geographically separated from the rest of the village, they nonetheless served their landlords and participated in the economic and ritual life of the village. Since 1952, the Noniyas have become increasingly independent of their old landlords—within the last three years they have built their own school and are now trying, in the face of some opposition from the Thakurs, to finance the continuation of the school. At Dashera last year, when I was visiting the village, I found that the Noniyas were celebrating their own Ram Lila, have built a temple in their hamlet, and were not participating in the general village *mela*. Both the temple and the celebration of their own Ram Lila, it seems to me, symbolize their independence from their former landlords. I still saw Noniyas in the main hamlet,

* Reproduced from '*The Economic Weekly*', special Number, Vol. XI, July 1959, pp. 963-967

and Noniyas still give the Thakurs outward signs of respect and deference, but this no longer symbolizes an actual social relationship, but is rapidly becoming a vestige.

The Chamars

On first appearance there is little change to be noted among the Chamars. They are still desperately poor and they complained bitterly of the abuses and tricks of the Thakurs. On my second visit I conducted a brief census of the Chamars, and several things quickly stood out which supported the Chamars' complaints. The census revealed three things: the number of Chamars working outside of the village has doubled in six years, rising from 36 in 1952 to 72 in 1959, this out of an adult Chamar population of about 225; there are now eight Chamar families who have migrated permanently to the cities whereas in 1952 there was only one Chamar who had done so; and in the space of five years at least five young Chamar brides have run away where in 1952-53 I could find only four cases of wives who had run away over a period of 30 years. These three facts pointed to one thing—the markedly deteriorated economic position of the Chamars in the village. All the Chamars testified to the fact that they had lost a good deal of land since 1953, their lot in the village was much harder, and although they could still work for the Thakurs, they couldn't get any new land to rent, and much of the land they had been renting and cultivating previously had been taken away from them by the Thakur landlords. The brides ran away because they weren't getting enough to eat in their husbands' homes.

Position Greatly Deteriorated

Previous to 1952 no Chamar owned land in the strict sense of the word; all was owned by the Thakurs. With Zamindari Abolition, however, those Chamars who were permanent tenants on the Thakurs' land were to become *Bhumidars*. In 1952 the Chamars of the village cultivated approximately 124 acres, most of this was as tenants-at-will on the *sir* land of the Thakurs. Only 12 of the 122 households of Chamars had any permanent cultivating rights in the land; the rest were *shikmi* tenants (tenants-at-will). Out of the 12 who did have permanent cultivating rights, ten had less than half an acre and only two had more than one acre. A few of the permanent cultivating tenants took advantage of Zamindari Abolition to get ownership rights in the land, but the rest were content to pay taxes to the Government without ownership. Three years ago *shikmi* tenants were supposed to become *sirdars* on the *sir* land which they had been cultivating. The Thakurs, however, were able to manage things so that very few of the Chamars got any rights in the land at all. In many cases they did not actually eject their Chamar tenants from their *sir* land, but it became widely known that the Chamars were not entered in the Government records as *sirdars* and the Thakurs still kept legal control of the land, so that the Chamar tenant could be ejected at any time. It appears it was the knowledge that they had no rights in the land and little hope of getting such rights, short of expensive and protracted litigation, rather than the actual loss of land, which drove many of the Chamars from the village into urban employment.

In some cases there was actual ejection. One family of Chamars who had served the same Thakur family as ploughmen for over three generations had part of their lands taken away by the Thakur. The father of the family continues to work for the Thakur but his two sons have now left for the coal fields of West Bengal.

The Chamars do not like working outside the village. They feel that the cities are unhealthy and dirty, they like working on the land, and they miss their families, friends and caste fellows when they go to the cities. In 1952 the majority of Chamars who worked in the cities from Madhopur thought of it as a temporary expedient, to pay off a debt, to buy a bullock, to pay for a wedding, or a new house. The fact that they thought of it as temporary is seen in their leaving their wives and families in the village. Now the families are beginning to go as well. There has always been some mobility among the Chamars, but previously this has been inter-rural, not rural-urban mobility on a permanent basis. In the past few years a new pattern of mobility is emerging.

Other Effects of Zamindari Abolition

The changes of the relations of the Thakurs and Noniyas and the Thakurs and Chamars are a direct result of the working of Zamindari Abolition. In the case of the Noniyas the act is having its intended result; with the Chamars it is not working as the framers of the act would presumably wish. But even though at the present it is bringing hardship, dislocation, and unhappiness to the Chamars, and one who is an admirer of the life in the Indian village can bemoan it, or curse the cleverness and unscrupulousness of the Thakurs, in the long run it may be the only solution for the Chamars. The brutal fact throughout most of Eastern U. P. is that there are just too many people on the land, in Madhopur there are over 2,000 people in the village with just over 1,000 acres, and someone has to get off the land.

Traditionally Thakurs are warriors and agricultural managers. As with many rural people in India, land was the principal source of income and status, and in the village today land largely determines a Thakur family's power and status within the village. In the past when a Thakur had some spare money, he would invest in land—this is still true today but to a much lesser extent as the price of land in and around Madhopur is high. Last year a man paid over Rs. 2,000 for half a *bigha* of rice land. However with Zamindari Abolition, under which a landlord must himself farm the land he has, and in a situation in which there will soon be a ceiling on the amount of land a person can farm, Thakurs are beginning to look to other ways of using their money. I would say the principal form of investment on the part of Thakurs today is the education of their sons, so that they may be able to work outside of the village and support their families through employment.

Another way Thakurs are using what capital they have is in investment in building and commercial activity. In the last five years, Thakurs have invested money in contracts to build irrigation channels, earth-moving jobs, and in *biri* manufacturing.

NON-AGRICULTURAL INVESTMENT

Two miles away from Madhopur on the Benares road are large patches of alkaline land, one on each side of the road. On one side, there are two new shops, a grain godown and a cycle shop, both owned and run by Thakurs. There are 13 buses a day which pass this little commercial centre, many of them stopping to take on or let off passengers, and there are many rickshaws waiting at the bus stop. Next to the already existing shops are the foundations for 12 more shops and a large sign proudly proclaiming a new bazaar which is to be built on the site.

Opposite, a local co-operative, formed by Thakurs of the area, is planning the building of a sugar factory. They are a long way from realizing the Rs. 60,000 they must raise in order to get the matching grant from the government, but the fact that they have formed a co-operative and have gotton some of money is a major change. It is important that it is the Thakurs and not, as one would expect, local merchant, groups who are taking the lead in this activity. Zamindari Abolition and the rising population are pushing the Thakurs into commercial activity, and although much of it is a minor sort, it is still a start. If and when the sugar factory is built it will be a major development for the area—it will enable farmers to get a higher price for their sugar crop (the sugar is now marketed in the form of gur) and it will provide some jobs for both the landless and the newly educated. In addition it will mean an expansion of transportation and marketing facilities in the region.

FROM RAIL TO ROAD

The second time I went back to Madhopur recently, I went by a different route as there is now regular bus service which goes near the village from Benaras except during and immediately after the rains. Three years ago a pontoon bridge was built across the Gumpti river and is in operation from the end of October until the middle of June. Formerly the trip from Benaras to the village took seven to eight hours by rail, *ekka* and foot, but now in the dry season it can be covered in two hours, an hour and half bus ride and half hour's walk to the village from the road.

This is not only a convenience for the villagers, but the establishment of the bus route indicates the shifting of the whole geography of trade for the village and surrounding area. Six years ago, those agricultural products of the village which were marketed, mainly *gur* and wheat, were sold through a bazaar four miles away, the *gur* or wheat being bought by the village shopkeepers and traders, loaded on camels, and taken for resale to the bazaar. A villager wanting a product not available in the village would go or send some one to the local bazaar, or would bring it from the District headquarters 25 miles away. Occasionally a villager would go to Benares for special things. Although this is the pattern which still largely prevails, there are indications that this situation will change.

There is talk that in the Third Five Year Plan a permanent bridge will be built upon the Gumpti, giving the area all-year-round access to Benares, which although mainly thought of as a religious centre, is more important to the villagers as a commercial and industrial centre, and will become increasingly so, if plans for the development of an industrial complex outside Benares at Mughal Serai are realized. For the people of Madhopur the bus and truck are definitely much more important than the railroad, and as this trend continues, a roadside bazaar will be much more important to them than the river and rail bazaar to which they were formerly linked.

A New Society ?

Is a new society emerging? Clearly I think there is a new rural as well as an urban society emerging in Northern India, as exemplified by the changes in Madhopur. The only comparable period of rapid social and economic change that Eastern U. P. went through was during the first 20 years of British rule from 1795 to 1815. During this period the basic social and economic structure which we know today seems to have been pretty much fixed. Madhopur is going through another period of change, but this change may not be all that the Planning Commission and those concerned with revitalization of village life may want.

In the late eighteenth and early nineteenth centuries the distinction between rural and urban, although it would be made, did not necessarily represent two different societies and ways of life. There was a continuum in social structure, values, religion, and outlook between the villager and the town dweller. There were groups in both city and village who were hinged together. The *Zamindar*, the priest, the merchant had relationships to the city, they moved freely back and forth. The city was a reflection and intensification of the village way of life. Villager and townman could freely communicate, as they were of the same culture.

Today I think this situation is changing. The hinges are no longer there. *Zamindars* face the choice of staying in the village and becoming progressively impoverished or moving into " white collar " urban employment. The priest faces the same choice and the merchant must learn new ways of doing business. The richer agriculturalist educates his son for urban employment, and perhaps for the first generation the son maintains his tie with the village, but after that it is gone. As for the landless Chamar who has lost his stake in the village, he can go to the city as part of the emerging working class. Politically the city was formerly the centre of the state, but the State was content to maintain law and order and extract revenue or tribute from the rural area. Now the city is still the political centre, but the goal is not only an extractive one, but one of guided social and economic change for the village; but just at the time when the State is becoming interested in the village for the villagers' sake, it would appear that the State is least able to affect the villager.

The Government is increasingly the only link between the two parts of the society, and although mechanical means of communication have increased, the cultural linkage between village and town are broken. Those groups which had been the links are gone. Through the working of land legislation and the rise of population, the pressure on land is increasing, the size of holdings is going down, there is less and less capital for investment in farming and what capital there is goes into education for urban employment or for non-farming activities.

In a generation's time, I think the village will be in the hands of small peasant proprietors, with a floating group of landless workers, counter-balanced by a modern industrial urban culture. A gap will have developed which is new to Indian history, and paradoxically enough India will develop a peasantry in the middle of the twentieth century such as we are familiar with in European history of the eighteenth and nineteenth centuries.

5

COMMUNICATION OF MODERN IDEAS AND KNOWLEDGE IN INDIAN VILLAGES*

Y. B. DAMLE

1. PROBLEM AND SCOPE OF THE ENQUIRY

THIS PAPER embodies the findings of a field study made of communication of modern ideas and knowledge into some Indian villages. The importance of the problem of communication both for theoretical and practical purposes hardly needs to be stressed. In an age which believes in mutual aid, both material and non-material, the problem of communication assumes all the greater significance.The pattern of communication both intranational and international in no small way determines intranational and international relations:

The diffusion into seven villages of the following modern ideas and kinds of knowledge was studied.

1. Information about the national political scene: knowledge of leaders, how many national leaders are known and by how many persons.
2. Knowledge of national policies: who rules the nation; division of the country; social and economic policies of the State; e. g., Five-Year Plan, extension projects, community development projects, national bonds and loans; secularism; different ideologies, e. g., the capitalist, the socialist, and the communist; abolition of untouchability and doing away with arbitrary differences between the two sexes and between different groups of people.
3. Knowledge about world political structure: awareness of the fact of the division of the world into two main camps, the American and the Soviet; knowledge of world leaders and also of foreign policies; knowledge about the location, meaning, and significance of Britain, U. S. A., France, Russia, China, Africa, Ceylon, Pakistan, Indo-China, etc.; knowledge about the leaders of these countries.
4. Knowledge of international policies and events: happenings in Korea; Geneva; American technical and financial aid; U. S. arms aid to Pakistan; Russian and American tensions; who are our friends and enemies; can world problems be solved with the

*Reproduced from "*Communication of Modern Ideas and Knowledge in Indian Villagers,*" by Y. B. Damle, pp. 1-22.

help of others; whom should we befriend; can India remain neutral; if not, whom should we join.

5. Awareness of modern ideas regarding caste and religion; extent of rationalism; awareness of the modern concept of essential quality of all human beings.
6. Impact of new ideas, of recreation; movies, radio, sports, etc.
7. How was this knowledge acquired: through contact with people, newspapers, lectures, political propaganda, etc.

This list of the items studied makes clear how the problem of communication has been tackled. Both intranational and international items of communication were analysed. Limited as the sample of each of these was, nevertheless, they brought out the relative predominance of knowledge of the former over the latter. To put it in another fashion, the perspective of the villages makes for greater communicability of certain items An analysis of the functional relationships which affect the communicability, of some ideas and the poor communicability of others would have implications for practical policy.

II. Methods and Procedure

The seven villages selected for study have different degrees of relationship with the city. Their spatial distance from Poona (their nearest city) ranged from one to eighty miles so the functioning of external agencies in some of the villages affected their reception of communications.

It was felt that the problem should be analysed from the structure-functional point of view in order to tackle adequately its different ramifications, particularly that of differential communication mentioned just above. The structure-functional point of view has been neatly elaborated by Merton in his book *Social Theory and Social Structure*. Its framework of analysis is utilised. This does not, however, mean that there is a complete and unqualified acceptance of Merton's position.

Different tools were used to obtain the necessary information, interviewing and observation were the main tools. The schedule containing the questions had sometimes to be kept in the background. Experience in the villages proves that greater information can be obtained by informal chats and discussions than by asking straight questions. The questions had to be mixed with a good deal of other conversation.

Choice of the Villages

Cities have always been properly regarded disseminators of ideas and knowledge. So in the choice of the villages to be studied the distance from Poona City was one of the most important considerations. The distances of the different villages selected for study are as follows :

1. Bopudi, on the outskirts of Poona City and now included within the City Corporation limits.

2. Subhashwadi (Manjri), 11 miles.
3. Muthe, 24 miles.
4. Andgaon, 26 miles.
5. Kondhur, 20 miles.
6. Ahupe, 80 miles.
7. Patan, 72 miles.

This lends itself to scale analysis, which is given later. The nearness or otherwise of a village to city would be of crucial importance in the process of communication.

III. Findings

Ambegaon Taluka: 1. Patan

Patan is 72 miles north-west of Poona City. To reach Patan one has to travel by a public bus up to Ambegaon (60 miles) and then trek the remaining 12 miles. Not even bullock carts can reach Patan since the path is through hills and jungles. In fact, the whole tract is formed by the ranges of the Sahyadri mountain. Patan is about 4,000 feet above sea level. The tract gets plenty of rain, ranging from 130 inches to 175 inches per year. It is primarily a rice-growing area and is famous for rice of good quality. Other cereals like nachani (*ragee*—a grain *cunosurus corocanus* of *elusine corocona*) and vari (the grain *coix barbata*) are also grown to supplement the diet of the people. In spite of this the people suffer from starvation for a couple of months a year. The village is surrounded on all four sides by hills and thus is isolated from the rest of the world. It is a tiny village with an area of 1·9 sq. miles and a total population of 51 persons.

Except for one household, that of the local Mahar who performed all sorts of functions from carrying message to scavenging, all other inhabitants are Mahadeo Koli. Mahadeo Koli is a Hindu tribe. Actually the epithet Mahadeo is derived from worship of the God Shankara, the Mahadeo (the big God). It is primarily an agricultural tribe. " It is probable that they (Kolis) are a mongrel race, and have sprung from alliances formed between Hindus and aboriginal tribes. " The Mahar is fed by every house in return for certain services he renders to the community.

Only one of the villagers is literate, and he left the village more than a year ago and went to suburb of Bombay to work as a labourer in a factory. Only four persons have seen a train. Only these four persons have had a ride in a motor bus, though the rest of the villagers have seen one as they have to go to Ambegaon every Wednesday to the weekly bazaar to buy everything from salt and oil to clothes. None of them have seen Poona.

The Patil (Headman), four other persons, and the Mahar were interviewed. It must be said that there was no difficulty whatsoever in interviewing.

1. These people know about independence though not about the partition of the country. Only the Patil had seen Mahatma Gandhi when he went to Bombay in his young days. None except for him,knows about Jawaharlal Nehru, his knowledge may be due to the functional relationship which such knowledge bears to the post of a Patil. He is paid Rs. 40/- per month by the Government for discharging functions like collecting land revenue, maintaining law and order in the village, and reporting to the Taluka authorities if anything serious happens in the village.
2. Only the Patil knew that Jawaharlal Nehru ruled India. He did not know anything more about national policies.
3. Knowledge of world political structure: Nil.
4. Knowledge of international policies and events: Nil.
5. Awareness of modern ideas on caste and religion: Nil.
6. Only the Patil has seen a mythological movie in Bombay. He has also heard a loudspeaker in a meeting. No impact whatsoever of any new idea.
7. Some of them have attended election propaganda meetings. However, they have no faith in pre-election promises. Only during epidemics do they get medical aid from Government. No agency of communication has reached the village.

Patan thus presents the spectacle of a relatively simple structure untouched by any innovation. The tribal social structure is devoid of any effective contact with the outside world. The structure is static. No new item has become either functional or dysfunctional.

Mulshi Taluka : 3. Kondhur

Kondhur is 20 miles south-west of Poona City. To reach Kondhur one has to travel by a motor bus up to Urwade—20 miles—and then walk 10 miles. Kondhur is separated from Muthe by the river Mutha. The distance is just 4 miles. Yet the village is turned into an island during the monsoon. The average rainfall is 130 inches per year. In addition to the natural isolation, cultural isolation impinges on the local inhabitants as the Sarvodaya Centre has not extended its field of activities to Kondhur.

The total population of Kondhur is 841. A primary school is functioning there. However, the total number of literates is only 25. Kondhur is a primitive and a traditional village. Only four persons have been educated in Poona. No innovation has reached Kondhur. Despite the wishes of the people, whatever changes have been introduced in Muthe have not been introduced in Kondhur. The discrepancy between subjective dispositions and objective consequences is heightened by the inadequacy of the social structure. The inhabitants of Kondhur had the requisite motivation to incorporate new items but lacked the means to put it into effect.

Six persons were interviewed. One of them was an influential land owner, another was the Patil, (Headman) and the rest were cultivators.

1. People have heard about Morarji Desai, the Chief Minister of Bombay, Nehru, and Gandhi.
2. Only two persons have heard about Five-Year Plan. People in general vaguely knew that the Indian Republic had declared itself to be a secular State. However, they did not at all approve. Secularism, they felt, is dysfunctional to the Indian social system. People also know that untouchability has been abolished by law but did not like it. This measure is dysfunctional to their social structure, which accords a lowly position to the Mahar (the untouchable). They knew about the partition of the country and the creation of Pakistan. Probably their knowledge of the happenings prior to the division of India makes them regard secularism as thoroughly dysfunctional.
3. Knowledge of world political structure: Nil.
4. Knowledge of international policies and events: Nil.
5. The people are aware of modern ideas about caste but strongly object to the same. A social structure which is based on a particular system of relationship between different castes would naturally regard any attempt to change the system of relationship as a serious threat to its existence. Abolition of differences based on caste is thus very dysfunctional to their prevailing social structure
6. Impact of new ideas of recreation: Nil.
7. New ideas and knowledge reached them through kinship and newspapers. Obviously, their reading of newspapers is not only very slight but also highly selective for world news was not noted or retained.

MUTHE

Muthe is 24 miles to the south-west of Poona City. A distance of 4 miles has to be covered on foot from Urwade to reach Muthe. Muthe is situated in the basin of the river Mutha. Its area is 4 sq. miles. The total population of Muthe is 1,490. The main occupation of the people is agriculture. Rice is the main crop. Pulses like beans are grown to a small extent. Trading in milch cattle is a subsidiary occupation of the people.

The Sarvodaya Centre was started three years ago. Since its inception medical care has been made available to the people of Muthe and neighbouring villages. The local medical officer in charge of the Sarvodaya dispensary, however, said that as many as 80 per cent of the people do not avail themselves of the medical facilities. In this context he made a very pertinent observation.

A mere provision of medical facilities is not adequate to solve the problems of villages (chronic poverty) as it reduced the natural immunity of the people of diseases. Besides modern medicines and treatment are so costly that the villages can ill-afford them. Economic improvement, improved sanitation, etc. would be more useful under the circumstances.

In short, medical care rendered in isolation becomes dysfunctional for the majority of the people. The centre helps in putting people in touch with the authorities relevant to improvement in cultivation. However, this is functional only for the upper stratum since it entails capital expenditure. It is dysfunctional for the majority of the people and thereby strains the social structure. This may bring about change in the desired direction, viz. an agitation to make such items functional for all.

The Sarvodaya Centre has undertaken some activities which are functional for all the people e. g. building of pucca wells, inoculation of people against cholera and plague, etc. The pit latrines and Khaddar are, however, functional only for a small group.

Interviews were held with four sets of people: (1) Mr. D. the local landlord and a popular person because of his helpfulness, (2) merchants and farmers, (3) the local priest, and (4) the medical officer in charge of the Sarvodaya dispensary, whose observations have already been recorded. Information, not to say a forthright analysis, came out not only on the problem on hand but also on the weakness of the social structure. It is recorded here since it throws a floodlight on the feelings of the people.

Mr. D. discussed the interrelationships among the different segments of the community and remarked that the Bara Balute system—a system which ensures occupational division of labour and interdependence is on the point of breaking down. He said " the Mahars no longer perform their traditional functions " and thus the first blow has been dealt to the system. Various factors—economic, political, legal—are responsible for this state of affairs. In short, the effort to register piecemeal improvement, e. g. abolition of untouchability, becomes positively dysfunctional for the entire system. It was further asserted by him that " people are craving for a change in their circumstances but they want such a change to be effected by some external agency. The springs of local leadership have almost dried out. " Inadequate social structure, structural constraints, and the impact of external influence on the marginal areas of the social structure are hindering any change for the better.

The most pertinent point made by the farmers and merchants concerned:

> the draining of Muthe of its youth and the consequent dissipation of the springs of enthusiasm and activity. Besides, the youths who go out to work come back alienated from the village folks. They are only worried about their own pleasure pursuits, develop a condescending attitude toward the people and do not mix with them. If anything, they have an adverse impact on the people. Being dissipated physically, mentally, and morally they cannot in any way become useful to the community

The pull of the cities thus proves tremendously dysfunctional to the entire system.

The local priest, who is well versed in the scriptures and is accorded respect by the people, pointed out that about four hundred persons have migrated to cities for employment. He further said: " these people cannot wield any influence on the village folk owing to their lowly occupational position. " They convey a good deal of information, but for that reason it does not bring about any change. To bring about change the persons who desire it must enjoy social esteem. Communication is also conditioned by status.

1. Most of the people know about ministers of Bombay State, Nehru. Gandhi, Namdeorao Mohol (the local Congress member of the Bombay Legislative Assembly).
2. People know about the Congress rule. It is through the work of construction undertaken by Government that they have an awareness of the Five-Year Plan, extension projects, community development projects. Whatever is visible impresses them. The people, however, feel that most of the improvements can be availed of only by the higher stratum. Thus improved methods of cultivation, medical facilities, communication, and transport can be used only by the richer section. These items are functional for a particular stratum and are dysfunctional for the system as a whole. People know about the abolition of untouchability but do not approve of it. This item is dysfunctional for them.
3. People in general know nothing about world political structure, not even about Pakistan. Except for the medical officer everyone else was in the dark about it.
4. The same holds good in respect to recent international events.
5. There is awareness of the new ideas relating to caste, religion, and rationalism, but there is no acceptance of these ideas. People feel that these ideas are not at all suitable for adoption by them under their present circumstances. Structural constraints and inadequacy of social structure prevent these ideas from being functional.
6. Traditional methods of recreation are in operation. The yearly fair held in honour of the local deity continues to be the clearing-house for ideas and objects. The fair is largely attended by people from the neighbouring villages. The old forms of recreation such as folk dances, wrestling matches, *tamasha* (a form of folk dramatics) persist even now. The Sarvodaya Centre made many efforts to replace tamasha, which sometimes verges on obscenity and indulges in rousing the sex impulses of the people, by plays which convey some moral, but such attempts have met with signal failure. The reason for this seems to be the insistence on the part of the people on allowing themselves indulgence in such

revelries once in a while to remove the monotony of drab existence. This is perfectly understandable in a situation in which sex is the main recreation, owing to the drab existence enforced on the majority of the people by force of circumstances. Moral preaching which is devoid of any consideration for the material aspects of well-being is dysfunctional to the system.

7. New ideas and knowledge reached the people through the Sarvodaya Centre, the local M. L. A. contact with Poona and Bombay through relatives and friends.

Muthe furnishes a classical example of the inability of an external agency to register any improvement in the life of a people by tinkering with the problem at a surface level. Neglect of structure is bound to lead such effort to failure. Neither the structural nor the functional aspect can be neglected. Structure also needs to be changed so as to be compatible with an adequate functioning of items of improvement. Equally important is the moral that structure needs to be strengthened from within and not from without. Communication of ideas and knowledge has constant impact on the social structure. To be able to withstand this impact successfully and to render it functional the system of interrelations between different components of a structure needs readjustment. In short, the dynamic aspect cannot be neglected.

POONA CITY TALUKA : 7. BOPUDI

Bopudi is situated on the northern border of Poona City. Its population is in the neighbourhood of 5,000. Since 1951 Bopudi has been included in the Poona City Municipal Corporation area. In fact, the village is next to Kirkee which has an ammunition factory and an ordnance depot. Naturally, the workers try to stay in the vicinity of the factory. During the last six years four other industrial works factories have been installed near Bopudi. Bopudi thus has become a factory workers' nest. Hardly 3 per cent of its inhabitants can be classed as cultivators. The original inhabitants, who were mainly agriculturists, have been swamped by the surging tide of factory labourers. The local Patil (the Headman) very much regretted the change and remarked that " it is very difficult for me to know who is who in the village. "...The nature of the work and the hours of work in the factories militate against any, composite life. There is a conglomeration of people, whose structural unity has been left undeveloped. The shifting nature of the population only heightens the process. The old structure has been submerged and a new one adequate to cope with the changing needs of the people has not been created. One illustration will suffice. The place still has the same sanitary facilities which it had eighteen years ago. The increase in the population has reduced these to a mockery. Structural development has not taken place at all. The sheer nearness of Poona City also accentuates this process. The city has become the centre of attraction in everything from education and entertainment to politics. Items like the school, market, cinem ahouses have ceased to be functional for a big sub-group. The impact of the neighbouring structure is simply overwhelming. So the already inadequate structure almost vanishes into thin air. There is no local leadership of any sort. People look toward the city for leads in every walk of life. The spirit of self-dependence has almost dried up. Naturally, the people made insistent demands on the municipal corporation for working out the necessary changes. A mobile dispensary has been started by the corporation and many people avail themselves of the medical facilities provided by the same. Recently, roads have been lighted by electricity. But many important needs such as good and adequate water supply, sanitary facilities etc., remain unattended to. Recently, a new school building was constructed by the corporation and a public library was also started. However, the response has not been encouraging as everyone depends on the same body to persuade and cajole them to make use of the same. Local action is conspicuous by its absence. And thus such items become non-functional, i. e. , irrelevant to the people.

Interviews were held with eight factory workers. Many others weie also present at the time of discussion. Many people have been educated up to vernacular second to fourth standards. Some of them read newspapers daily and as such were conversant with recent events and happenings. The growing unemployment has been worrying people considerably Pessimism and indifference on the part of the people toward events and happenings is the outcome.

1. There is awareness of the different political parties in India, e. g.the Congress, the Communist Party, the Socialist Party, the Hindu Mahasabha, etc. People know of Nehru, Azad, Morarji Desai, and some of the ministers of the Bombay State. Jayaprakash Narayan and Ashok Mehta—both of them are Socialist leaders.
2. There is awareness of national policies on the part of those who read newspapers, i.e. about 20 per cent of the people. People knew about secularism and abolition of untouchability etc. They felt, however, that " differences could not be obliterated unless groups like the untouchables became powerful—economically, educationally and politically. " Piecemeal improvement would not be of much use according to them. There was awareness of the different prevailing ideologies—the capitalist, the socialist, and the communist. No definite preference was expressed for any particular ideology. All that they desired was employment for all and better amenities of life.
3. Those who read newspapers and some others, too, know that India is friendly with China and the U.S.A. in spite of the arms aid to Pakistan. People know about England, though not about her leader. Division of the country is known to them as the same became dysfunctional for them owing to the influx of Hindu refugees. The refugees competed with them for jobs, housing, etc.

4. India's efforts for the establishment of peace are known to the people. There is a general feeling that India must avoid conflict.
5. People know about modern ideas relating to caste, religion, etc. but do not completely approve of them. They want to emphasise the importance of religious worship. They have a temple, which has become the meeting ground for people. The latent function of the temple as a meeting place has been transformed into a manifest function. Rationalism is accepted by the people for its utility and not as a value. There is a superficial acceptance of rationalism, but it is not ingrained in the people.
6. There are a couple of radio sets in the village. Most of the people have seen movies. There is almost no change in their methods of recreation.
7. Modern ideas and knowledge have reached them through newspapers and contact with Poona City. No political party works amongst them.

The stunted development of social structure in Bopudi constitutes the major drawback of the system. Modern ideas and knowledge cannot become functional in such a system. The impact of a powerful neighbouring structure perpetuates structural weaknesses of a system. Sometimes there is a possibility of an outward show of strength. Thus if Bopudi were studied superficially, the student might be impressed with the changes that have taken place. Analysing the situation from the structure-functional point of view, one learns the essential structural weaknesses and the consequent inefficient functioning or even dysfunctioning of certain items. Structure needs to be strengthened to ensure effective functioning of a system. Mere influx of ideas and knowledge fails to attain the desired consequences. The gap or discrepancy between subjective motivations and objective consequences arise out of the nature of a structure as is evidenced in the case of Bopudi.

IV. Concluding Remarks

Certain broad conclusions emerge from this study. These pertain to methodological, theoretical, and practical fields. As to methodology, it has been proved that the problem of communication can be adequately tackled from the structure-functional point of view. As is revealed by the scalogram, it is not merely the distance from or nearness to the city which facilitates communication of ideas and knowledge. Rather it is the nature of structure which also determines the qualitative and quantitative content of communication. This aspect needs further empirical study. Merton's paradigm is validated. As for the theory of communication of modern ideas and knowledge, the study reveals the necessity of analysing the dependent, interdependent, and independent variables. So many problems are posed. Is communication a one-way process? It is two-way? If so, what are the factors which make it so? Is there anything inherent in the socio-economic-political structure of a country which determines the content of communication of ideas and knowledge? Thus, for example, is it the realization of the structural weakness which makes for a wide dissemination of ideas relating to untouchability, caste, religion, etc.? At the level of reception of ideas it has been found that whatever is visible appeals to the people, e.g. the Five Year Plan, community development projects, etc. Then again it has been found that the structural constraints and inadequacies, whether natural or imposed by circumstances, e.g. by the impact of a powerful neighbouring structure, render certain ideas and knowledge dysfunctional. This naturally leads to a process of change. There are two possibilities in this connection: one is that the recipient structure may be modified or strengthened to render functional such items: the other is that the realization of the dysfunctional nature of such items may lead to their being discarded by the original disseminating agency and thus the re-establishment of a position of equilibrium may be facilitated even at the cost of a loss of face, e.g., what the medical officer in Muthe suggested in respect to the use of medicines and drugs amounts to this. Does communication follow the lines of stratification? This aspect also needs empirical investigation. As for the practical aspect, the study offers some suggestions. First of all, creating motivation without corresponding effort to create the necessary conditions for the fulfilment of the same leads to frustration. Otherwise, the usual spectacle of discrepancy between subjective motivation and objective consequences will persist. The needs and aspirations of the people ought to be considered before launching new ideas and knowledge. Actually, the necessary atmosphere can be created for the absorption of new ideas and knowledge—even some bitter pills like the new ideas relating to caste, religion, untouchability, etc., can be swallowed by first attending to the felt needs of the people. External agencies have very many limitations and these limitations cannot be got rid of except by fulfilling certain fundamental needs of the people e. g. by ensuring a higher standard of living to all the people. This would also presuppose an absence of any strings to any aid from such external agencies.

SECTION VIII

AGRARIAN UNREST

INTRODUCTION

THE PRESENT section contains five selections depicting the patterns of struggles that are found in agrarian India. Rural India, contrary to the general belief, is not inert. It is seething with discontent and conflicts. The old stable social structure of the village community with its varied institutions had experienced a severe jolt during the British period and is undergoing a very rapid, almost hectic transformation after Independence. The impact of elections based on universal franchise, of increasing competitive profit-oriented production by peasants and of the emergence of various new institutions and associations—political, economic, social and administrative, on various classes and castes, has resulted in a mobility and created a tension which is, in its intensity and depth, unparalleled in the history of Indian rural society. The five selections attempt to portray the most obvious types of tensions and conflicts that are rampant in rural India to-day. A systematic examination of the structural matrix which is generating these tensions and conflicts is absolutely essential if our approach to the study of the dynamics of rural society is to be adequate. To locate the reasons for these tensions, in the deterioration of individual psyche or the moral degradation of the people in general is, to my mind, a very cheap and superficial sociology. The causes of these great conflicts and tensions have to be located instead in the rapid structural transformation of rural society and the impact it is making on the various strata of the rural people and not in the goodwill or illwill of the individual or the groups. This point has to be emphasised and a profounder analysis of the roots of unrest have to be made because a massive propaganda advocating ethical explanations and panaceas as well as stricter coercive law and order measures by the government have been launched to overcome the growing agrarian unrest. It should be noted here that there are types and types of conflicts. While some of them have a historically progressive liberating influence, some others may work as a reactionary break on social progress. The papers included in this section are selected and presented with a veiw to indicate the lines on which the various types of struggles could be studied and to assist in the collection of data regarding the various struggles that have developed and have been growing in various parts of the country. It is unfortunate that systematic, properly classified and chronologically worked out data on the phenomenon of agrarian unrest as manifested in various fields has still not been collected. (*Author*).

1

INDIAN KISAN THEIR PRINCIPAL MOVEMENTS BEFORE INDEPENDENCE*

A. R. DESAI

WE WILL next briefly refer to the principal movements and organizations of the Indian kisans—peasant proprietors, tenants, and land labourers—during the British period.

It was after 1918 that the kisans began to develop political consciousness, take part in organized national struggles and subsequently even build up their own organizations under their own flag and programme, and organized struggles for the fulfilment of that programme under their own leadership.

There had, however, taken place before 1918, a number of peasant movements which were spontaneous, spasmodic, and having limited and economic aims. The period between 1870 and 1897 was interspersed with severe famines in India, among which those of 1870, 1896, and 1897, were most devastating. This led to great misery among the kisans in affected areas. Periodically occurring economic depressions also led to great hardships among them. As a result of this, occasional kisan struggles broke out against the zamindars, moneylenders, and the government.

In 1870, the Bengal tenants were hit hard by the economic depression accentuating their general poverty. Thousands of them 'came to consciously refuse rents, disobey the dictates of courts, obstruct their eviction and finally to fight with whatever weapons were available......A regular state of anarchy came to prevail in a large part of Bengal and Santal countryside.......... .' The rising was quelled by the government which, however, appointed an Inquiry Committee and subsequently enacted the Bengal Tenancy Act in 1885.

The slump in cotton prices after the end of the Civil War in America hit the Indian kisans hard. Their debt burden as a result became very heavy and, in the Deccan in 1875, the Maratha peasants rose against the moneylenders who, with the aid of Courts, threatened them with eviction. They raided the houses of moneylenders, destroyed documents of debts and even killed some of them. The riot was quelled. The government, however, recognized the necessity of relief to the peasants and passed the Deccan Agriculturists Relief Act in 1879.

A revolt of the peasants threatened with loss of their land to the moneylenders took place in the Punjab in the last decade of the nineteenth

*Reproduced from *Social Background of Indian Nationalism*, Fourth Edition, by A. R. Desai, pp. 188-194

century. To ease the situation, the government enacted the Punjab Alienation Act in 1902-3.

During the time of Lord Curzon, the resolution of the Government of India on Land Revenue Policy was adopted aiming at protecting the tenants from the heavy pressure of the demands of the zamindars.

The Indian National Congress ' did not lay as much stress on the need for relief for our peasants, during 1905-19 as it did on the needs of Indian industrialists, ' such as protection, etc. Especially, the Indian nationalists, on the whole, avoided reference to the mass of tenants living under the zamindari. ' Lord Curzon's challenge to Romesh Chandra Dutt, an ex-president of the Congress, that it was the government which had done more to protect tenants from the rapacity of the zamindars remained unanswered.'

In 1917-18 the struggle of the peasants of Champaran in Bihar, led by Gandhi, against the indigo planters, most of whom were Europeans, took place, where Gandhi employed his method of Satyagraha. The government appointed an Inquiry Committee with Gandhi as a member and, on the basis of the report published by it, it enacted a law which brought partial relief to the kisans. Professor Ranga, who was critical of Gandhi's leadership of the struggle, remarked: ' Just as the earlier Congress agitation led by Romesh Chandra Dutt against temporary settlements did not embrace the exploitation of our peasants by zamindars,so also this agitation led by the Mahatma in Champaran did not lead up to any fight against the main causes for the terrible poverty and sufferings of Champaran peasants namely the excessive rents and exorbitant incidence of debts......It does strike us rather significant that both he (Gandhi) and Rajen Prasad should have remained scrupulously silent upon the ravages of the zamindari system.........'

Thereafter, Gandhi organised the Satyagraha movement of peasants in Kaira against the collection of land revenue which they could not pay due to failure of crops.

These were some of the main kisan struggles before the Non-Co-operation Movement of 1919. The struggles lacked a political content and were often anarchic.

Sections of Indian kisans were aroused to political consciousness during the Non-Co-operation Movement. The Indian National Congress gave a slogan of non-payment of land revenue which had a great effect. The peasants interpreted the political struggle for Swaraj in terms of a struggle against the heavy land tax and sections of them sympathized with, supported, and participated in the movement. It was the first participation of a section of Indian peasants in an organized political movement.

During the period of the Non-Co-operation Movement, peasant struggles which were not organised by the Congress also broke out, such as the struggles in the Guntur District, Karnatak, and Oundh Rent Act of 1921 which partially met the demands of the peasants was enacted by the government.

The Moplah Rebellion of 1922 had both communal and economic roots. The economic discontent of the Moplahs, who were mainly Muslim agriculturists intensely exploited by the Nambudris who were Brahmin landlords in Malabar, was canalized by the Muslim communalists into communal channels with the result that a revolt predominantly economic in content but religious in form, broke out leading to tragic loss of life and property.

It frequently happened in India that, where the Hindus were landlords and the Muslims were peasants, often due to instigation of communalists, economic class conflict between them assumed communal forms.

Two more peasant struggles, one that of the Koyas in the Narsipatan Taluka, led by Sitaram Raju, and the other that of the peasantry of Sitapur, Rai Bareilli and other districts in the U. P. may also be mentioned. These struggles were, however, spontaneous in character, bearing striking resemblances to those of the nineteenth century.

It was after the end of the Non-Co-operation Movement that the process of the formation of independent class organizations of the Indian kisans started. Ryots' associations and agricultural and labour unions were formed in Andhra in 1923. Kisan Sabhas were started in some parts of the Punjab, Bengal, and the U. P. in 1926-27. In 1928, representatives of the Bihar and U. P. Kisan Sabhas presented a memorandum to the All-Parties Conference presided over by Pandit Motilal Nehru, which embodied such demands as universal franchise, fundamental democratic rights and national independence.

The Andhra Provincial Ryots' Association was started in 1928.

Two struggles of the peasantry of the Bardoli District in Gujarat broke out, one in 1928-29, and the other in 1930-31. The first was led by Vallabhbhai Patel and its success in persuading the government to concede most of the demands gave a strong impetus to the peasant movement.

In 1930, Gandhi, the absolute leader of the Congress, submitted his Eleven Points to the British government as a compromise. He was criticized by the left nationalists and socialists for not including in the Eleven Points the vital demands of the Indian working class and peasantry though they included the most crying grievances of the Indian capitalists. Professor Ranga remarked: 'Mahatmajee should certainly have asked for a considerable reduction of rents charged by zamindars, redemption of our agricultural indebtedness.........a minimum wage for our labour, nationalization of our key industries...... But he would not do it consistently with his class collaboration convictions and his anxiety not to divide our people into two political groups basing their difference on economic interests.'

The world agrarian and general economic crisis which occurred in 1929 hit the Indian peasantry hard. They were in a state of ferment. Section of them participated in demonstrations and meetings organized by the Congress. There were peasant movements in the U. P., Andhra,

Gujarat, Karnatak, and other parts of the country, both authorized by the Congress and unauthorised.

The process of independent organization of the kisans as a class gathered momentum after the end of the Civil Disobedience Movement. An impression grew among the radical nationalists and advanced elements in the kisan movement that the Congress leadership was solicitous of the interests of the capitalists and landed magnates. They felt that, to safeguard the interests of the kisans, their independent class organizations and leadership must be evolved. They also thought that the national struggle for Swaraj could be successful only if the kisans were drawn into its orbit, by taking up their own class demands. The Congress, Socialist Party, Communist Groups, and Left Nationalists like Jawaharlal Nehru, stressed the necessity of forming kisan organizations in the country.

The kisan movements began to gather strength in the thirties of the present century. The first Indian Kisan School to train active kisan workers in the methods of carrying on propaganda and organizational work was started at Nidubrole in 1938. The Madras Presidency Ryots' Association was formed in 1935. The Madras Presidency Agriculturist's Association was organized in 1937.

There were also attempts to organize the kisans on a communal basis. Sir Abdur Rahim and Faz-lul-Huq started in Bengal the Praja Party to muster the Muslim kisans. The party subsequently changed its name into Krishik Praja Party. It adopted a programme of agrarian reform and even abolition of the zamindari system. The party gained considerable strength among the Muslim peasantry of Bengal.

The Bihar Kisan Sabha which was started in 1927 developed into an extensive organization after 1934. This was due to the effort of Swami Sahajanand Sarswati. Bihar Kisan Sabha had been perhaps the strongest section of the All-India Kisan Sabha which was subsequently formed.

The Provincial Kisan Sabha was formed in the U. P. in 1935 with a programme which included the demand for the abolition of the zamindari system.

Kisan sabhas also began to spring up in other parts of the country.

The government passed a number of relief measures to alleviate the conditions of the kisans. In the U. P., five Debt Relief Acts were passed in 1934; in the Punjab, the Regulation of Accounts Act was passed in 1934; in Bengal, the Moneylenders Act was passed in 1933 and the Relief of Indebtedness Act in 1935. Since even this legislation did not appreciably improve the position of the kisans, their discontent continued to grow and find expression in the growth of the kisan movement.

The first All-India Kisan Congress which met at Lucknow in 1935 decided that the Congress should be established as the supreme kisan organization in the country. Jawaharlal Nehru expressed strong sympathies for and support to this Congress. The establishment of the All-India Kisan Congress, though not enveloping the entire kisan population of India, was an event of great historical significance. For the first time in the history of the Indian people, an all-India organization of the Indian peasantry came into existence with a programme of common demands and expressing the aspirations of the entire kisan humanity of this vast land. It revealed the birth of a new higher consciousness and a wider perspective which transcended the mere local perspective existing in the pre-British India among the rural population.

The All-India Kisan Sabha carried on wide educative and propaganda work among the Indian kisans. It also extended its organization in the country. The All-India Kisan Sabha asked for collective affiliation to the Indian National Congress. The Congress, however, did not agree to the suggestion.

On the eve of the elections for provincial legislatures held under the New Constitution in 1937, the Indian National Congress published an Election Manifesto which embodied democratic demands for civil liberties and a social and economic programme of radical improvement of the conditions of the kisans. The votes of the agrarian population, who were enthused by the manifesto, in favour of Congress candidates, played an important role in their successes at the polls.

The Congress governments which were subsequently established in a number of provinces, however, failed to meet the obligations made to the kisans. They passed some agrarian legislation in some provinces, (for details refer to Chapter X) which hardly affected the lower strata of the kisans. The dissatisfaction of the kisans with the Congress governments found expression in a number of protest meetings, conferences, and demonstrations. Further, they criticized the Congress governments for arresting a number of kisan leaders, banning kisan meetings, and even using police force against the kisans, especially in Bihar.

During the period of Congress governments, the kisan sabhas organized a number of meetings, conferences and kisan morchas, to bring pressure on them to implement their demands. The Right Wing leaders of the Congress and the Congress ministries disapproved of such extra-parliamentary forms of struggle when Congress governments were functioning.

During the period of the growth of the kisan movement since 1934, volunteers' organizations among kisans also sprang up in a number of places.

2

AGRARIAN UNREST AFTER INDEPENDENCE*

H. D. MALAVIYA

THERE WAS visible among the peasantry a growing restlessness which took the form of violent and deadly clashes between the zamindars and kisans every now and then. The peasants increasingly began to resist evictions and *begar*. The zamindars, having wealth and power, started to organise themselves and to resist the plans for zamindari abolition of Congress Ministries which had come to power after the 1946 General Elections. The forces of revolutionary socialism made full use of the situation and under the hammer and sickle flag, thousands of peasants were organised to forcibly sow or reap the fields which they claimed belonged to them, and from which the zamindars were forcibly evicting them.

Indeed, things seemed to be heading towards a show-down. For a time it appeared as though nothing will stop a bloody and violent conflict in the countryside. In the months preceding India's Independence on August 15, 1947, and in the period following it, the entire countryside in India witnessed ceaseless agrarian conflicts. To complete the picture we would give a brief account of the situation in Uttar Pradesh.

AGRARIAN VIOLENCE IN U. P. DURING 1947-49

Agrarian riots became marked in U. P. in early 1947. A party of zamindars attacked the residents of village Hamirpur in district Sultanpur, destroying the crops and looting the houses. A few months after one person was killed and five others received injuries when a party of men headed by a zamindar attacked the peasants of village Kaima in the same district. A few days earlier, the same paper has reported, parties of kisans and zamindars clashed over an agrarian dispute in village Bamori in Jhansi district, resulting in the death of two zamindars and injuries to half a dozen persons. Such clashes continued through 1948, and, it would appear, assumed serious proportions in 1949. In March 1949, an armed mob led by zamindars attacked kisans in village Shahpur in district Ballia, as a result of which one Socialist worker was reported killed, many injured, of which two were removed to the hospital in a serious condition. In village Shahwazpur in Ghazipur district, a mob of 2,000 attempted to rescue from a police party some " women members of the Communist Party for allegedly instigating villagers against a zamindar ", and was fired upon by the police. This was in July. In August , 40 zamindars armed with lathis attacked a meeting of kisans at village Rampur in Ballia.

*Reproduced from *Village Panchayats iu India*, by H. D. Malaviya, pp. 206-210.

The Secretary of the District Socialist Party was injured. Another worker of the Party "was caught hold of by zamindars when he lay wounded, who dragged him about. When he began to show signs of collapse they threw him away at some place outside the village. After this orgy of violence the zamindars looted the house of tenants of the village." There was trouble again at Tahirpur village in Ballia on September 8, leading to firing by the police resulting in one death and some injuries.

The eastern districts of U. P. were not the only areas of agrarian trouble. In April 1949, a deputation of peasants from village Bahroli waited on the Chief Minister, Pandit Govind Ballabh Pant, soon after which, on April 13, the zamindars attacked the *chammars* of the village, burning their houses, etc. The *National Herald* (of 4-5-49) reported a serious clash between kisans and landlords in village Amauli Kalan of district Barabandi. Towards the end of May there was trouble in village Johawanakati in district Rae Bareilly leading to police firing and three deaths. There was an agrarian riot in village Bishanpur in Malihabad sub-division of district Lucknow, following which a zamindar and 12 of his supporters were arrested. A week later there was an agrarian dispute in village Mastamall in Goshaiganj police circle of the same district resulting in one death and many injuries. The Press Trust of India reported from Banaras on June 27, 1949, the death of 8 persons and injuries to many in a clash between agricultural labourers and a party of zamindars on June 24, on the border of Mirzapur and Banaras districts. The trouble broke out when labourers refused to carry manure to the zamindar's land. Another serious agrarian riot was reported from Tanda in Faizabad district in which 2 men were killed and 8 injured seriously in a *lathi* fight between zamindars' men and tenants over the cultivation of paddy field. No wonder therefore, that a spokesman of U. P. Government said at Lucknow on August 4, 1949: "Agrarian riots in the rural areas of U. P. have shown an upward trend as a result of the increasing class consciousness among tenants and zamindars." He disclosed that the total number of riots upto July 15, 1949, was 2,057; for the corresponding period last year the figure was 1,878. A majority of them were attributed to property feuds and quarrels over possession of land. The spokesman said: "Though crime against person has decreased, crime against property has shown an upward trend."

Zamindari Abolition Averts Class Violence

It is clear from the foregoing that violence was in the air in post-Independence years in our countryside. The atmosphere was tense and the rural society had the germs within it which could lead to a bloody consummation. The incorporation of the demand for the abolition of the intermediary system in the Congress Election Manifesto of 1946, and the decision of the U.P. Assembly, on August 8, 1947, to abolish the zamindari system, contributed largely to pacify the simmering volcano that the countryside had become. Thakur Hukum Singh, then U.P.'s Revenue Minister, very rightly told Pressmen at Jhansi on December 10, 1946: "If the U.P. Government had not taken this drastic and revolutionary step, the politically and class conscious peasantry would have risen in revolt and whole of the province would have been in the grip of a great conflict."

THE ALL-INDIA KISAN SABHA IN POST-INDEPENDENCE YEARS

In subsequent years this policy of abolition of peasant exploitation by the landed classes was extended to other States. This, along with other socio-economic policies of the Congress and its Governments, have very largely contributed to the development of India on peaceful lines. The other trend, however, still persists. After the A.I.K.S. was split at Bihta in 1941, the different left groups never succeeded in uniting again in one organisation. In post-Independence years the Socialists organised their Hind Kisan Panchayat. The Revolutionary Socialist Party and other left groups constituted a United Kisan Sabha under the presidentship of the veteran revolutionary Shri Jogesh Chandra Chatterji. None of these organisations, however, have succeeded in making any headway. The parent body, the All-India Kisan Sabha, under Communist influence, has grown from strength to strength in post-Independence years. Some of the biggest organized kisan struggles were fought under its leadership between 1946 and 1950. Mention may be made of the struggle of the Warlis in Maharashtra during 1946-47. In Bengal, the *Tebhaga* Movement (that is, struggle for reduction of landlord's share of the produce from half to one-third) developed in most of the districts and succeeded in getting an assurance from the Government that it accepted the *Tebhaga* principle. In Andhra, throughout the zamindari areas, peasants began to occupy lands from which they had been removed and there were no-rent-campaigns in many estates. In Travancore, the peasants and agricultural workers, joined by demobilised army men, fought against the landed classes and there were armed clashes with the Maharajah's army, resulting in innumerable deaths. In Malabar also the Kisan Sangham became powerful and led many long drawn-out kisan struggles.

The most violent and bitter of these peasant struggles were waged in Telengana, Tripura and Manipur. The peasant armed struggle in Telengana took the form of guerilla action against the Razakars, and later against the forces of the Indian Union. A parallel government was established in about 2,500 villages and, according to Communist claims 10,00,000 acres of land were seized from the landed classes and distributed among the agricultural labourers and poor peasants. A regular guerilla fighting unit was organised and when routed in the plains they retired to the hills and forests and continued so till September 1951, when the violent movement was finally withdrawn. No exact figures are known of the total casualty in the Telengana area, but the death roll is supposed to be near about three to four thousand.

3

INTER-CASTE TENSIONS*

D. N. MAJUMDAR AND OTHERS

IN MOST of the villages in Uttar Pradesh, for example, the dominant element has been a particular caste, a Thakur, rarely a Brahmin or a Muslim pedigreed family who has ruled the village and has kept the various castes on the rails, by organising a kind of inter-dependent and symbiotic relationship with the dominant caste at the apex of the pyramidal social structure, and a traditional division of function and services between the castes. The customary code of rural life with its pattern of obligations, its stress and strain, its virtues and vices, has functioned to maintain a status structure, however inequitable its role might have been. There is to be noticed a passive conformity to the rural code of duties and services. Loyalty and co-operation that exist among the castes inhabiting a village have been, we are often told, always spontaneous, but a deeper knowledge of rural life reveals that this loyalty and co-operation are sometimes ordered. Political leadership has been on the caste pattern and in a village dominated by the Thakur, the leadership is in their hands. Consequent upon the abolition of the *zamindari* system and in villages with absentee landlords, the initiative for leadership has passed from the former leaders to the elders of the village, though even today the dominant caste or castes exert their influence and enjoy certain privileges. The village today in most parts of the country is becoming a venue for trial of strength among numerically larger castes and inter-village relations are being strengthened to keep the traditional status roles functioning. The lower castes in earlier days had some vertical mobility in the caste-ladder, but with the horizontal organisation in the villages today on intracaste level, social mobility is also tending to be horizontal, so that a Chamar or a Pasi need not look up to the higher castes in the village for recognition of their social claims or aspirations, but they find in their caste organisation the key to social capillarity. This is a development which has become manifest in the process of cultural change.

Chamars are considered the lowest caste and are regarded as untouchables. They are not allowed to touch the utensils or person of a Thakur. The same is true of the Bhaksors.

The Chamars are very dissatisfied with their present humiliating and degrading position in society. They were very often taken on *begar* (forced labour) by the Thakur landlords. Last year Gokaran Chamar was employed in digging a canal, earning about Rs. 2/-, according to the

*Reproduced from *Rural Profiles*, edited by D. N. Majumdar, pp. VII, 82-86.

amount of clay he dug. One of the Thakurs, Jaskaran Singh, took him forcibly to his house and made him work there the whole day. In the evening he gave him only 8 annas. There was another similar instance of *begar*. Makhana Chamar was going to his work. Raghubir Singh asked him to cut the *bandh* (dam) at the tank. Makhana was forced to oblige the Thakur. He worked at the tank without getting any money for the work he did. Apart from taking *begar*, the Thakur landlords also take away their (Chamar's) vegetables either forcibly or surreptitiously. Raghubir Singh, Ahibaran Singh and Maharaj Singh very often grab their vegetables. But now-a-days a Chamar resents doing *begar* for any one. He gives a flat refusal, even if money wages are offered. This is because the Chamars now work in the fields and so money does not matter much to them. A Chamar will only accept to work if he is in need of money.

Some of the Chamars are thinking of equality and assimilation with the higher castes. With this end in view they refuse to take food with the Dhobies and Bhaksors. They refuse to lift the *pattals* after the dinner parties of high caste people, and to eat the residual of food on the *pattals*. They accept only the *parosa* (servings) of fresh food.

Formerly the Chamars, Pasis and Bhaksors were not allowed to draw water from the wells in the village. They had to use the water from the *talab* (tank) even for drinking purposes. But now they freely use the wells along with people of the high castes. A Chamar is allowed to draw water from a Thakur's well now. The Thakurs, however, do not draw water from a well belonging to the Chamars. Today the Chamars have a say in the village *Panchayat* which they did not have some two years ago. There is a desire among the Chamars to lead a respectable life. That is why they refuse to work for the higher castes even when money wages are offered to them.

The lower castes are resentful of the unhelpful attitude of the higher caste people, who always try to humiliate them whenever they get the chance. Lakhai Chamar was once coming to the village with some tanned hides on the carrier of his bicycle. He had avoided passing through the village and had taken a longer route, outside the village. But while near the village, he espied a person who seemed to be a Brahmin. Lakhai rang his cycle bell vigorously to announce himself. The Brahmin let him pass. But when he recognized Lakhai as a Chamar he began shouting at him. Two other high caste passers-by stopped Lakhai. The Brahmin abused Lakhai and hit him on the plea that the hides smelt and had polluted him. After a good beating, Lakhai was asked to be more careful in future and avoid the Brahmin on the streets by taking a different route.

On another occasion Makhana Chamar was severly rebuked for touching a water bucket belonging to the *Sarpanch*, Jadoo Nath Singh. Sukhraj Singh caught Makhana touching the bucket and scolded him. Ahibaran Singh, Gajadhar and Jadoo Nath Singh joined Sukhraj Singh and threatened Makhana with a good beating. He was asked to get the bucket cleaned by a Nai and asked to be more careful in future. After finishing his work there, Makhana got a Nai to clean the bucket and hand it over to the Thakurs.

Chamars generally belong to the labour class. They do all kinds of work besides agriculture, for instance, repairing of houses, cutting wood for fuel, and working as labourers on daily wage. Very few own their own land, as they are usually agricultural labourers, working on other people's land on a daily wage of 8 annas or on Rs. 15/- to Rs. 16/- a month. Murari Singh has employed Gokaran Chamar, Makhana Chamar and Putti Chamar to work on his fields for a monthly payment of Rs. 16/- and one shirt a year, each. Some of the Chamars also cultivate land on *Batai*, giving half of the produce to the owner of the land. Chhota Chamar works on Ahibaran Singh's land on *Batai*. The Thakurs dictate the most ruthless terms to the Chamars who take their fields as share croppers.

Clashes: Ahirs *vs.* Thakurs

Last year an incident took place which shows that the relations between Thakurs and Ahirs are not as close and cordial as they profess them to be. Vishwanath Singh (Mukhia) told us that the Ahirs had called a meeting at *Holi* last year and decided they would not allow the Thakurs to carry the *phag* and sing the *kabirs* in their (Ahirs') *mohalla*. *Phag* is the procession of men who sing songs and play *Holi*. All the castes of the village are represented in the *phag*. *Kabirs* are sung by the Thakurs alone. When the Thakurs came to know about the decision of the Ahirs, they called a meeting of all the Thakurs and determined to carry the *phag* and *kabir* procession at any cost. So, on the *Holi* day the Thakurs took out the procession and went armed with *lathis* and *ballam* (spear). They sang the *kabirs* and marched through the Ahirs' *mohalla*, singing and playing *Holi*. None of the Ahirs came forward to face them or interfere with the procession. The festival was observed very peacefully. This year the Ahirs also took part in all the festivities of *Holi* without any grudge or ill-feeling towards the Thakurs.

Like the other lower castes, the Pasis have been making an attempt to rise in their social status. The attempt was first made in 1939, when Ajodhya Prasad (Pasi) of Girdhar-ka-Purva village, district Bara Banki, wrote a pamphlet. The pamphlet was published on 20th March, 1939. It said that the Pasis belonged to a high caste. They were the *Sewak* (servants) of the *jati* (caste system). They were the trusted confidants of the Thakurs. An appeal was made to the Pasis to cultivate cleanliness, to give up liquor and eating meat, to acquire good habits to live together in unity, and to educate their children. Moreover, the pamphlet urged the Pasis to try to rise in their social status. They should do no petty and humiliating work because they belonged to a clean caste. They should not accept *kachcha* food from the Thakurs or any other caste, except the Brahmins. As a symbolic expression of their claim to superiority, they were to wear the *janew* (sacred thread).

The pamphlet was circulated in the neighbouring villages to arouse enthusiasm among the Pasis. But this growing enthusiasm among the Pasis was curbed by World War II and the rigorous control of the Zamindari system. In 1949, when the rumour went round that the Zamindari system would be abolished, the matter was taken up again. In the last week of June, 1949, a meeting of the Pasis was called in Itaunja. Ajodhya Prasad (the author of the pamphlet) addressed the meeting. Chheda, Autar Divan, and Kali Din represented Gohana village at the meeting. The pamphlet was widely circulated.

Another meeting was called in July, 1949, in Gohana Kallan of eight or nine neighbouring villages. It was decided in the meeting that the Pasis would not accept *kachcha* food from any of the higher castes, except the Brahmins. Instead, they would accept only uncooked food or *seedha.* Immediately after the meeting, the Pasis started wearing *janew.* The Thakurs were infuriated when they heard of the Pasis' decision to refuse to accept *kachcha* food from them. They forbade the Pasis from grazing their cattle in their (Thakur's) fields and pastures.

In the last week of July, 1949, the Thakurs called the Village Panchayat in Gohana Kallan. The Thakurs decided to boycott the Pasis in every possible respect. Furthermore, they forced the other castes to socially boycott the Pasis and refuse to have anything to do with them. As a consequence, the Chamars refused to carry the carcass of the cattle belonging to the Pasis. The Bhaksorin refused to attend on a Pasi woman at childbirth. Similarly, the Nais would not shave a Pasi. The Barahai and Lohar both refused to provide agricultural implements to the Pasis. The Pasis were faced with a complete social boycott by all the castes.

In the second week of September, 1949, the Thakurs stopped all sorts of grants given to the Pasis, and took back their gifts of free land (*Mafi* land) for cultivation from them.

The Pasis reported this to the Police, and called a meeting of all the Pasis. Alam *Darogha* (sub-inspector) from the Mandion *Thana* took two constables with him to prevent any quarrel that might take place at the meeting. The Police inspector went to Vishwanath Singh (Mukhia) to ask the Thakurs to attend the meeting. Vishwanath Singh said that the Pasis would be sitting on *charpois* and *takhat* or cot and the Thakurs would be offended to sit with them. The Thakurs would go only if the sub-inspector undertook the responsibility of making all the Pasis sit on the ground. This the other refused to undertake. Hence none of the Thakurs attended the meeting.

Diwan Pasi (50 years old) addressed the meeting and said, "If the Thakurs do not want to see us wearing the *janew*, let them shut their eyes."

The Pasis had appealed to the Police to restore their land to them. The Police investigated into the matter and told the Pasis that the land belonged to the Thakurs and the Pasis had no legal claim on the land. This free grant of land depended solely on the pleasure of the Thakurs and hence their confiscating the land was justifiable. The Police could do nothing for the Pasis in this matter.

In the month of *Kartik* (Oct.-Nov.) the Thakurs forbade the Pasis from irrigating their fields with *Beri.* The Pasis were hard hit, especially the poor ones and they wanted to give in to the Thakurs. Bishambhar and Rameshwar, two poor Pasis of the village, urged the Pasis to end their strife and give in to the Thakurs. The more well-to-do Pasis like Lachchman and Chheda, were adamant and refused to budge an inch. Lootoo (the village *chowkidar*) acted as a spy, supplying the Thakurs with all the information about this rift among the Pasis. But the Pasis could not for long maintain their position. They had to bow down before the Thakurs. In order to please the Thakurs and win back their favour, the Pasis gave up wearing *janew* in the month of *Poos* (Dec.-Jan.). The Thakurs say they did not force the Pasis to give up wearing the *janew*, the Pasis themselves gave it up, realising the odds against them.

The foregoing description of functional relationship between castes indicate the dynamics of the caste structure in the rural setting. In a closed and symbiotic arrangement, co-operation and conflict both are manifest, but conflict does not assume ugly proportion, due to the social brakes applied by the dominant caste or castes. As leadership rests in the dominant castes and an interdependence in economic life becomes a necessity in a self sufficing economic unit like that of a village, the castes run on the rails and the passive co-operation of the numerous castes is equated with rural peace and tranquillity. To-day, after the abolition of Zamindari and the frequent contacts the villages have with urban and immigrant people, the cloak of solidarity has been pierced and the functional relationships have been undergoing reorientation. It is, as a social scientist put it, birth followed by decay and decay by rebirth. A new type of inter-caste relations is shaping in the villages, in which the old attitudes are being slowly transformed, and what is in the offing, is not tension or hostility, but greater concern for group survival, and an evaluative code of inter-caste patterns of behaviour.

There is a general complacency about our village solidarity and integration. We have idolised our village life and find human response in the cry of ' go back to the village. ' But we need to know what has been and what the village life is shaping into, before we fall a prey to panegyrics. We need to emphasise microcosmic study of Indian rural life to enable us to form correct perspectives about our rural life. Any action therapy must necessarily be oriented to the ' facts of rural life. '

4

PANCHAYATS AND VILLAGE CONFLICTS*

H. D. MALAVIYA

COMMENTING ON the Barabanki murders of two Uttar Pradesh M.L.As., New Delhi's esteemed *Hindustan Times* wrote: "The ancestors of quite a few big landlords were those who practised outlawry and later settled down under British rule as acknowledged leaders of the countryside. The temptation to revive the old profession is great at a time when zamindari has been abolished and elections to Panchayats, local bodies and legislatures provide the excuse for mobilising caste groups and goonda elements."

THE BARABANKI MURDERS

The Barabanki murders, in fact, underline, as nothing else does, the conflicts that currently prevail in our countryside, and brief account of the episode would be relevant for our discussion. In September, 1955, a Congress M.L.A., Shri Bhagwati Prasad Shukla, was murdered by unknown assassins while he was cycling to the District Court. Of this event, and the subsequent enquiries, we have hardly any information. A flood of light, however, has been thrown on the murder of a Socialist M.L.A., Mr. Avadh Saran Varma, and his companion Shri Siaram, at Village Baddupur in Barabanki district of U.P., in the third week of October, 1955. According to the special representative of *The Statesman*, "Mr. Avadh Saran Varma was alive when he was tied up to a pole and taken away by the armed mob to a grove about two miles from the scene of the attack and burnt along with the body of Mr. Siaram, the other victim of the Baddupur murders, according to eyewitnesses." The description underlines the intensity of the hatred of the armed party, who were, in point of fact, local ex-zamindars, mostly belonging to the Kshatriya caste, who were not taking kindly to the activities of Shri Avadh Saran and Shri Siaram, who by caste were *kurmis*, traditionally the most efficient cultivators in U.P.'s countryside and, by and large, tenants and agricultural workers. They were attacked when they were addressing a peasant gathering in a village where the Kshatriya landlords regarded their sway and superiority as by God ordained, and could not countenance such 'unruly' demonstrations by their erstwhile tenants and 'inferiors.' Reporting on the Barabanki outrage, the special representative of the *Hindustan Times* said: "The traditional agrarian tension which often follows a sharply

*Reproduced from *Village Pauchayats in India*, by H. D. Malaviya, pp. 707-715.

divided caste line, is being exploited by the parties, particularly in eastern districts, where pressure on land is extreme." And that, " Elections to Panchayats have accentuated caste rivalry, and caste considerations have been a major consideration in selecting candidates."

The Barabanki violence is thus representative of the new situation in our countryside. And what exactly is the essence of this situation ? Simply this, that the high caste authoritarianism of yore can no more work. The implementation of land reforms in particular, and the awakening of the Indian people in post-independence India in general, have created those conditions when the old hierarchical type of village structure, divided horizontally between a relatively small number of families at the top and a descending range of dependents—the poor petty tenants and agricultural labourers—at the lower rungs, can no more persist. For the top ones too much is at stake, not only their old economic power but also hitherto unquestioned social privileges, the exercise of all political power residing in the villages, their pride of place, etc. Those at the lower rung, strengthened as they have been economically by the abolition of landlordism and conferment of tenancy rights, and aware as they increasingly are of the equal rights granted to them in Republican India, are no more prepared to slave for the high-caste authoritarian as in olden days.

The New Co-relationship of Class Forces in Our Countryside

In point of fact, a new co-relationship of class forces is the new pattern in our villages. The landlords have been divested of their erstwhile privileges, but sufficient areas have been left to them for cultivation, and they now come into the category of substantial cultivators, the rich peasants so to say. In former days, the substantial tenant joined hands with the middling and the poor ones, as also the agricultural labourers, to fight against the excesses of the landlords, who, in the great majority of cases, were supported by the British regime—the judiciary, the police, and the hierarchy of revenue officials, from the District Collector down to the Kanungo and the village revenue record-keeper, who in most cases was a veritable villain. Now, in the new set-up of things, the ex-landlord turned into the substantial cultivator, as also the already existing substantial cultivator, both of whom, as coincidence would have it, generally hail from the so-called upper castes, have a common front against the middling and poor cultivators and the agricultural labourers, who generally belong to the so-called lower castes. These latter, however, have and are having as much right over the lands they cultivate as the substantial cultivators their erstwhile superiors and masters, and are no more prepared to be ordered about, suppressed and treated in the old way.

We have come across a profound observation on this new situation in our villages by Shri Tarlok Singh, Joint Secretary of the National Planning Commission, and a great student of our village affairs by his right. Says Shri Tarlok Singh: " Recent land reforms have tended to reduce inequalities in the ownership of land, but not sufficiently. The old leadership in the village has been losing its position and influence without substantial signs of a new leadership stepping into its place. The institution of caste has less of its social incidence, but it may well be that the economic incidence of castes, being due to lack or independent means of production and lack of alternative opportunity, is being accentuated, especially for the scheduled castes and other backward classes. There appear to be signs of increase in the productivity of land, but scarcely enough to make a large difference to the problems of rural poverty. The economy as a whole has gone forward, but the gap between population and production has not yet noticeably narrowed.

" In this situation, conflict of interest within the village community have sharpened and the process continues. There are now few values which can said to be common to the whole community, and certainly there is no common purpose which inspires all the sections equally. Many innovations benefit some, hurt others. As instances, one may cite the landlord's tractor and the electric connection which provides energy to the village entrepreneur's rice and flour mill. Progress and enterprise on the part of some proceed alongside growing poverty for others. The community as such seems to exert little influence on either trend."

These rampant and dormant conflicts in the villages have their full play in the Village Panchayats, in their elections as also in their functioning. We have before us a very large number of newspaper clippings from the daily and the weekly Hindi press of the States of Uttar Pradesh, Bihar, Rajasthan, Madhya Bharat, Vindhya Pradesh, etc. We will cite a few of these to illustrate the widespread nature of the conflict.

Conflicts in Uttar Pradesh Panchayats

On March 14, 1954, while the Adalati Panchayat of village Chabli in Agra District was in session, the Panchas quarrelled among themselves which culminated in a free *lathi* fight and breaking of heads. The Sarpanch of village Amarpur in Jhansi district was seriously assaulted with *lathis* on August 26, 1954, by some unknown persons as he was proceeding to another village and was admitted to the Civil Hospital in grave condition. Ulfat and Muloo, two kisans of Nagla Sheopur village in the Kampil police circle of Farrukhabad district in U.P., were shot dead by some unknown persons on June 9, 1955, while they were asleep on a *chabootra* in front of their house. Karan, who also sustained gunshot wounds, later succumbed to his injuries in hospital and another man lay in a precarious condition. The three deceased were related to each other and " the cause of the murder is said to be some old enmity over the possession of a 'plot of land." *Navjeevan*, an esteemed Hindi daily of Lucknow, reported in its issue of 19-6-'55 of the highhandedness and terrorism of ex-zamindars of Faizabad district. " An ex-landlord of Tanda tehsil got the hereditary lands of kisans cultivated by force in villages Hirapur, Jallapur and Sabukpur, with the help of *goondas* and the police." Further, on June 12, 1955, the ex-zamindars attacked with *lathis* a peasant meeting in village Abhari in Faizabad tehsil resulting in injuries to many kisans and kisan leaders. This attack took place even when the police was standing by. A day earlier, on June 11, Sarju Singh, a kisan worker was seriously assaulted by 25 *goondas* as he was proceeding from village Nandlal-Ka-Pura to Chaubepur, and was admitted in a serious condition to the hospital. Again, on December 6, 1955, an agrarian riot took place in village Hakimpur, 28 miles from Allahabad, in which the President and the Vice-President of the Gaon Sabha and a woman working in the field were killed. "The riot was the culmination of long-standing enmity between two groups of villagers. Recently allegations of theft and dacoity were made against one of the groups, about 76 members of which formed a riotous gang. They are alleged to have carried *lathis* and spears and made reckless attacks on members of the other group, killing 3 persons and injuring 25 others. They also looted, it is further alleged, about a dozen houses and took away clothes and ornaments."

Village Conflicts in Bihar

Let us now turn to Bihar. *Aryavarta*, a Hindi daily of Patna, wrote editorially on April 27, 1955: "Many Gram Panchayats are working ideally and we can have great expectations of them in future, but the same cannot be said of all Gram Panchayats. The establishment of many Gram Panchayats has resulted in worsening the conditions in the village because the race to occupy influential position in the Gram Panchayats has intensified village factions and quarrels." The paper then goes on to cite certain examples. Bihar, indeed, has traditionally been an area of agrarian tension and the village conflicts there have probably been more tense than elsewhere. According to a report, a *Pasi* of village Dhankaul in Pupri Police Station of Sitamarhi district was beheaded on July 27, 1954, following a dispute about possession. The Bihar papers also report of illegal acts of Panchayat officials and their punishment. Thus, the Panchayat officials of village Bhabanichak in Jehanabad sub-division of district Gaya conspired to get an innocent man hauled up for dacoity, and the Sub-Divisional Officer came to his rescue. According to a report from Daltonganj, the D.S.P. of Palamau district arrested an official and a member of Singasiya Gram Panchayat for involvement in a dacoity. Again, on a written complaint being filed against a village *Mukhiya* of Police Station Nangachia for taking bribes ranging from Rs. 3 to Rs. 10 from flood-affected people in exchange for extending to them flood-relief the Sub-Divisional Officer ordered an enquiry. On May 23, 1955, one Ramavatar Jayaswal filed a complaint in the court of S.D.O. of Sadar sub-division of district Purnea, against the *Mukhiya* of Barahara Gram Panchayat for beating. The complainant supported the rival of the

Mukhiya in the Panchayat elections. According to a report from Simmultala, district Monghyr, dated August 5, 1955, S. D. O. Jamui launched a case against a P. S. P. worker Shri Krishna Singh for assaulting the *Mukhiya* of Simmultala Gram Panchayat. The accused's party candidate was defeated in the Panchayat elections. According to another report, there was free fight in Gram Panchayat elections in villages Baro and Khaira of Nawadah sub-division in June 1955, resulting in injuries, to about two dozen people, two seriously. According to a message from Rajgir, dated November 10, 1955, one Adbul Ghafoor, *Mukhiya* of Bhui Gram Panchayat, was sentenced to a term of 1½ years for illegally registering a plot of land belonging to one Binda Upadhyaya in the name of his brother-in-law Najamuddin. There are many other reports of conflicts and fights in Panchayat elections.

According to a message from Chapra, dated June 11, 1955, the upper caste villagers of village Pabheja suddenly attacked the Harijans of the village. The reason was that the Harijans were being stopped from going to public places which they resisted. Again, on April 24, 1955, members of Islampur Gram Panchayat, and Mohanchak Gram Panchayat had a free fight over a dispute regarding fishing rights in a tank. Eight persons were injured.

More serious, however, have been the disputes between the tenants and the ex-landlords of the *Kayami Pattadars* of the abolished Permanent Settlement. We have referred in the Bihar Chapter (Book II) of the murders in Purnea district. Again, according to P. T. I. message from Muzaffarpur, dated August 25, 1955, the police opened fire in Madhipur Hazari village in the district, killing two men, when a crowd attacked them with spears. The police, it is stated, was trying to stop forcible harvesting of jute from land which was under dispute. According to a report from Nawadah, dated January 12, 1956, about 200 agricultural workers left their houses in village Goethadih after a clash between them and farmers over payment of wages. They were living in an open field outside the village, and a police force was rushed. This clash was the second of its kind in the village in the course of a month. According to Shri Keshav Ram, Secretary, Nawadah Backward Classes League, the cause of the trouble was the refusal of the cultivators to pay their agricultural labourers at the prescribed Government rates. He also alleged that some local leaders were preaching casteism and apprehended that this might worsen the situation.

Indeed, the story of village conflicts in Bihar can be endless and we would rather stop. The expropriated landholders are in no mood to take things lying down, and even Acharya Vinoba Bhave, during his Bihar Bhoodan tour, complained against them. Thus, addressing a prayer meeting at village Hansa near Samastipur in August 1954, Vinoba said he was grieved to hear that " some zamindars were harassing Bhoodan workers interested in stopping eviction and even dubbing some of them as Communists."

In Rajasthan

Almost an identical picture is seen in Rajasthan. The former Jagirdars and others with vested interests in land are doing their best to remain supreme in the villages and did their best to capture Village Panchayats in the elections last year. The Rajasthan dailies and weeklies (in Hindi), quite numerous and well-edited, abound in stories of excesses of ex-Jagirdars, and their high-handedness in Panchayats captured by them. According to the weekly *Marwar Sandesh*, (dated 25-8-'55), Jagirdar Abhay Singh of district Pali forcibly took away lands from long-standing tenants and converted them into his farm. All efforts made by the peasants to get redress from high authorities are defeated by the Jagirdar. Village folks who tend to sympathise with the ejected peasants are threatened with murder and other dire consequences. Such stories can be multiplied. According to another message on being defeated in Panchayat elections, the Jagirdars committed a most heinous crime in Khavaspura village of Jodhpur district. To avenge their defeat, the Jagirdars cut the nose and ears of Shri Sukhdeo, the President of Khavaspura Village Congress Committee and of Shri Bacharam, an elected Panch, and also extracted an eye of one of them. Another esteemed daily of Rajasthan has reported widespread efforts of former feudal landowners to act high-handedly and illegally in Panchayat elections and capture them. The incidents, into the details of which we need not go, relate to villages Panditjee-Ki-Gharni, Purala, Bairoo, Keroo, Banar, Gangano, Lorari, Nevra, Cheri, Bhikamkaur, etc., in Marwar (Jodhpur). Says the correspondent: " In the Marwar Panchayat elections democratic principles are being murdered in broad day-light......The feudal elements are doing their level best to save their fast-ending existence. At some places casteism is the medium for generating various evils. This effort to save their existence is proving a great obstruction in the development of healthy democracy." A correspondent of the same paper reported from Danta Ramgarh that in the forthcoming elections to Panchayats in villages Roopgarh and Khatu, a big confflict is expected between the Jagirdars and the peasants. These conflicts apparently continue in some form or other. For example, the body of the Up-Sarpanch of Shivrati Gram Panchayat in Bhilwara district, who had been a prominent social worker for the past 15 years, was found buried in a *nala*. He had been kidnapped 5 days before.

In Vindhya Pradesh

Elections to Vindhya Pradesh Panchayats towards the end of 1954 also revealed similar activities on the part of the divested owners. *Vindhya Panchayat*, a reputed weekly of State, devoted exclusively to Panchayat affairs, in its editorial of November 7, 1954, said: " Lots of complaints are pouring about the elections to the newly constituted Panchayats. Many illegal activities are going on and the officials must give attention to them. We accept that our village brethren are not as well aware of the processes of the law as they should be. This ignorance of the peasants is being fully exploited by the reactionary elements. Besides, the Jagirdars, *mahajans*, the *pavaidars* and *mukhiyas*, who had hitherto been dominant in village life, are not lagging behind in their scheming and cunningness. The masses should not allow such people to interfere in their activities and should elect the best people to Panchayats."

We have before us the files of *Vindhya Panchayat* and another leading weekly of the State, *Bhaskar*, also published from Rewa. While they contain commendable records of Panchayat work they also abound in reports of unfair dealings in Panchayats, of no-confidence motions against Sarpanchas, of factionalism in Panchayats, of interference in Panchayat work by village *Mukhiyas*, of wrong accounting of Panchayat funds, etc.

Rural Conflicts—Involved and Complicated

Compared to these States, the Panchayats in Madhya Bharat and Madhya Pradesh have had a comparatively smooth functioning. We have not been able to peruse the local press of other States. The general pattern, however, is ctear enough. In our countryside today live members of different groups with varying interests which conflict with one another. It is hardly a matter of belief or theory. It is a reality we see before our eyes. This conflict is visible in the hundreds of events taking place in the villages everyday. Panchayats have become the centres of these conflicts because they have become by far the most potent forum for the villagers, who had higherto been denied all avenues of self-expression. In other words, the new co-relationship of class forces in the rural India of today expresses itself in the Panchayats, which apparently seem to have become the centres of these conflicts. This conflict of diverse interests in the countryside is, however, not very sharp and clear-cut as, for example, the disputes that arise in industrial centres between the capitalists and the workers. The rural conflict is a highly involved and complicated affair. The broad lines indicated above may generally be true, but then it is not always essential for caste and property differences to be coincident in all cases of rural conflict. A host of other factors, old ties and loyalties, localism and parochialism—all intermingle and intertwine to produce a complex picture, to which the degeneration of the Indian as a man during more than a century of foreign rule, the narrowness of approach, the greed and jealousy, blind self-interest and all similar evil traits make a profound contribution.

5

PEASANTS AND REVOLUTION

HAMZA ALAVI

THE SITUATION IN India, at the turn of the century, was different from that of China. In India, inter-imperialist rivalry had long ended with the supremacy of the British. No war-lords or private armies roamed around the Indian countryside. The rising nationalist movement, with its modest constitutional aims, did not seek to arm itself as Sun Yat-sen's Kuomintang had done. Until the nineteen-twenties the nationalist movement stood isolated from the potent forces of the peasantry although there had been much peasant unrest and occasional uprisings. Nor was there that crucial contact between the Indian nationalists and the Soviet Union, which played such an important role in China, although the Russian revolution had made a big intellectual impact on the minds of many young nationalists such as Nehru.

The radicalization of the nationalist movement in India just before and especially after the First World War, increasingly began to draw the masses into the movement. Gandhi, above all, who emulated the simple life of the peasant and spoke his language and engaged in symbolic activities which captivated the peasant's imagination, played a vital role in mobilizing peasant support for the Indian National Congress. But if hemade the peasant speak for the Congress he did little to make the Congress speak for the peasant. When in 1921, during the first Civil Disobedience Movement, the peasant began to extend the struggle against British Imperialism to fight also the landlord and the moneylender, Gandhi invoked the principle of non-violence to call an abrupt halt to the movement. He was not prepared to go farther than to back, at certain times, a call to the peasantry to refuse to pay taxes; a slogan which evaded the issue of class exploitation in the village but was strong enough to rouse the peasantry. But, above all, his most powerful appeal to the peasantry was through the millenial concept of " Ram Rajya " (i. e. God's Kingdom) which would be established in India after the expulsion of the British.

Gandhi's accent on the peasantry in his political language did, however, lead many middle-class intellectuals to " go to the people, " very much in the spirit of Russian populism. The effect of this is described by Nehru: " He sent us to the villages and the countryside hummed with the activity of innumerable messengers of a new gospel of action. The peasant was shaken up and he began to emerge from his quiescent shell. The effect on us was different, but equally far reaching, for we saw for the first time, as it were, the villager......We learnt......"

---

*Reproduced from *Socialist Register* 1965.

The growth of an urban working-class movement, the new involvement with the peasantry, the ferment of new ideas, especially the impact of the Russian revolution, and the disillusionment with the Congress after Gandhi's decision to halt the Civil Disobedience Movement of 1921 and of 1930, each time precisely when the movement was gathering momentum, caused many middle-class intellectuals to shift leftwards in their outlook. In 1934 the Congress Socialist Party was constituted inside the parent organization. Several streams of ideas had influenced the young socialists; but in its early stages the influence of Marxist thinking was strong. Although the socialists had begun to take an interest in the problems of the peasantry they concentrated on fighting within the Congress for a recognition of peasant demands rather than on mobilizing the peasants themselves to fight for their demands. Isolated peasant struggles did, however, rise from their local roots, and some assumed a major importance. But little progress had yet been made to build up a class organization of the peasantry.

The Communist Party of India (a unified Party began to take shape only in the t'hirties) had, in the 'twenties, concentrated mainly on organizing the industrial working class. The peasant upheavals of the 'twenties did not produce a fresh orientation as in China. During the Civil Disobedience Movement of the 'thirties, when it could have developed peasant struggles, the Communist Party found itself crippled and isolated both by the fact that its main leadership was in prison, following the Meerut Conspiracy Case, and also because the Comintern line, at the time, did not premit its participation in a movement led by the Indian bourgeoisie. Thus very little work was done by them amongst the peasantry precisely at a time when it was in a ferment because of the economic crisis of the 'thirties and also the impact of the Civil Disobedience Movement.

In 1936 the Congress Socialist Party decided to admit communists to membership of the CSP. The coming together of the Left forces was the background to the setting up in 1936 of the All India Kisan Congress, which was later renamed the All India Kisan Sabha (i. e. Peasant Congress). Two other groups of peasant leadership also joined and later contended along with the socialists and the communists in the AIKS. These two groups as well as the socialists spoke in effect for the rich peasant and the middle peasant, and eschewed struggle for the special demands of the poor peasants. Thus Professor Ranga, one of their leaders, spoke of a " common front to be put up by both the landed and landless *kisans* " and the " common suffering of all classes of the rural public." Socialist Acharya Narendra Dev made this even more explicit in his Presidential address at the AIKS Conference in 1938. He said: " Our task today is to carry the whole peasantry with us....If romantic conceptions were to shape our resolves and prompt our actions, we would aspire to organize first the agricultural labourer and the semi-proletariat of the village, the most oppressed and exploited rural class...... but if we do so... the peasant in the mass would, in that case, remain aloof from the anti-imperialist struggle." If, for the socialists in the 1930s the postponement of the struggle for the poor peasants was a matter of political expediency, because of the primacy, as they understood it, of the anti-mperialist struggle, now the ideologues of Indian socialism have abandoned the struggle for the poor peasant altogether. Thus, Asoka Mehta, until recently the Chairman of the Praja Socialist Party (the heir of the Congress Socialist Party) and its most influential ideologue, wrote: "Should the Socialists, as the Communists are wont to do wherever they are in power, foment class conflict in villages even after landlordism is removed and use the wide array of tactics developed from Lenin to Mao Tse-tung to use one section against the other?......If that is the line chosen, democratic rights and socialist values cannot survive. Then must come the whole complex of communist paraphernalia: people's courts, liquidation of kulaks, forced levies and the attendant violence. The other alternative is to help the village to recover its community, solidarity and foster autonomy of the village community......The organic needs of village community cannot be met by sharpening class conflicts or party rivalries." Such an outlook acquiesces in and perpetuates the exploitation of the poor peasant by the rich peasant.

The Communists, on the other hand, did speak of setting up a separate organization of agricultural labourers and, in the *Kisan Sabhas* (peasant associations) they put a special emphasis on the organization of the poor peasantry. But, in practice, several factors stood in their way. Firstly, after the middle 'thirties they were guided by the "popular front" line of the Comintern and were not inclined to force the issue with their colleagues in the AIKS. Secondly, Indian Communists took an essentially "Menshevik" view of the revolutionary perspective in India. In the Joint Statement of Eighteen Communist Leaders issued at the time of the "Meerut Trial", which has been described as one of the most important documents of Communist policy, it was argued that because of an insufficiently developed industrial base an indefinite period would elapse between the "bourgeois-democratic revolution" and the "socialist revolution" in India. In effect this meant that the task of organizing the rural proletariat and the poor peasants did not have any special urgency for them. Finally, the Communists, like the others, had simply to face the fact that the poor peasantry, desperately exploited and literally starving, was, nevertheless, too strongly dominated by their masters to be able to emerge as an independent force. Thus the main direction of Communist practice also was similar to that of the Socialists and their other colleagues in the *Kisan Sabha*. They concentrated on agitation for broad peasant demands, especially for security of tenure, debt relief, and cheaper credit facilities, etc., and sought to influence Government policy rather than to bring about direct peasant action. This tradition largely continues to this day. But the Communists did lead many local struggles and two major uprisings of the peasantry, though both had a regional character.

Towards the end of the war and in the early post-war years, two outstanding peasant movements arose, which were led by the Communists, in both of which the poor peasant came to play an important role. The available published material about these movements is a little inadequate for one to base a definite analysis. But one can see several unique factors in each case which may go some way to explain why these movements, which fall outside the normal pattern, arose at all. The first of these was the *Tebhaga* Movement, which arose in what is now East Pakistan. *Tebhaga*, the slogan of the movement, was the demand for the reduction of the share of the proprietor from one-half of the crop to one-third. It may be added that the *jotedars*, the proprietors of the land, were in fact " occupancy tenants " (with transferable and heritable rights in the land) who paid a fixed-money rent to the Zamindars, the great landlords. Over the years the fixed-money rent paid to the landlords had become a relatively small part of the value of the crop. Thus it was the *jotedars* who appropriated the largest share of the crop. Their land was cultivated by *adhiars* or *bhargadars* who were the sharecroppers. The *Tebhaga* Movement had been preceded some years earlier by the great Bengal famine of 1943 in which three and a half million peasants had perished. In an account of the *Tebhaga* Movement, Bhowani Sen, who had led it, was struck by the difference in the peasants' behaviour at the time of the great famine of 1943, when millions of peasants had died without a struggle, and their militancy and courage in later years. But he did not attempt, in the article quoted, to explain why this was so, except for the comment that " the intolerable conditions of the *adhiars* (the sharecroppers) awakened them to a new sense of solidarity. " But the conditions could not have been more intolerable than they were in 1943. The *Tebhaga* Movement, officially, did not start until 1946. In fact the movement had been gathering momentum in 1945. Local Communist and *Kisan Sabha* cadres participated in it but the Communist Party did not put its full weight into the movement until the end of the war with Japan. When they did so in 1946 the movement went forward with tremendous force.

Altlough the great famine found the peasantry unprepared and unable to rise against profiteers and hoarders of food (much of the food having already vanished into the cities or military stocks), many of the unique features of subsequent years, which helped the rise of the *Tebhaga* Movement, arose as a consequence of the famine. Firstly, the weak peasant organizations were disrupted and disorganized by the overwhelming calamity of the famine. The Bengal peasant, used to semi-starvation, was just helpless in the face of the disaster, and evidently proved too weak to fight back. When the *Kisan Sabha* units had recovered from the initial blow, they were quickly drawn into famine relief work. It was only in the following years that a new determination gave impetus to their organization. Secondly, large numbers of students and persons from the educated middle classes were drawn into the voluntary relief work during the famine and into large-scale medical relief in the following year. This brought about a new contact between the peasantry and educated youth which provided social education for them both. This was a very important factor in creating new cadres for the Communist Party and the *Kisan Sabha*. Thirdly, a factor of vital importance was that following the famine the *Kisan Sabha* renewed its drive against hoarders and black-marketeers of food with fresh vigour. Now its hands were stronger because the authorities too began to view the activities of the hoarders with a fresh concern, because of the magnitude of the famine as well as the fact that in the spring and summer of 1944 the Japanese had invaded Assam and parts of East Bengal. The *jotedars*, rich peasants, who had the food to hoard and sell in the black market, could no longer count on the connivance of the authorities. The power of the *jotedar* was, thus, seen by the peasant to crumble in the face of the *Kisan Sabha* leadership, which gave the peasant a new confidence in that leadership and in the possibility of fighting back against the *jotedars*. An additional factor was that some tribal people, such as the Hajangs of North Mymensingh, who have a long tradition of militant struggle, participated in the movement. Finally, but not least, there was a change in the economic bargaining power of the sharecropper due to two factors. During the famine more sharecroppers had died than any other class because they had the least reserves with which to get through the famine. Apart from the millions who died, large numbers of them had drifted to the towns and cities to find jobs or to beg for food, and did not come back. The reduction in their numbers created a relative shortage of labour. Furthermore, the invasion of Assam and parts of East Bengal by the Japanese and the consequent military operations in the area, also opened up alternative avenues for employment for the sharecroppers. These factors greatly strengthened their economic bargaining position *vis-a-vis* the *jotedars*. The sharecroppers' economic dependence on the *jotedars* was weakened.

The crucial battles of the *Tebhaga* Movement were fought at harvest-time. But the fight did not always end there because the sharecroppers had to resist the attempts by *jotedars*, with the support of the police, to deprive them of their gains. This continuing struggle was led by peasant committees which became a power in the villages. They began to administer the affairs of the village and to administer justice. The Muslim League Government of Bengal which had, on the one hand, carried out repression of the movement, introduced, on the other hand, a bill in January 1947 to legalize the two-thirds share of the sharecropper. But the bill did not become law. The *jotedars*, through both Congress and Muslim League politicians, fought back.

By the summer of 1947, however, the movement collapsed. Bhowani Sen, the leader of the movement, asked the peasants not to launch direct action that year because after independence the new Governments of Pakistan and India were to be given the opportunity to fulfil their promises to the people. It was clear that these promises would not be fulfilled by them. Bhowani Sen's call merely formalized the fact that the *Tebhaga* Movement, which he had described as " one of the biggest mass movements of our time, " had come to an end.

In the article quoted above, Bhowani Sen, with much candour and political courage, lists the " Main Failings of the Leadership. " In his self-criticism he argues that the movement failed because it did not win the support of the " middle class " and the working class. Working class " support " could have been little more than a gesture of solidarity, for its size in the area in which the movement arose was insignificant. As regards the "middle class" Bhowani Sen writes; "Many of them are poor and petty *jotedars* who, while they recognize that the system is bad, feel that they would be done for if the system is liquidated without at the same time opening other avenues for their employment......We should have advised the *adhiars* (sharecroppers) to exempt petty *jotedars* from the operation of *Tebhaga* and concentrated against the richest and the biggest." As it stands, this argument is somewhat urealistic. What Sen says about the plight of the small *jotedar* is only too true. But if the movement had been strong enough to force the biggest *jotedars* to accept a one-third share of the crop, it would have been very difficult indeed to dissuade the sharecroppers who tilled the lands of small *jotedars* from demanding the same. However, Bhowani Sen's argument does point to the narrow base of the movement which failed to generate slogans which could have drawn in the active participation of the middle peasants who had not been unsympathetic to the movement in so far as it had challenged the power of the landlords and the rich peasants. There were two major changes in the situation also, which made it no longer possible for the *Tebhaga* Movement to continue. Firstly, with the end of the war with Japan, the authorities were no longer interested in supporting the anti-hoarding drives which had weakened and demoralized the *jotedars*. Now the full force of the Government's machinery of repression was turned on the poor peasant. With its limited class base in the village, the movement was not able to fight back effectively. Secondly, a deciding factor in the situation was that whereas the peasantry in the area in which the *Tebhaga* Movement arose, both the *jotedars* as well as the sharecroppers, were mostly Muslim, the cadres of the Communist Party and, of the *Tebhaga* Movement were mostly Hindu. With the approach of independence, the full force of Muslim nationalism was sweeping through Bengal, as through other areas with a Muslim majority in India. This tended to isolate the Hindu cadres. With the establishment of Pakistan, most of the Hindu cadres went over to India and the movement was virtually decapitated. It is now twenty years since the *Tebhaga* struggle had begun. But nothing like it has arisen again in the areas in which it had been the most powerful.

The other great peasant uprising in India, since the war, was the *Telengana* Movement. In its character and political objectives it was the most revolutionary peasant movement that has yet arisen in India. The movement had begun rather modestly in 1946 in the Nalgonda district of

Hyderabad State, which was ruled by the Nizam under British suzerainty. The movement then spread to the Warrangal and Bidar districts of the State. The Hyderabad State was dominated by a backward oppressive and ruthless aristocracy. The initial modest aims of the Telengana Movement reflected the broad demands of the whole of the peasantry against illegal and excessive exactions of the *Deshmukhs* and the *Nawabs*. One of the most powerful slogans of the movement was for writing off all peasant debts.

The repression let loose by the feudal lords and their governments was met by armed resistance by the peasantry. The movement then entered a new revolutionary stage. Local Communists had participated in the movement vigorously, although it did not receive the official sanction of the Communist leadership until later. By the time of the Second Congress of the CPI in March 1948 the Telengana Movement had already entered its revolutionary phase and was one of the factors which influenced the leftward swing in the Communist Party line at the Congress.

By 1947 the Telengana Movement had a guerilla army of about 5,000. The peasants killed or drove out the landlords and the local bureaucrats and seized and redistributed the land. They established governments of peasant " soviets " which were integrated regionally into a central organization. Peasant rule was established in an area of 15,000 square miles with a population of four million. The government of the armed peasantry continued until 1950; it was not finally crushed until the following year. Today the area remains one of the political strongholds of the Communist Party.

There are several special factors in the Telengana situation which at the time favoured the rise of a militant peasant movement and its subsequent transformation into a revolutionary movement. Firstly, the political situation in Telengana in 1946 provided the right political climate for such a movement. With the independence of India in sight the future of the Hyderabad State, and its place in the Indian Union, became a dominant political issue in the State. The nationalist movements in the subcontinent of India had looked to the eventual absorption of the " princely states " in free India or Pakistan, as the case may be. Hyderabad was the largest and the richest of them all. The majority of the population, which was Hindu, as well as its geography, favoured Hyderabad's union with India. The feudal aristocracy, both Hindu as well as Muslim, favoured the idea of an independent Hyderabad. So did the small Muslim middle class in the State which had enjoyed a favoured position there and had fears about its future in the Indian Union; they organized armed bands, called *Razakars*, to fight for an independent Hyderabad under the Nizam. Kasim Rizvi, the leader of the *Razakars* was looked down upon by the feudal lords, who considered him to be an upstart. But they used the *Razakars* against the peasants when the Telengana movement arose. The leadership of the Telengana Movement, in its first stages, had supported the idea of Hyderabad union with India; the Nizam's rule and the idea of an independent Hyderabad were identified with the feudal aristocracy of the State. The peasant movement, at that stage, thus drew great strength from the nationalist upsurge in the State. But later, when union with India seemed to be inevitable and it became clear that the Government of India would deploy far larger and more effective forces against them, the *Telengana* leadership, in panic, switched their political allegiance to the support of the Nizam and the demand for an independent Hyderabad. The Communist Party in Hyderabad was legalized for the first time and Communists and *Razakars* fought together against Indian troops. Now the movement was aligned with forces which it had fought in the past and it was running counter to the nationalist movement. This created agreat deal of political confusion and split in the Communist leadership of the movement. Nationalist sentiment, which was a powerful factor in the rise of the *Telengana* Movement, thus became an important factor leading to its eventual downfall. Secondly, the movement was initially successful because the feudal aristocracy was rather demoralized by the fact that union with India seemed inevitable, despite its desperate bid for autonomy. Moreover, the State apparatus was corrupt and inefficient. On the other hand there was general political unrest. The peasant movement, directed against the ruling aristocracy, drew much popular support and was able to withstand repression. But later it was confronted with a more powerful army of India and it also lost popular support. Thirdly, the movement developed its initial momentum from the fact that its demands were broad-based and it drew in the middle peasant as well as the poor peasant. Later on, when the peasant " Soviets " were set up and land was redistributed, conflicts of interest between different sections of the peasantry came to the surface. Some Communists argue that this was a hasty and ill thought out policy which the *Telangana* leadership sought to impose from above, instead of preparing the ground carefully and helping the peasantry to advance the movement from below. The disruption of their peasant base proved disastrous when they were under heavy military attack. Fourthly, amongst the special factors which favoured the rise of the *Telengana* Movement are those which favoured the guerrila struggle. Telengana is a very poor country, much of it covered by thorny scrub and jungle, interspersed with relatively more prosperous settlements in a few favoured basins with tank irrigation. It has also a substantial tribal population, among whom there is a greater sense of solidarity and a fighting spirit, than amongst stratified societies such as exist in richer areas. Thus, when an attempt was made in 1948 to extend the Movement to the neighbouring rich delta region of Andhra, it failed. However, it should be added that this failure was due also to the fact that by that time the movement had moved away from its broad slogans and had become " sectarian " and thus failed to draw the support of the middle peasant. By that time the Movement was also running counter to the nationalist sentiment on the Hyderabad issue.

The Tebhaga and the Telengana Movements had both risen from their local roots rather than from any initiatives of the Communist Party, although in both the Communists provided the leadership and played a vital role. After the Communist Party Congress of 1948 the Party was committed to launch insurrectionary forms of struggle. But it was not able to organize any movement on the scale of Tebhaga or the Telengana Movement. Between 1948 and 1952 the Communist Party was banned in many States. On the peasant front, as on other fronts, the party workers were subjected to severe repression. Most AIKS workers were either in jail or underground during this period and the organization virtually ceased to function. Despite this, local peasant unrest continued to manifest itself throughout India. But it remained localized and limited in scope. It was clear that peasant insurrections could not be launched merely by Party decisions, but required certain pre-conditions to exist before they could develop.

In the period which followed 1952 the *Kisan Sabha* and the Communist Party moved away from the idea of direct peasant action, except for demonstrations and agitation. They have put the emphasis, instead, on exerting pressure on the Congress Government for implementing effective land reform and on parliamentary political struggle for the Communist Party, which if brought to power would carry out a drastic land reform. At the Congress of the Communist Party in 1958 at Amritsar, the Party adopted the " peaceful road to socialism, " and at the Congress in 1961 at Vijaywada it put forward the concept of " *National Democracy* as the most suitable form to solve the problems of national regeneration and social progress *along the non-capitalist path* of development. " Thus they now seek to replace the present Government of " bourgeois-democracy in which the leadership of the national bourgeoisie is decisive " by a government of national democracy which is to be distinguished also from " *people's democracy* in which the leadership of the working class is decisive, that leadership having won the support of the overwhelming majority of the people. " National Democracy is distinguished from these two other concepts by the fact that in it " the proletariat shares power with the national bourgeoisie. " This conception does not appear to be very different from that of the Praja Socialist Party which is also prepared to share power with the Congress, in the hope of consolidating its left wing. The fundamental differences between the Praja Socialist Party and the Communists now seem to lie almost entirely in the field of international relations rather than domestic policy. " The effect of this realignment of political forces has been to limit the peasant movement to agitation about Government policies instead of undertaking any direct action.

Both the Communists and the Socialists are largely in agreement with the principles of land reform which have been adopted by the Congress. Their main criticism is directed at the manner of its implementation which defeats the objectives of the land reform. The Report of the Congress Land Reform Committee which was published in 1949 is a radical document. It took as its guiding principles the elimination of exploitation and giving the land back to the tiller. It sought to establish independent peasant landholdings and from that basis to develop a co-operative system of agriculture. That document, however, reflected the view of the Congress left wing rather than that of the main body of the Congress, much less the views of the various State Governments which were to undertake the land reform. The character of the land reform, as implemented rather unevenly in the various States over the last decade, is very different indeed from the recommendations of the Agrarian Reforms Committee. The actual result of the land reform is the subject of some controversy. The Chinese view is that it has " abolished only the *political privileges* of some of the local feudal princes and *zamindari* (*tax farming*) *privileges* of some landlords, " but that " the Indian feudal land system as a whole has been preserved. " Such a view underestimates the profound changes which have in fact taken place in the Indian agrarian economy over the last decade. Land reform in the different States of India has, to varying degrees, eliminated or limited exploitation by non-cultivating landlords and encouraged the growth of capitalist farming. The changes in the different States are too numerous and complex to permit an attempt to present them here even in outline. Moreover, although numerous studies have examined the changes in detail an over-all statistical picture of the present situation is still not available. (In the Third Five Year Plan, published in 1961, it was stated that a Report on the progress of land reforms was under preparation, but evidently it has not yet been published.) A few data may, however, help us to form a rough picture of the situation. Sulekh Gupta points to the fact that (in 1953-54) 75 per cent of the peasant households operate holdings of less than 5 acres. On the other hand, 65 per cent of the land was farmed by 13 per cent of the households; of the latter, at the top, 3·6 per cent of the households possessed 36 per cent of the land. Gupta points to the increasing disparity between the growing prosperity of capitalist agriculture and the stagnation and bankruptcy of the small peasant economy in which the vast mass of the peasantry live in increasing poverty. Gupta, perhaps, overestimates the extent of the capitalist sector. This picture is qualified by Bhowani Sen, who, while recognizing the trend towards the growth of the capitalist sector, also points out that " the *upper limit* of employment in India's capitalist cultivation is 16 per cent of the rural labour force (40 per cent of the agricultural workers—the rural proletariat)." The many survivals of the old system are pointed out by Sen and also by Kotovsky and Daniel Thorner, whose works provide a very useful survey of the land reforms. The existence of the survivals of the old system are also indicated by the continued emphasis in official documents, such as the Mid Term Appraisal Report on the Third Five Year Plan, on such questions as the problems of tenancy reform, security of tenure, regulations of rents, etc.

There are two aspects of the land reform which have a direct bearing on the question of political mobilization of the peasantry. Firstly, an upper stratum of tenants were able to acquire ownership of land and have become employers of labour. Kotovsky argues that " before the reforms, this stratum of tenants energetically advocated abolition of the *zamindari* system; it played an important role in the peasant movement ...After the reforms were put through it withdrew from active peasant movement. " Secondly one of the principal results of the land reform has been mass eviction of tenants on an unprecedented scale by land owners taking over land for " self-cultivation. " These peasants, deprived of their land and livelihood, might have been expected to become an explosive force in the countryside. The issue did in fact greatly agitate some local *Kisan Sabhas* and provoked some local demonstrations. But this burning issue did not develop into a militant movement. The peasants did not launch direct action to resist eviction. Indeed, during the period 1955-58, when the land reforms were in progress, " there was a temporary decline of the organized peasant movement." In criticising the Congress land reform the Communist Party has criticized its bureaucratic method of implementation which resulted in widespread evasion. The Party advocated instead the implementation of the land reform through peasant committees. But their appeal on this issue was evidently directed only towards the Congress Government because they took no steps to organize direct action by the peasants for the purpose.

The perspective that is being held out before the Indian peasantry today is one of " revolution from above " rather than " revolution from below." Although the Communist Party distinguishes between the "peaceful realization of the socialist revolution " from " the parliamentary way of the reformist conception, " it is clear that their commitment to a constitutional struggle leaves them with few alternatives of struggle beyond agitation to mobilize electoral support against the existing Congress Government. On the question of the ruling classes relinquishing power the Communist Party takes the view that " everything will depend on whether the force of peaceful mass struggle, isolating the ruling classes, compels them to surrender or whether they hit back with their armed might.... The class aspect (of the struggle) consists in *exposure* of capitalism... *showing how* the class aspirations of the national bourgeoisie conflict with the national aspirations... " (Emphasis added). As far as the peasant masses are concerned, however, the policy of agitation and " exposure " of the Congress Government has met with little success and has failed to mobilize a majority of peasant votes for the Left in the several elections that have been held in the decade and a half since independence. Nor has the agitational struggle generated a force which may isolate the ruling classes and compel them to surrender. This has been the situation, notwithstanding the fact that the Communist party has launched, from time to time, massive demonstrations in town and country on such issues as rising prices and for tax relief. Thus, one of the most successful mass demonstrations launched by the *Kisan Sabha* in recent years was the 1959 struggle in the Punjab against the "Betterment Levy," a tax which was levied on the enhanced value of land which has benefited from new irrigation. But if the *Kisan Sabhas* have had some success in launching such "mass struggles" they have had little success in launching any class struggles of the exploited peasantry. Moreover, success in such struggle, involving the entire peasantry, has not brought in its wake any substantial increase in electoral support. The reasons for this lie in certain power relationships which operate in the rural society and certain structural patterns of political behaviour of the peasantry which must be changed before any major advance can be expected in this direction.

The pattern of political behaviour of the peasantry is based on factions which are vertically integrated segments of the rural society, dominated by landlords and rich peasants at the top and with poor peasants and landless labourers, who are economically dependent on them, at the bottom. Amongst the exploited sections of the pesantry there is little or no class solidarity. They stand divided amongst themselves by their allegiance to their factions, led by their masters. Political initiative thus rests with faction leaders, who are owners of land and have power and prestige in the village society. They are often engaged in political competition (even conflict) amongst themselves in pursuit of power and prestige in the society. The dominating factions, who by virtue of their wealth have the largest following, back the party in power and, in return receive many reciprocal benefits. The opposition finds allies, generally, in factions of middle peasants who are relatively independent of the landlords but who often find themselves in conflict with them. Many factors enter into the factional picture; kinship, neighbourhood ties (or conflicts) and caste alignments affect the allegiance of particular peasants to one faction or another. But broadly, it does appear that in one group of factions the predominant characteristic is that of the relationship between masters and their dependants while other factions are predominantly those of the independent smallholders. The number of votes that the Left can hope to mobilize depends, in the main, not on the amount of agitation it conducts (although this must affect the situation partly) but on the relative balance of the factions. Above all, the decisive question here is that of winning over the votes of the large number of poor peasants and landless labourers who are still dominated by their masters. This cannot be done unless the factional structure is broken. For the allegiance of the poor peasants and the farm labourers to their masters is not merely due to subjective factors such as their "backward mentality," etc. It is based on the objective fact of their dependence on their masters for their continued livelihood. Thus, it seems hardly likely in the absence of any direct action by the peasantry or by action by a government, which might break the economic power of the landlords and rich peasants, that an effective electoral support can be won by the Left. This is a paradox of the parliamentary way, and a dilemma for Party which renounces direct action.

We have raised a number of questions in the above analysis. There is, however, one theme which runs through our discussion: the respective roles of the middle peasants, the independent peasant smallholders, on the one hand, and the various categories of poor peasants on the other.

We have found that the poor peasants are, *initially*, the least militant class of the peasantry. Their initial backwardness is sometimes explained in purely subjective terms such as servile habits ingrained in the peasant mind over centuries or the backward mentality of the peasant, etc. But in fact we find that when certain conditions appear the peasants are liberated from such a servile mentality very quickly. Clearly, the subjective backwardness of the peasantry is rooted in objective factors. There is a fundamental difference between the situation of the poor peasant and that of the industrial worker. The latter enjoys a relative anonymity in his employment and job mobility which gives him much strength in conducting the class struggle. Even in the case of the industrial worker, where his relative independence is reduced by such devices as tied housing, etc., his militancy is also undermined. In the case of the poor peasant the situation is much more difficult. He finds himself and his family totally dependent upon his master for their livelihood. When the pressure of population is great as in India and China, no great machinery of coercion is needed by the landlords to keep him down. Economic competition suffices. The poor peasant is thankful to his master, as a benefactor who gives him land to cultivate as tenant or gives him a job as labourer. He looks to his master for help in times of crisis. The master equally responds with a paternalistic attitude; he must keep alive the animal on whose labour he thrives. When in extreme and exceptional cases the exploitation and oppression is carried beyond the point of human endurance, the peasant may even be goaded into killing his master for his departure from the paternalistic norm. But he is still unable to rise, by himself, against the system itself. His dependence on the master thus undergoes a paternalistic mystification and he identifies himself with his master. But this backwardness of the peasantry, rooted as it is in objective dependence, is only a relative and not an absolute condition. In a revolutionary situation, when anti-landlord and anti-rich-peasant sentiment is built up by, say, the militancy of middle peasants, his morale is raised and he is more ready to respond to calls to action. His revolutionary energy is set in motion. When the objective pre-conditions are realized the poor peasant is a potentially revolutionary force. But the inherent weakness in his situation renders him more open to intimidation and setbacks can easily demoralize him. He finally and irrevocably takes the road to revolution only when he is shown *in practice* that the power of his master can be irrevocably broken and the possibility of an alternative mode of existence becomes real to him.

The middle peasants, on the other hand, are initially the most militant element of the peasantry, and they can be a powerful ally of the proletarian movement in the countryside, especially in generating the initial impetus of the peasant revolution. But their social perspective is limited by their class position. When the movement in the countryside advances to a revolutionary stage they may move away from the revolutionary movement unless their fears are allayed and they are drawn into a process of co-operative endeavour.

Our hypothesis, thus, reverses the sequence that is suggested in Maoist texts—although it is in accord with the Maoist practice ! It is not the poor peasant who is initially the leading force, and the main force of the peasant revolution with the middle peasant coming in only later when the success of the movement is guaranteed, but precisely the reverse. Evidently, a correct understanding of this sequence and the nature of the conditions required to mobilize the poor peasants must be vital to the formulation of a correct strategy *vis-a-vis* the peasantry.

Finally, we would like to end by emphasizing once again that our conclusions are purely tentative and are intended to open up a discussion of the problems by raising several questions rather than suggesting a fresh spirit of inquiry and, above all, from actual experience; and they will be proved by the success of those who lead the peasant struggle.

SECTION IX

LAND REFORMS

INTRODUCTION

THE PRESENT section is comprised of four sets of selections. Rural Society, as we have noted earlier, is in transition. Since Independence, the peculiar debacle that had developed in agrarian life as a result of the policies of the British rulers in India is attempted to be rectified by the Government of India. Land reforms, encouraging co-operation, establishing various kinds of village institutions, resurrection of cottage industries and creation of an adequate administrative machinery and a leadership which can reorganise the rural society are some of the measures adopted in recent times for this reconstruction.

The seven selections on the impact of Land Reforms indicate how the measures to reform land relations are creating a situation which, instead of improving the proprietary status of the vast bulk of the lower layers of cultivating tenants, are on the contrary creating a very dangerous trend, viz., that of enabling the old landowning classes to still retain their basic hold over land with only a small section of the upper tenants who are capable of purchasing the land benefiting by these reforms. It further creates a situation wherein the bulk of the lower tenants being uprooted as tenants and having lost tenancy protection are being transformed into land-tenants and having lost tenancy protection are being transformed into landless, unprotected, share-croppers leading sometimes to the creation of, as what one of the writers call, ' tenancy by backdoor.' Thus the seven studies cumulatively portray a trend of rural stratification which is fraught with grave consequences. They indicate a new polarisation of classes which if not porperly assessed, would nullify or vitiate most of the measures to reform agrarian society. A more methodical and extensive study of the impact of land reforms on the agrarian strata becomes urgent and immediately necessary for evolving a proper policy for reorganising the agrarian society.

(*Authour*)

1

IMPACT OF LAND REFORMS IN BARODA DISTRICT*

V. V. KOLHATKAR

AND

S. B. MAHABAL

CONCLUSIONS AND RECOMMENDATIONS

AS SHOWN above, our investigation has led us to conclude that the Tenancy legislation has not been able to achieve its major objectives. We are of course aware of the fact that the legislation was made applicable to the Baroda District only four years ago and, therefore, the experience in other districts where the legislation has been in operation for long may possibly be somewhat different from ours. But so far as the Baroda District is concerned, the recorded information in our questionnaires as well as other inquiries by our investigators reveal that the Act has been largely ineffective and landlords go on as merrily as ever.

We further believe that no alterations and improvements in the letter of the Acts is going to make them effective to any remarkable degree. The ineffectiveness of the Acts is not due to any faulty formulation of the Acts but to the very nature of the socio-agricultural conditions as they exist in reality. The bigger landlords are economically and socially in a far stronger position, than their tenants, and the weak tenants are not able to take advantage of the Acts due to the risk of courting hostility and opposition of the landlords. Our investigations have revealed that many of the tenants are ignorant about the benefits and rights conferred on them by the Act. And where knowledge exists, there is little hope that the tenants will be able to use it to their advantage. They are handicapped by their economic and social weakness. We come to believe, therefore, that, so long as the tenant is weak, no amount of refinement of the Tenancy Acts will be able to help him materially......

PROTECTED TENANCY

(1) Most of the existing tenants have gained the status of a protected tenant.

(2) There are no written tenancy agreements in most of the cases.

---

*Reproduced from *An Enquiry into the Effects of the Working of the Tenancy Legislation in the Baroda District* by V. V. Kolhatkar and S. B. Mahabal, pp. 50-52.

Security of Tenure

(3) There has been a sharp rise in the area under personal cultivation between 1948-49 and 1951-52, and a corresponding decline in the area under tenancy, thus indicating a large-scale eviction of tenants on the eve of the application of the Acts to the Baroda District and in the initial years following their application.

(4) Most of the cases of the termination of tenancy in the years 1949-50 to 1953-54 arose out of the demand for the land by the landlords for personal cultivation.

(5) There are reasons to believe that the personal cultivation for which the landlords terminated tenancies was not genuine.

Commutation of Crop-Rent into Cash-rent

(6) Only in about half the cases of tenancy studied, was rent being paid in cash; others are still on crop-share basis.

(7) In nearly 30 per cent of the cases, the tenants do not get any written receipts for payments made by way of rent.

Limitation of Maximum Rent

(8) Only in 32 per cent of the cases rent was reported to be within the maximum prescribed under the Acts.

(9) There has been no change in the practices of sharing the costs between the tenants and the landlords.

Purchase of Land by Tenants

(10) None of the tenants studied purchased land from the landlord.

(11) Out of the 248 tenants studied, only 21 received an offer from the landlord, to purchase the land. The offer was not accepted mainly because of lack of finance.

(12) In all, 82 cases of sale of land were situated. In 42 cases, the lands were offered to tenants and in 34 cases, the tenants accepted the offer and purchased the land.

(13) No landlord had to sell land because he held more than fifty acres and because his tenant demanded that he be allowed to purchase the land.

Improvement in Equipment and technique

(14) By and large, there has been no noteworthy improvement of or increase in investment of capital by the tenants that can be ascribed to the Tenancy Acts.

LANDLORD-TENANT RELATIONS

(15) There were few disputes that were referred to the Mamlatdars, and fewer still in which the initiative was taken by the tenants.

(16) Many of the disputes were initiated by the landlords and were mainly for taking over possession of the land for personal cultivation.

AVAILABILITY OF FINANCE

(17) Few landlords finance their tenants.

(18) Most of the tenants report that credit has become difficult for them.

OPINIONS ABOUT THE ACTS

(19) Majority of the tenants report that the Acts have benefited the tenants; but quite a substantial minority report that the Acts have benefited the landlords.

(20) The landlords, by and large, believe that the Acts have benefited the tenants.

2

CRITICAL EVALUATION OF TENANCY POLICY OF THE SAURASHTRA GOVERNMENT*

P. S. SANGHVI

THE CONDITIONS of tenants under feudal tenures and cultivators of former Crown lands before integration was more or less the same except for few big States. Four measures taken by Saurashtra Government, viz., conferring of occupancy rights, conversion of Bhag Batai into cash assessment in 800 Khalsa villages, gradual abolition of feudal levies and prohibition of veth or unpaid forced labour rendered some relief to the cultivators of Khalsa land and brought about considerable disparity in the conditions of Khalsa cultivators and tenants of alienated holders. This disparity combined with new hopes inspired by the Liquidation of the British rule and the powers of feudal princes, spurred tenants into action. The essence of their demand was that they should get the same treatment as Khalsa cultivators.

The landholders who were accustomed to rack-renting, forced labour and eviction-at-will and were beyond any judicial control in relation to their tenants, wanted to perpetuate these old conditions even after independence, and the establishment of the popular Government in Saurashtra. The desire to perpetuate the old conditions of pre-merger period had been the guiding force of all the activities of agitation of the landholders directed against their tenants and the Government.

In short, the desire of tenants to be treated on par with Khalsa cultivators and the attempts of the landholders to enforce old conditions of pre-Integration period formed the basis of the conflict between the two contending parties.

The demand for other khed land occupied a singular place in this conflict. As the landholders realised that it was impossible to realise the old exorbitant rates of rent, they advanced the plea that they were keen to 'personally' cultivate their land, hence the tenants should be evicted. It is evident that the demand for Gharkhed land did not originate from the genuine desire and love for the personal cultivation of land but it arose as a reaction to the restriction on the amount of rent and was primarily designed to circumvent the restriction on rent. A small section of small landholders, however, sensed the signs of new era and wanted to take agriculture as a profession.

In the course of our field investigation two forms under which the land-

* Reproduced from *Land Reforms in Saurashtra*, by P. S. S. Sanghvi, [Unpublished Thesis, Department of Economics, University of Bombay), pp. 103-107.

holders continued to exact the old levels of rent were discovered. In the alienated village of Rafarika, it was found on the basis of the records of the revenue department that 17 landholders were in possession of 407 acres of Gharkhed land. On enquiry in the village itself it was discovered that only one landholder really cultivated a piece of land of 20 acres. The rest of the 389 acres were defacto cultivated by tenants on the crop sharing basis. The levels of rent were the old rates of premerger period.

The landholders frankly admitted that they had leased the land because they did not know the art of cultivation. Some of them also added that they were not used to any form of physical labour for generations and now it was impossible for them to cultivate that habit. There was a tacit understanding between the tenants and landholders about the division of crop and their 'legal' status. Legally, the tenants were merely hired labourers of landholders. This legal facade helped the landholders to circumvent all tenancy legislation on fair rent and security of tenures. Tenants gave a very simple explanation for their complicity. They stated that they had neither sufficient land nor could they secure alternative employment. They complained that their holding were made too small due to allotment of Gharkhed land to support their families. The Local Revenue officials also knew about this phenomenon. They pointed out that it was impossible to prove that the terms of lease were in violation of tenancy legislation unless the tenants would be willing to complain against the landholders and prove against them in the court of law.

It was found that this form of concealed tenancy was widespread in Gharkhed holdings all over Saurashtra. Our field inquiries revealed that the officers of the Revenue Department were aware of this fact and generally expressed their inability to remedy the situation. Moreover, they objected to calling it 'concealed' tenancy because tenancy was technically not prohibited in Saurashtra till then.

It was also revealed that large holdings of 75 to 200 acres were in the possession of Girasdars as Gharkhed land. The land was cultivated by hired labourers under the supervision and guidance of the trusted and senior labourer who was paid somewhat higher than other labourers. The same type of bullocks and wooden ploughs were employed as are done by the tenants. Girasdars did not either employ large-scale production technique or investment as the capitalists did in their factories or contributed their own labour as the ordinary cultivators do.

Girasdars do not perform either the functions of entrepreneurs in the true sense or employ their own labour power but only live on unearned income. The so-called personal cultivation is rendered easy on account of ample availability of cheap landless labour. It is for this reason that the Congress Agrarian Reforms Committee defined a cultivator as one who performs some manual labour in the process of cultivations. But, this definition has not been recommended by the Saurashtra Agrarian Reforms

Commission nor has it been incorporated in the legislative measures of the Government of Saurashtra. It appears that the major portion of land in possession of landholders as Gharkhed is either under concealed tenancy or cultivating landlordism. Both the forms do not indicate any genuine desire of self-cultivation but reveal modified forms under which old exorbitant levels of rent are realised by the landholders. In fact they defeat the very spirit of personal cultivation and tenancy legislation.

3

EFFECT OF TENANCY ACT IN MAHARASHTRA*

V. M. DANDEKAR

AND

G. J. KHUDANPUR

THE MAIN facts brought out by this investigation are, firstly, the extensive resumption and changes of tenants that took place even after the enforcing of the Act showing that the protection given to the tenants could not be effective in practice; secondly, a more or less normal market in land showing that the provisions for promoting the transfer of lands into the hands of the tillers were not quite effective, and thirdly, an almost complete absence of any signs of lowering the share and cash rents or of any changes in the tenancy practices. As we have explained, the first two of these failures are attributable to certain inherent weaknesses of the original Act of 1948. The original provisions regarding the protection given to the tenant suffered from an important loophole, namely, that the tenant could surrender his land in favour of the landlord and when so surrendered the landlord could retain it without any restrictions. Similarly, the right given to the protected tenant to purchase on his own initiative, the lands cultivated by him was limited by an important condition that the purchase must not result in reducing the holding of the landlord below 50 acres. The latest amendment has remedied the original shortcomings in both these respects. The third failure, namely, the failure to regulate rent is, however, the most distressing for it is entirely a failure of implementation. As we have seen, in all the districts except Thana and Kolaba, the share rents have remained unchanged. The cash rents also have shown no signs of lowering. In fact, from the evidence we have presented, it is clear that at least on occasions when tenants were changed, there have been more cases of raising than of lowering the rents. The surprising element of the situation is that even the landlords reported to us the true rents they received and that they found no reasons to conceal the facts. Under the circumstances, many of our questions relating to the various specific provisions of the Act sounded extremely unrealistic. For all practical purposes the Act did not exist.

It is against this background that the implementation of the more comprehensive and far reaching provisions of the latest amendment must be thought out. As was pointed out, this amendment is not based on any concept of a normal landlord-tenant relationship; instead it seeks to

*Reproduced from *Working of Bombay Tenancy Act*, 1948, *Report of Investigation* by V. M. Dandekar and G. J. Khudanpur, pp. 187-194.

abolish this relationship altogether. Firstly, by protecting the tenant more securely than before and by reducing rents still further, it aims at cutting down the interest of the landlord to what might be called below economic levels. Secondly, by providing that on and with effect from a certain date, all the tenants will be deemed to have purchased the lands under their personal cultivation, it seeks to overcome inertia and to set in motion the necessary process of transfer of all agricultural lands into the hands of the cultivators. Strategically, this seems to be essentially a sound policy. It is necessary that in practice also the two aspects will be implemented as an integrated whole and not as two disjointed pieces. Otherwise there is a danger of regarding the provisions of protection and of regulation of rent as of only secondary importance in relation to the operation of the more resounding 'deemed to have purchased' clause; this would be natural because if the 'deemed to have purchased' clause succeeded, regulation of rent as also protection of tenant would both appear as either redundant or of only minor importance as they would concern only a small section of the peasantry. It will be natural therefore if, under the burden of implementing the 'deemed to have purchased' clause, the implementation of the clauses relating to the protection of tenant and the regulation of rent are somewhat neglected. Such a neglect may however make the implementation of the 'deemed to have purchased' clause itself more difficult. It is only through a firm enforcement of the clauses relating to protection of tenant and regulation of rent that the landlords may be induced to sell their lands or at least not create difficulties in the way of the implementation of the 'deemed to have purchased' clause.

On the other hand, it is important to realise that if for one reason or another, the 'deemed to have purchased' clause fails to take effect or if its effective implementation is delayed beyond a limit, all tenants will be reduced to the status of one year tenants enjoying an option to purchase or to quit, and that, therefore, the provisions of protection will become null and void. If protection clauses fail, the regulation will also become all the more difficult. It is obvious, therefore, that the two aspects, namely, cutting down the interest of the landlord and the transfer of lands hang together.

From this point of view, the failure to implement the earlier provisions of regulating rent deserves closer administrative attention. For, the new amendement requires a much more drastic reduction in the rents. The maximum rent is now defined to be five times the assessment or Rs. 20 per acre whichever is less but in no case less than two times the assessment. There is a further blanket provision that in no year the aggregate of the land revenue, local cess and the rent must exceed one-sixth of the value of the crop and the excess, if any, is to be deducted from the rent payable. Even if we leave aside this blanket maximum, the cash rents as prescribed above are likely to be very much below the prevailing cash rents. In Table 12·1, we give a classification of the cases of cash rents in our sample according to the prevailing rent as a multiple of the maximum rent prescribed by the amended provisions. In Table 12·2, we give the corresponding classification of the area of the plots concerned. It will be seen that it is only in the case of about 18 per cent of the area, that the prevailing rent does

Cases of Cash Renting Distribution According to the Actual Rent as a Multiple of the Prescribed Maximum Rent

District	Total No. of cases	Actual rent as multiple of prescribed maximum						Un-specified
		—1	—2	—3	—4	—5	More than 5	
W. Khandesh	50	25	13	5	2	1	3	1
E. Khandesh	75	8	22	12	12	8	12	1
Nasik	13	1	1	1	3	2	4	1
Thana	30	8	7	1	2	2	9	1
Kolaba	5	1	2	1	—	—	1	—
Poona	19	—	3	2	1	—	12	1
Ahmednagar	28	—	2	2	—	4	20	—
Sholapur	28	—	3	12	5	—	6	2
North Satara	12	3	1	2	1	1	3	1
South Satara	24	3	5	4	3	3	5	1
Kolhapur	41	2	2	8	6	—	20	3
Bijapur	85	8	17	11	9	8	27	5
Belgaum	65	10	16	11	4	4	18	2
Dharwar	72	14	20	12	7	8	10	1
Total	547	83	114	84	55	41	150	20

Percentage Distribution of the Cash Rented Area according to the Actual Rent as a Multiple of the Prescribed Maximum Rent

District	Total area (acres)	Actual rent as multiple of prescribed maximum						Un-specified
		—1	—2	—3	—4	—5	More than 5	
W. Khandesh	232	50·4	27·9	9·1	4·8	2·1	1·9	3·8
E. Khandesh	193	12·9	23·3	20·0	11·6	18·6	13·3	0·3
Nasik	48	12·8	22·5	26·9	19·8	3·4	13·5	1·1
Thana	60	46·1	22·3	0·8	1·2	4·5	19·0	6·1
Kolaba	6	9·1	63·6	21·8	—	—	5·5	—
Poona	69	—	19·2	1·7	0·9	—	77·6	0·6
Ahmednagar	93	—	2·4	10·8	—	10·0	76·8	—
Sholapur	214	—	29·8	44·7	21·3	—	4·1	0·1
N. Satara	18	29·4	2·3	22·6	11·3	2·8	28·2	3·4
S. Satara	76	15·2	18·6	43·0	3·3	6·9	12·9	0·1
Kolhapur	66	1·4	1·7	29·2	20·2	—	42·2	5·3
Bijapur	640	14·3	18·0	14·2	18·6	14·9	18·3	1·7
Belgaum	444	29·9	31·6	19·6	1·7	3·2	13·6	0·4
Dharwar	456	14·0	30·0	30·9	8·2	8·8	8·0	0·1
Total	2,615	18·4	23·9	21·3	10·4	8·0	16·8	1·2

not exceed the maximum prescribed by the amendment. In the case of about 24 per cent of the area, the prevailing rent is more than the prescribed but not more than two times the prescribed rent. In another 21 per cent it is between 2 and 3 times the maximum prescribed by the amendment. In the remaining nearly 35 per cent of the area, the prevailing rent is more than 3 times the prescribed maximum. Hence in these cases the cash rents will have to be brought down to less than one-third of the prevailing rents. In the case of more than half of this area the prevailing rents are in fact more than five times the prescribed maximum rents. Presumably much of this area is either irrigated or enjoyes certain other advantages. The amendment prescribing the maximum rents does not seem to make any allowance for such advantages and may require certain revision or adjustment.

The same is true of the prevailing rents. The new amendment seeks to abolish the share rents. As we have seen, 63·5 per cent of the tenant-cultivated area is at present share rented. The abolition of share renting will therefore be an extensive operation. Moreover the new level of rents will be considerably below the prevailing rents. As we have seen, nearly 80 per cent of the share rented area is rented for half share and a small fraction is rented for even larger shares. The new amendment prescribes that the aggregate of the rent, revenue and local cess will not exceed one-sixth of the value of the crop. This means that the rent is to be somewhere below one-sixth of the crop. Thus in the majority of the cases of share renting, the rents will be reduced to less than one-third of the prevailing levels. It will thus be appreciated that the reductions required in the prevailing rents are quite considerable and will need special effort for effective enforcement.

There are a large number of legal preliminaries to undergo before the implementation of the ' deemed to have purchased ' clause begins. They will naturally take some time. In the meanwhile, the regulation of rent must be immediately and firmly enforced. That alone will create conditions necessary for a smooth implementation of the ' deemed to have purchased' clause. Otherwise there is some danger of the tenants being induced to refuse to purchase the lands under their cultivation. Any large scale refusal on the part of the tenants will greatly impede the implementation of the ' deemed to have purchased ' clause and may lead to the most undesired consequences. Further even if the tenants initially agree to make the purchase, they will be making the payment of the instalments of the price over a period of more than ten years. They could be induced to make the purchase ineffective at any time during this long period and if a large number of purchases thus become ineffective, it may lead to all manner of complications in the situation. Underlying the failure to implement the provisions of the original Act, lies the basic fact that a majority of the landlords possess over their tenants an amount of social and political power. That they are willing to exercise such power to guard their economic interests is obvious from the large number of voluntary resignations induced from the tenants since the passing of the original Act. A successful implementation of any comprehensive land reform will depend upon a clear recognition of this fact.

Ideally speaking, for a successful implementation of the transfer of agricultural lands into the hands of the cultivators, the landlord must be put out of the picture as early as possible. This can only be done by paying him off in lump sum and assuming directly all responsibility of recovery of the instalments. Under the amendment, the Government does in fact assume the responsibility of recovering these instalments; in fact it is provided that arrears of instalments will be recovered as arrears of land revenue. This is satisfactory as far as it goes but in case of default in the payment of instalments, the purchase becomes ineffective, and the land reverts, it should be noted, to the landlord and not to the Government. Hence, in order to ensure that in practice no arrears of instalments will accumulate and no purchase will be declared ineffective on account of such arrears, it will be necessary to organise the necessary finance and credit through appropriate co-operative agencies.

It is obvious that in any case it will be impossible to pay off the landlords in a single instalment and that therefore payment will have to be spread over several instalments. From this standpoint it is important to note that the annual instalment which the tenant will have to pay over a period of 10 years is not likely to be much more than the rent he is currently paying. Thus, under the amendment, the maximum rent is fixed at five times the assessment which as we have seen is about half the current rent the tenant is actually paying for an average soil. On the other hand, the sale price is to be between 50 to 200 times the assessment plus the value of improvements. For an average soil, let us suppose that the sale price will be about 100 times the assessment. This means that for an average soil, the sale price will be about 20 times the maximum rent payable under the new amendment or about 10 times the actual rent being paid today. If this is spread over a period of ten years, the annual instalment of price will be just about the rent the tenant is currently paying.

For better lands, the sale price will of course be higher, say 200 or even 300 times the assessment; that is to say, the sale price may be 40 or even 60 times the maximum prescribed rent. But, as we have seen, for these lands, the currently prevailing rent is also more than four or even five times the prescribed maximum. Hence even in respect of these better lands, the sale price so determined will not be greatly in excess of say 10 or 12 times the current rent and hence the annual instalment will not be much more than the current rent. The net result of this operation will therefore be that the tenant will continue to pay more or less the same rent as he is paying today but that it will be called an instalment of price and not rent and after he has paid these regularly for a period of ten or twelve years, he will acquire the full ownership of the land.

The amendment prescribes that the prices will be between 50 and

200 times the assessment plus the value of improvements made by the landlord. There is thus a wide margin within which the Tribunals may fix the price. Certain working rules will therefore be necessary for the guidance of the Tribunals. It will greatly facilitate the operation if wherever possible the above relation between the current rent and the instalment of price is made an operative basis for the detemination of price. Wherever the rents currently being paid and received are not in dispute, the Tribunals may find it a very convenient rule. The tenants may also find it the most easy to comprehend. It certainly may be used for a popular exposition of the operation of the ' deemed to have purchased ' clause so that the tenants may not be misled by interested advice.

As pointed out earlier, organisation of appropriate and adequate finance will be necessary to facilitate the payment of instalments of price. For a successful implementation of the transfer of agricultural lands into the hands of the tiller, finance and credit will be needed for yet another and more fundamental reason. In the analysis of the cases of resumption and of change of tenants, it became clear that in a majority of these cases, the reason for the termination of tenancies was voluntary surrender or resignation by the evicted tenants. While discussing the nature of these cases, we suggested that, in large part, such voluntary resignations could have been under duress. The new legislation might be able to check to a certain extent such pressures acting upon the tenants and thus might be able to reduce the extent of such induced resignations. But the analysis of the cases of voluntary resignations also brought to notice a substantial number where the resignation or surrender could indeed be regarded as genuinely voluntary. Of particular interest among these cases are those where the tenants, surrendered the land because they said they were short of plough cattle. Such cases accounted for nearly 10 per cent of the area on which tenants were changed and about 2 per cent of the area which was resumed by the landlords. These cases, though not very extensive, point out to the moral that for a stable rehabilitation of the tenants on lands under their cultivation, something more than a mere granting of a legal title will be necessary. The need for more positive assistance will be paramount in those cases where, for one reason or another, lands will revert to Government and will be available for disposal by sale. Under the provisions of the Act, for the purpose of disposing of such lands, a high priority is rightly accorded to landless labour families. But to be effective in practice, such priority will have to be supported by finance and credit to enable the landless families to buy the land, to buy the necessary equipment and to bring and maintain the land under plough for an initial period of a few years.

The new legislation will be a great stride forward if it is successfully implemented; equally, its failure may lead to near chaos or disaster. The failure of earlier legislation is a warning that it will need more comprehensive supporting measures and greater administrative effort if this is to be avoided.

4

IMPACT OF LAND REFORMS IN GUJARAT*

M. B. DESAI

THE FOLLOWING main points emerge from the study of the working of the Bombay Tenancy and Agricultural Lands Act, 1948 :—

The inferior social status and the low standards of literacy of the tenants appear to be the two important contributory factors impeding the smooth and successful working of the provisions of the Act intended to benefit this class. Some of the significant provisions are relatively less known in districts such as the Banaskantha, Panch Mahals, and Surat where most of the tenants enjoy inferior social status and are relatively much less educated.

Some land transfers took place among the tenants during the years 1949-53. They are, however, not indicative of transactions between the landlords and the tenants in favour of the latter, because firstly, lands sold by tenants nearly offset those purchased by them, and secondly, land acquisition by tenants from landlords was relatively less significant than that from others. Expressed as percentage of the area under tenancy in 1953, during the 15 years of the working of the Tenancy Act of 1939, excluding the year 1951, the landlords resumed 1·5 per cent of the lands from tenants as against 0·8 per cent purchased by the latter from the former during the period 1949 to June, 1955, excluding the years 1950 and 1951, since the enforcement of the 1948 Act. Whereas there is a decline in land ownership in North Gujarat, tenants in South Gujarat acquired relatively more lands. Economic conditions rather than the benefits of the tenancy legislation seem to have been the factor responsible for the phenomenon. In almost all cases of purchases by the tenants, the prices were arrived at by mutual agreement.

It is similarly difficult to note any clear-cut tendency in mortgages both in the ryotwari and in the non-ryotwari tenures. It may broadly be said, however, that during the period under study, there was some decline in the area mortgaged by the tenants in the ryotwari villages.

The large shift in the area held under tenancy during the period 1949-53, indicates considerable uncertainty and insecurity of tenancy. Between North Gujarat and South Gujarat these fluctuations were less and tendency towards owner cultivation greater in the latter.

The outlay on irrigation cultivation by the tenants might be taken as one of the indicators of discrimination as between the owned and leased

*Reproduced from *Report on an Enquiry into the Working of the Bombay Tenancy and Agricultural Lands Act*, 1948 *in Gujarat* by M. B. Desai, pp. 94-96.

lands. It was found that owned lands in general were favoured for investment in irrigation extension. In the limited extent to which leased lands were irrigated, it was found that the landlords' initiative and effort were not significant factors towards such improvements.

There is no significant change for the better in the equipment of the landless tenants since 1949. The landowner-cum-tenant, on the other hand, bettered his position on this count during the period.

As against this, in the matter of indebtedness, the increase in both the long-term and short-term debts during 1949-53 was much lower for landless tenants and quite significant in the case of owner-cum-tenants. The explanation for this may partly be found in the superior credit-worthiness of the latter.

There has been extensive surrender of lands voluntarily aggregating to about 1 lakh acres upto June, 1955. In the absence of details, it is extremely difficult to precisely indicate how much of the surrender was genuinely voluntary.

Eviction of protected tenants during 1951-54 was considerable involving 27 per cent of the tenants. Similarly, during 1952-55, 38 per cent of the evictions arose due to failure by tenants to pay rent. About 6 per cent of the tenants examined failed to acquire protected tenancy rights due to faulty records. Another 13 per cent who were mere sub-tenants could not be covered by the legislation.

In the ryotwari villages crop-share as a mode of paying rent declined during 1946-53. By 1953-54 cash rent emerged as a predominant mode of paying rent. In the erstwhile non-ryotwari villages, crop-share continued to gain in importance till 1955.

The levels of rent over a period of time appear to be going down and give an impression of settling down to levels permissible under the Act. But the process is very slow and gradual, and is likely to take a long time. On the other hand, cases of rise in the levels of rent were very few and occurred only where the tenants were disadvantageously placed.

There is no marked difference in the overall crop pattern between the owned and leased lands. In view of the subsistence nature of farming, perhaps there is not much scope for such variations. The choice of crops is not influenced by the type of tenancy either.

There was no discrimination in the use of improved seeds as between owned and leased land and only a little preference in the application of manure in favour of owned land. Likewise, there was some discrimination by tenants as between owned and leased lands in the matter of land improvements. Lack of finance, fear of enhancement of rent and objection by the landlord were pointed out as impeding land improvements.

It might be stated in general that tenants have not yet grown conscious of the need for improving productivity. They are content with traditional farm practices and land improvements.

5

ON LAND REFORMS*

A. M. KHUSRO

DURING RECENT years the main instrument for the re-distribution of income, wealth, status, power, and opportunities has been thought to be land reform. In conjunction with other measures such as a more scientific use of agricultural inputs—water, better seeds, fertilizers and implements—land reform would also step up productivity. Several works are now available on the progress of land reforms and it is possible to study the impact of these reforms on the layers of income, wealth and power in rural society.

The abolition of Zamindari and Jagirdari was expected to transfer the real control of agricultural wealth (land) and the income as well as status derived from that wealth, from the hands of absentee intermediaries to those of actual cultivators. In certain areas like Hyderabad (now constituting a part of the States of Andhra, Bombay and Mysore) when jagirs were abolished, the citadels of power were liquidated, administrative control was taken over by the State proper, land revenue, which was unduly high, got reduced, and better administrative control was taken over by the State proper, and enhancing somewhat the real incomes of the other layers of the rural society. But in States like U. P. it is now a commonplace that owing to a loose definition of personal cultivation and the virtual non-existence of limits on resumptions of land, vast tracts were acquired by Zamindars who thereafter came to be called ' bhoomidars ' No doubt, many of them became managers of their large ' farms ' and took to tractors and other advanced methods of cultivation. This occurrence is by no means typical of U. P. and only goes to show that there are privileged groups in society which are not inimical to growth, so long as growth does not upset their existing prerogatives. So in these areas growth may indeed have occurred and even larger surpluses might have been generated, but this result has been achieved through large-scale evictions of tenants by the zamindars in the process of proving that a large area of land was ' Sir ' and ' Khudkasht ', i. e., their personal cultivation which admitted no tenants, since their own bhoomidari rights depended upon bringing such a proof. Such evictions militated against the egalitarian spirit of reform and led to a concentration of landed wealth and of the privilege and income derived therefrom.

The major objective of land reforms had been to make the tenant-

*Reproduced from Enquiry No. 4 article *Reflections on Redistributions of Income, Wealth and Opportunities in India* : 1950-1960.

cultivators secure in their land-holding by declaring them to be permanent, protected, and non-evictable tenants (subject to certain conditions). A further objective was to have rents reduced in their favour while they remained tenants and finally to help them purchase the holdings at extremely favourable prices (say about 40 % of market value) and become owners. All these measures were clearly re-distributive in character. While it is certain that some degree of benefit was derived from them, the picture of the implementation of these measures is disgustingly dismal. That consequent upon the passing of tenancy laws numerous evictions of tenants all over India became the rule, is a fact known to and investigated by almost all State Governments. A non-official enquiry into the working of the Bombay Tenancy Act came to the baffling conclusion that for all practical purposes the Act did not exist ! It would be appropriate to quote here some results of another non-official enquiry conducted in the ex-jagir areas of Hyderabad:

TABLE III

Protected Tenancies in 1954-55

	Still remaining	Purchased	Voluntarily Surrendered	Legally evicted	Illegally evicted	Others
Out of every 100 Protected Tenants created in 1951 :	45·39	12·42	17·83	2·58	22·14	0·12
Out of every 100 Acres of Protected Tenancy Created in 1951 :	49·82	14·94	20·76	1·96	12·62	0·006

Out of every one hundred protected tenants created in 1951, only 45·39 retained their protected status and remained on the land by the beginning of 1955. Another 12·42 % had purchased the land and became owners. Thus altogether about 58 % were still enjoying the fruit of the legislation, but the other 42 % had left the land. 2·58 % had been evicted under the law.......It appears that 17·83 % of the originally created protected tenants voluntarily surrendered their rights and handed their lands back......

Apart from these so-called ' voluntary surrenders ' the genuineness of which is most doubtful " one cannot learn without some surprise that as many as 22·14 % of tenants were illegally evicted." The results in terms of acreage are not very much different. But even so the conclusion emerges that the tenants who remained as protected tenants were of average size or slightly larger, 45 % of them holding 50 % of acreage. The same is true of tenants who became owners, 12 % of them holding 15 % of land. But tenants who did not receive protection and were evicted legally or illegally —were generally small men, forming about 25 % of the total but occupying less than 15 % of land. This conclusion was more pointedly borne out with respect to the Marathawada region. There, the enquiry goes on to state:

Those who remain on the land (23·80 %) are larger tenants accouning for 45·90 % of the total area under protected tenancies. Those who have purchased the land are also tenants having land much bigger than the average size, 2·12 % of them accounting for 5·28 % of the acreage. At the same time those who have been illegally evicted (51·80 %) are humbler occupants accounting for as little as 17·17% of the total protected area.

Thus, all in all, the smaller tenant has received much less protection and has suffered more than the bigger one.

But the story of land reform has advanced far enough for us to see clearly that only a small fraction of tenants has purchased ownership rights. The issue of ceilings on land was soft-peddled through the reluctance of most of the State Governments, and by the time this matter was taken up seriously even at the legislative level, vast transfers of land had already taken place, nominally splitting existing holdings into below-ceiling fragments, though effective management continued in much the same way as before. That land reforms, owing to legislative delays and administrative short-sightedness, have so far failed apart from exceptional cases, to promote any healthy structural change in terms of equity is a proposition which cannot easily be denied. The evidence that we have, goes to suggest that the effect of land policy in recent years has been in the direction of (i) reduction of power in the hands of jagirdars and zamindars, (ii) the emergence of a new managerial class of agriculturists through old-fashioned land reforms such as in U. P. or in Madras, (iii) large-scale evictions of tenants (and particularly smaller ones) in almost all States, and their merger in all probability into the ranks of labourers, (iv) enhancement of rents and a failure to establish a fair relation between rents and gross produce, (v) a general failure to make tenants own their holdings and be spared of rent payments, and (vi) a failure to bring about through ceilings a decrease in the inequality of wealth, income and power.

While land reforms generally affect the relation between landowners who lease out land and tenants who lease in, they leave practically untouched the very large group of owner-cultivators.

6

LAND REFORMS IN INDIA

I

Dr. P. C. Joshi

THE AGRARIAN structure which has been taking shape in India in recent years can be understood better in the background of India's agrarian history under the British rule. A brief historical retrospect of land relations during the pre-Independence period is, therefore, essential.

The land relations in a country are integrally related to the basic characteristics of its national economy, social structure and political system. In India, the most crucial influence on the development of agrarian relations in the modern period had been that of the colonial character of her economy. The main consequence of India's integration within the British Empire was that the historical process of evolution from a backward, pre-industrial economy to a developed, industrial economy was interrupted. On the contrary, this process was channelised into a new direction which was designed to bring India closer into the British colonial system. Consequently, the transformation of precapitalist agrarian relations which took place in the independent countries of the West could not take place in India in the same way. Her land tenures, on the other hand, were adapted and modified to suit the economic and political requirements of the British economy.

In their attempt to reorganise India's agrarian structure the British rulers established two main types of land systems in the country, viz. the Zamindari and the Raiyatwari. Under the Zamindari tenure the rights of property in land were conferred upon the native tax-gatherers who had so far never taken any interest in actual cultivation of the soil. As a result of this step, millions of persons who had been proprietors as well as cultivators of their lands from time immemorial were reduced to the position of mere tenants-at-will on their own fields. Under the Raiyatwari system, no intermediary proprietors were recognised, and the actual tillers of the soil were vested with a heritable and transferable right of property in their lands.

However, the proprietory rights, either of the Zamindars or of the Raiyats were not absolute. Under both systems the rights of the Britisth Government were supreme in so far as it was free to determine the amount of revenue assessment on land that was payable to the State. Moreover, the British administration also assumed the power to auction all lands the proprietors of which defaulted in the payment of revenue. The revenue demands were oppressive and extortionate both in the Zamindari and in the Raiyatwari areas. In Zamindari areas the consequent inability to meet these revenue demands led to the compulsory transfer of land on a vast scale from the traditional nobility to the more rapacious money-lenders and speculators. In the Raiyatwari areas also, the heavy pressure of revenue assessments led to the pauperisation of the Raiyat and to the alienation of his land in the hands of merchants and money-lenders. Thus, in both the areas there developed a class of intermediary proprietors between the actual cultivator of the soil and the State, which, through a process of sub-infeudation grew, into a hierarchy of non-cultivating landed interests. They all claimed a share of the gross produce of land leaving the cultivator barely with subsistence, which drove him further into the clutches of the money-lender and of perpetual debt. During the whole course of the 19th century, this became a vicious circle which denuded the agriculturist of the major part of the fruits of his labour.

Landed proprietors in India were thus, by and large, merely rentiers, who held landed property without ever being the managers of large scale agricultural enterprises. The actual units of cultivation were in most cases the small parcels of land, largely cultivated for subsistence by poor and oppressed tenants. The landlords generally leased out their holdings to these tenants from whom they extracted the maximum surplus produce, in kind or in cash, and squandered it away in conspicuous consumption. In spite of the juridical and other types of significant dissimilarities between the Zamindari and Raiyatwari land systems in both areas the pattern of land relations that developed in the wake of the British rule was characterised by semi-feudal land ownership which obstructed the development of productive forces in agriculture.

The landlord-tenant nexus was further consolidated by the pressure generated by the increasing penetration of colonial trade in agricultural produce. The growth of trade in raw materials in India and the inundation of the market with manufactured goods from Britain,on the one hand, undermined the foundations of village self-sufficiency by disrupting indigenous handicraft in both the cities and peasant homes, and, on the other hand, accelerated the penetration of commodity economy in rural areas. These changes created certain objective conditions and possibilities for the development of capitalist production inasmuch as the destruction of village self-sufficiency created a "commodity market" for capitalism, and the bankruptcy of large numbers of peasants and handicraftsmen created a "labour market" for it. These possibilities, however, only partially fructified; they did not lead the growth of a vigorous national capitalist system of production. The 'commodity economy' whose development was accelerated by British rule enabled the British rulers to subordinate and transform India's agricultural production according to their needs and requirements. The 'commodity market' created as a result of ruthless de-industrialisation did not become an 'internal market' of national industry, on the contrary, became an appendage of the 'internal market' of western capitalism. Further, the 'labour market' created as a result of widespread alienation of the peasants from land and of the artisans from native industry led only to pauperisation of the masses without proletarianisation (i. e. absorption in modern industry) as in the developed Western countries of the world.

The above process had far reaching repercussions on land relations and agricultural development. It led to excessive pressure of population on land since the ruined artisans and the impoverished, dispossessed peasants had no alternative avenues of employment. They had to fall back on land as tenants-at-will, sharecroppers and farm servants working on highly exploitative terms. The concentration of land in the hands of rentier land-owners enabled them to extract high rents from the tenants. Moreover, the seemingly large possibilities of receiving ever-increasing unearned rental incomes due to constantly growing pressure of population on land kept these land-owners away from productive and entrepreneurial activities in agriculture. Thus, the land-hungry and rack-rented peasantry constituted the vast army of unemployed manpower from whom high rents could be squeezed by leasing them lands on the most exploitative terms and conditions.

The absence of avenues for investment also arrested the flow of native merchant and commercial capital into industrial undertakings and diverted it into the rural sector. In fact, such diversion was encouraged deliberately by the British revenue policy which, through its practice of public auction of lands for revenue arrears provided ample opportunities for investment of money capital in land. The exploitative terms in which the tenants cultivated the lands provided further inducement for such investment.

In a nutshell, the development of a commodity economy under foreign rule, instead of paving the way for the growth of agriculture on modern lines, served to strengthen the depressive framework of landlordism by means of which economic surplus from the agricultural sector was extracted by a conglomeration of rentiers, merchants and userers. The utilisation of this economic surplus for conspicuous consumption and as usurious capital prevented productive investment in agriculture and, therefore, checked progressive agricultural development on the basis of modern farming methods.

Further, in all countries of the West, a radical transformation of the pre-industrial agrarian structure and a change from relationships based on custom and status to those based on contract proceeded simultaneously with their rapid economic development. But in India, with the modification of traditional, pre-British land relations, the new relationships which emerged carried forward certain basic features of the traditional social structure. The high-ranking castes traditionally dissociated from cultivation and direct management of land remained as land-owners and continued to appropriate rental incomes from land. The cultivating peasant castes and the depressed and untouchable castes, standing at the bottom of the social ladder, constantly swelled the ranks of tenants, share-croppers and farm servants. Even in those areas where the peasant castes occupied a dominant position as land-owners the big land holders among them preferred to abstain from direct cultivation and function as non-cultivating landlords employing labourers to run their farms or as pure rent-receivers.

To crown it all, the British Government which held the " commanding heights " of the national economy allied itself with the landlords, usurers and the trading classes and reduced them to mere cogs of its own massive machinery of economic and political exploitation. It tended to perpetuate the pre-capitalist forms of exploitation in the countryside which were the most corrosive elements in Indian agriculture. Thus the State, instead of actively encouraging the growth of a vigorous and free peasantry, acted as a barrier between the Indian peasant and agrarian revolution.

Consequently the agrarian structure which was handed over by the British to the Independent national government of India had been, in the words of Prof. Daniel Thorner, a ' built-in depressor ' which was a direct cause of the state of stagnation and backwardness of the agricultural economy.

This can be seen from the fact that " from 1890 to 1947 India's agricultural output rose so slowly that we are justified in speaking of stagnation ". Whatever increases occurred in output took place in industrial crops (cotton, peanuts, sugarcane, tobacco). It has been estimated that "......in the fortyfive years following 1900, population increased by 37·9 per cent, the acreage under cultivation increased by 18·4 per cent, food output remained stationery and the output of commercial crops went up by 59·3 per cent resulting in an increase of 12·6 per cent in the agricultural output." Thus, all the available evidence unmistakably points to the conclusion that " the agricultural economy of India was in a state of stagnation until about 1945. "

Sir Manilal Nanavati, in his Presidential address to the Sixth Conference of the Indian Society of Agricultural Economics at Banaras on December 6, 1945 presented certain telling facts and features of the state of the Indian rural economy which were a consequence, among other factors, of the persistence of an antiquated land system:

" ......During the last 75 years continuous deterioration in the conditions of the masses is taking place. In 1880 India had a surplus of food stuffs to the extent of 5 million tons and today we have a deficit of 10 million tons. The consumption of food was then estimated at 1½ lbs. per individual and now it is 1 lb. Nearly 30 per cent of the population in India is said to be suffering from chronic mal-nutrition and under-nutrition. The man-land ratio is steadily rising. In spite of the development of modern industries, deindustrialisation is still continuing. In 1880 industries absorbed 12·3 per cent of the population and now the figure is 9 per cent. In 1872, 56 per cent of the population depended on agriculture, this proportion has now increased to 73 per cent. " (Quoted in U. P. Z. A. C. Report, Vol. I. P 33).

The social and political consequences of the operation of this ' built-in depressor ' were no less serious. Landlord-tenant relations became a perpetual problem leading to widespread peasant discontent and disturbances. The U. P. Zamindari Abolition Committee Report (1948) succinctly sums up the agrarian situation in most parts of India on the eve of Independence as follows :—

" Our agrarian system has collapsed. It has become a drag on the development of productive forces in the country......Landlordism today has reached the state when it cannot be tolerated any longer, without putting our national interests in jeopardy....."

" The age-long simmering discontent bursting into acts of open defiance and sometimes of violence in our province and other parts of India has reached a critical state. Whatever forbearance and self-restraint we find in the countryside among the tenants is due to the hope that those who are running the State will undo the wrong done to them. Once that hope has gone, the tenant will be driven to desperation. The discontent may develop into revolt and our social security may be threatened by the outbreak of violence. Our scheme of Zamindari abolition contemplates payments of equitable compensation. If abolition may mean expropriation without compensation and quite possibly bloodshed and violence...... One can only hope that the entire landed gentry is not blind to the writing on the wall. "

However, the hope of the tenants in seeking the redress of the wrongs done to them from the then rulers was entirely misplaced. The tenant had to rise in revolt and resort even to violent struggle for the amelioration of his conditions. The series of peasant uprisings in the country throughout the period of British rule are a testimony to this constant struggle.

To sum up : " When the British withdrew from India in 1947, they left the country with perhaps the world's most refractory land problem. "

II

Evolution of the National Agrarian Programme

In the pre-independence period there were two divergent points of view on the economic development of India. The first was the institutional approach which regarded a radical change in the semi-feudal agrarian relations as an essential pre-condition for any kind of economic development whatsoever. The second, however, was the ' technological ' (or technocratic) approach which laid stress on the need for technical improvements in Indian agriculture without paying much attention to the fundamental changes in land relations.

The second approach dominated the thought and practice of the British administrators during the most part of the British rule in India. The preoccupation with the determination of principles on which the new land and revenue systems were to be based which characterised British policy in its early phase came to an end by 1856, by which time the essential foundations of the two land systems had been laid. In the years after the Mutiny in 1857, which was to a certain extent, the reflex action of British agrarian policy in its early years, the corner-stone of British policy became the preservation of the agrarian relations already established. They became sceptical about any radical changes in the land systems after the bitter experience of the Mutiny. Consequently, in the subsequent discussions on development of agriculture, there was a tendency to view the depressed state of Indian agriculture merely as a technological problem. Illustrative of this approach is the Report of the Royal Commission on Agriculture in India which was appointed in 1926, 'to make recommendations for the improvement of agriculture and to promote the welfare and prosperity of the rural population'. The scope of the Commission's enquiry, however, was circumscribed by its terms of reference which directed the Commission 'not to make recommendations regarding the existing systems of land ownership and tenancy or of assessment of land revenue and irrigation charges.'

In spite of such deliberate exclusion of the land-tenures and revenue assessment from the purview of the Commission, the British administration from time to time had sought to tinker with the agrarian structure on the fringes under the pressure of agrarian discontent and serious deterioration in the condition of the cultivating classes. A series of legislative measures were enacted in different provinces of India beginning with the Bengal Rent Act of 1859. All these laws, however, were designed to improve the position of only a limited section of cultivators below the landlord, leaving the basic structure unchanged. Many of them also became a dead letter and virtually inoperative because of the persistent evasion and lack of vigorous enforcement. Nevertheless, these measures provided some relief in the nature of 'first-aid' to a small group of tenants. At the same time, since these measures protected only the upper layers of the tenantry, viz., the occupancy tenants,* the majority of them remained virtually without protection against the rapacious landlords. Moreover, this limited protection led to widespread practice of sub-infeudation amongst the occupancy tenants as well, who abandoned the cultivation of their lands to lease them to sub-tenants on remunerative terms. Thus, even though, the beginning of providing relief to the tenantry had been made under the British rule, these had not proceeded far enough. Therefore, the relations 'which had sprung up by law, custom and usage between those who owned and those who operated the land with different degrees of rights' remained basically undisturbed.

The stagnation which set in the agricultural economy as a consequence was sought to be explained by the British administrators in terms of the low technological level of Indian agriculture and the schemes devised to break through such stagnation placed technological measures in the forefront and not the measures of reform and reorganisation of the agrarian structure.

*Amongst occupancy tenants were included only such cultivators who had continued to cultivate their lands on the payment of customary rates of revenue for a sufficiently long period and had not been in the meanwhile evicted from the particular farms, which they had held.

An inevitable corollary of the technological approach was an insular view of agricultural development. The British administration considered improvement of agricultural production in isolation from the needs of India's industrial development which was a *sine qua non* for initiating such improvement. Since India for them was only an agricultural colony they desired her to improve her agriculture without overcoming her industrial backwardness. But this was inherently impossible as is amply borne out by historical experience as well as by the current thinking in the country.

The nationalists in India, however, were opposed to the technological view adopted by the British. They continued to express dissatisfaction with the land and revenue policies of the British Government from as early a period as the late 19th century. Mr. R. C. Dutt was one of the first who voiced such criticism openly.

In the third decade of the twentieth century, as the national movement spread out to the vast masses in the countryside, the agrarian problem began to influence the course of political deliberations in the Indian National Congress as well. In the earlier phase of the movement, the Congress had been content merely by being critical of the glaring defects and injustices of the land system. Subsequently, however, in the face of the gathering storm of agrarian discontent, it was led to question the basic foundations of the prevailing land system and to plead for its radical reorganisation. Consequently the Indian National Congress which was a symbol of the united struggle of the Indian people for independence became wedded to the institutional approach. Further, as a national party reflecting the aspirations of the country for independent economic development, it naturally regarded agriculture and its problems in the broader context of the entire national economy.

A concrete proof of the sharp changes in the Congress view on the agrarian problem is available from the A. I. C. C. Resolution of 1929 which stressed the necessity " of a revolutionary change in the present economic and social order ", and from a series of resolutions passed thereafter at various sessions of the Congress. Important among these are the Karachi Resolution on Fundamental Rights (1932), the Resolution on Zamindari Abolition passed in April, 1935, at the U. P. Kisan Conference (under the Presidentship of Sardar Vallabhbhai Patel), the Agrarian Programme adopted at the 50th Session of the Congress at Faispur, and the recommendation of the National Planning Committee on Land Policy in 1938, which represent memorable land-marks in the evolution of a national agrarian programme.

Two Perspectives on Agrarian Re-Organisation :

The re-organisation of land relations could proceed, however, along two independent lines:

In the first place, the prevailing land system could be modified with a view to encouraging the erstwhile landlords who had so far been merely rent receivers to engage in cultivation and manage lands directly with hired labour along modern lines. They could be helped to consolidate the scattered units of cultivation under their tenants into large farming units and convert the ill-managed and ill-equipped fields into well-managed progressive farms. This would require the eviction of tenants from their lands and their re-employment as agricultural labourers on these modern farms. The development of these farms could be further buttressed with State assistance in the form of cheap credit and with the provision of other facilities at subsidised rates.

In the second place, the vast masses of tenant cultivators could be conferred the proprietary rights in their lands on easy terms, without allowing their eviction. This would wipe out the class of non-cultivating interests root and branch from the agricultural set-up, and would usher in small-scale peasant farming on a vast scale. Later, when the limited possibilities of small-scale cultivation had been exhausted, enlargement of the unit of cultivation with a view to modernisation of agriculture and application of scientific techniques could be brought about by means of co-operative farming.

These two perspectives broadly represented two alternative paths of pro-peasant and pro-landlord agrarian reorganization in India. It is worthy of note that there were sharp differences within the leadership of the Indian National Congress on the immediate policy as well as the future perspective of agrarian reform in India. There were radicals like Jawaharlal Nehru whose thinking and declarations showed a pronounced pro-peasant bias; on the other hand, there were conservative elements whose views and public pronouncements showed a pronounced pro-landlord bias. In view of the tremendous peasant discontent in almost all parts of the country and the necessity of rallying peasant support in the anti-imperialist struggle, the Congress organization and its leadership, however, was obliged to adopt a pro-peasant line through its resolutions and public pronouncements.

It is important to note that in the period before Independence, the Central task which confronted the national movement was the struggle for freedom from British rule. Until this task was accomplished, the blue print for India's economic development could not be drawn up in details. It was possible only to indicate its broad outline in a manner which would unite all sections and classes in the country in the struggle for freedom. Consequently, the basic questions which involved conflicts and antagonisms between various social groups in the country were not conclusively discussed and were even deliberately left vague. Congress policy and practice on the agrarian problem, therefore, reflects both before and after independence lack of consistency and singleness of direction which is a reflection of the contradictory pulls of a pro-landlord and a pro-peasant solution of the Indian land problem.

In the above background, we shall now review the course of land policy and the reform of the agrarian structure as actually carried out in the wake of freedom, during the last decade of planned economic effort.

III

Land Policy After Independence

Soon after independence the major task to which the independent national governments at the Centre and in the States had to address themselves was to prepare the blue-print for India's rapid economic development for its transformation from a backward and predominantly agrarian economy into an idustrially developed one.

The land problem was one of the key issues in economic development. A clear conception of the land relations which were to be adopted as the ultimate goal for the country and the stages by which this goal was to be realised became now an imperative necessity. Consequently, the unfinished debate on the basic issues of agrarian reorganisation was resumed within the ruling party and within the committees and commissions appointed by the Congress Governments with a view to suggesting an appropriate land policy for the country.

Land Reform Proposals in the Early Years of Independence

Closely following independence, the Congress Economic Programmes Committee (1947-48) put forward far-reaching proposals for changes in the agrarian structure.

(a) It enunciated the principle that " land should be held for use (as opposed to profit) and as a source of employment. The use of lands of those who are either non-cultivating landholders or otherwise unable for any period to exercise the right of cultivating them, must come to vest in the village co-operative community subject to the condition that the original holder or his successor will be entitled to come back to the land for genuine cultivation.

(b) The Committee further urged that in agriculture limits should be fixed for " the maximum size of holding...The surplus land over such a maximum should be acquired and placed at the disposal of the village co-operative. "

These proposals were of far-reaching importance inasmuch as they advocated a frontal assault on land concentration in the hands of a minority. Further, from the recommendations of the Committee, it logically followed that " all non-cultivating landholders would either have to become cultivators or they would lose their land. "

This approach was re-enforced and further elaborated in the Report of the Congress Agrarian Reforms Committee which had been appointed in December, 1947, by the then Congress President " to examine and make recommendations about agrarian reforms...... "

The Agrarian Reforms Committee in its Report, completed in July 1949, strongly asserted that " without comprehensive reforms in the country's land system, there cannot be any lasting improvement in agricultural production and efficiency. "

Among the recommendations made by the Committee for " comprehensive reforms in the land system " the following were the most crucial.

(a) The Committee was of the view that " in the agrarian system of India there is no place for intermediaries and land must belong to the tiller...... ". Consequently, as the first step, it proposed that " in future sub-letting of land will be prohibited except in the case of widows, minors and other disabled persons. "

(b) During the period of transition, however, the committee recommended " a set of rights for the actual tillers who are themselves not owners of land. Those who have been cultivating land continuously for a period of six years should......automatically get full occupancy rights. In the case of others, the Committee recommended, the owner may have the option, up to a certain period, to resume the holdings for personal cultivation. "

The Committee recommended definite safeguards against resumption by landowners. (1) " Only those who put in a minimum amount of physical labour and participate in actual agricultural operations would be deemed to cultivate the land personally. " (2) " The owner will have the option to resume the holding to the extent to which it is necessary to make his self-cultivated holding economic. He can, however, resume more land, up to the maximum prescribed, if thereby he does not reduce the tenants' holding below the economic. "

(c) The Committee recommended " that the tenant should have the right to purchase the holding at a reasonable price to be determined by regional Land Tribunal. The tenant should be assisted by a suitable financial agency in purchasing the holding. "

Further, it laid " special emphasis on immediate prevention of all evictions...... " All tenants, to whichever class they belonged, were to be protected from " rack-renting and illegal exactions ". Provision was to be made for " determination of reasonable rent as well as for the commutation of rents in kind into cash. "

(d) The next crucial step recommended by the Committee was the imposition of ceiling on land holdings. This was considered necessary for very sound reasons. " In the first place, the supply of land in relation to the number of people seeking it, is so limited that not to put a ceiling on individual holdings would be irrational and unjust. Secondly, under the present technique of cultivation the managerial capacity and financial resources of an average cultivator in India, the optimum size of a holding has to be fairly low. " In the opinion of the Committee, therefore, the optimum size should be " three times the size of the economic holding. "

In support of its proposal for a relatively lower limit of land holdings, the Committee further stated: " The optimum size of the farm is related to the technique used and as our effort should be to find gainful employment for as many as possible on land till industries develop to absorb the surplus population, the technique which may generally be used in agriculture is only better ploughs and bullocks with occasional assistance of tractors and other mechanised devices wherever needed."

It is clear that in the view of the Committee, large-scale mechanisation in agriculture in the immediate future was neither possible nor desirable. The main reliance for agricultural improvements was to be placed on labour-intensive methods supplemented by discriminating use of mechanical devices preferably of the non-labour displacing variety.

(e) Finally, on the most crucial and controversial question viz., the pattern of the agrarian economy, the Committee recommended a "composite" pattern "of individual farming assisted by co-operative organisation, co-operative joint farming, collective and State farming."

Firstly, it recommended 'restricted form of family farming for holdings between the basic and the optimum size.' Family farming was suggested for the basic (i.e., below the economic size holding) in the hope 'that the provision of multi-purpose co-operative societies would reduce to a very great extent the inefficiency involved in farming on such units.

Secondly, individual farming was not to be allowed on holdings which were smaller than basic holdings. This was so because there was a limit below which family farming even with all the co-operative aids ceased to be economic'. They were, therefore, in course of time, to be brought under a 'scheme of co-operative farming'.

Thirdly, peasant farming or capitalist farming was to be avoided on reclaimed land where collective farms with landless labourers should be organised.

While recommending a composite pattern of the agrarian systems and while conceding the possibilities of increasing the efficiency of Indian agriculture by means of the use of improved agricultural technique, better seeds and manure etc., the Committee was at the same time aware that "unless the unit of production was sufficiently large, the farmer would not be in a position to get the full advantage of the reform of land tenure......"

The enlargement of the unit of production could, however, be effected along two alternative lines, viz., that of private large-scale farming or co-operative large-scale farming. Since the committee had already ruled out the former alternative, it could be legitimately inferred that it was in favour of the latter. The Committee, however, refrained from expressing any categorical view in this regard.

The Report of the Congress Agrarian Reforms Committee was one of the most radical policy documents of the Indian National Congress in independent India inasmuch as its recommendations approximated to a very large extent to the objective of 'land to the tiller' and the abolition of non-cultivating interests from land.

According to the Committee's recommendations, "a tenant continuously cultivating a holding or a part of the holding for six years should automatically get the right of occupancy over it." A tenant was defined as " a person lawfully cutivating any land belonging to another person, if such land is not cultivated personally by the owner and if such a person is not:

(a) a member of the owner's family; or

(b) a servant on wages payable in cash or in kind but not a crop sharer or a hired labourer, cultivating the land under the personal supervision of the owner or any member of the owner's family; or

(c) a mortgage in possession ".

The above definition of the tenant would cover the vast masses of cultivating interests including those having the weakest position like ' the Adhiars in Assam and Orissa, Bargadars in West Bengal, Sikims in U. P. and Bihar, Warmadars in Madras, Verumpattamadars in Malabar and Kamins in East Punjab '. It is evident that the Committee's recommendations if implemented would extend security and protection to the vast masses of tenants.

The Committee had recommended that the maximum permissible individual holding should be three times the economic holding. It is noteworthy, that in matters of fixing ceilings a distinction was made between cultivating owners and non-cultivating owners of land. The former comprised those who did not lease out their lands and cultivated it all through. They were, therefore, allowed the right to own a holding three times the size of an economic holding. The latter (i.e., the non-cultivating owners), were those who had so far leased out their lands and, therefore, did not deserve the unrestricted right of having the maximum permissible holding by eviction of their tenants. They could, however, enjoy such right only if the tenant had an excess land over an economic holding. Further, if there was excess land even after the lessor had resumed land for making his holding equal to maximum holding, it was to remain with the tenant to the extent of building up a maximum holding for him. If there was excess land even after this, it was to be acquired by the village community. What is important to note is that from tenants with less than an economic holding, as was the case with overwhelming majority of tenants, the owner could resume nothing. It is evident that while the proposals of the Committee, if implemented, would not completely eliminate the non-cultivating interests from land, they would substantially restrict the area of their operations and protect and promote the interests of the cultivating peasantry.

On the whole, in the Committee's view, the landlord-tenant relations prevailing in Indian agriculture at the time of independence were to be substituted not by employer-employee relationships characteristic of large-scale capitalistic agriculture. On the contrary, the genuinely self-cultivating peasantry headed by a solid body of cultivators of optimum-sized holdings was to emerge as the vehicle of economic progress and stability in the rural areas.

Land Reform Proposals in the First Five Year Plan

The proposals of the Congress Agrarian Reforms Committee were, however, not the official policy of the Congress Government. The comprehensive framework of the official land policy was set out for the first time in the First Five Year Plan. In the Plan, an attempt was made to indicate the broad common approach for land reform programmes. The Plan also indicated the main stages in which the reforms were to be carried out.

Abolition of Intermediaries : It may be noted that schemes for the abolition of intermediaries were already being drawn up when the Plan was being formulated. The Plan recommended that the process should be expedited.

Tenancy Reforms : The main recommendations in respect of tenancy reforms were as follows :—

(i) Conferment of the right of occupancy on all tenants subject to the owner's right to resume a limited area for personal cultivation.

(ii) Resumption for personal cultivation should be permitted for the number of family holdings not exceeding three, which could be cultivated by adult workers belonging to the landlords' family with the assistance of agricultural labour to the extent customary among those who cultivate their own lands.

(iii) The owners should exercise the right of resumption for personal cultivation within a period of five years.

(iv) The tenants of non-resumable area or areas in which the landlord fails to exercise the right of resumption within five years should get the right of purchase, the price being determined in terms of the multiples of the rental value of land and payment being made in instalments. Government may establish direct contact with the tenants of the non-resumable area.

(v) A rate of rent exceeding one-fourth or one-fifth of the produce should be regarded as requiring special justification.

It was suggested that in order to stimulate the movement of the rural population to the urban area, leasing in future may be permitted with provisions for adequate protection to the tenants and it should generally be for a period of five to ten years and should be renewable, resumption being permitted if the owner himself wishes to cultivate the land. All leases were to be made through the village Panchayat, as direct landlord-tenant relationship was liable to several abuses.

Ceiling on Land Holdings : The principle that there should be an absolute limit to the amount of land which any individual may hold was accepted. This limit will be fixed by each State, having regard to its own agrarian history. A census of land holdings and cultivation was suggested with a view to collect relevant data. As an immediate step it was suggested that land management legislation should be undertaken by the States.

A distinction was to be made between land under the cultivation of tenants-at-will and that under the direct management of owners. For land with tenants-at-will, it was proposed that such tenants should be enabled to become owners of land cultivated by them.

Large farms directly managed by the owners were to be divided into two groups, viz.,

(i) Those which are so efficiently managed that their break-up would lead to a fall in production; and

(ii) which do not meet this test.

The farms falling in the latter category were to be taken over by the State for purposes of management either in their entirety or such portion thereof as might be in excess of a limit to be prescribed. The land brought under State management could be given for cultivation to agricultural workers, preferably in co-operative groups. The Plan expressed the view that these proposals " would provide for a large measure of redistribution of land belonging to substantial owners. "

Agricultural Workers : In addition to surplus lands coming under State management it was further recommended that plots of newly reclaimed land and cultivable waste land should be set apart wherever possible for the settlement on co-operative lines of groups of landless agricultural workers. Full support and assistance was also to be given to the Bhoodan movement by providing means of cultivation and other assistance to agricultural workers selected for the allotment of the donated lands. Provision for house sites and of small backyards for kitchen gardening was to receive special emphasis.

Co-operative Village Management : In the Plan, co-operative farming was viewed as a method by which small and middle farms could bring into existence sizeable farm units which would facilitate the application on a wider scale of scientific knowledge, increase in capital investment and rise in the productivity of land. It was, therefore, recommended that encouragement and assistance should be given to farmers to group themselves voluntarily into co-operative farming societies.

Finally, co-operative village management was defined as the ultimate goal towards which the country was to work. The concept of co-operative village management outlined in the Plan made due allowance for the rights of ownership as determined by the land reform legislation of a State. Even so, the village community was visualised to play an important role in the management of the entire area of the village, both cultivated and uncultivated. The actual cultivation could be arranged as might be feasible in family holdings, through small groups working blocks of land in the village on co-operative lines or through a combination of arrangements adapted to the operation to be carried out. The village community would discover the arrangements which served them best according to their needs and experience. There had to be a great deal of trial and experiment before patterns of organisation which best promote the interests of the rural population could be evolved.

The above, in brief, is the substance of the land policy as outlined in the First Five Year Plan. After its approval by the National Development Council and Parliament it was held up as India's national land policy and the State Governments were directed by the Central Government to draw up a phased programme for its implementation.

It can be seen that there were certain important differences in the land policy recommended in the First Five Year Plan from that embodied in the proposals of the Agrarian Reforms Committee.

It is noteworthy that the Agrarian Reforms Committee was far more inclined towards protecting the interests of the cultivating peasantry than towards giving concessions to the former landlords. It had defined a cultivator as one who 'put in a minimum amount of physical labour and participated in actual agricultural operations.' Further, as pointed out earlier, in respect of the right to hold a maximum of three economic holdings, it had distinguished between the cultivating owner who was free to exercise this right and the non-cultivating owner hitherto leasing out his land who would enjoy such right only if the tenant had an excess of land over an economic holding. Such a provision if enforced would seriously restrict if not eliminate the scope of eviction of tenants.

The Five Year Plan, on the other hand, appeared to make no such distinction between cultivating owners and non-cultivating owners in matters of resumption of land for personal cultivation or for fixation of ceiling on land holdings. Under the scheme proposed by the Plan the conferment of the right of occupancy on tenants was subject, without exception, to the owner's right to resume a limited area for personal cultivation. Consequently, according to Plan proposals, tenants were exposed to the risk of loss of rights over the lands hitherto under their cultivating possession as a sequel to the right of resumption granted to landlords. Further, the insistence on physical participation in agriculture was not laid down in the Plan as a *sine qua non* of personal cultivation. In fact, this condition was softpedalled in the Plan and in place of it, allowance was made for use of hired labour, by landlords although only 'to the extent customary among those who cultivated their own lands.'

Under the prevailing socio-economic set-up characterised by concentration of land ownership mostly in the hands of non-labouring upper castes, this concession could be stretched so far as to make cultivation with hired labour (with nominal and symbolic participation by members of the land owning family) fully compatible with the concept of personal cultivation. Thus, the absence of a rigorous definition of personal cultivation in the Plan created vast scope for the abuse of the right of resumption by landlords, causing a grave threat to the security of tenure of the large masses of tenants.

Similarly, the Agrarian Reforms Committee was opposed to subletting of land except in the case of minors, widows and other disabled persons. The Plan, on the other hand, was in favour of permitting of leasing in future with a view to stimulate the movement of the rural population to the urban areas. No discrimination, however, was suggested to be made in this respect between the mass of small holders being pushed to urban areas in search of employment, who may be entitled to protection and may be allowed to lease out their land under well-defined conditions and the large holders (absentee or otherwise) who were certain to misuse this right to sub-let in order to perpetuate landlord-tenant exploitation and in whose case, therefore, a total ban on sub-letting was an imperative necessity.

Further, the Plan did not provide a sufficiently wide definition of the term ' tenant ' so as to bring all possible categories of tillers (including share-croppers) leasing in land from the landlords. In particular, it did not take cognizance of the fact that as a result of this failure to define ' tenancy ' in a comprehensive manner, and further because of the possibility of a wide connotation of the form of personal cultivation, large masses of crop sharers cultivating the home farms etc., of landlords would remain outside the purview of the tenancy legislation. They could very well be treated as labourers or partners in cultivation and thus denied the rights of tenancy. The Congress Agrarian Reforms Committee, on the other hand, had clearly stated that: " By a tenant we understand a person lawfully cultivating any land belonging to another person, " and had included under this category crop sharers and even hired labourers cultivating the land under the personal supervision of the owner or any member of the owners's family.

Finally, the Agrarian Reforms Committee was categorically of the view that the ' non-cultivating owner discharging the function of the entrepreneur in agriculture has no place in our scheme '. It had stated its disapproval of ' capitalist farming ' as a general method of utilisation of agricultural resources on the ground that " it would deprive the agriculturists of their rights in land, turn them into mere wage-earners and subject society to capitalist control in such a vital matter as supply of food. " It would also create the problem of displaced *persons.* The Committee had, therefore, recommended the imposition of ceiling on all large holdings without exemption.

The Plan, on the other hand, recommended exemption of the efficiently managed holdings even though they might be cultivated by hired labour if their break-up was likely to lead to a fall in production. Only those large holdings which did not meet this test were to be wholly or partially taken over for purposes of management by the State. It did not suggest any definite and objective criterion for judging the efficiency of different types of large holdings. This recommendation of the Plan providing for exemption of big farms run largely by hired labour, (the landowners themselves playing only the managerial and entrepreneurial role) was in clear contradistinction to the earlier recommendation of the Plan according to which ' use of hired labour was to be permitted only to the extent customary among those who cultivated their own land '. Evidently, unlike the Congress Agrarian Reforms Committee, the Plan recommendations could be interpreted to favour protection and promotion of private large scale farming by former landlords and other owners of relatively large holdings, as against the continuance of landlordism based on extraction of rental income without any productive contribution in agricultural enterprise.

The First Plan proposal, therefore, registered a significant departure from the approach of the Congress Agrarian Reforms Committee. This is further borne out by the general survey of the land legislation enacted in different States during the Plan period.

IV

Survey of Land Legislation in States During the First Plan

The first step proposed by the Plan was the abolition of intermediaries between the cultivators and the State. The significance of the changes occurring as a result of this step in the intermediary areas can be appraised with reference to various categories of lands that were under the ownership and control of the intermediaries. They were as follows:

(1) village lands, forests, *abadi* sites etc;

(2) intermediary's home-farms, i. e., lands which the intermediary had the right either to cultivate himself or to let out to tenants;

(3) land other than the intermediary's home-farm which was under his personal cultivations;

(4) lands held by tenants directly from the intermediaries; and

(5) lands held by sub-tenants.

Common Lands : In the intermediary areas common lands such as waste lands, forests, *abadi* sites, etc. belonging to intermediaries were vested in the State Governments for purposes of management. Certain categories of nonagricultural lands, homesteads and buildings and in some cases tanks, fisheries and limited areas of pasture lands were, however, retained by the intermediaries.

Home-farms and Lands under Personal Cultivation : Home-farm lands and lands under the personal cultivation of intermediaries were generally left with them and lessees of home-farms continued as tenants under them. In some States, however, tenants of home-farms of intermediaries were also brought into direct relation with the State and the rights of intermediaries over these lands were abolished. In most of the States no provision was made for allotment of any land for personal cultivation to the intermediaries in addition to their home-farms and lands under their personal cultivation. In certain other States intermediaries were allowed to resume additional lands for personal cultivation. The abolition of intermediaries was based on payment of compensation to intermediaries for the loss of their rights in tenancy lands and common lands. The compensation was to be paid in cash or in the form of bonds. The rate of compensation was to be in inverse proportion to the area of land taken away from the landlords. As a rule, the amount of compensation was fixed as a multiple of the income of intermediaries from their estates. In most of the States higher multiples were allowed to persons in the lower-income groups. Abolition of intermediaries was to lead to increase in the amount of revenue accruing to the State. Compensation payments were to be financed out of these increases.

Land Held by Tenants directly from Intermediaries. In most of the States the tenants-in-chief holding land directly from an intermediary were brought into direct contact with the State and the rights of the intermediaries in their lands were acquired by the State. There were, however, certain exceptions to this rule. In the case of the latter only special categories of tenants were brought into direct relationship with the State. The remaining categories of tenants continued to hold land under the former intermediaries.

In some States tenants possessed permanent and transferable rights and it was not considered necessary to confer further rights upon them. There were other States where tenants were required to make payments in order to acquire rights of ownership. In certain other States either larger rights were conferred upon tenants or their rents were reduced without any direct payment being required of them.

The abolition of intermediaries brought about certain important changes in the agrarian structure of the former intermediary areas. As a consequence of the new laws, the ownership of vast areas of 'tenancy lands' was transferred from the former intermediaries to the State, and the landlords were deprived of the right of collecting rents on these lands. They were also relieved of the responsibility of paying land revenue on them. The rents realised by these intermediaries were invariably much higher than the revenues paid by them to the State. The landlords lost thereby not only their control over vast areas of land but also the sources of substantial rental incomes as well.

Further, as a sequel to the same process there emerged a body of tenants whose connexions with the former intermediaries were snapped and who enjoyed semi-proprietary rights (permanent and hereditary rights) over the lands under their cultivation. Under the new laws it was also open to the more affluent and substantial elements among them to purchase proprietary rights and thus consolidate their position as full-fledged peasant proprietors.

On the other hand, the provision permitted landlords to retain *Sir* and *Khudkasht* lands which enabled the large landowners to claim substantial areas of land even by evicting their tenants and thus remain at the top of the economic hierarchy in rural areas. It was generally assumed that the *Sir* and *Khudkasht* lands were under the ' personal cultivation ' of landlords.

Thus, the scheme of Zamindari Abolition was designed in such a manner that far from creating preconditions for the elimination of non-cultivating interests and the transfer of land rights to the actual tillers of these lands, a substantial part of the total land resources remained in the hands of erstwhile landlords who were themselves not the actual cultivators of these lands. On the abolition of intermediaries, the newly created land rights could broadly be classified as follows:

(a) former intermediaries who were recognised as landowners on their home-farms and lands under their personal cultivations;

(b) superior tenants who held lands now directly under the State;

and (c) inferior tenants who held lands from either the landlords or superior tenants.

It is evident that over large areas of land the problem of land to the actual tiller continued to be as serious as before. The tenancy legislation, as the following account will show, tackled this problem only partially.

Tenancy Legislation in Intermediary and Ryotwari Areas

In the intermediary areas tenancy reforms were proposed with a view to rationalise the rights and obligations of various classes of tenants. These in most cases formed part of the legislation for abolition of intermediaries. In the ryotwari areas, tenancy reforms constituted the core of the land legislation. The tenancy problem had been aggravated over past years and called for urgent attention both in the Zamindari as well as in the ryotwari areas. A number of factors had contributed to the gravity of the problem. Firstly, intermediaries very rarely took interest in the cultivation of their home-farm lands and in most cases these lands were leased to tenants. Secondly, even tenants holding lands under the landlords very often leased out their lands to sub-tenants. Thirdly, in the ryotwari areas of Andhra, Bombay, Madras, Mysore and in the States of peasant proprietorship like Punjab, parts of Rajasthan, Delhi and Manipur, a considerable proportion of land held by ryots or peasant proprietors was actually cultivated by tenants. Thus, the tenancy problem concerned generally the following classes of tenants:

(1) tenants of home-farm lands in the intermediary areas;

(2) sub-tenants in the intermediary areas;

(3) tenants holding land from the tenants in the ryotwari areas;

and (4) share-croppers who were in some areas not included in the definition of the term ' tenant ' though they had all the characteristic features of the tenants.

In respect of the above classes of tenants the following recommendations had been made in the Plan :—

(a) regulation of rent;

(b) security of tenure; and

(c) right of purchase for the tenants.

Regulation of Rent : The Plan had recommended that rent should not exceed one-fourth or one-fifth of the produce. The actual provision embodied in State legislations in this regard showed wide variations. In very few States the rents were brought down to one-fourth or less of the produce. In certain other States it was fixed at one-third of the produce while in some others it exceeded even one-third of the produce.

That the legislation in States did not always provide for scaling down of rents was only one aspect of the matter. It is noteworthy that even when land laws provided for reduction of rent it was difficult to enforce it. Further, the regulation of crop-share rent was beset with still more serious difficulties. In areas subject to heavy population pressure on scarce land resources, the enormous competition for land exercised an upward pressure on rents and in such a situation legislative provisions for reduction of rents remained more or less on paper. Rent regulation was itself dependent on the effectiveness of other related measures of land reforms (security of tenure, distribution of surplus land acquired from large holdings to the landless population, etc.) and upon the bargaining power and organised strength of the tenants to get these provisions actually enforced.

On the whole, during the period of the Plan the rental burden on the tenants might not have registered any serious increase; any appreciable scaling down of the prevailing levels of rent, however, appeared to be most unlikely.

Security of Tenure : Security of tenure for tenants had been one of the important recommendations of the Plan. The question of security for tenants was, however, interlinked with the question of landlords' right to resume land for personal cultivation. The nature and extent of restrictions on the right of resumption, therefore, constituted the core of the problem of security of tenure. Provision for security of tenure adopted by different States during the Plan showed very wide variations. They assumed mainly the following forms :—

(1) No right of resumption was granted to the landlords and the tenants holding land on a particular date acquired permanent and heritable rights.

(2) The londlord was granted the permission to resume land over a limited area subject to the condition that a minimum area or portion of land was left with the tenants.

(3) A limit was imposed on the extent of land which a landlord could resume for cultivation but there was no provision for the tenant to retain a minimum area for cultivation.

It is noteworthy that in their attempt to bring about an adjustment between the interests of the landlords and the tenants the provisions adopted in different States in many cases went against the interests of the tenants.

In the first place, while resumption of land was to be permitted only to those landlords who were keen to engage in personal cultivation, the definition of the term ' personal cultivation ' in most cases was kept so loose that in all cases it invariably included cultivation through farm servants or hired labourers. Further, under this definition crop-sharing arrangements having all the characteristics of tenancy could be ignored and crop-sharers could be treated as labourers or partners in cultivation. In no case did ' personal cultivation ' involve actual physical participation in major processes of cultivation. Thus under these provisions even those landlords who either let out their holdings to tenants-at-will and share-croppers or got them cultivated by farm servants or labourers were free to resume land for personal cultivation by disregarding the rights and interests of the actual tillers of the soil. Whatever limited safeguards were there in the legislations of certain States against indiscriminate resumption of land by landlords remained by and large on paper since the State Governments were not prepared to decisively interpose themselves between the landlords and the tenants with a view to protecting the interests of the latter. The tenants, on the other hand, had neither the bargaining power nor the necessary organisation to ensure the effective implementation of the beneficial features of the tenancy legislations. In fact, the scheme which was intended to grant greater security of tenure to the tenants, in practice served to aggravate the problem of insecurity of the large masses of tenants. Consequently, in the wake of resumption of lands by landlords, large-scale dispossession of tenants took place all over the country which to a large extent defeated the very purpose of tenancy reform. As has been very aptly remarked: " There have been more evictions and changes of tenants during the years following the tenancy legislation than in any previous period in recent history. " Further, " in a number of cases the superior economic and social position of the landowning class enabled it to secure voluntary surrenders of tenancies. "

Ownership for Tenants : The First Plan had recommended the conferment of ownership rights on the tenants of non-resumable areas of land. The provision incorporated in the land laws of different States in this respect were such that only a small section of the tenants could benefit from them and acquire ownership rights. In certain States the right of acquisition of ownership rights was granted to a limited section of tenants while the vast masses of tenants outside these categories were excluded from these rights. For instance, the right of purchase was available only to protected tenants in Hyderabad, to occupancy tenants in Madhya Pradesh and in Punjab only to those who had been in continuous possession for 6 years. In Bihar an optional right of purchase was given and the tenant could exercise it only after 20 years.

Again, the terms on which the rights could be purchased were not always favourable to and very often were beyond the reach of tenants. In these cases the advantages accruing as a result of acquisition of these rights were far outweighed by the burdens to be incurred and the payments to be made in the process of acquiring them. The compensation payable to the land-owners was generally recoverable in full from the tenants except only in a few States. It has been very aptly remarked: " All through the years the burden of maintaining these landlords has fallen upon the peasantry. Now they are called upon to bear the full cost of removing the burden. " It is no wonder that " judged by the amount of land purchased by tenants and the number of tenants who have been able to acquire ownership right " the scheme for conferment of ownership rights could not be said to have produced " significant results ". Even from the developmental point of view it was misconceived in as much as it envisaged the diversion and dissipation of the very limited financial resources of the tenants towards the purchase of land rights.

Ceiling on Landholdings : The recommendation of the Plan in regard to imposition of ceiling on land holdings was implemented only to the extent that ceilings on future acquisition of land were fixed in a number of States. In regard to the ceiling on existing holdings legislation was enacted only in a few States The postponement of the most crucial plank of the land reforms programme had very serious implications in as much as the effectiveness of the measures aiming at security of tenure for the tenants was vitally dependent upon the simultaneous imposition of ceiling on the area of land which any landholder could be permitted to retain. The postponement of ceilings on *existing* holdings enabled the landowners to frustrate the provisions which had been made to ensure security to the tenants since there was, in practice, no limit on the land area from which tenants could be evicted in the process of resumption of land for personal cultivation.

In a nutshell, the main developments as a sequel to the land legislations during the First Plan were as follows :

(1) In the first place, instead of the slogan of ' land to the tiller ' for all the classes of tenants being implemented, conditions were created only for certain special classes of tenants to enjoy security and proprietary rights over their lands. Over substantial areas of land (chiefly on the lands under the ' personal cultivation ' of landlords and also their home-farms) there continued to be ample scope for exploitation on the basis of landlord-tenant relationships.

The First Plan, therefore, failed both in its conception as well as implementation to eliminate the non-cultivating interests from land. The development of a free peasantry secure in its rights over lands under its cultivation remained an unfinished task.

(2) Secondly, by planning substantial areas of land in the hands of landlords as their *Sir* and *Khudkasht* and by giving legal and official sanction to entrepreneurial and supervisory role in agriculture (as distinct from the responsibility of genuine self-cultivations), the land legislations tended to favour the emergence of a class of capitalist farmers from among the ex-landlords and the upper strata of the peasantry.

This was the basic direction of change in the agrarian structure in the country as a whole notwithstanding the variations in each State in respect of the checks and safeguards provided against indiscriminate resumption by landlords and for the protection of tenants.

Land Policy During the Second Plan

The Second Plan reiterated as the immediate goal of land reforms " the establishment of an agrarian economy based predominantly upon peasant proprietorship." One of the foremost objectives of the Second Plan was the reduction in the inequality of distribution of income and wealth and a more even distribution of economic power. In applying this principle to the agrarian sector, the Plan stated: "In view of the existing pattern of distribution and size of agricultural holdings, redistribution of land in excess of ceiling may yield relatively limited results. Nevertheless, it is important that some effective step should be taken in this direction during the Second Five Year Plan so as to afford opportunities to landless section of the rural population to gain in social status and to feel a sense of opportunity with the other sections of the community. Reduction of disparities in the ownership of land is also essential for developing a cooperative rural economy, for cooperation thrives best in homogeneous groups in which there are no large inequalities."

In place of the vague concept of cooperative village management introduced in the First Plan, the Second Plan advanced the proposal for cooperative farming. The main task during the Second Five Year Plan was " to take such essential steps as will provide sound foundations for the development of cooperative farming, so that over a period of ten years or so a substantial proportion of agricultural lands are cultivated on cooperative lines." The approach of the Second Plan was further reinforced by the Resolution on the Agrarian Organisational Pattern adopted by the Congress Party in its Session at Nagpur.

Land Ceiling Proposals in the Second Five Year Plan

The major new development during the Second Plan was the more definite assurance for ceilings on existing landholdings. In the following the principal questions posed for consideration in the Second Plan are taken up for discussion one by one.

Land to which ceilings should apply: It was recommended that ceilings should apply to owned land (including land under permanent and heritable rights) held under personal cultivation. In regard to the important question as to whether ceilings should apply to holdings of individuals or to holdings of families, it was preferred that ceilings should apply to the whole area held by a farmer since in agriculture the appropriate unit was the family rather than the individual. In this connection the term ' family ' was to include husband, wife and dependent sons, daughters and grandchildren. The Plan, however, left the matter inconclusive and the final decision was to be taken by each State government. At the same time, the authors of the Plan were fully conversant with the fact that " if individual holdings are taken as the basis for the enforcement of ceilings, there would be greater scope for malafide transfers and special measures need to be devised to deal with the problem. In fact, it categorically stated that " during the past two or three years malafide transfers had been effected by landowners with the intention of circumventing ceiling on holdings " and recommended action to prevent such transfers in the future. It suggested that " transfers of lands which have already taken place should be reviewed. In respect of lands, if any, retained by a transfer the question should be considered whether the ceiling should be determined as if the transfer had not taken place. "

Level of Ceiling : In regard to the level at which ceilings should be fixed the Plan recommended : " In view of the fact that only a small fraction of agricultural holdings can be designated as large holdings, it will be convenient to place the ceiling at three times the family holding. If the ceiling is determined with reference to individual holdings, it might not be necessary to take further account of the number of members in an individual owner's family. On the other land, if the ceiling applies to the area held by a family it would be necessary to prescribe some method for taking account of the number of members in the family. " In this connection the Plan referred to the Committee of the Panel on Land Reforms which was of the view that " where the number of members of a family is larger than five the ceiling of the family holding may be raised to a maximum of six family holdings. "

The determination of the area which should comprise a family holding was also left to the discretion of each State " which was to specify according to the conditions of different regions, classes of soil, irrigation etc., the area of land which may be declared to be a family holding".

The Plan further suggested that " in those parts of the country where cultivable wastelands are available and a sufficient number of cultivators not easy to obtain a ceiling may not be necessary at this stage or may be set at a higher level than that suggested here. Similarly, there may be areas in which the level of the ceiling may be lower because of the high density of population. "

Exemption from ceiling : The Plan was of the view that the following categories of farms could be considered for exemption from the operation of ceilings :

" (1) tea, coffee and rubber plantations;

(2) orchards where they constitute reasonably compact area;

(3) specialised farms engaged in cattle-breeding, dairying, wool-raising etc.;

(4) sugarcane farms operated by sugar factories;

(5) efficiently managed farms which consist of compact blocks on which heavy investment or permanent structural improvement have been made and whose break-up is likely to lead to a fall in production."

It was at the same time indicated that the above were only general suggestions which should be adapted to the needs and conditions of each State.

Compensations : On the question of compensation to be paid to owners whose areas are acquired and the price of land to be recovered from persons to whom allotments are made, the major consideration to be kept in view was that any additional liability on the government and a high burden on the allottees should be avoided.

Schemes of Settlements : In respect of settlement on land acquired in consequence of the imposition of ceiling, displaced tenants, farmers with uneconomic holdings, and landless workers were to receive preference. Settlement as far as possible was to be made on cooperative lines.

The first thing that strikes one's attention in the above account is the glaring contradiction between the goals of land policy adopted by the Second Plan and the recommendations made for the realisation of these goals. This contradiction appears to be still more serious if we keep in view the trend of changes in the agrarian structure as a result of the policies adopted and implemented during the First Plan. As pointed out earlier, in the course of the First Plan, substantial land-owning interests had succeeded, by and large, in nullifying the beneficial features and provisions of the land reform legislations and had solidly entrenched themselves in the rural economy as the most privileged class of landholders. The benefits of tenancy reforms had accrued at best to the upper sections of tenants, who along with the erstwhile landlords now stood at the top of the economic hierarchy in rural areas controlling the vital nerve-strings of the rural economy. Further, even before the Second Plan had been framed, indications were available to the effect that large land-owners had been able to forestall ceilings. They had "effected innumerable partitions of family properties with the aim of making units of ownership appear smaller than they actually are, so that the landlords will be able to slip under the proposed ceilings." There had even been "many transfers to relatives outside the immediate family, to caste fellows and to friends." It was also reported that "in view of the special consideration urged for efficiently managed farms (the breaking up of which would presumably lead to a fall in output) some large owners have thought it wise to purchase tractors. Since the land reforms typically place the holdings of cooperatives and joint-stock companies outside their purview more than a few landlord families have transformed themselves into cooperatives. Some affluent landlords have also organised themselves into cooperatives for the production and refining of sugarcane."

Viewed in the light of the above developments which had occurred in the rural areas on the eve of the Second Plan the recommendations and suggestions made by the planners were hardly capable of achieving the goals which had been set for the Second Plan. Far from reflecting a determination and earnestness to formulate serious proposals for imposing ceilings on land holdings and to suggest effective methods of implementing them, the Plan left every major decision to the discretion of the State governments whose lukewarm support, if not antipathy, and resistance to every progressive and pro-peasant measure of land reforms had been fully revealed during the period of the First Plan. It was evident that the wide latitude given to State governments (in defining a family holding, in determining the level of ceilings, in deciding whether ceiling should apply to individual or family holdings, and in fixing exemptions or methods of distribution of surplus lands) was bound to open the door for endless manipulations and manoeuvrings, pulls and pressures, in a manner that the very object of ceilings was likely to be put in jeopardy and even defeated. As the following brief survey of the main features of the legislations for land ceilings in different States shows, the prospect of redistribution of land as a sequel to land ceilings was very remote.

In the first place, taking advantage of the recommendations of the Plan, the State governments did not adopt a uniform pattern for imposing land ceilings. These variations in pattern did not appear "to bear any correlation with variations in regional conditions in respect either of pressure of population on land or the density of population, or the average size of agricultural holdings or the non-availability or abundance of culturable waste land in the States. In most of the States, the level of ceiling was generally much higher than that proposed in the Plan. In some States, the ceiling was related to the level of income from land; in some others the concept of the standard area was adopted. Different ceilings were fixed for specified classes of land in some States; in some, it was related to the rental value or land revenue assessments. A few examples are enough to show that there was a general upgrading of the levels of ceilings in most of the States. In Bombay, it was proposed to fix ceilings at an area yielding a net annual income of Rs. 3,600; in Andhra it was to be imposed at an area yielding a net annual income of Rs. 5,400 as against Rs. 3,600 enacted earlier in the Hyderabad Tenancy Act. Subsequently, a bill for the entire State of Andhra Pradesh prescribed a uniform ceiling of 4½ times the family holding (i. e. 27 to 312 acres). In Bihar it varied from 30 acres of canal flow irrigated land to 90 acres of class II land; in Madhya Pradesh it varied from 28 acres of irrigated land to 84 acres of dry land; in Rajasthan the ceiling limit was 30 standard acres (one standard acre being equal to the extent of land yielding 10 maunds of wheat or other crops of equivalent value) for an average family of 5 members or less. Additional areas were to be allowed for each member in excess of 5 subject to an outside limit of 60 standard acres for the family. In U. P. the permissible area for a family of 5 members was 40 acres of class I land, 60 acres of class II land, and 80 acres of class III land. A family of 8 members or more was, however, entitled to 64 acres of class I land, 96 acres of class II land, or 128 acres of class III land. Kerala stands out as the only state where a relatively lower ceiling was fixed at 15 acres of class I land (7½ acres for bachelors). The effective ceiling was, however, likely to get further pushed up as a result of the other provisions of the ceiling legislations.

In some States the ceiling applied to land held by a person and in others to the area held by a family. The provision making the individual rather than the family the basis of ceiling was a clear indication to the large landowners as to what they should do in order to circumvent land ceilings and retain their hold over the maximum part of their landed property. No wonder that the landowners, forestalling these provisions effected partitions of family properties on a large scale so that even if ceilings were imposed, the ownership pattern would not be appreciably disturbed. Again, in those States where a person and not the family had been adopted as the unit, further allowance had been made for the size of a family.

In the States where ceiling applied to the aggregate area held by a family, each branch of the joint family automatically became the unit. Partition of family property was provided for even in those States where the family was taken as the unit for imposing ceiling. Thus in U. P., where the ceiling applied to the holding of a family (which included unseparated children), a child including grandchildren by a deceased male lineal descendant is deemed to be separate where the land is recorded separately in his name or where his share had been declared under a family settlement or a decree of court. Provisions of this type constituted very serious loopholes giving legal sanction to partitions effected deliberately with a view to evade land ceiling.

Another big loophole affecting the efficacy of land ceilings was the absence of adequate measures to prevent transfers of land effected with the same end in view. The main idea behind land ceilings was to use them as an instrument of re-distribution of land. This would be possible only if large holdings were cut down to a smaller size and the surplus acquired thereby distributed to the land-hungry population. Transfers made by landowners themselves would have the effect of reducing large holdings held by them without bringing about any alteration in the pattern of distribution of land. The main purpose behind transfers by landowners was to reduce the area available for redistribution. The Size of Holdings Committee of the Land Reforms Panel had, therefore, recommended that " any transfer or lease made after a given date should be disregarded in determining the surplus area. The date could be fixed by each State Government in the light of its own circumstances. "

Provisions for the review of transfers which were effected much before the introduction of the ceiling legislation were incorporated only in a few

States (viz., Bombay, Punjab, West Bengal and the Union Territory of Delhi). In other States there was either no provision for disregarding transfers or provision was made for disregarding only such transfers as were made after the introduction or enactment of the legislation. In Hyderabad, Bihar, Madhya Pradesh, Mysore and Orissa, no provision even for transfers effected after the enactment of the law was made. In Kerala, however, transfers effected after December 18, 1957, were deemed to be transfers calculated to defeat the provisions of the law and as such were to be invalid. Under the Madhya Pradesh Bill transfers and partitions made after the publication of the Bill (but before the commencement of the Act) were to be declared void if it was found that they were made to defeat the provision of the Act. After the commencement of the Act transfers could be made to specified categories of persons. A landholder was free to transfer surplus lands to such persons by sale during a period of two years from the commencement of the Act. Further, in most of the States there was no check against indiscriminate partitions of land amongst near and remote members of the family irrespective of whether they maintained or proposed to maintain any vital connection with land for pursuing agricultural activities. It had been widely known that in the recent past partitions of family property had been increasingly resorted to as an escape from land ceilings.

In the light of the above it can be said without exaggerating that just as during the First Plan the provision of resumption of land by landlords constituted the greatest source of threat to the security of tenants and served as the instrument for their large-scale evictions, similarly transfers and partitions of landed property could not but have served as the most effective method for evasion of land ceilings during the period of the Second Plan. This is fully corroborated by the experience, for instance, of Punjab and Hyderabad. It has been reported that in Hyderabad the surplus land now being found is very much less than the estimate that was originally made. This is said to be " because the Hyderabad law did not contain adequate provision with regard to transfers made with the object of evading law." Similarly, in regard to Punjab it has been reported that " according to the ownership pattern known to exist in 1956, about 50,000 landlords had between them nearly 4,00,000 acres of land which could be declared surplus. But because of the subsequent transfers a new law may be able to discover a surplus of only 1,50,000 acres."

Provision of exemption of certain categories of farm land from the operation of ceilings constituted another severe loophole in the legislation for land ceilings. These exemptions had been provided for in the case of almost all the States. Apart from transfer, these exemptions were bound to lead to a substantial reduction of the surplus land available for redistribution. It is common knowledge that, during the past years, there had been a veritable rage in the planting of groves, establishment of large-scale and mechanised farms and formation of co-operative societies by ex-landlords and by cultivators, largely with a view to forestall land ceilings. The provision for exemption of these various categories of farms from the operation of ceilings would pave the way for the landlords playing only the supervisory and entrepreneurial role in agriculture to dominate the rural economy and even the newly-formed co-operative societies.

Agrarian Structure as a Sequel to the Land Reforms

From the foregoing survey of land reform legislations during the last decade it is evident that the land reform programmes have consistently drifted away from the course of a radical solution of the land problem in the interests of the cultivating peasantry. This is further confirmed by an examination of the principal interest groups connected with land which have emerged in the rural areas as a sequel to the land laws proposed or enacted during the First and Second Five Year Plans.

Big Landowners : At the top of the hierarchy of landed interests stand the former landlords who have been able to retain ownership of large areas of land as their ' home-farms ' and ' land under personal cultivation ' by evicting from these lands the tenants in degrees varying from State to State, and also by successfully forestalling the legislation for land ceilings. The huge amounts of compensation provided (and partially paid) to them are expected to add substantially to their financial resources. The land legislations have created the preconditions for the utilisation of these holdings for purposes of large-scale farming by the former landlords.

Rich Peasants : The upper layer of the tenants having relatively bigger holdings and larger financial resources has been able, under the new land laws, to consolidate its position and purchase ownership rights. This section of the tenants has been the principal beneficiary from the tenancy reforms. In certain States the land revenue paid by them to the State has reduced to 50 per cent on the acquisition of full-fledged proprietary rights.

Inferior Tenants : These comprise the most numerous class of small cultivating interests whose economic status even after the land reforms remains as depressed as before. There has been no change in respect of the rent revenue payment demanded from them or the rights enjoyed by them over their lands. The only difference is that now they face directly, not the landlords, but the State. Even when they have been able to retain control over their lands which they cultivated, they do not enjoy the rights of transfer. In the absence of credit-worthiness based on land-ownership they are thus deprived of even the credit facilities offered by co-operative institutions. They have, therefore, no escape from the former landlords on whom they continue to be dependent in a number of ways.

Tenants-at-will, Share-Croppers and Farm Labourers : At the bottom of the scale are the tenants-at-will, share-croppers and farm labourers without any rights over the land of which they are the actual tillers. In areas where the pressure of population is acute, they continue to cultivate the home-farms and other lands of the landlords without enjoying any security. In other areas where the landlords have undertaken large-scale farming they have been the first to be evicted from the fields and have in most cases been re-employed on these very holdings on terms and conditions which are not entirely free from the semi-feudal hangovers.

Conclusion

It can be seen that the land reform measures during the First and Second Five Year Plans have proved to be favourable for the promotion of a class of capitalist farmers from the erstwhile landlords and the relatively better-off sections of the tenantry. This is evident from the fact that as between the rentier landlord leasing out his land to tenants or share-croppers, on the one hand, and the landlord undertaking cultivation through hired labour on the other, the land legislations offer support and protection to the latter and envisage the gradual restriction or dying out of the former. As between the upper strata of the tenants, on the one hand, and the vast masses of small and middle tenants on the other, the land reform measures are strongly biased in favour of the former. They offer only limited security and protection to the latter and that too with a view primarily to prevent the stresses and strains in rural areas developing into social explosions.

The above developments pose very serious problems for the future of India's economic planning, its goals of achieving rapid economic development in consonance with the establishment of a 'socialistic pattern of society' within the framework of a political democracy.

(1) In the first place, even from the narrow point of view of promoting rapid economic development in the rural sector, it may legitimately be asked whether the set-up emerging as a sequel to land reforms provides the most appropriate and favourable institutional framework. As pointed out earlier, the new element of dynamism introduced into the rural economy is constituted of the gradual emergence of a class of agricultural entrepreneurs and big peasants as the spearhead of the economic change and developmental effort. The prospects of this new class delivering the goods in the Indian context appear to be vitiated by certain fundamental limitations under which economic development has to be achieved in India in sharp contrast to the circumstances obtaining in certain countries of the West at the time of their economic growth. It seems necessary to stress that in these countries the *per capita* availability of land was large and the proportion of farm population to total population small. Under these circumstances there did exist, historically speaking, great scope for the growth and development of private large-scale farming. The dominant principle of land policy in these countries was, therefore, the 'maintenance of the climate of economic freedom' and 'flexibility in resource use' and the main stress was laid, with a view to increasing agricultural efficiency, on 'land utilisation' and 'farm management measures' rather

than on 'institutional reforms'. In an underdeveloped country like India, on the other hand, the importance of drastic institutional reforms (specially redistribution of land) has time and again been stressed as a *pre-condition* to any serious developmental effort. The main factors determining this sharp difference in emphasis are that in countries like India the man-land ratio is inordinately high; the agrarian structure is characterised by concentration of land at one pole and a vast, complete or almost complete landlessness at another; and finally, the prospect of siphoning away a substantial part of the surplus agricultural population into non-agricultural employment is, at least for the present, very remote. The institutional frame-work most appropriate to conditions prevailing in India logically appears to be that which maximises at once the scope for intensive use of its massive unemployed and idle manpower and most efficient and economical exploitation of land. The relevant question, then, is, how far does the consolidation of the emergent private large-scale farming as the dominant pattern of the Indian economy satisfy this dual conditions ?

(2) In the second place, the social goals of India's planned development as embodied in the concept of the 'socialistic pattern of society' are no less vital than the economic goals. In a country like India, 'for the larger part, inequalities arise from long-established features of a traditional society, such as feudal rights and tenures, or privileges and handicaps, associated with the social structure'. Apart from the grave disparities in landownership as reflected in the concentration of land at one pole and vast landlessness at another, specially significant has been the concentration of land in the hands mostly of the upper castes and dominant peasant castes to the exclusion of lower and backward castes from landownership. In this context, the significance of land reforms as an instrument of removal of economic disparities between different classes and the social upliftment of traditionally under-privileged sections of the rural society cannot be over-estimated. It is difficult at the same time to over-estimate the gravity of the consequences resulting from the failure of the land reforms and contributing to the accentuation of class and caste tensions in the rural areas. This implies not only that the inequalities associated with the traditional socio-economic structure are being basically preserved, but also that the opportunities for the traditionally privileged groups to spearhead and effect economic growth without drastic alterations in the existing socio-economic structure is widening, rather than narrowing, the social and economic distance between the different classes and castes in the rural society.

(3) Finally, the implications of these developments for the nascent Indian political democracy are also quite important. On the one hand, the new concentrations of economic and social power in the rural areas emerging as a sequel to land reforms and deriving economic strength from the forces of economic development during the last decade exhibit strong natural proclivities towards anti-democratic adaptations of the country's

political structure. On the other hand, the failure of the underprivileged sections of society to effect a significant advance in their economic and social position is bound to shake their faith in the effectiveness of the present democratic apparatus as an instrument of social and economic transformation in favour of the masses.

7

LAND REFORMS

DANIEL THORNER

LAND REFORM laws ostensibly passed for the benefit of the under privileged have not basically altered India's village structure. The small minority of oligarchs have had wit and resource enough to get around these laws in which, in any event, the loopholes were so large as to give them ample manoeuvring ground. By passing themselves off, whether legally or illegally, as tillers and cultivators, the village oligarchs have gone on running India's rural life. Their un-interrupted presence in power means that the forces of the " depressor " continue to operate strongly in the countryside.

If lasting agrarian progress is to be made on a wide front, and a proper basis laid for economic development, then the central elements of India's problem will require to be dealt with in a much more direct fashion. The States will have to surrender their claim, super-landlord style, to " rent " and devise a more suitable rational basis for obtaining their revenues from land. The proprietary rights (below those of the State) of non-cultivators will have to be so abridged that the existing gap between " right holding " and cultivation-in-the-fields can be closed. Thereby the older basis for capital-deprived cultivation and associated low-level production can be removed and a powerful impetus given to more effective and more efficient units of production in agriculture. In the process the older concentration of power in the hands of the village minority can be reduced and the nexus of forces constituting the " depressor " broken up. All of this is a tall order. It is easier to say, abstractly, that these steps should be taken than to suggest realistic ways, under prevailing Indian conditions, of actually putting them into effect.

We may begin, however, by putting forward one fundamental principle: lands and the fruits thereof are to belong to those who do the tilling, the tillers being defined as those who plough, harrow, sow, weed, and harvest. In consequence, the income from land of non-tillers is to be brought to an end (not necessarily overnight, but within a stipulated period of time). This will result in a major redistribution of rural income, to the advantage of those who work in the fields, and to the disadvantage of those who do not. In the process, income arising from property rights in land will dwindle and, in the course of time, fade away and disappear.

Before discussing how this principle may best be put into effect, let

---

*Reproduced from *The Agrarian Prospect in India,* by Daniel Thorner, pp. 79-84.

us first explore some of its possible implications. Control of a very considerable amount of land will pass from rent-receivers and other soft-handed folk to tenants, crop-sharers and labourers, i. e., those who have long been out in the fields beneath the hot sun, working the land. It is hard to think of anything more likely to lift up the spirits of masses of depressed or " backward " folk. Carried out properly, such a step might even lead to a real burst of enthusiasm, a genuine release of energy among the working peasantry. Their rights in land would increase and so would their share of the land's product. They would forthwith want more food, clothing and non-luxury housing materials; in time they would want other commodities, some of the better things of life; and more education for their children. In the language of the economist, there should be a very sizeable increase in effective demand; hence an improved rural market for urban manufactures, and an associated improved urban market for rural raw or semi-processed materials. With bigger and better markets for city and country products there would be more rural and urban employment. If we let our minds soar, we can conceive of a beneficial *upward* spiral of development. We could then cease to fear the current bugaboo of increased production—limited demand—falling prices. In short, there would be a solid institutional foundation for economic development. The attractive vista would be opened up of raising the existing low per capita, " social capital, " i. e., with more education and an improved grasp of the rudiments of science and engineering, the Indian rural and urban economy would be able to make better use of technological improvements and more complex forms of organization. As a long-term goal one could think of the displacement of cheap, half-hearted or incompetent labour, by a more rationally trained, better educated, and more competent labour force. Such a force is likely to be more efficient and more expensive; on both grounds employers would be driven to, and would benefit from the use of more labour-saving devices and the spurring of general technological development. The distant prospect is presented of India's engineering backwardness yielding to widespread modernization.

Let us now return to earth and explore further the practical side of carrying out the principle of land to the tiller-in-the-fields. Properly understood and executed, such a proposal could avoid bogging up in the ceilings issue and could escape the false dilemma of the land tenure reform *vs.* organization of production controversy. The essence of the proposal made here is quite simple: those who own land but don't work it would lose their (lucrative) paper rights; those who are already out in the fields working the land would gain the exclusive right to work that land, or, if they have weak rights, would gain the improved exclusive right. Thus the control of land would pass directly from non-tilling owners or tenants to working tenants (whether recognized leaseholders or customary tenants without formal documents), to cropsharers, and to farm servants and other regularly employed labourers. In the process, the existing work unit of the actual cultivator-in-the-field would become the *de facto* unit of ownership. Thus the existing cultivation pattern and the new ownership pattern would completely overlap and become identical. At the first instance there would arise neither the highly complex problem of organizing co-operatives nor the very thorny issue of imposing ceilings and redistributing land. Instead we would be executing a much more clear-cut and understandable programme; " Leave the land alone; redistribute the proprietors. "

One could think of a variety of measures which might give effect to such a proposal. Legislation might provide that at the death of non-tilling owners their rights in land could pass only to those who already are actual tillers. Or, to achieve more immediate results, legislation might lay down that no further transfers of agricultural land may occur except to those who are now tillers and who propose to work the land with their own hands. Or legislation might take away forthwith the rights in the land of the non-tillers. In this case, token compensation might be provided for former proprietors possessing ample means; rehabilitation grants could be offered to assist former proprietors of limited resources to take up other occupations.

If India's recent agrarian history demonstrates anything, it is that doing and saying nothing is preferable to taking small steps slowly and timidly. In Indian conditions if you do not totally reject the principle of non-working cultivators, you cannot prevent the village oligarchs from acting as landlords. As soon as you leave the door barely open for property income to non-working proprietors—which you do when you permit land ownership to exist unassociated with labour in the fields—you allow all the evils of concentration of power at the village level to come trotting back in. As long as some peasants are without land or very short of land, they will be at the mercy of those who are allowed to have land without working it. The whole world of organized subterfuge, with which so many villages are already replete, will continue unabated.

In basic concept the programme of abolishing proprietary rights is clearly and easily understandable at the village level. It is tangible and testable in village terms. Every peasant in the village knows who does what kind of work under what terms, in whose fields. Any outsider, even a " city slicker, " can soon tell who works in a village and who watches : all that is required is a glance either at the clothes (*safaid posh* don't dirty themselves in the fields), or at the forehead or back of the neck (you don't get a cracked sun-dried skin sitting on your shaded upstairs balcony); or by shaking hands (when a city person finds that *gaonwala's* hands are softer than his own, he can draw his own conclusion).

The proposal to take land away from those who don't work, and to leave it with those who do, is not new. Of all demands it is the one most frequently made in most parts of rural India by the working peasants themselves. It does not originate from outside, but from the very core of village realities. The heart of power, prestige, and standing in the village lies in land. Put land in the hands of those who are working it and you crack the existing concentration of power.

I do not intend to suggest that such a step will be a " cure all " to India's agrarian problem. If it is put on the statute book efforts will be organized to deal with it as with all other land reform laws, i. e., by evasion. It seems to me, however, that legislation of this type would prove the most difficult of all to evade. In one stroke it would establish the peasant's *legal* and *moral* right to the land he works; and it would encourage the working peasantry to join together to attain or protect the rights granted to them by law. The Indian rural scene, as I read it, is ready to yield to any *sustained* pressure for change. All sections of rural society are either hopeful or fearful of change. Even the Tanjore mirasdars, I believe, are prepared to give in; their strong language of recent months mostly represents an effort to extract the best possible terms from Government in exchange for the surrender of their highly privileged position. The most sustained resistance to change may possibly come from elements like the U. P.'s new *pakka haveliwale*, the bare *kisans* lately grown into *maliks*; newly won privileges are those given up most reluctantly.

It may appear to be a weakness of such a programme that it calls for no direct assault forthwith on the problem of economic organisation in agriculture. Fundamentally, however, the peasant families want land and they want land of their own. Their hunger for it is like that for water of travellers long lost in the desert and nearing a small, inadequate oasis. They see the water; they know it is not enough; but such as it is they must have it. Nothing else will do. In this setting the *agrarian* transformation must come first. Only then can there be a proper footing for the long needed rationalization of agricultural production. Until proprietary rights are ended, co-operatives won't stand a chance of working out successfully. Either they will fail or they will be dominated by the *maliks* and their friends.

In the last analysis the crucial question about these proposals is their bearing upon property rights. Much obscure and time-dissipating debate could be avoided if the participants would deal frankly with one central problem : where do they stand on property rights in land and the enjoyment of income based solely on such property rights. The fact is that all land reform from zamindari abolition downward amounts to an abridgement of property rights. The necessity for still further abridgement of such rights compelled the Central Government in 1955 to put through an amendment to the Constitution of India providing that the amount of compensation for property taken by Government could no longer be raised as a question in the Courts. The sanctity of property is also suffering from another attack: the cry for equality heard from all quarters today and the associated emphasis on the dignity of manual labour put in jeopardy the custom of permitting rentiers to derive an income solely from paper rights in land. It scarcely needs to be added that such rentiers have no place in a " socialistic pattern " of society, to which the Indian National Congress and the Government of India have formally committed themselves.

In the long run what holds out the best hope is any programme that will get the rural mass into motion, make them into a self-propelling force, generating their own energy. How often have we heard that in India everything is handed down from the top and that the process requires to be reversed. Whatever demerits our proposals may have, at least no one can say that they do not begin at the bottom.

A great deal of fundamental change is going on today among the working producers themselves—the labourers, tenants, and landowners. They are getting a better evaluation of themselves as people and of their economic contribution. They are casting a more realistic eye at the neighbours who have been riding on their backs. Land reforms have achieved less than was expected of them. Nonetheless, India's older agrarian order is on the way out.

SECTION X

COOPERATION, RURAL INDUSTRIES AND VILLAGE INSTITUTIONS

INTRODUCTION

AS OBSERVED earlier, Indian Rural Society is in transition. The Government is attempting to bring about a directed social change based on certain postulates. It has been trying to overcome the debacle of the Agrarian social order caused by the British Rulers. Along with Land Reforms, studied in the last section, the Government has been encouraging cooperation, building up various kinds of village institutions and has been striving to resurrect cottage industries. It is also endeavouring to create a new kind of administrative machinery which can reorganize the rural social system.

The present Section is comprised of three sets of selections giving a picture of these endeavours.

In the first set, there are three articles on 'Co-operatives'. Arun Chandra Guha in 'Cooperative as a Remedy' has given a vivid account of the 'cooperatives' as they are emerging in India after Independence. He has posed some crucial questions which deserve careful considerations. The selection from the famous General Report of the Rural Credit Survey entitled 'Village Cooperatives: An Analysis of Their Failure' though short, raises some of the most fundamental issues of social matrix within which the 'Cooperative Movement' has been developing in India. To Quote. "Failure of Cooperative Credit is explicable in terms of the total impracticability of any attempt to combine the very weak in competition with the very strong and expect them by themselves to create conditions, firstly, for their emancipation from the interests which oppose them, and secondly, for their social and economic development in the context of the severe disadvantages historically imposed by the structure of the type just described." According to the Report, there is a built-in social matrix wherein there is a great cleavage of interests in the village itself with big landholders, moneylenders, village traders etc., with their powerful institutional reserves on the one side and the medium and small cultivators on the other. Until new conditions favourable for the weaker sections are not created in rural society, the Cooperatives in the true sense cannot succeed. The creation of these new conditions will be opposed by the rural rich composed of big farmers, moneylenders and traders. Hence it shall have to be created by ruthlessly opposing them. This alone can inaugurate a new era of uninterrupted advance in agrarian India.

Has the 'State of Independent India' which claims to be a welfare state and which broadcasts that it represents masses, become an active agency undertaking the above mentioned task? Has it been adopting a bold and radical necessary policy which would make a qualitative break in the social set up by smashing the economic, social and political power of the rich? Has it been generating new institutional framework favourable to the poor?

Daniel Thorner provides one of the most comprehensive surveys of the cooperatives emerging after Independence. He concludes from his findings that the emerging cooperatives are controlled and run by the richer sections and are strengthening those strata.

The second set of selections deal with the trend of developments in Rural Industries. Rural Industries are supposed to be the next important source of livelihood and employment for rural masses. The selection from the Report of the Rural Credit Survey highlights the crucial obstacles to the growth of rural industries. The most important obstacle, according to the Report is the control over these industries by Karkhanadars, and a small-section of credit-providing, trading, and middle-men. The failure of the Government of India, after Independence, to vitalise Rural Industries is pithily indicated by the selection from the 'Report' of Balwant Rai Mehta Committee.

The third set of selections comprises two articles from the General Report of Rural Credit Survey. The first selection highlights the nature of administrative institutions which are emerging in Rural India and points out the following contradictions inherent in them. (i) The contradiction arising out of the needs of higher and lower echelons of administration; (ii) The contradiction between the requirements of showing certain achievements even though they are not. inherently possible; (iii) The liaison between administration and the rural rich and the upper caste groups in rural areas creating a situation whereby the proclaimed objective of fighting the rich is contradicted in practice; (iv) The supposed functional duty of Administrative machinery to encourage struggles of the weaker sections against a small minority of rural rich and thereby generating the ferment inrural areas and its Law and Order preserving role which opposes such a generation of ferment and thereby help and strengthen the rich. The second selection, while pointing out the inadequacy and inappropriateness of the extant rural institutions, points out how appropriate institutions cannot be created without breaking the influence of upper caste and upper classes over them. The article in fact warns that if this grip is not destroyed, these institutions will become instruments of the richer strata, and will be detrimental to the interests of the weaker sections of the rural people. Village Panchayats, Cooperatives, Schools and a large number of voluntary non-caste associations have been visualized as new associational devices by the Government. The effort on the part of the Government to evolve a web of institutional complex in rural areas is organized round two major devices called Panchayati Raj and Community Development Projects. We have separate sections to examine the functioning of these devices.

The three sets of selections in this Section, comprising seven readings, however, very pointedly reveal the malady that prevails in our Cooperative Movement, in the domain of Rural Industries as well as in the emerging administrative machinery and village institutions. Its chief features are —: (1) The cooperatives, village institutions and rural industries are becoming the preserves and the tools of the upper sections of the rural society who also happen to be the members of upper and intermediate castes; (2) The numerous associations, which have been emerging either as a result of new economic and political forces, or as a result of the Government's efforts to evolve agencies to implement its various programmes, have been found to have been monopolised by the very stratum from whose clutches the bulk of the people has to be liberated; (3) There is a peculiar liaison between the administrative officials and this upper stratum composed of both upperclasses and higher castes, resulting into the administration itself becoming a handmaid of this upper stratum.

All these are ominous tendencies from the point of view of a genuine reorganization of rural society. The implications of its role in influencing the patterns of social and cultural life in rural society are worth noting.

(*Author*)

Co-operation

1

COOPERATION AS A REMEDY*

ARUN CHANDRA GUHA

AFTER 15 years of intensive attempt to develop the country on a socialist or at least on an egalitarian basis, there is now a sort of pessimism as regards our progress in attaining the objectives. It is true both industrial and agricultural productions have gone up; it is true national income has also gone up; in social services like health and education we have made considerable progress. But now the question has arisen—how far we have been able to proceed towards an egalitarian society—if not towards a socialist society? That is the issue now before the nation. India has always depended on voluntary cooperation of the people. Under our Constitution, we accept the right of individuals to own and dispose of property; even for national and public purposes, property can be acquired only on payment of compensation; we cannot commandeer material resources and services.

India is still now a country with rural economy as its base. About 75% of our people reside in rural areas and depend on rural economy. In 1948, India accepted cooperatives as the institution for the social and economic development of rural areas. With that idea we have been trying to extend the cooperative movement in different fields. Previously cooperative was mostly limited to credit societies. But for the last few years, we have been trying to extend its scope to other spheres of nation's life, and consequently, service cooperatives, farming cooperatives, industrial cooperatives, cooperative warehousing and marketing and lastly consumer cooperatives have been initiated and encouraged. In statistics, our cooperative movement has made spectacular progress. The same progress has not yet been found in achieving the real purpose, i. e., of having established social justice. National wealth has increased but the distribution of wealth has not progressed according to our social ideas. Production of consumer goods has gone up. Here again the distribution of consumer goods has not flowed in the proper channel.

There is also the anomaly of price. The gap between the price received or the cost paid, by the producer and the price paid by the con-

*Reproduced from *Kurukshetra*, October 2, 1963

sumer has further widened. Even when certain agricultural commodities sell at a fairly high price in the urban market, the rural producers of those commodities do not get proper price. Urban intermediaries and commerce men grab a major portion of the price given by the urban consumers and deprive the rural producers of their due share in the price. This is particularly to be seen in vegetable and other easily perishable articles. It is not a rare sight that a good crop of vegetables and fruits would mean an uneconomic price for the producers. Sometimes it happens that the price a producer can get for his perishable vegetables and fruits is hardly commensurate even with his labour of bringing the vegetables from his village to the nearby market place.

We have initiated warehousing and cold storage with the idea of helping both the producer and the consumer. But we find just the reverse process in operation; through the actual working of these two institutions, it is the intermediary who gets the benefit. The producer is very often forced to sell the commodity almost at a distress price to the intermediary; and he keeps his stock in a warehouse or cold storage to be released at convenient times, when artificial scarcity of those commodities has been created. Even about the cooperative movement there is a general complaint; it is only the comparatively richer peasant who can get the benefit of cooperative credit and other assistances and the poorer peasant hardly gets any benefit. Similarly in the case of cottage industries or small-scale industries, the weaker elements cannot take advantage of the opportunities offered by the Government. It is the comparatively richer and cleverer section of the community that usually grabs the benefits. This has been the bane of our economic life.

Just at present we are passing through a sort of crisis. It is not the crisis of Chinese aggression, but it is the crisis of conflicts in our economy. The Prime Minister about three years ago wondered, where had gone the new wealth created by our Plans. Since then or even before that, inquiries and investigations have been going on; remedies have been suggested and tried; but the process of the rich becoming richer and the poor poorer goes on unabated. The crisis in our economy was highlighted by some conflicting statements made by some of our Ministers. From the same platform Shri G. L. Nanda and Shri S. K. Dey spoke in different strains. On the same issue, Shri Nanda and Shri S. K. Patil aired different ideas and policies. In spite of their differences, there is a common agreement between them on two points—failure to achieve certain objectives and no easy solution of the present difficulties. Ministers are the framers of our national policy and in a way the makers of the destiny of the nation. When they feel frustrated and openly declare a sort of helplessness on their part, the nation naturally gets perturbed.

One topic, which is today uppermost in the minds of almost everybody is the question of high prices. Year after year even the highest in the Government declare their solemn determination to hold the price line and year after year there has been palpable failure in this very important sector. It may be contested that Government was somewhat unrealistic in declaring their own determination to hold the price line and thereby they have created a false hope in the minds of the people. They ought to have realised, and told the people bluntly, that in a developing economy prices are bound to rise. But it does not mean any justification for runaway price rise; there is a limit to that. But what is the justifiable limit? Every year when a new tax is imposed, the price of any commodity goes up not according to the incidence of taxation, but by a multiple of the tax imposed. And even commodities, which have not attracted any new or an enhanced tax, also claim a higher price in the market.

I remember of an ordinary vendor giving a very simple explanation to this. This vendor has to maintain his family. If he has to pay a higher price for 2-3 or 4 commodities for his own family consumption, he must earn something more to pay for that higher prices. For that he tries to increase the price of all the commodities under him. How far is this justifiable and how is this preventable by the Government? An ordinary rural retail shopkeeper's economic argument may have some justification from the point of his own family budget, but from the national point of view, such a psychology can prove disastrous. We do not know if it is possible for the Government to control the retail shopkeepers in urban and rural areas, who may be tempted to indulge in small profiteering exercises.

But more dangerous is the tendency of the wholesalers to indulge in profiteering by creating an atmosphere of artificial scarcity, and the rise in prices is mostly due to such a tendency. It has been suggested that as a price stabilisation measure consumers cooperatives would be started in thousands for the distribution of the consumer goods at proper price. On theory this sounds quite good, but there are many practical difficulties. It is not easy to find suitable persons to establish and then to run thousands of consumers' cooperative stores with honesty and efficiency. Cooperative movement in India has suffered much from lack of that type of persons; and it cannot be claimed that now there is abundance of such persons. The record of cooperative stores in India is rather discouraging. Consumers' cooperatives were encouraged during the last War, i. e., when there was control due to a general scarcity of consumer goods. After the War, with comparatively abundant supply of consumer goods came the end of controls and the collapse of consumers' cooperative stores. This leaves an impression that these stores can work only when there is scarcity and control.

Apart from that, there is the question of the consumers' cooperatives getting their stores at fair price. Can the Government ensure that these cooperative stores will get all their stocks from a central or wholesale cooperative society which will receive the stores from the mills or the producing centres at regulated prices? The Government have no such machinery as yet and I do not think, they can give such an assurance to the primary consumers' cooperatives down to the rural areas—where about 80% of the consumers live. If the consumers cooperative stores are to get their stores from ordinary wholesalers, then their purchase price will entail something more than fair price of any commodity. In such a case the consumers' cooperatives cannot avoid profiteering and high prices.

Moreover, the hostility of the private traders—wholesalers or retailers is also there to create difficulties in the working of the cooperatives. The source of supply of stores being mostly in the monopoly possession of private traders, the cooperative stores have always to be cautious so as not to rouse their wrath. Further, the consumers' cooperatives will, even if they function properly, take the business of small retailers who will thus be thrown out of employment. Again millions of persons or families may be rendered paupers, and that will create another social problem just as the Gold Control Order has created. Then there is also the chance of spurious cooperatives—dominated by a handful of persons. Having secured monopoly supply privileges such cooperatives often indulge in profiteering tactics.

The services of cooperative societies have been invoked to ensure fair price to the producers and to supply commodities at a fair price to the consumers. For the last two years they had been trying to help the jute growers and seedlac growers through cooperative purchase. The purpose of such a cooperative is to ensure economic price to the producers; this is to be done by eliminating intermediaries and the profit they earn. But it is doubtful, how far the cooperatives have been able to eliminate intermediaries in the price support operation for jute and lac. According to our reports, in most cases the cooperatives purchase raw jutes, not from the producers themselves, but from the intermediaries (*beparies and fariahs*). If that is true, the cooperative societies have functioned only as an additional intermediary to the already existing 3 or 4 intermediaries between the jute producer and the jute mill. If the cooperatives are to help the jute growers or the lac growers, then it will be necessary for them to have net works of cooperative societies throughout the country and to make purchases direct from the agriculturists; but that is not done. May we hope that the Government will issue directives to the cooperative societies so that they may not make any purchases of raw jute from the intermediaries, and all purchases may be made direct from the growers. It is of vital importance that the Government and cooperative officials will work the societies in the true spirit of cooperation—and not for window-dressing and statistical satisfaction.

With all that said, we admit that the only machinery through which we can render assistance to the growers and relief to the consumers is the cooperative movement. Along with the consumers' cooperatives, there should be other cooperatives also to form a chain from the field and factory to the consumer's household. Some doubts may appear whether the chain of cooperative societies, covering the different tiers of our national economy, can properly function in our mixed economy set-up. We have already referred to the hostility of the private traders to cooperative movement. Production as also wholesale trade of consumers' goods being mostly in the hands of the private sector, the cooperatives at the lower or primary stage can have only a precarious existence. It will be very difficult for the cooperatives to compete with established commercial and industrial men who have all the material resources and the mental aptitude and shrewdness for a successful economic venture.

It is time for the Government to decide how far cooperatives should be allowed to proceed. Is it to be allowed to run the whole gamut of our economy? Or is it to work only within a very truncated scope? We expect the Government to make a proper assessment of the problem. It is often questioned that the Government or the governmental machinery including the Ministers and the permanent services are not really serious in implementing the economic measures implied in cooperative, Panchayat Raj, decentralised economy and all these things. We hope that this is a wrong appraisement; but that has to be demonstrated by specific performances. Declared policies proving unrealised, solemnly avowed objectives remaining unfulfilled, and defaulters or persons responsible for these failures getting approbation instead of being taken to task—all these create an atmosphere of doubt and suspicion about the bonafides of the Government and their officers, regarding all measures intended to affect rural economic development and to help decentralised economy and decentralised political authority.

2

VILLAGE CO-OPERATIVES—AN ANALYSIS OF THEIR FAILURE*

In considering the record of the co-operative credit movement in the Indian village, it has accordingly to be remembered that in India, as wholly distinguished from other countries, there has been the unique *combination* of the following features: (1) a socio-economic structure largely based on caste within the village itself, (2) the linking up of the upper parts of that structure to a cash economy and an administration centralized in the urban sector, and (3) the fact that the linking up took place as the outcome of three processes which historically happened to operate *together* in India, viz., colonial rule and administration, commercialization of agriculture and urbanization of industry.

In the sum total of the attitudes and environment, psychological, sociological and other, of co-operative societies, central co-operative banks, apex co-operative institutions, commercial banks, insurance companies and the Central Bank of the country, consists the climate of institutional credit; that climate in Indian conditions has been preponderantly 'urban'; it is not yet congenial to rural interests and the fulfilment of rural needs. It is in this climate that the rural producer is expected, by and large, both by co-operative theory and governmental policy, to combine with other rural producers, form co-operative associations at the village level and through them conduct his 'business' in so far as it concerns credit. He is expected to do this without financial assistance of a significant order from the State, but with a great deal of administrative advice and guidance from it. Having formed an association, he is left to face the powerful competition of private credit, private trade (often private money-lending-cum-trade) and private organisation of industry, all of them deriving strength and support from the urban apex--whether of commercial banking and finance or of export or wholesale trade. In the same context, the rural producer is expected to organize himself co-operatively for the promotion of the processing, marketing, etc., of his harvest. Added to all this is the cleavage of interests in the village itself, with the bigger landlord, the village moneylender, the village trader, etc., on one side and the medium and small cultivator on the other. Village leadership, vesting as it does in the former, usually operates partly for the advantage of the more powerful economic interests and partly in alignment

---

* Reproduced from *The General Report of the Committee of Direction of the All-India Rural Credit Survey*, Vol. II, pp. 272-279.

with the social institution of caste; and village leadership thus constituted and biased makes itself felt in every institution in the village including, of course, the co-operative society itself. In this combination resides the basic reason for the failure of the co-operative efforts at ' better business ' in its two-fold aspect of better co-operative credit and better co-operative economic activity.

The conclusion that the primary co-operative society had taken root in this country was premature then, and would perhaps be still premature now nearly forty years after the report of the Maclagan Committee. Indeed, it might not be wholly impermissible to detect a certain degree of truth in a description we have come across of Co-operation in this country as ' a plant held in position with both hands by Government since its roots refuse to enter the soil. ' More than the roots of Co-operation, it is the tentacles of private economy that have acquired grip in rural India.

The not-so-strong can combine co-operatively and get the same advantages as the strong. But the very weak are not in the same position as the not-so-strong; certainly not if the strong have, in addition, a whole reservoir of institutional strength from which they can add immeasurably to their own. This disproportion provides a key to the wholly different records of co-operative credit in the West and in India; for, Co-operation can succeed only if, between the forces of Co-operation on the one hand, and the opposing forces of private credit and private trade on the other, the disparity that ever tends to be present does not exceed certain reasonable bounds. In India, not only has there been too wide a disparity between the internal strength of the co-operative structure and the external forces pitched against it in competition; these latter have in many insidious ways entered into and vitiated the internal cohesion of co-operative bodies themselves. No more than an outline of how this has happened is attempted in this chapter.

The failure of co-operative credit is explicable in terms of the total impracticability of any attempt to combine the very weak in competition with the very strong and expect them by themselves to create conditions, firstly, for their emancipation from the interests which oppose them, and secondly, for their social and economic development in the context of the severe disadvantages historically imposed on them by a structure of the type described. The problem is not so much one of re-organisation of co-operative credit as of the creation of new conditions in which it can operate effectively and for the benefit of the weaker. The prevailing conditions cannot be transformed by the very persons who are oppressed and rendered weak by their existence. The forces of transformation have to be at least as powerful as those which are sought to be counteracted. Such forces can be generated not by Co-operation alone but by Co-operation in conjunction with the State.

3

CONTEXT FOR COOPERATIVES IN RURAL INDIA*

DANIEL THORNER

IN ORDER to find out how agricultural cooperatives were functioning —and were likely to function in the future—I decided to go and see things for myself. Accordingly, between December 1958 and May 1959, I visited some 117 cooperatives scattered throughout most of the States of India.

The particular societies which I visited were not selected by me. Rather, they were selected by the local authorities, but in no random sense. Since I was interested in the prospects for successful cooperation, I asked the local people (from the Cooperative Departments, in most cases) to take me to their best societies. Since they would want to show me their best, there would be no harm in asking them to do what they were, in any event, almost certain to do. Further, the places in which I halted while on tour were, wherever possible, well known for their achievements in the field of cooperation. Hence it was not by chance that my itinerary included Baroda, Salem, Kolhapur, Nilgiris, Mandya, and Anakapalla. In this way I saw not merely good cooperative societies, but the best of the best. These societies, however, did not constitute a properly drawn sample, whether of all coopertives or of good cooperatives. They are merely cases or illustrations which happened to be brought to my attention when I asked for the best.

As it happened, my field tour followed close upon an important shift in Governmental policy with regard to cooperatives. A decision had just been taken at the highest level to go no further with the integrated credit scheme which had been taken up at the recommendation of the Reserve Bank. As against the Reserve Bank's larger-sized societies, the new policy emphasised single village,multi-purpose service cooperatives. These, it was stated, ought to serve as a transition to cooperative joint farming. Since the implementation of the Reserve Bank programme had begun only three years earlier, the reversal had an upsetting effect on many cooperators. On the other hand, the Government's unprecedented stress on cooperation as an instrument of development made the subject a live one wherever I went.

THE LEADING COOPERATORS

When I arrived at the office of a village cooperative society, the first

*Reproduced from *The Economic Weekly* Thirtieth Annual Number, February 1962.

persons who came to meet me, or indeed were already waiting, were usually the members of the managing committee. In discussion I tried to ascertain the social make-up of the village and to find out which groups were represented in the cooperative and which in the managing committee. In quite a few places the people whom I met were anxious to impress upon me the importance of the heads of their cooperatives. They took pride in telling me that these cooperators were big men in trade, in Government contracts, in rice-milling, in land-holding, and in local politics. In general, I found that the heads of cooperatives were the big people of the villages and that they had their fingers in many other pies as well as cooperation.

For example, the leading figures of the multi-purpose cooperative at Saadhi in Baroda District of Gujarat are all landholders from the dominant local community, the Patels. They own enough land so that they do not have to work with their own hands. They have managed to get around the land reforms, and some of them were giving out land on 50-50 cropshare basis to the lesser folk of the village. Some of the leading figures in the cooperative appeared to be lending money informally on a private basis. The previous head of the cooperative had gone on to become the chairman (sarpanch) of the village Panchayat (the " council " of the village.)

Power Concentration in Single Family

One of the outstanding cooperative joint farms in Gujarat is located at Rasulabad, 10 miles north of Baroda. It seemed to be well run and the benefits of the members included purchase of school books for their children. But it was functioning as a one-family show, operated mostly on family land by one of the landlord families of the village. Three brothers from this single family were serving respectively as the Chairman of the Managing Committee, the Managing Director and the Farm Manager. More of the work of the farm appeared to be done by hired labourers than by the members themselves.

Sadoli in Kolhapur District affords a different kind of illustration of concentrated power of a single family. Seven brothers here constituted the village's leading family and wielded the greatest influence in the multipurpose cooperative. One brother was village *sarpanch*, another was director of a lift irrigation cooperative, while a third was director of a nearby cooperative sugarcane factory. In addition to owning more land than any other family, the seven brothers also owned 5 mechanical vehicles (tractors, bulldozer, car, lorry). During the busy season they employed more than 50 labourers. In the Sadoli multipurpose cooperative, half of the outstanding short-term loans (Rs. 95,000 out of a grand total of Rs. 191,000) had been made to only 11 members.

In Salem district of Madras, perhaps as celebrated as any in the State for work in cooperation, one family has dominated the movement for a generation. In 1959 one member of that family was simultaneously the president of no less than six cooperatives and the director of several others. The cooperative movement of the district seemed to be little more than an extension of his personality.

Work Done by Hired Labour

At a joint cultivation cooperative in Coimbatore District of Madras only 3 out of 28 members actually went out and helped till the society's fields. In another joint cultivation society in North Arcot, three-quarters of the members were absentees, and none of the full members living in the village actually did physical work in the fields. In both cases the cooperatives served as a form of organization whereby the full members could receive aid from the State and yet get their work done for them by the employment of hired labourers.

Nauranga in Kanpur District of the U. P. is perhaps the best-known in North India of the large-sized societies of the type recommended by the Reserve Bank. The society appears, however, to be under the wing of the local landlord, the ex-zamindar, who used to hold not only Nauranga but several other villages as well. He has been serving as a director of the new society assert that the big people, the ex-zamindars, get first preferential treatment from the cooperative, while application from the lesser folk are handled in dilatory fashion.

Chairman, Patel and Sarpanch—All Three in One

The chairman of a new, large-sized society in the Sehore area of Madhya Pradesh was simultaneously the village *patel* (headman of the village), the *sarpanch* (head of the Panchayat), and director of at least two other cooperative societies. He lived in a splendid house and was one of the three largest cultivators in the village, with four farm servants working for him full-time all year round.

In the Hyderabad District of Andhra the president of a new large-sized society founded in 1956 was a military contractor owning a mansion and a new car, while the secretary-treasurer was one of the largest landowners. Similarly, at a nearby and highly reputed single-village primary society, the president, in addition to being the largest holder in the village was also a P.W.D. (public works) contractor.

Mysore furnishes the example *par excellence* of leading families who completely control village affairs, including the cooperatives. These are the *mukhyestaru*, the local " all-in-alls. " To an extent perhaps unequalled anywhere else in India they are at one and the same time the principal landowners, chief traders, main moneylenders, shopkeepers, and village officials. The *mukhyestaru* have generally opposed the formation of cooperatives. Once these are established, however, they join the societies to take them over for their own purposes.

Masters and Servants

Let us now take a closer look at the range of activities of the bigger people who are so often found at the helm of the cooperatives. Their holdings, as we have noted, are likely to be the largest, or among the largest, in their villages. These they can either cultivate directly through hired labourers, or they can give them out for others to cultivate on payment of rent in cash or in kind. In actual practice the bigger people often do both. They keep some of their land directly in their own hands, and they give out the rest to others. To the extent that land is given out, they are likely to be giving out the most. As such, they wield great power. The little people, desperate to get land, cannot sit as equals with the important people who have significant amounts of land to give out. It is doubtful that they can work together on a cooperative basis.

Insofar as the large landlords are also big cultivators, they are the principal employers of agricultural labour. When the labourers are utterly landless, they are, with rare exceptions, not enrolled as members of the local cooperative. By contrast, there are numerous cases in which the labourers own tiny patches or take in bits of land on lease or cropshare. Some of these labourers may well have joined the cooperative. If so, there is almost certain to be a wide gap between them and the top people by whom they are hired. The employer is the master, and his hired labourer is the servant; in the languages of India there are no terms for distinguishing an employer-employee relationship from that of master and servant.

The relations of master and servant are typically complex. The labourer or his father may have borrowed money from the master, either in time of distress or for a major ceremony like marriage. Or the labourer may simultaneously by taking some pieces of land from the master on cropshare (batai). The masters may come from one caste and the labourers from another that ranks lower. The implications of caste differences and caste rivalries have been so widely commented on that we will not attempt to add anything to that subject here.

We cannot overlook, however, the question of attitude toward physical work in the fields. There is very little belief in India in the dignity of labour. For the most part, whoever can escape it considers manual labour an indignity. The surest way by which a family whose fortunes have been improving can stake a claim to higher standing in the village is for the members to abstain from manual labour. It is safe to say that in most of India the distinction between those who work with their own hands, and those who do not, cuts deep. It is idle to expect those who do not soil their hands, and their hired labourers who do, to work together in the spirit appropriate to a cooperative. Not only may the masters not be prepared to " work together, " they may simply not be prepared to work at all !

Moneylenders in the Societies

One cannot help but be impressed by the position occupied in the cooperatives by one or another type of person who lends money. The cultivator who also does some money-lending figures prominently in cooperatives in Baroda, Saurashtra, Hyderabad, and Rajasthan. The trader-cum-moneylender is found in societies in Saurashtra, Mysore, the Nilgiris, Nellore, and Kashmir. The formidable combination of the cultivating moneylenders-cum-trader dominates the scene in Mysore and coastal Andhra. If the aim of the cooperative credit societies has been to free the cultivators from the grip of the moneylenders, then the moneylenders do not belong in the societies, let alone in the leadership. How, then, have persons who lend money come to occupy so prominent a place in the cooperative movement?

Here we have to bear in mind that the need of the villagers to take loans is crucial and chronic. The bullock may die in the middle of the ploughing season; a son may be seriously ill; in the period between one harvest and the next, the foodgrains in the family jars may run out; etc. At such times the peasant must borrow and he cannot be choosy about rates of interest. He will have to pay whatever is asked. Hence, the lending of money is a very paying proposition. Bigger peasants whose crops have done well may find themselves with funds to spare. In such situations they may very well do a bit of moneylending. Among the well-off peasants, including those who are members of cooperatives, the growth of moneylending may almost be termed a natural process.

Persons well supplied with funds to lend are *ipso facto* important in the villages. If, as we have seen above, they are also active in cultivation or trade, they may be doubly important. As regards cooperatives, such persons may initially resist their formation. Once the societies are established, however, persons who lend may join the cooperatives, perhaps in order to get direct access to the society's funds. When an important person in the village wants to join the cooperative, it is usually hard to keep him out.

We must also note that it may be Government policy to bring the moneylenders into the cooperatives. Perhaps in no area of India in the 1950's did cooperatives expand so rapidly and achieve such complete coverage as in Saurashtra. In case after case among the best cooperatives, the leadership turns out to be the trader-moneylender.

Sahakari or Sarkari?

In many parts of the country the role of Government in the cooperatives is so great that the members consider the societies not as their own but as an instrument of the State. To them the cooperatives appear as a source from which they borrow Government funds. In Sehore District of Madhya Pradesh the Chairman and Secretary stated that they fostered this impression because it helped to facilitate recoveries of loans. Similarly, in a well-reputed society near Trivandrum, the members were stated to believe that the loans they got from the society were sums from Government. Their term for a loan from the society is, in Malayalam, *sarkar vaipa,* which means Government loan.

The State in which these attitudes and feelings are most pronounced is Madras. There the hand of the Cooperative Department bureaucracy seems to be everywhere, in the person of officials on deputation to run the affairs of local societies. The members of one of the best cooperative agricultural banks in Coimbatore District, for example, consider that the sums they borrow from the society are Government loans. The borrower feels (" has that fear ") that since the loan is from Government he must repay in time. The term in Tamil for a loan from the cooperative society is *sarkar kadan* (Government loan).

The societies in Madras appear to be bound down very closely by the Cooperative Department's book of rules and regulations. The consequence not only in Madras but in other States as well, is an inelasticity that has been the curse of the movement. In the Nilgiris, members of small and large societies feel that Government control is very rigid. In bad seasons they cannot count on the Government-controlled societies to see them through. Instead they must turn to the trader-moneylender, no matter how oppressive he may be; when they most need help, they get a kind of " cooperation " from him. But in their hour of need what they get from the cooperative society is a form of " non-cooperation. "

POLITICAL FORCES IN THE COOPERATIVES

The impact of politics upon the cooperatives seems to be getting heavier and more direct. In several States the leadership of the cooperatives is heavily sprinkled with active politicians. In Kashmir, Mysore and coastal Andhra, for example, there are many M. L. As. (members of the legislative assemblies) in the top cooperative posts.

Persons who succeed in becoming elected to the legislative assemblies are usually, if they are villagers, from the important and best-off families. They tend to use the cooperatives as levers or weapons in jostling for position with their rivals. Or they show their importance by the number of societies which they keep under their wings. In this connection it has to be borne in mind that the people in power in the capitals of the various States are pretty much the same people in the seats of power in the villages, only occupying larger chairs. When the Government decides upon a policy of vigorous support to cooperatives, then the people in power bring in their friends and loyal political supporters to implement the policy. Thus under the Congress regime in Saurashtra in the early 1950's Congress workers were encouraged to start cooperatives. During the Communist regime in Kerala, Communist workers were active in promoting cooperatives.

There is a danger that in this process the cooperatives may become political footfalls. No matter how well a society may be run, if it is the other party's or the other faction's society, then a change in State regime may take the ground from under its feet. A dramatic illustration of this is afforded by the Anthikad Toddy Tappers' Cooperative Society in Trichur (Cochin) Kerala State. Early in 1959 the local officers of the Kerala

Cooperative Department were proud of the success of the society; visitors were struck by the fact that 11 out of 12 of the directors of the society were themselves tappers who still climbed trees to bring down the toddy.

When the new anti-communist regime in Kerala assumed power after the elections early in 1960, one of its first main decisions was to end the system whereby toddy shops were given on negotiated contracts to the toddy tappers' societies. So intimate a relationship between politics and cooperatives does not augur well for the prospects of the movement.

RESERVE BANK 'S " INTEGRATED SCHEME OF RURAL CREDIT "

The most elaborate plan ever devised for the development of cooperatives in India was put forward at the end of 1954 under the auspices of the Reserve Bank. The basic features of this programme were spelled out in the General Report which constitutes Volume II of the Reserve Bank's All India Rural Credit Survey. Essentially, the Reserve Bank called for a more business-like approach to peasant farming. This was to be achieved by concentrating credit on the productive needs of farm business. The cooperatives were to make advances to the cultivators as producers of crops (not as owners of land). The loans were to be given on the basis that a crop was anticipated, and the amounts of the loans were to be related to the estimated outlay for raising the crop. The recoveries were to be made, as and when the crop was sold, from the proceeds of the sale.

The " integrated " aspect of the Reserve Bank's " Integrated Scheme of Rural Credit " is the effort to link credit and marketing. The credit cooperative was to finance its members on condition that the produce of the member is sold through the nearest marketing cooperative. One of these marketing societies was to serve a number of credit societies. The credit cooperatives were to arrange for collection and transport of the members' produce to the marketing centre. The sums due to the members for their produce were to be paid through the credit society, which would first deduct for outstanding loans. In this way the integrated scheme was intended to ensure recoveries of loans to members.

The scheme, of course, rests on the assumption that the members of the cooperatives produce crops primarily for sale. As it happens, the main crops of India are foodgrains, most of which the peasant families do not sell but retain for their own consumption. A system such as the Reserve Bank proposed would work best with growers of perishable cash crops like sugarcane or potatoes which require heavy investment and must be sold quickly after each harvest. But the areas under such special items are limited and they can never displace foodgrains as the dominant crop of the country.

We may also note that the Reserve Bank's scheme did not face up squarely to the credit needs of the peasantry to carry on their existence as social beings. From time to time the peasantry must spend on marriages, education, illnesses, funerals, journeys, pilgrimages, etc. Ceremonies and festivals are either the most solemn occasions of life, or occasions for the greatest rejoicing. The peasantry can and will do without neither. One of the main points made in the Rural Credit Survey was that the borrowings of the peasants must be understood as an overall " balancing factor. " Peasant families, the Survey Report observed, get accustomed to a certain level of living. They go on trying to live at that level whether or not in any given year their total resources are sufficient. When they fall short, they borrow. Their loans are a " balancing factor, " making up the difference between their total current needs and their total current resources.

It is the strength of the moneylender that he is prepared, at heavy cost to the peasant, to play the role of overall " balancing factor. " On this crucial ground, the Reserve Bank's integrated scheme, by contrast, offered him no competition. The Bank's scheme made rather vague and grudging allowance for " subsistence " needs in its system of crop loans : " Such needs will be automatically covered if the quantum of crop loans—at so much per acre of the particular crop cultivated—is properly fixed for each area after taking into account all relevant considerations. " (General Report, p. 433). One can roughly allocate manure on a crop acreage basis, but it is not so easy to do so with marriages! To be fair, the Reserve Bank did not really attempt to do so; but instead of trying to deal with such problems, the Bank fobbed them off with the suggestion that each credit cooperative should also sponsor a " mutual help " fund (" chit fund ").

In India, " chit funds " are known well only in the extreme South. There they are loosely organized, take many forms, and have a spotty record. The particular version that the Reserve Bank has suggested is exceedingly complicated and no indication is given that it has ever been tried anywhere. This seems surprising, in view of the importance which the Rural Credit Survey has attached to credit requirements for family living. Borrowings for " family expenditure " of all types, the Survey Report stated, many times overshadowed those for investment or for current production purposes (Survey Report, p. 402). To have put forward an intricate and untested scheme for dealing with these prime needs was neither businesslike nor responsible.

The Issue of Size

When it was put forward in 1954-55, the Reserve Bank's " integrated scheme " was well received. The Government of India accepted the main features of the programme and its implementation figured prominently in the Second Five Year Plan (1956-61). In the second half of 1958 the scheme fell into official disfavour, and the Government policy shifted to " service cooperatives. " The discussion of this change in policy has centred on the question of size, the Reserve Bank's " large-sized " societies (covering many villages) being contrasted unfavourably with societies limited to a single village (or, at most say three villages).

As we shall see, the question of size was not really the basic issue.

But it is convenient to take it up first. The Reserve Bank called for " larger-sized " societies so that each could afford to have a trained, full-time paid secretary. For this purpose it has been estimated that each society would have to make a minimum of at least Rs. 50,000 in loans per year. Judged by this criterion the traditional single-village primary societies were, in most cases, too small. Unless each of the societies had a properly trained secretary, the Reserve Bank argued, they would not be viable. Following the Reserve Bank's recommendations, the various States formed thousands of larger-sized societies by mergers of a dozen or so of the older-type single village societies.

From the time the Reserve Bank's proposals appeared, however, there were those who viewed with regret the way the scheme gave up the single village as the basic unit of rural credit. In their eyes a peasant cooperative did not have much meaning unless the members knew each other well and kept in personal touch. This could not be expected in a cooperative which covered a dozen or more villages. Rather such societies would tend to be not cooperatives but rural banks.

The Prime Minister, who had initially welcomed the Reserve Bank proposals, announced in 1958 that he had been mistaken. Mr. Nehru stated that he no longer agreed with the ideal of substituting bigger cooperatives for smaller ones. The bigger societies, controlled by an official, might do some good, but they would also do infinite harm in the sense that they would not teach people self-reliance. Rather, they would encourage the habit of looking to Government for everything. The Reserve Bank recommendations, Mr. Nehru lamented, had encouraged the tendency of Government officials to boss over the people. " We should try to get out of it as quickly as we can and aim at small cooperatives without official interference. "

Cooperatives and Land Reforms

When the All-India Congress Committee met at Hyderabad in October, 1958, they adopted a resolution calling for doubling of India's agricultural production in the next ten years. As might be expected, there were differences of opinion as to what would be required to reach so ambitious a target. An Agricultural Production Sub-Committee was set up to make specific recommendations. Meeting in New Delhi, November 6-7, 1958, the Committee drew up two parallel and linked three-year programmes, one involving land reforms, the other involving cooperatives.

Regarding land reform, the Committee recommended that comprehensive, thoroughgoing legislation should be enacted in all of the States by the end of March, 1959. These measures should include ceilings (limits on the larger holdings), which would result in surpluses being taken away from the bigger owners. Implementation of these laws should take no longer than three years, and should be completed by the end of 1961 (i.e., before the next general elections). The surpluses taken away from the larger holders, however, were not to be redistributed in tiny bits. Instead, in the interests of developing a more progressive and better-yielding agriculture, these were to be handed over for cooperative working.

During the same three years that the land reforms were to be implemented, the Committee recommended that multi-purpose service cooperatives should be formed to cover all the villages of India. These cooperatives should be small enough (covering only one or two villages) to allow for personal touch and intimate knowledge among the members. Such cooperatives, however, were not to be considered ends in themselves. If India's infinite number of small holdings were to be able to take advantage of modern farming methods, they would have to be brought together into larger units. Cooperative farming was inevitable, but it would have to come in stages.

The " service cooperatives " were to be the first stage. The next stage would be joint cultivation, in which small holdings would be thrown together to permit farming on a larger scale, while the property rights of the individual holders would remain separate. In his press conference on November 7, 1958, the Prime Minister emphasized the linkage among production ceilings, and cooperative farming.

> " We think that in every village there should be joint cultivation. Broadly, that is the approach and the question of ceiling is more tied up with cooperative farming. Otherwise there is the danger of production going down. "

TASKS OF THE SERVICE COOPERATIVES

In addition to providing credit, the service cooperatives are expected to collect, to store, and to arrange for the marketing of the produce of their members. Except for special crops in particular areas, cooperatives have had very little success in this field. Progress in the development of cooperative marketing may be expected to lag several steps behind the growth of cooperative credit. A large number of the private parties who lend money are also traders. It has been their custom to take their debtors' crops at prices below the going market rates. So long as substantial numbers of peasants depend for loans upon such traders, the scope for cooperative marketing will remain limited. (Cf. the position of the Shetkari Sahakari Sangh at Kolhapur and of the cooperative marketing society at Anakapalle.)

One way in which Government may try to strengthen the cooperatives is by making the societies the chief agents for the distribution of fertilizers and improved seeds. Such a favoured position, however, may not turn out to be an unmixed blessing. In practice the handling of seeds is a tricky matter. If the reputation of the cooperative is not to suffer, the right seeds must be ready at the right times, in the right places, in the required quantities.

To a considerable extent the problem is the same with fertilizers. It is also the case that for some years to come fertilizers are expected to be in short supply. The officers of the cooperatives may find the gratifications offered to them for special favours in the distribution of fertilizers almost irresistible. In this connection the diversion to cash crops of fertilizers provided for the Grow More Food campaign is worth recalling.

The service cooperatives have also been called up to promote such assorted activities as animal husbandry, contour bunding, consolidation of holdings, and more effective use of irrigation water. It is by no means clear how the efforts of the cooperatives along these lines will be integrated with the work already taken up by the community projects and the State agricultural departments. Half a century or more of experience in these fields shows that where achievements have been registered, they have followed upon sustained hard work on a full-time basis by qualified persons. It would seem unsound to expect much by way of accomplishment in these fields from the service cooperatives.

Cent Per cent enrolment

The goal of enrolling 100 per cent of the village families in the service cooperatives is relatively easy to attain. Saurashtra has shown how it can be done. There is no reason why similar successes cannot be scored in other parts of the country. In the abstract, the idea of having all the village families in the same cooperative might appear attractive. It would seem to represent a social advance by ensuring the inclusion of the bottom half of the population. Because of their weak economic position the labourers, artisans, cropsharers and village servants have generally been kept out of the societies and have failed to benefit from the cooperative movement. These are the elements in village society which have the greatest difficulty in making ends meet and consequently have the most trouble in repaying loans. It might seem heartless to leave them to the mercy of the moneylender while providing cooperative credit and other services to their betteroff neighbours. The fact remains, however, that simply bringing the weaker families into the cooperatives does not automatically improve their basic economic position. To gather all these insolvent people up into the cooperatives is doubtless a dramatic gesture. But it means that they carry all their unsolved problems with them into the cooperative. To enroll such families wholesale into the cooperatives before putting their affairs on a better footing is to invite the danger that they will drag the societies down with them.

It must also be realized that cent per cent village membership guarantees equally the enrolment of all the village traders, moneylenders, and landlords. Why should they stay out of the cooperatives when Government will be going to such trouble to funnel funds, supplies, equipment, and assistance through the new societies?

The Weak and the Strong

People like to think that a comprehensive, well supported, well-thought out Governmental programme of setting up cooperatives will change the pattern of village power. The evidence suggests that the structure of village power has imposed, and will continue to impose its own pattern on the cooperatives.

This is not to say that in recent years there have been no important changes in village life. A great deal has happened, but not enough to enable the mass of ordinary villagers to shake off grip of a few dominant families. The great zamindars of the north and once-haughty mirasdars of the south have lost much of their grandeur. A good deal of land has changed hands. Universal suffarage has come. Compulsory labour (begar) has mostly gone. Nonetheless, in areas where the former men of power have declined, others have risen up in their place. Newly-arrived men may show their strength by acting more arrogantly than effete aristocrats. In western Uttar Pradesh where the old zamindars have been brought down, the local Jats have talked of buying tractors and driving the Harijan labourers (Chamars) bodily out of their villages. In the south, landowning Thevars have been accused of burning down the quarters (cheris) of the labourers.

The fate of land reforms since 1947 furnishes ample testimony to the power of the little oligarchs who run village life. In the past dozen years the States of India have put on the statute books perhaps the largest body of land reform legislation passed in so brief a span of years in any country known to history. The village oligarchs have made a mockery of this legislation, devising 1001 ways of blocking or getting around the law. Their relations and friends in the State legislations have eased their task by putting numerous loopholes in the laws or adding crippling amendments.

Bombay in recent years was generally considered to have been the best administered of the States. The Bombay Tenancy Act of 1948 has been cited as a model land reform law. A detailed study made for the Planning Commission found the implementation from 1948 to 1953 to have been a dismal failure. The overriding social and economic power of the landlords against their tenants was so great that they did not even bother to take cognizance of the reforms. " For all practical purposes, " the authors concluded, the Bombay Tenancy Act " did not exist. " The top families in the Bombay villages were, in other words, able to disregard with impunity land reforms carrying the full sanction of the law.

In the eyes of the dominant families the ordinary people are inferiors, dependants, or servants. The little people lack land, education, influence, connections, staying power, resources. Often they even lack work. The top village families are not great lords, but they are strong enough to get the small folk to do their bidding. The dominant families try to abstain from the actual work of cultivation they get others to turn their sod and lift the water for their fields. Nevertheless, the dominant families consider themselves the principal " cultivators. " They are precisely the top groups who, according to report after report of the Planning Commission's Programme Evaluation Organization, have been securing for themselves the main benefits of the Community Projects: they see to it that their fields get the water first and foremost, and leave the rest for the ordinary, weaker folk. Where the Panchayats function, these *bare admi* are in the chairs. If labour is demanded in the name of village, the ordinary people must go out in the hot sun. The men from dominant families do not; they send money or lend the use of a tractor.

Firmly lodged in the chief positions of village power today, the dominant families stand ready to seize the lion's share of the vast programme of cooperative development. As the U.P. peasants say: " Jis ke pas Jitna hai, utna use milta hai " (to him that hath much, much shall be given).

Cooperative Joint Farming

It is hard to believe that the service cooperatives will provide a transition to joint farming. Here we have to note that the pressure for such group farming does not spring from India's villages. It is rather a policy laid down in New Delhi. The village strong have not asked for joint farms; they do not intend to surrender control of part or all of their land in favour of their tenants, cropsharers, labourers, or poorer neighbours. Nor, indeed, have these small folk demanded to be allowed to farm jointly with the bigger people. To the extent that the small people of the villages have asked for anything, it is to have in their own right some or all of the land now in the hands of the dominant families.

In the Indian framework today, if cooperative farming is to come, it would have to be imposed. The Government of India have made it clear—to all those willing to listen—that they do not intend to impose cooperative farming. Even if they were to try, there is no reason to believe that they could succeed. After all, to date, the Government of India have not been able to get the Panchayats, land reforms, or community projects to work along the lines laid down in New Delhi.

At the Centre, in the States, and in the districts, the administration is manned by men who do not believe in cooperative farming. If anything, they have less faith in this latest governmental policy than in Panchayats and community projects, to say nothing of their hostility to land redistribution.

There are, however, two kinds of cooperative farms which are likely to increase in number. First is the type so useful in evading land reform, the so-called cooperative which is really a single-family enterprise. Once a group of relatives convert themselves into an agricultural cooperative, they are eligible for such benefits as loans, subsidies or outright grants from Government; priorities in securing good seeds and scarce fertilizers; and the free services for several years of a trained secretary. The official review of the cooperative movement in Punjab for 1958-59 reported that:

> " ...a very large number of cooperative societies are, in effect, owned exclusively by influential families with a bogus membership of some outsiders to give them the appearance of cooperative bodies. "

A second type of which we may see more specimens is the kind of State-sponsored cooperative farms I found at Belligetti in Dharwar district (formerly in Bombay, now in Mysore), Kumbhapura in Mysore, Ashokpuri in the Etawah pilot project area (U.P.), and Jehangirpura near Bhopal

(M.P.). Here poor or previously uncultivated lands were made available by Government to special groups of Harijans, labourers, evicted peasants, or displaced persons. Situation, quality of soil, and availability of water were usually unpromising. The initiative in forming these joint farms had come from outside. The motive power to keep them going was furnished primarily by the State Governments which provided money, officers, supplies, and equipment. Joint farms of this description are expensive and unrewarding.

CONCLUSION

Experience in many countries has shown that cooperatives can serve as a means by which peasant cultivators can help each other to improve their position. But the success of rural cooperatives presupposes a modicum of social equality, political democracy, and economic viability among the villagers. These preconditions have not been present in village India and are still not present today. If the cooperative movement in India is to get anywhere, two things must happen first: (1) the power of the village oligarchs—the leading people, the *mukhyestaru,* to use the Kannada expression—must be curtailed; and (2) the Government must become an instrument of the ordinary people, and must be considered as such by the ordinary people.

What is happening in India today is that the cooperatives are being asked to create their own pre-conditions, to reconstruct village society so that the ordinary peasants can make effective use of the cooperative method. This is too much to expect. To rush ahead prematurely with cooperatives is to invite failure and give to cooperation a bad name.

FIELD NOTES

Chhota Nagpur

While driving north from Cuttack to Ranchi, I happened to meet a well-placed officer of the Government of Bihar. In his previous post he had spent the last few years trying to build up the cooperatives in the Chhota Nagpur Division. When he was first posted in Ranchi, there were about 60 village cooperatives in the area, and they were all unsuccessful. Before he left they had increased the number to about 70 but, he lamented, there still was not a single one among them that could be called successful. After I reached Ranchi, I told this story to the senior-most cooperative officer whom I met there. He at once offered to take me personally to a good cooperative in the Adivasi area. That afternoon we drove west from Ranchi along the first-class road that eventually reaches Daltonganj, the headquarters town of Palamau District. After driving about 30 miles we crossed over from Ranchi District into Palamau and three miles later we reached our destination, the village of Senha. This lies in a community development area, the Chandwa Stage I Block.

Senha is a small village with a total area of some 500 acres; of these about 200 are Government forest land. There used to be a major zamindar here, but he was successfully persuaded by Sarvodaya workers in 1953 to give his land as Bhoodan. In fact, we were told, nearly everybody in the village had surrendered their rights in favour of Acharya Vinoba Bhave; the only exceptions were two tenants, who clung to what they had. In due course the land gifts were properly registered and then the land was redistributed. There are 26 families in the village, of which 19 are Mundas, 3 are Oraons, another 3 are Ahirs (shepherds-cum-milkmen), and 1 a Brahman. Before Bhoodan, there were two or three families in the village which had no land. In the process of redistribution they were given land and the holdings of those with only tiny bits of land were enlarged.

The distinctive feature of Senha today is that it is a Sarvodaya village. The Sarvodaya worker who came to the village in 1953 to organize Bhoodan has never left. Instead he has continued to work there, has brought his wife and children, and seems to have settled down in Senha for good. His goal is to turn Senha into a 100 per cent Gramdan village, in which all the agricultural land will be worked as one joint farm. It was he who organized a cooperative society in the village in 1956, under the name, Senha Sarvodaya Sahjog Samiti, Ltd. He has persuaded practically all the villagers (excluding of course the two recalcitrant tenants) to join this Sarvodaya Samiti and to give the bulk of their land to the society. The Sarvodaya worker told me that Senha was the best Bhoodan village in Palamau, perhaps even the best Gramdan village in Chhota Nagpur. He used the terms Bhoodan and Gramdan interchangeably, telling me: " Bhoodan aur Gramdan eki chiz hai ." (Bhoodan and Gramdan are one.) In a few days, he told me, the President of the Bihar Bhoodan Samiti would be visiting Senha, and his (the Sarvodaya worker's) aim was to announce at that time that the village had agreed to 100 per cent joint cultivation.

The Sarvodaya worker could not wait to show me the pride of Senha, a large well which the villagers, under his direction, were trying to cut through rock, blasting when necessary. Sometimes, he said, they even worked right through the night. In any event the villagers had simple lives; they worked, ate, drank, made merry and slept. When we reached the well, we found it was already deep; they had worked their way down through much rock. At the bottom we found nearly a dozen men, the oldest of whom was a member of the cooperative society's board of directors (a Panchayatdar). It turned out that he was a Munda (his name was Delka Munda), and that one other director and the secretary were Mundas; another director was an Oraon; and the president, the treasurer, and the remaining director were Ahirs. The Sarvodaya worker had the title of " convener " of the cooperative.

Taking advantage of the fact that the villagers were glad to relax in the cool depths of the well, I asked them how they had been benefited from

Bhoodan. They said they were pleased to see the zamindar go. He and his agents used to be very severe with them, made them do unpaid work, and order them around: " Cha banao! Dudh lao! Pani lao ! " (Make tea! Bring milk! Bring water!). Now that the zamindars had gone the villagers had more land.

In view of the history of Bhoodan-cum-Gramdan in the village, I tried to find out from those present how, in their opinion, the land of the village was now held. Was it everybody's land? Was it their land? From the secretary of the society, who was with us in the well, I could only get vague answers. The oldest man present (Delka Munda, the Panchayatdar), was more positive: he answered in the affirmative to all three questions. Previously the land had been with the zamindars; now the land belonged to the village, to everybody, to us. " Gaon ko mila hai. " " Sub log ko mila hai. " " Hum log ko mila hai. "

When we tried to pursue the subject further, he explained that there was no difference among his three answers; they all meant the same thing. When we asked whether the land today belonged to the villages or to the Mundas, at first he replied that the land, he felt, was the land of the Mundas. He qualified this by adding that he was not sure he had understood the question. When the question was put again, he said he grasped it, and that, in his opinion, the land belonged to the village. He also said that there was no difference between the village and the people who made it up. The rest of the villagers in the well looked quite puzzled; clearly they could not make head or tail out of all this. From this discussion I was led to wonder how much clarity there was in their minds—or in anyone else's—about just who was the recipient, when such villagers made gifts of land " to the village. "

We climbed out of the well, in order to go to the house of the president of the society. As we started to leave, the Sarvodaya worker said briskly, " Kam kariye! " (Get to work). When we were at the top of the well, he looked down and saw that the Adivasis had still not moved; he shouted to the old man, ' Kam kariye, Delka Munda!"

We soon reached the house of the Nayak (headman), an Ahir by the name of Kewalal Mahto. When we did, the Sarvodaya worker instructed him to go and fetch up a cot (charpoy). After we were seated on it, the headman informed us that he had been president of the village Bhoodan group for the past five years. He was one of those, he told us, who had benefited from Bhoodan. When the lands of the zamindar were redistributed, he had got 7 acres. Of these, two acres were wet (paddy land), and the rest were dry. How much of this land, we asked him, was still with him. He answered that he had given the dry 5 acres to the Samiti for joint cultivation; he had retained for separate cultivation by his own family the two acres of paddy land. From this they got their food. In doing so he was merely following the general pattern in Senha; people kept in their own hands the good, paddy land; then gave the poorer dry land to the society. It was plain from the way he spoke that he was in no mood to give up his paddy land.

While we were talking about six p.m. a crowd of cattle and buffaloes came trotting by. The president interrupted the discussion by getting up, going over to his cattle shed, and starting to tie up his own animals. His lack of haste annoyed the Sarvodaya worker, who shouted to him brusquely: 'Jaldi Karo, Pradhan mantri!" (Hurry up, Chief Minister.) Just then a group of women returned from working in the fields and lined up before the Sarvodaya worker. He sent for a register and entered in it the number of hours that each woman had worked.

When we asked the president who now held the village land, he came back with a nice turn of phrase. There are no maliks (owners), he answered, or all are maliks ("Is gaon ke malik sub koi, nei to koi nahin").

As it was getting late, my companion and I got up, took their leave, and started back to Ranchi. While driving, we could not help but discuss the dominant man of the village, the forceful, hard-spoken Sarvodaya worker. It was plain to us that he planned, directed and personally supervised the work of the village. He was used to telling the Adivasis what he thought was good for them. While it might be too strong to say that he browbeat the villagers, he certainly was used to having his own way. The Adivasis had been freed of their zamindar, but did they now have a new kind of village super-headman?

Coastal Andhra

In the field of cooperation, coastal Andhra is a land of extremes. In the southern districts, cooperatives function at as low a level as can be found in India today; while in the northern district of Vizagapatam, the cooperatives rank among the country's finest. Since I entered Andhra from the south, the cooperatives in Nellore and Guntur districts which I visited first were the worst. In recording this opinion, it is only fair to add that the harshest judges of the working of cooperatives along the South Andhra coast were officers and directors of those cooperatives. They vied with each other in pointing out the most serious defects of their societies, perhaps partly in the hope that thereby they would bring closer the day when those deficiencies would no longer be present.

Nellore District has the panoply of agricultural cooperatives that is fairly common today: central cooperative bank, district marketing society, cooperative rural banks, large-sized societies, multi-purpose rural credit societies, and ordinary single village primary societies. When I asked cooperative officials how much the ordinary small and middle peasants benefited from the complex structure, they told me frankly, "Not much." The cooperatives furnish less than 10 per cent of the district's total rural credit needs. Less than one per cent of the main crop, paddy, is cooperatively marketed. To get a loan of more than Rs. 500, the peasant must not only have land, he must hold it as an owner. In practice all loans of more than Rs. 500 must be secured by unencumbered, immovable property. Credit continues to be linked to land assets, not to production.

The implication of this will be clearer when we review the current land-holding position in Nellore District. According to the senior-most cooperative officers and directors, half of the people in the district are not landholders and get little benefit from the cooperatives. On the other hand, the minority who have much land and good connections have many ways of securing substantial benefit.

The larger or largest landholders almost invariably provide the office-holders and directors of the cooperatives. Frequently they themselves and their family members are among the largest borrowers. Loans taken ostensibly for agricultural purposes may not be spent for that. District bank officers told me that of 128 loans given for pump sets in one year, only 8 were actually bought. The same position holds for loans to build wells. Instead, agricultural credit is being diverted to water, transport, mica, cattle or other business. This is so notorious that central bank directors told me that among the bigger people a cooperative rural bank or big society is no longer an aid in running a non-agricultural business, but a necessity. To start or to expand their private, non-agricultural business, the bigger people form a larger sized society or a cooperative rural bank. They know how to bring sufficient pressure from above on the local registrars and central bank officers so as to get what they want.

" *Emmelaitis* "

As in Coimbatore District the cooperative movement in Nellore plays a subordinate and secondary role to that of the private trading-money-lending-processing interests. Peasants repay their loans, reborrow, and hand the cash over to the private merchant-moneylenders, some of whom are owners of private rice mills, who use it in their own operations. Quite a number of these merchant-moneylenders are themselves substantial landholders who belong to or are heads of cooperative societies. The cooperative movement in coastal Andhra is permeated with politics, certainly with politicians. As the centre of the biggest cooperative operations (i.e., in the district marketing societies, the central banks, and the cooperative rural banks), one is almost certain to find in Nellore and neighbouring Andhra Districts one or more M. L.As. This condition, which affects not only parts of Andhra but many other areas of South India, may be called " emmelaitis ". So far as Nellore District is concerned, a number of the biggest names in Andhra Pradesh surely must know what is going on there, since they themselves hail from that district.

The cooperative movement of Vizagapatam District stands in sharpest contrast to that of Nellore. This is particularly true of the societies in Anakapalle and Yellamanchili Talukas, where a pilot project was undertaken in 1956, for the merger of about 150 small credit societies into less than thirty of the large-sized cooperatives recommended by the Reserve

Bank's Rural Credit Survey. The leadership of the pilot project has come from the Cooperative Central Bank of Vizianagaram.

In visiting four of these new large-size societies, I was struck at once by the fact that their heads and directors were agriculturists. They either went out to work in the fields with their own hands, or they have regular, direct, on-the-spot supervision on their labourers. From several angles of approach I endeavoured to ascertain whether there were among them any merchants, moneylenders, contractors, or other businessmen. The members of the Ankapalle cooperatives, I was repeatedly assured, knew very well that these business people were unsuitable for responsible posts in cooperatives; very few moneylenders were even members of the societies, and those who had joined were kept far way from the helm of affairs. As might be expected, some of the directors of the central bank and of the district marketing society were big people; among them, however, I could find only one solitary M.L.A. In the large-size societies at the village level, however, there were no giants; most directors were simply small or middlesized landowners.

They conceded that so far they had not done much for tenants and labourers. In the past, the main basis for loans had been the security of land. Hence well over half of the cooperative members had been landowners; many of these, of course, were small or tiny owners. Now, as part of the Pilot Project, the societies were shifting over to a new basis for credit. They were keeping comprehensive records of their members, showing the total income of each, indebtedness, expenses, etc. From these records the societies desired to arrive at a calculation for each member of "estimated surplus" or "saving capacity". On this basis they hoped to make more realistic loans, not only to owners, but to tenants and even labourers. They were already enrolling more tenants and labourers as members, and trying to give them larger credit than in the past.

Anakapalle Pilot Project

The societies in the Anakapalle Pilot Project are keeping other valuable statistics. Their tables of distribution of loans by size were particularly interesting. They show that, unlike the Kolhapur case, most loans are made in small and medium amounts; the total amounts lent in units of Rs. 500, Rs. 1,000, or more, do not seem disproportionate. This would tend to confirm my impression that, unlike Nellore, the big people in Vizagapatam are not in control of the societies and are not exploiting them for their own ends.

In contrast to many other parts of India, the cooperative movement in Vizagapatam does not seem to be subordinate to the sowkars, dalas, or other middlemen. If anything, the societies are gaining at their expense. The total amount of credit advanced at low rates of interest by the cooperatives has been growing rapidly. In the vicinity of Anakapalle the cooperatives are lending so much that they are causing a fall in the moneylenders' rates of interest. Whereas these used to run around 12 per cent,

18 per cent, 24 per cent, or more, now the big landlord-moneylenders are reported to be asking peasants to come and borrow at 9 per cent per year. Some of the big moneylenders are stated to be giving up their old profession and going in for cinema buildings and for P.W.D. contracts.

In its work at Anakapalle the Cooperative Central Bank has scored a number of important successes. In part, this is ascribable to the fact that the directors, officers, and staff of the bank itself are strong in character and competence. They have planned their work in a careful and methodical fashion; and at each stage they seem to have explained in a convincing fashion to the peasant members of the societies what they were about and why. Far from issuing premature press releases, they seem to have done their work quietly, without benefit of publicity.

There are some background reasons which may help to explain why the work has gone well. The Maharajah of Vizianagaram, quite some decades back, used to have the largest zamindari tract in British India. Long before the days of Bhoodan, he renounced his ownership rights in favour of the peasants, and thereby turned them into holders of raiyatwari rights. He performed a number of other notable acts, which helped to develop in Vizianagaram a spirit of public-mindedness and civic responsibility. We should also note that Vizagapatam is not a rich delta area, with the great extremes of wealth and poverty so frequently found in these tracts. Instead the soils of the district are on the poor side, and the water supply far from the best. There is a large mass of middle to small peasant holders. They are sufficiently spirited so as not to be intimidated by the big people; on the other hand, they are not so competitive, individualistic, or quarrelsome that they cannot cooperate with each other.

In one crucial sphere, however, the Anakapalle Pilot Project has progressed rather slowly, that is, in the linking of credit and marketing. As the Central Bank President himself stated, the total loans issued to members of the large-size societies in the year 1957-58 amounted to more than 100 lakhs of rupees; but the societies used the cooperative agency for the marketing of members' produce only to the tune of about Rs. 22 lakhs. In other words, the Reserve Bank's scheme of integrating credit and marketing still has a long way to go in Anakapalle. Here it should be noted that, like Kolhapur, Anakapalle is one of India's greatest jaggery centres. The trade is a lucrative one; to maintain their control of it, the private dealers will fight long and hard. As against the cooperatives, there are many points in their favour.

As we have seen elsewhere, the private traders can advance as much as they want to the peasant producers, and they can advance for any purpose. The cooperative marketing society at Anakapalle, which mainly handles jaggery, used to try to match the flexibility of the private traders in giving credit. The Reserve Bank, however, has called for the separation of the marketing function from the loan function. In deference to these orders from higher up, the Anakapalle Marketing Society no longer gives advances to the members of cooperative societies. In the last few weeks of the cane-cum-jaggery season, however, the peasants almost invariably need a final instalment of credit, to help meet the costs of converting their cane into jaggery. They used to get this from the Marketing Society. Normally they cannot hope to get it from their own cooperative credit society, because they have already borrowed from that society up to their limit. In this situation, they have had to turn to the private trader.

According to the Cooperative Central Bank, this is an important reason for the large gap between the total cooperative advances to members, and value of total produce marketed through the cooperatives. The Central Bank officers do not wish to question the principle of separating the marketing from the credit function. But they do feel that the principle should be applied at the right time. When the cooperative marketing society at Anakapalle was made to stop giving advances to peasants, there was no other cooperative agency ready to take over its credit function. There still is none. Had the marketing society gone on issuing credit as in the past, much more jaggery, they say, would have been cooperatively marketed.

Saurashtra

The work of organizing cooperatives has been given a high priority in Saurashtra. During the past ten years the authorities have been proceeding very rapidly toward their goal of having every village or group of villages served by a cooperative society. One is inclined to wonder whether the pace of activity in forming cooperatives in Saurashtra has been matched anywhere else in India. In many hundreds of villages of Saurashtra, the authorities told us, cent per cent of the cultivators were members of cooperatives. Thus in the district of Madhya Saurashtra, which includes Rajkot, there are said to be today 284 villages in which all the khatedars (holders of land) belong to cooperatives. We were told, in fact, that many of these cultivators were so well off that they did not really have to belong to any society. The cooperative organizers had nonetheless persuaded them or put pressure on them to join because the achievement of 100 per cent membership among cultivators looked so well on the records!

There are many reasons why Saurashtra should have provided favourable ground for cooperative organization. Saurashtra has been famous for its trading activity since remote antiquity. Its peasants, who grow money crops like cotton and ground-nuts, have a keen sense of business. As against the supply of credit at exorbitant rates from traders or moneylenders, they can easily understand the advantages of societies which provide them substantial credit at low rates. They also know the wisdom of prompt repayment of loans, to keep up the good reputation required for getting adequate credit.

The agricultural economy of Saurashtra is noteworthy for the relatively large size of holdings and for the relatively good condition of the livestock. Furthermore there are many non-agricultural activities in

Saurashtra—the area is perhaps less dependent on agriculture than any other sizeable region in India and these help to provide the cultivators with a good market or with supplementary sources of work or income.

As an area which was first organized into a State in 1949, Saurashtra came under a vigorous new administration. The shift from princely to popular rule also brought into prominence a relatively young group of political leaders and social workers. Determined to modernize their State, they pursued an energetic go-ahead policy. In this they had ample support from, and good connections in, the Central Government and Congress headquarters in New Delhi. To a considerable extent the momentum of their activity continued in the years after 1956, when Saurashtra was absorbed into Bombay State. Saurashtra today, it should be noted, is completely covered by community projects, either of the intensive block type or the national extension service.

Early in the 1950's the Saurashtra Government put down the near-rebellion of Bhupat and his friends among the former Princes. The land reforms in Saurashtra, principally girasdari abolition, constitute a major achievement. Parallel with their work in the cooperative field, the Saurashtra leaders have also been launching Panchayats. Today Saurashtra is covered with Panchayats and cooperatives; and at the village level, the same local leader is very often the head of both organizations.

Kevadra

One of the outstanding societies in Saurashtra is in the village of Kevadra, about 10 miles from Keshod, in the best-off district of Saurashtra, namely, Sorath. Accordingly, we drove down from Rajkot to Junagadh and then via Keshod on to Kevadra, by excellent roads all the way. In Kevadra the leading figure is Thakkerseybhai Dhanji. Up to 1949 he had been a moneylender-cum-trader. He also had a cloth shop in Keshod, while in Kevadra itself he operated, together with three partners, a mill to expel oil from groundnuts. The ordinary cultivators in Kevadra were at that time very short of credit; they had so little, in fact, that to get money they used to sell their standing crops at low prices to the moneylenders-cum-traders. A registrar of cooperatives came to Kevadra and told Thakkerseybhai he should start a society. He did so and, for some time, ran his own shop parallel with the cooperative. Then he closed down his shop, gave up moneylending, and applied himself only to the society. In 1952 he sold to the society at cost prices his oil mill and his huller for husking paddy. He has continued all along as head of the cooperative, while one of his partners is the secretary. Thakkerseybhai is also Sarpanch of the Village Panchayat.

The society today provides, we were told, all the agricultural finance of the 160 cultivators from Kevadra and one other nearby village who belong to it. They also get their seeds, fertilizer, and manure mixture from the society. Practically all of the members, we were informed, sell their cash crops through the society. The society also has a shop which sells cloth, sugar, gur, cereals, pulses, and other daily requirements. *To members* the society can sell on credit; this facility helps them to meet some of their non-agricultural needs for credit, e.g., the foodstuffs for a wedding feast. The area is quite prosperous, we were told, and cultivators usually can finance their personal needs from their own surpluses.

The groundnut oil mill which Thakkerseybhai sold to the society is reported to be very profitable. In the current year it is expected to make a profit of about Rs. 20,000; the price at which it was sold to the society is only Rs. 24,000. The mill employs a number of regular workers; the male employees are paid at the rate of Rs. 2 per day.

The Kevadra Society is distinguished by the fact that it has about 90 to 100 non-landholders as members. To them (Harijans, agricultural labourers, smiths and carpenters) the society is prepared to lend up to a limit of about Rs. 200. Out of its charity funds the society buys school-books for the children of its members.

For the past half-dozen years Thakkerseybhai himself has been cultivating land, and so has the secretary of the society. The actual work in the fields seems to depend on annual labourers who are called Sathis. They may be paid anywhere from Rs. 200 to Rs. 1,000 per annum; the average seems to be about Rs. 350 or 400. This is exclusive of food, cloth, etc. which are also provided by the cultivator. The Sathis are not paid a share of the crop, we were told, because of the legal restriction (which presumably endangers the holdings of those who get their land cultivated through cropsharers).

The officers of the Kevadra Society told us that there were 4 or 5 other cooperatives like theirs in Keshod Taluk, covering altogether 15 or 20 of the 52 villages in the taluk.

Thana-Pipri

From Keshod we proceeded to Vanthali, a neighbouring taluk in Sorath District, and visited the active society in Thana-Pipri. Like Kevadra, this cooperative has a wide range of activities in credit, marketing, agricultural supplies and sale of such consumer goods as cloth. Although it has just built a godown, it has not gone on to erect a processing mill; the officers hope to have by next year a ginning mill and an oil mill.

The Thana-Pipri Society was started in 1949, at the suggestion of a leading figure in Rajkot. From an original list of 50, the membership roll has steadily gone up until today it stands at 406. The cooperative covers three villages which have a total of 280 landholders (Khatedars); of these, 268 are in the society. The maximum which the society lends to a member is Rs. 1,500. At the time of our visit, 40 persons had received loans of this size. The total short-term loans made by the society amounted to Rs. 1,45,000; while the medium-term loans totalled Rs. 20,000.

The society has keen competition from local merchants in marketing groundnuts. The officers feel that they have had more success in the field of credit. Previously there used to be 15 moneylenders in Thana-Pipri, whereas now there are only 5. The founder of the society himself had been a trader (which in this area normally means moneylender as well). He told us that the society cannot lend much on a long-term basis to small cultivators. Previously, he said, they used to have to resort to the traders. Now there is a land mortgage bank which gives them up to 40 per cent of the value of their land. He also told us that the cultivators here usually had a surplus after they had sold their crops and paid off their loans to the society. This surplus they would draw on for weddings, other unusual occasions, and extra expenses. Then they would borrow again from the society for agricultural purposes.

Quite a number of the smaller cultivators and others go to the traders for their marginal requirements of Rs. 100 or so. If the society could lend these marginal amounts to them, he said, they would not go to the traders.

Vanthali

We went on from Thana-Pipri to the taluka town of Vanthali, which has a population of 14,000. Vanthali, we were told, has the richest land in all of Saurashtra. About 500 khatedars (landlords) live in Vanthali of whom 437 are members of the local multi-purpose cooperative society. The chairman of the cooperative is Muljibhai Patel, a well-known Congress worker. When we called upon him, he told us that one of the first two community project blocks in Saurashtra had been started in Vanthali. The community projects authorities indicated that a cooperative in Vanthali would be desirable. There was great opposition to this idea from some agriculturists who were simultaneously active in trading and moneylending. The other cultivators decided to take things into their own hands. Under the leadership of Muljibhai Patel, who holds 60 acres, they formed a society about six years ago. Muljibhai became the first Chairman and has held the post ever since.

The society has been particularly successful in the fields of credit, marketing, and sale of supplies. Last year the society advanced Rs. 2 lakhs to its members. The average loan amounted to Rs. 500. The maximum loan was Rs. 2,000, which was made available to 30 or 40 members. During the current year the society has sold as commission agents Rs. 16 lakhs of produce. The society handles, Muljibhai Patel told us, 90 per cent of the cash crops (cotton and groundnuts) of its members. As against the private traders, Muljibhai told us, the society gets the support of its members by giving them full weight for their produce and by paying them a slightly higher price. The society also makes available to its members a wide variety of supplies and services. The most interesting of these is protection against roaming cattle which are a great trouble in this area. For a small charge per acre the society has stationed men armed with guns who protect the members' fields against these animals and the shepherds who let them loose.

According to Muljibhai no member of the society now has to go for finance to a trader or moneylender. As a result he said, ten cultivators-cum-moneylenders who had previously opposed the society had now given up money lending. Today they only did cultivation and trading, because they could not compete in credit with the society. In fact, they had now become members of the society. The society proposes to expand its activities by going on next year to the building of a cooperative oil mill and other processing facilities.

In Madhya Saurashtra District we visited three well-reputed societies, each of which had its own interesting peculiarities. The first of these was the multi-purpose society at Sardhar which lies 17 miles to the east of Rajkot, on the highway to Bhavnagar. This society had the largest membership among those we visited in Saurashtra, namely, 551. Its total advances to members were correspondingly large, namely, Rs. 2·5 lakhs for short-term loans and Rs. 1·2 lakhs for medium-term loans. Further, against produce deposited with it for sale, the society had advanced another Rs. 2 lakhs. Four out of five members of the society, we were told, sold the great bulk of their cash crops through the society. The officers of the society assured us that in credit and marketing the old grip of the traders over the cultivators had been broken.

There are some limitations on the activities of the society which may be worth noting. The society lends only to members, but as members it has only khatedars (landholders). Further, the only loans which it has been making are for agricultural purposes. The normal limit of short-term loans is Rs. 750 while that for medium-term loans (three years) is Rs. 2,000. The members of the society can get loans from it for personal purposes only by entering some other reason on the loan application form. There is reason to believe that some have been doing this.

Non-landholders comprise somewhat more than 50 per cent of the 10,000 people who live in the 15 villages served by the Sardar Society. To date the cooperative movement has not reached these people and they continue to be dependent upon the traders-cum-moneylenders, whether registered or unregistered. We were informed that the secretary of the society, right from the start in 1955, has been a man of girasdar class. These ex-landlords have not always been noted for their cooperative spirit toward mere cultivators, let alone the less fortunate (possibly Harijan) agricultural labourers.

Sindhavadar

The society at Sindhavadar is stated to be the most active in Wankaner Taluk, but by contrast with the ones we visited in other talukas it is a modest operation. In an area of 4 villages it has 141 members; the total loans in the current year amount to Rs. 40,000. Loans have been made to 106 persons, the largest loan amounting to Rs. 650.

The secretary of the Sindhavadar Society since its inception in 1950 is an ex-moneylender-cum-trader. He said that he was acquainted with the Registrar of Cooperative Societies, who told him it was desired to start a cooperative society. He accordingly undertook the task, beginning with only 11 members. The president of the society is a Muslim who is active in the Wankaner Taluka Cooperative Bank; one of the members of the society's managing committee is Sarpanch of the Sindhavadar village Panchayat.

In view of the restricted scope of the society's activities we were not surprised to be told by non-members of the society that there was a good deal of informal moneylending in the village, on a person-to-person basis. Some of the bigger people in the village, including the Sarpanch, were stated to do this, but it was not clear what rate of interest they charged, if any. We were also informed that there was an intriguing system of lending money at what would appear to be no interest at all. Rather than take interest, the creditor would purchase his debtor's crop, but perhaps pay him only 30 per cent, 40 per cent or 50 per cent of the value.

One of the most active societies which we visited is at Kolithad in Gondal Taluk, 26 miles from Rajkot. This society provides credit, markets produce, sells foodgrains and agricultural supplies, processes groundnuts, and will soon be ginning cotton. In the 12 villages which it serves it has 522 members, all of whom are landholders.

Prior to 1950 there was nothing, we were told, by way of cooperation here. The idea of starting a society came from the Assistant Registrar who was the younger brother of one of the leading Patels in the village. They began with 25 members and a small amount of capital. Their work in credit and supplies went well. Some of them had been thinking about starting an oil mill privately, but they were persuaded by the Assistant Registrar to launch it on a cooperative basis. For a long time they were worried as to how they could raise the funds for so large a venture. In the end they spent Rs. 23,000 on land and buildings and Rs. 21,000 on oil mill machinery.

They met these expenses by putting everything they had into the oil mill, including their share capital, their deposits, borrowings, etc. The Saurashtra State Cooperative Bank in Rajkot has aided their venture by lending them Rs. 20,000 on a short-term basis, against the personal responsibility and signatures of the chairman and members of the managing committee of the Kolithad Society. In the first six months of operation the mill earned a net profit of Rs. 7,000. The society hopes to earn an equal amount in the next six months. They are worried, however, about competition from private mill owners in Gondal and Rajkot who, they say, offer a better price to the peasant producers but cheat on weight and by various deductions.

The head of the society, who is also village Sarpanch, told us that private moneylending had declined around Kolithad. Nonetheless, there were a number of well-off cultivators who were still lending privately. Formerly, these agriculturist-moneylenders had not been members of the Kolithad Society. There was no advantage in having them as members and they were not wanted. The pressure to enroll them came when the authorities in Rajkot raised the target of cooperative membership among landholders from 75 per cent to 100 per cent. Then they were taken in; some of them are now on the Society's managing committee. They are in a minority there, we were assured, and so cannot do any harm.

In considering these Saurashtra societies as a group one is led to wonder about the extent to which the cultivators in this well-off area are coming forward to cooperate in the use of their own resources; or whether they are showing more active interest in obtaining access, by following prescribed procedures, to grants, subsidies, loans, advances and other aid from the State. The principal activity of these societies is the fostering of cash crops. Under cooperative auspices land previously under foodgrains may be going over to cotton and groundnuts. In the context of India's food shortage this may not be an altogether desirable development.

One is tempted to refer to the Saurashtra societies as a case of the fusion of sarkari, sahakari and sowkari; and to wonder how stable, in the years to come, this mixture will prove.

1

RURAL INDUSTRIES*

THE WEAKEST spot in our programmes of community development is the development of rural industries for providing employment to the unemployed and the underemployed. From the data available, it appears that only 2·5 per cent of the families have been benefited by our activities in the 80 blocks examined by us. These figures are too generous in that the benefit of employment to one man has been equated to benefit to one whole family; also the employment has been assumed to be full employment. Even so, this additional employment introduced in the village is insufficient to set off the two years' increase in population. The training-cum-production centres have been the main channel of opening new rural industries. Figures available, however, show that more than 50 per cent of the persons passing out of such centres do not take up the profession to which they have been trained. These disquieting facts have to be faced and our present approach to the problem has to be revised radically.

To this end steps have to be taken for:

(i) carrying out a rapid local economic and technical survey in each block in the possibility of specific industries;

(ii) training for improvement of existing technical skills and introduction of new ones in consonance with the findings of (i) above;

(iii) establishment of pilot projects to demonstrate the technical feasibility and economic soundness of any particular industry or industries;

(iv) co-ordination of cottage, village and small-scale industries;

(v) rural electrification which could equally well serve irrigation purposes;

(vi) provision of credit for rural industry;

(vii) supply of raw material where necessary and of improved designs;

(viii) quality control and facilities for marketing; and

(ix) research, technical supervision and guidance.

---

* Reproduced from *Report of the Team for the Study of Community Projects and N. E. S.*, Vol. I, pp. 91-92. (Balwantrai Mehta Committee).

Cottage, village and small-scale industries need a very considerable co-ordination in their working. They have their appropriate place in the rural economy but sometimes are apt to cut into one another. At the all-India level, a number of such individual industries are promoted by all-India boards which sometimes are inclined to work in separate compartments. It should not be difficult to make some effort to pool funds, personnel, agencies of supervision and inspection and marketing arrangements so that inefficiency and waste can be minimised. The all-India boards, themselves should function through State boards nominated by the State Governments in consultation with them. The State boards in their turn should function through the various State departments concerned with the industry and through local representative organisations.

DIFFICULTIES CONFRONTING COTTAGE INDUSTRIES*

TAKING UP first those difficulties which are special to cottage industries, as distinguished from agriculture, three main items are obvious:

(1) Cottage industries have to face the competition of larger, better organized and technically much more competent units in the shape of the manufacturing industries situated in towns and cities.

(2) The market for cottage industries is much less assured than for the agricultural industry. Fortunately for the latter, food is firstly wanted by all, and secondly is still grown on land and not in factories. For cottage industries, on the other hand, the essence of the problem is to find a market and then not lose it to a more powerful urban competitor.

(3) The other important special problem for many cottage industries is the finding of the raw material. Thus, one of the greatest difficulties of the handloom industry, except perhaps in periods of control, has been that of the purchase of yarn. A number of weavers' co-operative societies, it is interesting to note, are little more than societies for buying yarn and distributing it among their members.

Apart from these items, all of them grave and all of them important, the nature of the difficulties seems essentially the same for cottage industries as for agriculture when looked at from the point of view of the reorganization and rehabilitation of the industry on a co-operative basis. The main and still largely unsolved problem for co-operative cottage industry is, we suggest, the same that has been faced by co-operative agriculture, namely, how to make a combination of the very weak strong enough in relation to the much stronger. Just as there is the moneylender in the sphere of agricultural credit, so there is the *Karkhanadar* for each important cottage industry, with the difference that he combines in himself the handicraftsman and the financier. The *karkhanadar* is himself part of a wider system of private finance. Thus a whole set of private creditors, financing agencies, marketing agencies, etc., deal with the individual small weaver, as do the private traders and private financiers with the cultivator. We would, in this connection, quote from a note which appears in the First Annual Report (1954) of the All-India Handloom Board.

" Since, according to the Fact Finding Committee's Report, the un-

---

*Reproduced from *The General Report of the Committee of Direction of the All-India Rural Credit Survey*, Vol. II, pp. 507-508.

organised condition of the industry is responsible for its abnormal high marketing costs and its consequent evils, it is but natural to accord pride of place to the organisation of the industry in all schemes aiming at the stabilization of the ancient industry and thereby ensuring the prosperity of the weavers." According to the Fact Finding Committee, the official agencies have fostered only co-operative organisations which have, speaking generally, suffered from financial weakness, inefficiency of management and inability to cope with fluctuation in yarn prices and with marketing of the finished product. The Committee has also emphasised the age-long social and business relations and, in most cases, ties of caste and creed between the master-weavers, sowcars and mahajans, on the one hand and the weavers on the other, which may have been primarily responsible for the half-hearted support accorded to the co-operative movement. It is also possible that the lack of credit facilities on social occasions such as marriages, *pujahs*, absence of any effective voice in the management of co-operative organisation and the smallness of the capital invested by him in the society did not evoke the enthusiasm of the weaver who preferred to eke out an existence as best as he could with the aid and support of the master-weaver or the sowcar mahajan. It is also not unlikely that co-operative organizations invited within their fold only the weavers and thus alienated the sympathy of the master-weavers and the mahajans.

"The next question of importance is the question of marketing. In so far as the independent weavers are concerned, they form the smaller proportion of the weaver population in the country; no tangible relief could be possible unless they join either the co-operative or any other organization which may be fostered. Their slender finances, chronic indebtedness and, therefore, complete dependence on the yarn dealer for the supply of yarn on credit leave them no option other than that of selling at the buyer's price. Unless, therefore, they are brought within the fold of such organisation as would supply them yarn on credit and take back the finished product at prices based on standard wages and replacement cost of yarn, they would in due course of time be relegated to the position of mere wage-earners.

"...The numerous types of middlemen and the functions of each has been dealt with fully by the Fact Finding Committee in paragraphs 60 to 63 of its Report, and the Committee has discussed the middlemen's profit in paragraph 124. The Committee has also come to the conclusion that 'there are far too many middlemen participating in the trade and that their efficiency and individual turnover are much lower than they should be. At the same time, there are many middlemen who appear to be keeping their heads above water by taking a proportionately higher share of the gross profits of the industry than the weaver himself.' The Committee has emphasised that the cost of marketing of handloom fabrics is 'prohibitively high and that the middleman is largely to be blamed for this.' 'The principal problem, therefore, so far as marketing is concerned, is how to reduce the marketing costs."

iii. *Problems of Administration*

1

PROBLEMS OF ADMINISTRATION*

(a) Village Leadership and Administration

It is not only the urban-induced power of the private moneylender and the private trader that affects the success of co-operatives when it manifests itself either inside or outside the society. Affinity is not confined to these two; it extends to the leadership in the village whether this is based on property or derived from connection with the administration. The bigger landlord has ways which conform with those of the moneylender, and indeed, as we have said, he is often the moneylender or trader himself. The village headman is also drawn from the same class, and it is usual for these to have connections which link them not only to the sources of finance but to the seats of administrative power. Subordinate officials, revenue and other—including those of the relatively low-paid co-operative department—have often no alternative but to stay with these village leaders and be dependent on them for ordinary amenities when they visit the village or camp in it for a few days. In this and other ways is initiated a process of association with those who wield power and influence in the village and who for that reason have their own uses as the local instruments of an administration which resides in towns and cities and which in varying degrees is inaccessible to the ordinary villager. This close conformity of association and interests between the subordinate officials of Government and the more powerful elements in the village is a matter to be borne in mind as of great significance in explaining the failure of implementation of the policies and directives, co-operative or other, emanating from the higher levels of the administration. Sometimes, temporarily overawed by superior official authority or enthused by missionary-minded officers, an important measure of co-operative policy, for example, may in fact be translated into practice in the village; but it is not often that the effect is lasting; frequently the directions merely remain on paper, especially where they involve some disadvantage to the more powerful in the village. Acting in concert with these, the subordinate official, whose functions take him to the village, creates for the benefit of the superior officers what might be called the illusion of implementation woven round the reality of non-compliance.

* Reproduced from *The General Report of the Committee of Direction of the All-India Rural Credit Survey*, Volume II, (a) pp. 277-278 and (b) pp. 525-528.

Several factors in the village help to create this effect, not least among them the powerful influence of caste. If the leader is of a particular caste, it is unusual for others of the same caste in the village to report to superior authority that things are otherwise than as reported by the leader and the subordinate official. This marked tendency towards the promotion of an impression of change around changelessness, of active obedience to behest around stolid resistance to instructions, which only the most persistent and detailed supervision from above can check, has always to be taken into account in assessing the worth of reports that the policies of Government have been put into operation in the village. The consideration is one which must qualify both satisfaction and belief when it is found stated, for example, of a particular area, that tenancy laws have been enforced, or that moneylenders are not operating without due authorization, or that co-operative societies are actively functioning from year to year. The *status quo* and the non-compliance are often achieved conjointly and at great effort by the leading elements in the village and the subordinate agencies of Government. The balance attained may be the result of some completely new alignment of forces, of some new distribution of perquisites or of some new passing of 'consideration'. The persons who suffer in this process are the weaker and disadvantaged elements of the village for whose benefit the directives and policies are conceived. Among the combinations of factors which thus operate against the interests of the bulk of those who reside in the village is the rigidity of caste feeling in conjunction with the power derived from money, land, leadership, and above all, the affiliation with the superior forces of urban economy. The rigidity of caste loyalty remains, while the original division of caste functions no longer does. The result is that the londlord who may also be moneylender, the moneylender who may also be trader and the educated person who may also be subordinate official, all these through their association with the outside urban world of finance and power wield an influence in the village which at many points is diverted from the good of the village to the benefit of the caste or even of a close circle of relatives.

(b) Problems of Quality of Administration

Besides Planning, an important aspect of the larger context with which we are concerned, by reason of the bearing which it has on our recommendations, is Administration. We have elsewhere made various suggestions which come under this head: organisation of training, strengthening of co-operative departments, formation of new cadres, etc. From the standpoint of a programme such as is here envisaged, the reorganisation required in respect of the co-operative departments alone will be considerable. But the administrative problem in the larger context, in so far as it has relevance to co-ordinated programmes of national development of which this may be regarded as a part, is much wider than re-organisation of cooperative departments or the training of the personnel of those and other departments and institutions. The particular items to which we propose to confine our brief remarks in this chapter are: (1) the selection and training of the personnel concerned with such programmes; (2) the effectiveness of implementation as ensured by supervision; and (3) the wider question of reorganization at different levels in the context of development.

As we have already emphasised, not only the training but also the recruitment of the personnel will have to be looked at from the point of view of the new functions. Thus, a capacity for sympathy, understanding and responsiveness, in the sense in which we have used those terms in relation to the rural environment and to the needs of different rural classes, should be among the qualities to which importance should be attached in recruiting new candidates. For, unless that capacity is initially present and is fostered and encouraged at all stages, the warning would be relevant that "to exchange the landlord for the tax-gatherer, the merchant for the agent of State monopolies and the moneylender for the State Bank official, may prove to be not progress but enslavement."

To the extent that official attitudes are rigid, unresponsive and unimaginative, they will stultify the progress in every one of the directions envisaged. In particular, they will be fatal to the objective of evolving State-partnered co-operative institutions, especially at the rural level, into fully co-operative institutions at the earliest possible stage. Moreover, it is here that the administrator and the official will be called upon to discharge the extremely difficult task of helping others to help themselves; in other words, while doing important work as an officer of government, yet so to perform it as to make himself dispensable within the shortest possible time.

Honesty and Efficiency

Besides sympathy and informed responsiveness, two important requirements are obviously honesty and efficiency. On the latter it is needless to dwell. There is evident in India today a sad lack of honesty in different degrees and at different levels of administration and governance. In a programme for the positive economic benefit of the weaker, in conditions in which certain sections of the rich and the powerful will ever be interested in the failure of the programme—both broadly and in the detail of its effect on themselves in so far as it is their position of vantage and their power of competition that will be sought to be weakened—it is more than ordinarily necessary that the strictest honesty should be enforced and dishonesty punished. The fact has to be faced that the sociological soil of India today is more favourable to corruption and oppression than to co-operation and planning. Corruption has its roots not only in men's characters but also, and from the point of view of social remedy more relevantly and more deeply, in men's institutions. In India at present, the largest single factor institutionally responsible for corruption may be said to be the lack of egalitarianism where this lack is most basically present, viz., in the Indian village. For, corruption is the exchange of some form of favour against the public interest for some form of satisfaction of private interest. The latter is offered by the man who wants the favour. But favour against the public interest implies that someone else is disadvantaged, viz., the man who cannot offer the satisfaction. This is the weak man. The greater the degree and extent of inequality between strong and weak, rich and poor, the greater the reason and the larger the occasion to seek favours. Perfect egalitarianism, if that were possible, might almost be said to be a perfect safeguard against corruption. These considerations make it all the more important to demand the highest standards of honesty not only of those concerned with the implementation of programmes of development, but also of those in public life, administrative and political, generally.

On the need for ensuring by efficient supervision that there has been actual implementation, we would observe that there are two big illusions in India which too often take away people's thoughts, often involuntarily, from the realities of action and effect. These are the legislative and administrative illusions. Legislation says, 'This shall be done,' and after such interval as may be dictated by propriety, expediency or sometimes sheer inefficiency, Administration answers back, 'That has been done.' While Legislation and Administration thus proceed from one exchange to another, the old realities often continue their former sway. In the context of development the failure to translate into administrative reality what has been laid down as governmental policy would vitiate all programmes except on paper. The utmost importance should therefore be attached and the strictest standards of efficiency enforced in the execution of policy, and in the supervision of execution, at all levels.

Rural Needs and Administrative Reforms

Many schemes and many suggestions for the re-organisation of the administrative set-up in order that the needs of independent India may be more effectively served are before the Government of the day. As in the reform of co-operative administration, so in that of general administration, especially in relation to the function of development, the main focus should be the village. It is necessary to emphasise this because, despite the welcome tendency to design certain important new measures of administration—such as National Extension—with the village in mind and round the village as centre, this requirement, which is basic to India's further development at this stage, is often lost sight of in the more comprehensive schemes of re-organisation. One sometimes comes across individual 'co-operators' who appear to think that co-operative re-organisation and development are best fostered by ensuring for its premier non-official bodies a continuity of political contacts at Delhi and a variety of international contacts at Geneva. But much greater than its need to go to the capitals of the world for guidance is the need of Indian co-operation to make, at long last, an effort to go to the Indian village for study and reflection and for genuine attempts to develop and reorganise. So too, for Indian administration as a whole, a vast field of research and action remains to be covered in the villages of the country. On lessons derived from rural India, rather than on those learnt from the unrelated experience of foreign, industrially more advanced and—in the socio-economic and political aspects—radically different countries, will have to be based both the assessment of administrative needs and the modification of structure to meet those needs. In the administrative structure itself are present two interrelated but not always coordinated aspects: the new and growing aspect of development and the old and 'basic' aspect of normal administration. The main task before the country being the bringing about of economic development in terms of simultaneous progress towards social egalitarianism, the prior function of the administrative structure as a whole—including the basic—may be said to be the promotion of conditions in which such development and progress will be possible. The indigenous situation, then, by which must be dictated all plans of administrative reorganisation, is wholly dissimilar to that, for example, of countries whose administration is geared to the free play of political and economic forces.

Considering the problem of administrative reform in the extended light of the analysis and proposals contained in this Report, the most important needs may be said to be these. There is first of all the need for Government to make its administrative role in the village more and more that of a beneficent authority and less and less that of the tax-gatherer which, for the most part, it has been till recently. Secondly, again in the village, there is the need for Government to assume the function of real partnership in economic development—especially of the middle and lower groups—and not merely that of administration on the one hand or of advice and 'extension' on the other. Thirdly, there is the need not only to simplify development administration at the village end, as in National Extension Service, but also to achieve effective co-ordination between (i) the different administrative agencies of development, including that of Local Self-Government and (ii) those agencies and the machinery of basic administration. A large field remains to be explored in connection with the more effective association of the local bodies of administration—*panchayats*, local boards, etc.—with local projects of planned development, e. g., those relating to minor irrigation, no less than roads, public health or primary education.

2

INAPPROPRIATE VILLAGE INSTITUTIONS*

(a) Inappropriate Extant Institution

An extremely important aspect of such an approach, in so far as the cultivator is concerned, is obviously the creation of an organization within the village which can be entrusted with the programme of production and other economic activities designed for the village as part of the bigger programme in the agricultural sector of the Plan. The search for such an organization may be said to be one of the main preoccupations of the Planning Commission. The position reached may be illustrated by the following extracts. These paragraphs appear in the Peoples Edition of the *First Five-Year Plan* (1953):

" It is greatly to be desired that in the agricultural part of the Plan, the village as a whole should be actively associated in fixing targets and working for their achievement. In recent years the State Governments have shown a welcome earnestness in establishing *panchayats* as civic bodies charged with general responsibility for the collective welfare of the village community. Many activities, such as framing programmes for production, obtaining and managing governmental grants for building roads, tanks, etc., introducing improvements in agricultural methods, organizing voluntary labour for community works and assisting in the implementation of legislation for economic and social reform, will fall within the purview of the *panchayat*.

" On the other hand, for the working of individual programmes of development, where the specific responsibility and liability of a member have to be ensured, a more binding form of association is necessary. Specific and practical tasks of reclaiming land, providing resources for better cultivation and for marketing the village produce are best performed through co-operatives. It is, however, very necessary that co-operative agencies in the village should have the closest possible relationship with the *panchayat*. Though in the discharge of their functions the two bodies have specific fields in which to operate, by having mutual representation and by common *ad hoc* committees for certain matters, it will be possible to build up a structure of democratic management through both the organisations. "

---

*Reproduced from *The General Report of the Committee of Direction of the All-India Rural Credit Survey*, Volume II, (a) pp. 521-523; (b) p. 520; (c) pp. 524-525.

'Village production councils' were the device thought of at an earlier stage as mentioned in the following quotation from the *Report of the Grow More Food Enquiry Committee*, 1952 :

"There are also village institutions that can be set up where they do not exist. *Panchayats* can be established under laws in force in States. And for every village or group of villages, according to conditions, there should be a multipurpose co-operative society for providing credit and supplies and giving other assistance needed by farmers including marketing. Close working relations should also be established with schools which can become useful centres of social education. On the question whether village *panchayats* or management boards or multi-purpose societies should be recognised as agents for implementation of development plans, opinion is divided. Some States favour the former and some the latter. There is also the Planning Commission's suggestion for village production councils. Each area should decide this on its own special needs and conditions. But it is worth emphasising again that no solution can be found to the problem of rural betterment unless local co-operation is secured to the maximum possible extent and the support of the best leadership is enlisted."

The Progress of the Plan (January 1954) contains the following passages which seem to indicate that village *panchayats* where possible, and *ad hoc* committees otherwise, are now favoured as instruments of development within the village :

"In the planning and implementation of the programme in the Community Projects and National Extension Areas the maximum use is being made of local popular organisations like *Panchayats* and Union Boards. Wherever *Panchayats* or Union Boards, organised along traditional lines, are effective, they are always utilised. In some areas, success has been achieved by entrusting developmental activities to *ad hoc* non-statutory bodies. These organisations have various names. In Madhya Pradesh they are called Gram Vikas Mandals; in Orissa, Gram Mangal Samities; in Madras, Gram Seva Sanghams, and in West Bengal, Palli Unnayan Samities. Participation of the people in developmental activities organised by these bodies is helping in the development of village leadership."

"Village *panchayats* have, thus, a vital role to play in the sphere of land reform and it is urgently necessary to establish a network of *panchayats* all over the country-side."

The problem itself was originally thus stated in the *First Five-Year Plan* (larger edition) in a passage in which the co-operative form of association, as a target if not an actuality, was considered to be the most desirable:

"According to their needs and experience, village communities will discover the arrangements which serve them best. There has to be a great deal of trial and experiment before patterns of organisation which will best promote the interests of the rural population can be evolved. Nevertheless, it is important to work towards a concept of co-operative village management, so that the village may become a vital, progressive and largely self-governing base of the structure of national planning and the existing social and economic disparities resulting from property, caste and status may be obliterated."

We have reproduced these extracts to illustrate the ineffectiveness of the search hitherto conducted for a body within the village which can assume responsibility for the execution of that part of the village plan which is concerned with agricultural production and development. If the analysis presented in this Report has some validity, the opinion may be hazarded that in most villages neither the *panchayat* nor an *ad hoc* committee would be an appropriate organization for being entrusted with this part of the task. Both these are likely to represent precisely those elements in the village which, by and large, operate against the interests of the middle and small cultivator. Here again, the more realistic approach seems to us to be to promote in the first instance those conditions which are necessary before such an organization can function successfully in the village in the context of better farm production and better farm business. For fulfilling this prior requirement, the effort on the part of the State, in the circumstances we have set out in detail, has to be a deliberate, concerted and nation-wide economic endeavour in combination, on a co-operative basis, with the weaker elements in the agricultural population itself. By and large, it is only State participation of this magnitude and direction that would constitute the needed approach. Into such an approach would then be fitted State activities such as National Extension and Community Development Project which, however important, cannot by themselves create conditions within the village which can be relied upon to retain their momentum after aid and supervision are withdrawn or reduced. The main task as recognized by the Plan is the generation within the village itself of forces which through their organic relation with village life and economy will continue to operate for the development and prosperity of the village. The creation of such forces by means which are not too costly in personnel and finance, which, in other words, can be adopted on a country-wide scale within a reasonable period, may be said to be the main problem of planning in relation to the important rural sector of the Plan.

(b) Want of Enthusiasm of the People

To the socio-economic problem which today confronts the country, the approach has necessarily to be constructive and constitutional; and if only for this reason—there are others such as, for example, are pertinent to the Indian tradition—the approach of violence and class conflict and of 'revolution' in terms of these two, is of course *a priori* excluded from consideration, but the gigantic constructive effort which this imposes on the State as well as the people and their institutions is the reverse of inaction, *laissez-faire* and lack of concerted purpose. All the more is it necessary, in such a context, to devise positive institutional modes of approach which, among other goals, lead to the resolution of conflict and mitigation of caste and class disparity, and the promotion of new factors of unity across the older divisions.

In the village itself, nothing is so important in this context as to build up a new loyalty of production—of common economic effort in the widest sense—across the loyalties of caste and the disparities of riches, influence and economic privilege. If the cultivators of the village, medium and small included, owned, if need be along with the State, the rice mill to which the harvested paddy was taken, if they converted their sugarcane into sugar in a factory which was co-operatively organized for them, if they were effectively served with both credit and marketing services by a rural co-operative society working in co-ordination with a co-operative marketing society at the erstwhile *mandi* and if in gradual process they combined to consolidate their holdings, or to organize a co-operative farm which reduced their expenses and increased their yield—in all these ways would be brought about a new sense of participation in common effort for the common benefit together with a new feeling of fellowship for those who shared the economic function, but not necessarily the caste, in common with themselves. In this new context, the association of the producer would not merely be with other producers, big or large, medium or small, but also with the State through their local representatives, i.e., the officials serving in the department or deputed to the society with whose guidance and alliance, together with the assistance of the finances made available by Government, the conditions and disparities of the older order could be made gradually to disappear. Only out of such association, socially and economically beneficent, with one another and with the State, would be born that enthusiasm for development which is recognized to be absent today in most villages in India despite large-scale efforts on the part of the Administration to improve the lot of the villager. This lack of enthusiasm may be illustrated from recent official experience. " In fact, " say the Grow More Food Enquiry Committee, with reference to that campaign, " the movement did not arouse nation-wide enthusiasm and did not become a mass movement for raising the level of village life. " " Measures of reform, " records the *Progress of the Plan* " have so far been enforced mainly through the revenue agency, but as the reforms take on a more radical character, it becomes more and more important that the people should be associated as fully as possible in their implementation. A new social and economic order cannot be built up without popular enthusiasm and the assistance of local leadership and initiative. " The recognition of the planning authorities that, for the next phase of the Plan, the design of development should be ' from the village upwards ' is itself evidence of the need to enlist the active interest of the villager in those measures for his economic benefit which today have failed to rouse him to whole-hearted participation.

This want of enthusiasm is a measure not of the smallness of governmental effort but of the vastness of the socio-economic disparity which the villager senses to be the main fact which conditions his life and which the policies and programmes of Government are seen by him to have left entirely unaffected. If, as may be assumed, in the larger context of the other disadvantaged groups in town and village, the next Five-Year Plan includes various programmes of economic amelioration, the same want of enthusiasm may be foreseen from these groups, if the same lack of effect is perceived by them to be inherent in the well-meaning and even costly efforts of the State conceived for the benefit of those very groups.

(c) Insoluble Problem in Present Conditions

The programme of development outlined in this Report—the development of co-operative credit, of co-operative marketing, processing and other economic activity, and of rural banking in order to facilitate the other two types of development—is concerned with the two main classes of rural producer: with the cultivator mainly, and with the handicraftsman incidentally. In the context of future planning, it may be assumed that, for the first, there will be an even bigger programme of agricultural production; and for the second, a large-scale programme for the development of cottage industries. For both, it may be further assumed that the next phase of the programme will be governed by the announced concept of planning upwards from the village. It is of the essence of such a concept that the new Plan will be no mere projection into the next five years of the many unfinished projects or continuing activities of the present Plan, but something else besides; for, such a projection of the present Plan, followed by its cutting up into local sections, would not constitute each such section a ' plan upwards ' from the particular locality, whether that locality be a village or a district. Mention has been made in the last chapter of the search for a suitable body inside the village which can take up and pursue a programme of agricultural development in which all the cultivators of the village can participate. This search for an appropriate village organization is symbolical of the wider effort to convert the present more or less super-imposed programme of economic improvement into something more in the nature of an organic development from within the village itself. From what point or nucleus shall this body of villagers be built up : from non-existent co-operative society, national production council, factious *panchayat* or, ignoring all these, from just an *ad hoc* committee in the village? The problem has not been solved because it is largely insoluble in present conditions. The search, as already indicated, is for something which can only emerge if the conditions requisite for it are first created by a State-partnered programme which, among other things, includes important aspects of agricultural economic activity besides credit-facilities for that activity; it will not materialize as the result of any mere programme for extension, supervision and administration. In the sphere of rural industry, the new Plan will come up, not only against a combination of all these obstacles, but in addition the fundamental difficulty of promoting and sustaining small units of production, which, in respect of most of the types of goods they produce, will be confronted with the competition of the much larger units of urban industry which are both better organized and, in their technical aspects, more advanced and progressive. It may be assumed that this effort will nevertheless be made and the needed lines of development formulated in the programme for the Second Five-Year period. About the supreme importance of such an effort there can be no doubt, for it will be directed towards the fulfilment of a vital requirement of both the unemployed and the underemployed in the rural area, whether cultivator, handicraftsman or labourer. Indeed, the accord of priority to rural industry over most forms of urban industry is already implicit in both Plan and Constitution. From the basic economic objective of increase of wealth, in conjunction with the basic egalitarian objective of reduction of disparity, it follows that, as between different forms of production of new wealth, those should in particular be encouraged and established which, in the very process or situation or production, tend to promote the distribution of the added wealth in the more needed directions, as distinguished from its further concentration at the relatively more saturated points. Such an approach, already implicit in the concepts and precepts of planning, if not in its practical expression, may be expected to be made explicit in the Second Five-Year Plan and substantially embodied in the new programmes it will lay down for the industrial, including agro-industrial, sector of rural production. We have throughout kept this important and inevitable, though still largely potential, development in view in designing the State-partnered credit structure, co-operative as well as commercial, of our recommendations. We have also, it may be recalled, as complementary to such a structure in the short-term sphere of credit, suggested the co-ordination of policies in respect of bodies such as the All-India Handloom Board, the All-India Khadi and Village Industries Board, the State Financial Corporations, etc., for the provision of the facilities needed in the context of the block and working capital requirements of State-sponsored, and possibly State-partnered, rural industries.

Section XI

PANCHAYATI RAJ

INTRODUCTION

LAND REFORMS, co-operatives, Panchayati Raj and Community Development movements, are supposed to be the four solid pillars on which a prosperous, dynamic and genuinely democratic rural social system is attempted to be built by the Government of Independent India.

Panchayati Raj is also claimed as a real democratic political apparatus which would bring the masses into active political participation and also would establish a genuine political control from below, from the vast majority of the weaker, poorer sections of Rural India. According to some it will " decentralize democracy. "

The present section is comprised of five selections on Panchayati Raj. The first selection of Hugh Gray entitled "The Problem" is a succinct presentation of significant issues connected with " Panchayati Raj. " It also briefly narrates the evolution of Panchayati Raj in India. The article by P. K. Chaudhari entitled " Panchayati Raj in Action—a study of Rajasthan", delineates the working of Panchayati Raj in the state where it was initiated first. It is an excellent study giving a very interesting insight into the functioning of Panchayati Raj and also raises some profound issues germane to this Institution.

The selection from 'A Study of Panchayats' by the Programme Evaluation Organization of the Planning Commission, and dealing with 'Structure of Panchayats' is an extremely valuable empirical study of Panchayati Raj organizational structure. It provides insights into the type of Leadership which is emerging in the Panchayat organization in the form of Presidents, Sarpanchas, elected Panchayati members and others. The control of Panchayats by rich landholding groups which also come from upper or upper intermediate castes raises some fundamental issues. Can an administrative machine, though elected on universal franchise, really become an instrument of the poorer sections, and adopt measures which will be at the cost of the richer sections, if the fundamental framework of socio-economic formation is perpetuated on exploitative class lines wherein a small section of the rich landowning class dominates and controls the economic life of the people ? In the context of class-relationship prevailing in rural society, will not the Panchayati Raj administrative organs, become tools to subserve the interest of the rich ?

The selections of Prof. Yogendra Singh and Shri. Uday Mehta, entitled 'Social Structure and Village Panchayats' and 'Panchayati Raj, its dangerous implications' respectively examine the functions and disfunctions of Panchayati Raj in the context of rural class structure in India.

A systematic elaborate set of inquiries on the basis of certain crucial hypothesis about the relation of Panchayati Raj and the class structure of Indian rural society will throw an illuminating theoretical light on the same problems which are now being examined by eminent scholars who are studying the relationships of Governments elected on the basis of universal franchise and the societies based on capitalist class-relationship wherein a small property owning class economically commands the majority of wage-earning sellers of their labour power.

The selections provide fruitful insights into some major trends developing in the Indian rural structure and also gives interesting procedural approaches for further investigations.

THE PROBLEM*

HUGH GRAY

THE INSPIRATION for Panchayati Raj is derived from the tradition of Panch Parameshwar, where God speaks through the Five, and official publications speak of ' Village Republics " as established historical facts, but do not list any sources for this well-established myth. By January 1957, every State had a Panchayat Act, and by September of that year 73 per cent of India's villages were covered by statutory panchayats with powers to enforce sanitation laws, to maintain the roads and protect the water supply. These were not autonomous bodies, and their activities were checked by State officials.

In India, most indigenous local consultative bodies seem to have had a caste origin. Within most castes, there were panchayats meeting to hear cases and arbitrate between fellow caste members involved in disputes, and punish offenders against caste rules and customs. Inter caste panchayats were also formed to hear disputes between members of different castes. There were also regional caste courts in some places hearing cases in which the people involved were from different villages. Disputes were also referred to Doras, Deshmukhs and Jagirdars for arbitration, and this was often paid for, an additional source of income to landlords. Before the introduction of British courts, justice was administered by the masters, or one's caste fellows.

The Indian Constitution deals with government at the Centre and State levels, and does not foreshadow Panchayati Raj as a form of political organization, except that States are directed in the Directive Principles to 'take steps to organise village panchayats...to enable them to function as units of self-government.' The declared aim, then, was the decentralising of democracy. There was also a more practical, immediate reason.

The main consideration which prompted their introduction seems to have been the need for provoking public co-operation and participation in national construction and development, in view of the slow momentum of economic growth compared with such countries as Israel, Yugoslavia and China.

The adoption by the Planning Commission of Panchayati Raj as the pattern of future political organization followed the report of the

* Reproduced from *Seminar*, ' Panchayati Raj ' September 1963.

Balwantrai Mehta study team, and experiments carried out in Andhra Pradesh and Rajasthan. Since 1959, ' democratic decentralization ' has been gradually extended throughout India. The Balwantrai Mehta report recommended the formation of a three-tier system of local government within districts, the three tiers to be indirectly elected and ' originally' linked. They were to be at village, block and district levels.

The report was enthusiastically received by the ruling party and its implementation recommended to all States, but States were left free to make their own variations on the general pattern. All States took as their top and bottom tiers the district and the village; at intermediate level, although most took the Block as unit, others (e.g. Mysore) took the taluk. At village level, all States decided on direct elections to the village panchayat, but again at the intermediate level, although most opted for indirect elections, some had direct. At district level, all elections are indirect.

In the State (Andhra Pradesh) where I was studying Panchayati Raj the Block is taken as the middle unit and direct elections are only at village level. The village panchayat is elected by secret ballot, the number of members proportional to the population. In Andhra, elections at village level are inevitably fought out on a caste basis in Congress dominated villages; the caste factor is intensified in these elections by the division of the villages into territorial wards.

In villages dominated by individual Congress landlords, or the Communist Party, there are no contested elections and the choice of the village panchayat is ' unanimous '. (In the State of Madras, this expression of 'concensus' receives a monetary award-so much for the ideal that democracy should extend rather than curtail the range of choices open to the individual!) After the village panchayat is constituted, its members elect a Sarpanch, and he becomes a member of the Panchayat Samiti.

The middle tier, the Panchayat Samiti, is composed (in Andhra Pradesh) of the thirty to forty directly elected Sarpanchas of the village panchayats, plus some co-opted members and members of the Legislative Assembly in whose constituency the Block is situated. Co-opted members are generally local politicians who are not interested in becoming Sarpanchas of their own villages, but wish to have a share in the power, patronage and perquisites deriving from Samiti membership.

At district level, the Zila Parishad consists of the presidents of all the samities, who are all ex-officio members, plus some co-opted members, M.L.A.'s, M.P.'s and such members of the Legislative Council and the all-India Council of State as have been directed by the State government to sit on the particular Zila Parishad. This provision was included to enable the Congress Party to assure themselves of a majority on any Zila Parishad which seemed likely to fall prey to another party.

The power wielded by a Zila Parishad chairman within a district depends on his personality, local standing, his skill in manipulating variables, and the interplay of his personality with that of the Collector. (In Andhra Pradesh, the Collector is chairman of the Zila Parishad standing committees, but the chairman of the Zila Parishad itself is a politician.) A strong Zila Parishad chairman, who belongs to a political faction within Congress opposed to that of the Chief Minister, is more likely to find himself with a strong Collector, than with one of his supporters. On the other hand, if the Zila Parishad chairman has powerful friends at State level, he can always get the Collector transferred elsewhere.

Under Panchayati Raj, the Collector's role is changing. Loud were the cries of nostalgia for the days of the British Raj when the Collector was a monarch in his own district, not a *primus inter pares* among district officers, heard at a recent seminar in Hyderabad, at which Collectors discussed their problems. But district officers are not the executive officers of Zila Parishads, and the Zila Parishad chairman's position is weak as compared with that of the Samiti presidents.

Real power in the three-tier system is at the middle tier, with the Samiti president, and he is the key figure in the whole set-up. He has no interfering Collector, and he is not only president, but chairman of all the standing committees. The senior official in the Block, the Block Development Officer, is his executive officer, and a word in the ear of ministerial friends can always secure the BDO's transfer, if he is not amenable to the president's wishes.

If the membership of samitis is analysed, one finds they consist almost entirely of members of the dominant landowning castes, whatever the political affiliations of the members concerned. More caste, more land, more money, more education are still the requisites for political success.

Panchayati Raj has provided a new framework for political and caste struggles between rival landlords (by this I don't mean feudal landlords but substantial landowners), jealous of their prestige and determined to maintain and, if possible, strengthen their district power networks. Needs have never been the ultimate criteria for help, except in the very broadest sense and in the individual instance there has always been patronage. Today, the Samiti president disposes not only of the Samiti jeep but of important sources of patronage, such as, for instance, the postings of primary school teachers. Through his political majority, the president decides who shall receive individual well subsidies and taccavi loans; these are rarely, if ever, given to political opponents. The prestige of the individual Samiti members depends on what they obtain for their villages in concrete physical benefits.

Like Panchayati Raj, Community Development benefits which have reached villagers through landlord representatives and officials who share the same socio-economic and educational background, have reinforced traditional authority. Officials do not consider it their role to nurture new sources of leadership, and subvert the class and caste structures, which in rural areas reinforce one another. Indeed, if they attempted any such thing they would find themselves quickly transferred. But with Panchayati Raj, certain changes have come about.

Panchayati Raj has brought politics down to village level, and made government more intelligible. 'You can talk to the Samiti President', as one villager said to me. Eventually, when the new ways of access to power are utilised by educated members of the lower castes, the traditional authority of the dominant landowning castes may be broken.

The aim of decentralising political power, has, to a great extent, been achieved. But the twin aim of arousing popular enthusiasm for community development has been less successful. One sees this by the amounts of money which lapse, particularly for roads and schools, when it is a question of the public's contribution amounting to 50 per cent instead of 25 per cent. (This is also partly a cause, partly a symptom of the failure of community development: what the leaders want is not necessarily what the villagers want. 'Who wants roads?' said a villager to me. 'I'll tell you, officials, politicians, landlords, but not us. Where there is a road the landlord will not have to pay us for taking his paddy on our bullock carts down to the main road.')

Where a 25 per cent contribution is expected, much more gets done, even though the public contribution in the forms of labour and material is often avoided. If villagers are asked if they favour Panchayati Raj, they tend to say 'YES,' because, it has brought more money to the village. Villagers do not yet feel that the Raj is theirs, they still think of it as the landlords, Landlords are better than officials, because they are people you can talk to easily, but the government is still of 'them' not 'us'.

Panchayati Raj has established a new forum in which the members of the dominant landowning castes fight each other for prestige and power. Before, they remained as lords of their villages or went to the Legislative Assembly; in between was a vacuum. In Andhra Pradesh, where the Congress Party is dominant, the Samiti presidency is fought for on a caste basis and a Reddi, Kamma or Velma almost invariably emerges as victor, except when a Brahmin successfully manipulates the caste factor in his favour. In districts where the Congress Party is in a minority, the caste factor is muted and the party cuts across caste, but the caste variable is always present, and manipulated, even by the Communist Party.

On the positive side, villagers are becoming election minded and beginning to realise that the whole of life is not dharma and karma, and that social plumbing is an everyday possibility: that if the ballot is secret, they can sometimes resist the landlords' pressure. They are not yet consciously participating in decision making processes, but they do realise that they have a vote to use, and that it is something which has a value because it represents a choice.

Whatever politicians may still be doing inside their houses, outside they will dine and accept alcohol from anybody. Political parties are ritual levellers, and the higher no longer dare to appear polluted by the lower who have votes to give them. This does not mean that the boundary-maintaining forces of caste are dead but that they are utilising more secular forms, and the dominant agricultural castes battle each other for control of the State governments and the new bodies set up by Panchayati Raj.

It is presumably the virulence of caste in political parties which has led thinkers such as Gore and Jayaprakash Narayan to reject them in favour of 'partyless democracy'. Jayaprakash Narayan would like to see a hierarchical structure replaced by a system of 'ever widening never ascending circles', with the individual at the centre of each circle and the world as the final circumference. He wishes to base political organization on small communities expressing the general will by consensus rather than through voting. Gram Panchayats would be formed by 'general consensus of opinion in the Sabha.'

Thinkers like Jayaprakash Narayan seem to assume that there is some straightforward, simple entity easily identified as pertaining to the common good, which can always be stripped naked by discussion and acclaimed by all. I would argue that there can only be common interests in egalitarian communities, which Indian villages are not. It seems to me that the stifling of the conflict of interests and opinions, serves not the emergence of synthesis from thesis and antithesis, but the interests of powerful individuals and groups. The consensus which emerges is always the view of the rulers, not the ruled.

For Community Development and Panchayati Raj, the main problem is to foster new sources of leadership from the peasant and artisan castes, and to thus break the iron stranglehold which the landlords have on village life. Only in this way can popular participation be obtained, when the leaders come from the majority castes, not the minority dominant ones.

The more political parties cut across caste and provide an alternative focus of loyalty, the more likely is this to happen. Will the Congress Party continue to foster new men only when it is in danger of losing district control. What is needed at the moment is more activity—including adult education—by political parties in villages, not less. The cries one often hears of, 'let us keep politics out of the villages' always means 'let us maintain the authoritarian hierarchical status quo', and calling this a village republic does not change its nature. Where there is democracy and voice, there are political parties. Only in totalitarian villages do elections not take place.

There must be no backtracking. Panchayati Raj is a great step forward in Asia's only democratic country. Within this new system of local government, democracy must be increased, not lessened, with direct elections and candidates from opposed political parties at every level.

And the immediate problem is still how to increase popular participation in decision-making and community development schemes—the undoubted social revolution is a slow one, and the sweeping away of the dominant castes' power, a long process. But there is no going back unless it were going back on democracy itself.

PANCHAYATI RAJ IN ACTION : A STUDY OF RAJASTHAN*

P. K. CHAUDHARI

PANCHAYATI RAJ institutions are more than mere agencies or limbs of the State Government; their purpose is not achieved with carrying out the development programmes and administrative tasks entrusted to them. They are organs of self-government at their respective levels. Mobilising popular enthusiasm and harnessing local manpower and other resources for development are thus their very *raison d'etre*. The functioning of Panchayati Raj has to be judged by the progress made towards achieving these vital objectives.

To bring about the direct and willing participation of the villagers in development, the planning process has to start from the village. Panchayati Raj institutions were expected to give the lead in this matter, but this they have failed to do so far. The so-called village production plans that we have now are nothing but paper plans prepared by the Village Level Workers in consultation with a few village elders and the sarpanch of the panchayat. No serious attempt has been made to prepare genuine village plans incorporating targets for each crop and for every family in the village.

Panchayat samitis and village panchayats are prompt to take up and execute programmes for which the Government provides loans, grants or subsidies so as to avail themselves of this assistance. But programmes which have to be carried out with local resources and initiative lag behind.

Panchayati Raj was inaugurated in Rajasthan on October 27, 1959. Elections to panchayat samitis and zila parishads were held the same month on the basis of the then existing village panchayats. In 1960 the village panchayats were reconstituted according to the one-village-one-panchayat principle. The State was divided into 7,394 panchayat circles, each with a population of 1,500 to 2,000. Fresh elections to these reconstituted panchayats were held in December 1960 and elections to panchayat samitis and zila parishads were completed by March 1961. It was without doubt a very bold step to introduce democratic decentralisation throughout the State at one stroke. It was a leap in the dark. But, after four years of working, it can be confidently said that Panchayati Raj has come to stay.

* Reproduced from *The Economic Weekly*, Special Number, Feb. 1964.

Though decentralisation has not yet succeeded in harnessing popular enthusiasm for development work, the execution and administration of development schemes entrusted to Panchayati Raj have been, by and large, satisfactory. The success of Panchayati Raj has to be judged by the extent to which the objectives set for it have been achieved. These objectives have been set out in the Third Plan as follows:

(i) Increasing agricultural production;

(ii) Development of rural industry;

(iii) Fostering co-operative institutions;

(iv) Full utilisation of local manpower and other resources and the resources, physical and financial, available to Panchayati Raj institutions;

(v) Assisting the economically weaker sections of the village community;

(vi) Progressive dispersal of authority and initiative, with special emphasis on the role of voluntary organizations; and,

(vii) Fostering cohesion and encouraging the spirit of self-help within the community.

Reluctance to Tax

One of the primary objectives of Panchayati Raj is to encourage people's participation in developmental activities. The efforts made by panchayat samitis to raise local resources is a measure of people's participation. Table 1 indicates the tax effort made by panchayat samitis in the last three years. Of the 232 panchayat samitis in the State, only 175 have so far imposed any taxes.

Cess on land revenue appears to be the most popular levy; nearly 67 per cent of the panchayat samitis have imposed it. It should be pointed out, though, that of the 26 districts in the State, in about ten of the bigger ones, which cover more than half the State, there used to be district boards before the introduction of Panchayati Raj. The district boards used to levy a cess on land revenue at the rate of 6 nP per rupee. When Panchayati Raj was introduced, the district boards were abolished, but Section 70(4) of the Rajasthan Panchayat Samitis and Zila Parishads Act, 1959 provided that "any taxes that were being levied and collected by an abolished District Board immediately before the date of its abolition shall, if such taxes are permissible under Section 33 of this Act, continue to be levied and collected after the constitution of a Panchayat Samiti for any area of the said District Board, by such Panchayat Samiti unless it decides otherwise by resolution. " So the cess on land revenue continued to be levied at the reduced rate of 5 nP per rupee by the successor panchayat samitis.

The cess on land revenue, therefore, cannot be treated as a fresh tax effort by the panchayat samitis, except in those areas where there were no district boards previously. The other taxes, namely, on profession and fairs, education, etc. can be taken as a measure of the effort made by the pachayat samitis to mobilise local resources. Table 1 also com-. pares the estimated annual income from taxes of the panchayat samitis with the actual realisation. It is seen that even in 1962-63 realisations including collection of arrears were only 50 per cent of estimated annual income. Thus panchayat samitis are not only reluctant to impose taxes, when taxes are imposed there is a tendency to put off collection.

Linking Taxes to Benefits

To encourage greater involvement of the population in the process of development it is necessary to overcome people's resistance to payment of taxes. The hope that the ushering in of Panchayati Raj will reduce this resistance has been belied by experience. The Study Team on Panchayat Finances appointed by the Government of India has suggested the imposition of compulsory taxes to augment the resources of panchayat samitis. But so long as villagers resist payment of taxes, compulsory taxes are no solution of the problem.

Nobody has yet made a proper study of why the villagers are averse to paying taxes. One of the main reasons, it is possible, is that they do not see any direct link between the taxes they pay and the benefits they get. If the resources could be collected in such a manner that the direct relationship between the benefits received and the taxes paid becomes evident to the villagers, their resistance to taxes will be reduced. One way of doing this is that the panchayat samitis should not impose any permanent taxes of a general or all-purpose nature. Instead, every year they should impose levies for specific projects, say, a school building, a village road, an irrigation dam, etc, and the funds so raised should be earmarked for and spent on these projects. Permanent taxes of a general nature may be raised by a body further removed from the people than the panchayat samitis.

Land revenue is one of the most important direct taxes paid by the agriculturist. But he has not the faintest idea as to how land revenue is being spent—whether he gets back even a part through the various schemes and projects executed in the village, and, if so, how much. Table 2 gives the figures of the State's land revenue collection during the last three years and the panchayat samitis' budget and expenditure. It will be evident that the budgeted annual income and expenditure of the panchayat samitis correspond very nearly to the land revenue collected. If all the land revenue collected from a panchayat circle is transferred to the village panchayat and all its development programmes are financed with it, the villager will readily perceive the relationship between the land revenue paid by him and the benefit that he receives. Besides, a surcharge on land revenue is long overdue and villagers will accept it more readily if the collections are spent on development schemes in the village.

PLANNING FROM BELOW

While preparing the State's Third Five Year Plan attempts were made to involve the panchayat samitis in the process. Before the State plans were finalised, proposals for development projects were collected from village panchayats at the samiti headquarters. But this was done without any indication of priorities. The State Government informed the panchayat samitis of the tentative schemewise allocation of funds that will be made available to them during the Plan period. The proposals received from the village panchayats were then sifted, modified and shaped into the block plan and forwarded to the State Government through the zila parishad. And at the State headquarters these proposals went through further modifications. Thus the process did not succeed to any great extent in incorporating the felt needs of the people in the Plan.

To achieve the direct and willing participation of the villagers in plan implementation, the planning process should start from the village. While drawing up the plan each village should be given an indication, as definitely as possible, of the resources that will be made available to it during the plan period and the local community on its part should make a firm commitment to implement the projects formulated on the basis of their felt needs. The State Government's Evaluation Organisation carried out a random survey to assess public opinion on the formulation of development plans. It revealed that an overwhelming majority of the people want the plan to be prepared at the local level. The results of the survey are given below :

	Percentage of Sample Families Giving First Preference for Formulation of the Plan by the Agency
Gram Sabha	42
Village Panchayats	49
Panchayat Samiti	5
State Government	2
Government of India	2

TABLE 1: Tax Effort by Panchayat Samitis

	1960–61	1961–62	1962–63
Number of Panchayat Samitis which impose taxes	129	159	175
Number of Panchayat Samitis which levied cess on land revenue	112	142	157
Number of Panchayat Samitis which levied education cess	11	23	26
Number of Panchayat Samitis which levied tax on professions	31	75	78
Number of Panchayat Samitis which levied tax on fairs	11	21	21
Estimated annual income of Panchayat Samitis from taxes (Rs. Lakhs)	29·74	37·89	41·88
Actual realisation (Rs. Lakhs)	9·42	15·50	20·60

TABLE 2: Land Revenue Collection and Panchayat Samitis' Expenditure (Rs. Lakhs)

	Land Revenue Collected	Panchayat Samitis' Budget	Panchayat Samitis' Expenditure
1960–61	715·16	831·31	803·16
1961–62	847·00	745·51	725·74
1962–63	875·00	745·43	724·47

FAILURE OF EXTENSION SERVICES

Panchayat samitis and village panchayats are prompt to take up and execute programmes for which funds are provided by the Government in the form of loans, subsidies, grants, etc, so as to utilise the assistance provided. But programmes which are to be carried out with local resources and initiative lag behind. Programmes like production of pure seed by registered seed growers, development and proper use of local manurial resources, use of improved implements, adoption of improved practices, etc, have not evoked sufficient response in the villages. This can be attributed to a very large extent to the failure of the extension services. Extension services were started in the blocks nearly a decade ago, but even now there is hardly any communication between the extension personnel and the villager. Impressive statistical figures are published from time to time by the Government regarding increased irrigation potential, distribution of fertilisers, use of improved implements, etc, but these achievements are seldom reflected in higher productivity on the fields.

The extension services should cater to the individual needs of the farmer, advise him on his problems and suggest solutions for his day-to-day difficulties. Today the approach of the extension services to rural problems is abstract and general. The extension personnel seldom go into the farmer's individual and specific problems. Unless this is done, little communication can be expected to be established between the farmer and the extension personnel. And without such communication being established our extension methods will never be able to make any impact on the rural scene.

ABSTRACT GENERAL APPROACH

Under present rules, the panchayat samiti vehicle can be used only when at least three extension officers go on tour together. So for touring the samiti area the extension officers generally form groups of 3 to 6 persons, take the samiti vehicle and go to the villages. They usually stop in a village for a short while, collect a few persons available on the stop or ask the sarpanch or a panch who is readily available to collect some people. Then they deliver harangues on their respective subjects in abstract and general terms. This method of extension has failed to make any impression on the agriculturist.

At times attempts are made to explain away this failure by putting the blame on the conservatism of the Indian farmer and his reluctance to adopt modern practices. It is difficult to subscribe to this view. The Indian farmer is not a fool. He is reputed for his strong commonsense. Take, for instance, the case of bullock carts. In rural India, the bullock cart is the only means of transport on which the farmer depends for moving his crops, manure and fodder and for visits to fairs and markets as well as for making social calls. The bullock carts used to have wooden or iron tyres, but in the last four or five years almost 90 per cent of the carts—bullock, camel or human drawn—in the State have been fitted with pneumatic rubber tyres. No extension officer or Government agency told farmers to adopt this modification in their age-old means of transportation. But they realised the value of this innovation and avidly seized upon it without any external agency urging them to do so.

Convincing the Farmer

What this example underscores is that a farmer has to be first convinced by practical demonstration of the value of any new method or practice before he can be expected to adopt it. The majority of our agriculturists belong to an income group just on or below subsistence level and it is wishful to expect them to indulge in the luxury of experimenting with new ideas on the strength of a few harangues from extension officers, whom they regard as youngmen, full of book-learning but ignorant of actual agricultural practices. It has been observed that whenever an enterprising agriculturist adopts a new agricultural practice and gets better yields from his field as a result, his neighbours adopt it without waiting for anybody to ask them to do so. It has been noted that the introduction of a new crop pattern in any locality by an agriculturist has a quicker and greater impact in the neighbourhood than the introduction of an improved practice of cultivation for the existing crop pattern in force in the area.

Demonstrations given in State-owned farms do not convince the farmer. The reason for this is obvious. The Government-managed farms are usually spoon-fed. Money and materials are spent on them freely. Rarely are any of these farms economically even self-supporting, not to talk of profits. Naturally, therefore, demonstrations given in the State farms do not carry conviction with the agriculturist.

Gaps in Administrative Procedure

The extension personnel are generally ill-equipped for the job they are entrusted with. Lack of practical field experience and adequate knowledge of local problems are their principal handicaps. Besides, the extension staff function under a dual control. The extension officers for agriculture, animal husbandry, co-operation, etc, are on deputation with the panchayat samiti. The Vikas Adhikari (Block Development Officer) has administrative control over them. Simultaneously they are under the technical control of the officers of their respective parent departments who are supposed to supervise and guide them in their technical work. Moreover, even though they are under the administrative control of the Vikas Adhikari, he cannot take any disciplinary action against them. Since they are on deputation with the panchayat samiti, all disciplinary action against them is initiated and taken by officers belonging to the parent department. This type of dual control encourages indiscipline among the extension staff and also contributes to their ineffective functioning.

Another important cause of indiscipline is the lack of clear demarcation of the spheres of action of the Pradhan (president of the panchayat samiti) and the Vikas Adhikari. At times conflicting instructions are issued to the extension staff by the Pradhan and the Vikas Adhikari. In case of friction between the two, the extension personnel are found to align themselves, some with the Pradhan and others with the Vikas Adhikari. This creates and impossible situation for the administration of the panchayat samiti.

District level extension officers are superimposed on the departmental cadre and function under the guidance and control of their departmental officers either at the regional level or at the headquarters. The district level officers, it has been noticed, evince less interest in their work in the field since the introduction of Panchayati Raj than they used to do before. They appear to feel that with the introduction of Panchayati Raj the onus of execution of projects has passed on to the popular representatives and Panchayati Raj institutions. The Government is conscious of this and various steps have been taken and instructions issued from time to time to ensure that the district officers take interest in their work, but till now these efforts, have not produced results. One suggestion that has been made is that the services of these officers may be transferred to the zila parishad and these officers placed under the administrative control of the zila parishad.

Village Production Plans

In the words of the Grow More Food Committee " no plan can have any chance of success unless the millions of small farmers in the country accept its objectives, share in its making, regard it as their own and are prepared to make the sacrifices necessary for implementing it." This can happen only when the extension agencies can assist every farmer with his production programme, otherwise, to quote Shri V. T. Krishnamachari, " these agencies will cease to command confidence."

The Third Plan outlay on agriculture is nearly double that provided in the Second Plan. During the First Plan agricultural production increased by 17 per cent and during the Second Plan by 16 per cent. It is proposed to increase agricultural production during the Third Plan by about 30 per cent and the yield per acre of foodgrains by about 16 per cent. This is a tremendous task. The only way these ambitious targets can be achieved is by involving all the cultivators, small and big, in the country. This can be done only by formulating effective village production plans.

Panchayati Raj institutions were expected to give the lead in this matter but this they have failed to do so far. The so-called village production plans that we have today are nothing but paper plans casually prepared by the Village Level Workers in consultation with a couple of village elders and the sarpanch of the village panchayat. No serious attempt has yet been made to prepare an authentic village production plan incorporating production plan targets for each crop and for every family in the village.

The village production plans, according to the Third Five Year Plan, should include two main groups of programmes :

(a) Programmes such as supply of credit, fertilisers and improved seeds, plant protection, minor irrigation, etc, for which a measure of assistance has to come from outside the village; and

(b) Programmes such as digging field channels for utilising irrigation from large projects, maintenance of bunds and field channels, digging and maintenance of village tanks, development and utilisation of local manurial resources, etc, which call for effort on the part of the village community or the beneficiaries.

In practice, the village production plans that are prepared at present do not take into consideration the productive capacities of the individual families in the village but are based purely on group (a) type programmes and are formulated on the basis of estimates or indications of the quantum of outside assistance expected to be made available during the agricultural season. No attempts have so far been made to incorporate in the village production plan group (b) type programmes which call for effort on the part of the village community or the beneficiaries. So the Planning Commission's directive " to give effect, in the field of extension, to the idea of working out village production plans so as to draw all the cultivators into the common effort, and at the same time, to make available to individual farmers in an efficient and organised manner the credit supplies, and other assistance needed " still remains on paper. As long as village production plans are not prepared on the basis of family units and in consultation with them, they will fail to involve the farmers.

No Place for Zila Parishads

In its present form the zila parishad as an institution appears to have become redundant. In spite of its status, it has played no effective role. One of the most important functions of the zila parishads, as provided in the Rajasthan Panchayat Samitis and Zila Parishads Act 1959, is to " supervise generally the activities of the panchayat samitis in the district and to advise the State Government on all matters concerning the panchayats and panchayat samitis ". The zila parishad's instructions to the panchayat samitis are all of an advisory nature having no sanction behind them. If the advice is not palatable, the samitis usually ignore it.

Zila parishads are also given power to scrutinise the budgets of the panchayat samitis under Section 37 (4) of the Act which reads as follows:

"The budget estimates as finally passed by the panchayat samiti shall be submitted by the Vikas Adhikari, on or before such date as may be prescribed, to the District Development Officer (i.e. the Collector), who shall, after scrutiny, place the same with his comments before the zila parishad within the prescribed time. If the zila parishad is satisfied that adequate provision has not been made in the budget estimates to give effect to the provisions of this Act, it shall have the power to suggest such modifications as may be necessary and return it to the panchayat samiti with its observations regarding the modifications to be made therein. The panchayat samiti shall consider such observations and pass the budget with such modification as it deems fit."

Thus the Act does not make it mandatory on the panchayat samiti to accept the modifications suggested by the zila parishad. And so the zila parishad is reluctant to issue any instructions which it knows may not be acceptable to the panchayat samiti. As for the zila parishad's function of advising the State Government on matters concerning panchayats and panchayat samitis, the position is no better. The advice is hardly ever acted upon by the Government.

Evils of Indirect Election

The pradhan of a panchayat samiti is elected by the sarpanchas of village panchayats in the jurisdiction of the samiti and the co-opted members of the samiti. In Rajasthan there are 7,394 village panchayats and 232 panchayat samitis. In 1960-61, 25 per cent of the elections of panchas and sarpanchas were unanimous; of sarpanchas, 38.8 per cent were elected unanimously. But unanimous elections of panchayat samiti pradhans were rare. In most cases, there were keen contests for the office of pradhans. The Congress contested the elections as a party. During these contests cases of forcible confinement and kidnapping of sarpanchas occurred on an alarming scale. The kidnapped persons were released at the place of the election just in time to cast their votes. In a few cases the sarpanchas were sent on pilgrimage to Hardwar, etc, or for sight-seeing to Kashmir at the expense of the prospective candidates for the office of pradhan so as to prevent them from coming under the influence of rival candidates.

These elections witnessed the worst features of indirect elections when the electoral college is small and the office is one of power and patronage. The assumption that direct election is more expensive than indirect election was disproved. None of the contestants for the office of pradhan spent less than what an average Assembly candidate spends (actual expenditure, not that submitted to the returning officer). Another unhappy feature of indirect elections also manifested itself—political and other pressures as well as money played a deciding role in them.

The elections have left such a bitter trail that every one in the state, irrespective of party affiliation, now wishes a change in the mode of election of the pradhan. The consensus of opinion is that the pradhan should be chosen either by direct election or the existing electoral college should be enlarged by including in it, besides the sarpanchas, the panchas in the panchayat samiti area.

Co-opted Members to Blame

Section 8 (2) of the Panchayats Act provides for co-opting certain categories of persons as members of the panchayat samitis to give adequate representation to weaker sections like women, scheduled castes, scheduled tribes, etc. It also provides for co-option of "two persons whose experience in administration, public life or rural development would be of benefit to the panchayat samiti ". The Act allows relaxation in the residential qualification for such persons who " need not reside in the block but they must be residing in the district in which the block is situated." The result is that a large majority of the persons co-opted are town dwellers.

Of the 232 panchayat samitis in the State no less than 60 have co-opted members as their pradhans. Of the co-opted persons who are pradhans, 80.5 per cent have been co-opted because of their experience in administration. Similarly, 33.3 of the chairmen of the standing committees on production are co-opted members. It is interesting to note that a number of co-opted members were defeated in the election of sarpanchas. Much of the doubtful tactics used in the election of pradhans are attributed to this particular type of co-opted members.

An enquiry by the State Government's Evaluation Organization into the nature of participation of co-opted members in samiti meetings is not very encouraging. Only about 10.2 per cent of the co-opted members participated actively in discussions at samiti meetings, while nearly 70 per cent of them had never participated at all in any discussion. Among co-opted members, of course, the most active are those who have been co-opted for their so-called experience in administration or social work. Co-opted members representing women, scheduled castes and tribes are the least active.

Politics of Standing Committees

Under Section 20 (1) of the Act every panchayat samiti is required to constitute standing committees for each of the following group of subjects:

Production programmes, including agriculture and other allied subjects;

Social services, including education, sanitation, communication and allied subjects; and

Finance, taxation and administration.

Panchayat samitis usually meet once every quarter. It is the standing committees which function throughout the year. As provided in the Act, the samiti delegates its powers and functions to the standing committee by a resolution and the decisions of the standing committee have the same legal force as those of the samiti unless it is revoked by the samiti within a month of the date on which it is taken.

The standing committee members are elected by simple majority and so normally the minority group in the samiti goes unrepresented on these committees which are monopolised by the majority group consisting of the supporters of the pradhan. The decisions taken by the standing committees are not always above reproach; very often they are influenced by factional and group considerations.

Members of panchayat samitis are generally more interested in transfers, postings and appointments of samiti staff than in developmental activities. This is what the State Evaluation Organisation has to say about the duration of meetings of the various standing committees: "On an average the meetings of the standing committees on Administration and Finance were the longest while those of the standing committees on Production were the shortest. It is interesting to note that a fairly large number of meetings of the standing committees lasted for only 15 minutes. Hardly any business could have been transacted in such meetings and they were just called to complete the formality of doing so ". Some statistics on the duration of the meetings of standing committees is given below :

	Duration of Meetings (in hours and minutes)
Standing committee on production	
Average	1.39
Longest	5.00
Shortest	0.15
Standing committee on social services	
Average	1.46
Longest	5.00
Shortest	0.15
Standing committee on administration and finance	
Average	2.62
Longest	6.45
Shortest	0.20

Role of Officials

After the introduction of Panchayati Raj, almost all appointments to the posts of Vikas Adhikaris have been made from the cadre of the State Administrative Services. The Vikas Adhikari is the chief executive officer of the panchayat samiti. But in practice he has no control over the samiti staff. Under Section 89 (2) of the Act he can punish only class IV staff; against the rest of the staff he can only record censures. But an appeal against such censure can be made to the standing committee of the samiti. Punishment of all other samiti staff is the sphere of the standing committee of the samiti.

This has created an anomalous position. The Vikas Adhikari is responsible for ensuring that "plans and programmes approved by the appropriate authority are executed efficiently" and for exercising "supervision and control over the acts of all officers and servants of the panchayat samiti and the staff working in institutions and schemes transferred by the State Government to the panchayat samiti in matters of executive administration". Yet he has been given no disciplinary control over the staff. As a result, the panchayat samiti gets paralysed when relations between the pradhan and the Vikas Adhikari are not cordial and when the pradhan is the chairman of the standing committee on administration which exercise disciplinary control over the samiti staff.

There is evidence of growing deterioration in the relations between officials and non-officials in the panchayat samitis. Instances of friction between the pradhan and the Vikas Adhikari are on the increase. Whenever the pradhan happens to be educated or assertive, conflicts with the Vikas Adhikari are frequent. A clear demarcation of the spheres of action and powers and functions of the two is urgently called for.

A panchayat samiti has a representative of the co-operative societies in the area as one of its co-opted members and the co-operative extension officer is placed under the administrative control of the Vikas Adhikari. In spite of this there is lack of coordination between the two. At the village panchayat level the situation is much worse. At times cooperatives and panchayats appear to work at cross purposes. Cooperative societies very often find place for persons losing panchayat elections. These persons then try to use the cooperative movement to regain political power. This is a reason why the cooperative movement is dominated by politicians.

Panchayats Lose Importance

The village panchayat is the corner-stone of Panchayati Raj. But in fact, village panchayats in the State have grown weaker than before the inauguration of Panchayati Raj. Some of the factors responsible for this are shortage of finance, increase in factionalism, and emergence of the sarpanch as a powerful personality on account of his membership of the panchayat samiti.

With the introduction of Panchayati Raj, village panchayats were reconstituted on the one-village-one-panchayat basis. Two consequences followed from this. First, with the reduction in size, the income of the village panchayats suffered proportionate decrease, while their overhead expenditure remained the same. Second, on account of the compact and smaller size of the panchayat contest for the offices became wider, keener and closer and gave rise to factionalism on a wide scale. The consequence of all this has been that the village panchayat as an institution actually suffered a setback after the introduction of the Panchayati Raj.

The Rajasthan Panchayat (Amendment) Act 1960 made provision

for gram sabhas. It is provided that " Every panchayat shall convene in such manner and at such times and intervals as may be prescribed, a meeting of all adult residents of the panchayat circle. At such meetings the programme and works undertaken by the panchayat and their progress shall be explained and the views of the residents thereon shall be reported to the panchayat at its next meeting. "

Though it has been decided to hold the meetings every six months, the institution of the gram sabha has yet to find its place in the Panchayati Raj system. The participants in these meetings are mostly passive, except when matters pertaining to the revenue or forest departments come under discussion. In such discussion they air their grievances without any inhibition.

Weaker Sections Have not Benefitted

Panchayati Raj has not brought relief to the weaker section of the community. There has been no perceptible increase in the flow of benefits of development to the economically and socially weaker sections of the village community. According to the 1961 Census, the State has a population of 21 millions, of which scheduled castes constitute about 3 million and scheduled tribes about 2.1 millions. Yet there is not a single scheduled caste pradhan in the whole State. Out of a total of 7,394 sarpanchas, the number of scheduled caste sarpanchas could be counted on one's fingers. And only in predominantly tribal areas do we find a few sarpanchas and pradhans belonging to the scheduled tribes. Rural leadership is still in the hands of the relatively well-to-do classes in the village which control all vantage positions in Panchayati Raj.

Another reason why the benefits of development in the rural areas have not percolated through to the weaker sections is that to take advantage of programmes like agricultural loans, subsidies, etc, one must possess land and immovable property to offer as sureties. If the weaker sections of the rural community are to take advantage of these development programmes, present rules in this respect will have to be changed.

3.

STRUCTURE OF PANCHAYATS*

SIZE OF THE PANCHAYAT UNIT

THE NUMBER of panchayats and the population covered by them in the fifteen evaluation blocks in which this study was conducted as also the number and population of those panchayats included in this study are shown in Table I. It will be seen that the average population of all the panchayats (including both single and multi-village) in the evaluation blocks is somewhat over 1,800. The corresponding figure for the 60 panchayats included in this study is somewhat over 2,600, with the averages for single village and multi-village panchayats being 1,929 and 3,520 respectively. The average for the panchayats included in the study is higher because panchayats below a certain size were excluded from the study. There are wide inter-State variations in the population covered by panchayats. In Kerala, for instance, the panchayats usually cover large populations, ranging from 5,000 to 15,000 in most cases, but going up to 30,000 in some cases. There are no villages in the usual sense in this area and the revenue 'village' which is a purely administrative unit generally has a population of 5 to 10 thousand and even more. The average population of the three panchayats in the State included in this study is above 1,000. In Madras similarly, the panchayats cover large populations because their jurisdiction generally extends over the revenue village and its attached hamlets. Other States in which the population covered by a panchayat is quite large are Assam, Orissa and Bihar. On the other hand, in Uttar Pradesh, Punjab, Bombay, Saurashtra and Madhya Pradesh the population covered by the panchayats is comparatively small. In Punjab panchayats can be formed in every village having a population of 500 and more. In Uttar Pradesh the lower limit is only 250 persons. But most panchayats cover much larger populations than this minimum figure. It may be added that the general trend in recent years has been to extend panchayats to smaller villages and generally to reduce the jurisdiction of the panchayats. This trend is noticeable in the panchayat legislation of several States including Bombay, Madras and Uttar Pradesh.

In view of the wide variations in the structure of the villages and their population in different parts of the country, it is not possible to indicate any figure as the most suitable for a panchayat. The figure of 5 to 10 thousand which may be necessary for Kerala where the density of population is very high, would be quite unsuitable in an area like

*Extract from 'A Study of Panchayats'—Programme Evaluation Organization, Planning Commission, May 1958.

Himachal Pradesh or even Orissa as it would result in the panchayats extending over a large number of villages and a large geographical area. But the question of jurisdiction of the panchayat is of considerable importance to the functioning of these institutions, and keeping extreme cases like that of Kerala aside it is useful to have a figure or preferably a range of figures, about the most appropriate size of a panchayat. The main consideration in favour of small panchayats is the existence of personal relations among the people and the opportunity for intimate contact between the panchayat and the village people. Meetings between the general village body and the panchayat which are provided in the Acts of some States to ensure such contacts are also feasible only where the total population covered by the panchayat is relatively small. It is claimed that such contacts make democracy at the primary level real to the people. On the other hand, administrative viability and efficiency require that the unit should have a minimum size, because if the panchayat is very small its resources would be too small for the responsibilities it has to bear. Even at present the internal resources of the panchayats are in some cases hardly sufficient for meeting the expenses of the most elementary administration. Further, too small a size would become a greater handicap as the development functions of the panchayats expand. Recognising the importance of size to the proper working of the panchayat the Report of the Second Five Year Plan recommends a population of 1,600 as the norm for a panchayat, to be reached, if necessary, by re-drawing the village boundaries. It is not possible to comment on the suitability of this or any other figure on the basis of the data of this study. As mentioned above most panchayats included in the study have considerably larger populations. There are only 22 panchayats having populations below 1,000 and these are located in a few blocks notably Sonepat and Batala in Punjab, Manavadar (Saurashtra), Mandya (Mysore) and Bhathat (U.P.). To judge the appropriateness of this norm, it would be necessary to study a large number of panchayats, both small and large.

Division into Wards

In some States e.g. Kerala, Orissa, Assam, Bombay and Madhya Pradesh the panchayat is divided into a number of wards in which different villages or sections of the same village are given adequate representation. This arrangement, however, does not exist in Bihar and Assam even though the panchayats in these States are large and cover many villages. Division into wards is a very useful device but it is liable to misuse. Wards are generally demarcated on the basis of population with more or less equal number of voters and where, the demarcation was carried out by the Revenue Department as in Chalakudy (Kerala), Kolhapur (Bombay), Erode (Madras) and Bhadrak (Orissa), it is considered fair by the people. But the division may be carried out in such a way as to perpetuate the domination of some group or faction. This is the complaint made by all the four panchayats in Morsi (Madhya

Pradesh) where the division was carried out by the old nominated panchayats.

COMPOSITION OF THE PANCHAYATS

Panchayats in all States are representative bodies elected on adult franchise. The nominated panchayats which were established in Madhya Pradesh in 1946 were replaced by elected bodies in 1955-56. In the Panchayat Acts of most States, there is provision to give adequate representation to scheduled castes and other under-privileged groups, either by reservation of seats or by nominating members from these groups. In Punjab, seats are reserved for the scheduled castes only where they form 10 per cent or more of the total population. In Kerala, this is done if this section of the population is 5 per cent or more,. In U.P. reservation of seats is generally in proportion to the population of these groups to the total population. In Bihar, where the Mukhiya alone is elected, he is expected to give adequate representation to the important castes including the scheduled castes. In a few States, notably Saurashtra and Madhya Bharat, women members were also nominated to the Panchayats. But in the two blocks Manavadar and Rajpur, studied in these States, it was reported by the P.E.Os. that women did not generally take interest in panchayat activities or even attend the panchayat meetings. This is unfortunate but not surprising in view of the inhibitions against participation of women in social activities. Generally speaking, the representatives of the scheduled castes also do not show enough interest. But it is reported by some P.E.Os. (e.g. of Punjab and U.P.) that election to panchayats on the basis of adult suffrage and election of scheduled caste members to these institutions has created among them a keen awareness of their rights.

Panchayats in most blocks do not have a nominated or ex-officio component. However, in the panchayats of Madhya Pradesh, the village patels were nominated by virtue of their office. This is reported to have been done with the idea that inclusion of persons having administrative experience and prestige in the village would impart strength to the institution and make it more readily acceptable to the people. But our very limited study suggests that this practice has not only not strengthened the institutions, but has actually hampered it. It is reported from all the 4 Panchayats studied in the Morsi block that the PATELS have influenced elections and have managed to get their own men elected on the panchayats. As a result, factional rivalries have become more acute and panchayat bodies have been rendered, more or less, ineffective. In Mysore also, where the village PATELS are nominated to all the panchayats and are frequently the presidents of the institutions, the panchayat system in the State is comparatively ineffective.

SIZE OF THE PANCHAYAT BODY

The strength of the panchayat varies greatly in different States. Thus, in the panchayats of U.P., the number of members of the institution excluding the Sabhapati varies from 15 to 30 depending upon the population. Considering that the jurisdiction of the panchayat is rather small, a fairly high proportion of the households are represented on the panchayat. The 6 panchayats studied in Bhathat block have nearly 10% of the households represented on them. At the other extreme is Kerala where panchayats with populations of even 10,000 have only 7 members; one additional member is added for every 2,000 persons, the maximum number being only 15. The strength of the panchayats selected for this study is shown in Table 3. A relatively large panchayat is, perhaps, somewhat better suited to represent different sections and interests in the population. If the number of members is very small in relation to the population they may remain unrepresented. Similarly, where the jurisdiction of a panchayat extends over a large number of hamlets e.g., in Madras, the body should be sufficiently large, so that all the hamlets can be represented. Of course, it should not be so large as to become unwieldy.

Panchayat and the General Body of the Village

A meaningful relationship between the panchayats and the village community as a whole can exist only where the jurisdiction of the panchayat is not too large, and is confined to one or a very few compact villages. Provision for contact between the panchayats and the general village body exists in the Panchayat Acts of a number of States including Punjab, U.P., Saurashtra and Bihar. Except the last, these are all States where panchayats have small jurisdictions extending over one or a very few villages. In both U.P. and Punjab, the panchayat is required to call meetings of the general village body, at least twice a year, inform it of its achievements and programme and present to it a statement of its financial position. In U.P., the budget of the panchayat has to be passed by the village body. In Saurashtra, any person of the village could attend the panchayat meetings. The meetings of the Madhyastha Mandal (State Panchayat Board) were also held in the villages and the people from the village as well as from the neighbouring villages were encouraged to attend these meetings.

The principle of consultation between the Panchayat and the village body is a commendable one. It is in accordance with traditions of western democracy and of the Indian village. The practice of village meetings could, if successful, bring the village people and their elected representatives closer together, and could promote understanding of the working of these institutions. However, experience has not been satisfactory so far. The village body meetings do not evoke any enthusiasm and are generally not effective. Most meetings are very thinly attended. In the panchayats studied in the block of Gorakhpur district of U. P., it was observed that there was no quorum in the village meetings, and the panchayat budgets could be passed only with the help of the clause which provides for the holding of a second meeting without the requirement of a quorum, if the first meeting could not be held for want of it.

METHODS OF ELECTION

In Kerala, Bombay, Punjab, Madhya Pradesh and Hyderabad elections to the panchayats are held by secret ballot. In Mysore, the method is followed, only if more than 10 members are to be elected. Other States follow the practice of open elections. Election by secret ballot is generally acknowledged to be preferable to open elections, but the latter practice is resorted to on grounds of economy and administrative convenience. It has its obvious disadvantages, however, which often over-shadow its merits. Under this system, free exercise of preference is not always possible. Thus a landless labourer or a member of the scheduled caste, would hesitate to express himself openly against a substantial cultivator whom he dare not annoy. The system also tends to aggravate group-tensions because group preferences have to be openly declared and the rival groups meet face to face.

ELECTIONS AND GROUPS OR FACTIONS

An analysis of the impact of election and functioning of panchayats on leadership patterns and group relationships in the villages, would require a much more detailed study than was possible in the course of this enquiry. However, the impressions gathered by the PEOs during the course of their enquiry indicate that in the 35 panchayats where elections were contested, group rivalries have come into existence or increased in as many as 12 panchayats. These impressions support the view that panchayat elections have an influence on group rivalries in the villages.

UNANIMOUS ELECTIONS

To avoid these rivalries many persons advocate unanimous elections. Such elections are by no means rare; they have been reported from as many as 21 out of the 56 reporting panchayats. However, unanimous election does not necessarily indicate solidarity in the village. It may only show the community's lack of interest in the panchayat. It was observed in two panchayats where there were unanimous elections, that the villagers had no knowledge of them. In another case, the election had been manipulated by interested parties. As the significance of panchayats is better understood, the number of unanimous elections may decline. While unanimity arising from a feeling of solidarity already existing in the village is most desirable, conscious efforts by officials to promote unanimous elections are not likely to lead to happy results. These may only have the effect of increasing corrupt practices and pressure tactics. As the experience of nominated panchayats and of nominated members in elected panchayats demonstrates, attempts to compromise with the democratic principle, however well-intentioned, lead to undesired consequences.

Political Parties in Elections

It is generally recognised that elections to panchayats should be free from considerations pertinent to wider party politics and should be influenced by purely local issues and the merits of individual candidates. This position obtains in all States except Kerala where wider issues are brought to bear on the local elections. In this State, the lack of real village units and the large jurisdiction of the panchayats have, in some measure, favoured this development; local bonds and intimate personal contact between individuals in well demarcated areas which are strong in other parts of the country are comparatively weak.

Caste, community and kinship play an important part in panchayat elections. As Table 3 shows the majority of panchayat members are from the dominant land owning high castes. The presidents of panchayats are, almost invariably, from such castes.

Personal Characteristics of Panchayat Members

In order to obtain an idea of the kind of persons who are returned to panchayats, data regarding the age, education, caste, ownership of land, aud economic and leadership status were obtained for all members of the selected panchayats who were resident in the selected villages. In case of the single village panchayats all members are included, but in case of the multi-village panchayats, members resident in villages not selected for the study are not included. Out of 614 members of these instiuttions data were obtained for 547. The results are presented in Table 3. Summary figures for panchayat members and presidents are as follows:—

Age: It will be noticed that in all blocks except Erode (Madras) and Morai (Madhya Pradesh) the majority of the panchayat members are above 40 years in age. In some blocks, like Batala and Sonepat (Punjab), Manavadar (Saurashtra) and Mandya (Mysore) more than 2/3rd of the members are in this age group. 39 per cent of all panchayat members are in the age group 25 to 40 years and only about one per cent are below 25 years of age. Election of older people to panchayats is in accordance with the traditions of the Indian village, in which leadership and decision making rest mainly with the older age groups; another factor favouring return of older persons to panchayats is their relative leisure. It will be seen from' the following paragraphs that the great majority of the members are from land owners' households. The older members of such households can have a certain degree of leisure because most of the cultivation work is done by the younger members. It is this type of persons—landholding, middle aged, frequently having younger people to look after cultivation—who take great interest in community affairs and are returned to panchayats in largest numbers.

Literacy: In the panchayats out of the 15 selected blocks, the literate members are larger in number than the illiterate. In three blocks Bhadrak (Orissa), Cachar (Assam) and Chalakudy (Kerala) all the panchayat members are literate. In all blocks, the percentage

TABLE 3

Particulars of Members and Presidents of the Panchayats.

Number of blocks	15
Number of Panchayats studied	60
Total number of	
(i) Members	547
(ii) Presidents	47

Sl. No.	*Particulars*	*Percentage of total number of members*	*Percentage of total number of presidents*
1	2	3	4
1.	AGE GROUP*		
	(i) Below 25 years	1·1	...
	(ii) 25 to 40 years	38·9	46·8
	(iii) 40 years and above	59·6	53·2
2.	EDUCATIONAL QUALIFICATIONS		
	(i) Illiterate	42·2	17·0
	(ii) Primary	36·4	44.7
	(iii) Middle	17·0	27·7
	(iv) Matric	2·9	8·5
	(v) Above matric	1·5	2·1
3.	OWNERSHIP OF LAND		
	(i) Land holders	88·1	95·7
	(ii) Non-land holders	11·9	4·3
4.	FINANCIAL STATUS		
	(i) Rich	32·5	89·4
	(ii) Others	67·5	10·6
5.	CASTE GROUP		
	(i) High	69·8	97·9
	(ii) Low	30·2	2·1
6.	WHETHER RESPECTED		
	(i) Yes	93·4	89·4
	(ii) No	6·6	10·6
7.	NUMBER OF PRESIDENTS WHO ARE CONVERSANT WITH THE PANCHAYAT ACT		
	(i) Yes	...	48·9
	(ii) No	...	51·1

* Age-group of 4 members is not available.

of literacy among panchayat members is significantly higher than among the adult males of the villages. The following figures showing literacy among panchayat members and among the adult male population in the block are of interest in this connection. The latter figures are of the Bench Mark Survey conducted in these blocks in 1954. (See p. 560.)

As might be expected, most of the literate members have had very little education, 63% have read only upto the primary standard and most of the remainder are below matric. The matriculates are only 2.9% of the total.

Sl. No.	*Name of the block*	*Percentage of literate members*	*Percentage of literates in the age group, 15 yrs. and above (B. M. S. data)*
1	2	3	4
1.	Bhadrak	100·00	28·2
2.	Batala	42·11	13·0
3.	Kolhapur	75·00	12·6
4.	Morsi	87·76	31·0
5.	Bhathat	41·29	10·2
6.	Manavadar	55·00	11·1
7.	Mandya	47·06	11·1
8.	Rajpur	60·00	30·6
9.	Erode	31·82	11·8
10.	Cachar	100·00	30·5
11.	Chalakudy	100·00	48·4
12.	Bodhan	61·53	8·1
13.	Pusa	88·37	22·2

Caste: In most panchayats, the majority of the members come from high castes or rather from castes which are the principal land-owning and cultivating castes of the area. In Cachar (Assam) there is no member from the low castes, while in Bhadrak (Orissa) and Erode (Madras) only 1 out of the 7 and 22 elected members respectively belong to low castes. In all three States there is no provision for reservation which is made in the Acts of most States, for adequate representation of the interests of these groups. In Manavadar (Saurashtra) the majority of panchayat members are listed as belonging to low castes. Actually, many of these belong to castes like Ahirs which are the dominant cultivating castes in the villages. This is borne out by the fact that majority of the members are landowners.

Ownership of Land: The great majority of members (82% of the total) are landowners. In Bhadrak, Mandya and Bhathat there is no member who does not own some land. In the last block, most of villagers have come to acquire land after the abolition of Zamindari. The number of landless members is appreciable in Erode, Manavadar and Rajpur, the figure being about 40 % in the first two cases and 35% in the last.

Wealth: While most of the members own land, only a few are considered rich by their fellow villagers. The word 'rich' is used here, in a relative sense, i.e., whether a person is considered so by the local people. Among the different centres, Manavadar has the highest percentage (60%) of rich members and Morsi the lowest (6.1%).

Leadership Status: Leadership status is even more a matter of public opinion than wealth. We collected information to find out to what extent, a member of the panchayat is also regarded as a 'leader' by the village people. These data show that in most panchayats, the majority (55%) of the members are generally respected in their villages. Another 34% are respected only by their own groups or factions. However, in Morsi (Madhya Pradesh) where the P.E.O. reported that the nominated Patels did not enjoy the confidence of the villagers, the majority of the members do not seem to have it either.

The Panchayat President

The president of the panchayat, who is known as the *Sabhapati* in Uttar Pradesh, *Mukhiya* in Bihar, *Sarpanch* in Punjab and by similar names elsewhere is by far the most important member of the institution. He is, in fact, its head and is often assigned a number of administrative and executive functions. In most States the execution of works programmes taken up on behalf of the panchayat is the responsibility of the President. He also plays an important role in the assessment and collection of taxes, levied by the panchayat. In some States, the president is empowered to exercise disciplinary control on the secretary and other staff of the panchayat. The working of a panchayat depends to a large extent upon his personality. One major difficulty in the functioning of the panchayats at present is that most presidents are not qualified by education or training to carry out adequately the functions, or to assume the responsibilities entrusted to them under the Panchayat Laws. As their level of education is generally low, the great majority of them do not fully understand their duties and responsibilities. Also, in most states no serious attempt has been made to enlighten them on the provisions of the Panchayat Act. About half the presidents of the panchayats studied, were not conversant with the Panchayat Act. The most notable attempt to educate the presidents and other members of the Panchayats was made in Saurashtra where training camps were organised for the purpose. The members of the Madhyastha Mandal (the State Panchayat Board) and the District Panchayat Mandals also played an active part in educating the panchayat members. Programmes of training panchayat members through Village Leaders' Training Camps were taken up in some other States also, including Uttar Pradesh and Madhya Pradesh, but sufficient efforts do not seem to have been made. It is obvious that the panchayats cannot work efficiently unless the presidents and members are given adequate training and are fully conversant with the provisions of the Panchayat Act.

As regards the election of panchayat presidents the system of direct election by the electorate prevails in Uttar Pradesh, Bihar, Madras, Assam and Saurashtra. In Bihar, the president (Mukhiya) alone is elected and he nominates other members of the panchayat. In U.P. where the president (Sabhapati) is directly elected, it is often his election alone that rouses the interests of the electorate. In three of the six Panchayats studied in the Bhathat block, the Panchayat presidents' election was contested. The main advantage claimed for the system of direct election of the president is that it brings out the real leader of the village. However, the system is not without its disadvantages. Thus it is reported from Erode (Madras), where both the president and the members are directly elected, that the president is not able to function effectively because the other members do not fully co-operate with him. The Madras Government have decided to replace this system by that of indirect election of the president. The Bihar system where the Mukhiya alone is elected has the added disadvantage that the functioning of the panchayat depends greatly on the personality of a single individual. The system of indirect election appears to be working satisfactorily in all the panchayats studied, except in those of Sonepat, where the P.E.O. feels that the president (Sarpanch) is often not the real leader of the village, and cannot function properly, because he is under an obligation to the members and has to support them even by going out of his way. He further reports that the system leads to aggravation of factioual rivalries within the village.

Data regarding the personal characteristics of presidents of the panchayats studied have been given on page 566. It will be seen that the majority of the presidents are above 40 years of age. Only 8 are illiterate, but most have had education only up to the primary or middle school stage. It is noteworthy that an overwhelming majority of the presidents are rich landowners, and belong to high castes. Presidentship of panchayats is concentrated in the more affluent class of cultivators even more than panchayat membership. Among the members, due to the reservation provisions and other reasons, there is still a considerable proportion of persons from the less favoured and less powerful sections of the community. But very few presidents belong to these sections.

THE PANCHAYAT SECRETARY

Most Panchayat Acts provide for the appointment of a panchayat secretary to maintain the records and account of the panchayats and to look after other routine duties. However, there is very great inter-state variation in matters like the method of recruitment of the secretary, his status as a government or panchayat servant or as a full or part time employee, his pay, educational qualifications and training etc. Some data on such inter-state variations are given in Table 4.

In several states including Punjab, U.P., Bihar, Orissa and Kerala, the secretaries are full-time persons. In Bombay, Hyderabad and Assam, on the other hand, they may be full-time or part-time. In Punjab and U.P. the full-time secretaries generally look after several panchayats. In Punjab the secretary is paid entirely by the panchayat. In U.P., on the other hand, he is a government servant who looks after the work of the

Nyaya Panchayat (Judicial panchayat), a number of Gaon Panchayats and performs, in addition, some of the functions of the Gram Sevak in some of the villages in his area. In Saurashtra also the panchayat secretaries are full-time government employees looking after the work of several panchayats. In this area, the 'A' and 'B' class panchayats were entrusted with the collection of land revenue. It was necessary for them to have whole-time persons to look after the work. For some time, the panchayat secretaries worked as gram sevaks, but the practice has been discontinued. In Bihar, Orissa, and Kerala the panchayat secretary who is a full-time government servant is expected to look after a single Panchayat. It may be recalled that in all these states, the panchayats have rather large jurisdictions. In Bihar, the panchayat secretary, who is called the gram sevak, is expected to attend to a number of duties like maintenance of agricultural and vital statistics in addition to his panchayat work. He is also actively associated with all development activities within the panchayat area. In Kerala, the panchayat secretary (called Panchayat Executive Officer) has been given extensive executive powers, with the result that the president and the members complain that they have no control over him. In Bombay, the panchayat secretary may be a full-time or a part-time worker whose salary is paid by the panchayat with or without some contribution from the Government. He is a servant of the panchayat and under the full control of the president. In Madras, panchayat secretaries are appointed in only class 'A' panchayats which have a population of not less than 5,000 persons and an annual income of not less than Rs. 10,000. But the smaller panchayats usually have clerks to look after the routine duties. In Mysore, no separate secretaries are appointed and the *Shanbhog* (Patwari) is expected to maintain the accounts of the panchayat on receipt of a small remuneration. A somewhat similar practice is followed in Madhya Bharat and Bhopal where the local school teacher (or in his absence another local person) is expected to maintain the panchayat records for an allowance of Rs. 10 per month. In all three cases, the results are reported to be unsatisfactory. The persons concerned do not take adequate interest in the work, because they are not under the Panchayat Department and the remuneration given is not attractive enough.

What type of candidates—what his calibre and qualifications are—come forward for the post of panchayat secretary is, in great measure, influenced by the system of recruitment and the pay of the post. Thus, in Kerala, where the panchayat secretaries are full-time government servants and have pay scales, they are all matriculates and above. Frequently, they are graduates, and they get a higher scale of pay than others. In States like U.P., Bihar and Saurashtra, where the secretaries are full-time government servants, matriculates or persons with somewhat lower qualifications are generally available for these posts. On the other hand, in Hyderabad, where the pay was only Rs. 12 per month the secretaries had generally low educational qualifications. In one of the panchayats in the Bodhan block, the secretary had read only up to the primary standard.

Many of the States have made arrangements for the training of panchayat secretaries. The duration of training varies all the way from six months in Saurashtra to 21 days in Kerala. The training system in Saurashtra was comprehensive and included instructions in the Panchayat Act, maintenance of records and accounts, as well as elements of agriculture, animal husbandry and social education. In Madhya Pradesh, the panchayat secretaries were given three months' training in the maintenance of records and accounts and organisation of social welfare activity.

The extent of control exercised by the panchayat on the secretary also varies from state to state. In general, this control is much less where the panchayat secretaries are full-fledged government servants or are looking after a number of panchayats than where they are servants of a single panchayat. The case of Kerala has been mentioned above. In U.P. also, even though the Act makes provision for control over the secretary by the panchayat and, especially, by the president, in practice there is very little control. On the contrary, it has been reported by the P.E.O., that under the pretext of ensuring that the provisions of the Panchayat Act and the rules and orders issued under it by the State Government are followed by the panchayat, he sometimes assumes the role of supervisory officer.

The extent of control over the panchayat secretary depends frequently upon the personality of the president. As the majority of the presidents are uneducated, they have to depend upon the secretaries for interpreting the rules and government orders. This dependence will continue until the president and the members are educated, have full training and can themselves understand their powers and obligations. In Punjab where the pay of the secretary is contributed by the panchayat, the extent of control is greater than in U.P. But even there, according to the P.E.O. the panchayat secretary is, in fact, controlled by the Government. In Bombay, on the other hand, where the secretaries are full or part time servants of a single panchayat, they are almost under the full control of the panchayat.

The question of the relationship between the panchayat and its staff including the secretary is of considerable importance. Two alternative points of view are possible on it: (i) that the panchayats should have full powers over their staff; and (ii) that the panchayats should be assisted by full-time trained executives who should be servants of a higher body. The first alternative is consistent with the autonomy of the panchayat and allows it fuller scope for development. But, for this alternative to work, the panchayat members and especially the presidents, should be persons of sufficient calibre who understand their powers and responsibilities. This condition is, unfortunately fulfilled in few instances only. We have already described the calibre and qualification of panchayat members and presidents. The secretary should, of course, be paid by the panchayat. It will, however, be seen in the Section on Resources, that the resources of the panchayats in most States are not large enough. Even in the few States like Punjab and Bombay where the income of the panchayat is adequate, the pay of the secretary and other staff takes up a substantial proportion of it. In many states it will be found that the panchayats can pay their secretaries, wholly or in large part, only if their jurisdictions are considerably larger. But then the panchayat may become too large for real democracy at the lower level. There are two ways out of this dilemma; either a higher body should subsidise the panchayat to enable it to engage a qualified secretary, or the secretary should be paid directly by the higher body. The second would reduce the control of the panchayat over its secretary. But in order to make the first solution practicable, the members of the panchayat and especially the presidents should be trained to discharge their responsibilities properly. The first step in real democracy has always been to train the immediate, if not the ultimate masters.

The higher body, the state government or the District Council could still assume responsibility for the training of the panchayat secretaries, and it may also require the panchayat to appoint their secretaries from among trained candidates only. The rate at which a programme of this kind can be worked out would govern the progress of the panchayats towards effective rural democracy.

Panchayat and Local Bodies

The relationship between the panchayat and higher level local bodies like the District Board, the Taluka or Tehsil Board or the Janpada Sabha is both important and difficult. This question as also the larger question of reorganisation of the local bodies are being considered by the State Governments. In some States, notably the former ' B ' State of Madhya Bharat, a system of interrelated democratic institutions with the panchayat at the village level and the Mandal Panchayat at the district level was tried. The arrangement has some similarity to the system of Panchayat Samities at the block level and Zilla Parishads at the district level which has been recently recommended by the COPP Team on Community Projects and N.E.S. This study is, however, concerned with the relationship between the higher bodies and the panchayats, only in so far as it affects the working of the panchayats. But our data are scanty, because the influence of local bodies on the working of the panchayats could be observed in only two blocks, Kolhapur (Bombay) and Morsi (Madhya Pradesh) and even in these it was not very marked. The main reason is that the Panchayat Acts in many States do not cover the relationship that should exist between panchayats and higher level local bodies. Moreover in most States the latter have been either dissolved or are in process of disintegration.

In Kolhapur the panchayats are under the dual control of the District Local Board and the State Government. The District Local Board is responsible for passing the budget, auditing the accounts and providing general guidance to the panchayats while the State Government exercises control mainly through the inspection carried out by the district level Special Officer for Panchayats. Apart from the disadvantages incidental to dual control, no other marked difficulty has been experienced in this case. In Morsi also, the panchayats are under the dual control of the Janapada Sabha and Social Welfare Department of the State Government. The Janapada Sabhas have not, however, done their duty satisfactorily. They did not pass the budgets of the panchayats studied, for a long period; nor did they make available to these the proceeds of the land cess granted by the State Government with the result that the panchayats could not undertake any activity. Further, it was reported, in 2 out of the 4 panchayats studied, that the politics of the Janapada Sabha intruded into the elections to the panchayats; group rivalries were intensified and the working of the panchayats adversely affected.

Panchayats and State Governments

Most States have an inspection organisation for inspection of the panchayats, audit of accounts and general guidance to them in working. There are Panchayat Officers at the District level with inspector level staff below them. There are some exceptions to this; however, in Mysore, the panchayats have remained with the Revenue Department and their inspection is looked after by the district and lower level officers of the Department. The arrangement has not been found to be satisfactory because the Revenue Officers being already over-burdened with other work have neither the time nor the will in taking an active interest in working of panchayats. Association of Revenue Deputy Collectors with panchayat work in Madhya Bharat was also found to be similarly unsatisfactory. In some States, notably Bombay and Madhya Pradesh, there is dual control of panchayats by the State Government on the one hand and a higher level local body on the other. This body is the District Board in Bombay and the Janapada Sabha in Madhya Pradesh.

The main difficulty reported by the PEOs about the inspection system is that inspector level staff have frequently very large jurisdictions, as a result of which inspection is inadequate both in frequency and intensity. Some PEOs have reported that some of the panchayats in the evaluation blocks have not been inspected even once since their formation. A number of panchayats included in the study have been inspected less than once a year. Thus, in Manavadar 2 out of the 4 selected panchayats have been inspected only once during the last 3-4 years. In Batala, none of the selected panchayats has been inspected more than twice since their establishment in 1952. The position regarding auditing of panchayat accounts is also unsatisfactory. It is reported from Bhathat (UP) that panchayat accounts have not been audited since the formation of the panchayats and it is only recently that a decision has been taken to audit them. In the Batala and Sonepat blocks of Punjab, auditing has not been done for the last 3-4 years. In both these blocks, the villagers appear to be rather conscious of this deficiency, as is seen from the fact that quite a proportion of the selected respondents have expressed the need for proper auditing of accounts as a step towards improving the functioning of the panchayats. (Table 11).

Mainly because of their large jurisdictions but at least partly because of their pre-occupation with administrative matters, the panchayat inspection staff in most States have not given adequate guidance to panchayats for improving their working. Their visits, not very frequent, are concerned primarily with administrative matters.

Education of members in the role and significance of these panchayats and guidance in the proper methods of functioning of these institutions should start with a brief initial training and should be followed by day to day advice by the secretary, and periodic, but not very infrequent, guidance from the inspector level staff. It has been mentioned above that arrangements for initial training of members through short training camps have existed only in a few States like UP, Saurashtra and that the panchayat secretaries are frequently untrained. With the inspector level staff also largely unavailable for this purpose, lack of arrangements for guidance of the members can be said to be complete.

Mention may be made here of a negative aspect of the State Government's relationship with the panchayats. In spite of the fact that wide powers and responsibilities have been given to panchayats in all States, *de facto* control has remained in the hands of government officials in many of them. In U.P., the panchayats cannot incur any expenditure except for very minor amounts, without the approval of the Panchayat Inspector and the Assistant Panchayat Raj Officer. In Kerala, the panchayats' power to sanction non-recurring expenditure is limited to Rs. 200. In a number of other States also control is exercised largely by the government and the powers of the panchayats are very limited. Such control might be justified under exceptional circumstances but when exercised in the day to day functioning of the panchayats it has the effect of only dampening the enthusiasm of the panchayat members and thwarting their initiative. Besides creating a feeling among the members that they have no real powers, it gives rise to the impression among the people that the panchayat is a part of government administration. A number of PEOs have reported the prevalance of this kind of feeling in the panchayat villages studied by them.

PANCHAYATS AND THE BLOCKS

Development of strong self-reliant democratic institutions at the base is one of the fundamental objectives of the community development and N.E.S. programme. The block pattern envisages that activity relating to development of panchayats should be coordinated at the block level, in the same way as in other fields like agriculture and cooperation. However, the block pattern had not so far provided an independent block level specialist on panchayats; it envisaged a common specialist for cooperation and panchayats. As a result, strengthening of staff in this field and coordination of work with that of the block staff did not take place to the desired extent. Even the jurisdiction of the panchayat inspector has continued to be different from the blocks in many States. The position of course varies considerably in different States, and in some, progress in coordination of activities has been much greater than in others. Thus, in U.P., the District Planning Officer who has overall charge of the community development programme and N.E.S. programme is also the district level officer for panchayats. The panchayat inspectors and the panchayat secretaries are under the control of BDO who might well be considered the block level officer for panchayats. The relationship has been carried further by making the presidents of all the panchayats in the block ex-officio members of the Block Advisory Committee. In Saurashtra, the B.D.O. was himself the panchayat officer for the block area. In other States also, steps have been taken for coordination between the panchayat and the project staff and with the recent revision in the block pattern which provides for an independent block level specialist for panchayats, this process will receive a great stimulus. Moreover, the reduction in the charge of the inspector and re-orientation of his functions, which are implied in this change should also help to reduce the deficiencies in inspection and in guidance to the panchayats.

As regards the role of the project staff in the functioning of the Panchayats included in this study, this appears to have been limited to carrying out certain development activities in the panchayat villages. The projects have given fairly large financial grants for execution of such development programmes. Data regarding financial assistance from the projects, the contributions by the panchayats and the *ad hoc* contributions by the people for these activities are given in the section on Resources. All these activities are properly the responsibility of the panchayats, and by undertaking them, the projects have done a job for the panchayats which they could not have done on their own.

However, the job has not been done with the panchayats, nor has it necessarily had the effect of strengthening the institution. As has been explained in the section on Functioning of Panchayats, *ad hoc* development committees as Vikas Mandals were formed in many States for execution of development works. In some areas, these committees were fully associated with panchayats; in others, the association was inadequate and in still others like Madhya Pradesh these committees functioned as rivals of the panchayats. In some States, the works were entrusted to contractors (who had also the responsibility for mobilizing popular participation) and the panchayats were not associated. The project staff were more concerned with execution of the works in specified periods than with strengthening of institution. As a result, the opportunities of strengthening the panchayat institutions, which availability of substantial financial resources offered, have not been fully or even adequately utilized.

Panchayats and the Gram Sevaks

Even though promotion of panchayat activity in his area is an important responsibility of the gram sevak, he is not formally associated with the panchayats in any State. In Saurashtra, the gram sevaks were made panchayat secretaries for a time but this arrangement could not be continued. In U.P. the gram sevaks are not given panchayat work but the panchayat secretaries are required to carry on certain development activities in some of their villages. The gram sevaks in their turn keep in touch with the panchayats and try to execute project activities, particularly construction programmes through the panchayat agency. In Bihar also the panchayat secretary is associated with development activity. However, in a number of other States of which Kerala is one example, the panchayat secretary is not connected with the block development programme in any way. Association of panchayats with development activities and active contacts between them and the gram sevaks are to the benefit of both, and the importance of these can be hardly overemphasised.

4

SOCIAL STRUCTURE AND VILLAGE PANCHAYATS*

A CASE STUDY ON CLASS RELATIONS IN RURAL POLITICAL PROCESS

YOGENDRA SINGH

SYSTEMATIC SOCIOLOGICAL study of the structure and process of Panchayati Raj has not been conducted so far. The studies have emphasised only partial factors either exogenous or endogenous that influence the working and growth of the panchayat system: mostly administrative, legal, economic and isolated institutional (leadership, factions, caste etc.) factors have been emphasised particularly in the context of their implication to the working of the panchayats. Inadequacy in such studies lies not in the wrong choice of variables for analysis but in the narrow theoretical frame of reference and conceptual categories, in terms of which facts are interpreted. *Diagnostic* and *didactic* orientation has predominated over the scientific and analytical. The first attitude emanates from an exaggerated claim for social sciences through *ad hoc* studies and surveys to suggest cut and dried formulae for the solution of problems of social planning and reconstruction and the second emerges from an essentially historical fact which profoundly affects the Indian elites 'image' about panchayats. The historical fact lies in the significance attached to panchayat system and village society by Mahatma Gandhi. The institution has thus come to symbolise not only a *structural innovation* but also a moral *commitment* and *an ideology*.

Sociological evaluation of working of panchayat system would not rule out the analysis of this institution from the standpoint of values or ideologies but they would constitute the subject matter of enquiry rather than be the tools or concepts employed for analysis. Such a study would attempt the establishment of relationship of the structure and value system implicit in this system with other systems at various levels of their structural and functional differentiation and growth. Panchayats would be treated as a sub-system of relationship and socio-political norms working within the structural framework of the large scale society, right from the *village* to the *region*, to the *state* and the *nation*. Reciprocity of relationship and the emerging consequences, both *intended* and *unintended*, of the mutal interaction of the various structural and normative ' types ' would indicate the overall process and problem of change.

***Paper submitted at the seminar on "Panchayati-Raj, Planning & Democracy", University of Rajasthan, Jaipur.**

Such comparison would not only bring to the surface the implications of panchayats on the village social structure in specific setting but would also point out the integral and differential aspects of the net balance of the forces of change that influence other major national institutions and processes such as democracy and planning. Questions to be asked would be: What is the structural and normative character of the indigenous system, where panchayats are introduced ? What is the degree of the correspondence or lag between the indigenous and introduced systems ? What bearing these structural and cultural innovations have upon the national society ? How is the process of change at various structural levels throwing up alternative and equivalent norms and roles ? And which factors promote or thwart their growth and institutionalisation ? If we intend to assess the system of village panchayats in terms of above queries, a more systematic theoretical frame of analysis would be required. Bailey* has recently made an attempt towards comparative structural analysis of political systems and values at the level of village, constituency and the state (F. G. Bailey, 1963) but fails to evolve a systematic method of enquiry for all the levels. Among the methods employed by him, he finds resemblance with anthropological method at his village level study, political science method at the constituency level study and historical method at the state level of analysis. This methodological eclecticism has thus led to a piece of work which has limitations of all the three types of studies without their advantages. For a better study this methodological multiplex is to be substituted by structural functional analysis as mentioned above. It will offer an integral view of all levels of social realities as well as all levels of structural complexities.

The application of the structural functional method in rural analysis has so far been confined to the study of the processes of change in caste stratification. This has led to the unfortunate neglect of the class structure and its consciousness in the rural society. The reason for the caste-centredness of the rural sociology in our country lies in its direct kinship with the works of British and Indian social anthropologists who have, through the study of caste, emphasised the cultural factors in social change rather than the role of economic and political factors and the interest-groups. Thus, ' casteism ', 'dominant castes', 'factions', etc. are some of the concepts which have been used as camouflage to divert the attention of sociologists from the strategic area of the class structure. Moreover, because of this neglect, structural functional studies tend to be more static and fail to interpret the relationship between economic status and political power. Study of rural social processes through class relations and its structure would introduce in structural functional analysis that methodological richness which would also bring about the much coveted synthesis between the dialectical and functional approaches to the understanding of the dynamics of social structure.

*Bailey F.G. : *Politics and Social Change,* Orissa 1959, Oxford 1963.

I

A micro-cosmic study from the structural point of view has been conducted in six villages of Eastern Uttar Pradesh where panchayats were simultaneously established in 1949 on the basis of adult suffrage rather than nomination of functionaries by Tehsildar as existed prior to it. Not only in the six villages but in the whole of the Eastern U.P., these elections projected very vigorously the latent class consciousness which was seething against the landlords who till then enjoyed supreme power in the villages. The nature of this class conflict was accentuated by the peasant movements against *rack-renting*, *sharecropping*, *elections*, etc. common in this area and which were led by congress leaderships since 1939 or even earlier. The first election in 1949 thus, marked a state of *initial euphoria* among the peasants and landless labourers to dispossess the traditional ruling elites from power. It was a confrontation of a *self-confidence populistic force* with a dominant class whose future was uncertain since the Zamindari Abolition Act was getting through the assembly. Zamindari was subsequently abolished in 1950. Yet the functionaries of the "Zamindar Association" gave a bitter fight to the peasant candidates in all the six villages. Zamindars, however, could only win in two villages out of the six. In other four villages the office of President went to peasants, one of them was an educated school teacher and the other three, semi-literate peasants. The offices of the *adalti* panchas, however, went in every village to landlords or the village *banias* due to literacy being a qualifying pre-condition for this office.

From 1949 to 1953 there followed a long period of internescine intrigues, faction-fights, in the four villages where the feudal group had lost. It was now that a conflict ensued between legal rights and social structural realities. The average landholding of ex-landlords in all the six villages compared six to twelve times that of the peasant holdings. Most of the peasants and agricultural labourers had to depend for the land for sharecropping, sub-tenancy, farm employment and money-lending etc. upon the feudal families. With these patronages the latter began to introduce internal dissension in the class solidarity of the village. In two villages they kept the village presidents engaged in one or the other litigation for the whole term of the panchayat; in the other two they systematically victimised the supporters of peasants village presidents. The landlords were educated, had acquaintance with the officers, were familiar with the pulse and rythms of bureaucracy; the peasants-presidents except the one (teacher) were unfamiliar with this milieu. Yet they kept the solidarity intact and did not break.

The pressure told upon the power aspirations of the peasant class, however, in the elections of 1953 when the ex-landlords changed their strategy of election along with pressure group tactics. They would quote illustrations of the lack of feuds and tension and developmental work (petty in nature though) done in those villages where ex-landlords were made presidents; they used mainly pragmatic arguments 'of peace in the village and general prosperity'. The result was, that in four villages out of six, ex-feudals became presidents defeating peasant candidates. The other two villages where peasant-presidents still kept the hold included the former educated teacher and a prosperous peasant, both again returned as presidents. The tension continued in these two villages. Even attempts were made to get the teacher dismissed from the higher secondary school of which the management was in the hands of the ex-landlords; but in these villages the traditionally dominant class was itself internally divided. In other four villages with the ex-landlords as presidents the conflict passed from *inter class level* to *intra-class structure*. In two villages even out of these four, the contestants were from among the ex-landlords themselves. In this situation, *peasants began to benefit from the faction rivalries among the group in power.*

The cycle in the dynamics of power was, however, complete in the third election of village panchayats in 1962 when in all the villages except one (where the teacher was president) ex-landlords were returned to the office of the village presidentship. In three of them the contest for presidentship was among ex-landlords themselves, in the other two they won against peasant candidates. Thus the process of regression in the power structure of the village had run a cycle.

This brief account of the political process in the six village communities may represent a unique situation which may not be identical to many others. However, the whole gamut of the change described above may be summarised in three stages which might have some degree of validity for other regions as well, (1) *the initial assertion of the exfranchised peasantry for its power in rural community*, (2) *the long drawn period of group conflict between the power climbers and the traditional power elites.* (3) *the withdrawal of the peasant leadership from the arena of power*. Now the question is, could this process be explained in terms of the social system as a whole ? What will be the advantages of such a *systematic approach over the eclectic ones employed so far* ?

II

Social processes can only analytically be isolated. In reality no single system of relationship or behaviour is free from the contingency of other relations and situations. Moreover, operation of any social system implies some pre-requisite processes and complementary roles. Whenever an old system or institution is replaced by a new one, the degree of its success, stability and growth would depend upon effective and quick development of these pre-requisites. Thus, the response of the existing social structure becomes a pre-condition for the success of an institutional innovation. In case of the above village panchayats we could classify following traditional structural institutions and forces into which the new system was introduced. (1) [the pressure of a traditional ruling elite, (2) vast economic and cultural gap in status between these *elites* and the new climbers, (3) persistence of a diffused form of institutionalised approval with some section of peasantry in the villages in favour of the traditional group, (4) lack of counter-balancing pressure from outside to reinforce the aspirations of the climbers (No help from political leaders, peasant associations, caste panchayats could be effectively available to these villagers), (5) direct conflict between legal or constitutional prerogative (voting power) with established social and economic scale of stratifications e.g. class structure and caste (particularly former) and (6) absence of effective complementary changes in the social structure along with that in power system. The Zamindari abolition was no doubt a very radical complementary change but this too in practice meant increased legal prerogatives than real (in terms of goods and services). A survey that was conducted about the benefits accruing to various classes as a result of Zamindari abolition, revealed that ex-tenants and labourers did not feel benefited by the measure. The rule for the acquisition of Bhumidhar's right in land on a lump sum payment of 10 years rent by the peasants drained off the resources even of the medium sized tenants who could have been the potential climbers in the rural power structure.

On the other hand the panchayat system though acclaimed by many as an indigenous institution was introjected into the village power structure with many radical nuances of modernity such as: (1) voting on the basis of civil status, rather than ascriptive status which prevailed in traditional panchayats; (2) introduction of a certain degree of bureaucratic rationality in the working of panchayats in place of the former traditional communal sanctions; (3) greater interlinkage of this institution with institutions of higher scale at the level of block, district and the state; and finally (4) introduction of an overall value system of a rational democratic polity. None of these sociological norms were present in the same form in the traditional village panchayats and the introduction of the new had a far reaching significance for the value system and social structure of the rural society. The above attributes of the new panchayat system required that proper institutional supports should have been forthcoming to reinforce its expected norms in the body politic of the villages. In technical sociological language it was necessary to assess the presence or possibility of the growth of the structural-functional pre-requisites for the success of panchayat system.

The nature and pattern of these pre-requisites would differ firstly, as the social structure and culture of the indigenous systems would differ and secondly, as the form and content of the institutional innovation would itself vary. For this matter, the delineation of the structural-functional pre-requisites of the panchayat system would require a thorough understanding of the nature of the village communities, as well as, of the panchayat system, its legal, social and political and cultural implications. On the basis of the existing knowledge about these, a fairly reliable formulation of these pre-requisites may be possible and in its background it may be further possible to analyse the significance of the case history of the panchayats mentioned above.

For a proper success in the working of the panchayats in the villages, the structural-functional pre-requisites could be (1) reduction in the nature of disparity in real income and land ownership of various groups; (2) greater occupational mobility in the villages; (3) rapid increase in the new types of economic activities (structural and infra-structural) to strengthen the base of rural economy and accelerate its social dynamics; (4) rational price policy to maintain a balance between rural-urban and agro-industrial sections and sectors respectively for control of the differential power and dependence relationship; (5) structural support to the specific and instrumental roles through reform in the indigenous sub-systems and support from large-scale social structures; (6) radical changes in the nature, and scope of communication system; (7) increased interaction among the various sub-structures of rural society (caste, kin-groups and lineages, etc.) through common participation at secular level of activities, cultural, economic and political, and finally (8) growth in equalitarian and secular symbolism (institutions, ceremonies, festivals, public gatherings, etc.) in the rural culture accompanied by its effective linkage with the culture of Indian nationalism.

These pre-requisites make it adequately clear as to how futile it would be to evaluate the success and failure of village panchayats in terms of its own organisation and working and to blame the institutions for many commissions and omissions for which it could not be held responsible. Moreover, it would also reveal the theoretical difficulties in the understanding of the processes and problems of village panchayat in terms of such sub-structures of this system as (1) problem of effective leadership; (2) lack of corporate (democratic) mechanism for decision-making; (3) existence of casteism and factions; (4) lack of effective administrative inter-linkage etc. etc. These are, in fact, consequences or functions of the interaction of the indigenous social structure and value system of the villages with the social structure and values of the village panchayats. These emanate from the total structural setting of the rural society and none of these alone could lend itself for correction and reconstruction for the desired working of the system as such. Why there has not arisen secular utilitarian and rational leadership in villages ? Why there is factionalism and groupism in the decision making processes of the panchayats ? Why new climbers to power cannot succeed ? Answer to these and scores of such questions lies not in the symptoms but in the texture of the body-social of the rural society. Hence the need for analysis not in terms of isolated institutions but the total rural social system.

In case of the six villages to which reference has been made in this paper, also in case of many others in the Eastern U.P., the effective existence of the structural-functional pre-requisites mentioned above has not been there. The average per household land-holding for ex-landlords in these villages is 28.5 acres and that of the ex-tenants only 1.6 acres. The average monthly income of the two compares as rupees 270 per month for the ex-landlords and rupees 60 per month for ex-tenants. The only economic innovation in the villages since 1947 has been cooperative brick-kilns which give seasonal employment to some agricultural labourers; most of the agricultural holdings including those of the ex-landlords are subsistence enterprises with little farm surplus which is consumed by industrial consumers' goods due to unfavourable price policy. No new roads except few shram-dana pavements have been constructed during the last thirteen years; no new primary schools have been opened since 1949 except a junior high school in one village; the adult education through night schools has never worked effectively; two new branch post-offices have certainly been opened due to large number of migrants in collieries, cloth mills, and for those gone for manual labour in Bihar, West Bengal and Bombay; in all these villages there are about 40 students reading in high school and intermediate colleges, about 15 are studying in degree colleges, there are 10 graduates and three post-graduates. Eighty per cent of these students who are studying in colleges and those who are graduates belong to ex-landlord families. There is no equalitarian interaction between ex-landlord families and ex-tenant families, complete hierarchical distance is maintained, even the very poor ex-landlord family, in fact poorer than average ex-tenant, maintains strict social distance from other classes, these ex-landlord groups have serious internal feuds and factions, but work as a consolidated front when the power or prestige of the whole class is threatened; at such occasions even traditional factions melt away contrary to the findings of Oscar Lewis.

In regard to the structural reinforcement from macro-social structure (at the level of block, constituency, state and finally national level) there has been no significant development. There is no interaction with political workers of the villages except during the periods of general elections; there is general unconcern with the block developmental meetings, police and revenue officers' visit to the village creates more stir in the villages than block development officers, involvement with national currents of events or even problems at state level is very little; not a single daily newspaper is subscribed by any member in any of the six villages; village panchayats have radio sets in four villages which are used only by the family members of the village presidents. The two macro-structures which influence village life are *judicial and administrative bureaucracy*, the influence of the latter is more effective and pervasive. Influence is unidirectional rather than reciprocal; between the administrative bureaucracy and the villagers the mode of relationship being more of *compliance rather than consensus*. The sociological value of this contact is not only limited but very often negative. It would be interesting to investigate how as the scale of bureaucracy moves from police administration to revenue to developmental the negative reaction of villages slowly diminishes though it is never absent. Just as villagers relationship to bureaucratic macro-structure is of indifferent compliance, the same to political macro-structure is that of skeptical-indifference.

There also exists an intimate relationship between the villagers cold and critical image about the political parties including the Congress and the sequential expropriation from them of the power in the village panchayats by the ex-landlords. As in course of the years following the abolition of landlordism the sting of oppression and control of the feudal group has waved from their memory and has been replaced by feline tactics of indirect control through manipulation of their emotions and interests. The average villagers' awareness about economic and material handicaps, has progressively increased and has created a kind of collective frustration which is evident in their reaction towards public policies and institutions. Feeling among them has gained strength that ultimately the C.D.P., the Panchayats and the assemblies etc. are for the privileged few. This feeling has further gained conviction due to consolidation of land holdings in the region (1956-57) which according to villagers has benefitted the big land owners (ex-landlords) only.

Now, this picture of the general condition of the villages deviates significantly from the various structural-functional pre-requisites and also from the norms implied by the new Panchayat system mentioned above. Obviously, looked at from this scale of evaluation, structure and process of Panchayat system has not made the expected impact on the rural society. Should we then consider Panchayat system a failure ? Far from it, the question should rather be asked, was there a better alternative ? Generally speaking, the answer to this question would be in the negative. Barring a few specific strategies about the implementation of the system and legal lacunae etc. the system as a whole had no alternative form of implementation. Within the structural framework of the rural society and its stratification system the process of gradual expropriation of the agricultural labourers and small peasants (ex-tenants) from power is a normal process and could only have been controverted by a very radical and harsher form of land reform which was perhaps repulsive to the collective conscience of the political leadership in power. A leftist version may perhaps be that this leadership itself is reactionary. The hypothesis is rather controversial, at best a truism from a sociological point of view. Leadership is itself a response thrown up by the society in the wake of the forces enshrined in new demands and innovations. At each level of socio-cultural adjustment the extent of deviation in the traditional and emergent form of leadership would invariably have its structural limit, assuming a normal or even accelerated process of social change.

However, in course of this discussion, we have now introduced in our analytical framework sufficient number of variables to sum up the implications of the facts presented in relation to the institution of village

Panchayats, its structure and process of change. Some of the broad inferences that could be drawn are as following:—

(1) The Village Panchayat system, like various similar social innovations in India has been introduced more as a radical cultural institution rather than structural. Its structural characteristics suffer from serious handicaps due to lack of complementary social changes. It has, so far, been instrumental in activising a process of social change only through alteration in the civic responsibilities and expectations of the villagers rather than changes in their class status and economic positions. Consequently, whenever, the inconsistency between the two becomes manifest through the interplay of politics-cultural processes of the Panchayats, it leads to either *violent group conflicts* or *regression in power*. In the cases quoted above, it has led to transition of power from the *climbers* to the *traditional elites.*

(2) Accompanying the former process, the intriguing problem of concentration of economic and socio-cultural benefits accruing from various institutional measures, e.g. C.D.P., cooperatives etc., to the substantially richer class of the villages is not surprising but is the normal consequence of the existing social conditions. It is unrealistic to isolate the aspects of economic and cultural power from the political, in order to justify the halfway measure of social change symbolised by the Panchayats or the Panchayati Raj. Panchayats have only succeeded in conferring upon the villagers certain legal rights which could not be put into effect for the absence of means to enforce them.

(3) Yet from one point of view the system can be justified viz. the integration of social structure. The case history of the power dynamics of the villages quoted here passes into three phases: (a) initial disequilibrium in power when power passes from traditional elites to the climbers; (b) period of acute group tension and conflict equivalent to the process of "*strain towards consistency*" and finally (c) the restoration of the equilibrium when the traditional elites come back to power. Thus, in the latest phase, social structure has gained a new level of social integration on a substantially different principle of cultural norms, adherence to which is more disguised than real. Hence from a strictly *sociological viewpoint* the change may even be desirable yet from an *ideological* point of view (grass root democracy, socialistic pattern, distribution of power etc.) it is not. Ideologically the requirement is not merely of integration but a certain level and form of integration which Panchayats have certainly not been able to achieve as yet.

(4) Both from cultural and structural point of view the Panchayats introduced radical and far-reaching measures of innovation. In view of it, not even the successes but also the failures of the system would have radical consequences for the whole rural society. This, however, is visible to even a casual observer of rural life, and the magnitude of this measure is bound to grow with administrative and economic diversification of rural

life. Mainly, the process is linked up with economic growth and increased social communication. But suitable checks on the class structure of the rural society would be imperative for the ideological success of the Panchayati Raj.

(5) Panchayats have been conceived not as isolated institutions but integral to the whole politico-ideological set-up of the Indian society. It was, therefore, expected that the administrative and ideological inter-linkages with institutions at the higher scale of operation and organisation in the country would reinforce this system. Due to unavoidable structural impediments this has not happened so far. For the same reason this process cannot even be expedited beyond a certain limit and should only grow steadily with overall process of social growth.

(6) Methodologically the analysis of the working of Panchayats offers better insight into the success and failure of the system if analysed from a dynamic class-structural point of view rather than through stereotypes of analytical categories like *caste*, *leadership* and *factions*. Analysed in this frame better insight is gained not only in the functioning of the system as such but also its interlinkage with other social structures and the social system as a whole.

5

THE IMPACT OF THE PANCHAYATI RAJ ON RURAL INDIA

UDAY MEHTA

AS WE OBSERVED in our earlier Section (Chapter on Impact of the British Welfare Measures on Rural Society), the Village Panchayat as a statutory institution, emerged for the first time under the British rule. The traditional village councils experienced a decay as a result of the Village administration by the agencies of the Central Government, extension of the jurisdiction of Civil & Criminal Courts to the rural areas, growth of modern education, communication, introduction of the novel land revenue system, police organization and such other factors during the British period. The British Government with a view to preserve and stabilize its political control over rural areas gradually adopted various measures for reorganizing the village panchayats. It appointed a special Commission on 'democratic decentralization' in 1909. This Commission stressed the need for revitalizing village panchayats for handling local affairs. Subsequently, various legislative Acts were passed in different provinces for the creation of local self-governing bodies in villages. Illustrative of this, are the Bengal Village Self-Government Act of 1919; Madras, Bombay and United Province Village Panchayat Acts of 1920; Bihar and Orissa Village Administration Act; Assam Rural Self-Government Act of 1926; Punjab Village Panchayat Act of 1935 and others. These new Panchayats were entrusted with such assignments as looking after village sanitation, lighting and were also empowered to try minor cases like theft, simple hurt, offence of cattle, trespass, etc. Various kinds of grants-in-aid, taxes, cesses, rates, tolls, fees, income from property, fines, donations and a portion of land cess were the general sources of income of Village Panchayats. There was no uniform practice for the establishment of Village Panchayats. Some provinces like Bengal, Madras, the United Provinces and the Punjab, declared specific areas as Panchayat areas. In Bombay, the Village Panchayats Act of 1939 made it compulsory to establish a Panchayat in a village with a population of 2000 or more. Thus it can be seen from the above perusal that the village Panchayat, as a formal statutory body, with officially sanctioned functions and powers and with specific financial allocation, emerged for the first time during the British period.

VILLAGE PANCHAYATS SINCE INDEPENDENCE

After independence, the development of village panchayats has received a fresh impetus. As per the Directive Principles of the Constitution (Article 40), the State is expected to take steps to organize Village Panchayats and attribute to them such powers and authority as may be necessary to enable them to function as units of self-government. Besides this Directive, the phenomenal increase in planned developmental activities after independence also brought home the need for the village panchayat as an integral part of decentralised administration. As a consequence, practically all the provinces took steps to improve the legislations with a view to promote rapid development of panchayats as well as entrusting them with greater responsibilities. Accordingly, almost all the provinces have enacted different legislations for providing requisite legal framework for the establishment of a village panchayat.

According to Nanavati and Anjaria, "The number of Village Panchayats increased from 83,093 in 1950-51 to 1,23,670 at the end of March 1956, and again increased to 1,64,358 at the end of March 1958. The number of villages covered was about four lakhs out of a total of about five lakhs of villages in the whole country. There has been good progress in the establishment of Village Panchayats in Uttar Pradesh, Punjab, Rajasthan, Kerala, Himachal Pradesh, and the erstwhile States of Madhya Bharat and Saurastra, where almost all villages are served by panchayats. The pace has been somewhat slow in Assam, West Bengal, Orissa, Mysore and Andhra; while in other States, progress has been steady. As regards the working of Village Panchayats, possibly not more than 10 per cent of the total number of Panchayats are functioning effectively, roughly half are average and the remaining 40 per cent are working unsatisfactorily." In the year 1965 there were 2,19,694 Village Panchayats functioning in the country covering approximately 99 percent of the entire rural population.

"The Village Panchayat Committee of the Congress Party, after a careful investigation of the working of Panchayats in 1954 made the following recommendations. The Panchayats provide a sound basis for the establishment of healthy, democratic traditions in the country. The Village Panchayats should not only serve as units of local self-Government but also as effective institutions for securing social justice and fostering corporate life, leading to conditions of fuller employment laid down in the Constitution. The State should therefore provide scope for the Village Panchayats to perform in the village society, functions such as credit, marketing, supplies, etc. The function of the Panchayats should include municipal, social, economic and judicial activities etc."

Similarly, the First Five Year Plan recommended that legislation should confer on the Panchayats specific functions relating to village production programmes and the development of village lands. The Second Plan further amplified this proposal, by classifying the functions as administrative and judicial. The functions in administrative sphere are defined as (1) civic, (2) development, (3) land management and (4) land reforms.

Secondly, with regard to finance it was suggested that " allocation to the Village Panchayats by the states may be in two parts, a basic proportion of 15 to 20 per cent of the land revenue and an additional grant extending upto 15 per cent of the land revenue on condition that the panchayat raises an equal additional amount by taxation or voluntary contribution."

The Second Plan also emphasised the need for creating a well organized democratic organization at the district level and suggested that the Village Panchayats should be organically linked with popular organizations at a higher level. Now we shall briefly refer to the recommendations of the Study Team on Community Projects and National Extension Service.

Recommendations of the Study Team on Community Projects and National Extension Service

Panchayati Raj in India owes its origin to the findings and recommendations of the Study Team on the working of Community Projects and National Extension Service under the auspices of the Committee on Plan Project, which is popularly known as Balwantrai Mehta Committee. From the point of view of the Mehta Committee the major shortcomings of the Community Projects and National Extension Service lies in its failure in generating the necessary enthusiasm among rural people for the programme and its implementation. According to the Committee, each development block has an Advisory Committee composed of the official and non-official representatives but they have no roots amongst the people and have no powers and responsibilities. All planning and execution is done by the block-staff, who are responsible for the proper and timely utilization of the block funds. In the opinion of the Committee the block administration functions more bureaucratically and has not imbibed the spirit behind the programme. For generating people's enthusiasm for the programme the Committee recommended that all development programmes in the block areas should be entrusted to representative institutions that can evoke local interest and initiative and the block staff and other officials should be placed at the disposal of those institutions. The Study Team also recommended for the provision of sufficient funds and sources of revenue for these local institutions to enable them to discharge their new duties. With this view in mind, the Committee suggested the formation of the three-tier system of local Government i.e. at village, block and district level. The three-tier system consisted of directly elected Panchayats at village level, Panchayat Samiti at block and Zila Parishad at district level. The Panchayat Samiti should have a life of five years, and should possess the power to scrutinize and approve the budgets of village panchayats. Its functions should include the development of agriculture, improvement of cattle, promotion of local industries, welfare work, public health, and administration of primary schools etc. As almost the entire rural development work would come within the purview of the Panchayat Samiti, the Study Team suggested the following resources should be assigned to them.

"(i) a percentage of land revenue collected within the block, which should not be less than 40 per cent of the State's net land revenue, (ii) cess on land revenue, etc. (iii) tax on professions, (iv) surcharge of duty on transfer of immovable property, (v) rent and profit accruing from property, (vi) net proceeds of tools and leases, (vii) pilgrim tax, tax on entertainment, primary education cess, proceeds from fairs and markets, (viii) share of motor vehicles tax, (ix) voluntary public contributions and (x) Government grants."

Further: "to ensure the necessary co-ordination between the Panchayat Samitis, a Zila Parishad should be established consisting of the Presidents of Panchayat Samitis, members of the State Legislature and of the Parliament, representing the area and the district level officers. The chairman of this parishad would be the Collector. The Parishad would have the power to examine and approve the budgets of the Panchayat Samitis. It would also generally supervise the activities of the Panchayat Samiti but it would not be invested with any executive functions."

The Central Government while accepting the proposals of the report recommended its implementation to all the States but the States were left free to make their own variations on the general pattern. All States that endorsed the proposal of the Centre adopted at their Zila and village level, the general pattern. At intermediate level, although most of the States took the block as unit, some States like Mysore and Gujarat opted for the taluk. At village level, all States favoured direct elections for the Village Panchayats, but again at intermediate level, most of the States preferred indirect elections, few having opted for direct. At district level, all elections are indirect.

It has been observed that, real power in the three-tier system is at the middle tier, with the Samiti President, and he is the key figure in the whole set-up. He has no interfering collector and he is not only president, but the chairman of all the Standing Committees. The senior official in the Block, the B.D.O. is his executive officer, and a word in the ear of ministerial friends can always secure the BDO's transfer if he is not alienable to the president's wishes."

Objectives of the Panchayati Raj

The main objectives of Panchayati Raj as laid down in third Five Year Plan are as follows:

(1) Increasing agricultural production,

(2) Development of rural industries,

(3) Fostering co-operative institutions,

(4) Full utilization of local manpower and other resources,

(5) Assisting the weaker sections of the community,

(6) Progressive dispersal of authority and initiative with emphasis on the role of voluntary organization, and

(7) Fostering cohesion and encouraging the spirit of self-help within the community.

The village production plans should include the following two programmes :

(a) Programmes such as supply of credit, fertilizers and improved seeds, plant protection, minor irrigation etc., for which major assistance has to come from outside; (b) Programmes such as digging field channels for utilizing irrigation from large projects, maintenance of bunds and field channels, digging and maintenance of village tanks, development and utilization of local manurial resources, etc. which call for effort on the part of the village community or the beneficiaries.

Now we shall birefly summarise the main functions of the three-tier system, at village, block and district levels respectively. This being the general pattern minor variation in the programme of activities do exist in different States.

At village level the main functions of the Panchayat are (a) provision of a water supply, (b) maintenance of minor irrigation, (c) school buildings etc., (d) family planning, (e) development and co-operation, (f) construction of wells, latrines etc.

Functions of the Panchayat Samiti

They cover agricultural improvement, development, co-operation, sanitation, primary education, social education, cottage industries, emergency relief. It works through Standing Committees for (a) production programmes, (b) social service and finance, (c) taxation and administration. Block Development Officers are regarded as on deputation to the Panchayat Samiti and are liable to be transferred in consultation with the pradhan. The Samiti pradhan exercises administrative control over the 'Vikas adhikari' (meaning development officer) and the staff within the block.

Functions of Zila Parishads

The functions of Zila Parishads include coordination and consolidation of the plans of the Panchayat Samiti, supervision of the activities, distribution among the Panchayat Samitis of the *adhoc* grants allotted to the district by the State Government etc. Pramukh of Zila Parishad can visit, guide and advise the Panchayat Samitis. Coordination between the work of the various departments is secured through the District Development Officer, who is normally the Collector and he is responsible to see that the amounts placed at the disposal of the Panchayat Samitis are being properly utilized and that the 'Vikas adhikaris' of this team are discharging their functions adequately as extension staff.

FINANCIAL RESOURCES

It can be seen from the perusal of the functions of the three-tier system that most of the functions of these three layers of the Panchayati Raj institutions are of a supervisory nature. "The district Panchayat acts as the agency of the State, the taluka Panchayat acts as the agency of the district Panchayat and the village Panchayat as that of the taluka Panchayat, for fulfilling certain previously laid down targets. Of course, the agency functions do not exhaust the list of all the responsibilities of various local institutions. There does remain the scope to initiate a limited programme of development on their own. As for the financing of the agency functions, it can be presumed that the principal agency will provide finance to carry out the functions which have been delegated to the lower agencies. It is mainly for the functions undertaken at the initiative of the village, taluka and district Panchayats that the problem of resources arises."

Further : "A review of the resources proposed to be made available to various local bodies in the Panchayat Raj Legislation shows that the main reliance is placed on land revenue. The total collection of the land revenue in a district will be distributed among various bodies in varying proportions. These bodies are also empowered to levy cess on land revenue at various rates. Besides land revenue, they also have a nominal share in forest revenue and a portion of royalty from sand and morveum etc. They can also levy a cess on water rates. But their main independent source of income viz. land revenue is a highly inelastic one."

The above observations succinctly sum up the position with regard to resources of the Panchayati Raj at various levels.

POWERS OF THE STATE

The State Government has reserved the right to cancel or reject any resolution or order passed by a Panchayat Samiti or in case of emergency the Collector can also suspend a resolution of the Panchayat Samiti and report the case for orders to the State Government. The State Government also retains the right to supersede or dissolve a Panchayat Samiti or Zila Parishad if it has failed to exercise, abuse or exceeded its power.

PANCHAYATI RAJ—GENERAL PATTERN

On January 12, 1958, the National Development Council endorsed the recommendations of the Balwantrai Mehta Committee. Since then Panchayati Raj is under implementation in Andhra Pradesh, Assam, Bihar, Gujrat, Madras, Maharashtra, Mysore, Orissa, Punjab, Rajsthan, Uttar Pradesh and West Bengal. The other States have either enacted or are in the process of enacting legislations to introduce a similar system. The Bihar Government have established the block as the primary unit of administration for all Government Departments and have assigned enlarged functions to the Block Advisory Committee. With regard to Gujarat, V. S. Vyas, remarks :

" In Gujarat, as in several though not in all States, the linchpin in the Panchayati Raj set-up is the district level institutions. All that has been done in the Panchayati Raj legislation is to give more powers to the district administration and to democratise the set-up at district level. There is hardly any significant change whether in the powers and responsibilities or in the composition of village Panchayats which have been in existence from 1958. At the taluka level, though a new democratic body has come into existence, it does not have any independent responsibilities at least none which cannot be borne by either the district or the village Panchayats."

In Madras, the local administration of the village vests in the Panchayats. Then there are Panchayat Samitis at Block level and Advisory Coordinating Committee at the district level. Most of the functions of the district local boards are taken over by the Block Panchayat Union. In Andhra Pradesh, Panchayat Samitis are established at Block level, and the developments are transferred to these Samitis. The relation of the Block Samiti with the village Panchayats are presumed to be of a coordinating and advisory nature. The District Committee is also assigned work of supervising and guiding the activities of the Samitis at the Block level. In Uttar Pradesh, the District Councils have gradually replaced the District Boards. This council is expected to handle all the departmental development activities of the Government. In Maharashtra Village Panchayat Mandals set up for every district are the main executing bodies of Government developmental programme. In Mysore, Taluka Boards function as advisory bodies for the Community Development Blocks in their areas. The District Development Council generally supervises the working of the Taluka Boards and provide guidance and assistance in co-ordinating their work. In other States also the three-tier system of the Panchayati Raj is based more or less on the above pattern.

We now propose to examine the functioning of the Panchayati Raj in action. We shall begin with Rajasthan where the Panchayati Raj was first initiated.

One of the important criteria for assessing the success of Panchayati Raj is the extent to which it has succeeded in fulfilling the objectives of village production plans and thereby increased village production.

P. K. Chaudhari makes very pertinent observations with regard to the functioning of the Panchayati Raj in Rajasthan. With regard to village production plans he points out "that the so-called village production plans that we have now are nothing but paper plans prepared by the village level workers in consultation with a few village elders and the Sarpanch of the Panchayat. No serious attempt has been made to prepare genuine village plans incorporating targets for each crop and for every family in the village."

Further: "Panchayat Samitis and Village Panchayats are prompt to take up and execute programmes for which the Government provides loans, grants or subsidies so as to avail themselves of this assistance. But programmes which have to be carried out with local resources and initiative lag behind."

With regard to the functioning of the Zila Parishad, the same author points out: "In its present form the Zila Parishad as an institution appears to have become redundant. In spite of its status, it has played no effective role. The Zila Parishads to the Panchayat Samitis are all of an advisory nature having no sanction behind them. If the advice is not palatable, the Samitis usually ignore it."

Further while narrating evils of indirect elections he remarks:

"In Rajasthan there are 7,394 village Panchayats and 232 Panchayat Samitis. In 1960-61, 25% of the elections of panchas and Sarpanches were unanimous; of sarpanches, 38.80% were elected unanimously. But unanimous election of Panchayat Samiti pradhan were rare. In most cases, there were keen contests for the office of pradhans. The Congress contested the elections as a party. During these contests, cases of forcible confinement and kidnapping of sarpanches occurred on an alarming scale. The kidnapped persons were released at the place of elections, just in time to cast their votes. In a few cases the sarpanches were sent on pilgrimage to Hardwar, etc., for sight-seeing to Kashmir at the expense of the prospective candidate for the office of pradhan so as to prevent them from coming under the influence of rival candidates."

Further: "These elections witnessed the worst features of indirect elections when the electoral college is small and the office is one of power and patronage. The assumption that direct election is more expensive than indirect was disproved. None of the contestants for the office of pradhan spent less than what an average Assembly Candidate spends (actual expenditure, not that submitted to the returning officer). Another unhappy feature of indirect elections also manifested itself—political and other pressures as well as money played a deciding role in them."

Standing Committees

It is the Standing Committee which is a real functioning body in the Panchayat Samiti. The Samiti has delegated its vital powers and functions to this body. With regard to the performance of these bodies the above author remarks: "Members of Panchayat Samitis are generally more interested in transfers, postings, and appointments of Samiti staff than in developmental activities. This is what the State Evaluation Organization has to say about the duration of meetings of the various Standing Committees. 'On an average the meetings of the Standing Committees on Administration and finances were the longest while those of the Standing Committees on production were the shortest. It is interesting to note that a fairly large number of meetings of the Standing Committee lasted for only 15 minutes. Hardly any business could have been transacted in such meetings and they were just called to complete the formality of doing so'.

Role of Officials

Implementation of 'Panchayati Raj' has caused deep apprehensions in the minds of the officials. According to Chaudhari, " there is evidence of growing deterioration in the relations between officials and non-officials in the Panchayat Samitis. Instances of friction between the pradhan and the Vikas Adhikari are on an increase".

" Whenever the Pradhan happens to be educated and assertive conflicts with the Vikas Adhikari are frequent. A clear demarcation of the sphere of action and powers and functions of the two is urgently called for."

With regard to the impact of the Panchayati Raj on weaker section of the rural population, the same author remarks: " Panchayat Raj has not brought relief to the weaker section of the community. There has been no perceptible increase in the flow of benefits of development to the economically and socially weaker section of village community. According to the 1961 Census, the State has a population of 21 millions, of which Scheduled Castes constitute about 3 millions and Scheduled Tribes about 2.1 millions. Yet there is not a single Scheduled Caste Pradhan in the whole of the State. Out of a total of 7,394 Sarpanches, the number of Scheduled Caste Sarpanches could be counted on one's fingers. And only in predominently tribal areas do we find a few sarpanches and pradhans belonging to the Scheduled Tribes. Rural leadership is still in the hands of the relatively well-to-do classes in the village which control all vantage positions in panchayati Raj."

Findings on the functioning of the Panchayati Raj in Mysore also broadly corroborate the above observations. Manu in this connection remarks that "under the Mysore Panchayati and Local Boards Act, Panchayati Raj institutions have been turned into bureaucratic cells. There is no organic link between different tiers of Panchayati Raj nor do the sources of revenue allocated to each bear any relation to the functions it has been charged with."

Further: " The Mysore Village Panchayats and Local Boards Act, 1959 is now four years old; the working of the Act has revealed glaring imperfections which affect the basic tenets of the Panchayati Raj like decentralization of decision making power, organic relationship between different tiers and democratisation of administration. The objective of increasing people's involvement in the development efforts of the State has not been attained because of the unrepresentative character of the District Development Council."

Now we shall examine the impact of democratic decentralization in Rajasthan and Andhra Pradesh as revealed by the survey conducted by the Central Institute of Study and Research in Community Development. The study of Panchayati Raj in Rajasthan and Andhra was done by Harold Hoffommer and D. C. Dubey.

With regard to Andhra Pradesh, the Report of the survey observes that "the fact that 35 percent of the people are still not aware of the programme of Panchayati Raj, is indicative of the ground still to be covered in acquainting all the villages with even a minimum awareness of the programme."

Further ; " Although 45 percent of the respondents are indicated by this analysis to know about the objective of the programme, typical comments indicate that this understanding is only at a first level, for example, most of these respondents regard the main objective of the programme as that of providing amenities for the village. They fail to see in Panchayati Raj the opportunities for developing agriculture and the other constructive phases relating to village life and welfare."

With regard to the areas of the functional leadership of the Panchayats in respect of various aspects of village life the study provides some interesting information. This can be seen from the table reproduced from the study as below.

TABLE I

Areas of Functional Leadership : Rajasthan.

(1)	Settling Disputes (with neighbours 76; within caste 32)	108	responses
(2)	Loan for Irrigation	91	"
(3)	Disease in standing crops	18	"
(4)	Sickness among cattle	15	"
(5)	Sickness of family	14	"
(6)	Loan for daughter's marriage	8	"
(7)	Planning of next years' crop	6	"
(8)	Selling crop	2	"

Areas of Functional Leadership : Andhra.

(1)	Settling disputes (with neighbours 71; within caste 42)	113	responses.
(2)	Loans for irrigation wells (Panchayat direct 18; Panchayat through village level worker 13)	31	"
(3)	Disease in standing crop	13	"
(4)	Sickness among cattle	9	"
(5)	Loan for daughter's marriage	6	"
(6)	Family sickness	3	"
(7)	Planning for next year's crop	3	"
(8)	Selling crop	1	"

Focus of Leadership	*Problem situation encompassed.*
(1) Family	Family discord, Planning next year's selling crop farm.
(2) Panchayat	Dispute with neighbours, Loan from Govt. (Irrigation, Wells)
(3) Extension Agency & Specialists	Disease in standing crop, Sickness in cattle, Sickness in family.
(4) Caste Group	Caste disputes.
(5) Money lenders	Loan for marriage of daughter, Selling crop.

(*Source*:'A Sociological Study of Panchayati Raj in Rajasthan and Andhra Pradesh', Harold Hoffsomer and D. C. Dubey, pp. 76 and 89.)

It can be seen from the above table that in Rajasthan as well as in Andhra Pradesh, the functional leadership provided by the Panchayats in such vital matters as planning of crop production is very inadequate. Only 6 respondents in Rajasthan and 3 respondents in Andhra Pradesh consulted the village panchayats in their planning for next year's crop. The reason underlying such poor response can be of a serious nature. The respondents in all probability might have a feeling that the panchayats have hardly any effective solution to offer them in this vital problem. The planning for crops involves the problem of existing structure of land holdings. The structure of land holdings in turn, depends on prevailing pattern of land-relations and ultimately upon prevailing system of property relations. The resolution of this problem is beyond the jurisdiction of Panchayats.

Similarly, the failure on the part of the large number of cultivators to consult Panchayats for crop sale also indicate the control of the money-lender over the peasants' crop. The cultivators because of their economic dependence on money-lenders have very little choice in selecting agencies for selling their crops.

With regard to the administrative framework of Panchayati Raj Vyas remarks: "What is being attempted in Gujrat, as in the other States, is the decentralization rather than devolution of power. The distinction is fundamental. Decentralization involves control by local branches of a Central department; while genuine devolution of power would mean transfer of control to lower levels of Government. Panchayati Raj Legislation aims at the decentralization of power of different Central departments. A simple test to distinguish between decentralization and devolution is to find out the agency which is the reservoir of power, though it might delegate some of its power to the talukas, district or State. As it is, the main source of power is the State which merely delegates its power to the lower limits.". Further, "The limits of this system of decentralization are better understood when it is realised that our economic planning is highly centralised."

In connection with Gujarat the author observes: " The absence of any provision for setting up Gramsabha is a real lacunae in Gujarat Panchayati Raj Act. Without effective control by the village people there is every danger of gram panchayats degenerating, literally in the rule of five persons. "

The implementation of the ' Panchayati Raj ' has led to the emergence of the novel forms of political tensions and conflicts in rural areas. The findings of the Report of Panchayati Raj Research Project conducted by the Department of Economic & Public Administration of the Rajasthan University has amply demonstrated this fact. The survey was conducted under the direction of Prof. M. V. Mathur (ex-member of the Santhanam Committee) on Panchayati Raj finances. Some of the findings of the Report are reproduced below.

LOCAL LEADERSHIP

Firstly, the introduction of Panchayati Raj has given a fillip to the emergence of a local leadership which though not independent from the State leadership is in a strong bargaining position vis-a-vis the political bosses at State level.

Secondly, the pradhan of the panchayat Samiti is an elected rival for the sphere of influence as far as the legislator is concerned. The former wields much more real power than the MLA and thus grows into a potential contender for the legislator's position.

Thirdly, the failure of public leaders in politicalizing Panchayati Raj affairs and their incapacity in generating loyalties based on platform of action and programme has revived and strengthened the traditional loyalties.

Fourthly, inadequate preparation of the large mass of really backward and downtrodden people in securing their due share in powers vested in these institutions has given an opportunity to the local vested interest to perpetuate itself with the aid of new resources provided by the State.

Fifthly, the wide gap between hopes raised by the slogan of Panchayati Raj and the actual sphere of work of these institutions has led to impatience and frustration on the one hand and in-built dynamism on the other.

Sixthly, the widespread tension between the administrative machinery and elected representatives and the usual tendency of the State Governments to protect the administrative wing has given rise to a deep-seated sense of hostility amongst the new and emergent leadership against the present new political monarchy.

Observations made by Hugh Gray, (fellow in South Asian Studies at the Oriental & African Studies, London,) who spent a year studying Panchayati Raj in Andhra Pradesh also corroborate the findings of the Report referred to above. According to him, " Panchayati Raj has provided a new framework for political and caste struggles between rival landlords (by this I don't mean feudal landlords but substantial land-owners), jealous of their prestige and determined to maintain and if possible strengthen their district power network. Needs have never been the ultimate criteria for help, except in the very broadest sense and in the individual instance there has always been patronage. Today, the Samiti president disposes not only of the Samiti jeep—but of important sources of patronage, such as for instance, the postings of primary school teachers. Through his political majority the president decides who shall receive individual well subsidies and taccavi loans, these are rarely if ever given to political opponents. The prestige of the individual Samiti members depends on what they obtain for their village in concrete physical benefits."

Further: "The aim of decentralizing political power has to a great extent been achieved. But the main aim of arousing popular enthusiasm for community development has been less successful. One sees this by the amounts of money which lapse, particularly for roads and schools, when it is a question of the public's contribution amounting to 50% instead of 25%."

According to Gray: "Villagers do not yet feel that the Raj is theirs, they still think of it as the landlords. Panchayati Raj has established a new forum in which the members of the dominant landowing castes, fight each other for prestige and power. Before, they remained as lords of their villages or went to the Legislative Assembly, in between was a vaccum. In Andhra Pradesh, where the Congress party is dominant, the Samiti Presidency is fought for on a caste basis and a Reddi, Kamma or Velma almost invariably emerges as Victor, except when a Brahmin successfully manipulates the caste factor in his favour. In districts where the Congress party is in a minority the caste factor is muted and the party cuts across caste, but the caste variable is always present and manipulated even by the communist party.

"Whatever politicians may still be doing inside their houses, outside they will dine and accept alcohol from anybody. Political parties are ritual levellers, and the higher no longer dare to appear polluted by the lower who have votes to give them. This does not mean that the boundary maintaining forces of caste are dead but that they are utilizing more secular forms and the dominant agricultural castes battle each other for control of the State Government and the new bodies set up by Panchayati Raj."

In his concluding remark the above author makes a very pertinent and revealing observation. According to him. "I would argue that there can only be common interests in egalitarian communities, which Indian villages are not: It seems to me that the shifting of the conflict of interests and opinions, serves not the emergence of synthesis from thesis and antithesis, but the interests of powerful individuals and groups. The consensus which emerges is always the view of the rulers and not the ruled."

The bureaucratic nature of the new power elite that has emerged as a result of the implementation of the Panchayati Raj is very ably depicted by 'Seminarists'.

The author observes that: " in Rajasthan, where the BDO is in many cases a junior I.A.S. Officer the president of the Panchayat Samiti writes his annual report. How impartial these reports are can easily be judged by the dilemma of the BDO. He is expected to carry the people with him but, more often than not, this simply means an ability to be tactful, without antagonising the unscrupulous. There is not a politician of consequence who is not either a building contractor or a road builder, an office bearer of the local cooperative. The BDO has to humour him or else he is easily transferred as tactless, inefficient bureaucrat lacking in the spirit of extension."

With regard to the impact of the Panchayati Raj on the weaker sections of the rural society the above author's findings deserve consideration.

He remarks: " The impoverished small cultivator who is sought to be put on his legs by Panchayati Raj is gullible enough to accept his old bare level of subsistence. No eggs for him, no fish for him, not even a reasonable quality of the paddy or wheat which he produces."

Further: " Firstly, Panchayati Raj is used more as an empty slogan to catch the fancy of the voter who has already exploded the myth of the common good....Secondly, democratic decentralization is not possible within the limits of perpetuating a regime. Not when Panchayati constituencies are delimited suitably to preserve group strength; elections are staged without adequate rules, administrators are either appointed or removed to suit the interests of political representatives, presidents of Zila Parishads are nominated and not elected; accounts are audited inordinately late, the collection of arrears of land revenue and loans is willfully postponed and schools and buildings and roads and wells are constructed in chosen constituencies. What earthly chance can the illiterate and backward, the gullible and innocent villagers have against the organised conspiracy ? Whether it is Bihar or Orissa, the Punjab or U.P. the story is the same."

The implementation of the Panchayati Raj has led to the strengthening of caste system. Number of scholars have pointed out this fact. Prof M. N. Srinivasa in his essay on 'Caste in Modern India', observes that the power and activity of caste has increased in proportion as political power passed increasingly to the people from the rulers and the establishment of the Panchayati Raj in Rajasthan and Andhra has given a new fillip to caste.

Characteristics of the Emerging Leadership in Rural Areas

Dr. Pradipto Roy, in a paper throws significant light on the new elite that has emerged in rural areas in recent years. According to him the main characteristics of the rural leadership today are as follows :

"In short, the characteristics that distinguish the emergent leaders who are participating in the new organizations from non-participants were–first, higher socio-economic level in a rational sense i.e. higher income, more material possessions and more education. The new participants as would be expected, had a higher level of contact with the extension agency and more secular orientation to life." Further in summing up the overall characteristics of the new leadership in rural areas the author observes : "The picture that emerges of the leader is a person of high economic status, some education, good contacts with extension agencies, a large family and a somewhat rational orientation to life."

Similar trends are also noticed by B. Ganguly in his paper entitled : 'The Emerging Leadership pattern under planning in Rural Bihar', submitted to the conference we referred above. He remarks: "Moreoever casteism has raised its head in a virulent form in recent years and sometimes second rate political leaders have been fanning caste tensions for getting support of voters. Zamindars, who were in most cases the natural leaders of the villages have lost their leadership and in their place have cropped up a class of semi literate leaders. In many cases the contractors, school managers, muharris, kutibs, karparardars, cooperative secretaries, and Banias are the village leaders. Mukhias, up-mukhias, sarpanches and Dalpatis very often crop up from the class of leaders who really belong to the Kamkanchana group, now clamouring for kirti. People of the 'Karma' and 'Dharma' groups are in the background. When MLAs and M.P.s take part in village politics, there is a better leadership no doubt, but party politics pollutes even the rural society. Even some Sarvodaya workers are hesitating to take up village leadership lest they might be corrupted by power and lest their participation in gram panchayats means lending whole hearted support to the Congress policy with which they are not in complete agreement."

The same author further observes that there were bitter quarrels and fights over Panchayat elections, often under the patronage of political parties. Mukhias, pramukhs and others were found to be more concerned with making contracts etc., than in promoting village welfare.

The studies conducted by the Planning Commission recently, further reveal that most of the Sarpanches in the villages surveyed by the Commission were recruited from upper caste.

We are reproducing below some more findings on the impact of the Panchayati Raj in rural areas. Recently a sample survey conducted by Prof. Y. M. Sirsikar, revealed that 'rural politics in Maharashtra tends to become more competitive than constructive' and traditional factors like caste, social status and wealth play an important role in Panchayat elections.

The survey has pointed out, ' the rural elite ', consisting of the well-to-do peasantry, lawyers with an agricultural background and a few businessmen, display an increasing power consciousness. Politics threatens to become more competitive than constructive. ' Ideology would seem to count less than power consideration. '

" The political structure in rural Maharashtra exhibits a mixed character, modern and traditional. The leaders are elected on party tickets by secret ballot and defined procedures. At the same time, traditional factors such as kinship and caste are in evidence and the party structure itself is threatened with infiltration by these traditional elements. "

Further the survey also shows that as many as 71.2 percent of the office bearers of Zila Parishads are drawn from the Maratha Caste. This means that the Marathas are 'heavily over-represented', since they constitute only 40 percent of the total population of the State. Brahmins hold less than four percent of the seats in the Panchayat institutions. This poor showing on their part is attributed to the shift of the Brahmin population from the rural to urban centres in recent years.

Referring to the age-group of leadership the survey reveals that 63.4 percent of the Panchayat officials belong to the age-group of 31-45, the younger ones (between 25 and 30 years) constituting only 9.8 percent. The percentage of office-bearers of up to 25 years is 3.6. Only 4.2 percent of the officials are above the age of 60.

Thus the leadership in rural Maharashtra at present appears to be concentrated in the hands of the 31-45 age-group.

The survey also points out that most of the leaders of Zila Parishads 'entered public life and political parties very recently—some not even more than a year prior to their election'. Referring to the education and social values of the new rural elites, the study reveals that there were no illiterates among the new rural leaders, though more than 30 percent had no English education. Only 25 per cent had passed the matriculation examination. There were a good number of graduates.

Another interesting revelation of the survey is the significant change in social values. For instance, against only 31·7 percent of the Panchayat officials being connected with temple or such other religious activities in their respective areas, 66.7 percent were found to be intimately connected with educational institutions. This indicates that education has become a matter of immediate concern for the rural leadership.

Another intensive inquiry into various Panchayat Samitis in the Punjab conducted by the Gram Swaraj Sangha concluded that these institutions have failed due to factionalism: " So long as there is a clash of interests—and it is idle to pretend that there is no such clash in the villages—such divisions cannot be wished away. "

The *Times of India* in its editorial points out, that the accumulating evidence shows that incompetence, moreover, is compounded by factionalism and that the Panchayati institutions (like all too many of the co-operative societies in the rural areas) are becoming instruments in the hands of the privileged sections in the countryside for their own advancement.

" Some months ago the Department of Economics and Public Administration of Rajasthan University completed a study of Panchayati Raj in the State; and its report is a sobering document. In the agricultural sector, the introduction of Panchayati Raj has had little impact on productivity; rather, it is ' bogged down ' in the complexities of distributing taccavi and other loans, and the recovery of these loans is disappointingly low. Democratic decentralization, it seems has generated development conciousness; but this has not led to the growth of social solidarity. In the sphere of social reform, it has had little direct impact, and its indirect impact has been negative. Clan and caste loyalties are finding renewed expession through Panchayati Raj institutions. If similar candid studies were conducted elsewhere, we might find that the situation in the other States is equally bad, if not worse. After all, Rajasthan continues to be hailed as a pioneer in democratic decentralization, one which has given a bold lead to the other States."

It can be seen from the above observations that the new leadership that has emerged in agrarian areas as a result of various Government developmental measures is essentially recruited from new landowning class. It has been also indicated that this leadership coming from higher income groups equipped with better education and with superior material resources at its command has acquired a more rational outlook on life. This new leadership is also bureaucratic and corrupt in character. The study conducted by the Planning Commission has also pointed out that most of the village sarpanches are recruited from upper castes. This leadership also exploits caste sentiments for promotion of its interests. Thus, the replacement of traditional leadership of Zamindars by a new land-owning class is a new phenomenon that has emerged in rural India after Independence. The above observations also reveal that the new land-owning class is emerging not only as an economic, but also as a political and social leader in agrarian areas. The above studies also indicate how this new leadership is slowly developing its grip over administrative authorities like Block Development Officer and other officials Thus the new land-owning class is emerging as a most powerful and potent force in agrarian India in recent years. The positive significance of the Panchayati Raj as per the strategy of the ruling class in India lie in accelerating this process in rural areas.

It may be noted here th t the Panchayati Raj as implemented by the Government of India is quite different from the one as visualised by Gandhiji and Vinobaji and other Sarvodaya leaders. The Panchayati Raj or ' Gram-Swarajya ' as envisaged by latter centred round the idea of reviving the self-sufficient village community with the spinning wheel as the base of the village economy. The social and economic life of the village community according to the concept of Gandhiji should be guided by the laws of morality. One of the most important ingredients of these moral laws is that every owner of property should consider himself to be a trustee on behalf of the people. The concept of gramdan, as evolved and propagated by Vinobaji represents the ideal image of such self-sufficient village community.

The Panchayati Raj as implemented now is the very opposite of this. Far from reviving the self-sufficient village community as cherished by Sarvodaya, it subjects every aspect of village life, agricultural production, animal husbandry and fisheries, education and public health, etc., to the direction and guidance emanating from the centre, as well as the State Head Quarters.

The establishment of socio-economic systems within the matrix of mixed economy as envisaged by the Indian Planning Commission makes it inevitable that the administration should have a large degree of centralization as it is impossible to build up a modern industrialized economy without having a centralized administration.

On the basis of the evaluations made by above official enquiries and the findings of the experts, the impact made by the Panchayati Raj on rural India can broadly be summed up as below:

(1) The implementation of the Panchayati Raj has given a new fillip to caste systems in Andhra and Rajasthan.

(2) The Panchayati Raj has further intensified the factional struggles and group rivalries among the contesting groups for power.

(3) It has given birth to a new variety of non-official bureaucrats in rural areas.

(4) It has further intensified the tensions and conflicts among the administrative personnel and taluk leaders.

(5) It has brought 'politics of manipulation' right up to the village level.

(6) It has successfully directed the mind of the rural people from resolving their basic economic and social problem to intrigues for power from village to taluka level.

(7) It has given rise to intensified form of nepotism and corruption through patronizing selected group of individuals.

(8) The ruling party has successfully created through Panchayati Raj an organised group of its supporters who form its social base today in rural areas.

(9) It has further generated power hunger and consequently power tensions in rural areas.

(10) The production plans which panchayats are expected to implement at the village level have largely remained only paper plans. Thus,

the Panchayati Raj like Community Development has proved a total failure in effectively enforcing production plans at village level and thereby contributing in increasing agricultural production.

(11) The Panchayati Raj has failed in benefitting weaker sections of the rural society.

(12) The new rural elite emerging from the higher income and more educated section of the rural society is dominating the Panchayati Raj today.

(13) The Scheduled Castes and the Scheduled Tribes members have no effective choice in Panchayat Samities which is a real governing body. To the best of our knowledge no scheduled caste member has been selected as the pramukh of the panchayat Samiti in any state. The Scheduled Tribes pramukhs are found only in tribal areas. Thus, the weaker sections of Indian rural society are left almost completely unrepresented in the Panchayati Raj institutions.

(14) Panchayati Raj has also failed in generating local enthusiasm for Government projects. This is evident from the fact that it has failed in enlisting the cooperation of the village people for the voluntary projects which demanded more contribution from the people in kind or cash. It has succeeded in undertaking only those projects which are mainly financed by the Government.

What are the implications of the above findings for rural India ? Can Panchayati Raj successfully resolve our agrarian problem within the matrix of the present social structure of rural society ? Can it successfully implement any production plan in the existing pattern of land relations ? Can it generate any sense of unity and cooperation and enthusiasm in class, caste and faction ridden rural society in India ? Is any 'democratic decentralization' possible in the hierarchically graded society ? Will it be too much to assume that in the absence of the basic prerequisites for effective application of 'democratic decentralization' the present programme of the Panchayati Raj only serves the function of expanding the social base of the ruling party and the Government by recruiting larger number of their supporters at different levels in rural society ?

Section XII

COMMUNITY DEVELOPMENT PROJECTS

THE PRESENT Section contains four selections. The selection from Sjt. Thirumalai attempts to provide a historical resume of the various types of efforts that have been made to bring about rural reconstruction from the time of British Rule and culminating in the most comprehensive and widespread effort now launched in the form of community development projects. Unfortunately, an exhaustive historical as well as theoretically oriented account of the various rural reconstruction measures in India is not available. The present Survey however provides a clue to more elaborate studies of such type. The other three selections try to provide an evaluation of the Community Development Projects both in terms of their practical achievement and theoretical postulates. More exhaustive studies of the Community Development Projects and other programmes in the background of agrarian transformation which has been taking place under the postulates of mixed economy have become necessary. Even the concept of village community as formulated in the development programme deserves scrutiny in the light of the industrialisation programme that has been inaugurated by the Government of India through its schemes of installing heavy industries, hydro-electric projects and transport and communication. (*Author.*)

1

HISTORICAL SURVEY*

S. THIRUMALAI

THE VERY FIRST type was, therefore, that of a single handed effort to construct a Model Village as a demonstration centre for neighbouring villages. After a brilliant initial success, such type of work has always ended in dismal failure with the slackening of individual effort and the waning of enthusiasm. The cost was also prohibitive.

The second type of rural uplift is characterised by co-operative effort by enthusiasts to enlarge the area of work and enlist the services of different departmental experts in their welfare work in the villages. As this type of activity required intense staff work, inspection and supervision, success could be obtained only in areas comprising a definite number of villages where the co-operative movement had gained in strength.

The third type of rural reconstruction was found in the work of the village *panchayats* in the period when they functioned efficiently in certain parts of the country. The latest type is that of the Community Projects which have been modelled on the Extension Services in Agriculture of the U.S.A.

STAGES AND METHODS OF RECONSTRUCTION

There have been six main stages of rural uplift work in India determined by the purposes and scope of work in relation to the agency of service. The first stage was marked by exclusive official effort. The main purpose of the work was confined to the sphere of public health and hygiene. The officers-in-charge of Government departments gathered the peasants whenever an epidemic broke out in an area and explained to them the measures they should take to combat the menace.

These sporadic meetings were not effective in awakening the rural conscience. In the second stage, work under reconstruction was extended to cover better education, better sanitation, cheap litigation, etc. The official agency of propaganda was strengthened, *ad hoc* officers being appointed to organise meetings. The methods of approach were made comparatively attractive and effective, through exhibits, posters, pamphlets and broad-sheets. The traditional institution of *panchayat* was encouraged and assisted to take up reconstruction work as then conceived. But still, the peasants were hardly touched by the propaganda machinery and little achievement could be recorded.

---

* Reproduced from *Post-war Agricultural Problems and Policies in India*, by S. Thirumalai, 1954, pp. 232-247.

In the third stage when the village *panchayats* languished, reconstruction work consisted in reorganising the machinery rather than improving conditions in villages. The fourth stage was marked by an enthusiastic revival of a general effort to uplift and intensification of the propaganda machinery and methods. Special efforts were made to improve the attractions and multiply the exhibits. The mobile van equipped with radio, loudspeaker, gramophone records and sets of exhibits from development departments, such as Industries, Agriculture, Veterinary, Hygiene, Cooperative, Education and Public Health formed the chief vehicle of propaganda. Villages were selected for reconstruction work and on-the-spot demonstrations were shown on what intensive efforts can achieve. The model village of Gurgaon, Rahi, Moga, Martandam, Vadmalaipuram, Partabgarh were the achievements of this stage. The degree of success in each centre depended upon the agency at work. The fifth stage has witnessed spectacular exhibitions on occasions of religious, or cultural festivals organised with greater precision and specialism. They have covered all aspects of reform in rural life, from agricultural improvements to physical culture, temperance, boy-scout camps, red cross displays, etc. In the sixth stage the concept of rural uplift has been widened and attempts have been made to bring into close contact the rural population by organising voluntary associations of landlords, tenants, labourers, etc. for the specific purpose of improvement in agriculture and corporate life.

In all these stages the chief limitation has been the absence of co-ordination of purpose and agencies at work. In recent times, there has been a widespread organisation of non-official social welfare agencies in the country. The States have also set up separate departments for comprehensive reorganisation of welfare work in villages. But still the structural organisation has not been found to be adequate for a readjustment of the problems under rural reconstruction. There has not been a comprehensive survey or handling of the rural problem as a whole.

Some Achievements

It is difficult to give quantitative data on the actual achievements in rural reconstruction in the country. However, an attempt is made to indicate the work done by some notable agencies by way of illustration.

Co-operative Schemes

The co-operatives have been utilised for reconstruction work in villages by almost every agency, official as well as non-official. But they have not been so far organised independently on a broad basis to serve as the single co-ordinating agency for purposes of rural development. Even the multipurpose societies which have been lately accepted as the model, have confined their activities to the economic needs of the village population, such as credit, supply, purchase and sale, distribution of controlled commodities, etc. Rarely have they covered the social and cultural requirements of the members.

Within the co-operative movement special types of societies have been organised for purposes of social welfare such as Education Societies, Better Living Societies, Health Societies, Veterinary Aid Societies, etc. These are found mostly in the Uttar Pradesh and the Punjab. Obviously their achievements must be small, due to the restricted scope of their functions.

SARVODAYA SCHEMES

The scheme of *Sarvodaya* is the embodiment of the principles on which the constructive programme of Mahatma Gandhi, the Father of the Nation, is based. The scheme is worked both by non-official agencies, particularly the organisations under the Congress Party as well as some of the State Governments as a humble tribute to the memory of the departed leader. The State of Bombay figures prominently in working the *Sarvodaya* schemes since 1948-49. The work is implemented by trained and trusted social workers designated as *sanchalaks* at the village level and the organisation comprises the Central State *Sarvodaya* Committee and area *Sarvodaya* Committees at the top. The schemes include plans relating to Education, Agriculture, Cow Protection, Village Industries, Public Health, Sanitation, Social Amenities and Social Welfare. Usually each centre selects one central activity such as colonisation and agricultural improvements or cattle breeding or hand spinning or basic education from which other parts of the programme derive their impulse. Emphasis is laid on Co-operative principles and methods in organising *Sarvodaya* activities and on inculcating habits of self-help, mutual aid, toleration and thrift among the people.

From the principles, methods and achievements, it can be inferred that the *Sarvodaya* Movement is a comparatively comprehensive effort in rural reconstruction. It attempts an integration with the co-operative organisations and non-official agencies in the sphere of rural reconstruction. The intimate association of the Movement with the name of Mahatma Gandhi and his work for the villages gives it a more popular appeal. The potentialities as an officially adapted movement by the States are yet to be evaluated.

THE FIRKA PLAN

Madras State has many pioneer schemes and achievements to its credit. But the *Firka* Development Plan as worked by the State since 1947, has provided another type of organisation for rural reconstruction. The scheme again derives its inspiration from the ideals of Mahatma Gandhi. Two significant features of this Plan which deserve special mention are the newly-oriented policy of viewing the welfare work programme from the community angle and the method by which villagers are taught, guided and encouraged to raise their standard of living and welfare. Government's role is mainly that of a catalytic agent. The scheme emphasises the perfect co-ordination of the work of departments like Agriculture, Industries, Irrigation, Veterinary, etc. Under the general Plan the five main centres of work are: Agriculture and Village Industries; Sanitation, Health and Housing; Village Education; Village Organisation; Village Culture. The *firkas* or regions selected for development work are placed under trained Rural Welfare Officers. The *Gram Sevaks* and social service volunteers provide the vital link in the implementation of the Plan. The advice of other constructive Institutions is also sought in training the workers.

The special achievement of the scheme is that the small grant of money by Government has acted effectively as a kind of tilting lever in obtaining a large measure of local contribution in money and in kind of labour. Some of the major achievements were in providing rural water-supply schemes, completing works of urgent importance and encouraging cottage industries. The excellent work and the results of the Madras *Firka* Development Scheme have been appreciated by the Central Government and they are anxious to see that other States copy this scheme.

Departmental Agencies

Though the activities undertaken under rural reconstruction may vary in the different States, the scheme is almost similar in all the States. The organisational set-up, however, is not uniform.

The development work includes encouragement to small-scale industries, construction of roads, distribution of medicines, village-sanitation, constitution of village *panchayats* and the running of night schools.

Community Development

The Community Projects recently initiated by the State are the result of the continuous emphasis that has been placed on Community Development in reconstructing agriculture. They are the beginnings of a bold venture to adapt advanced extension technique as conceived and applied in the West to local conditions and resources in the Indian Villages. They are the first centralised, extensive and co-ordinated plan for rural reconstruction, incorporated in the first National Five-Year Plan of the country.

The genesis of the Community Development schemes in the post-war period should, however, be traced to the establishment of new villages and townships in the scheme for Refugee Rehabilitation, formulated after partition. Among these the pilot development project at Mahewa in the Etawah District of the U. P. has earned public admiration for the enthusiasm and achievement in rural improvement.

COMMUNITY PROJECTS

The integrated scheme of Community Projects initiated by the State in 1952 for the transformation of the social and economic life of the villages proposes the establishment of a network of extension workers throughout the country over a period of ten years. The Community Project Area is conceived as being divided into 3 Development Blocks, each consisting of about 100 villages and a population of about 60,000 to 70,000. The Development Block is, in turn, divided into groups of 5 villages each, each group being the field of operation for a village level worker. The initial programme has been started with approximately 55 Projects. It covers an area of 26,950 square miles in 18,464 villages with a population of 15·19 millions. Agricultural production is the most urgent objective in the selection of the initial Projects. The criteria for selection of the Project Area or independent Development Block Area has been the existence of irrigation facilities or assured rainfall. Seven areas have been selected on the ground of their being inhabited predominantly by scheduled tribes. The main lines of activity in a Community Project is briefly divided into: Agriculture and related matters; Irrigation; Communications; Education; Health; Supplementary Employment; Housing; Training and Social Welfare. The organisational structure consists of the Central Committee (The Planning Commission), with an Administrator of the Community Projects, the Development Committee at the State level with a commissioner or a similar official as Secretary, at the District level, a Development Officer and at the Project level, an Executive Officer with 125 supervisors and village level workers. The essence of the programme is the ensuring of people's participation right from the start. The agency of the *Bharat Sevak Samaj* which has been inaugurated as the non-official counterpart of the Organisation is to become a major avenue for the mobilisation of voluntary effort on the part of the villagers. The contributions of the villagers may be in the form of voluntary labour or cash.

The estimated cost of a basic type of a rural Community Project is Rs. 6·5 million over a period of three years. The Central Committee has, however, decided that the Project should operate on a reduced total of Rs. 4·5 million. The cost is shared between the Centre and the State in the ratio of 75 : 25 in respect of non-recurring expenditure and 50 : 50 in respect of recurring expenditure. The entire expenditure of the development blocks is expected to be borne by the State at the end of three years. The Plan has provided for a little over Rs. 1,000 million for Community Projects and Rural Development. The financing of the operations under the Community Projects Scheme has been made secure under the Indo-American Technical Co-operation Fund. The contribution of U. S. A. to the Fund is 50 million dollars and the Government of India has agreed to contribute an equal amount, making up a total of 100 million dollars or about Rs. 500 million. The amount will be expended on the supporting projects such as the acquisition and distribution of fertilisers, iron and steel, project for ground water irrigation, for distribution of soil fertility and fertiliser use, for malaria control and for training of village level workers. Mention must also be made of the grants made by the Ford Foundation, totalling Rs. 23,030,000, towards the furtherance of community development and extension work in the country. Under this grant, 15 pilot community development projects and 25 extension training centres have been established. It is too early yet to indicate the achievements made by the Community Projects.

Provision has been made in the Plan for a systematic evaluation of the programme, anu the results of the evaluation should indicate the nature of adjustments in the future.

National Extension Service

Community development is the method and rural extension the agency through which the Plan seeks to initiate the programme of social and economic transformation. Extension work and community programme will run concurrently, the only difference being that the former, which is restricted in scope, will cover a wider region while the latter, aiming at all-round development, will concentrate on particular areas. A programme has been drawn up for 1,200 blocks covering 120,000 villages and nearly one-fourth of the population within the operation of the extension service.

Out of the 1,200 blocks, 700 comprising 70,000 villages and a population of about 46.2 million will receive intensive development under Community Programme, while 500 blocks covering 50,000 villages and a population of about 33 million will receive attention under National Extension Service.

Each N.E.S. Development block will have a small 'works" programme forming a nucleus of productive activities in respect of basic amenities. The N.E.S. programme has considerable potentialities for employment, both in the field of skilled and unskilled work. In the sphere of skilled work technical personnel numbering nearly 85,000 would be required in various categories, such as project executive officers, agricultural graduates, multipurpose village level workers, veterinary doctors, co-operative inspectors, school teachers, social education organisers, doctors, compounders, sanitary inspectors, health visitors, midwives, engineers, overseers, supervisors and mechanics.

2

COMMUNITY DEVELOPMENT PROJECTS —AN EVALUATION*

ADULT LITERACY CENTRES were started during the project period in all but 2 of the Evaluation Centres. 38.6 per cent of the sample villages reported this programme, village coverage by blocks varying from 8 per cent to 93 per cent with 6 centres reporting village coverage of over 58 per cent. From the reports received from P.E.Os., however, it appears that there is general lack of interest on the part of villages in this programme; and even when follow-up facilities are provided by way of rural libraries, the response is not enthusiastic. It has also been noticed that as soon as project grants cease, the literacy centres also tend to disappear. This lack of enthusiasm for literacy among adults constitutes a sharp contrast to their enthusiasm for primary education for their children and indicates some major deficiency either in the extension methods followed by social education officers or in the techniques adopted for imparting adult literacy.

As regards the benefits of the programme for the economically handicapped classes and the extent of the bridging of the distance between the better off and worse off sections of rural society, P.E.Os'; reports do not give room for optimism. It is true that some direct benefit has accrued to the handicapped classes by way of employment, drinking water wells, primary education, and rural housing. But these are not, with the exception of the last item and that too only in some areas, peculiar to the handicapped classes. Benefits of these programmes accrue also to the other classes in the villages. In addition the better off classes get loans, are more easily able to adopt improved practices, and otherwise derive larger benefit from the development programmes. The non-owner classes have not got the status that possession of land alone can give them, land re-distribution still remains in the realm of thought and discussion. Land reforms in the direction of ceiling on holdings, giving of land to the landless labourers, and co-operative farming are all still to be achieved in most of the evaluation block areas. Persons who can use credit productivity but do not have the assets that can make credit available are, generally speaking, handicapped by the absence of co-operative institutions lending supplies in kind and arranging for sales and recovery from sale proceeds. This system of what is called 'integrated finances' has been reported from one or two block areas, but is still in an incipient stage and in any case found only in limited areas. The result of all this

* Reproduced from *Evaluation Report on Working of Community Projects and N.E.S. Blocks*—Vol. I, Government of India, April 1957, pp. 17-21.

is that while some people are undoubtedly benefiting from the development programme and improving their economic and social conditions, these usually belong to those sections in the village who were already somewhat better off than their fellow villagers. This is a matter of concern for the future of the community development programme.

Finally, it must be pointed out that while there is reported to be some improvement in the working of Block and District Advisory Committees, it still remains largely true of the block areas that enough use is not being made of these agencies either in planning the programme or in creating the necessary atmosphere for implementing it. Officials are still not quite educated in seeing the possibilities of the immense help they can derive for the promotion of public participation by paying appropriate attention to these committees. The composition of these committees is still being determined in many cases on the basis of status and prestige rather than of functional competence or representation of organised village activity. What these committees need are members who have a vital stake in rural development and are, therefore, prepared actively to participate in C.D. and N.E.S. programmes and exert their influence in mobilising public co-operation for their implementation. What they also need are officials who have confidence in the sense of responsibility and capacity for public work on the part of the non-officials and are, therefore, anxious to enlist their active co-operation. Both these things are happening no doubt; but not yet in a measure that leaves an adequate enough impact on the rural community.

CONCLUSIONS

Several conclusions stand out from the survey we have made of the achievements of the community project programme. The more important of these are summarised below:

(1) Almost all villages have been covered by one or more items in the programme.

(2) Items involving physical change, especially constructional and irrigational activity, are widespread, and have contributed in some measure to the production potential and the social overheads of the block areas.

(3) Items involving physical change in production attitudes in agriculture and animal husbandry are comparatively successful, while it is not possible to say anything about changes in production attitudes among artisans due to the fact that programmes concerning cottage industries are neither widespread nor particularly successful.

(4) Items involving changes in standards or norms of living, especially in regard to primary education and drinking water are comparatively successful, while those concerning adult literacy and personal and environmental hygiene are not equally successful.

(5) Items involving change in social attitudes such as readiness to go in for or maintain community centres, youth clubs, and women's organizations are, generally speaking, not particularly successful.

(6) Items involving change in organisational attitudes in the economic field such as better understanding of the objectives and obligations of co-operation and readiness to make use of co-operative societies for purposes other than credit such as production and marketing are comparatively unsuccessful.

(7) Items involving change in organisational attitudes in the political field such as better understanding of the objectives and responsibilities of panchayat membership and readiness to use panchayats for planning and executing village development programmes are comparatively unsuccessful.

(8) The objective of inducing public participation and positive support has been comparatively successful in the case of constructional programmes, but not in the case of institutional programmes.

(9) While there has been considerable increase in rural consciousness of economic, and to a smaller extent, of social needs, the objective of stimulating continuing and positive effortbased on self-help for promoting economic or social development has been comparatively unsuccessful. Too much dependence on Government initiativeand assistance is still being exhibited by the vast majority of the rural population affected by the programme.

(10) The rural population in project areas is, generally speaking, now developing a feeling that Government is there not merely to rule but also to help. In fact, expectation of what Government can do to help has perhaps reached a stage beyond the current resources of Government. On the other hand, there has not taken place an equally strong sentiment of self-reliance and initiative, whether individual or co-operative. Unless, therefore, Government deploy more resources in rural areas and the people, in turn, show greater initiative and self-help, a situation is being created in rural India, which is bound to create serious difficulties.

(11) There is wide disparity in the distribution of the achievement and therefore of the benefits of community project programmes. This disparity exists as between different blocks in the project areas. Within the blocks, it exists as between the H. Q. villages of Grama Sevaks, the villages easily accessible to them, and the villages not so easily accessible. Within the villages, it exists as between cultivators and non-cultivators; and within the cultivating classes, it exists as between cultivators of bigger holdings and larger financial resources. This is a matter of serious concern not only in terms of regional and social justice but also in terms of the political consequences that may ensue in the context of the increasing awakening among the people.

(12) Orientation of the project staff in the objectives and techniques of community development and of the Five-Year Plan is neither adequate nor uniform in distribution.

(13) Advisory Committees at the block and district levels are still to play the role that was expected of them in the development programme. This is due partly to defective membership and partly to continuing reluctance of the official machinery to make full and positive use of the Advisory Committees.

(14) The transition from community project to the P.I.P. pattern has created a number of important problems of maintenance of facilities, satisfaction of demands and activising of project staff. These need to be solved urgently, if we are to activise both the project staff and the population of the project blocks which are now passing into 'post-intensive' phase. Only then can economic and social development of self-sustaining character be made possible for these areas.

3

COMMUNITY DEVELOPMENT PROJECTS—A SOCIOLOGICAL ANALYSIS*

A. R. DESAI

THE PRESENT paper attempts to make a sociological analysis of the Community Development Projects which have been sponsored by the Government of the Indian Union to assist the reconstruction of the agrarian economy and the rural society.

The Planning Commission in their First Five-Year Plan have described the Community Development Projects ' as the method through which Five-Year Plan seeks to initiate a process of transformation of the social and economic life of the villages. ' It is, according to an U.N.O. report, ' designed to promote better living for the whole community with the active participation and, if possible, on the initiative of the Community, but if this initiative is not forthcoming, by the same use of techniques for arousing it and stimulating it in order to secure its active and enthusiastic response. ' The Community Development Projects are of vital importance, according to Pandit Nehru, ' not so much for the material achievements that they would bring about, but much more so, because they seem to build up the community and the individual and to make the latter the builder of his own village centres and of India in the larger sense. '

The word ' Community Development ' itself is a novel nomenclature in India. As the Report of the Team for the Study of the Community Projects and National Extension Service (popularly known as the Balwantrai Committee Report) states, ' We have so far used such terms as rural development, constructive work, adult education and rural uplift to denote certain of its aspects. The word " Community " has, for the past many decades, denoted religious or caste groups or, in some instance, economic groups not necessarily living in one locality; but with the inauguration of the community development programme in this country, it is intended to apply it to the concept of the village community as a whole, cutting across caste, religious and economic differences. It is a programme which emphasises that the interest in the development of the locality is necessarily and unavoidably common to all the people living there. ' It is sociologically significant to note that to renovate the agrarian economy and the rural society through the active participation of millions

*Reproduced from *Sociological Bulletin*, Vol. VII, September 1958, No. 2, Indian Sociological Society, pp. 152-165.

of villagers, the sponsors of this movement could not find an appropriate term in any of the State languages of India to symbolize this vast process. We will examine the postulates underlying this new connotation of the term " Community " subsequently.

The Community Development Projects emerged as a result of inspiration from the following earlier experiments :

(i) Intensive rural development activities carried out at Sevagram and the Sarvodaya centres in the Bombay State; (ii) The Firca Development Schemes in Madras; (iii) Experiments to build up community centres for Refugees at Nilokheri and other places; (iv) And more particularly from the Pilot Projects at Etavah and Gorakhpur in the U.P. under the inspiration of Albert Meyers.

This idea also arose out of a realization that various efforts made by the Government departments such as Agriculture, Animal Husbandry, Co-operation, Health, Education and others which were carried on separately, should be co-ordinated to make them more effective. Further, according to the sponsors of the movement, this programme was launched with a view to changing the very philosophical basis of rural reconstruction. Most of the other institutions approached the village and rural reconstruction work in a philanthropic spirit. The Community Development Movement 'wants to create a psychological change in the villagers... It aims at inculcating in the villagers new desires, new incentives, new techniques, and a new confidence so that this vast reservoir of human resources may be used for the growing economic development of the country'.

The Community Development Programme was inaugurated on October 2, 1952. Fifty-five Community Projects were launched. Each Project Area comprised about 300 villages, covering an area of 450 to 500 sq. miles, i.e., about 1,50,000 acres with a population of about 2,00,000 persons. A project area was divided into three Development Blocks of hundred villages, each with a population of about 65,000 persons. Each Block was divided into about twenty groups, each containing five villages. Each group of villages was being served by a Gram-Sevak (the village level worker). Of the five villages, one generally became the headquarters of the Gram-Sevak.

The programme launched in 1952 was extended to wider areas at the end of the First Five-Year Plan. 603 National Extension Service Blocks, and 553 Community Development Blocks covering 1,57,000 villages and a population of 88.8 million persons were created. Nearly one out of every three villages in India was brought within the orbit of this Programme.

The Second Five-Year Plan proposed to bring every village in India under this scheme, 40 per cent of the area being brought under a more intensive development scheme. In all 3,800 additional Extension Service

Blocks will be set up, 1,120 of these being converted into Community Project Blocks. The ambitious scheme has, however, been subsequently modified.

The Community Development Programme is broadly divided into three phases, viz., the National Extension phase, the Intensive Community Development Project phase and the post-Intensive Development phase. Of course, it is not laid down that everywhere the first two phases must follow each other, the National Extension phase in some areas having been skipped over to usher in the Intensive Community Development Project phase. Usually, the period of the first and the second phase is to last for three years each.

In the first phase, the areas selected are subjected to the method of providing services on the ordinary rural development pattern with a lesser Governmental expenditure. In the intensive phase, the blocks selected are subjected to more composite and more intensive development schemes with larger Governmental expenditure. In the post-Intensive phase, it is presumed that the basis for self-perpetuation of the process initiated during the earlier phases has been created and the need for special Government expenses reduced. Slowly the areas are left in the charge of the Departments for the development.

In 1952-53 series of community projects, the provision per block was Rs. 22 lakhs for a period of three years. This was reduced to Rs. 15 lakhs for the 1953-54 series. The present provision for the N.E.S. stage of three years is Rs. 4 lakhs and for the Community Development stage is Rs. 8 lakhs, making up a total of Rs. 12 lakhs for six years. In other words, the annual expenditure per Block was reduced first from Rs. 7.3 lakhs to Rs. 5 lakhs and now to Rs. 2 lakhs.

An imposing list of activities has been prepared by the sponsors of the Community Development Projects. They include various items connected with the following eight categories of undertakings :

(1) Agriculture and related matters; (2) Communications; (3) Education; (4) Health; (5) Training; (6) Social Welfare; (7) Supplementary Employment; and (8) Housing.

The fourth Evaluation Report of 1957 adopted different criteria for classifying activities undertaken by the Community Development Projects. They divided the programmes of activities into the following major categories : (1) Constructional programmes; (2) Irrigational programmes; (3) Agricultural programmes; and (4) Institutional and other programmes. The detailed list of the various activities undertaken under each of these programmes is as under :

Constructional programmes: 'Kutcha' roads, 'Pucca' roads, culverts, drains, pavement of streets, school buildings, community centre buildings, dispensary buildings, houses for the Harijans and drinking water sources.

Irrigation programmes: Wells, pumping sets, tube wells and tanks.

Agricultural programmes: Reclamation, soil conservation, consolidation of holdings, improved seeds, manure and fertilizer, pesticides, improved methods of cultivation and improved implements.

Institutional and other programmes: Youth Clubs, Women's Organisations, Community Centres, 'Vikas Mandals,' co-operative societies, distribution stores, maternity centres, dispensaries, veterinary dispensaries, key village centres, panchayats, adult literacy centres, primary schools, 'dai' training centres, cottage industries, production-cum-training centres, demonstration plots, soakage pits, smokeless 'chulha'.

An elaborate organization has been created to implement Community Development Projects; it is known as the Community Project Administration. Originally functioning under the Planning Commission, it is now under the charge of the newly created Ministry of Community Development.

The entire administration is composed of four major types—the Central administration, the State administration, the district organization and the Project administration. The power and the control flow from top to bottom making it a hierarchic bureaucratic organization. At every level there is an Executive Officer, functioning with the aid of a Development Committee and helped by an Advisory Board. At the Centre, there is an Administrator, at the State level there is a Development Commissioner, at the district level there is a District Development Officer of Collector's grade and at the Project level a Project Level Officer equipped with a staff of some 125 supervisors and village level workers.

We will now survey the achievements of this programme. It is extremely difficult to give a total quantitative assessment of these achievements for a number of reasons. First, to the best of present writer's knowledge, such overall data have not been compiled. Second, it is not very easy to separate the achievements of the Community Development Projects from those brought about by other agencies. Some observers have pointed out that a number of activities attributed to the Community Development Project movement should, in fact, be credited to other agencies. We shall, however, accept for the purposes of evaluation, the achievement data in regard to constructional, irrigational, agricultural, institutional and other activities as collected by the Fourth Report of the Programme Evaluation Organization. It is a data carefully collected from seventeen Project units from different States studied by the Project Evaluation Organization.

The impact of the Community Development Projects has been subjected to analysis and evaluation by a number of scholars and organizations. Prof. Wilson, Prof. Carl Taylor, Prof. Oscar Lewis, Prof. Opler and his team, Prof. Dube, Prof. Mandelbaum and many others have attempted to assess the nature of the impact of the Community Development Projects on the life of the rural people. The Programme Evaluation Organization has also been doing assessment continuously and their Reports are valuable documents. The Bench Mark Surveys also provide insight into the working of the Community Projects. The popularly known Balwantrai Committee Report on the subject is one of the latest authoritative evaluation. Prof. Dube's *India's Changing Villages* is the latest comprehensive and systematic analysis of Community Projects, although based on a very intensive examination of only two different types of villages in U.P. It will be very difficult indeed to adequately indicate here the main findings of these studies and Reports separately. However, a certain general pattern of evaluation emerges which deserves our careful attention.

It should be noted at the very outset that all the scholars and organisations who have evaluated the Community Development Projects, fundamentally accept the major postulates of the economic policy of the Government of India and of the Five-Year Plans. Further, all these evaluators have assumed that the Community Development Movement is both desirable and appropriate as a technique of reconstructing the agrarian economy and society of India. Not one of them has even raised a single query or attempted to critically examine the major postulates of the Movement. It is, therefore, necessary to make explicit the major assumptions taken for granted by others. As Prof. Carl Taylor remarks: "The whole concept and plan of Community Development-Extension Programme is that local self-help Village groups will mobilize their natural and human resources for local improvements of all kinds and all technical agencies of Government will aid them in this undertaking." It implies, according to him (i) initiative of people in both formulating and executing the programmes. (ii) therefore the schemes of generating and organizing a large number of voluntary associations almost of primary group nature and also a wide variety of local institutions, (iii) reliance upon group work techniques, (iv) active participation of people in all the stages of implementation, resulting in local leadership, (v) governmental administrative machinery which acts as an assisting body. The personnel of the administrative machinery, at all levels, should not merely be equipped with administrative and other technical skills but must be fairly well-versed in social skills of evoking voluntary association and community participation.

The philosophy underlaying this Movement, in the context of the Indian agrarian society, therefore, implicitly accepts the following major sociological assumptions: (i) the individuals, sections, groups and strata forming the Village Community have a large number of common interests, sufficiently strong to bind them together; (ii) the interests of the various groups and classes within the village are both sufficiently like and common to create general enthusiasm as well as a feeling of development for all; (iii) the interests of the different sections of the community are not irreconciliably conflicting; (iv) the State is a super-class, impartial, non-partisan association and that the major policies of the Government are of such a nature that they do not further sharpen the inequalities between the existing social groups; (v) people's initiative and enthusiasm and active participation are possible in the extant village communities because they have common interests.

None of the scholars or the committees have critically inquired as to whether these assumptions about both the Village Communities in India and the Indian State and its governmental policies are valid or not.

However, we will review at present only the major findings of these scholars and committees regarding the operation of Community Development Projects and their impact upon the life of the rural people.

Prof. Taylor and most of the scholars feel that the Government machinery, though staffed by intelligent, hard-working and conscientious persons, has not still assimilated the true spirit underlying the entire programme. The Community Development-Extension Programme is operated more as an executive assignment. According to Prof. Taylor, the administration of the programme is predominantly based on aid from and reliance on the Government. The initiative of the people is still lacking. The Government machinery relies more on propaganda and spectacular results rather than on group work and voluntary creative participation. According to Prof. Taylor, a certain amount of active governmental participation was inevitable in a country like India during the earlier phases of the movement. But if that earlier phase was not crossed over and if the movement did not elicit active participation and initative from the people, the very basis of the Community Development Programme would crumble. The danger has been slowly raising its head.

Prof. S. C. Dube also comes to the same conclusion. " Planning so far appears to be from the top down ... It is necessary to examine the implications and results of the present trends in planning. Because of the unique curbs on Projects autonomy its officials hesitated to demonstrate much initiative. What was worse they tended on the official level to accept orders from above, i.e., from the State headquarters, without question or comment, and this despite pronounced private reservations. As an outcome of this trend the officials were oriented less towards the village people, and more towards the pleasing of their official superiors. " And further, " A large number of Project-sponsored activities are directed along the lines of traditional government ' drives ' rather than according to the proved principles of extension work. Visible accomplishments under such pressure and stimulation and completion of physical targets are greatly valued, and too little attention is given to the question of finding out if the movement is really acquiring roots in the village society. " According to Prof. Dube, government servants function as bureaucrats and have not become agents of change with an active social service mentality.

The Balwantrai Committee Report is critical of the structural foundation of the Community Administration. According to the Report :

" admittedly, one of the least successful aspects of the C.D. and N.E.S. work is its attempt to evoke popular initiative. We have found that few of the local bodies at a level higher than the village panchayat have shown any enthusiasm or interest in this work; and even the panchayats have not come into the fields to any appreciable extent. An attempt has been made to harness local initiative through the formation of *ad hoc* bodies mostly with the nominated personnel and invariably advisory in character. These bodies have so far given no indication of durable strength nor the leadership necessary to provide the motive force for continuing the improvement of economic and social condition in rural areas. So long as we do not discover or create a representative and democratic institution which will supply the 'local interest, supervision and care necessary to ensure that expenditure of money upon local objects conforms with the needs and wishes of the locality,' invest it with adequate power and assign to it appropriate finances, we will never be able to evoke local interest and excite local initiative in the field of development."

The report suggests that the elected Village Panchayat at village level and an elected Panchayat Samiti at the block level act as agencies to execute the Community Development Programme and the present Block level and Village level bureaucratic machinery be wound up.

In short the major criticism offered by scholars and Evaluating Committees boils down to the following major points : (i) its bureaucratic nature; (ii) absence of elective principle at any level in the machinery; (iii) decisions taken at the top and communicated below, almost like executive fiats; (iv) considerable confusion in the overall administration of the country, expressed in the relationship between the Project Administration and other Government departments; (v) considerable confusion and conflict with regard to powers and duties, and relative position and seniority within the staff of different departments as a result of their being interlocked with the Project Administration; (vi) duplication of work for a section of the administrative personnel and resultant overworking and the problem of divided loyalty towards functions; (vii) absence of social service mentality; and (viii) lack of social work skills among the staff.

In regard to the actual achievement of the Projects, within the cluster of villages operated by a Gram-sevak, his headquarter-village receives more benefits. Further, it has been found that bigger villages get greater benefits. Similarly, commercial belts receive more facilities than the non-commercial agrarian belts. As the Evaluation Report points out :

"There is wide disparity in the distribution of the achievement and therefore of the benefits of the community project programmes. This disparity exists as between different blocks in the project areas. Within the blocks it exists as between the H.Q. villages of Gram-sevaks, the villages easily accessible to them, and the villages not so easily accessible. Within the villages, it exists as between cultivators and non-cultivators; and within the cultivating classes, it exists as between cultivators of bigger holdings and larger financial resources and those of smaller holdings and lesser financial resources. This is a matter of serious concern not only in terms of regional and social justice but also in terms of the political consequences that may ensue in the context of the increasing awakening among the people."

Though this disparity of benefits is recognised, none of the scholars or evaluation organizations has made a systematic analysis of its consequences; its ecological repercussions are not even seen by them. The Indian rural society is undergoing transformation under the impact of numerous forces today. Government's programmes of industrialization electrification, land reforms, major irrigation works, export and import plans, taxation, commercialization and monetization of various sectors of economic life, and unification of the country through development of means of communication, are producing important changes in the agrarian areas also. The impact of urbanization and industrialization upon the pattern of rural life are being studied by a number of scholars. Unfortunately, however, none of the evaluators has analysed the impact of the Community Development Project upon the rural life from this wider perspective. Nor have these evaluators indicated the significance of this uneven growth of various regions, blocks, and villages.

The advantages of the improvement, as pointed out by the Community Evaluation Reports, are taken by larger cultivators. As Prof. Dube points out :

> " Although the ideal of the Community Development Project was to work for the many-sided development of the entire community, from the foregoing account of its work...it is clear that its significant and best organized activities were confined to the field of agricultural extension and consequently the group of agriculturists benefitted the most from them. A closer analysis of the agricultural extension work itself reveals that nearly 70 per cent of its benefits went to the elite group and to the more affluent and influential agriculturists. The gains to poorer agriculturists were considerably smaller.... For the economic development of this group, as well as for that of the artisans and agricultural labourers, no programmes were initiated by the Project. "

Similar observations are made by all Project Evaluation Reports as well as by scholars like Mandelbaum. This impact of the Community Development Project is fraught with serious consequences. It sharpens the gulf between the rich and the poor cultivators. It makes artisans and agricultural labourers relatively more handicapped than the cultivators and therefore generates greater inequality and wider chasm between the affluent farmers, the agrarian capitalist class on one hand and the poorer strata composed of poor peasants, artisans and agricultural labourers on the other. It implies that in the context of the economy which produces for market and profit, the poor farmers and other strata are made weaker in their competitive strength against the richer strata.

The organizations for rural change are dominated by the upper sections of the rural population. As pointed out by the Programme Evaluation Report, " When one considers the pattern of membership in village organizations, be they co-operative societies, *Vikas Mandals*, Gram Panchayats or Nyaya Panchayats, one clearly finds that the membership is confined to the large cultivators and that the smaller cultivators as well as landless agricultural labourers, have practically no stake in the organizations of the village. " As Prof. Dube has pointed out :

> " The Community Development Project sought the co-operation of the existing village institutions such as the village panchayat and the adalati panchayat schools and co-operative societies. Persons holding offices in these bodies or otherwise prominent in the activities were regarded as ' Village Leader', and the development officials made a special effort to work closely with them. Some others who had contacts with poli-

ticians and officials were also included in this category and were consulted in matters connected with the project.... Thus a group of village people having contacts with the world of officials and politicians largely came to be viewed as the local agents of change.... The first mistake was in assuming that these people were the leaders.... Because of their association with the officials and the urban ways of life these leaders as a group had come to possess a special status within the community, but the average villager did not trust them without reservations. Some of the common stereotypes regarding government officials applied in a modified form to these village officials who were recognised as having a semi-government status.... Among others included in the category of 'traditional leaders' were the important and influential people in the village. Naturally most of them were from the dominant landowning group. In identifying power and status with leadership, an important and emerging aspect of group dynamics was ignored.... The undue emphasis in working with 'traditional leaders' was construed by villagers as an effort on the part of the Government to maintain a *status quo* in the internal power relations within the village communities and indirectly as a step to support the domination of the landowning groups."

The same conclusion is drawn by almost all the evaluators. This reliance on the upper stratum of the village population by the Government has sociological significance which cannot be underestimated. Nay it has serious social implication in terms of the dynamics of rural society. It implies not merely a hold over the economic resources in that area by a small upper class, but also a hold over the political, social and cultural life of the community. It further means that in agrarian area, as a result of the functioning of the community development programmes, a stratum becomes strengthened economically and politically, and utilizes various institutions for its own end. It also means that in agrarian area, the Community Development Projects are creating an institutional and associational matrix wherein the Government buttresses the economically dominant classes, and in their turn, the economically dominant classes strengthen the power of the present rulers of the State. This development has dangerous significance for the all-round development of the rural society and also for the unprivileged strata of the agrarian area which constitute the bulk of the rural people. It is very unfortunate that the implication of this developmental tendency in terms of class polarization in agrarian area, and the role of the state as an agency of the upper stratum is not fully appreciated.

Almost all the evaluators have recognized that the contributions to be made by the village people are felt very burdensome by the lower sections of the people. *Shramdan* is the technique by which masses were asked to make contribution to the Community Development. Prof. Dube's observations on *Shramdan* as a voluntary movement of village self-help deserves attention :

"From a close observation and analysis of four *Shramdan* drives...certain points emerge that explain differences in reactions to *Shramdan*. The village elite, as well as the upper status groups have, on the whole, welcomed the *Shramdan* drives, and through them the construction and repairs of roads. They gained from it in two ways. First, the repaired and newly built roads facilitated the transport of their sugarcane and grain. Secondly, in these drives they could assert their position of leadership and prestige in the village.... as is explained at some length in Chapter VI, because of their status they assumed supervisory roles in this work, and left the hardest and less desirable part of the job to be done by the people of the lower status and lower income groups. Even this token participation won the praise and acclaim of the officials and outside political leaders. The poorer groups, on the other hand, had no practical and visible gain from these projects. Few among them owned bullock carts, and most of them did not have large quantities of sugarcane or wheat to be transported to the urban markets. Their work did not win much praise from outsiders. All that they got often was a formal acknowledgement from the lower officials and some village leaders. They not only had to work hard, but they also lost the wages for the day, which they otherwise might have earned. This explains why many of them viewed this thing as a revival of *begar*, a practice under which influential landowners and government officials compelled the poorer people to work without wages or at nominal wages and which is now prohibited by law."

New associations have been launched or some of the old associations performing those functions have been claimed to be revitalized. Youth clubs, women's organizations, community centres, schools, libraries, adult education classes and social education centres form the predominant type of institutions. These organizations have emerged only in a very few areas. Excepting some institutions like *Bhajan Mandalis* or *Akhadas* at some places, very few institutions have taken roots in the villages. A large number of these institutions are operating more as paper organizations. Almost all the evaluators have indicated the failure of this section of the Community Development Programme.

Almost all critics including Taylor, Wilson, the Balwantrai Committee, Dube and V. K. R. V. Rao indicate these trends. They criticise one aspect of the programme or the other. They suggest some symptomatic remedies to cure the ills. Prof. Taylor wants thousands of trained officers, equipped with social skills to make this programme a success. The Balwantrai Committee makes certain proposals for making Village Panchayats and Panchayat Samitis the instruments for operating the Community Development Programmes. It also wants to abolish two-phased division in the form of N.E.S. and C.D. with unequal financial allocations and creation of six-year unit with larger financial allocation. Further, it wants the C.D. Programme to concentrate more on select items like increase in production rather than cultural improvements. According to them, there is nothing wrong with the major premise of the Community Development Projects, nor is there any fundamental fallacy in the postulates of the Five-Year Plans. According to these evaluators, the failure of the C.D. Projects in essence is due to one or more of the following factors: ignorance, lack of will on the part of the personnel, faulty organizational principles, fatalism of the vast bulk of the people, lack of technical and social skills, or wrong choice in selection of items. According to Prof. Dube, the main obstacles are: " (i) the general apathy of a considerable part of the village population, (ii) suspicion and distrust of officials and outsiders; (iii) failure on the part of the Project to evolve effective and adequate media of communications; (iv) tradition and cultural factors. "

Are these costly projects, which do not fulful their proclaimed major objectives, worth continuing ? Are they not becoming agencies which do not merely defeat the very purpose for which they are ostensibly launched, but are actually playing the harmful role of strengthening the richer strata in the agrarian society ?

In spite of the fact that considerable factual material has been collected which indicates the class structure of the agrarian society, and which also points out how the agrarian proletariat, a large number of uneconomic holders, and an enormous group of ruined arusans constitute the bulk of the rural community, none of these evaluators confronts the question, viz., how can a programme which essentially supports the upper strata of the rural population and which primarily benefits this minority in strengthening it institutionally, be called a Community Development Programme ? The very name, to say the least, is deceptive.

Sociologically, the Community Development Programme is not merely proving futile in its acclaimed goals, but is becoming harmful.

4

COMMUNITY DEVELOPMENT—A CRITICAL REVIEW*

S. C. DUBE

SHRAMDAN—AN EVALUATION

THE COMMUNITY DEVELOPMENT PROJECT operated, as far as possible, on the principle of working in partnership with the people. It made outright grants covering the entire cost of a project only in a few exceptional cases. Generally people were expected to contribute money and labour towards the completion of the programmes instituted by the Project. As mentioned earlier they did contribute *shramdan*, or unpaid voluntary labour, as a part of their share in a number of projects. In public works, especially road-building, the importance of this type of contribution was greatly emphasized. Getting a specified piece of work done was only one of the major motives behind the *shramdan* drives; they were aimed also at encouraging the 'cult of dirty hands' and the 'dignity of labour,' and were expected to develop a spirit of co-operative teamwork among the people.

As in other villages of the Development Block, in Rajput Village and Tyagi Village the Republic Day celebrations included a '*shramdan* week', in which the village people completed a specified project wholly by their unpaid voluntary labour. This was an annual feature of Project sponsored development work in the villages. For other individual projects also the co-operation of the people was sought. Under the guidance of the Project, the people from Rajput Village built a 1½ mile long hard surface road, and a 2-mile long mud road. They repaired another road which was about three miles long. In addition, they also helped in the construction of two culverts. In Tyagi Village, *shramdan* was done mostly in connection with the paving of village lanes, renovation of wells, and construction of the school. Most of the unskilled work connected with these ventures, such as digging of earth, and carrying or carting earth and bricks, was accomplished in this way. A road, 2½ miles long, was repaired by the people.

THE RESPONSE

The Government of Uttar Pradesh lays great emphasis on mobilizing people's labour for development work. With this end in view, in its Panchayat Raj legislation it has made a provision authorizing village councils to secure five days of compulsory *shramdan* every year from

* Reproduced from *India's Changing Villages* (1958) by S. C. Dube, pp. 80-84.

residents of the village. The village council can impose fines on those who do not co-operate in *shramdan* projects organized by it. Very few village councils have so far taken recourse to this extreme method.

The method of *shramdan* is not new to these village communities. In Rajput Village, the people had given their enthusiastic support in the building of both the Sanskrit School and the Intermediate College. All segments of the village population had contributed free voluntary labour in this work. In building the village mosque, the Muslims of Tyagi Village had also depended in a large measure on the voluntary labour of their group.

Projects giving direct and immediate benefit to the people, such as renovation of wells and paving of village lanes, secured reasonable co-operation from most of the village people. However, the Project-sponsored '*shramdan* weeks', mostly to build or repair roads, did not receive the same enthusiastic welcome from them. Out of a random sample of 128 participants in a *shramdan* week organized separately in Rajput Village and Tyagi Village, only thirty-one had a clear or partial idea of the basic aims of the movement, the rest viewed it as a form of *begar* (forced, unpaid labour). A majority of these individuals said that they had participated in these drives only in compliance with the directions of the government and the leaders of the village.

From a close observation and analysis of four *shramdan* drives, two in Rajput Village and two in Tyagi Village, certain points emerge that explain differences in reactions to *shramdan*.

The village *elite* as well as the upper income and higher status groups have, on the whole, welcomed the *shramdan* drives, and through them the construction and repairs of roads. They gained from it in two ways. First, the repaired and newly built roads facilitated the transport of their sugarcane and grain. Secondly, in these drives they could assert their position of leadership and prestige in the village. Because of their status they assumed supervisory roles in this work, and left the hardest and less desirable part of the job to be done by the people of the lower status and lower income groups. Even their token participation won the praise and acclaim of officials and outside political leaders. The poorer groups, on the other hand, had no practical and visible gain from these projects. Few among them owned bullock carts, and most of them did not have large quantities of sugarcane or wheat to be transported to the urban markets. Their work did not win much praise from outsiders. All that they got often was a formal acknowledgement from the lower officials and some village leaders. They not only had to work hard, but they also lost the wages for the day, which they might otherwise have earned. This explains why many of them viewed the thing as a revival of *begar*, a practice under which influential landowners and government officials compelled the poorer people to work without wages or at nominal wages and which is now prohibited by law.

Regarding the utility of these road-building and road-repairing *shramdan* drives, even some of the village leaders were sceptical. Three out of the four projects observed by us were arbitrarily begun, without any consultation with the village people. The aims of the particular projects were not explained to those who were actually to work on them. Excessive reliance was placed on some established village leaders to bring a specified number of people with them for work. In two cases, in which new roads were to be constructed, the officials had not even done the preliminary measuring and marking. Several of the participants were picked up from their homes without any prior notice and more or less pressed into service. Unusual activity was shown by the officials when some important visitor was about to see *shramdan* in action; otherwise they were quite relaxed and slack. For these reasons, many responsible village people regarded the activities as a 'show', something which the officials had to do to justify their existence. To the credit of the officials it should be said that some of them worked as hard as most of the villagers themselves on these projects, and this won for them the appreciation and friendship of the people.

In conclusion, it may be said that projects emerging out of the felt needs of the people got their best support; those that were officially induced had only limited success. To develop *shramdan* into a powerful movement of village self-help, more imagination and careful planning than was displayed in these four drives are needed.

Comment

Although the ideal of the Community Development Project was to work for the many-sided development of the entire community, from the foregoing account of its work in two villages it is clear that its significant and best organized activities were confined to the field of agricultural extension, and consequently the group of agriculturists benefited the most from them. A closer analysis of the agricultural extension work itself reveals that nearly 70 per cent of its benefits went to the *elite* group and to the more affluent and influential agriculturists. The gains to poorer agriculturists were considerably smaller. Being suspicious of government officials they did not seek help from the Project as often. As this group had little influence in the village and outside, and was in no position to offer any material help in the furtherance of Project objectives, the officials largely ignored it. For the economic development of this group, as well as for that of the artisans and agricultural labourers, no programmes were initiated by the Project. Some programmes for the welfare of women, younger people, and the untouchables were undertaken, but their organization lacked imagination, and consequently they failed to make the desired impact. In the sphere of public health and sanitation some significant steps were taken, but they only touched the surface of the problem. They were far below the needs of the community, and did not in any appreciable measure change the attitude and outlook of the people towards nutrition, hygiene, and health. The social education programme made the least impact. It was treated as a stepchild, and was started more as a formal obligation than for its basic aims of awakening the community to its own needs.

An analysis of the motivation of village people in accepting the Project-sponsored programmes shows that they offered their co-operation mainly for the following reasons:

(i) *Economic advantage and convenience*: Several programmes in the sphere of agricultural extension, such as some new seeds and improved implements, were accepted for their visible economic advantage. Factors of convenience and practical utility governed the acceptance of certain items, such as the hand pumps and chaff-cutters.

(ii) *Prestige of the individual, family, kin-group, caste and village:* Co-operation with the Project opened up the possibility for some individuals to acquire a position of leadership in the village; others found it as a means by which they could assert their traditional leadership. Recognition by officials and outside leaders conferred a distinct honour on these individuals and enhanced their influence in the village. Adoption of 'progressive ideas' added to the prestige of the family, kin-group or caste also. Ownership of a tractor or an orchard added to the prestige of the family and the kin-group. Construction of new wells in their section of the village contributed in some measure to the prestige of the untouchable groups.

The building up of the reputation of the village was another significant motive in the acceptance of certain programmes. A village which built a new school, constructed a public building, or paved all its lanes could earn a reputation in the vicinity for being 'progressive'. Competition between individuals, families, kin-groups, castes and villages was also at the back of the acceptance of many programmes.

(iii) *Novelty of innovations:* Several items of the programmes, such as new agricultural implements and improved techniques, were tried out of curiosity. While a number of innovations were rejected because of their strangeness and people's lack of familiarity with them, some others were enthusiastically adopted because they were so novel.

(iv) *Compliance to the wishes of government and village leaders :* A large number of programmes in many spheres were accepted in a spirit of compliance to the wishes of the government and the influential village people. A remark heard often enough in these villages was 'if the government wants us to do a thing, we should do it.' The tremendous prestige of national leaders like Nehru and Pant, and the influence of local leaders like Thakur Phool Singh who were associated with the programme was also a reason for its acceptance by a considerable section of the village people.

The main obstacles in the way of the greater acceptance of the programme were :

(i) The general apathy of a considerable part of the village population.

(ii) Suspicion and distrust of officials and outsiders.

(iii) Failure on the part of the Project to evolve effective and adequate media of communication.

(iv) Tradition and cultural factors.

These factors have vitally affected the implementation of the programme.

Section XIII

BHOODAN AND GRAMDAN MOVEMENTS

THIS SECTION contains eight selections. An effort has been made to indicate the philosophical basis of the Bhoodan and the Gramdan movements which attempt to reconstruct the rural society on the " proclaimed philosophy " of Sarvodaya. The articles by Daniel Thorner, C. G. Shah T. K. Oommen and B. T. Ranadive provide a critical examination of both the philosophy and the actual achievements of the Bhoodan and Gramdan movements. They focus attention on one of the most spectacularly popular movements which has been launched in India and which is claimed to have endeavoured to bypass state efforts to overhaul the rural society. A methodological examination of the theoretical postulates as well as a systematic analysis of both the achievements and the failures of these movements has become very urgent. (*Author* .)

1

BHOODAN YAGNA*

ACHARYA VINOBA BHAVE

THE BASIS OF BHOODAN YAGNA

OUR WORK consists in changing the present social order from the very root. This is the secret of this Bhoodan campaign. That is why when people ask me whether this can be done by legislation alone, I reply in the negative. This is not a onesided movement. When it succeeds the State will change, the Government will change and the life-structure will change.

To the society which we seek to build up I have given the name "Samyayogi Society". I struck at this word from the Gita which teaches us to do unto others as we do unto ourselves. We should treat others in the same manner as we want to be treated by them. So also we must behave towards society as we aspire to be treated by it. When Hanuman met Ravana he placed before him the injustice of the latter's act in having stolen Rama's consort. He told him that he (Ravana) could easily see the error of his ways since he (Ravana) was himself a grahastha (householder). He asked him to visualise the situation in the event of his own wife being kidnapped.

In the Chapter on fasts ('roza'), the Holy Quran enjoins on all followers to observe fast during the month of Ramzan. Somebody raised a misgiving whether those who could not bear the pangs of hunger would be regarded as outcasts. The prophet spoke, "No, if on that day they feed a hungry man they would win the credit of a fast." Now what is grand about it ? The grandeur lies in your feeling what it is to suffer from pangs of hunger when you must take it that your duty lies in alleviating others' hunger. Gita has given it the name of *Atmopamya* (like-Self). This is not something particular to Hinduism alone. You will find it in all religions. This is termed the golden rule. In case one does not feel the pangs of hunger he cannot be enjoined to feed the hungry. If one does not feel the pangs of thirst he cannot be enjoined to slake the thirsty throat.

I ask the land-owners to imagine from their own experience the condition of those who own no land. I ask the property-owners to imagine from their experience the conditions of those who own no property. If you have any appreciation of their feeling it is enjoined upon you to distribute among them the extra that you have. This is your Dharma.

---

*Reproduced from the *Principles and Philosophy of the Bhoodan Yagna*, by Acharya Vinoba Bhave, 1955, pp. 1-5, 15-16.

The most essential requisite of a *Samyayogi* social structure is that all land, all property, and all wealth should belong to society. Only Vishnu can be the lord of Lakshmi, a seat which you have usurped. Bhartruhari has said that to us Lakshmi is mother, and we are her children. On the contrary, to-day we aggrandise ourselves as Her lord. I feel this injustice, and a denial of religion. It is not a single individual behaving thus, but the whole of society. Should somebody commit adultery it is his fault and not that of the society. But if the social structure be such that it grants the right of ownership of land to some, of ownership of property to others and so on, everybody would enjoy what he gets hold of. And all this is regarded sacred and holy ! Now the priests of Vaidyanathdam assaulted me. When I pondered over it I felt that they believed that we were out to destroy religion and they were out to protect it by the force of arms. Where religion enjoys such sanctions irreligion gets entrenched very deep.

What I want to inculcate among the people is that our body is made from and of society and for the service of the society. Service is thus a debt on our shoulders which we have to repay. We are distinct from our body. So when we are not the owners or masters of even our body, how dare we claim our right on other things as land and property ? Ganga loves all alike. She quenches the thirst of the lion as also of the cow. Should somebody claim his right upon such a beneficent Ganga, would we accept it ? If none has a claim on the Ganga, how can we have on land or property ?

I go on saying from village to village that if classes or differences had been dear to God's heart, He would not have provided everybody with one nose. He would have granted one nose to a poor man while ten or more to a minister. But he feels that everybody requires nose and should have equal right to breathe air. As none can claim ownership of air, water or sunshine, so also none can claim that of land. Should somebody claim it, that is due to wrong idea which is irreligious. Hence I have given it the name of moral revolution—*Dharma Pravarthan*. I want to root out the wrong ideas and erect the new society on the basis of religious ideas.

It is why I demand one-sixth of land. There are some 5 crores of landless people in our country. For them we require five crores of acres, about one-sixth of good land available in India. In case these calculations come out to be incorrect I would demand again more land. For what I want is that there must be a complete redistribution of land and property, as also of power.

Today we are busy in national planning. In fact we require a village planning. People of the village should exercise their own brains to do things. Should somebody err only one village would suffer. But when the stewardship of the whole country is entrusted to four or five persons the whole country has to suffer the consequence of their any single mistake.

But this will not be so when power resides in the village itself. If one village commits a certain blunder another would not repeat it. Hence, power should be distributed in every village. There must be decentralisation of power like the one set up by God. We do not want to imitate Russia or China in this. God does not reserve for Himself the store of wisdom, nor does he supply it according to individual needs. He distributes all unto all.

Still people have to co-operate among themselves. Co-operation is of two kinds. First is to give one's all and share with others. Second is that proverbial co-operation of the blind and the lame. Had the latter been the desired objective God would have bestowed four eyes to one, four ears to another and bid them co-operate. This amounts to a co-operative society of the disabled ! But God has not ordained this variety of society. He had provided everybody with all things and made them able and bid them co-operate. In other words, the wisdom of all should form one whole. Of course He could have made man all-sufficient and all-able. But He felt that life would then lose all charm.

We have to build up a society in which every calling is equally paid. Every calling has an importance of its own. That one work should be valued more than another is an injustice. Take for instance the work of a train-signaller. What great responsibility this carries ! A signaller's work is a responsibility of a type unique in itself.

It may be admitted that the responsibility implied in one work differs from that in another. But equal wages would have to be paid to all unless and until it is established that the one with a greater responsibility feels more hungry than the one with a lesser responsibility. It is wrong to pay according to the responsibility involved in a work or its extent.

In fact, objective is three-fold. Firstly, power should be decentralised from village to village; secondly, everybody should have a right on land and property; thirdly, there should be no distinction in the matter of wages, etc. With this aim in view, I have introduced the lever of Bhoodan in order that a Samya-Yogi order may be established. Hence I go from village to village. People ask me why I would not apply "pressure" over our Government to frame law accordingly. I am, in fact, not interested in it. What I am interested in, is in reducing the governmental authority itself and in the creation of a New Social Order. I have resorted to this problem of land with this objective.

We want to bring about an equilibrium or an equality in society. None can profit from an unequal and unbalanced society.

Samya-Yogi means "levelling" the field. That we have to do. Ours is not merely to distribute land but to level up the mental values of the entire society. With this mental approach you go from village to village and explain the idea. Go with a complete confidence in the heart of every one you approach.

Bhoodan Yagna: All-Comprehensive Programme

Bhoodan Yagna is an all-comprehensive movement directed to the reform in all walks of life. Today everyone thinks of himself alone and feels for his self only. But Bhoodan makes the people think and do just the opposite of what they do now. It makes the people look around and say " I will first think of my neighbour, and if he has no land, I must consider it is my duty to provide him with it. " In Bhoodan, distribution of land is not the only question.

It aims at the moral regeneration of the whole nation in fact. Through it we hope to solve the economic difficulties in our society. With all these hopes I am concentrating all my attention on it. If we succeed in this we are sure to succeed in everything else.

When village industries are encouraged, unemployment will disappear. Cottage industries can never prosper unless the land is equitably distributed. So Bhoodan takes in the programme for the revival of cottage industries also within it.

The great aloofness that we find in society today between the educated and the uneducated will not disappear unless both are made to join in common work. We have to inculcate in our people the habit and delight for doing manual work. The education that our children get now in schools, is devoid of any manual labour. They do not know how to earn their living and how to improve the country's economic conditions. So Shramadan (labour-gifts) is also initiated. This will bring an entire change to the whole life of the country. We have to reclaim and make the waste lands included in some of the gifts offered in Bhoodan, cultivable. Students can join this work and thus offer their share of gift of labour.

I am also claiming a share of the wealth in people's hand, through Sampattidan. Much wealth lies invested in gold and silver. It is wrong to keep wealth dead like this. The nation should get the benefit of it. That is why I ask those people who keep such wealth, to give a share of it for the good of society.

2

BHOODAN, ITS EVALUATION*

DANIEL THORNER

As CONTRASTED with the disappointing progress of legislative land reform the only alternative which has seemed to offer a promising way forward has been Acharya Vinoba Bhave's *Bhoodan* (land-gift) movement. The focus of this is on improving the position of the most submerged and dis-advantaged class in the countryside, the utterly landless. Assuming that there were 50 million landless peasants in India, Vinobaji set himself the task of collecting in land-gifts 50 million acres, so that one acre could be given to each landless peasant. With an average of five members, each such family, it was hoped, would end up with 5 acres. He called in Gandhian terms upon the landowners to feel compassion for the plight of the landless and to demonstrate their compassion by giving to the Bhoodan movement one-sixth of their holdings. Since roughly 300 million acres were under cultivation in India, such gifts, if made all over the country, would total up to the required 50 million acres. Under the guidance of Bhoodan workers these gifts would then be suitably redistributed.

The inspiration for Bhoodan had come to Vinobaji in 1951 when he was touring the Telengana districts of Hyderabad. This was the area where the Communists had recently called off an "activist" agrarian campaign during which a good few landlords had lost both their lands and their lives. Through Bhoodan Vinojabi aimed to show the peasantry that there was an efficacious alternative to the Communist programme. The movement got off to a good start; from 1952 to 1954 more than 3 million acres of land were received as Bhoodan. The largest part of this was collected in 1953 in Bihar, to which State Vinobaji had early shifted his headquarters from Hyderabad. He had, in fact, set up his camp in Gaya District, a long centre for Communist work among the peasantry. Vinobaji and his followers declared that they would make Gaya District the Bardoli of Bhoodan, a moving reference to the famous campaign of 1928 led by the late Vallabhbhai Patel among the Gujarati peasants of Bardoli district. The high hopes raised by the early progress of Bhoodan were soon brought into question, however, by sober assessment of the accomplishments of the movement, and by careful consideration of its basic nature and presuppositions.

In Bihar it turned out that much of the land donated as Bhoodan was rocky, barren, or otherwise agriculturally poor, or was under dispute

* Reproduced from *Agrarian Prospect in India* by Daniel Thorner, pp. 74-77.

in current litigation. In other States land donated was found to be just the excess, which under reform legislation already on the statue books or then before the legislatures, the donors shortly might have been required, in any event, to hand over by law. Even greater difficulties have been encountered, in practice, in distributing such lands as have been donated. Only a small percentage, in point of fact, has been turned over to the landless: out of a total of $3\frac{3}{4}$ million acres of land received by May, 1955, about 0.2 million acres have been redistributed, i.e. 5 per cent. Like ceilings, Bhoodan has received the verbal support of the Congress Party, particularly at the highest echelons. But district and taluka leaders have generally been far from enthusiastic. For political purposes they may associate their names briefly with the Bhoodan work. Some have attempted to gain control over Bhoodan redistribution so as to enlarge or strengthen their following. Vinobaji's resistance to these efforts accounts, in part, for the delay in redistribution.

A fundamental weakness of Bhoodan is that its appeal is directed not to the poor and landless (whose own interest naturally would lead them to welcome it), but to the rich and landed. These are the very people who, as we have shown in Lecture III, have succeeded to date in getting around or defeating all types of land reform. When the Bhoodan campaigners march into their village, these well-off folk make a good show by giving away a few patches of land. But they are careful to retain securely in their grasp the holdings and associated economic operations upon which their control of the village rests. The basic concept of Bhoodan, spreading the ownership of land, is a generous one; but even if realized in practice it would not amount to thorough-going land reform. For, like ceilings, Bhoodan fails to come to grips with the central elements in India's agrarian problem. These may be restated as follows:

(1) a peculiarly complex property structure topped by the State's claiming what amounts to a proprietary right to " rent ";

(2) the survival, despite land reforms and " abolition of intermediaries ", of a class of non-cultivating proprietary right-holders who continue to take substantial rents from the working peasantry—tenants, tenants-at-will, or cropsharers; where these proprietors cultivate by hiring labourers they pay low wages;

(3) the consequent persistence, after land reform, of a considerable gap between proprietary right-holding and the physical cultivation of land;

(4) the actual cultivation of land by tillers who are chronically and seriously short of physical capital and financial resources; severely limited use of improved implements; and low yields;

(5) in this setting the lack of impetus to economic re-organization; land remains subdivided and fragmented; the unit of production in agriculture is tiny.

These five elements form part of a rural context in which a small minority of villagers generally enjoy an effective concentration of local, economic, social and political power; while the great mass of peasants have to strive to carry on under conditions of multiple disadvantage. The landowners who form the core of the little oligarchies that run India's villages do not own all of the land of India's villages; more often than not, they have less than half. But the land under their control is likely to be most valuable in the village. Where land is generally given out to tenants or cropsharers, they are likely to give out the most; where servants or labourers are engaged to work the land, these landowners are likely to be the biggest employers. The same fortunate few are active in rural moneylending, marketing and processing (grinding, crushing, milling). In this setting the mass of weak and humble folk have to do the bidding of their more powerful neighbours.

3

SAMPATTIDAN AND BHOODAN MOVEMENT*

C. G. Shah

Motif of Bhoodan and Sampattidan Movements

The Bhoodan and Sampattidan movements, based on the theory of the possibility of the ethical transmutation of the heart of those who own land and wealth so that they would voluntarily relinquish a substantial portion of their possessions are, according to Jay Prakash, the decisive means to bring into being such an equalitarian society. The hearts of the wealthy classes, however callous they be at present, will thaw when incessantly stormed by powerful ethical appeals to their essential human nature and they must, in course of time, part with their surplus wealth for the benefit of the poverty-stricken section of the population. This would result in the diminution of the present staggering disparities of incomes between the members of the community and even their final disappearance. Thus an equalitarian society will be painlessly born.

Are not the wealthy also human beings and have, therefore, basically human hearts ?

Ideological Inspiration of the Movement

It must be noted that the ideology inspiring these movements is not a new one. It, historically, originated with the dissolution of primitive Communist Society and the rise of the class society when, as a result of the private ownership of the social means of production, exploitation and economic inequalities came into existence in the social world. Since then, every class society—slave, feudal and capitalist—projected groups of humanists who, not comprehending the economic genetic cause of these inequalities, viz., private ownership of the social means of production, engaged themselves in making perennial ethical appeals to the exploiting classes to use a portion of their wealth to alleviate the poverty of the exploited classes through philanthropic and charity schemes. The inherited religious and secular ethical literature of all peoples abounds in directives addressed to the wealthy classes to part with a good portion of their wealth to rescue the poor from want. Christ, Buddha and, in recent times, Gandhi, too, incessantly bombarded the auditory nerve of the rich exploiters with moral admonitions to that effect. The survey of all history, however, decisively proves that this technique of liquidating poverty and economic disparities rampant in the social world has decisively failed.

---

*Reproduced from *Sampattidan and Bhoodan Movement*, by C. G. Shah, pp. 3-16.

Characteristics of Bhoodan and Sampattidan Movements

The Bhoodan movement is distinguished from the Sampattidan movement, since the former aims at the redistribution of land, the basic means of production in agriculture, in contrast to the latter which aims at the redistribution, not of the basic means of production such as factories, and others but of the income derived by their capitalist owners on the basis of that ownership. This invests the programme of Sampattidan with a bourgeois class character since it endorses by implication capitalist private property in the means of production. It does not ask the capitalists to surrender this property which enables them to exploit the workers but appeals to them to set aside a portion of their profits born of this exploitation for relieving the distress of the poor. The right of the capitalists to own the means of production and thereby exploit labour and accumulate profit is implicitly, if not articulately, regarded moral and therefore sacrosanct. Immorality attaches only to the income from the exploitation not to the exploitation itself. Unlike in the sphere of agriculture the programme has for its objective a reshuffling of the income, not a redistribution of the means of production, the fountain source of that income. The bourgeoisie is only called upon to expand the scale of its charity and philanthropic activities. This reminds one of the incisive definition of charity given by Paul Lafargue, viz., " Charity is robbing wholesale and giving retail. "

Another striking feature of these movements consists in the fact that, regarding the method to achieve their objective, their sponsors—Vinoba Bhave and now Jay Prakash Narayan who has expanded the limited agrarian programme of the former into a universal socio-economic programme—exclusively restrict the means to that of the ethical reconstruction of the consciousness of primarily the wealthy classes. Even Gandhi, who equally stood for the preservation and perpetuation of the capitalist-landlord social system, while addressing moral appeals to the capitalists periodically reinforced this ethical weapon by strikes, peasant satyagrahas and others to exert pressure on them to redistribute their incomes to a little advantage of the masses. Surely he conducted those struggles within the matrix of the fundamental conception of the basic community of interests of the capitalists and the workers, the landlords and the peasants, and the resultant class collaborationist view, still he did not discard such episodic class struggles as pressure technique to back up ethical appeals. Jay Prakash, on the other hand, regards even such struggles as socially and morally disastrous for the creation of a non-violent equalitarian society. Addressing a gathering of industrial workers in Bombay he remarked:

" By persuasion and propaganda we can change the hearts of the people....The Bhoodan and Sampattidan movements will usher in the millennium in the country. There must be no class consciousness, there must be equality. This is my conception of a free state. The Sampattidan movement, if it succeeded, would in the very near future eliminate the profit making instinct of capitalists." He further said, "some businessmen and industrialists have expressed in favour of the Gandhian ideal of trusteeship and, I feel, the day is not far off when that ideal will be realised without the use of force or compulsion."

Limitations of Bourgeois Charity

The individual capitalists who succeed in the competitive struggle are compelled to set apart a big portion of the profits to renew, expand or rationalize their productive technique. If they fail to do so, they would be ruined in the further competitive struggle. It is the remaining portion of profit which they spend on themselves and sometimes for charitable and philanthropic work.

But this portion is a very small fraction of the total profit. Under pain of not losing in the competitive struggle the capitalist needs to spend a greater and greater section of the profit in the further investment in the means of production.

Compared to the increasing poverty which the capitalist system of production, governed by its own objective laws, generates, the meagre alleviation of working people's misery which the capitalists, even if they are universally surcharged with humanist emotion for the victims of their exploitation, could achieve, would be more than counterbalanced by the existing and new impoverishment which the system generates.

Even what charity or philanthropy the capitalists practise, is motivated mainly, consciously or sub-consciously, by individual or class interests. The chase for limelight drives some to start or endow institutions. Others build hospitals, for, disease is infectious and the poor when struck down with disease, can convince the rich of their common humanity by transmitting the infection to them. Some may construct workers' chawls, for, labour must be kept efficient for being exploited to the maximum, hence be provided with minimum housing. capitalist production needs trained cadres, therefore, technical and other educational institutions must be financed. Starvation is not infectious, therefore, no capitalist charity assures the starving that they will be provided with two square meals.

It is not the change of heart which supplies motif to capitalist charity and philanthropy. It is mostly craze for fame or conscious or unconscious class interest.

Is There a Free-Will for the Capitalist ?

There is a vital reason why the capitalist cannot help—there is no free-will for him—pursuing the road of ever increasing profit which is the fundamental urge of his psyche. Historical materialism alone can explain this phenomenon. According to it, the consciousness of man is primarily the product of the mode of his livelihood, therefore, of the position he occupies in the economic structure of society. In the existing capitalist economic structure of society, the capitalist starts with a definite amount of capital, buys means of production, hires and exploits labour, and annexes surplus value which via market is transformed into his profit. The original capital M returns to him, with the addition of this profit, as M. The motif of his entire economic activity is to transform the original capital into increased capital. It is an automatic chase for profit. Perennially engaged in this profit-chasing activity, he builds up profit-chasing instincts and exploitative psychology. The postulate of a common human nature of all men as such is a false postulate of idealistic psychology. Capitalist human nature with its profit-hankering and exploitative urges is quite different from the human nature of the proletariat when the latter liberates itself from the pressure of the capitalist ideology and which then becomes co-operative socialist. The mode of material living primarily moulds the psychology of the group and the class living in class society. There are only class men with class human natures in class society. An individual human with chemically pure human nature to which a pure human appeal can be addressed with a view to persuade him to act humanly and humanely is a myth of idealistic sociology.

The profit-chasing and greedy psychology of the capitalists is determined by the position they occupy in the capitalist economic structure, viz. that of exploiters of labour and chasers after profits. Marx, in Capital, explains this as follows:

" The simple circulation of commodities (as in the case of handicraftsmen), selling in order to buy, is a means of carrying out a purpose unconnected with circulation namely the satisfaction of wants. The circulation of money as capital is , on the contrary, and end in itself, for, the expansion of value takes place only within this constantly renewed movement. The circulation of capital has, therefore, no limits. Thus, the conscious representative of this movement, the possessor of money, becomes a capitalist. His person, or rather his pocket, is the point from which the money starts and to which it returns. The expansion of value, which is the objective basis or mainspring of the circulation, becomes his subjective aim. He functions as capital personified and endowed with consciousness and will. The restless never-ending process of profit-making alone is what he aims at.

" This boundless greed after riches, this passionate chase is common to the capitalist and the miser; but while the miser is merely a capitalist gone mad, the capitalist is a rational miser. The never-ending augmentation of exchange value, which the miser strives after by seeking to save his money from circulation, is attained by the more acute capitalist by constantly throwing it afresh into circulation. "

Thus the psychology of the capitalist human nature, his profit-making instincts, his exploitative impulses, his greed for more wealth, arise out of his specific activity in the cycle of capitalist production. It is the psychological outgrowth of his practice in the capitalist economic process. Till he is a capitalist, he will have his inescapable capitalist psychology. Gandhi's moral appeals to the capitalists for over two decades to change their hearts and act as trustees of their property did not affect them by an iota. If at all, they have during and after the second world war become more inhuman exploiters of the working people, more corrupt and brutal. And they cannot help behaving so since, as Marxist materialist psychology reveals, the consciousness of a class is the product of the material conditions of its existence.

Bourgeois Philosophy: A Product of Bourgeois Society

Regarding the futility of the moral appeals to the exploiting classes, Lenin used to narrate the story of Vaska the Cat. This cat had domiciled in the palace of Peter the Great, the Czar of Russia and used to commit depredations in the kitchen of the Great Czar. It used to invade and consume dishes destined for the royal stomach of the august Czar. The palace cook, a pacifist and like Jay Prakash, an exponent of the theory of the change of heart, used to make moral appeals to Vaska to abstain from its immoral bandit's activity. Vaska the Cat listened but went on eating.

So our capitalists and other wealthy classes will listen to the ethical admonitions of Jay Prakash Narayan, even extol and banquet him, but will go on exploiting and piling up wealth.

Their Role

The Bhoodan and Sampattidan movements are foredoomed to failure because they come in conflict with the laws of economy and psychology. Regarding the Bhoodan movement, the tempo of its advance has already slowed down. This is because the donation of land of big landowners was prompted not so much by any change of heart but by the strategic motive of safeguarding by far the greater amount of land owned by them by conceding a small portion of it mostly, fallow and uneconomic. This voluntary sacrifice on their part, in their view, would insure them against the kisan struggle which has been advancing with the slogan of expropriation of all their land. The chaotically collected land and their redistribution among the peasants, could hardly help the poor and miserable strata of the peasantry. In the absence of cheap credit for livestock, seeds and other prerequisites for agricultural operations, they could not utilise even the little advantage offered to them. Only the rich capitalist section could exploit such a situation and benefit by it. Further, since the motive inspiring the big landowners was not any change of heart but that of a strategic safeguard of their remaining land against any peasant demand for complete expropriation, the process of voluntary donation was bound to blow down and come at a deadlock at some stage.

A Brake on Socialist Movement

Though the Bhoodan and Sampattidan movements are, due to the abovementioned reasons, bound to prove futile from the standpoint of the objective which their sponsors have in view, they can do harm to the growing class struggle in the country. By sowing illusions among the backward sections of the exploited classes, they can paralyse them and disrupt the unity of class struggle which alone can liberate them from exploitation and poverty. They would also tend to kill the healthy class consciousness and the spirit of reliance on their own class action as a means of their emancipation. They would make them feel grateful to their capitalist and landlord exploiters. They would divert them from the road of class struggle, the only road to their freedom.

The sponsors of the movement eschew not only mass action, strikes and satyagrahas and others, but even legislative methods of securing favourable legislation in the interest of the poverty-stricken sections of population. The movement, therefore, sabotages both mass action as well as parliamentary struggles as means of securing economic relief for the masses. The programme of the movement is reduced exclusively to that of moral appeals to the wealthy classes. This is putting into operation the change of heart theory of Gandhi with a vengeance. This is even outdoing the Mahatma who, despite his class collaborationist theory, stood for organising strike and satyagraha struggle to back up his campaign of moral appeals to the rich. Jay Prakash Narayan may now claim to have purged Gandhism of its non-spiritual adulteration.

Class Struggle: The Only Way

The poverty-stricken Indian masses cannot, however, afford to be martyrs of such illusions in the present situation. Due to the organic crisis of the capitalist-landlord system, their poverty and misery are daily being aggravated. They cannot afford to listen to and be paralysed by illusions. Impelled by the biological impulse, the very will to live, they must discard the road of this fictitious solution of their poverty and advance on the road of the only real solution of that poverty, the road of class struggle.

4

THE GRAMDAN MOVEMENT*

MANMOHAN CHOUDHURI

THE LATEST PHASE OF BHOODAN

THE RENUNCIATION of private property in land on a mass scale through Gramdans is the latest and most significant development of the Bhoodan movement that is attracting widespread attention. Though the Gramdan movement began as far back as 1952 with the rather unexpected and spontaneous action of the villagers of Mangroth in U. P. it was only during and after Vinobaji's foot-march through Orissa, that the movement assumed mass proportions. We propose to briefly outline the genesis, development and future outlook of the movement in the following pages, with special reference to Orissa.

The first Gramdan in Orissa was obtained in Manpur, in the Cuttack district on 30th January, 1953 and shortly afterwards the movement caught on in the Koraput district where 26 Gramdans were received by the time Vinobaji entered Orissa on the 26th January, 1955. A few Gramdans had also been received in the districts of Balasore, Mayurbhanj, Ganjam and Sambalpur, but with Vinobaji's progress southwards, naturally, more attention was centred on Ganjam and Koraput, where Bhoodan workers from all over the province concentrated their efforts with the result that by the time Vinobaji left Orissa, the total number for the province reached 812 with 606 to the credit of Koraput alone. Since then the movement has continued to progress and the number of Gramdans has almost doubled, while the movement has spread to ten out of the thirteen districts in the province. We give below a district-wise break-up of the figures.

TOTAL GRAMDANS IN ORISSA AS ON 15TH DECEMBER, 1956

	District	Gramdans
1.	Koraput	1,226
2.	Balasore	185
3.	Mayurbhanj	62
4.	Ganjam	54
5.	Sambalpur	12
6.	Sundergarh	15
7.	Keonjhar	2
8.	Dhenkanal	1
9.	Puri	17
10.	Cuttack	1
	Total	1,575

*Reproduced from *Gramdan Movement*, by Manmohan Choudhuri, pp. 1-19.

The average population of a village in Orissa is a little more than three hundred. The villages received in Gramdan are generally the smaller ones, with an average population of one hundred and twenty. It is but natural that villages with a homogeneous population of peasants, labourers and artisans habituated to physical labour should be the first to offer themselves in Gramdan. The larger villages with high-caste families of sub-letting landowners, moneylenders, etc., are at present holding back. Kharka in Koraput district is the largest Gramdan village with a population of 900 while the smallest hamlet has a population of eight. The total population of all the villages is estimated at two lakhs.

Most of the villages in the Koraput district and elsewhere are Adivasi in character, each village being generally inhabited by a single tribe. This circumstance is doubtless one of the major predisposing factors, but there is a considerable number of villages with non-Adivasi and mixed populations. The number of such villages in Koraput exceeds 150 and is 80 in the Balasore district. All the villages in Sambalpur are non-Adivasi in character.

The movement has not been confined to Orissa but has simultaneously continued to spread in the other states also, so that there are already Gramdans in eleven of the states. A further development in Tamilnad is Grama Sankalpa, by which the villagers take a four-fold pledge:—

1. To give land to all the landless,
2. To eradicate untouchability and casteism,
3. To take to Khadi and Village Industries within a stipulated period, and
4. To have basic education in the village.

Twenty-six villages have already taken the pledge and the idea is spreading. This is in effect a combined pledge of Gramdan and subsequent reconstruction.

The Psychological Atmosphere

Gramdan on such a vast scale opens up the most exhilarating possibilities of social reconstruction and economic upliftment, of building up a new social order based on equality and co-operation. The voluntary renunciation of private property and eager acceptance of the new way of life of " getting along together ", unleashes undreamt of reservoirs of constructive social energy, repressed under the deadweight of an outmoded, exploitative and competitive social system. It is coming to be more and more generally recognised that popular enthusiasm and participation is an essential ingredient for the success of economic planning. Some of the spectacular results achieved in New China in recent years have been attributed, no doubt rightly, to the above causes. In any society this energy is generated on a considerable scale only when the underdogs, the under-privileged classes, get a feeling that they are getting a fair deal, that they are real participants in the rebuilding of a new order, not merely so many ' hands ' employed in renovating the old.

This has happened to a certain extent after the Communist revolution in China, but while the latter has succeeded in liberating the energies of the under-privileged masses, it has also, in the process of doing so, generated conflict and hostility on a considerable scale, the repercussions of which are being felt throughout the world to-day. It has brought into being forces that have complicated the problem of world peace.

Adherents of the democratic process have set their faces strongly against the fundamentally violent methods adopted in China and elsewhere, and it had seemed that planned progress in a democracy is bound to be a slow process and cannot hope to show the spectacular results achieved in the Communist countries. This has posed a fine problem for the underdeveloped and newly independent countries of the world. For them rapid economic progress is a *sine qua non* of their continued existence and yet, how far can they avoid being entangled in the methods of totalitarian regimentation, in their eager efforts to force the pace ?

Here the Gramdan movement provides an alternative. Here is a movement that has succeeded in at least subduing if not eliminating the individualistic traits in the peasantry, has put hope into the under-dog, and yet, while liberating the repressed creative energies, has not generated the least amount of friction and ill-will having based itself on the purely peaceful methods of persuasion.

Here the reader may pertinently ask, to what extent is the success of the movement due to the real psychological changes wrought in the minds of the people and how far due to the circumstances peculiar to the areas ? Is it not a fact that the movement has made considerable headway only among the backward Adivasis, and has demonstrably failed to catch on in the more advanced districts ? Is not land plentiful and cheap in the sparsely populated district of Koraput ? Have not the Adivasis very little attachment for land, and are in the habit of shifting cultivation?

It is a fact that the movement has had more success among the Advasis, who have a strong tradition of social cohesiveness. But this merely underlines the fact that even the backward classes in India have some valuable social traits highly useful for a new Sarvodaya or socialist order and the Gramdan movement is helping to preserve and canalise them. As a matter of fact, as we have noted earlier, quite a large number of villages with mixed and non-Adivasi populations have opted for Gramdan.

In this context it is significant that the movement seems to have caught on in the non-Adivasi and relatively more advanced state of Tamilnad, which has uptil now more than forty Gramdans to its credit.

Another predisposing factor in Koraput was the awakened consciousness of the people due to their participation in the national freedom struggle since the early thirties and the subsequent intensive constructive activities carried on there by a band of determined and self-less workers. Thus the psychological ground was being slowly prepared for more than two decades. In a way the psychological preparation has been going on in India since centuries, where numerous saints and social reformers have preached against untramelled individualism and Vinobaji's movement is a flowering of that long historical process, a culmination.

Several erroneous ideas are prevalent about the land situation in Koraput. An analysis of the statistics of 472 villages where land has been redistributed, shows that the average of cultivated and cultivable waste land per capita is only 1.33 acres. Taking into consideration the hilly nature of the area, this is not much. The people are not less attached to land than peasants in any other part of the world, and are as ready to fight and murder in disputes concerning land. Most of them are peasants with a settled life. One of the obvious reasons for their taking to Podu or shifting cultivation is that the money-lenders have filched their good lands in the valleys and have thus forced them to go higher and higher up on the hill-sides.

It is difficult to assess the actual depth of understanding in each and every village in a vast movement that has reached mass proportions. It is but natural that there should be all the gradations from the highest levels of understanding and ideological maturity to the lowest levels of hard mentality, and there have been a few dozens of regressions also. It is remarkable that the percentage of backsliders has been so small. An estimate of the degree of psychological change may, however, be formed from the results of land redistribution.

Land Redistribution

Redistribution work was carried on during the winter and summer of 1955-56 and with one mighty effort the work in 602 out of 850 villages donated by then was completed. The villagers themselves fixed the principles of redistribution, such as, which family was to get how much land per capita, etc., and the Bhoodan workers helped them with advice and in technical matters. The ideal, of course, was a thoroughly egalitarian distribution with shares in all types of land, to each family according to the number of its members. A good 20% of the villages strictly adhered to this ideal. But the majority of them preferred to give some extra land to the bigger landowners, amounting from one-and-a-half to three times the per capita average in the villages. In a minority of villages, they agreed to give even more than this to persuade a few recalcitrant big owners to join them. While as mentioned earlier, here were about 20 to 30 villages which went back on their pledge and refused to have any redistribution. There were also many cases in which former big owners refused to accept the bigger than the average shares so graciously offered to them by their fellow villagers.

These cases illustrate the changes wrought in the ownership pattern and the individual sacrifices made in the process of redistribution. Though the land is redistributed with full rights of cultivation, yet its ownership does not pass to the grantee, but rests in the village community. The individual farmer cannot sell or mortage his holding and the village community has the right and is expected to exercise it, to have periodical reconsiderations and reallotments, say every five or ten years. The Orissa Bhoodan Act, as recently amended recognises communal ownership of land in Gramdan villages.

Collective Farms

A certain percentage of land is generally set apart for collective farming. The average for the 472 villages in Koraput comes to just over 3% of the total cultivated land. The actual amount varies from village to village.

It may be asked, why no effort is being made to start collective farming, instead of redistributing the land ? The answer is simply this, that the Indian peasant in Koraput or elsewhere is not amply equipped to handle the organisational and technical problems involved in collectivisation. So it was thought best to lay stress on equalitarian distribution, coupled with non-ownership and encourage villagers to experiment with collective or community farming on a small scale, to gather experience. Very few of the villages have as yet taken up their collective lands in right earnest, but a few results stand out. In Manpur they have been cultivating their collective lands on a share out basis since three years. The first year they got a net produce of 230 mds. of paddy, which they credited to the village fund. The next year there were heavy floods which ravaged the crops. This year they expect a good crop. In Akili starting only last year they jointly cultivated the collective land, every adult, and even children working in the fields according to his or her capacity. The grain produce was credited to the village fund while the potato crop and other vegetables were distributed to all the families on a per capita basis, without taking into consideration the amount of labour contributed by them. Thus, the aged and the disabled also got a fair deal.

Principles of Reconstruction

Vinobaji felt the need of making an early start with the reconstruction work so that the popular enthusiasm may be caught and canalised while at its highest peak. Accordingly the Sarva Seva Sangh has shouldered the task of guiding the reconstruction programme, helped by the Navajivan Mandal, a constructive organisation working mainly among the Adivasis in Orissa.

Before going into the details of the activities we may do well to clarify some of the basic approaches underlying it.

Firstly, it should be emphasised that the ultimate objective is not mere material well-being, but an all-round development of human personality. It aims at creating a society of free individuals, willingly and freely working together for the common weal. So the reconstruction work is to be carried out in such a way that the villagers should first feel the necessity for any project and resolve to shoulder such responsibility as they can and the Sangh will help them to carry out their resolve. They should feel that it is their own decisions that are being carried out, something is not being bestowed on them from above. The Sangh is to be there as a guide and a helper, not as an overriding authority. The measure of the success of the programme is not merely in the physical targets achieved or the amount of money spent, but in the degree in which it succeeds in drawing out the capacities of self-help, initiative, co-operation and responsibility in the people.

Keeping the above objects in view and taking into consideration the realities and resources, a broad order of priorities was decided upon in which the various items of development work were to be taken up. The first ones were: (1) providing the landless who had now got land with bullocks and implements, (2) organisation of co-operative stores, etc., (3) irrigation and (4) Khadi. The next to follow were: (1) education, (2) village industries, (3) sanitation and health, etc. An effort was to be made to arouse the people in such a way that any one of the programmes taken up will get started on as wide a basis as possible over the whole area, thus giving it the shape of a popular movement. Thus, for instance, more than thirty co-operative stores were started within a short period of two months.

One of the fundamental principles of the Bhoodan movement is total social security, security for each and every individual in society. Gramdan lays the foundations for the construction of just such a social order in which the interests of all will be in harmony. So, after the abolition of conflicting interests in land, it is also essential that new industries and sources of employment be developed in such a way that they do not create conflict of interests in the system, that one's employment does not encroach upon the means of livelihood of another.

The Sarvodaya idealists are not opposed to scientific technology as such and in fact Vinobaji has welcomed the harnessing of atomic energy as he hopes that it will help in decentralising the industries by providing an abundance of electrical power. They are also not wedded to such utterly austere standards of life as people imagine.

In Orissa the rural population is one of the poorest in India and perhaps Koraput is the poorest district. It has been estimated that the average income of a rural family in Koraput is somewhere in the region of 225 rupees per annum. The desperate need of the moment is to increase their real income at least three times in the shortest possible time to make life just bearable for them.

But when faced with the stark realities of the situation we find that modern conventional technology can be of very little help. The people are undernourished and have lost any skill of the fingers that they had. For them, technological progress has stopped centuries ago. For them we have to invent a new technology that will take into consideration the disused state of their hands and minds and slowly put skill back into them so that ultimately their awakened intellect takes over command. We are forced to realise that there is no other alternative but to adopt the technology of small tools developed by the Gandhian research workers.

The Progress of Reconstruction

The Sarva Seva Sangh does not aspire to take up the responsibility for each and every village received in Gramdan. That responsibility rests ultimately with the people and the Government. It has taken up the responsibility for the villages in Koraput, Ganjam, Balasore and Mayurbhanj districts only. The areas have been divided into seven blocks, five in Koraput and one each in Ganjam and the Balasore-Mayurbhanj areas. The areas are further subdivided into centres, each serving a group of 15-20 Gramdan villages. 45 such centres have been opened. Each centre is in charge of a worker who looks after all the developmental activities in the region. There are in all 120 workers including 45 lady-workers working under the programme. Budgets and plans have been drawn up and funds obtained from the Government of India, the Orissa Government, the Sarva Seva Sangh and the Gandhi Nidhi.

But the actual progress of work has not been dictated by the cut and dried schedules and estimates of the budget, but has been moulded by the experiences gained from day-to-day and the objective realities of the situation as they were more and more clearly grasped.

Take for instance, the problem of irrigation. The people are extremely water-conscious and almost every other village has a pet irrigation scheme of its own, which is often a good hunch. Proposals were first submitted for small projects to irrigate a total of 5,000 acres in the first year. But it was soon apparent that it was hazardous to launch out on schemes without proper surveys and estimates. With the hands of the government departments full, enough surveyors or overseers were not available. So it was decided to open a training centre to train up a cadre of surveyors and engineers. The training classes have opened with twenty students who will do classroom work and field work for alternating periods of about three months, so that actual construction work gets as early a start as possible. The broad surveys of the countryside have revealed that soil conservation work is in some ways as important and urgent as irrigation schemes. So more emphasis will be laid henceforth on soil conservation and an effort made to make the villagers erosion-conscious.

Agricultural Improvement

The first programme taken up after the redistribution of land was distribution of bullocks to the former landless. 1091 pairs were distributed to 1,593 families in 200 villages, this year. In many villages, to which bullocks could not be supplied, the villagers helped each other with the existing bullocks. As cowkeeping is very indifferently done in Koraput, there is an overall shortage of bullocks in the district. While it is planned to distribute a similar number of bullock-pairs this year also, steps are being taken to educate the people in good livestock management and a cattle breeding centre has been opened.

A survey of the areas was jointly undertaken by the Director of Agriculture, Orissa, the Joint Director of Agriculture, Madhya Pradesh and the District Agriculture Officer, Koraput, and they have formulated proposals for a programme of agricultural development. According to this, six model agricultural farms will be started in the first instance, where improved methods will be first tried out under local conditions and then taught to trainees from the villages.

So far it has been possible to start only two such centres due to the lack of personnel. One plant nursery has also been started.

Agricultural implements worth a lakh of rupees donated by the Tata Steels have been distributed in the villages.

It is to be noted that when part of the land in a village is brought under irrigation the villagers agree to share the fields among all the families.

Gramdan opens up unlimited possibilites for crop planning, soil conservation and land management in general but we will have to wait a while for concrete results in these directions.

Co-operative Stores

In order to put an end to exploitation by moneylenders and traders, that has incidentally reached unbelievable proportion in Koraput and Ganjam, and also to put the villagers in control of their economic activities, stores were started in the villages on a co-operative basis. The villagers contributed a minimum of rupee one and eight annas per family in shares, etc., and the Sarva Seva Sangh advanced upto ten times the capital thus collected. Forty-seven stores have thus been opened. The total share capital collected exceeds Rs. 2,500. The amount advanced by the Sangh so far is Rs. 14,447. The total turnover by the end of May, 1956 exceeded Rs. 8,000.

The stores will help to make the villagers conscious of their economic plight. Now for the first time they will have an idea of the exports and imports from their villages and will be prompted to control them. The stores will also serve as marketing centres for the surplus produce of the villages and extend credit facilities, thus developing into multi-purpose co-operative societies. Steps are being taken to organise a central co-operative union for the entire Gramdan area.

The village stores are not as yet formally registered as co-operative societies and money has been advanced to them on good faith. These are often managed by totally illiterate villagers, yet the management has been remarkably honest and efficient and the losses sustained so far have been insignificant.

Indebtedness

The extortions practised by the moneylenders, especially in Koraput and Ganjam, had been on an unbelievable scale. The unjust debts piled on the peasants are enormous and efforts are being made to scale them down through negotiations. It is a happy augury that some moneylenders have agreed to scale down or write off debts. Some have even let go lands they had held on mortage for decades. But most of them are as yet hostile to Gramdan and have ceased extending loans to the villagers. Now the village stores are stepping into the breach by extending credit on bonded produce.

The only stable solution to the problem of indebtedness and insecurity is a village insurance scheme with annual premium contributions from every family that will cover cases of crop failure, accidents, fire, sickness, etc. These will be integrated into larger units that will be able to cover cases of major disaster affecting a whole village or a region. Vinobaji has this in mind as one of the ultimate modes of utilisation of Sampattidan. The Sampattidan movement has also made good progress in the Koraput district, with a promised total annual contribution valued at Rs. 27,400

Villagers labouring on development projects are encouraged to save and pool a part of their earnings to build up a village fund. They are readily accepting the idea.

Khadi and Village Industries

The villagers are eager to take up spinning, etc., but an early start could not be made due to the lack of accessories. A workshop for manufacturing charkhas and other accessories has been established at Rayaghada and is turning out about 300 charkhas monthly. 800 kisan charkhas have already been distributed in the villages and it is hoped that about 2,000 of them will be distributed by the end of the financial year. Cotton seeds have also been distributed.

It is proposed to encourage the villagers to take collective vows to have Khadi cloth only in their villages after, say, one year. Since more than a decade Khadi has taken root in some villages in the Koraput district. One who turns round may see and marvel at the facility with which even teenagers have taken to the processes. It is immediately evident that the spinner families are better clad than the rest. Khadi has helped them increase their standard.

Oil-pressing, pottery, soap-making, tanning and such other village industries will be gradually introduced and pilot schemes have already been started. These will be organised on a production for local consumption basis and only the surplus, if any, will be marketed.

EDUCATION

Though the problem of formal education has been shelved for a couple of years, yet in a real sense the whole scheme is one mighty educational effort. Through running their Grama Sabhas, managing their stores, working on engineering projects and in many other ways the people are learning things and their mental horizon is being widened as never before, because every scheme is based on the people's understanding and co-operation. Young men from the villages will be also trained in agriculture, cattle-breeding, carpentry, smithy, pottery, etc., at the various farms and centres and will carry on the activities in their own villages. It is proposed to even mobilise young men and women into labour corps to work on the various projects, living a disciplined life in camps and having a few hours of cultural and intellectual programmes. One such camp has been very successfully organised.

The urge for literacy is growing. Vinobaji laid great stress on it at every meeting in Koraput. Night schools for adults are being conducted by the workers. There are very few schools in the Koraput district. Literacy is only 5%. Education has to be provided for every child in every village and this will be according to the Basic system. A full-fledged attack on the front will be made only when the schemes that are to mitigate the desperate economic situation are well launched on their way. The immediate need is to ensure two square meals to everybody. Meanwhile efforts will be made to get " one-hour schools " started in every village to provide the modicum of the three R's to the children. Villagers undergoing the various vocational trainings will also be taught the three R's, so that they can start the ferment in their villages and run these one-hour schools.

The Adivasis have their own languages. Kandha, Saura, and Gadba are the important ones in Koraput. It is proposed to publish small booklets in these languages which will be useful for both children and adults. It is also necessary that the workers learn their languages to enter into their hearts. A manual in the Kandha language has been published while others are under preparation.

RESEARCH AND EXPERIMENT

The laboratory has been set up with two trained scientists. They are engaged at present on researches on the utilisation of forest products and testing of materials used in engineering projects. The research facilities will have to be extended by stages to ultimately cover the needs of all the branches of activities. Ultimately it will be possible to integrate the whole structure, down from the basic schools, upto the research institutes, into a full fledged rural university.

HEALTH AND SANITATION

The Adivasis have a surprising sense of neatness and beauty but are the victims of some insanitary personal habits mainly due to ignorance and poverty. Many do not even have enough clothing for a daily change, and wash. It will be easy enough to teach them better habits when they become a little better off.

Medical facilities in the areas are few and far between. Yaws are widely prevalent in the Ganjam-Koraput tract. Three doctors are at present employed on a campaign against yaws. Four sisters are working as injectors. They have treated and cured about 5,000 cases. Survey is being made as to the incidence of the disease in the area after which an intensive effort will be made with the help of volunteer doctors to eradicate the disease from the area within a short time.

All the lady-workers also help the villagers with advice, nursing and common medicines in cases of common ailments.

PROHIBITION

It is generally believed that it is impossible to make the Adivasis give up drink. But in point of fact thousands of them had given it up during the national movements. Vinobaji also laid great stress on it and the State Government agreed to enforce it in Koraput and Ganjam from April, 1956. It was already in force in Balasore. In Koraput prohibition has had phenomenal success and all the government officials have agreed that there are very few cases of contraventions. The reconstruction workers are also seeing to it that the villagers accept it whole-heartedly. Liquor had been a very convenient tool in the hands of the exploiters and its eradication will liberate the people in more than one way.

5

MYTH AND REALITY IN INDIA'S COMMUNITARIAN VILLAGES*

T. K. OOMMEN

THE introduction of *Panchayati Raj* in India marked an advance towards a decentralised democracy, a polity under which decision-making power is shared by the people's representatives even at the lowest level. Parallel to this political innovation another experiment in establishing self-governing village communities was launched by the *Sarvodaya* movement in *Gramdan* villages. This paper examines the working of government in three *Gramdan* villages in one state, Rajasthan. As a prerequisite to the present analysis it is necessary to understand the nature of the *sarvodaya* polity and the major assumptions on which it is conceived. It is as much my intention in this article to unfold the gap between ideal and actual as to discuss the implications of the assumption on which the *sarvodaya* political system is sought to be built.

THE POLITICAL PHILOSOPHY OF GRAMDAN

Gandhi valued individual freedom to the fullest extent, for he wrote: 'No society can possibly be built on a denial of individual freedom. It is contrary to the very nature of man.' But individual freedom is not conceded to be exercised for personal ends. On the contrary, individual freedom alone equips a man for the service of society and 'unrestricted individualism is the law of the beast of jungle'. Disinterested service to the group is the essence of the *sarvodaya* approach. The basic assumption in *sarvodaya* is that the individual is in harmony with the group. Inter-personal and inter-group antagonism is ruled out. Life is conceived as harmonious and co-operative, not conflicting or competitive; everyone will be thinking for the community as a whole. In fact J. P. Narayan calls it 'communitarian society', implying the primacy of the community over the individual. Differences are apt to occur even in such a society but they are by no means irreconciliable; since everything is orientated to the common interest there will be an all-pervading anxiety to arrive at compromises for the common good. An individual can discharge his duty to the community only when he is conscious of his rights and is willing to exercise them, participating in the community's decision-making process.

In order to realise this harmonious life all the coercive elements in society, including the state, should be done away with or minimised. 'I

*Reproduced from *Journal of Commonwealth Political Studies*, pp. 94-116.

(Gandhi) look upon an increase in the power of the state with the greatest fear because... it does the greatest harm to mankind by destroying individuality which lies at the root of all progress.' The state represents violence in a concentrated and organised form. The individual has a soul and is therefore changeable but the state is a soulless machine. Vinoba Bhave takes the same view. ' We should strive to create a state which would not need to exercise its coercive authority.'

If the state is not to exercise the coercive authority in society, who will do it ? Where will power in society be located ? In Gandhi's ideal state the individual rules himself in such a manner that he is never a hindrance to his neighbours. ' In the ideal state, therefore, (there is) no political power because there is no state.' The way out, as Vinoba sees it, is to create *swatantra janashakti* (the self-reliant power of the people). This power of the people is the opposite of the power of violence and is qualitatively different from the power of the state.

People's power is to be realised through self-discipline. This will do away with the distinction between the rulers and the ruled. In such a situation discipline from above is redundant; ' every man of society practises self-discipline and the values of socialism and co-operates with his fellowmen.' This brings one to the very heart of the problem of *sarvodaya* : *lokniti* or non-party and non-power politics as distinguished from *rajniti* or party and power politics.

How is *janashakti* to be generated and *lokniti* established ? Vinoba sees no difficulty in this. ' The power of government will be decentralized and distributed among the villages. Every village will be a state in itself.' Thus in the *sarvodaya* scheme a major part of the economic and political power should rest in the village and no power should be dominant in society. Government is by consent and consensus and not by bargaining and coercion.

It is important to strees the meaning of participation in the *sarvodaya* polity. Vinoba speaks of *kartritta vibhajan*, or the distribution of work among individuals without creating an administrative bureaucracy, the objective of which is to avoid concentration of power. Narayan rules out the significance of power in a *sarvodaya* polity when he notes : ' Majority and minority would have no relevance in a social context like that (*Gramdan*). Every one in such a context, in such a changed village, would be thinking not for himself but for the community as a whole '. This community orientation of the individual is crucial for it is through serving the community that the individual *participates* in community affairs. An important aspect of *sarvodaya* is ' a feeling in *every* individual that he is the servant of the community and it is his duty to do all that is possible for him to do to serve the community'. This would seem to imply active and equal participation by all individuals in the community decision-making process.

While *sarvodaya* aims to 'manufacture' an altruistic individual, the 'factory' in which this process will, it is hoped, take place is the small village. Man is a product of both nature and culture and the blending of the two is possible only in comparatively small communities. Narayan states it very clearly: 'self-government, self-management, mutual co-operation and sharing, equality, freedom, brotherhood—all could be practised and developed far better if man lived in small communities... it is undoubted that life in small communities, permitting and promoting personal relationships, will be more suited to the realisation of *sarvodaya* ideals.' The related goals of communitarian society and participating democracy alike are more easily secured when the community is small.

The leading notions contained in the foregoing discussion are : (i) the interests of the individual and the group are harmonious; (ii) it is possible to create a polity without power concentration; (iii) the smallness of the community facilitates the participation of all group members in the decision-making process. These notions are interrelated. Only when the interests of the individual and the group are identical does power dominance become meaningless and power dispersion possible. The index of equal power distribution among all members of the community is their equal participation in the decision-making process. All can equally participate only when the community is small enough to promote face-to-face interaction, informal relationships, intimate involvements. Communitarian society can operate only when the individual has close ties with the groups which surround him.

These conceptions are of course not peculiar to the proponents of *sarvodaya.* Several writers have stressed the notion that smallness and homogeneity of the community favour effective participation. It has also been argued that the loss of community, of an integrated and coherent belief system, has created malaise, anomie, and alienation which threaten the very operation of democracy. The underlying assumption in the argument is that community values are functional for political participation, that they are stronger in small communities, and that democracy can survive more easily in such 'integrated' social systems. Our evidence on the contrary suggests that community values are more often than not dysfunctional for the participation of individuals in secular political processes. The reason for this is to be discovered in the nature of the society itself.

The political process is not separated from other social processes. Role-relationships in non-western societies are diffuse and political roles are not always sharply differentiated from social and personal roles, with the result that an alteration in one role presses for concomitant change in other roles. The individual has total commitment and holistic orientation to groups. His loyalties, allegiances, and relationships to his group assume crucial significance in understanding the political processes in these societies. Moreover, the degree of attachment of the individual to his group is an important factor in facilitating or hindering his free action in the political context and in small communities the intensity of this attachment is likely to be great. Keeping this in view, we advance the hypothesis that the exclusive involvement of the individual with his group is dysfunctional for the effective operation of the secular political processes involved in the working of a self-governing community, particularly when this attachment is predominantly primordial. This hypothesis does not deny the importance of community values in maintaining harmonious relations between individual and group especially in the extra-political sector of life. It suggests, however, that, while certain aspects of community life facilitate some, not necessarily political, co-operative action, an ' overdose ' of the same will be dysfunctional in certain other, particularly political, spheres. The foundations on which rural community life in India is built are joint family, kinship, sub-caste, caste, territorial groups, and other in-groups. And 'no one can be regarded as an individual taken as he stands; he is always to be placed in terms of the group to which he belongs.' This article tries to explore how far the Indian individual with particularistic bases of life is capable of playing appropriate roles in the context of secular democratic political institutions.

Once certain ends are postulated the means of realising these ends should be identified. While *satyagraha* (non-violent persuasion) was the instrument devised by Gandhi to attain his ends, he did not rule out legislation. ' Legislation imposed by the people upon themselves is non-violence....' Vinoba while he wants to change men through *vichar shasan*, or peaceful conversion, recognises also a role for legislation: ' When every heart feels that the present order is unjust, when pity is created and there is proper understanding of the situation, then the light sort of legislation can come.' Proper preparation of the people and society is thus insisted upon as a pre-requisite for the introduction of law. Several states have passed measures to provide legal recognition for *Bhoodan* and *Gramdan* donations, but evidence does not suggest that the preparation has been everywhere adequate.

The leaders of the *sarvodaya* movement are not legislators. At the same time it cannot be assumed that the law makers are convinced followers of the *sarvodaya* philosophy. The passage of *Gramdan* legislation owes more to willingness to pay lip service to Gandhian ideals and readiness to recognise the popular acclaim which attaches to measures of agrarian reform. However, what is significant for the present analysis is not the motivation of the legislators but the use of law to help realise *sarvodaya* ideals.

The Universe and Method of Study

The three villages studied are Idanpura (Jaipur District), Sukpura (Nagour District), and Bhoodanpura (Baswara District) with populations of 336, 435, and 172 respectively. The villages are all very small but Sukpura has two and half times the population of Bhoodanpura.

Idanpura became a *Gramdan* village in 1959 and on 19 December 1960 the village was brought under the Rajasthan Gramdan Act 1960. On 5 July 1961 the *Gram Sabha* (village assembly) was established. The *Gram Sabha* came into existence in Sukpura only in 1960, although they had accepted *Gramdan* in 1958. While both Idanpura and Sukpura are multi-caste peasant villages, Bhoodanpura is a tribal village which came into existence in 1955 as a new colony for the rehabilitation of landless Bhils. All the land (264 acres) was donated by a former revenue officer of the *tehsil* in which Bhoodanpura is situated. The *Gram Sabha* started functioning on 3 December 1958.

The present study attempts to analyse both the formal and informal power structures and their interrelations. The most important of the formal power structures is the *Gram Sabha*. The analysis of the working of the three *Gram Sabhas* must begin by noting that they had been in operation at the time of this study for differing periods: Idanpura, 24 months; Sukpura, 35 months; Bhoodanpura, 52 months. These differences arise not only from the different starting dates but also because, for rather contrasting reasons, both Sukpura and Bhoodanpura have run smoothly over their whole periods, but in Idanpura the *Gram Sabha* had to be suspended.

It might be thought that the appropriate methods of analysis would be a comparison of *Gramdan* villages with neighbouring non-*Gramdan* villages of similar social structure, with a view to comparing the working of their systems of power. However, differences in political structure make meaningful comparison too difficult and the analysis is therefore limited to the *Gramdan* villages.

The major differences in form of government between the more general *Panchayati Raj* and the *Gramdan* systems may be noted here. Under the former (in Rajasthan at least) a number of villages come to constitute a *Vikas Panchayat* (Development Council) which engages itself primarily with problems of development. Representatives (*Panches*) are elected from the different villages and they, together with the *sarpanch* (president) who is directly elected from all the villages, constitute the executive committee of the *Panchayat*. A number of *Vikas Panchayats* combine to form a *Nyaya Panchayat* which attends to the administration of justice over its wider area. Each *Vikas Panchayat* nominates a member to the *Nyaya Panchayat*. Thus under the *Panchayati Raj* system the elected members are the decision-makers for the mass of voters and there is separation of powers between the *Vikas* and *Nyaya Panchayats*.

Under the *Gramdan* system, on the other hand, it is the *Gram Sabha* of ' all adult persons who either are residents of the *Gramdan* village or own land therein ' (Rajasthan Gramdan Act 1960, p. 6) which is the decision-making body. Each *Gramdan* village acts as a separate political entity and enjoys developmental and judicial powers. The Rajasthan Gramdan Act 1960 indeed gives still further powers:

1. Once donations of land are confirmed by law, the ownership of these lands, along with all common lands, is vested in the *Gram Sabha*;

2. The *Gram Sabha* is responsible for the payment of land revenue and other cesses on all the land in the village, including land under the private ownership of non-donors. Non-donors in the village pay the cess and taxes to the *Gram Sabha*;

3. The *Gram Sabha* is a body corporate having perpetual succession and a common seal with power to enter into contracts and to acquire, hold, administer, and dispose of both movable and immovable property;

4. The *Gram Sabha* has powers to borrow moneys on the security of *Gram Nidhi* (a fund raised through donations, bequests, gifts, or loans from the Central or State Government or any local authority or any person) or any other property vested in the *Gram Sabha;*

5. The *Gram Sabha* can remove the president and the executive committee from office;

6. The *Gram Sabha* has authority to deal with criminal and civil disputes and it can evict an allottee from land.

The *Gram Sabha* is thus a very powerful body with judicial and executive functions. No comparable institution operates in other villages. For while *Gram Sabha* meetings are required, even under the ordinary *Panchayati Raj* scheme, they are convened by the *Vikas Panchayat* only twice a year and then only to hear reports on and give formal approval to the work of the *Panchayat*. On the other hand, in *Gramdan* villages the executive committee is designed to carry out swiftly the policy decided by the *Gram Sabha* which is required to meet at least once a month.

With these points in mind, I shall try to assess the roles of *Gram Sabha* and the executive committee in the decision-making process. How far is the all-powerful village assembly capable of responding to the challenge put to it ? This analysis may at the same time also throw light on the validity of increasing decentralisation under the regular *Panchayati Raj* schemes.

Before we embark upon the analysis of the working of *Gram Sabha* it is necessary for two reasons to acquaint ourselves with the power structure in these villages: (i) the *power pool* may extend beyond the representatives on the formal power bodies, and (ii) the real power holders may not be on the formal power bodies. By ' power pool ' I mean the occupants of status positions who can exert influence in the community. The positions occupied may be hereditary and fixed (e.g. lineage headship) or elected and circulating (e.g. *Sarpanch*); they may be technically (*Gram Sevak* or village development workers) or ideologically orientated (*Shanti Sainik* or peace corps ' soldiers '). All these positions equip the occupant to exercise influence in the community. A particular person may occupy more than one position. The occupation of one position may facilitate the subsequent occupation of another (e.g. a lineage head may be elected *Sarpanch*). The group, which constitutes the power holders both real and formal, is viewed as a pool because at any one time all the persons who can be regarded as influencing the community life are drawn from it. Over a period new persons may be recruited and others ejected from it.

Rajasthan had a fairly developed feudal system and the *jagirdar* (landlord) and his caste (Rajputs) obviously wielded considerable influence; they continue to be influential today, abolition of *jagirdari* notwithstanding. Another group of men who counted in the village were the semi-officials who assisted the revenue officials of the *Raja* or the Government to collect land taxes and also derived prestige from these connections. Because of their positions they were looked upon as administrators of justice and conciliators of quarrels. They are known as *patels* in Idanpura, *mukhya* in Sukpura, and *gamati* in Bhoodanpura. Because these men were important and influential these titles came to be synonyms for prestige positions. While any important person may in this way come to be referred to by these terms, there remains a difference between the revenue *patel* and the ordinary *patel*. The number of *patels* in a village depends on the size of the village, the structure and functioning of caste groups, the number and size of the lineages.

Other traditional power positions are lineage headships and caste leaderships. When a caste is numerically inferior or depressed (untouchables) usually there will be only one person representing its interests in village affairs and he will be treated as the spokesman of the group by the villagers. It can happen that such a caste has no effective leader and then the group will tend to align itself with one of the factions in the village. When a caste is numerically superior or economically dominant it is very unlikely that the entire caste group will be represented by only one or even two persons. The usual pattern is that each *gotra* or even each lineage vies with the others for leadership in the village and each will have its own representatives.

With the introduction of *Panchayati Raj*, the co-operative movement, and community development programmes, new power positions have been created in rural India. In the *Gramdan* villages, too, statutory political bodies like the *Gram Sabha* executive committee, economic institutions like *Sahakari Samitis* (co-operative societies), *Gramodyog Vikri Bhandar* (village selling store), and social service and propaganda agencies like *Gram Seva Mandals* or *Sarvodaya Mandals* (village service councils), and *Shanti Sainiks* (peace corps) have opened up new power positions. Traditional and modern power positions in each of these villages must now be examined.

Power Personnel and Groups

Idanpura has 51 households drawn from the following caste groups: Ahir (peasants) 24, Rajput 9, Khati (carpenters) 6, Bhalai (previously leather workers and now rope-makers) 6, Brahmin 2, Jat (peasants) 2, Nai (barber) 1, and Kumbhar (potter) 1. The Rajputs claim common descent but belong to two lineages. The Khatis and Bhalais also have two lineages each. (A lineage is constituted by a group of persons who have common descent which can be actually traced.) The Ahirs of Idanpura belong to the Nandavanshi sub-caste which is an endogamous group. The sub-caste is divided into a number of exogamous *gotras* and each *gotra* has a number of lineages. The Ahirs of Idanpura belong to six *gotras*. The Gogad *gotra* has only two households, both of the same lineage. In spite of its numerical insignificance this is a major lineage for the revenue *patel* comes from this group. The Kudawat *gotra* is the most important numerically with 15 households belonging to two lineages. The non-revenue *patel* who occasionally challenges the revenue *patel* is from this group. Both lineages of this *gotra* are reckoned as major ones. The Totuwal *gotra* with 4 households is relatively insignificant. The Ganewal *gotra* has only one household but the leader of the neutral faction belongs to this. There are two other *gotras* with one household each making a total of 24 Ahir households. The *gotra* identification is observed to be very significant. Normally one refers to an Ahir not as such but by his *gotra* : e.g. Nathu Gogad.

Of the 165 adults in Idanpura, 22 persons, all male, constituted the power pool at the time of this study. The caste-wise distribution of power personnel and their membership of the executive committee of the *Gram Sabha* is presented in Table 1. The power pool includes the executive committee members, but the proportionate representation of different castes on the committee is shown separately since this is the most formal power-wielding body in the villages. The Brahmins are over-represented, the Ahirs are slightly under-represented, the lower caste Bhalai much more so. This is when all the power positions are equated. But in reality these positions have differing authority, meaning, and significance associated with them. The general position is that the Ahirs and Rajputs have a near monopoly of the power pool and the effective operation of other power-holders is possible only through alignment with them. The Ahirs are numerically superior and the Rajputs economically dominant. While the average land holding of households in Idanpura is 3·4 acres, the average holding of Rajput households is 5 acres.

Three power groups are active in Idanpura. A short description of the background of the faction leaders is in order ;

1. Ram Narain, Rajput, eldest son of the former *jagirdar*, lineage head, earlier treasurer of the *Sahakari Samiti*, former ward *panch* representing Idanpura.

2. Nathu, Gogad Ahir, lineage head, revenue *patel*, president of the *Sahakari Samiti*.

TABLE I. *Distribution of Power Personnel in Idanpura according to Caste*

Caste	Households	Adult population Male	Adult population Female	Power personnel (all male)	Representatives on the *Gram Sabha* executive committee
Ahir	24	46	43	10	5
Rajput	9	7	12	3	1
Khati	6	9	8	2	1
Bhalai	6	10	9	1	1
Brahmin	2	3	2	3	1
Jat	2	6	6	2	1
Nai	1	1	1	1	1
Kumhar	1	1	1	–	–
	51	83	82	22	11

3. Shuja, Kudawat Ahir, lineage head, non-revenue *patel*, former ward *panch* representing Idanpura.

4. Ganpat, Rajput, lineage head (second lineage of Rajputs), police constable

5. Bhuvana, Ganwal Ahir, member of the executive committee of *Sahakari Samiti*, member of the execuive committee *Gramodyog Vikri Bhandar*.

One faction is headed by Ram Narain and Nathu and includes as another leading figure Ram Dev, the educated village barber. Another group is led by Shuja supported by Ganpat. The third group, who style themselves neutrals, is led by Bhuvana who is the only one of his *gotra* in the village.

Early in 1961 Shuja was chosen by uncontested election as the ward member to the Bobas *Panchayat* of which Idanpura then formed a part. This success showed the strength his faction could mobilise. It was also needed if Shuja was to maintain his position *vis-a-vis* Ram Narain, for the latter was a candidate for the office of *Sarpanch*. In the event Ram Narain was not successful, votes from the other villages defeated him. But when in July 1961 the *Gram Sabha* was established in Idanpura Ram Narain became a leading contestant for the presidency. The Shuja faction opposed Ram Narain's candidature vigorously by putting a twenty-two year old Ahir matriculate of the Kudwat *gotra* as their candidate. (Ram Narain was thirty-seven and read only up to 7th standard of the Hindi vernacular.) While Ram Narain had never enjoyed the undivided loyalty of his village, he became particularly unpopular at this time. He was believed to have misappropriated the funds of the village co-operative society and the Block Development Officer concerned had filed a case against him, noting that his liability amounted to Rs. 3,040 and 98 maunds of wheat. In these circumstances even his supporters were not sure that he could win. This situation, combined with insistence on the principle of unanimous choice, led to the emergence of a compromise candidate,

Raghunathan, third son of the former *jagirdar* and brother of Ram Narain, who was 'unanimously' elected President. Ram Dev, the educated village barber and a supporter of the Ram Narain-Nathu group was elected Vice-President. Ram Dev had by now occupied a number of offices. He was the secretary of the *Sahakari Samiti*, Vice-President of the *Gramdyog Vikri Bhandar* Committee, member of the executive committee of the *Gram Seva Mandal*, and a *Shanti Sainik*. Of the remaining eight members of the Executive Committee one is the ineffective lower caste member and two are neutrals (one Ahir, one carpenter caste). The other five members belong to two factions, three to Ram Narain's and two to Shuja's. Thus the *Gram Sabha* executive committee included five members of Ram Narain's faction, two of Shuja's, and three of the politically neutral or ineffective group. (The other member is the *Gram Sahayak* or village aide who is an outsider and a paid employee.)

It is significant that neither of the *patels* (Nathu and Shuja) nor the leading descendant of the former *jagirdar* or the lineage head of the second lineage of Rajputs (Ram Narain and Ganpat)—all of whom lead the power groups in the village—are on the executive committee of *Gram Sabha*. Of the three lineage heads on the executive committee one is the untouchable and another is of the carpenter caste, both of whom are included to satisfy and silence the castes they come from and are not significant in the context of power in the village. The only lineage head from the Ahirs is Mahadev. Thus the traditional power personnel is almost totally absent from the formal political representative body. This does not mean that they have become irrelevant or unimportant in the power context of the village. In fact they remain the *power reservoir* of the village.

I use the term ' power reservoir ' to denote the persons or groups which are really powerful in a community. Power reservoirs may not be on the formal power bodies, such as the *Gram Sabha* executive committee in the present context, and yet they count in community affairs and may run the entire business from behind. Parallel to this, the concept of *power exerciser* is needed in order to denote those persons who may not be powerful in reality even though they handle power as a result of being office-holders. The power pool in a community is formed by the power reservoirs and power exercisers. The latter categories are not mutually exclusive; power exercisers may very well also be power reservoirs. A power exerciser may be able to use his position so as to become a power reservoir. On the other hand, without being a power exerciser one can be a power reservoir. If the power reservoirs are not also power exercisers or if the power exercisers are not falling in line with the power reservoirs, political instability is likely to ensue. Conversely, political stability is assured when power reservoirs are also power exercisers or power exercisers are under the thumb of power reservoirs.

That the power reservoirs of Idanpura are not on the executive committee of the *Gram Sabha* has already been noted. This was a sufficient reason (not a necessary one) for the perpetuation of restlessness in the political firmament of Idanpura. It culminated in July 1962 in the removal of Raghunathdan, President of the *Gram Sabha*, from office by a no-confidence motion. The motion was moved by the leader of the neutral group in a fairly well attended *Gram Sabha* meeting. The immediate reasons given for this move were that Raghunathdan had endorsed the illegal claims of one of his cousins to a portion of the pasture land in the village and that he had misappropriated funds of the *Gram Vikriya Bhandar* of which he had been for some time the manager.

There are 64 households in Sukpura, drawn from the following castes: Jats 39, Naiks (a detribalised untouchable caste) 12, Rajputs 9, Brahmin 1, Kayasth 1, Nai 1, and Chamar (leather worker) 1. The Naiks in Sukpura belong to two different lineages though they are formally represented as one group in village politics. The Rajputs of Sukpura belong to one lineage. There are a number of *gotras* from which the Sukpura Jats are drawn. The Bhamboo *gotra* have five households, all of the same lineage. This is a major lineage and includes a revenue patel. There are two households of the Shivar *gotra* who are affinally related to the Bhamboos. The Khileri *gotra* have 27 households and are drawn from five lineages, three of which have revenue patels and are reckoned as major lineages. One of the other two lineages has only one household while the other has seven. In spite of the numerical strength of the latter it is insignificant in the village power context. The remaining five Jat households belong to different *gotras* and are affinally related to Khileris.

21 persons constitute the power pool of Sukpura. A look at the caste composition of the power pool in Sukpura as presented in Table II is very revealing. The Jats have a virtual monopoly of the power positions and, of the 17 power positions they hold, as many as 11 belong to Khileri Jats. As in Idanpura, the Rajputs have their due share in the power pool and the lower castes are only nominally represented. Once more not a single power position is occupied by a woman. It is significant, however, that in the case of Sukpura members of the executive committee of *Gram Sabha* are *patels* of the village. The President, though a Khileri Jat, is not a power reservoir; his is the only household in his lineage and he did not hold any power position (such as *patel*) in the traditional context. He was in fact a compromise candidate. While the virtual Jat monopoly of the power pool could be explained in terms of their numerical strength, the Rajputs' economic dominance secures for them a proportionate share. (The average land holding of Rajput households is 50 acres whereas the average village holding is 30.5 acres.)

There are six *patels* in Sukpura of whom four are Jats (all of them revenue *patels*), one Rajput, and one Naik (lower caste) (both these being non-revenue *patels*). The power alignments are such that none of

TABLE II. *Distrjbution of Power Personnel in Sukpura according to Caste*

Caste	Households	Adult population Male	Female	Power personnel (all male)	Representatives on the *Gram Sabha* executive committee
Jat	39	71	60	17	5
Naik	12	14	15	1	1
Rajput	9	15	9	2	1
Brahmin	1	3	2	–	–
Kayasth	1	1	1	1	1
Nai	1	4	1	–	–
Chamar	1	1	–	–	–
	64	109	88	21	8

these *patels* can be taken to be the representative of the entire village. Thus, prior to the advent of *Gramdan* when the village was a ward under the Singhad *Panchayat*, it was Haridas (a compromise candidate) who was unanimously elected ward *panch*. But by the acceptance of *Gramdan* the necessity of establishing a *Gram Sabha* with an executive committee arose, which opened up possibilities for the representation of the *patels* on the committee in a formal official capacity. All the six *patels* have become members of the executive committee with Haridas as its President.

A short introduction to the faction leaders facilitates our analysis :

1. Haridas, Khileri Jat, former ward *panch* and the present president of *Gram Sabha* (Haridas' is the only household in his lineage).

2. Ram Suk, Khileri Jat, lineage head, revenue *patel*, executive committee member.

3. Mukunda, Khileri Jat, lineage head, revenue *patel*, executive committee member.

4. Narayan, Khileri Jat, revenue *patel*, executive committee member, member of the executive committee of *Sahakari Samiti*.

5. Chatura, Bhamboo Jat, revenue *patel*, executive committee member.

6. Nahar Singh, Rajput, lineage head, non-revenue *patel*, executive committee member, anti-prohibition secretary of the *Sarvodaya Mandal* executive committee.

7. Jetta, Naik, non-revenue *patel* of Naiks, executive committee member.

Ram Suk leads one of the Jat factions. There are 13 households in his group, of which one is that of the village barber. The remaining 12 are Jats belonging to two lineages. Mukunda is another Jat faction leader having the support of 8 households of which 6 are of one lineage. Narayan leads a numerically important faction of 12 households, 9 of which belong to one lineage. Chatura's faction includes 8 households, of which 5 are of one lineage, and also the Chamar household. Nahar

Singh is the spokesman of the Rajputs in the village. All the 9 Rajput households, except one, are related by blood. The Naiks have two leading lineages with 7 and 5 households. In spite of the occasional challenges to the chieftainship of Jetta, it is he who represents the lowest caste on the executive committee of *Gram Sabha.*

The structure and functioning of power groups in Sukpura, as in Idanpura, are such that the effective leadership exists only at the faction level. This means that the all-village leader has to be a compromise choice. To this extent any person elected as the representative of the entire village remains a mere power exerciser. The power reservoirs are at the faction level. In Sukpura, however, the choice of the former ward *panch* as compromise candidate for the presidency and the presence of all six *patels* as committee members has resulted in there being no change in the nature of the power structure or in the constitution of power personnel following the introduction of *Gramdan.* The *Gram Sabha* became a mere maintainer of the *status quo.*

Bhoodanpura is a tribal village newly established to rehabilitate the landless. Of the 36 households originally offered land only 30 have finally settled down. The 30 households are distributed into 8 clans. The power positions in this village are executive committee memberships in *Gram Sabha*, *Gram Sudhar* Committee, and *Sahakari Bhandar*. There are 9 *Lok Sevaks* in Bhoodanpura. The *patel* is newly elected and his position is not hereditary. Since the inhabitants are migrants and since the movement of kin groups was not wholesale, lineage headship as a power position is non-existent. Thus the two important hereditary positions, lineage headship and *patel,* do not exert any decisive influence in Bhoodanpura. Again, near economic equality obtains in the village since the lowest land holdings is 7 acres and the highest 9 acres.

12 persons form the power pool of Bhoodanpura. The distribution of power positions between the clans is shown in Table III. Of the 12, 10 are on the executive committee. As in Sukpura, the power exercisers are power reservoirs too. Once more, political stability results; the *Gram Sabha* has already worked for 52 months. While representation is distinctly uneven—the Nenamas over-represented, others not at all—unhappy political consequences seem to be avoided. This may be because all the competing clans are quite small in relation to the village as a whole. Indeed, apart from a few instances of friction, inter-group relations are harmonious. The coincidence of the power reservoirs and power exercisers and the number of small clans go some way to accounting for this, but there may be other factors, such as the absence of hereditary power positions, the absence of age-old friendships or enmities since the inhabitants are new migrants from different villages, near economic equality as between households, and the absence of territorial groupings which co-exist with clan-clusters. At the same time it is important to note that the power pool is quite limited in size.

TABLE III. *Distribution of Power Personnel in Bhoodanpura according to Clan*

Clan	Households	Adult population		Power personnel		Representatives on the *Gram Sabha* executive committee	
		Male	Female	Male	Female	Male	Female
Nenama	8	9	8	4	1	4	1
Bad	5	6	5	2	–	1	–
Damore	4	5	3	2	–	1	–
Lemberwara	3	4	3	–	–	–	–
Ratore	3	3	3	2	–	2	–
Dendore	3	3	3	–	–	–	–
Bamania	2	3	2	1	–	1	–
Kharad	2	3	2	–	–	–	–
	30	36	29	11	1	9	1

Our analysis of the power structure of the three villages points to the following conclusions:

1. Those who constitute the power pool are a minority and power positions tend to concentrate in a few hands;

2. Numerically superior castes (Ahir and Jats) and economically dominant ones (Rajput) have a preponderant place in the power pool;

3. If the power exercisers and power reservoirs are not the same, political instability can arise. Conversely, when they are the same, there is every possibility of political stability;

4. Extreme identification of faction leaders with their groups results in their becoming unacceptable to the village as a whole. This in turn leads to the selection as all-village leaders of compromise candidates who are usually mere power exercisers and hence ineffective;

5. Where hereditary power positions, age-old enmities, marked inequalities, and decisive numerical superiority of any single group are missing, harmonius inter-group relations are facilitated.

THE DECISION-MAKERS

The *Gram Sabha*, constituted by the entire adult population, is theoretically the decision-making body in a *Gramdan* village, and legislative, judicial, and executive powers are vested in it. By definition the executive committee of *Gram Sabha* is only to implement the decisions taken by the latter. But in practice the executive committee takes decisions on a number of policy matters. Table IV shows that in Idanpura and Sukpura meetings of the *Gram Sabha* are much less frequent than those of the executive committee. It is in the latter that the bulk of decisions are taken and the committee members are the men of influence. In Bhoodanpura on the other hand *Gram Sabha* meetings are more important. However, even here it is not safe to conclude that there is anything like mass participation in decisions. Although it is the usual practice that decisions made at executive committee meetings are endorsed by the signatures (or thumb impressions) of all those present, the same does not hold of *Gram Sabha* meetings; there usually only the *Khas Admi* (important persons) in the village will sign. This group may be taken as constituting the effective participators. The validity of this group as an operational indicator of political influence was supported by the opinion expressed by villagers and by other observations. By this test, Bhoodanpura, for all its advantages of smallness, fails to show any high level of participation or power dispersion.

TABLE IV. *Types of Meetings and Participation in Decision-making in Gramdan Villages*

	Duration of Working of *Gram Sabha* (in months)	*Gram Sabha* meetings	Average adult population signed %	Committee meetings	Average committee members signed %
Idanpura	24	5	17·5	20	60
Sukpura	35	9	6·9	29	65·7
Bhoodanpura	52	10	15·4	2	88·8

This group of those whose signatures are thought important is of course larger than the group of executive committee members but it may usefully be compared (Table V) with the membership of the 'Power Pool'. In Sukpura and Bhoodanpura the power pool is the larger; in Idanpura it is smaller. This difference is explained by two factors. In Sukpura and Bhoodanpura formal and real power are held on the whole by the same people; but evidently only a proportion of the power pool is of key importance. In Idanpura on the other hand there are many holders of formal positions of power whose signatures are taken as a matter of course while there is then a further group of people who really count and their signatures are obtained as a matter of necessity. Secondly, the Idanpura situation of tension and conflict leads to constant mobilisation of full faction strength.

TABLE V. *The Power Pool and the Decision-making Group in Gramdan Villages*

	Adult population	Adults in power pool %	Adults who singn in the *Gram Sabha* records %
Idanpura	165	13·3	17·5
Sukpura	197	10·6	6·9
Bhoodanpura	65	18·4	15·4

Sufficient has perhaps been said to throw serious doubt on the possibility of substantial dispersion of power even in small communities. It remains to examine the other assumption of *Gramdan* philosophy, that of harmonised interests, and in particular to consider evidence bearing on the counter-hypothesis that over-involvement of the individual in the group is dysfunctional for secular politics. Idanpura and Sukpura have each had their burning issue and it is instructive to examine these.

Idanpura has 272.24 acres of land. Of this 174.44 acres was in the private possessions of cultivators and the remaining 97.80 acres in Government ownership. The land in Government ownership was deemed to be common land and was used for such purposes as cattle grazing or burying the dead. The village had, however, no specifically demarcated pastureland according to the records of the land settlement. By early 1958 the Rajputs had managed to get 65.62 acres of this common land allotted to them. This posed a challenging problem for the *Gram Sabha* to tackle. In fact one of the main reasons which prompted the villagers to accept *Gramdan* was the assurance by *Sarvodaya* workers that there would be new arrangements for pastureland; by the time of this investigation in 1963 nothing had been done.

Of the 65.62 acres allotted, 37.51 acres had been secured by the Rajput lineage of which Ganpat is the head and the remaining 28.11 acres had been allotted to the lineage of Ram Narain. Though Ganpat and Ram Narain belong to the same *gotra* and believe themselves to be of the same ancestry they belong to different factions. Ram Narain was always looked upon as a *Neta* (leader) in the village; Ganpat on the other hand could not take such a large part in village politics because he was employed in Government service and consequently often away from the village.

When the land which was formerly used as pastureland was put under cultivation the villagers found it extremely difficult to graze their cattle. Naturally the problem was frequently discussed in the *Gram Sabha*. Whenever it was discussed Ram Narain with the characteristic technique of the village politician sought to impress upon the people that he was keen to act for the benefit of the entire village. He swore that he would return the land for the purpose of cattle grazing if Ganpat did so too. As compensation for the return of his 37.51 acres the *Gram Sabha* had agreed to give Ganpat 15 acres of single-crop land. However, he did not yield to persuasion. He was sure that he would lose nothing by being adamant. Ganpat knew that he could not cultivate the land singlehanded in the face of opposition from the entire village. He had seen that the most prudent step would be to share the benefit and then secure the co-operation and support of the faction to which he belongs. Accordingly, he distributed 31.5 acres to seven leading members of his (Shuja) faction, keeping only 6 acres for himself. He thus increased the involvement of his faction in the case, thereby preventing the issue of pastureland becoming one in which he and the rest of the village were on opposite sides. Ram Narain had to follow the same course. The villagers are now divided into two camps on this issue. While the problem confronts all of them equally, their factional identification makes it impossible for them to arrive at any solution agreeable to all. Both groups argue for the surrender of the allotted land by the persons belonging to the opposite camp. This is the burning problem more frequently discussed than any other in the *Gram Sabha;* yet in two years of the working of this institution no solution could be found.

The case illustrates that the nature of village politics is considerably conditioned by individual interests. Ganpat saw his interest as better served by a (no doubt temporary) distribution of 31 acres than by an exchange from which he would obtain only 15 acres. Ram Narain for his part would not risk making the first move. The villagers who identified themselves with the faction leaders also pursued their interests as they saw them. Yet pastureland is equally necessary for the entire village and hence to take sides with a person or group is to ignore the common interest. Initially the problem was one between two individuals on the one hand and the rest of the village on the other and both Ram Narain and Ganpat could have been persuaded or coerced into surrendering their allotted land had the villagers voiced their dissent together. Instead, the villagers, some for reasons of immediate gain, others from pressure of various kinds, allowed themselves to be ranged on the side of individual sub-groups, blocking a settlement of the dispute and ignoring a clear all-village interest.

Sukpura is situated in the arid zone of Rajasthan and the perpetual problem of the villagers is the scarcity of water. There are two main sources of drinking water: rain water collected during the monsoon and stored in deep tanks constructed in the form of wells, and ponds where rain water collects. The well-off households usually have water tanks of their own. The usual practice is that when water is available in the village pond all draw water from it. In addition, those who own tanks take water from the pond in big vessels drawn by bullocks and store it in their private tanks. The result is obvious. When the water in the village pond dries up (as it usually does) those who have tanks of their own continue to draw water from them while others have to go out of the village to bring water from a distance of four or five miles. In order to remove the difficulties arising from this situation the Rajput *patel* who is a member of the *Gram Sabha* executive committee proposed at the meeting on 31 January 1963 that tank owners should draw water from the village pond only for current consumption and not for filling their tanks. The subject was brought up at all nine meetings held up to the time (19 August 1963) when this study was completed. But no decision was taken during this period of about seven months and every time the discussion was postponed.

It is important to note that of the 19 private tanks in Sukpura 18 are owned by Jats and 5 of the 8 executive committee members are Jats. A decision to stop the drawing of water from the village pond to fill privately-owned tanks would affect their personal interest. Moreover, by taking such a decision the Jat committee members would risk becoming unpopular with their supporters. The rest of the population of Sukpura attribute the postponement of the decision to self-interest on the part of the Jats. To the Jats their attitude is natural for they are only maintaining the *status quo* or defending their own interests. And they believe that the proposal was made only to inconvenience them. This example clearly illustrates how the individual interests of committee members are a hindrance in the context of the welfare of the bulk of the population of the community. This case also shows that the individual's identification with the immediate group (here caste) beyond a certain point hinders his acting as an independent unit free of his traditional chains in the decision-making process.

The dysfunctional consequences of individual interests and the over-involvement of the individual with the group are illustrated in these two cases. I did not observe any similar instance in Bhoodanpura. At the time of the investigation in 1963 Bhoodanpura was eight years old. Because of the dispersed nature of the villages in this area, necessitated by the regional topography, the usual tendency is for people to form identifiable territorial units for residential purposes which usually coincide with clan clusters. But Bhoodanpura has drawn its population from 8 different villages between four and twelve miles away from the present site of the village. While 5 of these villages supplied only one household each, the remaining 25 households came from three villages with a distribution of 10, 8 and 7 households each. Bhoodanpura has four *Mohallas* or residential clusters which contain persons irrespective of their villages of descent, thereby negating the importance of old ties for neighbourhood formation. The absence of age-old ties also rules out clearly established friendship or enmity relations sustained for generations. The 30 households belong to 8 different clans and no single clan has decisive numerical superiority.

These facts are reported in order to highlight the nature of individual-group relations in Bhoodanpura. Individuals are certainly attached to their lineages and clans and to the villages they hailed from. But their kinship ties and time-old friendships or enmities do not have much significance in the political action context of Bhoodanpura for the simple reason that the entire kin-group or village did not move together to the new abode. I particularly emphasise this point because my observation in this connection is contrary to common arguments. As has been noted earlier (see Note 17), the usual argument is that the loss of community sentiment creates atomisation, alienation, and anomie which result in the formation of a rootless mass which can be manipulated by outside agencies and leaders, and hence poses a constant threat to democracy. But our evidence suggests that limiting community values at a certain level also facilitates the processes involved in the working of democracy. True, the total severance of community ties will perpetuate confusion and result in the creation of rootless individuals thirsting for a sense of belonging.

It is equally true that the over-involvement of the individual with the group prevents independent judgement and rational decision, which is equally detrimental for democracy. The complex task is to locate the point at which relations between the individual and the group will be functional for democracy.

That the *Gram Sabha* in Bhoodanpura had functioned for 52 months without any breakdown indicates that the existing conditions are favourable. Though the inhabitants are drawn from different villages and are distributed among different clans, they are not rootless. They are not deprived of a sense of belonging for they are sufficiently small in number and homogeneous to permit intimate face-to-face relationships. At the same time these community loyalties and values do not seem to inhibit their free action as independent individuals. They appear to be sufficiently attached to be adequately independent of group loyalties. Such a situation favours their effective participation in political activities, keeping the common end in view.

I have argued that the differentiation between power exercisers and power reservoirs caused political instability in Idanpura, that the *status quo* was maintained in Sukpura because the old power personnel had been recruited into the new formal power-wielding body, and that in Bhoodanpura favourable individual-group relations brought about political stability. Let us see how far the community view of the working of the *Gram Sabha* conforms with these conclusions.

TABLE VI. *Opinion of Household Heads on the Working of Gram Sabha*

	IDANPURA	SUKPURA	BHOODANPURA
Effective	8 (15.6%)	21 (33%)	—
Impartial	Nil	Nil	23 (77%)
Tolerable	2 (4%)	25 (39%)	7 (23%)
Not effective	27 (53%)	9 (14%)	—
Partial	9 (17.6%)	Nil	—
No response	5 (9.8%)	9 (14%)	—
	51	64	30

Table VI summarises the opinions of household heads on the working of *Gram Sabha* in their respective villages. The political restlessness of Idanpura is clear in the opinions expressed. 70.6 per cent of household heads expressed negative opinions ('not effective' and 'partial'). Only 15.6 per cent expressed satisfaction with the functioning of *Gram Sabha.* In Sukpura only 14 per cent associated negative sanctions with the working of *Gram Sabha.* 39 per cent said that it was 'tolerable', which indicates acceptance of the *status quo.* A clear difference is visible in Bhoodanpura. An overwhelming majority, 77 per cent of household heads, had the view that the *Gram Sabha* is working impartially. Even the phrases used by the people in different villages to denote their approval or disapproval are of importance. A reputation for impartiality is not easily gained by a decision-making body in a small community, particularly because of the over-involvement of the individual with the group. For reasons already given, Bhoodanpura was able to start with a clean slate. Thus the opinions expressed by household heads on the working of the *Gram Sabha* reflect to a large extent the political situation obtaining in these villages.

Conclusion

The evidence I have presented in this article reveals that a 'participating democracy' is far from existing in the *Gramdan* villages. While Sukpura and Idanpura are multicaste villages, Bhoodanpura is very small and occupied exclusively by one tribe. Even in such a village the proportion of persons who matter in the decision-making process is quite small. Sukpura's is the lowest participation and in this village the power exercisers and the power reservoirs are the same and hence the core or power personnel remains a small group. In the case of Bhoodanpura the absence of traditional power positions facilitated some power dispersion. But in Idanpura the traditional power holders are politically influential though several of them are not on the key power exercising body (the *Gram Sabha* executive committee). The number of adults in Idanpura is two and a half that in Bhoodanpura and yet a larger percentage of the population participate in the decision-making process in the former. There has been political instability in Idanpura since the establishment of *Gram Sabha* and the sharply divided power groups have always demonstrated their strength through the participation of the largest possible number of their members. Thus more and more people have had to be politically alert. In the light of this evidence I suggest that smallness and homogeneity in themselves are no guarantee for the participation of a greater segment of the population in the decision-making process; politicisation, however, may well have this effect.

It may be noted here that a large majority of non-participants are not aware of their political rights and they may not even think it appropriate for them to indulge in such activity which they see as belonging to certain persons or groups with prestige and prerogatives (*Jahagirdars, patels*, lineage heads, etc.). Even the nominal recognition accorded to them (as in the case of the lower caste member of the executive committee) is a great boon and they feel gratified and content. Therefore, unless the non-participants realise that it is equally their business to make decisions for the village and rebel against the existing power structure, there is little possibility of increased participation. In this sense also, then, it is political awareness which can bring with it increased participation.

The fact that the segment of the population participating in the decision-making process or forming the power pool is a minority suggests that there is great power concentration and that power dispersion has not been achieved. To this extent the situation obtaining in these villages is far from the *sarvodaya* ideal: the *janashakti* (people's power) is hardly generated and *rajniti* (power politics) still prevails. It can be argued that in small communities the participation of every individual in the decision-making process is not necessary since the communication channels are very informal and quickly effective. It may also be that, since each individual is no independent entity but has to be taken as a group member, it is sufficient if the spokesman or representative of that group participates in decision-making activities. This means that individuals should go by the commitments made by those who represent them, and the registering of individual opinions is not very significant. This assumes that the decision-makers are capable of looking beyond their immediate and personal interests and this assumption is in accordance with the concept of the communitarian society.

But this same ideal society emphasises the value of primary groups which in practice can be seen to make difficult that service to the community as a whole which is to be the proper role of the individual.

This is the basic dilemma involved in the attempt of *Sarvodayists* to achieve a participating democracy in a communitarian society. Recognition of this dilemma persuades me to agree with R. E. Lane that an 'overdose' of community values is antagonistic to the effective operation of a democratic political system. Community sentiments involve close and long-standing loyalties of locality and people but democracy based on such loyalties cannot be enduring. Community makes it hard for individuals to achieve status (political office in the present context) based on merit, and this almost undercuts the philosophy of a democratic system. Community is wedded to traditional ways and immobility and silences the critic, but without widespread innovation, mobility, questioning and criticism democracy cannot flourish. Community makes for solidarity relationships among men but for democracy to work men must be relatively free to combine and re-combine in a flexible fashion, and for this the individual should be a free-standing unit. These are the compelling reasons which dissuade me from believing that the weakening of the community is a threat to democracy.

But Lane's argument applies only to politics at the national level, whereas the present data refers to small communities. Moreover, Lane believes that the major flaw in the argument of the authors who see the weakening of community values as a threat to the future of democracy is that they view both national and local politics in the same perspective. Lane believes that 'in a village setting, a city-state, it is possible to combine these qualities of community with a trend of democracy, the town-meeting kind, or its extended version'. Only when a man enters politics at the national level must he '... shed the qualities of the community man and assume the lonely role of the independent, isolated individual'. Our evidence, on the other hand, suggests that even in small communities it is impossible to combine intense primary group sentiment with democracy. I am not suggesting that absolute individualisation and atomisation of the individual are prerequisites for democracy to operate in a community; I am only indicating that the individual should be emancipated from his slavery to the group if he is to act as a 'democratic man'. The problem is one of locating the degree of individual-group attachment which will be functional for democracy.

With this perspective in mind I suggest that the nature of individual-group relationships has to be recognised as an important dimension of politics in developing countries, especially in India where on the one hand authoritarian institutions like caste and joint family exert such influence and on the other there is eagerness to evolve a stable democratic political system. Less is to be expected from the attempt to cultivate harmony through smallness of community than from processes of 'political socialisation' which may emancipate individuals from particularistic moorings.

6

SARVODAYA*

B. T. Ranadive

Vinobaji is a sworn opponent of the institution of the state. He and his followers believe in a stateless society and claim to be working for it today. In this respect, he considers himself to be ahead of the communists because they want to abolish the state in future, while he wants to abolish it today. "The *puran wallahs* are *bhoot satyayug wadis* (believers in the state-free society of the past); the Communists are *bhavishya satyayug wadis* (believers in the state-free society of the future); while we are *vartaman satyayug wadis* (soldiers trying to build a state-free society in the present)." (*Vinoba and His Mission*, pp. 189-90.)

Vinobaji and his followers regard the state as an artificial product imposed on society and the source of the evil of centralised economic and political power. They seek to abolish the existing state without fighting against it. They look upon the state as an organ standing above society, not as the instrument of the ruling class to dominate society. For them it is not a product of certain historical conditions—a product which is bound to disappear when classes are abolished and exploitation of man by man is no more. That the state will wither away only as a consequence of new social relations and not till then, is not realised by them. They also fail to understand that before the state withers away the working class must take power and use the state during the transitional stage to build a new social order, organise economic life and punish those who seek to upset it.

Views on State

Vinobaji presents his thoughts on this subject as follows:

"Ethics and politics remain apart and follow different paths. That is why, I am out to establish a *pragya* as opposed to *rajya*, that is, I want a state where there is no government and people govern themselves." (*Ibid*, p. 166.)

Most of us believe that society will reach such a stage in the course of its evolution as would eliminate the necessity to run a government based on coercion or the power to punish. Even the Communists accept this as the ultimate objective....

But all of us know that under the existing situation, coercion-based

*Concluding portion of the article summing up the discussion on Sarvodaya and Communism. *New Age*, Vol. VII, No. 9, September 1958, pp. 1-14.

governments are a reality and will continue to be so for the present. We will have to admit that coercion has its place today. Nevertheless, the essential characteristic of a non-violent society would be that its greatest institution would be based on service. There shall be room for coercion and government in it, but that would be secondary. (*Ibid*, p. 121.)

The institution of ' government (state) is not a natural creation but an artificial one. But under present-day conditions man as soon as he is born comes under the control of the government. The government has such all-pervading power that it affects every aspect of a man's life. From his birth to his death man is affected by this institution'. (*Sarvodayache Adhar*, Marathi, p. 8.)

There is nothing more terrible than (the institution of) government. Present-day governments are wielding more power than any previous government in the past. Those in charge of the government say that they hold all power in their own hands to serve the interests of the people. The domination of society by government has made a handful the arbiter of the fates of the people. Today the entire world is quaking with fear. The representatives of various nations have kept in their own hands the power to do good or ill to their people. The common people are helpless and crippled; they think that they cannot do without the government. The people have got only the formal right to vote. This right is like the right of the sheep to elect a shepherd. It does not lead to any change in the conditions of the sheep. The people are deluded in this fashion, while the government gets more power concentrated in its hands.

The Communists agree that the institution of government should finally disappear but they say it should be strengthened today. The talk of strengthening the (institution of) government today is to advocate slavery. Therefore, the Sarvodaya thought advocates decline of the government today.

So far as the individual is concerned, every one should learn to control his mind and bodily organs. A new social order should be established taking into consideration that there is no conflict between the mutual interests of individuals. We should start working for the elimination of the government from today knowing that its existence is not at all necessary for us (*Ibid*, p. 30.)

Vinobaji's views, it is clear, sharply differ from the proletarian Marxist view of the state.

Anarchist Viewpoint

The state is not an organ of domination of one class over another; but an institution standing above society in which *a few individuals* get the power and dominate the others. The state is bad because it restricts the liberties of the individual by concentrating the economic and political power in the hands of a few *individuals*. It is not the conditions of economic exploitation, not capitalist exploitation, that creates the present state and concentrates economic power in the hands of a narrow class. But on the other hand, it is the state that concentrates power in the hands of a few individuals—such is the outlook of the Sarvodayaites.

This outlook is not new. It is the same individualistic outlook of European anarchists who thought only of the individual in relation to the state and forgot the class nature of the fight against capitalist state. Against the scientific conception of the disappearance of the state in a Communist society, the European anarchists of 19th century posed a crude type of anti-authoritarianism, demanding the abolition of the state forthwith and complete freedom for the individual from any kind of authority. They did not represent the revolutionary working class but the extreme individualism of *bourgeois* society.

Vinobaji's outlook on state, organisation, politics has many things in common with the individualist outlook prevalent among the followers of Bakunin and Proudhin in nineteenth century Europe. And that is but natural. For Vinobaji's Sarvodaya does not base itself on an oppressed revolutionary class, but on individuals—from all classes.

We have already seen Vinobaji's refusal to fight against the present national government. He raises this into a theory, promises the people to create a stateless society without a political struggle against the present ruling class. It will be thus seen that while the Sarvodayaites have taken the objective of a classless and stateless society from Marxism, they have not yet understood how to realise it. The abjuration of political struggle will only ensure the continuance of the present class domination. It will prevent the people from preparing the preliminary conditions for a classless and stateless society. The objective of classless and stateless society will prove to be unrealisable under the Sarvodaya practice.

With this outlook, Vinobaji does not see the need of the state of the working class operating during the transitional period to communism and classless society. For him all states are equally bad—and the working class state has no role to play in building the new order. When Sri Kripalani told the Bhoodanaites that they will have to take government in their own hands to carry the Bhoodan *kranti* to a successful conclusion, Vinobaji differed and categorically stated: 'I think it is not necessary to have political power in my hand; it is enough if I am able to control it.' As against *rajniti* (polity-state, political power) Vinobaji stresses *lokniti* (people's power to influence the state) and he thinks that a number of steps taken by the present government—like *khaddar* promotion, village industries, new education, etc., are the result of *Bhoodan*. (*Sarvodaya-ke Aur*, p. 48.) This is what he calls 'controlling the state'. This is enough to show that Vinobaji does not think it necessary to have a state of the oppressed class. The masses should not take charge of the state; they should control it from outside—all in the interest of the abolition of the state.

On the one hand Vinobaji wants to 'control' the present state; on the other hand, he wants to set in motion the process of its elimination from today—without a social revolution and elimination of classes from the economic structure. The revolutionary and scientific Marxian concept of the withering away of the state after abolition of exploitation and socialisation of production is replaced by the utopian concept of setting in motion the process of abolition here and now.

Attitude to Parties

Vinobaji's attitude towards political parties, elections, rule by majority shows that he takes an anti-political and anti-authoritarian stand on many issues. His criticism of the present-day state and society is generally made from the standpoint of the anti-authoritarian individual and not of the revolutionary working class.

His estimate of the world movement for democracy is as follows:

"For about a century past, the experiment of democracy is being tried in the world. There are different schools of thought; some are called rightists and other the leftists. And statesmen of the world are divided into different parties, groups or isms .... But when parties are formed on the basis of different views, they are even less concerned with ideology, than with organisation, discipline and propaganda. The party is an instrument of attaining political power. And power predominates while ideas become mere convenient trade-marks used for power-political rivalry." (*Vinoba and His Mission*, p. 251.)

This description of political parties does fit the ruling and opposition parties of the *bourgeoisie*, who promise all kinds of things to the masses but carry out the will of the capitalist class. But Vinobaji seeks to embrace in his description all political parties, including those who represent the interests of the working class and other downtrodden sections. The fight between these latter and the ruling parties of the *bourgeoisie* is not an unprincipled fight for power, but a fight for the emancipation of the oppressed classes. Because of his outlook on the state and political struggle Vinobaji misses this central issue of our times. The conflict between these he thinks has nothing to do with the struggle for a new social order. He sees in it only a fight for power between individuals.

He delivers the following judgment on India's political parties:

"The Congress cannot serve the people because the principle of service has become a joke for the Congress. They are concerned with power-politics. The Socialists are a better lot, but they are after power. The Communists are thinking only in terms of violence. In these circumstances, the Sarvodaya Samaj alone can deliver the goods." (*Ibid*, p. 51.)

Justifying abstention from politics, Vinobaji says:

"So long as a country is not free, all strength must be concentrated towards securing political power. But once the latter is attained, every effort must be directed towards the achievement of social and economic revolution. Hence, if you feel that strength lies merely in capturing political power, I must then say that you have missed the secret of Swaraj. You should, therefore, understand that those who offer life for a non-violent revolution based on Bhoodan Yajna, do not at all renounce their basic object of achieving radical social change. The Bhoodan movement seeks to wipe off the present party differences and establish what I call *lokniti* or discover the new dynamic of social action which is not a by-product of governmental policy". (*Ibid*, p. 292.)

Objection to Elections

Vinobaji objects not only to the existence of political parties but to elections as well:

"All of us should forget our differences of caste and religion, since they are not going to continue against the tide of time. Political parties and methods of elections bring the new differences which do not allow the servants of society to come together even for a good mission and serve the country which is weak and poor. Elections, a western import, has broken asunder every village and torn it into pieces. Country's strength is being lost in conflicts which are found even within a single party." (*Ibid*, p. 151.)

Any one who has carefully studied the results of the last two general elections will be impressed by the growing awareness of the Indian masses. The Congress party with its class rule, its selfish and corrupt administration is losing the confidence of the masses, who are moving to the left. In Kerala, the people have entrusted the Communist Party with the reins of administration. But Vinobaji sees in all this nothing but conflict and disunity of the village.

Suspecting political parties and all political activity, Vinobaji takes his stand against parliamentary government and rule by majority. He considers that the principle of the rule of majority has arisen out of an artificial political science. Describing the suffragette movement in Britain as the 'class struggle' of wives against husbands, he says:

The wives had to harass husbands by throwing eggs in parliament. In the end the husbands had to bow down to the wishes of the wives and agree to right to vote for them. We can never imagine such a conflict between fathers and mothers here. But the problem arose in England and the women had to fight. An artificial social science was born out of this imaginary conflict.

Political science came into existence to solve this conflict. It lays down that everything should be decided by majority. It started counting votes. If there are 51 votes in favour and 49 votes in opposition, then the former must have an overriding voice. I have also noted that in a murder case, an accused was hanged though out of the five judges two considered him to be innocent and only three considered him to be guilty. The majority verdict was carried out. In this way the policy of running the administration by majority vote and subordinating the minority to the vote of the majority arose out of this conception.... We have borrowed this conception of the rule of the majority from the British who ruled over our country. I do not say that we should not borrow good things from the West. But I think this wisdom of majority rule which we have taken from the West is not conducive to our interests. (*Sarvodayache Adhar*, Marathi, p. 14).

Elections are a western product; majority rule is a western concept unsuitable to India—such is the outlook of the leader of Sarvodaya. His criticism has little in common with Marxist criticism of *bourgeois* democracy—its formal character and limitations. Had Vinobaji taken note of the existence of classes he would have found that under the present conditions, it is a minority class that dominates the working majority of the toiling people. He would have found that in a capitalist society with means of production concentrated in the hands of a few people, majority rule remains formal while the exploiting minority continues to rule in reality. Instead of grasping these important truths, he objects to the very principle of majority rule as according to him it creates a conflict between majority and minority. Parliamentary system and elections are outright condemned in the name of social harmony between majority and minority.

What is Vinobaji's substitute for the rule of the majority?

We used to have a way out of the situation. We used to say the five *panchas* speak with the voice of the God. According to us there must be unanimity among the *panchas*. The rule of unanimity was the guiding rule for all administrative decisions. But now the new social science says that majority decisions must be given full sanctity.... It is this that has set aflame the world. (*Ibid*, pp. 16-17.)

In the ideal society of Vinobaji also decisions will be taken not by counting of hands but with the unanimous consent of all. Sometimes there may be sharp differences over questions of social welfare and well being—on such occasions a decision will be postponed in spite of the importance of the subject.

Compare the following written by Engels about Bakunin:

Now as the International, according to Bakunin, was not formed for political struggle but in order that it may at once replace the old state organisation as soon as social liquidation takes place, it follows that it must come as near as possible to the Bakuninist ideal of the society of the future. In this society there will, above all, be no authority, for authority—state—is an absolute evil. (Indeed, how these people propose to run a factory, operate a railway or steer a ship without having in the last resort one deciding will, without single management, they, of course, do not tell us.) The authority of the majority over the minority also ceases. Every individual and every community is autonomous; but as to how a society, even of only two people, is possible unless each gives up some of his autonomy, Bakunin again maintains silence. (*Marx-Engels Selected Works*, Vol. II, Moscow, p. 424.)

In the name of unanimity, a minority is to be given a veto over all social decisions—such is the conclusion of Sarvodayaite fear of majority rule. From where does this fear of majority come? It expresses an extreme individualist outlook which demands an end of all social restrictions in the name of individual freedom.

It will thus be seen that Vinobaji's outlook on state, parliamentary system, elections and majority rule is unsuited to build a new social order. It is not the outlook of a revolutionary class but of an individual impatient of all social restrictions which are inevitable in social co-operation. It stands in sharp contrast with the Marxian outlook which makes a devastating and revolutionary criticism of the present parliamentary system, the limitations of election when all means of propaganda are in the hands of the ruling class, the limitations of majority rule under conditions of class domination. From this, however, it concludes that a state guranteeing the rights of the masses can come into existence only when the economic domination of the exploiting capitalist class is replaced by the common ownership of the means of production.

Decentralisation

Similar erroneous views are held by the Sarvodayaites on other important questions also. The present-day centralisation of political and economic power evokes a justified protest from them. Their ideal society of the future will be based on decentralisation of political and economic power. But they understand decentralisation in a wrong way. They mean thereby avoidance of large-scale industry—as far as possible, i.e., avoidance of further scientific progress and increased human productivity as far as possible. 'As far as possible, every primary unit will produce its own necessities. This will protect its independence. It is common experience that concentration of wealth and power follows centralisation of production consequent on the use of big machinery. The tendency to dominate and exploit others increases. That is why the new society proposed decentralisation .... It is possible to continually improve machinery under a system of decentralised production.'

It is obvious that the ideal society will be based on minimum exchange, small peasant production in the villages, minimum use of large-scale industry and of big machinery and maximum of self-sufficiency. This type of decentralisation will only impede the progress in human productivity and set an absolute limit to it at an early stage. Restriction on the use of big machinery and application of science to social production will condemn society to a low standard of life. Society cannot implement the principle of 'from each according to his capacity, to each according to his necessity' unless labour productivity rises tremendously and there is plenty of everything to satisfy all the wants of the people. This cannot be had by artificially prohibiting the use of big machinery and large-scale industry. Small peasant individual production will prove ruinous to the declared objective of 'each according to his necessity'. Marxists have known these truths for more than a century and have tried to correct all those who ignored them.

Mental and Manual Labour

Because of this Sarvodayaites will be able to realise another cherished objective of theirs—the abolition of differences between manual and intellectual work. The condemnation of vast masses to mere mechanical and manual labour, and the monopoly of all intellectual activity by a handful is one of the evils of capitalist society—in fact of all societies based on the class rule of exploiters. Under a new social order, this evil must disappear. The Sarvodayaites, however, believe that the difference between intellectual and manual work will disappear if all do some kind of manual labour. The fact is that the difference will disappear only when productive work is shared by all and social productivity increases tremendously leading to considerable reduction in hours of work, giving the large mass of producers sufficient leisure to occupy themselves with intellectual activity.

So long as the major part of society spends the greater part of the day in raising the material means of livelihood, it cannot busy itself with intellectual activity and the difference between intellectual and manual work will not disappear. This will be the case under the new Sarvodaya Samaj because it will restrict the application of large-scale industry and big machinery to productive activity and thereby render it impossible to reduce the working day to any appreciable extent.

A higher standard of living, a higher cultural life accompained by reduction of the working day and spare time for intellectual activity became the basis of abolition of all difference between manual and intellectual work. This is rendered possible because no restriction is placed on the application of science to production.

The old mode of production must, therefore, be revolutionised from top to bottom and in particular, the former division of labour must disappear. Its place must be taken by an organisation of production in which, on the one hand, no individual can put on to other person his share in productive labour, this natural condition of human existence; and in which on the other hand, productive labour, instead of being a means to the subjection of men, will become a means to their emancipation, by giving each individual the opportunity to develop and exercise all his faculties, physical and mental, in all directions; in which, therefore, productive labour will become a pleasure instead of a burden.

Today this is no longer a phantasy, no longer a pious wish. With the present development of the productive forces, the increase in production which will follow from the very fact of the socialisation of the productive forces together with the abolition of the barrier and disturbances, of the waste of production and the means of production, resulting from the capitalist mode of production, will suffice, with everybody doing his share of work, to reduce the time required for labour to a point which measured by our present conception will be small indeed. (*Anti-Duhring*, p. 438.)

Two conditions are essential to abolish the difference between intellectual and manual labour. First, everyone must share productive work; secondly, there must be tremendous increase in productivity leading to reduction of working day, so that productive labour ceases to be a burden and sufficient leisure is left for all to pursue intellectual activity. The Sarvodayaites take note of only the first condition; they neglect the second. In fact their very conception of decentralisation which restricts large-scale industry will prevent them from realising the second condition.

Large-scale Industry

The Sarvodaya demand for ending the present concentration of economic power is perfectly correct and justified. But unfortunately they identify concentration of economic power with large-scale industry. Firstly, it is not the size of the industrial unit that leads to concentration but private ownership of big units that is responsible for it. The socialisation of means of production will end this concentration once and for all. Secondly, under capitalism, private-owned large-scale industry gets concentrated in big cities and towns. The cities monopolise technical and scientific advance while the countryside remains backward, leading to the well-known antagonism between town and country.

This concentration of economic activity in the cities is both harmful and unnecessary. No equitable social order is possible without abolishing it. There will be no quarrel with the Sarvodayaites if by decentralisation they only mean the abolition of the present antagonism between the town and the country. It presupposes the most equal distribution possible of modern industry over the country; not the maximum restriction of large-scale industry. But they wrongly identify large-scale industry with centralisation and instead of demanding dispersal of industry over the countryside to break the centralisation in towns, they demand restriction of large-scale industry as much as possible. Their plan will perpetuate backwardness in rural areas and veto further increase in labour productivity both in towns and the countryside. The correct way to ensure decentralisation is to socialise the means of production and disperse advanced technique and industry all over the country so as to end the economic monopoly of the town.

Linguistic States

Apart from these erroneous conceptions concerning the ideal order, on important political questions of the day also Vinobaji often takes a stand hardly distinguishable from that of the Congress government. One of the most outstanding issues of recent times was the demand for linguistic

States and government attempt to suppress the popular movement in Maharashtra and Gujarat. He had the following to say in this connection:

People of the country have today compartmentalised themselves into the people of particular provinces, some magniloquently calling themselves Andhraites, some Kanarese and still some others as Bengalis, etc. etc...Those who transcended the heights of humanity have now reduced to believing to be something short of and separate and distinct from Bharatiya—the Indians ! Surely, we are presently witnessing a farce when, on the publication of the States Reorganisation Committee's Report, the people of one province have been dancing with joy while those of the other are doomed into dejected moods. (*Vinoba and His Mission*, p. 148.)

How is it that Vinobaji with his large-heartedness could not see that great injustice was done to the people of Gujarat and Maharashtra when only they were denied a linguistic State of their own ?

In the course of the agitation for linguistic State in Bombay, the Congress government resorted to brutal firings and killed more than a hundred innocent people.. One expected Vinobaji with his profound belief in non-violence and truth, with his great sympathy for the *daridra narayan*, to voice his protest against the wanton killings, at least to insist on judicial inquiry. Instead, he said something which gave a complete alibi to the Congress government :

I am very sad over the recent disturbances in the country as a result of the proposals of the reorganisation of States....During the last five or seven years, the police have fired a number of times. In some cases, no inquiries were held. I do not want to say whether firing is advisable or not. I do not want to say that firing should not be treated as something common or natural. If there is violence on the part of the people, the government also resorts to violence. Both sides believe in ' minor violence '. (*Ibid*, p. 164.)

It seems to be an unwritten axiom with him not to embarrass the Congress government by outspoken comment on its methods and policies. It is obvious that he cannot agree with them.

Private and Public Sectors

Writing about private and public sector, he says :

The government tells us that we should organise on socialist pattern and for that the sphere of private sector should be reduced and of the public sector widened. I do not quite understand the proposition of a conflict between the two sectors. If anybody asks me whether the work of fingers is more valuable than that of the hand, what reply can I give him ? As though the hand represents the public sector and the fingers the private sector ! Well, their work is the same. Then where is the difference and how has it come ? Should the business community apply its time and talent for the benefit of society, private business becomes public as well. (*Ibid*, p. 280.)

And again :

Our ancients have had great trust in the businessmen. They have great powers and shall put them into use to save the world. They should become mixed in it like sugar in milk .... In his (Gandhiji's) name I call upon the business people to come forward and save the world. They know what *vaishya dharma* is; if only they combine their love and simple life with organising ability for social good, the government will get freed from all its fears. (*Ibid*, p. 280.)

Sometimes Vinobaji hits out with unusual candour against the same elements : " We consider stealing to be a crime, but connive at those who encourage this anti-social activity by amassing heaps of money. We condemn the thieves to rot in a prison house but let their creators roam about in complete freedom. They even occupy seats of honour and respectability. Is this justice ? " (*Ibid*, p. 274.)

Then again :

The highly expensive administration and other departments of the government are known as ' services '. And there are services galore : civil service, medical service, educational service. The officials of the civil service are paid four figure salaries, while their masters, the poor of the country whom they profess to serve have to live on a pittance of annas eight a day. It is a tragic paradox that those who earn lakhs are called servants, while those who produce food for the nation are regarded as self-seekers who work to further their own interest. What is one to say of these ' services ' ? If words are not to be deprived of their meaning, then this is nothing but cant and hypocrisy. (*Ibid*, p. 275.)

From time to time Vinobaji makes such passionate protests on behalf of the common man.

Despite his differences with the Communists, Vinobaji has friendly feeling for them. With his broad-mindedness and tolerance he tries to understand their viewpoint : ' I want to assure my Communist friends that I bear no ill-feeling towards them. On the other hand, my feelings are good. God made a mistake in not equipping the breast with a window to know the inside of our heart. Had there been one you would have found that I am full of love towards the Communists.' (*Ibid*, p. 239.) ' Some people say that the Communists are destructive. I don't think so. It is book of the great seer Marx that has converted innumerable people. Yet the Communists affirm that they have no faith in change of heart. It is here I differ from them. I tell those friends that you are a living instance of heart-conversion. ' (*Ibid*, p. 189.)

' I have got quite a few friends among the Communists. I have got regard for them. They had their doubts about me in the beginning but now they have realised that I am striving for change of heart and that I am their friend. ' (*Sarvodayache Adhar*, p. 44.)

Conclusion

The discussion on Sarvodaya conducted in the pages of *New Age* has been very helpful in clarifying the issues. Our contributors have written on different aspects of Sarvodaya and examined its position in relation to Marxism. Some have dealt with the philosophical basis of Sarvodaya while others have discussed its methods and ideals. Some have seen too close a similarity between Marxism and Sarvodaya; while a few have perhaps paid a little less attention to its social origin. On the whole, however, our contributors have maintained a high level of discussion and have enabled our readers to increase their understanding of the Sarvodaya movement and philosophy.

In conclusion, we might say that the Sarvodaya philosophy and ideology of Vinoba Bhave is an amalgam of several elements forming part of Indian social existence. The land problem facing Indian society, plays an important role in the immediate practical activity of the Sarvodaya workers. Under the impact of advanced Communist thought, the Sarvodayaites are thinking of an ideal society without classes, without the state, a society, based on the principle ' from each according to his capacity, to each according to his necessity. ' They quote Engels and they want a society in which administration of men will be replaced by administration of things.

At the same time, they reject all political struggle on principle. In fact, they reject all struggle in the name of a new constructive satyagraha. Vinobaji's thoughts on parliament, majority rule, political parties do not conform to reality and cannot be described as contributing to the progress towards a new social order.

Ignoring class realities the Sarvodayaites concentrate only on propaganda to change the hearts of men. Their criticism of present society, their attack on private property in land and the injustices of the present order arise out of a sincere desire to do good to the people. Yet for remedying the evils they do not look to the future but look backwards, to small-scale production, to practical village self-sufficiency and thereby express their fear of science and large-scale industry.

Their understanding of the state and its disappearance is erroneous. They do not want to struggle against the state and yet they seek to eliminate it here and now. Rejecting the motive force of social change—the mass struggle—they have made their ideals and immediate aims unrealisable.

The practical results of the Bhoodan and Gramdan are already there to show how little they could achieve in spite of state patronage—or perhaps because of it.

They consider themselves to be the followers of Mahatma Gandhi. And yet they have rejected precisely, that heritage of the Mahatma which made him a leader of the people—political mass struggle. One sympathises with the honest band of selfless workers who are working with

Vinobaji. One has got great regard for the earnestness of purpose that dominates Vinobaji's activities. One sincerely hopes that through their activities they can bring some relief to the village population of our country. Their great ideals, however, will be unrealisable unless they change their outlook and lead the masses against existing inequality and injustice.

Once again Lenin's appraisal of Tolstoy has some relevance here:

His (Tolstoy's) unswerving repudiation of the private ownership of land conveys the mentality of the peasant masses at the historical moment when the old, medieval system of landownership, both the landlord estates and the official 'allotments' has definitely become an intolerable hindrance to the country's further development and when the old system of landownership must inevitably be thoroughly and ruthlessly shattered. His unceasing denunciation of capitalism, prompted by the most deep-felt sentiments and most passionate anger conveys all the horror felt by the patriarchal peasant, against whom a new, invisible and mysterious enemy was advancing from somewhere in town, or from somewhere abroad, smashing all the 'foundations' of rural life, bringing unprecedented ruin, poverty, death from starvation, degradation, prostitution and syphilis—all the evils of the 'epoch of primitive accumulation' intensified a hundred-fold by the transplanting to Russian soil the very latest methods of robbery devised by Mr. Coupon.

But at the same time, the ardent protestant, passionate denunciator and great critic revealed in his works a failure to understand the causes of the crisis and the means of escape from the crisis that was advancing on Russia such as is characteristic only of the patriarchal naive peasant and not of the European-educated writer. For him the struggle against the feudal and police state, against the monarchy, became the repudiation of politics, led to the doctrine of 'resist not evil', and resulted in complete divorcement from the revolutionary struggle of the masses in 1905-1907. He combined the struggle against the official church with the preaching of a new, purified religion, that is, a new, refined and more subtle poison for the oppressed masses. His repudiation of the private ownership and land led not to the concentration of the entire struggle on the real enemy, on landlordism and its political instrument of power; i.e., the monarchy, but to dreamy, vague and impotent longing. He combined denunciation of capitalism and the misery it caused the masses with utter apathy towards the world struggle for emancipation waged by the international socialist proletariat. (*Articles on Tolstoy*, pp. 18-20.)

SECTION XIV

RURAL SOCIETY IN TRANSITION

INTRODUCTION

THE PRESENT section is comprised of nine selections. They, in their totality, indicate some of the major trends of transformation in rural society. The trends may be briefly summarised as follows: (i) The rapid transformation of the agrarian society from the subsistance-based traditional society to a market-based, profit-oriented, commercialised agrarian sector of the total Indian society; (ii) the rapid introduction by the Government of modern urban techniques and devices to completely transform the existing loose, scattered and underdeveloped colonial agrarian economy into a well-knit compact one and its organic integration into the total national economy; (iii) attempts by the Government to cripple or eliminate some of the classes while at the same time strengthening or creating another group of classes in agrarian India and (iv) the emergence of a complex network of various associations and institutions within the agrarian society having close links with and being shaped by urban influences.

The crucial questions which emerge are: Whither Indian Rural Society? What are the basic trends of development within it? What social strata have been benefiting from the growing changes? What type of social structure, institutional matrix, associational web, leadership pattern, ideological currents and cultural developments have been taking place there?

The article in this section, by the author himself, draws attention to some of the salient features of this transition. Thirumalai's article indicates how family, caste and the institutional life of the village have been undergoing changes. Professor Mandelbaum points out how the attempts made by the Government of India adversely affect the lower strata of the agrarian society. Dr. Majumdar's article portrays how the old social stratification and spirit underlying it are in a fluid condition resulting into the growth of an atmosphere of intense tension in the agrarian areas. Prof. Gadgil's article pinpoints how the Government measures have failed to touch the core of the agrarian problem, namely the problem of the unit of agricultural production.

The papers by Profs. Gadgil and Daniel Thorner, indicate a significant unhealthy trend which deserves to be carefully investigated. This trend, if true, requires to be counteracted if the direction of development of rural society is to be a progressive one. Agricultural production in India today suffers from numerous maladies, the most outstanding of which are the uneconomic holding, sub-division and fragmentation of land, inefficient farming as a result of the miserably small unit of production, extensive class stratification, over-pressure on agriculture, lack of alternative occupation for the vast bulk of the population and defective property relations.

The Government's agrarian policy based on the postulates of a mixed economy which keeps the entire agrarian sector as private enterprise really cannot resolve any of these problems. This policy only aggravates the major contradictions of agrarian society, economic, political, social and cultural. It operates in a manner which strengthens the upper stratum to the disadvantage of the lower ones. It thereby creates a situation of greater and greater social tension and collision instead of higher and higher social harmonies and progressive growth of toiling sections of the rural community. Does not this policy require complete overhauling from its base upwards?

The articles by Dr. Yogindra Singh and Prof. Weiner and Kathleen Gough describe the new political leadership that is emerging in U.P. and West Bengal and Kerala. They reveal that political controls are increasingly being monopolised by the upper stratum of the agrarian society. This dominant section has been slowly fusing economic control, political power and cultural instruments for its own advantage. The other two articles by Professor Lucio Mendieta Nunez and by the author also indicate the direction in which Indian rural society has been moving during the present transition.

It is the author's modest suggestion that a more thorough, a more intensive and a more comprehensive study of the major features of transition which Indian rural society is experiencing has become urgent on a macro-Indian scale. Some of the abovementioned crucial questions have to be considered on an all-India basis if the real phase of the transition is to be understood. Burning problems like those of co-operative farms, private property in land, role of profit incentive and free market, impact of the Welfare State on the matrix of functionally planned private economic sector and the feasibility of the crucial, decisive and, above all, progressive transformation of the entire Indian economy along with its rural part require to be boldly confronted. It is the basic task of the sociologists to anwer the most fundamental historical question: Can an economically underdeveloped and predominantly agrarian country accomplish the historically necessary task of successfully growing into a highly advanced industrialized country through the instrumentality of a Plan which is based on the postulates of private property, profit incentive and the principle of mixed economy? Can capitalism resolve the agrarian problem in an underdeveloped country? (*Author.*)

1

TRENDS IN RURAL CHANGE*

S. THIRUMALAI

THE MAIN changes are noticed in the caste, the joint family system and village administration through *Panchayats* which together formed the base of the old social edifice. The rise of internal markets, assisted by the extension of railways and roads, and the expansion in foreign trade of agricultural commodities transformed the old self-sufficient economy of the village based on barter into a market economy, based on cash. With the gradual urbanisation of the village, the rigidity of the division of labour among the community softened. The old caste barriers to economic mobility have been slowly giving way. The expansion of towns, the diversification of employment opportunities in trade and services and the glamour and attractions of city life have created a steady drift towards the city. This has been responsible for loosening the hold of the joint family system on the members. There has also been continuous drain on the intelligentsia among the rural population. The two World Wars drew from the village population into military service hundreds of thousands who imbibed a new outlook on life. After their return from the distant theatres of war they have added a new ferment to the social urges of the rural community, already seething with discontent under the pressure of poverty. The advent of freedom with a new promise and hope, the acceleration of economic and social reform measures, resulting in the abolition of large landed estates and the protection of the rights of the tenants and labourers, the political enfranchisement of the vast population under adult suffrage, have all widened the horizon of economic standards in the village and have further complicated the problems of adjustment and of devising a new social order for the villages.

SOCIAL CUSTOMS

The significant among the factors of change in the social order have been the rise in the age of marriage, the improved status of women, the lesser vogue of caste despotism and of *purdah*, the removal of the disabilities of sections of population under caste hierarchy and in general, the realignment of family relations. But it must however be said that while glimpses of change in outlook are noticed among the educated in the village community, in respect of social disabilities, the old order is kept intact in the observances of the privileges. Untouchability, access to

*Reproduced from *Post-War Agricultural Problems and Policies in India*, by S. Thirumalai, pp. 224-226.

places of public convenience as wells, etc., and public worship were the three crucial barriers and all the three have given way under legislative compulsion and educative propaganda. The inner change of heart, which is the result of enlightened education, is yet far from achievement. In one respect no change is visible. The tanner and sweeper still live on the outermost fringe of the village, often on opposite sides, though the *Brahmin* is losing his halo and the untouchable, the stigma. The two tests of free association in a modern society are food and marriage. In the village, they are still as strong a barrier as they were and education has done nothing to weaken them. The cow is more the object of veneration, than a problem in economic improvement.

Standard of Living

In objective terms a standard of living consists of three main elements: (1) the level of consumption or the composition of goods and services of a specific quantity and quality consumed by an individual, family or group within a given period; (2) social services and free services, particularly those which relate to health, education and recreation, and (3) working conditions which affect not only the worker's health and earning capacity but also the size and regularity of his income. As a dynamic concept, it implies in the first place the eradication of poverty among the rural community and in the second, improving the content of living of all categories of workers with regard to consumption, social and free services and conditions of work.

Examined on the basis of the above terms, it would be difficult to answer the question whether there has been an improvement in the standard of living of the rural community. While the view is often held that the rise in prices during the war period ushered in a period of prosperity, evidence is lacking as to the category of the population which was actually benefited and the extent of increase in prosperity. While a relative improvement in the standard of living of the strata of economic landholders may be accepted, the available data indicate that there has been a deterioration in the other sections of the agricultural population who form the majority.

2

SOCIAL ORGANIZATION AND PLANNED CULTURE CHANGE IN INDIA*

DAVID G. MANDELBAUM

THE LARGE-SCALE development plans which are now under way in India are, in the main plans for technological and economic change. As these plans become realised, they cannot but have effect on social organization and be affected by it. Such reciprocal influence is now being felt in various spheres of Indian society. Certain broad trends of this interaction can be stated, as they are seen in the joint family, in caste structure, in village organization and in relation between villagers and government.

The joint family has long been the common form of family organization in India, sanctified in scripture and sanctioned in secular law. It consists typically of a set of men, related as fathers and sons, or brothers, together with their wives and children. The several nuclear families thus grouped together form a single unit of consumers and often also a single producing unit. The property of all is held in common under the trusteeship of the senior male; every male child is entitled to a share of the joint family property. All in the joint family are fed from a single kitchen and receive money from the family purse. Among cultivators, all in the joint family work together for the family's crop.

Formation and fission go on now as they have before but the regular tendency is toward smaller joint families. Many factors are involved in this, among them the increased chances for a man to earn a living as an individual rather than as one of a joint family team, and the decreased willingness to be subservient to the head of the family or to pool both effort and income. An added impetus toward splitting the larger joint families has come about in those areas where land reform measures have been introduced.

A common feature of these measures is to set a limit to the amount of land which any family may own. Hence in these circumstances the men of a large joint family hasten to split up into nuclear families when such reform measures are brought about lest they be restricted to a holding uneconomical for a large family group. With formal separation there tends to be separation in fact also, at least in so far as the joint family is a producing unit. But in many cases the larger family group is a much more efficient producing unit than is the small family group.

---

* Reproduced from *India's Villages*, A collection of articles originally published by the *Economic Weekly*, Bombay, pp. 13-14.

This is especially true where continuous work is required, as where ripening crops must be watched against animal and human predators and when field labour must be quickly mobilized and intensively worked, as at harvest.The larger joint family is also more apt than the smaller to be able to raise the capital necessary for implements and animals. Thus one rather unforeseen, though by no means inevitable, consequence of land reform may be a hastening of the push toward smaller families with some consequent decline in agricultural efficiency.

Caste structure has close ties with village economics. In the classical system of relations among castes in a village, the *jajmani* system, the various non-cultivating castes provided specialised services for the cultivators and received foodstuffs in return. The economic interdependence is strictly regulated by social and religious patterns which both keep the caste groups segregated in certain respects and require communication and interchange in other respects. Caste ranking and economic status were, and for many villages still are, closely linked. Caste rank is particularly manifest through ritual symbols: a group which was economically well off could acquire ritual hallmark to raise its relative position in the hierarchy.

The results of the development programmes of the last century in the fields of transportation and communication, in the spread of Western education, in the frequent switch from subsistence crops to cash crops, have all had consequences on village caste relations. But the criteria of ritual rank are not greatly changed—the eating of meat and the performance of menial services are still stigmas of lower rank—and ritual rank remains a main concern in the village. While there may be some relaxation of the taboos on inter-dining among castes there is no easing of the prohibition of intermarriage.

As the newer development programmes take effect there often is some levelling of economic differences among the villagers. The less high castes, newly advantaged, jockey for higher ritual rank and may attempt to use their new political franchise to gain both economic and ritual prerogatives for their caste.

One exception to the levelling effect of the newer development programmes must be noted. The lowest caste, those who are mainly landless labourers, often gain nothing at all from the irrigation projects and the redistribution of land. They have nothing to begin with, nothing which can be improved, no means of getting an economic start and so they remain economically as well as socially disadvantaged. The gap between them and the other villagers frequently widens rather than diminishes on account of development projects.

The changing nature of caste has effect on village social organization and on agricultural output. The social and economic systems were both relatively stable over many centuries partly because they reinforced each other. Now that both are being modified though still closely connected, changes in one may accelerate changes in the otner. Thus the *jajmani* system of traditional, personal, exchange relations is being replaced by contractual, impersonal, pecuniary relations. Many cultivators who could summon sudden aid if quickly needed from among their traditional associates of other castes now can hire labour only if they have the cash. This process is a familar one and has been going on in India for a century or more. But in recent years the full effect of the change is being widely felt.

As the rights and obligations of one village caste to another tend to lapse, so does the whole village drift away from the ceremonial order within which these reciprocal patterns were organized and reinforced. The traditional caste system provides for a division of labour, the traditional ceremonial order stipulates how and when the various divisions co-operate and are rewarded. With the loosening of the system of economic cooperation under religious auspices there is not usually available as effective a plan of village co-operation under purely economic or political auspices, and agricultural output may decline for this reason.

Governmental agencies, of both the central and the state administrations, have attempted to encourage the growth of a new social organization in the village which would be able to cope with modern problems and could make the transition from the old order to some new procedure. Legislation has been passed in some provinces and funds provided to enable village councils, *panchayats*, to be formed and to function. In name, these are the same as the traditional councils which have for centuries adjudicated disputes among villagers. In manner of composition, in function, they are very different. The members of the new *panchayat* must be elected, must electioneer; in the old, they were accorded place by universal respect and could hardly keep that respect if they pressed their claims. The old councils were arbitrary, conserving agencies whose prime function was to smooth over or settle village friction. The new *panchayats* are supposed to be innovating, organizing bodies working for changes rather than conserving solidarity.

Where they have been installed, the new *panchayats* seem generally to be off to a shaky start. There is some tendency for them to become the battle-ground of village factionalism. Factionalism has long been a frequent disrupter of joint village action. The traditional ceremonial order provides opportunities for the healing of factional breaks by mandatory co-operation towards common ceremonial goals. With the passing of the old ceremonial order, there is not the same rejoining of those whom factional disputes have rent asunder. And village elections may become little more than ways of crystallizing each opposing and non-co-operating faction. In some villages the new *panchayat* is less a forum for factionalism than it is an empty form set up for the satisfaction of visiting officials. In such villages the older *panchayat* continues to function much as it has before.

But as a social form, it is not felt adequate by many villagers to deal with the new economic and technological influences—the procuring of irrigation water or of fertilisers, for example—and these influences reach even to relatively remote villages. Hence there is widely in Indian villages today a process of social change from the traditional forms and orders to some other forms. The newer forms may not be those proposed by legislators and planners but they are also not, it seems probable, a mere recasting of the older social system.

3

FLUIDITY OF STATUS STRUCTURE IN INDIA*

D. N. Majumdar

We have made sweeping generalisations regarding rural life and its problems. We have depicted village life as if the pattern was similar in all parts of the country. We have ignored the facts of alien invasions, different governments, varying religions and multiple levels of culture, as if they had little or no effect on our rural life. It is true that all parts of the country were not equally touched by social upheavals, invasions or conquests, but today we are becoming more and more aware of specific differences in different parts of the country. We know, however, the basic similarities in all villages and the personalities of villages as well. We know the common problems, and we also know the rough and ready prescriptions for our rural ills. What is needed in rural studies, today, is the shaping of effective scientific techniques of rural analysis to understand the problems of rural life in their wider contexts.

The status structure of our villages is in a fluid state. While still clinging to the traditional ways of eking out an income, the villager is today experiencing the impact of technology and competitive economy. Land is not in abundance, while the size of the family is on the increase. The artisan castes, no longer can secure a minimum level of living, out of their traditional occupation in the village and from the *jajmans* whom they still cater to. They either migrate to centres of greater opportunities, or live a precarious existence. More people today are in the grip of the money-lender than ever before and co-operative societies cannot as yet size up the want and poverty of the villages. The channels of rural finance have changed their course. The abolition of the *zamindari* has dimmed the halo around the heads of the high caste men. They are nervous about losing their rights—which they have enjoyed from time immemorial—and they are not prepared to give in without a struggle. Fighting tooth and nail they are trying to maintain their hold on the village. If they have lost some rights, they still have wealth, and that means power. Why should they not use their wealth in new ways to strengthen their position of importance? So that many of them have adopted money-lending as their profession, which till now was the much-maligned monopoly of the village-Bania. The breakdown of the status relations has deprived the artisan elements of the village of concessions in kind which helped now and then to relieve their chronic distress. They still yoke themselves to the village economy but they have been caught in deep furrows.

---

* Reproduced from *Indian Rural Profiles*, Ed. by D. N. Majumdar, Pp. V-VII.

The relationship of status factors to the acceptance of innovations in dress, food and farm practices is important in the context of social change. A number of investigations carried out in various parts of the world on farm practices, for example, 'have high-lighted farm-ownership, education, income, size of the farm and social participation as being associated with the adoption of improved farm practices.' Contacts with urban centres, and improved communications are helping adoption of innovations. Leaders in community affairs are not useful in dissemination of new farm practices. 'On the other hand innovators are not likely to be leaders in community affairs.' This is an area of study that must be given due consideration in planning and action research.

We are apt to isolate village leadership in its traditional setting. In the Indian villages of the past, leaders were born, but now in the new set-up it is not so. The frequency of leadership from sections or castes other than the dominant one, requires evaluation. Goods, today, are not necessarily delivered through the traditional leaders. The new leaders may not even be from the status groups, neither have they jumped into the scene by the spin of the coin. The social awareness of the people is the medium which fashions new leadership.

We have simplified the social structure of our country by equating it with the magic word 'caste'. Caste is no doubt a complex structure, but it is also a dynamic one. Three significant periods in caste history are worth mentioning. Caste as it was in the time of Manu, a fluid structure, flexible and mobile; vertical as well as horizontal features characterised caste as is understood in the context of *anuloma* and *pratiloma* marriages, i.e., marriages prescribed and those forbidden. This was the formulative period of the caste constitution. Caste in the medieval period became rigid and stereotyped. The rigidity encouraged fission, but circumscribed the chances of fusion. The challenge of the rigid caste system was met by religious revivalism in which sectarian and other types of castes emerged to accommodate deviants and aspirants after social status. A critical evaluation of the caste structure at this period would show the caste system as a cross between 'feudalism' and, the 'schism of the soul' to use a Toynbean phrase. Today caste-structure is fighting a battle of survival, as it were, and is mobilising forces and factors, that were once dormant or unintegrated. The saving factors are the not-too-clear lines of demarcation among the castes, between the higher and intermediate and between the latter and lower castes. The intermediate castes most of whom are artisans, usually bridge the disparities between the two ends of the caste ladder. The new trend in caste dynamics today, is a concerted move on the part of the backward and socially non-privileged castes to rearrange themselves on a horizontal plane instead of pressing their claims for accommodation in the hierarchical ladder. The hitherto voiceless castes are becoming articulate, even vocal, and are not prepared to accept the status differentials. The new orientation in the attitude of the non-privileged castes has already made social distance ineffective in many ways. If the trend continues, and it is likely to continue, it certainly augurs well for the future of the Indian caste structure.

4

ORGANISATION OF AGRICULTURAL PRODUCTION*

D. R. GADGIL

THE SUBJECT I have chosen for the address is usually discussed under the broad heading land reform or agrarian reform. There are many aspects of agrarian reform and I shall deal only with what I consider to be the core of agrarian reform in India, namely, organisation of agricultural production with particular reference to the size and structure of the unit of agricultural production.

The main constituents of the programme of agrarian or land reform currently undertaken by the State in India are classified as follows in the Progress Report for 1953-54 of the Five-Year Plan:—

(1) The abolition of intermediaries;

(2) Tenancy reforms designed:—

   (a) To scale down rents to 1/4th or 1/5th of the produce;

   (b) To give tenants permanent rights subject to the landlord's right to resume a minimum holding for his personal cultivation within a limited time;

   (c) To enable tenants (subject to the landlord's right of resumption for personal cultivation) to acquire ownership of their lands, on payment of moderate compensation to the landlord spread over a period of years;

(3) Fixing of ceilings on holdings;

(4) Re-organisation of agriculture including the consolidation of holdings, the prevention of fragmentation and the development of co-operative village management and co-operative farming.

Many of the items included in the above have been subjects of attention and activity on the part of governments for many decades past. However, a number of important elements are of recent introduction and the programme has begun to look like an integrated attempt only within the last few years. An important feature which has received emphasis only since the attainment of Independence is the abolition of intermediaries, popularly regarded as equivalent to the abolition of zamindari.

While emphasising the primary importance of the abolition of zamindari it is necessary to remember that, in India, it affects, in the main,

* Presidential Address, Fifteenth Annual Conference, the Indian Society of Agricultural Economics, Bombay.

the distribution of the total agricultural product and not the size and organisation of the unit of agricultural production.

This is because, in the first instance, the abolition of intermediaries does not mean the break-up of large farms or farming estates or the redistribution of land and secondly because, even if this had been a part of the programme, there are, in fact, with the exception of a small number of regions, no large farming estates in India. The very description of the reform as abolition of intermediaries, emphasises this aspect of the redistribution of the product and reduction of the burden on the actual cultivator. It is conceived of essentially as establishing, as far as possible, a direct relation between the actual tiller of the soil and the State.

Tenancy reform or tenancy legislation has a much wider sphere of operation than legislation for the abolition of intermediaries.

Tenancy reform also, it will be obvious, does not affect the size and shape of the agricultural holding. It brings about, in the main, a redistribution of the total produce in favour of the tenant and also gives him a sense of security regarding the future which should react favourably on the economic and technical operation of the tenant cultivator. However, there is one important difference between tenancy reform and the abolition of intermediaries. The latter is, for the most part, a once-for-all operation; the former, on the other hand, has not only continuous effect but has further to adapt itself constantly to a changing situation. In consequence though tenancy legislation may not operate directly on the unit of agricultural production, the framing of tenancy legislation is always influenced by total land policy including policy relating to the size and structure of the unit of agricultural production. In India, tenancy legislation has to concern itself with problems such as those of sub-letting or of the alienation, transfer or inheritance of land; and all of these have relation with objectives of policy relating to the unit of agricultural production.

The fixing of ceilings on holdings is likely to affect the size of the unit of agricultural production much more directly than either the abolition of intermediaries or tenancy reform. Before proceeding further I may note that the omission to distinguish clearly between the ownership holdings and the cultivating holdings leads often to a confusion in thinking and exposition of the subject of land reform in India.

The immediate effect of the adoption of a ceiling for the future, on size of the production unit would, on the other hand, be negligible, except to the extent that it would encourage actual or notional division of existing large holdings among family members so as not to be affected early by the operation of the legislation. The long-term effects are problematical and would depend on the extent to which the existing or future situation otherwise favoured the formation of very large holdings.

Even the comparatively large estate of Kashmir and Telengana do not or did not contain elements of direct cultivation large enough for redistribution to effect sensibly the problem of the small peasant holding, in even restricted areas. Elsewhere the contrasts are much less glaring. The concept of the ceiling, if it is to be used in India must, therefore, be different in content and operation from that in countries with large landlord estates. plantations or latifundia.

The concept of the economic holding or a minimum holding called by any name, like the concept of the ceiling, can form the basis of an immediate operation of reorganisation or can be confined to setting a limit to future transactions. In the latter alternative it may act as an effective means of preventing a worsening of the existing situation and may partly even help to improve it gradually in the future. These effects will, however, become apparent only slowly over a series of years and a limit for the future cannot help towards reorganisation, if the existing situation in itself is extremely unsatisfactory. A minimum holding or a floor has not been used in any State in India yet for bringing about immediate reorganisation of production units in lands included in units below the minimum size.

Consolidation as practised in India affects powerfully the internal organisation of a holding, though not usually its total size. The process of consolidation may lead to some saving in the land surface used for such purposes as boundaries or roads and may thus enable formation of a pool of land for specific common purposes. But the saving effected in this way is not likely to yield substantial acreage for distribution among existing holders. Co-operative farming or co-operative village management are yet chiefly in the stage of thought. What little action has been taken is experimental and nowhere has any legislation been formulated or contemplated which bases itself on the formation of co-operative farming units for at least a part of state policy relating to land management.

Legislation on land reform is essentially a matter for governments of States. Therefore, the programme is usually framed in the context of particular problems of each State. The activity of the National Planning Commission affords the chief occasion and instrument for integrating policies of different State Governments and for formulating a common Indian policy. Considerable importance, therefore, attaches to the views regarding land policy contained in the First Five-Year Plan. It is difficult to piece together in a consistent whole the ideas contained in the chapter on Land Policy of the Plan. The problems of the policy are divided into two aspects: Land Management and Land Reform. It is evidently considered that there is some conflict between the two; for, it is said that " Land Policy should include both elements but should maintain a balance between the two."

The suggested land reform policy is again not uniform; it is evidently to change with size of land owning. The most important result is that the tenants of small and middle owners are recommended much less protection than the tenants of large owners. As middle owners are defined as owners of land upto three times the family holding the field of tenancy protection is thus seriously narrowed. The main reason given for the maintenance of a large class of tenants-at-will in this way is that otherwise movement of people from agriculture and rural areas into other occupations and towns may be seriously checked. It is fortunate that most State Governments have paid little attention to this recommendation in their legislative programme.

In relation to the landless worker the main concrete reference is to the Bhoodan movement. " It offers the landless worker an opportunity not otherwise open to him. " This can be only interpreted as meaning that the State itself considers it neither necessary nor possible to do anything for him. It is added that the problem of the landless worker must be considered in terms of institutional changes which would create conditions of equality for all sections of the population. The essence of these changes is described as a system of co-operative village management. Co-operative village management is referred to in the Plan in other context also. For example, after having formulated the important and unexceptionable proposition that " the basic condition for increase in agricultural production is increase in the unit of management of land" this also is said to be possible only through co-operative management at the village level. With regard to the small and the middle farmers again it is recommended that they should be encouraged and assisted to develop their production and organise their activities on co-operative basis. With this emphasis on co-operation it would be expected, that co-operative organisation or co-operative village management would be described in specific detail and a programme sketched out for establishing it. The following extract summarises the ideas of the Planning Commission on co-operative village management.

" Broadly speaking, however, we envisage that the village panchayat should become the agency both for land reform and for land management in the village. In the first place it should be the body concerned with the management of land taken over from substantial owners, and also of village waste lands. The leasing of lands by small and middle owners should also be done through the panchayat and not directly. In this way the village panchayat may be able to provide cultivating holdings of economic size, at any rate for landless cultivators. The exercise of these functions would naturally lead on to the wider conception of the co-operative management of the entire land of the village and the undertaking of activities for creating non-agricultural employment in the village."

It is not necessary to comment on the above except to note that it does not deal with the problem in the comprehensive manner that might have been expected, that it is over-optimistic and also that the working model presented is obviously unsuitable and inadequate in most respects. Moreover, no concrete programme is provided for progress in the direction of co-operative village management even according to ideas contained in the Plan, beyond the Rs. 50 lakhs provided for study, training and experimentation. It would not be unfair in the circumstances, to suggest that the Plan proposes little of importance in relation to land management and that we have at present no effective programme in contemplation for dealing with what the Planning Commission itself recognises as the basic problem, viz., that of " the increase in the unit of management of land ".

Not only is the subject treated unsatisfactorily in the Plan but also the subsequent activities of the Planning Commission and the Central Government do not indicate that it is currently held in importance or receives any special attention.

The Community Projects are supposed to be the special field of the Planning Commission and great reliance is placed on them in relation to agricultural development in the future. Not only do these projects pay no attention to land reform or land distribution but even experimentation in relation to land management appears to find no place in them. The complete absence of any attention to it in the programme of community projects is evidenced by its not having been necessary to devote any attention to the subject in the Evaluation Report on the first year's working of these projects. And the later report of the Evaluation Organization, " Community Projects—First Reactions " contains enough evidence to show how the project authorities completely ignore land management and land reform problems. In regard to co-operative organizations we have the following comment in the Evaluation Report. " While in the very initial stages of the formulation of community plans this aspect of mutual dependence between community development and co-operative organization was not so explicitly stated, during the course of the year increasing emphasis was placed by the Community Projects Administration on promotion of cooperative organizations." (p. 39.) The co-operatives to which increasing attention is reported are still the credit, purchase and sale and other organizations and not experiments in increasing scales of land management. The putting forward more recently of agricultural extension as the panacea for all rural ills is, perhaps, a reflection of the same attitude. It appears to be considered by the Planning Commission, as by many foreign experts, that all that is required to increase agricultural production in India adequately is to arouse enthusiasm and to transfer techniques. The problem as to whether conditions in the field are such as to favour generation of enthusiasm and the acquisition and continued practice of new techniques does not evidently need prior consideration. Finally, it is reported that in some States, the Central Government, presumably acting through the Planning Commission, was responsible for persuading Governments to modify their original ideas regarding immediate operation of a ceiling on holdings. All in all, one gathers the impression that while in its theoretic formulation the Planning Commission may recognize the existence of the problem of land management it is not ready to give this recognition any immediate or concrete form.

As indicated above, the Planning Commission appears content to operate with the existing unit of agricultural production and does not propose to change in any radical manner the organization of land management and operation. The Congress Agrarian Reforms Committee also formulates its actual programme very largely in terms of the peasant farm and it does not appear to consider that a programme of reorganization involving large numbers of families and a considerable land surface is insistently called for. The experts appear to talk almost exclusively of the peasant unit and their ideas of land reform are confined mostly to abolition of intermediaries and dealing with large estates. In the circumstances, it becomes necessary to examine existing conditions carefully, especially with a view to throwing light on the strength and efficiency of the independent peasant farm as the unit of land management and agricultural production.

It is generally known that the size of the large bulk of farms in India is very small and that numbers of them cannot be called family farms in any valid sense of that term. However, no attempt is usually made to indicate with figures the dimensions of the problem. I shall, therefore, note certain salient features of the situation very briefly. My concern is with the unit of land management, the cultivated holding, and data relating to ownership of land are not relevant to my purpose. The data required are those relating to size, scale of operations and of investment, receipts and employment, etc., from farming, of the independent farming units.

According to the Survey a little over half of the cultivators reported a value of gross produce of farm business lower than Rs. 400 for the year.

This then is a useful starting point of the description, that half or more of the farm units, i.e., independent units of land management in India may have a gross produce of farm less than Rs. 600 a year. The next step is to assess the relative importance of farming activity to the farm family. In the total number of cultivators reporting less than Rs. 400 of value of gross produce during the year two divisions were made representing those with a value of gross produce below Rs. 200 and those with a value of gross produce between Rs. 200 and Rs. 400. The former formed slightly more than 29 per cent of the total cultivators and the latter group 21 per cent. Those reporting value of gross produce less than Rs. 200 reported total farm expenses which exceeded their value of gross produce and those in the latter class reported total farm expenses that were on an average only about Rs. 60 less than the average value of gross produce. The average reported cash receipts from sale of crops and fodder in the two classes were about Rs. 20 and Rs. 70 respectively and both classes reported cash farm expenses that were more than Rs. 50 on an average than the average cash receipts from sale of crops and fodder. Making all allowances for errors in reporting, etc., it is clear that the cultivators included in these groups earn little, if any, net cash income through their farming activity and the main advantage derived by them from farming is some contribution in kind to family living.

In the main, however, cultivators in the lower strata have much lower values of gross produce than those in the upper.

Of the total borrowings of even the middle four deciles more than half represented borrowing for family expenditure items; for the last three deciles the corresponding proportion was almost 60 per cent. The capacity of the average cultivating family to undertake capital expenditure was obviously extremely limited. The average expenditure undertaken on all items such as bunding, reclamation, irrigation sources, implements, etc., including expenditure on repairs, maintenance and replacement was about Rs. 22 for families of the lowest three deciles and Rs. 51 for families of the middle four deciles; the corresponding amount was Rs. 311 for families of the first decile. But if this expenditure is taken together with expenditure on purchase of livestock by the respective groups of deciles and the total calculated on a per acre basis the expenditure incurred actually increases as one goes down the groups of deciles. This means that while the total outlays of the families of the middle and lower deciles are small and are known to be inadequate their burden in terms of per acre costs rules high.

It is not necessary to labour the point further. What I want to emphasise is that the size of farming business of at least half the cultivating families in India is such that it is futile to consider them as independent units of land exploitation in any plan for a developing economy. It is irrelevant in the light of the data cited above to talk in terms of family farms or economic holdings. Even the definition of basic holding of the Congress Agrarian Reforms Committee cannot cover these units. Therefore, a land policy for a developing economy must face up to the serious problem of the reorganization of these units. A vague recognition of these facts is seen in the general comments made in various contexts by numerous experts and committees on the "non-creditworthy" or the "marginal and submarginal" groups. This recognition must become more explicit and must lead on to a realisation of the inability of any supply or credit reorganization to deal with fundamental defects of the small size and turnover of the existing basic units and of the large numbers involved in any scheme of reorganization.

There appears at present general agreement on the nature of the problem and the main approach to its solution. The following statement by the Prime Minister, Pandit Jawaharlal Nehru, may be taken as representative of this.

"As agriculture is the principal occupation of the great majority of our people, it must be the first concern of the State. The abolition of the zamindari system has been the first reform and this must be expedited.

But it must be remembered that this by itself is no solution of the problem. Even before this abolition a very large proportion of land was self-cultivated. An addition to it, without any further reforms, will not help much. The small subsistence farm makes progress difficult. We have to think, therefore, and think soon, of other and further steps. There should be a diversion of a part of the agricultural population to other occupations. There should be a development of cottage and small-scale industries. But essentially the problem of agriculture needs co-operative cultivation and the application of modern techniques. This does not mean necessarily mechanising agriculture all over India, though some degree of mechanisation is taking place and is desirable. But there is no escape from some form of co-operative cultivation, if we are to make agriculture progressive."

Considerations of production economy do not seem to indicate any particular figures or proportions in this context. However, data from the Rural Credit Survey may be set out to illustrate the relative proportions involved. These data relate to all the cultivated holdings in the 600 villages selected for the survey in 75 districts. The cultivators were arranged, for the purpose, in order of the size of their cultivated holdings. When so arranged it was found that the first 10 per cent or decile of the cultivators held more than 25 per cent of the total land surface in almost all districts and held more than 30 per cent of it in 51 of the 75 districts. The first 30 per cent of three deciles taken together held more than 50 per cent of the land in almost all districts and in 48 districts they held more than 60 per cent; in no district was this proportion larger than 85 but in 6 it varied between 75 and 85 per cent. The middle four deciles held between 25 and 35 per cent of the total cultivated land in the large majority of districts. The holdings of the last three deciles included less than 10 per cent of the total cultivated land in the majority of districts; but in 27 out of the 75 districts they held between 10 and 15 per cent. Taking the broad division of cultivators into the upper half and lower half the relative size of their holdings of total land surface would be approximately 3 : 1.

The above taken together with the data relating to occupational distribution of families should give an idea of the overall dimensions of the problem. We may assume that about 60 per cent of families in rural India are cultivators in the sense of operating some cultivated land and that of the non-cultivators at least half depend for their support on agriculture and land. This gives about 80 per cent of rural families as interested in land management units and policy. We may, on the basis of data set out before, consider about half of the cultivators as having unsuitable units for independent land management, the proportion cannot at a minimum be put at less than a third of the cultivators. If we take the former figure the cultivating families together with the landless interested in reorganization, will form about half the total number of families in the countryside, and, if the latter, about 40 per cent of them. Working with the data for existing distribution of cultivating holdings and assuming a transfer, because of the operation of the ceiling, of the order of 5 per cent of the total cultivated land, we have the following figures of the extent of land surface and number of families affected by reorganization; if, half the units cease to be independent, about 50 per cent of rural families and 30 per cent of the cultivated land; and if, about one-third of cultivators are so affected, about 40 per cent of the rural families and about 15 per cent of the total land surface. These calculations are so broad as to be almost notional and they have been indulged in at this place only to give some idea of the dimension of the problem.

The two fundamental steps in reorganization of land management units in India are: (i) redistribution of the land surface and: (ii) formation of the larger consolidated units out of the pooled resources of the uneconomic units and surplus available for redistribution. The first step is an essential preliminary in almost all programmes of land improvement and agricultural development. Its importance is universally recognized in connection with the consolidation of fragmented holdings. It is, however, necessary from other points of view also. One can view the process of consolidation in a wider context as part of the process of a rational layout of the total land surface for agricultural and other utilisation.

This task is no doubt of vast dimensions. But tasks of somewhat similar dimensions have been undertaken in other countries and the total work indicated above is not more complicated or larger than the process of consolidation undertaken currently by many State Governments in India. As I visualise it the first stage in the process will be that of determining the general layout and the second of locating in this layout the independent farm units now fixed in location and made impartible, and the co-operative estates or farms.

The formation of larger units out of pooled land and other resources will have two aspects, one compulsory and the other voluntary. I have assumed that once the floor has been defined independent units of farm management smaller in area will not be allowed to exist. Obviously the enforcement of this must be by some sort of legislation. The measure of compulsion may vary. In the early stages the step may be initiated, as in some programmes of consolidation, only on the motion of a minimum number of families involved.

Both these tasks, that of redistributing the land surface and the formation of a small number of co-operative farms in each village are immense in extent and complexity. I would argue that not only are they a *sine qua non* of any programme of land reform but also that they are not beyond our capacity, if a sincere and concentrated effort is made. Consolidation is already generally accepted as a necessary part of the programme by everybody. The formation and proper functioning of co-operative farms is undoubtedly less generally accepted as part of universal policy and is somewhat more difficult. It is, however, equally necessary. I shall, without elaborating them, briefly state a number of reasons in favour of this proposition. In the first instance, without co-operatives, collectives or state farms, an economic reorganization for operation of the existing numerous small units is impossible. Secondly, except as member of a co-operative the small farmer can never be in a position to avail himself of technical, financial, or other external aid of which he stands in need, more than anybody else. The findings of all studies, whether, e.g., of the Rural Credit Survey or the Evaluation Organization are that the bigger man gets the greater profit out of everything, government loans, co-operative finance or other financial or technical assistance of any type. One need not go into the reasons for this state of affairs; it is, however, clear from the studies that the scattered, weak units cannot really be helped effectively unless they come together. Also, as long as there is no consolidation of these weak units the balance in rural society will always remain against them. Any close study of the effects of recent land reforms legislation reveals large variations in its results, dependent chiefly on the strength of tenants and smaller holders in a locality or region. In a large number of instances legal protection and other devices prove constantly fruitless because of the strength and ingenuity of the strong. It is sad to record that large deflection of original intentions, brought about by the strong, has been reported even in the working of the Bhoodan movement. The moral is that unless the weak acquire economic strength by joining together they could never stand up and get full advantage of state policy and state legislation. The formation of a small number of co-operative farming societies of the smaller holders and the landless in each locality is a necessary step in this direction. It will be noticed that I consider redistribution as only a part of the process in the formation of the large co-operative farms. I cannot see any virtue in merely tenancy co-operatives which perpetuate the smaller units of management. Leaving scope for allotments or kitchen gardens would be welcome but the main cropping operations must be in terms of the large units. The experience elsewhere, such as with the Ejido in Mexico, emphasises importance of this.

I do not think that widespread formation of such co-operatives is an impossible undertaking. In the initial stages the progress may be slow but once the movement gathers momentum the field could be covered fairly quickly. Wide extension of the activities of State governments in rural areas together with efforts made by the Central Government in directions of Community Development and National Extension already provide comparatively large staffs in the field; the work of this staff would come to have real meaning and purpose only if it is linked to a programme of the formation and operation of such co-operatives. Instead of chiefly conducting propaganda they would find in these co-operatives numerous local units which could prove centres of demonstration and experimentation. All governmental information and propaganda, aid and assistance could be directed towards and routed through these co-operatives. The special terms of assistance, etc., laid down for these co-operatives should combine the features of the programmes envisaged in the draft outline of the Five-Year Plan for the Registered Farms and for the Co-operative Farming Societies. Instead of receiving very little or nothing of government protection and assistance this step would ensure that the most disadvantaged received, as they should, the highest priority and the greatest assistance.

Therefore, in concluding I shall content myself with reiterating the following basic propositions. That in relation to land management we are following, in this country today, a policy mainly of drift; that a programme of economic development requires more positive approach in respect of agricultural productive organization and units of land management; that a very large number of existing cultivating holdings are extremely unsuitable for functioning as independent units in a programme of agricultural development and that a rational layout of the land surface for its proper utilisation and a programme for the creation of large consolidated holdings are essential ingredients in any agricultural and land development policy. I may add finally that it would be impossible to deal with this problem except in term of bold steps and very large and strenuous effort. However, these would be no more radical and strenuous than those undertaken by many other countries in analogous situations, as evidenced, for example, by the Mexican Agrarian Revolution which redistributed land in favour of the Ejidos or the transformations brought about in countries of South and East Europe both during the inter-war years and in the period after the Second World War.

5

THE CHANGING POWER STRUCTURE OF VILLAGE COMMUNITY–A CASE STUDY OF SIX VILLAGES IN EASTERN U. P.*

YOGENDRA SINGH

AS A SOCIOLOGICAL concept, 'power' occupies a very basic and central place in the study of the dynamics of social systems. From one point of view, all processes of social change, social crisis or equilibrium and disequilibrium of society can be interpreted and analysed with reference to and within the matrix of changing structure of power. Theoretically the concept of power has been discussed and applied by social and political philosophers, psychologists and sociologists in different connotations with emphasis on its different dimensions. An attempt to classify them may involve major difficulty of arbitrary and rather unwarranted pooling up of otherwise different independent and heterogenous marginal concepts of power, yet some of the theoretically well delineated uses of the concept of power may be grouped as: (a) political philosophical; (b) individual psychological and (c) sociological. The political philosophers and scientists right from Plato and Aristotle upto the present day have generally analysed power in relation to the theory of state and the forces tending to generate these political systems. Their discussion of power has often run into the danger of rectification of the concept (Hupe: *Power & Community*, 1956) which complicates its theoretical significance. The individual psychological approach accounts for power either as an attribute of personality (Adler 1929) or gift of God and Charisma (Max Weber 1947).

As different from these approaches which suffer from the inadequacy of systematic causal analysis of power in relation to the integrated elements of social structure as well as personality system the sociological approach to power analysis (R. K. Mukerjee 1923, Russel B. 1938, Hainer and Shils 1939, Mannheim K. 1950, F. Hunter 1952, and Oesar and Emery 1954) emerges from the assessment of its functional role as a perpetuative and cohesive element of social structural configuration. It is treated not only as identical to a political system but also as the integrative principle of social structure and stratification (Parsons 1949). Its sociological analysis, therefore, includes the whole gamut of the interacting personal, social, historical and economic forces of society which result

*Reproduced from Ph.D. dissertation *The Changing Pattern of Socio-economic Relations in the Countryside: A Survey of Selected Villages in Eastern Uttar Pradesh*, by Yogendra Singh, University of Lucknow, 1958.

into mode of social relationship of 'Superordination and subordination' or of 'Control of interests' and structure of people controlled and controlling—the power personnel.

POWER STRUCTURE UNDER FEUDAL-SOCIAL ORGANISATION

Prior to the abolition of landlordism, the power structure of the village was founded upon the zamindari system on the one hand which represented the material and economic interest or expectation system of the community, and the village panchayats and caste panchayats on the other which symbolised the basic social dimensions of the rural polity.

Agriculture being the main economic occupation of the villagers the nature of the rights in land represented the nature of the mastery of the economic expectations of different segments of the community by a person or a group of persons who held that right and in Uttar Pradesh with the tedious and long history of its land-settlements the zamindars and the taluqdars were such persons who had supreme control over this right and thereby had a command over the economic expectations of the rest of the members in the rural community. Thus, the zamindari system had a very vital role to play in the power-system of the villages, so much so that it itself grew into a power institution and influenced the selection of leadership and occasionally it also defined the role of the caste and community panchayats in the village. A systematic analysis of the relationship between the zamindari system and the power-structure of the village should, therefore, be the focal point of any comprehensive study of rural pattern of power.

The caste organisation is another face of the social system which determines the social, behavioural, ritualistic and traditional expectations and interests of the villagers. It had, therefore, simultaneously with the zamindari system evolved its own structure of power personnel and thus needs separate treatment. Yet, at another level the rural structure of power expressed and institutionalised itself in the form of the village panchayats. Long before the establishment of the systematic formal village panchayats by the State, the council of elders from all caste groups constituted the village panchayat, which under the zamindari system was deeply overshadowed by the authority of the collective body of the zamindars. But in spite of this loss of its original status, it maintained its separate status and constituted a stable structure of power. The zamindari system, the village panchayat and the caste system, thus, appear to be three overall institutional determinants of the power system of villages before the abolition of zamindari because the village members usually had to refer to the zamindar and the village panchayat (Council of elder zamindars and a few other elders from other castes) in case, economic and political interest was involved and to their caste leader in case any problem of social, cultural, ritualistic nature was involved. It is, however, not claimed that these three institutions of the village exhausted all the power generating situations in the villages but it simply represents the three broad dimensions of the rural order which encompassed other power agencies of a more generic nature such as the ecclesiastical power vested in the priest which is common to all the village members or the power of custom, tradition and the folk mores which each member of the community obeys unconsciously and the violation of which may create serious schism in the life of the community. Another point which is worth the emphasis is the functional interdependence and the overlapping nature of these three institutions of power. The zamindari system, the village panchayat and caste panchayat as the three levels of the structure of power did not enjoy a state of complete insularity or independence but a status of relative dependence, adjustment and symbiosis. Above all this there was, however, the power of the police and the state upon which all the others were not only dependent but sometimes also derive their authority. This was specially true of the zamindari system and the village panchayat.

1. Zamindari System and Power Structure

The relationship between the power-structure of the villages with the system of zamindari was inter-woven with the particular type of right of property or right of ownership in land, which the landlord enjoyed to the exclusion of the other members of the village. There is a long-drawn controversy in respect of the type of land right before the establishment of the zamindari settlement and particularly it centres around the communal versus the peasant proprietorship in land over which the zamindari tenure is supposed to have grown later. Sir Henry Maine mentioned that in the past, villages organised along a patriarchal family head were cultivating land jointly and there was communal ownership of land. On the other hand Dr. R. K. Mukerjee and Altekar have strongly refuted this view. Baden Powell, however, has given an ethnological explanation of the land rights, changing with pressures and pulls of different racial immigrations and conquests. He accepts the peasant proprietorship in the pre-Aryan time which still persists in the South in the form of ryotwari village tenures but in northern India he maintains a state of juxtaposition of insurging Aryans over the native settlers which created a different type of village tenure which he calls "joint-village tenure". He, however, recapitulates the whole process saying 'the right to land grew out of two ideas, one being that a special claim arises, to any object or to a plot of land by virtue of the labour and skill expended on making it useful or profitable, the other that a claim arose for conquest or superior right.' In the northern India he mentioned that the landlord type of land right developed because of the conquering clans imposing their right over the native settlers of the soil at one place or by grant of the king at the other or by extension of the clan-cultivation at a third place. In the whole eastern region of Uttar Pradesh to which this study extends, two major forms of village-land tenure were to be found : (1) the taluqdari type and (2) the joint village type or joint zamindari type.

Out of the sample villages studied, four villages, that is, Chaukhara in Basti district, Mahadeva in Gorakhpur, Dumahi in Deoria and Niamtabad in Benaras district belonged to the second type of the joint-villages mentioned above, and two were taluqdari villages, that is, Itaunja in the Lucknow district and Belaha in Gonda district which show the same origin through conquest by a chief. In the above four villages excluding Dumahi where Bhumihars had zamindari right, all the zamindars were Chattris (Rajputs) who claimed descent from some ancestor of the past who had conquered a whole territory from original settlers and ruled over them as an overlord. For example in the village Chaukhra the overlord clan was of Kalhans Chattris who came from Gahumunj Baghlana in West Rajasthan at about 1544 century A. D. and usurped the land-right from the original settlers perhaps the Bharas and Tharus and established their power; Mahadeva village in Gorakhpur was likewise usurped by the Sarnet Chattris who entered the district in 1400 A. D. and drove away the Domkatars and Bharas. In Dumahi village, however, the Bhumihars had their lordship—whom Mr. Hooper calls of indigenous origin but the Gazetteer of the North Western Provinces mentioned the probable date of their immigration between 950-1100 A. D. The Bhumihars, however, are popularly known sometimes belonging to Rajput clan and at other to Brahmin caste. The two taluqdari villages, Itaunja and Belha, were also annexed by conquest, the former by Suryabansi Chattris in 13th century A. D. by defeating the strong domination of the Kurmis and Muraos and latter by Janwar Chattris who came from Pavagarh in Gujrat in 1374 A. D. and established a kingdom by usurping the right of the original settlers who were Tharus, Doms and Pasis. Thus, the account of the ethnological and historical origin of all the sample villages under investigation shows that the origin of the overlordship and feudal socio-economic structure had taken root long before the zamindari system was formally recognised by the British through revenue settlements. This overlordship of the upper caste clans had taken place some four hundred years ago and most of these overlords were Rajputs, or the Mohammadans who were at the head of the rural society.

The dominations of these castes over the original tillers of the soil both from the economic as well as social point of view vested enormous power into their hands. Where such a power was diffused into the whole communal body of the clan the system was of the joint zamindari type of settlement and where it was under a single landlord or taluqdar it was called taluqdari village. With the establishment of the Companies rule in Uttar Pradesh these overlords were recognised as taluqdars or zamindars and a regular settlement was effected with them as the taluqdar or zamindar of their respective landholdings and the estate.

The nature of the power which the landlord or the taluqdar wielded over the other groups in the village community was primarily based on his judicial rights in land ownership. He alone was the proprietor oi

'Malik' of the land and all others were his tenants or 'Ryots' holding the right to cultivate from him and paying land rent for it. The zamindar was also the owner of the village habitation—site, the village grove, pasture land and village ponds.

The timberland and the village pasture land being the property of the landlords the villagers had to pay a price for its utilization which varied from ceremonial gifts and offerings to regular payment of rent in cash or kind. The functionary castes and artisans and merchants used to pay in terms of their services and other gifts. Thus, the proprietary right in land held by the zamindars, had placed them in an unique power-position. They had not only the economic and feudal style power over their tenants but they enjoyed the privilege of holding all other castes and classes into a subjugate feudatory relationship based on economic and social reciprocation and obligation. Thus, their economic status or the proprietary right in land was a fundamental source of the power-institution in the villages. 'The zamindar had great power over his ryot; the interference of law was but partial; the zamindar could do much without law and the reliance of ryots was much more on custom than on law'.

However, this relationship which was the result of the economic power of the landlord had given shape to a regular power-structure in the villages. 'The landlords were the law in the villages for all practical purposes beyond the caste councils. The landlords maintained their own courts and record-room and dealt summarily with offenders through the strength of their dependent followers. One or another landlord always held the office of police headman, Mukhia.'

The exact structure of this power differed from the Joint Zamindari villages to Taluqdari villages. In the Joint Zamindari villages the total body of proprietors was divided into Thoks, Thoks into Pattis and it was actually these different Thoks headed by one or more Lambardar which acted as an independent unit of power. The tenants, village Bania and functionary castes were divided according to Thoks and hence used to always belong to the power jurisdiction of the Thok concerned. Thus in one Joint Zamindari village there could be more than one such units of power. In the four villages under Joint Zamindari each one had two Thoks, hence two rival power groups.

The jurisdiction of these zamindari power groups was : (a) collection of rent, (b) collection of house tax, (c) distribution of pasture land and timber to their tenants at the occasion of death, birth or marriage and (d) to hear appeals against the caste panchayat of their tenants belonging to different castes. The body of power personnel consisted of (a) the Lambardar, (b) the elders from the various landlord households and (c) the Godait (the lower caste messenger-cum-orderly). Sometimes the village Patwari's and Chaukidar's help was also taken although these were responsible directly to the 'Mukhia' or the police headman, one for each village appointed by Government from among the landlords.

In the Taluqdari villages where there were sub-proprietors (*Thekedars*), a similar divided pattern of power used to exist (as in Belha village in district Gonda) but in other villages Taluqdar's officers used to exercise power over the villagers on behalf of the Taluqdar, who used to only hear appeals in more complicated and important cases.

2. The Village Panchayat

The growth of the well delineated structure of village panchayat in the villages of Eastern U. P. had been complicated and overshadowed by the domination of the feudal element in the village polity. Hence, like the villages in the southern India or Punjab although these villages had a village level panchayat, with its defined jurisdiction and power personnel yet it had very plastic structure. The body of the village panchayat was constituted of the Lambardars from different Thoks of the landlord shareholders, the elderly leaders of various caste panchayats and the 'Chaukidar'. Thus, whereas the zamindari system used to divide the village from the point of view of structure of power into Thoks and Patti (Thola and Pana of Jat village : Oscar Lewis) which exercised power over the tenants and functionary castes in agrarian relation to it, with such power personnel of its own as 'the Lambardars' the collective body proprietors and co-proprietors and '*Godait*' (messenger), the village panchayat was a broad based structure of power, rather a federation representing all rural sub-structures of power, i.e., the caste panchayats and the Thok and Patti of the zamindari system. The jurisdiction of the village panchayat consisted of (a) upkeep and preservation of general law and order in the village; (b) hearing appeals against caste panchayats and (c) also against the body of landlords of a particular Thok.

Theoretically, therefore, it occupied a very powerful and supreme status in the structure of rural power but in practice it was always oscillating for authority between the rival strong factions of landlord Thoks and it seldom succeeded in a broad-based exercise of power. Generally it used to remain dormant in the structure of rural polity and used to take a manifest structural form when the prestige or security of the village as a whole was in danger. It was at such occasions alone that the village panchayat in these villages used to activise or attain its supremacy as an institution of power.

3. The Caste Panchayat

The caste panchayats, however, have been a well-known and indispensable institution of power in the villages all over India. They were mainly responsible for the preservation of the caste system against the onslaught of hostile forces. This role of old panchayats has occupied the attention of people from different disciplines (Blunt, Risley 1908, Mathai 1915, Altekar 1927, Mukerjee 1920, Malaviya 1956 etc.). In course of the extension of the British system of judiciary and the infeudation of the rural polity the caste panchayats lost most of their original complexion. In the eastern region of U.P. perhaps these caste panchayats were extremely powerful, before the arrival of the feudal clans when the agrarian pattern was also on the line of communal ownership. The landlord clans deprived the caste panchayats of many of their rights through feudal superposition of power. The British system of judiciary and police organization also deprived them of some of their powers.

On the eve of the abolition of feudalism the village had very weak and loose panchayat organisation. The officials of the caste panchayat such as the " Choudhari " (President), " panch " (member of panchayat executive), " Charidar or Sipahi " (Messenger) existed on hereditary basis in all lower and intermediate castes. The organisation of these power personnel, however, went across the village boundaries and consisted of ten to twenty villages. The area of power was confined to: (1) safeguarding the commensal and connubial rules of the caste, (2) punishing any gross moral, social and economic deviation of the members of caste, and (3) resisting against any threat extended towards the prestige, security and vital interests of the caste by external enemy castes or groups.

In course of the abolition of landlordism and introduction of the new elected panchayat system, it is now the third aspect of the caste panchayats which has come to be highly activised with the result that formation of strong caste factions and the process of horizontal mobility in the caste organisation has become a common pattern of rural caste organisation. During the period of zamindari, much of this element of ' Casteism ' in caste panchayats was suppressed by the strong power groups of landlords. The caste panchayats were a secondary and ignored institution of power. Now they have become potential instruments controlling the mode of social, economic and power relations of the groups in the village community. They are also the source of a good deal of social tension and ferment in the rural social structure.

Thus, the general pattern that emerges from the study of the power system of village before the abolition of landlordism is, that the mastery of economic resources, and its centralization in certain class remained by far the most important source of power. Thus, the economic system of zamindari, in course of time, effected a metamorphosis in the social system as well as power system of villages. The village panchayat remained generally a tool in the hands of landlords and could not develop as an effective instrument of power. The caste panchayats of course represented a parallel and widespread power system but this tool had, in matters outside caste rules, to be subjugated to the power of landlords. The other interesting point that comes out is that the village settlement and its land tenure had deep relationship with not only the power structure of the village but also its social system. This pattern does not emerge as clearly through the study of one village as through the study of a whole region (eastern U.P.) and also its historic-political, ethnological and economic history. The pattern of leadership was structured around the system of zamindari on the one hand and caste on the other. Hence the circulation of leaders and their selection was relatively closed. The opportunity for vertical mobility of power status was substantially blocked on the basis of caste status on the one hand and economic status on the other.

THE NEW PATTERN OF POWER

In course of the national movement for political independence, the significance of landlordism as a social, economic and power system responsible for the perpetuation of a highly reactionary, exploitative and conservative mode of social and economic relationship in villages was adequately realised. Consequently after the realisation of political independence the first major step that the new government took was to abolish the system of zamindari as well as its nuclei of power in villages. The functional relationship between the system of zamindari and the subsequent rural power structure was understood and systematic attempt was made to exterminate and replace both the institutions. This attempt in U. P. was symbolized into the U. P. Panchayat Raj Act 1948 and the U. P. Zamindari Abolition Act 1951.

Previously the system of zamindari as an economic institution had evolved an elaborate juridical structure, in terms of land rights, village settlements, village offices (Lambardar, Mukhia, Patwari, etc.) and in due course of its existence a number of customary and conventional rights, and power obligations had developed around this otherwise a purely juridical economic system. The power structure during the zamindari system, therefore, both in the form of village panchayats as well as caste panchayats had generally a non-juridical and customary mode of existence. This had introduced elements of regional variations in its pattern although its basic ethos was the same in all eastern U. P. villages.

The new legislations of village panchayat for the first time introduced a systematic and comprehensive juridical base of a new power structure. Earlier in 1920 British Government had introduced an act for establishing village panchayats but therein, the village officers were to be nominated and consequently it could not free itself from the influence of zamindars. There was no provision of election and adult franchise. Hence it could not elicit popular support and response of the people. The act of 1948 on the other hand introduced many very revolutionary ideas and practices. Each adult member of the village (with the exceptions as laid down in the Act) was given the right to vote; election was to be held by show of hands; women for the first time secured the right of active participation in the village affairs, the procedure of the village panchayat was to be maintained in writing and the office of the panchayat was linked with the overall judicial and revenue administration of the state. The traditional role of economic status and caste status for village offices was for the first time theoretically and legally abolished.

The legislation for the abolition of zamindari system which followed later further removed the bottlenecks in the path of rapid rural democratization. With the abolition of intermediary rights in land the majority of rural households of ex-tenants were rendered free from the sphere of economic and social subjugation to the ex-landlords; the office of the 'Lambardar' and 'Mukhia' was abolished; the village ponds, village pasture land, and groves and other 'Aabadi' land till now the property of landlords became the property of the village community, to be controlled and administered by the elected office-bearers of the panchayat. The village Chaukidar instead of being responsible to the 'Mukhia' (headman) who used to be a landlord, became responsible to the office of the elected 'President' and other village panchayat officers.

Thus, from the sociological viewpoint extremely radical steps were taken to transform the complexion of the village community in the mould of a highly democratic pattern of social, economic and power structure. These steps were also at the same time in conformity with the overall goal of national social planning which aimed at the establishment of a parliamentary democratic socialist republic.

Thus, from the statutory point of view the basis of the old pattern of rural group relations was rendered outmoded and the old power pattern was to be replaced with a completely new one. The new power system, however, acknowledged not the household but the individual as unit of participation; the objective was implicitly to infuse the values of individualism, secularism and liberalism. Hence, the purposive denial of caste in the selection of power personnel. The value of ascriptive-status was under this system to give way to achievement principles; the sociological significance of which was far-reaching and deeper. It was from a broad-based point of view an attempt to transform the very basis of traditional rural world-view.

These implications of the new power system are, however, of theoretical and juridical nature. The actual extent of realisation could not be possibly foreseen unless with reference to empirical structures of the village community. The attempt in the following passage is towards the same end.

The primary objective of the new system of power (through Gaon Panchayat and Nyaya Panchayat) was to democratize the base of power on the basis of people's acceptance. The selection of leaders under this system in principle has to be on the basis of individual merit and not on the basis of class or caste. Thus, each qualified member of the village community was supposed to gain a new status deriving it from the value system of democratic society. But the leadership pattern as it emerged after the first elections in the villages demonstrates that the goal of diffusion of power in each class and caste of the village community has not succeeded. The figures of the elected leaders show that the key offices of village president and vice-presidents in almost all the six villages are with the upper castes. In four of the villages the same come from the class of ex-zamindars and in the rest of the two they belong to substantial class of farmers. Even in regard to the office of membership in the village executive council and panchayat court 52·6 per cent of these belong to the upper caste, 15·7 per cent to intermediate and only 22·4 per cent to the lower caste. Some 9·3 per cent of these offices, however, are occupied by members of other communities.

The class background of these elected leaders reveals yet another significant trend of concentration of offices. As many as 53·3 per cent of the leaders are from ex-landlords or big farmers, 40·4 per cent belong to intermediate class cultivators and only 6·3 per cent belong to the class of agricultural labourers. This pattern of distribution of offices among the various castes and classes is also, however, substantially disproportionate to their population and the numerical strength. The upper castes which constitute only 20·6 per cent of the village population occupy 52·6 per cent of panchayat offices, the intermediate and lower castes constituting 25·4 per cent and 33·0 per cent of the population respectively, occupy only 15·7 and 22·4 per cent of the village offices. Similarly on the basis of class as well the big farmers who constitute only 16·0 per cent of the population in villages own 53·3 per cent of the village panchayat offices, and cultivators and agricultural labourers comprising of 42·4 and 21·2 per cent of village population command 40·4 per cent and 6·3 per cent of the offices respectively. The adverse position of the agricultural labourers among the classes and the lower castes men in the caste hierarchy in the matter of power distribution is, therefore, clearly substantiated. The significant paradox that needs explanation and analysis is as to why in spite of numerical strength the members of lower castes and classes have failed to come into power in villages. It may, however, be incidentally pointed out that invariably in the villages of eastern U. P., the caste and class categories are found to be subsumed together, i. e., the upper castes also generally belong to the upper class, and the intermediate and lower castes to the same class categories respectively and hence the explanation applicable to the phenomenon of caste concentration of power will implicitly also explain the reasons of its class-concentration.

The important reasons that come into the purview of observation for the class and caste concentration of power in villages, in spite of statutory effort for its diffusion, is economic. The abolition of the intermediary right in land could not abolish the huge difference in the economic status of the various castes and classes in villages.

Taking the ownership of land as an index of economic status in village it may be found that even after the abolition of landlordism huge disparities persist. The average landholding and ex-zamindar household compares very highly with that of an ex-tenant in the villages, the two being 63·0 and 1·2 acres respectively in village of Itaunja, 5·0 and 1·1 acres in Belha, 25·0 and 1·8 acres in Chaukhara, 5·0 and 0·3 acres in Mahadeva, 14·0 and 2·5 acres in Dumahi and 17·0 and 3·5 acres in the village of Niamtabad. The minimum range of disparity is of five times and the maximum goes as high as sixty-three times. Similarly on the basis of caste the upper castes comprising 26·0 per cent of rural population own 54·9 per cent of total village land, whereas the two percentages are 25·4 and 29·3 for the intermediate caste, 33·0 and 9·6 for the lower castes and 25·6 and 6·2 for Muslims and other communities.

Thus, the big farmers and moneylenders of the villages still continue to master the economic, social and other expectations of the majority of the people through money-lending and illegal transfer of land for sub-letting and share cropping. Therefore, this class continues to succeed in creating a nucleus of supporters in the election of village panchayats. The chain of cumulative causation is complete when the economic deprivations of a certain class or caste leads to, perpetuates and enhances its subsequent social, cultural and political or power deprivations.

Moreover, in the process of the abolition of landlordism the new pattern of land tenure which was introduced recognised only Bhumidhari right as the right in land ownership. The ex-tenants were given the option to purchase this right from the Government only through the payment of ten times of the existing rental value, which rendered most of the village peasant poor and indebted, thus additionally increasing the economic dependence of this class on the substantial class of ex-landlords and money-lenders. Hence the failure in the realisation of the goal of democratic power structure and social and economic system in villages to a very substantial degree rests upon the economic fetters which still bind and coerce most of the rural population to owe allegiance to a group or class of people who continue in power and, against whom they are waging a relentless battle for the realisation of new status and mode of relationship rendered possible by new legislation.

There is nevertheless, overwhelming evidence to demonstrate that the groups, classes and castes who were politically and socially suppressed so far are making substantial efforts to come out on top of the power structure of the village. During the panchayat elections in almost every village the key offices, which for feline tactics ultimately went to the upper class, were keenly contested by the lower and intermediate classes. The result has been that the village community is at present subdivided into rival factions, political groups and cliques and the social tension has mounted up. The whole life of the village community is in tremendous ferment.

An attitude study of 736 heads of the households in these villages regarding the role of factions, castes and classes in the panchayat elections has brought into light very interesting results. About ninety per cent of the people, in spite of their different class and caste backgrounds, have expressed the view that there is a tendency among the people in villages to support candidates in panchayat elections primarily on the basis of faction alliances and for reasons of belonging to the same caste and class. With regard to the particular caste or class that influences the selection of leaders in village panchayats or holds command over it each caste and class group thinks that it is the other caste or class which holds the most powerful status. Such a pattern of subjective and attitudinal response is demonstrative of the fact that in the village community almost every class and caste group has a feeling of deep insecurity and a clearly delineated pattern of power structure has not yet emerged. The present favourable power position of the upper caste and class groups is, however, a temporary phase and shall have to give way in the impact of the new liberal secular forces that are emerging.

The actual shape of this secular or democratic pattern of rural polity as it would emerge in times to come still remains elusive and hazy for a clear realisation, but the new trend of the dynamics of power and group relation in villages does not lend support to the view that in near foreseeable future group-oriented pattern of power domination in terms of caste faction and household alliances will be replaced by individual oriented liberal pattern of power domination. Although in theory individual as a unit has been vested with the right of social, economic and political participation, yet, not the individual but the household still remains the unit of social interaction in the village community.

Thus, some of the salient trends of the present power dynamics in the rural communities may be summarised as follows:

1. The upper castes (Rajputs, Brahmins, Bhumihars) and classes (ex-landlords and money-lenders) continue to hold power in villages. The only difference from village to village may be that in the one, domination may be direct and manifest and in others, it may be indirect and latent.

2. Increased competition for power has been energised from the section of lower caste and class groups on an organised basis. This tendency is relatively more true for the caste groups rather than class groups. At the caste level this participation takes the form of faction alliances. This has not only sub-divided the village community but also increased social tension and insecurity in village life.

3. The secular democratic value system which had been anticipated to work as the basis of the new power system of villages, has not as yet succeeded in finding acceptance or root in the rural value system and social structure. Not the individual but household or allied groups of households or faction still remains the unit of social, cultural and political participation in villages.

4. The village polity still continues to be deeply affected and determined by the pattern of economic deprivations and privileges of the vari-

ous castes and classes. The power system has a tendency to incline in favour of the groups who can control the economic expectations of the people in villages. From this point, however, any future dynamics of rural power system will be in direct response to the economic change introduced and the pattern of rural economic growth.

6

POLITICAL LEADERSHIP IN WEST BENGAL: THE IMPLICATIONS OF ITS CHANGING PATTERNS FOR ECONOMIC PLANNING*

MYRON WEINER

THE PROCESS by which a new leadership is emerging throughout Asia provides us with one key to understanding the dynamics of social and political change. With the achievement of independence new leaders emerge with new interests and demands. How well these fragile democracies will be able to withstand the pressures exercised by new leaders and new groups is one of the fundamental questions of our times. It is the purpose of this paper to explore the changing pattern of leadership in a single state in India during the past forty years and to suggest the kinds of demands likely to enter Indian political life as a result of these changes. Finally, we shall ask what effect these demands are likely to have on the freedom with which economic planning may be pursued by the Indian government in the years ahead.

Our study is based upon the following reflections:

Under western colonial rule the countries of Asia have experienced a quiet but profound change in the character of their political leadership. One could view the nationalist struggle in India, as elsewhere, not only as a struggle by Indians to replace their British rulers, but as a struggle by one group of Indians—a western-educated class of journalists, doctors, lawyers and administrators—to replace an older leadership of maharajas, landlords and hereditary administrators. To understand modern India, one must understand the new leadership, the social background from which it derives, the groups with which it is associated and whose interests it articulates, the values and ideologies it propagates, and the influence which it wields.

This new leadership has itself been undergoing many changes. The late 19th and early 20th century leadership which participated in the Indian National Congress, India's paramount nationalist organisation, was largely drawn from middle income groups in the coastal cities of Calcutta Bombay, Madras and their environs. In the 1920's major changes occurred within the nationalist government movement. Not only did the advent of Gandhi mean a change in style by the nationalist movement, from the two strands of modern liberalism and violent extremism to non-violent civil disobedience built upon mass participation, but a change oc-

*Reproduced from *The Economic Weekly*, Special Number, July 1959, pp. 925-933.

curred in the character of the leadership. The leadership which arose in the 1920's did not come so exclusively from Bengal, Madras and Bombay but from Gujarat, United Provinces, Bihar, Andhra and the Central Provinces. The new leadership came from the hinterlands away from the main centres of western intrusion. Such changes in the geographic backgrounds of leaders, along with changes in social origin, are often critical factors in the kinds of political conflicts and public policies which emerge.

Finally, it is assumed here that public policy in India is not simply made by a handful of men who attempt to enforce their decisions upon a static population. Between the top decision makers and the masses are an array of intermediate leaders, some of whom communicate governmental decisions to the masses, others of whom attempt to influence policy, administration and the selection of personnel on the basis of the interest of the groups to which they belong and identify. Much of the thinking about political leadership in India and elsewhere in Asia and Africa focuses on the elite-mass dichotomy. This dichotomy finds a central place in the thinking of Tareto, Mosca and Lasswell, but while it now plays a secondary role in the analysis of American and European political systems, it occupies a central place in popular and even scholarly thinking about non-European political systems. This image of the political process fails to take into account the great changes which have occurred in India since the 1920's and fails to explore the linkage between the top leadership in India—the Prime Minister, cabinet members, and State Chief Ministers—and the masses.

Middle Strata of Leadership

This study, therefore, is an attempt to explore the social and geographic origins of this intermediate leadership, and the ways in which this leadership has been and is changing. By intermediate leadership we refer to those leaders who serve as a link between the social system and the governmental structure. What characterizes this leadership is that it has a "constituency", not simply an electoral constituency, but some group affiliation—a trade union; a peasant, refugee, caste or tribal organization; a business chamber; or a civic association.

Our inquiry into this middle strata of leadership in India has led us to focus our attention on a single state, West Bengal. West Bengal is by no means a "typical" state, but for that matter one can find unique as well as "'typical" features of every Indian State. But the most salient fact about the uniqueness of West Bengal for our study, however, is the extent and duration of the Western impact. The East India Company established itself in Bengal in the latter part of the 18th century. British policy during the 18th and early 19th centuries resulted in the elimination of Moghul rule, the establishment of a new landlord class, the introduction of English in a newly created system of Anglo-Indian schools and a major university in Calcutta, and the rise of new westernized occupations associated with activities of the British—administration, medicine, law, and journalism. Bengal was perhaps the most active of the earliest nationalist centres. Bengalis were among the leading moderates who led the Indian National Congress in the latter part of the 19th century, and they were also among the leading terrorists who threw bombs at the British in the first decade of the 20th century. Not until the early 1920's when Gandhi and a new national leadership arose, did the position of Bengal in the national movement recede. Bengal was further weakened by the partition of 1947 when some 40 millions of people in East Bengal became part of Pakistan while some 27 millions of people in West Bengal remained part of India. But even with partition, West Bengal continues to remain one of the most politically active states in India. It is possible that Bengal's early access to western ideas, her higher degree of political organization, and her relatively high level of industrialization may foreshadow developments elsewhere. But this is speculation. It is enough at this stage to indicate the pattern of development in one state and leave to other researchers the task of developing comparative data.

Analysis of 408 Bengali Leaders

Our inquiry is based upon an analysis of 408 Bengali leaders in the Western Bengal Legislative Assembly and Council (1957-), the Indian Parliament (1952-57), the West Bengal State Congress Committee (1958), the Executive Committee of the Praja Socialist Party (1958), the Executive Committee of the Communist-sponsored peasant organization, the All India Kisan Sabha (1958), and the Executive Committee of the Marxist Left peasant organization, the United Kisan Sabha (1958). Our sample thus includes members of the four major political groups in West Bengal; the Congress Party (198), which controls the state government, the Communists (85), the Socialists (36), and the various splinter Marxist Left parties (42), plus independents and members of smaller parties (47). How involved these leaders are with various interest groups in West Bengal is indicated by the following statistics. Ninety-nine are involved in civic activities at the local level, 33 are in religious and caste bodies, 83 are in peasant associations, 38 are in trade unions, 14 are in credit societies and co-operatives, 35 are in cultural and professional bodies, 11 are in business chambers. One hundred and nineteen members of the sample are also active in institutions and local government. Of the 408 individuals in our sample, 315 hold public office in Parliament, the West Bengal Legislative Assembly or the West Bengal Legislative Council. The data employed in this study was derived from published who's who and interviews conducted in Calcutta in 1957 and 1958.

We shall focus on the one fundamental issue before us: How has this leadership been changing, and what effects do these changes have upon political demands and public policy? We are faced at the outset with a serious methodological problem. While data on the present leadership is available, direct data is not available for those who were active in politics in the 1920's or 1930's, or even the 1940's. Our study would have to be terminated even before we began it not for the fact that Indians, like most other Asians and Africans, are recruited into politics in their early 20s or younger. Those who are today on the 60s entered politics in the 1920's, those who are 50 entered in the 1930's and so on. By exploring the differences between age groups it thus becomes possible for us to see the ways in which political recruitment has been changing over a forty-year period.

In our sample we have the ages of 340 individuals. Of these 84 were born before 1900, 98 were born between 1900 and 1909, 101 were born between 1910 and 1919 and 57 were born after 1920.

Ruralization of Elites

As might be expected in a largely agricultural country, most political leaders were born in villages. However, through the forty years the number born in Calcutta and other urban centres had declined, while the number born in villages has increased. Fifty per cent of the sample born before 1900 came from villages, while 74 per cent of those born after 1920 were of village origin (see Table I).

Table I

Age and Birthplace of 340 Political Leaders in West Bengal

	Calcutta (per cent)	*Towns (per cent)*	*Villages (per cent)*
Before 1900	21	29	50
1900—1909	16	23	61
1910—1919	16	13	71
1920—1939	11	15	74

The trend is thus toward more ruralization of the elite rather than less. (The question might be raised as to whether the rise in rural born leadership might not merely indicate that urban areas have more village-born leaders than earlier.) That this is not true is proven by the fact that only 11 of the 36 members of the Legislative Assembly representing urban areas were born in villages. Other criteria of "ruralization", such as occupation, parental occupation, and source of income, all tend to substantiate our conclusion. Of the 214 assembly members for whom occupation data was available 12 per cent of the oldest group reports agricultural occupations compared with 37 per cent of the youngest.

The trend runs counter to the increasing urbanization of West Bengal, and likewise runs counter to the increasing urbanization of political leadership in industrialized countries of the West. In India, rural powers—

princes and landlords—were so protected by the colonial power that they did not participate in nationalist politics. Nationalist leadership arose in urban centres where western ideas of democracy and representation were introduced, and where the new universities created a class of lawyers, doctors, clerks and other middle class occupations. Not until the 1920's when the nationalist movement tried to win support for independence from the rural population did more rural leaders enter politics. But the trend toward the emergence of a new rural leadership had begun even earlier with the gradual emergence of a new rural middle class only partially involved in land ownership. The smaller landlords or their sons who became rural lawyers, teachers and shopkeepers soon became as intensely patriotic as their urban brothers.

Most of the rural seats in the Legislative Assembly are now represented by rural-born members. Only 33 out of 168 rural seats in the Legislative Assembly have urban-born members. By contrast, 14 out of 29 rural MP seats are still held by urban members. The trend in both the Assembly and in Parliament, however, is for more and more of the younger members to be rural born. While only 56 per cent of the MLAs born before 1900 come from rural areas, 79 per cent of those born after 1920 are rural. Since 77 per cent of the Assembly seats are from rural constituencies, it is possible to conclude that the rural areas are now producing enough of their own leaders to fill the seats in the Legislative Assembly. This is yet to be reflected in the selection of members of Parliament where 78 per cent of the seats are rural, but only 41 per cent of the seats are held by rural-born members. On the basis of what has already happened in the West Bengal Assembly (where 68 per cent are rural-born), one could predict that rural-born representation in the Parliament in New Delhi from West Bengal is likely to increase.

Rural-Urban Separation

What does this growing self-sufficiency in rural leadership indicate? It suggests that urban discontent may not so easily overflow into rural areas. With rural areas increasingly providing their own leaders, both rural leaders and rural voters are more likely to be conditioned by what is going on in rural areas than by discontent in the cities. Bad urban conditions may, of course, affect rural conditions as well. The absence of industrial growth may lessen job opportunities, increase rural overcrowding, and lower rural living standards. But the mere fact of urban discontent by itself may not affect rural leadership or voting behaviour. It was possible, for example, for Calcutta to elect a majority of its Assembly representatives from the Communist Party in 1957, but for the rural areas to elect Congressmen. And it is possible too that this rural-urban political split in West Bengal may persist for some time, precisely because of the self-sustaining nature of both rural and urban political leadership.

To the extent that rural and urban areas of West Bengal separate politically, each with their own leadership, their own interests, and their own voting patterns, then West Bengal will simply be following a pattern already established in other growing industrial areas of the world. Democratic Chicago versus Republican "downstate" and Democratic New York versus Republican "upstate" simply indicate that rural and urban areas often have conflicting interests, outlooks and leadership. The later development of rural interests in India, which runs counter to the timing of such developments in the West, is the consequence of a complex series of factors related to western domination; but equalization of rural-urban interests in West Bengal does seem to be occurring and may portend a pattern likely to develop in other parts of India.

It is popularly believed in Calcutta, especially by the intellectuals of that city, that as Calcutta goes so goes all of West Bengal. Since Calcutta turned against the Congress Party in 1957 elections, many Calcutta intellectuals believe that rural Bengal will follow suit in the 1962 elections. The data provided here concerning the rise of a rural elite into political positions suggests that the influence of Calcutta and of her politicians upon rural areas is decreasing. Many Bengalis are living with an image of the political process of an earlier era when intellectual ferment in Calcutta overflowed into the rural areas as urban nationalists journeyed to the rural areas to organize the peasantry on behalf of the national movement. Calcutta's influence on rural areas is still great. Her newspapers are read by many of the literate leaders of the rural areas. Rural elites have often studied in and have friendship ties with Calcutta. But today, Calcutta provides *influence*, not *leadership* for rural West Bengal.

Built upon this outdated image of the political process is another view that India's parliamentary system is simply the "plaything" of urban intellectuals. It is true that half of the West Bengal Cabinet is urban-born, that 17 out of 22 members of the Executive Committee of the Praja Socialist Party in West Bengal are urban and only one out of four Bengali Ministers in New Delhi is rural, but the legislature is already under rural control, rural representation in Parliament is increasing and it is likely that rural influence will continue to increase.

Characteristics of Rural Leaders

Who are those rural politicans and what interests do they represent? By all measurements, Congress is the most rural party in West Bengal (see Table II). In our total sample of 192 Congressmen for whom place of birth was available, 119 were born in villages, 39 in towns and 34 in Calcutta. The village bias is heaviest in the Legislative Assembly (95 out of 133) and least in Parliament (only 15 out of 39). These rural-born Congressmen invariably represent rural constituencies. One hundred and sixteen of the Congress MLA constituencies (86 per cent) are rural and almost all the 116 Congressmen from rural constituencies give rural addresses as their permanent address. In short, the vast majority of

TABLE II

Birthplace and Constituency of West Bengal Members of the Legislative Assembly

	Birthplace							*Constituency*						
	Village		*Town*		*City*		*Total*	*Rural*		*Mixed*		*Urban*		*Total*
	No.	*%*	*No.*	*%*	*No.*	*%*	*No.*	*No.*	*%*	*No.*	*%*	*No.*	*%*	*No.*
Congress	95	(71)	26	(19)	12	(9)	133	116	(86)	6	(4)	13	(10)	135
Communists	20	(56)	8	(22)	8	(22)	36	19	(50)	3	(8)	16	(42)	38
Socialists	13	(72)	3	(17)	2	(11)	18	11	(61)	1	(6)	6	(33)	18
Marxist Left	7	(64)	3	(27)	1	(9)	11	9	(75)	0	—	3	(25)	12
Total	135	(68)	40	(20)	23	(12)	198	155	(77)	10	(5)	38	(18)	203

Congressmen in the Assembly were born in villages, represent the constituency in which they were born, and continue to reside within their constituency and, in some instances, even in the village of their birth.

Place of birth of Communists was only available for the 43 Communist MLAs and MPs. Of these, one-half were village born, one-fourth from towns and another fourth from Calcutta. Of the 38 Communists in the West Bengal Legislative Assembly, only 19 are from rural constituencies. Among the seven Communist MPs, only two are village-born. Data on the exact birthplace of Communist workers in the All India Kisan Sabha was not available, but it is interesting to note that as many as 12 out of the 44 for whom district of birth was known were born outside of West Bengal (mostly in East Bengal). A rather large number of Communist workers among peasants apparently come from outside of the areas in which they work, in contrast to the Congressmen who are invariably part of the local rural gentry.

The Socialists and Marxist Lefts in the Assembly occupy proportionately more rural seats than the Communists, less rural seats than Congress. Of the 30 MLA seats held by Socialists and Marxists, 20 are rural (See Table II).

INTEREST GROUP AFFILIATIONS

What are the interest group affiliations of rural politicians? The interest group affiliations of MLAs indicate the extent to which rural representatives tend to be well established in their communities. Eighty-five of the 168 rural MLAs have been active in local government, and 62 in local civic associations. In contrast only 12 of the 38 urban MLAs have active in local government and only nine in local civic associations. Many of the rural representatives are also active in caste, tribal and religious associations (20) and credit and banking associations (10). There are few rural MLAs who have not had a record of activity in local government, local civic associations, caste, tribal and religious bodies, credit and banking associations or co-operatives. In contrast, many of the 38 urban MLAs (19 of whom are members of the Communist or Marxist Left parties) have no group affiliations other than the party to which they belong and the trade unions, peace fronts and other associations dominated by their party.

One striking difference between Communists and Marxist Leftists on the one hand and Congressmen on the other is the extent to which one is deeply involved in various kinds of occupational interests, such as unions and peasant associations, while the other is more involved in local government, local civic activities, various caste, religious and tribal bodies. Congressmen are active in school boards, village panchayats, charitable organizations, tribal and scheduled caste societies, Muslim associations, temple boards and host of other bodies in the local community. These bodies, public and private, are the structures of power and influence in rural India and it is in these that the Congress party demonstrates so clearly the sources of its voting power in West Bengal. Few Assembly members have built their electoral careers on trade union and peasant organisation work, and the fact that so few non-Congressmen are elected from outside of Calcutta is a demonstration of this fact. Even opposition legislators in rural areas must build themselves through local government and civic activities. If Congress wins votes in West Bengal, in large measure it must be contributed to the fact that Congress is better entrenched in such local activities than are other parties.

Economic Conflicts in Rural Areas

All this suggests that class conflicts within rural areas are not so great as to disrupt the unity of local civic bodies. Were economic conflicts within rural areas clearly articulated, then peasant organizations, bodies of agricultural labourers, tenant associations and the like would be growing sources of power and would provide the base by which politicians could obtain power. This has not happened in West Bengal and the Congress Party, with its commitment to harmonizing divergent interests, profits from rural unity. For some time but with little success the Communists and the Marxist Left parties have endeavoured to cultivate class struggle. But in recent years, there have been indications that these parties intend to imitate the Congress by working within local bodies, credit societies, co-operatives, and village panchayats—a recognition by the Communists of the essential character of rural society in West Bengal.

Table III

Occupations of Rural Members of the West Bengal Legislative Assembly

Agricultural Occupations[1]		Non-Agricultural Occupations	
Peasant	1	Journalism	4
Farmer	40	Medicine	19
Landowner	11	Business	13
		Law	22
Total	52	Teaching	14
		University teaching	3
		Clerk	3
Political Workers[2]			
Political workers, trade		Total	78
union workers, social workers	38	Grand Total	168

[1] Categories as enumerated in the West Bengal Legislative Assembly Who's Who by each Assembly member. "Farmer" is more likely to refer to landowner than tiller.

[2] Since these 38 political workers list no other occupation, one can assume that for most of them their major source of income is from land holdings. I have verified this from personal observation but can give no precise statistics.

The rural leadership in the Legislative Assembly is made up of small landholders (52 out of 168), and middle class professionals (78), who hold positions as doctors, merchants, lawyers, teachers, journalists and clerks (see Table III). It is this well-established group, relatively high in income, occupational status, education, and in some instances, caste from which political leadership is derived.

Leadership and Planning Process

What effect will this increase in rural leadership have upon the freedom with which economic planning may be pursued? At present, it is possible for India's planners to plan on a highly rational and relatively non-political basis. Planners assess resources, needs and targets, and then proceed to allocate those resources to best achieve those targets. The demands of various political groups for special attention have thus far been of minor importance. Planners work within a *relatively* free atmosphere as far as political pressures are concerned. What pressures exist are slight compared with those present in American, British, or Japanese politics, and slight compared to what they are likely to be a few decades hence as interests in India become more articulate. We have noted that rural leadership is derived from community associations which often unite the community, not class associations which divide. Intermediary landholders, large peasants and non-agricultural middle classes are sources of local leadership. Poorer tenants and sharecroppers might oppose this leadership, but have yet to show any disposition to do so and attempts by Communist and Marxist Left peasant associations to win their support have been without success. Rural demands are likely to be directed at winning government assistance, rather than expressions of political conflict within the rural community. This pattern may change, in which event the predictions which follow will have no validity. But at this time there is no evidence that conflicts within the rural community are of any magnitude.

Demands upon government have focussed on two issues: government taxation, and allocations of government revenue. Attempts by government to increase rural taxes (such as irrigation taxes) are likely to meet with increased opposition. Demands from rural areas for more government expenditure for agricultural development, irrigation schemes, roads, rural industries, medical and public health programmes, credit facilities and the like are already present and are sure to increase. Already, criticisms within the Indian Parliament have been made that the Second Five-Year Plan has had an industrial urban bias and that increased attention, i. e., expenditure, must be given to rural areas in subsequent plans. To the extent that rural areas increasingly articulate their interests, it will become more and more difficult for planners not to take these demands into account. During the past few years planners have had and perhaps for a few years longer may continue to have opportunities for rational planning which may rapidly diminish.

Demands within Congress Party

Were rural demands rising outside the Congress Party fold, it might be possible for the government to resist pressures as it has so successfully resisted pressures from many urban groups. But demands within the Congress Party are more difficult to resist. In some States, such as in Rajasthan, rural-urban conflicts have taken the form of Congress Party-government conflicts. In other states, such as in West Bengal, growing rural and urban demands have forced the state government to exert pressure on New Delhi for more financial support. The growth of rural political power has the effect of straining centre-state relations. For West Bengal, like other states, has the constitutional authority to tax agriculture, but agriculture is poor and politically powerful. On the other hand, West Bengal's industrial sector is relatively wealthy, but only the centre has the authority to tax industry and income. The State government thus increasingly turns to the Centre for financial help. The result is that growing rural demands on the state are deflected into state-centre conflicts.

Congress governments have thus far resisted urban demands for lower food prices, higher wages, more consumer goods and more employment. a factor not unrelated to the growing weakness of Congress in India's major urban centres. To resist rural demands is more difficult, for Congress depends so heavily upon the rural areas for votes. The rural leadership and particularly the rural gentry have thus far effectively delayed or through influence on local administration effectively delayed or through influence on local adminstration effectively negated legislation creating ceilings on land holdings. In both land reform and tax policy the rural leadership has demonstrated its capacity to prevent or invalidate government action. The possibility now exists that the rising number of rural Congress leaders combined with the decreasing number of urban Congress leaders may result in a situation in which this rural leadership could do more than negate, policies, but may make more demands on government. Already there are reports of increasing pressures from rural MLAs on the departments of Public Works, Fisheries, Agriculture, and Community Development. Social service expenditures for health programmes, schools, fisheries, agriculture, etc., per capita are even now higher in West Bengal than any other state (Rs. 6·12 in West Bengal, Rs. 5·94 in Bombay, Rs. 4·19 in Madras and Rs. 2·37 in U. P.).

Hard Choice

We are admittedly now entering speculative realms, but is it far-fetched to assume that the growing numbers of rural MLAs, MPs and political workers will affect the relative freedom with which policy makers now operate? If political demands increasingly enter into economic planning, what effect might this have upon the democratic structure? Government planners will be placed with some hard choices. They are likely to be under pressure from growing rural interests to modify their plans. At this point they must either modify what they conceive to be highly rational plans based solely upon economic considerations, or alternatively they must adopt authoritarian measures to minimise the influence of these political pressures. In short, there is likely to be a price for democracy which planners have not yet had to pay. Indian government officials rightly pride themselves on their eagerness to plan for economic growth within a democratic framework, but thus far these two values have hardly come into conflict with one another. So long as many government officials look upon democracy as a way in which the population is exhorted to freely participate in activities leading toward the goals of national unity, economic development and rural reconstruction, then democracy appears to harmonize with a highly economic and rational view of the planning process. But as organized demands increase and politicians begin to view democracy as a threat to this highly rational and what in their minds is a "responsible" view of planning and the country's long term needs, many a politician in the higher echelons of government may consider sacrificing democratic institutions.

But the dilemma may very well never take this form. At the moment control of the central and state governments is largely in the hands of those who come from urban areas and have an urban outlook and an urban committal to giving priority to industrial development. The rise of rural leadership in the Assembly and in political parties has yet to be reflected in actual control of the governmental machinery on the state and national level. The demands of rural areas for greater allocations of government expenditures and the demands of rural leaders for greater access to power will be difficult to reject, not only because of the growing importance of rural leaders in a system in which universal suffrage flourishes, but also because of the rural populist ideology of many urban leaders who, stepped in Gandhian lore, look upon villages as the 'real' India, and as the repository of India's national heritage. Few urban politicians would be willing to argue the case for increasing rural taxes, in spite of the low taxes now paid. Nor can the urban politician modify the system to diminish the role of rural representatives, since the electoral system is built into the constitution. The urban politicians' control over national and state governments, and the urban-industrial emphasis of planning may indeed undergo great changes.

7

VILLAGE POLITICS IN KERALA*

KATHLEEN GOUGH

PALAKKARA LIES four miles from Ambalapuram, a town and district capital in Central Kerala.** Its population has increased from 1,289 to 1,932 between 1949 and 1964, largely through natural increase, but partly as a result of the construction, in 1958, of a block of government offices in an adjacent village. This event brought several new families of government servants and uprooted landless labourers to live in Palakkara. The increase has made the village very crowded, while the entry of a few rather wealthy families has raised the price of land. About 60 per cent of men in Palakkara work in Ambalapuram or neighbouring towns; less than half did so in 1949. Their work ranges through a great variety of wage or salary occupations.

Parambur, the second village, lies in a rural area in the foothills of the Western Ghats in North Malabar, sixteen miles east of a coastal town which is also the district capital. There is wet paddy farming in the valleys, as in Palakkara, but the bulk of cultivation is of hillside gardens of cashewnuts, coconuts, arecanuts and pepper. About 63 per cent of the men are landless agricultural labourers, in contrast to Palakkara's 24 per cent. About 88 per cent of men have more or less traditional rural occupations. Parambur's population has increased less than Palakkara's in the past fifteen years—namely, from 1,320 to 1,510. Its economy has also changed less, although there has been expansion of cashewnut farming on formerly waste lands.

"AS BAD AS EVER"

When I asked middle-aged people in both villages, "Do you feel better or worse off now than when I saw you in 1949 ?" the most characteristic answer was a laugh and "As bad as ever". There were, in fact, modest improvements in both villages' public property and services. Palakkara has electric street lights, better country roads, a radio house, reading room, children's playground, and some minor irrigation developments. Parambur has several new roads, replacing mountain footpaths—one of the first things I was told is that it is now possible to get a jeep from the main road to the largest paddy-flat, and that two have been down there, one, the Block Development Officer's, and the other,

* Reproduced from *Economic Weekly*, February 20 and 27, 1965.

** I have used pseudonyms for all proper nouns except the names of famous leaders, to protect the identity of my informants.

a Congress Party speaker's. Parambur also has a small reading room and a large co-operative society building. Both villages have more frequent bus services to the town. In both, more of the children are in school.

Regarding private wealth, the real wages of landless day labourers—the poorest stratum of the employed—have no doubt somewhat increased. Yet there is if anything more insecurity of employment than formerly in this class. Many families still suffer acutely for two to three months during the monsoon, and some of the less fortunate are almost destitute most of the time. Demands and expectations in this group have risen enormously, and there are perpetual complaints against employers.

At the opposite end of the scale, Palakkara's " upper class " consists of some 26 families of small landlords, of owner-cultivators possessing more than five acres of land, of higher ranking government clerks, and of small businessmen (a spinning mill owner, a jewel-cutting shop owner, and a lorry-owner)—employing more than a dozen workers. Seventeen of these families are indigenous to the village. Most of them have improved their wealth since 1949 through a fortunate combination of farming with white-collar jobs. Palakkara's only indigenous landlord is a Namboodri Brahman whose forebears were village headmen. The family contains no educated urban workers, and has been obliged to sell some gardens since 1949. Its members still own about 60 acres. In spite of lower rents and higher labour costs, the head has been able to hold on to a modest affluence by personally farming a portion of the estate.

Increased Wealth

Among the dozen bigger landlords of neighbouring villages, the impression I received was one of increased rather than of decreased wealth. In 1949, for example, a wealthy Namboodiri family of an adjacent village owned 600 acres of coconut gardens and wet paddy land. They were obliged by the Communist Agrarian Relations Bill of 1959 to sell 150 acres to tenants. The rest has been parcelled out among relatives and brings a rich livelihood, most of it is now being farmed, with hired labour rather than through tenants. The family's wealth has been further increased by professional employment, and by investment in shop buildings and rental houses in the town.

Similarly, Parambur's one very wealthy landowning joint family, of Nayar caste, has retained or increased its wealth through a combination of subdivision of the property to maximize holdings under the land laws, of personal farming of large acreages, of professional employment, and of intensive cultivation of plantation crops such as cashewnuts, which are exempt from land-ceilings. The net effect in both areas is that while landlords are deeply concerned about threats to their estates from future land laws, few have suffered so far from the ceilings imposed either by the Communist Agrarian Relations Act or by the subsequent, and much more moderate, Land Reform Act of the Congress government of April 1964.

It is in the middle ranks in both villages that economic deprivation is most bitterly lamented. These ranks include small owner-cultivators having less than five acres, tenant farmers, village craftsmen and other village servants, petty brokers of cash crops or livestock, and individual keepers of small grocery stores or of tea shops. Palakkara's "middle class" also includes lower ranking clerical workers, "peons", and workers in restaurants or in industries. While there is minor variation, in only a few special cases has the livelihood of these families substantially improved since 1949. Among the latter are, for example, half a dozen enterprising carpenters and masons who have gained wealth from the new government building, and half a dozen workers in a metal parts factory whose Communist union has secured substantial wage increases. The rest complain of low wages, high prices, loss or subdivision of land plots, unemployment of some members, heavy indebtedness, poor food and frequent illness, and inability to maintain the most modest middle class standing in spite of hard work and thrift. For such people, the picture is further darkened by a sense of loss of morale and of local co-operation, of growth of corruption and cut-throat competition for land, jobs, influence and education. They feel that they have been left behind by the few fortunate rich, yet are threatened by the unskilled manual labourers, who, under Communist influence, grow ever bolder in their demands. An elementary school teacher summed up the position when he said, " Seventeen years ago we had troubles but we told you it was a transition period. At least we had hope. Now we do not know what lies ahead—we are looking into darkness."

Castes and Religious Groups

The two villages encompass the main ethnic groups of Kerala. We may divide these into five broad categories. Among Hindus, the Nayars and their congeners (including the small castes of Namboodri Brahmans and Temple Servants), have traditionally been a landed aristocracy of government servants and religious specialists, about 19 per cent of the people. Below them come the Iravas and a number of allied castes (25 per cent), occupied as tenant farmers, landless labourers, artisans, or in the coir and cashewnut industries. With the mobility of wealth that market relations have brought to Kerala, some Iravas have become merchants, landlords or small industrialists, while many Nayars are now wage-earners. At the bottom of the caste scale fall the Harijans, some 9 percent of the people. They are landless labourers in villages or on the tea and rubber plantations.

Muslims, concentrated in North Kerala or Malabar, form 20 per cent of the people. They have progressed less rapidly than Hindus or Christians in education, and include, as well as rich merchants, many poor and preliterate labouring families in the ports and inland bazars.

Christians form 24 per cent of the people. They are divided into

Roman Catholics (about 90 per cent) and several sects of Syrian Christians and Protestants. Much of the modern capitalist enterprise of Southern Kerala has been carried out by Christians, but Christians span the class structure and include almost every occupation.

Palakkara contains 94 households of Nayars and allied high castes. In traditional parlance they are the " good " or " clean " castes, and the Nayars proper have been the dominant caste in this village. The bulk of Nayars descend from seven ancient matrilineages, whose ancestors owned some land and leased more from the Nambodri Brahman landlord and head of the village. Today, only about a dozen Nayar families retain paddy fields or more than a single garden, the majority being clerks, mill-hands or urban service workers. Correspondingly, more than three-quarters of Palakkara's wet land and almost half its dry land is now owned by absentee landlords, chiefly Christian merchants or Nayar or Brahman professional men of the town.

Palakkara's 51 Christian households rank socially, and in some contexts ritually, between the Nayars and the Iravas. Their ancestors moved to Palakkara from a nearby Christian village eighty years ago, and they were never fully integrated into its traditional social life. Unlike the aristocratic Syrian Christians and the older Catholic families of Ambalapuram, Palakkara's Christians are believed to have once been Harijans and Iravas who were converted to Catholicism within the past two hundred years. Only three of Palakkara's present-day Christians have wealth and high school education, and they have arrived since the government offices were build in 1958. The rest are tenant farmers, brokers, or semi-skilled manual workers in the town.

Irava and Harijan Groups

The 115 households of the " Irava group " were once tenant cultivators and village servants under the Brahmans and Nayars. I have included among them the small service castes who rank close to the Iravas, such as Smiths, Astrologers, Masons, Barbers and Washermen. Some retain their traditional occupations; others trade, or fill town jobs of the same type as the Christians. Some half dozen have completed high school and now hold clerical posts.

The Harijans of Palakkara, finally, comprise 33 households of the Vettuvan and Parayan castes. Once agricultural serfs, hereditarily bound to Nayar and Brahman households, they are today mainly coolies or landless labourers. Most of the younger children are in elementary school, but none has attended high school.

The Irava and Harijan groups traditionally comprised the polluting castes. There was wide social distance between all of them and the Nayars. Within this category, however, the Iravas and their congeners were sharply separated from the Harijans—a fact today reflected in the government classification of the Irava group as " Backward Classes " but not as Harijans. In Palakkara the social distance between Iravas and Christians has always been much less than between either of them and, on the one hand, the Nayars, or on the other hand, the Harijans.

Simpler Caste Structure

Parambur's caste structure is simpler. There are no Christians, and only one house of Harijans. The vast bulk of the village falls into either the Nayar group (53 houses) or the Irava group with 132. As in Palakkara, the Nayars have been the dominant caste of small land-owners and tenant cultivators, leasing some lands from a leading family. A hundred years ago, the leading Nayars were a Parambur matrilineage, formerly village headmen under the local Rajas. With the mobility of wealth brought about by export crop farming in the late nineteenth century, the local headman's lineage lost most of its land to a bigger landlord lineage of a village five miles away. This lineage made wealth in the timber trade and " ate up " the surrounding villages. Today one of its branches occupies a large house on a hill-top overlooking Parambur, and the lineage as a whole owns much of the village land. The local Nayar households, of lower social status, own small plots or lease gardens from the landlords, or in some cases work as coolies. The majority of the Iravas are landless agricultural coolies or very small tenant farmers. In both Nayar and Irava castes, a few men are cash crop merchants, shop-keepers, school teachers, hand-loom weavers, bus-drivers, postmen or constables.

Finally, on the eastern boundary of the village, near the river bank, live 25 households of Muslims, culturally and economically affiliated to the small Muslim bazar town across the river. Sixteen years ago Parambur's Muslims were ' timber coolies ' for Muslim merchants. They swam down-stream with logs to the port, returning with trade goods. In the past five years timber transport has been taken over by lorries. Parambur's Muslims are therefore very poor and insecurely employed. They pick up day jobs as coolies for Nayar farmers or Muslim merchants across the river, or peddle dried fish between coast and interior.

How the Parties Came

When I came to Palakkara in 1948, there was only limited franchise and political parties had not galvanized social life. Cochin and Travancore, as native states, had played less part in the Independence struggle than had Malabar, and its excitement had scarcely penetrated the village. A few Nayars belonged to Cochin Praja Mandal or States Congress Party, but most were cold to the Congress Party because it had recently opened temples to the lower castes. In these latter castes four youths, the only ones to have passed through Primary School, supported the Indian Socialist Party. They were a Carpenter, Two Astrologers and a Washerman. Starting out as Congressmen after Independence, they had become disgusted with what they regarded as Congress corruption, its favouring of wealthy and high caste supporters, and its failure to control the prices of food.

About six youths, Nayars and Iravas, supported the Communists. They worked in a textile mill and belonged to the AITUC union, were rebellious against caste restrictions, and in town demonstrations, marched proudly behind the flag. They sat in low caste teashops, played cards on the road, and tested the Temple Entry Act by bathing together in the village temple tank. Most Nayyars, especially women, condemned them as crazy and sinful, shaking their heads over the supernatural dangers, to the village of youth who transgressed religious laws. When a slimy, noxious weed appeared in the tank in the dry season, Nayar women stayed away and blamed it on the deity's wrath against the Communists.

Most of the Iravas were accepting of the Communists, but disinterested. For the past ten years, Palakkara Iravas had belonged to the Sri Narayana Guru movement (SNDP), a famous caste association based on the creed " one god, one caste, one religion " The SNDP required monogamy of Iravas, Sanskritization of their religious rites, repudiation of caste inequalities, and a kind of Protestant (and indeed capitalist) ethic of thrift and independent enterprise. Under SNDP influence the Iravas paid monthly dues to their statewide association, attended its temple in a nearby village, and employed its Irava priest to perform Sanskrit life-crisis rites. They had ceased to take part in animal sacrifice or other "low caste " ceremonies at the village temple festival. The Iravas had, in fact, partly abstracted themselves from Palakkara's traditional caste system—both economically through wage work, and also morally through the SNDP. They did not, however, attack Nayar dominance head on, but lived in a kind of quiet, back-to-back relationship with the Nayars, fulfilling their tasks and keeping social contacts to a minimum. While few could vote, Iravas tacitly supported Irava candidates who were recommended by the SNDP and who ran as Congressmen or Independents. The Christians, similarly, were deeply involved in their parish church in the next village and supported only church-approved Christian candidates, who at that date ran chiefly as Independents.

Party Tactics

In 1948, Palakkara's Harijans had no interest in political parties. All were pre-literate and worked only within the village. Engaged in relations with small owner-cultivators, they had never been contacted by the Communist peasant unions which, on the larger estates, were in this turbulent period attacking the privileges—and the granaries—of wealthy landlords.

Just beyond the southern boundary of Palakkara lived a strange young man called " Communist Namboodiripad ". Aged 25, he was the younger son of a landlord house in a neighbouring village. As a boy he had served as priest in one of Palakkara's temples. At 13 he ran away because his father would not allow him to attend high school and learn English. Vishvanathan joined and worked for the Congress youth movement, lived in the Congress Party office, ate in the houses of Christian,

Muslim or Hindu party workers, and somehow pulled himself through high school. At 19 he quarreled with the Congress Party because, he said, local leaders were absconding with its funds. He was inspired by a speech by A. K. Gopalan, the Communist peasant-organizer, followed him on a demonstration, was arrested, and soon joined the Communist Party. "I came to know that only thus could we stop the inequalities." He was instructed in Marxism by a local Namboodiri leader, who seems to have stood to him as a *guru*. Following party policy, Vishvanathan later joined the British army and fought in the Burma campaign, but was court-marshalled and imprisoned for organizing strikes in protest against British officers' superior conditions. Returning to Kerala, he formed trade unions among factory and plantation workers. In 1948 he married (within the caste but without dowry), obtained a share of family property, and settled on the edge of Palakkara. I saw him only twice, for he was usually underground or in prison. He had almost no contact with Palakkara people. Most thought him mad, and he thought them hopelessly backward.

When I returned to Palakkara in 1964, I found more than half the village supporting the Leftist Communists. Vishwanathan is now President of the local panchayat board. In his party he is prominent on the district committee. Palakkara is now considered a hot-bed of Communist influence in the mainly working class neighbourhoods which surround Ambalapuram.

Political Consciousness

The change to widespread political consciousness came in Palakkara with the introduction of universal franchise and the entry to the village of units of the Congress and Communist parties at the end of 1951. Political interest much increased when, in 1953, Palakkara became one of seven wards in a newly organized panchayat, whose board members were for the first time elected through universal franchise. Four of the wards elected Communists; three of them, Congressmen. Palakkara elected as ward member Gopalan, a young Nayar ex-constable who was by that time one of three Communist Party members in Palakkara. Panchayat elections were not held again until December 1963; the elected board was suspended during the Chinese Emergency and its functions carried out by a government Panchayat Inspector. In 1963 the panchayat elected a new board of eight members, six of them Communists or independents with CP support. Two additional nominated members, representing women and Harijans, were Leftist Communist supporters. Palakkara's Gopalan was re-elected, and Vishvanathan for the first time became panchayat president in his role as ward-member from the next village. The Communists have steadily increased their support; by 1963, only 337 Palakkara people voted for the Congress candidate, and 513, for the Communist.

The parties came to Parambur in a different way. There, as in Palakkara, half a dozen educated and prosperous Nayars (teachers, landlords and owner-cultivators) joined the Congress Party during the Independence movement on nationalist ideological grounds. The difference from Palakkara was that Parambur lay in a region dominated by very large landowners. Its tenants were swept up in the peasant unions of the mid-1930's. These unions were led by A. K. Gopalan and other eminent mass leaders, then of the Congress Left. They agitated against the landlords for lower rents, fixity of tenure, and the abolition of feudal levies. They also attacked the landlords' right to administer village justice and to impose beatings and fines.

The unions were extremely active until World War II, and in Parabur mobilized 200 Nayar and Irava tenants. Their activism seems to have been related to the growth of export crop farming, the consequent monetization of tenancy and labour relations, the increasing gap in wealth between the great landlords and their masses of impoverished tenants and labourers; and therefore, the labourers' increasing resentment against the old-style levies in kind and against the landlord's paternalistic " justice". Village members of the *karshaka sangams* almost all became Communist supporters when their organizers left the Congress and joined the CPI in 1939. From about 1942-6, *sangam* activism subsided, partly because the war-boom brought gains to the cultivators, and partly because the CPI ceased its most militant forms of agitation while collaborating with the Allied war effort. The sangams were revived in 1946 and reached the peak of their militancy in 1948. Following CPI national policy, they harvested crops for the benefit of the tenants, ransacked granaries, and waylaid grain lorries to distribute food to the landless. Parambur itself actually had rather little violent " trouble ". The local landlord, an Independent MLA of understanding and high character, adopted the enlightened policy of freely distributing stocks of grain to his tenants. But in some neighbouring villages there were bloody encounters between tenants and police, arrests, and two famous cases of martyrdom of Communist leaders. The period became burned into the memories of villagers as one of bitter class struggle between the landlords and the Communist-led tenantry.

When I reached Parambur in mid-1948 the main battles were over. Most Communist Party members were in jail or undergound. I was, however, well aware that most tenants secretly supported the CPI. Parambur, like Palakkara, had its budding Communist leader, Parameswaran, a Nayar youth of 27. But whereas Vishvanathan looked for his following to urban factory workers and rubber plantation workers of several miles away, Parameswaran's was already established in his village.

After 1951, party units developed in Parambur much as in Palakkara. In 1953 the village became a ward of a larger panchayat, first of three and later of eight villages. From the first, the panchayat elected a

Communist dominated board. In December 1963, the Communists further increased their vote, securing seven seats out of eight. Parameswaran has been the ward-member for Parambur since 1953. In 1963, 490 people voted for him, and 227 for the Congress candidate.

PARTY UNITS IN THE VILLAGES

The structure and activities of village units of the Congress and Communist parties in some ways resemble each other. This is natural, as both participate in the electoral system. In each party, village units are responsible to higher committees of the party which tend to parallel the main administrative divisions of the state and nation. Thus, Congress Party members of a ward, which is usually coterminous with a village, elect delegates to a committee of the *mandal*, which is usually coterminous with the panchayat. Mandal committee members elect delegates to committees of the district, state and nation. The Communist Party is similarly constituted, except that the CP seldom has an independent unit at the level of the village or panchayat-ward. Its smallest unit is a branch, which (as in the case of Palakkara and Parambur) is often drawn from a whole panchayat. Branch members elect delegates to committees of the district, state and nation.

When we look into matters, important differences emerge. An obvious one is that in each village, the Congress Party has a large number of enrolled members—76 in Palakkara and 99 in Parambur—but a relatively small number of firm supporters. The CPI, by contrast, has only two or three party members in each village, but a large number of followers. There are several reasons for this. One is that the CPI has apparently, in most periods, restricted its membership to a small organization of trained and proven Marxists, appropriate to a revolutionary party with secret activities. Party members told me that this was necessary because most ordinary men, engaged in everyday relationships, could not be trusted to be loyal to the party if they got into difficulties. Party members must be ready to suffer hardships and observe strict codes of conduct which tend to set them apart from others. Even in the past decade of parliamentary participation, demonstrations against Congress policies have often landed them in prison. Many were there for brief periods during my stay, after organizing demonstrations during the food crisis. Party members who drink heavily, steal, gamble or otherwise create public trouble, or who criticize party leaders or policies to outsiders are subject to temporary or permanent suspension. There are similar rules of conduct for Congress members, but my impression was that they are less strictly observed. The risks and discipline required of C.P. members cause some men to abstain from joining who would readily be accepted. A Nayar factory worker who had supported the C.P.I. for 17 years told me, for example, that Gopalan often urged him to join it. He refused because, he said " The party takes the whole man. " He was also afraid of endangering the educational chances of his younger brother, who held a government scholarship.

Party Membership

From 1957-9, during the period of Communist rule, efforts were made to widen the party membership and to create a "popular" democratic party. CPI membership in Kerala is said to have reached 60,000. After 1959 it dropped again to about 25,000—people say, because "bogus members" who merely wanted favours from the government changed sides when it fell, and because the party grew weaker as a result of the ever-widening Right/Left division. When the split finally came, in April 1964, the Leftists appear to have carried off a large majority of Kerala CP members, although they had only a minority in the leadership. In both Palakkara and Parambur two or three members had tacitly left the party during the Left/Right dispute. Because the leadership was too busy arguing to maintain close contact with the villages, they simply stopped paying dues. All were, however, Leftist supporters after the split had occurred, and said that they would probably try to rejoin after its policy became clarified.

As a party permanently devoted to parliamentary democracy, the Congress has enrolled as many members as possible. It was said to have about 15 lakhs in Kerala. In both villages almost all were primary or "Four-anna" members. Only the ward-presidents and one or two others were "active members" who had fulfilled the criterion of paying Rs. 10 to the party or of enrolling 50 primary members.

In fact, primary members in the Congress Party are in some respects comparable to a category of villagers called "Communist *anubhavis*" (supporters), a phrase heard on everyone's lips. A Communist *anubhavi* is one who is not afraid to publicize his Communist allegiance. He is close to the local party unit, canvasses in elections, and takes part in public demonstrations. If suitably qualified, an *anubhavi* may run for office in the panchayat with CPI backing—three or four had done so, and won, in both the panchayats where I worked. I had the impression that Communist *anubhavis* work harder for the party than do Congress primary members. Many of the latter pay their 4 annas and then remain in a kind of sleeping partnership, attending party meetings only when required to vote for the active members who enrolled them. The fact that locally prominent men wish to have a large number of personal supporters who will vote them on to the *mandal* or some higher Congress committee seems, indeed, to be the main reason why so many primary members are enrolled. Several Congress district secretaries with whom I talked admitted this openly, and I noticed that two automatically referred to primary members as "bogus members". It will be interesting to see whether the new ruling of June, 1964, which forbids primary members to vote for Congress office-bearers above the level of the Community Development

Block, will affect enrollment in villages. Perhaps not, for village primary membership seems to be already mainly relevant to the election of "small big men" at the panchayat level, rather than to elections to the district or state committees.

Communist *anubhavis* are also often members of Communist labour unions. In Parambur about 100 *anubhavis*—small tenant farmers—belong to the peasant union which dates back to the 1930's. They pay dues to the union, elect their own officers, and attend meetings at which they evaluate and criticize the achievements of Communist Party members of the panchayat board. Palakkara formed a similar peasant union of 40 members for the first time in 1963, during the panchayat election drive. In both villages, however, the events surrounding the Left/Right split had so absorbed the energies of party members that they allowed their *sangam* work to lapse, and the peasant unions were temporarily inactive. When I left in September, Leftist party members were beginning to reorganize the tenants to demand their legal rights under the new Congress Land Reform Act, and to prepare them to argue for these rights before the government constituted land tribunals.

Peasant Unions

Peasant unions are naturally the most prominent kinds in villages. In Palakkara, however, about thirty men belong to one or another AITUC industrial union. By contrast, villagers' support for Congress unions was very weak. The Congress Party does have its kisan unions, but I was told they are insignificant in Kerala and that, after the CPI, only PSP has any strength in peasant organizations. The Congress party also, of course, runs unions in almost all industries and on the tea and rubber plantations. In Palakkara, about six men and an equal number of women belonged to recently organized Congress unions, in a local undershirt factory for women and in a newly started spinning mill. Both of these factories refused admission to known CPI supporters, so that to-date the CPI had been unable to establish unions there. Unionism was in general, however, a much more lively interest of Communists than of Congress members.

Within each village, the two parties tend to carry out the same range of formal and informal activities, but with different emphases and goals. Most of these differences spring from the contrast between the Congress as a democratic party which has tried to "absorb" the traditional power structure and gain maximum consensus while only gradually changing the *status quo*, and the CPI whose village members (in spite of a decade of parliamentarism) have retained the outlook of Marxist revolutionaries.

In each village both party units, of course, carry on the political tasks of fund-raising and propaganda through public speeches and door-to-door canvassing. These activities are intensified just before an election, and tend to lapse in between. On the whole, CP canvassing appeals to the class interests of the propertyless and the desire for radical changes leading to greater economic and social equality; Congress canvassing, to self interest and to the desire for public welfare of a more traditional kind. CPI canvassers rely much more on rousing public speeches, demonstrations of protest, organization for militant struggles, and solidarity with charismatic leaders who have conducted such struggles. Congress workers rely more on quiet appeals to the vested interests of those who own property, however little, and for the rest, on personal influence and friendship and on favours, monetary or otherwise, to potential party supporters. It is true, however, that this contrast has to do not only with ideology but with whether or not the Congress is already in power, for the 1960 "liberation struggle" against the Communists did involve large and vociferous demonstrations of an unusual kind.

POLITICAL FAVOURS

Moreover I do not mean merely to echo the Communist allegation that the Congress gains its supporters through bribery, corruption and general appeals to self interest, while the Communists gain theirs through idealistic dedication to the working classes. It is more complicated than that CP supporters, like Congress, do gain personal favours from party members and did so especially during the period of CP rule. Occasionally such favours involve acts which are, strictly speaking, illegal. Most often they are a matter of favouritism in the use of personal influence and the distribution of scarce resources which party members control. An example of the former would be the fact that in Palakkara, with the recent overcrowding, many landless families have encroached on government wasteland by the roadside and built small huts there. Leaders in both parties have provided legal aid, and tried to influence employees of the village land-office and the district revenue department, to make such claims "stick" on behalf of their own followers, but to have followers of what each calls the "anti-party" evicted. Examples of mere favouritism are the fact that in Parambur, in the CP period, the panchayat board saw to it that Communist supporting landless labourers were the first to receive gifts of free housing from the government. Similarly, in both villages co-operative societies have given jobs as clerks and fair-price shop managers to supporters of the party whose members happen to dominate the co-operative society's board. The Communist panchayat boards have in both villages also given contracts to build roads and irrigation works to Communist-supporting contractors and labourers.

The difference is that in the case of the Congress Party, my evidence suggests that only propertied persons are likely to join and support it for the sake of either class interests or ideological conviction, whereas propertyless people (as well as many of the propertied) join or support the party *in the first place* to gain good personal relations with, or favours from, party leaders. Communist supporters usually become so because they believe in the party's policies and in the benefit it may bring to their *class*, whereas personal favours come to them as secondary rewards. Instances to the contrary are, of course, available. Thus the managers of two large firms in Ambalapuram—a textile store and a transport company—are said to have switched to the CPI during 1957-59 to gain contracts from municipal and state governments, and then to have reverted to the Congress after 1959. In general, however, in the neighbourhood of these villages, it is assumed that property-owners, and those who have special relations with them, will support the Congress, and the rest of the propertyless, the Communists.

Other activities of the parties show the same kinds of surface similarities, with underlying differences which stem from their different ideologies and class-bases. Both parties stress that in addition to political canvassing it is their members' duty unselfishly to "serve" the public. But Congressmen tend to see their duty in terms of voluntary philanthropy or bringing "help and benefits" to the village; Communists, in terms of "conducting struggles" against the wealthy, or forcing benefits out of the government on behalf of the poor. Thus in Palakkara, Congressmen were proud that wealthy, urban members of their party had recently built a clinic within the boundaries of the panchayat; and that after the death of Pandit Nehru, the Palakkara Congress party unit gave a mourning feast, prepared in the Congress office, to the villagers as a whole. The Communists, by contrast, are proud that in both villages, their agitations have wrung higher wages and fixity of tenure out of the landlords, and have lowered the house-taxes of people of low incomes, and raised those of middle incomes.

Benefits for the Poorest

By virtue of their control of the panchayat board, the Communists have, of course, brought certain "benefits" to each village with the aid of government funds. But these again have tended to be heavily biased in favour of the poorest sections of the villagers. Examples would be a new road in the Harijan quarter, or a new tank for the low caste washerwomen, while the high caste tanks went unrenovated—benefits which in themselves made it necessary to "conduct struggles" against the privileged before they could be achieved.

Similarly, when communist members do undertake private philanthropy they tend to do it for the lowest and poorest (their own followers), whereas the philanthropies of Congressmen usually end by benefiting the upper and middle ranks of the villagers. The clinic, for example, must charge fees to cover its expenses. These, although small, are prohibitive for the poorer people. Congress members in the village raised funds to build a reading room in the Nayar area, which is—quite naturally—attended only by literate people, mainly from that area. By contrast, the Communist ward member runs a drama club which is located in a mixed street of Iravas and Christians, and is patronized by mainly pre-literate Iravas, Harijans, and a few Communist-supporting Christians and Nayars.

THE LEADERS

The origins and social networks of village party leaders cast light on their influence and roles. In both panchayats, the top Communist leaders have a double advantage. They come from ancient, high caste, local families who were formerly prominent landlords and village headmen. At the same time, they promulgate policies designed to aid lower caste and poorer villagers in their struggles against the privileges of the very classes from which their leaders came.

In the Palakkara panchayat, Visvanathan, the panchayat president, is a Brahman from a formerly wealthy—and still moderately prosperous—village headman's family. Gopalan, the Palakkara Communist ward-member, comes from the most ancient, and by far the biggest, Nayar matrilineage in the village. His ancestors were once prosperous military commanders of Palakkara's Nayar soldiers and also bailiffs of the Brahman village headmen to whom these Nayars were attached as retainers. Gopalan's lineage, and he himself, are now almost landless, but their ancient name and overwhelming numerical preponderance over the other Nayars of the village give his leadership a kind of local authenticity.

In Parambur, Parameswaran, the Communist ward-member and former panchayat president, hails from Parambur's former village headman's lineage, who lost much of their land in the nineteenth century to an "alien" lineage of Nayars.

All three of these men broke completely from orthodox but educationally backward families in their adolescence. They left their villages and underwent a kind of *brahmacharyam*, submitting to the rigours of party discipline and elders' intellectual training, the alienation of imprisonment, and the uncertainties of poverty or of hiding out in the homes of Communist supporters—often of the lower castes. Their marriages and return to their villages shortly preceded the beginning of the Communists' parliamentary period in 1951. With their honourable family histories, local origins and intimate knowledge of the villagers, yet their revolutionary convictions and identification with the lowly, they were ideally suited to guide the ferment toward social and economic equality which was beginning in the lower ranks of their local societies. The fact that all hailed from "feudal" families which had experienced loss of land to the new capitalist classes of cash crop farmers and merchants perhaps aided their identification with the poor. It also helped them to attract some followers from their own caste and class similarly situated to themselves. It need hardly be mentioned that E. M. Sankaran Namboodiripad and A. K. Gopalan, the two Communist leaders in Kerala who tower above all others in the popular imagination, come from similar Brahman and Nayar backgrounds and had similar, if more spectacular, personal careers.

Newer Type of Supporter

Such men still hold the reins in both the panchayats and, I believe, in a large proportion of the Communist-dominated panchayats of these areas. A newer type of Communist and C. P. supporter is, however, appearing on panchayat boards and in district offices. The panchayat to which Palakkara belongs has five such men on its board, and the Parambur panchayat, four. They come from the Irava group; they lack both the aristocratic traditions and the revolutionary experience of their high caste mentors; but they are locally born and have a primary or high school education. Occupationally they include private school teachers, unionized factory workers, village teashop keepers and landless labourers. They obviously illustrate the push toward local power and social equality on the part of propertyless, but increasingly educated, low caste people which the older high caste Communists helped to liberate.

The Congress Party's village leaders have similar social origins to the Communists, but different networks of relationships. Until recently, Congress leaders in both neighbourhoods came from ancient, high caste, local landlord families of the same traditions as those of the Communists. Where these were not already Congressmen, the Congress Party immediately after Independence seems in fact to have co-opted the rural gentry and tried to take over their bailiwicks intact. In both neighbourhoods the top leaders of those days were men of the wealthiest Nayar or Brahman landlord families; their subordinates, junior men of their own lineages or heads of lesser landlord lineages of the locality. Visvanathan's elder brother won a place as a Congress candidate on the Palakkara panchayat board in 1953, and in Parambur Parameswaran has been opposed by Congressmen of his own lineage. The difference between such men and the Communists was, of course, that while sometimes reformist in outlook, they had never broken sharply with the conservative values of their castes and families. They relied for followers on traditional kinds of authority, rather than on revolutionary experience coupled with rejection of such authority.

Two Changes

In the past few years, two changes seem to have occurred on the local scene and in the Congress Party's policies. One is that capital owners such as bankers, merchants, industrialists and export-crop planters—often Christians or 'upstart' Hindus, but sometimes drawn from the older landed gentry—are gaining influence in the higher ranks of the party. The other change is that, with the modern pressure of the propertyless toward social and economic equality, multitudes of villagers now refuse to support their own local landlords of Congress persuasion. The party must, therefore, seek other kinds of candidates for the panchayat elections. In the neighbourhood of Parambur its choice has tended to fall on Nayar, Irava or Muslim owner-cultivators or village merchants.

In the more urban neighbourhood of Palakkara, it has fallen on Christian or Nayar owner-cultivators, white-collar workers, store-keepers or mill-owners, most of whom work in the town.

Most of these men lack the aristocratic mode of life of the old-style landlords, as well as their traditional authority. Engaged in private enterprise, they have a more bustling manner and egalitarian etiquette. Although most have moderate to great wealth, some of the lesser leaders are of poor or low caste origin.

Congress Disadvantages

In Palakkara, a disadvantage of these men is that their top leaders are not locally born. The president of the Congress *mandal* is a Christian of 24 whose father came to live in the panchayat 20 years ago. The family, located in Ambalapuram, are extremely wealthy owners of rice and oil mills, a timber business, and stores for electric and motor parts. The *mandal* secretary is a Nayar timber merchant with a workshop making plates for electric switches. This man hails from 60 miles away and arrived three years ago. When I first met him, he did not know how many wards there were in the panchayat or who headed some of them, although he was collecting petitions to the district Collector to complain about the Communist panchayat board's failure to clean out the public wells.

A second disadvantage was the Congress leaders' alleged involvement in the use of improper political influence and in corruption. The president was accused of using his party-role to obtain government licences and subsidies for his various businesses. Both president and secretary had founded a farming cooperative of 46 local small landowners. The group had received Rs. 20,000 from the Community Development Block to buy improved tools and fertilizers on condition that they engage in joint cultivation. In fact, no joint cultivation was done, most of the labour being by coolies, and a large part of the grant was said to have been "swallowed" in personal expenses.

It must be said that Communists, too, are often accused of double-dealing with government agencies as well as with the public. A Congress member in Ambalapuram accused Visvanathan of pocketing funds from rubber workers' unions, although I never heard this allegation in Palakkara. Gopalan was accused of making money illegally out of a government cement permit, and Parameswaran, of having shared surplus funds from the Communist government's housing scheme with the coolies to whom the houses were allotted. In the Parambur panchayat, 100 Iravas formed a co-operative to make jaggery and sell it to the local Communist-run multipurpose cooperative. In fact the group used their government toddy-tapping permit in order to sell the fermented liquor illegally to the public. They paid the cooperative manager the amount he might have made if he had bought the jaggery and sold it at standard prices.

There does, however, appear to be a difference of scale between the corruption of which Congress and Communist members, respectively, are accused. Congress members are more often initially engaged in substantial private business than are Communists, and so have far greater access to government contracts and the "gravy" that comes with them. Under a Congress State Government they also, of course, wield greater influence to obtain such contracts.

The Congress leaders of other villages of the Palakkara mandal are locally born and of modest means. Palakkara's own Congress ward president is a Nayar owner-cultivator, formerly a motor-mechanic but now a paid party worker. He comes from a smaller lineage than Gopalan, and is an inconspicuous figure in the village. His secretary is the Carpenter-school-teacher who, seventeen years ago, belonged to the Indian Socialist Party. The teacher's elder brother, and actual carpenter and a Congressman, receives contracts through the timber merchant who is the mandal secretary. Earlier he gained wealth through the new building associated with the government offices, and he is now the most prosperous carpenter in the village. My point is that even when the village Congress leaders are locally and humbly born, their concern with private enterprise cuts them off from the mass of propertyless labourers. Their ties to more powerful Congressmen outside their village tend to be at least partly a matter of personal financial advantage, and, directly or indirectly, bind their interests with those of the wealthiest urban capitalists.

A similar though less mercenary situation exists in Parambur. The village Congress president is a Nayar owner-cultivator of modest means. He comes from the same lineage as Parameswaran and ran against him unsuccessfully in the panchayat elections. Balachandran's disadvantage is that, while evidently honest, he has no strong networks of influence in the village except with his own kin and labourers. His father was a bailiff for the wealthiest local landlord and, on their behalf, opposed the rise of the peasant union in the 1930's. His mother's brother was a former village headman, loyal to the British and to the landlords. Balachandran in his turn tends to be viewed as a party-functionary who canvasses on behalf of the landlords, cash crop merchants, store-keepers and more prosperous cultivators who finance the local party unit. In the wider neighbourhood, the Congress mandal treasurer is a member of one of the two greatest Nayar landlord lineages of the region, as well as the owner of two cloth stores. Such a man, however well intentioned, naturally tends to protect the claims of both landlords and merchants against those of landless labourers and small tenants. Towering above him in the town sixteen miles away are higher-echelon Congressmen involved in the really big money of textile manufacturing, whose long arm of influence was said to reach into the legislature, and even the cabinet.

THE VOTERS

Most men in both villages have a definite party allegiance. More than half of those over thirty have maintained the same allegiance for a decade. I found none who had shifted from Communist to Congress since 1957; a number have switched from Congress to Communist in the same period. This paper concerns only men, for I found it more difficult to discover the political allegiances of women. Most women are said to vote as their husbands or other close kinsmen do, but I am unsure how true that is.

"Party allegiance" means the party for which a man said he voted in the state and national elections, or for which he was reliably reported to work. The data were collected by myself and my research assistances, from the individuals or from their close friends or kinsmen. I realize that some of my information may be false. If anything, it errs by favouring the Congress Party. Some men with government jobs fear what is called "police verification". They believe that if they are reported to be Communist supporters, they or their kin may lose their employment. For this reason some men who wish to enter the army or to become postmen or police constables even enroll as Congress members to impress the authorities, while voting for the Communists.

In addition, some men who gave their normal allegiance as Congress actually voted for Copalan, the Communist candidate, in the panchayat elections, because he was a kinsman, or a lineage-mate, or because they admired him personally. These facts partly explain why my own figures show a more even breakdown between Communist and Congress supporters, while those for both men and women voters in the panchayat elections favour the Communist more strongly. Moreover, I was unable to obtain the information for 32 male voters, while 28 more said that they had "no politics" but may actually have voted in the panchayat as in State and national elections.

CASTE AND PARTY ALLEGIANCE

Table 1 shows the male voters of Palakkara by party allegiance and caste-category. The table shows a moderately strong and highly signi-

TABLE 1

Caste and Party Allegiance—Palakkara Men

	Communist	*Congress*	*PSP*	*No politics*	*Unknown*	*Totals*
Nayar Group	46	131	1	5	7	190
Christian	45	20	0	6	7	78
Irava Group	100	44	1	15	14	174
Harijan	38	7	0	2	4	51
Total	229	202	2	28	32	493

ficant association between caste and party affiliation, with higher castes favouring the Congress. I have not yet analysed my figures for Parambur, but the trend is in the same direction and is, if anything, more pronounced. The Parambur picture is complicated, however, in that some of the Muslims support the Muslim League. I was unable to discover exactly how many, because in the last panchayat elections the League had an alliance with the Communists and supported Parameswaran as its candidate. Some Muslims are actually Communist rather than League supporters, but I am unsure how many. Only two Muslims support the Congress. In Parambur as in Palakkara, a much larger proportion of the "Nayar group" than of the "Irava group" support the Congress.

The correlation between caste rank and party support raises the question of "casteism" in Kerala politics. The leadership of the Congress Party has been *internally* divided—and in late 1964, finally split—between competing groups dominated by Iravas, Nayars and Christians. The League is an openly communal party. The Communist Party is sometimes accused of favouring Iravas and Harijans as *castes*, and it has in the past at times made electoral "adjustments" with the League.

I cannot argue the question here except to acknowledge that all the parties, in their effort to control more seats, jockey for influence with one or another of the communal associations (Nayar Service Society, SNDP, Muslim League and Catholic church). What I wish to point out, however, is that in these villages I found that once they have begun actively to support the Communist Party, men have greater *political* allegiance to it than to their caste or to any organized communal association. Communist supporters are also in general men who wish to abolish both inter-caste competition and social inequalities between the castes. Space prevents me from quoting the many instances in which this was illustrated, but I may mention one. The Irava Congress Chief Minister, R. Sankar, fell from office in September. Communist supporting Iravas, as well as Nayars, in Parambur rejoiced exceedingly. Some went sixteen miles to the town to join the celebration with bonfires and fireworks. Irava coolies jubiliated that "Now our EMS (a Brahman) and AKG (a Nayar) may come back to power." It was only among Congress supporters that I heard discussion of the communal implications of Sankar's fall and of the secession from the Congress Party of the 15 dissident Nayar and Christian legislators of Central Kerala, who later formed the nucleus of the Kerala Congress Party.

The Communist Party's problem seems to be, therefore, not what to do about communalism among its own followers, but about that of the poorer classes of Muslims and Christians who are more influenced by their own religious leaders than by the class doctrines of the Communists. Of late this problem has become less acute with regard to the Christian poor, for since 1960 many have disregarded Church teaching and come to support the Communists. Palakkara is especially instructive. Most of the Christians still attend the Catholic church, but a majority now openly support the Communists, as their priest told me he was aware, " What can I do about it ? " he asked. " They are good people: I leave them alone. " Still other Christian tenants and workers of this area (though not in Palakkara) support the Karshaka Tozhilali Party of Father Vadakkan, a class conscious organization which has come increasingly to align itself with the Communists.

Communists and Muslim League

Among the Muslims, however, many of the poor still appear to be without politics or to support the conservative leadership of the League. The question for the Communists is whether to sacrifice principle and maximize their chances in any given election by making " adjustments " with the League, or to reject its communalism and make a drive to convert its followers.

Leftists differed on this question. Parameswaran said mildly that he supposed the Leftists must ally with the League to win the elections, but admitted that this made his life more difficult. Between elections he worked to persuade Parambur Muslims that the League was against their interests, but at election time had to announce alliance with its leaders. He saw that electoral alliances freeze the *status quo* of the parties and turn the Communist Party into a machine rather than a revolutionary movement. In Palakkara, Vishvanathan's approach was one of hard-boiled cynicism. " We must use them (the conservative League leadership) to smash the Congress and then we can easily smash them. " When I discussed this view with Leftist supporters in both villages I met some troubled reactions. A teacher said with disgust, " It is bad—it is cheating the people. It is simply telling lies to the people. " He added that electoral opportunism and deceiving those who do not agree with them are the worst faults of the Communists and the main reasons he did not try to join the party. " What is your idea ? " he asked sadly. " My idea is that we would get rid of *all leaders*. All are old-fashioned, corrupt. We should raise up a new leadership from the schools and countryside. " This view was shared by some other Leftist *anubhavis* who were disillusioned by the vaccillations of policy and internal disruptions of the Communists. Nevertheless, there was no doubt that they would go on supporting the Leftists unless a more principled leadership appeared with the same programmes. Writing in February, 1965, it is interesting to note that to-date the Rightist Communists appear to have taken a more principled position than the Leftists with regard to the coming elections. I do not know what effect this is having on Leftist supporters. I am doubtful, however, if many village Leftists will switch to the Rightist party, for they doubt the Rightist party, for they doubt the Rightists' general intention to press for revolutionary changes.

Caste and Class

The correlation between caste rank and party support rests chiefly, it seems, on two factors, neither of which signifies competitive " casteism " in the usual sense of the term. One is that caste rank is still closely related to socio-economic class, and the Congress/Communist cleavage is at least partly based on class. The other factor is that the Communists have, more than all other parties, attacked the traditional religious and social rank discrimination between high and low castes. It has been the Communists in Kerala, above all, who have visited Harijan houses, fraternized in low caste tea-shops, and upheld irregular marriages between persons of high and low caste.

A Palakkara Nayar Congress supporter commented wryly on this. " See this Vishvanathan, what a clever fellow he is ! He will go even to the very huts of Vettuvas, and enter in when they are eating. And he will say, ' What, man, what is this you are eating ? Is it good or is it bad, what you are getting from your landlord ? Let me taste that *kanji* ? ' And he will taste it. Then these Vettuvas think, ' Who is this Namboodiri ? He is coming into our huts and eating our food ! ' And then they will adore him like a god—is it not natural ? And they will think, ' Surely we must do everything for this Namboodiri. ' " The appraisal, although cynical, hits on an important reason why so many Palakkara Iravas and Vettuvas do "adore" "our Vishvanathan", and follow him for other reasons than the meagre economic benefits he has been able to confer on them. This was shown, I think, on another occasion when I asked a wretchedly poor Irava coolie woman why she voted for the Communists. Had they helped her in any way ? She answered soberly, " Nobody really helps us. But we feel that the Communists are thinking of us. They are friendly, and have good hearts. "

Table 2 shows the male voters of Palakkara by party allegiance and occupation. I have ranked occupations into four categories, based on rough estimates of household income, including income from land and other property. Category I contains landlords, businessmen employing more than 12 people, bigger store-owners, owner-cultivators with more than five acres, and white-collar workers of higher grades. Category

Table 2

Occupation and Party Allegiance—Palakkara Men

	Communists	*Congress*	*Others*	*Total*
Category I	4	45	2	51
Category II	94	126	25	245
Category III	40	18	8	66
Category IV	91	13	27	131
Total	229	202	62	493

II contains owner-cultivators of smaller holdings, lower grade clerks, skilled urban workers, highly skilled craftsmen and village servants, and businessmen with 5 to 12 workers. Category III contains tenant-cultivators, petty brokers, individual shop-keepers and the less skilled village servants. Category IV contains unskilled day labourers and the unemployed.

The table shows a moderately strong and highly significant association between occupation and party affiliation.* Although the association between occupation and party is slightly stronger than that between caste and party, there is no satisfactory way of assessing whether the difference between the two associations is significant. Nevertheless, Table 2 supports my view that although both Congress and Communists Parties have originally been led mainly by high caste men drawn from landowning families, the contemporary struggle between them is based substantially on a struggle between propertied and propertyless classes. There is no doubt that the trend in Parambur is the same.

The Issues

Among pre-literate and propertyless Communist supporters, economic issues are prominent. In both villages the poor cite benefits received during Communist rule in 1957-59. They included debt-relief, fixity of tenure, a ten cent plot for landless labourers, higher agricultural wages, free housing for the homeless, lower food prices than subsequently, ceiling on land ownership, and for tenants, the prospect of buying some land. Some of these benefits were carried over into the Congress period after 1960, but most have been seriously diluted or made impracticable by the more moderate Land Reforms Act of 1964. The runaway rise in food prices in summer 1964 confirmed the poor in their belief that the Congress is opposed to their interests—although few needed the confirmation after seeing " their " government ejected in 1959. The food crisis since September, followed by the arrests of their leaders, can only have deepened their bitterness.

" Equality ", often talked of, vaguely defined, is the objective of the village poor, and they believe that the Communists will bring it. It means the end of *mudalalithwam* (capitalism, or more literally, " rule by big men "), which to the poor means both rule by the Congress government and the more immediate exactions of the landed, mercantile and industrial rich. " Equality " means the end of the rank distinctions, of privilege and etiquette, and of all traces of the religious discriminations of caste. But it also—and in a quite simple and literal way—means equality of wealth; land, wages and profits, they believe, should be equally divided, and there should be no more rich and poor.

*Chi square for Table 1 is 92,239, significant at better than the ·001 level; for Table 2, 104·524, significant at better than the ·001 level. Phi was used as a non-parametric measure of association. The association between caste and party is ·46, and between occupation and party, 49

Among party members, educated Communist supporters, and the younger and more informed labourers, discussions entered realms of theory embodied in the Tenali draft platform, which cannot be reproduced here. Briefly, one thing was certain to them; the Congress is the captive of the national and imperial bourgeoisie, and cannot bring socialism to India. It must be removed, " somehow ". The Rightist Communists were seen as revisionists who had surrendered revolutionary ideals, and, on the national scene, were " compromising " with the Congress.

Left Communist Stronghold

There were no Rightist Communists in Palakkara, and only one in Parambur; Communist supporters followed the Leftists for two reasons. First, both their own local leaders, and also E. M. Sankaran and A. K. Gopalan, the most popular state leaders, were Leftists. For most people, this was evidence enough where their own allegiance should go. Second, there was a popular revulsion against any hint of compromising radical programmes. Significantly, Leftist village Communists and their supporters, in August-September 1964, did not want a United Front with the Rightists. As a party member in Parambur put it, " Yesterday we ate from the same leaf with the Rightists, but today they call us Chinese dogs. Why should we join with them tomorrow ? As for the Samyukta Socialist Party, they were seen as " not a party at all ", but an opportunistic clique, and " even more reactionary than the Congress ". For this reason I heard, and heard about, covert grumblings among some village Communists in late August and early September as electoral alliance began to be talked of. Among the pre-literate, less sophisticated Leftist supporters, uninitiated in party-manoeuvres, the reaction was still stronger: the Leftists should go it alone with their own programmes and methods and win or lose the elections on the merits of their appeal to the people. I do not know how these villagers, with their urgent need and simple revolutionary fervour, have reacted to the recent vaccillations over a United Front.

Not a Live Issue

The Chinese invasion was not a " live " issue among the less educated Communist supporters. China was far away, and the details unknown to most people. When I suggested that non-Communists accused the Leftists of national betrayal, the most common response was that this accusation was designed to confuse the real local issues of land, wages and prices. In Parambur a tenant farmer did try to come to grips with the issue. He told me, " Often in our country two men plant cashewnut trees on a hillside. Eventually they meet near the summit. Each knows his trees and they do not worry about it. The trouble comes in the next generation. And then it is very, very difficult to draw a boundary on these hills. I am thinking that the Chinese and Indian quarrel is of this kind." He thought that it should be arbitrated in the same way that a village arbitrator (*madyesthan*), disinterested, but with friendly ties to both parties, would try to settle a local boundary dispute.

Among Leftist party-members and those in their confidence, there seemed to be more deep-seated anxiety about China and a greater range of disagreement. A prominent woman Leftist told me with fears that China had betrayed the Indian Communists and India must defend herself at all costs. It was right for India to buy weapons from any country—even the United States—provided she paid for them, although meanwhile, negotiations to settle the border issue were essential. At the other extreme was a Leftist who told me that both India and China had been at fault and the border should be internationally arbitrated, but that China's actions should not deter the Leftists from pressing towards socialist revolution in India. His personal view, which he distinguished from part policy, was that Indian revolution should not, and could not in the nature of things, be instigated by a foreign power, but that when it began, "certainly we shall need and will receive all help from our Chinese comrades." Most Leftists to whom I talked took a less definite position. Most held that (1) China had been largely at fault on the border, but China was not out to conquer India, and international arbitration, not war preparations, was the answer; (2) in general the Chinese line on world socialism was correct, the Russian, revisionist, and Khrushchev, "not at all a Marxist"; and (3) it was unlikely that India would reach socialism through the present electoral process, but that its channels had not been exhausted and the time for revolution was not in sight.

The Congress Supporters

Among persons who supported the Congress, there seemed to be a wider range of reasons and of political positions. Two types of reaction were common among lower caste Congress supporters. One was that of the younger or middle aged man who, through personal enterprise or the patronage of superiors was improving his lot in society. Such men saw the Communist poor as thriftless and parasitic. Why should they clamour for equality and free benefits, when everyone knew that life was a struggle and men advanced through perseverance ? A second type of Irava or Harijan Congress supporters, usually older men, comprised those able to retain security and favour through traditionally "moral" relationships, for example, loyalty to a long-term employer.

Among high caste, but less educated and less prosperous Congress supporters, there was often a wish to hold on to traditional caste privileges, which the Communists were out to destroy. With this frequently went the view that the individual's own property and status had been undermined by Communist assaults. This was especially true of Nayar owner-cultivators and small non-cultivating landowners who had been impoverished by the Communist land act—obliged to give fixity of tenure to a recalcitrant labourer, or to sit quiet while a tenant withheld or delayed his rent. For such men Communism meant violence, irresponsibility, and even plain robbery, and support of the Congress, the only hope of stemming the frightening tide of rebellion.

A small number of prosperous, high caste Hindu or Christian landlords and merchants opposed both Congress and Communist policies, but voted for the former as the lesser evil. For them socialism was a farce and democracy (as a lawyer landlord put it) "the anarchical nonsense of the multitude". Such men had opposed Independence in the first place, and would have preferred India to be ruled by the army, or Kerala to be under permanent President's rule.

For all of these people, support of the Congress meant, primarily, opposition to the Communists. Their objections to the Communists were regularly coupled with two other highly charged accusations: atheism and national betrayal. There was also a more discriminating category of men, most of them white-collar workers, who expressed positive faith in democracy and socialism. Most were pre-Independence Congress supporters or, if young, were informed about and proud of the Freedom struggle. Some of these men had opposed the 1959 "Liberation Struggle" against the Communists because they considered it undemocratic. Some approved of both the Communists (Land and their Education Acts), and opposed Communism chiefly because they thought it involved oppressive dictatorship. For such men, eager to maintain faith in the electoral process, the factionalism, corruptions and economic failures of the Congress in Kerala were extremely distressing. Memories of the Independence struggle, and reverence for Gandhi and Nehru, were the mainsprings of their support. As one Nayar put it, " In my youth I have touched the robe of Mahatma Gandhi when he came to visit my high school. From that day I vowed that I would not depart from this Congress. "

Working Out of the Party Conflict

The party-conflict is the deepest in both villages, and ramifies through almost all institutions. It takes two forms: (1) a long-term struggle for power between propertied and propertyless classes, with the Communist Party usually championing the propertyless, and the Congress Party, or individual Congress Party members, usually defending the traditional rights of property-owners but sometimes nervously challenging them or conceding points to the propertyless; and (2) a struggle between actual local political factions (which are not solely based on economic class) for control over available resources, goods and people. These two types of struggles are not always mutually compatible. In different contexts now one, now the other, predominates.

Struggles to control land are naturally prominent in both villages. On the "class struggle" front, the Communists try to get land or its produce away from landowners and give it to tenants and labourers. Visvanathan, for example, fought a struggle in court against his own elder brother, a Congress candidate in the 1963 panchayat elections and a Congress ward representative on the previous panchayat board. The struggle was to have sixty Harijan families, domiciled on the latters' land, provided with 10-cent plots and new small houses when they were evicted from their old sites in order that a spinning mill could be built. Each brother employed a "party lawyer" who takes cases only from members or supporters of the party that he himself favours. It is struggles of this type which bind the landless, as a class, ever more closely to the Communist Party, and alienate them from the Congress Party. On the "party factional" front, however, both local party units try to obtain plots of waste or government land to house their own supporters or to augment the gardens which their supporters, already own. With the acute shortage of land in Palakkara, this often means struggling through the courts or through influence with government officials, to have supporters of the "anti-party" evicted.

IN FACTORIES AND OFFICES

In the urban context of which Palakkara is part, struggles inside factories and government offices resemble those over land. From the class-angle, both NGO's and factory workers press for higher pay from their employers. Factory owners are almost all Congress supporters, while government has usually, and of late, been a Congress government. In both contexts Communist unions wage the most uncompromising struggles. On the party-factional front there are, however, rival Congress unions which compete with the Communist ones for influence among workers and for some measure of benefits from employers. These unions sometimes ally with the Communists in strikes, but sometimes reach separate compromises with the management. In Palakkara, Congress unions are widely regarded as "management unions". Thus, the Congress-supporting Christian owner of a local handloom mill closed down the mill in the Communist period because the Communist union demanded higher wages and various other concessions. When Congress came to power he reopened the building as a power-mill in which village women now make undershirts for very low wages. In 1963 a Communist union formed in the mill, with local party instigation, but its registration was legally suspended after the owner had fought a battle in the courts. In 1964 the Congress *mandal* secretary was forming a new union among the women, to "get some help and benefits" from the management in the form of tea-breaks and medical care. As he was himself a businessman and as the mill-owner was a Congressman, local Communists thought his actions completely bogus. A Congress supporter remarked that there was always an element of self-interest in all union organizers' activities, Congress or Communist, but that the secretary might sincerely help the women in order to gain their votes,

Control of Public Funds

Another area of party conflicts is that for control over public funds obtained from local taxes or provided to the village by government agencies. The most important are (1) the panchayat budget, (2) special-purpose grants from the block development office, and (3) loans and grants to cooperative societies. The first set of funds concerns such matters as road maintenance, rural sanitation, electric lighting, public wells, etc. In all panchayats, parties campaign strenuously to gain control of the panchayat board, and whichever party wins tends to favour its own followers in the distribution of public benefits. In Palakkara and Parambur, where Congress supporters have consistently lost the panchayat elections, they have tended to seek control of alternative funds through cooperative societies and block development projects. In general, block development funds tend to go more often to individuals and groups who support the Congress Party, because such individuals usually have a better credit rating, and security is required for loans from the development fund. There is therefore a growing tendency for the Communist party units to ignore or to fight the block offices on the theory that they are unable to help the poor.

Party conflict erupts, again, over the control of churches, mosques and temples. This may seem strange, for the authorities of all these institutions charge the Communists with atheism. Some are, indeed, militant atheists. Visvanathan is said to have made a microphone speech two years ago in the middle of the village goddess festival, beseeching the people to abandon such foolishness. But I found that many village Communist members are vague about belief and quietly practice religious observances. Gopalan worships at a shrine dedicated to the spirits of his parents, and goes on pilgrimage to Rameswaram. Parameswaran made a vow to Kondungalur Bhadrakali when he had smallpox, and fulfilled it a year ago.

Religious Institutions

What seems to happen in the case of religious institutions is that movements form among lower ranking Communist supporters for more democratic control of the institution, which are partly *sui generis* and partly indirectly stimulated by Communist teachings about equality. The Party itself may be unconnected, or its members may take individual stands. In Palakkara, for example, the Harijans last year staged a campaign to perform their own annual temple festival inside the village Bhagavadi temple, with appropriate Sanskritic rites, rather than performing it with traditional rites to a Harijan diety several hundred yards away. Their unsuccessful petition to the Congress-dominated Nayar temple committee to be allowed to do this was signed by eleven Nayar Communist members and party supporters, but the party members did not actually attend the festival when it took place outside the locked temple gate. In Parambur, a struggle was being carried on by Communist-influenced Muslims against elders of the mosque to stop the latter from making propaganda for the Muslim League in the Friday sermons. In the town near Palakkara, a similar struggle was occurring inside the Chaldean Syrian churches between a conservative faction who support a Middle Eastern patriarch now living in America, and a leftwing faction who support an indigenous patriarch. I was told that although the parties may not be directly "behind" this schism, members of the American faction tend to support the Congress, and those of the left wing, the Communists. The interesting point is that even where the parties do not themselves engineer fission, the different value-premises of their supporters cause the fundamental conflict to ramify through every aspect of public life.

The same kind of conflict occurs in connection with the caste associations of Nayars and Iravas. As Communism gained strength in Palakkara, Irava allegiance to the SNDP weakened, and the local branch faded out a decade ago.. In 1959, however, an Irava government servant came to live in the village and tried to restart a branch with the aid of the Congress Party unit. The group's aim seems to have been to raise the educational standards of Iravas and try to "rescue" them from Communism. Funds were collected from Ambalapuram Irava businessmen to build an office and reading room. When the office was half erected, Palakkara Iravas voted in a local Communist President and office bearers, and physically drove off the Congressmen. The sponsors withdrew their funds in dismay, and for five years the building has stood uncompleted. In a nearby village, Communist Iravas "captured" the SNDP temple and reading room some years ago through elections, and have turned both into multi-caste facilities used mainly by Communist subscribers. Carpenter-Blacksmith and Irava-Christian marriages have been conducted in the temple. The branch retains its allegiance to Sri Narayana Guru, but operates autonomously. Its members have broken their connection with the statewide Congress leadership of the SNDP, in response to a hullabaloo at the election of the State leaders in 1962. Communist SNDP members, who appear to be the majority of the rank and file, accuse the Congress leadership of having held on to its power by fraud and police intimidation at the elections. Since 1962 many SNDP local branches have dissociated themselves from the official body. The SNDP was never strong in North Kerala and appears to have virtually disappeared.

Nayar Service Society

The Nayar Service Society, beginning in 1924, expanded greatly in the 1950's. It became a powerful corporation owning schools, colleges, a hospital, rubber plantations, a sugar mill, and areas of forest land which have been newly colonized by Nayars. Always a secular organization, its goals have been Nayar education, the development of capitalist enterprise and economic and political competition with Christians and Iravas under the new democratic dispensation. As a joint-stock company, it jockeys with the SNDP and with Catholic corporations to obtain educational and development funds from the government. In rural areas its branches have tried to revive ancient Nayar art forms, temple organizations and caste assemblies. They thus foster Nayar separatism from the lower castes while easing the transition from "feudal" dominance to capitalist competition. At the same time they recruit a portion of the electorate for support of NSS-sponsored candidates for state and local offices. While superficially similar to the SNDP, the NSS, a high caste organization, has never had its crusading faith in social equality nor its popularity among the poor. Its leadership influences right wing pressure groups both inside and outside the Congress Party and was, of course, with the Catholic hierarchy, instrumental in ousting the Communists from office. N. S. S. and a portion of the Catholic church are now dominant power-groups in the new Kerala Congress Party.

Constant Tension

The NSS made its debut in Palakkara two years ago under the influence of an RSS-supporting leader from Ambalapuram, but with the sponsorship of the Palakkara Congress unit and the Congress-supporting Nayar village temple committee. An initial meeting was held and plans made to start a reading room and local office. Evidently, Congress members hoped to use the NSS and its urban sponsors as an educational and financial bulwark against the Communists. At the first meeting, however, Gopalan cheerfully turned up with his followers and, playing on his panchayat authority and lineage membership, got himself elected to the executive committee. The urban sponsors appear to have withdrawn, and the NSS has made no further headway in Palakkara.

All of these power struggles between Congress and Communist factions occasion a constant state of tension in both villages. Villagers on both sides lament that the tensions produce stalemate in many activities and prevent the village from carrying out its goals of production increase and public welfare. The stalemate is especially noteworthy in land-relations. With the seesaw changes in land laws under the successive Communist, PSP and Congress ministries between 1957 and 1964, conflict and litigation have increased phenomenally. Some tenants in 1964 refused to pay their rents at all, hoping the government would change before the Congress Act of 1964 was fully implemented. Land revenue had not been collected for two years. Landlords tended to lose interest in the care of their land, and to exploit tenants and labourers to the maximum, fearing that their land might be taken from them within the next few years. Several village projects, too, were abandoned or delayed by the mutual sabotage between the parties. So demoralizing was this state of affairs that I had the impression of witnessing a terminal period of some kind in Kerala's political relations, although I had no idea what would follow it. The sudden collapse of the Congress government, the alarming food crisis in the period of President's rule, the new fissions and vacillations in both the Congress and left-wing parties, and the arrests of the Leftist leaders, must have greatly increased the villager's frustrations.

Covert and Restrained

It must be said that most of the time, tensions between the parties remain remarkably covert and restrained. In Palakkara, however, with its overcrowding and unemployment they do periodically erupt in violence. Each party faction has a few expert fighters as henchmen. Fights are most likely to occur just before or after an election, and several took place in 1960. A series of episodes also occurred in 1964 soon after the panchayat elections. A mixed party of Nayar and Irava men attended the wedding of a Palakkara Nayar in a village some miles away. Coming home in the private bus (actually, a borrowed police-van) a drunken Nayar accused the Communist panchayat board of incompetence, and a fight broke out between the factions. For several weeks thereafter Congress and Communist supporting Nayars hired Christian and Irava men from Ambalapuram or elsewhere to beat members of the "anti-party" of each on their way home from work in the dark. Four such incidents occurred, two on each side, before the conflict temporarily subsided. The injured persons filed complaints at the police station but no action was taken, although "investigations" were going on. I was never able to discover the extent of responsibility of the local party leaders for these incidents. Each faction leader denies his own responsibility for such assaults, attributing the blame to lesser individuals, while accusing the other party's leaders of financing and engineering counter-assaults, and sometimes of bribing the police to take no action. My information suggests that party leaders of both sides may occasionally hire henchmen to carry out assaults on party-enemies, but that most such assaults are made by *ad hoc* groups of faction supporters who feel that they are defending the pride and interests of themselves and their party. It is interesting to notice that whereas some decades ago, Nayars of opposed lineages sometimes employed their hereditary lower caste tenants and labourers to fight for them, today they may employ lower caste political supporters of the village, or even politically unaffiliated mercenaries, to prosecute their inter-party feuds.

Mutual Restraint

In spite of these eruptions, a cheerful, kindly temper, social endurance, mutual restraint, and orderly prosecution of routine tasks prevailed in both villages most of the time. In the midst of hunger, unemployment, and the general struggle for survival, such personal strength could only evoke admiration. I am unable to "explain" and can only pay tribute to these individual moral qualities, but may suggest some social reasons why, in spite of the basic cleavage, the parties do not engage in more continuous and overt conflict.

One reason is, of course, that some relationships do cross the party cleavage, and in individual cases prove temporarily stronger than party-allegiance. In Palakkara, Ammini was a strong-minded, dominant Nayar Communist supporter who had made an unorthodox marriage with an Irava factory worker. Early in the fights referred to, she boasted to me that her husband was a henchman of the Communist faction, and could beat any Congressman within miles. But when her own father's brother's son, a Nayar Congressman, was hospitalized after being beaten by an Ambalapuram Communist Christian, Ammini became subdued and hastened to tell me that her husband was not involved, and that "some outside people have bad customs and are giving blows without reason". She blamed it on alcohol, but from that day withdrew her support of the vendetta.

Similarly, neighbours and occupational companions, as well as kinsmen, often have reciprocal interests in helping each other out in emergencies, and personal friendships which override party. Moreover, most people simply do not wish to be at loggerheads with others most of the time. Parameswaran an unusually affectionate and mildmannered leader prided himself that he had no personal grudge toward the younger lineage-brother who ran against him as Congress candidate for the ward. They greeted each other on footpaths and had never broken the pattern of mutual visits and help at life crisis. Visvanathan did stay away from his family for most of two decades, but in the end went home to make peace with his mother.

Present System Cannot Continue

Everyone, moreover, especially the panchayat board, has an interest in maintaining peace and at least trying to carry out public development projects. The panchayat board wishes to be re-elected; its members wish their panchayat to be a credit to them and a rival to other panchayats. They do not want to be accused of trouble-making and continuous negativism. That is why panchayat board members always claim to outsiders that in their panchayat "party really does not matter" and that all of them represent the panchayat as a whole, rather than their separate party factions. In fact, of course, they do both, prosecuting the party conflict when it is a question of defending their own supporters, and co-operating for the panchayat when they need to wrest money from the government or to satisfy an impatient public. Parameswaran, for example, had a hard time explaining to his own followers, as well as the Congressmen, why two minor irrigation projects failed because of poor engineering. He is now struggling to persuade higher officials to finance some needed adjustments.

This does not mean that the present system in Kerala can continue indefinitely. My own impression is that the Communist period so deepened the existing class struggles and liberated propertyless people from their old ties of subordination, that traditional relations of private property, tenancy and wage labour cannot now be made to work harmoniously. Especially if the economy does not rapidly develop and spread its benefits, the poor will now, of their own initiative, sabotage efforts aimed at restoring the classrelations of pre-1957. The arrest of Leftist leaders will not, therefore, solve the political crisis in Kerala. Deeper measures, aimed to harness rather than repress the striving of the common people, will be needed to bring this about.

8

IMPACT OF GOVERNMENTAL MEASURES ON RURAL SOCIETY*

A. R. DESAI

THE PAPER represents an attempt at a brief review, in a very broad outline, of the changes that have been taking place in the rural life of India under the impact of the various measures of the Indian Union Government.

The choice of the subject has been prompted by the following considerations:

INDIAN SOCIETY IN TRANSITION

Indian society has been experiencing one of its greatest transitions in history since the advent of the British rule. Its technological foundation, its economic structure, its social institutional framework based on the caste-system and the joint family, its political organization, its ideological orientation and cultural value systems have been undergoing a qualitative transformation. As the British rulers generated changes in Indian society basically to serve their own interests, these changes were not uniform or symmetrical and, therefore, created specific types of contradictions and antagonisms within Indian society.

After the withdrawal of the British from India the Indian people have entered a new phase of existence; independence has released their initiative and creative energies. The Government as well as other agencies have been evolving and operating various schemes to bring about changes in the social, economic, political and cultural life of the people. The study of these changes is fascinating and instructive as it gives glimpses of the social change affecting one-fifth of mankind.

Among the various agencies attempting to alter the social life in India at present the state has acquired signal significance as a factor ushering change. It has been effecting social changes by creating, to use Talcott Parsons' phraseology, "situations in which people must act" as well as by operating on 'subjective' elements—their sentiments, goals, attitudes and definitions of situations.

STATE OF INDEPENDENT INDIA—ITS GOAL

The Constitution of the Indian Union has already formulated the goal towards which Indian society is to develop.

---

*Reproduced from *Transactions of the Third World Congress of Sociology*, Vol. I-II, pp. 267-277.

The Legacy of British Rule

Before we survey the measures adopted by the government of the Indian Union to realize this goal, it is necessary to visualize concretely the type of rural social structure which it inherited from the British rulers and which became the basis on which it operated.

(a) The British rulers, as is now well-known, had dealt an almost fatal blow to the rural organization which existed for centuries on the foundation of an almost independent and autarchic village community, collectivist in spirit, based on the village possession of land and unity of agriculture and industry, producing for local needs and functioning through three main institutions, viz., the Joint Family, the Caste and the Village Panchayat, and paying tribute to the state or the intermediary collectively and in kind out of the actual produce.

(b) They introduced situations "which were external to the social system as a whole" and "independent of the internal institutional structure, or the immediate situations in which large masses of people acted," by almost destroying the collectivist through hierarchic foundations of the social order and by introducing the individualist, competitive *gestalt* within it. They introduced private property in land through *Zamindari* and *Ryotwari* land tenures. They substituted in place of payment of revenue in kind by the village community on the basis of a definite share from the produce, one in cash from the individual, with the inevitable result that the motif of the entire agrarian economy shifted from production for use to production for market, first to secure cash for the payment of revenue and secondly to adjust to the new setting introduced by the British. Thus the agrarian economy was enmeshed into the web of the Indian and world market. By ruining village artisan industries through pushing their own machine-made goods, they destroyed the self-sufficiency of village life. They undermined the authority of the caste and the village *panchayat* by bringing the village under the rule of laws made by the centralized state and depriving the old institutions of their penal powers.

(c) While Britain thus destroyed the old economic and social equilibrium by introducing capitalist economic forms in India, no new equilibrium emerged, since she thwarted free economic development in general, and industrial development in particular, which would have militated against imperialist economic interests. The Indian rural scene as a result of this underwent a transformation based on increased impoverishment of the mass of the rural population, an increasingly deteriorating agrarian economy, sharp changes in rural class structure and fossilization of rural, social and cultural institutions.

(d) This resulted in the lop-sided and unbalanced position of agriculture in the national economy, mass ruination of artisans, over-pressure on land, increasing diminution in the size of the holdings, growth of subdivision and fragmentation of land leading to the alarming increase of uneconomic holdings, low yields, rise of massive indebtedness of the peasant population, extending grip of moneylenders, traders, landlords and substantial farmers over poor peasantry, steady passing of land from cultivators to creditors and resultant growth of absentee landlordism and rise in the number of landless labourers. In the *zamindari* areas, the letting and sub-letting of land resulted in the extensive growth of functionless non-cultivating rent-receivers creating a chain of intermediaries (tenants, sub-tenants and sub-sub-tenants) whose cumulative burden had to be borne by the actual tiller of the soil.

(e) In the social sphere, the operation of the laws which transformed land into a commodity capable of being bought, sold, mortgaged, leased and partitioned, in the economic context described above, engendered centrifugal tendencies in the joint family and led to its increasing disintegration. According to the Report of All India Agricultural Labour Enquiry Committee, the average size of the rural family has dwindled to 5·01 persons. The consequences of the shrinking of family in terms of human relations, emotional and attitudinal imbalance deserve to be stressed.

(f) The caste system experienced a peculiar jolt under the impact of the British rule. Caste ranking and economic status have been closely co-related. "Caste rank is particularly manifest through ritual symbols; a group which was economically well off could acquire ritual hallmark to raise its relative position in the hierarchy."

The impact of the British rule and the developments that took place under it were different on different castes. Some of the upper castes of the old social order acquired control over land and became land owners. Some of these took to trading, moneylending and such other business. A number of the intermediate castes, as a result of the operation of the laws of market economy, acquired lands and developed into substantial farmers or rich tenants. Many other castes and sub-castes, having lost their occupational security and having no alternative means of employment, took to agriculture, becoming small farmers or agricultural labourers, or vegetated in their traditional occupation. The scheduled castes, depressed classes and aboriginal tribes were more and more transformed into agricultural labourers, agrestic serfs or bond-tillers.

Thus, in the rural area, as a result of the dynamic but increasingly deteriorating economy, a profound socio-economic transformation took place during the British rule. Certain castes acquired a monopoly of economic power and resources. Certain other castes belonging either to upper or intermediate categories struggled to wrest control from the successful caste groups. Other castes suffered a further decline in their economic status. The agrarian area became a vast cauldron of fiercely competing units where the old hierarchy of caste system based on birth, status and ritual hallmarks, was being transformed into a new hierarchy based on the increasing monopoly of wealth, power and culture. However, it should be noted that this competition predominantly operated within the matrix of the caste structure. Castes were competing with castes. There were shifts of power from some of the upper castes either to other upper castes or to some of the intermediate castes. The economically weak lower castes, though they became still weaker in this conflict, also initated and developed struggles for the removal of their disabilities and the betterment of their conditions. It was unfortunate that this historical process of occupational changes of castes and their new correlations was not properly observed and its significance evaluated till very recently.

RURAL INDIA

A brief picture of conditions in the rural area will assist us to understand the nature of the legacy inherited from the British period by the government of the free Indian Union.

Land concentration, predominance of uneconomic holdings, a third of the agricultural population reduced to the level of agricultural labourers, a large portion of the non-agricultural rural population also living in a precarious condition, dependent on the prosperity of agriculture, and, further, a substantial section of even the agricultural owners and agricultural tenants on medium or small-sized farms desperately struggling for survival on meagre agricultural production—such has been the picture of rural social life in India.

Provision for employment for millions of peasants who are unemployed but whose unemployment is disguised, as also for the ruined and unemployed non-agricultural section of the rural people; adequate wage for the agricultural labourers; proprietary rights and economic units of cultivation for the tenants; and economic holdings for the lower and middle strata of peasantry, along with proper credit facilities, marketing opportunities, suitable conditions for growing crops in a manner which would enable them to compete favourably with the prosperous and rich farmers—these are some of the fundamental requirements of a vast section of the rural people. In addition to these, they need to be provided with better seeds, fertilizers, adequate supply of water and better transport and marketing facilities. In short, the fundamental task confronting new government was to provide proper opportunities to all agricultural producers to compete on equal terms in the market.

As Chester Bowles very aptly sums up "Land inequality is a bottleneck clogging the creative energy of the people; a bottleneck that must be broken" and further "Land reform is not a solution of course; it is the first essential step to agricultural improvement, to consolidation of fragmented holdings and to the development of village co-operatives."

MEASURES ADOPTED BY THE GOVERNMENT OF THE INDIAN UNION

The government of the Indian Union has adopted a number of measures to reconstruct rural social life. They can broadly fall into the following categories:

(a) *Measures Affecting Political Life, Their Impact.* The granting of universal franchise to the people by the state has been one of the most significant events. Millions of individuals, irrespective of caste, rank, sex or any other differentiation, have secured the right to vote. Thus the entire rural population has been brought into the political whirlpool. Of the two-hundred million voters, the overwhelming majority belongs to the rural areas. The picture and some of the results of the first election are now available. Implications of such elections in generating various currents have now become more distinct. The very organization brought into being conducting elections in 1951 had great impact on the rural people. Ninety-thousand polling stations were established; 224,000 polling booths built. A systematic campaign was launched to explain the mechanics of voting to the people. Balloting was spread over one hundred days. Voting by party symbols printed on voting papers of different colours was evolved to suit the illiterate masses. Symbols having caste or religious significance were not permitted. About 1,800 candidates contested the 497 seats in the House of People, and over 15,000 candidates for the 3,283 seats in twenty-two assemblies. Numerous parties organized their propaganda campaigns. The four largest parties had secular politico-economic programmes. Numerous minor parties on provincial level sprang up. A total of 106 million people voted in the elections.

This single measure of the government generated powerful social and political ferment in rural India, the implications of which are too profound to be fully comprehended. It exposed the rural populations to the battery of ideas formulated in their programmes by various political parties and groups. It created a new type of social and cultural climate and process. Political discussions, meetings, processions and demonstrations were unprecedented events, new phenomena in the life of the countryside. The election processes agitated extensively for the first time the almost inert life of the rural people and created a new mobility, physical, mental and emotional, among them. It created conditions for the rise of numerous institutions of political, economic and cultural significance, some of them progressive, others reactionary (caste, communal, semi-feudal, social and economic and others). During the elections, economic issues came to the forefront and divergent class interests were revealed. Even propaganda carried on to work up caste sentiments had to resort to distinct economic appeals. Even voting on the basis of caste loyalties disclosed that specific castes usually aligned with specific political and economic parties. It is unfortunate that sociological and anthropological literature which is mounting up in India has not paid proper attention to this aspect of the contemporary rural life almost electrified by the elections and resultant mass political awakening of the rural people.

The effects of this development on different age groups, different sexes, different castes and provincial groups, as well as on different classes have to be assessed. It has created a situation, a climate, in which various ideologies and outlooks, passions and emotions, will ally, clash, modify one another or even result into various amalgams. In centuries of its existence, the rural community never lived such rich turbulent life, never experienced such unique events. The entry of the rural millions in the orbit of active politics as a result of the grant of universal suffrage and elections is a veritable new point of departure in the history of rural society pregnant with incalculable possibilities.

(b) *Measures Affecting Economic Life :* The government of the Indian Union has taken various measures to reconstruct the economy of India on the basis of what it describes as the principle of Mixed Economy. To reconstruct rural economy it has adopted measures which can be broadly classified into the following categories:

(a) *Measures to extend and improve the extant agriculture.*

(i) Reclamation of certain lands for cultivation.

(ii) Construction of major and minor irrigation projects, some of them of multi-purpose nature.

(iii) Production of improved seeds, fertilizers, and tools as well as insecticides.

(b) *Measures to reform land relations* :

(i) Vesting of the estates of the intermediaries (*Zamindars*, Taluqdars and others) barring certain properties such as home farm lands, homesteads and others in the state on the basis of payments of compensation to the intermediaries.

(ii) Placing of limitations on future acquisitions of lands by different classes of people.

(iii) Tenancy reforms designed to reduce rents, give security against eviction, and give tenants an opportunity to acquire permanent rights over the land by payment of fixed compensation subject to landlord's right to resume cultivation of a certain area for his personal cultivation.

(iv) Restrictions on sale and mortgage, letting and subletting of lands.

(c) *Measures to protect farmers from the oppression of Creditors*:

(i) Numerous measures to regulate private moneylending.

(ii) Measures to scale down debts, etc.

(d) *Measures to bring about an all-round development of rural areas, resulting in the strengthening of the national economy as a whole* :

(i) Establishment of Community Development Blocks and National Extension Services.

(e) *Measures creating new organizations to assist the process of the betterment of the life of the rural people* :

(i) Establishment of co-operative societies, Vikas Mandals, Gaon or Gram (Village) Panchayats as well as Nyaya Panchayats.

(f) *Measures to assist some of the small-scale and cottage Industries in Rural India.*

We shall briefly indicate the effects of these measures on rural life of the people as well as their impact on different classes of rural society.

No measures have been evolved which would provide employment on a sufficient scale to solve even to a reasonable extent this major problem of the rural society, or which would give better conditions of living or land to the agricultural workers comprising about one-third of the agrarian population. As David G. Mandelbaum has rightly pointed out " The lowest castes, those who are mainly landless labourers, often gain nothing at all from the irrigation projects and the redistribution of land. They have nothing to begin with, nothing which can be improved, no means of getting an economic start and so they remain economically as well as socially disadvantaged. The gap between them and other villagers frequently widens rather than diminishes on account of development projects. "

As irrigation facilities, seed, fertilizers and improved tools, are not given gratis but are to be paid for, the advantages of these facilities are taken predominantly by those who have financial resources to purchase them. As the Community Project Evaluation Report points out the advantage is taken mainly by substantial farmers.

The measures to abolish intermediaries suffer from two basic defects. The compensation to be paid to the intermediaries runs to 550 crores. It is a huge burden on the community. These measures also permit large tracts of land to remain in the hands of *Zamindars* and others as personal property. Further, as the compensation to be paid by tenants is very heavy, only substantial tenants can purchase proprietary titles of the lands taken from the intermediaries.

With regard to tenancy legislation it may be observed that " about 50 per cent of tenants on small plots, where fleecing by landlords can be as serious as on large, were not covered " and further, " tenancy regulations are unworkable because the landlord is still left in a powerful position," and still further " ever since tenancy legislation has been first talked about, the alert landowners had been carrying out widespread eviction in order to remove many of the occupancy claims. "

Measures adopted to check the ravages of the moneylenders have hardly borne fruit. The report of the Rural Credit Survey very convincingly brings this out. These measures have been effectively circumvented and the moneylender is still supreme as he alone holds the key to finance necessary for meeting both the consumption and the production needs of the lower strata of the rural society.

Institutions established by the government like Co-operatives, Vikas Mandals, Gram Panchayats and Nyaya Panchayats are also assisting in practice only the richer sections of the rural population and are further controlled by them. The Community Project Evaluation Report very significantly discloses this in the following words : " When one considers the pattern of membership in village organizations, be they co-operative societies, Vikas Mandals, Gram Panchayats or Nyaya Panchayats, one clearly finds that the membership is confined to the larger cultivators and that the smaller cultivators as well as agricultural labourers have practically no stake in the organization of the village. "

With regard to the Community Development Projects and their impact on rural life, the Evaluation Report has brought to light the following facts :—

(a) The advantages of improvements are taken predominantly by substantial farmers. (b) The contributions to be made by the village people are felt as very burdensome by the lower sections of the people. (c) The organizations emerging in these areas for bringing about rural change are dominated by upper sections of the rural population, the poorer ones having " no stake in them ". (d) The initial enthusiasm born of great hopes in the projects is slowly declining among the lower strata of the population.

Growth of Social Cleavage in Rural Areas

To sum up, as a result of the government measures to reconstruct economic life of the rural people, great changes have taken place in the socio-economic structure of the rural society. Some of the old classes (feudal and semi-feudal) have been largely crippled; some (substantial farmers) have been strengthened. Middle and lower sections have not benefited. The process of economic disintegration of these sections is advancing. (i) The measures have resulted in transforming many *zamindari* type of landlords into a class of substantial farmers and capitalist agriculturists. (ii) By numerous tenancy and other laws referred to above, the government is helping to create a class of prosperous peasants out of substantial tenants or a section of the medium-sized cultivators.

This class of prosperous peasants only can take advantage of the numerous facilities, such as improved seeds, better fertilizers, irrigation, efficient tools, better roads and also improved marketing facilities, thereby improving their production and sale of the product.

On the other hand, the vast mass of unemployed persons, large sections of the owners of uneconomic holdings, the mass of poor peasants and agricultural labourers, either remain unaffected by these measures or are adversely affected.

A sharp conflict of interests and a resultant social cleavage are developing in the rural areas as a result of the measures of the government, Central and State. On one side there are prosperous peasants, landlords, village moneylenders and traders and the richer sections of the rural people. On the other, the middle and small cultivators, the mass of land labourers and ruined non-agrarian population.

As observed earlier, social castes and economic classes are closely correlated. As a result of this, the conflicts of these classes even take the form of conflicts of castes. Thus rural areas are seething with new caste tensions, sometimes visible in elections, sometimes in economic struggles, sometimes in the struggles in local organizations.

These new patterns of tensions are slowly emerging in the open. The tensions are becoming more widespread and are moving unfortunately in the direction of sharper conflicts.

CONCLUSION

The rural life of India is undergoing transformation under the impact of Government measures. The types of changes that are taking place have been narrated in their broadest outline. What will be the direction and tempo of these changes ? Will the democratic political objective fit in with the newly-emerging class and social antagonisms in Rural India ? Will rural social life experience another round of tensions and antagonisms ? Can these contradictions be resolved without changing the very motif and mode of production ? What institutional transformation will be required to establish both economic prosperity and social harmony in the rural life? These are some of the fundamental questions posed before all social scientists.

The rural change that is generated by the Government measures is tending to sharpen the contradictions among various classes in the rural society and in the context of caste and other institutional background is slowly unleashing tensions, antagonisms and collisions, the implications of which have to be properly comprehended if the direction of the development of one-fifth of mankind is to be assessed and influenced.

9

CHANGES IN AGRARIAN ORGANIZATION*

LUCIO MENDIETA Y. NUNEZ

DR. S. C. DUBE, in a clear, interesting and systematically developed study, under the title of " Social Structure and Change in Indian Peasant Communities ", presents a general panorama of the Indian population in this century.

The population of an Indian village is united by three different bonds of solidarity: (a) family ties, (b) the caste system, and (c) territorial affinities.

The caste system is the most important and over-rules family and territorial ties; in order to understand the extent and depth of its influence, it is only necessary to know that internal relationships within the castes are subject to rules governing matrimony, meals, physical contact and occupations and that these rules are obeyed because they are considered to be of divine origin.

Castes have remained as exclusive groups throughout the ages, since strict endogamy is observed.

The influence of the castes in social relationships is, accordingly, very great in India, although sometimes of a negative character. " The taboos of the Indian caste system, " asserts Max Weber, " inhibit social intercourse much more than the Funy-Schi system of Chinese belief in spirits hindered trade. " Nevertheless, according to this same author, " the railways will gradually render caste taboos illusory. "

The interesting paper by Dr. S. C. Dube on present-day India confirms the study made by the great German sociologist at the end of the last century. In effect, according to S. C. Dube, the social structure of India is subject to considerable changes under the impact of Western culture and civilization. Modern systems of transport and communications, modern technology, industrialization and Western type education during the last 10 years have combined to produce the following obvious changes :

(1) The social position of the individual in India is dependent upon his caste; but at present that system of class distinction is being superseded by another rival system by which the individual's position in society is determined on his own personal merit.

(2) This change in class distinction is more apparent when a person

* Reproduced from *Transactions of the Third World Congress of Sociology*, Vol. I-II, pp. 225-230.

moves from country to town since, on establishing himself in the city, he has to accustom himself to urban customs.

(3) There is a noticeable weakening in the authority of the individual castes in rural India.

(4) A certain individualism has developed within the family.

(5) Western forms of life and modern technology have been accepted by the upper strata of society as they have the opportunity of acquiring them.

(6) On the other hand the lower strata are, in a way, conservative because of their lack of education and poverty.

(7) Notwithstanding the relative conservatism of the lower classes, it appears that the social structure of the village is in a state of dissolution and disintegration.

The work of Dr. Tarlok Singh of the New Delhi Planning Commission complements the information given by Dr. Dube.

Dr. Tarlok Singh discusses the "Landless Labourer and the Pattern of Social and Economic Change" and explains in detail in this valuable work the effect upon India of what is known as "the impact of the West". This impact is particularly noticeable in the villages and has developed slowly and indirectly.

(a) The products of Western industry introduced into the villages of India by pedlars diminished the demand for home-produced goods. Many craftsmen who used to make such local products became redundant and turned into farm workers without land of their own.

(b) Western ideas on ownership and finance changed the self-sufficient spirit in the village for an acquisitive, profit-seeking spirit, with the exploitation of the weak by the strong under the guise of legality. Wealth and self-seeking replaced the community spirit in the scale of values.

(c) These conditions created an internal capitalism represented by foreigners and by Indian traders and landowners who promoted the feudal conditions by means of latifundism and monetary loans.

(d) New techniques diminished the opportunities for work in a growing population, thus accentuating the effect of Western economic influence and Indian capitalism.

(e) As a result of all this, in the last 60 years, the population dependent upon agriculture has increased. It is calculated that it increased from 193 to 250 million between 1931 and 1951.

(f) Under Western influence, the bonds created by the social castes are tending to decrease, and some castes have disappeared altogether; but this has created the problem of providing work for men who were formerly employed within the strict caste system.

The increase in the number of agricultural workers in India without land of their own is a problem which requires early solution. For this reason a democratic planning scheme is being put into practice and is founded on various definite points which tend to explain what should be done. Dr. Tarlok Singh is working on this. But can a Sociological Congress embark upon the study of these questions which properly belong to politics ? We think not; the role of sociology should be defined as the study of prevailing social conditions for the purpose of obtaining scientific theories capable of serving as a basis for action; but sociology cannot indicate the precise terms for this action since they are dependent upon political conditions and the economic and social potentialities of each individual country.

Dr. A. R. Desai, of the Department of Sociology of the University of Bombay, with his work on " The Impact of the Measures Adopted by the Government of the Indian Union on the Life of the Rural People ", confirms the concepts we have just put before you. He describes firstly the changes which took place in Indian society under the influence of Western culture and civilization during the period of British rule and the effects—mostly negative—of the measures adopted by the present Government of the Indian Union to reconstruct the country on new social and economic bases. The study of the effects of these measures certainly comes within the scope of sociology since they form part of the social structure of India and the failure of many of them shows how daring and dangerous it is to prescribe them.

The study now being made by Dr. Desai of the results of the contact between Western culture and civilisation and Indian culture, under British rule, to a large extent confirms and also complements the information given by Doctors S. C. Dube and Tarlok Singh :

(a) Western culture dealt a mortal blow to the rual organization of India, based on an autarchical village community, with common ownership of land.

(b) It destroyed the collectivistic spirit and introduced individualism and competition.

(c) It introduced private ownership, letting out of land and individual cash taxation.

(d) In this way, agrarian economy based on the satisfaction of the needs of the family changed to an economy based on satisfaction of the demands of the market.

(e) It destroyed the self-sufficiency of rural life, at the same time ruining the small village industries by the introduction of machine-made products.

(f) The mass of craftsmen—deprived of their crafts by the articles imported from modern British factories—turned to agriculture, thus increasing the volume of labourers without land and accentuating the pressure of the rural population on the land. The size of small holdings diminished, and uneconomic properties increased in number.

(g) It increased the power of moneylenders, tradesmen and landowners over the poverty-stricken farmers.

(h) It increased the number of tenants and intermediaries (farmer-tenants, sub-tenants, sub-sub-tenants, etc.) supported by those who actually cultivated the ground.

(i) It decreased the power of the caste and reduced the size of the family.

(j) All this produced considerable impoverishment of the masses and internal lack of balance in the rural structure of India. To remedy this situation the Government of the Indian Union has put various measures into practice: (a) measures of a political nature establishing universal suffrage which gave rise "to considerable social and political quickening in rural India"; (b) measures of an economic nature such as irrigation projects, the introduction of better seed and fertilizers, reforms in letting arrangements to protect the tenant and cut out intermediaries, protection of the peasants against abuse by creditors, economic development of rural zones and the creation of co-operative societies and assistance to the small rural industries.

But these and other measures have failed because they only benefit those farmers who are in a sound economic position. No measures have been taken to allocate land to rural workers who have none, or to provide them with employment. The protective measures are easily circumvented; the co-operative societies only favour the clever farmers. The plans for rural economic development do not favour those who have nothing and, on the other hand, the subscriptions required to put them into operation overburden them.

To sum up, according to Dr. Desai, the governmental measures adopted in India have produced changes in the rural community which tend to intensify the opposition between classes in the rural communities and also between castes, thus causing tension, antagonism and clashes.

What sociological conclusions can be obtained from the three studies we have mentioned? What can the sociologist advise in regard to the changes which are taking place in the rural community of India?

The experience of the Indian people, like that of other peoples as history shows, supports the following generalization: whenever peoples of different culture and civilization come into contact, the most advanced tends to dominate and exploit the least developed. When these latter gain their independence, their upper classes who succeed in assimilating the civilization of their rulers, replace them in ruling and exploiting the masses.

The failure of the measures adopted by the Government of India to help the rural working class in the face of the changes in agrarian economic structure brought about by British rule and Western culture and civilization, in the same way as similar failures suffered by other peoples, serves as a basis for this further generalization : the upper classes of a country, who hold the economic power, tend to circumvent all the protective measures devised by the Government to help the working classes or to turn these same measures to their own profit.

From a strictly scientific point of view this is what, in our opinion, the Third World Sociological Congress can prove by way of general conclusions on the interesting studies submitted by Doctors Dube, Singh and Desai with regard to the changes in agrarian economic structure in India.

Although it is certain that sociology must study prevailing conditions, it does not follow from this, affirms the talented French sociologist, Emile Durkheim, " that we should give up trying to improve them : we would feel that our speculations were not worth the trouble if they had no more than a speculative interest. " " Science, " he adds, " can help us to find the road we should follow and to determine the goal towards which we blindly struggle."

With the support of the abovementioned theories the sociologist can recommend, also in a general way, that in all those countries where peoples of different civilizations come into contact with each other, the Governments should not adopt empirical action in favour of the economically and politically weaker rural classes, but action planned on the basis of investigations and research carried out by scientists experienced in the social sciences so that the political action guides the changes in agrarian economic structure efficiently, preventing abuses, social inequalities and injustices.

SECTION XV

VILLAGE STUDIES IN INDIA

Introduction

The present section consists of four selections. Professors Srinivas, Dube, Atal and Ramkrishna Mukerjee in their articles have highlighted the need for methodical, scientific and extensive study of Agrarian India which is comprised of nearly five lacs of villages, experiencing transformation under the impact of directed social change ushered in by the Government since Independence.

Professor Srinivas rightly warns against " the unstated but none-the-less real and deep seated assumptions " among the educated people including scholars " that what is written is true, and the older a manuscript, the more true its contents ". He strongly urges scholars to realise that Indology is not merely a study of India's past based on uncritical acceptance of the "vast body of written literature, sacred as well as secular as true. " According to him Indology can develop only if along with the " book view " of India, comprehensive study of contemporary Indian reality is carried out. According to him empirical study of the present society would help to give a new meaning even to some of the elementary but key concepts like Varna, Caste, Joint Family and Hinduism. This may lead to the overhauling of the present notions of historical epochs of Indian Society. Professor Srinivas strongly pleads for scientific, empirical village studies to correct the " book view " and " upper-caste-view " of many phenomenon of Indian Society.

Professor Dube in his study justifies the changed focus of Social Anthropologists from tribal studies to village studies. He examines the criticism levelled against the type of village studies undertaken by Social Anthropologists. While admitting the validity of some of the points, he strongly makes out a case for such studies. He acknowledges the need for a clear conceptual framework for studying both the structural matrix of the village community and the change it is experiencing. He proposes certain interesting steps to evolve a methodology of study. He also points out the areas of study. According to Professor Dube, a systematic study of village communities " will provide the requisite background data from which more purposeful planning can emerge ".

Professor Atal enumerates the eight factors which have facilitated the inclusion of a new dimension in the form of rural study in Anthropology. He briefly reviews the rural studies made by Social Anthropologists and points out how they have helped to expand the horizon of an understanding of village social life. He further indicates how these studies have helped to generate certain concepts which are proving valuable as tools for fruitful explorations in rural social structure.

Professor Ramkrishna Mukerjee's approach to Rural Studies is qualitatively different from the earlier three scholars. In his article, he provides an historical evolution of village studies in India. He draws attention to the forces and factors which led to the study of villages. Professor Ramkrishna Mukerjee while tracing the various streams of village studies points out the major limitations of the studies made by economists as well as Sociologists/Social Anthropologists. He shows how economists have ignored the socio-cultural matrix of the village community, while Sociologists and Social Anthropologists have not taken into consideration the economic and class matrix while conducting the village studies. He strongly feels that this mechanical exclusion of one or the other aspect of social reality and dichotomising of social world of village life has created a peculiar distortion in our comprehension of rural social structure and rural social change.

According to Professor Mukerjee "the two streams of village studies carrying the imprint of economists or social Anthropologists/Sociologists, respectively must meet at relevant sites ". He raises a very significant point for controversy. Are the two streams not meeting because they have different presuppositions about the social world ?

These four selections from four distinguished scholars are presented to stimulate further discussions on the various methodological issues involved in Rural Studies. (*Author.*)

1

VILLAGE STUDIES AND THEIR SIGNIFICANCE*

M. N. SRINIVAS

A VAST BODY of written literature, sacred as well as secular, is available to the student of Indian social institutions, and the existence of this literature has exercised a decisive influence on the analysis of Indian sociological problems. For instance, references to caste and kin relations in literature have been treated as historical data and conditions obtaining today have been compared and contrasted with conditions alleged to prevail in historical times. The law books (Dharma Sutras and Dharma Shastras) have been assumed to refer to laws which were actually in force among the people and it has not been asked whether the laws did not refer to merely what a particular lawyer considered desirable or good. Even for the major lawyers it is not known when exactly they lived, it being not uncommon for one scholar's estimate to differ from another by as much as three centuries. This is especially so in the case of the earlier lawyers. Dr. I. P. Desai writes, " A further difficulty in the development of Hindu law is the lack of agreement among scholars regarding the dates of various works...There is no agreement regarding the time sequence (of the various authors). Buhler considers Gautama as the earliest Dharmasastrakar and Apastamba as the latest, while Jayaswal reverses the order, considering Apastamba as the earliest and Gautama as the latest Dharmasastrakar. " (*Punishment and Penance in Manusmriti*, Journal of the University of Bombay, XV, part I, July 1946, p. 42.) The provenance of a lawyer, and the sanction behind the rules enunciated by him are frequently far from clear if not unknown.

It is pertinent to mention in this connection that there is among our educated people, an unstated but none-the-less real and deep-seated assumption that what is written is true, and the older a manuscript, the more true its contents. Learning is almost synonymous with pouring over palm leaf mss. This bias in favour of literary material is most clearly seen in the syllabuses of Indological studies in our universities. Indology has come to be regarded as knowledge about India's past. Any suggestion that Indology should include the study of tribes and villages which are in existence today would be regarded as too absurd to merit consideration. Caste in the Vedas and in Manu ought to be studied but caste as a powerful force in modern Indian life ought not to be. Such a separation between the past and present is not healthy.

---

*Reproduced from the article "Village Studies and their Significance", from *Rural Profiles*. Edited by D. N. Majumdar, pp. 95-100.

The observation of social behaviour is everywhere a difficult undertaking and, in certain respects, observing one's own society is far more difficult than observing an alien society. In the case of Indians, there is the additional difficulty that ideas which are carried over from literary material, and from the caste to which one belongs by birth, vitiate the observation of field-behaviour. An example of such a failure to understanding the factual situation is provided by the way in which the idea of *Varna* has vitiated the understanding of caste. According to the *Varna* scheme, there are only four castes and a few other groups, while actually there are, in each linguistic area, several hundred castes, each of which is a homogeneous group, with a common culture, occupation or occupations and practising endogamy and commensality. The castes of a local area form a hierarchy. There are several features of this hierarchy which run counter to the hierarchy as it is conceptualised in the idea of *Varna*. Firstly, in the *Varna* scheme, the four all-India castes occupy definite and immutable places, while, in caste at the existential level, the only definite thing is that all the local castes form a hierarchy. Everything else is far from certain. For one thing, the hierarchy is characterised by uncertainty, especially in the middle region which spans an enormous structural gulf. Each caste tries to argue that it occupies a higher place than the one allotted to it by its neighbours. This arguability has an important function because it makes possible mobility, and castes are mobile over a period of time. There is occasional leap-frogging inside the system, a caste jumping over its neighbours to achieve a high position. Another important point is that the hierarchy is local, varying from one small local area to another, if not from one village to another. Two groups bearing the same name and living in the same linguistic region often occupy different positions in their respective local hierarchies and differ from each other in some customs and rites. The Kolis of Gujarat are a case in point.

It is clear that the idea of *Varna* is far too rigid and simple to cover the immensely complex facts of caste. But the idea of *Varna* helps to make the facts of caste in one region intelligible all over India by providing a conceptual frame that is simple, clear-cut, stable and which, it is imagined, holds good everywhere. And it helps mobility too, for ambitious castes find it less difficult to take on highsounding Sanskritic names with the name of one of the *Varnas* as a suffix, than to take on the name of a local higher caste. But all this is lost sight of because varna is treated as describing caste accurately and fully. This would not have happened if we Indians had not taken it for granted that the idea of *Varna* derived from literary material, adequately explained the facts of the caste system. The only cure for this literary bais lies in doing field-research. The field-worker, confronted by the bewildering variety and complexity of facts as they actually are is forced to relate what he sees to what he has assumed it to be, and the lack of correspondence between the two, results in his attempting to reassess the written material.

In every part of India only a few castes at the top enjoyed a literary tradition while the bulk of the people did not. Under British rule the top castes supplied the intelligentsia which acted as the link between the new masters and the bulk of the people. And the new intelligentsia saw the social reality through the written literature, regarding the deviations from the latter as aberrations. This group also perpetrated an upper caste view of the Hindu social system on the new masters and through them, the outside world. Conditions prevalent among the upper castes were generalized to include all Hindus. For instance, women are treated much more severely among the higher castes than among the lower, but his distinction was ignored by the early reformers. They talked about the plight of the Hindu widow, the absence of divorce, the harshness of the sex code towards her and so on, but on all these matters the institutions of the lower differ in important respects from those of the higher castes. The point I am trying to make is that the observation of Hindu social life has been, and still is, vitiated by the book-view and the uppercaste-view. A sociological study of Indian sociologists would yield interesting results.

An emphasis on religious behaviour as such, as distinguished from what is written in the religious books and the opinions of the upper castes, would have provided us with a view of Hinduism substantially different from that of the philosophers, Sanskritists and reformers. I shall try to explain what I mean by an example. In the summer of 1948, I went along with the elders of Rampura village to the temple of the deity Basava to watch them consult the deity about rain. The priest performed *Puja*, chanting *Mantras* in Sanskrit, and then the elders began to ask the deity to let them know whether it was going to rain or not in the next few days. I was expecting them to behave as I have seen devotees behave in the temples of the upper castes, viz., stand with bowed head and folded palms, shut eyes, and utter words showing great respect for, and fear of, and dependence upon, the deity. I was completely taken aback to find them using words which they used to an equal, and a somewhat unreasonable equal at that. They became angry, shouted at the deity, taunted him, and went so far as to say that they considered even the government more worthy of confidence than him. And they were deadly serious all the time. Nothing could have been further from an urban Hindu's ideas of what the proper relationship was between man and god.

It is frequently said by apologists and reformers that Hinduism is not a proselytizing religion like Christianity and Islam. This again is not strictly true. Besides the Buddhists and Jains, the Lingayats, who began as a militant reformist sect in the South in the twelfth century, A. D., secured converts from all the castes from the Brahmin to the Untouchable in the early days of their history. The Lingayats are a well-organized sect, and they have monasteries scattered all over the Karnatak.

In southern Mysore, for instance, the monasteries have a following not only among Lingayats but among a number of middle-range non-Brahminical castes with whom they are in continuous contact, and over whose life they exercise some kind of direction. The head of each monastery collects a levy from each of his followers through a hierarchy of agents. It is important to note that this is not confined to the Lingayats though they are the best-organised of the sects. The Brahmin followers of the great theologian and reformer, Sri Ramanujacharya, have a monastery at Melkote, about 26 miles from Mysore City, and the monastery has a following among the people in the surrounding towns and villages. Thus, both Brahmin and non-Brahmin sects have deeply influenced the people at large through organizations which have existed for hundreds of years. Still one frequently reads in books on Hindu religion and philosophy that Hinduism is unique in that it is not a proselytizing religion. It is true that Hindus do not try to convert Christians or Muslims, but in a sense conversion is going on all the time within Hinduism. The lower castes and tribal people have been undergoing Sanskritization all the time, and sects, Brahminical and non-Brahminical, and Vaishnavite and Shaivite, have actively sought converts. Persecution for religious views and practices has not been unknown.

The studies of village communities which are currently being carried out in the different parts of the country provide the future historian with a vast body of facts about rural social life, facts collected not by travellers in a hurry, but by men who are trained to observe keenly and accurately. These studies constitute therefore valuable contributions to the social, political, economic and religious history of our country. Their value is further enhanced when it is realized that the changes which are being ushered in Independent and Plan-conscious India herald a complete revolution in our social life. It is true that in historic times India has been subject to invasions by diverse peoples including the Mughals and British, and that British rule inaugurated changes the fulfilment of which we are observing now, but the break with the past was never as complete and thorough-going as it is today. We have, at the most, another ten years in which to record facts about a type of society which is changing fundamentally and with great rapidity.

Historians have stated that a knowledge of that past is helpful in the understanding of the present if not in forecasting the future. It is not, however, realized that thorough understanding of the present frequently sheds light on the past. To put it in other words the intimate knowledge which results from the intensive field-survey of extant social institutions does enable us to interpret better data about past social institutions. Historical data are neither as accurate nor as rich and detailed as the data collected by field-anthropologists, and the study of certain existing processes increases our understanding of similar processes in the past. It is necessary to add here that great caution has to be exercised in such a task, for otherwise history will be twisted out of all recognition. But once the need for extreme caution is recognised, there is no doubt that our knowledge of the working of historical processes will be enhanced by this method. The universities are the proper organisations to conduct this research, and the government can help by giving money to the establishment of teaching and research posts in social anthropology and sociology. Too much stress on utilitarian research will defeat itself, and will further lower intellectual standards.

2

THE STUDY OF INDIAN VILLAGE COMMUNITIES*

S. C. DUBE

IN THE last decade there has been a noticeable shift in the orientation and the focus of interest of social anthropology in India. Anthropologists are no longer concerned primarily or even mainly with the study of tribal cultures; in increasing numbers they are now operating nearer home in village communities where they have discovered challenging possibilities of theoretical and applied social science research. This is a very welcome trend indeed, and augurs well for the future of social research in the country.

This development is not without its critics and detractors. There are those who criticize the utility of village studies, as also that of much else in anthropology, on the ground that such studies, howsoever intimate and intensive, do not add in any appreciable measure to our knowledge of the socio-cultural systems of the country, nor even to the understanding of the processes and trends of the society at large. An extreme view goes to the extent of questioning their validity as diagnostic or even illustrative case studies. It must be conceded immediately that the village communities studied so far and those being studied currently, do not approach anywhere near a statistically acceptable sample for the country as a whole. But such critics appear to ignore certain essential characteristics of anthropological research. What we lose by not working on an extensive and statistically adequate sample, we more than compensate by acquiring depth and coverage of overt and covert norms in our analyses. Survey research of the extensive type does yield certain data that conform to the rigid tests of validity and reliability but its coverage must of necessity be limited. In its very nature it cannot explore the depths and covert aspects of behaviour which the anthropologist can in his study of single communities. To attempt the study-task of such magnitude we could only look upon it as an ideal for the distant future involving an enormous investment of men and money. Even if the money were to be found, we simply do not have the trained personnel to undertake the adventure. The intensification of such research must be phased carefully. We would not lose much by waiting to go on the job on a massive scale only after we have evolved a clearer and more coherent theoretical frame of reference. In the meantime anthropologists can remain unrepentent advocates of single village studies, in the

* Presidential address delivered to the Social Anthropology Section of the Indian Sociological Conference, held at Agra, on February. 8, 1958.

same way as there are devoted students of family and kinship, for the village as a culture-bearing unit does mirror certain significant aspects of the region and the nation. Empirically derived meaningful concepts and hypotheses for more extensive survey research can emerge only from such investigations. In order to avoid a mechanical and overly schematic approach to the study of regional similarities and differences in the country, it is most desirable to continue with the anthropological tradition of single village studies. With the increase in the volume of such studies order would eventually emerge out of the apparent anarchy that prevails today.

A more valid criticism of the present trend is that some anthropologists have tended to ignore basic sociological realities by viewing the village as a biotic community, although in essence it is a synthesized community. Because of their theoretical and methodological orientation towards tribal studies some anthropologists indeed have tried to study village communities in a biotic frame of reference regarding it as an isolate; in consequence the unity of the village has been emphasized more than its extensions. It must be admitted that any efforts to understand the village without reference to its extensions in time and space in the social, cultural, and ideological contexts are bound to be partial and incomplete, and it is necessary to evolve an approach that would take account of the historical and regional determinants that shape and condition the culture of a village. Here too most of the fears of our critics are somewhat imaginary; the two major studies of Indian village communities published within hard covers to-date contain unmistakable evidence of the anthropologists' awareness of the problem and have sought to study single village in the background of the wider universe of Indian civilization.

A third criticism voiced by more discriminating social scientists points out certain inherent weaknesses in our initial approach in this direction. Our studies are often modelled on similar studies done elsewhere in the world, and lack a coherent frame of reference relevant to the structure and organization of Indian Society. While our descriptive categories are satisfactory, our analytical categories leave much to be desired. On the whole the organization of such research on an India-wide basis lacks planning, and we have not evinced enough interest in evolving or rigidly defining the criteria on which we select village for community study. It should be conceded that the critics have a point of unmistakable validity here. We can explain our position by suggesting that initial efforts in any new direction are necessarily exploratory in nature or by emphasizing that our need for facts is so great that almost any type of study should be welcome, but these and such other explanations would not constitute a justification of our position. That we have lacked theoretical sophistication we should admit. With humility and critical self-evaluation we should proceed to chalk out the lines of further action,

The concepts of Great and Little Traditions, *Sanskritization*, and universalization and parochialization offer us a good starting point, and from here we should build step by step a series of hypotheses and concepts that would ultimately lead to meaningful generalizations regarding the structure and processes of Indian Society.

The structural-functional and themal approaches provide us with more or less satisfactory conceptual tools for the study of village communities. A little more critical examination of the complexities introduced into such studies by the fact of their belonging to the complex web of the Indic civilization would yield the required refinements and correctives. The study of change in village communities, significant as it is both in its theoretical and applied aspects, needs a more rigorous framework. To ensure comparability of data it is necessary to evolve certain common categories of investigation, processing, and analysis covering this broad area of research.

Redfield's folk-urban continuum provides one such conceptual framework. Analyses of Indian materials within this frame of reference, however, have pointed out some of its shortcomings. The fabric of contemporary Indian Society is the result of so many divergent patterns of inter-action between local, regional, and classical cultural influences, that the folk-urban continuum concept cannot cover them all adequately. Redfield himself has been among the first to recognize this inadequacy and to suggest an alternative approach. The concept of Great Little Traditions, to which a reference has been made earlier, provides an approach for the study not only of the structure and integration of Indian Society but also for the analysis of change as a broad historical process. Srinivas' useful and much-discussed concept of *Sanskritization*, although it is independent of and was developed before Redfield's formulation, fits well into this conceptual scheme. Similarly, Marriott's *Universalization* and *Parochialization* concepts are refinements within the same general theme.

While the broad framework provided by these concepts is simple and attractive, operationally they are not without inherent contradictions and difficulties. There is apparently no precise definition of Great or Little Traditions. To define the Great Tradition as the corpus of beliefs, rituals, and social patterns embodied in the sacred canonical literature does not take us very far. Even the clarification that it often emanates from the little traditions of the little communities and is abstracted and synthesized by the urban *Literati* does not help our understanding very substantially. It is difficult to reduce the inviolable central core of the more or less static ideas of a Great Tradition to a list of traits and complexes; nor is it easy to classify them, with any degree of precision, as universals, alternatives, and specialities. The concept must also allow for a wide nebulous area covering ideas and institutions that are not accounted for by the sacred or near-sacred texts. This only adds to our difficulties in using the concept as an analytical tool. Where there are more than one Great or near-Great Traditions, each with its canonical texts and ethical codes, the situation becomes all the more confusing. In such a situation we have no criteria for determining the elements which could be said to be basic to the Great Tradition. Scriptures and sacred texts themselves often illustrate certain aspects of evolution and change in society and there is by no means unanimity among them. When conflicting ideal patterns are laid down by the sacred texts, and there is no universality in the acceptance of one in preference to the others, the efforts to find the Great Tradition would be fruitless. It may also be added that the Great Tradition-Little Tradition frame of reference does not allow proper scope for the consideration of the role and significance of regional, western, and emergent national traditions, each of which is powerful in its own way. Some of these considerations would apply also to Srinivas' concept of *Sanskritization.* In our study of Indian village communities, therefore, it may be useful to consider the contextual classical and local traditions, as well as the regional (culture-area), western (ideological-technological) and emergent national (nativistic-reinterpretational-adaptive) traditions.

The urgency with which the study of the changing village scene in India is being pressed in the wake of the national development programme should not seduce us into adopting short-cuts of questionable validity for the study of culture change. It is doubtful if the plethora of spurious and superficial writings emerging from such efforts would provide any meaningful leads to the community development planners and administrators. A good study of change invariably follows a good structural-functional-themal study of a society, and together these need sustained work by trained social scientists. Promise of quick results by adoption of short-cuts would not be anything more or better than anthropological quackery. For a little immediate gain we shall only be discrediting the profession in the eyes of the discerning planner. Our time-consuming methods may arouse some impatience in those who subsidize our research, but our ultimate results are bound to be of constructive help to them.

It is hoped that the observations made above will not be construed as a plea for letting the anthropologists pursue their own pleasures. Nor is there any denial of the urgency and importance of the study of change. Its critical significance is evident.

Earlier it has been suggested that we need to evolve a clear conceptual framework for the study of change, and that it is necessary to have some agreement on the broad categories covering data collection, processing, and analysis to ensure the comparability of the materials.

To place the study of change in one particular community in the proper perspective, it will be necessary to relate its changes to the wider national, regional, and local area developments. An historical survey of the major trends would prepare the ground for the characterization of change, and would help in determining its cumulative, concentrated, or sporadic nature. In this context it would be useful to examine also the involvement of the community in this process, and to determine the areas most or least affected by the trends. Concepts of change and its conscious formulation too would merit a serious examination.

As the second step in such research it would be essential to discover and identify the reference groups, and the agents and carriers of change. Who provides the model for change? And who are its promoters? It would be most useful to construct a typelogy of the agents and carriers of change as individuals and groups, and to examine the sponsor-recipient relationships in all their ramifications. The motivations of the innovators as well as of the acceptors and rejectors would constitute a legitimate field for investigation. It would only be logical to extend the research also to the techniques of effecting change by analyzing the communication channels and appeals that are employed for the purpose.

The dynamics of change can be best studied in the context of the kinds of changes that are taking place in the community. It would be necessary to distinguish between planned and unplanned change, and to assess the relative importance of both. This study would also involve the examination of the mechanics of change, and a microscopic analysis of the selectivity in and sequence of change. This would entail a study of the patterns of change in reference to their spread within and outside the community. In the cultural context the logic of the acceptance or rejection of particular items will have to be examined; the sequence of change, both in its ramifying and non-ramifying aspects, will have to be closely watched and analyzed.

Finally, the community attitudes and reactions to change will have to be given an adequate coverage. This would necessitate research into valuation of change, associated aspirations and fears, and assignment of responsibility for change. The attitudes to change will have to be studied in reference to moves to facilitate, block, or reverse change. Such analysis, it is hoped, would help us in making justifiable predictions regarding prospects for further change.

The numerous calls to social engineering, while adding to the general recognition of the utility of anthropology and sociology in development planning, have tended to confuse the role of the anthropologist. Our role should be viewed essentially as one of the analyst, and not that of the therapist. The temptations to the student of village India to assume the mantle of an action engineer will be many, but it is doubtful if we are cut out for such a role by our orientation, training, and experience. What the enlightened administrator expects of us is not so much of glib advice, but substantial additions to the existing knowledge of the village communities to enable him to formulate informed policies. Good base-line studies of village culture and social organization, followed by penetrating enquiries into the directions and content of change claim top priority on our time and research energy. To aid the administrator further, within this general framework we can undertake more focussed investigations in areas which have a direct bearing on day-to-day action programmes. Serious analytical studies in the fields of group dynamics, leadership and decision-making, communication, and cultural factors governing acceptance or rejection of the externally induced programmes of change will have to be taken in hand without delay. Those of us who are oriented to the finer points of methodology could make a valuable contribution by introducing refinements in evaluation techniques. The more action-minded could participate in the training programmes for the extension agents, and in the formulation of pilot action-research projects. The need for independent evaluation of the state-sponsored development projects, preferably without requiring financial support from the government, cannot be over-emphasized, and we need a great deal of illustrative as well as diagnostic case material. To these, it is hoped, we shall now turn with proper equipment of theory and methodology.

There can be no doubt that village studies in this country have a future. Our teething troubles over, we have now to devote ourselves to the tasks of developing a proper conceptual frame of reference testing our methodological tools, formulating clear hypotheses, and the going into the field for a spell of good solid field-work. In doing this we shall not only satisfy our over-developed sense of curiosity and make valuable theoretical advances, but shall contribute our bit towards understanding the complex factors involved in the problem of the emotional integration of India, and will provide the requisite background data from which more purposeful planning can emerge.

3

RURAL STUDIES : INDIAN VILLAGE*

YOGESH ATAL

IN THE earlier phases of the development of Anthropology, tribal societies of far-off lands, isolated from the main links of modern civilisation, were the subject-matter of its study. This led to a rather unfortunate assumption on the part of common man that Anthropology is the study of tribes. But "Anthropologists are no longer concerned primarily, or even mainly, with the study of tribal cultures; in increasing numbers they are now operating nearer home in village communities where they have discovered challenging possibilities of theoretical and applied social science research." (Dube, 1958.) Basically Anthropology studies Man—and He should be studied at all levels of cultural development. Keeping this aim in view, Anthropology has extended its frontiers to include not only the rural studies, but also urban societies, determination of national character, and analysis of complex cultures. "Today all over the world, Anthropology has embraced the whole human society." (Ishwaran, 1960:5.) It studies "just every thing human". (Redfield, 1956.)

The tools of research that were sharpened in the microcosms of little tribes could be used for the study of the "village" communities, easily and most effectively, with only slight modifications, and quite in consonance with the techniques of other social sciences. The concept of "Ideal Folk-society" developed by Redfield was tried out in analysing the cultures of Latin America, but there it was found almost non-operational. While re-examining it Redfield thought that there was nothing wrong in the concept itself. The communities that one wanted to fit into the conceptual framework were remote in several of the characteristic traits from the ideal type. The later studies proved that the folk societies tend to lose increasingly their basic traits when they come into contact with other advanced cultures. Folk societies, thus, gradually transform themselves into village communities and isolate themselves from the ideal types, say, the one constructed by Redfield. As a result of the processes of culture-contact it is today hardly possible to get any pure, unaffected, and completely isolated "primitive" community. The culture-contact gives rise to a continuum, technically known as the "Folk-Urban continuum". The intermediate category between the two polar types presents the "peasant society" or the village-community.

Thus, the processes of change initiated and accelerated by contact have opened new vistas of study. They presented new problems of

* Reproduced from *The Eastern Anthropologist*, Vol. 14, pp. 249-257.

analysis and research methodology. It was apparent that the holistic approach that could be successfully employed in the study of isolated and remotely situated small tribal communities was not possible here. The 'whole' of the village community was not complete. It was a part of a wider 'whole'—of a greater society. In order to apprehend the village in its totality, it was deemed essential to take cognizance of extraneous forces and factors that affect the life-ways and work-ways of the community.

In the past few years, the programmes of directed and planned change in the underdeveloped countries have immensely increased the possibilities of modifying the form and structure of the village communities. It was therefore considered desirable to record the existing structure of the rural society which would later help the evaluation of the impacts of the development programmes of planned culture change. Some "challenging possibilities" of applied social science research were easily discernible and they provided enough incentive to the social scientist to undertake such studies.

In the Indian context, there is one more factor. Indian society is caste-structured. Knowledge about caste was nothing but "Book-view" and the "Upper caste-view" (Srinivas, 1955). What type of caste organisation is prevalent today? Which of the frontiers have had the largest impact of changes, and in which part of the country or which section of the society (rural or urban)? These were some of the pressing problems of theoretical interest and practical significance which demanded a more thorough and intimate enquiry in specific and limited fields in the different parts of the country.

In brief, following factors may be listed which have facilitated inclusion of a new dimension of study in Anthropology:—

1. Attempts to redefine Anthropology as the Science of man at all levels of cultural development;
2. Recognition of the fact that simple, isolated tribal folks are only an ideal construct and that culture-contact has already broken their isolation. Some writers go to the extent of saying that "they were never isolated";
3. The fact that the majority of world population is rural and it demands attention for systematic study;
4. Attraction toward research possibilities of the new field of study.
5. Facilities for research in terms of proximity, easy accessibility and therefore involving comparatively lesser expenditure than in the study of Tribes;
6. Need for the systematic and scientific study of Indian social structure as it exists today to provide authentic, factual material for the posterity, to reconstruct the past, and to enable the planner in his formulation of plans and projects;

7. Need for the study of changing situation in the village communities brought about by external agencies directly or indirectly, planned or non-directed; and
8. Applicability of the traditional anthropological methods of research to the analysis of rural society.

Economists and Sociologists have been engaged in the study of rural society and it could be said that the entrance of Anthropology in this field is an encroachment or an undesirable intrusion upon others' fields. But this is rather an overstatement. Neither Economics nor even Sociology attempts to intensively study any particular village community. Whatever is being written on rural society is only an outcome of the shuffling of data obtainable from official records like the Patwari Registers, census reports, etc. They give their generalised statements for the country as a whole without caring to go into the intricate details which lay hidden and remain unnoticed to the superficial observers. "Survey research of the extensive type does yield certain data that conform to the rigid tests of validity and reliability but its coverage must of necessity be limited. In its very nature it cannot explore the depths and covert aspects of behaviour...." (Dube, 1958:2.) To the advantage of the planner they can yield general data but the analysis of human factors is beyond their scope. Thus, although the field is common, methods and techniques of study are different. Keeping this difference of techniques in view, if Rural Sociology has to be differentiated from anthropological studies of village communities, it is proposed that the generalised analysis on national level based on books and statistics be designated as *Rural Sociology* and the intensive study of particular village communities based on anthropological techniques of research be known as *Rural Anthropology*. Fortunately in India there is no need for such a distinction. Both Sociologists and Anthropologists are jointly exploring the Village Community with a largely common methodology. Rural India provides a good meeting ground for the two disciplines. This effective communication is indeed a healthy trend and one should welcome this happy "merging".

The year 1955 was of immense significance for Indian anthropology and sociology. In that year, for the first time four books and several papers on Indian Village were published. These studies were made by Indian as well as American and British social scientists. Dube's *Indian Village*, Majumdar's *Rural Profiles* (ed.), Marriot's *Village India* (ed.), and Srinivas' *India's Villages* (ed.) were the major publications of the year. The same year a conference was also held under the Chairmanship of Dr. (Mrs.) Irawati Karve at Madras, in which Professor Robert Redfield also participated. The much-discussed concept of *Sanskritisation* proposed by Srinivas in *Religion & Society in Coorg* was reiterated by him who thought the discussions had reinforced his belief in its validity. The proceedings of the conference have been published in a book entitled *Society in India.* Later, *Twice Born* (Carstairs; 1957), *India's*

Changing Villages (Dube, 1958), *Caste and Communication in an Indian Village* (Majumdar, 1958), *Caste and the Economic Frontier* (Bailey, 1957) and *Village Life in Northern India* (Lewis, 1958) were added to the Library of Indian rural studies. Albert Mayer's book *Pilot Project, India* (1958) summarises the main achievements of the Etawah Project. *An Introduction to Rural Sociology in India*, an anthology edited by A. R. Desai, appeared in a revised and enlarged version in the year 1959. Recently Adrian Mayer's work "*Caste and Kinship in Central India* (1960) has come out. Besides these major publications, several research papers based on field work in rural areas have appeared in various journals. The yearly sessions of the Indian Sociological Conference have also included discussions on varied and important problems of Rural Analysis. University departments of Anthropology and Sociology have been and are undertaking various projects for conducting researches in the rural areas. The Research Programmes Committee of the Planning Commission, Government of India, is also promoting rural research through such centres.

The study of Indian Rural Society has helped in developing certain analytical categories. Srinivas has pointed toward a social process, which he christened as *Sanskritisation*, through which the lower castes try to bring about changes in their life-ways to obtain greater ritual purity, and thereby attain a higher status in the ritual hierarchy of castes. He has also analysed the process of *Westernisation* which simultaneously operates in a society. N. Prasad has tried to elaborate the concept and suggested the term *Kulinisation* for the same. Majumdar through *Desanskritisation* suggests a reverse process by which the Brahman castes also try to identify in some matters with other castes. Ishwaran considers the concept of Sanskritisation as "misleading" and asserts "A thorough understanding of the Hindu culture could only be had by referring to *Brahmanisation* but not sanskritisation. (1960:9.) Chauhan (1959) while suggesting the limitations of the concepts of sanskritisation and Westernisation mentions the other processes which are simultaneously at work. Efforts have also been made to analyse the hierarchical aspects of caste and the factors leading towards the dominance of a caste. The very concept of caste has been re-examined in an effort to make it more precise, less open-textured so to say. Marriott discovered the processes of Universalisation and Parochialisation (1955) which explain the complexity of Indian civilisation and the communication channels that exist between the Great and Little traditions of the country. To avoid the limitations of the polar distinctions, Dubey is busy in conceptualising the total realm of Tradition into a five-fold division. According to him, " In our study of Indian Village communities...it may be useful to consider the contextual classical and local traditions as well the regional (culture-area), western (ideological-technological), and emergent national (nativistic-reinterpretational-adaptive) traditions. " (1958:10.)

The most significant problem which has attracted the attention of a number of social scientists is that of the representativeness of a village. Can a village represent the whole nation ? It could be said that as every one who is a resident of India is Indian so also is every village in India an Indian village. But the problem is not so simple. Every village has a distinct " personality " of its own. It has its distinctive structure, network of kinship-affiliations, caste-composition and dominance, and leadership patterns. The south Indian village is different in many respects from a north Indian village. Even in north or south India no specific homogeneity in the village organisation is to be discovered. In Marriott's Kishangarhi, " Marriage. . . is oriented to flow in a single direction only. " There is no possibility of " marriage by exchange " there. But in Rajasthan this practice is observed and is locally known as " Anta Santa ". The system of *Seem Seemna Bhaichara* found in villages around Delhi is peculiarity of this region alone. In the villages of Mahakaushal, it was found that it is the parents who will touch the feet of their daughter as a mark of respect. Similarly the brothers would respect their sisters irrespective of age-considerations. The elder sisters, in the same vein, touch the feet of their younger sisters. But in Rajasthan, it is always the daughters who would touch the feet of their parents. Similarly the younger sister has to bow down to her elder siblings. These instances prove that while in Mahakaushal sex of the child or the sibling has an important role to play in commanding respect, in Rajasthan it is not so relevant as the factor of Age is. To give another example, the Telis are oil pressers and traditional confectioners in Mewar. Their '*pakka*' preparations are acceptable even to high caste Brahmans. But in Mahakaushal the idea of Telis being confectioners will be abhorred. In Mewar, the role of midwifery is traditionally assigned to the Barber woman (*Nain*). In Mahakaushal two different castes have their role at the time of delivery. The Basor woman performs the surgical operation, and after the preliminary purificatory rites, the Nai-woman takes over. Similarly, differences in dialects, in dressing-patterns, in details of ritual observances, in kinship terminology and usages and in the economic sphere could be located. In such situations, when a village in the neighbourhood of Delhi is compared with that of Mexico, the utility of such a comparison is uncertain and the representativeness of the compared villages very much open to question. From this point of view the very title of the book viz., *Village Life in Northern India* is dubious.

In spite of all these considerations one moot question still remains : Is the significance of a village study confined only to the village studies or can the results of the research be used for a wider area ? To put it in other words, whether the village represents its own confines or a region (or area) bigger than that? In the fifth session of the Indian Sociological Conference held at Lucknow (1960) Brij Raj Chauhan raised the same question in a different manner. According to him, the question as " to what extent any village in India can be considered as representative of the country...can lead to four facts :

1. Any village selected at random represents the nation;
2. There are various types of villages in the country and one village may represent other villages of its own type;
3. A village happened to be studied may be only selectively representative with reference to the item selected for study;
4. It may be possible to find a representative village for the country.

On the basis of Census of India—1951, Chauhan created a *Hindupur* village. In terms of size of the village, sex-ratio, distance from a city, and availability of modern means of transport (bus and rail) Hindupur represents the Indian village. " Hindupur is the name given to the village that is 18 miles from the rail, 6 miles from pucca road, 4 miles from Kachcha road and 33 miles from a city. With 269 males and 260 females it is inhabited by 529 persons." When some of the Indian villages reported on in Anthropological literature were compared with this " Ideal type " or, Average Type of Hindupur, the following facts emerged in regard to the size of the village.

1. All the villages so compared " fall above the category of small villages thereby excluding 68% of the villages in India ";
2. Villages of Mohana (Majumdar), Namhalli (Beals), Kishangarhi (Marriott), Kasandra (Steed) and Ranikhera (Lewis) having a population between 575 and 1,100 " are fairly near the mark of Hindupur and these villages represent 18.5% of the villages in India".
3. Rampura (Srinivas) and Madhopur (Cohn) of the population of 1,523 and 1,852 respectively, "represent 10% of villages".
4. Shamirpet (Dube) village of the size of 2,454 represents only 3.5% of the villages in India.

Similarly these eight villages were compared with Hindupur on the remaining three counts.

Here it is necessary to mention that Hindupur is Chauhan's own creation. He " has not visited this village and in fact does not know whether such a village exists at all ". This is the magic of Census figures and statistical computations. Chauhan, however, believes that " for every region perhaps a picture of villages like Uttarpur, Madhyapur, Bangpur, Rajput, etc., will aid in furthering our knowledge and ignorance (*sic*) with regard to the efficacy of studies of single village communities for making nationwide conclusions."

Social scientists have reacted differently towards this effort of constructing an Ideal type in terms of limited factors, based on methods of statistical computations alone. There are certain theoretical difficulties in accepting Hindupur as a representative Indian village. The selection of the four factors on the basis of which this Ideal village was invented has been governed by the considerations of convenience and personal preference. The village as a socio-cultural entity cannot be deduced from quantophrenic rhapsodies. Possibly Asiapur (Asian village) and Vishwapur (universal village) can also be constructed as ideal types for Asia and the world in the same manner as Bangpur for Bengal and Hindupur for India. It is quite possible that the ideal village of Australia or Iraq may have closer identity with Hindupur or Rajpur. In that situation what would remain specifically Indian in Hindupur to justify the prefix "Hind"?

Secondly, where the suggestion for making 'purs' for Rajasthan, Madhya Pradesh etc. is offered, probably it is overlooked that the provinces are organised for administrative purposes and their boundaries are defined mainly geographically. But cultural boundaries do not necessarily coincide with the geographical.

It also appears that Chauhan wants to conceive of Indian Village as a concept. It has happened in the history of Anthropology earlier also; it is implicit in the effort of persons like Tylor, Morgan and Frazer to make anthropology the study of culture and not of cultures. Relevant data suitable enough to be fitted into the scheme of the cultural construct were collected from different cultures "torn out of their cultural context with little reference to their meaning". They were all in search of an ideal pattern of culture which, in extremist hands, split up into the schools of evolutionism and diffusionism. The number of village studies done so far in India is quite meagre and not quite adequate to yield nation-wide generalisations. "In order to avoid a mechanical and overly schematic approach to the study of regional similarities and differences in the country, it is most desirable to continue with the anthropological tradition of single village studies." (Dube, 1958 : 3.)

However, if we want to understand Indian village as a concept, we have to get hold of those points of comparison which are significant and distinctive of Indian culture. The factors that are analysed in establishing Hindupur as *the* Indian village do not give any idea of village as a culture-bearing entity. Their Indianness is accidental, and by no means refers to the specificities of our villages.

In spite of all this, the Hindupur proposal has certainly provided stimulation and food for thought. Perhaps, it serves to point out that thinking in terms of *the* Indian village, or talking about the nationwide representative character of a single village is fruitless. Statistical calculations alone cannot offer any answer. Although Shamirpet, Rampura, Mohana, Ranikhera, Namhalli, Kasandra, Kishangarhi, etc. are different in more ways than one, from the Ideal type, Hindupur, they nevertheless represent the tradition of Indian villages in many respects. In every village in India, there is something which distinguishes it from the villages of the other countries of the world. If the two village studies of different countries are to be examined, at least this could easily be said that both these villages do not belong to the same country or culture. It, therefore, is implicit that each village has a certain measure of representativeness; the difference may be a matter of degree in which, and the area that, it represents.

And moreover, representativeness is always relative. When Man is related to the Animal Kingdom he is supposed to have those characteristics which are found even in a protozoon. But the similarity in the characteristics would go on increasing as he is classified as a vertebrate, a mammal, an eutherian, a primate and ultimately a Homosapien. He would be having all the characteristics of his species and, therefore, would truly represent it. But nonetheless he also represents other subdivisions to which he belongs in degrees that go on reducing as he departs from his station in the scheme. In the same way the village would represent in many respects its own region, then its province, then the nation, the continent and the world.

Representativeness should be based on similarities of cultural traits and complexes, and aspects of social organisation. Size of the village, distance from the city etc., should be given a secondary importance. It is apparent that proximity to the city in terms of communication may not be coexistent with physical distance. It should not be difficult for the social scientist to assign relative significance to sociological contexts over biological and geographical ones. Thus, caste-system, concepts of ritual purity and pollution, agriculture, hereditary occupational-specialization, temple worship and polytheistic beliefs may be some of the factors on which the representative type may be constructed. Of course, this would necessitate undertaking of more village studies and developing an elaborate methodology of comparative approach. The villages and Institutions of the same and of different culture-areas will have to be investigated in order to assess the range of similarities and differences.

The following hypotheses are proposed for determining the representativeness of an Indian Village:—

1. The language (or dialect) of a village can most adequately represent the linguistic area to which it belongs;
2. The ritual hierarchy of castes in a village could be representative of the culture-area or sub-culture-area to which the village belongs. However, it has to be remembered that it would only represent the ritual hierarchy of those castes which are found in the village.
3. In the same sub-cultural and the linguistic-area, social behaviour, ritual belief, customs and traditions, peculiarities of economic organisation, dressing and decoration patterns would tend to be similar;
4. From the point of view of caste-dominance, there could be wide-range dfferences between the village and the region. The

caste which is regionally dominant may not necessarily have the same degree of influence and dominance in all the villages of the region;

5. Along with regional similarities in a social institution found to be present in all the villages of a given region, local variations are also associated. The complete understanding of the structure and functioning of that institution is only possible when all its variations and ramifications are recorded. This requires the study of the institution in more than one village. In such a situation, the very fact of the presence of an institution in the village is not sufficient to justify its regional representativeness.

If, on the basis of these and other similar hypotheses, new researches are directed the regional ideal types could possibly be formulated. Once the problem of regional representation is solved, we shall be better equipped for the national Ideal type. It has to be specifically pointed out here that the concepts of "region" and "area" are also not sociologically well-defined. Attempts towards defining these concepts will facilitate proper examination of the issue of representativeness. Once good research data from Rural India are accumulated for comparative purposes, the ground will be prepared for thinking in terms of Indian Village as a concept.

4

ON 'VILLAGE STUDIES' IN INDIA*

PROF. RAMKRISHNA MUKHERJEE

I

THE DETERIORATION in India's rural economy, set in a century earlier and spreading insidiously over the subcontinent because of the lack of effective checks (Dutt, 1950), came up clearly on the surface from the beginning of the present century. The end of the First World War unveiled the abject poverty, squalor, and disorganization of village societies; the rumblings of rural discontent began to reach the ears of the Government and the educated public in towns and cities.

The Government had to take a serious note of the imminent agrarian crisis leading to the appointment of the first Royal Commission on Agriculture in 1926. Sympathetic private bodies and individuals also became interested, rendering a political and/or economic slant to the situation.

It was in this critical phase of India's history that "village studies", in the sense the label is employed today, took its birth in order that facts and figures could be gathered for an objective understanding of how the rural folks live, what are their wants, and why are they obliged to lead a subhuman existence.

Contextually, the Indian National Movement played a significant role. For one of its fruitful bye-products was to create interest of social scientists in "village studies". The mass movement of 1920's, led by Gandhi and based essentially on the rural question, synchronized with series of "village studies" carried out in different parts of India. Patel has succinctly summarized the situation.

"With the end of the First World War, the beginning of an agrarian crisis was accompanied by the entry of peasants into the political arena, as exemplified during the Champaran and Kaira campaigns led by Gandhiji. As a result, the cultivator of the soil began to attract considerable attention from students of Indian society. G. Keatings and Harold Mann in Bombay, Gilbert Slater in Madras, and E. V. Lucas in the Punjab, initiated intensive studies of particular villages and general agricultural problems. The results of these investigations evoked great interest and stressed the necessity for still further study." (Patel, 1952:1.)

In 1930's many more scientists, administrators, and politically imbued

*Published in the *Indian Journal of Social Research*, Vol. IV, No. 2 (1963), (Ed.) G. C. Hallen.

social workers joined forces. "Village studies" began to be carried out extensively all over India by organizations and individuals.

The Punjab Board of Economic Enquiry went on organizing village surveys conducted by individual workers (since 1920's). The Bengal Board of Economic Enquiry was set up and it undertook village surveys (1935); some in collaboration with the Indian Statistical Institute, Calcutta (Chakravarti, 1937). Tagore's Visva-Bharati organized village surveys around Santiniketan, Bengal, under the auspices of the Visva-Bharati Rural Reconstruction Board and at the individual initiative of Sri Kali Mohan Ghosh (data partly processed in Mukherjee and Mukerjee, 1946; Mukherjee, 1957; & c.) Professors Bhattacharya and Natesan of Scottish Church College, Calcutta, published accounts of village life in Bengal as collected by their students from respective villages (1932). The same was done by Professors Thomas and Ramakrishnan of Madras University (1940) with reference to the south Indian villages previously surveyed under the guidance of Gilbert Slater. The Cochin State published accounts of individual villages under the authorship of T. K. Sankara Menon (1935). Subramanian published the survey of a south Indian village under the auspices of the Congress Economic and Political Studies (1936), Gujarat Vidyapeeth persuaded Prof. J. C. Kumarappa to undertake the survey of Matar Taluka in Gujarat (1931), and his work synchronized or was followed by those of G. C. Mukhtyar (1930), J. B. Shukla (1937), and others in Gujarat. Village surveys were also taken up in Maharashtra by the Gokhale Institute of Politics and Economics, Poona (Gadgil and Gadgil, 1940, and others). And so it went on with studies undertaken by organizations and by individuals themselves.

Significantly, for these studies the field under focus was the economic life of the people; so that the pressing problems of rural society could be exposed in bold relief. Slater, one of the pioneers in "village studies" in India, wrote in his introduction to the study of "some South Indian Villages":

"Villages came before towns, and even in the most industrialized countries, where all economic questions tend to be studied from an urban point of view, it is well to be reminded that the economic life of a town or city cannot be understood without reference to the lands which send its food and raw materials, and the villages from which it attracts young men and women. The importance of rural activities and of village life in India, in view of the enormous preponderence of its agricultural population over that engaged in mining, manufacture, commerce and transport, is not likely to be overlooked and last of all in southern India, which has no coal mines and no great industries like cotton manufacture in Bombay and jute in Bengal." (Slater, 1918:1.)

Mann wrote in the Preface to his second study of Deccan village :

"The study of rural conditions by close inquiry into the circumstances of a single unit, be it village, parish, or estate, has come to the front prominently in recent years as a method of social and economic investigation. And by the use of this method, if the villages to be studied are well chosen, a very much more intimate acquaintance with the actual conditions of life than by any other method can be obtained." (Mann and Kanitkar, 1921: iii.)

Kalelkar wrote in his introduction to J. C. Kumarappa's "An Economic Survey of Matar Taluka":

"If there is one thing that characterises the educated man in India and distinguishes him from his confrere elsewhere it is his abysmal ignorance of the actual rural conditions in his own country. There are some people who are anxious to see India industrialized. There are others who will be content if India got back her own. But neither of them have secured the bedrock of statistics collected from the mouths of the peasants themselves. The present survey is unique in this respect." (Kumarappa, 1931: vii.)

Economics and material well-being of the rural folks had thus become the preoccupation with those undertaking "village studies", as the situation then dictated.

In 1940's also the orientation of social scientists towards "village studies" remained virtually the same as before. Only it could be noticed that henceforth they began to launch *extensive enquiries* by covering large tracts in the light of the picture of rural society already built up by means of the ever-increasing numbers of isolated "village studies". Concurrently, they were often found to concentrate on specific aspects of the "rural problem" in a particular area.

Thus the Indian Statistical Institute, Calcutta, undertook series of sample surveys of Bengal villages in order to ascertain the effects of the 1943 famine on rural society (Mahalanobis *et al*, 1946); to estimate the extent of rural indebtedness or to portray the condition of agricultural labourers in society (Indian Statistical Institute, 1948); and so on. Other organizations also made similar attempts, the details of which are not of immediate concern (e. g., Iyengar, 1951).

Likewise, the Government Departments, Central and Provincial, undertook extensive studies such as the Agricultural Labour Enquiry of the Ministry of Labour, Government of India, since 1948 (published from 1954 onwards). And individuals also contributed their mite in this venture. For example, Sayana of the Bombay School of Economics and Sociology undertook sample survey of Telegu-speaking districts of the Madras Province, along with the collation of relevant data from official and non-official sources, in order to study the "Agrarian Problem of Madras Province" (Sayana, 1949).

The upshot was that by 1950 the minimum of basic knowledge had been accumulated, at any rate, to attempt estimating the national income of rural India with reasonable precision, to formulate plans and programmes for India's rural development, and to sponsor studies on an all-India scale for the planned development of India in the future.

This is evident from the reports of the National Income Committee set up by the Government of India in 1949 (e. g., *The First Report* 1951), from the precise formulations of rural economic problems in the *plans* propagated by the Government of India or private bodies, from the inauguration of the Government of India National Sample Survey in 1950 (viz. *General Report No.* 1, 1952), etc. etc.

II

This course of development and outcome of "village studies" meets evidently an important need of the country and the government. So it may not be fortuitous that from a different ulterior motive it was brought up by the British East India Company as early as in 1689.

Those were the days when the Directors of the Company were becoming interested in controlling land and people in India instead of indulging in mere trading activities along with contemporary European and Indian rivals. Pursuantly, they wrote to their agents in India:

"The increase of our revenue is the subject of our care, as much as our trade; 'tis that must maintain our force, when twenty accidents may interrupt our trade; 'tis that must make us a nation in India; — without that we are but as a great number of interlopers, united by his Majesty's royal charter, fit only to trade where nobody of power thinks it their interest to prevent us; — and upon this account it is that the wise Duch, in all their general advices which we have seen, write ten paragraphs concerning their government, their civil and military policy, warfare, and the increase of their revenue, for one paragraph they write concerning trade." (Quoted by Mill, 1858-i, 87-88.)

In the present context, the aspirations of the East India Company for political power over India, as narrated elsewhere (Mukherjee 1958 a), do not concern us. What, however, would be of interest to note is that after the futile attempt of the Company in this direction at the end of the seventeenth century the successful attempts made since the middle of the eighteenth were followed by increasing awareness of the foreign power to know more and more about life and living in the sub-continent. Because, for good or bad, for the welfare of the people or for the exploitation of the masses, it is necessary to know at the outset how the society is organized and how the people live.

Here, therefore, we need not dwell upon the policy which sponsored from the beginning of the nineteenth century the extensive (although sketchy) collection of information on how the Indian people live in villages. Such as the Company's requisition of the services of Dr. Francis Buchanan from 1800 in order to report on the conditions in towns and villages in Madras, Mysore, Bihar, Bengal, etc. (Buchanan-Hamilton, 1807).

We need not also refer to the genuine interest in the welfare of the people which prompted a number of foreign administrators and scientists to undertake relevant investigations in villages and in broader regions, mainly from the beginning of the twentieth century. Such as the study of British administrator in India on the economic life of a Bengal district (Faridpur) in the first decade of the present century which he undertook on his own initiative and as a labour of love (Jack, 1916).

What we must note, instead, is that infrequent and usually a generalized version of the situation as they were, these efforts built the monumental gateway to the path of development of " village studies " in India.

The path. however, remained narrow and not yet fully reinforced even after several decades of conducting "village studies". Because in all these days engrossing attention was showered on rural "economics". A change in the depth of focus of the pictures emerging from the investigations was therefore called for.

Namely, to the poineers in the field the individuals and the social groups were living entities with reference to the economic activities they were engaged in. The *institutional* approach, in the sense it endeavours to portray the "organized, purposeful system of human effort and achievement" (Malinowski, 1944: 51), was possibly not deliberated. It was spontaneous as one might expect in unsophisticated keen observers. But in the course of development of "village studies" during 1920-50 the emphasis was laid increasingly on purely economic categorization of rural society; and even the *social relations* which the villagers had evolved with reference to their economic organization were not attended to properly or at all.

Such as the number of gainfully occupied persons in a village their affiliation to respective sectors of the national economy (as agriculture, handicraft production, etc.), the type of job they performed (such as non-manual or skilled manual occupation, etc.), and their activity status (as employer, employee, own-account worker), were the usual subject-matter for analysis. But the bearing of the presence of these individuals in society in terms of the relations which had emerged among themselves on account of their work and earnings, the relations which had crysalized within and between the societal groups incorporating one or the other of these persons, and such other facets of social relations evolving out of the economic organization of society were hardly touched upon.

Or, the income distribution, landholding, the expenditure pattern, and such other economic attributes of the villagers were often treated in meticulous details; but the social relations the rural folks had developed with respect to such economic attributes were, almost invariably, lost sight of. Similar examples may be cited in numbers.

As a result, even in terms of only such organized, purposeful systems of human effort and achievement as refer to the economic sphere of society not enough has been learnt so far as how the relevant individuals, the co-resident and commensal kingroups (viz. residential family-units), the kingroups of larger dimensions, or other varieties of societal units characterized by the involuntary and voluntary groupings of the villagers are integrated with one another with reference to the economic appellations of their constituent members.

Indeed, we know very little today about the structural and functional alignments in village society consequent to the economic activities of the people, not to speak of other aspects of their life. For the preoccupation of the social scientists with the "economics" of rural society, which became more and more pronounced since 1940's, began to push the living persons in the background; and instead of presenting the villagers *as social beings* presented them (with increasingly finer precision no doubt) as abstract economic and statistical categories.

III

To be sure, there was, there is, and there will remain the need for such specialized studies. But equally, it began to be felt, there is the need to take up "village studies" from *another* perspective; the perspective formulated and interpreted by cultural and social anthropologists and sociologists in contradistinction to that evolved by the economists from an earlier period.

This felt-need began to be satisfied by the publications coming out since 1950's. The late Professor Majumdar, one of those who undertook the task, had aptly described the situation.

"Of late, in India, we have a spate of literature on our rural life. Some have been written by foreign scholars, some by Indians. Some of these studies have been monographically oriented, as for example, Srinivas's "Mysore Village" or Dube's "Indian Village". Some are problem oriented, as one discovers in the various anthropologies published in anthropological or social science journals or in the *Economic Weekly*. The West Bengal Government has published a volume of essays on Indian village life and problems edited by M. N. Srinivas. McKim Marriot has edited a series of articles on Indian rural life, under the title *Village India*, while the Ethnographic and Folk Culture Society, Uttar Pradesh, has published a volume on *Rural Profiles*, the first of a series of village studies. All these indicate the interest the anthropologists are taking in rural assignments. Some of these studies are intimate, intensive and competent, some are superficial; and no doubt, some have raised our expectations, for they have focused attention on the many problems of rural life which demand priority in the context of the planning for the countryside, which is the avowed goal of our planners." (Majumdar, 1958: 326-327.)

It is not the contention of the writer to comment on the writings of individual anthropologists and sociologists who have thus given a *new look* to "village studies". Obviously, at the initial stage of such a venture there would be some hasty generalizations, occasionally narrow specialization, or, infrequently, dogmatic adherence to an intriguing concept. But these are minor blemishes on the edifice that is being built by this attempt; an edifice which will serve the purpose of presenting, eventually, a balanced view of the forces at work in rural society and a harmonious picture of the course of life pulsating therein.

I thus comment on the lack of a balanced view of the dynamics of rural society and on the incomplete picture of rural life we are presented with even after this new venture. And I note, concurrently, that this will have to be achieved. There is an important reason for subscribing to this viewpoint.

Namely, although most of the studies falling under the recently sponsored scheme are of substantial worth, they swing to specialization similar to those of contemporary economists but at the other extreme. The twain do not meet. Or they meet seldom, and there again in most instances inconsequentially. A composite picture of rural society has, therefore, yet to be exposed.

Thus, with reference to the same subject as "village study", an economist may be found to dwell on the theme of "proletarianization" of the mass villagers as indicate of the dominant phenomenon in rural society. Whereas a social anthropologist or sociologist would be complimentarily concentrating his attention on the role of *dominant caste* in a village, on *casteization* or *sanskritization* of the rural folk, etc.

Is there a link between the two processes or are they independent of each other? And if a link is there, what does it stand for *vis-a-vis* the dynamics of rural society? Would it not be useful to explore that link for a harmonious picture of the life pulsating in a village?

In the same way as for the above example, with respect to village as an entity the economist may speak of "closed" versus "vulnerable" economy and elucidate the concept of pointing out "sub-marginal" productive and service enterprise in a "self-subsisting economy". The social anthropologist or sociologist, on the other hand, may treat the village as a unit *hierarchically structured* and may elucidate rural life as a "concept" based on kinship ties, caste-wise integration, and the *jajmani* system. But is it not possible to combine the two aspects of rural society and obtain thereby a fuller understanding of the course of life therein?

Similarly, an economist interested in the *social accounting* of a village may discuss the problem of evaluation of "non-monetary income and outgoings in family-household enterprises" while a social anthropologist or sociologist who considers the village as a "constellation of values" may elaborate on the particular value system of rural folks, on the concepts of *parochialization* versus *universalization*, etc. But, again, would not the superimposition of these two facets of rural life yield a better harvest?

Or, both being concerned with explaining current changes in village society, an economist may point out the growing phenomenon of *entrepreneurship* in rural areas and the emergence of a *class* in village society with improved means and techniques of production and distribution, etc. Whereas a social anthropologist or sociologist may describe the content of the "urbanization process" in rural areas against the schematic formulation of *rural-urban continuum* and may ascertain the role of "village elite" in that context. But there, again, it may be desirable to bring the two sets of phenomena in focus simultaneously so as to appreciate the crucial character of the emergent leadership in rural society.

Many more instances could be cited to illustrate how even the complimentary aspects of village life are emphasized unilaterally by the economists and the social anthropologists or sociologists in two different directions, without attempts being made to link up the two equally useful lines of study. And, then, there are obviously such other aspects of village life as fall under the respective fields of specialization of an economist, a social anthropologist or a sociologist.

The upshot is that today we encounter, virtually, two different worlds of concepts and models, of analysis and interpretation, and of idioms of expression and inference concerning the same topic as "village study".

IV

No doubt, the separation and the current parallel development of these two perspectives in "village study" substantiate the fact that this branch of study has passed its stage of adolescence and has attained adulthood. So that the *social* investigation of villages may be conducted on its own merit as already accorded to the economic *investigation* of the same. For, on the one hand, both would enrich our knowledge of the social organism under reference, and, on the other, there are certain distinctly important nuances of life and living in a village which can be elicited by only one of the two approaches respectively.

Thus, when describing the economic structure of a village, Dube concentrates his attention on the relation between the caste-affiliation and the occupation of respective villagers (Dube 1955: 57f). Thereby he certainly departs from the no less useful procedure followed by economists; such as the relation between land ownership utilization and occupation of the same villagers, their activity status with reference to different sectors of the national economy, etc. But the picture Dube presents by following this line of analysis is an addition to our store of knowledge regarding village societies which was lacking in the picture presented by economists, although some of them may have noted the caste affiliation of villagers as merely one of the many ways of classifying a village society or may have mentioned in passing the association of *some* castes with *certain* facets of its economic organization.

Also, while noting as above the utility of "village studies" by social anthropologists or sociologists we may comment on the usefulness of exposing by means of relevant conceptual tools the specifically *social* characteristics of village society. Such as the relative position of a village in the spectrum of *rural-urban continuum;* or the working of a particular process of acculturation in rural society under the labels of *sanskritization, parochialization*, etc.; and so on.

And, concurrently, we may note the distinct importance of portraying the peculiar and specific *way of life* of a village, as Rosser has done for instance. (Rosser, 1960: 77-89.)

Briefly, therefore, there is no ground to denounce, or even undermine, the intrinsic merit of "village studies" usually conducted by social anthropologists and sociologists. But, all the same, the point remains that the two streams of "village studies" carrying the imprint of economists or social anthropologists/sociologists, respectively, must meet at relevant sites. Alternatively bridges will have to be built at the places if confluence of the streams cannot be achieved.

For it is the causal or concomitant relations among *economic* and *social* (including *ideological*) traits of a people which lead to the emergence of specific societal organizations and the formulation of distinct ideological orientations of their constituent members. Also these are the relations which either maintain the current structural and functional alignments in society or engineer their respective courses of change or transformation. So that, until and unless the "economic" and "social" perspectives towards "village studies" meet at critical points, it is not possible to obtain a composite understanding of village life and a balanced view of the dynamics of village society.

Evidently, the demand may not be met in a single study unless it is an omnibus one. For we find that, justifiably, specialized studies in the economic or the social field call for respective volumes. Pursuantly, specialized investigations in the above respect also should be included in the curriculum for "village studies".

V

The aim, thus outlined, is not of mere academic interest to one with a squeamish taste for the *total* knowledge. This is also not the means to feed a doctrinaire because of his preoccupation with the finding of so-called "economic" motivation to each and every societal manifestation. On the contrary, it has a distinct usefulness. Because it meets one of the imperative requisites to appreciate the governing processes within a social organism by the cross-fertilization of the "economic" and the "social" factors instead of depending upon the subjective assumptions and interpretations of either of the two schools of social scientists to *fill in the gap* in this respect.

Moreover, the need for such an attempt, is underlined in the context of our present-day situation, as Professor Firth had noted very forcefully more than a decade ago.

"India is beginning to learn the lesson that the price of political freedom is economic responsibility. The sympathy extended to her in her struggle for independence is needed in manifold measure now, in her struggle to abate the grinding rural poverty of so many of her people. It can hardly be denied that some solution of the pressing agrarian problem of India is crucial to the survival of her present political system. More than that, it is crucial to the survival of many of her citizens."

"Most of the books and articles about the agrarian problems of India that reach the Western reader are analyses of a general kind. They tell us of India—and leave us with a feeling of ignorance as to just how these problems affect different groups and classes of the people in different places. They talk of economics—and leave untouched those social alignments and social values which give the economic system its meaning. Or they talk about the social background as something which simply inhibits the development of free economic enterprise and efficiency—in terms of caste taboos and sacred cows and sacred monkeys—and leave untouched the solid satisfactions to be found in the family and kinship system, in the caste associations and reliances, and even in the complex ritual evaluations of animals which share with man something of what he believes to be the divine spirit." (Firth, 1952: v.)

In the light of our achievements till today as regards the *motivation to change* in rural society, the words of Professor Firth ring a topical note. For, even after half a century's efforts to understand and appreciate village life in India, we are not certain, as yet, as to which are the *soft spots* in the social organism through which a desired course of change could be introduced in rural society. (Mukherjee, 1962.)

For instance: is it the "proletarianized" rural mass and/or the *numerically* "dominant caste" placed low in the caste hierarchy which is to be the harbinger of a *new life* in villages? Alternatively, would the charge devolve upon the landed gentry and/or the top-ranking caste Hindus?

Likewise, would the carriers of *new values* to rural society be the growing "rural intelligentsia" or the dumb millions who have their "education" in the hard way? And should we go on considering, similarly, other distinctly "social" and/or distinctly "economic" groups in society in order to unravel the course of change therein?

Or, instead of such formal and mutually distinct economic and social categorizations of the rural folk, is it a symbiosis of their various economic and social attributes which should lead us to the diagnosis of relevant soft spots in the social organisms under reference?

Evidently, in consideration of its theoretical value as well as its practical implications, a course of research in this direction has been called for since a long time. But, falling in no-man's land between "economics" and "social anthropology or sociology" as two different disciplines of study, its progress has been halting and hesitating. So that achievements in this line have been very little so far; in quantity, at any rate.

From among the economists, possibly the investigations of J. P. Bhattacharjee (1958) and of Baljit Singh (1961) stand out in this respect. From the other side, A. C. Mayer's *Land and Society in Malabar* (1952) falls in the line; his *Caste and Kinship in Central India* (1960) is also not out of the path. *Six Villages of Bengal*, surveyed during 1941-45 and published as late as in 1958, was also a feeble venture of the present writer in this field; leading him at a later date to discuss *The Dynamics of a Rural Society* (1957). F. G. Bailey's *Caste and the Economic Frontier* (1958) is a distinct contribution in the same field; and his explorations in the wider field of *Tribe, Caste, and Nation* (1960) follow therefrom.

Contextually it should be noted that some studies of social scientists in East Pakistan (formerly a part of the Indian sub-continent) also give the in dication ofa similar orientation. Such as of Husain as an economist (Husain 1956), and of some social anthropologists as found in the volume *Social Research in East Pakistan* edited by Pierre Bessaignet (1960).

Thus, irrespective of the relative merits of these studies, we find that attempts have been made in the desired direction in the last ten or twelve years. But such studies remain intermittent and relatively scarce. Should we not, therefore, undertake more such studies; and with, possibly, pointed relevance?

VI

The question may be raised at this stage of our discussion as to which of the two schools of specialists, viz. economists and social anthropologists or sociologists, should undertake the task.

This is a moot question. But it is also a question that we are facing frequently these days on other courses of social research because of the significant development of different disciplines of study under the banner of social sciences. And so a quick answer may be provided as that inter-disciplinary research in the fields of economics, social anthropology and sociology, and psychology is the *sine qua non* of the present-day position of "village studies" just as it is with respect to almost all other aspects of the study of social beings.

But the answer, however perfect, may not be the most practicable one; in a large number of cases, at any rate. Alternatively, therefore, we may note that as the study of group relations evolved in a society with respect to all the activities of is constituent members falls directly under the terms of reference of social anthropology and sociology, the task should- devolve upon them particularly.

Even so, the question would not be fully answered. Because we should note concurrently that if the term of reference to the economists be acclaimed as the study of relations among men with respect to material goods and services instead of as that between man and material goods and services (Sweezy 1956:4-5), they could not also be exempted from shouldering the burden. And if the psychologists are not to indulge in researches on human beings in a rarified "personal" situation only, they would also have to accept the responsibility equally with economists, social anthropologists, and sociologists.

Thus the frontiers of the three disciplines meet in the field of "village study", and so scientists duly equipped to cross the no-man's land between the disciplines should also be forthcoming.

The question therefore does not boil down to which discipline should undertake the task or that it can be accomplished only by interdisciplinary research. Contrariwise, the question throws up the challenge to create interest among those belonging to any one of the disciplines to assume the responsibility and equip themselves accordingly.

So that where the necessary facilities are available, inter-disciplinary research may be undertaken for this course of "village study". And if such facilities cannot be provided with, as it is likely in many instances, duly-equipped scientists from any one of the disciplines must undertake the task as a distinct course of research.

I am inclined to the view that thereby we shall fulfil a very important objective of social research, both theoretically and as applied.

REFERENCES

AGRICULTURAL LABOUR ENQUIRY, REPORTS, since 1954, Ministry of Labour, Government of India, New Delhi.

AIYAR, S. SUBBARAME, 1952, *Economic Life in a Malabar Village*, University of Madras Economic Series, No. 2, Bangalore City.

BADEN-POWELL, B. H., *The Indian Village Community*, London, John Murray, 1872.

BADEN-POWELL, B. H., *The Origin and Growth of Village Communities in India*, London, Swan Sonnesnsheir, 1899.

BAILEY, F. G., 1958, *Caste and the Economic Frontier*, Oxford University Press, India.

BAILEY, F. G., 1960, *Tribe, Caste and Nation*, Manchester University Press, U. K.

BENGAL BOARD OF ECONOMIC ENQUIRY, 1935, *Enquiry on Rural Indebtedness, The Preliminary Report*, The Calcutta Gazette, Government of Bengal.

BESSAIGNET, PIERRE (Ed.), 1960, *Social Research in East Pakistan*, Asiatic Society of Pakistan, Dacca.

BHATTACHARJEE, J. P., *et al*, 1958, *Sahajapur*, West Bengal, Agro-Economic Research Centre for East India, Visva-Bharati University, Santiniketan.

BHATTACHARYA, N. C., and NATESAN, L. A. (ed.), 1932, *Some Bengal Villages; An Economic Survey*, Calcutta University, Calcutta.

BUCHANAN-HAMILTON, FRANCIS, 1807, *Manuscripts* in the Commonwealth Office Library, London.

CHAKRAVARTI, N. C., 1937, *The Report on the Survey of Hand-Loom Weaving Industry in Bengal*, Board of Economic Enquiry, Government of Bengal.

DESHPANDE, S. R., and GHURYE, G. S., 1927, *A Survey of* 154 *Families in Four Villages of the Kolaba District*, Indian Journal of Economics, April number.

DUBE, S. C., 1955, *Indian Village*, Routledge & Kegan Paul, London.

DUBE, S. C., Presidential Address to the Social Anthropological Section of 1958, *The Study of Indian Village Communities.*

DUTT, ROMESH, 1950, *The Economic History of British India* (2 vols.), Routledge & Kegan Paul, London.

First Report of the National Income Committee, April 1951, The Department of Economic Affairs, Ministry of Finance, Government of India, New Delhi.

FIRTH, RAYMOND, 1952, "Introduction" to A. C. Mayer's *Land and Society in Malabar* (referred below).

GADGIL, D. R., and GADGIL, V. R., 1940, *A Survey of Farm Business in Wai Taluka* Gokhale Institute of Politics & Economics, Poona.

General Report No. 1 on the First Round, October 1950-March 1951, The National Sample Survey, 1952, The Department of Economic Affairs, Ministry of Finance, Government of India, New Delhi.

HUSSAIN, A. F. A., 1956, *Human & Social Impact of Technological Change in Pakistan*, Oxford Cumberlege, Dacca.

INDIAN STATISTICAL INSTITUTE, 1948, Reports submitted to the Government of Bengal on the Rural Indebtedness Inquiry and the Agricultural Labour Enquiry, Calcutta.

IYENGAR, S. K., 1951, *Rural Economic Surveys in Hyderabad* (1949-51), Hyderabad.

JACK, J. C., 1916, *The Economic Life of a Bengal District* (*Faridpur*), Oxford University Press, U. K.

KUMARAPPA, J. C., 1931, *An Economic Survey of Matar Taluka*, Ahmedabad.

LUCAS, E. V., 1920, *The Economic Life of a Punjab Village*, Lahore.

MAHALANOBIS, P. C., MUKHERJEE, R., and GHOSH, A., 1946, *A Sample Survey of the After-Effects of the Bengal Famine of* 1943, Statistical Publishing Society, Calcutta.

MAJUMDAR, D. N. (ed.), 1955, *Rural Profiles*, Ethnographic and Folk Culture Society, Lucknow.

MAJUMDAR, D. N., 1958, *Caste and Communication in an Indian Village*, Asia Publishing House, Bombay.

MALINOWSKI, B., 1944, *A Scientific Theory of Culture and other Essays*, North Carolina University Press, U. S. A.

MANDAL, G. C., and SEN GUPTA, S. C., *Kashipur, West Bengal* (1956-60), Visva-Bharati University, 1961.

MANN, H. H., 1917, *Land and Labour in a Deccan Village*, University of Bombay Economic Series No. 1, Bombay.

MANN, H. H., 1921, *Land and Labour in a Deccan Village*, University of Bombay Economic Series No. 2, Bombay.

MAYER, A. C., 1952, *Land and Society in Malabar*, Oxford University Press, U. K.

MAYER, A. C., 1960, *Caste and Kinship in Central India*, Routledge & Kegan Paul, London.

MCKIM MARRIOT (ed), 1955, *Village India*, The University of Chicago Press, U.S.A.

MILL, JAMES, 1858, *The History of British India*, James Madden, London.

MUKHERJEE, P. K., 1959, *Economic Surveys in Under-Developed Countries*, Asia Publishing House, Bombay.

MUKHERJEE, P. K. & GUPTA, S. C., 1959, *A Pilot Survey of Fourteen Villages in U. P. and Punjab*, Asia Pub. House, Bombay.

MUKHERJEE, RAMKRISHNA and MUKHERJEE, MONIMOHAN, 1946, *A Note on the Concentration of Agricultural Wealth in Bengal*, "Sankhya"—The Indian Journal of Statistics, Calcutta, Vol. 7, Part 4.

MUKHERJEE, RAMKRISHNA, 1957, *The Dynamics of a Rural Society*, Akademie Verlad, Berlin.

MUKHERJEE, RAMKRISHNA, 1959, (a) *The Rise and Fall of the East India Company*, Verlag der Wissenschaften, Berlin.

MUKHERJEE RAMKRISHNA, 1958, (b) "Six Villages of Bengal", *Journal of the Asiatic Society of Bengal*, Vol. XXIV, Nos. 1 and 2, Calcutta.

MUKHERJEE, RAMKRISHNA, 1961, "Caste and Economic Structure in West Bengal in present times" in *Sociology, Social Research and Social Problems in India*, (ed.) R. N. Saksena, Asia Pub. House, Bombay.

MUKHERJEE, RAMKRISHNA, 1961, "A Note on Village as Unit or Variable for Studies of Rural Society", *Eastern Anthropologist*, Vol. XIV, No. 1, Lucknow.

MUKHERJEE, RAMKRISHNA, 1962, "Sociologist and Social Change in India Today", *Sociological Bulletin*, Decennial Symposium Volume, March & September issue, Bombay.

MUKHERJEE, RAMKRISHNA, 1962, "A Minority/Marginal Group in Calcutta", contributed to the Fifth World Congress of Sociology, Washington.

MUKHERJEE, RAMKRISHNA, 1962, "On Rural-Urban Differences and Relationships in Social Characteristics", contributed to the Unesco Rural-Urban Seminar, New Delhi.

MUKHTYAR, G. C., 1930, *Life and Labour in a South Gujarat Village*, Bombay.

PATEL, S. J., 1952, *Agricultural Labourers in Modern India and Pakistan*, Current Book House, Bombay.

PUNJAB BOARD OF ECONOMIC ENQUIRY, 1920's and since, Village Surveys by M. B. Ahmed, R. L. Bhalia, F. L. Brayne, A. Das, L. N. Dawar, R. Narain, B. M. Raj, R. Singh, S. Singh, S. G. Singh, and others, Government of Punjab Publications, Lahore.

RANADE, V. G., 1927, *A Social and Economic Survey of a Konkan Village*, The Provincial Co-operative Institute of Bombay, Rural Economic Series, Bombay.

ROSSER, COLLIN, 1955, "A 'Hermit' Village in Kulu", *India's Villages*, (ed.) M. N. Srinivas (referred below).

SANKARA MENON, T. K., 1935, "Economic Survey of Nayerambalam Village".

SANKARA MENON, T. K., 1935, "Economic Survey of Eruttampadi".

SANKARA MENON, T. K., 1935, "Economic Survey of Antikkad."
(All three publications of the Cochin State).

SAYANA, V. V., 1949, *The Agrarian Problems of Madras Province*, Madras.

SHUKLA, J. B., 1937, Life and Labour in a Gujarat Taluka (Olpad), Bombay University Economic Series No. 10, Bombay.

SINGH, BALJIT, 1961, *Next Step in Village India*, Asia Publishing House, Bombay.

SLATER, GILBERT, 1918, *Some South Indian Villages*, Madras University Economic Studies No. 1, Madras.

SRINIVAS, M. N., (ed.) 1955, *India's Villages*, Government of West Bengal Publication, Calcutta.

STEVENSION-MOORE, J., 1898, "Report on the Material Conditions of Small Agriculturists and Labourers in Gaya", Calcutta.

SUBRAMNIAN, N. S., 1936, *Survey of a South Indian Village*, Congress Economic & Political Studies No. 2.

SWEEZY, PAUL M., 1956, *The Theory of Capitalist Development*, Monthly Review Press, New York (Fourth Printing).

THOMAS, P. J. and RAMAKRISHNAN, K. C., (ed.) 1940, *Some South Indian Villages: A Re-survey*, Madras University Economic Series No. 4, Madras.

SECTION SIXTEEN

THEORIES OF AGRARIAN DEVELOPMENT

INTRODUCTION

THE END of the second world war inaugurated a new chapter in the social drama of mankind. The colonial and the semi-colonial peoples of Africa, Asia and Latin America, exploited and oppressed under direct or indirect rule of Imperialist Western countries, exhibited a new dynamism. A large number of these peoples forced the imperialist masters to abdicate their political rule and entered into a new epoch of political freedom. One-third of the world broke away from the capitalist mode of production and took to non-capitalist socialist path of modernization and industrialization. The mainland China, North Korea, North Vietnam, Eastern Europe including Yugoslavia, and subsequently Cuba launched the experiment of development on the non-capitalist path. Many other countries of Asia, Africa and Latin America, while freed from the direct political tutelage of Imperialist masters, have been reshaping the economy and society on capitalist mixed economy postulates.

The world is witnessing what Prof. Horowitz has characterized as "three worlds of development". (1) The development in the highly industrialist neo-capitalist western countries headed by the U.S.A. giant. (2) The development in the countries, which have taken to non-capitalist path and which are attempting to reshape the economies and societies on the postulates of central planning, based on nationalization of major and key means of production and production basically oriented to the assessed needs of the people rather than geared to the profit-need of the private owners of the means of production. (3) The 'Third World' as it is now popularly described comprised of underdeveloped and developing ex-colonial and semi-colonial countries of Asia, Africa and Latin America which are reshaping their economy and society on the basis of mixed economy postulates fundamentally on capitalist lines.

The developmental processes in the 'third world' of underdeveloped but developing countries have revealed trends which are alarming. The pace of their development is considerably slower and is creating a condition whereby these countries will lag behind the advanced countries further and further. The pattern of urbanization that is taking place is extremely unsatisfactory and has not generated that momentum in the countryside which would affect the overwhelmingly agrarian basis of these countries, so necessary for the take-off of development. The efforts to reconstruct the agrarian economy and social structure are causing some of the gravest dilemmas. The elementary bourgeois-democratic tasks like solution of agrarian problems, or provision of education, medical facilities, adequate job opportunities or nationality problems are not merely not fulfilled but their solutions are receding into the background and are becoming outside the pale of practical resolution. The governments, which started their appeal on populist-socialist slogans are slowly losing their mass appeal and are facing the growing opposition and struggles from various sections of the people. The states are increasingly throwing away their democratic-populist masks and are revealing their totalitarian dictatorial real face to protect the propertied classes in the face of growing restlessness of the toiling masses.

Eminent thinkers have started probing deeply into the grim, tragic and dramatic developments that are taking place in these countries. The earlier rosy, optimistic portrayals are slowly assuming darker and pessimistic hues. *The Asian Drama* by Gunnar Myrdal, and the works of eminent scholars such as Peter Worsley, Wertheim, Horowitz and others indicate the same anxious forebodings about the fate of the 'third world'.

In this section Prof. Dantwalla, Prof. Dandekar and Dr. Surendra Patel, experts on Indian agrarian problems, provide valuable factual basis of agrarian development in India and have, according to their assessments, raised some of the most crucial issues confronted by Planners of the country. Prof. Baran, who unfortunately expired prematurely, is well known for his classic analysis of underdeveloped countries. His selection raises some of the basic questions connected with the problem of development on the basis of mixed economy postulates. Prof. Wertheim and Earnst Germain are internationally famous theoreticians who have examined the underlying assumptions of the developmental philosophies of the third world. The two articles selected from a journal, the mouthpiece of one of the most distinguished International Marxist organizations, also provides a panorama of the colonial revolutions and problems of the path of development.

I have contributed a paper which was presented to the 1st World congress of Rural Sociology held in France in 1964. In it an attempt is being made to examine the social implications of the developmental policies based on reliance on rich farmers.

The ten selections of this section will, I am sure, stimulate a very keen controversy about some of the vital problems of transformation affecting the Third World. They will, I trust, raise some fundamental questions connected with developmental processes. They will also pose some of the basic methodological issues connected with type of researches which are being conducted with regard to the changing agrarian structures of India and other underdeveloped countries.

1

AGRICULTURE IN A DEVELOPING ECONOMY —THE INDIAN EXPERIENCE*

M. L. DANTWALLA

A LITTLE more than a decade has elapsed since this country launched upon a programme of planned economic development. According to the estimates of the Planning Commission, an investment of 10,110 crore rupees has been made in the economy between 1951 and 1961. The Third-Five Year Plan envisages an investment of another 10,000 crore rupees during 1961-65. It is legitimate to expect that all this investment and the organizational effort that goes with it, would not only accelerate the pace of economic development, but, in the process, also alter the structure of the economy. It would be interesting therefore to examine the nature and extent of change in the structure of the national economy during the last decade, by reference to some of the conventional economic indicators.

For the purpose of this Address, I should like to focus attention on the impact of the process of growth on the agricultural sector. The literature on the economics of growth visualizes a certain role for agriculture in the process of economic development, stage by stage, but a little more precisely in the early stage of development. Not that all writers are unanimous on the subject, but most of them agree on the importance or the crucial role of agriculture.

As a background to our main factual analysis of India's experience, it would be interesting to review briefly, first, some of the theories on the role of agriculture in economic development, and then, the thinking of the Indian planners on the subject, as revealed in the successive Five-Year Plans.

THEORETICAL VIEWPOINTS

The primacy of agricultural development is emphasized by some writers, because agriculture is not only the most populous but also the most depressed sector of the economy in most of the developing economies. This view is sometimes carried to the extreme of opposition to industrial development. It is argued that "the policy of industrialization will intensify the tendency for savings to be drained from the countryside by making investment in urban industries more attractive",[1] and thus

*Reproduced from R. R. Kale Memorial Lecture 1964.

1 Oshima, Harry, 'A Strategy of Asian Development', *Economic Development and Cultural Change*, April 1962.

widen the range of inequality between the urban and rural standards of living. "Problems of over-population and unemployment, very low incomes, excessive urbanization, food shortages as well as certain social and political considerations would suggest that the policy of industrialization is premature and undesirable at the present stage of Asian development."[2] The importance of increased supply of food and other wage goods is emphasized by a group of thinkers not merely on welfare grounds, but as a necessary investment in human capital. The 'consumption multiplier', it is argued, is not less crucial than the conventional investment multiplier in the strategy of development.

Priority for agriculture is also favoured on the ground that the creation of investible surplus is technologically easier in agriculture and has much shorter gestation period. Increase in agricultural production in the initial period of development can be brought about through the application of resources which have a low opportunity cost and make no inroads on the critically scarce resources necessary for industrial development.[3]

The point of departure comes on the question whether the economic surplus in agriculture should be retained within it for improving the standard of rural living or should be siphoned off for urban, industrial development. Those who advocate the latter are interested in agriculturists either forcibly or through lower prices.[4] The non-violent strategy is expounded thus: "Increase in the output of foodgrains and other agricultural commodities sufficient to lower their price will make the terms of trade unfavourable to agriculture. The fall in agricultural prices will be steep, due to the fact that the demand for food is not infinitely elastic. If agricultural prices are depressed relative to non-agricultural prices, agricultural surpluses will go into the hands of non-agriculturists."[5]

As against the agriculture-first school, those who emphasize the role of rapid industrialization in economic development argue that most of the underdeveloped countries are, in fact, so termed because of the predominance of agriculture in their national economy. The path of progress, therefore, must inevitably lie in the direction of a shift of resources, both capital and labour, from low-productivity enterprises to high-productivity enterprises. Agriculture is admittedly a relatively low-productivity sector even in most of the advanced countries; as such, the strategy of economic development would consist in gradually reducing the preponderance of the agricultural sector in the national economy through a process of industrialization. This, in any case, would be necessary

[2] *Ibid.*

[3] Johnston, Bruce, and John Melier, 'The Nature of Agriculture's Contribution to Economic Development', Food Research Institute Studies, Nov. 1960.

[4] Khan, N. A., 'Resource Mobilization from Agriculture and Economic Development in India', *Economic Development and Cultural Change*, October 1963.

[5] *Ibid.*

inasmuch as with rising incomes, the community's demand-pattern will undergo a change in favour of industrial products.

International comparisons of shares of major sectors in national product "reveal a negative correlation between the level of income and agriculture's share in it, and a positive correlation between the level of income and the share of non-agricultural commodity production. As the level of per capita income increases, the share of agriculture in national product drops and that of industry rises."[6] Analysis of long-term trends also confirms the results obtained by cross-country analysis. Thus, Prof. Kuznets found that with the secular rise of product per capita and per worker, the share of the agricultural sector in total product declines and the share of the manufacturing sector rises. The analysis in terms of distribution of labour force in the different sectors of the national economy suggests a significant positive association between the rate of growth in per capita and a shift away from agriculture in the structure of the labour force. One is therefore led to argue that "if real income per capita is to grow rapidly, the accompanying changes in the occupational structure of the labour force should be equally large. In the sample of eighteen countries, the total shift in the percentage distribution of labour force (including unpaid family labour) among the three major sectors (agriculture, manufacture, services) tends to be large in countries with high rates of growth of per capita income and vice versa."[7]

These conclusions, however, should not be interpreted to imply that a mere re-deployment of labour force would automatically, so to say, lead to higher per capita income. Kuznets' analysis has also revealed that a mere shift of the industrial structure of underdeveloped countries towards the pattern of developed countries—retaining the contrast between the high, relative, per-worker product in the manufacturing and service sectors and the low one in the agricultural sector—will not reduce the international differences in per-worker product. "To put in simply," he says, "the major source of international differences in countrywide output per worker (and per capita) between developed and underdeveloped countries is not that the full-time labour force of the former and of the latter are distributed differently among the several industrial sectors.... It is rather in the fact that within each sector proper—within agriculture, within mining, within manufacturing, within transportation and trade, etc.—the product per worker in the underdeveloped countries is so much lower than in the developed." As a matter of fact, Kuznets himself has elsewhere argued: "Agricultural Revolution—a marked rise in productivity per worker in agriculture—is a pre-condition of the

6 Kuznets, Simon, 'Quantitative Aspects of Economic Growth of Nations', *Economic Development and Cultural Change*, July, 1957. The subsequent observations are also based on this article.

7 *Ibid.*

industrial revolution in any part of the world."[8] Whatever be the motive or objective of economic development, welfare of the rural community or its surplus-generating-potential for overall economic development, there appears to be a fair degree of consensus regarding the crucial importance of agriculture in the initial period of economic growth.

II

PLACE OF AGRICULTURE IN INDIA'S FIVE-YEAR PLANS

In the light of the foregoing discussion on the role of agriculture in economic development, it would be useful to review briefly the views of the Planning Commission on this question as stated in the successive Five-Year Plans. Writing about the pattern of priority in the First Five-Year Plan, the Planning Commission states: "The conception of priorities over a period has to be a dynamic one, the emphasis as between different sectors shifting as development in those taken up initially prepares the ground for development in others." Having laid down this broad principle, the Planning Commission proceeds to state: "For the next five-year period, agriculture including irrigation and power must, in our view, have the top-most priority. For one thing, this emphasis is indicated by the need to complete the projects in hand, and further we are convinced that without a substantial increase in the production of food and of raw materials needed for industry, it would be impossible to sustain a high tempo of industrial development. In an underdeveloped economy, with low yield in agriculture, there is of course no real conflict between agricultural and industrial development. One cannot go far without the other; the two are complementary. It is necessary, however, on economic as well as on other grounds, first of all to strengthen the economy at the base and to create conditions of sufficiency and even plentitude in respect of food and raw materials." Consistent with this approach, in the total Plan outlay of 2,356 crore rupees, as much as 15·1 per cent was allocated to agriculture and community development and 28·1 per cent to irrigation and power (16·3 per cent to irrigation, 11·1 per cent to power and 0·7 per cent to flood control, etc.) as against 7·6 per cent to industry and mining (6·3 per cent for large and medium industries and 1·3 per cent for small industries).[9] It should, however, be mentioned that the Planning Commission, at that stage, held the following view: "The progress in industries, especially large-scale industries, would have to depend, to a great extent, on effort in the private sector, while the State would concentrate on the provision of basic services like power and transportation." Though it was stated, that the State had also "special responsibility for developing key industries and heavy industries like iron and steel, heavy chemicals and manufacture of electrical equipments with-

---

[8] Kuznets, Simon, *Six Lectures in Economic Growth.*

[9] For the statement of outlay in the public sector under the three Five-Year Plans, see Table 1.

out which development in the modern world is impossible," no significant allocation was made for the development of these key industries in the public sector.

Agricultural production during the First Five-Year Plan increased substantially, though in retrospect it appears that the bulk of it was due to an increase in the acreage and to good weather conditions. At the

TABLE 1 : **Outlay* in the Public Sector in the First, the Second and the Third Plan.**

Head	*First Plan* (1951—56)		*Second Plan* (1956—61)		*Third Plan* (1961—66)	
	Outlay	*Percentage*	*Outlay*	*Percentage*	*Outlay*	*Percentage*
Agriculture & Community Development	357	15·1	568	11·8	1,068	14
Major & Medium Irrigation	401	17·0	486	10·1	650	9
Power	260	11·1	427	8·9	1,012	13
Village & Small Industries	30	1·3	200	4·1	264	4
Industries & Minerals	149	6·3	690	14·4	1,520	20
Transport & Communications	557	23·6	1,385	29·9	1,486	20
Social Services & Miscellaneous	533	22·6	945	19·7	1,300	17
Inventories/Miscellaneous	69	3·0	99	2·1	200	3
Total	2,356	100	4,800	100	7,500	100

* Planned, not actual. *Source*: Five-Year Plans.

end of the First Five-Year Plan, food-grain production had increased from 55 million tons to 65 million tons, exceeding the target of 61·6 million tons laid down for the last year of the Plan. Prices of agricultural commodities also declined sharply. The comfortable situation on the agricultural front induced the Planning Commission to shift the emphasis towards industrialization, while formulating the Second Five-Year Plan. One of the major objectives of the Second Five-Year Plan was stated to be "rapid industrialization with particular emphasis on the development of basic and heavy industries". The other objectives mentioned in this context were a sizeable increase in national income, large expansion of employment opportunities and reduction of inequalities in incomes and wealth, but there was no specific mention of the development in agriculture. Arguing the case for rapid industrialization, the Commission state: "Low or static standards of living, under-employment and unemployment and, to a certain extent, a gap between the average and the highest incomes are all manifestations of basic under-development which characterizes an economy dependent mainly on agriculture. The core of development is thus rapid industrialization and diversification of the economy. But, for industrialization to be rapid enough, basic industries like iron and steel, non-ferrous metals, coal, cement and heavy chemicals as well as industries which make machines for making machines have to be developed rapidly." The approach of the balanced growth was not given up. It was stated that balanced pattern of industrialization requires well-recognized effort to utilize labour for increasing the supplies of much-needed consumer goods in a manner which economizes the use of capital.

Consistent with this view, the percentage of the developmental outlay (Rs. 4,800 crores) allocated to industry and mining was increased to 18·5 per cent (from 7·6 per cent in the First Five-Year Plan) and that for agriculture and community development was reduced to 11·8 per cent (from 15·1 in the First Plan). There was a similar reduction to 19 per cent from 28·1 per cent in outlay allocated for irrigation and power. The targets of agricultural production for the Second Five-Year Plan were also relatively modest. For example, the production of food-grains was to be increased from 65 million tons in 1955-56 to 75 million tons in 1960-61, an increase of 10 million tons in the five years of the Second Plan as against an increase of 14 million tons achieved during the First Five-Year Plan. Soon after, however, it was realized that the target for food-grain production in the Second Five-Year Plan was rather low and was raised to 80 million tons, without however, making any addition to the financial allocation for agricultural development.

Though in the last year of the Second Plan, food-grain production nearly reached the revised target, in the preceding years, shortages were experienced resulting in a substantial increase in food-grain prices. The Third Plan, therefore, restored the primacy of agriculture in its development programme. Unlike in the Second Plan, the achievement of self-sufficiency in food-grains and increased agricultural production to meet the requirements of industry and export, found place in the principal objectives of the Third Plan. It was stated that in the scheme of development in the Third Plan, the first priority necessarily belonged to agriculture. The experience during the period of the first two Plans, especially the Second, had shown that the rate of growth in agricultural production was one of the main limiting factors in the progress of the Indian economy. This, however, did not imply relaxation of emphasis on the development of basic and heavy industries. As a matter of fact, there appears to be a degree of ambivalence regarding the relative importance of agriculture and industry. On the one hand, it was stated: "The development of agriculture based on utilization of manpower resources of the countryside and the maximum use of local resources holds the key to the rapid development of the country." On the other, it was also stated: "There is no doubt that industry has a leading role in securing rapid economic advance." This was sought to be reconciled by the following statement:

"The growth of agriculture and the development of human resources alike hinge upon the advance made by industry. Not only does industry provide the new tools, but it begins to change the mental outlook of the peasant."

Allocation of financial outlay to the different sectors in the Third Plan does indicate a slight shift in favour of agriculture. The share of agriculture and community development in the total financial outlay was increased from 11·8 per cent in the Second Plan to 14 per cent in the Third, while the percentage allocated to major and medium irrigation was slightly reduced. The percentage share of organized industry and minerals was stepped up from 14·4 to 20 per cent. It was, however, stated: "In formulating agricultural production programmes for the Third Plan, the guiding consideration has been that the agricultural efforts should not be impeded in any manner for want of financial or other resources. Accordingly, finance is being provided on a scale which is considered adequate and further assurance is given that if for achieving the targets of production, additional resources are found necessary, this will be provided as the Plan proceeds." During the first two years of the Third Plan, progress of agricultural production was very unsatisfactory and when national emergency was declared, after the invasion of the northern frontier, the National Development Council sanctioned supplementary allocation for minor irrigation and soil conservation.

Viewing the three Five-Year Plans together, one can state that the only period during which the importance of agricultural development was not sufficiently appreciated was at the time of the formulation of the Second Plan. It may be perhaps more appropriate to say that during that period, the importance of the basic and heavy industries in national development came to be emphasized for the first time. It was interpreted as 'neglect' of agriculture. In this connection, it is important to mention that the allocation of only 6·3 per cent of the total financial outlay in the First Plan to the development of large and medium industries in the public sector was altogether too meagre and its step-up to 14·4 per cent in the Second Plan was, in a way, a correction of the 'neglect' of industrial development in the First Plan. It is interesting to note that, in retrospect, even the critics of the heavy-industry bias of the Second Plan agree that it would have been worthwhile to have endeavoured to establish a steel mill during the period of the First Plan.

In this connection, it is necessary to emphasize that it is inappropriate to judge the priorities accorded to different sectors, only by reference to the composition of planned public outlay or investment. Apart from the considerable non-monetized investment, particularly in the agricultural sector, so characteristic of underdeveloped economies, the quantum of private investment in different sectors constitutes an important component of the total investment in which the ultimate output would depend. According to the estimates given in the Third Five-Year Plan, during the period of the First Five-Year Plan (1951-56), the private-sector investment came to 1,800 crore rupees as against 1,560 crore rupees of public sector investment. The corresponding figures for the Second Plan period (1956-61) are 3,100 crore rupees and 3,650 crore rupees. It may also be noted that during the period of the Second Plan, private investment in agriculture and community development came to 625 crore rupees as against public investment of 210 crore rupees. In the case of major and medium irrigation, however, as expected, there was no private investment against an investment of 420 crore rupees by the public sector.[10] Further, as Reddaway has rightly pointed out, "The only way of judging whether a development plan is well-balanced is by considering the flow of output of the various goods and services. Investment is simply one means of securing this balance and the character of the development cannot be judged by the way in which this one means is allocated between various industries.[11] "The capital expenditures", he says, "are a very important means of helping to attain this output, but they are not objectives in themselves; if some other method of raising output could be discovered during the Plan period (e.g. by the use of better seeds instead of costly irrigation schemes), then, the essence of the Plan can be fulfilled even if the capital expenditure were far below the original figures."[12]

Professor Reddaway has elaborated this point thus: "A five-year plan normally shows two main sets of figures: targets for the outputs of various commodities which should be attained in the last year of the plan, and plans for capital expenditure to be done in the whole period of the plan. Of these two, the capital expenditure is the thing which calls for direct and immediate action, and it tends, therefore, to be regarded as the essence of 'the Plan'. This is, however, to mistake the means for the objective: the fundamental objective of the Plan is to attain the higher levels of output, and it is these levels of future output which have to be kept in balance as between one product and another, if the Plan is to be a coherent one."

III

After this rather prolix introductory background, we may concentrate on our main theme: the impact of the growth-process on Indian agriculture. Let us begin with the examination of the relative growth-rates in the agricultural and non-agricultural sectors of the economy. To keep quantitative analysis within a modest limit, ours will be only a two-sector analysis: agriculture—including animal husbandry, forest

10 See Table 2.

11 Reddaway, W. B., *The Development of the Indian Economy*, p. 161.

12 *Ibid.*, p. 189.

TABLE 2 : **Investment (Private and Public) in the First, the Second and the Third Plan**

Head	*First Plan Investment*				*Second Plan Investment*				*Third Plan Investment*			
	Public (a)	*Private (b)*	*Total*	*Percent-age*	*Public*	*Private*	*Total*	*Percent-age*	*Public*	*Private*	*Total*	*Percent age*
1	2	3	4	5	6	7	8	9	10	11	12	13
Agriculture & Community Development	234	363	597	18·0	210	625	835	12	660	800	1,460	13
Major & Medium Irrigation	250	(b)	250	7·2	420	(b)	420	6	650	(b)	650	6
Power	203	23	226	6·7	445	40	485	7	1,012	50	1,062	10
Village & Small industries	31	101	132	4·0	90	175	265	4	150	275	425	4
Organized industries & Minerals	62	392	454	13·5	870	675	1,545	23	1,520	1,050	2,570	25
Transport & Communica-tions	421	78	499	15·0	1,275	135	1,410	21	1,486	250	1,736	18
Social Services & Miscell-aneous	359	553	912	27·0	340	950	1,290	19	622	1,075	1,697	16
Inventories	—	290	290	8·6	—	500	500	8	200	600	800	8
Total	1,560	1,800	3,360	100	3,650	3,100	6,750	100	6,300	4,100	10,400	100

Note :—Investment should be distinguished from outlay. The former represents expenditure on the creation of physical assets, the latter corresponds to revenue expenditure on Plan schemes.

(a) The break-up of investment in the private and the public sector for the period of the First Plan is not availabe. The break-up given in column 2 corresponds to the break-up of public outlay. The break-up in column 3 is worked out under the assumption that its pattern was the same as in the Second Plan (column 7).

(b) Included under agriculture and community development.

Source : *Third Five-Year Plan*, Tables on pp. 32, 33 and 59.

and fisheries—and the rest of the economy which, for the sake of convenience, has been termed non-agricultural sector, unless otherwise stated.

Several factors influence the relative position of the two sectors in the process of development. Firstly, the growth-rates in the two sectors may vary. The impact of the differential growth-rates on per capita (or per worker) income will be modified by the sectoral transfer of labour-force. The change in the terms of trade will further alter the income-parity ratio of the two sectors. We shall first briefly review the experience in regard to these three dominant factors during the last decade.

GROWTH-RATES

A variety of statistical data, not always easily comparable, is available on growth-rates in agricultural production, and productivity.

We have the unadjusted and the adjusted figures of annual production in absolute terms. We have also the Index Numbers of Production, Area and Productivity which claim that they remove the non-comparability due to changes in statistical coverage and methods of estimation. As the measurement based on two specific points (years) would be influenced by seasonal conditions which are important in agriculture, linear growth-rates and compound rates have been calculated. One series is based on the three-year moving-averages of the index numbers for the period 1949-50 to 1961-62 and the other for the period 1952-53 to 1961-62.[13]

TABLE 3 : **All-India Compound Growth-rates in Percentages**

	1949-50 *to* 1961-62 (*Average* 1949-50 *to* 1959-62 = 100)	1952-53 *to* 1961-62 (*Average* 1952-53 *to* 1954-55 = 100)
Food-grains	3·45	2·46
Non-food-grains	3·57	3·88
All crops	3·49	2·94

The table reveals that agricultural production increased at the compound rate of about 3·5 per cent during 1951-61. If, however, a three-year average centred on 1951-54 is taken, the increase amounts to only three per cent per year.

The better results in the 1949-50 series are believed to be primarily due to the larger contribution of the increase in area. As there are grave doubts about the Index Number Series of Area (which incidentally is used as a deflator for calculating the Index of Productivity) it would be

[13] *Growth Rates in Agriculture* (Mimeo.), Economic and Statistical Adviser, Ministry of Food & Agriculture, Govt. of India.

advisable to avoid going into the question of relative contribution of Area and Productivity to the growth in production.

For industrial growth, we have the Revised Series of Index of Industrial Production with the Base: 1956=100. After shifting the base to 1951, we get a linear rate of growth of 9·7 per cent per year.[14] That the growth-rate in the industrial sector should be higher than that in the agricultural sector, is to be expected in a developing economy. What is somewhat unexpected is the wide divergence between the two.

The national income data provide another source from which the sectoral growth-rates may be derived. The net national output in 1948-49 prices originating from the agricultural sector increased from 43·8 abja* rupees (annual average of 1949-52) to 57·6 abja rupees (average of 1959-62) resulting in an increase of 31·5 per cent during these years (Table). For the corresponding period, the increase in the net national output in the rest of the economy (termed the non-agricultural sector) was from 45·6 abja to 68·3 abja, resulting in an increase of 49·8 per cent. If these figures are viewed from another angle, 37·8 per cent of the total

TABLE 4 : Growth in National Output.

	1949-52*	1959-62**	*Increase*	*Increase percentage*	*Share in total increase*
	Constant prices (1948-49)				
Agriculture@	43·8	57·6	13·8	31·5	37·8
Non-agriculture@@	45·6	68·3	22·7	49·8	62·2
Total	89·4	125·9	36·5	40·8	100·00
	In current prices				
Agriculture	48·0	66·7	18·7	39·0	42·1
Non-agriculture	47·2	72·9	25·7	54·4	57·9
Total	95·2	139·6	44·4	46·6	100·0

* Three-year average centred round 1950-51.

** Three-year average centred round 1960-61.

@ Includes animal husbandry, forest and fisheries.

@@ The rest of the economy.

increase in national output during the period was contributed by the agricultural sector and the remaining 62·2 per cent by the non-agricultural sector. It is apparent that the rate of growth was relatively small for the agricultural sector as compared with that for the non-agricultural sector. This would make the income-parity ratio between the two sectors

14 Moving average is not taken. The Index covers only the organized industry.

* Abja = 100 crores or 1000 millions.

less favourable to the agricultural sector over the decade; other factors such as labour-force movement and terms of trade remaining the same. This picture is slightly altered when the national output is measured in current prices. Under this method of calculation, the output in the agricultural sector shows an increase of 39 per cent as against an increase of 54·4 per cent in the non-agricultural sector. In other words, 42·1 per cent of the increase in the national output during this period was contributed by agriculture as against 57·9 per cent by the non-agricultural sector. The contribution of the agricultural sector to the total increase in national output was relatively larger (42·1 per cent) when measured in terms of current prices instead of constant prices (37·8 per cent). This difference can be attributed to the change in the terms of trade in favour of agriculture (Price-parity ratio 102·72).*

Labour-force : The changes in the composition of labour-force between 1951 and 1961 as revealed by the population census, are presented in Table 5. There were, however, some drastic changes in the concepts and definition used in the two censuses, and extreme caution is needed in drawing conclusions based on these figures. Particular mention may be made of the marked increase in the labour-participation rates from 39 per cent in 1951 to 42·98 per cent in 1961. On the whole, it can be said that the increase in the labour-force between 1951 and 1961 revealed by the table exaggerates the situation due to an underestimation by the 1951 census and overestimation by the 1961 census. Anyway, the most significant factor which emerges from the table is that the proportion of the labour-force employed in agriculture remains almost the same (72·13 in 1951 and 71·79 in 1961) over the decade. This would imply that the change in the relative position of the two sectors due to differential growth-rates would not be affected by this factor inasmuch as there was no change in the disposition of the labour-force.

Terms of trade : The third factor which would affect the relative position of the two sectors would be the change in their terms of trade. Various methods have been used to determine the terms of trade: (a) of the agricultural sector *vis-a-vis* non-agricultural sector; and (b) of the farmers in terms of the ratio of prices received to prices paid. The usual method used for the former is to study the relative movements

*

	Price Indexes 1949-52	1959-62		
Agricultural	100	107·45	$\frac{107·45}{104·60}$	= 102·72
Non-Agricultural	100	104·60	$\frac{107·45}{105·84}$	= 101·52
Total	100	105·84	$\frac{104·60}{105·84}$	= 98·82

TABLE 5 : **Population and Labour-Force by Sectors**

(*Figures in million*)

Year	*Population*	*Working force*	*Agricultural workers**	*Non-agricultural workers*	*% of agri. workers to total workers*
1951	356·88	139·52	100·63	38·89	72·13
1961	438·31	188·42	135·26	53·16	71·79
Change 1961-51	81·43	48·90	34·63	14·27	(–) 00·34

*(1) The term " agricultural workers " includes : (a) ' cultivators', or the industrial category I of the 1961 census; (b) 'agricultural labourers', or the industrial category II of the 1961 census; and (c) workers engaged in ' livestock, forestry, hunting and plantations, orchards and allied activities ' but not those engaged in mining and quarrying, or, in other words, only a part of the industrial category III of the 1961 census.

(2) The 1961 data are taken from : *Census of India*, Paper No. 1 of 1962, 1961 Census : Final Population Totals.

in the prices of agricultural and non-agricultural commodities and the ratio between the two. This should not be strictly termed as terms of trade inasmuch as the weights used in the construction of the wholesale prices would be very different from the weights of the commodities entering into the trade between the two sectors. In any case, information regarding the movement in the prices of these two groups of commodities would be of some interest and is given in Table 6.

By and large, the movements in the prices of the two groups of commodities have been on parallel lines. In the year 1955, however, the index for the agricultural commodities declined by as many as 12 points from the base year but that for the non-agricultural commodities fell by only one point. From this year onwards, the rise in the price index of the agricultural commodities has been somewhat steeper than that of the non-agricultural commodity price-index. In the year 1961, the two indexes stood almost at the same level.

Information regarding the ratio of prices received to prices paid by the farmers is available only for a few regions. (see Table 7.) The Punjab Board of Economic Enquiry has been compiling this information for the last 25 years. Similar information is available for the last decade in some other states like Assam, Kerala, Orissa and West Bengal. Extreme caution should be exercised in making use of this information without a detailed scrutiny of the methods and techniques used in the construction of the index. The differences in the crop patterns of these regions are significant. Orissa, Assam and West Bengal are predominantly rice-growing areas, while the major crops in the Punjab are wheat

TABLE 6 : **Index Numbers of Wholesale Prices of Agricultural to Non-Agricultural Commodities.**

(*Base* : 1951-53 = 100)

Weights	*Agricultural commodities* (680)	*Non-agricultural commodities* (320)	*All commodities* (1000)
1950	113	99	109
1951	122	117	120
1952	102	104	102
1953	107	99	104
1954	99	100	100
1955	88	99	92
1956	102	105	103
1957	109	108	109
1958	112	109	111
1959	118	111	116
1960	124	121	123
1961	126	127	126

Source : *Economic Survey*, 1960-61, Directorate of Economics and Statistics, Ministry of Food and Agriculture, p. 56.

and gram. Kerala's 'agriculture' is dominated by coconut, tapioca and pepper. Weights given to different commodities in the construction of the indexes of prices received naturally vary, as they should. But the marked variations in the weights given to commodities entering into the indexes of prices paid, particularly in regard to family consumption—

TABLE 7 : **Index numbers of parity between prices received and prices paid.**

Year	*Assam* (1944- = 100)	*Kerala* (1952-53 = 100)	*Punjab* (1938-39 = 100)	*Orissa* (1939- = 100)	*West Bengal* (*Previous year* = 100)
1951-52	131·6*	—	91·7	—	—
1952-53	103·9	—	98·5	110·02*	—
1953-54	102·1	95·2	101·2	103·02	—
1954-55	99·6	85·2	89·9	113·81	101·1*
1955-56	96·4	82·4	99·1	126·24	98·9
1956-57	106·7	83·4	102·7	135·54	—
1957-58	118·6	81·9	96·9	123·92	—
1958-59	109·3	83·0	103·2	121·84	107·3
1959-60	99·1	92·8	94·8	—	98·2
1960-61	107·3	92·1	95·3	—	102·6
1961-62	115·5	88·8	87·8	—	98·7
1962-63	105·6	84·1	84·9	—	97·9

*Calendar years, e.g.. 1951 is identified as 1951–52 and so on, in column one.

Source : Directorate of Economics & Statistics, Ministry of Food & Agriculture, Government of India.

e. g., 48 per cent for clothing in the Punjab and eight per cent in Bengal—are difficult to explain. Similarly, the basis for weights given to commodities purchased for farm production is quite arbitrary in some cases. Apart from the technicalities of the construction of the index numbers, the method of collection of the data and their dependability leave much to be desired. However, for the sake of completing the record of available information, the parity indexes for these states are given in Table 7.

The statistical evidence regarding the terms of trade, apart from its inadequacy and qualitative deficiencies, does not lead to any firm conclusions. The sectoral national-income estimates in constant and current prices, indicate a positive shift of the terms of trade in favour of agriculture. Perhaps there is something in the national-income-estimation procedures, which has such a built-in bias. The question needs a more careful and critical examination. Conclusions based on the wholesale-price index, would depend upon the year from which the trend is measured. Of the 12 years for which the data are given in Table 6, in 7 years, the price index was favourable for agriculture, and the positive difference in its favour was, on the whole, larger than the negative difference against it. The data on the parity of the prices received to prices paid for Kerala and the Punjab definitely indicate that the terms of trade have gone against the former; Orissa shows exactly the opposite trend, and West Bengal a mixed trend.

The experience of the progress in the agricultural and non-agricultural sectors during the period 1951-61 may be summed up as follows:

(1) The gross product derived from the agricultural sector increased at the compound rate of 2·7 per cent; the growth-rate in the non-agricultural sector was 3·76 (1948-49 to 1960-61 National Income Statistics).

(2) The proportion of workers engaged in the agricultural sector* declined fractionally from 72·13 in 1951 to 71·82 in 1961. Consequently, there was an insignificant increase in the proportion of the work-force engaged in the non-agricultural sector, from 27·87 in 1951 to 28·18 in 1961.

(3) The incomes per worker in the two sectors in 1951 were 431 rupees and 1,165 rupees respectively@@. In 1961, they had crept up to 437 rupees and 1,297 rupees respectively. As a result, the income parity of the workers in the two sectors declined from 0·37 : 1 to 0·34:1. It should be mentioned that the paltry rise of only six rupees in the per-agricultural-worker income is, in some measure, due to the sharp increase in the agricultural work-force, a part of which may be purely definitional. If the 1961 participation-rate is applied to the 1951 population-data, the work-force in 1951 would be larger and the per-worker income would be smaller (approximately Rs. 392). In that case the

* Including livestock, forestry, fishing, plantations, orchards and allied activities but not mining and quarrying.

@@ See Table 8.

increase in the per-worker income in agriculture, during the decade, would amount to 45 rupees.

IV

We may now examine some facets of the situation as it will emerge after a ten-year period ending 1971 and a 15-year period ending 1976, under certain specific assumptions. The projection examines the impact on the per-worker-income ratio of the two sectors under following assumptions:

(1) Population will grow at the compound rate of 2·35 per cent during this period;

(2) The growth-rates in the two sectors will be the same as observed during the decade 1951-61; and

(3) The proportion of workers engaged in the two sectors will remain the same as in 1961.

The result of the projection shows that after a ten-year period, i. e. in 1971, the per-worker-income ratio in the agricultural and the non-agricultural sector will decline from 0·33 : 1 in 1961 to 0·30 : 1 in 1971, and to 0·29 : 1 in 1975 (see Table 8.)

Apart from the deterioration in the relative position of the worker in the agricultural sector, as revealed by the above projection, the implications of our assumptions, that the ratio of the work-force in the two sectors will remain constant, need to be examined. On this assumption, the work-force in agriculture would expand from 135·3 millions in 1961 to 170·7 millions in 1971—resulting in an increase of 35·4 millions; in 1975 it will reach 191·7 millions—resulting in an increase of 56·4 millions in 15 years. The current pressure of population on land is already excessive, and one of the objectives of planned economic development is to reduce it. As we saw in Section III, we have not succeeded in doing so during the last decade. The abovementioned calculations indicate the magnitude of the task the agricultural sector will have to face in the next decade in regard to the employment situation.

Faced with this situation, it will be convenient to argue that the transfer of workers from agriculture to industry should be accelerated. But the industrial sector faces an equally difficult task. Under the assumption of no change (from 1961) in the proportion of workers in the two sectors, by 1971, the non-agricultural sector will have to find employment for 13·8 million people. If the income-parity ratio is not to deteriorate for the agricultural sector, it will have to take in additional five million persons. If the workers' proportion in agriculture is to come down to 65 (instead of 71·8 in 1961), the total absorption by the non-agricultural sector will have to be of the magnitude of 28 million workers in 1971. We have not worked out the capital requirements of employing such a large number in industries. It will depend on the pattern of

TABLE 8 : Employment, Output, Income Per Worker, and Income Ratio in Agriculture and the Rest of the Economy, 1951, 1961, 1971, 1975.

Year	*Total work-force*	*Workers in agriculture*	*Workers in non-agri-culture*	*Output in agriculture*	*Output in non-agri-culture*	*Agri. output per worker*	*Non-agri. output per worker*	*Income ratio Agri. 1 Non-agri.*
1	2	3	4	5	6	7	8	9
		In millions		In Rs. abja, 1948-49 prices		Rupees		
1951	139·52	100·63	38·89	43·4	45·3	431	1165	0·37:1
1960-61	188·4	135·3	53·1	59·1	68·9	437	1297	0·34:1
1970-71	237·7	170·7	67·0	77·14	99·70	452	1488	0·30:1
1970-71*	237·7	165·6	72·1	77·14	99·70	466	1383	0·34:1
1975-76	266·9	191·7	75·2	88·13	119·93	460	1595	0·29:1

Assumptions : (i) Population increases at the compound rate of 2·35 per cent per year; (ii) Work-force increases in both sectors at the same rate as that of population; (iii) Proportion of workers in the agricultural and the non-agricultural sector remains the same as in 1961 (71·8 and 28·2); (iv) Output in the two sectors increases at the same rate as experienced during 1948-49 to 1960-61 (agri. 3·7 per cent per year compound, non-agri. 3·76 per cent, National Income Data); *(v) In row IV in the Table, figures are worked out on the assumption that the ratio of the agricultural and the non-agricultural income in 1971 remains the same as in 1961.

industrialization, a discussion on which will lead us into the controversy of employment-oriented *v.* surplus-generating industrialization.

The situation as is developing presents an awkward dilemma for the planner. If industrialization is not speeded up, the employment and the income situation in the agricultural sector will become explosive. With the acceleration in the rate of population-growth in the current decade, if the growth-rate and the rate of labour-transfer remain the same as in 1951-61, there will be an increase in the per-worker income in the agricultural sector of only six rupees in 10 years (1971). The situation will improve only if the growth-rate is significantly stepped up or there is a massive transfer of workers from the agricultural to the non-agricultural sector or both. The experience of the first three years of this decade has demonstrated how difficult it is to step up the growth-rate in agriculture. I am not suggesting that this experience of the first three years would be typical for the entire 1961-71 decade. Far from it; but neither would any facile optimism be in order. It is also necessary to point out that there are limits to the expansion of agricultural commodities from the demand side as well. Though in the context of the present shortage this aspect of the problem may not be immediately relevant, its relevance for long-term planning should not escape attention. Agricultural surpluses can be quite embarrassing, not only in the developed countries, but also in the developing ones. Not only are the export prospects of primary commodities somewhat dim, but the income-elasticity of domestic demand also will, sooner or later, begin to exercise a curb on expansion. As and when this happens, the gains of improved production may be lost through adverse terms of trade. Transfer of workers from agriculture to other sectors of the economy—which themselves are not free from the gnawing problem of unemployment and under-employment—is also not easy. Apart from the social and the psychological problems involved in it, the magnitude of capital requirements for employment in large industries, and organizational effort that would be needed if employment is to be found in decentralized and small-scale enterprises, would be stupendous. The situation demands a highly competent and wise economic statesmanship.

2

REFLECTIONS ON NEW STRATEGY FOR AGRICULTURAL DEVELOPMENT*

V. M. DANDEKAR

IT IS customary for a President to begin his presidential address by expressing his gratitude to the members of the Society for having elected him to this august position and to say how greatly honoured he felt for the same. I should follow this customary practice. However, to say that I feel greatly honoured is a gross understatement of what I feel and what I felt when all this happened. As you know, it all happened at the last Conference. You will remember that last year when Professor Karve, at the end of a wonderfully irrelevant preamble, proposed my name for the Presidentship of this Conference, all of us were taken by surprise and you had voted me into the presidentship before you had recovered from the shock. Now that the thing is over, let me confess that I was equally surprised and that it took me some time to realize that I was honoured. Let me now proceed to unburden myself.

The Draft Outline of the Fourth Plan has been published and I suppose propriety requires that I take congizance of the same and say something on the plan proposals on Agriculture. You will remember that last year, the Ministry of Food and Agriculture published its own "Approach to Agricultural Development in the Fourth Five Year Plan" and requested our Society to organize four regional seminars on the subject. We did this and duly submitted our report to the Ministry. It therefore seems almost obligatory that I should now devote my address to the proposals on Agriculture as they appear in the Draft Outline.

The new thing about agricultural development in the Fourth Plan is the New Strategy. You are going to discuss it during the next two days and I do not want to anticipate that discussion. Therefore, I shall address myself to a rather different question. It is not quite an integral element of the New Strategy. Nevertheless, it is central to planning for agricultural development. In the Draft Outline, it is recognized as such. Let me quote:

> "Agricultural development has suffered on account of incomplete planning, particularly at the local levels. The central fact to be kept in view is that agriculture lies, almost entirely, in the private, unorganized sector. Agricultural production is, in consequence, primarily the result of individual planning or decisions taken and effort

---

* Presiedential Address, 26th All India Agricultural Economics Conference, Ludhiana, 1966.

put in by...farmers...who control thc aetual production process...An agricultural plan becomes a plan in the true sense of the term and the targets acquire real meaning, validity and sanction, only if the national goals or broad targets are concretized into a set of specific programmes through village, block and district plans and are accepted by the farmers as their own and there is a joint commitment on the part of the farmers, their institutions (co-operatives and panchayat raj), the State governments and the Centre to play their respective roles." (p. 118.)

Admittedly this is a crucial fact. Agricultural production rests in the hands of millions of farmers. Therefore, without their full acceptance of our plans, the planning would be reduced to a fruitless exercise of our proposing and the farmers' disposing. How do we then secure their acceptance? One of the means suggested is what is called complete planning particularly at the local level. Let me quote:

"In the Fourth Plan, an attempt was made in May 1965 to indicate production goals, programme targets and outlays to each State. The intention was that each State would break them up into district programmes and targets and the latter would further break them up into block programmes and targets. It was also proposed that an agricultural planning cell should be set up at each State headquarters with wholetime officers of the various departments concerned to work out clearcut programmes and give technical guidance for the further break up to block level...: When the overall plans of States for the Fourth Plan period are formulated, within the framework which they provide, steps should be taken to draw up district and block plans for agriculture and other sectors. These will serve as the basis for intensifying production effort at the village level." (*loc. cit.*, pp. 181-182.)

Let us get this idea clear. The wholetime officers sitting in the Ministry and in the Planning Commission would indicate production goals, programme targets and outlays to each state; the wholetime officers sitting at the state headquarters and in the proposed agricultural planning cells in the states, would break them into district programmes and targets, and would give techinical guidance for their further break-up into block programmes and targets; the latter in turn would serve as the basis for intensifying production effort at the village level. Once this was done, the national targets would be accepted as their own, by millions of farmers with whom rest the actual production decisions and the targets would thus acquire real meaning, validity and sanction; finally a joint commitment would emerge in which the farmers, their institutions and governments in the states and at the Centre would play their respective roles. Amen.

We are told that this was not done in the Third Plan and that it was partially responsible for the shortfall in agricultural production. I suppose we should believe. However, it would be only fair to say that the concept of preparing district and block plans, by splitting the national and state plans, has existed ever since the beginning of the First Plan and that exhortations to that effect have been made since then in almost identical terms. I suppose I am also right in believing that ever since the establishment of community development blocks and especially during the Second and the Third Plan periods, block plans prepared along these lines were a part of the essential stationery of the Block Development Officers. Nevertheless, it did not help to enthuse the farmers or to induce them, to use another phrase, "to take the right decisions consistent with national goals and policies". What then is the basis of these expectations and hopes being placed in the local plans of this variety?

I suppose you will want me to dismiss these phrases as part of that hocus-pocus which somehow seems to be so necessary to make a five-year plan stand together. I would be happy if that was all. But, I am afraid, it is worse than that. I think these expectations and hopes are genuine and sincere. Thus viewed, they appear to me to be characteristic expressions of our long-standing attitudes towards farmers and rural people generally and of our assessment of their intelligence. We think they are children. It is high time we realize that they are adults. If we do not, the danger is that farmers may begin to treat us like children.

In order to secure greater participation of the farmers in our plans, we have tried yet another, and it seems to me, a more sensible approach, namely the establishment of panchayat-raj institutions at the district and the block level. In fact, in the matter of plan implementation, especially at the local levels, this is the single, most important thing which we have tried to-date. Nevertheless, I must ask: Does the establishment of panchayat-raj institutions at the district and block levels alter the relations between the plan and the farmers? I am afraid, it does not, and I see no reason why it should.

The panchayat-raj institutions are local governments at the district and block levels. That is how they are conceived and that is how they are constituted. Their purpose is to bring the popular government closer to the people. In the field of development, they secure association of the popular representatives with the administrative agencies in charge of the plan-implementation. This is obviously necessary and desirable. However, this in itself does not alter the central fact that while the plans are prepared by government, the production decisions rest with the individual farmers. Even if the panchayat-raj institutions prepared their own plans for the districts and the blocks, that would not alter the basic situation because the plans would still be prepared by certain organs of government while the production decisions would continue to be with the individual farmers. As I said, panchayat-raj institutions are popular governments at the local levels. But we must clearly reckon that these local governments are no more and no less popular than the governments in the states and at the Centre. Therefore, the agricultural plan does not acquire any real meaning, and the targets set out in it do not acquire any greater validity and sanction just because the district-and block-level programmes are implemented by panchayat-raj institutions or even if certain aspects of the local programmes were worked out by these bodies. This has been the experience over the last five years. It could not have been otherwise.

In our anxiety to involve the farmers somehow in the plans of agricultural development, we have used some less reputable means. We have used national emergencies to sell our agricultural plans to the farmers. Our performance during these periods was utterly childish. We thought that if we declared an emergency, even the crops would set aside all considerations of season and weather and would, indeed, grow faster and taller. But it was worse than being just childish. It was sinful. We wanted to take advantage of the patriotic feelings of the people—it was said in so many words—to sell our plans to them. It did not work. We could have seen that it would not work if we had realized that farmers were not children but that thev were adults.

How do we then secure the participation of the farmers in our plans of agricultural development? Before we may answer this question, let us check what is the initial difficulty. Why is it that our plans for agricultural development are not plans in the true sense of the term? Why is it that the targets set out therein lack real meaning, validity and sanction? I shall begin with a few preliminary propositions.

A plan is a plan in the true sense of the term when it is essentially a plan of action on the part of one who makes the plan. In the present context, if a government has prepared the plan, it must be a plan of action by government and other public authorities. The reason why our plan for agricultural development is not a plan in the true sense of the term is that it is not essentially a plan for state action. It is much more or much less than that. In fact, it covers many fields and areas over which the government has little authority to make decisions or initiate action. Consequently, many targets set out in the plan lack real meaning, validity and sanction.

Take for instance our targets of agricultural production, crop by crop. Admittedly, this is a matter primarily governed by the decisions made by millions of individual farmers. It is not therefore very meaningful to fix plan targets in this field. Even in respect of the so-called physical programmes, all targets are not equally meaningful. For instance, a plan target in major irrigation, in the sense of creating a certain irrigation potential, has a clear meaning; but the plan target for minor irrigation, as it includes investment decisions of individual farmers in digging of wells etc., is not equally meaningful. The targets for production of nucleus or foundation seed of improved varieties are meaningful; but the targets for bringing certain acreage under improved seed are a fiction. Targets of production and import of chemical fertilizers are meaningful; but the targets of organic manures and green manuring are worse than fiction—they deserve to be dumped into a compost pit,

Nevertheless, we have been planning in terms of these targets, because our plans include not only plans for government action but also our expectations and hopes as to how the millions of farmers would respond to these actions. I think it is essential to make a distinction between the two, and distinguish planning from speculative thinking about the future, and plan targets from statistical projections or economic forecasts. I am not saying that speculative thinking about the future and informed projections and forecasts are not useful. Such projections or forecasts are valid and useful even in a completely unplanned economy. They should certainly be useful in a planned or a partially planned economy. But they are not valid plan-targets because they lack sanction.

Let me therefore suggest that our plans for agricultural development should be confined to those fields and those items over which the government has authority to make decisions and initiate action and that our plan targets should be in terms of state action. As I have already indicated, there are many matters on which the government and other public authorities can make decisions and which affect agricultural production. For instance, through construction of irrigation works, government can bring more land under assured irrigation. Through increased domestic production or imports, government can make larger quantities of chemical fertilizers available to the farmers. Through fundamental research in agricultural sciences, the government can breed new high-yielding varieties and develop more efficient cultural practices. Government can spread this new knowledge among farmers either through formal education or through extension services. Government can make production credit available to the farmers, and with appropriate price and distribution policies, government can affect the relative profitability of different crops to the farmer. Agricultural planning, in the real sense of the term, should be confined to these and such other areas in which the state has a clear authority to make decisions and initiate action.

The state has no such authority in the field of agricultural production because, admittedly, the ultimate decisions here rest with the farmer. He decides how much irrigation water to use, how much fertilizer to buy, which crops to grow and which cultural practices to follow. He must be willing to receive and adopt new knowledge, and he must be careful to use production credit for production purposes. There are innumerable such decisions which rest with millions of farmers and which affect the agricultural production. There can therefore be no plan-targets in these fields and no schemes and programmes to achieve them. Nevertheless, this is precisely the content of our agricultural production programmes in the districts and the blocks. We witness the district and block agricultural officers and the extension workers under them running around with targets of agricultural production, crop by crop, targets of areas to be sown under different crops, targets of areas to be sown with improved seed, targets of areas to be brought under new minor irrigation, targets of green manuring, and targets of compost pits to be dug. In all these cases, the officers and the extension workers know full well that what they can do in the matter of achieving these targets is extremely limited and that the final decisions lie with the farmers. But they receive orders from above in terms of these targets, and they must report the progress in terms of these targets. In consequence, a whole make-believe world is created in which targets are determined and progress is reported in terms of items over which the parties concerned have no authority or control whatever. No one believes in these figures and nevertheless everyone must engage himself in so much paper-work which is worse than wasteful—for it is intellectually corrupting. This must stop.

Let us then ask: What is it that the state can do in respect of all such items in which the ultimate decisions lie with the farmers? As I see it, there are three functions which the state can perform in this sphere. They are: (1) to educate and to improve the farmer as a farmer; (2) to reorganize the production apparatus in agriculture so as to enable the farmer to take better care of his land and water resources; and (3) to create appropriate institutions in order to improve the decision-making in agriculture. These are the three functions which the state can perform in this sphere and these should constitute the essential elements of the district- and block-level programmes for agricultural development. The first is a task of education. The second is a task of much detailed work on the ground. The third is a political task. We have neglected all the three because of a mistaken belief that we could achieve the production targets directly without bothering to improve the man, to improve the land and to improve the institutions governing the relation between man and land. Let me consider these one by one.

As I said, the first is the task of education—of adult education to adult farmers. Indeed, this is the legitimate function of agricultural extension. But our extension service has not been oriented to dissemination of knowledge. Instead, it has been geared to the administration of certain schemes and programmes which, we expect, will achieve the production targets directly. In consequence, the extension worker today need know little about agricultural technology and farm economics; what he must know are the details of official schemes and the rules and procedures of granting loan and subsidy assistance under them. This is what he extends to the farmer. This has created wrong motivation among farmers and wrong orientation among the extension workers.

There is a new variety of extension men we are now training in the universities. They need know even less of agricultural technology and farm economics. They are masters of extension as such. Hence their expertise is mainly in sociology, psychology, social psychology, educational psychology, group dynamics, leadership structures, motivational patterns and several other luxuries. With so much sophisticated extension education, I am afraid, they will have little to extend except themselves.

Let us for a moment ask ourselves, what is the fundamental task before us. A major plank of the New Strategy is greater application of the latest advances in agricultural sciences. How do we achieve this? The programme administration seems to have a pretty simple notion about it. Apparently, a major scientific break-through has occurred and the advances achieved thereby are available in neat, ready-to-serve packages. All that is needed now is smart salesmanship backed by credit. Permit me to say that this is essentially a foreign concept propagated by foreigners and accepted by administrators who are equally foreign to their people. It is founded on the presumption that production targets can be achieved without bothering to improve the man, without educating the farmer as a farmer, and without his intelligent participation in the process. This is wrong. What we have before us is a task in education, not in programme administration or in sales promotion. I wish I am able to carry to you my conviction that this is a fundamental task and that it must be approached in a fundamental manner.

To be sure, the importance of education to farmers is now recognized. In fact, in the Draft Outline, there is a paragraph devoted to it. It is observed that "it is inherent in the process of transformation of traditional agriculture into modern agriculture that the primary producer —the farmer—should be enabled to understand and adjust himself to new technology". With this objective in view, it is proposed to provide special facilities for farmers' education. However, I am not sure that much thought has been given to the content of this education. It is obvious that this education must focus on explaining to the farmer, the essential difference between traditional and modern agriculture. Let us see what it is.

As I view it, the essential difference between traditional and modern agriculture is the difference between certain basic attitudes to life. We may conveniently classify them into three: (a) difference between traditional and modern attitudes towards Nature and man's place in it; (b) difference between traditional knowledge and modern science; and (c) difference between traditional and modern attitudes to certain economic aspects of human life and endeavour. It is essential that the farmers understand these differences. Let me consider them one by one.

The traditional attitude towards Nature is one of awe, a subconscious fear that to disturb Nature would ultimately bring disaster, and hence a conviction that man must make his living by working with Nature. The attitude arises because of lack of knowledge regarding the working of Nature. It is one of the functions of education to explain the working of Nature and to indicate the possibilities of modifying and harnessing it in the interest of man. In the context of adult education to farmers, the simplest way to do this is to explain to the farmer the working of several natural phenomena, especially biological phenomena, which affect his everyday life—facts of plant and animal ife, difference between health and disease, and the basis of the universal struggle for existence and survival that goes on mercilessly in the kingdom of Nature. It is thus that the farmer will realize that this is a struggle which man must win if he has to survive, and know that modern science has placed in his hands the necessary tools.

The second aspect requiring education is the difference between traditional knowledge and modern science. Traditional knowledge is authoritarian in the sense that it is handed down from one generation to the next by the authority of tradition. On the other hand, modern science is experimental. Every bit of it is supposed to be verifiable by experiment or observation, and it is the privilege of every man to put it to such a test and to reject it if not verified and to publicize his findings in a manner that they in turn may be verified. This difference between traditional knowledge and science is likely to be overlooked by official extension agencies, because within the official hierarchy, knowledge and all that passes under that name, moves from the Secretary to the Deputy Secretary or from the Director to the Deputy Director until to the last functionary at the village level, all along fully protected and secured with the sanction of authority. As a consequence, when his turn comes, the last extension-man at the village level himself tries to pass on to the farmer, the little piece of knowledge or information, in an equally authoritarian manner. It is often believed that this is how it should be. For instance, it is said that if the farmer knew the experimental basis of the agronomic recommendations and knew the wide variability to which the results were liable, it would make it even more difficult to secure his acceptance of the new technology. It is, therefore, suggested that the new technology to be recommended should be presented to him in the simplest and in the most categorical manner. This is plainly wrong. It does not work either. The farmer soon discovers the large variation to which the results of the recommended practices are liable, and the extension man has no more than mere apologies to offer. It is not only wise but also essential that the farmer is informed fully about the experimental nature of all agronomic recommendations.

The third aspect requiring education is the difference between the traditional and the modern attitudes to certain aspects of human life and endeavour. In contrast to traditional attitude in this respect, the modern attitude seeks to distinguish the behaviour of man as a consumer and his behaviour as a producer, and advocates that the latter behaviour should be governed primarily by economic considerations. In the context of a farmer, this means that the farmer should be able to make a distinction between his household and his farm, between his mother and his cow, and should be able to look at the farming as a business requiring decisions on economic considerations. I have in mind decisions in relation to new inputs and new technology as also in relation to alternative investment choices. The extension worker today has neither the basic knowledge of the issues involved nor any relevant data to base his extension advice on. The farmer has certainly some notion of the governing considerations. However, a systematic formulation and conscious realization of the same on his part are needed.

These are then the three aspects which require education in order to prepare the farmer for a transition from traditional agriculture to modern agriculture. It is necessary to establish appropriate institutions which will impart this education to adult farmers in an informal manner. It is obvious to me, and I suppose you will agree with me, that this is not a function which can be trusted to programme administration. I do not therefore favour the proposal, made in the Draft Outline, to locate the farmers' education centres at the Gram Sevak Training Centres. The Gram Sevak Training Centres are too much programme oriented. They are also too few in number being just 100 in the whole country. There will have to be many more farmers' education centres, ideally at least one for each block. I think that an agricultural high school, which has a reasonably good farm attached to it, offers the most suitable base to locate a farmers' education centre. There are several reasons for this choice. In the first instance, it will place these centres firmly within the educational environment and at the same time sufficiently close to the ground. Secondly, because many of the students in the high school will be sons of farmers from the surrounding area, it will provide culturally and emotionally a most satisfying ground for the adult farmers to meet. Thirdly, the location of a centre at a high school and consequent visits of groups of farmers to the place will unavoidably affect the formal teaching in the high school and will orientate it towards agricultural problems of the local area. Fourthly, I envisage that the teaching staff giving formal courses in the high school and giving informal instruction in the farmers' education centre form a common pool so that, as far as possible, all members of the teaching staff participate both in the formal teaching in the high school and the informal instruction in the farmers' education centre. This is bound to improve the quality of instruction in both the courses. Finally, I imagine that the teaching staff will have opportunity to try out the new technology on the farm attached to the high school and satisfy themselves about the merits of what they recommend. Lack of such facility is the most serious handicap of the present-day extension-worker. He is a talking machine without competence, facility or responsibility to practise and demonstrate what he preaches.

Having thus located the farmers' education centres at the agricultural high schools, I suggest that courses of varying durations, say from one to ten or twelve weeks, should be offered to farmers in the area. In view of what I have already said, I suggest that the instruction should include three types of courses: Firstly, it should cover basic facts regarding plant and animal life, reproductive processes, plant and animal diseases of common occurrence with special emphasis on their bacterial and virus origins, disease control, hygiene, public health and family planning. A small laboratory should offer facilities to test soil, water, blood, urine, stool, sputum, sections of diseased plants and animals, etc., and the farmers should have an opportunity to view, first-hand, these natural phenomena through a microscope. Instruction in such basic scientific aspects requires many aids. However, if for reasons of economy, we must choose one single instrument, it seems to me that the microscope is the most potent of them all. It offers a real peep into the working of Nature and lays bare many of her secrets. Its impact is direct and immediate, because the experience is first-hand. Other media of communication such as posters and screen have of course their uses. But they are a poor substitute for the microscope.

A second set of courses to be offered should cover detailed instruction in the management of soil and water and in crop and animal husbandry appropriate to the region. Emphasis should be on the difference between the traditional practices and the new technology being recommended and the experimental basis of the new recommendations should be fully explained. The agricultural farm attached to the high school should prove useful for this purpose. Besides, the farmers should be deliberately encouraged to record systematically the results of any trials they might conduct on their own farms with the recommended practices or any other practices they might evolve as superior, and to report them in a seminar. In fact, in each agricultural season, a systematic programme of experimental trials on recommended practices and any other practices reported by the farmers as superior, should be executed with active participation of the farmers, and the results discussed in a seminar of the participating farmers. This proposal, should be distinguished from the existing programme of co-ordinated trials conducted all over the country to determine the adaptability of different strains of crops. It should also be distinguished from the programme of tests and demonstrations on farmers' fields in order to convince them about the efficiency and superiority of certain recommended practices. The purpose of a systematic programme of experimental trials to be conducted and reported upon by the farmers under the guidance of the farmers' education centres is educational and hence more fundamental, namely, to inculcate in them the spirit of scientific enquiry, careful experimentation and observation, systematic recording of results, and objective discussion. I am aware that the spirit of scientific enquiry is not a common commodity. I know that it cannot be cultivated in all minds. However, I know equally well that its occurrence is not more common among the university-trained than among the illiterate. It must be a function of education and instruction to discover and encourage wherever it exists.

Another purpose of involving the farmer actively in a programme of experimental trials and of creating a systematic record of the results is to feed the research stations and laboratories with problems back from the field. At present the traffic is very much in one direction—from the research stations to the farmer. This needs to be corrected.

A third set of courses to be offered should cover the economic aspects of farming. We must admit that in spite of much effort in farm-business surveys and farm-management studies, we have as yet very little to offer to the farmer. Recent trends in university-level courses in farm management also seem to take us further away from the decision-making processes of a farmer. I suppose we should be very humble in this field. I suggest that we should encourage and assist a few farmers in each area to maintain faithful records on cost and returns in their farm business. Such records should constitute the teaching-material in the courses on farm economics. These records should be analysed and their economic meaning should be discussed in active participation of the farmers. The aim should be to create cost-and-return consciousness among the farmers. In the process, we shall have ample opportunity to learn some farm economics ourselves.

This is broadly the content of the courses which, I suggest, should be offered to groups of farmers who will visit the farmers' education centres located at the agricultural high schools. The instruction should be completely informal and, I emphasize, it must not lead to any certificate or diploma recognizable for a government service. Depending upon what we have to offer, I think a number of farmers in the area will show interest and will actively participate. But I shall be satisfied even if only a few hundred farmers in each area join this movement, because later they will constitute the most natural and the most effective media of communicating the new attitudes and the new technology to the other farmers in the area. Let us be quite clear on one point: If we are looking for a technological transformation in agriculture, it will be brought about not by the efforts of a programme administration, nor by the activities of a politician, but by assiduous and scientific attention to their farms by a few professional farmers in each local area. All that the government, both in its administrative and in its political wings, at the centre as well as at the local level, can do in this respect is to create conditions to promote such attitudes and scientific interest among farmers. I believe, the programme of adult education to farmers along lines I have indicated, will initiate the process.

Let me now move on to the second of the three functions which I said the state should perform at the local level, namely, reorganizing the production apparatus in agriculture so that the farmer may take better care of his land and water resources. There are two proposals appearing in the Draft Outline which are relevant to what I wish to suggest. One appears in the section on Soil Conservation. There it is admitted that "so far, soil conservation has been limited to erosion control measures in widely dispersed cultivated areas", and it is proposed to undertake soil conservation programmes in the Fourth Plan "on the complete watershed basis". It is suggested, for instance, that in ravine lands, major emphasis would be given to the treatment and protection of agriculturally productive tablelands and stabilization of marginal lands. In arid and semi-arid areas, the minor irrigation programme would be effectively correlated with soil-and-moisture-conservation programmes with emphasis on contour bunding, controlled grazing, and pasture development. The second proposal appears in the section on what is called Ayacut Development to be undertaken in irrigated areas. The essential ingredients of this programe are: "crop planning, regulation of irrigation water, land shaping and consolidation of holdings, soil surveys, arrangements for supply of inputs, extension and demonstration, credit, co-operatives, storage and marketing, communications and agro-industrial development." While I wholly appreciate the importance of all the ingredients mentioned in this long list, I suggest that we should have a small pause, for mere breath, after soil survey. Otherwise, I am afraid, the concept may degenerate into one of those intensive and integrated approaches.

You will then see that the two proposals, one under Soil Conservation and the other under Ayacut Development, in fact, constitute a single programme directed to improving the use, promoting conservation, and facilitating development of the soil and water resources of the country. I believe that planning for this purpose is the essence of area-planning and that, wherever necessary, the area-planning in this sense, must cut across political and administrative boundaries between states, between districts, between development blocks, between villages and finally between individual proprietary rights. I do not know whether, in the two proposals made in the Draft Outline, it is intended to cut across these political and administrative boundaries and especially across the existing layout of the individual proprietary rights in land. If it is not, most of the ingredients of the two proposals will be found operationally ineffective.

This requires, what I have called, reorganization of the production apparatus in agriculture. As soon as I say this, you may expect me to advocate co-operative or collective farming. However, what I have to say is somewhat different, and I wish to emphasize the difference. All along, we have assumed that the programme of cooperative farming is directed, in the main, towards the solution of problems presented by the class of small or uneconomic cultivators. Thus the starting point of co-operative farming is a class of cultivators. To be sure, their lands come along; but judging from the manner in which we have debated the question whether co-operative farming requires pooling of lands, I presume that the lands come along only incidentally. As soon as we agreed that the pooling of lands was essential, we moved to the position that not only lands but all production equipment and resources belonging to the members must also be pooled. So once again, the lands come only incidentally as part of the total production equipment. It is not my intention here to examine these propositions and to describe the many futile complications they have led us into. My purpose in mentioning these is only to request you to forget them all for a moment, because, in common with the two proposals made in the Draft Outline, central to my concept of reorganizing the agricultural production apparatus, is not a class of cultivators, but a block of land with its soil and water resources.

Consider, for instance, a block of irrigated land consisting of, say, a few hundred acres. The proprietary rights in the land in this block were most probably established long before irrigation came in and so, I suppose, must be much of the physical layout of fields and plots on the ground. When irrigation came in, the physical layout of the proprietary rights was regarded inviolable and the irrigation channels were laid out accordingly. As we can see, they are not designed to achieve the most efficient distribution of water. Some of the lands are uneven, and levelling would greatly improve the utilization of water. But it is not done because the existing layout of the proprietary rights comes in the way. The cultivators in the block are usually free to cultivate whatever crops they choose, and the crops often require varying quantities of water at varying intervals. This leads to innumerable disputes, unauthorized breaches into the water channels and consequent waste of water. There are no proper paths laid out to reach all the fields, and one person's crop stands in the way of another person's harvesting and removing his crop from his field. This results in unduly late harvesting and consequent damage to some crops, or else disputes about trespassing. If one sees these people closely, working in the fields and moving around, one notices that they are causing innumerable such inconveniences to one another. The irony of the situation is that every one realizes this and yet every one feels so helpless about it.

Let us for a moment suppose that this block of land covering possibly a few hundred acres, was all owned by a single proprietor. Suppose further that the proprietor knew something about the soil and water conservation or that he had employed a good farm-manager. In such a case, I imagine that the proprietor or the manager would have surveyed the block of land, determined the contours and levels, and laid out the irrigation channels, fields, foot-paths and cart-tracks accordingly. He would have levelled the fields and he would have divided the entire block of land into suitable sub-blocks for cultivation of different crops in appropriate rotations. In short, he would have developed the block of land and achieved a more efficient use and conservation of its soil and water resources.

Let us now ask: Why cannot we do this to the block of land on which a number of individual proprietors are sitting in a disorderly fashion causing inconvenience to themselves and damage to the soil and water resources? Let me tell you immediately that the individual proprietary rights are not coming in the way and that we do not have to abolish them and rush to co-operative or collective farming. It is only the existing layout of these rights that comes in the way. All that we have to do is to inform and convince the proprietors that they have been sitting in a disorderly manner and that it is possible for them to sit in better order and to greater mutual convenience and benefit. This requires a certain amount of detailed physical planning on the ground and a certain effort of educating the people concerned. We have as yet done nothing in this direction. I suggest that we should make an early beginning.

Let us see what are the necessary steps. As I have said, the starting point is a block of land which is likely to be benefited by such a reorganization. I shall later describe how to locate such blocks. Let us for the time being begin with the existence of such a block. The first step then is to appoint a Farm Planning or an Area Planning Officer. Whatever his name and title, we should understand that he is one who knows that farm planning has to be done on the farm. In other words, the farm planning that he will do is not of the linear programming variety. Secondly, even if we may call him an officer, we should understand that he is an agricultural technician. Within the sphere of agriculture, I suppose, his expertise would be in agricultural engineering. His job will be to survey the block of land for its soil and water resources, determine contours and levels, treat the entire block of land as a single farm, and plan the layout of the fields and plots, irrigation channels, footpaths, cart-tracks and the like. He will not, of course, plan any farm houses and cattle sheds because, as we know, the block of land is in fact not a single farm. Having prepared the ground layout, he will prepare and submit a project report indicating the necessary development works which must be executed. These will include levelling, bunding, minor irrigation works, irrigation channels, paths, and the like. In consultation with an agronomist, he will also divide the whole block into sub-blocks indicating which crops may be grown in which rotation. Having done this, the development and utilization plan for the block of land will be published.

Then must begin the process of education and persuasion. Its purpose is to secure the consent of the persons concerned to the proposed plan and to a scheme of redistribution of the land among themselves. The principle of redistribution should be that everybody should get back as far as possible an area approximately equal to or equal in value to his original holding within the block and that any marginal losses should be fully compensated by those who gain thereby. You will thus see that in its formal procedures, the programme is similar to one of consolidation of holdings though, in their content, the two programmes are, of course, fundamentally different. I am aware that the acceptance of the development and redistribution plan will require considerable education and persuasion. In the initial stages, we may have to offer certain incentives such as contribution to the development costs and technical assistance for subsequent management. However, I believe that once a beginning is made and the advantages are demonstrated, the resistance will diminish. I shall presently suggest more concretely how a beginning may be made.

For the time being, let me proceed on the assumption that the plan is accepted by the people concerned. The next step will then be to get the essential development works executed as speedily as possible and with as little disturbance to current cultivation as possible. As soon as this is completed and the land is divided into plots according to the planned layout, it will be redistributed according to an agreed scheme with full proprietary rights as before.

You will thus see that co-operative or collective farming is not a necessary part of the reorganization of the production apparatus I am proposing. Indeed, the reorganization I am suggesting is a physical reorganization of the production units on the ground and it is completely compatible with individual ownership and management of land. Nevertheless, it seems to me that it will be necessary to create, among the cultivators in the reorganized block, an appropriate organization to look after those aspects of their farm business which obviously require joint attention. For instance, in the context of an irrigation block, management of water and enforcement of an agreed cropping-programme will obviously require joint decision and action. Division of a block into sub-blocks and agreeing to a certain cropping-programme in each sub-block may be useful even in an unirrigated block of land, for that will greatly facilitate cultivation, protection and the watching of crops. Spraying and dusting of crops with pesticides and weedicides may also have to be enforced jointly. The maintenance in good repair of all development works such as bunds, irrigation channels, roads and paths must, of course, be a joint responsibility. In sub-marginal lands suitable for developing only as pasture and woodlands, the joint management may have to be extended to certain production aspects as well. For instance, for pasture cultivation, it may be convenient to plough and sow with improved grasses an entire block of land without dividing into separate plots. Rotational grazing will also have to be managed jointly. For woodland development, suitable blocks of lands may be planted, protected and exploited jointly. The particular activities where joint decision and action are necessary and beneficial will of course depend upon the nature of the land use. However, nowhere will it be necessary to abolish individual proprietary rights in land. All that will be necessary is to set up appropriate organizations among the cultivators to look after those aspects of land management which require joint attention. I shall shortly come to the form of such organizations.

Let me first discuss the more practical question how we may make a beginning along these lines. I think, all new irrigation projects offer the best opportunity to make a beginning in this direction. A new irrigation project transforms, overnight, dry land into irrigated land and thus brings immense benefits to the persons whose lands are irrigated. It changes the pattern of land use and hence offers an opportunity to rationalize the entire layout on the ground. Thus viewed, an irrigation project, whether major, medium, or minor, should constitute not just an irrigation project but a comprehensive land-and-water-development project in the area. This means that the project should concern itself not only with the construction of irrigation works and distributaries as at persent, but also with the preparation of an efficient layout for the whole area commanded by the irrigation works, complete with levelling, bunding, field channels and roads, and execute the necessary works. For this purpose, the project authority should acquire necessary control over the whole concerned area for a brief period and after executing the works return the lands to their owners in a reorganized layout. This might add to the construction cost of the project somewhat, but it will ensure speedy completion of all preparatory work necessary for an efficient use of the new water-resources.

The reason why I suggest we should begin with the new irrigation projects is that they give us a ready opportunity and a certain authority to move in this direction and introduce a new concept of physical planning at the ground level. There is yet another consideration in my mind. It is not quite germane to my main theme this morning. Nevetheless, I shall mention it because, I think, it should receive urgent attention. I have in mind the question how we may ensure a more equitable and a wider distribution of the benefits of development undertaken at the cost of the whole community. Irrigation projects provide a glaring example of what might happen otherwise. At present, the benefits of these works are distribution extremely unequally. At one extreme are the farmers whose lands receive the new irrigation waters. Overnight, the productivity and security of these lands is enhanced several-fold and their owners reap the windfall gains. At the other extreme are the people who are displaced by the irrigation works. They lose everything and are moved several miles away from their ancient homes. In between lie the farmers whose lands lie just outside the command area. They watch their neighbours grow rich overnight.

Such are the glaring inequalities which a new irrigation project creates in the rural area. The project is executed at the expense of the entire community but its benefits are confined to a few. All attempts to recover even a part of the cost through betterment levy have proved ineffective. Those who get, get it free. There is also no sustained effort to secure for the community at least a part of the gains flowing from such works through appropriate taxation of agricultural incomes. Thus the inequalities initially created by the irrigation works, grow year by year. The New Strategy to be adopted for agricultural development during the Fourth Plan, will accelerate this process, because the strategy requires that those who have water should receive preference while giving the high-yielding seed, fertilizer, credit and extension advice. The hope is that this minority will then grow all the food that the country needs. They may as well do this. In the meanwhile, and subsequently, they may blackmail the country and extract more and more advantages. They may tell us that betterment levy, irrigation charges, agricultural income-tax are all disincentives to greater production and therefore none of these must be levied. We must listen. But, they may very well grow food enough for the whole country. If and when they do, we shall wonder how those millions who could not participate in the production process, would buy the food they need. This is a sure method of creating a surplus in the midst of poverty.

But this is a subject you are going to discuss during the next two days and I must not anticipate your discussion. All that I need emphasize for my present purpose is that irrigation works create glaring inequalities in the rural areas and that, once created, the inequalities grow at an accelerating pace. We should see therefore if we could do something initially to ensure that the benefits of irrigation would be distributed somewhat more widely and equitably than at present. If we adopt the project approach involving a fresh layout and a redistribution of the proprietary rights, it may be possible to distribute the benefits more equitably than at present, provided we adopt this as a deliberate policy. We may then be able to give a fairer treatment to the persons displaced by the irrigation works and settle them within the areas commanded by the irrigation works. We may also be able to accommodate within the commanded area a few farmers from the neighbourhood. This means that the original owners of the lands now being irrigated by the new works would get back not their entire lands but only a part of them. Let us say, for purposes of illustration, that the original owners would get back only half the area but now fully developed by the new works. The remaining half would then be available for settling the displaced persons and for sale to farmers in adjoining areas. It is through such sales that a part of the initial development costs could be recovered. In the scheme of redistribution, it may also be possible to reduce somewhat the existing inequalities within the project area. For instance, to those who have very small holdings in the commanded area, their entire lands might be returned fully developed while a proportionately larger cut might be made in the larger-sized holdings. These are matters of detail. The main point to remember is that we need explicitly introduce the principle that the benefits of development undertaken at the cost of the whole community must be distributed more widely and equitably and that those who receive the benefits must pay at least part of the costs.

The irrigation works create the most glaring inequalities but offer the best opportunity to establish this principle.

The point is extremely important. However, as I said, it is not germane to my main theme this morning. I must, therefore, return to my theme and say that the new irrigation projects offer us an excellent opportunity to make a beginning with a new concept of physical planning on the ground. Once we achieve success in a few such areas, agriculture there will be so visibly different from agriculture elsewhere that it will provide a standing demonstration of the new concept. We shall then be able to move with greater ease in areas which are already irrigated and where vested interest is entrenched. We may be able to move even in dry areas where the benefits of reorganization may not be equally obvious, and in submarginal lands where there is no conscious recognition of the fact that so much land resource is being under-utilized or, in fact, is being wasted. We shall thus be able to extend the operation to a number of areas with very different resources of soil and water. In anticipation, we should make an immediate beginning in the identification of such blocks of lands where the reorganization is likely to be beneficial and start preparing detailed plans for the same.

I imagine that we may have to undertake this work in three stages. In the first stage, we may aim at demarcating large geographical areas which are suitable for comprehensive planning for development of their land and water resources. I presume that in most cases these will be areas corresponding to river valleys, basins, watersheds, etc. These are easily identifiable, but unfortunately have not been so identified until now. Our thinking on regional planning is still too much conditioned by the administrative boundaries of districts and tahsils. These areas, therefore, need to be demarcated and given concrete identity by putting together all the relevant agroclimatic facts relating to them. I suppose this is a task for the geographers. In the second stage we must undertake detailed topographical survey of each such region and work out plans for the development works that must be carried out in order to improve the use, conservation and development of the land and water resources of the region. This must be the task of the civil engineers assisted by agronomists and soil scientists. The aim must be to prepare and keep ready to be executed, a programme of productive rural works in each region. In the absence of such a ready programme, we are today wasting what little effort we are making in the direction of utilizing our vast manpower. In the third stage, we must move closer and within each region, identify smaller blocks of land inside of which reorganization of the physical layout of the fields, etc., will prove beneficial, and prepare detailed plans for them. This is the task of agronomists assisted by civil engineers. Once we have such detailed plans ready for any block, the process of education and persuasion must begin in order to secure the consent of the cultivators for the plan of reorganization. They stand to benefit but they must be convinced of the same. This is a task of the social-political workers assisted by economists and other social scientists who are willing to work close to the soil and the people.

This brings me to the third and the last of the tasks which, I suggest, the state should undertake at the local level, namely, to create appropriate institutions in order to improve decision-making in agriculture. We require such institutions among farmers to deal with those aspects of their farm business where joint decision and action are needed. I have already indicated a number of such functions in connection with the farm management within a reorganized block of land. Those are all functions directly concerned with the efficient management and use of the land and water resources in the block. There are a few ancillary functions as well where joint decision and action are beneficial, for instance, provision of essential supplies, services and credit, and processing and marketing of farm produce. It is now generally agreed that these latter functions should be looked after by co-operatives of farmers. I fully agree with this accepted policy. I shall not therefore elaborate on it any further. Instead, I shall briefly discuss the form of organization necessary to look after the management of soil and water resources in a reorganized block of land.

My first reaction is that this should also be left to some kind of a co-operative organization of the farmers concerned. However, I can see the difficulty. A co-operative form of organization requires that the membership be voluntary. Obviously, this will not do for an organization which must make day-to-day decisions regarding the soil and water management in a given block of land and must enforce them. All cultivators of land within the given block must therefore of necessity be members of the proposed organization. This means, I presume, that the proposed organization must be a statutory body established by law as, for instance, is a village panchayat. I suggest that in every block of land where the physical layout on the ground is proposed to be reorganized, simultaneous with the process of reorganization, should be set up a democratic statutory authority. Its jurisdiction should extend to the block of land and its functions should be confined, at any rate initially, to the management of soil and water in the block. It must have financial powers to raise resources to meet its expenses and it should be serviced with competent technical staff. Later, it may be possible and advisable to expand its functions to cover provisions of essential supplies, services and credit to the farmers in the block and to arrange for the processing and marketing of their produce.

Let me emphasize that the basis for the establishment of such statutory bodies is a plan to reorganize the production structure, the physical layout on the ground, in a block of land. It is the reorganized layout which creates the necessary physical conditions where joint decision and action become both inevitable and beneficial. Without such a necessary physical structure, even a statutory body will have no functions to perform in the field of agricultural production. This is precisely what has happened to village panchayats today. We have charged them with several functions in the field of agricultural production, such as preparation of production plans, securing minimum standards of cultivation, bringing under cultivation waste and fallow lands, preservation and improvement of village forests, promotion of co-operative management of land, so on and so forth. In the absence of a rational production structure on the ground, none of these functions make any sense.

Friends, I am aware that I have taxed your patience too long. Let me therefore sum up. I have only two simple points to make. One is that I fully approve of one of the elements of the New Strategy, namely, greater reliance on agricultural science and technology. I believe that this has two corollaries which we have neglected so far. Firstly, we need a vast and an enlightened programme of adult education oriented to cultivate necessary scientific attitudes among farmers. Our approach so far has been too much administrative and too little educational. Secondly, we must create opportunities for the technically trained and scientifically oriented personnel to perform technical and scientific functions. We have too few persons in this class at all levels and we are wasting them all, from top to bottom, in preparing meaningless plans and trying to administer them. The programme of adult education among farmers and the programme of physical reorganization in agriculture with a view to more scientific management of our agriculture will both provide, I expect, ample opportunity for the technically competent persons to demonstrate application of agricultural sciences to agricultural production. My second point is that I fully sympathize with the Minister in his feeling of helplessness when he realizes that the actual production decisions in agriculture, in fact, rest with millions of farmers. However, I submit, the alternative is not to take these decisions in our hands. This is not only because it is politically not possible, but because we really do not know enough and we need the active participation of the farmers in the process of decision-making. For this purpose, two conditions must be satisfied. One is to reorganize the production structure on the ground and thus create necessary physical environment wherein the farmers may meaningfully participate in the new kinds of decisions needed for agricultural development. Second is to establish statutory authorities competent to make and enforce such decisions, close enough to the ground so that each such decision necessarily affects every farmer in the area and each farmer in the area necessarily participates in the making of every such decision.

These are the two simple points I wanted to make and I realize that I should not have taken so long over them. I am grateful to you for your patience and indulgence.

3

THE STRATEGY OF AGRICULTURAL ADVANCE*

SURENDRA J. PATEL

PERHAPS YOU are now expecting that the remaining lectures will recommend measured dozes of palatable tonic to strengthen us for accomplishing the transition outlined earlier. Let me warn you beforehand that towards this objective, I have no cure-alls, no impressive armoury of gimmics or shortcuts; not any conclusive answers, or even the basis of searching them, to our contemporary concerns. Perhaps all this will come to you as anti-climax. I intend to take some of the main issues, and discuss them in the framework of a longer-term outlook. In essence, the exercise may help, I hope, explore the problems, raise some questions, suggest broad approaches but leave most of the technical details to be settled. The task of formulating precise blue-prints requires a body of settled knowledge and convictions as its basis. Here, I am merely using this platform and your presence to talk aloud, to explore the issues which have been bothering my mind and put before you the broad conclusions they seem to suggest. But there is no finality, even in my own mind, about them; I only hope that they may provoke some discussion from which an approach may emerge.

There is one more qualification I wish to make. Those who may find my discussion of policy issues too thin or brief may please remember that I am attempting to cover a wide canvass in the course of only two lectures. I will have to be selective, emphasizing only what appears to me relevant; other issues, perhaps no less urgent or important, are left untouched for want of time and space.

Bearing these limitations in mind, I will take up the main policy issues involved in a rapid agricultural and industrial growth, and pass on to a discussion of raising the necessary resources and training the skilled manpower, and the broad framework of approach to socialist transformation of our institutions.

Food supplies, together with public finance and foreign exchange, have formed the unholy trinity which has plagued our planning efforts from the beginning. Commissions and expert groups have followed one another in succession. Recommendations have been made. In times of a little bit of luck, the problems have appeared to have been nearly solved, but the ugly reality has continued to raise its head again, adding pressure for the appointment of yet another expert group.

---

* Reproduced from *The India we want* by Surendra J. Patel, Manaktalas, Bombay.

Nowhere have the pressures been more critical than on the food front. The food-crisis has been now a hardy triennial.[1] It was our good fortune, it seems in retrospect, that it made its appearance in the early or the middle stage of the Plan, rather than at a time when a new plan was being adopted. For whenever it has come, it has created a crisis of confidence in the country; voices have been raised condemning nearly every side of planned development, and even those who wanted India to abandon planned development altogether have found sympathetic audiences. Fortunately, as I said, the kindly clouds have so far not failed to drench our parched soils and produce a bountiful harvest just as the nation was about to decide the dimensions of its new plan. That intense questioning then looked like a nightmare and the ambitious horizons of the new plan were accepted with measured confidence. But I wonder what would have happened if the heavens missed, even once (as they seem to have done this year), the finesse of timing!

1. The Target of Agricultural Growth

What I have proposed earlier is a transition from agricultural scarcity to surplus by rasing per capita agricultural output 2·2 times over the next four to five decades. This would entail about a five-fold expansion of total agricultural output in 40 to 50 years at an annual growth-rate of 3·5 to 4·5 per cent. While the notion of a five-fold expansion may sound over-ambitious, I would like to emphasize that when translated in terms of an annual growth-rate, the task posed only slightly more ambitious than our past performance since 1950. The annual growth-rate being proposed to be raised from about 3·5 per cent in the past to 4·5 per cent at the maximum; and if this were to be continued for eight five-year plans, we would be producing enough food and other agricultural supplies for the people. The ugly sight of poverty, malnutrition and near starvation would have been permanently effaced.

While not much more ambitious than the recent performance, it need not be overlooked that these goals are far more ambitious than proposed by Professor W. Arthur Lewis only a decade ago. In outlining growth prospect for the 25 years between 1955 and 1980, he assumed that "even with the best effort" food output could be raised by only about 45 per cent, or at an annual growth-rate of only 1·5 per cent.[2] Professor Lewis was unsure about the ability of the developing countries to raise their output; he thought that an annual growth-rate of 4 per cent for total output "is so difficult to obtain that it is really an ambitous target".[3]

[1] The graph of agricultural output since 1950 looks like a step-ladder poised upward rather than a wave-like movement around a straightline as was the case between 1900 and 1950.

[2] See his "Indian Economic Prospects for 1980—The Need to Develop Export of Manufactures", in *Capital*, December 1954.

[3] See his address delivered in October 1960 at a special convocation of Williams College, Williamstown, U.S.A. and printed in Institute of Development Economics, *Economic Digest* (Pakistan), Vol. 3, Number 4, Winter 1960, p. 3.

He was particularly uncertain about India, when he counselled that it should aim at even a lower rate of growth—only 3·2 per cent.

I am citing this not to question judgements, but merely to underline that how far removed from reality were the judgements current only a decade ago. Our past performance has been significantly above these prescriptions; and with a proper development strategy, we can certainly improve upon our modest achievements. A healthy sense of realism may then help reassure us that the targets I am suggesting are not really fanciful. In fact, we had aimed much higher—5·5 per cent per year—for the Third Plan; the Ford Foundation team had suggested an annual growth-rate of as high as 8 per cent for cereals. Perhaps if we could achieve these goals earlier at a higher growth-rate, it would indeed be even better for our people. The general possibilities are there. But they do need fashioning appropriate policies to attain the feasible.

A five-fold increase in agricultural output would require a major transformation of its structure. Foodgrains output need not rise to the same extent. An expansion of 3- to 4-fold in it, with a part of it being for feeding grains for animal husbandry, should be enough; its share in total agricultural output would fall from nearly three-fourths at present to about one-half. Other sectors (such as dairy and other products of animal husbandry and fishing, fruits, vegetables, oilseeds and sugarcane and agricultural raw materials for industries) would increase over six times, thus providing a balanced diet and a broader raw material base.

2. The Present Agricultural Setting

A review of our agriculture at present may be of some help in assessing the feasibility of these targets. The main features are familiar to you all, but permit me to summarize some of the more important ones briefly. In this, I intend to concentrate only on the major elements—conditions of production on the one hand, and agrarian relations on the other.

(a) *Conditions of Production*

(i) The gross cultivated area in the country comes to a little over 150 million hectares,[4] of which 14 million are cropped more than once; the net cultivated area is about 131 million hectares. Of the gross total, 113 million hectares, or about three-fourths, are used for growing all kinds of foodgrains.

(ii) The ratio of land cultivated per head (land/man ratio) comes to 0·37 hectare. This is lower than the world average (0·47)—a fact which has given currency to the notion that ours is a crowded country suffering from acute shortages of land. It is well to remember, however, that our land/man ratio is slightly higher than in Europe excluding the Soviet Union (0·35), nearly twice as high as China (0·18), over four times as high as Taiwan, South Korea and North Vietnam (0·08), and in

[4] The arable land, including land left fallow, is estimated to be 161 million hectares.

fact six times as high as in Japan (0·06).[5] The comparison should provide some sense of realism to the cries of land shortage in India.

(iii) Some 28 million hectares, or over one-fifth of the total under cultivation, are being irrigated. It may be useful to have an approximate idea of the relative extent of irrigation facilities in India. 175 million hectares of cultivated land all over the world are provided with some form of man-made irrigation; and of these as many as 74 million hectares are in China. India alone thus accounts for under one-third of the irrigated area in the world excluding China—a fact which cannot be dismissed lightly.

(iv) In addition to the irrigated area, there are about 30 to 40 million hectares (the estimates are very approximate) which have assured rainfall. These together with the irrigated area account for 45-53 per cent of net cultivated area, and as high as 51-58 per cent of the gross cultivated area. Even if we take the lower estimates of land with assured rainfall, we have thus nearly one-half the total cultivated area which does not seriously suffer from the lack of an adequate supply of humidity (or water) to the soil for raising the necessary crops.

(v) But we know that areas with assured water supply are usually cultivated more than once and more intensively, so that their crop-yield is on the whole nearly twice as high—and often more—as in lands with uncertain rainfall. An estimate based on these approximate indicators would then suggest that two-thirds or more of our agricultural output originates on the area which has adequate water supplies. If aridity, or lack of water, is a problem for land in India, it is closely limited to about one-half of the area and less than one-third of the output. This fact has considerable significance for the strategy of agricultural development we are going to present later on.

(vi) Let us look at what this land produces. Nearly three-fourths of our people toil in one capacity or another year round to raise the crops. All their labour produced upto 85 million tons of cereals (counting rice in paddy form) as an average for 1961-1962, or only 9 quintals per hectare of land.[6] We have the doubtful distinction of having among the lowest productivity per hectare of land. In comparison, the yields are two to three times in Europe, South Korea and Malaya, four to five times in Egypt, Taiwan and Japan. The land that was characterized as "Shashya Shyamala" by Bankim and "Sare Jahan se achchha" by Iqbal does not produce enough to deserve the poets' affectionate words.

(vii) The characteristic feature of our agriculture then is not a relative shortage of land, but land which for a number of reasons pro-

[5] The basic data used in this and the following page are taken from United Nations Economic Commission for Asia and the Far East, "National Development Perspectives of Agriculture in the ECAFE Region" in the *Economic Bulletin for Asia and the Far East*, June 1965.

[6] The figures would be lower if rice output is counted, as in India, in the milled form.

duces an incredibly low level of output per unit. We have acres and acres of land which grow only one-half, one-third or even one-fourth of their potential. This may be termed "excess capacity" in agriculture.

In recent discussion of development, we have become conceptually accustomed to the idea of surplus manpower in agriculture; and all sorts of models have been built to utilize its potential for development based on varying assumptions as to its marginal productivity and cost. I would like to suggest that the notion of "excess capacity" in agriculture as defined above has a much greater relevance for accelerating development than of surplus manpower.

Excess capacity in agriculture is defined here as land yielding less than its technical potential at a given point of time. Conceptually speaking, this is not much different from what we understood as excess capacity in industries. In both cases, there is unusual or under-utilized equipment (factories in industry and land in agriculture); increase in output could be achieved without increasing capacity but, by the supply of certain necessary current inputs or by the removal of bottlenecks (supplies of raw materials, manpower, skills, working capital, energy, transport, etc.) The major elements in an adequate utilization of capacity in industry are thus not altogether different from those in agriculture. But the share of agriculture in the output of the developing countries and the possibilities of raising the outputs are so large that its potential contribution to overall economic growth through an adequate utilization of its "excess capacity" is much greater than that of industry or of surplus manpower. But owing to misplaced emphasis, we hear a lot about the latter and little about the former.

(viii) Surely some suggestions as to the reasons for the low yields is in order. The low level in areas where the rainfall is inadequate and uncertain and in the lands of marginal productivity is understandable. But as emphasized earlier, this does not relate to nearly one-half of the area with assured water-supply; and it produces two-thirds of our output. The low yield, I suggest, does not arise from the fact that our soils are so poor, or our farmers lazy, or ignorant or illiterate; it represents the result of a number of factors which have combined to keep the level of our agricultural techniques low. The vast revolution in agricultural techniques which has recently helped to raise output per hectare two to four times in Europe, Egypt, Taiwan and Japan, has similarly bypassed the Indian farmer. As a result, the yields per unit of land have remained virtually unchanged over as long a period as we have historical data for.

This technical backwardness is summarized in many elements; for instance, poor seeds, inadequate weeding, absence of proper fertilizer inputs (especially of the chemical fertilizers), poor insect control, improper storage, and so on. Among them, perhaps the most important reflector, however, is the low level of fertilizer inputs. Let me give you some comparative data. For each hectare of land, we put in 3·5 kgs. of plant nutrient, against 75 kgs. in Egypt, 85 kgs. in western Europe, and as high as 190 kgs. in Taiwan and 310 kgs. in Japan (see Table 6). Particularly striking is the fact that the Egyptian farmer uses twenty-one times more fertilizers per hectare and the Taiwanese fifty-four times. Surely, the low level of chemical fertilizer consumption in India cannot be explained away by the fact that this western innovation is difficult to use in India, if the Egyptians and the Chinese in Taiwan have mastered it. This element is of particular significance for the future strategy of agricultural development in India.

(ix) Similarly, India's relative cattle wealth is also not inadequate. Per head of our population, there are 0·35 cattle units compared with a world average of 0·34, and that for Europe of 0·33.[7] But like the land under cultivation, our cattle population also suffers from excess capacity — that is, for various reasons, their output per unit is very low.

(x) The list is getting long, but you would perhaps let me emphasize one more feature of Indian agriculture, which has a considerable significance to a proper understanding of what has too often been termed "India's food crisis". The marketed surplus of foodgrains in India is about one-third of the total output, or some 25 million tons out of the recent average of 80 million tons.[8] Only 15 out of 355 districts are reported to produce nearly one-third of our marketable supplies.[9] A fall of total output by 5 per cent or a rise in demand by the same percentage in the face of stagnant supplies creates a relative shortage in marketable supplies by as high as one-sixth to one-fifth. Add to this the near certainty of big speculative gains by withholding grains by traders till prices rise; and we have all the makings of a major food crisis with minor disturbance in supply/demand relations.

I am not advancing this as a major discovery of this decade. The elements have been well-known, and so are the remedies—building up of buffer-stocks. But the implementation has been singularly ineffective, despite all the fanfare. It is an irony that we get all set to build stocks precisely when this is impossible—in times of shortages. The inverse correlation between the stress on stock building and the possibility to do so—a good harvest year—reveals weaknesses in implementation.

(b) *Agrarian Relationship*

Behind every grain of foodgrains supplied lies the living reality

[7] For details, see *ECAFE Bulletin*, June 1965, *op. cit.*; all animals converted to comparable cattle units at these ratios:

horse = 1·0
cattle = 0·8
pig = 0·2 and
sheep and goat = 0·1

[8] Including rice in milled form.

[9] See "More Food Less Dogma" in the *Economist* (London, April 24, 1965), p. 416.

of the Indian peasant, too often dismissed as the pack-animal of human history. His interest in his work, his share in the fruits of his labour—in short, his incentives form an important element in understanding the reasons why agricultural techniques in India have remained virtually unaltered.

(i) For this, let us briefly summarize the main features of the agrarian society we inherited at the time of our Independence.[10] The pre-nineteenth century rural society in India was built upon two main pillars: self-sufficient village communities in which the cultivators and artisans exchanged their products on the basis of traditional arrangements. The structure disintegrated under the impact of more than a century and a half of British rule. On the eve of Independence, over 70 per cent of our agricultural population had no rights on land; two-fifths of it were landless labourers and one-third dwarf-holding labourers, both of whom worked under serf-like conditions on lands owned by a relatively small number of landowners. This large body had no fixity of tenure or rent, or of income. I had occasion to remark in the study just cited:

> "No wonder that the cultivators in India are poor and that the per acre productivity is very low and falling. In a social context wherein exploitation of persons, desperately seeking to subsist, is placed at a higher premium than of the soil itself, widespread emergence of improved methods of cultivation is clearly out of the question."

(ii) This hard reality formed the bedrock of all expressions on the ultimate reorganization of our rural society. Nowhere were these aspirations more clearly stated than in Panditji's immemorable words:

> "Whose freedom are we particularly striving for, for nationalism covers many sins and includes many conflicting elements...... It is obvious that there are serious conflicts between various interests in the country, and every law, every policy, which is good for one interest may be harmful for another...... Nothing is more absurd than to imagine that all the interests in the nation can be fitted in without injury to any.
>
> "If an indigenous government took the place of the foreign government and kept all the vested interests intact, this would not even be the shadow of freedom...... The whole basis and urge for the national movement came from a desire for economic betterment, to throw off the burden that crushed the masses, and to crush the exploitation of the Indian people. If these burdens continue, and are actually added to, it does not require a powerful mind to realize that the fight must not only continue but grow more intense. Leaders and individuals may come and go; they may get tired and slacken off; they may compromise or betray; but the exploited and

[10] For details, see the author's study, *Agricultural Labourers in Modern India and Pakistan* (Current Book House, Bombay, 1952).

suffering masses must carry on the struggle, for their drill-sergeant is hunger. Swaraj or freedom from exploitation for them is not a fine paper constitution or a problem of the hereafter. It is a question of here and now, of immediate relief. Roast lamb and mint sauce may be a tasty dish for those who eat it, but the poor lamb is not likely to appreciate the force of the best of arguments which point at the beauty of sacrifice for the good of the elect and the joys of close communion, even though dead, with mint sauce.

(iii) These ideas were incorporated in official pronouncements and policy resolutions. You are all familar with the details. But what has been the actual progress? Perhaps the best summary is to quote at length from the latest official statement as contained in the Third Plan: Mid-term Appraisal (New Delhi, 1963), pp. 98-101:

"The main aspects of land reform are the abolition of intermediaries, tenancy reform, ceiling on land holdings and consolidation of holdings.

"Abolition of Intermediaries—The programme for the abolition of intermediaries has been mostly completed.

"Tenancy Reform—Comprehensive legislation for tenancy reforms has been enacted in several States. In some States the existing provisions for security of tenure are of temporary nature and comprehensive measures have not yet been enacted or enforced, although ejectment of tenants has been stayed temporarily. In Andhra area, an interim legislation provides for stay of ejectments. In Telengana area, to which the Hyderabad Tenancy and Agricultural Lands Act applies, some of the principal provisions have not been enforced pending enactment of tenancy legislation for the entire State of Andhra Pradesh. In Bihar, tenancies are still generally regulated under the Tenancy Act of 1885 with some modifications. In Madras, the present legislation is of a temporary nature and comprehensive proposals for tenancy legislation are still under the consideration of the State Government. In Mysore, the Land Reform Act was enacted in 1960 but its implementation was stayed pending its amendment to incorporate the recommendations of the Government of India. The Amendment Act has yet to be promoted. In Orissa also, the Land Reform Act, 1960 has not yet been enforced due to the pending amendments. Delays in enacting comprehensive legislation create a great deal of uncertainty which is inimical to efforts to increase agricultural production.

"Security of Tenure—Effectiveness of the provisions of security of tenure centres on the issue of resumption and the safeguards included in the legislation to prevent voluntary surrenders which have taken place on a considerable scale in several States. The right to resume land for personal cultivation for which a provision still obtains in several States, has tended to create uncertainty and to diminish the protection afforded to tenants. It had been recommended in the Third Plan that in view of the period that has already elapsed, there should be no further right of resumption except for owners holding land equivalent to a family holding or less. With regard to surrenders, as stated in the Plan, most voluntary surrenders of tenancies are open to doubt as bonafide transactions and this has been confirmed by such enquiries and investigations as have been undertaken. Recommendations have been made in the Third Plan to meet the problems of surrenders. Only in Bihar, Madhya Pradesh, Mysore, Manipur and Tripura, provisions have been made for the regulation of surrenders on the lines suggested in the Plan. In Gujarat and Maharashtra, surrenders are to be registered but other measures suggested in the Plan have not been adopted. On the whole both administrative and legislative action taken so far have fallen short of the recommendations in the Plan in several States.

"Problem of Implementation—A number of surveys of land reform undertaken in different parts of the country through the Research Programmes Committee of the Planning Commission have brought out the extreme importance of effective implementation of the legislation which has been enacted. Failures in implementation take away some part of the benefits of the progressive land reform legislation which States have undertaken. A major obstacle in implementation arises from the fact that a large proportion of leases are oral and tenants cannot prove their title through documents. In a number of States, such as Andhra Pradesh, Assam, Bihar, Kerala, Madras, Mysore and Orissa, the land records do not contain information about tenants and share-croppers. There are States also in which records of tenants and share-croppers are maintained, but these are often deficient. An up-to-date and correct record of tenancies is a necessary condition for the implementaton of land reform legislation. With a view to expediting preparation and correction of records it was agreed that such schemes might be included in the plans of States and would receive assistance from the Central Government. In some States, provision to this effect has been made in the annual plans, but practical action still lags behind."

Against the noble words in which the aspirations were framed, the actual account of what in fact has happened makes a sober, depressing reading. In its main elements, it is almost like a dreary diary of a do-little. The recent report by Mr. Ladjinsky serves to emphasize the significance of land reform for increasing agricultural output.[11]

It is a sad comment on India's socialist pronouncements that lands much less publicly committed to socialism, such as post-war Japan and Taiwan, have accomplished a more radical reorganization of their agrarian relationships; and as a rich reward, have registered appreciable progress in their agricultural output. Our continued difficulties in raising agricultural output serve to emphasize that repetitions of pious declarations will not somehow produce results. Without a reconstruction of

11 See his Report which was published in the *Mainstream* (New Delhi), March 13, 20, 27, 1965.

the land relationships, it will be impossible to attain major progress in agricultural output, let alone create a just and fair society. Some of the main elements in this reorganization, required as the minimum steps, are discussed later on.

3. Revolution in Agricultural Techniques

An analysis of the future strategy of agricultural advance in India can be helped greatly by a full grasp of the main landmarks in the development of agricultural techniques. If we could turn our time-machines backwards, we would find that at the mid-point of the last century the gap between the actual and the possible output per hectare of land was very narrow indeed. In western Europe, the yield of wheat, taken as an approximate general indicator of productivity of the soil, was 8 to 10 quintals per hectare—or about the same as in Attica at the height of the Greek civilization over two thousand years ago, and in India and the other developing countries now.

True enough, many changes in agricultural techniques had taken place since the beginning of cultivation; but they consisted mainly in introducing the domestication of animals, or new implements, or new plants. All those increased the possibility of extensive cultivation and added to the range of the crops grown. There was also the development of irrigation, of contour-bunding of some selection of seeds, etc. But they had limited influence on raising yields per hectare—certainly much less than what was to follow in the century since 1850.

In the first half of the eighteenth century a number of innovations were introduced: new root crops, the practice of hoeing and tilling, drainage of heavy soils, and some improvements in stock-breeding. One thinks of the name of Tull, Townsend and Blackwell in England, and of course of Arthur Young's classic work, *A Course of Experimental Agriculture*, published in 1770—only six years before Adam Smith's *Wealth of Nations*; he was appointed the Secretary of the newly-established Board of Agriculture in 1793 and had considerable influence in popularising the new innovations. But these barely went beyond the very well-to-do "gentlemen" farmers, and their impact on raising yields per hectare for the country as a whole was marginal. The average yield in Europe at mid-point of the last century was still no more than 8 to 10 quintals per hectare.

This is not surprising at all when it is recalled that agriculture was still not subjected to the scientific approach. Little was known of what made the plants grow the way they did; the soils were classified by colour and not their content; and sickness and disease were considered the exclusive prerogatives of man and animals. Young Louise Pasteur was about to make his sensational announcements that the grape-vines in France were affected by diseases that could be cured or controlled; and Sir John B. Lawe and Justus von Liebig had just begun their experiments in the use of fertilizers on plants on their window-sills in the forties of the last century. The beginning was being made—slowly and hesitatingly—towards a fuller understanding of the growth of plants and its relation to the supply of plant nutrients from the soil, air, sunshine and moisture. But it was to take more than half a century before these results widely influenced the practice of cultivation.

For one thing, the supply of mineral phosphates was limited in the most advanced countries. Nitrates were a rarity and little was known of their use. The German chemical industry was to succeed in their large-scale synthetic production during the first World War when the country was cut off from Chilean sources. This was less than half a century ago. It has been recently estimated by the FAO that more than one-half the increase in yields in agriculture has directly resulted from the increased use of chemical fertilizers.[12]

The study of soil and the techniques of its classification and enrichment were begun by the Russian pioneer, Dokuchaev, towards the end of the last century. It was to make remarkable progress thereafter.

Darwin's Origin of Species and Pasteur's discoveries had given a great stimulus to the study of plant genetics and plant pathology. But operational successes in the evolution of new seeds suited to varying conditions of heat, light, moisture and soil, and resistant to frost, pests and diseases were to come in the twentieth century; little of the modern science of agrobiology was known in the nineteenth century. The widespread use of chemicals for the control of plant diseases and pests, and of weedicides for the preferential growth of selected plants is even more recent.

The use of concentrated protein-rich food, such as oil cakes, had just started to spread in Europe in the closing decades of the last century. Now, with vitamins and minerals added, and differentiation of animal breeds for different functions—producing meat or milk—animal husbandry has taken a long stride from its pastoral origin. Animal farms which gave title to children's classic tales have now been taken over by animal factories.

The age of animals as the motive-power began to recede during the twenties. Tractors, harvesters and combines lend now a different silhouette to the farms in the industrial countries. Fears are already being expressed for the extinction of the horse, like that of the Dinosaurs, as a specie, since the tractor and the car have taken over as the motive-power and since it cannot compete with the cow in milk and meat.

All these details add up to an impressive transformation of agricultural techniques—more recent in their historical origin than industrial techniques. In the process yields per hectare of land have risen significantly in northwestern Europe and Japan—from 8 to 9 quintals to 40

[12] FAO, *The State of Food and Agriculture* (Rome, 1963), pp. 135 ff.

quintals or above; and fertilizers formed the spearhead of this advance.[13] Let me emphasize: the same hectare now produces nearly 5 times more.

Malthus was worried about the elasticity of the human stomach, the voracity of its demand and the prolific productivity of the poor; but he rarely questioned the bearing capacity of the god-given land. An acre was an acre. But it took only a little over half a century to raise the ceiling of its output five times above where it had remained stubbornly fixed for at least two to three thousand years. Not being a technician, I would dare not guess how high it would go in the years to come; but also not being a man of faith, as Malthus was, I would desist from believing that the heights have been reached.

This rapid raising of the ceiling, this vast gap between the actual and the potential yields have combined to alter the frame of reference for agricultural growth.

This change has special significance for the developing countries, particularly those like India which have limited possibilities in extensive cultivation. Let me explain this in a comparative way. In the economic growth of Europe in the 19th century, virgin lands were an imperative necessity. At that time, the margin between the actual and possible output per unit of land was small. No wonder, over those years Europeans flocked to the Americas, Australasia and South Africa.[14] The agricultural output from these areas fed the growing urban and industrial centres in Europe. Extensive cultivation thus played a strategic role in 19th century economic growth.

But with the rise in the ceiling of output per unit of land, this is no longer necessary. The Soviet Union made a heroic dash for extensive cultivation of the virgin lands during the fifties, but many are now wondering whether the exhausting effort was worth the additional output—particularly if you could get it on the soil nearer your homestead.[15]

[13] FAO, *The State of Food and Agriculture*, 1963, p. 136; the significance of fertilizer use is clearly reflected in the chapter title, "Fertilizer Use: Spearhead of Agriculture", Chapter IV, pp. 135-175. The chapter contains a great deal of details and analysis on the key role of fertilizers; for an earlier discussion of the subject, see also ECE, *Economic Survey of Europe in* 1959, Chapter VII, pp. 7-8, 15-19, 46-50; also see ECAFE, *Economic Bulletin for Asia and the Far East, June* 1965.

[14] In comparison, the migration of the Chinese and the Indians over the last two centuries are minor movements.

[15] For details see the author's study, "What is holding up Agricultural Growth?" in the *Economic Weekly*, Annual Number, 1964; pp. 327-341. N. Khruschev is reported to have stated in a speech at Novayya-Kharkova that: "The conditions that have risen this year require that we make an all-out effort for increasing yields (on existing lands) ......If we are now giving first priority to fertilizers and only second priority to irrigation, it does not mean that we are underestimating the importance of irrigation. It is because a solution of both tasks simultaneously is beyond our capabilities." See the *New York Times*, International Edition, Octo ber 1, 1963

This candid admission has even a greater relevance to the conditions of agricultural advance in India.

The growth of the immense potential of intensive cultivation offers the most powerful tool to the planners in the developing countries. Their yields per hectare are very low; and consequent total output of food supplies is not adequate to feed the peoples at a satisfactory level of diet. Much of our poverty and malnutrition springs from this low. Low yields are in this sense no doubt highly deplorable.

But they need not depress an economist or a planner. The fact that they are low and the knowledge that they can be raised 3 to 5 times suggest at once the journey that was inconceivable earlier but possible now. Raising the yields three to five times would be enough, as indicated earlier, to provide all the food and agricultural output we need at the highest income levels for our expanding population for the next half a century—without adding an extra acre to the area under cultivation.

With this background, we can perhaps now turn to investigating the main elements of the strategy for agricultural advance in India.

4. Towards a More Intensive Agriculture

India is admittedly a country where the possibilities of extensive cultivation are limited. We may by improved techniques of crop rotation and fertilization succeed in reducing the land left fallow; extend the area under irrigation, particularly of uncultivated soils; add some more acres through schemes of land reclamation and soil conservation and turn marginal lands more productive; increase the extent of double-cropping, which if water were available, has a great potential in our climate. All these measures are important and need no doubt to be pursued. But the final solution of our agricultural problems lies in intensive agriculture, in raising the low level of yield per hectare. The strategy for such advance may be conveniently discussed under two headings: the technical and the institutional aspects.

(*a*) *Technical aspects*

(i) India in world comparison: The main features of Indian agriculture, noted earlier, may be summarised here for convenience. This is done in Table 6, where the agricultural operations in India are compared with those in the United States, Europe (excluding the Soviet Union), Egypt, Taiwan and Japan.

The size of the total population and the arable area and the land/man ratio are all approximately the same in both India and Europe; but the latter produces two and a half times as high net agricultural output per head or per unit of land. India uses only 3·5 kg. of plant nutrients or net chemical fertilizers per hectare, mostly concentrated on market gardening and commercial crops. The rest of the land is fertilized by occasional bird-droppings and the nitrogen mercifully mixed with falling rain water. The European farmer on the other hand uses 85 kg. of net

TABLE 6: COMPARATIVE DATA ON AGRICULTURE IN INDIA AND SELECTED COUNTRIES AND AREAS, 1960

Item		*India*	*United States* 1960	*Europe*[a] 1960	*Egypt* 1960	*Taiwan* 1960	*Japan* 1960
Population (million)	...	430	181	424	26	10·6	93
Arable land (mil. ha.)	...	161	127	153	2·6	0·9	6·1
Arable land (ha. per capita)	...	0·37	0·27	0·36	0·1	0·08	0·06
Net domestic products ($ billion)	...	29·9	397	...	(3·4) b	1·7	47·5
Net domestic product ($ per capita)	...	75	2,200	...	130	150	495
Agricultural output capita ($ billion)	...	14·4	16·2	34 a	1·1	0·45	5·0
Agricultural output ($ per capita)	...	35	90	80	40	45	55
Agricultural output ($ per ha.)	...	90	130	200	400	500	820
Fertilizer input (million) c	...	0·56	7·26	12·90	0·19	0·17	1·84
Fertilizer input (kg. per ha.)	...	3·5	57	85	74	190	310
Fertilizer cost ($ million) d	...	140	1,820	3,200	48	41	460
Fertilizer cost ($ per ha.) d	...	0·9	14	21	18	46	75
Fertilizer cost (cents per dollar of agricultural output)	...	1·0	11·2	9·4	4·4	9·2	9·2

SOURCES : Based on FAO Production Yearbook 1961; OEEC, General Statistics, 1961, No. 4; United Nations, Yearbook of National Accounts, 1962; United States, Statistical Abstract, 1963, p. 613.

NOTE : The data on arable land not always comparable owing to inadequate average of fallow and double-cropped area; the derived figures are therefore to be treated as orders of magnitude only.

a. Excluding the USSR; net value of agricultural output per each inhabitant of the OEEC countries, with a population of 305 million, was $ 87; for other countries with 119 million people it was assumed on the basis of approximate estimates to be $65. The average for the whole region would therefore come to about $80 per capita.

b. Approximate estimate.

c. Plant nutrients in terms of nitrogen, phosphate and potash.

d. At an estimated price, paid by the farmers, of $25 per 100 kg. of plant nutrient.

chemical fertilizers per hectare, or 25 times higher than in India;[16] the additional cost of this input is more than amply repaid by additional output—per each dollar worth of additional fertilizer cost, the European farmer obtains over 6 times more output.

It may be suggested that the comparison with the European farmer, living in highly advanced industrial countries, is unfair to the Indian peasant. In Europe, much of the new knowledge and techniques are part of daily life; whereas these have to be acquired by a process of unlearning followed by learning in India. We have therefore also provided data for Egypt, Taiwan and Japan, all non-European countries. The land/man ratio in these countries is extremely low—from one-fourth to only one-sixth of India's. These are the classic examples of overcrowding; but their agricultural output per head of population is higher. Per hectare of land, Egypt produces four and a half times, Taiwan five and a half times and Japan nearly ten times as much as India. The difference can hardly be explained by the Indian farmer being more Asian, lazy, less hard-working, unintelligent or less enlightened; or by our soils much less fertile. Surely not.

What is then the source of such marked differences in soil productivity? Many factors related to history, culture, climate, tradition, institutions etc. do have a certain degree of difficulty to measure influence. But the most important recognizable and easy to observe difference is in the input of chemical fertilizers per hectare—3·5 kg. in India against 74 kg. in Egypt, 190 in Taiwan and 310 in Japan. While we have been hoping that eulogies of our past history and exhortations to "grow more food" may produce good harvests, our Asian brothers in Japan and Taiwan have proceeded somewhat differently—they have simply littered their soil with the newly discovered nutrients. They have not allowed their pride in Asia's past shy them away from what may be considered a west European invention—the chemical fertilizers.

There are other factors of course such as more labour inputs, better preparation of the soil, proper water control, careful weeding, use of insecticides and so on; but they are all associated with new techniques, of which fertilizers form the spearhead. In all the three cases, additional cost of fertilizers is repaid ten times over in the bountiful harvest; it is in reality no longer an additional cost, but like the seeds, an integral input of agricultural operations.

Some such approach is needed in India.

(ii) Line of Advance in India: These elements have great importance in India. We have talked at length about the Japanese method of cultivation, but without the use of extra fertilizers it is like Ramayana without Rama.

[16] Throughout the discussion, chemical fertilizers are expressed in terms of plant nutrients.

Let me illustrate the possibilities in India through a simple arithmetical exercise. Assume that we keep the foodgrains area constant at 110 million hectares, and devote any increase in area to other crops; that irrigation is extended from 28 million hectares at present to at least 50 million hectares, of which 80 per cent (as at present) would be for growing grains; and that the input of chemical fertilizers per hectare of land is raised to 200 kg. for irrigated foodgrains area, to 40 kg. for non-irrigated foodgrains area, and to 150 kg. for all the non-foodgrains area. This would imply an average consumption for the country of some 130 kg. per hectare—or nearly one-half above the present west European and the Egyptian level, but much lower than the levels in Taiwan and Japan.

With such inputs, suppose further that we succeed in raising yields on irrigated land to the average in Egypt, Taiwan and Japan—say 40 quintals and on non-irrigated land to double the present level. The resultant agricultural output of India would approximate the figure shown in the table below.

Given these assumptions—and none of them is unreasonable—we could raise the average yield to 20-25 quintals and total grain output to 225 to 275 million tons; even if accomplished by 2000—and it can in fact be done even earlier—it could raise per capita gross availability of foodgrains from 185 kg. per year to 250 to 300 kg. or by one-third to one-half. This would be adequate for human, animal and industrial consumption and for seed requirements.

If we assume that the productivity of the soil under other crops may go up at least 3 times and that the area sown with them (including double cropped) may increase by 75 per cent, their total output may rise 5 to 6 times. They would then come to occupy about one-half of the weight in the index of agricultural output—that is, a structural transformation of Indian agriculture would also have been accomplished along these lines.

MAIN ELEMENTS IN AGRICULTURAL ADVANCE

Main Crops	*1960* mi. ha	*Future: 1980 or say, 2000* Area mil. ha.	Fertilizer kg. per ha.	Yields quintals per ha.	Output mil. tons	Fertilizers needed mil. tons
Foodgrains						
Irrigated	22	40	200	40	160	8·0
Other	88	70	40	9–16	65–115	2·8
Sub-total	110	110	110	20–25	225–275	10·8
Other crops	40	70	150	...	...	10·5
TOTAL	150	180	120	...	...	21·3

All these would require raising total fertilizer consumption from half a million tons in 1960 to over 21 million tons by whatever year is chosen as the terminal point of this transformation. Whether this is ambitious may be judged in comparison with the recent targets. The Third Five Year Plan aimed at producing 1·5 million tons of chemical fertilizers (plant nutrients), and the outline of the Fourth looks up to a total of about 4 million tons by 1970. Each five-year plan implied a two and a half to three times increase. At that rate, it would require only 10 more years, or two five-year plans, to reach the suggested level of 21 million tons. Even if the plans are staggered, the goal is thus not out of reach by, say, 1980—or later if you are very cautious.

But the economist will surely ask: Can we afford it, even if it were physically possible?

(iii) Estimates of Costs: In the first place, fertilizer inputs need not be regarded as capital costs. Like seeds they are inputs incorporated in a magnified form in the output which comes a few months later. But their capital costs, usually counted together with industrial investments, should be considered.

The input cost of fertilizers at Rs. 1,200 (or $ 250) per ton of plant nutrient would be about Rs. 25 billion. But fertilizers alone do not constitute the whole story. There are a number of other improved inputs which are needed if the full benefits of increased fertilizer use are to be reaped. These inputs, together with fertilizers, constitute an inseparable whole, including the use of improved variety of seeds, a minimum application of selected fertilizers (up to 80 to 100 kg. of plant nutrients per hectare), deep ploughing and thicker sowing, and proper and timely weeding and use of weedicides and insecticides.

The cost of all these new inputs is not easy to estimate. The experience in Europe suggests that the cost of all other inputs (excluding seed and feed) is approximately equal to that of fertilizers.[17] The total of new inputs in India may thus be estimated at say Rs. 50 billion. Against this, the net agricultural output could rise in the process from Rs. 68 billion to at least Rs. 268 billion, or by Rs. 200 billion—that is, each additional unit of input would have produced four times increase in output.

Capital costs are not easy to estimate. But according to a recent estimate for the Fourth Plan, reported in the *Capital* of 15 April 1965 (p. 518), the cost of 5 giant factories producing 1.75 million tons of plant nutrients was reported to be Rs. 2,023 millions, or little over Rs. 1,100 per ton. The FAO estimates capital costs to vary between $450 to $1,000 (or Rs. 2,150 to 4,800) per ton of output.[18] Even if the cost is taken at

17 See ECE, *Economic Survey of Europe in* 1960, Chapter III, pp. 6-7.

18 The capital requirements for a nitrogen plant have been estimated by the FAO to be $30 to $50 million for a plant with an annual capcity of 50,000 to 70,000 tons; of these $20 to $30 million may be foreign exchange cost. See FAO, *The State of Faod and Agriculture*, 1963 (Rome), p. 172; nitrate plants used only as an illustration of the relationship between capital and imports costs for all other plant nutrients.

Rs. 3,600 (or $750) per ton of capacity, and at an assumed equivalent investment cost for assuring other supplies, the total would be Rs. 144 billion, or equal to India's national income in 1960. These costs would of course be lower if the lower estimates of capital costs are found to prevail; if the capital costs of plant construction estimated for the Fourth Plan are taken as a basis, the investment for the proposed expansion of fertilizer output would come to only one-third of the figure mentioned here. But, for the purpose of illustration, we may use here the cost figures based on the obviously higher FAO estimates.

In addition, there are costs for irrigation for the suggested extension of 22 million hectares. Again using heroic estimates—Rs. 1,200 (or $250) per hectare—this may be totalled at Rs. 24 billion.

All in all, the capital costs of providing the required expansion of irrigation facilities, of fertilizer supplies and of all other essential inputs would come to Rs. 165 to Rs. 175 billion; of this Rs. 25 billion or less than one-sixth would be for irrigation, that is, exclusively for agricultural investments intended to supply the requirements of chemical fertilizers and other inputs. These sums may sound very large, but it is well to keep in mind that most of the capital costs suggested are really for industries—a point which clearly emphasizes the interdependence of agriculture and industry.

Can we afford these investments ? Perhaps the best way of answering the question is to compare them with our past experience. Between 1950 and 1965, we have spent about Rs. 25 billion in agriculture alone, of which about Rs. 6 to 7 billion in the First Plan and nearly Rs. 19 billion between 1955 and 1965. The annual rate of agricultural investment is now perhaps running at Rs. 3 billion, or over 2 per cent of the national income. Of the total of Rs. 25 billion, Rs. 13 billion or more than one-half of the total, was devoted to irrigation (major and minor) alone. The area under irrigation was planned to rise from 20 million hectares in 1950-51 to 36 million by 1965-66, or by 16 million hectares at an annual addition of over 1 million hectares.

In comparison, the irrigation investments proposed here are Rs. 25 billion, or twice what we undertook between 1950 and 1965. If the other agricultural investments were to continue to form the same proportion to irrigation as in the past, the total called for would be Rs. 50 billion. We may make provision for raising the share of the non-irrigation sector somewhat higher—from one-half to say around 60 per cent. In that case the proposed agricultural investments would come to a round sum of Rs. 60 billion.

Let us be ambitious and decide that all this should be accomplished in only 20 years, that is by 1985. Even if the investments are spread evenly—and phased to rise with our rising income as they should be—they represent no more than Rs. 3 billion per year, or equal to the present level. But rising income in the period would mean that this simple average, even if it increases only in line with income, could be raised at 7 per cent-per year to four times its present level—or to some Rs. 12 billion. In that case, we could invest in agriculture during the whole period Rs. 140 billion, or Rs. 80 billion more than the modest sum suggested here. We could in fact do much more—that is, finance from this simple model of growth even a major part of the industrial investment which is mainly intended for agriculture.

Obviously the exercise has no more than illustrative merit. The estimates of capital costs for fertilizer output are certainly nearly three times higher than reported for the Fourth Plan. Even then, the exercise does show that no outrageous demands are really being made on our growing resources. All this suggests that perhaps the time has come to look at investment in a slightly different manner than we have done so far. Our pre-occupation with static analysis has presented investment as a cost, as a benefit foregone, and this is not far from reality if we are dealing with fixed magnitudes at a point of time.

But growth, development, change, advance—all these imply change over a period. If a certain level of investment is deemed essential to obtain a certain increment in incomes, not to undertake it means foregoing the increment in income. Looked at from this view, not to undertake the investment (rather than undertaking it) is a real cost for the nation.

At the danger of stretching the argument too far, let me illustrate. Our net agricultural output is estimated to be Rs. 68 billion; the twenty-year programme suggested by us could, if successfully implemented, raise it to Rs. 268, or by Rs. 200 billion in the end-year. But the increment in that year alone, is higher than the capital costs proposed for the whole period.

This all goes against the currently accepted notions of capital costs and benefits. But if we must measure costs and benefits, there is much to be said in favour of the above view, which emphasizes the role of investment as a generator of income. Not investing then would appear as growth foregone—a real national loss indeed, something which no planner can afford, once he deals with a period and not a point of time. Thus, in a dynamic sense, not investing is a cost and investing a real gain.

There are problems of phasing, time-lags, implementation, etc. But approached in this general manner, we may be able to look at the ability of the developing countries to invest from a slightly different angle. I hope to develop this point further in the next lecture.

(*b*) *Institutional Aspects*

The crucial role of fertilizers and other inputs has been emphasized above. It can hardly be imagined that any amount of exhortation can effectively substitute for their supplies. But nor can it be suggested that even on the wild assumption of their ready availability, the illiterate and impoverished peasant will, from one day to another, take to them without the introduction of many other supplementary measures.[19] The water resources need to be effectively controlled; illiteracy rapidly eliminated; the road and electricity networks extended; human and animal diseases fought; and the new techniques popularized through rural stimulation, community development, and extension services. All these, in varying measures, stimulate, reflect or accompany agricultural development. But if the barriers of century-old conventional wisdom are to be broken it is essential above all to organize agrarian relationships along new lines; these include stabilization of farm prices, extension of marketing and credit facilities on cooperative lines, introduction of a system of adequate incentives, guaranteed tenure at fair rents, and organization of schemes for the popularization and the distribution of the necessary inputs.

Even when the importance of fertilizers and all other modern inputs is accepted and decisions made concerning their production, they would be of little use if the farmers were not to receive them in right quantities, at the right time, and under right terms. In short, the question is the desire and the ability of the peasants to absorb them. Indian farmer is no less intelligent than his average counterpart anywhere else; nor has the middle-class cant about our "spiritual" heritage sufficiently overwhelmed him so as to be indifferent to material problems, such as raising the level of the output so that his family may eat better, dress better and be housed in more adequate dwellings. He has demonstrated, despite all dissertations to the contrary, his innate will, his desire to progress, given the opportunity. What is needed is a careful assessment of his ability, possibility, and opportunity of fulfilling his desires.

The last fifteen years have witnessed an important debate between what I may call, for convenience, the structuralists and the technocrats in the country on the subject. On the other hand, there are impressive arguments, developed over the last 40 years in India, in favour of a thoroughgoing form of the agrarian structure as a pre-condition for agricultural growth. The Indian peasant is poor, he is crushed under the burden of heavy indebtedness and high rents, receiving little of the fruits of his labour which are snatched away by the moneylenders and landlords, virtuosos in unscrupulous extortions. He is too feeble to protest, for he may be turned out of his land in favour of the more willing. The main theme is well known, and I shall not belabour it. The conclusion is inescapable; unless the agrarian relations are reorganized, little progress can be expected.

As pointed out earlier, much has been talked about our land reforms. Big landlords or intermediaries have been more or less abolished, but as

[19] Professor K. N. Raj, in his lectures to the Indian Council of World Affairs in 1964, pointedly drew attention to the institutional factors which hold back agricultural progress. See his "Development and Economic Policy-I" in the *Mainstream*, Vol. III, No. 6, October 10, 1964.

we all know, these touched a small part of the agrarian society. The bulk of our peasantry consists of landless agricultural labourers and dwarf-holding labourers or small-holding tenants. After fifteen years of public devotion to land reforms we have little success to report about any major change in their position—a change which would alter their outlook of helplessness. Laws have been passed, but the unlettered farmer has neither the ability, nor the knowledge, nor the means to defend himself against the conflicting interpretation of cleverly-drafted clauses. He often gets himself caught in the legal mesh, from which he is unable to extricate himself.

In the slow agricultural progress of the country, the strong advocates of land reforms see a full vindication of their view. But like the peasant, they find themselves helpless when faced with a balance of power in the country in which the legislation at the State level, often landlords themselves, stubbornly refuse to obliterate their vested interests. All this has left the protagonists of the land reforms sulky, frustrated and repeating the old arguments with renewed vigour.

On the other hand, the technocrat brushes aside these arguments as oldfashioned in the first place, and major land reforms not likely to be implemented under the present balance of power in any case. Why then wait, he asks impatiently, and suggests a rapid increase in the supplies of improved seeds, fertilizers, insecticides and so on. He imagines the farm as a factory where you put in a, b and c, gather a few hands to operate the machines and you would surely have the finished products coming off the lines.

There is much in these arguments which merits close consideration. But one essential element is apparently overlooked; a farm is not a factory, and a farmer not a worker and an entrepreneur (what a glorified term for the poor fellow) rolled into one; he has neither the fixity of tenure nor of income, nor much control over the fruits of his operations. Increase in the supplies of technical inputs without strengthening the base of the agrarian society to utilize them is likely to benefit only the rich and well-to-do peasants. Even when this would succeed in raising their agricultural output, its influence on widening the economic inequality in the countryside, creating a basis for social tension, and over the long run limiting the expansion of the rural market (a factor of major significance in the years to come) need not be overlooked.

So far we have treated the outlook, assumptions and arguments of the structuralists and the technocrats in two separate compartments. Up to an extent, this is not unjustified; but only up to an extent. The outlook of the structuralists is mainly determined by the vision of a fair and just society, and naturally they want to restore to the peasantry their fair place in a new society. Even when their arguments about the strict casual connection between a fundamental reform of the agrarian structure and its reflection in increased output may lack convincing content, there is little doubt that these sensitive elements, more than any other, reflect the whole body of our national and peasant's aspirations; they are closer to the feelings of the most neglected sectors and have become the reflectors and vehicles of the peasant's frustrations, discontent, uneasiness, agony and quite often their fury. These cannot be dismissed lightly, particularly when they concern at least half of our population.

The technocrats on the other hand have solid arguments in the simple mechanics of agricultural growth. Their aims are relatively short-term; to a people suffering from chronic food shortages, they sound like sweet music. More fertilizers, more other inputs, better seeds, regulated water supply; provide these to whoever wants them and there cannot but be an increase in output. Even if the immediate beneficiaries are the well-to-do farmers, there would at least be an increase in output; the resultant intensification of agricultural inequalities and longer-term problems leave them relatively unexcited. Impatiently, they often retort citing Keynes: "In the long run, we are all dead." And yet, sustained growth and structural transformation are essentially long-term problems, and planned socialist development—India's national objective—is not just output increases, though it requires it.

I have tried to present the issues as they apppear to me. And yet I wonder whether these are separate issues. There is perhaps need for some rethinking on the subject, and I would like you to bear with some of my thoughts before you label them in a hurry.

In the field of agriculture, possession of land was an important element in all forms of earlier proposals—whether it was to be allotted to the individual peasant as in the nineteenth-centry Europe, or it was to be nationalized and organized into collective farms or into communes as in the Soviet Union and the other socialist countries; between these two extremes, a number of propositions combining a selected mixture of the two with the particular conditions of the country concerned were advanced. At the same basis of all these was the conviction that the level of output was integrally related to the organization of agrarian relations; the view had at one time an iron-bound logic. But is it really true to say now that the history of agricultural growth over the last hundred years in various parts of the world has so far given a convincing answer to the exact form of organization of land relationships which is most conducive to the growth of output? We have examples of plantations owned by expatriates where labourers work under semi-serfdom; of Egyptian landlords only a few years ago working the rack-rented fellahins to semi-starvation; individual peasant proprietors; and individual collective farms or communes; among each of these forms of organization, we find units with the highest as well as the lowest level of productivity of the soil; it was the highest where the agricultural operations were modernized, and the lowest where they were not.

The main consideration, it would seem to me, is to devise a form of organization under which the techniques can be changed and inputs enlarged in the shortest possible time.

This then requires a peasant body which sees its own interests being served by rapid growth — that is, as the economist would term it, an organization of proper incentives; and the availability of new techniques in readily applicable forms (including the physical supplies of inputs). It is at this point where I feel the main considerations of the structuralists and the technocrats can perhaps converge. The former requires an assurance to the farmer of unhindered occupancy at well-defined fair cost (whether rent as a tenant or tax as an owner); and the latter the organization of supplies and the distribution of new inputs in right quantities, at the right time and on right terms[20].

I am not dwelling at length on the former, not because it is less important but mainly because it is an area in which there is a consensus of opinion. The task of its full and effective implementation is, however, not very far from complete and needs to be undertaken immediately.

The latter is a somewhat new consideration and may therefore be discussed in some detail. A really intensive agriculture in India requires a vast increase in inputs. For fertilizers alone, we have been thinking of raising the consumption from just about one-half million tons to over 20 million tons as rapidly as possible. And then there are other inputs, such as improved seeds, insecticides, weedicides, etc. All these will no doubt present major problems in the organization of their output and distribution.

Can we perhaps think in terms of the socialization of the provision of these agricultural inputs and the new agricultural techniques? The idea is to nationalize or socialize, as you may prefer, the process rather than the place (soil) of production. The extent of such socialization in the first instance would be controlled by the physical availabilities; but the distribution need no longer be determined by the financial or other resources of the individual farmer—whether large or small, rich or poor, producing the necessary crops or not. This being a new area, socializing it will not be faced with the same obstacles from the vested interests, as, say, in socializing trade in foodgrains.

As remarked earlier, only 15 out of 355 districts are reported to produce one-third of the marketable surplus of grain, and around one-half of the cultivated area produces at least two-thirds of our output. These dictate a strategy of a concentrated rather than a scattered application of new inputs.

It is well known that the maximum benefit from the new techniques can be derived only when they are used in combination at concentrated points. Improved seeds, a minimum application of 80 to 100 kg. of plant nutrients per hectare, deeper ploughing, thicker sowing, adequate weed-

[20] For details see National Council of Applied Economic Research, *Factors Affecting Fertilizer Consumption: Problems and Policies* (New Delhi, 1964).

ing, timely water use, proper pest control, timely harvesting and proper processing and storing—all these main elements in the new agricultural techniques have to be tried together. Without that, the experience in many countries suggests that the results are far from satisfactory.[21]

But the concentrated use is something which we are not doing in India. Once the fertilizers are produced or imported and distributed, it is entirely up to any individual farmer to use them any way he pleases. The results usually are not worth the social cost of procuring these new inputs, which being scarce in supplies and highly productive in their impact on output command, as the economists would say, a much higher "shadow price".

A socialization of the distribution of the new inputs at once offers the possibility of concentrating them at the right place, under the right technical conditions and thus deriving the maximum national benefit. At the same time, such a policy ensures that they are not used at random by the well-to-do peasants only, who can afford them, and thus succeed in raising their relative level of income. Our present policy provides more to those who already have, and not the other way round if the objective of removing the inequalities of income is to be taken seriously. The policy suggested here would seem to serve at the same time interests of a higher output and of socialization of the process of production.

The experience in India clearly shows that the productivity of the soil does not rise with the size of the farm. Thus, there is no technical or economic reason for the farmer with a larger farm and higher means to get for his exclusive use and benefit the scarce supplies of the new inputs. These, as emphasized earlier as the active agents of raising agricultural output, should be used with the maximum national benefit in mind.

There are many problems connected with organizing the distribution of these supplies; the particular agency to be used, the terms of credit, etc. All these require careful consideration. The main purpose of socialization, however, is to achieve their concentration at the desired points and on the desired crops on the one hand, and eliminating an individual farmer's strong economic or social position as the basis for acquiring much of the scarce growth-stimulating inputs. The coverage of socialized distribution can be extended as the supplies improve.

Can this be done? There would of course be administrative and financial problems, and these need to be thought out in detail. But let me point out that the development blocks "covering almost the entire rural area of the country" now number over 5,000; and these are being geared to serve as vehicles "for increasing output".[22] Without being

[21] For details see ECE, *Economic Survey of Europe in* 1959, Chapter vii, pp. 15-19, 46-50.

[22] Government of India, *The Third Plan: Mid-term Appraisal* (New Delhi, 1963), p. 85.

sure whether they are so far effective towards this end, can it be suggested that these be turned into instruments for increasing output and that the socialized distribution of inputs be carried through them—from concentrated points in the initial phase to expanding their spread as the supplies rise? This is only a suggestion for consideration; there may be other ways of achieving these ends more effectively.

There is one consideration to which I should draw attention. While a socialization of inputs would strengthen the position of weak farmers, their concentration in the early phase would lead to accentuating regional disparities of agricultural income, particularly if this were to take place in only one or two states in the beginning. But we have suggested a very rapid expansion of the supplies, and it should soon be possible to assure more balanced state-wise—yet concentrated district-wise—distribution. Even then, there is little doubt that areas with irrigation facilities and assured rainfall would no doubt benefit more than the other ones, where water supplies are generally limited. It would necessitate consideration at a national level of directing some of the other investment funds—say for industrial development—to areas which would suffer from relative "neglect" in agricultural development.

But the policy of socialization of inputs would seem to serve both the overall national interest of maximum benefit from existing limited supplies and of the creation of a more just and egalitarian framework which is a pre-requisite for a rapid upsurge of agricultural output. I must emphasize however that this is only a suggestion for your consideration.

4

RELIANCE ON RICH FARMERS FOR DEVELOPMENT: ITS IMPLICATIONS

A. R. Desai

The present paper attempts, in a very broad manner, to analyse the character of changes that have been taking place in underdeveloped but developing countries of Asia after the end of World War II. It attempts to locate the trends of changes as revealed in those countries which have liberated themselves from European colonial rule and have been trying to refashion their economies and their social structures with a view to accelerating their overall development. The analysis is restricted to those countries which after liberation have chosen to develop broadly on capitalist lines through the operation of functional plans and not on the basis of centralised structural plans and on socialist lines. Thus the paper excludes the analysis of changes that have been taking place in countries like China, North Korea, North Viet Nam and others.

With a view to appreciating the nature of changes that are taking place in the countries of Asia it is necessary to have, as a starting point, some preliminary background of these countries to locate and assess the changes.

II

Basic Features

The countries of Asia, barring Japan, till the end of the Second World War exhibited the following characteristics:

(A) All these countries were either directly ruled by European Imperialist countries like Britain, France, Holland, Belgium, Spain, Portugal and others or were indirectly regulated by them. These countries were kept predominantly as appendages of the western powers, operating as agrarian, raw material producing areas subserving the interests of the colonial masters. Some of the countries were turned into colonies round some important commodity like oil. The extraction, refinement and final processing of this commodity were largely the preserve of foreign oil monopolies. Some of the smaller countries produced commercial products like tea, coffee, jute, sugar, rubber or some mineral products. These products were grown mostly through large European owned estates organised in plantations. Barring a few which introduced improved, modern techniques of production, most of the estates carried on operations through small cultivators who were expected to grow the products and supply them to the plantation owners. The third group of Asiatic countries like India, Pakistan, Burma, Indonesia and others produced a wide variety of crops, basically food crops, and operated on the basis of nonmechanised, rimitive, inefficient family farm methods. These countries also included a small but growing sector of agrarian production concentrating on non-food commercial crops like cotton, jute, tea, coffee, oilseeds and a few others.

(B) The second feature of the colonial and semi-colonial Asiatic countries lay in the fact that they were deliberately kept agrarian and underdeveloped by the European rulers. Industrial development was not merely not permitted in these countries but was deliberately hampered. Development was permitted only in those sectors which either supplied the requirements of the foreign rulers or did not fundamentally challenge their commericial, industrial or financial empires. The limited commercial, financial and industrial development that was permitted was basically owned and manned by the branches of some of the important corporations of the European countries. Indigenous companies had a very subordinate position in the commercial, industrial and financial set-up of these countries. They were more in the nature of feeder groups attached to the giant European companies, or competed very unfavourably with them. The distorted and lopsided development of these countries, under the direct and indirect impact of foreign rulers, created a unique pattern of social development, exposed these countries to the influences of the western capitalist mode of social relationships, destroyed the peculiar type of equilibrium which existed, introduced capitalist economic relationships but only to a limited extent, created an indent on the agrarian social structure which disfigured it and made these countries a wild agrarian hinterland of foreign industry and foreign capitalist organisations and thus brought them into the vortex of modern economic relations without allowing the consequences of these trends to mature in the form of a fully industrialised society, with the agrarian sector as a healthy but subordinate part.

This feature has to be noted by scholars for two reasons. (1) The underdeveloped countries on the eve of their independence were not backward in the sense that they exhibited characteristics of old feudal traditional society. These countries were a part of the world capitalist colonial system and hence they had acquired distinctly new features. Their development now depended on different approaches and forces than the ones which operated to transform feudal Europe into capitalist industrial Europe. Unfortunately this distinction is ignored by a large number of scholars under the influence of the Rostow model of development. (2) This feature has to be noted for another reason: Many scholars try to discuss the problems of development of these underdeveloped countries on the assumption that forces like private incentive for profit, "betting on the richer sections" to take initiative and then spreading the improvement like an 'oil stain' are the only way to lift them to a developed stage. Their basic analysis operates within the framework of a concept of unilinear-evolutionary development. They presume that these countries are only lagging behind the developed countries in terms of time. They will pass through the same stages of development which Europe did during the last three hundred years.

These two major assumptions have coloured the approach of a large number of scholars and have made them oblivious to the fact that the underdeveloped countries are not the same as pre-capitalist underdeveloped feudal countries, but are the distorted, agrarian counterpart of the world capitalist system. They forget that these colonial and semi-colonial underdeveloped countries have been and are in a qualitatively different phase where the normal path of industrial development, as was pursued in West European countries, cannot be adopted as a means to bring them to a developed stage.

(C) The third feature of the underdeveloped colonial and semi-colonial countries is summed up in the observation that "in many non-western countries, the protracted colonial or semi-colonial expansion has not furthered, but retarded economic development". As Prof. Wertheim has indicated in his work *East-West Parallel*, "for many of those countries, the traits mentioned by Sauvy still apply: one-sided economic structure, high percentage of agriculturists, low standard of living and nutrition, low degree of mechanisation." Further this colonial and semi-colonial expansion has generated numerous currents which have upset the old pre-industrial sets of interactions. By not permitting industrial growth in those countries, it has 'petrified' many social institutions. However, by introducing money economy and exchange it has also disrupted many traditional bonds and values. It has transformed land into a commodity and thereby initiated a new stratification system by " mobilising landed property", thus destroying the traditional protection and security surrounding the individual. It has further led to the process of atomising and proletarianizing peasant population, with the consequent ferment among them in the competitive-capitalist matrix unparallelled even in their past histories. The colonial and semicolonial expansion by the European capitalist powers also led to the ruination of handicrafts and artisan industries. It has brought the agrarian economy and society, though lop-sidedly into the vortex of the world market. By preventing the growth of alternate occupations it has brought about excessive pressure on agriculture, leading to subdivision and fragmentation of land, transforming cultivable lands into tinier and tinier plots. It has forced agriculture to remain technically inefficient, incapable of utilising technological and scientific improvements, and operated predominantly by small peasants, tenants or landless labourers on uneconomic units of operational holdings. These processes, in the context of land becoming a commodity and the agrarian population being brought in the network of monetary transactions both for payment of revenue in cash and for other purposes, created a peculiar type of stratification, which was new to these countries and which had a tremendous impact on the trend of development in the agrarian sectors. Colonial and semi-colonial expansion had thus created problems of technical and institutional improvements in agriculture and also of removing the increasing pressure on agriculture. It also made rapid industrialisation of the countries imperative as a basic pre-requisite for absorbing a big proportion of rural population into secondary and tertiary occupations.

The above characteristics of the underdeveloped countries are the result of colonial and semi-colonial expansion of the western capitalist countries and therefore have to be viewed as peculiar to modern underdeveloped countries.

(D) The emergence of a new pattern of stratification in the agrarian area was another feature which developed in these countries as a result of these countries being shaped as colonial or semi-colonial territories. The colonial and semi-colonial policies created a peculiar class configuration in agrarian areas, composed of the following:

(1) *A class of proprietors of land* (*landlords*) composed of the following categories: (i) old feudal tribute gatherers transformed into absentee landlords; (ii) a new group of moneylenders and traders, who extended their grip over the crops, land and even persons of the agrarian population by providing loans and credit so necessary for farmers in the new setting; (iii) a small group of companies, or persons operating as plantation or mine owners, mostly composed of Europeans; (iv) a small group of rich farmers, which emerged in the context of growing market economy. However, it should be noted that the majority of even rich farmers, operated on small farms on the basis of family labour or by utilizing the cheap abundant labour of tenants or the agricultural proletariat.

(2) *A class of small peasants*, the majority of whom hold tiny, uneconomic holdings. The members of this class have been in the process of becoming poorer and poorer and of being transformed into tenants or landless labourers. They have been perpetually in debt. Having hardly any resources, or sufficient land, they could not undertake improvements in agriculture. This class of petty-peasants operating on small-uneconomic farms slowly grew into nearly eighty per cent of the total proprietary class in agrarian areas of Asia.

(3) *A class of tenant farmers*, operating as tenants on the land of proprietors. The majority of this class was composed of small, inefficient cultivators working on uneconomic holdings.

(4) *A growing class of agricultural labourers*, composed of those whose sources of livelihood was predominantly selling their labour, a class which has been growing during this period.

(5) *A fifth category of agrarian population* was composed of *ruined artisans and others* who eked out their livelihood in agrarian areas by

methods which defy imagination. This category also contained a large section of unemployed in the agrarian areas, who finding employment neither in rural areas nor in urban areas constituted a floating vegetating population.

This stratification developed as another peculiar feature in all colonial and semi-colonial countries of Asia on the eve of their independence from European powers. The proportion of small farmers, tenants, agricultural labourers and ruined artisans may vary from country to country, but they constitute the majority of the rural population in all the colonial and the semi-colonial countries. The group of big landlords or rich farmers constitute a very small minority in Asiatic countries. Within this group, the proportion of big absentee landlords, composed of feudal tribute gatherers, moneylenders or traders, has always been larger than that of rich farmers who cultivate or supervise cultivation and who in some cases make use of modern technical and scientific inputs.

All the Asiatic countries exhibit the abovementioned features in various degrees. These features have to be borne in mind if the changes in the character of agriculture after the Second World War, particularly after these countries secured independence from foreign rule are to be understood. We will now observe the changes in the character of agriculture taking place in the underdeveloped but developing countries of Asia. As pointed out earlier, we will restrict our observation to countries which have not taken the socialist path of developing their economy.

III

Major Approaches to Change

The leaderships of these underdeveloped countries have been trying to adopt various measures to bring about changes in their economic and social set-up. They are trying hard to elevate the state of their economy and social structure from one of underdevelopment to one of development. With a view to achieving this they have started various measures to bring about transformation in agriculture.

We will briefly indicate the types of changes that are being introduced. We will then take India as an illustration for pointing out how far these changes are being effected and with what consequences to the social structure.

The changes that are being brought about can be listed as follows:

(1) Changes brought about by making the technical basis of agriculture scientific and efficient. For instance, improved seeds, fertilizers, irrigation facilities through various major hydro-electrical projects and minor irrigation projects, supply of electricity, improved ploughs and other implements including even use of tractors where possible and other measures are being adopted in these countries, to raise the productivity of land and increase the quantity and improve the quality of agricultural production.

(2) Efforts to eliminate the subsistence orientation of production and to bring agricultural goods to wider and wider markets, by building roads, marketing facilities, standardizing weights and measures and creating facilities for marketing. Efforts are also being made to protect the agriculturists by price regulation.

(3) Efforts to change the class-relationships in the agrarian area, by land reforms and other institutional means. Measures to remove absentee feudal landlords, eliminate tenancy and curb the moneylenders are being adopted.

(4) Efforts to provide various agencies like co-operative societies, land mortgage banks and other institutions to enable peasants to combine, and to provide them with the necessary credit and marketing prerequisites for making their agriculture efficient.

(5) Efforts to introduce educational facilities as well as public health measures to improve the skills and general health of the population in agrarian areas. Efforts to regulate the birthrate by spreading ideas of family-planning and birth control techniques.

(6) Efforts to evolve new voluntary institutions and associations to generate a new approach and atmosphere in the traditional rural setting and to counteract the effects of petrified old social institutions and values.

(7) Efforts to industrialise the countries to supply alternative employment to the already surplus population as well as to the population that will be rendered superfluous as a result of improving technical efficiency of agriculture. In order to transform the agrarian colonial and semi-colonial underdeveloped countries into developed ones, it is necessary that the percentage of population dependent on agriculture be drastically reduced. At least fifty per cent of the population of the country must depend upon non-agricultural vocations. It means relieving agriculture of nearly 20 to 30 per cent of its operators and provision of alternative employment for them. Industrialisation, demands machinery and other capital goods. These countries are dependent for such capital goods on more advanced countries. This implies creating a surplus of agricultural production for export to discharge the interest and capital liabilities to these countries created as a result of importing these capital goods.

The leaderships of the countries we are concerned with here are trying to reconstruct the economies and societies of these countries on the basis of private enterprise, operating with the profit incentive as the motive of production. State intervention and participation in the economy and social life is more to create adequate facilities or generate a regulative mechanism which would soften the ravages of unrestricted operation of the market mechanism in the context of imperfect and unequal competition. The object of the state intervention is not to supplant the competitive system,

The rich farmer is conceived as the lynchpin of agrarian development by the leaders of these countries. According to these leaderships the progressive rich farmer would initiate the great transformation in agricultural production. The fundamental strategy in all the underdeveloped countries, is to create conditions for helping rich farmers as the key figures of agrarian transformation. The rich farmer is the pivot round which the entire strategy of agrarian reforms has been developing. Even in the context of the total developmental schemes, the rich farmer is depended on to usher in new technical scientific agriculture as well as generate capital formation in the countryside. The leaderships of these countries, who are worried about the take-off problem, tend to look upon rich farmers as specific agents for introducing the innovations wanted. As Professor Wertheim has pointed out: "It is the advanced farmers who are almost automatically being selected as such. It is they who show a greater responsiveness to all kinds of innovations and technical improvements, and who are much easier to approach for governmental agencies and special services. Such an approach starts implicitly from the assumption that advanced farmers will set an example to the poorer sections, who are expected to follow the model which they are able to observe from close by. The innovation is intended to spread like an oil-stain, to other layers of rural society. It is this approach which could be called 'betting on the strong'."

The "progressive rich farmers" is the agent through whom agrarian innovations have to be launched. This is the fundamental strategy in all underdeveloped countries like India, Indonesia and others under the leaderships of non-communist governments. We will observe the changes in the character of agriculture in Asia that have been taking place during the last fifteen years by taking India as the example. India is among the most densely populated of these countries. She contains nearly half the population of this part of Asia. She is conducting experiments to change the rural areas on the basis of an organised conscious effort reflected through its plans. We will observe the changes that have taken place in India after independence and draw a few conclusions of a sociological nature for further discussion.

IV

India is second-most populous country of the world. According to the 1961 census the country's population is 43,90,72,893. The average density of population was 312 per square mile in 1951 while it has become 370 per square mile in 1961. "The births have occurred at an average rate of 40 per thousand per annum, deaths at an average rate of 27 per thousand per annum and the natural increase of population at an average rate of 13 per thousand per annum." Out of the total population of India in 1951, 82·7 per cent lived in rural areas and 17·3 per cent in urban areas. In 1961, after 10 years of planning, 82 per cent lived in villages and 18 per cent in urban areas. It can be easily seen that a decade of planning has not made a major dent on the percentage of population living in rural areas. About 70 per cent of the people depend for their livelihood on land and agriculture and ancillary activities account for half the country's national income.

India ranks first in the world in the production of groundnuts and tea and enjoys a virtual monopoly in the production of lac. It is the second largest producer of rice, jute, raw sugar, rapeseed, sesamum and castor seed. Out of the total geographical area of the country of 80·63 crore acres the net area sown in 1950-51 was 29·34 crore acres and in 1958-59 it was 32 crore acres. Out of this area 3·25 crore acres were sown more than once in 1950-51; this proportion rose to 4·87 crore acres in 1958-59. The area irrigated is 16·1 of the total area in cultivation. Between the period 1951 to 1959 there was an increase of 68 lakhs acres in net irrigated area. That nearly 84 per cent of the area sown was unirrigated and dependent mainly on rains deserves to be noted. The decade of planning has increased the proportion of irrigated area by a very small percentage. This is another feature worth noting. About 75 per cent of the total sown area is under food crops. It is also interesting to observe that the area growing non-food crops generally enjoys greater irrigation facilities. This point needs to be stressed because even after a decade of planning cultivation of crops remains largely on the same inefficient level. To meet the increased demand for food India has to import food from other countries. This is a peculiar situation. India, and probably most of the Asiatic countries, are increasingly becoming more and more dependent both for industrial goods and food supply on the industrialised countries.

That an agrarian country is unable to produce enough cereals for the population is itself indicative of the inefficient and backward modes of production in agriculture. The growing dependence for even cereals on foreign countries reveals that agriculture is not becoming efficient. Efforts to improve agricultural production by introducing improved implements, fertilizers, better seeds, irrigation facilities, insecticides and other methods have been to some extent extended. But the increase is comparatively negligible and affects only a very small area of cultivated land and the facilities are used by a small sector of rich farmers. We have observed how limited has been the spread of irrigation during the last fifteen years. Similarly the other modern inputs in agriculture are also applied on a very small scale. Further they are utilised more in the growth of commercial crops and by richer farmers who can afford to purchase them.

These observations are borne out by the following data gathered by the tenth and twelfth rounds of the National Sample Survey conducted during 1955 and 1957.

"In about 97 per cent of the villages tilling was done with the help of animals. Only 0·4 to 0·9 per cent of the villages had the power-driven system, whereas in 1·3 to 2·3 per cent of the villages the mixed system prevailed. Non-chemical manures (cow-dung, green manures, composts, etc.) were used in 64 per cent and 75 per cent respectively of the villages in the twelfth and eleventh rounds whereas chemical manures were used in only 0·1 per cent villages for each round.

"Chemical as well as non-chemical manures were used in 29 and 21 per cent, respectively, of the villages of these two rounds. As regards irrigation about 22 per cent of the villages received water from wells, about 10 to 12 per cent of the villages received canal and river water, about 6 to 8 per cent from tanks and a few others from tube wells and anicuts. In about 21 per cent of the villages, the mixed system of irrigation was in vogue. Thirty-four to 36 per cent of the villages had none of these systems of irrigation and probably had to depend on rains for watering the fields."

The above figures indicate that technical improvement of agriculture is proceeding at a very slow rate. A decade of planning has not made a very appreciable indent on the technical efficiency of agricultural production. With a view to understanding the character of changes in agriculture we should also take note of the peculiar type of stratification which has been growing under the Plans.

According to the eighth round of the National Sample Survey "over one-fifth (23 per cent), that is about one and a half crores of households, did not own any land. About a quarter of all rural households (24 per cent) had land less than one acre. A little less than half of the rural households had thus either no land or owned less than one acre, their share being only a little more than one per cent of the land owned by all rural households. About three-fourths of all households had either no land or less than 5 acres and their share was about one-sixth of the area. At the other end, about one-eighth of the households had more than 10 acres each, with a total share of about two-thirds of the whole area, and about one per cent of the households owned more than 50 acres each and together accounted for nearly one-fifth of the area."

That nearly half the cultivators of India have become almost landless destroys the image created of India as a land of peasant proprietors. Nearly 75 per cent of the cultivators own less than 5 acres of land and the fact that a large proportion of the cultivated lands are dry lands having single crop and limited irrigational facilities means that even the 25 per cent of cultivators who own between one and five acres are uneconomic peasants. Even among the 25 per cent of the cultivators who own more than 5 acres of land, hardly 10 per cent could come within the category of groups having sufficient land to produce profitably.

V

Implications of Relying on the Rich Farmer

The leaderships in the underdeveloped countries of Asia are adopting various measures to improve agriculture. But these measures have benefitted and strengthened only a small rich section of the agrarian population. This class has been thriving (in the context of the competitive, profit-oriented, market-based framework) at the cost of the uneconomic farmers. This class has been benefiting by ousting the rest of the poor peasants. This class is pushing out a large section of poor peasants and even landless labourers from the ambit of profitable economic relationships. The Plans, by strengthening the rich farmers, by relying upon these farmers to improve agriculture, are actually generating a process of disintegration, ruination, pauperization and proletarianization of the vast majority of agriculturists. The presence of the large numbers of unemployed makes labour abundantly cheap, and in the context of the family farm as the unit of agriculture leaves little incentive even to the rich landlords to introduce technical improvements in production. Thus the Plans by helping the rich farmers have been indirectly creating the very condition for preventing the use of technical innovations. During a decade and a half of planning on the basis of making rich farmers the lynchpin of agrarian development, the leaderships in these underdeveloped areas have started not developmental currents in their economic and social systems but what Prof. Wertheim calls "involutionary trends" which are likely to inaugurate a new epoch of tensions and explosions. A developmental pattern based on "betting on the poor" is essential if these involutionary trends are to be halted.

A proper sociological understanding of the various aspects of change in the character of agriculture in Asiatic countries is possible only if the implications of reliance upon richer farmers are appreciated. In the context of an ocean of poor peasants operating on miserably uneconomic holdings an ever-growing number of landless labourers and ruined artisans and a vast backlog of unemployed and underemployed, the significance of strengthening the rich require more careful scrutiny. This is the crucial sociological inquiry that is needed.

Proper understanding of the implications of relying on rich farmers is necessary for another reason. The richer landowing groups in various Asiatic countries come from certain upper castes or certain regional, racial or religious groups, while landless labourers, small farmers and ruined artisans belong to lower castes or specific regional or religious or racial groups. The efforts to boost the richer landowing groups may have far-reaching consequences in terms of strengthening certain castes or religious, regional or racial groups. The economic tensions may as a consequence lead to social, religious, regional and racial tensions.

A proper study of the social impact of the change in character of agriculture should begin with examination of the implications of the major assumption of "relying on rich farmer" which is at the centre of all efforts to develop agriculture in the developing countries of Asia.

5

BETTING ON THE STRONG*

W. F. WERTHEIM

THE DIFFICULTY of bringing about a 'take-off' in the non-Western world is realized more and more clearly by modern economists. The impossibility of simply copying the Western model of economic development is hardly challenged any more. It is the omnipresent rural poverty combined with a rapid natural increase which reduce to nought any attempt at bringing about a take-off by conventional means. Even the numerous economists who do not share the pessimistic outlook of the late Professor J. H. Boeke as to the capacity of Asian societies to overcome the present impasse, have to acknowledge the 'vicious circle' character of the actual state of the rural economy. Radical innovations are needed to increase agricultural *per capita* production. But poverty and ignorance are severe impediments to introducing innovations. Lack of response from the poor masses to all well-intentioned governmental measures is among the most serious obstacles to economic development.

This is why many of those who are seriously concerned with the 'take-off' problem tend to look for specific agents for introducing the innovations wanted. It is the more advanced farmers who are almost automatically being selected as such. It is they who show a greater responsiveness to all kinds of innovations and technical improvements and who are much easier to approach for government agencies or special services. Such an approach starts implicitly from the assumption that the advanced farmers will set an example to the poorer sections, who are expected to follow the model which they are able to observe from close by. The innovation is intended to spread, like an oil-stain, to other layers of rural society.

It is this approach which could be called: ***betting on the strong.***

It is obvious, that the underlying philosophy of this approach is an inherent belief in gradual evolution. It is assumed that the process of spreading knowledge and technical progress cannot be but a gradual one, and that the best agents for this evolutionary process have to be looked for among the most advanced individuals in rural society. In the village sphere this group generally consists of those well-to-do farmers who have enjoyed sufficient education or had enough contacts with urban elements to respond positively to all kinds of suggestions for the improvement of their production techniques.

---

*Reproduced from *East-West Parallels* by W. F. Wertheim, pp. 259-277.

In the former Saurashtra State in Western India even a special registration of so-called 'progressive farmers' had been introduced, as the prospective agents of a Community Development Scheme. I quote from an official government report:

A Progressive Farmer should:

(1) possess at least 2 acres of land for irrigation and eight acres of land for dry farming and if irrigation is not possible in any area, he should have 16 acres of land for dry farming;

(2) have at least one pair of good bullocks;

(3) have at least one cow preferably of good Gir breed or of local breed or he should arrange to have one as early as possible in case he has none;

(4) have planted at least five trees on his farm or should have given an assurance of doing so at the earliest;

(5) have dug at least two systematic compost pits either on his *wadi* of field, or he should give an assurance of doing so at the earliest;

(6) have taken all possible measures to prevent erosion of his land;

(7) have adopted improved agricultural practices by taking advantage of agricultural research;

(8) be a member of any one cooperative society or should enrol himself as such within a year of his having been registered as a progressive farmer; and

(9) use improved and selected variety of seeds for sowing.

These progressive farmers were afforded preferential treatment by the governmental services.

Progressive farmers should...be given preference in the matter of supply of improved seeds, fertilizers, technical advice and guidance and other facilities available from the State. Every progressive farmer will thus serve as an experimental and research centre spread all over the rural areas, and will be an effective instrument of propagating improved agricultural practices. Such a scheme has certain definite advantages over any scheme worked by the department in that the agriculturist will have greater faith and confidence in the results obtained on the fields of his fellow-cultivators which he will readily adopt.

The special reliance on the 'progressive' farmer is typical of the general Indian approach to rural society. Dube also found, in his survey of the Community Development Scheme as applied in a certain village, that the Project hoped to be able to work intimately with a smaller group of individuals who were expected to function as local agents of change. For this purpose persons occupying existing positions of leadership in the village as well as traditional leaders were to be used. The underlying assumption in this approach was that if leaders could first be converted to the ideology of change, the task of converting the rest of the community would be greatly facilitated. Implied in this assumption was the belief that people normally looked to this group for guidance and would automatically start emulating their example once they adopted the new practices. It was also hoped that by making them a link between the officials and the people some of the difficulties in communication would be appreciably reduced.

Dube also points out, that among those included in the category of 'traditional leaders' were the important and influential people in the village. Naturally most of them were from the dominant land-owning groups.

I remember once having read that an Indian writer divided the rural people into two types: the hens and the ducks. The hens are those, who run, who are 'progressive'. The ducks are the mass of the people. They move slowly and heavily. The Indian authorities rely on the hens: they are *betting on the strong*.

The *betting on the strong* principle has been, for a long time, a controversial issue in the literature devoted to Indonesian economics. In his doctoral dissertation of 1910 based on printed sources and not on personal experience in the colony, J. H. Boeke had expressed a distrust of the 'well-to-do Natives', among whom many *hadjis*, as agents for economic development. Their progress would only amount to a situation in which 'the rich grow richer and the poor grow poorer'.

Paradoxically enough, Boeke himself, after a prolonged stay in Indonesia, reversed his stand in 1927. At that time he did not see any possibility of promoting native welfare except through the intermediary of a small elite, consisting of 'the vigorous, energetic, advanced elements' in Indonesian rural society. These wealthier landowners working their way upwards should not be blackened and branded as usurers and bloodsuckers.

These elements of rural society should be approached by the specialized welfare agencies in a way which Boeke called 'person-centered'. Not compulsion, but patient persuasion should be the method used by the welfare agencies; and the effort should not be directed towards the poor masses, in order to get certain 'objects' done, but towards individuals differentiating themselves from the mass by certain personal qualities. The basic assumption, is, evidently, that the improvement of native welfare cannot be but slow, gradual process. The person-centered welfare policy should be led, above all, by 'faith and patience'.

At the time when Boeke expressed these thoughts, the Agricultural Extension Service in the Netherlands East Indies had already embarked upon a policy which was also primarily directed towards the more advanced farmers, whose example was expected to spread automatically, according to what was called an 'oil-stain system'.

It is of minor importance that Boeke, adding a new paradox to the existing one, appears in his later publications to have reversed his stand once more. Promoting the economic welfare of the masses did not seem to him to be any longer within the range of human possibilities, when he, in 1948, declared the poverty of the masses of Asia unchangeable, at least as far as the densely populated areas are concerned. Probably this explains why also the gradualistic approach to rural society, via well-to do advanced farmers, no longer occupies an essential part in his later publications.

What matters more is how the oil-stain approach, actually applied by the Agricultural Extension Service in Indonesia, worked out in practice. The fruits of such a policy, as recorded by H. Ten Dam in a study of Western Java village Tjibodas, are far from promising. In this village it is with the large landowners–comprising roughly one and a half *per cent* of the total village population—that the representatives of the government agencies came into personal contact. It is they who profited most from all kinds of facilities provided by the Agricultural Extension Service. It is they who, through a co-operative society in which they had the largest stakes, got artificial fertilizers and chemical preparations, needed for the cultivation of profitable commercial crops, such as potatoes and cabbage, at prices set by the Extension Service.

There was a group of smaller independent farmers with economic holding, of whom a number attempted to follow the example of large landowners. If they grew cabbage and potatoes, their profits were frequently lower than those of the large landowners since they had to pay higher commercial prices for fertilizers and chemicals. The prices they had to pay for these items were excessive because they obtained them from large landowners, who in turn bought them at reduced prices from the Extension Service.

But even when taken together, the large landowners and the independent farmers do not exceed ten per cent of the total village population. The great majority, the farm hands and the part time farmers with uneconomic holdings who have to work for the larger landowners as wage labourers or share-croppers, do not profit at all from the manifold innovations introduced in local agriculture. They simply lack the amount of land and the capital needed for imitating the farming methods introduced by the Extension Service. The oil-stain stops at the ten per cent level. Ten Dam even mentions the possibility that the farm hands are worse off since the creation of the co-operative, 'since relations with the co-operative are much more businesslike and impersonal than the master-servant relations between a farmer and his hired hands'.

Tjibodas is certainly an extreme case in certain respects. In most other villages of Java the percentage of landless people and of peasants with uneconomic holdings is decidedly lower, and the antithesis between the landed and the landless may be less sharp. But the general tendency pointed out by Ten Dam, is manifest in many parts of Java.

Boeke's prophecy, pronounced as early as 1910, appears to have come true: as a consequence of a policy of *betting on the strong* the rich grew richer and the poor grew, if not poorer, then at least more numerous—and more restive.

This is exactly what happened in India whenever the *betting on the strong* approach was attempted. Dube assesses the results of the Community Development Project in the villages investigated by him, as far as the agricultural extension work is concerned, as follows:

A closer analysis of the agricultural extension work itself reveals that nearly 70 per cent of its benefits went to the *elite* group and to the more affluent and influential agriculturists. The gains to poorer agriculturists were considerably smaller. Being suspicious of government officials they did not seek help from the Project as often. As this group had little influence in the village and outside, and was in no position to offer any material help in the furtherance of Project objectives, the officials largely ignored it. For the economic development of this group, as well as for that of the artisans and agricultural labourers, no programmes were initiated by the Project.

Dube points out the mistake inherent in the assumption that 'progressive farmers' would be the 'accepted leaders' of village society. The village looked to them for guidance in its general relationship with the urban areas and the officials, and their help was sought in legal matters, in contacting and influencing officials, and generally in facing problems that arise out of contact between the village and the outside world. They were not necessarily looked upon as leaders in agriculture, nor were they in any sense decision makers in many vital matters concerning the individual and his family. Because of their association with the officials and the urban ways of life these leaders as a group had come to possess a special status within the community, but the average villager did not trust them without reservations.

Since most of these 'traditional leaders' chosen as a link between the officials and the people were from the dominant landowing group, the undue emphasis in working with 'traditional leaders' was construed by some villagers as an effort on the part of the government to maintain a *status quo* in the internal power relations within village communities and indirectly as a step to support the domination of the landowing groups. Thus the policy of the government on the subject of leadership seemed contradictory and confusing.

But the main obstacle to the oil-stain effect can be reduced to the obvious cause that following the example of the 'progressive farmers' presupposes the possession of sufficient land and capital, besides the required 'progressive' outlook and a mental preparedness to follow the example of the 'strong'. Those possessing uneconomic holdings are excluded anyway from that possibility. They are more likely to be forced, in the long run, to sell their holdings in order to pay off debts. The larger landowners, profiting from technical innovations, may be tempted to extend their holdings; a ' progressive ' outlook as far as farming technique is concerned, is by no means a guarantee for a 'progressive' outlook as far as principles of social justice are concerned.

The prospect is still more complicated by the existence of a large category of landless farm hands. Can they be expected to profit from the improvements in farming techniques, introduced by their wealthier master-landowners ? First, it is not at all certain that the larger landowners working with paid labour will be among those readily accepting innovations. According to Dube, ' most substantial landowners, until recently, did not take enough personal interest in what was being done in their fields. The work was largely left to unskilled labourers, who preferred working along traditional lines.' But even apart from that, in a situation in which there is no dearth of cheap labour, the type of improvement profitable for a landowner will at best aim at increasing the productivity per acre; there is no incentive at all to increase *per capita* production. And if the production per acre is being raised, it is not at all certain, that real wages for the landless labourers (or the shares for the sharecroppers, where such sharecropping contracts are legally allowed or illegally practised) will reflect the upward trend of production. There is a wealth of evidence to indicate that on the average real wages in rural India have not appreciably increased since independence. Over against certain local increases of rural employment opportunities, largely as a consequence of the introduction of irrigation works, we have to take account not only of the strong social, political and economic position of the land-owning castes in the countryside, but of the rapid natural increase of the population in the rural areas.

Only by absorbing most of the natural increase of the rural population in non-agricultural occupations could a mounting productivity per surface area, in the long run, be turned into higher real wages for agricultural labour, through a raising of *per capita* production. In order to make mechanization of agriculture profitable the absolute number of people dependent on agriculture would even have to be reduced, except inasfar as a reclamation of waste lands could increase the total cultivated area. But even the former condition—an approximately stationary population engaged in farming—is far from being realized in most parts of India, since urbanization and industrialization are developing much too slowly to be able considerably to reduce the percentage of the total population employed in agriculture, let alone to absorb the natural increase.

It has been suggested that, for some decades before the war, ' the farms appear to have retained an approximately constant or slightly increasing proportion of the population'. And as far as available sources indicate, after a period of accelerated migration to urban centres during the war and the partition disturbances, the percentage of urban population in relation to total population has again remained nearly constant in the period 1951-1961. And it is not very likely that in the Indian villages the percentage of those primarily dependent on agriculture would have been appreciably reduced during that period.

The conclusion to be drawn from this constellation is obvious. Modern farm techniques are not likely to spread in a situation in which cheap agricultural labour is abundant. The gains to be derived from 'community development' largely aimed at the 'progressive farmers' will predominantly accrue to a restricted landowning group. A *betting on the strong* policy is likely to amount to a policy of *the devil take the hindmost.* In countries where these 'hindmost' are restricted in numbers, a large proportion of them may be driven away from the countryside to seek employment in an urban sphere; the remaining ones may, if they are not too numerous in comparison with the land surface available for cultivation, profit in the long run from the increased productivity per surface area and eventually learn improved farming techniques from the more prosperous farmers.

But in countries where the 'hindmost' form a large majority, either as peasants with uneconomic holdings or as landless labourers, the *betting on the strong* policy cannot work. The large masses of the rural population are, for the time being, tied to their traditional rural occupations as farm hands or sharecroppers, which means that a gradual oilstain-like spread of modern farming techniques to them is out of the question. These poor masses form a drag upon any attempt to solve the rural problem in a gradual way. Tarlok Singh recognizes that the Indian Five-Year Plans 'were weak in dealing with the problem of landless labour, but it was thought that with the growth of the economy as a whole, increase in the productivity of land, development of cooperation and changes in the agrarian structure, this problem might become more manageable.' In actual fact this proved to be a miscalculation. The problem has become less and less manageable, since this neglected sector had a stagnating effect upon the whole economy.

Where the actual trend could, rightly, be termed one of 'involution', a policy based on evolutionary principles is bound to fail.

The underlying philosophy of the Indian Community Development Program has been aptly circumscribed by Phillips Ruopp:

The development differs radically from the cataclysmic, with the latter's delusive appeals to violent action. Development is gradual, but it is not a gradualness that lends itself as an excuse for inaction. It means growth, but it must be growth cultivated by unequivocal and constant witness to justice, liberty, and compassion.

On the basis of the foregoing analysis we should reconsider this thesis in the light of actual experience in countries like Indonesia and India, which shows that a 'pre-take-off' situation is not necessarily one of 'accelerated development' but sometimes rather the reverse.

The inappropriateness of the *betting on the strong* principle finds a fitting parallel in international economics. Britain was the first country to develop modern industry. It aspired to becoming 'the workshop of the world'. Far from actively supporting the other countries' attempt at following its example, it tried to prevent the spread of industry. Any effort at industrial development outside Britain had to be achieved by a long term policy aimed at outdoing Britain's initial advantage and at protecting the newcomer's home industry against foreign competition. This is the way Germany, the United States, and Canada succeeded in building up an economic apparatus of similar strength as Britain. Instead of *betting on the strong*, in international economics *betting on the backward* appeared a more promising policy to make the backward strong. If the *betting on the strong* principle held true, it would amount, on a world scale, to further developing the already developed countries under the assumption that the thus acquired economic potential would automatically spread to the underdeveloped part of the world and that the backward countries would be able to follow the example of the developed ones.

Actual developments prove, time and again, that no automatical spread of the industrial potential to the underdeveloped part of the world is bound to occur. Despite a prevailing official international ideology stressing aid to be extended by developed countries to the underdeveloped ones, in actual practice the industrial world has not shown any great desire actively to promote the industrial advancement of the non-industrial world—though the experience in the Western world should have made clear long ago that the dwellers of a modern industrial country are, in the long run, far better customers for industrial goods than an impoverished peasantry. The gap between the price level of industrial goods and of raw materials has tended to increase since the end of the Second World War, and at the same time the cleavage between the welfare level of the industrial and the non-industrial world, if anything, has widened even further. The term 'countries in a process of accelerated development' amounts to a euphemism. If 'automatism' is allowed to work, the only effect is, as in the Asian countryside, that the rich become richer and the poor become, if not poorer, then much more numerous—and much more restive. No advanced country is willing to part with its monopolistic advantages, in the same sense as no advanced farmer is prepared to part with his virtual monopoly in the realm of agriculture.

The analogy extends still further: in the cases in which non-industrial countries have succeeded in releasing a true take-off, they have done so largely on their own strength and with limited foreign assistance. In order to achieve this end, they had to curb the power of those foreign interests which were interested in essentially preserving the *status quo*. The amount of state interference needed to achieve a certain amount of autarchy and economic independence has considerably risen since the first competitors of Britain started on the road towards industrial development. The industrial revolution in Russia, the only major country which has thus far completed a take-off in the twentieth century, was even accompanied with a political and social revolution of an unprecedented magnitude. Only by a complete overhaul of the existing social structure and by an all-out mustering of the potential productive forces could the backwardness of the Russian economy be overcome. And the amount of directed planning, revolutionary zeal, lasting endurance, and inventive capacity needed to effectuate a true take-off in China appears again by far to exceed all previous instances.

The parallel with the agrarian situation in Asian countries seems obvious. If an evolutionary way out of the agrarian impasse is blocked because of involuntary tendencies, only a revolutionary response to the existing challenge seems appropriate. No more than in the realm of overall industrial development is an evolutionary course in the Asian countryside, via capitalistic enterprise, within the range of possibilities. Those who tend to view the formation of a class of capitalistic farmers as a pre-condition for further advances on the road to socialism and collectivism overlook the true character of the 'dialectics of progress'.

...Without a radical social revolution no progress in the economic field can be achieved. In this revolution an essential role has to be played by the poor peasantry.

...It would be perilous to speculate about the ultimate shape which the agrarian revolutions in Asian countries will assume. It is probable that the actual content of each revolutionary development will depend on the special rural and political conditions in the relative country and on the time factor, that is to say, on the moment when the revolutionary movement will occur. But this much could be stated, that the pre-condition to such an agrarian revolution will be the elimination of the well-to-do farmers as a power group. No truly effective agrarian reforms or co-operative movements will be possible if these *kulak* are allowed to counteract or dodge the reforms, or to compete with the co-operative society. Because of their strength they are dangerous to any movement pursuing a policy which aims at improvement of the living conditions for those who form the poor majority in the village...

Betting on the strong is bound to fail in the prevailing conditions of most countries of Asia. The policy to be pursued instead is one of *betting on the many*—who will be made strong, mainly through organization and intensive education toward efficiency and self-reliance.

But only through a grasp of the basic idea of the dialectics of progress could be acquired a firm belief that the backward masses actually are a potential strength; and that they will soon be able to outdo the former *kulak* not only in devotion to society but in technical and administrative ability as well. Since the beginning of the twentieth century throughout the non-Western world those who are *betting on the many*, that is to say, who truly believe in human beings and promote their emancipation from all kinds of bondages, are patently on the winning side.

6

THE POLITICAL ECONOMY OF BACKWARDNESS*

PAUL A. BARAN

THE CAPITALIST mode of production and the social and political order concomitant with it provided, during the latter part of the eighteenth century, and still more during the entire nineteenth century, a framework for a continuous and, in spite of cyclical disturbances and setbacks, momentous expansion of productivity and material welfare. The relevant facts are well known and call for no elaboration. Yet this material (and cultural) progress was not only spotty in time but most unevenly distributed in space. It was confined to the Western world; and did not affect even all of this territorially and demographically relatively small sector of the inhabited globe. Germany and Austria, Britain and France, some smaller countries in Western Europe, and the United States and Canada occupied places in the neighbourhood of the sun. The vast expanses and the multitude of inhabitants of Eastern Europe, Spain and Portugal, Italy and the Balkans, Latin America and Asia, not to speak of Africa, remained in the deep shadow of backwardness and squalor, of stagnation and misery.

Tardy and skimpy as the benefits of capitalism may have been with respect to the lower classes even in most of the leading industrial countries, they were all but negligible in the less privileged parts of the world. There productivity remained low, and rapid increases in population pushed living standards from bad to worse. The dreams of the prophets of capitalist harmony remained on paper. Capital either did not move from countries where its marginal productivity was low to countries where it could be expected to be high, or if it did, it moved there mainly in order to extract profits from backward countries that frequently accounted for a lion's share of the increments in total output caused by the *original* investments. Where an increase in the aggregate national product of an underdeveloped country took place, the existing distribution of income prevented this increment from raising the living standards of the broad masses of the population. Like all general statements, this one is obviously open to criticism based on particular cases. There were, no doubt, colonies and dependencies where the populations profited from inflow of foreign capital. These benefits, however, were few and far between, while exploitation and stagnation were the prevailing rule.

But if Western capitalism failed to improve materially the lot of the

* *The Manchester School*, January 1952. Reprinted by permission of The Manchester School and the author.

peoples inhabiting most backward areas, it accomplished something that profoundly affected the social and political conditions in underdeveloped countries. It introduced there, with amazing rapidity, all the economic and social tensions inherent in the capitalist order. It effectively disrupted whatever was left of the 'feudal' coherence of the backward societies. It substituted market contracts for such paternalistic relationships as still survived from century to century. It reoriented the partly or wholly self-sufficient economies of agricultural countries towards the production of marketable commodities. It linked their economic fate with the vagaries of the world market and connected it with the fever curve of international price movements.

A complete substitution of capitalist market rationality for the rigidities of feudal or semi-feudal servitude would have represented, in spite of all the pains of transition, an important step in the direction of progress. Yet all that happened was that the age-old exploitation of the population of underdeveloped countries by their domestic overlords, was freed of the mitigating constraints inherited from the feudal tradition. This superimposition of business mores over ancient oppression by landed gentries resulted in compounded exploitation, more outrageous corruption, and more glaring injustice.

Nor is this by any means the end of the story. Such export of capital and capitalism as has taken place had not only far-reaching implications of a social nature. It was accompanied by important physical and technical processes. Modern machines and products of advanced industries reached the poverty-stricken backyards of the world. To be sure most, if not all, of these machines worked for their foreign owners—or at least were believed by the population to be working for no one else—and the new refined appurtenances of the good life belonged to foreign businessmen and their domestic counterparts. The bonanza that was capitalism, the fullness of things that was modern industrial civilization, were crowding the display windows—they were protected by barbed wire from the anxious grip of the starving and desperate man in the street.

But they have drastically changed his outlook. Broadening and deepening his economic horizon, they aroused aspirations, envies, and hopes. Young intellectuals filled with zeal and patriotic devotion travelled from the underdeveloped lands to Berlin and London to Paris and New York, and returned home with the 'message of the possible'.

Fascinated by the advances and accomplishments observed in the centres of modern industry, they developed, and propagandized the image of what could be attained in their home countries under a more rational economic and social order. The dissatisfaction with the stagnation (or at best, barely perceptible growth) that ripened gradually under the still-calm political and social surface was given an articulate expression. This dissatisfaction was not nurtured by a comparison of reality with a vision of a socialist society. It found sufficient fuel in the confrontation of what was actually happening with what could be accomplished under capitalist institutions of the Western type.

The establishment of such institutions was, however, beyond the reach of the tiny middle classes of most backward areas. The inherited backwardness and poverty of their countries never gave them an opportunity to gather the economic strength, the insight, and the self-confidence needed for the assumption of a leading role in society. For centuries under feudal rule they themselves assimilated the political, moral, and cultural values of the dominating class.

While in advanced countries, such as France or Great Britain, the economically ascending middle-classes developed at an early stage a new rational world outlook, which they proudly opposed to the medieval obscurantism of the feudal age, the poor, fledgling bourgeoisie of the underdeveloped countries sought nothing but accommodation to the prevailing order. Living in societies based on privilege, they strove for a share in the existing sinecures. They made political and economic deals with their domestic feudal overlords or with powerful foreign investors, and what industry and commerce developed in backward areas in the course of the last hundred years was rapidly moulded in the straitjacket of monopoly—the plutocratic partner of the aristocratic rulers. What resulted was an economic and political amalgam combining the worst features of both worlds—feudalism and capitalism—and blocking effectively all possibilities of economic growth.

It is quite conceivable that a 'conservative' exit from this impasse might have been found in the course of time. A younger generation of enterprising and enlightened businessmen and intellectuals allied with moderate leaders of workers and peasants—a 'Young Turk' movement of some sort—might have succeeded in breaking the deadlock, in loosening the hide-bound social and political structure of their countries and in creating the institutional arrangements indispensable for a measure of social and economic progress.

Yet in our rapid age history accorded no time for such a gradual transition. Popular pressures for an amelioration of economic and social conditions, or at least for some perceptible movement in that direction, steadily gained in intensity. To be sure, the growing restiveness of the underprivileged was not directed against the ephemeral principles of a hardly yet existing capitalist order. Its objects were parasitic feudal overlords appropriating large slices of the national product and wasting them on extravagent living; a government machinery protecting and abetting the dominant interests; wealthy businessmen reaping immense profits and not utilizing them for productive purposes; last but not least, foreign colonizers extracting or believed to be extracting vast gains from their 'developmental' operations.

This popular movement had thus essentially bourgeois, democratic, anti-feudal, anti-imperialist tenets. It found outlets in agrarian egalitarianism; it incorporated 'muckraker' elements denouncing monopoly; it strove for national independence and freedom from foreign exploitation.

For the native capitalist middle-classes to assume the leadership of these popular forces and to direct them into the channels of bourgeois democracy—as had happened in Western Europe—they had to identify themselves with the common man. They had to break away from the political, economic, and ideological leadership of the feudal crust and the monopolists allied with it; and they had to demonstrate to the nation as a whole that they had the knowledge, the courage, and the determination to undertake and to carry to victorious conclusion the struggle for economic and social improvement.

In hardly any underdeveloped country were the middle-classes capable of living up to this historical challenge. Some of the reasons for this portentous failure, reasons connected with the internal make-up of the business class itself, were briefly mentioned above. Of equal importance was, however, an 'outside' factor. It was the spectacular growth of the international labour movement in Europe that offered the leadership that was denied to them by the native bourgeoisie. It pushed the goals and targets of the popular movements far beyond their original limited objectives.

This liaison of labour radicalism and populist revolt painted on the wall the imminent danger of a social revolution. Whether this danger was real or imaginary matters very little. What was essential is that the awareness of this threat effectively determined political and social action. It destroyed whatever chances there were of the capitalist classes joining and leading the popular anti-feudal, anti-monopolist movement. By instilling a mortal fear of expropriation and extinction in the minds of all property-owning groups the rise of socialist radicalism, and in particular the Bolshevik Revolution in Russia, tended to drive all more or less privileged, more or less well-to-do elements in the society into one 'counter-revolutionary' coalition. Whatever differences and antagonisms existed between large and small landowners, between monopolistic and competitive business, between liberal bourgeois and reactionary feudal overlords, between domestic and foreign interests, were largely submerged on all important occasions by the over-riding common interest in staving off socialism.

The possibility of solving the economic and political deadlock prevailing in the underdeveloped countries on lines of a progressive capitalism all but disappeared. Entering the alliance with all other segments of the ruling class, the capitalist middle-classes yielded one strategic position after another. Afraid that a quarrel with the landed gentry might be exploited by the radical populist movement, the middle-classes abandoned all progressive attitudes in agrarian matters. Afraid that a conflict with the church and the military might weaken the political authority of the government, the middle-classes moved away from all liberal and pacifist currents. Afraid that hostility toward foreign interests might deprive them of foreign support in a case of a revolutionary emergency, the native capitalists deserted their previous anti-imperialist, nationalist platforms.

The peculiar mechanisms of political interaction characteristic of all underdeveloped (and perhaps not only underdeveloped) countries thus operated at full speed. The aboriginal failure of the middle-classes to provide inspiration and leadership to the popular masses pushed those masses into the camp of socialist radicalism. The growth of radicalism pushed the middle-classes into an alliance with the aristocratic and monopolistic reaction. This alliance, cemented by common interest and common fear, pushed the populist forces still further along the road of radicalism and revolt. The outcome was a polarization of society with very little left between the poles. By permitting this polarization to develop, by abandoning the common man and resigning the task of reorganizing society on new, progressive lines, the capitalist middle-classes threw away their historical chance of assuming effective control over the destinies of their nations, and of directing the gathering popular storm against the fortresses of feudalism and reaction. Its blazing fire turned thus against the entirety of existing economic and social institutions.

The economic and political order maintained by the ruling coalition of owning classes finds itself invariably at odds with all the urgent needs of the underdeveloped countries. Neither the social fabric that it embodies nor the institutions that rest upon it are conducive to progressive economic development. The only way to provide for economic growth and to prevent a continuous deterioration of living standards (apart from mass emigration unacceptable to other countries) is to assure a steady increase of total output—at least large enough to offset the rapid growth of population.

An obvious source of such an increase is the utilization of available unutilized or underutilized resources. A large part of this reservoir of dormant productive potentialities is the vast multitude of entirely unemployed or ineffectively employed manpower. There is no way of employing it usefully in agriculture, where the marginal productivity of labour tends to zero. They could be provided with opportunities for productive work only by transfer to industrial pursuits. For this to be feasible large investments in industrial plant and facilities have to be undertaken. Under prevailing conditions such investments are not forthcoming for a number of important and interrelated reasons.

With a very uneven distribution of a very small aggregate income (and wealth), large individual incomes exceeding what could be regarded as ' reasonable ' requirements for current consumption accrue as a rule to a relatively small group of high-income receivers. Many of them are large landowners maintaining a feudal style of life with large outlays on housing servants, travel, and other luxuries. Their ' requirements for consumption' are so high that there is only little room for savings. Only relatively insignificant amounts are left to be spent on improvements of agricultural estates.

Other members of the 'upper crust' receiving incomes markedly surpassing 'reasonable' levels of consumption are wealthy businessmen. For social reasons briefly mentioned above, their consumption too is very much larger than it would have been were they brought up in the puritan tradition of a bourgeois civilization. Their drive to accumulate and to expand their enterprises is continuously counteracted by the urgent desire to imitate in their living habits the socially dominant 'old families', to prove by their conspicuous outlays on the amenities of rich life that they are socially (and therefore also politically) not inferior to their aristocratic partners in the ruling coalition.

But if this tendency curtails the volume of savings that could have been amassed by the urban high-income receivers, their will to re-invest their funds in productive enterprises is effectively curbed by a strong reluctance to damage their carefully erected monopolistic market positions through creation of additional productive capacity, and by absence of suitable investment opportunities—paradoxical as this may sound with reference to underdeveloped countries.

The deficiency of investment opportunities stems to a large extent from the structure and the limitations of the existing effective demand. With very low living standards the bulk of the aggregate money income of the population is spent on food and relatively primitive items of clothing and household necessities. These are available at low prices, and investment of large funds in plant and facilities that could produce this type of commodities more cheaply rarely promises attractive returns. Nor does it appear profitable to develop major enterprises the output of which would cater to the requirements of the rich. Large as their individual purchases of various luxuries may be, their aggregate spending on each of them is not sufficient to support the development of an elaborate luxury industry—in particular since the 'snob' character of prevailing tastes renders only imported luxury articles true marks of social distinction.

Finally, the limited demand for investment goods precludes the building up of a machinery or equipment industry. Such mass consumption goods as are lacking, and such quantities of luxury goods as are purchased by the well-to-do, as well as the comparatively small quantities of investment goods needed by industry, are thus imported from abroad in exchange for domestic agricultural products and raw materials.

This leaves the expansion of exportable raw materials output as a major outlet for investment activities. There the possibilities are greatly influenced, however, by the technology of the production of most raw materials as well as by the nature of the markets to be served. Many raw materials, in particular oil, metals, certain industrial crops, have to be produced on a large scale if costs are to be kept low and satisfactory returns assured. Large-scale production, however, calls for large investments, so large indeed as to exceed the potentialities of the native capitalists in backward countries. Production of raw materials for a distant market entails, moreover, much larger risks than those encountered in domestic business. The difficulty of foreseeing accurately such things as receptiveness of the world markets, prices obtainable in competition with other countries, volume of output in other competition with other countries, volume of output in other parts of the world, etc., sharply reduces the interest of native capitalists in these lines of business. They become to a predominant extent the domain of foreigners who, financially stronger, have at the same time much closer contacts with foreign outlets of their products.

The shortage of investible funds and the lack of investment opportunities represent two aspects of the same problem. A great number of investment projects, unprofitable under prevailing conditions, could be most promising in a general environment of economic expansion.

In backward areas a new industrial venture must frequently, if not always, break virgin ground. It has no functioning economic system to draw upon. It has to organize with its own efforts not only the productive process within its own confines, it must provide in addition for all the necessary outside arrangements essential to its operations. It does not enjoy the benefits of 'external economies'.

There can be no doubt that the absence of external economies, the inadequacy of the economic millieu in underdeveloped countries, constituted everywhere an important deterrent to investment in industrial projects. There is no way of rapidly bridging the gap. Large-scale investment is predicated upon large-scale investment. Roads, electric power stations, railroads, and houses have to be built before businessmen find it profitable to erect factories, to invest their funds in new industrial enterprises.

Yet investing in road building, financing construction of canals and power stations, organizing large housing projects, etc., transcend by far the financial and mental horizon of capitalists in underdeveloped countries. Not only are their financial resources too small for such ambitious projects, but their background and habits militate against entering commitments of this type. Brought up in the tradition of merchandizing and manufacturing consumers' goods—as is characteristic of an early phase of capitalist development—businessmen in underdeveloped countries are accustomed to rapid turnover, large but short-term risks, and correspondingly high rates of profit. Sinking funds in enterprises where profitability could manifest itself only in the course of many years is a largely unknown and unattractive departure.

The difference between social and private rationality that exists in any market and profit-determined economy is thus particularly striking in underdeveloped countries. While building of roads, harnessing of water power, or organization of housing developments may facilitate industrial growth and thus contribute to increased productivity on a national scale, the individual firms engaged in such activities may suffer losses and be unable to recover their investments. The nature of the problem involved can be easily exemplified; starting a new industrial enterprise is predicated among other things upon the availability of appropriately skilled manpower. Engaging men and training them on the job is time-consuming and expensive. They are liable to be unproductive, wasteful, and careless in the treatment of valuable tools and equipment. Accepting the losses involved may be justifiable from the standpoint of the individual firm if such a firm can count with reasonable certainty on retaining the services of those men after they go through training and acquire the requisite skills. However, should they leave the firm that provided the training and proceed to work for another enterprise, that new employer would reap the fruits of the first firm's outlays. In a developed industrial society this consideration is relatively unimportant. Losses and gains of individual firms generated by labour turnover may cancel out. In an underdeveloped country the chances of such cancellation are very small, if not nil. Although society as a whole would clearly benefit by the increase of skills of at least some of its members, individual businessmen cannot afford to provide the training that such an increase demands.

But could not the required increase in total output be attained by better utilization of land—another unutilized or inadequately utilized productive factor ?

There is usually no land that is both fit for agricultural purposes and at the same time readily accessible. Such terrain as could be cultivated but is actually not being tilled would usually require considerable investment before becoming suitable for settlement. In underdeveloped countries such outlays for agricultural purposes are just as unattractive to private interests as they are for industrial purposes.

On the other hand, more adequate employment of land that is already used in agriculture runs into considerable difficulties. Very few improvements that would be necessary in order to increase productivity can be carried out within the narrow confines of small-peasant holdings. Not only are the peasants in underdeveloped countries utterly unable to pay for such innovations, but the size of their lot offers no justification for their introduction.

Owners of large estates are in a sense in no better position. With limited savings at their disposal they do not have the funds to finance expensive improvements in their enterprises, nor do such projects appear profitable in view of the high prices of imported equipment in relation to prices of agricultural produce and wages of agricultural labour.

Approached thus via agriculture, an expansion of total output would also seem to be attainable only through the development of industry. Only through increase of industrial productivity could agricultural machinery, fertilizers, electric power, etc., be brought within the reach of the agricultural producer. Only through an increased demand for labour could agricultural wages be raised and a stimulus provided for a modernization of the agricultural economy. Only through the growth of industrial production could agricultural labour displaced by the machine be absorbed in productive employment.

Monopolistic market structures, shortage of savings, lack of external economics, the divergence of social and private rationalities do not exhaust, however, the list of obstacles blocking the way of privately organized industrial expansion in underdeveloped countries. Those obstacles have to be considered against the background of the general feeling of uncertainty prevailing in all backward areas. The coalition of the owning classes formed under pressure of fear, and held together by the real or imagined danger of social upheavals, provokes continuously more or less threatening rumblings under the outwardly calm political surface. The social and political tensions to which that coalition is a political response are not liquidated by the prevailing system; they are only repressed. Normal and quiet as the daily routine frequently appears, the more enlightened and understanding members of the ruling groups in underdeveloped countries sense the inherent instability of the political and social order. Occasional outbursts of popular dissatisfaction assuming the form of peasant uprisings, violent strikes or local guerrilla warfare, serve from time to time as grim reminders of the latent crisis.

In such a climate there is no will to invest on the part of monied people; in such a climate there is no enthusiasm for long-term projects; in such a climate the motto of all participants in the privileges offered by society is *carpe diem*.

Could not, however, an appropriate policy on the part of the governments involved change the political climate and facilitate economic growth ? In our time, when faith in the manipulative omnipotence of the State has all but displaced analysis of its social structure and understanding of its political and economic functions, the tendency is obviously to answer these questions in the affirmative.

Looking at the matter purely mechanically, it would appear indeed that much could be done, by a well-advised regime in an underdeveloped country, to provide for a relatively rapid increase of total output, accompanied by an improvement of the living standards of the population. There are a number of measures that the government could take in an effort to overcome backwardness. A fiscal policy could be adopted that, by means of capital levies and a highly progressive tax system, would syphon off all surplus purchasing power, and in this way eliminate non-essential consumption. The savings thus enforced could be channelled by the government into productive investment. Power stations, railroads, highways, irrigation systems, and soil improvements could be organized by the State with a view to creating an economic environment conducive to the growth of productivity. Technical schools on various levels could be set up by the public authority to furnish industrial training to young people as well as to adult workers and the unemployed. A system of scholarships could be introduced rendering acquisition of skills accessible to low-income strata.

Wherever private capital refrains from undertaking certain industrial projects, or wherever monopolistic controls block the necessary expansion of plant and facilities in particular industries, the government could step in and make the requisite investments. Where developmental possibilities that are rewarding in the long-run appear unprofitable during the initial period of gestation and learning, and are therefore beyond the horizon of private businessmen, the government could undertake to shoulder the short-run losses.

In addition an entire arsenal of ' preventive ' devices is at the disposal of the authorities. Inflationary pressures resulting from developmental activities (private and public) could be reduced or even eliminated, if outlays on investment projects could be offset by a corresponding and simultaneous contraction of spending elsewhere in the economic system. What this would call for is a taxation policy that would effectively remove from the income stream amounts sufficient to neutralize the investment-caused expansion of aggregate money income.

In the interim, and as a supplement, speculation in scarce goods and excessive profiteering in essential commodities could be suppressed by rigorous price controls. An equitable distribution of mass consumption goods in short supply could be assured by rationing. Diversion of resources in high demand to luxury purposes could be prevented by allocation and priority schemes. Strict supervision of transactions involving foreign exchanges could render capital flight, expenditure of limited foreign funds on luxury imports, pleasure trips abroad, and the like, impossible.

What the combination of these measures would accomplish is a radical change in the structure of effective demand in the underdeveloped country, and a reallocation of productive resources to satisfy society's need for economic development. By curtailing consumption of the higher income groups, the amounts of savings available for investment purposes could be markedly increased. The squandering of limited supplies of foreign exchange on capital flight, or on importation of redundant foreign goods and services, could be prevented, and the foreign funds thus saved could be used for the acquisition of foreign-made machinery needed for economic development. The reluctance of private interests to engage in enterprises that are socially necessary, but may not promise rich returns in the short-run, would be prevented from determining the economic life of the backward country.

The mere listing of the steps that would have to be undertaken, in order to assure an expansion of output and income in an underdeveloped country, reveals the utter implausibility of the view that they could be carried out by the governments existing in most underdeveloped countries. The reason for this inability is only to a negligible extent the non-existence of the competent and honest civil service needed for the administration of the programme. A symptom itself of the political and social marasmus prevailing in underdeveloped countries, this lack cannot be remedied without attacking the underlying causes. Nor does it touch anything near the roots of the matter to lament the lack of satisfactory tax policies in backward countries, or to deplore the absence of tax 'morale' and 'discipline' among the civic virtues of their populations.

The crucial fact rendering the realization of a developmental programme illusory is the political and social structure of the governments in power. The alliance of property-owning classes controlling the destinies of most underdeveloped countries, cannot be expected to design and to execute a set of measures running counter to each and all of their immediate vested interests. If to appease the restive public, blueprints of progressive measures such as agrarian reform, equitable tax legislation, etc., are officially announced, their enforcement is wilfully sabotaged. The government, representing a political compromise between landed and business interests cannot suppress the wasteful management of landed estates and the conspicuous consumption on the part of the aristocracy; cannot suppress monopolistic abuses, profiteering, capital flights, and extravagant living on the part of businessmen. It cannot curtail or abandon its lavish appropriations for a military and police establishment, providing attractive careers to the scions of wealthy families and a profitable outlet for armaments produced by their parents—quite from the fact that this establishment serves as the main protection against possible popular revolt. Set up to guard and to abet the existing property rights and privileges, it cannot become the architect of a policy calculated to destroy the privileges standing in the way of economic progress and to place the property and the incomes derived from it at the service of society as a whole.

Nor is there much to be said for the 'intermediate' position which, granting the essential incompatibility of a well-conceived and vigorously executed developmental programme with the political and social institutions prevailing in most underdeveloped countries, insists that at least some of the requisite measures could be carried out by the existing political authorities. This school of thought overlooks entirely the weakness, if not the complete absence, of social and political forces that could induce the necessary concessions on the part of the ruling coalition. By background and political upbringing, too myopic and self-interested to permit the slightest encroachments upon their inherited positions and cherished privileges, the upper-classes in underdeveloped countries resist doggedly all pressures in that direction. Every time such pressures grow in strength they succeed in cementing anew the alliance of all conservative elements, by decrying all attempts at reform as assaults on the very foundations of society.

Even if measures like progressive taxation, capital levies, and foreign exchange controls could be enforced by the corrupt officials operating in the demoralized business communities of underdeveloped countries, such enforcement would to a large extent defeat its original purpose. Where businessmen do not invest, unless in expectation of lavish profits, a taxation system succeeding in confiscating large parts of these profits is bound to kill private investment. Where doing business or operating landed estates are attractive mainly because they permit luxurious living, foreign exchange controls preventing the importation of luxury goods are bound to blight enterprise. Where the only stimulus to hard work on the part of intellectuals, technicians, and civil servants is the chance of partaking in the privileges of the ruling class, a policy aiming at the reduction of inequality of social status and income is bound to smother effort.

The injection of planning into a society living in the twilight between feudalism and capitalism cannot but result in additional corruption, larger and more artful evasions of the law, and more brazen abuses of authority.

There would seem to be no exit from the impasse. The ruling coalition of interests does not abdicate of its own volition, nor does it change its character in response to incantation. Although its individual members occasionally leave the sinking ship physically or financially (or in both ways), the property-owning classes as a whole are as a rule grimly determined to hold fast to their political and economic entrenchments.

If the threat of social upheaval assumes dangerous proportions, they tighten their grip on political life and move rapidly in the direction and military dictatorship. Making use of favourable international opportunities, and of ideological and social affinities to ruling groups in other countries, they solicit foreign economic and sometimes military aid, in their efforts to stave off the impending disaster.

Such aid is likely to be given to them by foreign governments regarding them as an evil less to be feared than the social revolution that would sweep them out of power. This attitude of their friends and protectors abroad is no less shortsighted than their own.

The adjustment of the social and political conditions in underdeveloped countries to the urgent needs of economic development can be postponed; it cannot be indefinitely avoided. In the past, it could have been delayed by decades or even centuries. In our age it is a matter of years. Bolstering the political system of power existing in backward countries by providing it with military support may temporarily block the eruption of the volcano; it cannot stop the subterranean gathering of explosive forces.

Economic help in the form of loans and grants given to the governments of backward countries, to enable them to promote a measure of economic progress, is no substitute for the domestic changes that are mandatory if economic development is to be attained.

Such help, in fact, may actually do more harm than good. Possibly permitting the importation of some foreign-made machinery and equipment for government or business sponsored investment projects, but not accompanied by any of the steps that are needed to assure healthy economic growth, foreign assistance thus supplied may set off an inflationary spiral increasing and aggravating the existing social and economic tensions in underdeveloped countries.

If, as is frequently the case, these loans or grants from abroad are tied to the fulfilment of certain conditions on the part of the receiving country regarding their use, the resulting investment may be directed in such channels as to conform more to the interests of the lending than to those of the borrowing country. Where economic advice as a form of 'technical assistance' is made a prerequisite to eligibility for financial aid, this advice often pushes the governments of underdeveloped countries toward policies, ideologically or otherwise attractive to the foreign experts dispensing economic counsel, but not necessarily conducive to economic development of the 'benefited' countries. Nationalism and xenophobia are thus strengthened in backward areas—additional fuel for political restiveness.

For backward countries to enter the road of economic growth and social progress, the political framework of their existence has to be drastically revamped. The alliance between feudal landlords, industrial royalists, and the capitalist middle-classes has to be broken. The keepers of the past cannot be the builders of the future. Such progressive and enterprising elements as exist in backward societies have to obtain the possibility of leading their countries in the direction of economic and social growth.

What France, Britain, and America have accomplished through their own revolutions has to be attained in backward countries by a combined effort of popular forces, enlightened government, and unselfish foreign help. This combined effort must sweep away the holdover institutions of a defunct age, must change the political and social climate in the underdeveloped countries, and must imbue their nations with a new spirit of enterprise and freedom.

Should it prove too late in the historical process for the bourgeoisie to rise to its responsibilities in backward areas, should the long experience of servitude and accommodation to the feudal past have reduced the forces of progressive capitalism to impotence, the backward countries of the world will inevitably turn to economic planning and social progress, propelled by enlightened self-interest, should prove unable to triumph over the conservatism of inherited positions and traditional privileges, if the capitalist promise of advance and reward to the efficient, the industrious, the able, should not displace the feudal assurance of security and power to the well-bred, the well-connected and the conformist—a new social ethos will become the spirit and guide of a new age. It will be the ethos of the collective effort, the creed of the predominance of the interests of society over the interests of selected few.

The transition may be abrupt and painful The land not given to the peasants legally may be taken by them forcibly. High incomes not confiscated through taxation may be eliminated by outright expropriation. Corrupt officials not retired in orderly fashion may be removed by violent action.

Which way the historical wheel will turn and in which way the crisis in the backward countries will find its final solution will depend in the main on whether the capitalist middle-classes in the backward areas, and the rulers of the advanced industrial nations of the world, overcome their fear and myopia. Or are they too spell-bound by their narrowly conceived selfish interests, too blinded by their hatred of progress, grown so senile in these latter days of the capitalist age, as to commit suicide out of fear of death ?

7

THE CRISIS OF GROWTH OF THE COLONIAL AND SEMI-COLONIAL COUNTRIES*

ALL THE partial, conjunctural phenomena of the economies of the colonial and semi-colonial countries are overshadowed by a general phenomenon: the commencement of the liquidation of the imperialist and semi-feudal regimes, the beginning of a transformation of the old economic and social structure, a movement for agrarian reform and industrialization.

Just as, in the imperialist countries, the governments try to sustain the economic conjuncture by direct and permanent intervention, so, in the colonial and semi-colonial countries, it is the masses who sustain the process of structural change, who force nationalizations, or who simply prevent the stabilization of imperialist and capitalist domination.

Since the end of World War II, this process has already given birth to the workers' states of China, North Korea, North Vietnam, and Cuba, and it never stops spreading and deepening. It is that which gives drive to the crisis of imperialism, beyond any temporarily favourable conjuncture in the imperialist countries themselves, and which definitively gives to the crisis of the capitalist regime as a whole.

While the workers' states and the advanced capitalist states have to various degrees been experiencing and are still experiencing a rapid economic growth, the colonial and semi-colonial countries observe an increase in their lag behind the production, and consumption levels of the advanced countries. As a result, they are passing through a real economic and social crisis which underlies the colonial revolution—the dominant fact of the last decade, which will doubtless still dominate the coming one.

Granted, if we speak of an economic crisis, we must specify that it is a matter of a crisis *sui generis*, a crisis of insufficient growth, and not one of classic overproduction, even though certain symptoms (slump in the sales of certain products, mass unemployment, drop in the real wages of the toilers, etc) are common to both types of crisis. Despite this crisis *sui generis*, the increase in industrial production, i.e., the process of industrialization, goes on, but at a rhythm inferior to that of the advanced countries, totally insufficient to modify the country's structure, and above all impotent to improve the masses' standard of living.

Thus industrial production in Latin America has risen from the index

*Reproduced from Fourth International No. 12, Winter 1960-61.

number 91 in 1950 to 100 in 1953 and 136 in 1958. This increase, however, remains very much lower than that of the Europe of the Six, not to speak of Japan or the USSR and China. Most underdeveloped areas in the world, moreover, have had an increase in production less than that of Latin America; that is especially the case for the Indian peninsula and South-east Asia.

The more and more inadequate growth that has marked the economy of the colonial and semi-colonial countries has both conjunctural and structural causes. The first concern the trend to a fall in the prices (and sometimes even in the volume) of exported raw materials, which form the main element of export for these countries. The second concern the main consequences of the feudo-capitalist structure of these countries which acts as a powerful brake on a rapid industrialization.

13. The Imperialist System and the Colonial Revolution

The profits reaped by imperialist capital invested in the backward countries, which play an important role in the metropolitan countries, prevent possible primitive accumulation in the colonial and semi-colonial countries. To the contrary of what is currently said by the propagandists of imperialism, it is the backward areas of the world which partly finance the advanced zones.

Traditionally, it is the export of raw materials, which has enabled the economies of backward countries to profit partly from the resources of the capitalist world market. The unfavourable evolution of the terms of exchange, however, limit even this possibility.[8] The situation is aggravated by the development of the production of raw materials in the imperialist countries themselves (oil and synthetic fibres; etc), and by the development of raw materials in new zones such as Africa (especially coffee, cotton, cocoa, copper, tin, aluminium, etc.)

Furthermore, there was, especially after the Korean war, a conscious and organized effort by imperialism to drive down the prices of raw materials. The United States, as a means of pressure, used mainly its own internal resources, especially agricultural surpluses, products of the unheard-of growth of the productivity of farm labour, together with its own mine and oil production, etc. For the raw materials which the United States and the other great imperialist powers do not produce in the metropolitan countries themselves, they resorted to the organization of big consumers' markets to impose their conditions and prices on the producing countries. Such is the case of the International Tin Council,[9] The International Sugar Agreement, and agreements about coffee, cotton, etc

[8] According to information issued by the G A T T, between 1953 and 1958, the proportion of the manufactured articles that the non-industrialized regions as a whole could pay for by means of their exports fell from 90% to 64%.

[9] In cases like that of tin, the United States resorted to the formation of big stocks at low prices, which are kept down by foreign-exchange operations and the pressure of these stocks on the market when prices tend to rise.

Some of the counter-measures decided on by the bourgeois or petty-bourgeois nationalist regimes of the semi-colonial countries were to limit the repatriation of the profits on foreign capital, to establish different foreign-exchange systems, and to take protectionist measures in favour of local industry, particularly to raise the prices of imported manufactured products. But imperialism actively intervenes to force open the gates that are closing against its expansion. It profits by the crises, the bottlenecks, and the threatening deficits in the balance of payments of the semi-colonial countries to impose a "freedom" from all economic and financial controls. In Latin America especially, the Eder Plan (Bolivia), the Klein-Sachs Plan (Chile), the Prebich Plan (Argentina), and then the direct intervention of the International Monetary Fund, by forcing the liquidation of foreign-exchange controls, showed to what a degree imperialism considers it necessary to keep these economies open to its exploitation, and to what a point it needs this in order to defend the dollar.

When imperialism tries to pacify the contradictions thus exacerbated, by means of alleged plans of "aid", it can in reality solve none of the problems raised. The aid of imperialism is the equivalent of only a small part of the surplus-value that it is itself extracting from the backward countries. To ensure their industrialization and their overall economic development, the colonial and semi-colonial countries would need not only to capitalize all the surplus-value produced in the country and obtain fair prices for their raw materials, but also to receive aid in the form of net investments of an amount at least ten times greater than the total sum of the "aid" given annually today by all the imperialists and all the workers' states.

Certain regions of the "third world" have received investments and undergone a not unimportant industrial development: such as the Union of South Africa, the two Rhodesias, the ex-Belgian Congo, Argentina, Brazil, Mexico, and Chile, as well as India and other areas of Asia. Venezuela and the oil-producing countries of the Near East have received very important royalties which, however, have not calmed social contradictions, but have rather accentuated the polarization of the classes, and the explosiveness of their internal situation.

Agrarian reform or the struggle for agrarian reform raises the problem of the incorporation of more than half of humanity in civilized life. It is shaking the power of the native landowners or white settlers who hold the best lands (especially in Algeria, Kenya, Southern Rhodesia, and South Africa), it enters into direct conflict with the system of capitalist plantations, and knocks down the age-old partitioning walls that cut the communal or tribal communities (in Tropical Africa, Peru, Bolivia, and India) from the rest of the world.

The awakening of these populations, who generally comprise the majority of the peasants in these countries and occupy most of the lands, (though not the most productive ones), requires great investments to bring them out of their backward state. The long stagnation of the Bolivian agrarian reform is a proof of this. The reform itself and the problems of economic development that it raises cannot be solved within the framework of the capitalist regime. It requires the expropriation and expulsion of the present masters, a wide-scale plan of investment based on the millions of small peasants to whom the land they till is granted. The development of the agrarian reform for this reason accentuates the crisis of the imperialist system and offers an objective—and to a growing degree, even a subjective—support to the proletarian and revolutionary forces that are driving toward the world-wide liquidation of capitalism.

The other great economic process set going by the colonial revolution is industrialization and general economic development. Like agrarian reform, it has its roots in the masses' deep desire to change their living conditions. And, like agrarian reform, it soon runs up against capitalism itself, the one-sided division of labour imposed by imperialism, the narrowness of the internal market, the Balkanization of Latin America, the Arab world, and Tropical Africa, the penury of capital, and the repatriation to the imperialist countries of an important part of the surplus-value produced in the colonial and semi-colonial countries. Capitalism is unable to incorporate broad strata of the population in the internal market by wrenching them out of their vegetative existence by means of the agrarian reform.

Only accumulation by the State can partly solve this problem, especially by the expropriation of the foreign enterprises and of the native landowners. Thus social surplus production can be concentrated in the hands of a workers' and peasants' government, which will use it both for economic development and for the improvement of the masses' standard of living, by means of a large-scale mobilization of the productive forces that are drowning in the immense masses of unemployed or insufficiently employed toilers. This is the alternative that is posed to the colonial revolution, which has already entered on this road through the Chinese revolution, which today is reaching Cuba, and is beginning to open up paths for itself in some areas of Africa.

14. Feudo-Capitalist Structure, an Obstacle to Rapid Industrialization

Beside the conjunctural factor represented by the reversal of terms of exchange at the expense of the colonial and semi-colonial countries beginning with 1952-53, the feudo-capitalist social structure of these countries remains the principal brake on rapid industrialization. In general, especially in Negro Africa and in Southeast Asia, the extreme poverty of the peasants who form the overwhelming majority of the population and who either still live under primitive conditions or have the blood squeezed out of them by the alliance of landowners, usurers, and tradesmen—produces the lack of a sufficiently broad domestic market to stimulate the private development of big industry. The Balkanization of these regions—

Latin America, Negro Africa, and the Arab countries—still further limits the domestic market. It follows that the limited, are invested especially in land speculation, trade, and usury, or else are exported.

Such is the explanation of the mystery of countries such as those that are big oil producers (Venezuela, Iraq, Iran, Saudi Arabia, Kuweit, Qatar) which in the last decade have accumulated thousands of millions of dollars in royalties without for all that having gone through a genuine process of industrialization. Most of this considerable capital has gone on works of substructure or on prestige building (at Caracas, Teheran, and elsewhere), on the mass importation of luxury products, and on the creation of industries that are simply complementary to oil production (refineries, ports, chemical plants). In countries like South Vietnam, South Korea, Turkey, and Pakistan, which during the same period received several thousand millons of dollars in American aid for essentially strategic reasons, this waste has been repeated on an even vaster scale.

The initiatives taken by the native national bourgeoisie, even in countries where it is relatively strongest (India, Argentina, Brazil, Mexico) have been limited to the sector of consumers' goods. The effort to create a national heavy industry, in direct opposition to and competition with the imperialist countries, has generally had to be entrusted to the State. It runs up against more and more powerful social and economic obstacles as the shift is made from plans or preparations to carrying them out in reality, and is frequently brought into question again by fractions of the dominant classes (Turkey under Menderes, Argentina under Frondizi, etc.)

In countries such as Mexico, Egypt, Indonesia, or Bolivia, where important interests of imperialism have been expropriated but where the capitalist management of economy has been maintained, this nationalized property is tending to become the business domain of private property and the source of private enrichment of functionaries and bureaucrats—which sows failure and casts discredit upon the nationalized property, and unfits it for being a source of accumulation for economic growth.

The agrarian reform contemplated by these regimes, as in Egypt, Mexico, Betancourt in Venezuela, or Nehru in India, is only a capitalist repurchase of lands and an attempt to alleviate contradictions in the countryside without solving the fundamental problem of conveying the land to those who till it, and without making investments aimed at developing agricultural production. The bourgeoisie itself, under the pressure of imperialism, is shaken by internal contradictions. Frondizi's attempt to develop heavy industry by leaning upon imperialism has been perhaps achieved at the cost of the short-term prospects of light industry—which was developed during Peron's government—to the extent that it tends toward the accumulation of capital by means of an increased exploitation of the working class and of the popular strata, i.e. a limitation of the domestic market for light industry.

It is the working class which has simultaneously led a permanent struggle against these plans of industrial demobilization and really defended against the bourgeoisie itself the level of industrialization already reached.

The attempts to overcome Balkanization through regional agreements are only ineffective measures—as were the previous agreements concerning Central America and Latin America, which only serve to maintain some privileges of regional trade that existed prior to the agreements with the I M F. Generally speaking, even among semi-colonial countries, the differences are so great that regional agreements will mean privilege for the more developed countries, which would be in a position to block the attempts of industrialization of the more backward countries.

15. Economic Effects of the Colonial Revolution

The colonial revolution has not failed to influence the capitalist economic system as a whole, and it will continue to undermine it in the coming years. Its effects are felt both directly in the colonial and semi-colonial countries and in the metropolitan countries themselves.

In the underdeveloped countries, the colonial revolution, by stimulating the masses' aspirations for well-being, hinders or prevents capitalist financial and economic "stabilization", undermines the rate of profit, and renders any long-term private investment more and more speculative and risky. By exerting a powerful pressure in favour of the industrialization of this zone, the colonial revolution tends to reduce the outlets still open to the metropolitan capitalist countries, which have for that matter already suffered amputations from the destruction of capitalism over a vast zone of the world. It likewise stirs up new competitors to the metropolitan industrial producers, and, to the degree that it spontaneously tends to ally itself with the workers' States, it threatens other capitalist outlets which will be taken over by exports from the USSR, the German Democratic Republic, Czechoslovakia, etc.

In the advanced capitalist countries, it reduces the possibility of finding in exports to overseas countries the safety valve against a tendency to overproduction inherent in capitalist production. By lessening or wiping out the income from capital investments exported to the colonial and semi-colonial countries, it shakes the equilibrium of the balance of payments, reduces the bourgeoisie's margin of manoeuvre in its struggle against the proletariat, and tends to force it to a policy of austerity that runs the risk of setting off a social crisis.

These economic effects of the colonial revolution, however, make themselves felt only in the long run, and precisely to the degree that it succeeds in detaching the colonial and semi-colonial countries from the world capitalist economy as a whole. Now during the whole first phase, imperialism has tried to conserve what is essential in its positions in underdeveloped countries by transferring the power there to the national bourgeoisie. Such a transfer is a very hard blow for imperialism only in the sole case that it is accompanied by a nationalization of foreign capital invested in the country and by a basic reorientation of its foreign trade. Despite some spectacular nationalizations in the last decade (Iranian oil industry, Suez Canal), in general most countries drawn into the colonial revolution have not by-and-large detached themselves from the world capitalist economy. This is the main factor that has uptil now limited the immediate economic effects of the colonial revolution on the economy of the metropolitan capitalist countries.

In this connection, the experience of the Cuban revolution. For the first time, this revolution, before even giving itself a proletarian leadership, has ended up in the nationalization of the principal foreign capital invested in the country, as well as in a fundamental reorientation of Cuba's foreign trade toward the workers' States. If the immediate economic effects of these developments on the U. S. or European capitalist economy are insignificant, they are nonetheless of historic importance as a sketch of a future general tendency. To the degree to which, in the coming decade, the colonial revolution goes beyond the stage or bourgeois-democratic leadership in several countries, its economic effects on the metropolitan capitalist countries will become more important. And if entire blocks of the "Third World" (India, Brazil, the Middle East) were to escape from the capitalist world market, these effects would become disastrous.

The colonial revolution today is expressing in an acute form the world crisis of the capitalist system. But this crisis is transformed into a crisis of the world capitalist economy only to the degree to which it undermines the economy of the most important industrial capitalist countries: the U.S.A., the Common Market, Great Britain, Japan. Experience permits us to declare that in the short run this degree is determined more or less exactly by the degree to which the colonial revolution goes beyond democratic-bourgeois leadership.

16. Factors Which Have Heretofore Limited The Economic Effects of the Colonial Revolution

The main paradox of the last decade lies precisely in the fact that, despite a capitalist world market that unites the underdeveloped zone with the industrialized zone, despite the enormous advances of the colonial revolution, and despite the global evolution of a correlation of forces unfavourable to capital (which more and more undermines the long-term security of investments), the advanced capitalist countries have been able to enjoy relatively rapid industrial growth. In the last analysis, this can be explained only by the fact that there enter into play a series of factors which momentarily limit the economic effect of the colonial revolution on the metropolitan capitalist economy. Most of these factors have already been pointed out by the Vth World Congress theses on economic and political perspectives:

(a) The maintenance of important imperialist positions in the countries where the colonial revolution has begun This applies to capital investments and outlets for industrial products. The most striking case is that of Iraq, where, despite the beginning of the revolution, important dividends are still flowing to the city. In all, Great Britain continues each year to get income of some £350 million ($980 million) from its foreign investments. As for outlets, in 1959 53% of British exports, 44% of French exports, 27% of Italian exports, and 25% of West German exports, still went to colonial and semi-colonial countries and the British dominions.

(b) The replacement, inside the underdeveloped zone, of lost outlets by new outlets. Thus the losses of outlets suffered by Great Britain, France, and the Netherlands in their former colonies have been in part offset by a boom in exports to other "associated" territories (for Great Britain, especially Australia, South Africa, Canada, and the Central African Federation; for France, especially Negro Africa and Algeria; for the Netherlands, the Dutch West Indies) or to the colonial or semi-colonial zones of their partners.

(c) The replacement of exchanges with the colonial and semi-colonial countries by exchanges among the industrialized countries. In a general way, since 1953, the exchanges among the industrially advanced capitalist countries have been developing more rapidly than the exchanges between advanced capitalist countries and underdeveloped countries. Two phenomena have often been striking in this connection.

The U. S. A. has become an important market for most of the colonialist powers which have there found again part of the outlets lost elsewhere:

Percentage of Total Exports Sold to the U. S. A.

Country	1928	1938	1950	1959
Great Britain	6 %	4 %	5 %	11 %
France	6 %	6 %	4 %	8 %
Italy	11 %	8 %	6 %	12 %
Netherlands	4 %	3 %	5 %	6 %
Belgium	8 %	7 %	9 %	14 %

As for Japan, it is currently sending 30% of its exports to the U.S.A.

Exchanges within the Common Market are developing much more rapidly than between the Common Market and the rest of the world.

(d) The replacement of formerly imported products by domestic products (and outlets). This applies both to the development of synthetic or nationally new raw materials industries (oil in Italy, France, Germany, the Netherlands; methane gas in Italy, and France; uranium in the U.S.A., Canada, and France, etc.) and to the steady replacement of purchases abroad of foodstuffs or textiles by national manufacture of synthetic textiles and durable consumers' goods industries.

8

THE INDUSTRIALIZATION OF BACKWARD COUNTRIES

ERNEST GERMAIN

1 THE THEORETICAL SETTING OF THE PROBLEM

"POVERTY BREEDS POVERTY": this simple formula which has become a platitude still summarizes all the wisdom of most economists on the subject, bourgeois and Marxist alike. What they mean, in Marxist terms, goes more or less like this. Backwardness means a low level of productivity, a low level of productivity stems in the last resort from a low level of fixed capital equipment and of industrialization. But industrialization means (under capitalism) capital accumulation, and in any case a larger social surplus product. The poorer a country, the greater the part of its current production that is necessary (and barely sufficient) to maintain the mass of the producers at a low level of subsistence. Hence, the poorer a country, the lower its rate of capital accumulation, the lower is social surplus product. Hence, the poorer a country, the slower is industrialization: poverty breeds poverty.

We shall return in a moment to one of the main links in this chain of reasoning: "the poorer a country, the smaller its surplus product." This formula is correct only as a most sweeping historical generalization, i.e., if for example a purely feudal society is compared to modern industrial capitalism. It ceases to be true if one compares the *relative* poverty of present-day societies, which are all more or less products of *combined development*. But in any case, the traditional emphasis of the reasoning lies on the supply side of fixed capital equipment, not on the *demand* side.

It has been the merit of Professor Nurkse,[1] whatever mistakes he also makes in the assumption of a low social surplus product in backward countries, decisively to change this emphasis, and to rediscover a truth long known to Marxists (e.g., Lenin and Trotsky in their writings on Russia before 1914), i. e., that the real vicious circle of poverty works the other way round.

It is not because a country is poor that it lacks financial resources for industrialization; it is because a country is poor that it lacks *a market which makes industrialization a profitable business from the capitalist point of view*. Because of the absence of this market, capital (the social surplus product) is invested in other fields than industry (trade, buying and speculation in real estate, hoarding, or, paradoxically, capital export). Therefore, the level of industrialization remains low, the level of productivity of labour remains low, and the country remains poor, which means that there is no stimulus for private industrial enterprise ; "Proverty breeds poverty."

In his recently published and to a large extent very valuable book, Paul A. Baran, who is one of the rare American Marxists to teach at a University (Stanford) draws an impressive picture of the social surplus product in backward countries.[2] He mentions the huge part of the agricultural product appropriated by landlords and money-lenders (usually up to 50% of the national agricultural product in many backward countries, and as agricultural production itself represents more than 50 % of the national product of such countries, this reveals the existence of a social surplus product of the order of 25-30% of the total product!) He further mentions the income of the great number of intermediaries between the countryside and the city, and inside the city itself, whom he aptly describes as *lumpenbourgeoisie*, a group so numerous that, even if it is not composed of individually prosperous persons, it absorbs quite a fraction of the national product. He finally mentions government income and native capitalist income, as well as income of foreign-owned plantations, mines, and other enterprises, which in some countries (e.g. Rhodesia), represents a huge fraction of the national income.

We may therefore say that the central problem is not that of *creating* resources which make industrialization possible, but one of *reallocating* existing resources in order to industrialize the country. Or more correctly, the problem is that of creating social and economic conditions which make such a reallocation possible. Such conditions require the suppression of colonial rule, the expropriation of foreign capital (at least in cases where such capital already occupies an important place in the economy), and a radical agrarian revolution, which suppresses the income and even the very class of landowners—money-lenders—compradores. As a general historical rule, one may add that the existing weak native industrial class also becomes an obstacle on the road to industrialization, and has to be disposed of.

Once however this social revolution has been accomplished (as for example by the October Revolution in Russia, by the Jugoslav revolution of 1941-1946, or by bureaucratic-military means, with a limited mobilization of the masses, in the "people's democracies" from 1945-48), the problem of reallocating national resources to further rapid industrialization is still not solved at all. On the contrary, the obstacle now seems even more formidable than before.

For the revolution itself carries through a reallocation of resources of its own, and in a most peculiar manner. As a backward country is a predominantly agrarian country, the fate of the revolution depends on the willingness of the peasant to accept the new order. The peasant, who, to quote Khrushchev, knows how to count, will accept the new order only if he is better off than before. He will be better off only if he has to give, to the state and the city in the form of taxes and costs of industrial goods purchased, a smaller part of his income than he gave before to the landlord, the money-lender, and the merchant. In other words: the first economic result of the successful colonial revolution is to diminish the social surplus product, or to hand part of it over to the agricultural petty commodity producers.

This fact has been empirically proved both in Russia under the NEP and in the "people's democracies" under various policies of slow collectivization. Everywhere, the peasantry appears as the main if not the only class of society which substantially increased its standard of living after the revolution. This increase in its standard of living now creates of course a market sufficiently large to make rapid industrialization possible. But at the same moment that the problem seems to be solved on the demand side, it pops up again on the supply side. Although the general standard of living of the peasantry (up to 80% of the population of a backward country!) has only been moderately increased, this increase is enough to absorb not only the greater part of the former surplus product, but also the greater part of the new potential surplus which results from a first substantial increase in the general level of production and productivity.

This is of course no paradox: as the social product is composed of the income of the producers plus the surplus product, any increase in the former has for result a decrease of the latter.

For that reason, traditionally, bourgeois and Marxist economists alike thought there were only two solutions to this problem: either massive foreign aid or "primitive socialist accumulation" (the phrase was coined by the Soviet economist Preobashensky, who was temporarily associated with the Left Opposition). Either an advanced industrial country would give the backward country an important part of the resources necessary for industrialization (in the form of massive cheap credit, or more directly in the form of capital equipment, railways, ships, airplanes, prefabricated houses, and, not to be forgotten, technicians and scientific personnel); or the backward country would have to cut back extensively the standard of living of its population, above all its peasant population, in order to free the resources necessary for industrialization. Apologists of the tragic Stalinist experience with industrialization of this kind even added the theorem: "The more backward the country and the quicker the industriaization, the greater must be the setback in general consumption, and the harsher must be the dictatorship which has to force people to work under those circumstances."

Of course, Trotsky and the main economic specialists of the Left Opposition (e.g. Rakovsky and Piatakov) never accepted these theorems. They always pointed out that a *parallel and harmonious increase* in production and popular consumption was a necessary condition for socialist industrialization. Today their concept is widely accepted. Tito has made it his own. Polish economists like Lange have stated it in unmistakable terms. We have still, however, to try to find a theoretical foundation for this political advice. This is what we shall attempt, as a first tentative sketch, in this article.

2. The Theoretical Solution of the Problem

In the framework of a workers' state, the problem of industrializing a backward country involves solutions for every element of the reproduction process; supply (production and import) of the fixed capital equipment necessary; supply of a regular flow of raw materials; increase of the number and qualifications of industrial workers; adequate distribution of the social product between industry and agriculture, and the two sectors of industry, in order to prevent disequilibriums, shortages, and bottlenecks, e.g., in the food supply in the supply of agricultural raw materials, etc. All these problems are interrelated. Inadequate supply of industrial consumer goods to the village, for example, could become one of the main reasons for a slower rate of development of agricultural production, especially of agricultural raw materials for industry, and thereby reduce the general rate of growth of industrial production.

We shall not go into all these problems here, but concentrate on the main field, that of the adequate distribution of social product (or income) i.e., that of the rate of accumulation.

The mistake committed by the Stalinist planners during the first Five-Year Plans, and even more—and with less excuse—by the apologists who try today to justify the wrong course followed, is a confusion between *maximum* and *optimum* rate of accumulation. Or rather: these planners started from the wrong assumption that the maximum rate of accumulation is also the optimum rate, at least in the short run.

Even if we define the optimum rate of accumulation from a purely economic point of view, i.e., as the rate which enables the *maximum increase in the social product* (or income) in a given period, this identification is completely wrong. It is all the more wrong because no Marxist can give such a purely economic definition to that central notion. He cannot leave out *living class forces*. He can never forget that any rate of accumulation which creates demoralization of the proletariat through hunger, political apathy, tendency to flee from the factories and the city, etc., cannot be called "optimum" from the point of view of working-class revolutionists.

It is interesting however to beat the apologists of a maximum rate of accumulation even on their own field, i.e., the purely economic result, in tons of steel, cement, coal and cotton goods. The mistake made has its roots in the *absurd assumption that the productivity of labour is independent of the level of consumption* of the producer. We say that this assumption is absurd not only in the long run, but even and especially in the short run. The whole history of modern industry has shown that any sharp decrease of the standard of consumption of the workers results in a decrease of per capita productivity. And the poorer the country and the lower its initial level of consumption, the stronger this interrelation will be.

One could of course point out that this decrease will translate itself into a decrease of *production* only if one assumes that the fixed capital on which the producers operate remains unchanged. It is evident that the goal of a maximised rate of accumulation is precisely to increase the supply and quality of fixed equipment of industry. If the workers tend to make less efforts, because they eat less and live under worse conditions, then, so the argument will continue this decrease of per capita productivity will be ten times overcome by the increased productivity resulting from the introduction of better machinery.

It is at this point that our concept of *optimum rate of accumulation* becomes all-important. Let us assume that with a given quantity of fixed machinery, 1000 workers produce over a given period a value of $1,000,000 when their real wage is $500 a year (we should not forget that we are concerned with workers in backward countries!). If we double the value of capital equipment in the course of three years, the product of these workers could, for example, treble and be worth $3,000,000 (first hypothesis) on condition that their real wage is not changed or even that it increases.[3] If, however, in order to double the value of the capital equipment, we first cut the real wages of the workers to $250 a year we might find that the final product will not be $3,000,000, but only $1,500,000 (second hypothesis). Production has, of course, still increased. But we have caused a terrible waste of wealth. For had we increased the value of capital equipment by only 50%, instead of by 100%, in order to leave real wages where they were before, or to increase them even by a given percentage, then the total final product would have been say $2,000,000, instead of $1,500,000 (third hypothesis).

The first hypothesis is the ideal one; it presupposes more or less unlimited resources freed for the given project. The second and the third hypothesis are both trying to divide *limited* resources in a given way. The second hypothesis, the one of the maximum rate of accumulation, does not lead to maximum expansion of production. The third hypothesis, with a lower rate of accumulation than the second one, leads to a bigger expansion of production under given conditions, and is, therefore, the *optimum* rate of accumulation (or the optimum division of the social product, of the social income, etc.)

In real fact, it is of course not very easy to determine this optimum rate. It can be discovered only by trial and error. But what we should understand from the start is the fact that in a backward country, with a generally low standard of living of the workers, the maximum rate will *never* be the optimum rate, i.e., will always result in a level of productivity of labour *below* the level rendered possible by a given set of machinery and a given level of qualification and cultural background of a working class.

We may add that we have *understated* our point. For a "purely economic" solution leaves out a serious social consideration, with important economic repercussions. Any attempt to impose a maximum rate of accumulation results in a lowering of an already low standard of living. As the workers do not accept this without resistance—even be it passive—it is necessary to drive them back to the production line by force and keep them there by constant supervision. In order to achieve this result, a huge army of gendarmes, bureaucrats, and supervisors of all sorts must be built up and kept supported, generally at far above the subsistence level down to which the producers have been forced.

But this in turn means a large increase of unproductive consumption in society, lowering thereby the fraction of the social product ready to be used for productive accumulation.

A "maximum rate of accumulation" is "maximum" only if we "forget" the huge waste it involves; in fact, it may be lower, after a decade, than a level which would have allowed an increase in workers' consumption, would thereby have much more quickly increased the social average productivity, and would have enabled society greatly to reduce the funds for unproductive consumption of policemen, uniformed or not.

Just to show the reader that all these considerations are not purely theoretical, we shall limit ourselves to a single example, but a decisively revealing one. There were in 1928 3·1 million workers and employees (technicians and engineers with university degrees not included) in Soviet industry. In order to achieve the First-Year Plan, figures worked out at that moment estimated the manpower necessary for attaining the production goals at 4·1 million workers and employees (i.e., an increase of 1 million, or 33%). In fact, in 1932-3, *without* all the goals of the First Five-Year Plan having been achieved, 6·7 million workers and employees were working in Soviet factories, an increase of more than 110% over the figure of 1928, and of 65% over the planned number of workers! What should have been produced by 4 million workers needed 6·7 millions to be manufactured, i.e., *per capita* productivity was *more than* 50% *below the planned level.* The maximum rate of accumulation was far from being the optimum rate, far from maximizing the social product.

We now understand how wrong are those who excuse the Stalinist variant of industrialization by the argument that, anyway, as the war danger was growing, as the country was weak and surrounded by enemies, it was necessary to industrialise as quickly as possible.[4] In reality, what we are trying to prove is that a "maximum" rate of accumulation produces a *slower* overall rate of growth of the economy than the "optimum" rate. It was that point that Trotsky, Rakovsky, and other Marxist critics of Stalin's economic policy did not cease to make between 1928 and 1940, and the now existing factual material completely confirms the accuracy of their criticism.

It is interesting to note that Professor Baran is carried by his theoretical elan to a thesis quite similar to ours when he writes:

> While the maximization of the rates of growth—if such be the requirement of the concrete situation—is tantamount to a minimization(?)

of current consumption (or, conversely, maximization of the economic surplus), it would be erroneous to equate such minimization of consumption conducive to speediest growth with its reduction to some rock-bottom levels. In view of the obvious relation *between consumption standards and the ability and willingness* to work on the part of the population, minimum consumption compatible with maximum output (and growth) may, and in most underdeveloped countries will, require a more or less substantial increase of the existing consumption standard. Given a small initial output and accordingly limited possibilities for such an increase, it will have to be differentiated. (...) Accordingly, while it might be thought at first that maximization of the rates of growth calls for plowing back into the economy all increments in output resulting from current investment, in actual fact some splitting of these increments so as to increase *both* investment and consumption may be a more effective, or even the only possible, method of attaining the *largest possible increase* in production. (*Op. cit.*, p. 270).

However, in a passage describing concretely the Stalinist industrialization policy of the period 1928-1937, Professor Baran cannot shake off his old apologetic hide, and we are confronted with various platitudes like the "war danger" which made necessary a "rapid rhythm" of industrialization etc. Professor Baran even tries to make us believe that the "inconvenience" caused by the desperate attempt of maximization of the rate of accumulation was only of short duration. He therefore conveniently quotes the crop figures of 1937, without adding that those figures remain exceptional, not only for the period 1928-1940, but even for the period 1928-1953, if we take into consideration the increased territory and population of the USSR! He also forgets to add that Soviet livestock for 25 *years* fell below the 1928 level, and that we had to wait till 1956(!) in order to find a number of milch-cows equal to that of 1928 (which does not mean equal per capita of Soviet population, given the important increase during this quarter of a century). It is impossible to cover up the tremendous price Soviet economy had to pay for Stalin's attempt to "maximize" the rate of accumulation by brutally lowering the consumption levels of workers and peasants.

3. An Interesting Theoretical Sideline

Up till now, we have always considered economic growth and industrialization as a result of the increase in the real supply of fixed capital equipment, machinery, buildings, power works, etc. Professor Nurkse, however, has made another and interesting contribution to the theory of industrialization of backward countries by concentrating attention on one of the most striking characteristics of backwardness: *rural overpopulation.*

This phenomenon has, of course, long been known to economists and especially to Marxists. More than half a century ago, Lenin and Trotsky made of that rural over-population, and the pressure it exercises on land

and land rent, one of the main links in the chain of arguments explaining backwardness: the preference given by capitalists to the buying of land over industrial investment, the land rent allowing a higher average return than industrial profits.

But whereas the problem of rural overpopulation has always been considered from the point of view of an easy supply of manpower for *urban industry*, once the industrialization process got into motion, Professor Nurkse now has stressed a new and strikingly important aspect of the problem. Economic growth, he says, is essentially an increase in the average productivity of labour. No Marxist will quarrel with that definition. But in a country with a huge population of underemployed peasants (it would be more correct to say village inhabitants), it is not necessary to start with huge capital investment in order to achieve a substantial increase in the average productivity of labour.

For what else is underemployment if not the fact that in such backward countries half or two-thirds of the population, living in the village, are only really working 150 or 200 days a year![5] The rest of the year, they do nothing. Now if it were possible to give them something to do during the rest of the year, some productive purpose which does not need huge fixed equipment, their annual production, and thus their annual productivity, would tremendously increase. In fact, while doing nothing, they continue to eat. It would be sufficient to give them a little bit more to eat, while getting them to work, in order to treat the largest part, if not the whole, of their increased production as social surplus product, as a social investment fund. And once this surplus product has been created, the basis is laid for large-scale industrialization, not by lowering but by increasing the standard of living of the working population, at least in real terms.[6]

At first sight, there seem to be different "catches" in this line of reasoning, but Professor Nurkse deftly does away with them, one by one. How is it possible, we may ask, to give a huge amount of new jobs to the overpopulated countryside, if the land is already fully occupied? To this there are different answers. First of all there is no underdeveloped country in the world, not even Indonesia, in which the land is "fullly occupied" from an economic point of view. Possibilities of increasing agricultural production by fertilization and irrigation operated with relative low-cost methods (from shoveling the mud out of river beds for use as fertilizers to the digging of thousands of small canals, the drilling of thousands of cemented water pits, etc.) are everywhere present.[7]

Professor Nurkse does not add, but this we may do in his place, that these jobs are not limited by *natural* but by *social* conditions, as long as landlordism and capitalism are not overcome. For opening up these tremendous and relatively "cheap" opportunities for the big mass of unemployed peasants means must be found—means of concentrating the marketable food supplies in the hands of central authorities and/or of peasant cooperatives, means of concentrating the peasants themselves, either by appeal or by coercion, means of *planning* these thousands of local projects in a way that their results are split up between the producers themselves and the community, and not siphoned away by landlords, money-lenders, usurers, black-marketeers, compradores, or capitalists.

We shall see further on that these social preconditions are all-important for the success of these experiments.

A second question which crops up is the question of equipment. Professor Nurkse of course knows very well that millions of underfed underemployed peasants cannot start to "produce" a social surplus product with their bare hands. His solution is : a) to import a large mass of cheap simple tools and b) to have them produce these tools themselves.

The investment workers, before they start building a piece of fixed capital such as a road, could, after all, sit down and make the most necessary primitive tools with their own hands, starting if need be from scratch. They could make their own shovels, wheelbarrows, carts, hoists, and other things to help them build the road. (p.44).

As we shall see, this is precisely the way the Chinese Communists have conceived the "acceleration" of their "uninterrupted revolution" in 1957-8!

But there remains a third, and formidable, difficulty. An underdeveloped country is characterized by very low standards of living, especially of food supply, in the countryside. Underemployment means that the working peasants have to share their meagre pittance with practically unemployed sons, nephews, and uncles living with them. Now the whole theory of the "accumulation fund hidden in underemployment" hinges on the *stability* of peasant consumption. If the working peasants increase their food consumption from the moment their nephews, sons, and uncles are mobilized to build irrigation trenches, water pits, and roads, then of course the problem of *feeding these newly occupied workers* will appear. There will be a deficit of the food balance of the country, and the increase in real wealth created by the products of these workers might be wiped out entirely by the need to import supplementary food.

Professor Nurkse states the problem admirably. But he does not solve it adequately, for somewhat sinister formulae like "the saving *has to be made*" are not solutions. He tries to introduce a difference between densely and sparsely occupied countries. In fact the solution he indicates for sparsely occupied countries only, applies for all of them: the supplementary amount of workers must be occupied in such a way as to make possible, among other things, *a substantial increase in agricultural production*. Any other solution would *impose* the process of growth on the peasantry through various forms of "forced savings", and then we should again be up against the old problem of estimating the negative results of such a decline in the standard of living.

Is it possible substantially to increase agricultural production in the backward countries? Of course it is. And it is at this point that Professor

Nurkse makes his most substantial mistake, when he minimizes or even excludes this possibility in the densely populated countries. As a matter of fact, two of the most densely populated backward countries of the world, India and China, are most susceptible of mobilizing the biggest "accumulation fund" from a heavy increase of agricultural production.

For if we look closer at those various "low-cost local investment projects", made possible by drawing on the underemployed village populations, we find that nearly all of them tend to increase agricultural productivity. Irrigation, regulation of local rivers, flood control, road building, local iron foundries, manufacture of agricultural implements of a more modern though still simple type, local building industries helping the peasants to build better houses for themselves and stables, or better stables, for their livestock—all these projects tend to prepare larger harvests. What is more, they permit almost immediate results in elevating living standards in the countryside. Thereby they enable the mobilization of a big—and growing—part of the increased surplus product for purposes of national economic growth. If they are better fed, better clothed, and better housed, the sons, nephews, and uncles of the toiling peasants will work without resistance the second year on provincial and national roads, and not just local ones. They will without resistance build local foundries in order to manufacture not just agricultural implements but machinery of various sorts, i. e., means of production. The initial impetus will have been given. By "building" Professor Nurkse's conception into our general theoretical solution, and correcting it in that sense, we get a clearer picture of the possibilities of initially industrializing a backward country, without (sufficient) foreign help and without pushing down the standard of living of the working population.

We should like to emphasize a warning: the setting to work of the village unemployed on local investment projects is no panacea for solving the industrialization of backward countries. It is only a relatively cheap means of giving that industrialization *an initial push*. If a correct balance between the local "low-cost" investment projects and the "high-cost" "modern" industrialization projects is not struck, the economy will rapidly run into the classic difficulties of Soviet Russia during the NEP.

Local industries, built with ancient technology and locally manufactured equipment, are of low productivity. As long as they are an absolute addition to national wealth, and a school of industrial technique and habits which makes the transition of the peasant towards the modern factory, easier, they are of tremendous importance. But from the moment productivity in agriculture starts to rise rapidly, the well-known phenomenon of the scissors will appear. Agricultural prices will fall in comparison with the prices of (scarce) industrial consumer goods and means of production. At the same time, the peasantry will accumulate money and cry for cheaper industrial goods. There will be a political risk of alienating the peasantry from the workers' regime; there will be the economic danger of an artificial withdrawal or even decrease of the agricultural surplus. The investment fund mobilized through the voluntary mobilization of the rural unemployed has to be transformed into modern fixed equipment, ready to deliver cheap industrial goods, to the countryside. Modern steel works will progressively take over from the local foundries. Both processes, intertwined in the beginning, will become unravelled: the local low-productivity projects will wither away.

4. The Pragmatic Approach: India

Did the authors of India's First Five-Year Plan know and understand Professor Nurkse's theory? If they did, they did not show any sign of it. But it is a fact that, following a theory of long standing, very dear to bourgeois economists, they concentrated the effort of their plan on agriculture, and introduced the novel feature of thousands of "local community-development" projects. Dr. D. K. Rangnekar, in a recently published general appraisal of the problems of India's economic growth, writes on the subject:

"Community project" is a comprehensive description for several aspects of rural development with the broad objective of transforming the agriculturist and initiating a social revolution (?) in the 560,000 villages. With the help of a Rural Extension Service of trained village workers, the community projects, seek to bring new methods, new ideas, and new knowledge to almost every aspect of the peasant's life. The impact of the programme is expected to be felt in road communications, school education, housing and sanitation, community recreation and entertainment, farming methods and techniques, supplementary or fuller employment (in village crafts and other commercial and professional services). The villagers themselves are to build and construct, change and improve, as a community. The object is to galvanize the whole of the rural population into activity on a voluntary basis under state guidance and assistance (p. 70).[8]

Our Indian comrades will soon show us their final estimate of the First Five-Year Plan. But there is no doubt that it was a complete failure. On the industrial field, development was very slow, in fact slower than in colonial countries like Rhodesia or the Belgian Congo. The problem of rural unemployment was not even scratched. As for agriculture, although there was a certain increase in the production of food-grains, it barely kept up with the population increase. Per capita food production *fell*, from a pre-war average index-figure of 100, to 87 in 1947-48, 85 in 1948-49, 84 in 1950-51 and 82 in 1951-52, and remained at approximately these levels in 1954. With regard to average yields per *acre* and agricultural productitivity, the low pre-war level was barely maintained, notwithstanding huge and extremely costly multiple-purpose irrigation schemes. As for the "social revolution" in the village, it is sufficient to state that the planned expenditure on social services, worked out at less than 1 rupee (a rupee is worth something like 1sh 6d or 20 US cents) per head (and per *five years*!) of the population. And this incredibly meagre sum of less than 1 rupee per head was expected to provide for education, hospitals, dispensaries, community services, etc., all of which were woefully lacking. In the base year of the Plan, 1950-51, there was, for example, 1 rural dispensary for about 105 villages and 56,400 persons; at the end of the Plan there would be only a slight change: 1 dispensary will serve about 95 villages and 54,000 persons (id, pp. 82-3).

What are the reasons for this dismal failure? They should not be sought in the fact that a large part of the accumulation fund went into agriculture, although the balance for a healthy development seems to have been upset at the expense of industry in that First Plan (the Second Plan upsets the balance at the expense of agriculture; but that is another story). The real keys for the failure are twofold: an inadequate accumulation fund on the one hand; social conditions in town and especially countryside which make an adequate use of even that inadequate accumulation fund impossible.

During the First-Five Year Plan, "investment" (in the bourgeois economic sense of the word, i.e., including stock formation) was only 7% of the national income, and fixed capital formation only between 4 and 5·5% of the national income (*op. cit*., p. 231). As Dr. Rangnekar himself states, a net domestic capital formation rate of 15-16% of the national income is considered the necessary minimum for a rapid economic development (*op. cit*., p. 281). Not only was this rate not approached, but the relatively small increase in the national income over the five-year period, which he estimates at 18% (or 3·5 % per annum), was wiped out by population growth and increase of consumption (of the better-off social classes, we should add). There was no perceptible increase of the rate of accumulation during the five-year period itself.

This low level of accumulation has, of course, essentially *social* roots. It is not so much a question of lacking resources, as of lacking *mobilization* and reallocation of existing resources. Dr. Rangnekar carefully avoids making this point, but he himself gives all the facts which point in that direction. He indicates for instance (p. 224) that at least 500 million rupees a year are spent for importing and hoarding gold. This, he says, is "only" 0·5% of the national income, which gives the percentage by which investment would increase if social control would do away with that habit. The true figure, however, should be that of the *total* private gold hoard of India, which is estimated at 50 or 60 times that figure. It would have enabled thereby at least *doubling* the accumulation fund (total net investment during the five year period being estimated at 30 billion rupees). And China's quick economic growth was made possible precisely by a rate of accumulation double that of India.

Gold hoards are only one example. The skimming off the increased cream of agricultural productivity by landlords and money-lenders is another.

> The same class of agriculturists which has benefited from the recent turn in prices appears to have started or increased money-lending operations, presumably as a sequel to the new legislative curbs on professional money-lenders. (...) The yield from such operations is known to be incredibly high, probably ranging from 12 to 40%, and in some cases perhaps 100% or more (id., p. 55).

It is difficult to evaluate the part of the agricultural product which is appropriated by the landlord-money-lender class, and siphoned away from the accumulation fund. But this percentage can be considered very high.

> Cash rents were not very common, but where the practice existed the rents were extremely high. Division of crop was the most common practice, and the landowner would get about half of the yield for providing land and seed, and sometimes even more. (...) Where the landlord provided cattle and implements as well as land and seed, the landowners would receive 40-60% and even 80%(!) of the yield (id., p. 59).

And there is no doubt in our mind that this problem of the scarcely initiated agrarian reform is the key to the deficiency of both the accumulation fund and of agricultural productivity:

> The unsatisfactory forms of agrarian structure, reflected in maldistribution of land ownership, insecurity of tenure and high rents, uneconomic size of farms and fragmentation of holdings, tend in a variety of ways to impede investment. The existing system reduces living standards below the level which might be attained even with prevailing farm methods. It holds back investment both by reducing farmers' funds for investment and by reducing incentives to develop production (*ibid.*)

Needless to say, this "vicious circle of poverty" is closed by stating that this extreme misery of the great mass of the peasants removes any incentive for the development of a strong class of industrial capitalists, catering to a broad internal market for mass production goods. Poverty not only breeds poverty; it also breeds backwardness!

The problem can be reduced to a single formula: the First Five-Year Plan failed not because priority was given to agricultural development but because the landlord-money-lender-compradore system makes the mobilization of a great accumulation fund and the voluntary mobilization of the rural underemployed (conditioned by a quick increase in their standard of living) impossible. India is losing its struggle for industrialization because it has not yet accomplished its basic social revolution. And when the Second Five-Year Plan tried to increase substantially the rate of accumulation, this became completely dependent on foreign credits, led to a rapid exhaustion of sterling reserves built up during the war, and made the Indian government scale down its ambitious objectives as soon as it became evident that foreign assistance would be less than expected.

REFERENCES

1. Ragnar Nurkse: *Problems of Capital Formation in Underdeveloped Countries*, pp. 163, Oxford, Basil Backwell, 1953.
2. Paul A. Baran: *The Political Economy of Growth*, pp. 308, New York, Monthly Review Press, 1957.
3. In order to leave out complicated calculations of value production, we may assume that these workers produce some very rare industrial equipment, for which the social need remains unsatisfied even if production increases ten-fold, so that a tripling of production means a tripling of value produced, social *average* productivity of labour remaining unchanged outside this sector. The assumption is only apparently unreal; in fact, in the initial stages of industrialization, most heavy industrial plants operate precisely under such conditions.
4. These apologists of course also "forget" that Stalin opposed a quick increase in the rate of accumulation between 1924 and 1927; that thereby four years had been lost; and that the division of the accumulation fund of the First Five Year Plan over the time-span 1924-1932, instead of being concentrated in 4 years, would have enabled to realize exactly the same projects at a considerably lower expense of hardship, sacrifice and...loss of productivity of the workers and peasants.
5. The First Five-Year Plan of India estimated the number of under-employed adult males in Indian agriculture at the staggering figure of 70 million people!
6. In money terms, of course, increased agricultural production could mean, under conditions of stable currency, lower agricultural prices, and even lower money income of the peasants. This would be of no consequence, if at the same time a constant flow of industrial consumer goods, at falling prices, would be directed towards the villages.
7. In India, only 15% of the arable land is irrigated; in China only 45%.
8. D. K. Rangnekar: *Poverty and Capital Development in India*, pp. 316, Oxford University Press, 1958.

THE COLONIAL REVOLUTION*

Its Balance-Sheet, Its Problems, and Its Prospects

I GENERAL CONSIDERATIONS

1. The Causes which Maintain the Upsurge of the Colonial Revolution.

The continuing rise of the colonial revolution in the last decade has been in striking contrast with the prolonged stagnation of the revolutionary workers' movement in the advanced capitalist countries.

The upsurge of the colonial revolution in this postwar period is produced by a whole series of causes which were lacking or ceased to exist with the same intensity as previously in the advanced capitalist countries.

The process of relative capitalist stabilization in these countries has occurred simultaneously with the worsening of the economic and financial situation in most of the colonial and semi-colonial countries.

Capitalism in the advanced countries has profited by the mass injection of American capital and by the enormous worldwide needs in reconstruction and industrial development created by the war, to set in motion a new cycle of expansion on a higher level of productivity. The colonial and semi-colonial countries, on the contrary, having quickly exhausted the capital accumulated during the war and the first years thereafter, saw themselves more and more left behind by the advances both absolute and relative, achieved by the advanced countries.

The economic evolution of the colonial and semi-colonial countries, marked by a process of industrialization which though jerky and uneven, has not ceased on the average to be continuous, has favoured the industrial expansion of the advanced capitalist countries.

At the same time the capitalist countries have profited both by technological and scientific advances to increase their independence from certain imports of agricultural products and raw materials and by the fall in prices of such imports, to maintain a favourable balance of trade toward the dependent countries and a better protection against inflation. The dependent countries, on the contrary, have seen their balance of trade deteriorate and are struggling against the feverish upthrusts of endemic inflation.

The lag of dependent countries after advanced countries is aggravated in terms of both absolute production and per capita production by the fact that the production of the dependent countries is increasing at a faster rate than their production.

*Reproduced from Fourth International No. 12, winter 1960-61

At the basis of these developments lie the facts that the dependent countries have a different social and economic structure, and are historically belated. For a country to be able to catch up with the present development of the advanced capitalist countries it is necessary to have as starting-points a developed economic substructure, technically skilled manpower, and a very high per capita rate of investment.

Now the dependent countries are structurally handicapped in this race. They lack an adequate economic substructure, have a relatively low national income at their disposal, and do not accumulate sufficient capital, both because of their present limited income and because of the fact that a large part of the surplus-value created goes back to the imperialist countries and that a large part of the capital belonging to the native oligarchies tends to be directed toward usury, trading profits, and rent.

In any case the rate of accumulation of 15 to 20 % of the national income considered necessary for large-scale industrialization proves to be, in these countries, beyond their present practical possibilities. Even this rate, in most of these countries, would be insufficient if it were not backed up by other resources.

In the case of countries whose structure is already capitalist, these resources would normally have to come from foreign capital, in the form of public investments (for the substructure) or private reinvestments on the spot. Such resources, even if they were found—despite capital's reservations about investment not producing the average rate of profit—would have to be immensely higher than the total of current annual expenditures going to the "under-developed" countries (including from the USSR): from $ 4,000 million to over $ 20,000 million, if not considerably more.[1]

It is excluded that capitalism can agree to such an effort. Under these conditions—and without at all minimizing imperialism's new attempts "to aid" on a broader scale the so-called "underdeveloped" countries (India, Latin America, Africa, the Arab countries)—what must be foreseen is rather that the gap, both absolute and relative (in the meaning indicated), between these countries and the advanced countries will be aggravated in the years to come.

This means that these countries' economic and industrial development, which nevertheless will not fail to be steady, will be accomplished under conditions that are highly explosive and very different from those of the advanced countries, with real depressions, and not just recessions, unemployment, and inflation.

It is this different economic situation—resulting both from the historical tardiness of the dependent countries compared to the advanced

[1] United Nations experts have put forward the estimate that the sum annually needed to promote, within 35 years, a doubling of the living levels of populations now having at their disposal $100 per capita per annum (i.e., some 1,600 million people), would reach $20,000 million. But other estimates raise this sum to $50,000-$60,000 million, and even more.

countries launched on a new cycle of expansion, and from the obstacles set up to their development by their economic and social structure, feudo-capitalist, and indeed in places tribal with capitalist infiltration—which fundamentally explain the gap between the powerful and constantly renewed revolutionary activity of the masses in the dependent countries, and the decline of the revolutionary workers' movement in the advanced capitalist countries.

Another cause that is at present stimulating the upsurge of the colonial revolution is obviously the decline of imperialism in comparison with the rising power of the workers' states, and the new relationships established in this postwar period by the leading strata of the colonial revolution with imperialism on the one hand and the bureaucracy of the workers' states on the other. These leading strata, Bonapartist in function, composed mainly of elements who aspire to a national economic development, profit by the existence, the power, and the increased possibilities of the workers' states, as well as by their antagonism toward imperialism, precisely to increase their Bonapartist role and to advance far in their efforts to free themselves from the direct grasp of imperialism.

The colonial revolution is not finished by the attainment of its primordial goal: formal independence from imperialism. It continues with the search for a general liquidation of the whole aftermath of imperialism, and of all structural economico-social fetters on a rapid economic development and industrialization. The essential need, felt in a constantly more imperious and irresistible way by the masses of the dependent countries, is rapidly to reach the level of the advanced industrial countries and to make up their historical lateness.

It is for this reason that in a general way the national anti-imperialist phase of the colonial revolution, during which bourgeois and petty-bourgeois leaderships have been phased that brings forward the imperative economico-social needs of the dependent countries. This is particularly the case with the formally independent countries of Latin America, the countries of the Middle East and North Africa, India, Pakistan, Indonesia, Ceylon, etc. In Cuba the logic of the process of the permanent revolution has already caused that revolution to break through the limits of capitalism.

Under these conditions the colonial revolution occupies the vanguard place in the world revolution and operates as its main force, including for the reawakening of the revolutionary struggle in the advanced countries. As a result of the historical lateness of the revolution in the advanced capitalist countries, which is the result of the dialectical interaction of the betrayals of the leaderships and the new economic evolution of capitalism, the colonial revolution is objectively the driving force of the world revolution, combined with the rising force of the workers' states.

The reawakening of the revolution in the advanced capitalist states, particularly of Europe, has every chance of appearing historically as the result, at least in part, of the exterior pressure of these combined forces, in a new economic conjuncture less favourable than at present to capitalism in these countries.

II. THE COLONIAL REVOLUTION AND IMPERIALISM

Under the irresistible drive of the masses, pushing the colonial revolution steadily to a more advanced position, imperialism sees itself forced to resort to more indirect and flexible forms of dependence. All the recent examples given by British, French, and Belgian imperialism clearly show this tendency: the promotion of territories that yesterday were still colonies to the status of self-government, or of dominions within a more and more flexible association with the metropolis; and states that formally are completely independent.

Imperialism—at least its more clear-sighted wing—is at present seeking to safeguard what is essential in its economic position through a transfer of power to the native elites, which it is trying to develop and bribe, thanks to its political and economic power. This wing is aware of the impossibility of ruling for long either in the form of direct European domination or in the more flexible form of native governments that are not broadly independent.

Wherever native elites exist—intellectuals and various other categories of actually or potentially bourgeois or petty-bourgeois elements—imperialism is endeavouring to base itself on them by granting them political power, either immediately or in stages, and by bribing them by associating them in a joint economic exploitation of their respective countries. But the big difficulty for imperialism in this enterprise is the lack of native strata sufficiently developed to play such a part, in face of the impetuous movement of the masses, who from now on demand living conditions which capitalism cannot ensure.

For imperialism, the economic and in part strategic importance of the colonial and semi-colonial countries does not cease to be still vital (both for its supplies of raw materials and for the export of its industrial products and even of capital, the importance of this last factor having, however, diminished by comparison with the two others). Furthermore, the strategy of atomic war, which favours surprise attack, and raises the problem of survival, leads to the dispersal of bases around the world.

In the decisive race in which, by the force of events, imperialism finds itself setting out against the workers' states, the maintenance of its influence, over dependent countries will take on an importance still greater than in the past. For this competition—supposing that it stays "peaceful" for a period—involves a race even hotter than in the past for economic power, the most important reserve of which still remains the resources and the industrialization of the dependent countries.

In the decade that is beginning, imperialism enters this race handicapped from several points of view: compromised by its past in the eyes of the masses; incapable, by its structure, of granting effective aid; divided within its own ranks among powers that have re-established and surpassed their past potential and are throwing themselves into keener competition precisely in the field par excellence for accumulation: the industrialization of dependent countries.

The only chance for imperialism in this field lies in the help that can be brought to it by the colonial bourgeoisie in formation. The next stage of the colonial revolution depends on the race in time between the formation of such strata, to which imperialism conduces by every means, and the revolutionary movement of the masses looking for radical solutions and therefore a radical leadership.

But even the transition via a native neo-bourgeois leadership can turn out historically to be of short duration and finally also economically ruinous for imperialism. For any important development of a native bourgeoisie cannot but diminish in the long run that share of the surplus-value still cornered by imperialism.

III. THE COLONIAL REVOLUTION AND THE WORKERS' STATES

In the present historical phase of the formation, side-by-side with capitalism, of a system of workers' states, the alliance between the colonial revolution and this system of workers' states ought to be establishing itself quite naturally and almost automatically. The convergence of interests in the common struggle against imperialism is obvious, and ought to give rise to an active and unconditional support of this struggle by the workers' states.

Furthermore, in the field of economic exchanges, the workers' states will gradually have the possibility of advantageously replacing the "aid" granted by imperialism, and of diverting the present circuits with imperialism into their own orbit. The workers' states can grant low-cost financial and technical aid for the real economic development of the dependent countries, and without imposing political conditions.

They can furthermore establish—though this case may not be general —trade relations on the basis of the complementary nature of their economies: agricultural products and raw materials coming from the dependent countries against material for industrial equipment coming from the workers' states. The development of such relations with the dependent states in a historic perspective will make clearly apparent the enormous possibilities potentially possessed by the workers' states in this field and the fatal risks run by imperialism in the eventuality of a prolonged "peaceful competition". It is only the nature of the political regime in the present workers' states, degenerated or deformed by the bureaucracy, that limits the possibilities to be exploited, and handicaps and deforms the *de facto* alliance between the colonial revolution and the workers' states.

Naturally, no objection could be raised to the economic aid which the bureaucracy of the USSR or of the other workers' states is granting to the bourgeois regimes of the dependent countries so that they may momentarily resist imperialism or develop more freely. But to the degree to which this aid is granted in exchange for the "neutralist" policy of the colonial bourgeoisie and that the Communist Parties in the dependent countries find themselves forced to subordinate their autonomous class policy to the requirement of the diplomacy of the workers' states, this runs the risk of ending up practically in the consolidation of bourgeois regimes which invariably turn against the workers' movement in their own countries, and, at a more distant stage, against the workers' states themselves. From this point of view, the examples provided recently by Nehru, Sukarno, Nasser, Kassem, and other beneficiaries of the aid of the workers' states, speak eloquently.

Still, the aid of the workers' states can objectively help the process of the masses' becoming mature and consequently appear to capitalism to be an objective threat. This explains, among other things, the attitude of certain bourgeoisies, such as those of Brazil and Bolivia. The objective alliance between the colonial revolution and the workers' states is expressed in all its dynamism by the case of Cuba, where the Soviet bureaucracy found itself forced to over-ride the policy of peaceful co-existence to offer its missiles for the defence of the revolution. In its new stage, the colonial revolution is factually joining forces with the workers' states despite the efforts of the Soviet bureaucracy and petty-bourgeois leaderships to prevent it.

IV. THE ROLE OF THE NATIONAL BOURGEOISIE

The native comprador oligarchies, obtaining their income from trading profits, land rent, usury, or acting as functionaries at the service of imperialism, are strata now in decline in the dependent countries, to the advantage of new social formations, which are reflecting the process—steady, in spite of everything—of economic and industrial development in these countries. It is these strata which, directly or through their petty-bourgeois demagogues, are at the present stage-cornering for themselves the leadership of the colonial revolution.

The importance of these strata, called national bourgeoisies, is highly variable in the different dependent countries according to the degree of economic development achieved.

In cases such as India, Argentina, Brazil, and Chile, the matter is one already of a genuine class, sufficiently powerful and conscious to take direct political power, even if it risks losing it momentarily to the benefit of other fractions more tied up with the oligarchy and imperialism.

In the case of other Asiatic and Latin American countries, the importance of the national bourgeoisie compared to the comprador oligarchy is less.

In certain cases its power is often exercised through Bonapartist political regimes (such as Sukarno, Nasser, Kassem, Nkhrumah, et al) which are operating historically for the benefit of the national bourgeoisie.

In other cases, which can turn out to be frequent in Africa, the very weak formation of native elites, other than the tribal chiefs and the functionaries at the service of imperialism, can give birth to new comprador bourgeoisies closely associated with imperialism for the economic coexploitation of their own countries.

Everywhere the principal instrument for the development of the national burgeoisie proves to be Bonapartist political power. It is this power that renders it possible to face simultaneously the oligarchy, imperialism, and the masses, and to find the important amounts of capital required for building the substructure and the financing of large-scale enterprises. It is furthermore through the exercise of the political power and the economic functions of the state that the cadres of this bourgeoisie are partly formed, by the enrichment of functionaries, their infiltration in the enterprises, their corruption, etc. The Bonapartist state becomes, under these circumstances, a genuine nursery for capitalist development in the dependent countries.

The ideology which best corresponds to the Bonapartist state is the *defacto* dictatorship of the Single Party, which boils down to its leadership taking power. In the case that this party is truly proletarian and socialist through its programme and ideology, such a dictatorship, based on the masses organized in democratic committees or communes, would unquestionably have a historically progressive meaning. But the pretext of the so-called classless colonial society currently used by certain people to justify in Africa the Bonapartist dictatorship of the Single Party, engaged in a capitalist economic development and without democratic control by the organized masses, is to be rejected.

Though it is true that the multi-party regime of socialist democracy cannot be transplanted, just as it is, into a society scarcely emerged from tribalism, it would be impossible for all that to neglect the need for such a possible Single Party to have a class character with proletarian ideology and programme and to base itself on the masses democratically organized in peasant communes and urban committees which control the government and hold the power.

In any case the International cannot give up the conception according to which the right to have several workers' parties represents an essential guarantee of a genuine socialist democracy.

No illusion is permissible about the real tendencies of the national bourgeoisie. Although in its formation it is obliged to struggle to a certain extent against imperialism and the oligarchy, to ally itself with the proletariat and its trade-union organizations, and to advocate and even put into practice for a certain period nationalizations and a "mixed" economy, it invariably tends, precisely through its increase in strength, to act like the classic bourgeoisie of the advanced countries: to turn against the workers' movement and to draw closer to imperialism both by "freeing" its "mixed" economy (in order to attract foreign capital and to stimulate native private capitalist initiative) and by lining up diplomatically with imperialism. Nehru's India, one of the first countries that obtained its independence and formed a serious national bourgeoisie, is the mirror in which there is already clearly reflected the national bourgeosie's inevitable historical evolution, regressive and counter-revolutionary on a relatively short-term basis. (Other examples are: Tunisia, Egypt, Ghana, Argentina, Brazil.) The greatest danger lying in wait for the colonial masses in revolution is to be lulled by the mystique of national unity with their bourgeoisie and to sacrifice to this mystique their autonomous class policy and organization.

V. THE CAPITALIST ROAD OR THE SOCIALIST ROAD?

The colonial masses' aspiration to political independence and rapid economic development is everywhere profound and irresistible.

The national bourgeoisie is trying to fufil this mission, both to profit by it itself and to pacify the masses. But it stumbles over the impossibility of attaining the goal of rapid economic development by capitalist roads.

The national bourgeoisie shows itself everywhere unable to nationalize definitively (after a few stages that turn out to be necessary) the essential part of the surplus-value extorted by the imperialists in the dependent countries, as well as the land rent of the native feudalists, and to valorize the enormous resource represented by the unused manpower of these countries. Nowhere has it been able or willing to expropriate without indemnity the imperialist enterprises in agriculture, mining, and trade; to expropriate without indemnity the feudalists and give the land to the peasants; to nationalize and plan the economy, and mobilize for its service the masses of the country.

Now the agrarian question is fundamental everywhere. The land for the most part is everywhere hoarded by the native feudalists, colons (big settlers), or foreign imperialist firms, and only a part of it (whose importance varies according to each concrete case) is cultivated on a private basis by native peasants or collectively in tribal reserves (of Negro Africa, for example).

Even these free peasants who are neither serfs nor share-croppers nor rural labourers are for the most part poor peasants compared to the standards of the peasants of the advanced capitalist countries, and have to struggle desperately to continue to exist as peasants. From this there arises the primordial importance of a radical agrarian reform, accompanied by the effective material and technical aid of a genuine proletarian state.

The agrarian reform is above all the distribution of the land according to the free will of those who till it. According to the concrete case, this can take the form of the distribution of the lands of the feudalists and the colons to landless or almost landless peasants, accompanied by effective aid by the state to the peasant cooperatives; or else the form of a collective management of the land right from the beginning by communes on a village or broader scale, and collectives of agricultural workers and share-croppers of the great plantations and estates; or, most frequently, a mixed system.

For economic development, the national bourgeoisie counts only on the main contribution of foreign capital. Now its volume and the conditions for granting it render it an illusion to expect an even slightly rapid industrialization of the dependent countries so as to catch up with the advanced countries. The comparative examples of China and India become decisive in this field (without insisting on that of the USSR). The example of Jugoslavia is another. The Chinese experience is extremely valuable as an indication of a specific road for the rapid and balanced economic development of a colonial country that starts out from a very low level of the productive forces.

The organisation of peasant masses into communes contains elements that might be able to be profitably applied in other cases, especially where the communal traditions of the peasants are still relatively strong. The political and economic organization of the commune permits productively employing the whole available labouring mass by using the productive means and forces on the spot and thus beginning the rapid and balanced economic development of the country.

The setting up of the communes in general might be criticized only from the viewpoint of their possible bureaucratic administration, which would have the tendency not to take sufficiently into account the masses' living conditions and the need for their voluntarily joining this new type of economic and social organization. But in the case where the bureaucratic excesses might be limited—thanks mainly to the democratic organization of the masses managing the communes—the communes as an institution might turn out historically to be one form for the rapid, balanced, and more productive development of the "underdeveloped" countries, by using fully and judiciously all the available resources, and a school for a more communal social life.

The Jugoslav example on its side is valuable as an experiment in the rapid development of an "underdeveloped" country in which private small farm property predominates, thanks to an economy which, while being a workers' economy in its nature, remains open to the advantages of the world market, and thanks also to the close democratic association of the producers in the control and even the management of the economy (workers' councils.)

The "underdeveloped" countries, far from being caught in the dilemma of either stagnation or a capitalist-type development thanks to the contribution of foreign capital, have the real possibility of taking, according to their concrete case, the "Chinese road" or the "Jugoslav road" or any combination of the two, rid of their negative elements.

But the primordial condition for such a possible development is the setting up of new economic and social structures of the socialist type.

This means that the struggle for real liberation from imperialism, and for economic development and industrialization, is inseparable from the struggle for the socialist revolution. Only those dependent countries which have known how to combine the anti-imperialist struggle with the struggle for the socialist revolution have been able really to break loose from the imperialist system and to open wide the road to their rapid development and industrialization.

VI. THE PERMANENT CHARACTER OF THE COLONIAL REVOLUTION

Instinctively, the masses who have thrown themselves into the anti-imperialist struggle against direct or indirect imperialist domination, are pushed toward goals that lie beyond that of formal independence. In the present international and national contexts of the colonial revolution, it has inexorably a tendency to develop as a permanent revolution, putting more and more in the forefront the economic and social goals of the broad peasant and worker masses who are carrying it forward: agrarian reform, nationalization and planning of the economy, emancipation of women.

In this process the clash with the national bourgeoisie also becomes inevitable at a given stage of the struggle. Though the bourgeoisie in the dependent countries inevitably sets out on a sort of *de facto* united front of all the social classes (except the feudalists and the comprador bourgeoisie) against direct or indirect imperialist domination, the deepening of the struggle no less inevitably differentiates this front along class lines. The national bourgeoisie soon finds itself at grips with the radicalism of the movement of the peasant and worker masses who aspire to agrarian reform, nationalization and planning of the economy, and the emancipation of women—all objectives incompatible with the regime of the national bourgeoisie. This obliges the bourgeoisie to turn against the mass movement and to resort to a regime that is, whether overtly or not, dictatorial.

The prestige acquired by the national bourgeoisie during the phase of the united anti-imperialist struggle can—in the absence of a genuine revolutionary mass party—with credit for it among the masses and allow it temporarily to stop the revolution halfway (e.g, Nehru, Sukarno, Bourguiba, Nasser, Kassem, Nkhrumah, et al). Thence arises the need never to subordinate the autonomous revolutionary movement of the masses to the political leadership of the national bourgeoisie, never to "prettify" it, never to stop criticizing and exposing it, while agreeing to give critical support to all concrete anti-imperialist measures that it might be led to adopt, to the degree that it continues to have credit among the masses of workers and poor peasants.

The prominent role now played in the colonial revolution by the national bourgeoisie, or by petty-bourgeois formations with an ideology that is in the last analysis bourgeois, is partly the result of the policy of

Stalinism, which has subordinated the autonomous revolutionary movement of the masses to the interests either of the metropolitan bourgeoisie or of the colonial national bourgeoisie. If this policy is not radically opposed, and if a stop is not put to treating the revolutionary movement of the masses simply as a contributory force to the game of the bourgeoisie and its relations with the Stalinist bureaucracy, there is a risk of enormously slowing down the progress of the colonial revolution to a higher level.

10

A SOCIOLOGICAL APPROACH TO THE PROBLEMS OF UNDERDEVELOPMENT*

W. F. WERTHEIM

THE PURPOSE of this essay is to try to give a sociological description of those countries, areas and communities which are usually regarded as 'underdeveloped' technically and economically.

This is no simple task. For indeed, far from showing uniform traits, it is on the contrary the great diversity of the 'underdeveloped' world which impresses us. This is understandable considering the fact that only a few centuries ago the whole inhabited world was underdeveloped judging by present European or North American standards. Not until the Industrial Revolution did what Romein calls the Western European Deviation from the Common Human Pattern[1] begin to stand out clearly.

On closer scrutiny, however, the Common Human Pattern turns out to be a 'mosaic of cultural patterns'[2]—in the 'underdeveloped world' practically uninhabited desert regions can be found side by side with unimaginably densely populated river valleys, where wet rice cultivation is the prevailing means of existence; nomadic tribes practising cattle breeding or hoe-culture side by side with peasant populations which for tens of centuries have been living within an organized state structure; isolated little mountain peoples living close to nature side by side with groups of small traders and artisans huddled together in closely built-up, stinking urban quarters; peoples which for centuries have been living under an omnipotent colonial authority side by side with only recently discovered tribes without the slightest notion of the existence of a world outside their own. A sociological approach to this 'underdeveloped world' would be more in place in an encyclopaedia of eighteen volumes than in an article of eighteen pages.

What then does lie within our scope? At most an attempt to seek, not the diversity, but the common characteristics of this underdeveloped

---

* Reproduced from *East West Parallels* by W. F. Wertheim, pp. 3-20.

1 Jan Romein in co-operation with Annie Romein-Verschoor, Aera van Europa: De Europese geschiedenis als afwijking van het Algemeen Menselijk Patroon (Era of Europe: European history as a deviation from the Common Human Pattern, Leiden, 1954). See for an English version of the basic idea also Romein's paper mentioned on p. 6, note 1.

2 Expression used by A.J.F. Kobben, in a critical appraisal of Romein's Common Human Pattern concept from the point of view of a cultural anthropologist, 'Het A.M.P. en de volkenkundige' (The C.H.P. and the cultural anthropologist), Mens en Maatschappij, Vol. 32 (1957), pp. 193 ff.

world. In practice this must amount to emphasizing such sociological aspects as are closely connected with the distinctive feature of this particular part of the world—namely the low level of its technical and economic development.

The first and most obvious economic characteristic of such countries, areas and communities is low productivity per head of the population. This is in turn a consequence of the low degree of mechanization of labour coupled with lagging technical development. Next is an economic structure which, according to our present standards, is onesided with a strong emphasis on primary production, in the first place agriculture. The economic superstructure, and connected with it the sectors of 'secondary' and 'tertiary' production—however one may circumscribe these—has reached only a limited development. The low mechanization and the predominant role of agriculture again generally result in a great dependence on natural forces and climatic conditions and in the great vulnerability of the most elementary means of existence. The dependence of agriculture on the cycle of nature furthermore causes a large number of man-hours per year to remain unproductive—and this sometimes applies even more forcibly to woman—hours.

This links up with the phenomenon we call, according to our present standards of efficiency, 'hidden unemployment'—wisely ignoring how much of our present expenditure of time will be deemed inefficient according to the norms of the future.

This brief summary of some essential economic traits also indicates in which direction we must seek the sociological characteristics of our underdeveloped societies. First of all the low per capita productivity of labour and the dependence on natural forces engenders in intense feeling of insecurity. For the large majority of the members of the community the margin between production and the minimal necessities of life remains alarmingly narrow. This sense of insecurity leads in turn to an attitude to life which attaches great value to behaviour in accord with ancient traditions. Disasters and bad harvests are regarded as normal; the only possible way to meet them is by maximum solidarity and mutual support. Such a society affords little room for adventurous individualism. In such an environment religious or quasi-religious ideas tend towards acceptance of suffering and of the ever-recurring disasters as an inevitable fate. Ignorance of technical means to avert natural disasters furthers the use of expedients which we, from the viewpoint of our present knowledge, designate as magic. In the religious sphere, too, the emphasis lies on a collective following of traditions rather than on personal experience.

The changing cycle of nature leads to a labour ethos which is essentially different from our Western-industrial ideal of constant and continuous labour. Neither labour nor time are measured in standardized units. Labour is performed discontinuously—in some seasons with great intensity, while in others the expenditure of labour is characterized, according to the standards of the urban observer from an industrialized world, by an extremely uneconomic management of time.

The loyalties of the rural inhabitant of the underdeveloped world are in general confined to a circle with which he is familiar, in conformity with his limited mental horizon. His relations to his fellow humans are not abstract, but concrete and personal. Even in the urban centres the modern, impersonal business relationship is unknown. Trade is carried on in the traditional way, in an atmosphere of genial haggling which leaves the man to man relationship intact. But wherever people face one another not as equals, traditional authority based on birth can be exercised and accepted in a way which approaches the absolute.

If one compares the abovementioned characteristics of the underdeveloped world with the traits Romein calls typical of the Comman Human Pattern, one is struck by their great similarity to his description.[1] Romein mentions in particular the attitude of 'the C.H.P.-man towards nature', which does not objectify but is subjective, i.e. experiencing and enduring. He points furthermore to the habit of thinking in images, i.e. concretely instead of abstractly, and to the character of community life which is organized instead of organizational. He also mentions the absence of a conscious struggle against natural disasters and, in connection with this, the predominance of a religious-magical world of ideas. He stresses the absence in the underdeveloped world of time as an economic commodity. Finally he points out the absolute character of authority.

So it appears that Romein, with his concept of the Common Human Pattern, has succeeded in most strikingly characterizing whatever the pre-industrial world, in spite of all its diversity, has in common.

But if the above outline should be considered too vague, since it describes underdeveloped society only in qualitative terms, we could try to approach it in quantitative ones. We can do this in the main by falling back on Alfred Sauvy's attempt to enumerate the demographic aspects of the underdeveloped world.

In his Theorie generale de la population this French demographer mentions ten tests for recognizing the underdeveloped countries.[2] These are:

1. High level of mortality, especially of infant mortality; low average expectation of life, between thirty and forty.
2. High birth rate, not far from the physiological fertility limit; at least the absence of birth control.
3. Insufficient nutrition, on the average below 2500 calories per day, and a diet especially weak in proteins.

---

[1] Jan Romein, 'The Common Human Pattern; Origin and Scope of Historical Theories', *Journal of World History*, Vol. 4, no. 2 (1958), pp. 449, ff; also published in *Delta*, Vol. 2 (1959), pp. 5 ff.

[2] Alffred Sauvy, Theorie generale de la population, Part One: Economie et population (Paris, 1952), pp. 241-242.

4. High percentage of illiterates, often close on eighty per cent.
5. High percentage of peasants or fishermen.
6. Lack of opportunity for employment as a result of the absence of means of production.
7. Inferior position of women; no outdoor labour for women.
8. Child labour from the age of ten or less.
9. Absence or weakness of middle classes.
10. Authoritarian regime in various forms: absence of democratic institutions.

There is something to be said against several of these descriptions, notably against the general character which is ascribed to these demographic traits. Thus for example, though a high birth rate is characteristic of the large majority of types of 'underdeveloped' countries—as is shown by a comprehensive and comparative study by Frank Lorimer c.a., *Culture and Human Fertility*—there are some striking exceptions particularly in Africa.[1] Insufficient nutrition is acceptable as a general characteristic, but point seven—the absence of outdoor labour for women—is very controversial. In the 'underdeveloped' countries many peoples can be found among whom the women fulfil a vital function in agriculture, in gathering forest products or in fishing. The subordinate position of women is therefore rather an urban phenomenon and widespread in oriental commercial districts. For rural societies this subordination of women certainly cannot be taken as an omniprevalent characteristic.

But the strongest objections arise when Sauvy asserts that these ten tests apply nearly as well to the underdeveloped countries of 1952 as to the Western countries at the time before economic development started. For when we subject the quantitative aspects of the underdeveloped countries to a closer investigation we realize with a shock that the identification of the pre-industrial 'West' with the present 'East' does not hold good in every particular, and that the present specific problems of the underdeveloped countries are partly due to the very existence, in the middle of the twentieth century, of an 'underdeveloped' part of the world side by side with a 'developed' one.

For the Common Human Pattern as sketched by Romein is connected with a certain stability of social relations which, in spite of all the uncertainties of material existence, continues to dominate the activities of life. The ten demographic characteristics of Sauvy reflect a certain long-term equilibrium. The high birth and mortality rates on the one hand ensure a safe old age for the parents despite the high child mortality, and on the other hand prevent a too sudden disturbance of the equilibrium between population and means of subsistence. And insofar as the modest though

[1] Frank Lorimer c.a., *Culture and Human Fertility : A Study of the Relation of Cultural Conditions to Fertility in Non-Industrial and Transitional Societies* (Unesco, Paris, 1954); for divergent birth rates in African areas see p. 118.

constant population increase drew too heavily on the productive capacity of pre-industrial man, there were 'the there Fates'—famine, epidemic, and war—which bursquely restored some of the demographic equilibrium.[1] According to Sauvy's calculations, the world population from the beginning of our era until 1950 or thereabout did not on an average increase faster than at a rate of one per thousand a year.[2] And even from about 1650 to the middle of the nineteenth century the average annual increase was still no higher than four or five per thousand.[3] But one of the most important differences between the mediaeval West and the present-day East is that Sauvy's first demographic 'test'—high mortality—is no longer valid otherwise than in a relative sense. For although mortality, and notably child mortality, is in general still considerably higher in the 'underdeveloped' than in the 'developed' part of the world—all the more so if one takes into account the composition of the population according to age groups, since the percentage of young people is as a rule much higher than in Western countries—the rapid decline that has gone on in mortality while all other structural traits of the underdeveloped country are retained lends the present problems in those areas their specific character. This is because the rapid decline in mortality, due not to internal factors but to intervention from outside, has brought about the present 'population explosion'.

Therefore the preceding description of the social structure of the underdeveloped countries is too static. In order to be complete it would simultaneously have to do full justice to the fact that for the first time in world history a situation which until recently formed the Common Human Pattern is now experienced as underdevelopment, as a pathological deviation. And it is not only the leading groups in the developed world, with their sense of responsibility for world events, who want to eliminate or reduce the gap between the two types of society. In the underdeveloped world itself, too, awareness of 'underdevelopment' and dissatisfaction with this state of affairs is beginning to penetrate more and more deeply and more and more widely. This is the biggest essential difference with the pre-industrial West.

The existence of a developed part of the world presents a challenge to the part which is not yet developed. It sets in motion processes which irreparably destroy the relative equilibrium within the societies hitherto corresponding with the typology of the Common Human Pattern. For the same reason it is impossible to approach the underdeveloped societies sociologically in terms of static structures and conditions. It is the task of the sociologist to awaken understanding of the dynamic processes taking place in those societies. In order to approach these he will yet again have to use qualitative terms.

---

1 Alfred Sauvy, *Fertility and Survival: Population Problems from Malthus to Mao Tse-tung* (New York, 1963), p. 38.

2 Sauvy, *Fertility and Survival*, *op. cit.*, pp. 27-28.

3 *Ibidem*, p. 26.

True, there are some quantitative indications of the presence of new dynamic factors. For example, if we once again look at Sauvy's ten tests we see the decline in mortality is not the only quantitative pointer to the existence of such dynamic tendencies. Thus the percentage of illiterates in the underdeveloped world has been rapidly decreasing since the end of the Second World War. Also those young governments which have not succeeded in changing the economic structure noticeably nor in raising nutrition above the 'underdeveloped' level, often score big successes in the spheres of hygiene and education and thereby, voluntarily or involuntarily, arouse the revolutionary forces which want to abolish the underdevelopment at an accelerated tempo.

But when one describes the 'underdeveloped' areas euphemistically as countries in a process of 'accelerated development' one simply overlooks the most essential element of what is actually going on in those areas.

For—and now I shall try to describe these processes in qualitative terms—in the first instance the economic influence which the developed world exerts on the underdeveloped world has often been inhibiting rather than stimulating. The present underdeveloped world presents a picture not only of backwardness, but also of artifical petrification in that underdeveloped state. In this artifical situation there are tensions—social, psychological, ideological and also purely economic and technical—which make the present conditions in that world differ so widely from the Western pre-industrial world that they are poles apart. For as J. H. Boeke has justly argued all his life, the present 'East' is not characterized by a pre-capitalist economy, but by the existence of a pre-capitalist system side by side with a high-capitalist one mutually influencing one another.[1] The capitalist system, an extension of the Western industrialized world, has for many years influenced the rural East and put its stamp on it.

In this interaction capitalism, coming from outside, was in the main the active factor, the indigenous rural society in the main the passive. The West appeared in the East in various guises—as the colonial ruler who brought into existence a stratification according to race: as the colonial administration which introduced medical and hygienic provisions—such as mass inoculation against smallpox; as the plantation owner in search of cheap land and cheap labour; as the engrosser and money-lender who brought the money economy deep into the interior; as the missionary who founded schools or hospitals.

A perceptive analysis of the social processes set in motion by these contacts has been undertaken by the American social anthropologist Clifford Geertz for pre-war Indonesia. In a recent book which elaborates ideas previously forwarded in a series of mimeographed studies he has described such processes in Central and East Java.

---

[1] J. H. Boeke, *Economics and Economic Policy of Dual Societies as Exemplified by Indonesia* (Haarlem, 1953). For a discussion of Boeke's views see *Indonesian Economics: The Concept of Dualism in Theory and Policy* (The Hague, 1961).

One of his main conclusions is that the processes set in train by the sugar plantations must be characterized, for the great mass of the Javanese peasants, not as a 'development'— evolution— but as the opposite— involution.[1] The rapid growth of the population caused by improved hygienic conditions resulted in increasing pressure on agricultural land. The plantation economy led to an artificial preservation of the traditional forms of communal land tenure, and to a capitalist stimulus introduced in this way the population could react only by a rigidifying of traditional structures and institutions. Thus a social pattern emerged which Geertz has defined as a 'shared poverty system',[2] in which at least some sort of security is sought by spreading out the available goods over as many people as possible.

Raised to an extreme, the density of the population makes it more and more difficult to find elbow room for economic and social renewal in the countryside. Technical renewal usually boils down to the release of labour, and in a chronic condition of hidden unemployment there is not the slightest incentive to this. On the contrary, the 'shared poverty' system serves, at any rate to provide a minimum of social security for the many economically weak members of the village.

Originating in rural society, the 'shared poverty' pattern also spreads to Eastern urban society. Of this Geertz has also given striking illistrations in an analysis of life in the town of 'Modjokuto'.[3] The lack of opportunity for employment in the town, the growing stream of impoverished rural inhabitants moving there, and the generally low standard of living lead to the available opportunities for work being spread over large numbers of applicants each of whom has too little to do and is living on the very margin of minimal subsistence. The innumerable street-vendors, pedicab drivers, 'peons' and little clerks in the offices all testify to the same system, in which social justice takes precedence over inefficiency and a minimum output per head is put up with so that the available means of subsistence can be spread out over a maximum number of people. In urban industry too, the efficiency and viability of an enterprise suffer from the social pressure of the environment, which demands that the factory owner takes on and maintains so many male or female workers that each has too little to live

[1] Clifford Geertz has launched this concept of involution in the *The Development of the Javanese Economy : A Socio-Cultural Approach* (mimeographed paper, M.I.T., Cambridge, Mass., 1956), pp. 29 ff., 112-113 (note 24). The effect of the sugar plantation economy upon traditional agriculture in Java has been analysed by Geertz, *The Social Context of Economic Change: An Indonesian Case Study* (mimeographed paper, M.I.T., Cambridge, Mass., 1956), pp. 29 ff. The basic ideas have recently been elaborated in much greater detail in Geertz, *Agricultural Involution*: *The Processes of Ecological Change in Indonesia* (Berkeley/Los Angeles, 1963).

[2] Geertz, 'Religious Belief and Economic Behavior in a Central Javanese Town: Some Preliminary Considerations', *Economic Development and Cultural Change*, Vol. 4 (1956), p. 141.

[3] Modjokuto—a fictitious name for a small town in the Western part of East Java.

and too much to die while there is no incentive to and possibility of further investment left.

Hence the paradox that the same capitalism which in the West formed a stimulus for technical development, in the East has in many cases had the opposite effect, because the colonial or semi-colonial form in which capitalism appeared there often had a petrifying effect on the social institutions and consequently paralysed economic-technical adaptability.

Since the decline in mortality occurred before the industrialization, Eastern society was forced into an attitude of passive resistance which for many years excluded active adaptation. And this while the dynamic development in the demographic sphere—a population growth of hitherto unprecedented rapidity, in Java as early as the first half of the nineteenth century, in other non-Western areas some time later—presents a challenge to which the correct answer would have to be at least as dynamic as the original stimulus. For it is clear that, if the cause of 'underdevelopment' lies in low per capita productivity, development can never be achieved in any other way than by increasing this labour productivity. A purely passive resistance, either in the form of 'shared poverty' or in that of birth control (in Sauvy's terminology: 'the demographic solution') or emigration, can provide no more than temporary relief and by no means removes the cause of the 'disease'—on the contrary, it tends only to divert the energy necessary to give the correct answer: the 'economic solution' to use Sauvy's terminology again.[1]

Now it becomes clearer why there are still so many countries for which Sauvy's ten tests are largely valid. In many non-Western countries the protracted colonial or semi-colonial expansion has not furthered, but retarded economic development. Consequently for many of those countries the traits mentioned by Sauvy still apply: one-sided economic structure, high percentage of agriculturalists, low standard of living and of nutrition, low degree of mechanization. If, however, we want fully to understand the social processes in these areas we must also take into account the positive dynamic forces which are also operative there. For simultaneously with the petrifaction of many social institutions a process is found which has a solvent effect on those institutions. The penetration of monetary exchange has disrupted many traditional bonds, has mobilized landed property and thus uprooted the traditional protection surrounding the individual. A process of atomizing and proletarianizing of the peasant population is going on as a result of which the traditional structures, preserved in a petrified form, are often no more than an empty shell. Both a rural and an urban proletariat have begun to move. Dissatisfied with the present, they no longer regard poverty and destitution as inevitable, partly as a result of visual confrontation either in reality or via the film with the way of life of the neighbouring whites—colonial administrators or businessmen. And the small clerks crowding urban offices have also become a tur-

[1] Sauvy, *Fertility and Survival, op. cit.*, pp. 105 ff., 185 ff.

bulent element in society. These groups, moreover, freely make use of modern forms of organization (trade unions, peasant organizations, district associations) which replace the community bonds rooted in tradition.

For this reason, too, present Asian society cannot be put on a par with the pre-industrial West. Although in Western history expressions of social dissatisfaction also occurred again and again, they usually sought an outlet in religious, messianic movements which turned away from reality.

In the present underdeveloped areas the dissatisfaction expresses itself in new forms often derived from the modern West. The loyalties of the present rural population in the East are no longer predominantly particularistic. Even though their new ideals, whether these present themselves in a nationalistic, a religious, or a socialist or anti-imperialist garb, can not yet be called 'universalistic' in a true sense, their universe is still an expanding one. Even if the society itself does not yet harbour a social dynamic sufficiently powerful to bring about economic and technical innovations, there is an inner, psychological motive force which contrasts sharply with the traditional, fatalistic-religious attitude to life.

A philosophically resigned East exists nowadays almost exclusively in the imagination of sentimental Westerners.

A review of the actual sociological aspects of the underdeveloped part of the world cannot be confined to the broad mass of agriculturalists and townspeople. It must embrace the elite groups which in the present situation contend with each other and with the foreign rulers for supremacy.[1] Naturally, modern industrial culture influences these groups even more than it does the mass of simple peasants and workers.

In the attitude and way of life of these groups there are still many remnants of the traditional pre-industrial society. Their behaviour shows many relics of aristocratic-traditional life patterns, while their loyalties towards relatives or persons belonging to the same ethnic group also frequently display particularistic traits. On the other hand these groups are often more strongly affected by universalist or quasiuniversalist ideals which can serve to bridge traditional local particularisms. It is especially this class of two conflicting worlds meeting within one and the same person which causes a certain lability in social norms and attitudes to life. The phenomenon of corruption, so widespread in the present underdeveloped world, should also be seen in the first place as the expression of a chronic conflict between universalist norms and particularist loyalties. Purely economic factors such as low remuneration, or exorbitant power for individual civil servants in deciding matters involving large interests, play only a secondary role in this respect. Nor is the pre-industrial pattern of nepotism and 'squeeze' the decisive point, but the marginal position between traditional-particularist and modern-universalist norms. Even more than

[1] For a more detailed treatment of the elite in Asian countries see the fourth paper of this volume. The corruption issue is dealt with in the fifth paper.

the great mass of the people, the new leading group moves on the borderline between two worlds. In many underdeveloped areas this leading group fulfils a dynamic and revolutionary function—but it is able to do so only because and insofar as the social dynamic has to a certain extent also affected the masses.

At this point the question arises, to what extent the social dynamics in Asian countries can be expected, in the near future, to take a similar course as previously in the West.

According to Romein's view of Western modern History as a deviation from the Common Human Pattern, the new way of life which originated in the West gradually spreads to other parts of the world. As a result, the original deviation is gradually developing into a new Common Human Pattern. The prospect, in that case, would appear to be such that, despite many retarding or impeding factors, the dynamics of development in Asia could be expected, in the long run, to create a counterpart of Western society.

But in addition, Romein has formulated in one of his pre-war essays which, unfortunately, has never been published in an English translation,[1] a hypothesis on the way human evolution tends to proceed.

Contrary to the nineteenth-century belief in a unilinear evolutionary pattern according to which any human society develops through a series of distinct, identical phases, Romein tries to establish a different pattern of evolution, which he calls a 'dialectical' one.

He demonstrates, with a wealth of examples drawn from human history, that far from developing in a gradual way, human history progresses with leaps and bounds, comparable to the mutations known from the world of living nature. A next step in human evolution is not at all likely to occur within the society which has achieved a high degree of perfection in a given direction. On the contrary, the progress once achieved in the past is liable to act as a brake upon further progress. Both an atmosphere of complacency and vested interests tend to oppose further steps which might involve a complete overhaul of established institutions or equipments.

Therefore, further progress on the road of human evolution is, time and again, much more likely to occur in a more backward society, where resistances against social change are weaker. Romein shows that leadership in human evolution perpetually sifts from one society to another, after over-specialization has led yesterday's leader into a blind alley. He draws his examples both from the realm of technique (including arma-

[1] Jan Romein, 'De dialektiek van de vooruitgang: Bijdrage tot het ontwikkelingsbegrip in de geschiedenis' (The dialectics of progress: a contribution to our understanding of evolution within history), forum, Vol. 4, Part Two (1935), pp. 752-777 and 828-855; reprinted in Romein, Het onvoltovid verleden: Cultuur-historische studies (The Imperfect Past: Studies in cultural history, Second Ed., Amsterdam. 1948), pp. 13-69. A German version has been published with the title 'Dialektik des Fortschritts', in Mass und Wert, Vol. 2 (1939), pp. 305 ff.

ments and warfare) and the birth of social institutions. A few of his most striking illustrations of his thesis are the following: retardation in the introduction of electric lighting in London, which was the first city to develop illumination with gas and to carry it forth to a remarkable perfection; the lagging behind of the productivity of collieries in Britain, France and Belgium, the countries which were the first to develop large-scale coal mining; the advantage of late-comer Japan over Britain as far as modernization and rationalization of textile industries is concerned; and finally the occurrence of the proletarian revolution in backward Russia contrary to the prophecies of those Marxists who had expected this revolution to take place in Germany, at that time industrially the most developed country. The general design of his argument is to show that backwardness may, under certain circumstances, act as an advantage and a spur to further effort, whereas rapid advance in the past may act as a brake. This is what he calls 'the dialectics of progress', or the 'law of the retarding lead'.

Romein's thesis, which could be substantiated with many more instances from the history of mankind, seems to me highly relevant to the problem as to how far repetition of a Western pattern of evolution is to be expected in Asian countries. If Romein's view of the way human evolution proceeds is essentially correct, this means that it would be futile to look for a pure copying, in Asia, of patterns familiar from the West. Even though the general trend in Asia may, in general terms and to a certain extent, run parallel with recent Western developments, the statement that the 'Western deviation' is going to develop into a Common Human Pattern may be accepted only in its most general sense. The rate at which social change occurs, and the exact shape which it takes, will vary from one single society to another. It is, more in particular, the time factor which is subject to significant variations.[1] If it is true, as elaborated by Romein, that under certain circumstances an initial handicap may function as an advantage, short-cuts and the skipping over of phases are possible in human history. This means that mankind is able to repeat a certain process within a much shorter period than in a parallel case, thus avoiding the many detours which had to be made in the original model.

This insight has an enormous importance for our theoretical approach to modern Asia. For it enables us to keep clear from any forced search for institutional parallels, even though the general direction of developing trends may be largely comparable. If human evolution is not, as a matter of course, a gradual one, then actual processes need not necessarily be developments in the direction which we have witnessed in the West. They may even present 'involutionary' trends as defined by Clifford Geertz. For example, if we evaluate the present trends of development in the majority of Asian cities and small towns, we may be forced to conclude that,

[1] I may refer to the eighth paper of this volume, dealing with urban characteristics in Indonesia.

for the time being, these do not move in the direction which urbanization has taken in the West, but exactly in the opposite one.

On the other hand, factors of stagnation may be compensated for by other dynamic factors that can occasionally lead to a development which should no longer be called 'evolutionary' but 'revolutionary'. In such a case the period within which a social process is completed would be appreciably abridged in comparison with the original model, though numerous remnants of the pre-revolutionary structure may stay on for a long time, representing a cultural lag in comparison with the main body of society. Such a revolutionary process may even take the social structure beyond the point achieved by the society which had taken the lead in the first instance, in particular if, according to the 'dialectics of progress', 'involutionary' factors are retarding a continuous growth in the advanced society.

In practice this might imply that modernization and industrialization in Asia need not necessarily follow the course taken in the West, via private capitalistic enterprise. Certain phases from Western development can be skipped over, taking a definite Asian society beyond the level of technical and institutional perfection achieved in the countries which, in the past, led the way towards modern industrial development. But even so, the new type of society produced in Asia may show, for a long time to come, a combination of elements which are hyper-modern with other ones which represent, in our Western history, a much less advanced phase of social development.

This view of social transformation appears more enlightening than a theory such as Rostow's which takes a universal pattern of economic development for granted, though even he acknowledges that there is no need for a growing society to recapitulate the course of events in the older industrial societies.[1] The stereotype of a perpetual transition via a take-off period of a relatively short, equal duration (two or three decades) into a phase of 'self-sustained growth' does not take account of the differential inherent in the time-factor; it neglects the possibility of short-cuts from a backward state into a more advanced one; and it overlooks the 'involutionary' elements within Western society by viewing the 'self-sustained growth' as proceeding more or less automatically, if necessary without appreciable interference by the government. Rostow recognizes, that Britain's lead was gone, as soon as the United States and continental Western Europe had 'completed their take-off'. But in his view this is not a dialectical process, but simply an equalization of chances for 'a latecomer

[1] See for example W. W. Rostow, 'The Take-Off into Self-Sustained Growth', *The Economic Journal*, Vol. 66 (1956), pp. 25 ff.; Rostow, *The Stages of Economic Growth: A Non-Communist Manifesto* (Cambridge, 1960); 'Rostow on Growth', *The Economist*, August 15 and 22, 1959.

For a critical appraisal of Rostow's and Gerschenkron's schemes I may refer to Witold Kula, Les debuts du capitalisme en Pologne dans la perspective de l'histoire comparee (Rome, 1960).

with a big unapplied backlog of technology available'. In Russia nothing extraordinary has happened, according to Rostow: the take-off had occurred before the Revolution; at present 'Russia closes the technological gap on the West; China, India, Brazil and others promise to repeat the trick again on the older mature powers, including Russia, in the next half century or so.'[1]

It may be difficult for a Western scholar to imagine that the type of social development with which he is familar is not the most advanced one conceivable: and that the advantage achieved by the West, which is, by the way, rather a recent phenomenon in world history, is not likely to be permanent. Rostow's theory aims clearly at explaining away the specific upsurge of the Soviet Union under communist rule by defining its development as fitting within the usual pattern and the usual timetable.

But then, a scholarly attitude is always characterized by a relativistic attitude which does not put one's own society, nation or race in the centre of the world. A deeper concern with the social dynamics of the Eastern world might rescue us, Westerners, from complacency—the most retarding factor in human evolution.

[1] '*Rostow on Growth*', *loc. cit.*, p. 413.

BIBLIOGRAPHY

Agarwal, A. N. and Singh, S. P. : *Economics of Underdevelopment.*

Agricultural Production Team (sponsored by Ford Foundation): Report on *India's Food Crisis and Steps to Meet It.*

Altekar, A. S. : *A History of Village Communities in Western India.*

Aykroyd, W. R. : *The Nutritive Value of Indian Foods and the Planning of Satisfactory Diets.*

Baden-Powell : *Land Systems of British India; The Origin and Growth of Village Communities in India; Village Community in India.*

Bailey, F. G. : *Caste and the Economic Frontier.*

Baker, O. E. : *Agriculture in Modern Life.*

Baran, Paul A. : *The Political Economy of Growth.*

Basu, T. K. : *The Bengal-Peasant from Time to Time.*

Belden, J. : *China Shakes the World.*

Bews, J. W. : *Human Ecology.*

Bhattacharjee, Jyotiprasad : *Mechanisation of Agriculture in India—Its Economics; Sahajpur: Socio Economic Study of a West Bengal Village.*

Bhave, Acharya Vinoba : *Bhoodan to Gramdan; The Principles and Philosophy of the Bhoodan Yagna.*

Bose, A. : *Social and Rural Economy in Northern India*, Vols. 2.

Brayne, F. L. : *Better Villages.*

Burns, W. : *Technological Possibilities of Agricultural Development in India.*

Carstairs, G. Morris : *The Twice Born.*

Childe, V. G. : *Social Evolution; Man Makes Himself; What Happened in History; History.*

Choudhuri, Manmohan : *The Gramdan Movement.*

Clark, Grahame : *From Savagery to Civilization.*

Coon, C. S. (Ed.) : *General Anthropology.*

Curwin, E. C. : *Plough and Pasture.*

Dantwala, M. L. : *India's Food Problems.*

Dandekar, V. M. and Khundanpur, G. J. : *Working of Bombay Tenancy Act*, 1948—*Report of Investigation.*

Dange, S. A. : *India from Primitive Communism to Slavery.*

Darling, Malcolm Lyall : *The Punjab Peasant in Prosperity and Debt; Wisdom and Waste in the Punjab Village.*

Datta, Bhupendra Nath : *Dialectics of Land-Economics in India.*

Datta, Dvijdas : *Peasant Proprietorship in India*; *Landlordism in India.*

Davis, Kingsley : *The Population of India and Pakistan.*

De-Castro : *Geography of Hunger.*

Desai, A. R. : *Social Background of Indian Nationalism*; *Rural India in Transition.*

Desai, M. B. : Report of an Enquiry into the working of the Bombay Tenancy and Agricultural Lands Act, 1948 in Gujarat.

Desai, Ramanlal V. : *Grammonnati* (Gujarati).

Development Department (West Bengal) : *India's Villages* (A collection of Articles originally published in the Economic Weekly of Bombay).

Dhillon, Harvant: *Leadership and Groups in a South India Village.*

Digby, William : *Prosperous British India.*

Dube, S. C. : *Indian Village; India's Changing Villages.*

Dubois, J. A. : *Hindu Manners, Customs, and Ceremonies.*

Dutt, Romesh C. : *Famines in India; The Economic History of India under British Rule.*

Engles, F. : *Origin of Family, Private Property and State.*

Epstein, S. : *Social Change in South India.*

F. A. O. Publications : *Essentials of Rural Welfare; Training Rural Leaders; The State of Food and Agriculture; Farm Mechanization; The Consolidation of Fragmented Agricultural Holdings.*

Fei, Hsiao-Tung : *Peasant Life in China.*

Forde, C. D. : *Habitat, Economy and Society.*

Gadgil, D. R. : *Planning and Economic Policy in India.*

Ghoshal, U. N. : *The Agrarian System in Ancient India.*

Ghurye, G. S. : *Caste and Class in India; The Scheduled Tribes.*

Gillatte, J. M. : *Rural Sociology.*

Gupta, S. C. : *An Economic Survey of Shamaspur Village (Dist. Shamaspur, U.P.)—A case study in the Structure and Functioning of a Village Economy; Indian Agrarian Structure—A Study in Evolution.*

Gyan Chand : *India's Teeming Millions.*

Hall, William F. : *Agriculture in India.*

Hanson, A. H. : *The Process of Planning—A study of India's Five Year Plans*, 1950-64.

Harrison, Selig S. : *India—The Most Dangerous Decades.*

Hayes, A. W. : *Rural Sociology.*

Herskovits, M. : *Man and His Works.*

Hobhouse, L. T., Wheeler, G. C. and Ginsberg, M. : *The Material Culture and Social Institutions of Simpler People.*

Holmes, R. H. : *Rural Sociology.*

Hopper, D. : *Allocation Efficiency in Indian Agriculture.*

Hough, Eleanor M. : *The Co-operative Movement in India.*

India, Government of : *Census of India*, 1951, 1961; *Report of the Team for the study of Community Development Projects and National Extension Service*, Vols. I, II and III; *Regional Variations in Social Development and Levels of Living*, Vols. I and II.

India, Government of, Ministry of Food and Agriculture : *Indian Agriculture in Brief; Agricultural Development—Problems and Perspectives; Approach to Agricultural Development in the Fourth Five Year Plan; Growth Rates in Agriculture*, 1949-50 *to* 1964-65; *Bibliography of Indian Agriculture Economy*; *Report of the German Agricultural Delegation to India on Co-operative Farming, Farm Machinery, Fertilizer, Land Consolidation and Dairy Processing.*

India, Government of, Planning Commission : *First Five Year Plan; Review of the First Five Year Plan; Second Five Year Plan; Appraisal and Prospects of the Second Five Year Plan; Reappraisal of the Second Five Year Plan; The New India: Progress Through Democracy; The Third Five Year Plan; The Planning Process; The Fourth Five Year Plan—A Draft Outline; The Fourth Five Year Plan; Report of the Team for the study of Community Projects and National Extension Service*, Vols. I-III; *Land Reforms in India.*

India, Government of, Ministry of Food and Agriculture : *Report of the Committee on Large-sized Mechanized Farms, First Report* 1961, *Second Report* 1964; *Agricultural Legislation in India*, VI (Land Reforms).

India, Government of, Ministry of Labour : *Report of the Agricultural Labour Enquiry.*

Indian Society of Agricultural Economics : *Selected Readings; Bhadkad; Seminar on Rationale of Regional Variations in Agrarian Structure of India.*

Karve, Iravati : *The Indian Village; Kinship Organization in India.*

Khusro, A. M. : *An analysis of Agricultural Land in India by size of Holdings and Tenure; Economic and Social effects of Jagirdari Abolition and Land Reforms in Hyderabad.*

Khusro, A. M. and Agarwala, D. M. : *The Problem of Co-operative Farming in India.*

Kolb, J. H. and Brunner, E. : *A study of Rural Society.*

Kolhatkar, V. V. and Mahabal, S. B. : *An enquiry into the Effects of the Working of the Tenancy Legislation in Baroda District.*

Kosambi, D. D. : *An Introduction to Indian History.*

Kotovosky, G. : *Agrarian Reforms in India.*

Kumarappa, J. C. : *Why the Village Movement?*

Ladejinsky, W. : *A Study on Tenurial Conditions in Package Districts.*

Landis, P. H. : *Rural Life in Process.*

League of Nations : *European Conference on Rural Life*, 1939; *Intellectual Aspects of Rural Life*; *Recreation in Rural Areas.*

Lewis, J. P. : *Quiet Crisis in India.*

Lewis, Oscar : *Village Life in Northern India: Studies in a Delhi Village*

Lewis, Oscar : *Group Dynamics in a North Indian Village : A Study in Factions; Village Life in Northern India.*

Loomis, C. P. and Beegle, J. A. : *Rural Social Systems.*

Madan, B. K. (ed.) : *Rural Social Systems.*

Maine, Sir H. : *Village Communities in the East and West*; *Ancient Law.*

Majumdar, D. N. (ed.) : *Rural Profiles; Caste and Communication in Indian Village.*

Majumdar, R. C. and Others : *An Advanced History of India.*

Majumdar, R. C. and Pusalkar A. D. : *The History and Culture of the Indian People.*

Malaviya, H. D. : *Land Reforms in India; Village Panchayats in India.*

Malenbaum, W. : *Prospects of Indian Development.*

Mann, H. H. : *Life and Labour in a Deccan Village.*

Marriott, McKim : *Village India.*

Marx, Karl : 'Articles on India, *Capital*, Vol. I

Mason, Edward : *Economic Development in India and Pakistan.*

Mathai, John : *Village Government in British India.*

Mayer, A., McKim Marriot and Richard L. Park (eds.) : *Pilot Project, India.*
Mayer, Adrian C. : *Caste and Kinship in Central India.*
Maynard, J. : *The Russian Peasant and other Studies.*
Menon, Sankara, T. K. : *Economic Surrey of Nayerambalam Village.*
Mookerji, Radhakamal. : *Ancient Indian Education.*
Morrison, Theodore : *The Economic Transition in India.*
Mukerjee, Radhakamal : *Land Problems in India; Regional Sociology.*
Mukherji, P. K. and Gupta, P. K. : *A Pilot Survey of Fourteen Villages in U. P. and Punjab.*
Mukherji, Ramakrishna : *The Sociologist and Social Change in India Today; The Dynamics of Rural Society; Rise and Fall of East India Company.*
Murphy, G. & L. B. : *In the Minds of Men.*
Myrdal, G. : *Asian Drama,* Vols. I, II and III.

Nair, Kusum : *Blossoms in the Dust.*
Nanavati, M. B. & Anjaria, J. J. : *The Indian Rural Problem* (VI Éd.).
Natarajan, I. : *Peasant Uprisings in India* (1850-1900).
Nehru, S. S. : *Caste and Credit in Rural India.*
Nelson, Lowry : *Rural Sociology.*

Parameswaran, S. : *The Peasant Question in Kerala.*
Park, Richard L. and Tinker, Irene : *Leadership and Political Institutions in India.*
Patel, S. J. : *Agricultural Labourers in Modern India and Pakistan; The India We Want.*
Peake, H. J. : *The English Village; The Origins of Agriculture.*
Peake, H. J. and Fluere, J. H. : *Peasants and Potters.*
Philips, C. H. (ed.) : *Politics and Society in India.*
Piggot, Stuart : *Pre-Historic India.*
Potter, D. C. : *Government in Rural India.*
Premchand Lal : *Reconstruction and Education in Rural India.*

Quinn, J. A. : *Human Ecology.*

Raj, K. N. : *Indian Economic Growth: Performance and Prospects; India, Pakistan and China.*
Ranade, V. G. : *A Social and Economic Survey of a Konkan Village.*
Ranga, N. G. : *Kisan Speaks; The Modern Indian Peasant; Peasants and Progress; Kisan Handbook; History of Kisan Movement.*
Rao, V. K. R. V. : *Agricultural Development in the Fourth Plan.*
Rao, B. Sarveswara : *The Economic and Social Effects of Zamindari Abolition in Andhra.*
Raper, A. : *Preface to Peasantry.*
Reserve Bank of India : *All India Rural Credit Survey,* Vol. 2, General Report.
Retzlaff, Ralph : *Village Government in India.*
Robertson, T. : *Human Ecology.*
Rosen, G. : *Democracy and Economic Change in India.*

Sanderson, Dwight : *Rural Sociology and Rural Social Reconstruction.*

Schultz, T. W. : Transforming Traditional Agriculture.

Seebohm, F. : *The English Village Community.*

Sen, S. R : *The Strategy for Agricultnral Development and Other Essays on Economic Policy and Planning.*

Shah, C. G. : *Marxism, Gandhism and Stalinism.*

Shelvankar, K. S. *The Problem of India.*

Sims, N. L. : *Elements in Rural Sociology; The Rural Community: Ancient and Modern.*

Singer, Milton : 'Cultural Values in India's Economic Development', *Economic Development and Cultural Change*, VII (Oct. 1958), 1-12.

Singh, Baljit : *Next Step in Village India.*

Singh, Baljit and Singh, V. B. : *Social and Economic Change.*

Singh, Tarlok : *Poverty and Social Change: A study in the Economic Reorganization of Indian Rural Society.*

Singh, Yogendra : *The Changing Pattern of Socio-Economic Relation in the Countryside: A survey of selected villages in Eastern Uttar Pradesh.*

Sinha, M. R. (ed.) : *A Decade of Economic Development and Planning in India.*

Slater, G. : *Some South Indian Villages.*

Smith, T. L. : *The Sociology of Rural Life.*

Sociology, The Third World Congress : *Transactions*, Vols. I and II.

Sorokin, P. A. : *Principles of Rural-Urban Sociology.*

Sorokin, P. A., Zimmerman, C. C. and Galpin, C. J. : *A Systematic Source Book in Rural Sociology*, Vols. I, II and III.

Spate, O. H. K. : *India and Pakistan.*

Spence, L. : *Introduction to Mythology.*

Srinivas, M. N. : *Religion and Society Among the Coorgs of South India.*

Srinivas, M. N. (ed.) : *India's Villages.*

Stalin, J. V. : *On the Peasantry.*

Stamp, L. Dudley : *Our Underdeveloped World.*

Steevenson-Moore, J. : *Report of the Material Conditions of Small Agriculturists and Labourers in Gaya.*

Stites, R. S. : *Arts and Man.*

Subbarao, B. : *The Personality of India.*

Subramanian, N. S. 1936 : *Survey of South Indian Village*, Congress Economic & Political Studies No. 2.

Sumner, W. G. and Keller, A. C. : *The Science of Society*, Vols. I, II, III & IV.

Taylor, C. C. : *A Critical Analysis of India's Community Development Programme; Rural Sociology.*

Taylor and Others : *Rural Life in the United States.*

Thirumalai, S. : *Postwar Agricultural Problems and Policies in India.*

Thomas, W. I. and Znaniocki, F. : *The Polish Peasant in Europe and America*, Vols. I and II.

Thorner, D. : *Agricultural Co-operatives in India; The Agrarian Prospect in India.*

Thorner, D. and Alice Thorner : *Land Labour in India.*

Turner, Ralph : *The Great Cultural Traditions*, Vols. I & II.

United Nations : *Land Reforms—Defects in Agrarian Structure; Processes and Problems of Industrialization in Under-developed Countries.*

Vinogradoff, P. : *The Growth of Manor.*

Weiner, M., *The Politics of Scarcity.*

Yagnik, I. K. : *Peasant's Revolts.*
Yakovlev, Y. A. : *Red Villages.*

Zimmerman, C. C. : *Consumption and Standards of Living.*
Zimmerman, C. C. and Framption, Merle E. : *Family and Society.*